**Disorders of elimination**
307.60     Functional enuresis
307.70     Functional encopresis

**Other Disorders of Infancy, Childhood or Adolescence**
313.89     Reactive attachment disorder of infancy and early childhood
307.30     Stereotypy/habit disorder
313.23     Elective mutism

## ORGANIC MENTAL SYNDROMES AND DISORDERS (NON-SUBSTANCE-INDUCED)

**Organic Mental Syndromes whose etiology or pathophysiologic process is either noted as an additional diagnosis from outside the mental disorders section of ICD-9-CM (DSM-III-R Axis III) or is unknown.**

293.00     Delirium
294.10     Dementia
294.00     Amnestic syndrome
293.81     Organic delusional syndrome
293.82     Organic hallucinosis
293.83     Organic mood syndrome
           Specify: manic
                    depressed
                    mixed
294.80*    Organic anxiety syndrome
310.10     Organic personality syndrome
           Specify if explosive type
294.80*    Organic mental syndrome NOS

**Dementias Arising in the Senium and Presenium**
Primary degenerative dementia, senile onset
290.30     with delirium
290.20     with delusions
290.21     with depression
Mutli-infarct dementia
290.41     with delerium
290.42     with delusions
290.43     with depression
290.40     uncomplicated

**Organic Mental Syndromes (whose etiology or pathophysiologic process is either noted as an additional diagnosis from outside the mental disorders section of ICD-9-CM or is unknown)**
293.00     Delerium
294.10     Dementia
294.00     Amnestic Syndrome
293.81     Organic Delusional Syndrome
293.82     Organic Hallucinosis
293.83     Organic Affective Syndrome
294.80*    Organic Anxiety Syndrome
310.10     Organic Personality Syndrome
294.80*    Organic Mental Syndrome NOS

## PSYCHOACTIVE SUBSTANCE USE DISORDERS

**Psychoactive Substance-Induced Organic Mental Disorders**

Alcohol
303.00     intoxication
291.40     idiosyncratic intoxication
291.80     withdrawal
291.00     withdrawal delirium
291.30     hallucinosis
291.10     amnestic disorder
291.20     dementia associated with alcoholism

Barbiturate or similarly acting sedative or hypnotic
305.40     intoxication
292.00*    withdrawal
292.00*    withdrawal delirium
292.83*    amnestic disorder
292.82*    dementia
292.90*    flashback disorder
310.90*    residual disorder

Opioid
305.50     intoxication
292.00*    withdrawal
310.90*    residual disorder

Cocaine
305.60     intoxication
292.00*    withdrawal
292.81*    delirium
292.11*    delusional disorder
292.90*    flashback disorder
310.90*    residual disorder

Amphetamine or similarly acting sympathomimetic
305.70     intoxication
292.00*    withdrawal
292.81*    delirium
292.11*    delusional disorder
292.90*    flashback disorder
310.90*    residual disorder

Phencyclidine (PCP) or similarly acting arylcyclohexylamine
305.90*    intoxication
292.81*    delirium
292.11*    delusional disorder
292.90*    flashback disorder
310.90*    residual disorder

Hallucinogen
305.30     hallucinosis
292.81*    delirium
292.11*    delusional disorder
292.90*    flashback disorder
310.90*    residual disorder

Cannabis
305.20     intoxication
292.81*    delirium
292.11*    delusional disorder
292.90*    flashback disorder
310.90*    residual disorder

Tobacco
292.00*    withdrawal

Caffeine
305.90*    intoxication

Other drug or unspecified psychoactive substance
292.81*    delirium
292.82*    dementia
292.83*    amnestic disorder

# ABNORMAL PSYCHOLOGY

FIFTH EDITION

# ABNORMAL PSYCHOLOGY

## The Problem of Maladaptive Behavior

**Irwin G. Sarason**
*University of Washington*

**Barbara R. Sarason**
*University of Washington*

PRENTICE-HALL, INC., ENGLEWOOD CLIFFS, N.J.

**Library of Congress Cataloging-in-Publication Data**

Sarason, Irwin G.
  Abnormal psychology.

  Bibliography: p.
  Includes indexes.
  1. Psychology, Pathological.   I. Sarason,
Barbara R.   II. Title.   [DNLM: 1. Psychopathology.
2. Social Behavior Disorders.   WM 100 S2425a]
RC454.S28   1987        616.89        86–25136
ISBN 0-13-000381-6

Editorial/production supervision: Dee A. Josephson and Marina Harrison
Interior design: Berta Lewis
Cover design: Suzanne Behnke
Manufacturing buyer: Barbara Kelly Kittle
Photo research: Ilene Cherna
Photo editor: Lorinda Morris
Cover art: "Family of Harlequins" by Pablo Picasso
          1908
          Giraudon/Art Resource

Printed in the United States of America
10  9  8  7  6  5  4  3  2  1

ISBN 0-13-000381-6   01

Prentice-Hall International (UK) Limited, *London*
Prentice-Hall of Australia Pty. Limited, *Sydney*
Prentice-Hall Canada Inc., *Toronto*
Prentice-Hall Hispanoamericana, S.A., *Mexico*
Prentice-Hall of India Private Limited, *New Delhi*
Prentice-Hall of Japan, Inc., *Tokyo*
Prentice-Hall of Southeast Asia Pte. Ltd., *Singapore*
Editora Prentice-Hall do Brasil, Ltda., *Rio de Janeiro*

*To three individuals whose ability to adapt we admire (in order of their appearance) Sue, Jane, and Don*

# CONTENTS

# 8

## SEXUAL VARIATIONS AND DISORDERS     208

# 12

## CAUSES AND MARKERS OF SCHIZOPHRENIA     319

# 13

## BRAIN DISORDERS AND CHANGES RELATED TO AGING     345

# PREFACE
# TO THE FIFTH EDITION

In addition to providing the reader with a preview of coming attractions, the preface to a book that has been revised several times provides the authors with an opportunity to give their reasons for selecting the attractions and presenting them as they do. In addition, it lets them say something about the new and revised material and the material that has been retained from the previous edition.

This edition retains the same organizational structure of the fourth edition. We continue to believe that students must be helped to go beyond the mere acquisition and cataloging of facts. For that reason, we continue to emphasize the integrative and generative contributions of the major theoretical perspectives of abnormal psychology. Throughout the book, we refer as appropriate to the following theoretical perspectives: biological, psychodynamic, learning, cognitive, humanistic/existential and community and discuss how they have shaped research in psychopathology and contributed to therapeutic interventions. Our aim is to help the student appreciate the role theory plays in research and clinical practice. The use of these perspectives is complemented by our use of the concepts of stress, coping, and vulnerability as an organizational focus. With these concepts we are able to provide an overall organizing structure that draws on characteristics of both the person and the environment and helps students develop a theoretical framework within which they can integrate the diverse disorders which provide the subject matter of abnormal psychology.

Nevertheless, research advances have led us to elaborate or modify certain aspects of this approach in the fifth edition. For example, we now explain in greater detail how such variables as social support influence both the coping process and the individual's vulnerability to disorder. In clarifying its role as a stress moderator, we expose the important link between social support and the individual's social skills repertory. Thus, while our approach to maladaptive behavior is basically the same as in previous editions, with an emphasis on maladaptation as a product of interactions among relevant factors, we have refined it and sought to extend its usefulness.

It goes without saying that one of our aims is to provide students with a stimulating up-to-date and informed account of abnormal psychology, its causes and relevant treatments. This edition incorporates the categories of the 1987 revision of the *Diagnostic and Statistical Manual* of the *American Psychiatric Association* (DSM-III-R). Thus, students will benefit from changes in classification based on clinicians' and researchers' experience with the DSM-III-R's predecessor, DSM-III, which first appeared in 1980. While we believe that DSM-III-R represents significant advances in diagnosis, we recognize that it is not the final word on classification and that both it and its predecessor stirred up considerable controversy. For example, many clinicians feel that the DSM-III approach is not sufficiently based on available theories of psychopathology. We introduce the student not only to DSM-III-R but to the orientation that produced it.

This edition emphasizes research methodology and

empirical findings more than did the fourth edition. We make extensive use of the many feedback loops that exist among theoretical concepts, clinical practice, and scientific investigations. Students usually understand that scientific advances influence theory and clinical practice, but the impacts of theory on scientific work through identification of variables that require controlled study are often less apparent to them. We highlight these relationships at relevant points throughout the book.

In addition to providing state-of-the-art reviews of numerous research topics, we have also provided accounts of the important relationship between research design and the resulting empirical evidence. The evidence can't be better than the design out of which it emerged. Evidence that arises from research with a faulty design can be the source of misinformation and confusion. These unfortunate effects can be avoided if the data are examined critically in the light of the research that produced it.

In this edition, we review research methods specific to several particular disorders, as well as general methodological issues. We discuss such topics as what is involved in carrying out a clinical trial, pitfalls in interpreting long-term outcome studies, how to plan high-risk studies, and how to use the balanced placebo design. Several recently developed methodologies are influencing research design in abnormal psychology and we introduce students to them. They include the use of the research interview in the diagnostic process, meta-analysis, and the concept and identification of markers of behavior disorders. For example, in schizophrenia attentional deficits assessed using the Continuous Performance Test may serve as markers of a vulnerability to schizophrenic disorder.

We review a wide variety of topics that provide clues to better understanding and treatment of maladaptive behavior. Perhaps foremost among these is the biology of abnormal behavior, but there are major advances in several fields. The latest information is presented on the genetics of alcoholism and autism, the role of specific chromosomes in Huntington's disease, the technology of noninvasive measurement of blood pressure and heart rate, and the roles of alpha and beta receptors and biological rhythms in depression. We deal extensively with the rapidly developing fields of health psychology and behavioral medicine. For example, recent work on psychoimmunology and psychological factors in coronary heart disease (such as anger and whether the individual is a "hot" or "cold" reactor) is described and illustrated. We also review recent evidence about another area of advance and ferment, the epidemiology of maladaptation. Students of abnormal psychology need to know about the epidemiology of specific types of maladaptive behavior and should be aware of what is involved in doing epidemiological research.

Often neglected in textbooks of abnormal psychology, is any discussion of the effect of the disordered behavior on other family members. This edition uses dramatic personal accounts to clarify this impact on parents, children, and siblings. We have also added several new boxes, for example, one on disordered attachment in children and one on paranoid disorders. The material on anorexia nervosa and bulimia has also been expanded as research on these disorders has grown.

As in previous editions, we continue to emphasize how the important roles played by the major theoretical perspectives influence work on abnormal psychology. For example, the cognitive perspective, which views the person as an information processor, is helping us to better understand several specific clinical problems. Recently, it has directed our attention to the roles of distorted self-schemata and attributions in both depression and anxiety. We review the theoretical and clinical background of the biologically based concepts of schizophrenic spectrum disorders and Types I and II schizophrenia and discuss the recent eruption of interest and research on dissociative disorders. We also explore recent developments concerning theories of intelligence that may have important clinical implications. We have mentioned only a few of the new or expanded topics covered in this edition.

We have also made several pedagogical changes that will enhance the student's interest and involvement in abnormal behavior. We have revised some tables and graphics and added new ones. We think they will make learning easier. There are frequent tables that contain concise summaries of the key features of particular disorders (for example, one table lists the key triggers of migraines); other new tables permit easy contrast between disorders that are in some ways similar. We have also added many graphic interpretations of research findings, so that students can grasp their basic meaning without the distraction of digits and decimal points. To aid students' integration of material, our chapter summaries are now organized as study outlines. The extensive use of color in this edition will also help students' learning and make for a visually appealing book. The use of color will be especially valuable in the many examples of the art productions of deviant individuals.

One feature of this edition that is not new is our commitment to providing students with a text that is clear and not loaded with jargon. We have written in the simplest language that will do justice to the topics covered. Our preoccupation with a simple, interesting writing style doesn't have anything to do with undervaluing the capacities of students to deal with sometimes complex topics. On the contrary, we are continually impressed with how quickly students are able to get to the core of an issue if its presentation has not been obscured by "sophisticated," or jargon-filled writing. Regular readers of professional and scientific literature know what a breath of fresh air it is to hit upon a book or article that is simple, to the point, and possibly even has a touch of humor. Through clear exposition, simple language, relevant case studies, and stimulating illustrations and examples, we hope to involve students in the subject matter of abnormal psychology and to help them achieve an integrated view of current knowledge about maladaptive behavior. We have tried to achieve a proper balance of clinical and research emphases and to avoid oversimplifying the complex realities of disordered behavior.

In addition to the book itself, students should find the optional study guide a valuable learning tool. We believe instructors will be pleased with the instructor's manual and test bank as well as Prentice-Hall's telephone testing service and floppy disk testing available for the Apple and the IBM PC. In addition, we are offering an interactive study guide to accompany the text, as well as Prentice-Hall's Educational Assistance/Film Policy and Gradebook software.

We appreciate the assistance of the many people who have helped to make this book as up-to-date, authoritative, and appealing as possible. We have benefitted from the insights and suggestions of many of our colleagues both at the University of Washington and elsewhere. We are indebted to the many researchers who shared their as yet unpublished findings with us. We are especially grateful to Robert L. Spitzer for his willingness to provide us with the several preliminary versions of DSM-III-R that preceded its final format. We also wish to thank the following reviewers whose suggestions and comments were very helpful: Professor Anne Harris, Arizona State University; Professor Scott Henggeler, Memphis State University; Professor Robert Lueger, Marquette University; Professor Tom Marsh, Pitt Community College; Professor Linda Musum-Miller, University of Arkansas at Little Rock; Professor Clive Robins, New York University; Professor Michael D. Spiegler, Providence College; and Professor Robert Tipton, Virginia Commonwealth University.

As usual, it has been a delight to work with John Iseley and the Prentice-Hall team. Carolyn D. Smith and Ilene McGrath; preparation and editing of the text increased its readability. Dee Josephson and Marina Harrison outdid themselves as our production editors. Lorinda Morris, our photo researcher, was resourceful and creative.

This edition was begun in Seattle and completed in Wassenaar, The Netherlands. We very much appreciate the work setting and hospitality provided for us by the Netherlands Institute for Advanced Study while we were in residence at that marvelous and unique institution. Less unique, but still helpful, were the various express delivery companies of the United States and The Netherlands without whose services this edition would never have been published on time. We also wish to note the contribution of Betty Johnson. At every stage of writing this book, she performed amazingly. She repeatedly transformed garbled pages full of arrows, inserts, and indecipherable scrawl into readable copy even when the creators of that confusion were 6,000 miles away. We appreciate both her contributions to this book and her good humor. We also appreciate the help of Nancy Whitney who spent many hours locating references for us, and David Pierce, who made it possible for us to meet production deadlines by sorting some 9,000 index cards with accuracy and dispatch.

Irwin G. Sarason
Barbara R. Sarason

# 1

# ABNORMAL BEHAVIOR

*Bob Cates had felt tense, anxious, and worried a lot of the time during his entire stay at the large university he attended. There seemed to be so much to do. However, in his senior year, despite the fact that he was usually an energetic person, even small things seemed to require a major effort. He felt particularly overwhelmed at pressure points like taking exams, writing papers, and having to say things in class.*

*For reasons that were not clear, Bob became increasingly depressed and began to feel that he couldn't go on much longer. His classes, and life in general, seemed less and less worth the effort they required. He couldn't concentrate on his school work and spent several hours each day sitting in his dormitory room—sometimes just staring into space.*

*Bob's friends noticed the changes in his behavior and mood and were concerned. As a result of their encouragement, Bob went to the University Counseling Service and had a series of sessions with a counselor. The questions that passed through the counselor's mind included the following.*

*What is Bob experiencing at the present time—what is he feeling and thinking about?*

*How serious is the problem that he presents, and to what degree is he aware of its seriousness?*

*What are the causes of Bob's problem—is it due to something that has arisen in his current situation or is it a continuation of a long-term, perhaps lifelong, pattern?*

*What can be done to help Bob overcome his unhappy state?*

What is going on in a particular person's life that results in unhappiness and disordered behavior? What can be done to alleviate the problem? These questions are the focus of abnormal psychology. In the case of Bob Cates, the problem was part of a long-term pattern but was also related to things that were going on in his current life situation. His parents had always emphasized the importance of hard work and achievement. His excellent high school record showed the degree to which he had learned to strive for success. What seemed to have happened at the university (many of the facts were far from clear) was that for the first time he began to question the values on which his need to achieve was based. As the counseling proceeded, he came to see that in many subtle ways his parents had shaped him to be a "producer." During his junior year, when he was beginning to think about what to do after completing his education, Bob began to feel that he could never achieve as much as his parents wanted him to. This thought had a nagging, depressing effect on

him. The future seemed hopeless, and he felt helpless to do anything about it. After several counseling sessions Bob admitted that he had had suicidal thoughts, although he had never seriously considered taking his own life.

## ■ WHAT IS ABNORMAL BEHAVIOR?

How abnormal is Bob Cates? While there is no basis for concluding that Bob is "crazy," he definitely had serious difficulty adjusting to college. Just how much pressure his parents actually placed on him is not answered by the available information. The fact that he spent hours just sitting in his room, together with his suicidal thoughts, suggests that he was experiencing adjustment difficulties that were much greater than those that are typically experienced by college students.

In this book we will see cases of abnormal behavior that are both more and less serious than that of Bob Cates. Because our goal is not simply to describe abnormal behavior, we will review the theoretical frameworks within which instances of human failure, inadequacy, and unhappiness have been conceptualized. At the same time, we will review basic research that is pertinent to theories of abnormal behavior. This review of existing theory and research will give us a general framework within which to interpret the wide variety of human problems that find expression in abnormal behaviors. This framework emphasizes the roles played by stress, coping skills, and personal vulnerabilities.

Mental disorders, like anything unusual, may make us uncomfortable and even a little frightened. A mentally ill person should not be seen as evil, however, merely as different. Abnormal psychology deals with how it feels to be different, the meanings that get attached to being different, and how society deals with people whom it considers to be different. The spectrum of differentness is wide, ranging from reality-defying delusions and severe debilitation to worries and behavioral quirks that we would be better off not having but that do not interfere significantly with our daily lives.

An example of this milder end of the spectrum is a man who was an outstandingly successful district attorney, was elected governor of New York on three occasions, and was almost elected President of the United States in 1948. This man, Thomas E. Dewey, reached the pinnacle of success, displaying such qualities as rectitude, efficiency, precision, and a nearly limitless capacity for hard work. Yet it was just this combination of traits that made Dewey seem too good to be true.

For example, he was never late or absent in his first twelve years of schooling. He lacked a sense of humor and seemed to enjoy life only when he was achieving some goal. He also had personal rigidities that restricted the spontaneity that is so important in public figures. For example, he had a phobia about germs. When he toured prisons, he would not touch a doorknob without first wiping it off with a folded handkerchief concealed in his palm. He also drank three quarts of water a day because of its presumed healthful effects. Dewey achieved much, but had he been less rigid he might have achieved even more; perhaps more important, he might have been a happier person (R. N. Smith, 1982).

An example of a much more severe abnormality is Joan Houghton, whose break with reality required intensive treatment during a five-week period of hospitalization. After her recovery she wrote an account of her experiences.

> My mother and I sat next to each other in the waiting room while my father investigated admission procedures. A young man was seated near us. Perspiration dripped across his brow and down his cheeks. In silence I took a tissue from my purse, moved close to him and gently wiped the moisture from his face. I reassured him that everything would be fine.

> Soon my father rejoined us. We went together to a small room where I met Kay, the psychiatric social worker assigned to my case, and a psychiatrist (whose name I don't recall). We talked a few minutes. I was presented with a piece of paper and instructed to sign my name. Obediently, I wrote, "Saint Joan" on the paper, not realizing that I was voluntarily admitting myself to a state mental hospital . . . At the time of my hospitalization I had both a sense of death and a rebirth about me. My first psychotic episode appeared as a private mental exorcism, ending with the honor of sainthood and the gifts of hope and faith. (Houghton, 1982, pp. 548–549)

Although Houghton's recovery enabled her to obtain a job at the National Institute of Mental Health and to write sensitively about her experience, she faced many barriers that made the recovery process more difficult than it had to be. Her ordeal continued after her discharge from the hospital.

> The crisis of mental illness appeared as a nuclear explosion in my life. All that I had known and enjoyed previously was suddenly transformed, like some strange reverse process of nature, from a butterfly's beauty into a pupa's cocoon. There was a binding, confining quality to my life, in part chosen, in part imposed. Repeated rejections, the awkwardness of others around me, and my own discomfort and self-consciousness propelled me into solitary confinement.

> My recovery from mental illness and its aftermath involved a struggle—against my own body, which seemed to be without energy and stamina, and against a society that seemed reluctant to embrace me. It seemed that my greatest needs—to be wanted, needed, valued—were the very needs which others could not fulfill. At times, it felt as though I were trying to swim against a tidal wave. (Houghton, 1980, p.8)

The following incident illustrates what swimming against that tidal wave was like.

> One Sunday I went to church alone after being absent for several weeks. The minister (who knew of my history, faith, and strong belief in God) began his sermon with reference to the devil. He said, "If you ever want to be convinced of the existence of the devil, you should visit a mental institution." To illustrate his point, he described people who had lost control of their bodily functions, who screamed out obscenities. I left church after the sermon, drove home vowing never to return to that church as long as that minister preached from the pulpit. At home, however, I began to replace my anger with doubt. Maybe I misunderstood.

> At my invitation the minister visited our home to discuss his philosophy about mental illness and the mentally ill. His visit was our last encounter. Not only did he see evil in mental illness but he conveyed an unforgiving attitude to those who have the misfortune of residing in mental hospitals. (Houghton, 1980, p. 10)

## The Stigma of Abnormal Behavior

As Houghton's account makes clear, people who are noticeably deviant may experience prejudice and discrimination. However, it is not clear whether the stigma associated with mental disorder—the sense of disgrace, or the reality of rejection—is experienced by most people who are known to have a history of mental disorder, regardless of whether they have recovered or not, or only by those who continue to engage in abnormal behaviors. In general, the more visible the abnormal behavior, the greater the probability that the person will experience prejudice and rejection.

For many years researchers have studied public attitudes toward abnormal behavior. The evidence shows that people know more about behavioral abnormalities today than they did twenty years ago and that overt rejection of the mentally ill has declined. Nevertheless, ex-mental patients who continue to be identified as such by their behavior or history are not treated in the same way as ex-medical patients when it comes to housing, school admission, jobs, or general goodwill. Many people continue to be frightened of former mental patients, although it is becoming less socially acceptable to say so.

Some segments of the mass media may contribute to the public's fear of mental disorder. One study showed that 17 percent of prime-time television programs involve the theme of mental disorder and that 3 percent of the major characters have some sort of mental disorder (Gerbner and others, 1981). Of these characters, 73 percent are portrayed as violent, compared with 40 percent of normal characters. Eighty-one percent of them fall victim to violence compared with 44 percent of normal characters. Of women who are depicted as mentally ill, 73 percent are violent compared with 24 percent of normal characters. Among all prime-time characters portrayed this way, one-fourth will be killed and one-fourth will kill someone else. Highly publicized acts, such as that of would-be presidential assassin John Hinckley, further reinforce the stereotype that mental disorder equals violence.

TV also builds misconceptions concerning what behaviors are normal or typical (Gerbner and others, 1981). More than three-quarters of all dramatic characters are shown eating, drinking, or talking about food—often more than once. Alcohol is mentioned in 80 percent of prime-time programs, aside from the commercials (see Figure 1–1). A child may see ten scenes of alcohol consumption on TV during one day's viewing. The world of soap operas literally floats in alcohol, and it is liquor, not oil, that greases the wheels of "Dallas." An average of nearly three 1-minute periods per each 21-minute program show an alcohol-related event—a rate of about 6 per hour. Another recent study has shown that televised violence and crime have significant effects on crime rates (Hennigan and others, 1982).

## Adaptive and Maladaptive Behaviors

The bulk of the behaviors studied by abnormal psychology are related to human failures and inadequa-

(a)

(b)

(c)

**FIGURE 1–1**
Television and the movies influence people's views of what behaviors are acceptable and desirable. An example of this influence is the media's portrayal of alcohol consumption. (Phototeque)

(a)

(b)

(c)

**FIGURE 1-2**
Maladaptation can arise in a variety of situations and can vary in severity. (a) The homeless man lying on the street in the first photo is unable to function well in society, his level of adaptation is very low. (b) This man, who suffers from an obsessive compulsive disorder is a "checker," someone with a need continually to check on the status of a situation. Here he is checking his front door—for the tenth time—to make sure he has really locked it. (c) Some of the students in this photo may also be functioning maladaptively. They may be so worried about getting a good score that they cannot concentrate on their performance on the test. Although this is a much milder level of maladaptation, it may still be very important to some of the students. (Lenore Weber, Taurus Photos; Laimute Druskis; Will McIntyre, Photo Researchers)

cies. These failures in living are due mainly to failures in adaptation (see Figure 1–2). Adaptation involves the balance between what people do and want to do, on the one hand, and what the environment (the community) wants, on the other.

Adaptation is a dynamic process. Each of us responds to our environment and to the changes that occur within it. How well we adapt depends on two factors: our personal characteristics (skills, attitudes, physical condition) and the nature of the situations that confront us (for example, family conflict or natural disasters). These two factors jointly determine whether we survive, are content, and prosper, or whether we fall by the wayside. Because nothing—neither ourselves nor the environment—stays the same for very long, adap-

tation must take place all the time. The extremely rapid rate of change in the modern world puts a particular strain on our ability to adapt. Moreover, successful adaptation to one set of conditions is not a guarantee of successful adaptation to others.

**Adaptation and Adjustment** A distinction is sometimes drawn between adaptation and adjustment. Adaptation refers to the survival of the species, whereas adjustment refers to individual mastery of the environment and the sense of being at peace with oneself. In many instances this is a valid and useful distinction. In certain cases, however, it oversimplifies the human situation. Unlike those of animals, the adaptive successes and failures of human beings cannot be measured simply in terms of the survival and reproduction of the species. For most people in the modern world, concerns about quality of life and level of contentment far overshadow the need to satisfy biological requirements. Human beings have developed subtle language forms, a refined level of thinking, superior problem-solving skills, intricate social relationships, and complex communication processes, all of which affect behavior and its interpretation. Individuals' feelings of failure may damage their social relationships, and the human gene pool might be significantly affected by the failure of such people to marry and have children. On the other hand, many individuals with certain types of inadequacies, who would probably be unable to hold their own in a subsistence economy, can survive and reproduce in the modern world because of social institutions such as welfare programs, Social Security, and health insurance.

Biological factors aside, how we live and how we feel about the way we live are important factors in human adaptation. For us, adaptation refers to people's ability or inability to modify their behavior in response to changing environmental requirements. In this book, therefore, we devote most of our attention to people's personal and social adaptations.

**Maladaptive vs. Deviant Behavior**  All maladaptive behavior is deviant behavior. However, deviant or unusual behavior is not necessarily maladaptive. This can be seen in the case of Albert Einstein. At the age of 12 Einstein decided to devote his life to solving the "riddle of the huge world." Early in his career, while working as a patent office examiner, he wrote five papers that eventually changed our view of the universe. Although public recognition of the importance of Einstein's theory was many years away, his ability to think about the properties of matter in a completely new way began almost at once to influence the thought of physicists. Other kinds of deviant behavior, such as wearing very bright ties, refusing to travel by airplane, drinking ten cups of coffee a day, and needing to read in bed for two hours before falling asleep, are not as productive as Einstein's behavior and may seem odd or annoying, but people who act in these ways do not need major rehabilitative efforts to live happy, productive lives.

Describing behavior as maladaptive implies that a problem exists; it also suggests that either vulnerability in the individual, inability to cope, or exceptional stress in the environment has led to problems in living. Students of maladaptive behavior are especially interested in behavior that is not merely different or deviant but also represents a source of concern to the individual, to his or her family and friends, or to society. This means, for example, that students of maladaptive behavior direct more of their attention toward people with very low IQs than toward those with high IQs, or toward those who are not happy rather than toward those who are.

There are many causes of maladaptation. In some instances—for example, in certain forms of brain damage—an organic cause is uncovered. In other cases, undesirable present or past social relationships—for example, an incestuous relationship—may be implicated. In still other cases, a combination of these factors along with a stressful event, such as the death of a loved one or the birth of a child, plays a decisive role.

Maladaptations range from chronic fears that are troubling but not disabling to nearly complete loss of orientation, severe distortion of reality, and inability to communicate. The individual may be unhappy about his or her maladaptive behavior, or the community may be worried about what might happen if the person is not removed from society. Throughout this book many different kinds of maladaptive behaviors will be described, along with the social reactions they evoke.

## ■ STRESS, COPING, AND VULNERABILITY

When we talk about how well people adapt, it is important to consider the conditions under which the adaptations are made. The same person may handle a frightening or difficult situation well at one time and maladaptively at others. Some people may behave adaptively in a situation that others handle poorly. Why is this the case? Three concepts—stress, coping, and vulnerability—help us understand these differences in behavior. Seven-year-old Denton may adapt well when he has a sympathetic teacher, when his parents are getting along well, and when he is healthy. However, if he has a teacher whom he hates, if his parents bicker half the night and are on the edge of divorce, and if he is constipated, he may become much more upset about not being a starting player on his soccer team than we might have predicted. If Mrs. Block has just lost an important client for her firm and comes home to find that someone has smashed into her car as it sat parked in the carport, and then her 12-year-old child tells her he has left his violin on the school bus, she may not respond as constructively as she might have under other circumstances.

Stress refers to people's reactions to situations that pose demands, constraints, or opportunities. For example, a person could feel stressed by seeing a child fall into a rapidly flowing river, by being awakened by a fire alarm and smelling smoke, or by being promoted to a new job with more responsibility. People are likely to experience psychological stress when they have to deal with an unexpected or unusual change, such as a natural disaster. They are likely to experience even greater stress than usual when the change occurs at the same time as a severe life crisis (such as the death of a loved one) or at the beginning of a critical developmental period (such as adolescence).

Coping refers to how people deal with difficulties and attempt to overcome them. Coping skills are the techniques that are available to an individual in making such attempts. A number of general skills are useful in handling stressful situations. These include thinking constructively, dealing with problems as they arise, behaving flexibly, and providing feedback to oneself about which tactics work in a given situation and which ones do not. How useful any particular skill will be depends on the nature of the situation and on the individual's vulnerabilities and assets. Having an effective repertory of coping skills strengthens a person's sense of self-control and self-direction. By gaining greater control over our behavior, we may be able to alter environmental conditions that influence us.

Vulnerability refers to how likely we are to respond maladaptively to certain situations. An individual can be an effective coper in one situation but not in another. Vulnerability may be increased by having a particular kind of heredity such as a schizophrenic parent, by certain personality characteristics such as a tendency to worry or feel anxious, by the lack of certain skills such as the ability to make decisions calmly, or by a buildup of unexpected negative experiences. Some people are more vulnerable in all situations because they deal less effectively with what happens to them in daily life. Others are more vulnerable simply because of a combination of recent stressful events. Certain people are more vulnerable in particular kinds of situations that remind them of former problems or difficulties. For example, upon seeing a child swept away in a river, a person who has seen one of her younger brothers killed in an accident when she was 5 might freeze, while soneone who has not had such an experience would be able to act in time to save the child.

Certain life conditions in and of themselves increase people's vulnerability and their risk of maladaptive behavior. They become part of a high-risk group of people who, because they share these life conditions, are more likely than the rest of the population to experience the negative effects of stress. Population groups that may be at high risk for certain conditions include children and adolescents, the aged and the disabled, and disadvantaged minority groups.

Stress, coping, and vulnerability interact (see Figure 1-3). The greater the stress, the less vulnerability is required for a person to display maladaptive behavior.

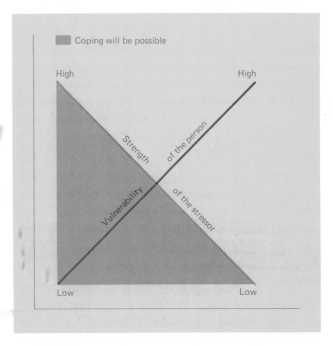

**FIGURE 1-3**
The interaction between stress and vulnerability determines whether coping will be possible. Whether a person has adequate coping skills determines whether coping will occur.

The less severe the stress, the greater the vulnerability needed to produce maladaptive behavior. The better people's coping repertories, the less likely they are to fall apart in situations in which they are vulnerable. Generally, it is easier and more effective to help people learn better ways of dealing with stress than to prevent the stresses to which they are vulnerable. Chapter 5 presents a more in-depth view of the effects of stress and the variety of ways people deal with them.

Clinical interventions are ways of helping people cope with stress more effectively. The intervention selected for someone who is experiencing a short-term crisis, such as the serious illness of a loved one, might be a tranquilizing drug. In this case, the tranquilizer reduces vulnerability to intense anxiety experienced over a period of time. In other cases, insight into the person's desires, motivations, and conflicts is needed in order to help the individual cope more effectively with stress and become less vulnerable to the crises that are the inevitable ingredient of every human life. Sometimes the person needs to learn new skills or behaviors that are effective in dealing with difficult situations. For some people, the way they think about a situation needs to be changed. If a low grade makes you think, "I'm dumb; it's no use trying to finish this course," the results may be very different than they would be if you thought, "I didn't study very effectively; I'd better organize my work better and check with the professor before the test to ask about the points that aren't clear." The particular approach taken by the clinician depends on his or her assessment of the factors in a given case and on the psychological perspective or viewpoint he or she favors.

In this book we will present a number of perspectives on why maladaptive behavior occurs and how adaptive behavior can be substituted for it. Running through our discussion of abnormal psychology will be a consideration of the effects of stress and individual vulnerability on the outcome of any particular situation. The more we understand what causes an individual to feel stressed, and the more we can identify the factors that produce vulnerability, the clearer the sources of the maladaptive behavior will be and the more likely we will be to come up with effective treatment procedures. That is what the study of abnormal psychology is all about.

## ■ REASONS FOR CLINICAL CONTACTS

Some people seek professional help because they are dissatisfied with themselves and with certain aspects of their lives; others do so because of concerns expressed by family members, friends, or co-workers; still others are forced to see clinicians because they have gotten into trouble with the community.

### Personal Unhappiness

In the following case, personal unhappiness seems to have been the factor that led the person to seek help.

*Jack Farmer is a 35-year-old executive in a large multinational corporation. From all outward appearances, any differences he might have from other people are positive. Whatever weaknesses he has are minor. For example, his coordination in physical activities, such as playing tennis, is probably below average. The opinion of members of his company and community is that Jack Farmer is a very well-functioning individual. While he and his wife and two children get along reasonably well, Jack has some concerns that have shaped his family role, particularly as his children approach high school age. These concerns have to do with the burdens of family responsibility, especially the need to ensure his family's happiness should anything happen to him. He has occasionally commented to his wife that television commercials about the need to have plenty of life insurance seem to have been written specifically with him in mind. However, Jack is concerned about more*

*than money. He feels that he should be a closer friend to his children and less distant from his wife than he often is. He is also very concerned about the issues of nuclear waste and pollution of the natural environment. His concerns often cause him to feel blue and hopeless about the future.*

*One Sunday Jack read a newspaper article about a local mental health center that had opened recently. The article pointed out that the center's services were not restricted to severely disturbed individuals, that perfectly normal people who have hit a rough spot in their lives might find it valuable to talk with an expert about their personal problems. After several weeks of internal debate ("Could I be a little crazy?" "I'd be ashamed if my friends ever found out that I went to a shrink"), Jack decided to go to the mental health center.*

By conventional standards Jack Farmer's case is not serious. He sought help because of personal dissatisfactions and concerns. Wrestling further with his personal tensions seemed worse to him than his fear of being stigmatized if he sought professional help.

### The Concerns of Others

Sometimes it is difficult even for professionals to decide what the dividing line should be between maladaptive and merely unusual behavior. In the following case, there was no agreement about whether the woman concerned was psychotic (out of touch with reality) and needed institutionalization, or whether her behavior was simply unusual and presented no hazard to her or her family.

*Mary Waverly was in her late twenties. A university graduate, she had run a successful boutique in a large western city until shortly before the birth of her daughter, who is now 2 years old. During the year before Mary's daughter was born, Mary's mother had been treated for cancer. She died when Alice, her granddaughter, was fourteen months old. During the baby's first year and a half, she had surgery several times to correct a birth defect.*

*Recently Mary's husband attempted to have her committed to a psychiatric hospital. He said he was concerned about their daughter's welfare. Mary had become a religious fanatic. Although she came from a very religious family, until recently, when she joined a cult group, her behavior had not seemed unusual. Since joining the group she had refused to have sexual relations with her husband because he was not a "believer." Although she seemed to take good care of her child, she made all decisions only after listening to the "voice of the Lord."*

When Mary Waverly was examined, her judgment did not seem impaired, her intelligence was above average, and her religious thoughts, although they took up a great deal of her time, did not seem to differ from those of other enthusiastic converts to a cult group. A pediatrician examined her daughter and reported that she was well cared for. A question was raised about what Mrs. Waverly might do if she thought God told her to harm her child or someone else. Neither of the clinicians who examined her was willing to give a definite answer.

Mrs. Waverly didn't think she had a mental disorder and didn't think she needed treatment. One of the clinicians agreed. He believed that her behavior was unusual but that she was not mentally ill. Another clinician thought she was a paranoid schizophrenic who should be hospitalized for drug therapy. What should be done when professionals disagree? In this case, after hearing the conflicting views Mr. Waverly decided not to press for hospitalization.

## Legal and Community Problems

Mild personal maladaptations like Jack Farmer's affect the lives of the individual and possibly a small number of other people. Mary Waverly's behavior was a matter of concern to her husband because he was worried about the possibility that she might harm their daughter. In the case of Charles Clay, a legal problem arose over something he had done.

*Charles Clay, aged 45, owned what had been a successful 24-hour-a-day grocery store. Now, however, he was having increasing difficulty containing his anger toward his customers. Until five years ago he had been a cheerful, friendly merchant. Then his wife died, and his personality seemed to change. Increasingly he worried that people were trying to shoplift his merchandise. (There was a problem with a few high school students who frequented his store after school.) As time went on, he began to confront customers with his suspicions and even to demand that some of them submit to being searched.*

*Not surprisingly, Clay's business began to decline. When this happened, he got very angry and even more suspicious. The culminating event occurred when a woman entered the store, walked around for a few minutes, and then bought a newspaper. When Clay tried to search her (at the same time yelling, "Don't tell me you were just looking around!"), she ran from the store and summoned the police. The police investigation led Clay to seek advice from his lawyer, who had been a friend since high school. Although Clay insisted that "there is nothing the matter with me," his anger and*

*suspiciousness bothered the lawyer. Using tact and persuasion, the lawyer got Clay to agree to visit a psychiatrist. Unfortunately, the visit did not work out well. Clay was reluctant to talk about his concerns and was angered by what he viewed as the psychiatrist's inquisitiveness. He refused to return for a second visit. Nevertheless, the lawyer was able to get Clay out of trouble with the police. Unfortunately, several months later Clay was arrested and convicted of physically attacking another customer.*

Many people saw Charles Clay as having problems that he refused to recognize. In spite of the social consensus about the maladaptive quality of his behavior, he gave himself a clean bill of health. In part because of his failure to perceive his own behavior accurately, Clay eventually got into trouble with the law. His first contact with the police did not result in formal charges; the community's agents recognized his psychological difficulties, and the focus of their attention was on helping a citizen with his personal problems. The second contact, however, resulted in punishment for a crime. Society had decided that Clay was not going to help himself, and it moved to protect itself.

Gross failure to see one's behavior accurately as was the case with Charles Clay is characteristic of several of the most serious forms of maladaptive behavior. In such cases, it is a highly positive development if the person begins to suspect that his or her behavior is contributing to difficulties in getting along with other people.

## ■ THE EPIDEMIOLOGY OF MALADAPTIVE BEHAVIOR

The aim of **epidemiological research** is to obtain information about the physical and psychological maladaptations of populations and groups. Epidemiologists are especially interested in identifying the environmental causes of particular conditions, especially those associated with a community's way of life. The Broad Street pump incident is one of the most famous examples of epidemiological inquiry and its use in furthering public health. In 1848, during a severe cholera epidemic in London, a study of the disease's distribution within the city was carried out. The study showed that the outbreak had a geographical center, a water pump in Broad Street (see Figure 1–4). It was further found that two groups—inmates of an institution and employees of a brewery—did not develop the illness in anything like epidemic proportions. Each of these groups had its own well, and brewery workers drank beer rather than water at work. On the basis of this

**FIGURE 1-4**
Epidemiological detective work can reveal the source of disease. (New York Public Library Picture Collection)

information, the Broad Street pump was dismantled and the epidemic brought under control. This example is especially interesting because it shows how epidemiological work can contribute to human well-being even when the cause of a condition is unknown—the microorganisms that cause cholera had not been identified in 1848.

## Prevalence and Incidence

Epidemiologists conduct surveys to estimate the extent of a health problem. Two types of information are obtained in these surveys. **Prevalence** data describe the frequency of occurrence of a given condition at a particular point in time. For example, if on a given date 100 cases of depression were counted in a community of 1,000 people, the prevalence rate would be 10 percent. **Incidence** data relate to the number of new cases of a specific condition that arise during a particular period. For example, if ten people who had not been de-

pressed at the time of the prevalence study became depressed during the next year, the incidence rate would be 1 percent. Epidemiological research has identified a number of factors that must be attended to in order to ensure the accuracy of survey results. These include representative sampling of the population, clearly worded questions, and careful training of interviewers (Eaton and others, 1984).

The scope of mental health problems is reflected in facts that were uncovered in a recent survey of nearly 10,000 people living in Baltimore, Maryland; New Haven, Connecticut; and St. Louis, Missouri (Myers and others, 1984). The findings suggest that at any given time about 29 million Americans—nearly one in five adults—suffer from mental disorders ranging from mildly disabling anxiety to severe schizophrenia. Anxiety disorders (not depressions, as was previously thought) are the most common psychiatric problem, occurring in about 8 percent of those surveyed. Abuse or dependence on drugs afflicts about 6–7 percent of the population (most of these cases involve alcohol). Mood disorders, which include depression and alternating periods of depression and mania (intense excitement), affected 6 percent of the adults studied. Schizophrenia, the most severely disabling of mental illnesses, was found in about 1 percent of the population.

The same survey showed that, while the overall rates of mental illness for men and women are similar, the most common diagnoses for women are phobias and depressions, whereas for men the most common diagnoses are alcohol abuse and dependence on drugs. The study also found that the rate of mental disorders drops sharply after 45 years of age. Other evidence suggests that the prevalence of persistent and handicapping mental health problems among children aged 3 to 15 ranges from 5 to 15 percent (Commission on Mental Health, 1978). A recent epidemiological study showed that, in addition to those with diagnosed mental disorders, another 15 percent of the population show high levels of demoralization and unhappiness that are not accompanied by a diagnosable disorder (Dohrenwend and Dohrenwend, 1982). It must also be noted that the lives of 30 to 40 million people are affected because of their close ties with mentally ill individuals. (*Research on Mental Ilness and Addictive Disorders*, 1985).

Table 1-1 lists several factors that are significantly related to the presence of mental illness. It seems clear that interpersonal, economic, and educational factors play important roles in the frequency of abnormal behaviors. There is also evidence that people who have good coping skills and supportive friends and relatives are less likely to suffer psychological distress than those who do not (Horwitz, 1984).

---

□ **TABLE 1-1**
**Factors Associated with Rates of Diagnosed Mental Disorder**

---

1. *Age.* Younger people have higher rates than older people.
2. *Marital Status.* Separated, divorced, and single people have higher rates than the marrried and widowed.
3. *Education.* Less educated people have higher rates than people who have more education.
4. *Personal Income.* The lower the income, the higher the rates.
5. *Employment Status.* Unemployed people have higher rates than employed people.
6. *Contract with Friends.* Lack of social contacts is associated with relatively high rates.
7. *Satisfaction with Relationships with Friends and Relatives.* The greater the satisfaction, the lower the rates.
8. *Marital Happiness.* The greater the degree of marital happiness, the lower the rates.

---

Based on Leaf and others, 1984.

## Cause and Prevention

A major epidemiological challenge in abnormal psychology is the need to move from obtaining accurate and meaningful estimates of different types of maladaptation to determining their causes and preventing them. Epidemiologists were acting to prevent illness when they traced cholera to the Broad Street pump. The challenge to abnormal psychology is whether the same kind of detective work can prevent and eventually aid in unraveling the complex cause-and-effect relationships involved in maladaptive behavior. For example, we know that there are significant correlations between depression and being female, between suicide and being an older white male, between drug addiction and being a member of an urban black group, and between schizophrenia and failure. Why do these relationships exist? Answers to questions like these should lay the groundwork for better treatment and prevention.

One can compare the types and recorded frequencies of disorders in a population by using statistics from different periods. However, these comparisons are sometimes confusing, because in addition to any real changes that may occur, statistics reflect many other things, such as changes in diagnostic criteria as well as social and political changes. **Diagnosis,** or the way disorders are defined and patients labeled, changes from time to time, and as a result different frequencies are reported for certain disorders.

The effects of social changes, together with changes in diagnostic fashions, can be seen in the following examples.

1. The number of cases diagnosed as alcoholism has increased sharply, to the point where alcoholism is now one of the most frequently used diagnostic categories.
2. The number of children who receive treatment for childhood disorders has increased sharply.

In the first case, in many states alcoholism is now treated as a maladaptive behavior rather than as a crime. This means that many people who would have been dealt with by the criminal justice system are now showing up as mental health cases. In the second example, facilities for treating children are more available, and a variety of effective psychological methods now exist to deal with many childhood problems; as a result of both of these factors, figures showing increases in treatment for childhood disorders do not necessarily indicate any change in the prevalence of such disorders.

Many other examples of the effect of social change on statistics could be cited. In the past, many old people who could not care for themselves ended up in state mental hospitals. The recent use of nursing homes for this group has reduced the rate of hospitalization of the elderly for mental disorders. However, there have been increases in admission rates for younger age groups, probably also as a result of social change. The age groups under 24 have shown the greatest percentage increase in mental hospital admission in recent years. At present the 25–44-year-old age group has the highest rate of admissions (2,727 per 100,000 population), followed by the 18–24-year-old group (2,299 per 100,000). Figure 1–5 shows the percent distribution of admissions to mental health facilities by age.

Another variable that affects the number of cases reported is the availability of mental health services. Not only does the number of beds reserved for patients with mental health problems (often called psychiatric beds) vary from one state to another (see Figure 1–6), but the total number of such beds has declined. To some extent the decrease in hospital beds is linked with

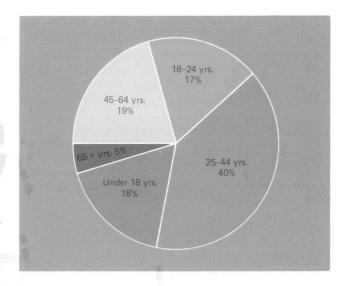

**FIGURE 1–5**
Percentages of people in different age groups who are treated at different types of clinical centers. The percentages do not add to 100 because of rounding. (adapted from Rosenstein and Millazo-Sayre, 1981)

**FIGURE 1–6**
The number of hospital beds reserved for mental health patients varies widely. This map shows the beds available per each 100,000 of state population in the United States (Redick and others, 1984, p. 22).

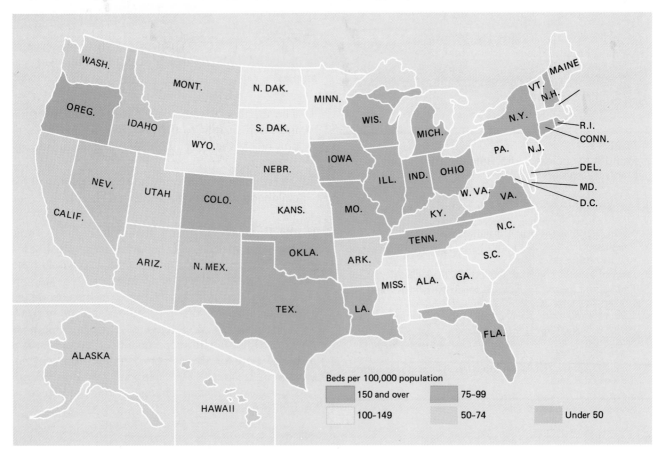

(a)

(b)

(c)

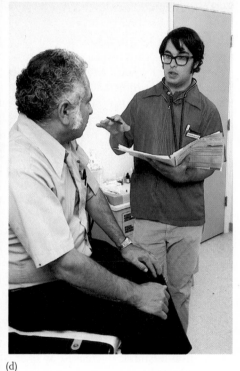

(d)

(e)

**FIGURE 1-7**
Many communities have several mental health services available to residents. Community mental health centers (a) provide many services, ranging from traditional, individual, group, and behavioral therapy (b), to supportive activities that help integrate isolated people into the community, as well as day hospital centers that permit structured activities and socialization for clients (c). With this kind of help, families often are able to care for the mentally ill at home over a long period. General medical hospitals (d) often have mental health units that provide emergency care and long-term treatment, while private practitioners (e), such as clinical psychologists and psychiatrists, treat many people who seek help in coping with the problems of daily life. (Johnnie Walker, The Picture Cube; Stacy Pick/ Stock, Boston; Joseph Nettis, Photo Researchers; Michael Heron, Woodfin Camp & Associates, Michael Heron, Woodfin Camp & Associates)

an increase in low-cost community-sponsored outpatient facilities in many areas. These offer crisis intervention or short-term treatment focused on specific problems for which appropriate help might not have been available in the past.

The number of community treatment and care facilities has increased over threefold since 1955, and the trend toward treating people in the community is now firmly established. Of the estimated 3.6 million people served in mental health facilities in 1975, over 65 percent were treated on an outpatient basis (outpatient psychiatric clinics and community mental health centers combined). Figure 1–7 shows the variety of mental health facilities that are available today.

# ■ SOURCES OF HELP

## Types of Treatment Facilities

There are dramatic differences in the statistics on the populations of mental hospitals before and after 1955, the year in which the National Mental Health Study Act became law. This act, together with later legislation, led to a national commitment to treat psychiatric patients in the community if at all possible. Community-based treatment became a more realistic possibility for some disturbed individuals because of an increase in the availability of community facilities, changes in state laws regarding involuntary hospitalization and retention of disturbed individuals in mental hospitals, and the discovery that a variety of drugs effectively control much of the violent and bizarre behavior associated with mental patients. Between 1972 and 1982 there was a drop of almost 50 percent in the number of beds reserved for patients with mental health problems. The number of beds in state and county mental hospitals decreased by over 61 percent, but the number of beds in private psychiatric hospitals and in the psychiatric units of general hospitals increased by about 30 percent each year (Redick and others, 1984) (see Figure 1–8).

In recent years there has been a movement to **deinstitutionalize,** or return to the community, mental patients whose problems can be expected to continue for long periods. Under the banner of community-based care, many such people now live in nursing homes, boarding houses, residential hotels (often in undesirable neighborhoods), and subsidized apartments. This change, based partly on concern for the civil rights of the individual, is also a result of scientific advances like the use of antipsychotic drugs. These make it possible for many people to function adaptively enough so that they don't need to be institutionalized, although many

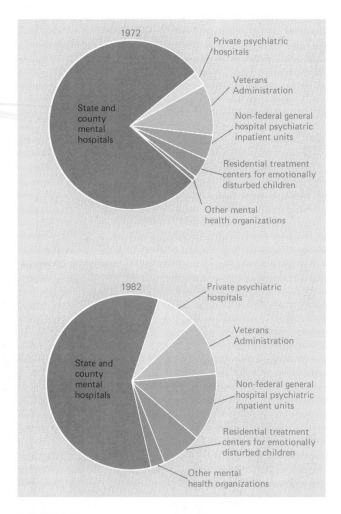

**FIGURE 1–8**
The rate per 100,000 population of hospital beds available for patients whose primary problem is a mental disorder.

of these individuals still behave in a marginal, ineffective fashion.

Most authorities agree that one in five people engage in some form of maladaptive behavior, although only a small percentage of these people come into contact with mental health services. This is true despite the fact that a recent survey of the utilization of both general medical and mental health services showed that during the six-month period studied, 16 to 25 percent of the visits to these services were for psychological problems, and a large proportion of those cases were handled by mental health specialists (Shapiro and others, 1984). The number of workers involved in providing services for these troubled people is well over 400,000. When the income losses of the clients are added to the salaries of health care personnel, the cost of mental health care comes to tens of billions of dollars per year.

## Types of Mental Health Specialists

Most of the behavior patterns with which this book deals are of special interest to three groups of mental health specialists: clinical psychologists, psychiatrists, and psychiatric social workers. A **clinical psychologist** is a psychologist with a graduate degree, usually a Ph.D., who specializes in abnormal behavior. Clinical psychologists are trained to diagnose and treat personality problems that are not medical or organic in nature. They also plan and conduct research investigations. A **psychiatrist** is a physician (an M.D.) with post graduate training and experience in treating emotional disorders. Psychiatrists have legal responsibilities in commitment proceedings and in the supervision of mental hospitals. Somatic therapies, such as drugs and electroconvulsive therapy, are administered by psychiatrists. A **psychiatric social worker** holds a graduate degree in social work and is trained to work with families and help them utilize social agencies or other community resources to get practical help with such things as finances, as well as mental health care. Psychiatric social workers are most often concerned with the link between a person who displays problematic behavior and his or her home environment. The activities of psychiatrists, clinical psychologists, and social workers often overlap. For example, all three are trained to conduct psychotherapy and counseling.

This account by a clinical psychologist accurately reflects the diversity of activities in which most clinicians engage.

*I wish the time passed more slowly because there is just so much to do. From talking to my clinician friends I know I'm not alone in feeling that way. Part of the problem is that most of us don't just do one thing. Sure, some do mainly therapy and others are primarily diagnosticians. But most of us do many things.*

*Take me, for example. I work in a big-city general hospital that has two wards for psychiatric cases and a large outpatient clinic. Many of these patients are not in very good contact with reality. In some cases police officers picked them up because they were wandering aimlessly around town in the middle of winter, in the dead of night. In other cases, they are people who have had some recent situational stress and are just not able to come to terms with it.*

*In still other cases, physicians who have patients on other wards in the hospital ask us for help. Yesterday, for example, a surgeon referred a case to me because the patient, who is supposed to undergo abdominal surgery tomorrow, has been in such a psychological panic that the doctor felt something had to be done—and he didn't know what to do. So far, I've talked with the patient*

*twice. Really, all I did was listen and let her ventilate her feelings. You'd be amazed how much just listening in a sympathetic and supportive manner does to help a person who is going through a stressful situation. When I told the surgeon that this patient was very worried about getting too strong a dose of anesthetic and dying, he was amazed. He said the patient had never mentioned that worry to him.*

*About 20 percent of my time is spent dealing with problems that nonpsychiatric physicians need help with. Perhaps 30 percent is spent doing therapy either on the wards or in the outpatient clinic. Another 20 percent involves administering psychological tests to patients with particular problems. The rest of the time I do research. That's what usually gets squeezed out when a number of pressing clinical problems arise. That's when I most need a time-stretcher. But all the pressure is nothing compared to how much I like what I'm doing. I wouldn't trade with anybody.*

The work of professionals in the mental health field is especially challenging because it requires the ability to think on one's feet, correctly and quickly size up a problem ("Is this person depressed enough to be thinking about suicide?"), and devise appropriate and sometimes unusual treatment plans for clients. This means that while clinicians strive for complete objectivity in their work and try to use proven techniques, they often must devise on-the-spot tactics to deal with the particular problem confronting them.

Clinicians emphasize the clinical or case study method, which involves an in-depth study of the individual. Each case seems to be different because of the particular circumstances surrounding the case and because troubled people more often than not leave out important information in telling their stories to clinicians. Complicating each case is the client's frequent failure to remember significant experiences and the feelings and thoughts related to them. Each case study thus is unique, although with experience clinicians become sensitive to commonalities that aid them in understanding and helping people.

## ■ RESEARCH IN ABNORMAL PSYCHOLOGY

The scientific method has greatly increased our understanding of abnormal behavior, how to treat it, and how to prevent it. As a consequence, observation and fact have replaced belief and hope in efforts to help people who suffer from behavior disorders.

Some scientists have contributed to clinical progress either by accident or as an offshoot of some other interest. For example, some advances in the development of tranquilizing drugs came from the observation that drugs that were being used for other purposes also decreased anxiety. However, most of the scientific information on which contemporary abnormal psychology is based comes from in-depth studies of deviant people. Although researchers may differ in their interpretation of data, they agree that careful observation is essential for scientific progress.

## Observing Behavior

Certain sciences, such as astronomy and anatomy, are basically descriptive in nature. Scientists in those two disciplines concentrate on using careful observations to describe heavenly or earthly bodies. Psychologists also do research that is descriptive in nature. By describing various behaviors and the specific circumstances under which they seem to occur, researchers can obtain important information about cause-and-effect relationships. Observation and description are often the first steps in the scientific process; eventually they lead to the formulation of hypotheses that can be tested experimentally and applied in clinical situations. As can be seen in the following description, observation plays an important role in psychological treatment.

> I noticed that Mr. R. never looked directly at me. He answered my questions but always looked the other way. He seemed terribly shy and afraid. I was tempted to ask him what he was afraid of, but decided not to because he might take my comment as a criticism.

Some clinicians might have decided to ask Mr. R. about his apparent fearfulness. However, all would agree on the importance of carefully observing and noting his anxious behavior.

Some observations are easier to make than others. It doesn't take years of scientific training to evaluate objectively how well or poorly a dog or a tulip has adapted to its environment. In a sense, the researcher is a disinterested observer in the world of the robin and the redwood. For example, the behavior of lemmings, which periodically throw themselves into the sea in what appears to be mass suicide, arouses no public outcries.

People cannot be completely disinterested observers of themselves, however. Personal values, goals, and interests, together with cultural norms, influence our judgments about the success or failure of human adaptation. For example, in a society that did not make judgments about the private sexual activities of its members, homosexuals would be seen as unusual but not as objects of concern. On the other hand, a society that believes homosexuality to be undesirable and illegal creates for itself, in a manner of speaking, a problem of maladaptation. Maladaptation therefore is neither a universal nor a timeless concept. Behavior that may be quite adaptive in one society may be a failure in another.

With this in mind, how do scientists study human behavior objectively? They record responses, describe events and the conditions surrounding them, and then draw inferences about causes. In order to overcome the effects of personal bias, several observers make reports on each of the individuals or events under study. Reliability increases when these observers have a common frame of reference, agree on which particular aspects of behavior they want to emphasize, and do not have to draw too many inferences from their observations. Observational methods are used in specially created laboratory conditions as well as in naturally occurring situations.

Observation is more than simply using one's eyes in a seemingly straightforward way. Certain questions must be asked first: What types of responses should be selected for observation? How capable is the observer of making reliable and unbiased observations? Will the observer's presence influence the behavior that he or she wants to study? Is it preferable to observe behavior within naturally occurring settings or under controlled laboratory conditions? Should observations be limited to motor responses (walking, running), verbal responses (phone conversations, requests for help), or expressive behavior (smiling, crying)? How long a period is needed for reliable observation? Is time sampling needed—that is, should observations be gathered during several different time intervals? Even mental patients who hallucinate frequently do not engage in this kind of behavior all the time; time sampling can provide data on the conditions under which certain types of responses are most likely to occur.

Reliable observations can provide useful records of both the incidence of behavior in a given environment and the events that elicit and maintain it. An example of how observational research can correct common-sense but incorrect assumptions is found in a study of the frequency of interactions between patients and staff on a mental hospital ward (Eldred and others, 1964). One might assume that the staff members' goal of helping their patients would lead them to spend most of their time interacting with the patients. However, as Figure 1-9 shows, the rate at which staff members interacted with other staff members was approximately double the rate at which they interacted with patients. The low rate of interaction between patients also seems surprising, but it is typical of the social isolation found on the wards of many mental hospitals.

Although they are subjective and therefore are sus-

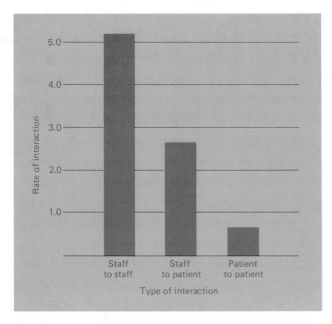

**FIGURE 1-9**
Rates of interaction for different patient and staff relationships. (adapted from Eldred and others, 1964, p. 4)

ceptible to personal bias, **self-observations** can be useful in clinical research. For example, a patient who had been admitted to a mental hospital because of depression was asked to keep track of her mood (level of sadness) and activity (number of social exchanges with hospital staff or other patients). Figure 1–10 shows a progressively less depressed mood and increased social activity during her first 15 days of hospitalization. In this case, there was good agreement between the pa-

tient's self-observations and the observations made by the hospital staff. This will not always be the case. As we all know, the people with whom we come into contact in our daily lives may not see us as we see ourselves (see Figure 1–11).

Self-observations are useful in keeping records of the responses to clinical treatment. In the case of the patient whose self-observations are recorded in Figure 1–10, the treatment was complex, consisting of a benign hospital environment, daily individual and group psychotherapy, and medication. It would be interesting to compare the self-observation records of groups of comparable patients whose treatment consisted of only one of these elements—the hospital environment, psychotherapy, or medication alone—as well as all the possible combinations of these treatments.

Studies conducted in ongoing clinical settings often do not permit complete control over all relevant factors. Although the inability to exercise full control over the situation may pose some methodological problems, the fact that research is conducted in the "real world" probably increases the applicability of the findings. A study entitled *On Being Sane in Insane Places* provides an example. The researcher wanted to know what happens when people who have been diagnosed as mentally ill begin to act completely sane after they have been hospitalized (Rosenhan, 1973). Are they immediately recognized as sane and released from the hos-

**FIGURE 1-10**
The mood and activity changes in a patient treated for depression. The patient's mood ratings are based on her self-observations.

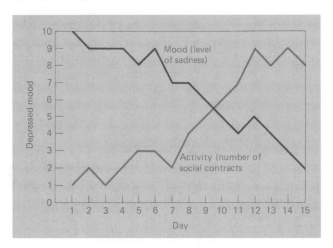

**FIGURE 1-11**
"You are fair, compassionate, and intelligent, but you are *perceived* as biased, callous, and dumb." Drawing by Mankoff; © 1985 The New Yorker Magazine, Inc.

"You are fair, compassionate, and intelligent, but you are *perceived* as biased, callous, and dumb."

pital, or does the label "mentally ill" affect the way their behavior is perceived by the staff?

Eight normal individuals were admitted to mental hospitals when they telephoned the hospitals and complained that they were hearing voices. They falsified their names and occupations (several were psychiatrists or psychologists) but otherwise gave their true life histories, except for their description of their "symptoms." All except one received a diagnosis of schizophrenia, a serious behavior disorder that is characterized by disorganized thought processes and inappropriate emotional responses. Once they had been admitted to the hospitals, however, the "patients" acted as normal as possible.

Were these "patients" immediately detected as impostors? Not at all. No staff member in any of the hospitals ever expressed any suspicion of them. (It is interesting to note, however, that other patients on the wards frequently suspected that the false patients were impostors.) Although the false patients were soon highly motivated to obtain a release from the hospital, their hospitalization periods ranged from 7 to 52 days, with an average stay of 19 days.

The hospital staff members were understandably conditioned to see their patients as mentally ill, since most of their patients are truly disturbed, and this conditioning strongly influenced their perceptions of the false patients. They sometimes saw evidence of mental illness in the most innocent behaviors. For example, at one hospital mealtimes were the most exciting events of the day, and patients would often start gathering before it was time to eat. One psychiatrist pointed to a group of patients waiting outside the lunchroom and remarked to a group of staff members that this behavior reflected the unconscious "oral-incorporative needs" that are symptomatic of schizophrenia. If patients became justifiably angry with staff members, their anger was almost always attributed to their illness rather than to the behavior of the staff. A later examination of hospital records also disclosed that because the clinicians who wrote the diagnostic reports were aware that the false patients had complained of hearing voices, they often distorted the facts in the patients' life histories to fit their belief that the patients were schizophrenic.

Thus the label of schizophrenic persisted long after the behaviors that led to the original diagnosis had ceased. Every false patient except one (who was still diagnosed as schizophrenic) was discharged with the diagnosis of **schizophrenia in remission** which meant that the disorder was assumed to be present but not in an active form. Perhaps one of the most damaging effect of labels like "crazy" and "mentally ill" is that the patients themselves may come to accept them and be-

have accordingly. The effects of labeling (having a diagnosis attached to the individual) influence the observations of both patients and clinicians and also influence how those observations are interpreted.

The value of observations is greatest when what is to be observed is defined explicitly. Four types of data are of special interest in observational research:

1. The stimuli that elicit particular types of responses—for example, the influence of family members' behavior (such as criticism or hostility) on a person who is prone to become depressed.
2. The subjective response to the stimuli—for example, the person's feelings when he or she is criticized.
3. The behavioral response to the stimuli—for example, the person's level of social activity after receiving criticism.
4. The consequences of the behavior—for example, how does the environment respond when the person behaves in a depressed manner?

The types of observations made and the observational methods employed depend on a number of factors, including the hypothesis being investigated and the situations in which the observations must be made. Observations might be made by means of hidden videotaping equipment, by visible observers who do not interact with the people they are studying, or by participant observers who become actively involved in the behavior they are observing. Each of these methods has its advantages and disadvantages. For example, secret videotaping allows us to observe behavior without the knowledge of the individual who is being observed, but many scientists object to this technique on ethical grounds. Participant and nonparticipant observation have been used by anthropologists and sociologists as well as by psychologists. However, any observer may affect people's behavior simply by being present. Participant observers may damage their objectivity by becoming overinvolved with the people they are studying. Nonparticipant observers may come to superficial conclusions because they are not involved enough. Each of these techniques can be valuable, and each has both supporters and critics.

## The Role of Theory

Scientists like to proceed from observation to theory because they want to figure out why or how a particular phenomenon occurs. Behaving just as lay people would, they use reason, logic, and sometimes simple guesswork to arrive at an initial, tentative explanation.

However, whereas casual observers may be satisfied with such a tentative answer, scientists recognize it as only tentative and go on to test their understanding by means of additional observations. They formulate an "if . . . then . . ." hypothesis that can be tested (for example, "If children are frustrated, then they are likely to behave aggressively"). They then proceed to collect the observations needed to either support or refute the hypothesis. If the hypothesis is supported by their observations, they return to their original "Why?" question and attempt to formulate increasingly broad concepts and principles that go beyond their observations. This is the way theories are developed.

Good theories have a number of functions. First, they are able to incorporate many existing facts, observations, and relationships within a single, broad explanatory framework. Second, additional hypotheses may be derived from the theory and tested, and may lead to new observations. In this way theories provide a foundation on which to build knowledge. If new observations do not support the theory, it may be modified or discarded. However, it will still have served a valuable function by leading to the discovery of new knowledge and to the development of an even better and more inclusive theory.

In order for a theory to be useful, it must be capable of being tested and refuted. It should be able to specify the types of relationships that are not possible as well as those that are. If it seems able to account for everything and anything, even seemingly contradictory facts, it is not a good scientific theory. The essence of the scientific method is systematic observation and the use of objective procedures to identify cause-and-effect relationships.

## The Research Journey

Saying that research goes from observation to theory is a little like going on an automobile trip. There is a lot more to the journey than knowing where one is and where one wants to go. What route should be followed? Will there be detours? Would bad weather make a difference? How should one prepare for the trip? Following are some of the important steps in the scientist's research journey.

1. *Specifying the topic as clearly as possible.* Suppose you are intrigued by psychotherapy. Why are you drawn to that topic? Is it because you think verbal interchanges are crucial to achieving therapeutic change? Or are you more interested in the interpersonal relationship between client and therapist?

2. *Reviewing the relevant literature.* Some library work can save a researcher a lot of time and frustration. Studying the pertinent books and journals can answer many questions: How have other people dealt with this idea? What were the outcomes of their research?

3. *Defining the variables.* A variable is any aspect of a person, group, or setting that is measured for the purposes of the study in question. **Independent variables** are manipulated by the researcher in order to investigate their effects on particular outcomes, which are called **dependent variables**.

4. *Developing a specific hypothesis.* A hypothesis is a statement to be proved, an idea that has been formulated so that it may be evaluated using scientific methods. A hypothesis is a kind of educated guess that states a predicted relationship between events or variables. It is typically stated in the form, "If A occurs, then B will occur."

5. *Selecting a research strategy.* What plan of action will permit the hypothesis to be tested? Does the researcher plan to see each subject on one occasion (for example, at the beginning or end of psychotherapy), or will several observations be necessary in order to test the hypothesis? Should an experiment be conducted? Conducting an experiment means systematically varying one or more conditions for some groups but not for others. Is experimental research possible in a particular clinical setting?

6. *Conducting the study.* The research should be carried out objectively enough to permit others to repeat (replicate) it. Therefore, all the steps in the research process must be specified. For example, how was the sample of subjects selected? Were the subjects chosen on the basis of age, sex, or intelligence? If so, the selection variables must be specified.

7. *Analyzing the results.* How did the group or groups perform? What is the likelihood that the results are due to chance? An analysis of research results usually includes making a distribution of the scores obtained by subjects; calculating relevant **descriptive statistics**, the numerical measures (scores) that enable a researcher to describe certain aspects of subjects' performance (for example, the mean or average); and calculating **inferential statistics**, the statistics that are used for judgments about the probability that the results are due to chance.

8. *Reporting research findings.* Writing up a piece of research not only permits communication of ideas and findings to others but also forces the researcher to think through all that he or she has done and the meaning that might be attached to it. Going public serves an important communication function. The

scientific journey would be much less valuable if research results were not written up and published.

## Types of Research

In evaluating a hypothesis it is important to decide on the observations that are relevant to it and the conditions under which those observations should be made. The conditions might be the same for all subjects or different for designated groups. In **assessment** studies, the conditions are the same, the aim being to gather information under standard conditions for purposes of description and prediction. In **experimental** studies, the conditions are varied so as to test hypotheses about the effects of the conditions.

**Assessment Studies**   The purpose of **assessment** is to provide an objective account of behavior at any given time. Assessment methods range from recording how often certain responses occur in natural situations to noting the types of behavior displayed in specially created settings such as interviews. Assessment is not simply a measuring device; it is a general approach to observing and interpreting behavior. As such, it extends beyond traditional procedures such as interviews and tests in much the same way that the concept of I.Q. and the judgments based on it extend beyond the tests used to measure it.

Assessment data can be used in a number of ways. They might be used to predict future behavior, to identify correlates of present behavior, or to measure the likelihood of a positive reaction to therapeutic procedures. For example, a study of junior high school students might indicate the type of person who is most likely to engage in antisocial behavior in the future; a comparison of the assessed characteristics of depressed individuals might point out those who are most likely to commit suicide; and a comparison of the personality traits of people who respond positively to psychotherapy and those who respond negatively might help in screening candidates for therapy. Assessment research ranges from in-depth studies of one or a few people to surveys of large populations.

When people are assessed, several kinds of data are usually gathered, including age, sex, personal history, and number of previous hospitalizations. This information can be intercorrelated and the degree of relationship among the items determined. This type of study—called a **correlation study**—can be useful in a limited way. Correlational studies tells us only that two factors are related; they do not tell us how or why. Just knowing that variables A and B have a high degree of association does not tell us whether A causes B or B causes A, as Figure 1–12 humorously illustrates. Per-

**FIGURE 1–12**
"Which is it—do people hate us because we dress this way, or do we dress this way because people hate us?" (By permission of Sidney Harris and *Saturday Review World* © 1987 by Sidney Harris)

haps another variable, C, has caused the correlation between A and B. There is also a fourth possibility, that the correlation is simply a coincidence with no causality involved.

For example, a study done in eleven countries found that anxiety was positively correlated with the rate of alcoholism (Lynn and Hampson, 1970). In other words, the more anxiety the population attributed to itself, the higher the alcoholism rate. This is a provocative finding, but its meaning requires extensive inquiry. Does it mean that anxiety causes alcoholism, that alcoholism causes anxiety, that some other factor (such as income level or marital status) might cause both alcoholism and anxiety, or that the relationship between anxiety and alcoholism is accidental?

Despite their limitations, correlational studies have much to contribute to the study of abnormal behavior. This is particularly true when, for either practical or ethical reasons, it is not possible to manipulate conditions experimentally. Suppose, for example, that we wanted to study the possibility that having been abused as a child increases the likelihood that one will abuse one's own children. It would be highly unethical as well as impractical to subject an experimental group of children to severe abuse and then wait twenty years to see whether or not they beat their own children. However, information about such a correlation could be of great value in understanding the causes of abuse, and could perhaps be used in selecting high-risk parents for programs designed to prevent abuse.

As an alternative, we might find ways to measure the amount of abuse parents received when they were children as well as the extent to which they now abuse their own children. For each of a large group of parents, we could obtain a score for each of the two abuse variables—each parent's reports of being abused as a child and some measure of his or her abusiveness as a parent—and then determine what kind of relationship, if any, exists between the two sets of measures. The knowledge that being abusive and having been abused are correlated provides a potentially useful clue to how child abuse could be prevented. Perhaps parental counseling and training for people who were abused as children would have preventive value.

If we find a positive correlation, we might be tempted to conclude from the data that child abuse is caused by parents' having been abused as children. This is certainly a possibility, but there are other possible explanations for the positive correlation. It may be, for example, that guilt about abusing their own child causes parents to exaggerate the extent to which they were abused as children. Another possibility is that some other variable that was not measured in the study (such as some form of psychological disturbance) actually caused the person to be a target of abuse as a child and causes him or her to become a child abuser as an adult (Belsky, 1980). We simply cannot be certain which of these and other possible causal relationships may account for the positive correlation between recalled childhood experiences and present adult behavior.

One way to deal with a problem of this kind is the **longitudinal study**, whose goal is to observe and record the behavior of people over long periods—perhaps twenty or thirty years. This type of study is costly, time-consuming, and often frustrating to the investigator, who may not live to see the study completed. There are other problems as well. The nature of the group under study may change greatly as people move or die. The methods chosen at the beginning of the study may become outdated. The importance of new variables that were ignored in the study may become recognized by the scientific community. For these reasons, few longitudinal studies are done. Nevertheless, because they deal so directly with the developmental process, the value of such studies is widely recognized.

One type of research that avoids some of these problems but still has longitudinal features is the **follow-up study**. In such studies, people are given an initial assessment and are contacted months or years later to see whether there have been any changes in their behavior during that time. Follow-up studies are used to assess the effects of different therapeutic approaches as well as to observe the development of particular conditions. For example, a follow-up study might be carried out to determine how well people who have been discharged from a mental hospital have adjusted to life in the community.

The **cross-sectional study** is a useful way to assess the views or status of one or more groups of people at any given time. Cross-sectional studies are the most common assessment method used by social scientists. Because no follow-up is required, these studies are less time-consuming and expensive than longitudinal studies. A public opinion poll is an example of a cross-sectional study that is carried out in the field. Developmental psychologists often use the cross-sectional approach in the laboratory or in natural settings to compare children's behavior, attributes, abilities, and concerns at different ages.

**Experimental Studies** Experimental research involves the observation and assessment of behavior, but with an important additional ingredient. **In experiments**, variables can be manipulated. This degree of control is impossible in many real-life situations. Because experimenters can control variables in a laboratory, they can more easily isolate and record the causes of the behavior they observe. For certain purposes research with animals is valuable because it permits the manipulation of experimental variables and the control of unwanted factors to an extent that usually is not possible with people (see Box 1–1).

The variables that are manipulated by researchers in experiments are **independent variables; dependent variables** are any observed changes in behavior that are due to the manipulation. Psychological experiments are designed to discover relationships between environmental conditions and behavior. For example, an experiment might be done to discover the relationship between the temperature in a room and people's performance on a test. In this experiment the independent variable would be the temperature. The experimenter would use a different temperature for each experimental group. The dependent variable would be the test scores. If the average test scores for the groups were different, the experimenter would conclude that this result was related to the different temperatures in the rooms in which the groups worked. Asking people how they felt under both conditions

# ■BOX 1–1 UNDERSTANDING ABNORMAL BEHAVIOR THROUGH ANIMAL RESEARCH

(a)                (b)

**FIGURE 1–13** (a) All monkeys go through a clinging stage, but monkeys who are reared without their mothers show a greatly prolonged period of clinging. (b) A young monkey, still in the clinging stage, can be an effective therapist for an older monkey who was reared in isolation. (University of Wisconsin Primate Laboratory)

For obvious reasons, certain types of experimentation cannot be carried out using human subjects. For example, it would be impossible—and unethical, even if it were possible—to try to observe and control the course of a person's life. However, the telescoped life span of nonhuman primates like monkeys makes it possible to study the long-term consequences of early experiences. Under controlled conditions these experiences can be observed either as they unfold or after experimental manipulations. Animal studies permit levels of control and ways of carrying out experimental manipulations that are not possible with humans. As a consequence, animal experimentation plays an important role in the study of abnormal behavior.

Animal studies can be used to investigate both biological and social factors in behavior. One example of research with a biological focus is the investigation of the effects of drugs. Researchers have fed monkeys large doses of drugs that are believed to cause depression and have noted their effects on the animals' behavior. Such experiments have shown that depression-inducing drugs lead to decreases in the general activity and exploratory behavior of monkeys.

A group of drugs called amphetamines, which function as stimulants, produce psychotic symptoms in people. If the effects of amphetamines on animals were known, animals that had been in-

jected with amphetamines could be given antipsychotic drugs to determine whether they are able to counteract the amphetamine's psychosis-inducing action. Research has shown that rats and humans exhibit some similar symptoms when treated with amphetamines, and we now know that certain antipsychotic drugs are effective in reversing the effects of amphetamines on rats.

People who abuse amphetamines frequently engage in ritualized, stereotyped behavior such as repetitively disassembling complex objects like radios. Not surprisingly, reassembly of such objects requires more concentration than they can muster. Rats that are given high doses of amphetamines develop a similar syndrome called **stereotypy**. They pace back and forth, sniffing the corners of their cages and chewing repetitively on the bars. Studies are being conducted on the brains of rats treated with either or both amphetamines and antipsychotic drugs. These studies will help identify the areas of the brain and the mechanisms that are related to the drug effects.

Animal subjects have been used in another aspect of research on amphetamines and other stimulants. In a number of studies, stimulant drugs have been shown to increase an animal's sensitivity to reinforcement. That is, the drug increases the effects of reward and possibly even punishment so that the animal learns habits more quickly and with greater success. This finding is provocative, because stimulant drugs often make hyperactive children more responsive to reward and punishment.

In the course of their research on dogs, Samuel Corson and his co-workers (1976), noticed that some of the dogs were quite restless and were not very responsive to rewards and punishments. They administered a variety of drugs to the dogs with no beneficial effect until they tried amphetamine. The researchers found that the stimulant medication quieted the dogs and that, like hyperactive children, they were then better able to learn. An examination of the hyperactive dogs' brains showed that they were deficient in certain neurotransmitters, chemicals that make possible the movement of nerve impulses. The identification of this deficiency opens up the possibility of a better understanding of the nervous system abnormalities that cause hyperactivity and the way therapeutic drugs like amphetamine act to alleviate this condition.

Another example of animal studies with a biological focus can be seen in the work of Harry Harlow and his co-workers. They were interested in the effects of early experience on the later development of monkeys. Infant monkeys show a number of innate behaviors, such as clinging and sucking.

When the infants are separated from their mothers and reared with other young monkeys, their clinging behavior lasts much longer than it does for mother-reared monkeys (see Figure A). Young monkeys also begin to show innate fear behavior when they are about two months old. When they are reared with other monkeys, the fear behaviors do not disappear but last into adulthood (Suomi and Harlow, 1978).

When infant monkeys are not only separated from their mothers but reared in isolation for six months, they show several disturbed behaviors. They suck themselves, constantly rock back and forth, and are very timid. When their isolation ends, they behave very aggressively toward other monkeys. The research showed, however, that monkeys that are reared in isolation for six months can later develop normally if they are "treated" by therapist monkeys. The most successful therapist monkeys were three-month-olds who still showed a great deal of clinging behavior. They clung to the isolates affectionately (see Figure B). The isolates soon responded, and within six months their behavior was hard to distinguish from that of their therapists (Suomi and Harlow, 1972).

would be simpler, but the results would not be nearly as accurate or objective.

A study by Abrams and Wilson (1979) illustrates the power of the experiment in identifying a factor that is relevant to a particular type of behavior. The researchers were interested in the relationship between alcohol consumption and social anxiety in women. The subjects were paid female undergraduates selected from volunteers who reported only moderate drinking. Two independent variables, alcohol dose and expectancy, were manipulated by randomly assigning subjects to one of four groups: expect alcohol and receive alcohol, expect alcohol and receive placebo, expect placebo and receive alcohol, or expect placebo and receive placebo. (A **placebo** is an inactive substance whose effect on a person's behavior depends on his or her expectations.) The experimental manipulation was **double-blind**; that is, neither the subject nor the experimenter knew what the subject was drinking. All of the subjects were told that both alcohol and nonalcohol groups would be tested in the study and that they had been randomly assigned to either the alcohol-only group or the tonic-only group. Under the guise of preparing for a breathalyzer test, the subjects gargled with a mouthwash that reduced their sensitivity to taste. The drinks were mixed from labeled bottles in full view of the subject, and the glasses in the "receive placebo" group were

surreptitiously smeared with vodka. Finally, the breathalyzer was altered to give false feedback.

After the drink manipulation and the breathalyzer test, the subjects were placed in a controlled social interaction with a male confederate. The dependent variables included physiological measures of anxiety (heart rate and skin conductance) taken before, during, and after the interaction; self-report measures of anxiety taken before and after the interaction; and observer ratings of the anxiety shown by each subject during the interaction.

The experiment showed that women who believed that they had consumed alcohol, whether or not their drinks actually contained alcohol, showed significantly increased levels of physiological arousal compared with those who believed that they had drunk only tonic water. According to ratings made by observers, subjects who believed that they had consumed alcohol showed greater discomfort in the social interaction (see Figure 1-13). This experiment highlights the decisive role that subjects' expectations can play in their behavior and in their ability to cope.

There are two general types of experiments. The first type is the **hypothesis-testing experiment**, in which the researcher makes a prediction based on a theory and then conducts an experiment to see whether the prediction is correct.

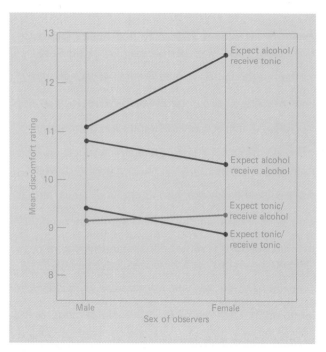

**FIGURE 1-14**
Mean discomfort ratings by drink content, expectancy, and sex made by observers who rated videotapes of subjects' social interactions. [From Abrams, D.B. and Wilson, O.T. (1979), Effects of alcohol on social anxiety in women. *Journal of Abnormal Psychology, 88,* 161–173. Copyright (c) 1979 by the American Psychological Association. Reprinted by permission of the author.]

*I'm interested in determining whether, if children have an early close, secure relationship with an adult, what psychologists call attachment, they will have fewer problems getting along with other children when they enter school. My hypothesis is that if children are securely attached when they are very young, their social skills will be better and they will be less likely to be described as having behavior problems.*

*I have some records of nursery school children's behavior in a situation designed to measure attachment. In that research setup, a young child and his or her mother sit together in an attractive room with some playthings. Then a "stranger" (a research worker) comes into the room and sits down. After a while the mother leaves; she comes back a short time later. The way the child behaves, both while the mother is gone and when she returns, is a measure of attachment. If, the child does not cling to the mother when the stranger enters, and if the child continues to play with the toys, is not distressed when she leaves, and greets her warmly but does not cling to her when she returns, the child is said to be securely attached.*

*Now those children are in first grade and I am asking their teachers to rate their behavior in class, how well*

*they are learning, and how they get along with other children. I'm also doing some behavioral observations in the classroom and giving each child a simple social skills test during an individual session. The ratings, observations data, and tests will be my dependent measures. My independent variable will be the attachment ratings for the children when they were 18 months old.*

The second type of experiment, the **behavior-change experiment**, is concerned primarily with the development of therapeutic techniques. It is also designed to test a hypothesis, but in this case the goal is to make an immediate contribution to the development of practical rehabilitative techniques. For example, a behavior-change experiment might test the hypothesis that supervised work experiences are significantly more effective than group psychotherapy in changing the attitudes and behavior of convicted criminals. The researcher who wrote the following account is studying schizophrenics. However, his goal is a very practical one: to improve the social skills of schizophrenics.

*I'm trying to devise procedures that will help hospitalized schizophrenics return to the community more quickly and be more effective when they make their return. My approach is to start with one obvious deficiency of schizophrenics: inadequate social skills. They just don't do a very good job of relating to other people. What I've been doing is finding out, by asking them questions and observing them, what social lacks schizophrenics have; for example, they have a lot of trouble introducing themselves to strangers and making small talk. I'm modeling—that is, demonstrating—for them various ways of being effective in social situations. I also have a control group that doesn't get the social skills training, as well as a group that participates in discussions about how to handle social situations but gets no modeling. If I'm on the right track, follow-ups should show that the modeling group is better able to adjust back into the community than the control group and maybe also better than the discussion group.*

## Ethical Aspects of Research

Regardless of the scholarly reasons for doing research, researchers should not place people in either physical or psychological jeopardy without their informed consent. Subjects should be informed regarding what the experiment is about and any hazards associated with participation in it. They also must be clearly told that they are free to withdraw from the experiment at any time. If deception must be used, the subjects must be completely debriefed after the experiment, and the entire procedure must be explained to them. Special measures must be taken to protect confidentiality.

As a result of the increasing emphasis on the protection and welfare of both human and animal subjects used in psychological research, psychologists now must restrict their experimentation with certain groups of people who are not in a position to give their consent, such as children, the mentally retarded, and seriously disturbed mental patients. When such people, or others who are not able to give their consent, are involved, consent must be obtained from their parents or guardians. Strict guidelines are also being developed for research in prisons. No prisoner can be forced to participate in research or penalized for refusal to do so, and in the case of rehabilitative programs, prisoners must be permitted to share in decisions concerning program goals. Researchers must adhere to the ethics of research or risk serious legal and professional consequences.

# ■ STUDY OUTLINE

### WHAT IS ABNORMAL BEHAVIOR?

1. Abnormal psychology deals with how it feels to be different, the meanings that get attached to being different, and how society deals with people whom it considers to be different.

2. Overt rejection of abnormal behavior has declined, yet there is still prejudice toward people who are noticeably deviant or have a history of mental disorder. Television and other mass media build misconceptions about what behavior is normal and what is abnormal.

3. **Adaptation** is an ongoing process that involves a balance between what people want and what their environment wants. How well a person adapts depends on his or her personal characteristics and the nature of the situations confronting him or her.

4. Maladaptive behavior not only is deviant but also causes concern in the individual, his or her family and friends, or society. Maladaptation has many causes and can range from mildly troubling fears to severe distortion of reality and inability to communicate.

### STRESS, COPING, AND VULNERABILITY

1. **Stress** refers to people's reactions to situations that pose demands, constraints, or opportunities. It is increased by unexpected change, severe crises, or critical developmental periods. **Coping skills** are techniques, such as constructive thinking and flexibility, that enable people to deal with stress, giving them some control over their behavior and over the environment.

**Vulnerability**, or the likelihood of maladaptive responses, is affected by heredity, personality, lack of certain skills, negative experiences, and certain life conditions.

2. Stress, coping, and vulnerability interact and affect a person's adaptive behavior. Clinical intervention can help people cope with stress.

### REASONS FOR CLINICAL CONTACTS

People may seek professional help because they are unhappy, because others are concerned about them, or because they are in trouble with the community or the law.

### THE EPIDEMIOLOGY OF MALADAPTIVE BEHAVIOR

1. Epidemiologists seek information about the physical and psychological adaptation of groups, especially environmental causes of conditions associated with a community's way of life. They obtain two types of information: **prevalence data**, or the frequency of occurrence of a condition at a given point in time, and **incidence data**, or the number of new cases occurring during a given period. Comparisons of statistics from different periods are confusing because of changes in the definition and labeling of disorders, as well as social and political changes such as divorce, care of the aged, and availability of mental health services.

### SOURCES OF HELP

1. Federal and local laws now encourage psychiatric treatment within the community rather than in large institutions. Community care for chronic patients is supplied by nursing homes and other special residences and is facilitated by antipsychotic drugs. Only a small percentage of people who engage in maladaptive behaviors are in contact with mental health services.

2. **Clinical psychologists** have postgraduate degrees and specialized knowledge of abnormal behavior. They diagnose and treat nonmedical personality problems and do research. **Psychiatrists**, or physicians who specialize in emotional disorders, have legal responsibilities in commitment proceedings, supervision of mental hospitals, and administration of drugs. **Psychiatric social workers** have graduate degrees in social work. They work with families and help them utilize community resources. Clinicians from all these fields are trained to do therapy and counseling.

### RESEARCH IN ABNORMAL PSYCHOLOGY

1. Observation and description of behavior, either under controlled laboratory conditions or in natural settings, can lead to inferences about its causes. Per-

sonal biases can be counteracted by the use of more than one observer. Self-observation can also be useful in clinical research. The data obtained in these ways include the stimuli that elicit particular responses, subjective and behavioral responses to particular stimuli, and the environmental consequences of certain behaviors.

2. To develop theories about why particular phenomena occur, scientists apply reason, logic, and even guesswork to their observations in order to arrive at a tentative explanation that can be tested with further observations. Good theories lay a foundation on which to build further knowledge; they must be testable and capable of being refuted.

3. The steps in scientific research are: (a) specifying the topic; (b) reviewing the literature; (c) defining the variables to be measured—both **independent variables**, those that are manipulated by the researcher, and **dependent variables** or outcomes; (d) developing a hypothesis; (e) selecting a research strategy; (f) conducting the study; (g) analyzing the results (which involves calculating **descriptive statistics**, or numerical measures, and **inferential statistics**, which are used in judging the probability that the results are due to chance); and (h) reporting the findings of the research.

4. **Assessment studies** describe and predict behavior under specific conditions. They include correlational, longitudinal, follow-up, and cross-sectional studies. **Correlational studies** tell the degree of relationship among various factors; they can be useful when it is not possible to manipulate experimental conditions. **Longitudinal studies** record behavior over long periods. In **follow-up studies**, people are contacted some time after an initial assessment to determine whether there have been any changes in their behavior. **Cross-sectional studies** assess one or more groups at a particular time.

5. In **experimental studies**, independent variables are manipulated and changes in behavior (the dependent variables) are observed in order to discover their relationships to the independent variables. In a **hypothesis-testing experiment** the researcher makes a prediction based on a theory and then conducts an experiment to see whether the prediction is correct. **Behavior-change experiments** test hypotheses that are related to possible therapeutic techniques.

6. Various ethical considerations in psychological research involve disclosing the nature of the experiment, protecting subjects' anonymity, obtaining the consent of the subjects, and not forcing participation.

# 2

# THE HISTORICAL BACKGROUND OF ABNORMAL PSYCHOLOGY

## ■ HISTORICAL VIEWS OF ABNORMAL BEHAVIOR

At this point, what you know about abnormal psychology could be compared to what you would know about your friends if all you had was current information such as their majors in college and how they furnish their rooms. To really know them, you would need to know a lot about what their life was like before you met them. The same is true for the study of abnormal psychology. Until you learn about its origins and history, you will be unable to understand it fully.

You may feel that an excursion into history is irrelevant. Because modern techniques are no doubt much more effective, enlightened, and sophisticated than those used in earlier times, why not concentrate on them instead of getting bogged down in accounts of the past? The trouble with this approach is that it misses important links between the past and the present. Much of what seems modern is an outgrowth of the past, not a rejection of it. In abnormal psychology, as in other fields of study, there are fewer completely new ideas than one might think. A review of the history of abnormal psychology provides a context within which the modern discipline can be understood.

People have always been concerned about their physical well-being, their social relationships, and their place in the universe. They have posed many questions about these issues and have evolved theories about them. Some of those theories seem almost universal.

They can be observed in many parts of the world and in many periods of human history. Perhaps the greatest benefit of studying the history of abnormal psychology is the awareness that certain theories of deviance have emerged over and over again.

One ancient theory that is still encountered today holds that abnormal behavior can be explained by the operation of supernatural and magical forces such as evil spirits or the devil. In societies that believe in this theory, therapy generally involves **exorcism,** that is, removing the evil that resides in the individual through countermagic and prayer. Although this view is most prevalent in nonliterate cultures, it is still found in industrialized societies and often exists side by side with more modern approaches. For example, many people who use folk healers also seek assistance from health care professionals (Ness and Wintrob, 1981). Professionals can improve the effectiveness of the help they provide by understanding what folk healers do and why patients seek them out.

In many societies the **shaman** or medicine man, a magician who is believed to have contact with supernatural forces, is the medium through which spirits communicate with human beings (see Figure 2–1). Through the shaman, an afflicted person can learn which spirits are responsible for his or her problem and what needs to be done to appease them. To accomplish this, the shaman conducts a seance in which he displays intense excitement and often mimics the abnormal behavior that he seeks to cure. Through mystical

**FIGURE 2–1**
A shaman anoints a man with holy water as the latter embarks on a pilgrimage. (Karl Muller, Woodfin Camp & Associates)

utterances and violent movements, and by acting out his dreams, the shaman reveals messages from the spirits. Often the liberation of an evil spirit from the patient's body is expressed through what appears to be the actual expulsion of an object, such as a stone, from the patient's ear or mouth. These rituals are based on specific theories about magic as the cause of abnormal behavior and the basis of therapeutic change.

It is tempting to view seemingly primitive beliefs about mental illness as part of the dead past. Yet the fact is that even in a relatively advanced and enlightened society like the United States there is a wide range of views about the causes of personal problems. The following case, reported in 1977, concerned a 33-year-old man from a rural area near Little Rock, Arkansas.

> *The patient had been having seizures recently and had become increasingly irritable and withdrawn from his family. When he could no longer be detained safely on the neurology service, he was transferred to the psychiatric ward, where he became increasingly more agitated, confused, and almost delirious. He became very fearful whenever people approached him, and he began to hallucinate. He finally slowed down after being given 1000 mg. of chlorpromazine (a tranquilizer), but the necessity for bed restraint remained. All neurological findings, including a brain scan, proved normal. After two weeks of hospitalization the patient suffered a cardiac arrest. All efforts to revive him failed. An autopsy provided no reason for the death. After he died, the patient's wife told staff members that her husband had been seeing a "two-headed," an older woman considered by the community to be a witch who cast spells and healed people. The widow stated that her husband had angered the two-headed and that she had caused his death. (Golden, 1977, p. 1425)*

Reports of "two-headeds" in Africa and other places describe them as people with voodoo powers that are able to cause sickness, insanity, and death. The power of such beings apparently is related to the victim's belief in them.

Another recurring theme in the history of abnormal behavior is the belief that individuals behave strangely because their bodies are not working right. Such people have something wrong with them, an organic defect that affects a specific organ rather than the whole body. The source of the presumed defect varies according to the nature of the abnormality, the society's cultural beliefs, and—particularly in the modern era—scientific knowledge.

The finding of ancient skulls with holes in them that were not caused by battle wounds has led some writers to conjecture that abnormal behavior was sometimes treated by means of a procedure called **trephination.** In this technique a sharp tool such as a stone was used to make a hole in the skull about two centimeters in diameter (see Figure 2–2). Evidence that trephination was performed as early as 3000 to 2000 B.C. has been uncovered in eastern Mediterranean and North African countries. Studies of trephined skulls suggest that the operation often was not fatal, a remarkable achievement given the difficulty of the procedure. Trephination may have been done to permit demonic spirits to escape. However, because of the absence of written records and the fact that our only data are the trephined skulls themselves, we need to be cautious in speculating about their significance.

A third general approach reflects what might be called the psychological perspective. According to this point of view, behavioral disturbances are caused by inadequacies in the way an individual thinks, feels, or perceives the world. According to the psychological perspective, people are at least potentially capable of examining their own thinking and modifying their behavior in light of that examination. Many modern psychotherapists see their task as helping people learn to think more rationally about themselves and their social relationships.

All three of these perspectives—mystical, organic,

**FIGURE 2–2**
The technique of trephining involved chipping a hole in the person's skull. The healing that took place on this skull shows that some individuals actually survived the operation. (Courtesy of American Museum of Natural History, photo by T. Bierwert)

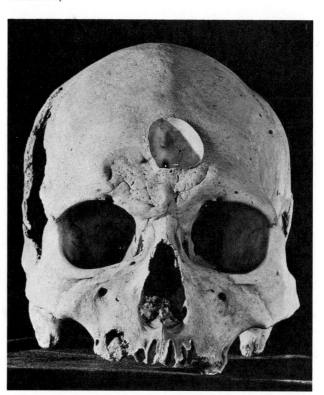

and psychological—have recurred throughout the history of Western civilization, beginning with the Greeks.

## The Ancient Greeks

The earliest writers about the psychological and organic approaches to deviance were the philosophers of ancient Greece. At the height of their civilization, the Greeks emphasized rational analysis of the natural world. The concepts of motivation and intelligence were among those that they invented in their efforts to explain the behavior they observed in everyday life. We tend to see the modern era as the period in which human beings have sought to push back the boundaries of human understanding through the application of reason. The main difference between us and the ancient Greeks is that we have access to all the knowledge that has accumulated in the past 2000 years, as well as the tools of the scientific method.

Even in ancient Greece, however, knowledge evolved over a period of several centuries. At the time that Homer created the *Iliad* and the *Odyssey* (about 800 B.C.), disturbed or psychotic behavior was interpreted as a form of punishment for offenses against the gods. ("Those whom the gods would destroy, they first make mad.") In the battle scenes in the *Iliad,* Homer typically described his heros as suddenly possessed by feelings of power that are engendered in them by the gods. States of insanity were believed to be created in the same way. Therapy took place in a group of temples dedicated to Asclepius, the god of healing. Each temple was a mazelike structure in which mental patients walked and slept and ultimately reached the center. In the process it was believed that Asclepius attended to their dreams and healed them.

In the centuries after Homer the idea that a person's life is in the hands of the gods gradually declined, at least among educated citizens. The Greek philosophers became increasingly curious about aspects of the individual that might explain normal as well as abnormal behavior. Extreme mental deviations and disorders came to be viewed as natural phenomena for which rational treatments might be developed.

Hippocrates (460–377 B.C.) looked to the brain in his efforts to explain why people behave as they do. He described the brain as the interpreter of consciousness and the body's most important organ. (Before Hippocrates' time it had been widely believed that the heart was the seat of mental and emotional life.) Hippocrates described epileptic seizures, concluded that they were caused by a diseased brain, and also wrote about depression, states of delirium, psychosis, the irrational fears that we now call phobias, and hysteria (organic symptoms in the absence of an organic disturbance).

He and his followers became known for their ability to recognize and treat mental illness. Their therapeutic techniques consisted of rest, bathing, and dieting. There is even a record of Hippocrates appearing as an expert witness at the trial of an insane person. Today physicians continue to pay their debt to Hippocrates by taking the Hippocratic oath when they graduate from medical school (see Figure 2–3).

Three other Greek philosophers—Socrates (470–399 B.C.), Plato (427–347 B.C.), and Aristotle (384–322 B.C.)—also deserve mention for their contributions to abnormal psychology. Socrates was interested in self-exploration and considered reasoning to be the cornerstone of the good life and personal happiness. He believed in using inquiry to further knowledge; his goal was to teach by asking questions instead of giving answers. Today this procedure—called the Socratic method—is a valuable teaching tool as well as a component of the scientific method.

Socrates' most famous student, Plato, developed the **organismic point of view.** In his view, behavior is a product of the totality of psychological processes. Like many modern writers, Plato believed that disturbed behavior grew out of conflicts between emotion and reason. In contrast to those who saw abnormal behavior as having a physical cause, he stressed the power of ideas, going so far as to say that the mind is the only true reality of human existence. According to Plato, the ideal individual is, above all, guided by reason. In his *Laws,* he expressed the belief that people who have lost their reason should be separated from society: "No lunatic shall be allowed to be at large in the community; the relatives of such persons shall keep them in safe custody at home by such methods as they contrive, on penalty of fine."

Aristotle, a pupil of Plato and the teacher of Alexander the Great, wrote extensively on the nature of reasoning and consciousness and also sought to analyze human emotions. He described and speculated about a number of emotional and motivational states, including anger, fear, envy, courage, hatred, and pity. He believed that anger occurred when a person was subjected to what he or she experienced as injustice or wrongdoing; he saw fear as the awareness of danger with an expectation of loss, defeat, or rejection. Like most of the Greek philosophers, Aristotle placed the highest value on reason and its application. He also believed that the various forces in the body need to be in balance for reason to prevail (see Figure 2–4).

The rational approach of the Greek philosophers laid the groundwork for modern science. It led to attempts to classify abnormal behavior according to some consistent scheme. It temporarily replaced magic and religious explanations of abnormal behavior with a

FIGURE 2-3

Hippocrates, an older contemporary of Plato, was born in 460 B.C. He attended the medical school on the island of Cos and traveled to many cities both to practice and to teach. Over the centuries his fame grew. His writings include material that today would be called textbooks, articles, case histories, and speeches. The following comments reflect his belief in the value of trying to understand mental life in terms of the physical functioning of the brain:

And men should know that from nothing else but from the brain come joys, laughter, and jests, and sorrows, griefs, despondency and lamentations. And by this, in an especial manner, we acquire wisdom and knowledge, and see and hear and know what are foul and what are fair, what sweet and what unsavory . . . and by the same organ we become mad and delirious and fears and terrors assail us, some by day, and dreams and untimely wanderings, and cares that are not suitable and ignorance of present circumstances, disquietude and unskillfulness. (The Bettmann Archives)

quest, through observation and reason, for natural causes. Except for a break during the Middle Ages, that quest has continued until the present time.

## The Middle Ages

A host of changes accompanied the decline of ancient Greek culture and the rise and fall of the Roman Empire. Perhaps the most obvious causes of these changes were the invasions of Western Europe by barbarian tribes and the growth of the Christian religion. The invaders, whose ideas were primitive compared with those of the Greeks and Romans, caused great social unrest; the Christian religion served to comfort people in troubled times. The church also acted as a unifying force when the civil government of Rome finally fell.

The unrest of the Middle Ages was intensified by nearly constant warfare as well as by the Black Death and other epidemics that came without warning and wiped out hundreds of thousands of people. During this period fear and terror spread like brush fires, causing many outbreaks of group hysteria. The nature of those outbreaks varied. Some groups of people behaved like packs of wolves (lycanthropy); others danced in the streets, making spiderlike movements (tarantism).

During the early Middle Ages the importance of the Christian spirit of charity, particularly toward stigmatized groups such as the severely mentally disturbed, cannot be overestimated. For example, in Gheel, Belgium, the church established a special institution for the care of retarded and psychotic children. As they

**FIGURE 2–4**
A pleasant and diverting environment has often been thought of as a way to help the mind regain its proper balance. This sixteenth-century engraving by the Dutch artist Lucas Van Leyden shows David, the shephard boy, playing his harp in an effort to use music therapy to decrease the symptoms of depression shown by Saul, King of the Israelites. Saul, seated at the right, shows behavior that is typical of a depressed person. He is hunched over, has a doleful expression, and is staring into space instead of responding to what is going on around him. (Stadt Bibliothek, Nurenberg)

**FIGURE 2–5**
One place where moral therapy has survived is Gheel, Belgium. Founded after the miracle cure of five "lunatics" at the shrine of St. Dymphna in the thirteenth century, the colony has continued its work to the present. Over 2000 patients like this man live in private homes under few restrictions; there they work with the inhabitants as everyday tasks until they have recovered. (Karales, Peter Arnold)

improved, the children were often placed with sympathetic families in the neighborhood of the institution (see Figure 2–5). Also during this period, music and dance were thought to cure insanity by restoring the chemical balance within the body (see Figure 2–6).

One figure in the early Christian era, the theologian and philosopher Saint Augustine (A.D. 354–430), stands out because he helped lay the groundwork for modern psychodynamic theories of abnormal behavior. Writing extensively about feelings, mental anguish, and human conflict, he was perhaps the earliest forerunner of today's psychoanalysts. It was not so much the topics he dealt with as the way he approached them that most resembles the psychoanalytic method of today. Saint Augustine used introspection, or examination of his own thoughts, feelings, and motives, to discuss mental processes like the conflict between pleasure and discipline. He worked almost ruthlessly toward a complete, if painful, self-analysis, and in his *Confessions* he revealed his innermost thoughts, temptations, and fears.

By demonstrating that introspection and exploration of the individual's emotional life could be valuable sources of psychological knowledge, Saint Augustine made an important contribution to modern abnormal psychology. Unfortunately, these efforts were not followed up during the later Middle Ages. As the church's control and influence increased, so did its role in governmental affairs, and it was religious dogma, not civil law, that became the supreme voice of authority. The church came to control the practice of medicine, defining its goals and prescribing treatments for various conditions. To the degree that this control reflected a feeling of charity toward people suffering hardships of various kinds, the church played a positive role. To the degree that it was intolerant, authoritarian, and repressive, its role was decidedly negative.

The legacy of rationality that the Middle Ages had inherited from the Greek philosophers was soon aban-

**FIGURE 2-6**
In this engraving, the insane are shown being led through a dance in an effort to improve their mental condition. (The Bettmann Archive)

doned. Demonology and superstition gained renewed importance in the explanation of abnormal behavior. Church authorities felt the need for a definitive document on the apprehension and conviction of witches and sorcerers, whom they saw as the primary agents of evil. That need was met in 1484 with the publication of *Malleus Maleficarum (The Witches' Hammer)*, by Fathers Henry Kramer and James Sprenger, a highly influential work that became a basic reference for investigators of diabolical phenomena.

In the late Middle Ages, while many people continued to take a benign, naturalistic view of mental illness, anti-intellectualism and belief in magic and witchcraft increased. It is difficult to draw firm conclusions about the mental status of the witches who were put on trial during the Middle Ages, since the available evidence is sparse and scattered. However, recent research has shown that many of the "witches" who were put on trial in New England during the sixteenth and seventeenth centuries were persecuted social outcasts rather than people suffering from mental disorders (Demos, 1982; Schoenman, 1984; Spanos, 1978).

History does not move in a simple, uncomplicated way. As we look back on the past, certain broad patterns, such as the authoritarian rigidity of the Middle Ages, stand out. Yet there were many serious efforts to care for mentally troubled individuals. For instance, Paracelsus (1493–1541) vigorously attacked such notions as possession by the devil. Like the Greeks before him, he pictured maladaptations as natural phenomena, although, as a believer in astrology, he felt that such phenomena lay within the stars and planets, not

within the individual. In the sixteenth century another rational thinker, Juan Huarte (1530–1589), wrote one of the first treatises on psychology, *Probe of the Mind*. In it he distinguished between theology and psychology and argued forcefully for a rational explanation of the psychological development of children.

In addition to thoughtful individuals like Paracelsus and Huarte, there were some relatively enlightened governments. In England, for example, the Crown had the right and duty to protect the mentally impaired, who were divided into two categories: natural fools and persons *non compos mentis*. A **natural fool** was a mentally retarded person whose intellectual capacities had never progressed beyond those of a child. **Persons non compos mentis** did not show mental disability at birth. Their deviant behavior was not continuous, and they might show long periods of recovery. (For reasons that are not clear, by the fifteenth century the term **lunatic** had replaced the phrase *non compos mentis* and **idiot** had replaced *natural fool*.)

There is also evidence that hearings to judge a person's mental status and legal competency were held as early as the thirteenth century (Neugebauer, 1979). Such examinations were designed to assess a person's orientation, memory, and intellect. The following description of Emma de Beston, which dates from 1383, is typical of the reports that were based on such examinations.

*The said Emma, being caused to appear before them, was asked whence she came and said that she did not know. Being asked in what town she was, she said that she was at Ely. Being asked how many days there were in the week, she said seven but could not name them. Being asked how many husbands she had had in her time she said three, giving the name of one only and not knowing the names of the others. Being asked whether she had ever had issue by them, she said that she had had a husband with a son, but did not know his name. Being asked how many shillings there were in forty pence, she said she did not know. Being asked whether she would rather have twenty silver groats than forty pence, she said they were of the same value. They examined her in all other ways which they thought best and found that she was not of sound mind, having neither sense nor memory nor sufficient intelligence to manage herself, her lands, or her goods. As appeared by inspection she had the face and countenance of an idiot. (O'Donoghue, 1914, pp. 127–128)*

## The Renaissance

The Renaissance was a period of increased humanism, curiosity about nature, and interest in scholarship. Yet persecution of people whom society did not like continued. Figure 2–7 is an example of the less than compassionate view of insanity that was commonplace. Many medical authorities devoted much time to investigating skin blemishes, which were believed to indicate points of contact with Satan. The idea of magical cures embodied in shamanism survived in the popular therapy of removing stones from the head (see Figure 2–8).

Although the influence of *Malleus Maleficarum* continued to be felt for centuries, the idea that irrational behavior could be explained rationally gained renewed attention. It followed that detailed descriptions of the behaviors in question were needed. Johann Weyer (1515–1576), a physician, was one of the major contributors to this development (see Figure 2–9). In an age of unbridled superstition, Weyer's enlightened humanism undoubtedly saved countless mentally ill people from death at the stake. Weyer had the courage to insist that witches were mentally disturbed individuals rather than creatures of Satan. He vigorously asserted the need to treat such people medically rather than theologically.

On the basis of careful psychological examination of mental patients, Weyer described a wide range of abnormal behavior, including paranoia, epilepsy, psychosis, depression, and persistent nightmares. In *The Deception of Demons* he specifically attacked the preposterous claims of *Malleus Maleficarum*. He argued that clinical treatment must be oriented toward meeting the needs of disturbed people rather than merely following rules of institutions like the church. He spent much time talking with and observing his patients because he felt that he could not treat psychopathology without firsthand knowledge of it. The knowledge gained in this way led him to the conclusion that inner experiences (such as psychological conflict) and disturbed relationships with others were significant causes of mental illness. Weyer's writings represent a major step toward the separation of abnormal psychology from theology.

## The Age of Reason and the Enlightenment

The seventeenth century, known as the Age of Reason, and the eighteenth century, known as the Enlightenment, have been so labeled because during these two centuries reason and the scientific method came to replace faith and dogma as ways of understanding the natural world. During these two centuries major advances were made in such diverse fields as astronomy, biology, and chemistry. The aspect of the scientific

**FIGURE 2–7**
This sixteenth-century woodcut shows a method for curing insanity. An insane man's head is held in an oven while demons and troublesome thoughts exit though the top of the oven.

**FIGURE 2–8**
This early sixteenth-century painting by Hieronymous Bosch shows an operation for stones in the head. An old phrase that is used even today describing a mentally unbalanced person is "He has stones (or rocks) in his head." In the sixteenth and seventeenth centuries quacks took advantage of this superstition and pretended to cure insanity by making a superficial incision in the patient's scalp and "extracting" small stones that were supplied by confederate standing behind the patient. (Scala/Art Resource)

Joannes Wierus
J. dictus Piscinarius, Med. D. natus 1515. Archiat. Duc. Clevof. 1588.

**FIGURE 2–9**
Jonann Weyer, sixteenth-century physician, emphasized psychological conflict and disturbed interpersonal relationships as a cause of mental disorder. (The Bettmann Archive)

method that received the greatest emphasis was the need to support assertions with observations of natural phenomena.

Although human emotions and motivations are less accessible to direct observation than the moon, the stars, and the human circulatory system, a number of philosophers and scientists focused on the subjective experiences of human beings. Baruch Spinoza (1632–1677) anticipated modern approaches to psychology and physiology with his argument that mind and body are inseparable. In terms that were reminiscent of much modern writing in psychology, Spinoza wrote about psychological causation and the roles of emotions, ideas, and desires in human life. He even re-ferred to unconscious mechanisms that influence behavior. Spinoza's main contribution to abnormal psychology was his argument that psychological processes, though they are not directly observable, are equal in importance to the material processes of the natural world. William Harvey (1578–1657), best known for his work on the circulatory system, also wrote about the relationships between the psychological and physiological sides of life.

Among the most perceptive observers of the human experience have been playwrights, novelists, and poets. During the Age of Reason a number of authors probed especially deeply into the problems of human motivation and emotions. The clearest examples can be found in the plays of William Shakespeare (1564–1616), particularly *Hamlet*. Hamlet wants to take revenge on his uncle but consistently hesitates to act. Psychoanalysts have interpreted this hesitation as a reflection of Hamlet's neurotic conflicts concerning his mother, who had married the uncle after the death of Hamlet's father. Another literary work that dealt with human emotions was *The Anatomy of Melancholy*, by Robert Burton (1577–1640) (see Figure 2–10). In this book Burton focused on the emotional core of depression and called attention to an observation that clinical workers have often made: depressed people tend to be very angry not only with themselves but with all others as well. Burton, a professor of divinity at Oxford, based

**FIGURE 2-10**
The title page from Burton's book, which was written under the name of Democritus Junior. At the top center is a picture of Democritus the Elder in his garden, a portrait of the author at the bottom. The three larger pictures on each side illustrate some of the causes of melancholy. Jealousy, love, and superstition are on the left; solitude, hypochondriasis, and mania are on the right. At the bottom are two herbs, borage and hellebore that are thought to help cure melancholia. Originally published in 1628, reprint from Tudor Publishing Company [Farrar and Rinehart], New York, 1927. (National Library of Medicine)

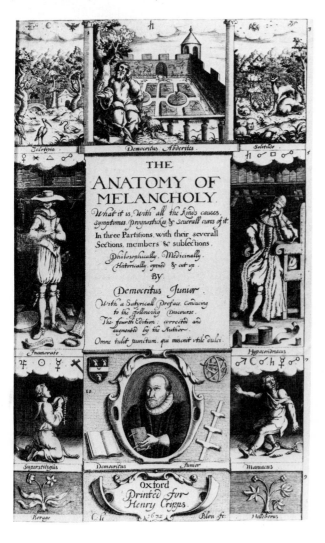

his description and analysis of depression on his own experience.

These developments mirror the longstanding conflict between the psychological and physical explanations of abnormal behavior. However, during the seventeenth and eighteenth centuries both groups—those who analyzed subjective experience and those who sought to identify physical defects—finally rejected the idea that demons and supernatural forces were the causes of abnormal behavior. As a consequence, by the end of the eighteenth century superstition had been almost totally replaced by a commitment to rationality, scientific observation, and humane treatment of the mentally ill.

In England the movement toward humane treatment gained impetus as a result of the psychotic breakdown suffered by King George III in 1765. This event precipitated a constitutional crisis and made many people aware that even prominent individuals were not immune to mental derangement. Madhouses had existed in England for many years, but only in 1774 did Britain pass its first parliamentary act licensing such institutions and regulating the admission of patients to them.

In the early nineteenth century a new approach to abnormal psychology emerged. Franz Joseph Gall (1758–1828), a physician, studied the brains of different kinds of people (young, old, deranged) and gathered evidence suggesting that brain size and mental development are related. On the basis of this evidence he formulated the theory of **phrenology**, according to which discrete psychological "faculties" were located in specific areas of the brain. Gall believed that bumps and indentations on the surface of the skull were accurate reflections of the underlying brain parts. Figure 2–11 shows a device that was used to measure these irregularities. Interest in this now-discredited theory lasted a long time: the journal of the Ohio State Phrenological Society was published until 1938, and the British Phrenological Society was in existence until 1967.

Another approach was developed by the Scottish physician William Cullen (1712–1790), who believed that neurotic behavior was caused by defects of the nervous system. Cullen's therapeutic efforts seem naive, but they were a logical outgrowth of his organic orientation. He treated his patients with cold dousings, bloodletting, vomiting, special diets, exercise programs, and physiotherapy. Like most of his contemporaries, Cullen used severe restraints and straitjackets to control violently disturbed individuals.

An even more famous example of the quest for organic explanations of abnormal behavior is the career of a Viennese physician, Franz Anton Mesmer (1734–1815). In 1774 Mesmer heard of the work of some Eng-

**FIGURE 2-11**
The Lavery electric phrenometer, invented in 1907, was designed to measure bumps on the head.

lish physicians who were treating certain diseases with magnets. He then treated a patient by making her swallow a preparation containing iron and attaching three magnets to her body, one on her stomach and two on her legs. Following her dramatic recovery, Mesmer speculated about the mechanisms that had brought about the cure. We would all agree with his first conclusion: the favorable result could not reasonably be explained by the action of the magnets alone. But Mesmer, a flamboyant and ambitious man, went on to assert that the magnets had simply reinforced or strengthened the primary cause of the cure: his personal or animal magnetism.

While Mesmer's idea of animal magnetism seems ridiculous today, it fit reasonably well with some of the scientific beliefs of his time. In the eighteenth century it was widely believed that the planets influenced both physiological and psychological aspects of behavior. Mesmer contended that all human beings were endowed with a special magnetic fluid, a kind of sixth sense that, when liberated, could cure and prevent all illnesses (see Figure 2–12). Furthermore, he was convinced that he possessed an unusual abundance of the fluid. Mesmer believed that a gesture with his hands was enough to make his patients feel the transmission of his magnetic force.

Mesmer's patients entered a thickly carpeted, dimly lit room amid soft music and perfumed air. They held hands, forming a circle around the **baquet,** a tub filled with magnetized water. Mesmer entered, dressed in an elegant cloak and carrying a sword. These dramatics were deliberately created to accomplish the emotional crisis needed for the cure.

Many testimonials claimed that Mesmer's treatment had been helpful. However, the mechanism of his therapy had more to do with the power of suggestion than with the planets. His animal magnetism was a forerunner not of an organic cure, but rather of a complex psychological means of influencing attitudes and behavior. Mesmer thus was an important figure in the history of hypnosis, a clinical technique that, while far removed from Mesmer's *baquet,* still relies on sug-

**FIGURE 2-12**
Mesmer treated his patients using a *baquet*, a round tub in which he placed bottles of magnetized water. This eighteenth-century engraving shows patients using rods and ropes connected to the tub to touch the afflicted areas on their bodies. (New York Public Library Picture Collection)

gestion as a means of influencing the patient's state of awareness.

## The Reform Movement

Along with the growth of a scientific attitude toward mental disorders, there was an increase in compassion for people who suffered from them. Philippe Pinel (1745–1826), a leader in the reform of French mental hospitals, had expressed great sympathy for the plight of the deranged. He firmly believed that they required humane care and treatment. Although this orientation is widely accepted by both professional workers and the public today, Pinel's ideas were far from commonplace in his time. Pinel had to fight against the view that institutions for the insane are needed more to protect society than to help the deranged.

An interesting aspect of the growth of Pinel's humanism was the influence of Jean-Baptiste Pussin, a former patient at a hospital where Pinel worked. After being discharged Pussin was given a job at the Hospice de Bicêtre, where he eventually became superintendent of the ward for incurable mental patients. Recent research has shown that it was Pussin, not Pinel, who removed the chains from patients at the Bicêtre (see Figure 2–13). Pussin forbade cruelty toward patients and routinely dismissed attendants who mistreated them. Pinel learned much from Pussin, and when he was appointed head of the Salpêtrière, he insisted that Pussin come with him.

Other reformers in Europe and America also had to fight many battles to achieve their goals. An example of the less-than-humane methods that they opposed was the use of ships of fools, or ships whose captains were paid to take the mentally ill away from the offended community. The community usually managed to ignore the fact that the lives of the passengers often ended at the bottom of the sea thousands of miles from home.

An important step toward humane treatment of the mentally ill occurred on May 25, 1815, when the British House of Commons ordered a "Parliamentary Inquiry into the Madhouses of England." One of these, the Hospital of St. Mary of Bethlehem in London, had become known for the noise and chaos prevailing within it. The activities in this "madhouse" were of such great interest to the public that visitors often came to observe the antics of the patients. Tickets were even sold to this popular tourist attraction (see Figure 2–14), from which the word *bedlam* is derived. A full-scale investigation was initiated after incidents of physical abuse at Bethlehem Hospital were revealed by a citizen's committee, which rallied public support for enlightened legislation on behalf of the mentally ill.

One of the leaders of the reform committee was William Hone, a political satirist. Hone described the formation of the committee as follows.

*I was at a Coffee Shop in Fleet Street sitting next to Alderman Waithman, when the illustrator, George Cruikshank, came in. We talked, as we often did, on the subject of madhouses, of the abuses and cruelty to the patients—*

*I then proposed forming a committee to investigate the Lunatic Asylums.*

**FIGURE 2-13**
Philippe Pinel is often pictured as he liberated mental patients from their chains. Recent research suggests that his assistant, a former patient in his hospital, actually was the first to unchain the patients in the large hospital directed by Pinel. (WHO photo)

*Thus self-authorized, we knocked at the door of one Asylum after another. George Cruikshank drew the pictures and I took notes.*

Cruikshank's graphic portrayals of the inhuman conditions endured by the mentally ill were a major factor in bringing about reform (see Figure 2–15).

By the middle of the nineteenth century, the growing acceptance of humanitarian ideas had led to a broad recognition of the need to reform social institutions. Vigorous movements were begun to establish protective and benign asylums for the mentally ill. These movements were given impetus by Pinel's *Treatise on Insanity,* in which he called for the application of scientific principles in place of guesswork in arriving at treatments for disturbed behavior. Classifying his patients according to observable characteristics, such as melancholy and delirium, Pinel sought to devise specific treatments for them. For example, here is how he described the optimal treatment of melancholia and depression.

*Patience, firmness, humane feeling in the manner of directing them, continuous watchfulness in the wards to*

**FIGURE 2-14**
It may be difficult to believe that a mental hospital would sell admission tickets, but this is exactly what was done until the late nineteenth century at Bethlehem Hospital in London (see part a of the figure). Visitors were charged a penny a visit, for which they could view the antics of the inmates and tease them to their hearts' content. Part of the figure shows one artist's conception of Bethlehem Hospital as it was in 1710. Note the visitors looking at the patients through the barred windows. (Cornell University Library)

*prevent outbursts of anger and exasperations, pleasant occupations varied according to differences in taste, various types of physical exercise, spacious quarters among trees, all the enjoyments and tranquility of country living, and from time to time soft and melodious music, all the easier to obtain since there is almost always in these establishments some distinguished musician whose talents languish for want of exercise and cultivation.* (Pinel, 1809, pp. 258–260)

The sometimes huge asylums for the insane that were built in the nineteenth century came into exis-

**FIGURE 2-15**
George Cruikshank's dramatic pictures of the mistreatment of mental patients helped bring about reform legislation. His portrait of William Norris, who was bound by footlong chains to an iron rod at the head of his bed for 12 years, is an example of those illustrations. (Cornell University Library)

and organized physical and mental activities (see Figure 2-16).

**The Reform Movement in America** The eighteenth century was not a good time to be insane in the fledgling British colonies; often the mentally ill simply languished in jail. Gradually, however, a reform movement took hold in the colonies. Virginia's royal governor, Francis Fauquier, persuaded the House of Burgesses to build a hospital for "ideots and lunaticks"; the hospital opened on October 12, 1773 (see Figure 2-17).

Benjamin Rush (1745-1813), a signer of the Declaration of Independence, is often credited with the founding of American psychiatry. Although the treatment methods that he advocated (bleeding, purging, and water cures), seem more like punishment than like therapy, his work took place in a hospital rather than in a custodial institution. The Pennsylvania Hospital, where Rush introduced his new treatment methods, was the first hospital in America to admit mentally ill patients.

The lack of humane treatment and decent facilities for the insane in America (see Figure 2-18) appalled Dorothea Dix (1802-1887), a Boston schoolteacher who devoted much of her life to visiting institutions for the indigent. By 1847 she had visited eighteen penitentiaries, 300 county jails and houses of correction, and 500 almshouses where the mentally ill were kept. Through her personal efforts 32 mental hospitals were constructed.

**FIGURE 2-16**
This lithograph, called Lunatic's Ball, shows a dance that was held for patients at a county asylum in 1848. The contrast between this illustration and those of Bethlehem Hospital illustrates the advances made in the 1800s. Note also the continued belief in the beneficial effects of music and the arts, also illustrated in FIGUREs 2-4 and 2-6. (Katherine Drake, *Lunatic's Ball* [1848] The Royal College of Psychiatrists, London)

tence because it was felt that the only way to treat mentally disturbed people was to isolate them from the damaging influences of family, friends, and community. Accompanying this view was the belief in **moral treatment**. This approach sought to control and rehabilitate the patient through a fixed schedule that encouraged regular habits; kind treatment with a minimum of restraint; a daily visit from the hospital superintendent, who assumed the role of persuader and inspirational leader; calm, pleasant surroundings; accommodations that separated patients with different degrees of disturbance; proper diet; some medication;

(a)

(c)

(b)

**FIGURE 2-17**
A reconstruction of the Public Hospital for Persons of Insane and Disordered Minds in Williamsburg, VA, America's first public institution exclusively for the mentally ill, recently opened for public viewing. In the eighteenth century the inmates inhabited bare, depressing cells. By the mid nineteenth century, comfortable housing had become an important part of treatment (Colonial Williamsburg Photograph)

**FIGURE 2-18**
The crib was one of the prescientific "therapies" for violent patients that Dorothea Dix sought to abolish. (The Bettmann Archive)

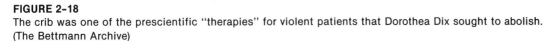

At the turn of the century an American business-man named Clifford Beers recorded his experiences as a mental patient in *A Mind that Found Itself*, published in 1908 (see Box 2–1). After his recovery Beers became determined to make changes in the conditions of mental hospitals, and his book helped him gather support for a citizens' reform group, the National Committee for Mental Hygiene (now called the National Associa-tion for Mental Health), which was founded in 1909. The group promoted social programs aimed at pre-venting mental illness as well as ensuring humane treatment of the mentally ill.

Despite the progress toward more humane treat-ment of mental patients in the nineteenth century, the mentally ill continued to be persecuted well into the twentieth century. An example is provided by Albert

---

## ■ BOX 2–1 A PROTEST THAT HAD AN EFFECT

Clifford Beers's book, *A Mind That Found Itself*, is the story of his treatment in mental hospitals dur-ing a period of psychosis. Its description of what Beers endured gripped the imagination of readers and helped gain popular support for the American mental health movement. After his recovery Beers carried on a lifelong crusade that helped revolu-tionize the care of the mentally ill (see Figure 2–19). In the following excerpt Beers describes how he was restrained in a camisole or straitjacket, a can-vas device that was used to restrain unruly pa-tients. In this case Beers believed that the attending physician had laced the jacket unnecessarily tight because of his anger at Beers's behavior.

*No incidents of my life have ever impressed themselves more indelibly on my memory than those of my first night in a straitjacket. Within one hour of the time I was placed in it I was suffering pain as intense as any I ever endured, and before the night had passed it had become almost unbearable. My right hand was so held that the tip of one of my fingers was all but cut by the nail of another, and soon knifelike pains began to shoot through my right arm as far as the shoulder. After four or five hours the excess of pain rendered me partially insensible to it. But for fifteen consecutive hours I remained in that instrument of torture; and not until the twelfth hour, about breakfast time the next morning, did the attendant so much as loosen a cord.*

*During the first seven or eight hours, excruciating pains racked not only my arms, but half of my body. Though I cried and moaned, in fact, screamed so loudly that the attendants must have heard me, little attention was paid to me. . . . I even begged the attendants to loosen the jacket enough to ease me a little. This they refused to do, and they even seemed to enjoy being in a position to add their considerable mite to my torture.*

FIGURE 2–19
Clifford Beers became an effective advocate for human treatment of mental disorders after his own experiences in a mental institution. (National Mental Health Association)

*After fifteen interminable hours the straitjacket was removed. Whereas just prior to its putting on I had been in a vigorous enough condition to offer stout resistance*

---

> *when wantonly assaulted, now, on coming out of it, I was helpless. When my arms were released from their constricted position, the pain was intense. Every joint had been racked. I had no control over the fingers of either hand, and could not have dressed myself had I been promised my freedom for doing so.*
>
> *For more than the following week I suffered as already described, though of course with gradually decreasing intensity as my racked body became accustomed to the unnatural positions it was forced to take. The first experience occurred on the night of October 18th, 1902. I was subjected to the same unfair, unnecessary, and unscientific ordeal for twenty-one consecutive nights and parts of the corresponding twenty-one days. On more*
>
> *than one occasion, indeed, the attendant placed me in the straitjacket during the day for refusing to obey some trivial command. This, too, without an explicit order from the doctor in charge, though perhaps he acted under a general order.*
>
> *During most of the time I was held also in seclusion in a padded cell. A padded cell is a vile hole. The side walls are padded as high as a man can reach, as is also the inside of the door. One of the worst features of such cells is the lack of ventilation, which deficiency of course aggravates their general unsanitary condition. The cell which I was forced to occupy was practically without heat, and as winter was coming on, I suffered intensely from the cold. (Beers, 1981 [1907], pp. 107, 110–111)*

Deutsch, who published a shocking exposé of the mistreatment of patients at the Philadelphia State Hospital for Mental Diseases during the 1940s.

> *The male "incontinent ward" was like a scene out of Dante's Inferno. Three hundred nude men, stood, squatted and sprawled in this bare room . . . Winter or Summer, these creatures never were given any clothing at all . . . Many patients . . . had to eat their meals with their hands. There weren't nearly enough spoons or other tableware to go around . . . Four hundred patients were herded into one barn-like dayroom intended for only 80. There were only a few benches; most of the men had to stand all day or sit on the splintery floor. There was no supervised recreation, no occupational therapy . . . Only two attendants were on this ward; at least 10 were needed. The hogs in a near-by pigpen were far better fed, in far greater comfort than these human beings. (Deutsch, 1948, pp. 49–50)*

Today such conditions are unlikely to exist, and many institutions provide a high standard of care. Figure 2–20 shows scenes from contemporary mental hospitals.

## ■ PSYCHOLOGICAL VS. ORGANIC VIEWS

The causes of abnormal behavior have yet to be determined fully, and debates on this issue recur continually. Is abnormal behavior caused by disturbances in bodily functioning or by subjective experiences, thoughts, and motivations? This question remains high on the agenda of contemporary clinicians and researchers, and the way it is approached today owes much to the way it has been phrased over the years, particularly during the nineteenth century.

### The Psychological Approach

Eighteenth-century theories emphasized **rational thinking** as the way to achieve personal and social adjustment. During the first half of the nineteenth century, however, the role of **irrational thought** in both normal and abnormal behavior attracted much more attention. This took place as part of the so-called Romantic reaction against the views of philosophers and scientists who gave little weight to the role of emotions, motivations, and internal conflicts in human behavior. Many clinical workers and researchers began to view internal conflicts as a major cause of personal unhappiness and failure to adapt socially. This focus on emotion and irrational feelings laid the groundwork for Sigmund Freud's theories about mental processes and their relationship to disturbed behavior.

The reaction against pure rationalism directed more attention to the inner life of the person than to any other aspect of human existence. The German psychiatrist Johann Christian Heinroth (1773–1843) theorized that mental illness resulted from internal conflicts between unacceptable impulses and the guilt generated by those impulses, and that the individual is often unaware of these conflicts. What distinguished theories like Heinroth's from those of his predecessors was their attempt to provide an account of the whole person, the inner life, and the mental stresses and strains that underlie observable behavior. This was in contrast to the rationalist view that the scientific study of abnormal behavior required meticulous observation and

(a)

(b)

(c)

**FIGURE 2-20**
Present day mental institutions range from barren facilities for "warehousing" (b) patients, to pleasant and stimulating (c). Sometimes the uncontrolled behavior of patients makes it necessary to confine them to isolation rooms (a); however, in well-run hospitals, the time of such confinement is kept to a minimum. (The Bettmann Archive; Michael O'Brien, Archive Pictures Inc.; Peter Arnold, Inc.)

description of disordered behaviors and classification of those behaviors.

Heinroth's ideas are strikingly similar to Freud's notion that impulses clash with conscience and result in anxiety, unhappiness, and socially inappropriate behavior. Freud, like Heinroth, recognized that this clash might take place at an unconscious level and that awareness of these conflicts was a means of understanding and resolving them, and hence a way of correcting maladaptive behavior. Despite these similarities, Freud seems to have been only slightly acquainted with Heinroth and the other participants in the Romantic reaction. One reason for this was that by midcentury, long before Freud's work began, the pendulum had begun to swing in a quite different direction—toward the search for biological causes of abnormal behavior.

## The Organic Approach

Just as Heinroth was the champion of the psychological approach to abnormal behavior, another German psychiatrist, Wilhelm Griesinger (1817–1868), led the search for bodily causes. He argued that most mental disorders were caused by the direct or indirect influence of disturbances in brain function. While he was a staunch advocate of humane treatment and was himself a sensitive observer of human conflict, Griesinger firmly believed that the organic, rather than the psychological, origins of human maladaptation and unhappiness were predominant. His slogan was "mental diseases are brain diseases."

Behind this perspective was the assumption that the material (brain cells) almost invariably causes the mental (personal unhappiness). The major implication of this viewpoint was that it was necessary to find out more about how the body (particularly the nervous system) works. One way of doing so was to dissect the brains of mentally disturbed individuals after their death. Researchers reasoned that the aberrant behaviors exhibited by those individuals had been caused by structural abnormalities in the brain. Through direct examination of the brains of such people, they hoped to discover relationships between the brain and behavior. From this point of view, introspection as a path to understanding psychological disturbance held little appeal. Nor was there much interest in how thought directs observable behavior.

Emil Kraepelin (1856–1926), who was influenced by Griesinger, also believed that abnormal behavior was caused by organic disturbances. Kraepelin's major contribution was his attempt to construct a classification system that would encompass most of the disorders that required treatment and hospitalization. He distinguished between two especially serious and debilitating conditions, dementia praecox and manic-depressive psychosis, and believed that they were specific diseases with specific organic causes.

## The Approaches Converge

Toward the end of the nineteenth century, important developments took place on both the physical and psychological fronts. The French neurologist Jean Martin Charcot (1825–1893) continued to believe that organic disturbances were of crucial importance, but he used a psychological approach in studying and treating his patients. The patients in whom Charcot was most interested were **hysterics,** people who suffered from organic complaints for which no organic causes could be found. Hysterics complained of loss of sensation in the skin, pain in various parts of the body, blindness and other visual impairments, tics, muscular contractions that resembled epileptic seizures, difficulty in walking, or paralysis. In addition to this wide variety of inexplicable symptoms, Charcot observed some psychological consistencies in hysterical patients, notably what he called *la belle indifference:* although a person who had become paralyzed could be expected to be de-

pressed about it, Charcot's patients seemed unconcerned about their condition. Charcot also noticed that hysterical patients had their own incorrect theories of bodily functioning and that their physical symptoms were compatible with those theories. He diagnosed many of these cases as "traumatic paralysis."

Despite his orientation toward organic causes, Charcot became impressed with his psychological observations and came to the conclusion that mental states were indeed related to hysterical symptoms. He therefore developed a technique for hypnotizing hysterical patients. While they were in a hypnotic trance, he suggested to them that their symptoms (for example, paralysis of a part of the body) would disappear. In many cases the symptoms disappeared completely. Charcot also was able to induce hysterical symptoms in normal individuals by giving them appropriate suggestions while they were under hypnosis.

Throughout France and Europe Charcot gained great prestige; he was referred to as the "Napoleon of neuroses." He became known as a charismatic clinician and teacher (see Figure 2–21). The following account describes some of his "miraculous" cures.

> Many patients were brought to Charcot from all over the world, paralytics on stretchers or wearing complicated apparatuses. Charcot ordered the removal of those appliances and told the patients to walk. There was, for instance, a young lady who had been paralyzed for years. Charcot bade her stand up and walk, which she did under the astonished eyes of her parents and of the Mother Superior of the convent in which she had been staying. Another young lady was brought to Charcot with a paralysis of both legs. Charcot found no organic lesion; the consultation was not yet over when the patient stood up and walked back to the door where the cabman, who was waiting for her, took off his hat in amazement and crossed himself. (Ellenberger, 1970, p. 95)

One of Charcot's students, Pierre Janet (1859–1947), extended his work and concluded that hysteria was due to a splitting off from conscious experience of certain ideas that continued to influence behavior. He observed that under hypnosis many patients recalled upsetting events that seemed to be related to the onset of their symptoms. He found that in some cases, when patients expressed the strong feelings they had experienced when the events originally took place, their symptoms weakened temporarily or disappeared.

Besides strengthening the view that psychological causes played a role in a significant number of behavioral disorders, Charcot and Janet helped broaden the scope of behavior that was studied by abnormal psychology. Their patients, though they were troubled

**FIGURE 2-21**
This portrait of Charcot shows him lecturing to a group of colleagues at the Salpêtrière, the same institution where Pinel had unchained the patients. In this scene Charcot is demonstrating the typical behavior of a hysteric, using a female patient as an example. Notice her fainting posture. Such dramatic behavior is typical of a hysterical episode. (Andre Brouillet, *Charcot at Salpêtière* [1887] National Library of Medicine.)

people who needed help, were not thought of as insane or crazy.

One of the many clinical workers who came to France especially to study with Charcot was Sigmund Freud (1856–1939). Freud had received his medical training as a neurologist and initially believed that the ultimate causes of abnormal behavior were biological. Like Charcot, however, he chose to explore aspects of mental life that seemed to be related to psychological discomfort and maladaptive behavior. Also like Charcot, Freud became increasingly interested in noncatastrophic conditions such as hysteria and phobias.

## ■ THE STAGE IS SET

The history of abnormal psychology is the story of how communities have responded to people who were different and did not fit in. The ups and downs, the advances and retreats, leave us with a feeling of cautious optimism about the power of the intellect to comprehend and devise ways of helping individuals who are unable to adapt to community norms.

Ideas about abnormality are almost never brand new. As we have seen, they have a past that in some cases is very long. Moreover, they are often complex. Attitudes toward deviant individuals have always reflected the social dynamics that prevailed at the time. An example of the link between what is going on in a society (its values, prejudices, and the like), and how it conceives of mental illness has been provided by studies of the role of women in the nineteenth century. Theories that asserted that there were sex-based differences in the tendency to engage in abnormal behavior were clearly an outgrowth of cultural stereotypes and the social status quo. Not only were women regarded as subordinate to men, they were also believed to be more prone to nervous and emotional disorders. Biological factors were assumed to play a role in these differences. Some of Freud's writings reflect this sexist assessment; for example, early in his career he assumed that the strong sexual repression he observed in women was the cause of what he viewed as their intellectual inferiority (Ellenberger, 1970).

Because we are so close to our own times, we tend to lose sight of many of the basic assumptions and beliefs that direct the thinking of our contemporaries about a wide variety of topics. If we look back at earlier periods, these assumptions and beliefs are easier to see, and they often seem strange. For example, during the 1880s and 1890s Freud's developing theories had to compete with ideas that seem naive today. One such idea was the notion that masturbation is a sign of a serious personality disorder. People who masturbated were described as moral degenerates, as deceitful, selfish, and full of cunning. Excessive masturbation was believed to result in "masturbational insanity" (see Figure 2-22). Another popular idea was that there was a

**FIGURE 2-22**
This illustration from a textbook entitled *The Secret Habits*, published in 1830, shows a masturbator in a state of physical collapse. Note the rolled-back pupils often used in representations of insanity. (D. M. Rozier, "Des Habitudes Secretes" [1830], from Oskar Diethelm Historical Library, Cornell University)

connection between blushing and psychological functioning: excessive blushing indicated inner moral failings, whereas inability to blush reflected psychological weakness (Skultans, 1979).

Policies regarding the treatment of abnormal behavior have been influenced by the public's concerns and priorities. For example, the American public puts a premium on speed and often seems to feel that a quick solution is best. Thus in the 1960s and 1970s public opinion favored a drastic reduction in the number of residents in mental hospitals. Because an effective system of halfway houses and other support services had not been established, masses of hurriedly discharged mental patients had to make their own way into unprepared and largely hostile communities. Few were able to make the transition successfully.

This book is devoted to modern theory, research, and practice concerning abnormal behavior. Everyone has read dozens of newspaper and magazine articles describing breakthroughs that will soon eliminate certain types of mental disorders. Too often the solutions

do not materialize, because the breakthrough has been interpreted too simplistically. As the scientific method has uncovered information on a variety of fronts, the need to recognize the complexity of most forms of maladaptive behavior has become clearer.

## ■ STUDY OUTLINE

### HISTORICAL VIEWS OF ABNORMAL BEHAVIOR

1. One of the oldest theories of maladaptive behavior attributes it to supernatural and magical forces. In societies that accept such beliefs, therapy generally involves exorcism of the evil spirits by a **shaman** or medicine man.

2. Maladaptive behavior has also been explained by the presence of organic defects that affect only a specific organ, not the whole body. **Trephination,** an extremely ancient therapy that apparently involved the release of evil spirits through a hole made in the skull, is based on the organic approach to abnormal behavior.

3. A third general approach to abnormal behavior is the psychological perspective. According to this point of view, behavioral disturbances are caused by inadequacies in the way an individual thinks, feels, or perceives the world.

4. In ancient Greece during the ninth century B.C., therapy took place in the temple of the god Asclepius. Hippocrates recognized the importance of the brain in explaining abnormal behavior and developed a therapy based on resting, bathing, and dieting. The trend toward rational explanations of behavior was strengthened by Socrates, Plato, and Aristotle. Socrates saw reason as the cornerstone of the good life. Plato developed the **organismic point of view,** which explains behavior as an expression of the totality of a person's psychological processes; he said that disturbed behavior grew out of internal conflicts between emotion and reason. Aristotle analyzed the emotions and wrote extensively on the nature of consciousness.

5. During the Middle Ages there were many instances of shocking treatment of the mentally ill as well as humane attitudes toward disturbed individuals. Superstitious beliefs in devils and demons were strengthened under the auspices of the Catholic Church, but at the same time the idea of Christian charity encouraged more humane treatment of the mentally ill. Saint Augustine's *Confessions* serve as a prototype of modern psychological tools like introspection and self-analysis. Paracelsus and Juan Huarte attacked superstitious beliefs, and some governments were relatively enlightened in their treatment of the mentally ill. Neverthe-

less, the best-selling book of the time was *Malleus Maleficarum (The Witches' Hammer)*, a treatise on diabolical phenomena.

6. Although it was characterized by increasing humanism and scholarship in many areas, the Renaissance was not a period of major change in people's attitudes toward maladaptive behavior. However, in *The Deception of Demons* Johann Weyer called for the separation of abnormal psychology from theology.

7. In the seventeenth century (the Age of Reason) and the eighteenth century (the Enlightenment), reason and the scientific method finally supplanted superstition as the primary ways of understanding human behavior. Baruch Spinoza argued that internal psychological processes were just as worthy of scientific examination as directly observable natural processes. At the same time, the belief that neurotic behavior was caused by physical defects remained current, leading to Franz Anton Mesmer's idea of animal magnetism and eventually to the use of hypnosis in treating psychological problems.

8. The movement toward more humane treatment of the mentally ill began in France with Philippe Pinel, who developed his **moral treatment** at the end of the eighteenth century. William Hone and George Cruikshank spearheaded a governmental review of conditions in London's Bethlehem Hospital in 1815. Benjamin Rush, Dorothea Dix, and Clifford Beers led the reform movement in America.

## PSYCHOLOGICAL VS. ORGANIC VIEWS

1. The causes of abnormal behavior have not been established, and the debate over the relative importance of bodily functioning and psychological experiences continues. The eighteenth-century emphasis on **rational thought** was answered by the romantics' emphasis on the role of **irrational thoughts**. According to Johann Christian Heinroth, mental illness was caused by internal conflicts between unacceptable impulses and the guilt aroused by those impulses.

2. Wilhelm Greisinger led the search for the bodily causes of mental problems; he said that "mental diseases are brain diseases." Emil Kraepelin also stressed organic causes, but his major contribution was a classification system for disorders that required hospitalization. Jean Martin Charcot continued to believe in organic causes, but he treated his patients from a psychological perspective. Pierre Janet first made the observation that hysteria seemed to develop in response to past traumatic events that the patient could recall under hypnosis.

## THE STAGE IS SET

1. Attitudes toward deviant individuals reflect the social dynamics of the time, that is, the society's prevailing values and prejudices. Policies regarding the treatment of abnormal behavior are influenced by the public's concerns and priorities.

# 3

# THEORETICAL PERSPECTIVES ON MALADAPTIVE BEHAVIOR

In Chapter 1 we said that stress, ways of coping, and vulnerability play important roles in maladaptive behavior. Stress arises when we must respond to challenges that are unexpected or for which we do not feel prepared. The beginning of a new school year, a death in the family, and living in an area with a high crime rate are examples of such challenges. People respond to stress by trying to do something about it. How they respond reflects the effectiveness of their coping skills. For example, a person might install an alarm system after a neighbor's house has been robbed. Some people, however, choose less constructive responses. They may deal with the stress of living in a crime-ridden area by buying guns and vicious dogs or by never leaving their houses after dark. Abnormal psychology deals with behavior that results from failures to cope constructively with the demands, constraints, and opportunities that we all experience as we go through life.

The failures to adapt that are the concern of abnormal psychology usually cannot be explained by the presence of stress alone. It is necessary to investigate the coping styles and vulnerabilities of people who exhibit such failures if we are to understand their maladaptive behavior and help them correct it. There are large differences in how well particular individuals cope with stress. We are all vulnerable to experiences that are related to sensitive areas in our personalities. When these personally relevant buttons are pushed, our capacity for handling stress declines and we feel less competent and content than usual. The war hero who falls apart when his wife threatens to divorce him, the child who is the delight of her teachers but cannot get along with her playmates—both show that an individual may be more vulnerable to certain situational and developmental challenges than to others.

A variety of theories have been offered to explain the vulnerabilities and coping failures that increase the likelihood of personal breakdown. In this chapter we will review the major theoretical approaches as they apply to the relationships among stress, coping, and vulnerability and to other important aspects of maladaptive behavior.

## ■ THE ROLE OF THEORY IN ABNORMAL PSYCHOLOGY

Everyone wants to know why things happen. Scientific theories are created to organize what we know and explain what it means. Theories are never complete, because there are different ways of looking at what we do know and also because there are some pieces missing from our knowledge. Even an incomplete theory is useful, however, if it provides a perspective for examining the information we have. A good theory will also help us decide what new information we need.

Clinical workers and researchers operate on the basis of formal theories, but they also use informal theories or hunches based on past experience. A psychiatrist, clinical psychologist, or social worker who is assigned a case will use a particular theoretical perspective to analyze the available information. Theoretical perspectives serve as lenses that reflect and shape our conceptions of human nature. Thus according to one theoretical perspective a bad cold may be thought of as a viral infection; according to another it may be simply "God's will"; and according to your mother it may be "your own fault for getting your feet wet."

The diversity of theories in abnormal psychology is wide. We will review six theoretical perspectives that are particularly influential today: (1) the **biological perspective,** which emphasizes the role of bodily processes; (2) the **psychodynamic perspective,** which emphasizes the role of anxiety and inner conflict; (3) the **learning perspective,** which examines how the environment influences behavior; (4) the **cognitive perspective,** which looks to defective thinking and problem solving as causes of abnormal behavior; (5) the **humanist–existentialist perspective,** which emphasizes our uniqueness as individuals and our freedom to make our own decisions; and (6) the **community perspective,** which is concerned with the roles of social relationships and the impact of socioeconomic conditions on maladaptive behavior.

Which of these theoretical perspectives is right? In Jewish lore there is a story about a couple who came to their rabbi for marriage counseling. The rabbi interviewed each partner separately and then met with them together. They asked him who was right and who was wrong. The rabbi told the puzzled couple, "You are both right." The rabbi's observation also applies to these theoretical perspectives. Each one deals with pieces of reality, but the pieces are often quite different. Some theories are more pertinent to an understanding of the causes of stress, others to the ways in which we cope, and still others to the nature of human vulnerabilities. Consequently, there is no reason why we should commit ourselves to a particular theoretical position and feel called upon to explain all abnormal behavior in terms of its concepts. With a topic as complex as abnormal behavior, it is a good idea to remember that even a respected theory may be too simple an explanation.

There are many examples of the dangers of adopting too rigid a theoretical position. Consider the case of the elderly. The relatively high incidence of severe behavior disorders in older people represents a major social problem. A high percentage of these disorders are related to bodily changes that are part of the aging process. However, it would be a mistake to say that psychotic behavior among old people is due simply to deterioration of the brain and disorders of the circulatory system. Two people with the same type of brain disorder might behave quite differently, depending on their life histories, self-concepts, present circumstances, coping styles, and worries about death and dying.

It is also important to note that theories are not static. In the previous chapter we saw that through the centuries explanations of deviance have undergone wide swings. New facts exerted an influence on existing theories, but so did people's beliefs, which may or may not have scientific validity. Besides accommodating new facts or changes in public attitudes, a new theory may be developed as a reaction to weaknesses in a currently popular theory. Although all of the basic theoretical viewpoints discussed in this chapter are important and are actively used and researched today, it is worthwhile to keep in mind that each was a reaction to the situation prevailing at the time that it was initially proposed.

# ■ THE BIOLOGICAL PERSPECTIVE

In our review of the history of abnormal psychology in Chapter 2, we saw that the idea that bodily disturbances cause disordered behavior has been around for a long time. It is not surprising that the biological perspective gained renewed popularity in the eighteenth and nineteenth centuries, when great leaps forward in anatomy, physiology, and genetics made it seem reasonable that a biological cause might eventually be found for every disorder, be it physical or behavioral.

Major impetus for the biological point of view came from findings about the relationship between bodily infections and defects, on the one hand, and disordered behavior, on the other. Perhaps the most dramatic of these was the discovery of the link between syphilitic infection in early adulthood and general paresis, a serious deterioration of the brain that often appeared when the infected person reached middle age.

Recent information about the role of biological factors supports the argument that such factors are important to some, but certainly not all, mental conditions. Modern advances in several areas of biology and medicine have continued to motivate researchers. For example, equipment and techniques like the PT scan and the CT scan, which make it possible to see how the brain works without the use of surgical or other invasive procedures, are beginning to permit previously unthought-of studies of the relationships between behavior and the brain. And research on heredity and genetics has shown that certain chromosome defects are responsible for metabolic disorders, such as phenylketonuria, that in turn lead to specific forms of mental retardation. The list of behavioral problems in which biological processes play at least some role is lengthening, as is the list of biologically based therapies.

Most people distinguish between the body and the mind, although the meanings attached to these words vary widely. **Body** refers to organs, muscles, bones, and brain; **mind** usually refers to attitudes, feelings, and thoughts. We generally speak as if the worlds of body and mind were totally separate, as if the body were something in which the mind rides around, like a car. However, the separation between body and mind is an intellectual invention rather than a reality. Cognitive and bodily processes are closely intertwined, though how much weight one assigns to each process in accounting for maladaptive behavior depends on one's view of human beings. New evidence may alter the prevailing views from time to time.

At its most extreme, the biological viewpoint assumes that all maladaptive behavior is due to a disordered body structure or function. Such a disorder can be explained by an inherited defect, by a defect acquired through injury or infection before or after birth, or by a more or less temporary physiological malfunction caused by some condition that is present at a particular time. A less extreme view, which still emphasizes the importance of biological functioning, recognizes that maladaptive behavior is a joint product of three types of disordered processes: in the body (for example, a hormonal deficiency), in psychological functioning (for example, a tendency toward shyness), and in the social environment (for example, a high unemployment rate in the community).

## Biological Determinants of Abnormal Behavior

A number of biological factors influence the behavior of organisms. How we behave and think depends not only on the action of each by itself but also on the interrelationships among them. Genetic factors, the brain and nervous system, and the endocrine glands all play important roles in psychological processes and have been shown to be involved in abnormal behavior.

**Genetic factors**   Few fields have expanded as rapidly as genetics. Evidence that genetic abnormalities account for a significant number of medical problems has led researchers to seek hereditary roots for maladaptive behavior as well. Available evidence suggests that genetic factors may play a role in such diverse disorders as schizophrenia, depression, criminality, and mental retardation.

A major factor in some genetic abnormalities is irregularities in the structure or number of an individual's chromosomes. **Chromosomes** are threadlike bodies that are present in pairs in all body cells. Humans have 46 chromosomes in each cell. Chromosomal abnormalities, or **chromosomal anomalies,** are likely to produce abnormalities in the brain. For instance, in Down syndrome, a type of mental retardation, there are three #21 chromosomes instead of two.

Arranged linearly along the chromosomes are the **genes,** each of which occupies its own characteristic position or **locus.** Faulty genes, or genes that are defective in some way, can exist in the absence of obvious chromosomal deviations and may cause metabolic or biochemical abnormalities. Particular genes influence behavior through a long series of steps. Their influence may be modified by events that happen before and after birth, as well as by the actions of other genes. The basis for gene action is a complex substance, **deoxyribonucleic acid (DNA),** that is found in the chromosomes. The discovery that DNA is the means by which genetic information is transferred led to the discovery of how genes work.

Behavior is not inherited. What we receive from our parents are molecules of DNA. Your DNA may carry the blueprint for a strong, sturdy body, but this will not automatically make you an athlete. For example, your nutrition, the amount of exercise and training you get, and your motivation, as well as any illnesses or injuries you experience before or after your birth, will all influence how your genetic predisposition toward physical strength is expressed. Sometimes a specific gene is present that has been identified as causing a certain characteristic or disease, yet the person may show no sign of the problem or perhaps only mild symptoms. The term **penetrance** has been used to refer to the percentage of cases in which, if a specific gene is present, a particular trait, characteristic, or disease will actually manifest itself in the fully developed organism.

The extent to which genes affect behavior has been a subject of debate for at least the last two centuries. In the nineteenth century fierce battles were fought in what has come to be known as the nature–nurture controversy. Heredity (nature) and environment (nurture) were seen as separate and distinct forces that worked in an either/or fashion. Either nature determined a certain behavior, or nurture did; you couldn't have it both ways. More in line with reality, however, is the view that the interaction of many forces—in particular the interaction between the information carried by

genes and that provided by the environment—determines behavioral patterns.

A young but rapidly developing field is **population genetics,** the study of the distribution of genes throughout groups of people who mate with each other. Such information is used in predicting the incidence of certain genetically carried disorders. (For example, Tay Sachs disease is a form of retardation that is caused by genes carried by some Jews whose ancestors came from a particular area of Europe.) Related to population genetics is **behavior genetics.** Research in this field involves breeding animals selectively and uncovering the effects of inbreeding on behavior patterns such as those related to emotionality and maze learning. Horse breeders who attempt to raise Derby winners by mating the fastest mare to the fastest stallion are essentially behavior geneticists.

Research on the effects of inheritance on human behavior usually takes one of two forms: analysis of family histories and twin studies. Pedigree and family tree studies begin with an individual who manifests a particular trait. His or her relatives are then assessed to see whether they have the same trait. When such an analysis is carried out over at least two generations, some inferences about family genetics can be drawn. Twin studies are a more direct way of studying the effects of heredity on behavior. **Monozygotic** (identical) twins have been compared with **dizygotic** (fraternal) twins with respect to a variety of behaviors. Because monozygotic twins develop from the same fertilized egg, they have identical genes and hence identical heredities. Dizygotic twins, on the other hand, are the products of two entirely different eggs. If monozygotic twins exhibit a particular behavior disorder more often than dizygotic twins do, the identical heredity of the monozygotic pair may be the important factor.

The degree of **concordance** in twin studies refers to the relationship between twins or other family members with respect to a given characteristic or trait. If both twins show the trait, the pair is described as concordant. If they do not, the pair is described as discordant. For example, studies have shown that the concordance rate of schizophrenics is high for monozygotic twins and drops precipitously for dizygotic twins of the same sex. The drop is even greater for dizygotic twins of opposite sexes. The fact that the concordance rate is not 100 percent for monozygotic twins suggests that environmental influences play a role. Although there is a very strong suggestion of a genetic component in schizophrenia, we must not forget that experience can lessen or emphasize the effects of any hereditary tendency.

The latter point is illustrated by a recent study of a

set of identical triplets, all of whom suffered from serious chronic disorders (McGuffin, and others, 1982). Two of the brothers had periods of auditory hallucinations and other clear schizophrenic symptoms. Between these periods they functioned at a low level and were unable to work. The third brother also had psychotic periods (although not as clearly schizophrenic), but he was able to function at a relatively high level and could hold a job between his psychotic episodes. His IQ was higher than that of his brothers, and his relationship with his father was much less stormy than theirs. This case demonstrates that even when people have identical heredities, their levels of functioning may vary in important ways.

**The Brain and Nervous System** The nervous system has two major divisions: the **central nervous system,** which includes all the nerve cells (neurons) of the brain and spinal cord, and the **peripheral nervous system,** which includes all the neurons connecting the central nervous system with the glands, muscles, and sensory receptors (see Figure 3–1). The peripheral nervous system also has two divisions; the **somatic system,** which transmits information from sense organs to the muscles responsible for voluntary movement, and the **autonomic system,** which directs the activity of the glands and internal organs.

The fundamental unit of the entire nervous system is the **neuron,** or nerve cell, which has a long extension called the **axon** and several shorter extensions called **dendrites.** The function of nerve cells is to transmit electrical impulses to other nerve cells and to structures outside the nervous system (such as muscles and glands). A typical nerve cell receives a messenger chemical, or **neurotransmitter,** from other nerve cells through specific receptor sites on its dendrites. It changes the chemical signal to an electrical signal and sends the electrical signal through the axon. When the electrical signal reaches the tip of the axon, the nerve cell releases molecules of neurotransmitters that pass through a tiny region called the **synapse** and are taken up by specific receptors on the dendrites of adjacent nerve cells. This process can be repeated many times to transmit signals throughout the nervous system (see Figure 3–2).

The brain is easily the most complex structure in the body (see Figure 3–3). Its two cerebral hemispheres are highly developed centers for processing sensory information. The **cerebral cortex,** the convoluted layer of gray matter that covers each hemisphere, controls our distinctively human behavior. The cortex has areas that monitor hearing, vision, body sensations, and other processes. Disturbances in specific parts of the brain

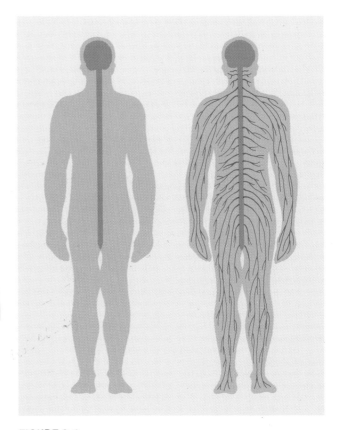

**FIGURE 3–1**
The central nervous system and the peripheral nervous system. The central nervous system (CNS) (left) consists of the brain, brain stem, and spinal cord; the peripheral nervous system (PNS) (right) includes all nerve fibers extending to and from the rest of the body. The CNS acts on the world through the PNS (a brain without a mouth cannot speak); it also learns about the world through the PNS (a brain without eyes cannot see).

(caused, for example, by tumors) will result in specific behavioral deficits (for example, loss of speech). Electrical stimulation of certain areas of the cerebral cortex also produces specific motor responses or sensory effects.

The brain and its neurons are active continuously. This activity occurs spontaneously as well as in response to external stimulation. The activity of nerve cells generates electrical energy, and the voltage differences between cells or regions can be amplified and measured as brain potentials. A record of these brain

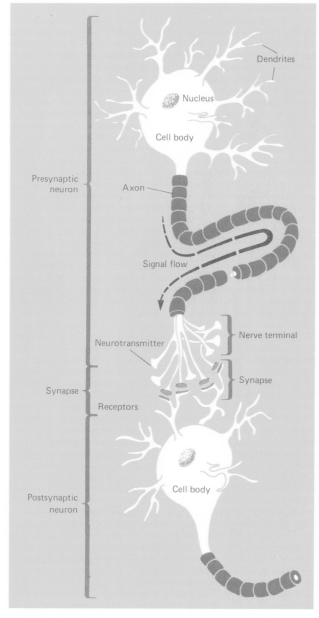

**FIGURE 3-2**
The relationship between a pair of typical neurons. A neuron consists of a cell body and two types of extensions—dendrites and an axon. Specific receptors or dendrites receive neurotransmitter molecules from the axons of adjacent neurons. This sets up an electrical impulse in the receiving neuron that is transmitted through the neuron to the nerve terminal at the tip of its axon. The arrival of the impulse at the nerve terminal causes the release of neurotransmitter molecules (shown by dots), which diffuse across a small gap (the synapse) to receptors on the dendrites of the next neuron. The process can be repeated many times to send signals throughout the brain and the rest of the nervous system.

**FIGURE 3-3**
The human brain. (a) View of exposed human brain during surgery. (Photo by Alexander Tsiaras, Science Source, Photo Researchers). (b) The surface of the left hemisphere with major areas and their functions labeled (from W. C. Wittrock and Jackson Beatty, Joseph E. Bogen, Michal S. Gazzaniga, Harry J. Jerison, Stephen D. Krashen, Robert D. Nebes, Timothy J. Teyler, THE HUMAN BRAIN. (Englewood Cliffs, NJ: Prentice-Hall, Inc., 1977). (c) A midline view of the right hemisphere with major areas/structures and their functions labeled. (Ibid)

potentials, called an **electroencephalogram** (EEG), shows a pattern of brain waves. Researchers have found that most behavioral states have distinct brain wave patterns. For example, beta waves dominate during wakefulness, whereas theta and delta waves characterize deep sleep. Researchers have also been able to correlate brain wave patterns with psychological functions such as dreaming and attention, and with abnormalities caused by tumors or by the unusual electrical activity found in epilepsy (see Figure 3–4).

There is abundant evidence that various behavioral deficits result from defects in the central nervous system, but many questions remain unanswered. Fre-

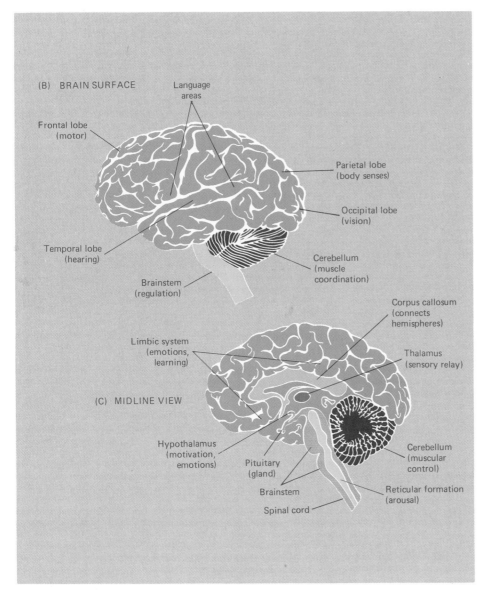

**FIGURE 3-3b and c**

quently, neither the particular type of deficit nor the available information about possible organic damage is sufficiently clear-cut to permit a high degree of certainty about the causes of the behavior. A person who experiences memory losses and thought disturbances may have fallen on his or her head, but the actual effects of the fall on brain tissue may not be obvious. In such a case, clinicians exercise caution in weighing the relative importance of organic damage and psychological factors. Full understanding of the brain's role in abnormal behavior will require extensive research on the interrelationships among psychological and biological processes.

The time and effort required for such research is illustrated by recent studies of the frontal lobes, the largest and most impressive parts of the brain. It is only natural to assume that such a large area would perform some important function. For many years it was assumed that the frontal lobes must be a "seat of intelligence." In recent years this view of the frontal lobes has been modified considerably. The frontal system now appears to be an important coordinator of emotion, volition, judgment, and creativity. A more refined charting of the functions of the frontal system is currently under way, and the results indicate that the frontal system may be quite important in major mental illnesses such as schizophrenia and affective disorders. For example, signs of damage to the frontal lobes have been noticed in schizophrenics. Much more research will be needed to determine whether some schizo-

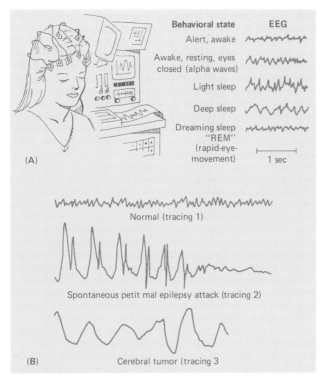

| Behavioral state | EEG |
|---|---|
| Alert, awake | |
| Awake, resting, eyes closed (alpha waves) | |
| Light sleep | |
| Deep sleep | |
| Dreaming sleep "REM" (rapid-eye-movement) | 1 sec |

(A)

Normal (tracing 1)

Spontaneous petit mal epilepsy attack (tracing 2)

(B)   Cerebral tumor (tracing 3

**FIGURE 3-4**
An EEG and three EEG tracings. (a) An electroencephalogram (EEG) uses scalp electrodes to measure the activity of specific types of neutrons. Particular EEG patterns are associated with certain behavioral states as depicted here. (Wittrock and others, 1979). (b) EEG tracings from patients who have different disorders are often visually distinguishable from one another and from those of normal subjects. Tracing 1 show a normal EEG. Tracing 2 shows the onset of wave and spike, discharges that are characteristic of petit mal epilepsy, a disorder in which sudden transitory disturbances of brain function may cause brief periods of loss of consciousness. Tracing 3 demonstrates the slow wave activity that is often associated with a cerebral tumor.

phrenics do indeed have defective frontal-lobe functioning or whether there is a breakdown in the communication between their frontal lobes and other important systems.

An important part of current brain research concerns recently identified systems within the brain. For example, work on the basic psychology and biology of motivation has resulted in the discovery of the brain reward system in higher animals. The brain reward system involves the hypothalamus and structures of the limbic system. The **limbic system** is part of the primitive, lower part of the cortex and is associated with emotional and motivational functions; the **hypothalamus,** located above the roof of the mouth, plays a role in motivation and emotions but also has connections with many other areas of the brain. Activation of the

brain reward system by electrical stimulation produces an intense feeling of pleasure that is much more powerful than ordinary reinforcers, such as food and sex. In experimental work with rats it has been found that if an electrode is implanted so that an animal can deliver a weak shock to its own brain reward system by pressing a lever (electrical self-stimulation), it will do so at a very fast rate. If the animal is starved and then given a choice between food and electrical self-stimulation, it will self-stimulate until it starves to death.

Early researchers who studied the brain reward system had no idea that their work might be related to addiction to substances like opium, but unexpected recent evidence is rapidly changing the situation. Researchers have discovered that there are chemical receptors on neurons in certain regions of the brain that respond to opiates. In fact, the greatest concentration of these opiate receptors is in the brain reward system. Moreover, the brain produces substances called **endorphins** that activate these receptors; they are even more powerful analgesics (pain relievers) than opium and, when administered directly, are addictive.

The endorphins work like keys in a lock. They fit only into sites, or receptors, that are specifically designed to accept them. Because the endorphins are similar to opium and related chemicals, knowledge of how they work may lead to a better understanding of drug addiction and its treatment. There are, of course, equally important environmental, psychosocial, and personality factors that influence the actual addictive behaviors. If scientists can create nonaddictive chemicals that function like the opiates, they may be able to ease pain of all kinds, including the pain connected with stopping a heroin habit. Before this can happen, however, much more information about the brain reward system and endorphins is needed.

**The Endocrines**   Several glands, including the pituitary, thyroid, adrenal, and gonadal (sex) glands, as well as the part of the pancreas that produces insulin, make up the endocrine system (Figure 3–5). These glands are ductless: the endocrines, unlike the salivary glands or the tear glands, have no ducts for delivery of the substances they produce. Instead, they discharge those substances directly into the bloodstream, which carries them to all parts of the body. Hormones secreted by the endocrine glands act as chemical messengers (the word "hormone" is derived from a Greek word meaning "messenger"). They correlate our reactions to external events and coordinate bodily growth and development.

Hormones are very potent, so it takes very little of them to exert an influence over their specific target cells. Cells that respond to hormones are genetically

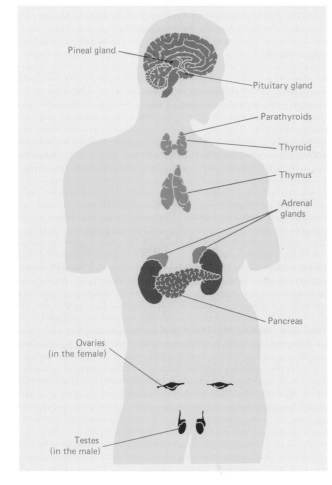

**FIGURE 3-5**
The endocrine glands and their location in the body.

endowed with special surface molecules, or "receptors," that detect even very low hormone concentrations. Once these cells receive a hormone, they initiate a series of adjustments within the cell that are dictated by the hormone. Hormones will usually increase the cell's activity temporarily.

In the study of abnormal psychology there is particular interest in the role played by the endocrine glands in dealing with stress. The word **stressor** is often used to refer to a condition that makes it harder to achieve or maintain biological and psychological adaptation. Examples of stressors to which the endocrine glands respond are biological factors such as disease germs and psychological experiences such as receiving an insult or engaging in combat. The hormones secreted by the glands help us mobilize our physical resources to deal with stressors by fighting or escaping.

The stress response involves the pituitary gland and the part of the adrenal gland called the **adrenal cortex.** In times of stress the brain is activated and sends messages to one of its structures, the hypothalamus, which is close to the pituitary gland. The hypothalamus releases a substance called **corticotrophin-releasing factor** (CRF), which goes to the pituitary to form and

release another chemical, **adrenocortico-trophic hormone** (ACTH). ACTH is released into the bloodstream and can go directly to the adrenal cortex, where it causes the adrenal cortex to form and release **adrenal corticosteroids,** which affect the brain's and the body's response to mental and physical stress. Some researchers have used the level of these steroids as an indicator of the degree of stress experienced by the individual.

## Research on Biological Factors and Abnormal Behavior

The enormous growth in knowledge about biological processes has strengthened beliefs concerning their relationship to abnormal behavior and has stimulated two promising lines of research. In one, an effort is made to determine the causal role of biological factors in maladaptation. The study of identical triplets mentioned earlier illustrates this approach, as does research on certain forms of mental retardation that are clearly related to biological defects, and research on the connection between biochemical factors and depression. In the triplet study, the fact that the three brothers showed important differences in behavior, intelligence, and social adaptation serves as a stimulus for further research aimed at identifying variables that might account for the differences among people who have identical genes.

The other line of biological research has a therapeutic orientation. Drug studies illustrate this approach. Although the pill that will cure mental illness, like the process that will turn lead into gold, has not yet been invented, great strides are being made in biological therapies.

### Psychoimmunology: A Search for Causes

*Fred Jackson, a 50-year-old divorced high school teacher, had had a series of infections and fevers, swollen lymph nodes, and a nagging cough ever since his high-school-age daughter had died four years previously. Recently he had experienced severe respiratory difficulties, as a result of which he had been hospitalized. The three months prior to the hospitalization had been particularly stressful because of disagreements with the school principal, who seemed always to be annoyed with him. While he was in the hospital, treatment with antibiotics resulted in some symptomatic improvement, but he continued to feel weak and the lymph node swelling persisted. A lymph node biopsy showed the existence of a cancerous condition.*

*His physician was not sure whether it was related to Jackson's physical condition, but the doctor concluded, after several conversations with his patient, that Jackson had not yet gotten over his daughter's death. Jackson seemed to work very hard at denying his grief over the daughter's death. He never expressed the feelings that the doctor felt would be normal under the circumstances.*

Many physicians have noted associations between significant losses, like a daughter's death, and subsequent illness. The association often seems greatest when the person experiencing the loss is unable to express strong emotions, for example, the grief that normally accompanies personal tragedies. Cases like Jackson's have led researchers to the hypothesis that the stress evoked by major losses and separations disrupts the body's immune system and thereby contributes to a host of physical illnesses.

The immune system has two major tasks: recognition of foreign materials (called **antigens**), and inactivation and/or removal of these materials. The immune system influences a person's susceptibility to the course of a disease. It consists of several distinct groups of cells called **lymphocytes**. Recent research has provided a preliminary understanding of how stress and emotional factors lead to hormonal changes that can sometimes decrease the efficiency of the immune system and thus increase susceptibility to disease.

The first demonstration of a relationship between bereavement and alterations in the functioning of the immune system was a study of 26 surviving spouses of patients who either had been fatally injured or had died after a prolonged illness (Bartrop and others, 1977). Although the effects were not large, the evidence suggested diminished immune system functioning among the survivors. Subsequent research has shown that bereavement associated with the death of a spouse is associated with a suppression of immunity and that the absence of a supportive social network contributes to suppression of the immune system (Laudenslager and Reite, 1984). Furthermore, certain psychological states, such as loneliness, depression, and feelings of helplessness, have a negative impact on the immune system. In this connection it is noteworthy that Jackson's divorce had occurred a year before his daughter's death. The divorce had greatly restricted his social network. He had fewer contacts with other people and lacked social relationships that made it easy for him to express his grief, loneliness, and anger at the terrible things that had happened to him.

**Psychoimmunology** is a new field of study that links psychological and immunological events. While much research in this field involves the relationship between experimentally created stress and the immune systems of animals, increasing emphasis is being placed on studies of humans. There is reason to believe that behavioral factors can alter immunity and susceptibility to disease through direct central nervous system mechanisms and disruptions in the way the endocrine sys-

tem functions (Jemmott and Locke, 1984). The challenge facing psychoimmunologists is to specify the mechanisms involved in the process that begins with a major stressful life event and ends with disease and perhaps even death.

The search for psychological factors in the onset of cancer has focused increased attention on the immune system. One difficulty in studying the development of cancer is that it occurs over a relatively long period; consequently, patients are not studied until clinical symptoms are evident. However, studies have suggested that the loss of a close and important person is associated with reduced immune competence, which contributes to the onset of cancer (Laudenslager and Reite, 1984). These results are reinforced by the finding that lack of social support or close interpersonal ties is also associated with the occurrence of cancer. In one study, almost 1,000 medical students were interviewed and then their medical records were monitored for ten to fifteen years (Thomas and Duszynski, 1974). Those who originally reported that they had few family ties were the most likely to have developed cancer during the fifteen year period. Stress in general appears to be involved in the development of cancer, and lack of social support is associated with greater stress impact.

**Psychopharmacology** is the study of the effects of drugs on behavior. This fast-growing area of investigation requires the skills of the chemist, physiologist, and psychologist. For many years chemicals have been known to influence behavior—for example, to reduce pain and induce sleep. Only in recent years have chemicals been used extensively in treating maladaptive behavior. Several kinds of psychoactive drugs (antipsychotic, antianxiety, and antidepressant drugs) are often highly effective in reducing particular types of maladaptive behavior. Figure 3–6 illustrates how the use of antipsychotic drugs allows many individuals to be treated as outpatients instead of during long stays in mental hospitals.

Psychopharmacologists study five major types of drugs. Some of these are therapeutic agents and others are important because of the social and health problems arising from their illegal use. In addition to the three types of psychoactive drugs already mentioned, psychopharmacologists study substances that have pain-relieving properties (such as opium) or that influence perceptual processes (such as LSD). These drugs do not create new responses in the organism; they simply modify processes that are already going on. They exert their effects by blocking or modifying certain biochemical and physiological processes, particularly those involved in neural transmission within the brain.

The biological perspective has proven fruitful because of the therapies, such as drugs, that it has pro-

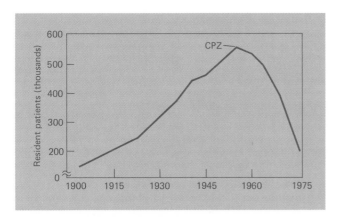

**FIGURE 3-6**
The introduction of antipsychotic drugs resulted in a sharp decline in the number of patients in mental hospitals. This figure shows the number of resident patients in state and county mental hospitals before and after the introduction of chlorpromazine, a drug that is particularly effective in treating schizophrenia. Prior to the introduction of the antipsychotic drugs, there had been a steady increase in the number of hospitalized mental patients. The use of those drugs has greatly reduced and even eliminated hospital stays for many individuals. (Based on data from National Institute of Mental Health)

duced, and also because of the questions it has raised. If the bizarre behavior of schizophrenics can be muted or eliminated by certain chemical compounds, can schizophrenia be regarded merely as a sign of a specific chemical disorder in the nervous system? Unfortunately, this sort of question can almost never be answered in a true-or-false fashion. For example, there are also instances in which purely psychological treatment of schizophrenics has led to marked reductions in bizarre behavior.

To what degree can maladaptive behavior be viewed as a disease? The boundaries between health and disease are far from clear, partly because of the roles played by psychological, social, and cultural factors. Given the multiple factors that affect people, an extreme organic perspective is likely to be simplistic. More likely to stand the test of time is a model that views maladaptive behavior as a product of these interacting factors. Although it does not provide a final answer, the biological perspective has enhanced our understanding of one of these sets of factors.

## Integration of Biological and Psychological Systems

Virtually all fields of science and technology are marked by progressively increasing levels of specialization. This means that some people have much deeper knowledge

about particular problems than others. As researchers involve themselves in the complexities of specific areas, they may tend to lose sight of the relationship of "their" topic to other topics.

The need for an integrated view of biological systems is illustrated by the endocrine glands. Traditionally, the endocrine system was viewed as separate from the nervous system but parallel to it in its activities. The traditional view also held the pituitary to be the "master gland" of the endocrine system. However, research has shown that certain pituitary cells are themselves subject to control by the hypothalamus in the brain. Specific neurons exert potent control over the pituitary. Thus, the brain in general, and the hypothalamus in particular, is the real "master gland" of the endocrine system. Awareness of the entire process by which the brain integrates the needs of the body with the demands of the environment has led to greater emphasis on neuroendocrine functions.

The organism behaves as an integrated unit. Exactly how the integration is achieved is an important but difficult question to answer. In an organism as complex as a human being, everything is related to everything else. These interrelationships extend beyond purely biological systems; each system enters into relationships with the behavioral and mental spheres of life, and those are not always one-way relationships. The amounts of certain chemicals in our bodies influence how much we are in contact with reality and how happy or sad we feel. However, our experiences and psychological reactions seem to influence how our immune system functions. An important goal in the study of the relationships between bodily systems and behaviors is to develop a theoretical framework that encompasses all of these types of relationships.

From the standpoint of abnormal psychology, it is important to relate biological processes to maladaptive behavior. Theories about these relationships range from those that reject the importance of the relationship for most disorders, to those that see value in exploring them but do not draw many firm conclusions, to those that argue that mental illnesses are diseases in the same sense as cancer or high blood pressure. However, there is growing evidence that cancer and high blood pressure are not pure illustrations of physically caused conditions. Most diseases are probably caused by multiple determinants, including physical, environmental, psychological, and hereditary factors. Disentangling these various kinds of causes from one another can be a difficult scientific problem.

It is clear that mental illness has multiple causes, and that these, like cancer and high blood pressure, are only partially understood. The biological perspective implies that many types of abnormal behavior are due largely to factors beyond people's control—that they are due primarily to the type of brain and body people are born with and the environment in which they are nourished. While this point of view may seem extremely deterministic, it is not totally so. Most theorists recognize that, to varying degrees, biological systems have plasticity. For example, the brain has built into it the ability to adapt and change in response to injury or changes in the environment. The limits that biological processes place on behavior and the degree to which those processes can be influenced represent topics of current research and theory.

## ■ THE PSYCHODYNAMIC PERSPECTIVE

The **psychodynamic perspective** is based on the idea that thoughts and emotions are important causes of behavior. Sigmund Freud, the originator of this perspective, believed that eventually all behavior could be explained by bodily changes; however, because so little was known about the relationships between the body and the personality, he actually gave biological factors little emphasis (Sulloway, 1979). Most of his followers also have paid little attention to biology and have not thought of it as an important factor in the development of behavioral problems.

Psychodynamic approaches to behavior assume that, to varying degrees, observable behavior (overt responses) is a function of intrapsychic processes (covert events). Not all psychodynamic theorists emphasize the same inner events and the same sources of environmental stimulation, but they do agree that personality is shaped by a combination of inner and outer events, with emphasis on the inner ones.

Because thoughts and feelings are not directly observable, psychodynamic theorists must infer them. They relate their inferences about inner processes to important features of overt behavior. The following account by a psychotherapist illustrates how this is done:

> By the fourth session I realized that he had never mentioned his father. It seemed as if there wasn't and never had been a father. I asked myself: How could it be that this man who is so unhappy and has so many problems fails to even mention his father? I guessed that he was either so ashamed of his father that he couldn't talk about him or he harbored so much anger toward him that consciously or unconsciously he couldn't deal with it. I decided to wait and see what would happen rather than push the client in the direction of talking about something that was very sensitive for him.
>
> During the ninth session he told me about a dream he had had the night before. A large dark man sat at a table and a small child watched from a corner as the man ate great quantities of food and ordered a small, frightened woman to bring him more and more. After he ate each helping he would raise a gun and shoot down a few people who were standing in a row against the wall.
>
> The client reported how frightened he had felt during the dream. As we discussed his associations to the dream, it became clear to me that the man in the dream represented his father. After several more sessions he told me he felt very angry with me because I constantly told him what to do and verbally cut him down. After pointing out that in reality I had said almost nothing, I asked him if I seemed like the man in the dream. Finally the dike burst. For the rest of the session and the next one all of his seething hatred toward his father came out. He blurted out that when he was a child he had seen his father strike his mother several times. When he saw this happen, he had wanted to kill his father.

Apart from the contribution that psychodynamic theories have made to our understanding of human behavior, they seem especially influential because they are the systems out of which all types of psychotherapy developed. While clinical psychoanalysis as developed by Freud is infrequently used today, its basic elements and the theory of mental events underlying it have greatly influenced the development of the entire field of psychotherapy.

### Freud and Psychoanalysis

Sigmund Freud, a Viennese neurologist, is clearly one of the most influential writers of this century, admired for his wit, intellect, and willingness to revise and improve his theories as his clinical experience grew. Freud began his practice at a time when there were few effective forms of treatment in most fields of medicine (see Figure 3–7). Effective treatment generally depends on an understanding of the causes of a disorder, and at that time, although accurate diagnoses could sometimes be made, little was known about the causes of disease, whether physical or mental. A disorder that was particularly common during the late 1800s was hysteria, the presence of physical problems in the absence of any physical causes. Like other well-trained neurologists of his time, Freud originally used hypnosis to help his hysterical patients loose their symptoms. Then a friend, Joseph Breuer, told Freud that while under hypnosis one of his patients had recalled and understood the emotional experience that had led to the development of her symptoms, and that her symptoms had then disappeared. For a time Freud and Breuer used this method of recapturing memories with some success. However, because some patients were not easy to hypnotize and sometimes the positive effects did not

**FIGURE 3-7**
Sigmund Freud and his future wife, Martha Bernays, in September of 1885. Freud, a promising physician, had not yet begun his psychoanalytic inquiries. At the time that the photograph was taken, he was experimenting with cocaine. After taking repeated small doses of cocaine, Freud found that it was able to relieve depression as well as stimulate his capacity for concentrated work. He wrote an article in which he recommended the use of the drug as a stimulant, as a local anesthetic, and as a means of withdrawal from morphine addiction. Although these ideas seemed useful at the time, today we know more about the problems associated with cocaine use. (Photo from Sigmund Freud Copyrights Ltd., The Bettmann Archive, Inc.)

last long, Freud began to develop his method of psychoanalysis, in which the patient recaptures forgotten memories without the use of hypnosis.

## Freud's Theories of Personality

Freud's theories of personality seem complicated because they incorporate many interlocking factors, but two basic assumptions underlie them all: psychic determinism and the conscious–unconscious dimension.

The principle of **psychic determinism** states that all behavior, whether overt (a muscle movement) or covert (a thought), is caused or determined by prior mental events. The outside world and the private psychic life of the individual combine to determine all aspects of behavior. As a clinical practitioner, Freud sought to modify unwanted behavior by identifying and eliminating its psychic determinants.

Freud assumed that mental events such as thoughts and fantasies vary in the ease with which they come to the individual's awareness. For example, aspects of mental life that are currently in awareness are **conscious.** Mental contents that are not currently at the level of awareness but can reach awareness fairly easily are **preconscious.** Mental contents that can be brought to awareness only with great difficulty are **unconscious.** Freud was interested mainly in how these unconscious mental contents could influence overt behavior.

Freud was especially intrigued by thoughts and fantasies that seem to go underground but then reappear at the conscious level. He asserted that the level of intrapsychic conflict was a major factor in determining our awareness of particular mental events. According to Freud, the classic example of intrapsychic conflict results when a young boy desires to take his father's place in relation to his mother but at the same time feels love and affection for his father. Freud believed that the greater the degree of intrapsychic conflict, the greater the likelihood that the mental events connected with it would remain unconscious. The more massive the unconscious conflict, the greater the person's vulnerability to stress. Freud believed that behavior disorders that occur after childhood are caused by a combination of early traumatic experiences and later experiences that trigger the emotions and unresolved conflicts associated with the early events.

Freud contended that hidden impulses or drives are involved in human conflict. He referred to these drives as **libido** and believed that they were a form of psychic energy analogous to the individual's supply of physical energy. Just as some people are more athletic, some have stronger libido. Freud also believed that the psychic energy or drive level of the individual sets up an inner state of tension that must somehow be reduced. In general, libido can be seen as desire for pleasure, particularly sexual gratification.

One novel feature of Freud's theory was his emphasis on sexuality. This emphasis was no doubt related to the often prudish, repressive atmosphere of Vienna at that time. The concept of sexuality within psychoanalytic theory is very broad and, rather than referring only to sexual intimacy, can be equated with the individual's total quest for pleasure and gratification. Freud also saw the process of development as being expressed in sexual terms.

**Stages of Psychosexual Development** Freud's theory of personality development placed tremendous emphasis on the effects of experiences that occur during the first five years of life. During this period children pass through a number of stages during which their libido is focused on a series of pleasure-giving or erogenous zones in the body. Those zones are the mouth, the anus, and the genitals, resulting in the **oral, anal,** and **phallic psychosexual stages.** In the phallic period, which occurs at about age 3, the child's pleasure in touching his or her genitals is accompanied by fantasies related to the sexual and aggressive impulses the child feels toward his or her parents. The child then enters a more or less sexually inactive latency period, which lasts until adolescence, when the sexual impulses are once again activated. If all has gone well to this point, the individual reaches the **genital stage,** in which pleasure comes from a mature heterosexual relationship.

What happens to children during these psychosexual stages helps mold their adult personalities. If they are unsuccessful in resolving the psychosexual conflicts that accompany a given stage or are severely deprived or overindulged, they may become fixated at one stage or another. **Fixation** is an arrest in personal development caused by the unresolved difficulties experienced at a given stage. Moreover, even if people resolve their conflicts successfully, severe difficulties later in life may cause them to **regress,** or adopt some of the feelings or behaviors of earlier, more satisfying stages.

In well-socialized adults the self-centered sexuality of earlier psychosexual stages blossoms into mature love and the individual becomes capable of genuine caring and adult sexual satisfaction. Freud's ideas about psychosexual development are undoubtedly the most controversial aspect of his theory. Although many theorists agree that childhood experiences are very important in personality development, many of them reject Freud's assertions about childhood sexuality.

**The Psychic Apparatus** For Freud, the mental world of the individual is divided into three structures: the **id,** the **ego,** and the **superego.** A basic distinction is made between the ego and the id. The id is a completely unorganized reservoir of psychic energy. The ego, on the other hand, is a problem-solving agent. Whereas the id is concerned simply with maximizing pleasure, the ego's efforts are directed toward maximizing pleasure within the constraints of reality. The id says, "I want it now." The ego says, "Okay, but first we have to do our homework" or "No, that's illegal." The ego performs the valuable functions of avoiding danger or coping with it when avoidance is not possible. There are three major sources of danger for the individual: the environment, his or her id impulses, and guilt. Guilt comes from the third structure of the psychic apparatus, the superego, which represents the person's moral code and reflects social values as expressed by parents, schools, and so on. The superego uses guilt to keep the id in line. The superego might say, "You know that's wrong" or "Work is more important than pleasure" (see Figure 3–8).

In early infancy the id is in control of all phases of behavior. Freud described the thought processes of the infant as **primary process thinking,** or thinking that is characterized by inability to discriminate between the real and the unreal, between the "me" and the "nonme," as well as by inability to inhibit impulses. Primary process thinking reflects uninhibited adherence to the **pleasure principle**—the immediate satisfaction of needs and desires without regard for the requirements of reality. The desire for immediate gratification that characterizes primary process thinking is dominant in childhood. Thus, most children, when given a piece of candy, eat it immediately, whereas an adult might wait until after lunch. A child who can't get immediate gratification often shifts its goal in order to achieve gratification in some other way. Thus, a baby that is crying for its bottle may gratify itself at least temporarily by sucking vigorously on its thumb.

**Secondary process thinking** is characteristic of older children and adults and is dependent on the development of the ego. The adult has learned to wait for gratification. Saving money for a goal—a new stereo system, a nest egg for old age—rather than going out for an expensive dinner on payday would be an example. The adult is also less likely than the child to substitute another object for gratification. An adult will generally keep working for the originally desired object even if setbacks occur.

Primary process thinking is still found in adults. It can be seen in cartoons, in dreams, in the parent who feels better after coming home and hitting the children because her boss criticized her on the job, and in the person who eats a pint of ice cream out of the container right in front of the refrigerator. However, maladaptation is considered to exist only when the primary process plays an overriding role in the adult's behavior.

**Anxiety** Freud defined **anxiety** as a response to perceived danger or stress. He distinguished between two kinds of anxiety-provoking situations. In one, of which birth might be the best example, anxiety is caused by stimulation that exceeds the organism's capacity to handle it. In the other, Freud assumed that psychic energy (libido) accumulates if inhibitions and taboos keep it from being expressed. This accumulated energy may

**FIGURE 3-8**
The id, ego, and superego can give very different messages. See if you can identify which is the source of each message in this cartoon. The answers are at the bottom of this page. (*New Yorker* magazine.)

build up to the point where it may overwhelm the controls of the ego. When this happens, a panic or traumatic state results. Psychoanalysts believe that these traumatic states are likely to occur in infants and children who do not know how to cope with much of their environment.

Anxiety often arises in anticipation of danger rather than after a dangerous situation has actually occurred. Anxiety, like physical pain, thus serves a protective function by signaling the approach of danger and warning us to prepare our defenses. Anxiety can also indicate inability to cope with danger, however. The meaning of anxiety is a central problem of psychoanalysis.

**Defense Mechanisms**   Freud believed that the ego was not helpless in the face of the demands of the id, the outside world, and the superego. Anxiety alerts the

individual to danger, such as the presence of an intense unconscious conflict or unacceptable wish. If this anxiety cannot be managed by direct action, so that the wish can be gratified, the ego initiates unconscious defenses in order to ward off awareness of the conflict. A variety of defensive responses to perceived danger are possible. Since everyone experiences danger, the use of these responses, called **defense mechanisms,** clearly is not a special characteristic of maladaptive behavior. Defense mechanisms are used by all people, either singly or in combination, at one time or another. The level of adaptive behavior depends on the repertory of defenses available to the individual under study (see Figure 3-9).

The most important and basic of the defense mechanisms is **repression.** Freud called it the cornerstone on which psychoanalysis rests. Repression, like other defenses, is directed at both external dangers, such as fear-arousing events, and internal dangers, such as wishes, impulses, and emotions that cry out for gratification but arouse guilt. Repression reduces anxiety by keeping anxiety-laden thoughts and impulses out of the

Answers: a, c ego
b superego
d id

**FIGURE 3-9**
Freud never cataloged all the defense mechanisms, but he recognized that his use of repression as an all-encompassing concept needed clarification. In 1936 he focused on this need: "There are an extraordinarily large number of methods (or mechanisms, as we say) used by our ego in the discharge of its defensive functions. My daughter, the child analyst, is writing a book about them." (S. Freud (1936), 1964, p. 245) Shortly afterward, Anna Freud, who played a creative role in adapting analytic therapy for use with children, published her book, *The Ego and the Mechanisms of Defense.* There she defined and illustrated most of the defense mechanisms that are still referred to today. This photo shows Signmund and Anna Freud in Paris in 1938. (UPI/Bettmann Newsphotos)

person's consciousness. Thus, a boy who experiences sexual desire for his mother and fear of retaliatory castration by his father could repress (render unconscious) both his unacceptable desire and his fear. The effort required to achieve such repression sometimes makes other behavior less effective. The person is, in a sense, preoccupied with the effort to maintain the repression. Sometimes repressed thoughts and wishes leak out and are expressed indirectly.

Repression is often described as motivated forgetting. It is necessary to distinguish between two kinds of forgetting: forgetting neutral mental content such as an unimportant telephone number is not the same as forgetting a traumatic childhood experience. Psychoanalysts are not nearly as interested in neutral material as they are in personally significant events. For instance, a recent college graduate may forget to go for a job interview if she is afraid that she will fail and not be hired, or a man may forget to attend the wedding of his brother to a woman that he himself was attracted to. In each case, the forgetting is real. The person is not making an excuse but actually is unaware of the engagement at the time. Figure 3-10 lists some other defense mechanisms.

## Clinical Psychoanalysis

**Psychoanalysis** is both a theoretical perspective and a clinical technique. As a clinical technique, it takes time. One of its conditions usually is that both patient and analyst make a commitment to the process for an indefinite period. Freud believes that much unhappiness and ineffectiveness are caused by forgotten conflicts that occurred long ago. Many a psychoanalyst has commented that a lifetime of difficulty cannot be straightened out in a few months.

Today most psychoanalysts are physicians who receive special training in the field of psychiatry and even more specialized analytic training. Some people without medical training, including psychologists, are also qualified to do psychoanalysis. All psychoanalysts believe that the roots of maladaptive behavior may be found in early childhood experiences and in infantile thoughts and feelings that persist into later life. They believe that insight into what went on in childhood enables the individual to adopt more mature and effective ways of living a happier, more productive adult life.

Many of Freud's ideas emerged from his studies of the dreams, fantasies, and memories of his patients. He developed the technique of **free association,** which calls for patients to express their thoughts and feelings as freely as possible during psychotherapy. With censorship (defense) reduced in this way, Freud hoped to gain a clearer picture of the conflicts underlying maladaptive behavior. As his work proceeded, it occurred to him that dreams might provide evidence about the workings of unconscious impulses. Clinical psychoanalysis places great weight on the interpretation of dreams and other types of fantasy and their relationship to thought and behavior (see Figure 3-11).

Psychotherapists agree that not all cases of maladaptive behavior are suitable for psychoanalysis. There are several reasons why psychoanalysis might not be recommended for certain people. For example, a person might not have adequate financial resources to pay for the many sessions needed, or might lack the necessary intellectual resources, particularly the verbal skill

Freud mentioned a number of defense mechanisms but he devoted most of his attention to repression as an all-inclusive defense. His daughter, Anna Freud, defined most of the concepts we refer to today as defense mechanisms.

## DISPLACEMENT

A shift of feelings and attitudes from one object to another, more acceptable substitute.

Examples:

A man is criticized by his boss and then feels angry. He comes home and yells at his wife (yelling at the boss might be too dangerous).

A young girl feels sexually attracted to her older brother. She finds a person in her office who has the same dry sense of humor and curly hair as her brother and quickly becomes very attracted to him.

## INTELLECTUALIZATION

Dealing with problems as interesting events which can be explained rationally and which have no anxiety or emotional content attached to them.

Examples:

A woman whose husband has just died discusses the inadequacy of America's mourning rituals, rather than her anger at her husband for leaving her.

A man who has just seen a bank robbery in which five people near him were gunned down talks about how interesting it was to observe the variety of ways that the people present reacted to the murders.

## REACTION FORMATION

Expressing an unacceptable impulse by transforming it into its opposite.

Examples:

A person who is attracted by the excitement and brutality of war becomes an overly zealous pacifist.

A mother who feels angry and rejecting toward her child checks many times to see if the child is all right during the night and worries excessively about her safety on the way to and from school.

## DENIAL

Refusal to acknowledge the anxiety-arousing aspects of the environment. The denial may be related only to the emotions connected to an idea or event or it may involve failure to acknowledge the event itself. Denial is most often seen in psychosis. It is seen in adults only under very severe stress.

Examples:

A husband, when told that his wife has incurable cancer, remains convinced that she will recover.

A student who has to take a final exam on material she doesn't understand, tells herself the exam is really not important and goes to a movie instead of studying the material with which she is having trouble.

## PROJECTION

Characteristics or impulses that arouse anxiety are externalized by attributing them to others. Psychotics are particularly likely to use projection.

Examples:

Nazis in Germany who started World War II insisted that they did so because of aggressive threats from other countries.

A man who has a strong desire to have extramarital affairs but feels guilty about it constantly accuses his wife of being unfaithful to him even though he has no evidence.

## REGRESSION

Going back to earlier ways of behaving that were characteristic of a previous development level. Typical of people who go to pieces under stress.

Examples:

A wife goes home to her mother every time she and her husband have a quarrel.

A student consoles himself, whenever things get rough, with several hot fudge sundaes, repeating behavior learned when his mother gave him ice cream to make him feel better after a scraped elbow or a disappointment.

## SUBLIMATION

A socially useful course of action developed when more direct forms of gratification are blocked.

Examples:

A teenager with strong aggressive feelings expresses them without danger by becoming a football player.

Someone with strong erotic feelings expresses them in a socially approved way by becoming a painter of evocative nudes.

**FIGURE 3-10**
Some defense mechanisms used in addition to repression.

to engage in the required level of communication. Freud believed that the most severe mental disorders, psychoses, could not be treated successfully with psychoanalysis. In addition, some analysts believe that people over the age of 40 lack sufficient flexibility for major personality change, and some personal problems are of such pressing urgency that there is not enough time to complete a lengthy psychoanalysis.

## The Neo-Freudians

Theorists who follow Freud in general terms but disagree with certain of his ideas are often called **neo-Freudians** or neo-analysts because they have sought to revise most of Freud's basic ideas. Among the early neo-Freudians were Carl Jung (1875–1961) and Alfred Adler (1870–1937), both of whom were originally members of

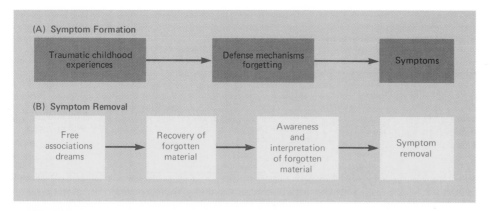

**FIGURE 3-11**

Processes hypothesized by Freud to be involved in symptom formation and removal. Symptoms (abnormal behavior, worries, unhappiness) result from traumatic childhood experiences that are detended against and forgotten but continue to exert unconscious influences that distort behavior, thought, and emotions. In the accepting, benign atmosphere of the psychoanalytic session, clues to the forgotten material come to the fore and are interpreted. Realization of the infantile quality of the forgotten material permits the individual to give up the symptoms.

Freud's inner circle of supporters. Both men had much more optimistic conceptions of human nature than Freud did. Jung did not think that all behavior is determined by earlier events. His emphasis on the need to emphasize spiritual qualities as well as rational ideas and his interest in Eastern religious thought have made him popular with many people today. Adler believed that people could be changed for the better through the creation of social conditions designed to develop realistic and adaptive lifestyles. For example, children have to be helped to overcome the inferiority that they naturally feel in comparison to adults. Consequently, Adler attached great importance to training parents in effective child-rearing techniques, and to the early education of children. He was a strong believer in the need to prevent psychological disorders rather than simply treat them after they occur.

Erik Erikson (b. 1902) is a central figure in contemporary psychoanalytic theory. His theory is a psychosocial one that emphasizes the "mutual fit between the individual and environment—that is, of the individual's capacity to relate to an ever-changing life space of people and institutions, on the one hand, and, on the other, the readiness of these people and institutions to make him part of an ongoing cultural concern" (Erikson, 1975, p. 102). Erikson stresses the role Freud assigned to the ego, but he gives it additional qualities such as the needs for trust and hope, industry, intimacy and love, and integrity. He thinks of the ego as a strong creative force that can deal effectively with problems.

Of special interest to psychologists is Erikson's idea of stages of development. Unlike Freud, who believed that development was essentially completed early in life, Erikson sees development as a lifelong process

consisting of eight stages. The first four stages occur during infancy and childhood, the fifth during adolescence, and the last three during adulthood and old age.

The neo-Freudians helped broaden the perspectives of psychodynamic theory, particularly through their emphasis on the role of distorted interpersonal relationships in maladaptive behavior. They insisted that disordered behavior and thought must be viewed as outgrowths of the individual's efforts to cope with personal crises in a world peopled by others. The neo-Freudians deemphasized the role of biology in personality and instead looked to the social environment for explanations of maladaptive behavior.

## Evaluating Psychoanalytic Theory

Psychoanalytic theory contains many ideas about the nature of perception and thought, human development, psychopathology, and treatment. However, its formulations are difficult to study scientifically because the events they hypothesize are not directly observable. Because psychoanalytic theory contains many general and somewhat unclearly defined concepts, it is hard to evaluate objectively. It seems to be better at explaining what has already happened than at predicting future events.

Because psychoanalytic concepts are difficult to prove experimentally, some researchers have tended to reject them out of hand. Others recognize that certain psychoanalytic concepts are vaguely stated and in fact untestable, but nevertheless they feel that scientific investigations should be conducted whenever possible.

Is psychoanalysis a theoretical framework within which human behavior can be studied scientifically, or is it a therapeutic method? These two possibilities are not inconsistent, as Freud pointed out on several occasions. A full evaluation of psychoanalysis will be possible only when its effectiveness as a therapy for maladaptive behavior has been objectively assessed and its links with the scientific method have been strengthened.

In recent years two research areas pertinent to the psychoanalytic perspective have seemed particularly promising. One concerns efforts to relate hypothesized psychodynamic processes to specific areas of brain function (Winson, 1985); and the other seeks to test experimentally such specific psychoanalytic concepts as primary process thinking, repression, and the superego's role as censor (Erdelyi, 1985; Bowers and Meichenbaum, 1985).

## ■ THE LEARNING PERSPECTIVE

*Give me a dozen healthy infants, well-formed, and my own specified world to bring them up in and I'll guarantee to take any one at random and train him to become any type of specialist I might select, doctor, lawyer, artist, merchant-chief, and yes, even beggar-man and thief, regardless of his talents, penchants, tendencies, abilities, vocations, and race of his ancestors. (Watson, 1925, p. 82)*

For John B. Watson (1878–1958), the founder of behaviorism, development was a thoroughly mechanical affair. The complete personality—by which Watson meant the whole system of overt behavior—was built up out of the conditioning process. Although many contemporary learning theorists are not as confident as Watson about the simplicity of the processes of behavior acquisition and behavior change, the behavioristic approach continues to exert a powerful influence.

Just as dissatisfaction with a narrow biological orientation was one factor in the development of the psychodynamic perspective, the **learning perspective** developed in part because psychologists found many of Freud's ideas about the mind vague, complicated, and untestable. These theorists thought that the same behavior studied by Freud could be explained in a simpler fashion and in a way that would make it possible to study them experimentally.

Both the psychoanalytic and behavioristic approaches to behavior are deterministic, but each finds the source of behavior in a different place. (**Determinism** means that every event or act is caused by what has happened before, not by the decisions of the individual.) Learning psychologists view behavior as a product of stimulus–response (S–R) relationships, not of intrapsychic events. They do not delve into the past or try to get people to figure out why they are the way they are. To change behavior, learning psychologists concentrate on changing the relevant aspects of the environment, particularly sources of reinforcement.

A **reinforcer** is an event whose occurrence increases the probability that a certain stimulus will evoke a certain response. Reinforcers reward the individual for doing the right thing or not doing the wrong thing. If the reward is desirable enough, the individual is likely to keep on performing properly as long as the response is reinforced. The response can be either an approach response (asking for another glass of milk) or an escape or avoidance response (running from a pursuer or refusing to go out at night). A **positive reinforcer** increases the probability that the proper response will be made by giving the individual something pleasant. A **negative reinforcer,** on the other hand, increases the probability that the proper response will be made by taking away something unpleasant as soon as the proper response occurs.

**Punishment,** another way of changing behavior, is an unpleasant consequence for a wrong response. For example, a wife may positively reinforce her husband for not drinking by having sex with him only when he is sober; she may negatively reinforce his drinking by stopping her nagging when he stops drinking; and she may punish him for drunkenness by locking him out of the house. Figure 3–12 illustrates the differences between reinforcement and punishment and contrasts them with **extinction,** still another way of changing behavior.

Positive and negative reinforcers and punishment have been applied to a variety of situations. Smiles, gold stars, and hugs are often highly effective in stimulating productive behavior in schoolchildren, and frowns or scolding may be used to discourage undesirable behavior. However, punishment, a negative consequence of behavior that is intended to discourage its repetition, is not very effective when used alone. It may cut down on undesired behavior, but it does not necessarily stimulate productive activity, since the person does not learn an acceptable substitute behavior.

The use of reinforcement in research on maladaptive behavior has followed two general paradigms: classical conditioning and operant conditioning.

### Classical Conditioning

In **classical conditioning**, the response that an organism automatically makes to a certain stimulus is transferred to a new stimulus through an association between the two stimuli. The most famous classical conditioning experiment was Ivan Pavlov's (1849–1936) investigation of salivation in dogs. Pavlov placed a hungry dog in a harness and turned on a light at certain

| | DEFINITION | EXAMPLES |
|---|---|---|
| POSITIVE REINFORCEMENT | "Stamping in" any behavior by using a desired reinforcer as a reward. | Giving a child candy when he brings in a homework assignment.<br>Saying "good girl" when the baby swallows a spoonful of cereal. |
| NEGATIVE REINFORCEMENT | "Stamping in" any behavior by removing an aversive stimulus when the behavior occurs. | Ceasing to scold a child when he hangs up his coat after throwing it on the floor.<br>Allowing a child to go out if the child is having a tantrum because she must stay home. |
| PUNISHMENT | Aversive stimulus given as a result of an undesired behavior in an attempt to suppress that behavior in the future. | Slapping a child for swearing at you.<br>Sending a child to her room because she broke her brother's toy. |
| EXTINCTION | Suppressing behavior by removing the reinforcers for it. | Ignoring a child when he has a temper tantrum.<br>Removing all rock records from the record collection if your roommate, who likes only rock music, plays the stereo too often for your comfort. |

**FIGURE 3-12**
Some mechanisms of behavior change.

intervals. The dog did not salivate in response to the light, which was the **conditioned stimulus (CS)**. After a few such trials, meat powder was delivered immediately after the light had been turned on. Since the dog was hungry, it salivated—an **unconditioned response (UR)**—upon presentation of the **unconditioned stimulus (US)**, the meat powder. After a number of trials in which turning on of the light was followed by delivery of meat powder, Pavlov found that the dog salivated when the light was turned on even if food did not follow. A **conditioned response (CR)** to the light had been established (see Figure 3–13).

In some classical conditioning experiments, the US is painful. Unpleasant US's are used when the goal is to strengthen **escape** or **avoidance responses**. Conditioned responses that are not reinforced periodically through the presence of the US become weaker and ultimately disappear from the organism's repertory of responses. This disappearance of a previously learned response is called **extinction**.

Students of maladaptive behavior have been intrigued by the process of classical conditioning because it seems to explain fear, anxiety, and other types of emotional reactions. Some of these reactions may come about because of accidental classical conditioning. A child who has been bitten by a dog may fear all dogs and, through generalization, other types of animals as well. Classical conditioning is also the basis for some therapies. An example is **systematic desensitization**, a therapeutic procedure whose goal is to extinguish a conditioned response. This procedure might be used to help a woman who has been afraid of cars ever since she was injured in a serious auto crash. At first she was merely uncomfortable in a car, but finally she became so fearful that she could not even look at a picture of a car. A diagram of the classical conditioning situation would look like this:

Unconditioned stimulus → Unconditioned response
*Car crash and injury*        *Fear*

Conditioned stimulus    → Conditioned response
*Car*                              *Fear*

Through a series of steps that break down the bond between the conditioned stimulus and the conditioned response and substitute another conditioned response, the woman's unrealistic fear could be removed. First she would be taught to relax, then to imagine she was looking at an automobile ad in a magazine. Her relaxed state would counteract the anxiety response. Once she could do this successfully, she might be asked to look at a real car, to touch a car, to imagine herself in a car, and so on. At each step she would relax first and then experience the conditioned stimulus. In this way a new conditioning bond would be built up between a car and a relaxed state.

**FIGURE 3–13**
Ivan Pavlov (the man with the white beard) stands in his laboratory beside a dog in the apparatus he used in his famous studies of classical conditioning. (Culver Pictures, Inc.)

## Operant Conditioning

In **operant conditioning,** the organism must make a particular response before the reinforcement occurs. The organism "operates" on its environment and produces an effect. A rat in a Skinner box, a device developed by B. F. Skinner (b. 1904) (Figure 3–14), will press a bar repeatedly if this activity is reinforced by pellets of food falling into a dish. Whereas classical conditioning makes use of natural as well as contrived responses, operant conditioning deals with responses that occur relatively infrequently prior to being reinforced.

A diagram of operant conditioning looks like this:

Response→Reinforcement→Increased probability that the response will be repeated

For example, in teaching a child to talk, parents reward the child with smiles and hugs whenever it says a desired word. These parental behaviors are positive reinforcements; they increase the chance that the child will repeat the word.

We hear over and over again how complex human behavior is. With pride we point to our lofty thoughts, fine feelings, and obscure motives. But learning theorists see human behavior as complex for other reasons. Even the simplest act can be seen as a chain of responses, each of which needs to be learned. Few of us get things right the first time. Children are particularly likely to become discouraged and give up if reinforce-

ment is withheld until they do something perfectly. Thus, **shaping**—obtaining the desired response by reinforcing successfully better approximations of it—is one of the basic processes in operant conditioning.

Considerable thought and planning are needed to decide what sorts of reinforcers are best for achieving particular behavior-shaping goals. In some situations an effective reinforcer may be rejected for purely practical reasons. A teacher who wanted to control disruptive behavior in the classroom probably could not use candy as a reinforcer, because it might have an undesirable effect on the pupils' appetites. In addition to deciding which reinforcers would be most effective and practical, it is necessary to decide on a **schedule** for reinforcing particular types of responses. The following case, which involves shaping verbal behavior in a 13-year-old boy with a suspected hearing problem, illustrates these elements.

*Benjie, who wore a hearing aid, had never been observed to make verbal responses (except for occasional grunts). He did not smile, cry, or interact meaningfully with others in any way. A reinforcement program was instituted in which candy was used as both a positive and a negative reinforcer. In addition to negative reinforcement (removal of a previously earned piece of candy), mild punishment (a slap on the hand) was used. This was how the operant treatment of Benjie began:*

*a. The experimenter sat across from Benjie and said, "Do you hear me, Benji? If you do, nod your head." The*

**FIGURE 3–14**
B. F. Skinner, one of the most influential psychologists of the twentieth century, is shown here demonstrating the famous Skinner box used in many of his operant-conditioning experiments. (Courtesy of B. F. Skinner)

*experimenter nodded his head in the hope that Benjie would imitate him. Initially, Benjie made no head-nodding response.*

*b. Next, the basic procedure remained the same; however, candy was made contingent on the head-nodding response. Soon, Benji was making 100 percent imitative head-nodding responses.*

*c. In the next procedure, the experimenter stood behind Benjie when giving the verbal cue. Benjie responded by nodding his head. This was the first indication to the experimenters that Benjie did, in fact, have the ability to hear verbalizations given at a normal conversational volume. From that point on Benjie did not wear his hearing aid in the laboratory or at home. (Knowles and Prutsman, 1968, p. 2)*

*Discouragingly, Benjie made no discernible progress in vocalization. Because he seemed unresponsive to rewards,*

*the experimenters decided to try a food deprivation schedule as a means of modifying Benjie's behavior. At breakfast, as soon as he made a sound he received a bite of food. This procedure proved to be effective. When he was hungry, he would make sounds at the command, "Benjie, tell me something." Eventually he came to respond to the command even when he was not hungry. After several months Benjie responded with a vocal sound every time a verbal command was directed toward him.*

## Modeling

Reinforcement is not always necessary for learning to occur. Modeling can be used to change behavior because people are able to learn by watching how other people do things. Opportunities for observational learning arise when another person—a model—performs some response or group of responses. The observer does not need to have had practice in making the observed response and does not necessarily have to be reinforced in order to learn it. Exposure to models whose behavior and skills we admire plays an important role in our personal development and contributes to our self-esteem (see Figure 3–15). Models may have desirable or undesirable effects on those who observe their behavior.

Clinical studies support the conclusion that observational learning plays a part in the acquisition of maladaptive behavior. Anxiety in patients can often be traced to modeling experiences. A severe phobia, for example, may represent an exaggeration of a major or minor fear observed in a parent. Watching television is basically a symbolic modeling experience, especially for children. Significant links have been established between aggression displayed on television and aggressive behavior in viewers (Parke and Slaby, 1983). However, because television is not a systematically programmed modeling technique, controlled laboratory studies are needed to specify what is going on when modeling effects occur. Noticeable and sometimes dramatic changes in behavior can result from modeling experiences. Terms like **vicarious learning, social facilitation, copying,** and **identification** have been used to characterize this process.

Modeling exposes the observer to the specific responses displayed by the model. Even more important, it provides the observer with food for thought. A child who observes continual arguing between parents forms a concept of what marriage is like. Poor people who observe the parade of commercials on television think that most other people are free from financial worries. Modeling, then, not only illustrates possible overt behavior but also contributes to the formation of concepts, attitudes, and needs. **Role playing,** or practicing

**FIGURE 3-15**
Modeling behavior can occur at all ages. As a childhood playmate of former President Lyndon B. Johnson, Sherman Birdwell obediently followed Johnson's lead. As an adult, Birdwell spent long hours working for Johnson at menial jobs in Washington, D.C. His speech and posture still seemed to be modeled after Johnson's. (LBJ Library)

*in situations that required putting one's best foot forward. In the institution he was given the opportunity to observe job interview behavior as modeled by persons (noninmates) who were effective in this area. On several occasions John observed simulated job interviews and then practiced being interviewed himself. After leaving the institution, he found that the modeling experience had helped him. He reported that while waiting for an actual job interview he had remembered and thought about the behavior he had observed. He then mentally rehearsed how he might handle himself when confronted by the personnel manager. He was hired, he felt, because of the new skill and security he brought to the previously traumatic job interview situation. His increased skill and security seemed to result from his having a better idea of what to expect in a job interview.*

## Learning and Mediational Processes

Over the years there have been many theories about the learning process. In general, these theories can be divided into two camps. The first says that covert events such as thoughts and feelings do not count because they cannot be directly observed and measured. This group, led by B. F. Skinner, believes that unless all references to inner processes are avoided, it will be impossible to develop a truly scientific approach to behavior. This strict environmentalist approach bases explanations of behavior only on observed events. From this perspective, therapy involves manipulating the person's environment so as to reinforce adaptive responses and extinguish maladaptive ones. Learning theorists who support this viewpoint, often called **radical behaviorists,** describe people as being more or less at the mercy of their environment.

Learning theorists of the second camp feel that environmentalism may be adequate to explain the behavior of pigeons and laboratory rats but is not sufficient to explain the complexity of human behavior, especially the qualities that distinguish humans from less complex animals. Members of this group, called **social-learning theorists,** emphasize the idea that a number of factors combine to shape social behavior and mediate the influence of learning experiences. Although social-learning theorists generally agree that covert events serve as mediators between external stimuli and overt behavior, the nature of the process is not clear.

An area of research that has received considerable attention from social-learning theorists is modeling. The modeling approach does not consider either practicing of the desired behavior or immediate reinforcement of that behavior to be necessary for learning to take place. What a person observes can be essentially stored away and brought out in the form of a behavior

behavior shown by a model, is another important learning technique.

The way in which modeling and role playing can strengthen adaptive behavior is illustrated by the case of John R., an unemployed 18-year-old who had been institutionalized for stealing a car. Therapists noted that his problem was not simply a failure to adhere to social norms but a weak behavioral repertoire.

*A particularly serious deficiency was his fear about and inadequacy in job interview situations. He had never had an opportunity to observe the effective behavior of others* when a situation occurs that is similar to the one faced by the model. Thus, although they recognize the importance of past events in the formation of present behavior, social-learning therapists focus on the current maladaptive behavior that troubles the client.

# ■ THE COGNITIVE PERSPECTIVE

*People are disturbed not by things, but by the views which they take of them. (Epictetus, first century A.D.)*

If Epictetus were alive today, he would be a cognitive psychologist. The word "cognitive" comes from the Latin word *cognitare*, meaning "to have known." Cognitive psychology deals with human beings as information processors and problem solvers. The cognitive view seeks to account for behavior by studying the ways in which the person attends to, interprets, and uses available information.

The **cognitive perspective** in abnormal psychology has grown out of new directions in learning and psychodynamic theory. Some learning theorists have become increasingly interested in what goes on in the individual between the application of a stimulus and the response, and certain psychodynamic theorists have emphasized the need to focus on thinking and problem solving as well as on feelings and emotions (Bieber, 1980). This perspective has been given added impetus by a group of clinicians (such as Albert Ellis and George Kelly) who have derived cognitive theories from their own therapeutic experiences with clients.

Like the psychodynamic perspective, the cognitive perspective is concerned with internal processes. Rather than stressing urges, needs, and motivations, however, it emphasizes how people acquire and interpret information and use it in solving problems. Unlike psychoanalysis, it places great emphasis on mental processes that we are aware of or can rather easily be made aware of, as opposed to hidden motivations, feelings, and conflicts. Its approach has been contrasted with the learning perspective's emphasis on the external environment as a prime cause of behavior. Typically, the cognitive perspective pays more attention to our present thoughts and problem-solving strategies than to our personal histories. However, histories of cognitions are now receiving some attention (Sarason, 1979). The relationships among emotions, motivations, and cognitive processes are also being studied more intensively. The overlap between the cognitive perspective and other approaches is becoming more evident.

A special emphasis of the cognitive perspective is the concept of the person as information processor. According to this view, people are continually collecting, storing, modifying, interpreting, and understanding both internally generated information and environmental stimuli. Humans are viewed as active, selective seekers, creators, and users of information, and behavior is viewed as both a product and an initiator of mental acts and environmental changes. The mental life of the individual is conceived of as consisting of **schemata** (plural of schema) that contain information in particular domains such as parents, work, and pets. Through their influence on cognitive processes, schemata enable people to identify stimuli quickly, cluster them into manageable units, fill in missing information, and select a strategy for obtaining further information, solving a problem, or reaching a goal.

From a clinical standpoint, self-schemata are especially important. They organize and guide not only our social experiences but any experiences that are personally relevant. Personally relevant experiences are often laden with emotions and are likely to reflect an individual's prior learning history. Self-schemata are capable of distorting a person's perceptions of reality. Schemata that concern our self-evaluations influence not only how we feel about ourselves but also how we relate to others. For example, **self-efficacy** refers to the strength of our convictions about our personal effectiveness. People may imagine potential difficulties as more formidable than they are in reality if they perceive themselves as ineffective in important types of situations. Inappropriate or maladaptive behavior in those situations may confirm the individual's self-perception as inadequate, helpless, or cowardly. This confirmation may cause the person to avoid problematic situations or reduce his or her task-relevant efforts. A vicious cycle is thereby created and perpetuated (Turk and Salovey, 1985).

## Cognitive Approaches to Personality

The cognitive perspective on personality has led to a variety of theories. Among the best known of these are those of Dollard and Miller, Kelly, Rotter, and Bandura.

**John Dollard and Neal Miller** John Dollard (1900–1980) and Neal Miller (b. 1909) tried to relate human learning to psychodynamic processes as well as to external events. Although thinking, feeling, perceiving, and other covert processes cannot be observed, they can be inferred. They are usually called **hypothetical constructs** (because there is no way to prove that they really exist) or **intervening variables** (because they are presumed to intervene between environmental stimuli and behavior).

Dollard and Miller (1950) thought they saw parallels between learning theory and Freudian theory in the area of personality development. For example, the reinforcement principle and Freud's pleasure principle have the same general function: people are more likely to do what makes them feel good. Dollard and Miller also made use of cognitive concepts by describing maladaptive behavior as a joint product of unfortunate life experiences and maladaptive thinking. They viewed gaining insight into the roots of one's own behavior as acquiring self-awareness responses. Despite their preference for describing behavior in terms of habits and learning, they emphasized the individual's cognitive resolution of conflicts.

Dollard and Miller suggested that the use of labeling, a cognitive device that enables one to classify emotional responses, is a way of controlling one's own reactions in a particular situation. This sort of labeling can help a person cope with what otherwise might be a stress-producing situation. For example:

> [A young man] had invited a girl whom he particularly liked but did not know very well to a formal dance. The girl had declined the invitation but said she would be glad to go to dinner before the dance. Trapped by her suggestion and his attraction to her, he had agreed to take her to dinner. The boy found the dinner rough going. He was immediately attacked by a stomach-ache so severe that he thought he would be forced to leave the table.

He was able to use an understanding of his reactions and a cognitive technique learned in psychotherapy to improve the situation.

> He recalled that aggression against a woman frequently took gastric form in his case. Could it be that he was angry at the girl, and if so, why? He realized immediately that he was angry and had repressed his anger. He had felt exploited by her suggesting dinner when she could not go with him to the dance. He was just being used to fill in a chink of time before the dance. When these thoughts occurred, ones contradictory to them came up also. The girl did not seem like an exploitative type. Maybe she wanted to show that she really liked him. There would, after all, be another dance, so why not ask her then and there for another date. This he did, and she accepted with evident pleasure. The combination of this lack of cause for aggression and hope of the future brought relief; the stomach-ache disappeared. . . .

> Once the stomach-ache was labeled as aggression-produced, the rest of the solution appeared rapidly. (Dollard and Miller, 1950, p. 443)

**George Kelly** The product of George Kelly's (1905–1966) extensive study of the nature of personal experience was his psychology of **personal constructs.** Kelly (1955) concluded that people's personal constructs re-

flect how they interpret or develop ideas about themselves, the world, and future events. Personal constructs are the way in which each person builds his or her own reality by sorting people and events into categories. Kelly believed that each person is constantly engaged in problem solving and that personal constructs are an important means of organizing information about interpersonal relationships.

There are wide differences between the personal constructs of different individuals. People may perceive the same event in entirely different ways. For example, suppose two lovers break up. One observer may describe the event as simple incompatibility, while another may believe that one person "jilted" the other. Another might say that the breakup was due to "parental meddling;" still another might see it as a "blessing in disguise."

Kelly was not a supporter of the concepts of hidden psychodynamics and the unconscious. He often referred to what he whimsically termed "Kelly's first principle": "If you don't know what is wrong with clients, ask them, they may tell you." Although he recognized that we might not be aware of all of our personal constructs at any given time, he tended to reject Freud's belief that the greater part of mental life is hidden from view. He also tended to reject the emphasis placed by psychoanalysis on what happened to a person in the past. For Kelly, the important thing was the distinctive set of personal constructs that guide a person's life at the present time.

Kelly stressed the role of personal constructs as causes of emotional reactions. We feel anxious when we don't know how to handle a situation, when we become aware that our system of constructs does not encompass a problem that has arisen. Thus, Kelly believed that cognitions precede emotions. He saw psychotherapy as a way of demonstrating to clients that their constructs are hypotheses rather than facts. Once clients realized this, he encouraged them to test their constructs so that the maladaptive ones could be replaced with more useful ones.

**Julian Rotter** A social-learning theorist who has stressed the cognitive perspective for many years is Julian Rotter (b. 1916). Like other social-learning theorists, Rotter believes that the problems of maladjusted people originate in their relationships with others. However, he also emphasizes that people's behavior is strongly influenced by how they expect a situation to turn out. Many people are convinced that they are unable to obtain the gratifications they desire. As a result, they learn how to defend themselves against anticipated failure rather than how to achieve their goals. In addition to having low expectations for success in particular situations, such as on a job, maladjusted people generalize these expectations to other areas of life.

**Albert Bandura** In addition to his emphasis on social learning theory, Albert Bandura (b. 1925) has more recently emphasized the symbolic and cognitive aspects of learning as opposed to the stimulus–response aspects (see Figure 3–16). According to Bandura (1982), we can solve problems symbolically without having to resort to trial-and-error behavior because we can foresee the consequences of our behavior and act accordingly. For example, we buy fire insurance because we think about what might happen if our house burned down. Similarly, in preparing for our first winter camping trip, we assemble protective gear because we can anticipate the effects of a blizzard. The ability to anticipate consequences operates in more routine behaviors as well as in special instances like these.

Bandura (1978) has become interested in studying self-regulation or learning by internal reinforcement as opposed to the idea of modifying behavior by external reinforcement alone. Many cognitive psychologists are developing techniques by which people who lack behavioral self-control can be helped to acquire it. The

**FIGURE 3-16**
Albert Bandura's work on modeling, as well as his more recent work on self-regulation, has been important not only theoretically but also in the development of new therapeutic approaches. (Courtesy of Albert Bandura)

following examples illustrate techniques for strengthening self-control that make use of cognitive mechanisms.

1. A student studies every night even though no test has been announced.
2. A heavy smoker teaches herself nonsmoking behavior.

In the first case, the student may motivate himself by means of cognitive representation of future consequences. That is, he may think about how bad he would feel if he scored poorly on the next test or how stressful it would be to try to learn all the information the night before the test. Another motivation may be his own goal-setting behavior. He wants to receive a high grade for the course. Whenever he feels like turning on the television set or stopping for a snack, he visualizes how he will feel if he attains his goal. When people evaluate their own behavior in this way, they tend to persist until they achieve their goals.

In the second example, each time the former smoker has the impulse to smoke, she may imagine an X-ray of lungs afflicted by cancer, or she may see herself coughing and unable to breathe. Such self-generated cognitive mechanisms would provide negative reinforcement for her thoughts about smoking.

In addition to their application to the self-control of behavior, cognitive mechanisms are important in problem solving. If you were an engineer designing a bridge, you wouldn't try out different construction methods until you arrived at one that didn't collapse. Instead, after considering information about materials, climatic conditions, and the technical data on different designs and then performing complex cognitive operations, you would come up with a plan. Or suppose you have a chance to get a job as a summer trainee with a firm you'd like to work for after graduation. It would be a good experience, but the pay is low and it would mean moving to another state for the summer. Your finances would be stretched and you would have to work part time for the next winter to make up for the extra cost. You couldn't simply try out the job. Instead you would probably do some financial figuring, see what jobs are available in town, and after thinking about all the options and consequences, make a decision.

**Cognitive Therapies** The idea that maladaptive thoughts are the cause of maladaptive behavior and that people must be taught new ways of thinking has been used as a basic approach by many therapists. Several forms of therapy are based on the cognitive perspective.

**Rational–emotive therapy,** developed by Albert Ellis, is based on the belief that behavior depends more on individual belief systems and ways of interpreting situations than on objective conditions. Ellis contends that all effective psychotherapists, whether or not they realize it, function as teachers for their clients. They help their clients to review, reperceive, and rethink their lives; to question their irrational beliefs; and to modify their unrealistic and illogical thoughts, emotions, and behaviors. Ellis regards both intense emotions and maladaptive behavior as the modifiable consequences of thoughts. He admits that faulty beliefs are probably formed in childhood. However, he feels that finding out how people got to be the way they are is less important than helping them respond more constructively to their present situation.

In rational–emotive therapy the clinician explains and demonstrates productive thinking, persuades the client to think and behave in more effective ways, and discusses homework assignments. Through such assignments the client might practice ways of behaving more assertively with co-workers or family members without alienating them (Ellis, 1962, 1970; Smith, 1982).

George Kelly used a variety of tactics to help his clients explore and modify their personal constructs. Most often he used a traditional interview format in which he and his client talked about specific personal constructs and the roles they led the client to play in social relationships. In addition, he used **fixed-role therapy,** in which clients experimented with (by acting out) new roles that might result from particular revisions in their personal-construct systems. Kelly believed that people have difficulty simply trying out new ways of behaving; hence he was very supportive of these experimental efforts (Niemeyer, 1986).

Aaron Beck (1976) also thinks that the job of the therapist is to help clients restructure their thinking and replace maladaptive thoughts with thoughts that are more helpful in coping with stressful situations. Beck's work was originally focused on the cognitions of depressed individuals; but recently his approach has been extended to the problem of anxiety (Beck and Emery, 1985). Beck thinks that people's emotions and behavior are based largely on the way they view the world. In his view, depressed and anxious people exaggerate their difficulties and minimize the possibility that anything can be done about them.

## ■ THE HUMANISTIC–EXISTENTIAL PERSPECTIVE

The humanistic–existential perspective presents a sharp contrast to the theoretical approaches described so far. Its roots are found in a number of philosophical and religious systems that have stressed the dignity, inherent goodness, and freedom of human nature. The growth of this perspective within psychology was partly a product of this tradition and partly a reaction to the less flattering conceptions of human nature that are characteristic of psychoanalysis and radical behaviorism.

One of the central assumptions of the humanistic view is that in every person there is an active force toward **self-actualization,** toward being "all that you can be." When the human personality unfolds in a benign environment that gives these creative forces free rein, the positive inner nature of the human being emerges. Human misery and pathology, on the other hand, are fostered by environments that frustrate the individual's tendencies toward self-actualization.

Closely related to the humanistic movement is the existential perspective, which became popular in Europe as psychologists and philosophers sought to understand how the horrors of World War II could have occurred and how certain people were able to rise above them and find meaning in life. While the humanistic theories focus on the process of self-actualization, existential theorists emphasize self-determination, choice, and the responsibility of the individual to rise above environmental forces. "We are our choices," maintains the existentialist. "Our existence and its meaning are squarely in our own hands, for we alone can decide what our attitudes and behaviors will be."

Humanistic–existential theorists believe that scientific psychology is missing the mark when it dwells only on observable behavior and neglects the person's inner life. They believe that inner experiences and the search for the meaning of existence are the core of the individual's being-in-the-world and hence should be the focus of psychology. They therefore regard introspection as a valid and, indeed, indispensable source of psychological information.

### Maslow's Hierarchy of Needs

Abraham Maslow (1908–1970) was a leader in the effort to integrate a humanistic philosophy into the traditional scientific approach. His vehicle for accomplishing this was the **hierarchy of needs** (1968). Figure 3–17 shows Maslow's hierarchy as a five-layer pyramid. The needs in each layer must be satisfied before those in the next higher layer become important.

Maslow assumed that needs direct behavior. When we are hungry (need food), we direct our behavior toward getting food. When the most basic requirements, or **deficiency needs** (the two lower levels of Figure 3–17), are not met, they exert a dominant influence over our thinking and behavior. Physiological needs include those for food, water, and air. Safety needs take in freedom from pain, fear, and insecurity. When these basic needs are satisfied, we can turn to the needs at

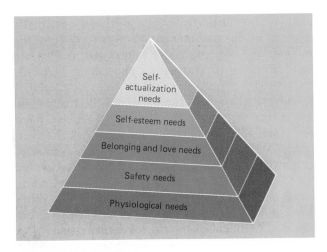

**FIGURE 3-17**
Maslow's hierarchy of needs.

higher levels of the pyramid. Needs for identification with others and the feeling of being loved come next. When these are satisfied, the person's need to feel competent and in control of the environment becomes important. Finally, when all these needs are met the person can turn to **self-actualization needs,** which refer to problems that we create for ourselves. The artist must paint and the scientist must inquire if each is to attain self-actualization. Maslow saw self-actualization as the realization and fulfillment of people's most distinctive potentialities.

Maslow viewed neurotics as people who have been prevented or are preventing themselves from attaining their basic needs, which means that they are also barred from self-actualization. As a result, they feel threatened and insecure. To correct this situation, therapists must give their clients enough respect and love to satisfy those basic needs. In addition, the client must be encouraged to display affection toward the therapist and others. Once this reciprocal relationship has been established, the client can begin the process of growth.

## Rogers' Conception of the Self

Along with Maslow, Carl Rogers (b. 1902) is one of the leaders of humanistic psychology (see Figure 3–18). The centerpiece of his perspective on personality is the self-image (1951, 1959, 1980). Rogers relates the ability to achieve self-understanding and self-actualization to the individual's self-regard and perception of acceptance by others. An adult who felt wanted and highly valued as a child is likely to have a positive self-image, to be thought well of by others, and to have the capacity for self-actualization. Optimal adjustment results in what Rogers calls the fully functioning person and is characterized by a low level of anxiety. Anxiety is due to uneasiness or tension resulting from inconsistencies between people's self-perceptions and their ideas of what they would like to be.

Although the ways in which they conceptualize behavior contrast sharply, both Rogers and Freud developed their theoretical positions on the basis of similar observational data: the behavior of clients and therapists in psychotherapy. However, Rogers rejects the psychoanalytic notion that people are irrational and unsocialized by nature. He asserts, on the contrary, that each person is basically rational, socialized, and constructive.

For Rogers, psychotherapy is a situation in which anxious, troubled people with low self-regard and distorted perceptions of themselves and the world seek help. Rogers thinks that healthy people are those who move away from roles created by the expectations of others, that is, from pretending to be something they are not. Instead, they learn to trust themselves and reject the false selves that they have created. Neurotic and psychotic people, on the other hand, have self-concepts that do not match their experiences. They are afraid to accept their own experiences as valid, so they distort them, either to protect themselves or to win approval from others. A therapist can help them give up these false selves.

The task for Rogerian therapists is neither to provide interpretations nor to give advice. Rather, the therapist must accept clients as having worth and dignity in their own right despite their problems. This acceptance means that the therapist must understand the client's feelings, no matter how positive or negative they are or how much they contradict the therapist's own attitudes.

## The Existential Point of View

Existentialists believe that people are free to choose among alternative courses of action. If this is true, why are so many people unhappy and dissatisfied? Why does maladaptive behavior exist? For one thing, not everyone chooses wisely. A person can choose to act either authentically or inauthentically. To act **authentically** means to freely establish one's own goals. To act **inauthentically** means to let other people dictate those goals. For each person there are also certain givens that place definite limits on what he or she may become. These may be characteristics that are present at birth, such as learning ability, physical appearance, or the presence of a disabling disease, or they may be environmental, including the influence of parents and later of school. These expand or contract the individual's chances for fulfillment based on the qualities present at birth. Other unavoidable givens are guilt, which comes from failure to fulfill all possibilities, and dread of nothingness, which means not only death but also alienation from the world.

Rollo May (1958), a prominent existential therapist, believes that anxiety is created when a person is faced with a fundamental choice or question. A person who has been rejected may use anxiety constructively by questioning the other people involved. However, the person may also avoid questions because they are too embarrassing, thus blocking further development.

If anxiety is not used constructively, it causes guilt. According to Freud, guilt results when one ignores cultural prohibitions. May thinks of guilt as the response of a person who is able to choose but fails to do so. Anxiety may be produced by such events as not being accepted into medical school after years of planning for a career as a physician, or being rejected by a lover who announces that he or she is in love with someone else. The primary task of the therapist, according to May, is to help empty, lonely people expand their experiences and fulfill their own uniqueness, that is, to help them make constructive choices.

## ■ THE COMMUNITY PERSPECTIVE

Most people see mental illness as a personal health problem or as a character defect. In contrast, from the **community perspective,** maladaptive behavior results from inability to cope effectively with stress. It is not viewed as a disease or problem that exists only within the individual; instead, it is seen as at least partly a failure of the individual's social support system. This system includes the person's spouse, parents, siblings, relatives, friends, teachers, employer, religious adviser, and others, as well as community organizations and government agencies.

Community psychologists do not deny the role of life history or genetic makeup in causing maladaptive behavior, but these are not seen as necessarily sufficient to produce such behavior. For example, a schizophrenic may develop hallucinations for many reasons: biochemical factors, traumatic early experiences, or unusual social relationships are all possibilities. However, the presence of an especially strong stressor or the breakdown of the person's social support system may be equally important in producing the schizophrenic behavior.

The community approach attempts to reduce maladaptive behavior through preventive measures, by intervening in people's lives before catastrophes occur. Such measures include a variety of special programs: discussion or mutual support programs for recently separated, divorced, or widowed people; preschool enrichment programs for children from low-income, single-parent homes; day-care centers for the care of elderly people who need help in solving problems of living. Implicit in community psychology is the belief that the effects of social disorganization (such as slums, bad schools, and high unemployment rates) are a major cause of many personal problems. For this reason, mental health professionals with a community orientation tend to become involved in efforts to change society by lobbying for legislation and becoming actively involved in community affairs.

Community psychologists study the social environment and factors related to it, such as socioeconomic status. When the living places of people who are identified as psychologically and socially impaired are plotted on a map, it can be shown that the frequency of such problems is much higher in certain areas than in others. **Social-causation theories** argue that the poor schools, crime, poor housing, and prejudice often found in low-income, deteriorating neighborhoods may increase the stress experienced by already vulnerable people. The **social-selection theory,** on the other hand, argues that lower socioeconomic groups show a greater incidence of maladaptive behavior because people who do not function well tend to experience downward social mobility.

Those who believe in the community perspective are more likely to support the social-causation theory. They point out that, while social selection may be a factor, the theory does not rule out the stress-producing situations of lower-class living that may aggravate existing disorders. Lower-class people may have less power to control their environment as well as fewer resources for dealing with stress. For a variety of reasons, not the least of which is the difficulty of carrying out controlled research in community settings, one cannot completely rule out either the social-selection or the social-causation theory. One or the other might apply to certain types of disorders. In either case, psychologists with a community perspective see a need to develop special programs aimed at counteracting undesirable aspects of urban life such as poverty and overcrowding. Such programs would improve the lives of the general population as well as those of people with specific psychological problems.

## Social Roles and Labeling

All individuals belong to social groups. These groups shape people's behavior by providing the distinctive reinforcement, punishments, and models that are part of life in a particular cultural setting. The members of a social group share a set of meanings or symbols, experience a feeling of unity, and participate in a network of mutual obligations. The group or groups to which a person belongs influence nearly every aspect of his or her life.

**Social roles** are particular functions that a person plays as a member of a social group. Some writers have maintained that we always attempt to project an image and that, in fact, we have no true self. This position is presented by Erving Goffman (1959), who argues that in all of our encounters with other people we adopt particular roles. Each role is accompanied by a script that includes different actions and signals. In effect, we vary our behaviors continuously as the situation requires. This viewpoint implies that there is no such thing as a fixed personality.

Less extreme than this position, and more widely accepted, is the composite position: there is a basic personality that is overlaid with situational role playing. Research has shown that a number of factors influence the roles people play in social relationships. These factors are often important because they serve to label an individual in a particular way. **Labeling** occurs whenever people are categorized on some basis, whether that basis is relevant and fair or not. Labels can be destructive because they draw attention to one aspect of the person while ignoring other aspects that make him or her unique. (Would you like to be labeled as a slob simply because you don't like to put your shoes away at night?) Some labels, such as "good student" and "loyal friend," are desirable, but many others carry negative social connotations. For example, the role of mental patient is widely viewed as socially unacceptable, and the

label of mentally ill often causes permanent damage. The damage takes many forms, including discrimination by others and feelings of self-doubt and inadequacy.

In an experiment that demonstrated the effects of labeling on people's behavior (Farina and others, 1971), the subjects were psychiatric patients who had been hospitalized in the past but at the time of the study were outpatients living in the community. They were told that the study was designed to find out whether prospective employers would be less likely to hire former psychiatric patients than to hire individuals without a known history of mental illness. Half of the subjects were told that the interviewer knew their true status; the other half were told that the interviewer thought they were former "medical" patients. The interviewer (who was actually a confederate of the experimenter) worked with each subject on a cooperative task. The subjects who thought they had been described as medical patients made higher scores on the task, rated the task as easier, and thought the interviewer appreciated them more than did those who had been labeled as psychiatric patients. The interviewer, who did not know what the subjects had been told, rated the mental-patient group as more anxious, tense, and poorly adjusted than the so-called medical patients. This experiment demonstrates that knowing how one is labeled can change one's behavior even if the label is known to be false.

## Contributions of the Community Perspective

What we know at present supports the emphasis that community psychology has given to the role of the social environment in emotions and maladaptive behavior (Gottlieb, 1985). For example, children's levels of distress and oppression increase sharply when they live in an environment in which adults express high levels of anger and behave aggressively. There is some evidence that this responsiveness to family discord is greater for boys than it is for girls (Cummings and others, 1985; Farber and others, 1985).

Rutter and Quinton (1984) studied 137 psychiatric patients who had children under the age of 15. They found that there was a high rate of psychological distress among the patients' spouses, which could be attributed to the tense family environment. In the children there was a significant increase in the rates of disturbances (assessed by questionnaire) and psychiatric disorders (assessed by interview). The disturbance was greater when the children were exposed to hostile behavior on the part of their parents. One-third of the children of psychiatric patients were found to have a persistent psychiatric—usually conduct—disorder that was derived not from the parental illness itself but from the associated disturbance within the family. (A conduct disorder is one in which a child or adolescent habitually violates the rights of others through violent or antisocial behavior.) Evidence of this type suggests that once serious disorders are established within a family, these are incorporated into the child's personality and functioning, and the child's disordered behavior may continue even when the parental disorder improves.

The community perspective has been influential in producing creative new approaches to maladaptive behavior and in reaching segments of the population whose psychological needs have been ignored. It has been effective both in changing the perspective of academic thinking and in altering social policy.

# ■ THE VALUE
# OF AN INTERACTIONAL APPROACH

We have reviewed six widely varying perspectives on the causes and treatment of maladaptive behavior. You may be wondering how these perspectives relate to the rest of the book. Which one is emphasized most? We think you should know our biases and how our views will affect what you learn in this book.

We have attempted to use the most valuable contributions of each viewpoint in our discussions of abnormal behavior. Abnormal behavior can result from any or all of a large number of factors. One perspective may contribute more than another under one set of conditions; under a different set, another viewpoint may be more useful. Our approach, which is shared by many other psychologists, is interactional. The way a situation influences behavior depends on the particular vulnerabilities, capabilities, and preoccupations of the person experiencing the particular set of conditions. These conditions and the person's characteristics can be thought of as interacting or combining to produce a special product, the individual's behavior. For example, there is evidence that many people do not become depressed for either purely mental or purely environmental reasons (Oatley and Bolton, 1985). A full understanding of depression requires information about both the person's mental state and the state of his or her social and community ties. Depression can be viewed as despair over a severe loss or disappointment from which, for a longer or shorter time, there seems to be no escape. Recovery from this crisis depends on whether the situation changes and how the person's cognitions about the situation change.

Clinical interventions that help people cope more effectively with stress can also take many forms, depending on the client's problems and vulnerabilities and on the theoretical viewpoint of the clinician. For example, a tranquilizing drug might be prescribed for someone who is experiencing a temporary crisis such as the serious illness of a loved one. In that case, the tranquilizer reduces the person's vulnerability to intense anxiety experienced over a limited period. In other cases, insight into the client's desires, motivations, and conflicts is needed in order to help him or her cope more effectively with stress and be less vulnerable to the crises that are the inevitable ingredients of every human life. In still another case, a person might never have learned the behavior needed to cope with a given situation. The best procedure in such a case might be to teach that behavior. Or perhaps the client is in an intolerable situation—for example, he or she is the child of an abusive parent. In such a case, the child's environment must be modified by removing the parent or helping the parent avoid abusive behavior. Or it may be that a person habitually misinterprets situations; here, retraining in how to think about problems might be appropriate.

Each of us has expectations and goals that color our thoughts. A stamp collector probably has different thoughts when going to the post office than a noncollector does. Our thoughts serve as **mediators:** they provide links between informational inputs and behavioral outputs, just as an intermediary in the business world links a manufacturer and a retailer. Several theories of abnormal behavior deal with the mediating process, though there are differences of opinion about which ones are most important. The various theoretical perspectives reflect these differences by focusing on such different mediators as chemical processes in the body, drives and emotions, thinking styles, values and needs, or the social milieu.

Each of us confronts diverse situations each day. They provide us with information (pleasant, unpleasant, frightening, worrisome) and often call forth certain reactions. The information available to us influences our way of looking at things. At the same time, our personal characteristics—our skills and vulnerabilities—help determine how we handle the situations to which we must respond. The authors of this textbook are interested in what makes an individual vulnerable to particular situations, what kind of stressors cause maladaptive behavior to appear, and how people can build coping skills that enable them to deal better with stressors and compensate for their vulnerabilities.

# ■ STUDY OUTLINE

### THE ROLE OF THEORY
### IN ABNORMAL PSYCHOLOGY

Clinicians use a number of theories to explain vulnerabilities that lead to maladaptation and to plan therapies. Existing theories are continually changing, and new ones emerge frequently.

## THE BIOLOGICAL PERSPECTIVE

1. The biological perspective emphasizes the idea that bodily disturbances cause disordered behavior. Irregularities in the genes may be responsible for some maladaptive behaviors. Through a substance called DNA, people may inherit a *tendency* toward a particular characteristic or disease. Research on heredity in humans makes use of family histories and twin studies.

2. Another biological determinant of behavior is the brain and nervous system. Disturbances in specific parts of the brain can result in specific behavioral deficits. Researchers use electroencephalograms to analyze the brain wave patterns that are characteristic of different behavioral states. Research on the brain reward system, particularly substances called **endorphins,** may lead to a better understanding of drug addiction.

3. The **endocrine system,** which consists of various glands, affects the body's responses through the secretion of hormones. The pituitary gland and the adrenal cortex play roles in biological and psychological adaptation to stress.

4. **Psychoimmunology** links psychological and immunological events. It has been noted that bereavement and other stressors are frequently followed by illness, possibly caused by an alteration in the immune system. **Psychopharmacology** is the study of the effects of drugs on behavior.

## THE PSYCHODYNAMIC PERSPECTIVE

1. The psychodynamic perspective is based on the idea that thoughts and emotions are important causes of behavior. Clinicians must infer these covert, unobservable thoughts and emotions from overt behavior.

2. According to Freud's method of **psychoanalysis,** it is important for patients to be helped to recapture emotionally laden memories that have been forgotten.

3. Freud's theory of **psychic determinism** states that all behavior is caused by prior mental events, which may be conscious (the individual is aware of them), preconscious (the individual can be made aware of them easily), or unconscious (they are difficult to bring to awareness). The level of awareness of mental events is determined by the amount of intrapsychic conflict surrounding those events.

4. During the first five years of life, the **libido** focuses on specific erogenous zones, resulting in the **oral, anal,** and **phallic** psychosexual stages, which eventually lead to the mature **genital** stage. Unresolved conflicts may cause a person to become **fixated** or arrested at one stage or to **regress** to a previous stage.

5. Freud believed that the mental world is divided into three structures: the pleasure-seeking **id;** the **ego,** which avoids or copes with danger; and the **superego,** which represents the society's moral code. During infancy, **primary process thinking,** characterized by the **pleasure principle** and desire for immediate gratification, is dominant. Later, **secondary process thinking** develops and gratification can be postponed. Some primary process thinking is found in adults.

6. **Anxiety** is a response to perceived danger that exceeds the organism's capacity to handle it. Because anxiety arises in anticipation of danger, it can serve a protective function.

7. The ego initiates **defense mechanisms** to ward off awareness of conflict. The most important of these mechanisms is **repression,** which reduces anxiety by keeping thoughts and impulses out of awareness.

8. In clinical psychoanalysis, the causes of maladaptive behavior are sought in early childhood experiences through such techniques as free association and the analysis of dreams, fantasies, and memories.

9. Neo-Freudians, including Jung, Adler, and more recently Erikson, have revised some of Freud's ideas and broadened the psychodynamic perspective. However, psychoanalytic theory remains difficult to evaluate scientifically.

## THE LEARNING PERSPECTIVE

1. According to the learning perspective, behavior is a response to stimuli in the environment. **Positive reinforcers** increase the probability of particular responses by giving a reward for those responses; **negative reinforcers** take away something unpleasant; **punishment** gives an unpleasant consequence for the wrong response; **extinction** suppresses behavior by removing the reinforcers.

2. In **classical conditioning,** the response that is automatically made to a particular stimulus is transferred to a new stimulus through contiguity. In Pavlov's experiment based on the salivation of dogs, the light was the **conditioned stimulus,** the salivation was an **unconditioned response** to the food, which was the **unconditioned stimulus,** and the eventual salivation in response to the light alone was the **conditioned response.** Some maladaptive behaviors can be explained in terms of classical conditioning.

3. In **operant conditioning,** the response must precede the reinforcement; the organism operates on the environment and produces an effect. Using operant conditioning, B. F. Skinner taught rats to press a bar in order to receive food. **Shaping** of behavior involves reinforcing successively better approximations of a desired response.

4. Learning also occurs through **modeling,** or watching how other people do things, and **role playing,**

or practicing the observed behavior. Models may have both desirable and undesirable effects on anxiety and fear, personal development, and self-esteem.

5. **Radical behaviorists** like B. F. Skinner believe that all behavior can be affected by manipulation of the environment. **Social-learning theorists** believe that cognitive factors also influence behavior.

### THE COGNITIVE PERSPECTIVE

1. The cognitive perspective focuses on how people acquire and interpret information and use it to solve problems. In this view, mental life consists of **schemata,** which contains information that people process in order to select strategies for solving a problem or reaching a goal. Self-schemata contain personally relevant information as well, including emotions, which can distort perceptions of reality.

2. John Dollard and Neal Miller combined elements of the psychodynamic, learning, and cognitive perspectives. They saw maladaptive behavior as the joint product of unfortunate life experiences and maladaptive thinking.

3. George Kelly believed that emotional reactions are based on **personal constructs;** that is, each person builds a view of the world by sorting people and events into categories. He saw the role of psychotherapy as replacing maladaptive constructs with more useful ones.

4. The social-learning theorist Julian Rotter believes that maladjustment problems are based on relationships with others and that behavior is influenced by how one expects a situation to turn out. People attempt to defend themselves against anticipated failure.

5. Albert Bandura believes that people can solve problems symbolically by foreseeing the consequences of their behavior. He has focused on **self-regulation** through the use of internal rather than external reinforcement.

6. There are several cognitive therapies. In **rational-emotive therapy,** developed by Albert Ellis, people are helped to question and modify their belief systems. George Kelly developed **fixed-role therapy,** in which people explore new ways of behaving. Aaron Beck, who has focused on depression and anxiety, believes that therapists can help people restructure their thoughts so as to cope better with stress.

### THE HUMANISTIC-EXISTENTIAL PERSPECTIVE

1. The humanistic–existential perspective focuses on self-examination and the desire for freedom. In the humanistic view, there is a force toward self-actualization, or being "all that you can be." Existential theorists emphasize **self-determination.**

2. Abraham Maslow established a five-layer **hierarchy of needs**—physiological, safety, belonging and love, self-esteem, and self-actualization. Lower needs must be satisfied before higher needs become important. Maslow viewed neurotics as people who have not satisfied the lower levels of needs, especially those for belonging and self-esteem. They thus are prevented from seeking self-actualization.

3. According to Carl Rogers, personal adjustment depends on people's self-image. Therapists can help them accept themselves for what they are.

4. Existentialists believe that people are free to act either **authentically,** establishing their own goals, or **inauthentically,** letting others dictate their goals. Innate or environmental factors may limit or expand their potential for fulfillment. Rollo May believes that anxiety, which is caused when a person faces an important choice, either results in personal growth or may cause guilt. Therapists can help people make constructive choices.

### THE COMMUNITY PERSPECTIVE

1. Community psychologists see maladaptation as resulting from the failure of social support systems. These systems can reduce such problems through preventive intervention, including special programs in the community. Community psychologists are likely to support **social-causation theories,** which argue that low socioeconomic status and poor living conditions cause stress that leads to psychological and social impairment; the **social-selection theory,** on the other hand, says that maladaptive behavior can lead to downward social mobility.

2. Behavior is shaped by a person's social group and the roles he or she plays within that group. Behavior is also affected by **labeling,** or categorizing people on some general basis.

### THE VALUE OF AN INTERACTIONAL APPROACH

The interactional approach uses contributions from all of the six perspectives discussed in the chapter. Every person confronts diverse situations each day. The resulting behavior depends on the meshing of personal vulnerabilities and strengths, coping styles, and characteristics of the environment.

# 4

# CLASSIFICATION AND ASSESSMENT

*Robert Frank, a 37-year-old married man, came to a community mental health center because some of his thoughts had been bothering him.*

*For as long as he can recall, he has been introverted and somewhat fearful of people. He has desired social contact but, because of his fearfulness, has usually been unsuccessful in forming relationships. At the time that he came to the center, he was keeping certain disturbing thoughts to himself. In the past he had discussed these thoughts with his wife and with clinicians at a mental hospital. He thinks he is being spied upon by some unknown group, which he believes to be a government intelligence agency. He also feels that his television set is providing him with special messages and that an attempt is being made to control his will and thoughts. He has a job in a large corporation. In the judgment of his supervisor, he has performed well in the past but recently his work has deteriorated somewhat.*

*Frank has been hospitalized on two occasions, after which he seemed to make a good adjustment to the community. Six months ago his mother's death upset him greatly. During the past few months he has increasingly restricted his social activities to members of his family and has been somewhat withdrawn even with them. He came to the community mental health center because the voices were becoming louder and more persistent. His discomfort level was increasing, he realized that he was becoming more incoherent, and he wanted to avoid another hospitalization if at all possible.*

The clinical worker who talked with Frank wanted to get all this background information so that she could recommend the most practical and effective therapeutic program. She went through a series of steps in which information about Frank was gathered and interpreted. To increase the accuracy of their interpretations, clinicians often make use of the experiences of others in evaluating behavior. Classification systems are particularly valuable because they represent attempts to organize what a great many clinical workers know about the various types of problems they deal with.

The classification of personal problems is based on assessments of what clients say and how they behave. Both present life conditions and past experiences are taken into account. Classification is not simply an intellectual exercise, however. It has far-reaching effects on the lives of people who exhibit maladaptive behavior and on the activities of clinical workers.

## ■ CLASSIFICATION

The need to classify various types of personalities and personal problems has been recognized for a long time. Since the time of Hippocrates, classification systems have continually been revised to incorporate new knowledge and changing viewpoints. Nevertheless, the classification of abnormal behavior is still in an early stage of evolution, partly because of the arbitrary nature of the process of attaching labels to people. For example, there is no precise point at which an excessive drinker becomes a full-blown alcoholic, or when the tension you feel when you are alone in a strange room becomes the intense dread known as claustrophobia.

A classification statement or **diagnosis** places a disorder within a system of conventional groupings based on significant similarities in symptoms. Most classification systems are organized in hierarchical fashion. Thus, in the system that is used to classify animal life, human beings are members of the species *sapiens*, genus *Homo*, which is a subdivision of the family Hominidae, of the order *Primate*, of the class Mammalia, of the phylum Chordata, of the kingdom Animalia. Similarly, manic behavior is a subdivision of bipolar disorder, which in turn is one of the major disorders in the family of mood disorders.

General use of a widely recognized classification system is very important. If every clinical worker made up his or her own system, communication problems would be enormous. It would be difficult to make use of research data on effective treatment, for example. Classification systems are also useful for statistical purposes. Government and other planning agencies need records of how often various types of maladaptation occur. Without such records, it would be impossible to say whether the incidence of certain forms of maladaptation was increasing or decreasing. Moreover, to the extent that the categories used in established classification systems are distinctive and can be rated reliably, they contribute to the planning of treatment programs and facilities.

The idea of classifying maladaptive behaviors has been criticized on several counts. Most important to many people is the fact that a diagnosis puts a label on a person. Labeling might make it difficult for a former patient to get a job, gain admission to a professional program, obtain custody of a child, and the like. Another argument is that many diagnoses are not useful because the diagnostic categories are imperfect and the same label may be assigned to behaviors that appear similar but have different causes and different treatments.

On balance, the case for classification is a strong one. It is easy to defend the idea that each patient is unique, yet nothing can be done to help an individual without referring to general principles. What is known about an individual case, however detailed, can be utilized only if the case is viewed within the context of existing knowledge. At the same time, general principles will have validity only if they are based on observation of individuals.

There are two major sources of unreliability in diagnoses. One concerns clinical judgment: differences in therapists' clinical training and theoretical orientation may lead to different diagnoses. The other major source of unreliability is the fact that diagnostic labels are attached to people, and no two people (or their problems) are alike. The same person might even describe his or her problem differently on two separate occasions. Diagnosticians may change their original assessment of a case, or two people with similar problems might describe their conditions differently and therefore be classified differently.

Ambiguities and inconsistencies also arise because most clinics and hospitals are burdened with more cases than they can handle. Leisurely and protracted study aimed at accurate classification is often impossible. Another factor is the range of problems treated by a particular clinical facility. The staff of a facility that treats a narrow range of disorders may tend to describe and interpret its cases differently than the staff of a more broadly based institution would. Diagnostic methods will achieve a firmer scientific basis as assessment becomes more standardized and less susceptible to distortion by such factors.

### The Roles of Stress, Vulnerability, and Coping Resources

The authors' approach to abnormal psychology has some definite implications for the process of classification. This approach argues that abnormal behavior must be understood in the context of three factors: the stress in a person's life, such as a recent bereavement or loss of a job; the person's vulnerabilities, such as a tendency toward low self-esteem that may have been engendered by early childhood experiences; and what the individual has going for him or her, such as coping skills, intellectual ability, and family and friends who are willing and able to help.

Classifying abnormal behavior should be a matter of drawing a picture of a person rather than simply marking a point on a graph. In classifying a person who is experiencing a problem, we want to know not only what the problem is (for example, Frank's belief that he is being spied on) but also the context of the problem. The context includes (1) recent experiences that may have aroused stress and led to the worsening of his condition, (2) his vulnerabilities or weaknesses, and (3) his assets or strengths. The fact that Frank has experienced long periods of good adjustment (for example, being able to hold a job) is encouraging and should not be ignored. Optimally, the way we classify people should tell us something about their future prospects and likely responses to therapeutic efforts.

### ■ DSM-III AND DSM-III-R

The most commonly used classification system for abnormal behaviors is the revised third edition of the American Psychiatric Association's *Diagnostic and Statistical Manual of Mental Disorders* (DSM-III-R). This manual, published as DSM-III in 1980 and later revised is used as a basis for communication among clinicians, for the maintenance of statistical records on the incidence of various types of problems, and for the planning of therapeutic programs. DSM-III-R might best be viewed as a set of guidelines for characterizing clinical problems, and it is concerned primarily with the description of these problems. Its categories take note of the etiology, or cause, of the disorder when it can be identified, as well as the subjective experiences of clients (for example, how worried or angry they seem to be) and their assets and liabilities. Thus, DSM-III-R provides information about the context in which abnormal behavior occurs as well as a description of the behavior in question.

DSM-III and DSM-III-R differ from earlier classification manuals in their emphasis on describing clinical problems rather than interpreting them. This change came about as a result of widespread concern that psychiatric diagnoses are often unreliable because they are based on guesses about the underlying causes of problems. The clinicians and researchers who developed DSM-III introduced more precise language into the classification system, increased its coverage to include additional types of maladaptive behavior, and provided more examples of the various categories. As a consequence, DSM-III-R is about ten times longer than DSM-II, which was published in 1968.

Although it represents an advance in clinical classification, no one believes that DSM-III-R is the final word on the subject. Among its limitations is its continued reliance on impressionistic clinical judgments (for example, in estimating the severity of a disorder). An improved manual, DSM-IV, is scheduled to appear in the 1990s.

### The Multiaxial Approach

DSM-III-R uses what is called a **multiaxial classification system**. This means that each case is not merely assigned to a category (for example, schizophrenia); instead, it is characterized in terms of a number of clinically important factors, which are grouped into the following five **axes**.

□ AXIS I contains the **primary classification** or diagnosis of the problem that requires attention (for example, fear of heights).

□ AXIS II classifies any **developmental and personality disorders** that begin in childhood or adolescence and usually persist in stable form into adult life. Examples are mental retardation and personality disorders such as an unwarranted tendency to interpret the actions of other people as threatening.

□ AXIS III refers to any **physical disorders** that seem relevant to a case (for example, the client's history of heart attacks).

□ AXIS IV rates the severity of **psychosocial stressors** in the client's recent past that may have contributed to the clinical problem and might influence the course of treatment (for example, divorce, death of a parent, loss of a job). Whether the stress is acute or chronic is also noted.

□ AXIS V contains a global assessment of **psychological functioning, social relationships, and occupational activities** attained by the client. Ratings are made for both current functioning and the highest level of functioning during the past year. The behavior of two severely disturbed people would probably be interpreted differently and even treated differently if one had a history of good relationships with others and an excellent work record while the other had a history of social inadequacy and inability to hold a job.

The case presented at the beginning of the chapter might be classified as follows.

□ Axis I: Paranoid schizophrenia
□ Axis II: Avoidant personality disorder
□ Axis III: No apparent medical problems
□ Axis IV: Extreme
□ Axis V: Some difficulty

The more complete the available information about a given case, the more reliable the clinical categorizations and ratings will be. Often, particularly in acute or emergency cases, a classification is made even though there are big informational gaps. In these cases, the classification is considered to be tentative and may be revised as more information is acquired.

## The Major Diagnostic Categories

The first three axes constitute the official diagnostic categories of the American Psychiatric Association. Axes IV and V are regarded as supplementary categories for use in clinical and research settings.

DSM-III-R lists factors that are known to be relevant to particular diagnostic categories. These include the typical features of the disorder, the age at which it usually develops, its likely progression or outcome, the amount of social and occupational impairment involved, possible complications (for example, suicide attempts by depressed individuals), aspects of a person's life that increase the risk of a severe disorder, sex differences, and relevant family patterns.

**Axis I Categories** Axis I includes all the major clinical disorders except personality and specific developmental disorders. These disorders are broken down as follows.

□ ORGANIC MENTAL DISORDERS. Transient or permanent brain dysfunction attributable to such factors as the aging process or ingestion of a substance that affects the brain—for example, psychoses due to effects of excessive intake of alcohol, difficulty in directing attention, memory loss.

□ SUBSTANCE USE DISORDERS. Personal and social problems with use of certain substances—for example, dependence on and abuse of heroin, marijuana, and tobacco.

□ SLEEP AND AROUSAL DISORDERS. Insomnia or difficulty in going to sleep or staying asleep, excessive daytime sleepiness, complaints of sleep disturbance without objective evidence, impairment of respiration during sleep, disturbance of the sleep–wake schedule, sleepwalking, sleep terrors.

□ SCHIZOPHRENIC DISORDERS. Chronic disorganized behavior and thought of psychotic proportions (delusions, hallucinations), incoherence, and social isolation.

□ DELUSIONAL (PARANOID) DISORDERS. Well-organized system of delusions (often of being persecuted) without the incoherence, bizarreness, and social isolation seen in schizophrenia.

□ PSYCHOTIC DISORDERS NOT CLASSIFIED ELSEWHERE. Includes schizophreniform disorders (similar to schizophrenia but currently of less than six months' duration), brief psychosis in reaction to a particular stress and schizoaffective disorders (a combination of disorganization and delusional behavior with feelings of depression and elation).

□ MOOD (AFFECTIVE) DISORDERS. Depression or manic excitement, or both.

□ ANXIETY DISORDERS. Anxiety, tension, and worry are major aspects of the clinical picture, with psychotic features (delusions, hallucinations) absent. Included also are post-traumatic (reactive, stress-caused) disorders. These may be brief or chronic.

☐ SOMATOFORM DISORDERS. Physical symptoms for which no medical causes can be found. These symptoms are apparently not under voluntary control and are linked to psychological factors or conflicts.

☐ DISSOCIATIVE DISORDERS. Sudden, temporary change in the normal functions of consciousness (for example, loss of memory, sleepwalking).

☐ GENDER AND SEXUAL DISORDERS. Deviant sexual thoughts and behavior that are either personally anxiety-provoking or socially maladaptive.

☐ FACTITIOUS DISORDERS. Physical or behavior symptoms that are voluntarily produced by the individual, apparently in order to play the role of patient, and often involving chronic, blatant lying.

☐ IMPULSE CONTROL DISORDERS NOT CLASSIFIED ELSEWHERE. Maladaptations characterized by failure to resist impulses (for example, pathological gambling, chronic stealing of desired objects, habitual fire-setting).

☐ ADJUSTMENT DISORDER. Maladaptive reactions to identifiable life events or circumstances that are expected to lessen and cease when the stressor ceases. The reactions may be dominated by depressed mood, anxiety, withdrawal, conduct disorder such as truancy, or lessening in work or job performance.

☐ PSYCHOLOGICAL FACTORS AFFECTING PHYSICAL CONDITION. Used to describe what have been referred to as either psychophysiological or psychosomatic disorders. Common examples include migraine headaches, painful menstruation, asthma, and duodenal ulcer.

**Axis II Categories** The disorders listed on Axis II begin in childhood or adolescence and continue into adult life without much change. Axis I and II are separated so that when adults are evaluated, these continuing characteristics, which may affect personality or cognitive, social, or motor skills, will be taken into consideration. Axis II contains two major categories, *Developmental Disorders* and *Personality Disorders*. In some instances, the classification statements of Axis II are used to provide additional information about the primary diagnosis of Axis I. In others, the disorder referred to on Axis II is the individual's major problem.

DEVELOPMENTAL DISORDERS. These include *Mental Retardation*, a significantly subaverage level of general intellectual functioning; *Pervasive Developmental Disorders*, in which there is an impairment in social interaction and communication that is accompanied by odd stereotyped behavior; and *Specific Developmental Disorders*, in which there are problems in particular aspects of speech, academic skills such as reading or arithmetic, or physical coordination.

PERSONALITY DISORDERS. These are characterized by enduring, inflexible, and maladaptive patterns of relating to, perceiving, and thinking about the environment and oneself. They cause impairment in social and occupational functioning. Personality disorders may resemble personality characteristics that occur in people who are functioning adaptively. They may also resemble many different behaviors associated with anxiety disorders, psychoses, or mood disorders.

Axis II may not distinguish clearly enough between personality styles or traits that are commonly seen in the general population and the rigid and clearly maladaptive personality styles that lead to personal unhappiness or ineffectiveness. Imperfect as it may be, however, the attempt to include personality factors in psychiatric classification is a step forward.

## Evaluation of DSM-III

Although much more research evidence is needed if one is to make a definitive evaluation of DSM-III, some of its strengths and weaknesses can already be identified. DSM-III-R attempts to correct some of these. One of the major objectives of DSM-III was to be quite specific about the criteria for using the various diagnostic categories. It seems to have succeeded in achieving this objective. By emphasizing descriptions of behavior rather than ideas about its cause, DSM-III also seems to have succeeded in reducing the amount of inference needed to make a particular diagnosis. In working toward these objectives, DSM-III and DSM-III-R have taken a primarily descriptive, rather than theoretical, approach to abnormal behavior. Table 4–1 illustrates DSM-III's emphasis on specifying criteria.

In addition to increasing the dimensions used in describing particular disorders, DSM-III greatly increased its coverage of the range of disorders. This increase is especially evident in the way it deals with childhood disorders.

DSM-III sought to increase its reliability by focusing on observable behavior rather than requiring inferences about what is going on inside the individual. Research studies have suggested that there may be adequate agreement in making Axis I and Axis V classifications but that there is less agreement for Axis II and Axis IV classifications (Spitzer, Forman, and Nee, 1979;

## TABLE 4-1
Diagnostic Criteria for Separation Anxiety
in Children

A. Excessive anxiety concerning separation from those to whom
the child is attached, as manifested by at least three of the following:

(1) unrealistic and persistent worry about possible harm befall-
ing major attachment figures or fear that they will leave and
not return

(2) unrealistic and persistent worry that an untoward calami-
tous event will separate the child from a major attachment
figure, e.g., the child will be lost, kidnapped, killed, or be
the victim of an accident

(3) persistent reluctance or refusal to go to school in order to
stay with major attachment figures or at home

(4) persistent reluctance or refusal to go to sleep without being
next to a major attachment figure or to go to sleep away
from home

(5) persistent avoidance of being alone

(6) repeated nightmares involving theme of separation

(7) complaints of physical symptoms, e.g., stomachaches, headaches, nausea, vomiting on many school days, or on other
occasions when anticipating separation from major attachment figures

(8) recurrent signs or complaints of excessive distress in anticipation of, during or following separation from major attachment figures, e.g., temper tantrums or crying, pleading with
parents not to leave, extreme homesickness (for children
below the age of six, the distress must be of panic proportions)

(9) recurrent instances of social withdrawal, apathy, sadness, or
difficulty concentrating on work or play when not with a
major attachment figure

B. Duration of disturbance of at least two weeks.

C. Not due to a Pervasive Developmental Disorder, Schizophrenia, or any other psychotic disorder.

D. If 18 or older, does not meet the criteria for Agoraphobia with
or without panic attacks.

*Source:* American Psychiatric Association, 1980, pp. 53, 55.

Spitzer and Forman, 1979). Some of the changes in
DSM-III-R are intended to increase the reliability of
classification.

Related to the matter of reliability is the degree to
which most clinicians would agree that the diagnostic
categories are the "right" ones, that is, that they are
meaningful and important. The developmental disorders included in Axis II exemplify these problems. To
what extent should children's reading and arithmetic
difficulties be regarded as clinical problems? The inclusion of these developmental problems in a psychiatric classification system seems questionable.

It is possible that DSM-III's comprehensiveness is
a mixed blessing. Research on agreement among clinicians in classifying patients has shown that there is
a high level of agreement on broad general diagnostic

categories, such as depression and juvenile delinquency, and low reliability for finer subdivisions within
these general categories (Rutter and Shaffer, 1980).
Much research will be required in order to determine
the breadth and specificity needed to maximize the
value of DSM-III and its revision (Williams, 1985).

DSM-III aroused considerable controversy (Klerman, 1984). Its supporters point to its recognition of
the multiple problems that produce abnormal behavior, its effort to specify the bases for a particular classification, its superior reliability compared with DSM
II, and its use of the concept of multiaxial classification. Critics argue that it pays too much attention to
how a person appears at a particular point in time (for
example, upon admission to a clinic or hospital) and
not enough to his or her prior history and developmental crises. DSM-III has also been criticized for providing little information about the causes of abnormal
behavior. Several writers argue that the manual ignores
etiology and that both description and inferences about
the processes involved in maladaptive behavior are
needed (Bayer and Spitzer, 1985; Vaillant, 1984). The
revised manual (DSM-III-R) attempts to address these
criticisms; for instance, it contains a list of defense
mechanisms that can be referred to in case studies.

By introducing axes that pertain to severity of stress
and previous level of adjustment, as well as to long-
lasting personality patterns, DSM-III recognized the
need for integrating what is known about people's vulnerabilities, assets, and stressful life events with what
is observed in their behavior. No doubt modifications
of the existing axes will be made in the light of research
findings and the needs of practicing clinicians. For example, Axis V provides a global rating of the individual's highest level of adaptive functioning, but greater
specificity would probably make this axis more useful.
Separate ratings of level of adaptive functioning for social and occupational contexts would provide for more
detailed characterization of an individual's problems.
Separate ratings on Axis V for the past week and the
past year might also be helpful (Williams, 1985).

Despite criticisms like those just noted, there seems
little doubt that DSM-III was an improvement over
previous diagnostic systems. Many of its limitations
grew out of limitations in our understanding of what
mental health and mental disorder are (Persons, in
press). Any classification system can be no better than
available knowledge and attitudes about what is being
classified. As we will see later in the chapter, experts
who have devoted their entire careers to studying a
specific topic such as schizophrenia have strong differences about what types of behavior should be studied.

The following comments by an experienced clinician show that even the concept of classification is controversial.

*You would think that after working with troubled people for twenty years I'd know what their major problems are and what I should be diagnosing. Yet I'm not really sure what diagnosis is, what it should be, or how it can do more than just name and pigeonhole. I classify cases because it helps me keep records and communicate with other clinicians. At the same time, my major job is to treat people, to decide what I can do that will help them figure out what they should do to make their lives happier and more worthwhile. People are more different than they are similar. Two people may come in with a similar symptom, like delusions of grandeur, but the mechanisms that produce the symptom may be different. I wish diagnosis helped me better understand the basis for the conditions I diagnose.*

DSM-III's greatest contribution may turn out to be the new knowledge that results from the arguments it has stimulated.

## ■ RESEARCH ON CLASSIFICATION

Research on the classification of abnormal behavior has focused on the role of clinical judgment in classification and on the effects of the labeling process. Information is also needed on how complex a classification system should be. How many categories should it have? Which variables must be assessed in making a diagnosis? Which ones should be optional? In what way should an individual's life story be taken into account in assessing his or her present behavior? The psychoanalytic perspective might lead to the conclusion that information about early childhood is essential to assessment, whereas a behavioristic viewpoint might emphasize a detailed description of present-day behavior. A diagnosis is not simply a label that is attached to a client by a clinician; it is a complex product of present knowledge and opinion about maladaptive behavior. As such, diagnosis is not an immutable process. Rather, it changes with advances in knowledge and alterations in what society defines as a problem.

### Clinical Judgment

A variety of data go into classification statements. In arriving at a diagnosis, the clinician goes through a series of problem-solving and decision-making steps. The more complete and standardized the data and the more explicit the intervening cognitive steps, the greater the reliability of the diagnosis. This holds true whether we are talking about a clinician making a diagnosis on two different occasions using the same data or about two clinicians making independent diagnoses on the basis of the same information.

Studies of clinical judgment have been carried out in order to determine just how the clinician's role affects the reliability of classification. One study showed that 5 percent of the disagreements and inconsistencies among diagnosticians are due to inconsistencies in the way patients behave and describe their problems; 30 percent are due to inconsistencies in the diagnosticians' integration of the available information; and 60 percent are due to inadequacies in the diagnostic system itself, which in this case was DSM-II (Kendell, 1975). There is evidence that when diagnostic criteria are described clearly and intensive training is given in their use, and when the clinicians using them employ comparable methods, the reliability of diagnoses increases significantly (Endicott and Spitzer, 1978; Grove and others, 1981).

Additional factors affect clinical judgments. One of these is the fact that certain disorders are more easily classified than others. For example, diagnostic reliability and stability is higher for organic brain disorders than for schizophrenia, and it is higher for schizophrenia than for depressive disorders (Tsuang and others, 1981; Wing and others, 1974). In addition, irrelevant or tangential information, such as labels, may throw a clinician off course; moreover, the attitudes and characteristics of diagnosticians often influence the judgments they make.

Contributing to unreliability in classification are differences in clinicians' training, theoretical outlook, and expectations about deviance. Research on the effects of such factors is illustrated by a study by Langer and Abelson (1974) in which clinicians viewed a videotaped interview. Half of the clinicians were told that the man being interviewed was a job applicant, the remaining half that he was a patient. At the end of the videotape all the clinicians were asked to complete a questionnaire in which they evaluated the man. An additional factor in the study was the theoretical orientation of the clinicians. One group consisted of psychodynamically oriented therapists, the other of behavior therapists. The results showed that, while the ratings of the behavior therapists were unaffected by the labels attached to the man, the psychodynamically oriented therapists described him as significantly more disturbed when he was labeled as a patient than when the label of job applicant was used (see Table 4–2). The research did not provide information about the basis for the labeling effect and why it influenced one type of clinician more than another. The study does, however, demonstrate that labels can be used to organize

Terms Used by Behavior Therapists
and Psychodynamically Oriented Therapists
in Describing Interviewee

### Interviewee Labeled as "Job Applicant"

| Behavior Therapists | Psychodynamic Therapists |
| --- | --- |
| "Realistic" | "Attractive" |
| "Pleasant" | "Conventional looking" |
| "Fairly sincere" | "Straightforward" |

### Interviewee Labeled as "Patient"

| Behavior Therapists | Psychodynamic Therapists |
| --- | --- |
| "Relatively bright" | "Considerable hostility, repressed or channeled" |
| "Responsible" | "Tight defensive person" |
| "Easy manner of speaking" | "Conflict over homosexuality" |

Based on Langer and Abelson, 1974, p. 8.

information. The use of particular labels may lead even experienced clinicians to view the same event in different ways.

## Clinical Judgments Over Time

Because views of abnormal behavior change over time, the topics clinicians explore and the importance they attach to them vary. One investigation examined the topics mentioned in clinical descriptions made during two decades, 1932–1941 and 1947–1956, and found significant differences (Kuriansky and others, 1977). There were consistent, and in some cases dramatic, increases in the percentage of cases that showed particular clinical deviations or indicators. For example, the problems of suspected delusions, severe work impairment, and extreme social isolation were mentioned more than twice as often in the second decade as in the first. In contrast, the frequency of a history of paranoid thinking and suspected hallucinations increased only slightly.

These findings and the ones mentioned previously show why research on clinical judgment is needed. It is encouraging that work on this topic is increasing and that some practical conclusions can already be drawn. For example, the more closely clinicians stick to clients' words and behavior and the less abstract their terminology, the more reliable classifications they can be expected to make. There is also reason to believe that the more aware clinicians are of the biases they may intro-

duce into the clinical situation, the more likely they are to control these biases.

## Transnational Differences

In a study of the use of diagnostic labels by British, American, and Canadian psychiatrists, striking differences among the three countries were found (Cooper and others, 1972; Kendall, 1975). In one case, the percentage of psychiatrists diagnosing schizophrenia ranged from 2 percent in the British Isles to 69 percent in the United States. American psychiatrists tended to rate behavior disorders as severe more often than the British and Canadian psychiatrists did. One observation that was common to the three countries was the agreement about the nature of clinical problems decreased when the language used was technical and increased when the language was simple and referred to specific responses made by patients. Psychiatrists in the three countries differed in how often they used the various classification categories, in part because of the type of training they received and the theories on which that training was based.

In sum, research on clinical judgment has identified factors that reduce its usefulness (theoretical biases, training differences) and methods that can improve its reliability (clearly stated diagnostic criteria, standardized procedures). The available evidence suggests that even though they may not carry out formal research projects, clinicians use a research process in making their judgments. Like more research-oriented scientists, clinicians make observations, integrate them, and draw conclusions on the basis of the evidence they have gathered.

Evidence gathered in formal research on clinical judgment has helped identify factors that contribute to disagreement and error in day-to-day clinical research. Among them are the following.

1. *Patient factors.* The patient is not a constant. In fact, the patient may contribute to differences in clinical opinion by behaving in different ways at different times. If one clinician assesses an individual who is in the midst of an alcoholic delirium whereas another clinician's assessment is carried out several days after the delirium has lifted, differences in classification would not be surprising.

2. *Method factors.* Clinicians who use different assessment techniques might describe people who are actually similar as being different.

3. *Criteria factors.* Clinicians who have different standards for classifying cases might differ in their diagnoses.

4. *Clinician factors.* Clinicians differ in how they assess data. Personality differences, as well as differences in training and theoretical orientation, influence the clinician's information processing.

Clinicians differ in how they process information and in how much they can keep track of. The computer may prove to be a valuable aid to clinical assessment because it is capable of scanning and retaining larger amounts of information than a human diagnostician can. Whether or not clinicians are aided by computers, the process by which they form judgments and make decisions is an important part of research on classification.

# ■ ASSESSMENT: THE BASIS OF CLASSIFICATION

While efforts are made to improve classification systems, clinical workers must employ currently available methods in their work. The major methods used to assess behavior in clinical settings include interviews, psychological tests, behavioral assessment, cognitive assessment, and bodily assessment.

## Interviews

The interview continues to be the most widely used assessment tool. Clinical interviews are of two types: assessment and therapeutic. The purpose of the **assessment** or **diagnostic interview** is to gather information and assess behavior. On the basis of the client's verbal and nonverbal behavior during the interview, the interviewer tries to figure out why the client is seeking help and what might be done from a therapeutic standpoint. The **therapeutic interview** occurs after a preliminary assessment has been made. Its aim is the actual modification of maladaptive behavior and attitudes.

Interviews usually involve two individuals, the interviewer and the client, although other people, such as family members, are sometimes included. Family members may also be interviewed separately. Treatment decisions are often based largely on the data gathered in an assessment interview, which may begin as a telephone call and then be followed up in a face-to-face setting.

**Content of the Interview** Assessment interviewers seek to identify problems and determine the nature and extent of maladaptive behavior. Typically, interviewers begin by trying to find out how the client describes, understands, and interprets his or her problem. In some cases, the complaint is nonspecific, such as "I feel tense

and worried all the time." In other cases, it may seem deceptively clear, as in "My child is hyperactive—I can't control him." Then the interviewer may inquire into the history of the problem. In the course of obtaining this information, the interviewer may get a better understanding of the stressing agents that were present in the client's life as the problem was developing.

Assessment interviews generally are relatively unstructured. Depending on the problem and how it is described, the interviewer may have to move back and forth among a number of topics. However, an attempt is made to answer the following questions:

1. *Who is the client?* That is, what is his or her name, age, ethnic and cultural background, marital status, and occupation? What led to his or her decision to obtain help from the clinic, hospital, or private consulting office?
2. *How does the client think and feel about life at this time?* What are the client's preoccupations and feelings?
3. *What is the history of the problem and the client's developmental background?* Depending on the particular problem, an inquiry might be made into the physical and emotional climate of the home during the client's infancy and childhood, as well as the client's sleep patterns, physical and motor development, and sexual and social development.
4. *What is the client's present psychological state?* What is noteworthy about the client's speech, thought, judgment, cooperativeness, and social skills?

During an assessment interview, many aspects of behavior must be observed and noted. These include the client's general appearance and grooming, voice and speech patterns, and the kinds of thoughts described, as well as facial expression, posture, and style of movement.

People with serious problems state facts, opinions, attitudes, and, in some cases, distortions and lies. They behave in a variety of ways: they may sigh, gesture, avert their eyes, tap their feet, smile, or grimace at the interviewer. As a consequence of this flood of responses, the interviewer usually can extract and use only a small percentage of the data presented during the interview. On the other hand, some clients hesitate to discuss their problems openly and provide very little information. Answers to questions such as, "How does your wife get on your nerves?" can differ widely in honesty, clarity, and feeling. Unanticipated reactions by the interviewee must also be noted.

Interviewers need to observe the relationship between their clients' verbal and nonverbal behaviors. Often what interviewers hear contradicts what they see. The client's verbal manner may be calm and dispassionate even though tension is evident from nonverbal signs such as sweating and hand-wringing. In some cases, gestures, movements, and facial expressions yield clues to the sources of a client's anxiety. Experienced clinicians are adept at observing nuances of behavior that clients are unaware of or believe they are suppressing successfully, as can be seen in the following interview.

> During the interview she held her small son on her lap. The child began to play with his genitals. The mother, without looking directly at the child, moved his hand away and held it securely for a while. Later in the interview the mother was asked what she ordinarily did when the child played with himself. She replied that he never did this—he was a very "good" boy. She was evidently entirely unconscious of what had transpired in the very presence of the interviewer. (Maccoby and Maccoby, 1954, p. 484)

Another interviewer recorded the frequency of a client's "blouse-clutching" behavior during an assessment interview (see Figure 4–1) and noted a particularly high frequency of this behavior during one portion of the interview. The client had at that time been describing how, at the age of 8, she and her twin sister had been told that they had "killed their mother" during their birth.

**The Interview as a Behavior Sample**   Every type of assessment involves taking a behavior sample for the

**FIGURE 4-1**
Frequency of one nonverbal response (blouse clutching) during an interview.

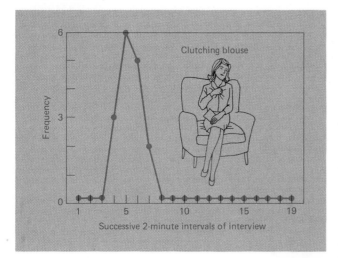

purpose of predicting future behavior. Much of the behavior that is sampled in an interview is self-description. To facilitate the planning of treatment, the interviewer must establish valid relationships between the responses made during the interview and the interviewee's behavior in current or future life situations. If the interview behavior is not representative of the client's characteristic response tendencies, inappropriate treatment decisions may be made. The interviewer attempts to construct a situation that, within a short period, provides reflections of complex lifelong patterns.

In most applied settings assessment interviewers make mental and written notes, subjectively interpreting the behavior sample as it unfolds. Are they accurate observers of the interviewee's behavior? Do they unduly influence the behavior of the person being interviewed? These questions arise frequently in discussions of interviewing. Interviewers don't always note or interpret correctly much of what goes on in an interview. In one study, for example, videotapes of interviews of psychiatric patients by medical students were compared with the reports the interviewers presented to their supervisors. In more than half of the verbal reports, there was some distortion of what had occurred. In addition, almost half of the materials that are considered vital to an evaluation was omitted from the reports. Students who were at the end of their psychiatric clerkships did not perform better as interviewers than those who were just beginning that part of their training (Muslin and others, 1981).

A truly objective evaluation of an interview cannot focus on the interviewee alone. Each interview involves a developing and distinctive relationship between the interviewer and the interviewee, and their characteristics jointly influence what takes place during the interview. Research supports clinical impressions that the interviewer is a major factor in the interview (see Box 4–1). The interviewer's behavior may influence the data obtained in an interview as well as how those data are analyzed. This is true for both assessment and therapeutic interviews.

**The Standardized Interview**   We noted earlier that standardized procedures increase the reliability of classifications of abnormal behavior. This makes a lot of sense, since standardization guarantees that clinicians will at least ask the same questions of each person they interview. An argument against standardized interviews is that they do not give the clinician the flexibility needed to form a productive relationship with a client. However, there is no reason why a clinical worker could not use a standardized format in one interview and a more flexible one in another.

# ■ BOX 4-1 THE ROLE OF THE CLINICIAN IN ASSESSMENT INTERVIEWS

This case study describes an initial assessment interview. Because the client was unique, the assessment did not proceed in a standard way.

The interviewer knew nothing about Robert Hatton except that he was 19 years old, had just begun his studies at a large university, and had a skin condition of apparently recent origin. The skin condition included redness, breaking out in large welts, and itchiness. Hatton had come to the Student Health Service for the skin condition, but the ointment prescribed gave only minor, temporary relief. The physician who had treated him recommended that he talk with a clinical psychologist who was on the staff of the Student Health Service.

The first thing Hatton mentioned to the psychologist was the skin condition, how annoying and disruptive it was because of the incessant itching, and his puzzlement at being referred to a psychologist. During the initial interview he sweated a lot, occasionally had to catch his breath, and tapped his foot continually. Noting the stigma Hatton seemed to feel about talking with what he called "a mental specialist," the psychologist made the following analysis of the situation: "If Robert's skin condition does have a psychological component, he has to learn that it is okay to talk to me. My main job right now is to listen and not to ask a lot of questions that make Robert think he's crazy."

The psychologist did ask some questions ("Have you had skin problems in the past? Under what circumstances?" "How do you like it at the University"), but mainly she listened patiently, avoiding making quick judgments about what the client had to say, and carefully observed what the client said and did, as well as what topics seemed to be upsetting to him. While avoiding aloofness, the psychologist maintained a detached but friendly attitude. When the client expressed concern about his ability to succeed at the university, the clinician did not say, "You're obviously intelligent enough to be very successful at this university," even though Hatton's vocabulary and manner of expressing himself were obviously outstanding. ("What good would it do if I told Robert what all his friends and relatives tell him? What he is saying is that he's scared and really is worried about flunking out. I've got to let him know I realize what he is going through. The flip reassurance of other people hasn't done him one bit of good.")

The interview was uncomfortable for both Hatton and the psychologist. Hatton was tense, and there were long pauses during which he seemed unable to think of anything to say. Each of these pauses posed a conflict for the interviewer. ("If the pause is too long and too uncomfortable, he might decide not to come to see me again. On the other hand, what clients say after pauses is often very significant. I've got to steer along just the right path with Robert.") The interviewer increased her level of activity whenever she detected that the client was experiencing too much anxiety or felt that he needed a show of interest and support.

The clinical psychologist had seen many cases in which physical problems (such as skin conditions) were related to the stress of university life. But she did not want to pigeonhole Hatton. Her main goal in the intake interview was to establish a relationship of mutual trust with him. She liked him, wanted to help him, and thought she could. But the first task was to accept him as a likable, unique person and hope that he would want to come back. Apparently her approach worked, because Hatton came back four times, as a result of which much information was brought out and the clinical picture became clearer. What emerged was a person of exceptional potential for whom the university was an intense stress because of the need he felt to be worthy of all the sacrifices his family was making for him. While he wanted to reward his parents for their help, he was also deeply angered at the way in which they blithely assumed he would make Phi Beta Kappa if he avoided being lazy.

On the basis of the series of assessment interviews, the psychologist pieced together a picture of an intense stress reaction because of all the pressures to which Hatton felt he was being subjected. The psychologist did not know for sure what had caused the skin condition, but she felt that it might have been an accompaniment of the anxious thoughts connected with going to the university. Her recommendation was that Hatton be seen by a psychotherapist who might help him decide on his own goals in life, rather than uncritically accepting his parents' goals for him. After a series of twenty therapy sessions, Hatton was much less anxious, his skin condition was no longer in existence, and he felt more accepting of both himself and his parents.

---

Standardized interviews are used to determine whether specific symptoms are present. Standardization is achieved by providing the interviewer with a glossary of symptom definitions, a series of questions that are pertinent to symptoms, a set of topics about which information should be obtained, and cut-off points that indicate when to stop probing on a particular topic. The clinician also is given instructions for rating the presence and severity of symptoms in numerical terms. Most structured interviews permit the interviewer to depart from the standardized form under specified circumstances. The interviewer also has the option of pursuing lines of inquiry (including a return to a former line of questioning or a jump to a completely different section) that are suggested by the client's responses.

A basic requirement of structured interviews is that interviewers be trained in their use. For example, a structured interview that was developed in England, the Present State Examination (PSE), requires that interviewers take a one-week course in its use and that they conduct at least 20 interviews under supervision before using the technique independently (Wing, 1983).

### The Diagnostic Interview Schedule
The Diagnostic Interview Schedule (DIS) illustrates the potential of the standardized interview (Robins and others, 1981). The DIS is designed to permit diagnosis of selected DSM-III categories such as panic disorders. Panic disorders are recurrent anxiety attacks that often occur unpredictably, though certain situations, such as riding on a bus, may become associated with a panic attack. Panic attacks are noted for their frequency, severity, and symptoms, which include sweating, trembling, faintness, and heart palpitations. The section of the DIS that pertains to panic disorders provides answers to the following questions and offers procedures for deriving the appropriate DSM-III classification.

- □ Did a panic attack occur?
- □ How many attacks have occurred?
- □ What are the symptoms?
- □ Are the attacks repetitive rather than isolated?
- □ Are the attacks characteristic of the person's life rather than confined to a brief, atypical period?
- □ At what age did the attacks begin?
- □ Are the attacks explainable as symptoms of another disorder?
- □ Is the person tense, nervous, or high-strung between attacks?

The DIS has continued to evolve and now includes procedures, probes, and criteria appropriate for use with specific clusters of symptoms. New clusters are added periodically. For example, certain anxiety, stress, and eating disorders are included in the latest DIS format, Version IV, which not only describes symptoms but provides information about recent and past life experiences that are associated with their onset. For bulimia, whose main symptom is binge eating, questions are asked about the types of food eaten, the respondent's mood during and after the binge, the environment in which the eating is done, how the binges are terminated, associated weight gain, and efforts to prevent weight gain. The onset and most recent occurrence of the disorder are determined from the dates of the first and most recent binges.

The DIS can be employed by professional and nonprofessional interviewers who have been trained in its use. The types of questions used are illustrated in Table 4-3. Training (a week-long course), supervision, quality control in the use of the interview, and periodic retraining sessions are emphasized. Programs for computer scoring of interview data are available. Studies are being carried out to determine the feasibility of using computers either to directly administer the DIS or to aid the interviewer in administering it.

Research has shown that both professional and nonprofessional DIS users tend to agree with each other and with the impressions gained by clinicians in more usual psychiatric interviews (Helzer and others, 1985). However, while the goal of an instrument like the DIS is to assess the occurrence of specific symptoms, deciding whether that goal has been achieved is not a simple matter since there is no objective and absolute standard against which to measure results. Nevertheless, clear specification of diagnostic definitions is a major achievement because it makes possible uniform diagnostic methods for diverse populations and places.

Instruments like the DIS, based on specific clinical criteria, have the potential to make comparability across studies a reality. However, much more research will be needed to determine whether this potential can be fully realized. Research on the DIS and similar instruments is proceeding at an accelerating pace. One of the findings of that research is that lay interviewers (that is, nonprofessionals) are able to use the DIS in a reliable

---

□ **TABLE 4-3**
**Examples of Questions Used in Standardized Interviews**

---

How old were you the first time you were bothered by these particular fears?

Has there ever been a period of two weeks or more when you felt worthless, sinful, or guilty?

Have you ever gotten into physical fights while drinking?

For how many weeks, months, or years did you continue to have no interest in an activity that had meant a lot to you before?

Has there ever been a period of two weeks or more when you had a lot more trouble concentrating than is normal for you?

Has there ever been a period of two weeks or more when you wanted to die?

---

fashion and that their judgments tend to agree with those of professionals (Anthony and others, 1985; Wittchen and others, 1985).

## Psychological Tests

Although there is agreement about the need to develop valid ways of characterizing individuals, clinicians disagree on how this can best be accomplished. Because no single assessment tool is considered foolproof, assessment is commonly approached in more than one way in order to yield a more complete and accurate description of the individual. Over the past several decades an array of techniques for classifying behavior have been developed, mostly in the form of psychological tests.

Psychological tests differ from interviews in that they restrict the client's freedom of expression. Just as it is easier to quantify and compare scores on a multiple choice test than on an essay test, the responses obtained on psychological tests can be more readily quantified and compared than the more open-ended and unstructured responses obtained in interviews. To achieve a well-rounded picture of the individual, most clinicians interpret quantified psychometric results in light of behavioral observations made in less restricted situations. We will discuss three types of psychological tests: intelligence tests, personality inventories, and projective techniques.

**Intelligence Tests**  Intelligence tests were the first widely recognized psychological assessment tool. During the latter part of the nineteenth century, intelligence was equated with fast reflexes and sensitivity to the environment. Efforts to assess intelligence relied heavily on sensory and other discrimination tasks. The English scientist Francis Galton sought to evaluate intelligence by measuring such things as reaction time, ability to discriminate between weights, sensitivity to pain, and ability to differentiate tones.

*The Binet Tests.*  In the late nineteenth and early twentieth centuries, the French psychologist Alfred Binet developed a series of tests that differed noticeably from those that had previously been used to measure intelligence. Binet viewed intelligence as something that grows with age; older children are, on the average, more intelligent than younger ones. He sought to measure reasoning, ability to understand and follow directions, and the exercise of judgment or good sense. The child's score on the original Binet test was expressed as a mental level corresponding to the age of normal children whose performance reached the same level.

Later the term "mental age" was substituted for "mental level" and an intelligence quotient (IQ) was computed by dividing the person's test score, or mental age (MA), by his or her chronological age (CA) and multiplying the result by 100. In equation form,

$$IQ = \frac{MA}{CA} \times 100$$

The current test, called the Stanford-Binet scales, has undergone periodic revisions (Terman and Merrill, 1937, 1960, 1973). The Stanford-Binet still uses the term "IQ," but the score is derived from norms based on how much the individual's score deviates from the mean score for a particular age.

In its first three editions the Binet test yielded one overall score. Use of the Binet-type tests declined, partly because the tasks on the Binet scales did not lend themselves to separate, reliable, quantitative analyses. Perhaps the most important reason for the relative decline in the use of the Binet scales was that they were designed primarily for work with children. As a result of these criticisms, the fourth edition (Stanford-Binet, 1985) yields several different scores, and many of the items have been rewritten to appeal to adults as well as children.

*The Wechsler Tests.*  David Wechsler (1955, 1958) regarded the Binet tests as deficient because they produced only a single score. He believed that intelligence is an aggregate of abilities and should be measured as such. The *Wechsler Adult Intelligence Scale* (WAIS-R), published in 1981, consists of eleven subtests, of which six are verbal and five nonverbal. An important advantage of a test like the WAIS is that in addition to being able to compute a score for the entire test, one can score each of the subtests separately.

Three IQs are obtained on the Wechsler scales. **Verbal IQ** reflects level of attainment on subtests dealing with general information, comprehension, ability to think in abstract terms, and arithmetic. **Performance IQ** reflects level of attainment on tasks requiring solution of puzzles, substitution of symbols for digits, and reproduction of designs. The third type of IQ is the **Full Scale IQ,** which represents the total score on the test.

The success of Wechsler's Adult Intelligence Scales led to the development of the *Wechsler Intelligence Scale for Children* (WISC) (see Figure 4–2). In 1974 a revision of the children's test, WISC-R, was published; in this version not only were the test items improved, but the group whose score formed the norms or comparison group for evaluating performance was more representative of the total population (Kaufman, 1979). For use with even younger children the *Wechsler Preschool and Primary Scale of Intelligence* (WPPSI), was developed.

**FIGURE 4-2a**
The Weschsler Intelligence Scales contain a variety of subtests. This photo shows subtests from the performance section of the revised Weschsler Intelligence Scale for Children (WISC-R). (Courtesy of The Psychological Corporation)

**FIGURE 4-2b**
This child is working on the Object Assembly subtest. (Courtesy of The Psychological Corporation)

*Controversies in Intelligence Testing.* For many years intelligence testers have employed the Wechsler, Binet, and similar batteries in making clinical assessments. Recently, however, new theories have been suggested that may lead to different approaches to the assessment of intelligence. Cognitive and developmental psychologists have sought to create models of the structure of intelligence. Jean Piaget directed attention to how cognitive behavior changes in the course of a child's development. He suggested that the child passes through a series of cognitive stages, each of which is distinguished by the appearance of concepts that the child was unable to grasp earlier. Piaget was interested not so much in the correctness of children's responses as in the way they reason in arriving at the response. For example, if a child was asked whether a hammer is more like a nail or more like a screwdriver, Piaget would focus on whether the child selected a nail because a hammer and a nail are often used together or a screwdriver because both it and the hammer are tools. Most 4-year-olds would give the first answer, whereas older children would give the second. According to Piaget, as children become older they progress to symbolic thought and later to a final stage, that of logical, rational thought.

Cognitive psychologists have also studied how individuals with widely differing scores on intelligence tests solve problems. One of the most dramatic differences in problem-solving skills seems to deal with strategies of learning or **metacognition.** Low scores on intelligence tests are related to deficiencies in these strategies. For example, most people learn a variety of memorization strategies without any particular instruction. Those who are retarded need to have these strategies explicitly taught and explained to them. Teaching the strategies to retarded individuals improves their performance on a particular task, but the training cannot readily be applied to other tasks.

Biological factors also play a role in intelligence. One theorist who emphasizes such factors is Howard Gardner (1983). Gardner believes that there are a small number of separate human intelligences, each of which is controlled by a specific region of the brain. His list includes the ability to use language, the ability to reason logically or mathematically, spatial skills, bodily talents like dance or mime, awareness of one's own feelings, and the ability to understand the feelings of others. Gardner describes his theory by saying that "the normal human being is so constituted as to be sensitive to certain informational content; when a particular form of information is presented, various mechanisms in the nervous system are triggered to carry out specific operations upon it. And from the repeated use of, elaboration of, and interaction among, these various computational devices, eventually flow forms of knowledge that we would readily term 'intelligent' " (Gardner, 1983, p. 279).

Neuropsychologists are interested in differentiating among intellectual functions and identifying their biological bases. For example, one group of researchers studied the effects of lowered oxygen intake on the performance of members of an expedition to Mt. Everest (West, 1984). Using a neuropsychological test battery and tests of memory and coordination, they measured the expedition members' performance at various altitudes on the mountain and one year after the expedition. There was a significant decline in verbal learning, verbal expression, short-term memory, and finger-tapping speed at high altitudes. Memory, verbal expression, and learning had returned to pre-expedition levels a year later, but most of the subjects still showed impairment in finger-tapping speed. Although the reason for this finding is unclear, it is likely that prolonged severe oxygen deprivation was related to a continuing dysfunction in the cerebrum.

The Kaufman Assessment Battery for Children (K-ABC) is designed to incorporate new ideas from cognitive psychology and neuropsychology into the assessment of intelligence (Kaufman and Kaufman, 1983). The K-ABC consists of 16 subtests, some for older and some for younger children. The tests fall into several categories: sequential processing, such as remembering a series of digits or hand movements; simultaneous processing, such as arranging a series of related pictures in the correct order; and tests that measure school experience more directly, such as naming pictures of well-known places and objects (see Figure 4-3). Many of the tests do not require a verbal response, and those that do require a few words at most. In most cases, the child can respond by pointing or in other nonverbal ways. The test has been described as a way to learn more about the child's approach to problem-solving and learning tasks. The test's emphasis on short-term memory has been questioned by some critics, but the Kaufmans argue that what is being measured is not memory as such but the sequential and simultaneous processing abilities that are defined as intelligence by cognitive psychologists.

Although the K-ABC tests have been described as being particularly fair to minority children, scores on these tests show the same black–white differences that are seen on other intelligence tests. However, the K-ABC tests do demonstrate that if parental education is taken into account there is little racial or ethnic difference on many nonverbal reasoning tasks. When the education of the parents is taken into account, blacks of preschool age and Hispanics of preschool and school age perform as well as whites. These similarities are due primarily to the tests' emphasis on short-term memory.

**Personality Assessment** Research on personality has stimulated the development of a variety of tests, rating scales, and questionnaires aimed at measuring personality differences. These devices can be useful shortcuts to understanding behavior. Think how long it takes you to get to know a person; in many situations psychologists do not have that kind of time.

Personality tests and other assessment methods are used in clinical settings in making diagnoses, in deciding whether treatment is required, and in planning the treatment to be used. Personality tests are also used in selecting employees. A third major use of personality measures is in psychological research, where the tests may be used as either independent or dependent variables. For example, as independent variables, scores on a measure of test anxiety—that is, the feeling of tenseness and worry that people experience before an exam—might be used to divide people into groups according to how upset they get while taking exams. Researchers have investigated whether more test-anxious students behave differently than less anxious ones in an experimental situation. A less common use of personality tests is as a dependent variable. One group of subjects might see a war movie showing violent battle scenes while another views a nature film. A personality test might then be used to determine which group had the higher aggression score.

*Personality Inventories.* The success of intelligence tests in predicting future achievement led researchers to try to develop similar ways to measure personality. But personality isn't something that can be measured by a total score that is high, medium, or low. The testlike measures used in personality assessment are meant to indicate the types of characteristics that combine to make up an individual's personality.

Rather than testing general knowledge or specific skills, **personality inventories** ask people questions about themselves. These questions may take a variety of forms. When taking such a test, you might have to decide whether each of a series of statements is accurate as a self-description, or you might be asked to respond to a series of true–false questions about yourself and the world. Several inventories require the respondent to rate a set of statements on a scale based on how well they reflect his or her characteristics. Modern personality inventories yield several scores, each of which is intended to represent a distinct aspect of the personality.

The diversity of items found in personality inventories is illustrated by the following statements, which

**FIGURE 4-3**
Some of the tasks from the Kaufman-ABC. In the Face Recognition subtest, the child is shown a picture of one or two faces such as (a) for 5 seconds. The child is then asked to select that face or faces from a group picture such as (b). The Gestalt Closure subtest, illustrated by (c) consists of a series of partially completed drawings. The child's task is to name the object pictured, in this case a bicycle. In the Word Order subtest (d) the child is shown a group of pictures and asked to touch them in the order they are named. Later the task is made more difficult by having the examiner name the items and then ask the child to do another task before pointing to the pictures in the correct sequence. (American Guidance Service, Inc.)

are drawn from the *Minnesota Multiphasic Personality Inventory* (MMPI) (Hathaway and McKinley, 1967). The test taker responds to each statement with "True," "False," or "Cannot say."

a. I believe there is a God.

b. I would rather win than lose a game.

c. I am worried about sex matters.

d. I believe I am being plotted against.

e. I believe in obeying the law.

f. Everything smells the same.

The MMPI, the most widely used personality inventory today, was developed at the University of Minnesota during the 1930s in response to the need for a practical, economical means of characterizing the personalities of psychiatric patients who had been given different diagnoses. It originally consisted of nine scales related to different groups of clinical disorders: hypochondriasis (Hs), depression (D), hysteria (Hy), psychopathic deviate (Pd), masculinity–femininity (Mf), paranoia (Pa), psychasthenia (Pt), schizophrenia (Sc), and hypomania (Ma). The more recently developed social introversion (Si) scale is now considered to be part of a standard 10-scale battery. There are also numerous special scales.

In developing each clinical scale, Hathaway and McKinley, the authors of the MMPI, looked at how groups of individuals with the appropriate diagnosis responded to the items on the MMPI. They also gave the test to people who were not psychiatric patients. The latter group included college students, nonpsychiatric patients, medical personnel, and visitors to the University of Minnesota Hospital. The responses of this normal group were compared with those of people who had been diagnosed as having a particular psychiatric disorder, such as a schizophrenic disorder. Items on which the scores were significantly different for the two groups came to constitute the scale for the disorder in question—in our example, this would be the schizophrenia scale. A high score on this scale indicates that the person's responses were similar to those of the schizophrenics in the original group tested by Hathaway and McKinley.

In addition to the clinical scales, there are three control scales. The L (or Lie) scale was devised to measure people's tendency to make themselves look good by attributing socially desirable characteristics to themselves. One L scale item is "I never tell a lie." An answer of "True" to this and similar items would cast doubt on how honest the rest of the person's answers are. People with high L scores appear impossibly good and virtuous.

The F scale was included to reflect people's carelessness and confusion in taking the MMPI. High scores on the F scale indicate that people described themselves as having a number of rare and improbable characteristics. For example, one F scale item is "There is an international plot against me."

The K scale is more subtle than the L and F scales. Its construction was based on the observation that some open and frank people may obtain high scores on the clinical scales while others who are very defensive may obtain low scores. The K scale was devised to reduce these biasing factors. People who get high K scores are defensive; they tend to answer "False" to items like "I feel bad when others criticize me." K corrections are made on a number of clinical scales in order to compare the scores obtained by people who differ in these tendencies.

Table 4–4 describes the MMPI's clinical and control scales. The principal application of the MMPI is in deciding how to classify a given case. In general, the greater the number and magnitude of deviant scores on the MMPI, the more likely it is that the individual is severely disturbed. In making diagnostic decisions, the MMPI user must be adept at interpreting not only the scores on the individual scales but also the pattern

□ **TABLE 4-4**
**The MMPI: Clinical and Control Scales**

The name, abbreviation, and number of each scale is given. (Clinical workers typically refer to the scales by number rather than by name or abbreviation.) Interpretations of high scores for the scales are also given.

**Clinical Scales**

| Name and Abbreviation | Scale Number | Interpretation of High Scores |
|---|---|---|
| Hypochondriasis (Hs) | 1 | Bodily preoccupation; pessimistic |
| Depression (D) | 2 | Depressed; lacks self-confidence |
| Hysteria (Hy) | 3 | Psychologically motivated physical symptoms; lacks insight |
| Psychopathic deviate (Pd) | 4 | Antisocial tendencies: impulsive |
| Masculinity—femininity (Mf) | 5 | Sex-role conflict |
| Paranoia (Pa) | 6 | Suspiciousness; resentful |
| Psychasthenia (Pt) | 7 | Anxious; insecure |
| Schizophrenia (Sc) | 8 | Bizarre thinking; withdrawn |
| Hypomania (Ma) | 9 | Excessive psychomotor activity; unrealistic goals |
| Social introversion (Si) | 0 | Social anxiety; shy |

**Control Scales**

| | | |
|---|---|---|
| L scale | — | Need to present unrealistically favorable impression |
| F scale | — | Severe psychological disturbance |
| K scale | — | Defensive; inhibited |

of those scores in a particular person's profile. For example, the assessor cannot assume that a high score on the schizophrenia scale indicates the presence of schizophrenia. Other psychotic groups may show high elevation on this scale, and schizophrenics often score higher on other scales than on the Sc scale.

*Rating Scales.* There are many other personality assessment techniques. The **rating scale** is one of the most venerable and versatile of these. Rating scales present respondents with an item (a concept, person, or situation) and ask them to select from a number of choices. The rating scale is similar in some respects to a multiple choice test, but its options represent degrees of a particular characteristic.

An example of a rating scale item is "To what degree are you shy?" People might be asked to place this item on a scale ranging from "Not at all" to "Extremely." They can do this graphically by placing a check mark at an appropriate point on a continuum:

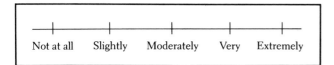

| Not at all | Slightly | Moderately | Very | Extremely |

Unlike the MMPI, which can be used only for self-reporting, rating scales can be used to rate other people's behavior as well as one's own. For instance, a teacher might use rating scales to rate his or her students. In this case the item above might read "To what degree is this student shy?"

Rating scales, like self-report questionnaires, are not immune to inaccuracy. One possible biasing factor, the **halo effect,** results when an individual rates a person more favorably than is realistic on a specific characteristic because the rater has a generally favorable reaction to the person (Cooper, 1981). Other methodological problems include the tendency to want to say only nice things about oneself or someone else, and the tendency to use the midrange of the scales. Research has shown that many of these problems can be reduced through careful wording of items, instructions to the rater, use of minimally ambiguous concepts and scales, and in some cases, actual training in making ratings.

An example of the use of rating scales in clinical work is the assessment of children's ability to pay attention to what is going on around them and to exercise self-control. The degree to which children possess these abilities is an indicator of their personal development. Many clinical problems in children are related to the inability to delay responding until the desired time, to plan activities, and to engage in socially appropriate behavior. Kendall and Wilcox (1978) devised a convenient series of rating scales to assess children's self-control. Their measure, the Behavior Rating Scale for Children, has proven reliable and can be used in a variety of settings and by untrained observers such as parents.

The Behavior Rating Scale for Children presents the rater with 33 questions, each of which is responded to on a 7-point rating scale (1 = always, 7 = never). The following are some representative items from the scale.

- ☐ Does the child sit still?
- ☐ Does the child disrupt games?
- ☐ Does the child think before he or she acts?
- ☐ Does the child grab for the belongings of others?
- ☐ Is the child easily distracted from his or her work or chores?

*Projective Techniques.* One group of assessment specialists believes that the more freedom people have in picking their responses, the more meaningful the description and classification that can be obtained. Because personality inventories do not permit much freedom of choice, some clinical psychologists prefer to use **projective techniques,** in which a person is shown ambiguous stimuli and asked what he or she thinks they are about. Some clinicians believe that projective techniques are very sensitive to unconscious dimensions of personality. Defense mechanisms, latent impulses, and anxieties have all been inferred from data gathered in projective situations.

The *Rorschach inkblots,* developed by the Swiss psychiatrist Hermann Rorschach (1932–1942), consist of ten cards, half colored and half black and white (see Figure 4-4). The test is administered by showing the cards, one at a time, and asking the person to describe what he or she sees in them. There are no right or wrong answers. After the person has responded to the inkblots in a free-association manner, the examiner asks questions about particular responses ("What gave you that impression?" "What made it seem like a———?"). Besides recording what is said in response to the inkblots, the examiner also notes the person's mannerisms, gestures, and attitudes.

Rorschach developed the inkblot test as part of an experimental effort to relate perception to personality. He believed that people's responses to inkblots could serve as clues to their basic personality traits. However, negative research findings have caused many users of projective techniques to become dubious about the validity of the Rorschach inkblots as perceptual indicators of personality. Even if the inkblots are useless for this purpose, however, the test can be used in analyzing people's social behavior and the content of their verbal productions. Attempts to elicit assistance from the examiner and the use of stereotyped verbal responses are examples of the types of behavior that can be observed in the Rorschach situation.

Like the Rorschach test, the *Thematic Apperception Test* (TAT) employs ambiguous stimuli to which people can respond in a free manner. The TAT uses pictures that show people engaging in a variety of activities; hence, it is less ambiguous than the Rorschach inkblots (see Figure 4-5). The total test consists of 30 picture cards and one blank card, although in most test situations not all of the cards are used. The cards are presented one at a time, and the person is asked to make up a story describing the scene in each picture, the events that led up to that scene, and the events that will grow of it. The person is also asked to describe the thoughts and feelings of the people in the story.

Henry A. Murray (1943), the author of the TAT, de-

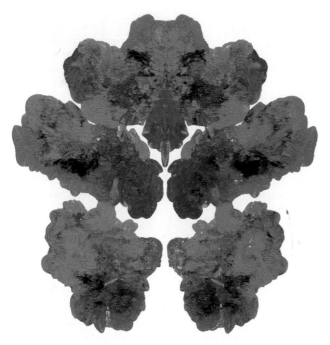

**FIGURE 4-4a**
This inkblot which is similar to those used in the Rorschach test, produced a variety of responses, including: 1. "Looks like a long tunnel or channel in the center." 2. "On its side, I see a crabby old man frowning, with a long nose. I don't like him." 3. "There is a head of a camel in the middle there—no body, just the head."

**FIGURE 4-4b**
As the client responds to the Rorschach card, the clinician records both verbal responses and behavior. (Sepp Seitz, Woodfin Camp & Associates)

scribed the picture in Figure 4–5a (Card 12-F) as a portrait of a young woman, with a weird old woman grimacing in the background. Following is a story about that picture that was told by a 37-year-old woman who was diagnosed as a paranoid schizophrenic and was also

depressed. How might it be interpreted? Note the perceptual distortion that changed the usual mother–daughter relationship into a father–son relationship. (The examiner's questions are indicated in parentheses.)

> *It's an old man standing behind a young man thinking, or knows what this young man should do, what he has ahead of him. He is very tired [old man] and the young man has a lot more—I can't explain it. The young man hasn't had the experience and gone through as much as the old man. That's all I think of now. (Relationship?) There is no relationship. I said father and son though didn't I? (Related?) No. (Happening?) They're both concentrating on life. (Explain?) Well, the old man, as I said, is concentrating on what the young man has ahead of him. (?) Whatever he chooses. (What did old man go through?) Whatever he chooses. (What did old man go through?) He looked like he had gone through suffering. (Explain?) Suffering from living. (?) Working hard. (Else?) No. (?) Well, I thought of other things. The trouble he'd had. (?) Family troubles. (Story!) They lived way out in a lonely place, worked and existed. Nothing much to do, and they became very tired, and that's all.* (Schafer, 1948, pp. 188–189)

This is the response to the same card that was given by a 27-year-old married woman who would probably be diagnosed as having an anxiety disorder. How does it compare with the first response?

> *[Shakes head, swallows.] The old woman must be either the mother or the grandmother of the young woman. The young woman has a strong face. She has lots of character. The old woman has a sly expression on her face or around her mouth. If it wasn't for that expression on her face, I might try to interpret it. I can't imagine why she looks that way. The old woman looks like she worked hard all her life. (?) I don't know, just can't imagine. If this old lady had a different expression on her face, say, one of worry . . . (?) Then I'd say she must be cherishing a lot of ambitions for this girl. Maybe she would be hoping that the girl would do things she always wanted to do. Maybe her ambitions would be realized in this woman.* (Schafer, 1948, p. 258)

Clinical interpretation of a TAT story usually begins with an effort to determine the character with whom the person seems to have identified. Attention is paid to such variables as the person's behavior in the testing situation, characteristics of his or her utterances, the way the stories are told, the stories' emotional tone, and the conscious and unconscious needs that are revealed by the story content.

Whereas Rorschach viewed his test as an experimental perceptual task, Murray conceived of the TAT as a probe of the unconscious. Most contemporary users of projective techniques consider them to be

**FIGURE 4-5a**
Cards from the Thematic Apperception Test are more structured than the Rorschach stimuli yet they also produce many different responses. This card, produced the two very different stories in the text. (Reproduced from Murray, 1943)

**FIGURE 4-5b**
As the client looks at the card and tells the story, the clinician not only records the story itself but notes behavior such as pauses, facial expressions, and changes in tone of voice. (Sepp Seitz, Woodfin Camp & Associates)

methods of tapping unconscious processes, an emphasis that is derived largely from the influence of psychoanalytic theory. Some psychotherapists use TAT responses as clues to hidden problem areas that require in-depth exploration.

In addition to the Rorschach and the TAT, many types of tasks are used as projective stimuli. In a **word-association test,** for example, a list of words is presented one at a time, and the person is asked to respond with the first word or idea that comes to mind. Clinicians are most interested in how long it takes a person to respond and how unusual the associations are. The **sentence-completion technique** is a logical extension of word associations. Here the subject is presented with a series of incomplete sentences and asked to complete them. Sentence-completion methods are typically analyzed in terms of the attitude, conflicts, and motives reflected in them. The following are typical sentence stems.

- □ I worry about _____.
- □ My mother _____.
- □ What makes me mad is _____.
- □ My greatest regret is _____.

Other widely used projective methods include asking people to draw pictures of themselves and others, to finger paint, and to tell stories. These approaches have been used as means of increasing knowledge about fantasy, its determinants, and its behavioral correlates. At times their clinical use has been based more on theoretical usefulness than on objectively demonstrated validity. Researchers who are concerned with the evaluation of clinical tools continue to study these techniques.

## Behavioral Assessment

Consider the case of a 7-year-old boy who, according to his teacher, is doing poorly in his schoolwork and, according to his parents, is difficult to manage at home and doesn't get along with other children. Among the types of assessment that might be considered in this case are the following: (1) a measure of the boy's general intelligence, which might help explain his poor schoolwork; (2) an interview with him to provide insights into his view of his problem; (3) personality tests, which might reveal trends that are related to his inadequate social relationships; (4) observations of his activities and response patterns in school; (5) observations of his behavior in a specially created situation, such as a playroom with many interesting toys and games; (6) an interview with his parents, since the boy's poor behavior in school may be symptomatic of problems at home; and (7) direct observation of his behavior at home.

Making all of these assessments would be a major undertaking. Because of the variety of data that are potentially available, the assessor must decide which types of information are most feasible and desirable under a given set of circumstances. In most cases, the clinician is interested in both subjective and objective information. Subjective information includes what clients think about, the emotions they experience, and their worries and preoccupations. Interviews, personality inventories, and projective techniques provide indications of subjective experience, although considerable clinical judgment is needed to infer what is going on within the client from the way he or she responds to a test. Objective information includes the person's observable behavior and usually does not require the assessor to draw complex inferences about such topics as attitudes toward parents, unconscious wishes, and deep-seated conflicts. **Behavioral assessment** is directed toward this type of observation (see Figure 4–6).

Behavioral assessment has grown out of the behavioral-therapy movement. It is often used to identify response deficits, which are then treated through the use of behavioral methods such as reinforcement schedules and modeling. Clinicians often use behavioral observations to get information that cannot be obtained by other means. Examples of such observations include the frequency of a particular type of response, such as physical attacks on others or observations by ward attendants of certain behaviors of psychiatric patients. In either case, observational data must meet the same standards of reliability as data obtained by more formal measures.

**The Assessment Focus**   The following are some of the questions that are likely to be covered in behavioral assessments. Notice the absence of references to unconscious motivations or intrapsychic tensions.

Cary Wolinsky, Stock, Boston

**FIGURE 4–6a**
This child's aggressive behavior in a playroom situation is being rated by observers through a one-way mirror. Behavioral observations made in a standardized situation are helpful to clinicians because the controlled environment makes comparisons among children more meaningful. (Cary Wolinsky, Stock, Boston)

**FIGURE 4–6b**
Children's behavior can also be observed in a natural setting. Aggressive behavior on a playground can be rated by observers. Because the situation is less standardized and other children are involved, these naturalistic ratings may be less easily compared. At the same time, the observed behavior may give important information about the child's everday behaviors. (Tom Tucker, Photo Researchers)

1. What is the problem as described by the clinician?

2. Who are the people involved in the problem (parents, spouse)?

3. Under what circumstances is the problem most in evidence?

4. What reinforcers contribute to maintenance of the problematic behavior?

5. What is the developmental history of the problem?

6. What are the assets and liabilities of the client's behavioral repetoire.

7. How modifiable are aspects of the client's situation that bear on the problem, and how can modification be made?

The value of behavioral assessment depends on the behaviors selected for observation. For example, if the goal of assessment is to detect a tendency toward depression, the responses recorded should be those that are relevant to that tendency, such as smiling, motor activity, and talking. In one study of severely depressed individuals, daily observations of these types of responses were useful in judging how well clients were responding to treatment (Williams and others, 1972).

**Baseline** or **operant observations** are a type of behavioral observation that is becoming increasingly popular. These are recordings of response frequencies in particular situations before any treatment intervention has been made. They can be used in several ways. Observations might be made simply to describe a person's response repertory at a given time. For example, the number of aggressive responses made by children of different ages might be recorded. Such observations also provide a baseline for judging the effectiveness of behavior modification techniques. A similar set of observations made after behavior modification procedures have been used, could be compared with the baseline measurement as a way of determining how well the therapy worked.

**Behavioral Assessment by Nonprofessionals**  A study of distressed and nondistressed married couples shows how behavioral assessment can be used in the home (Jacobson and others, 1980). Two groups of subjects were studied: couples whose marital difficulties had led them to seek professional help, and volunteers whose marital lives appeared to be satisfactory. The couples were instructed to complete a comprehensive behavioral checklist for 15 consecutive evenings. Each spouse recorded the behaviors of his or her partner. In addition, they made daily ratings of their overall level of satisfaction. Table 4–5 gives examples of items from the spouse observation checklist. On days when their

□ **TABLE 4–5**
Examples of Items from the Spouse-Observation Checklist (Adapted from Jacobson, Waldron, and Moore, 1980)

| Type of Behavior | Item |
| --- | --- |
| Shared activities | We sat and read together.<br>We took a walk. |
| Pleasing interactive events | Spouse asked me how my day was.<br>Talked about personal feelings.<br>Spouse showed interest in what I said by agreeing or asking relevant questions. |
| Displeasing interactive events | Spouse commanded me to do something.<br>Spouse complained about something I did.<br>Spouse interrupted me. |
| Pleasing affectionate behavior | We held each other.<br>Spouse hugged or kissed me. |
| Displeasing affectionate behavior | Spouse rushed into intercourse without foreplay.<br>Spouse rejected my sexual advances. |
| Pleasing instrumental events | Spouse played with the children.<br>Spouse did the dishes. |
| Displeasing instrumental events | Spouse yelled at the children.<br>Spouse left a sink full of dishes.<br>Spouse talked too much about work. |

partners engaged in fewer displeasing behaviors, the couples who were experiencing marital difficulties reported their happiest days. Happily married couples' satisfaction levels were not altered by negative behavior on the part of the partner, although they were enhanced by positive events. Thus, the types of spouse behavior that correlated with daily satisfaction differed for distressed and nondistressed couples.

## Cognitive Assessment

Just as it is important to know what a person does and how his or her behavior affects other people, it is also necessary to assess the thoughts that may lie behind the behavior. **Cognitive assessment** provides information about thoughts that precede, accompany, and follow maladaptive behavior. It also provides information about the effects of procedures whose goal is to modify both how someone thinks about a problem and how he or she behaves.

An example of cognitive assessment is provided by Krantz and Hammen's (1979) study of the distortions in thinking that play a role in depression. Their work grew out of research and theory suggesting that depression-prone individuals tend to commit certain errors in thinking that stimulate feelings of depression (see Chapter 10). Krantz and Hammen developed a questionnaire consisting of several stories that dealt with interpersonal relationships and achievement of goals. For each story the subjects answered questions pertaining to the central character's feelings, thoughts, and expectations. The answers were scored for various types of distorted thinking (for example, a tendency to draw a general conclusion either from a single incident or from no evidence whatever; failure to attend to relevant aspects of a situation; and distortion of an incident or its significance).

On the basis of the subjects' interpretations of the central characters, Krantz and Hammen were able to show that subjects who were depressed were more likely than nondepressed subjects to make certain types of thinking errors. Their findings, together with those of other researchers, suggest that people with a tendency toward depression are particularly prone to accept more responsibility than they should in difficult situations, as well as to feel more self-blame and to expect the worst.

Cognitive assessment can be carried out in a variety of ways (Kendall, 1985). For example, questionnaires have been developed to sample people's thoughts after an upsetting event. Beepers have been used to signal subjects to record their thoughts at certain times of the day. There are also questionnaires to assess the directions people give themselves while working on a task and their theories about why things happen as they do.

Cognitions play an important role when a person is trying to concentrate on an intellectual task (see Figure 4–7). Anyone who has taken exams knows that worrying about one's ability, the possibility of failure, and what other students might be doing interferes with effective performance. Whereas thoughts that reflect worry have undesirable effects, thoughts that are directed toward the task at hand are helpful. The Cognitive Interference Questionnaire (Sarason and Stoops, 1978) was developed to assess the degree to which people working on important tasks have thoughts that interfere with their concentration. Subjects respond to the questionnaire by indicating how often thoughts like the following ones enter their minds while they are working on an assigned task.

☐ I thought about how others have done on this task.
☐ I thought about things completely unrelated to this task.
☐ I thought about how poorly I was doing.
☐ I thought about something that made me angry.
☐ I thought about something that happened earlier in the day.

The assessment of thoughts and ideas is a relatively new development. It has received impetus from the growing evidence that thought processes and the content of thoughts are related to emotions and behavior. Cognitive assessment provides information about adaptive and maladaptive aspects of people's thoughts and the role their thoughts play in the processes of planning, making decisions, and interpreting reality.

Tests that measure maladaptive behavior are beginning to focus on the situations in which the behavior

**FIGURE 4–7**
People have different kinds of thoughts while taking an exam. Worries or thoughts that are unrelated to the exam interfere with good performance. (Stephen Collins, Photo Researchers)

occurs and on how a particular individual deals with difficult situations. The approach helps relate certain difficulties to particular types of treatment. Such tests are designed to measure stress, coping skills, and social or interpersonal skills. It is likely that in the near future, many of these tests will move from experimental to clinical use as research data accumulate.

## Bodily Assessment

An individual's expressive behavior may reveal his or her feelings and motivations, and clinicians pay particular attention to these nonverbal messages. Bodily functions may also reflect motivations and concerns, and some clinicians pay attention to these as well. Sophisticated devices have been developed to measure such physiological changes such as pupil dilation, blood pressure, and electrical skin responses under specific conditions.

### Measurement Techniques
In one study, homosexual and heterosexual men were shown pictures of nude males and females. Since pupil dilation is a sign of interest and arousal, the researcher recorded changes in the size of the men's pupils while they looked at the pictures. The heterosexuals all showed change in pupil size (from a previous control period) when they were shown pictures of females; the homosexuals' pupils enlarged when they were shown pictures of males. Measurement of pupil dilation is a novel approach to assessment, and it requires careful evaluation. It may open up useful paths to the identification of personal preferences and response tendencies (Janisse, 1977).

Pupil dilation is just one response that is affected by the balance among various components of the autonomic nervous system. Technological advances are making it possible to monitor an individual's physiological state on a continuous basis. Sweat, heartbeat, blood volume, the amounts of different substances in the bloodstream, and blood pressure can all be recorded and correlated with the presence or absence of certain psychological conditions such as stress. Although the automated assessment of bodily processes that are pertinent to behavior disorders is just getting under way, this approach seems promising.

An example of the use of automated assessment can be seen in the measurement of blood pressure. It is now possible to measure blood pressure while a person is engaged in everyday activities. This represents a considerable advance, since resting blood pressure readings may not give a full picture of changes in pressure or provide an accurate 24-hour average (Harshfield and others, 1982). Ambulatory monitors can show changes in a patient's blood pressure throughout the day and

during sleep (see Figure 4–8). Such data are useful in diagnosing cases of high blood pressure in which cognitive and behavioral factors play important roles. They may also be important in the selection and evaluation of treatment programs.

Figure 4–8b shows the pattern of blood pressure changes for a 45-year-old woman during a typical day. The patient had been diagnosed as having chronically elevated blood pressure, but as the figure shows, the readings actually covered a wide range. Other studies of patients who had been diagnosed as having high blood pressure have shown that blood pressure readings taken in the doctor's office may be significantly higher than readings taken during normal activity, even though the office readings are usually taken after a period of rest.

A final example of the assessment of bodily functioning has aroused controversy in the study of criminal behavior. The **polygraph,** or lie detector, measures emotional responses through physiological reactions (heartbeat, blood pressure, breathing, and galvanic skin response). Its use has been criticized because it violates the right of privacy and the right to avoid self-incrimination. In addition, questions have been raised about its reliability and validity. Research may provide answers to these questions and may also suggest novel applications of the polygraph in the field of mental health. For example, it may be possible to use the polygraph to determine what situations or topics caused a particular emotional reaction on the part of a client. This knowledge might provide some clues about areas that should be explored during therapy.

There are probably over 4,000 polygraphic examiners currently practicing in the United States. However, the validity of their procedures is still not universally accepted because of gaps in available knowledge about conditions under which the polygraph is likely to be accurate or inaccurate (Lykken, 1981).

It can be assumed that changes in the physiological reactions measured by a polygraph indicate psychological tension. In one study (Abrams, 1973), the polygraph was used in much the same way that a word-association test would be used. Stimulus words—some neutral, some thought to be especially relevant—were read to each of twenty psychiatric patients while they were attached to a polygraph. Figure 4–9 shows a typical set of polygraph tracings. Respiration is at the top, galvanic skin response (GSR) in the center, and a combination of heartbeat and blood pressure at the bottom. Stimulus word 23, *window,* was included as a neutral word. However, instead of the expected lack of response, the patient showed a definite reaction to it. On the other hand, while there is a response to *sex,* it does

**FIGURE 4-8a**
The portable blood pressure monitor allows a person's blood pressure to be recorded automatically at predetermined times without interfering with his or her normal daily activities. (Courtesy of Spacelabs)

not compare with the GSR to *window*. The patient later disclosed that he had considered committing suicide by jumping out a window. Word 26, the therapist's name, resulted in a large GSR, a slight rise in blood pressure, and suppression of breathing. In contrast, the patient reacted relatively little to neutral word 27, *pen*.

**Biofeedback,** which is described in Chapter 7, is being used increasingly often in the treatment of certain bodily complaints. The patient receives continuous reports of a particular index of bodily functions, such as blood pressure, and is helped to find ways of bringing the index within normal limits. Thus, the opportunity to monitor one's own behavior and bodily functioning can have a therapeutic effect.

**Bodily Assessment and Emotions** Do different emotions produce different patterns of physiological arousal? An early clinical study suggested that this might be the case. The subject was a man whose throat and esophagus had been so badly burned in an accident that he could no longer swallow. A "window," or fistula, had been cut so that food could be fed directly into his stomach. Through this fistula it was possible to watch what happened in his stomach when the man was emotionally aroused. When he reported that he was angry, the researchers could actually see acid pouring

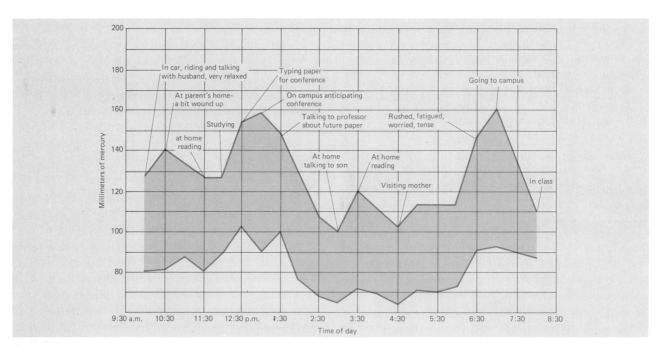

**FIGURE 4-8b**
An ambulatory blood pressure monitor was used to record the changes in a 45-year-old woman's blood pressure during a one-day period. The top line charts systolic blood pressure and the bottom line diastolic blood pressure. The systolic pressure represents the higher point in the blood in the blood pressure cycle as the heart contracts and sends the blood through the circulatory system. The diastolic pressure represents the low point in the pressure cycle, which occurs as the heart fills with blood. (Werdegar and others, 1967, p. 103)

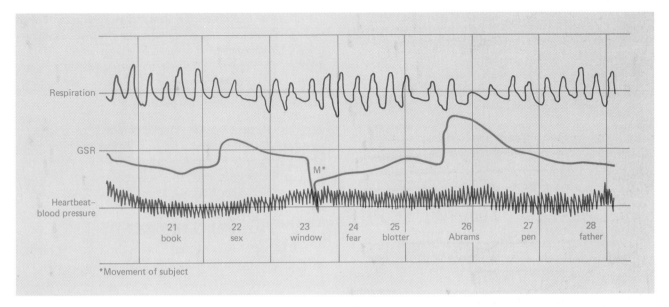

**FIGURE 4-9**
Polygraph tracing for one psychiatric patient. Stimulus words are numbered. (Abrams, 1973, p. 95)

in and the stomach lining becoming thick with blood. When he was fearful or anxious, the scene was quite different. There was a decrease in stomach acid and contractions, and the lining grew pale as a result of a decrease in blood volume. In this patient the physical patterns associated with anger and fear seemed to be quite different (Wolf and Wolff, 1947).

However, the results of more than 30 years of research using increasingly sophisticated techniques for measuring physiological arousal have led ost investigators to conclude that there are no distinct patterns of arousal related to specific emotions. Although some differences have been found between strong anger and fear, there is no evidence that other, more subtle emotions like jealousy and love are different at a physiological level.

People do differ widely in their patterns of general arousal. For example, all people don't express the same pattern of bodily arousal when they are afraid. Some show marked changes in heart rate or blood pressure and only minor changes in other responses such as muscle tension and respiration. Others show different patterns. Researchers have learned that no single measure is appropriate for all subjects; it is important to measure as many physiological indicators as possible.

As theories of maladaptive behavior become more comprehensive and more firmly based on scientific findings, approaches to classification can be expected to change. Assessment and classification methods help clinicians describe disordered behavior and plan therapeutic interventions to change it. What is assessed and how people are classified and treated depend on what we know about the factors involved in abnormal behavior.

## ■ STUDY OUTLINE

### CLASSIFICATION

1. The **classification** of personal problems is based on assessments of what clients say and how they behave. It takes into account life conditions and past experiences. A classification statement or **diagnosis** places a disorder within a system of conventional groupings. Classification is useful for statistical purposes and enhances communication among clinicians and researchers.

2. Good classification characterizes a personal problem within the context of the person's stresses, vulnerabilities, and assets such as coping skills and support system.

### DSM-III and DSM-II-R

1. The most commonly used classification system for abnormal behavior is DSM-III-R, the revised third edition of the American Psychiatric Association's *Diagnostic and Statistical Manual of Mental Disorders*. It describes clinical problems rather than interpreting them, and is considered more reliable than earlier editions.

2. DSM-III-R uses a **multiaxial classification system** that characterizes each case in terms of a number of factors. Axis I is the primary diagnosis; Axis II clas-

sifies developmental and personality disorders that begin in childhood or adolescence and persist into adult life; Axis III refers to relevant physical disorders; Axis IV rates the severity of psychosocial stressors, and Axis V provides a global assessment of functioning.

3. Axis I includes organic mental disorders, substance use disorders, sleep and arousal disorders, schizophrenic disorders, delusional disorders, psychotic disorders not classified elsewhere, mood disorders, anxiety disorders, somatoform disorders, dissociative disorders, gender and sexual disorders, factitious disorders, impulse control disorders not classified elsewhere, adjustment disorder, and physical conditions affected by psychological factors.

4. Axis II includes disorders that begin in childhood or adolescence and continue into adulthood. There are two general categories of disorders classified on this axis: developmental disorders and personality disorders. Developmental disorders include mental retardation, pervasive developmental disorders, and specific developmental disorders. Personality disorders include a number of sometimes overlapping categories. Personality disorders differ from personality traits or syles because in personality disorders the behavior is more rigid and maladaptive.

5. DMS-III-R has provided more specific criteria for using the various diagnostic categories and has reduced the amount of inference needed to make a particular diagnosis. It also has increased its coverage of the range of disorders. Further research is needed to evaluate its reliability.

### RESEARCH ON CLASSIFICATION

Research has shown that unreliability in classification is due to inconsistencies in patients' behavior, unreliability of classification systems, differences in assessment techniques, and differences among clinicians in training, theoretical orientation, and personality.

### ASSESSMENT: THE BASIS OF CLASSIFICATION

1. The basis of classification is assessment. The major assessment methods include interviews, psychological tests, behavioral assessment, cognitive assessment, and bodily assessment.

2. **Interviews** can be used for both diagnosis and therapy. Interviewers typically observe nonverbal as well as verbal behavior. In assessment, the clinician tries to use the interview as a sample of the client's behavior. Standardized, structured interviews like the Diagnostic Interview Schedule increase the reliability of results.

3. The three general types of **psychological tests** are intelligence tests, personality inventories, and projective techniques.

4. The first standardized **intelligence tests** were developed by Alfred Binet to measure the reasoning ability and judgment of children. Some of these tests expressed the score as an intelligence quotient (IQ), derived by dividing **mental age** by chronological age and multiplying by 100. The current Stanford-Binet scales use an IQ score based on deviations from a norm. The revised Wechsler Adult Intelligence Scale (WAIS-R), originally developed to overcome some of the shortcomings of the Binet test, can be broken down into **Verbal IQ, Performance IQ,** and **Full-Scale IQ.**

5. Low test scores have been shown to be related to deficient learning strategies, or **metacognition.** The Kaufman Assessment Battery for Children (K-ABC) is designed to reduce cultural bias in intelligence tests by tapping a variety of basic cognitive processing abilities.

6. **Personality inventories** ask people questions about themselves. They usually yield several scores, each representing an aspect of personality. The Minnesota Multiphasic Personality Inventory (MMPI) is a widely used personality inventory. Another technique is the **rating scale,** in which the test taker chooses options representing degrees of a particular characteristic; these can be used to rate someone else's behavior as well as one's own.

7. In **projective techniques** people are asked to respond to ambiguous stimuli; these responses often express unconscious feelings. In the Rorschach inkblots, the individual is asked to tell what the ten inkblots look like in a free-association manner. In the Thematic Apperception Test (TAT), which consists of pictures of people in various situations, the individual makes up stories to explain what is going on in each picture. Other projective techniques are **word-association tests** and **sentence-completion tasks.**

8. In **behavioral assessment,** which has grown out of the behavioral therapy movement, the direct observations are made of a person's behavior. **Baseline** or **operant observation,** establishes the frequency of a particular behavior before treatment is begun. Nonprofessionals and clients themselves can be trained to do behavioral assessment.

9. **Cognitive assessment** provides information about thoughts that precede, accompany, and follow maladaptive behavior, as well as about the effectiveness of various treatment procedures. The individuals being assessed may be asked to complete questionnaires, write down their thoughts at various times, or respond to stories.

10. **Bodily assessment** involves determining a person's inner state by measuring bodily functions such as pupil dilation and blood pressure. Sophisticated devices are now being used to monitor these functions. The **polygraph,** or lie detector, is a highly controversial device that measures heartbeat, blood pressure, respiration rate, and galvanic skin response. **Biofeedback** gives a patient continuous reports of his or her bodily functioning and provides an opportunity to monitor behavior.

# 5

# VULNERABILITY, STRESS, AND COPING: MALADAPTIVE REACTIONS

*One morning, while brushing her teeth, Sheila Mason noticed a small lump on her gum. It didn't hurt, but she was sure that it had not been there before. She wondered whether it might be related to an upset stomach or a cold, but there had been no recent changes in her diet and she felt fine. She was worried about the lump, but at the same time she didn't want to bring a trivial symptom to the attention of her physician or dentist. After three days the lump was still there. It was no bigger than it had been when she had first noticed it, and it still didn't hurt. Sheila concluded that it was not her responsibility to decide whether or not the lump was a trivial symptom. That was the professionals' job. Having decided to get an expert to look at the lump, Sheila was left with only one question: Should she call her physician or her dentist?*

*Grace Dolby, married and the mother of two children, felt a small but noticeable lump in her right breast. Her first reaction was one of alarm bordering on panic, but she said nothing to anyone for two months. Grace was usually outgoing and cheerful, but during those months her husband, Jack, noticed that she had become moody, tense, and depressed. At times she also seemed distant and preoccupied. Toward the end of the two-month period, Grace's moodiness and distance from others (including her children) increased. Her sleep became fitful, and she had frequent headaches (even though previously she had almost never had them). If her husband insisted that she tell him what the matter was, her reply was always, "Nothing's the matter. I'm perfectly normal." Finally, one evening during lovemaking Jack felt the lump in her breast, and despite Grace's protests that it was "nothing" he insisted that she see the family physician.*

Just about the only thing that Sheila Mason and Grace Dolby have in common is that they discovered lumps that worried them. The two women dealt with their worries in quite different ways. After some doubt about whether she should undergo a clinical examination, Sheila made a rational decision to seek help. She realized that there was a possibility that the lump could be serious but that she could not evaluate the possibility herself and that the longer she waited, the worse it would be.

In contrast, Grace Dolby seemed unable to act realistically and decisively. She first attempted to cope with the discovery of the lump in her breast by trying to deny that it was really there. But this was not completely successful. She then tried to tell herself that it "wasn't anything." The stress aroused by her discovery could be reduced only temporarily by denial and secrecy. She was still unable to deal with the reality of the lump.

Such a situation would be stressful for anyone. Most people who find themselves in such a situation go to a doctor immediately. Grace Dolby's response to her stressful situation is considered maladaptive mainly because it did not work: the lump (or reality) did not go away. In fact, Grace's behavior simply increased the amount of stress she experienced. A clinician working with Grace would want to understand the personal needs, motivations, and dispositions that combined with the situation (discovery of the lump) to produce her decision not to act. What made Grace Dolby so much more vulnerable to stress than Sheila Mason?

In this chapter we describe ways in which people react to stress. We emphasize examples of maladaptive behavior in response to two types of situations: those, like Sheila Mason's and Grace Dolby's, that arise suddenly, and those that develop more gradually and represent turning points in life, such as making a career decision. We examine the concept of stress, explore the different ways in which people handle it, and review three clinical conditions (adjustment disorders, posttraumatic disorders, and dissociative disorders) in which stress plays an identifiable role. Even though the behavioral reactions observed in the three conditions seem quite different, stress plays a crucial role in each, and its removal is often followed by improvement.

Because this is the first chapter in which we study particular disorders in some depth, it is worthwhile to anticipate an observation that has been made many times by both experienced clinicians and students: the various disorders are not conveniently arranged so that they have mutually exclusive features. Stress is the main topic of this chapter, but we will also refer to stress as we discuss other forms of maladaptation. What is distinctive about the disorders discussed here is that the exact sources of stress are more evident than they usually are in most forms of abnormal behavior. In the next chapter, where we review the anxiety disorders, we will find it more difficult to specify the exact sources of stress that result in intense anxiety.

# ■ VULNERABILITY AND COPING

In Chapter 1 we said that the term "stress" refers to situations that pose demands, constraints, or opportunities. However, a situation that is stress-arousing for one person might be a neutral event for another. Whether a certain situation is stressful for us or not depends on how we appraise it and how we rate our ability to deal with it. There are two stages in the appraisal of any situation. During **primary appraisal,** individuals interpret a situation as either threatening or harmless. During **secondary appraisal,** they consider the kind of action that is called for, as well as the nature and potency of their resources for managing or coping with it. The extent to which people feel threatened depends on their estimate of these resources, which in turn is based largely on the information provided by the environment and by their own experiences and characteristics.

## Vulnerability and Adjustment to Stress

People differ not only in the life events they experience but also in their vulnerability to them. A person's **vulnerability** to stress is influenced by his or her coping skills and the social support available. Vulnerability increases the likelihood of a maladaptive response to stress. For example, unloved children are more vulnerable and generally at greater risk of developing behavior disorders than those who are loved (Werner and Smith, 1982).

**Coping skills** are characteristic ways of dealing with situations. Successful copers are not just people who know how to do things. They also know how to approach situations for which they do not have a readily available response.

The characteristics that people bring with them to life experiences (their expectations, fears, skills, hopes) influence how much stress they feel and how well they cope with it. Experience and success in coping with similar situations, well-founded self-confidence, and the ability to remain composed and "think on one's feet" instead of falling to pieces when faced with a problem, all contribute to realistic appraisals of and responses to situations. These characteristics are products of personality development, which, in turn, is influenced by social relationships.

Figure 5-1 traces the steps involved in reactions to stress. On the right side of the figure are the four major types of overt reactions or **behavioral coping:** matter-of-factly confronting the situation, feeling anxious, be-

coming angry, and being defensive. Behavioral coping is what we actually do when confronted with a demand, constraint, or opportunity. Notice that the word "coping" appears twice in Figure 5-1, on the right side (C) and on the left (A), in the term **coping resources.** This term refers to capabilities, not to what a person will actually do in a given situation. People frequently fail to use their knowledge and skills in handling stressful situations. When this happens, we wonder why the person's coping resources were not enough to permit effective behavioral coping.

A task-oriented, matter-of-fact response to a tough situation is usually more effective than becoming anxious, angry, or defensive. Failure to be task-oriented can happen for a variety of reasons. It could be that we simply lack the coping resources we need if we are to take a matter-of-fact approach. In that case, the situation is beyond our capabilities. It could also be that certain elements of the situation prevent us from taking a constructive approach to it. For example, a man might have the coping resources needed to be assertive with other men but not with women. His vulnerability with regard to women might keep him from complaining about being shortchanged by a waitress, whereas he would be quick to complain if he were shortchanged by a waiter. In trying to identify the basis for a particular behavioral coping response, it is necessary to analyze carefully what is going on in the situation, together with the person's assets and liabilities (coping resources and vulnerabilities). In addition, attention must be paid to how the person sizes up the situation (primary appraisal) and his or her coping resources (secondary appraisal).

Personal vulnerabilities and past experiences influence how much stress we experience in a given situation and how we deal with it. For example, Grace Dolby had had many experiences that involved doing something about a physical symptom (high temperature, skin rash). The lump in her breast, however, was different because of its life-threatening implications. Her mother had died when Grace was 4 years old, and Grace was concerned about depriving her children of the maternal love and attention that she had missed as a result of her mother's early death. Perhaps her intense concern about abandoning her children made Grace particularly vulnerable to her symptom and resulted in her denial of its significance.

Like Grace, many people with bodily symptoms either fail to attend to them or misinterpret them. A common response to the chest pain of a heart attack is denial of its significance. It has been estimated that 80 to 90 percent of people who experience such pain attribute it to other causes, usually indigestion (Hackett and Cassem, 1975). Once the possibility that it might

**FIGURE 5-1**
The stress process: ways of dealing with demands, constraints and opportunities.

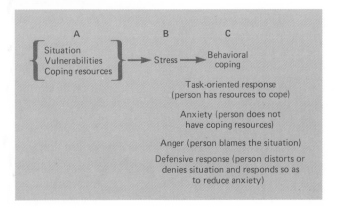

be a heart attack strikes them, they think, "It couldn't be happening to me." This thought alone seems to be enough to keep them from seeking medical help. Even some physicians, who should know better, have gone jogging when they experienced chest pains in order to "prove it's nothing." Thus, there is a common tendency to deny the true significance of pain despite its severity, intensity, or duration.

This is true for psychological pain as well. Many people deny the reality of an unhappy or unsatisfying marriage rather than seek counseling or even a divorce. People who have lost their jobs may blame their employers instead of recognizing their own inadequacies as employees. They may put off looking for work because they "deserve a rest," denying even to themselves that they are afraid of being fired again.

Particular conditions might arouse stressful reactions in some people but not in others. At a memorial concert honoring the famous jazz musician Louis "Satchmo" Armstrong, his widow was stricken with a fatal heart attack as she played the final chord of a song that was identified with her husband, "The St. Louis Blues." According to a newspaper report, a 38-year-old father collapsed and died when his efforts to revive his 2-year-old daughter, who had fallen into a wading pool, failed. The report suggested that the girl had fallen into the pool while the father's attention wandered. An obituary noting the sudden death, at 51, of the newly appointed president of a television network stated that he was on his way to attend the funeral of his father, who had died the day before. Each of these examples suggests the importance of the appraisal process for each individual who experiences a particular type of event.

Another example of the importance of the appraisal process is found in hospitals, places to which we turn in times of great stress. Hospitals are supposed to be places where people can recover from illness, but in fact hospitalization can be a highly stressful experience. For instance, the continuous monitoring of a patient's physical status in the intensive care unit can be a highly stressful experience. The knowledge that one has a condition that is serious enough to require placement in an intensive care unit may be even more stressful. Probably the most stressful aspect of hospitalization for both the patient and for family members is the frequently occurring uncertainty about what the outcome of the treatment may be (see Box 5-1). Under such conditions frustrations from dealing with bureaucratic hospital procedures can be stressful even to a patient who is familiar with hospital routines and who has excellent coping skills.

Heightened stress levels have detectable, although usually not immediately noticeable, psychological consequences. For example, a significantly higher percentage of depressed and suicidal people than of people with other disorders have had undesirable recent experiences. The undesirable events that contribute most to depression include the departure or loss of significant people in one's life during the previous year (see Chapter 10).

Stress can also have delayed effects that tend to be obscured by intervening events. George Brown and his co-workers (Brown and others, 1975) conducted a study of depression in working-class English women. One factor that significantly distinguished depressed women from women with other types of psychiatric disorders was the high number of cases in which the woman had

## ■BOX 5-1  TWO WEEKS IN THE HOSPITAL

John A. Talbott, the author of this account, was not just "any" patient. At the time of the accident he was President of the American Psychiatric Association. Although as a physician he was familiar with medical procedures, being a patient gave him a quite different view of his condition and treatment than he would have had as a hospital staff member. The effect of injuries and the hospitalization itself may be stressful (see Figure 5–2), but this account shows how hospital procedures and medical personnel can add significantly to the problems of hospitalization.

"On November 30, 1981, while standing on the sidewalk near the Museum of Natural History in New York, I was hit by one of two cabs that had collided at the nearby intersection. . . . It was early in the morning. My physical injuries were substantial. . . . but in retrospect, it was the way I was subsequently *cared* for, rather than treated, that sticks most in mind. . . ."

Some of Talbott's experiences show how interpersonal interactions can add to stress. For instance:

"Each morning a new nurse would bounce cheerily into the room, introduce herself, and take a history. I assumed on the second day that my first day's nurse had the day off. But by the third or fourth day I realized that some bizarre rotational

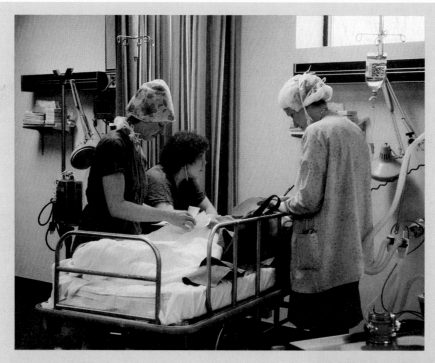

FIGURE 5–2
In addition to the patient's stress and the pressures under which caregivers work, the anxious relatives and friends must meet coping challenges as well. (Milton Feinberg/Stock, Boston)

system ensured that no nurse would ever get to know me, my needs, and my care, since I'd never see the same one twice.

One evening I received no dinner. After calls to the kitchen from the nursing staff produced no result, they urged me to call—"they'll listen to you, you're a doctor." The nutrition person announced that it was too late for dinner, they were already immersed in setting up the breakfast trays. I asked if it wasn't possible to alter the routine so that I might be fed before 10 p.m. She then blew up at me for not undestanding all the pressures she was under, and only after I reminded her that I was the patient, and her job was to help patients, did she apologize and relent.

Finally, the day arrived, my few meager belongings marking a two-week stay were packed, and I was ready for the trip home. I eagerly awaited my physician's arrival to deliver some parting words—I awaited his optimistic view on my recovery, his good cheer, his clinical enthusiasm. Instead, he said he hoped he'd be able to "save" my leg, since the damage done was extensive, the healing complicated, and the prognosis uncertain. But, if he wasn't, all sorts of things could be done, including bone grafts. And if worse came to worse there was always the possibility of an amputation. But I shouldn't worry, that wouldn't happen for a while. When my wife arrived I was in tears.

Going home was no picnic—with an enormous, heavy cast and limited energy, I could barely make it to the bathroom—but it was home, without the surly aides, constantly rotating nurses, inadequate medication, dashing house staff, uncoordinated treatment team, incredibly unappealing food, and dehumanized physicians."

(Talbott, 1985, pp. 2, 31)

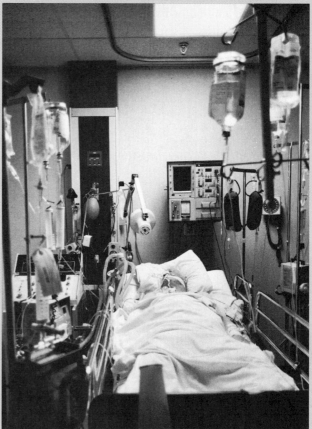

FIGURE 5–3
A hospital intensive-care unit, although it contains a variety of life-saving equipment, can be a frightening place that increases the stress already experienced by a patient. (Ken Karp, Photo Researchers)

lost her mother in early childhood. While loss of one's mother at an early age has many immediate effects, such delayed reactions during the middle years of life suggest that even though a person may seem to have successfully gotten through a period of stress, its effects may remain latent for a long time.

The psychological disorders discussed in this chapter begin with a specific event that has definable characteristics and has special meaning for the individual. This event is appraised or processed by the individual. As a result of the appraisal, the person's emotions or thoughts (fears, plans) are aroused and coping strategies are considered. The end product is some response that reflects the level of stress as well as the person's resources and vulnerabilities.

## Coping Techniques

In coping, people use their personal resources to master a problem, overcome or sidestep an obstacle, answer a question, or resolve a dilemma. Successful copers are not just people who know how to do things. They also know how to probe situations for which they do not have a readily available response. Different coping strategies are effective in different types of situations. People who are generally successful copers have a varied array of personal resources, which include the ability to:

1. seek pertinent information.
2. share concerns and find consolation when needed.
3. redefine a situation so as to make it more solvable.
4. consider alternatives and examine consequences.
5. use humor to defuse a situation.

A growing body of research is devoted to the question of how people can be helped to cope with stress more effectively. One finding of this research is that what you don't know *can* hurt you. People who know what to expect beforehand are better able to cope with stress than people who do not know what lies ahead. Many surgical patients, for example, suffer unnecessarily because they have not been warned that they will have considerable pain after the operation. It has been shown that patients are less anxious and recover faster when they understand beforehand how the surgery will be done and have a clear idea of what the recovery process will be like. In one study, the subjects were patients who were about to undergo a stressful diagnostic procedure that required the insertion of a tube through the mouth and into the gastrointestinal tract (Shipley and others, 1978). Three groups of patients viewed a videotape of the procedure before going through it themselves. Some subjects saw the tape once, others

saw it twice, and still others saw it three times. A control group did not see the tape at all. The patients who saw the tape three times experienced the least distress, and those who saw the tape once or twice experienced less distress than the control group.

Learning the specific skills needed in stressful situations also helps individuals cope more effectively. Many people enter dangerous situations without proper training. For example, many hiking and mountain climbing accidents are a result of poor training and preparation. Besides learning specific skills, individuals can be trained for stressful situations by being put through a series of experiences that are graded from relatively low to relatively high in stress. In addition, observing a model who copes with stress in an effective way can help people who are about to enter a strange or dangerous situation.

People sometimes fail to cope with stress because a high level of arousal interferes with their ability to concentrate on adaptive thoughts. These people do not observe their own thoughts, feelings, and behaviors in challenging situations, and they fail to engage in constructive problem solving. Learning general skills for coping with stress involves learning how to think constructively, solve problems, behave flexibly, and provide feedback to oneself about which tactics work and which do not (see Table 5-1).

The following are examples of useful statements that people can make to themselves in preparing for and dealing with stressful situations. Such statements have been used in training programs directed toward strengthening cognitive skills. In this training, the statements are modeled for each participant, who is then given an opportunity to rehearse them while imagining being in stressful situations.

### PREPARING FOR A STRESSFUL SITUATION

☐ "I should work out a plan for dealing with this problem."
☐ "I'm not going to worry about what happens; I'll just prepare myself in the best way I can."

### CONFRONTING A STRESSFUL SITUATION

☐ "I'm just going to take one step at a time. I can do it."
☐ "I want to be sure to stick to what's really important."

### COPING WITH FEELINGS OF BEING OVERWHELMED

☐ "Sure I'm scared—but that's normal."
☐ "I know I'm afraid, but I've got to do things that will help me cope."

1. *Be task-oriented.* Focus only on the task confronting you. It is not productive to spend time with thoughts or feelings that are unrelated to accomplishing the task. Being task-oriented means that you are concentrating completely on the job at hand. Negative or disruptive thoughts and emotions are the enemies of task orientation.

2. *Be yourself.* Don't role play. You will be more effective acting naturally than trying to fit a role. Place your confidence in *yourself*, not in the role.

3. *Self-monitor.* Pay attention to the way you are thinking and feeling in a given situation. It is important to learn about what causes stress for you and about your personal reactions to stress. Effective self-monitoring is your early warning system. It can alert you to the necessity of using the other coping skills to prevent a blowup.

4. *Be realistic about what you can achieve.* Know your own limits as well as your strengths. At times, laughter is the best medicine—don't lose your sense of humor.

5. *Have a constructive outlook.* Try to look for the positives in the people around you. Don't be too quick to conclude that people are behaving the way they are just to upset you. Put yourself in the other person's shoes—from that point of view his or her behavior may make perfect sense.

6. *Use supportive relationships.* Compare notes, blow off steam, and get support from your friends. Don't draw into yourself when you are feeling stressed. Remember that we all get by with a little help from our friends.

7. *Be patient with yourself.* Don't punish yourself for not achieving perfection. Your mistakes should be learning experiences, not times for heavy self-criticism. Keep your expectations of yourself at a reasonable level.

### REINFORCING SELF-STATEMENTS

□ "I controlled my tension—and I did it."

□ "I must be pretty good to be able to handle a crisis like that one."

People who cope effectively with stressful situations have learned to direct their thoughts along productive lines and to avoid being distracted by fear and worry. Actors, quarterbacks, and other people who are often in the limelight soon learn that attention to the task at hand is more constructive than self-preoccupied thoughts ("There are 100,000 people out there waiting for me to fumble that ball"). They also learn to anticipate problems that might complicate a stressful situation and to think about the best way to deal with them. Actors come to accept that they will occasionally get their lines mixed up and that deemphasizing their mistakes and moving on to the next line reduces the impact of their errors. On the other hand, the thoughts of some people who are prone to reactive disorders are saturated with self-blame and catastrophizing ("The worst will surely happen").

Researchers have analyzed the components of stressful situations and have taught people to be cognitive rather than emotional in responding to them. For example, anger-provoking situations are highly stressful to many people. Novaco (1975) trained people to avoid being overwhelmed by their anger by focusing on their own reactions and keeping their minds on the task at hand. He emphasized the following steps.

1. *Preparation for provocation.* The person imagines situations in which anger might arise and rehearses thoughts that would foster adequate coping. ("I'll just stick to the issues; no need to get angry." "Easy does it.")

2. *Impact and confrontation.* The person imagines that the provocation is actually occurring. ("Think of what you have to do.")

3. *The post-impact period.* The person imagines that the provocation has occurred, notices the emotional reactions that follow, and rehearses thoughts aimed at reducing emotionality. ("My anger is a signal of what I need to do.")

4. *Feedback.* If being made angry is highly stressful and leads to inadequate coping, the person is encouraged to engage in thought redirection. ("Thinking about it only makes it worse. I can shake it off.") If the person does a good job of avoiding intense feelings of anger, self-reinforcing thoughts are brought to mind. ("I'm doing better at this all the time.")

Through this type of cognitive training, people who were prone to anger have achieved better control over their temper and reported increased feelings of self-satisfaction.

## Social Support

"It isn't what you know, it's who you know" is a somewhat cynical saying, but there is some unintended wisdom in it. The traditional Danish proverb, "No one is rich enough to do without a neighbor" makes the point more positively. Recent research on social support has focused attention on the positive side of social relationships, or those interpersonal ties that are desired, rewarding, and protective.

Our social network includes people on whom we can rely, people who let us know that they care about, value, and love us. Someone who believes that he or she belongs to a social network experiences **social support**. Evidence is increasing that maladaptive ways of thinking and behaving occur disproportionately among people with few social supports. The amount and adequacy of social support available to a person plays a part in both vulnerability and coping (Sarason and Sarason, 1985). Vulnerability to physical and psychological breakdown increases as social support decreases. That is, social support serves as a buffer against the upsets of living in a complex world. Not only is social support very helpful during a period of stress (it is nice to know that there are people pulling for us in a tough situation), but it is also helpful in times of relative calm. It gives us the security and self-confidence to try out new approaches and gain additional coping skills. With an expanded repertory of coping skills, we are in a better position to handle demands, frustrations, and challenges when they do arise.

Research aimed at measuring social support is under way. The Social Support Questionnaire (SSQ) provides information about how much social support people have and how satisfied they are with it (Sarason and others, 1983). Table 5-2 lists some of the items on the SSQ. One interesting finding of research using the SSQ is that there is only a moderate correlation between the Availability and Satisfaction scores. There appears to be no minimum number of social supports that ensures satisfaction for everyone. For some people, a small number of close friends and relatives is satisfying, whereas others seem to need ties to many different people.

---

□ **TABLE 5-2**
**The Social Support Questionnaire**

---

The *Social Support Questionnaire* (SSQ) consists of 27 items, four of which are presented here. After answering each item, the test taker is asked to indicate his or her level of satisfaction with the support available by marking a 6-point rating scale that ranges from "very satisfied" to "very unsatisfied." The SSQ yields scores relating to *Availability of* and *Satisfaction with* social support.

Whom do you know whom you can trust with information that could get you in trouble? (This item is completed as an example.)

| ____ No one | A) R.N. (brother) | D) T.N. (father) | G) |
| | B) L.M. (friend) | E) L.M. (employer) | H) |
| | C) R.S. (friend) | F) | I) |

Whose lives do you feel that you are an important part of?

| ____ No one | A) | D) | G) |
| | B) | E) | H) |
| | C) | F) | I) |

Whom can you really count on to distract you from your worries when you feel under stress?

| ____ No one | A) | D) | G) |
| | B) | E) | H) |
| | C) | F) | I) |

Who helps you feel that you truly have something positive to contribute to others?

| ____ No one | A) | D) | G) |
| | B) | E) | H) |
| | C) | F) | I) |

---

Research with the SSQ has also revealed relationships between social support and physical health. In general, people who have had many recent undesirable experiences are more likely to get sick than those who have been more fortunate. However, people who have high levels of social support are less vulnerable to illness even when they have experienced a recent misfortune (Sarason and others, 1985).

Maladaptive ways of thinking and behaving are more common among people who have few social supports, particularly within their families. After an extensive review of the relevant literature, Bowlby (1973) concluded that, rather than sapping self-reliance, strong family ties seem to encourage it. Self-reliance and reliance on others are not only compatible but complementary. The "apron strings" become a hindrance only when the family exerts too much control over a person's life. However, even though lack of social support in one's early years can be damaging, the possibility exists that new social relationships can have stress-buffering and therapeutic value. Psychotherapy, from this perspective, is a special social relationship directed at helping people face and overcome obstacles.

Social support facilitates coping with crisis and adapting to change. One study examined the role of social supports in the lives of pregnant women (Nuckolls and others, 1972). The women were assessed in two ways: frequency and severity of recent life changes, and availability of social supports—people with whom the women were close, from whom they obtained affection, and on whom they could rely. Women who had many social supports experienced significantly fewer complications during childbirth than women who had relatively few supports. This relationship was particularly dramatic among women who had experienced recent negative life changes. For this group, 91 percent of women who were low in social supports had birth complications; the comparable figure for those who were high in social supports was 33 percent. This study, together with other evidence, suggests that close social ties have a protective function.

Why do some people have many rewarding ties that help them smooth out the rough spots in their lives, while others are lonely and socially isolated? Are the number and quality of social ties simply a matter of luck? There is evidence that people with high and low levels of social support as assessed by the SSQ differ in the social skills needed to attract the interest of others (B. R. Sarason and others, 1985). When engaging in a conversation with a stranger, people who are high in social support feel more competent, comfortable, and assured than people who report having few social supports. In addition, people who are low in social support tend to be perceived by others as being less interesting, dependable, friendly, and considerate than people who are high in social support. They are also less wanted as friends and co-workers and report feeling more lonely. There appears to be a strong link between social skills and social support. People with low levels of support may not believe that other people could be interested in them. This belief would tend to increase their vulnerability to stress especially in situations that called for interactions with other people. Training in social skills might not only increase their interpersonal effectiveness but also help reduce their perception of social isolation.

# ■ STRESS AROUSAL

The reason it is important to build up a person's resources for behavioral coping is that stress has undesirable effects on behavior, thought, and bodily functioning. Uncomfortable psychological feelings are present when people experience stress, and there is a strong tendency to avoid situations that bring about distress. Blood pressure, hormone levels, and brain waves are also affected by stress. Very high levels of stress can result in trembling, stuttering, and a decline in the effectiveness with which tasks are carried out.

There is often little consistency in people's reactions to stress. That is, one person might react to stress primarily in a bodily way, another might develop psychological symptoms (such as excessive worry), and yet another might show a profound deterioration in performance. Responses to stress involve bodily, psychological, and behavioral systems, but the correlations among these systems is often low (Burchfield, 1985). Table 5–3 lists ways in which the three systems may react to stress.

A variety of circumstances can evoke stress and require the individual to adjust to it. Two broad types of stress-arousing conditions that require adjustment are (1) situations that arise in life, often unexpectedly, and (2) developmental transitions. The death of a close friend illustrates the need for a situational adjustment; going to college is an example of a transitional adjustment.

## Stress-Arousing Situations

Events and circumstances that arouse stressful responses have varying characteristics. As the following newspaper article suggests, even the weather is capable of arousing stress.

> SALT LAKE CITY—(AP)—A thick, clammy fog has been hanging over the Salt Lake Valley for more than a

□ TABLE 5–3
Some Psychological, Bodily, and Behavioral Reactions to Stress

### Psychological Responses

feeling upset
inability to concentrate
irritability
loss of self-confidence
worry
difficulty making decisions
racing thoughts
absent-mindedness

### Bodily Responses

rapid pulse
pounding heart
increased perspiration
tightened stomach
tensing of arm and leg muscles
shortness of breath
gritting of teeth

### Behavioral Responses

deterioration in performance effectiveness
smoking and use of alcohol or other "recreational" drugs
accident proneness
nervous mannerisms (foot tapping, nail biting)
increased or decreased eating
increased or decreased sleeping

*month, and mental-health officials say it's starting to drive people nuts.*

*Since December 6, Salt Lake has had just three days without fog.*

*Kent Griffiths, director of Cottonwood Hospital's counseling center, says the weather has angered and frustrated people in a way he's never seen before. Griffiths says his and other mental-health centers have reported heavy workloads, with many persons complaining about the fog.*

*Rick Bangerter, assistant director of the Salt Lake County Crisis Intervention Center, says there was an 8 to 10 percent increase in calls over the holidays, with many callers saying the weather was getting them down.*

*"My personal opinion is that it's having an effect on people who are susceptible to stress and it may be the straw that is breaking the camel's back," Bangerter said. (Seattle Times, January 23, 1981, p. A1)*

**Characteristics of Stressful Situations** Some crises develop suddenly, whereas others develop gradually even though they may seem to hit us suddenly. Following are some of the ways in which challenging situations and circumstances vary.

1. *Duration.* Stressful situations differ in duration. A job interview lasts for a short time, whereas a marital quarrel might last for hours or days.

2. *Severity.* Situations vary in the severity of the circumstances confronting the individual. In general, a minor injury is easier to cope with than a major injury.

3. *Predictability.* In some cases we know what is going to happen (predictability is high), whereas in others predictability is low. The amount of stress caused by a request to give an oral presentation in class would depend on whether the request was made on the spot or was a previously given assignment.

4. *Degree of loss of control.* One of the most upsetting aspects of a situation is the feeling that one is unable to exert any influence on the circumstances. For example, earthquake victims can do nothing to prevent or control the quake's initial impact and aftershocks.

5. *The individual's level of self-confidence.* Lack of self-confidence often results in reduced personal effectiveness, even though the person may really know how to handle the situation. For example, a recently divorced woman may feel ill at ease in social situations that she was able to handle very well during her marriage.

6. *Suddenness of onset.* Suddenness of onset influences how prepared we are to cope with a particular situation. An accident is usually completely unexpected, whereas the crises of adolescence build up gradually.

Although stress is a highly personal response, a number of situations almost always lead to stress for the majority of individuals. Accidents, natural disasters, and military combat are examples of situations that typically evoke high levels of stress and may result in post-traumatic stress disorders.

**Natural Disasters** are sudden, violent natural events such as hurricanes, floods or earthquakes that cause death, injury, and property loss. They include both natural disasters and accidents. **Accidents,** or disasters caused by human activity, occur in varied settings. Their psychological impact comes from actual physical injury or threat of injury and from the possibility of loss of life. An accident can happen to anyone, and whether we are directly involved, know someone who is in-volved, or merely see a report on TV of a disaster such as an airplane crash, it exerts an impact on us.

An airplane crash has some special features that must be recognized if its victims are to be psychologically helped. The passengers on a flight are usually strangers to one another, often come from a variety of areas, and are far from home. Whereas natural disasters are frequently perceived as "acts of God," air crashes engender reactions of anger and, even more striking, of guilt on the part of some survivors.

Along with passengers and crew members, other groups may feel the emotional effects of an airplane crash. These include ground crew members, air controllers, and relatives and friends of the victims. There may also be serious long-range problems related to airplane crashes. Survivors and crew members are likely to experience such chronic problems as psychological withdrawal from their work, family life, or society in general, as well as physical symptoms and habitual anxiety. Special problems may be felt by certain groups, such as children, the elderly, and ethnic minorities.

Survivors often torture themselves with such questions as "Why didn't I do more to save those who perished?" and "Why did I survive when others did not?" Victims may experience an "anniversary syndrome"—episodes of depression and anxiety on the anniversary of the disaster. This may happen without the victim's understanding the source of the strong feelings that well up at about the time of the anniversary.

After the collision of a commercial airliner and a small private plane, wreckage and bodies fell into a suburban area (see Figure 5–4). Efforts were made to obtain information about witnesses' psychological reactions and to help them return to normal as quickly as possible. The following account of the experience of a young couple illustrates some of the psychological, behavioral, and bodily reactions found in disaster victims.

*At first they responded with great reservation, saying that they had been eye witnesses to the crash from their home in North Park. They added that although their house was still intact, there had been approximately seventeen bodies scattered around their yard, trees, and roof. They had decided that they never wanted to live in the house again and had called the Salvation Army for help in finding a new home. After some initial reluctance to talk at all about their reactions, they began to freely disclose every detail. They were obviously quite anxious and angry, focusing their hostility at the media, police, and the councilman who was present. Recurrent images of bodies lying around their home were reported by the man, as were obsessions with the details of the tragedy. (Where did the body come from that hit their car and did $700 worth of damage? Did he die on impact or before?*

**FIGURE 5-4**
Sometimes death strikes suddenly. This passenger jet has just collided with a small plane near the San Diego airport. The photographer snapped it as it plunged toward the ground in a crash that killed all 136 passengers aboard. The two passengers in the small plane were also killed. (UPI Bettmann Newsphotos)

*Was he on the ground and, if so, how could he have hit from that angle? Why did they put a sheet over him when there were so many other bodies and parts lying around and when "gawkers" just kept lifting the sheet off anyway?) He had attempted to remain busy and mentally occupied in order to keep his mind off these images. The woman experienced multiple somatic disturbances including, most prominently, anorexia, nausea, and frequent sighing respirations. They both talked intensively and openly for an hour and a half; at the end, both agreed that they felt better having had the opportunity to get some of these thoughts out in the open.* (Shuchter and Zisook, 1984, p. 296)

As more becomes known about what disasters like airplane accidents do to people, steps can be taken to improve the effectiveness of personnel who have the job of dealing with them. Training in the ability to recognize emotional problems and provide emotional support would be of great value in the efforts of such personnel to reduce both the short-term and long-term effects of these events.

**Natural disasters** (floods, earthquakes, and the like) threaten people's homes and property as well as their physical well-being. When there is warning of a disaster, the impending threat exerts a strong psychological influence. The disaster itself is extremely stressful because one has no control over it. The immediate post-disaster period can also be very emotionally arousing. Some survivors have difficulty picking up the pieces of their lives. Others may be troubled by strong feelings of guilt because they survived while others did not.

Military personnel in **combat** must deal with the constant fear of capture, death, or mutilation. Loss of sleep, physical exhaustion, separation from family, and concern about the killing of others heighten the stress of war (see Figure 5–5). Stress reactions are also seen in wartime when soldiers who are not yet in combat think about what may be in store for them.

In his book *A Rumor of War*, the Pulitzer Prize-winning journalist Philip Caputo has written a sensitive account of his experience as a Marine Corps lieutenant in the Vietnam War. In the following excerpt Caputo describes in an especially clear way the intrusive thoughts aroused by being in combat and seeing death all around him.

*I did not go crazy, not in the clinical sense, but others did. Malaria and gunshot and shrapnel wounds continued*

**FIGURE 5-5**
The stress-producing experiences of combat are clearly reflected on this soldier's face. (Frank Johnson, UPI/Bettmann Newsphotos)

*to account for most of our losses, but in the late summer the phrases acute anxiety reaction and acute depressive reaction started to appear on the sick-and-injured reports sent out each morning by the division hospital. I noticed, in myself and in other men, a tendency to fall into black, gloomy moods and then to explode out of them in fits of bitterness and rage. It was partly caused by grief, grief over the deaths of friends. I thought about my friends a lot; too much. That was the trouble with the war then: the long lulls between action gave us too much time to think.* (Caputo, 1977, pp. 190–191)

Caputo also describes the anger aroused by the combat experience.

*One of its symptoms is a hatred for everything and everyone around you; now I hated myself as well, plunging into morbid depressions and thinking about committing suicide in some socially acceptable way—say, by throwing myself on an enemy hand grenade. At other times, I felt urges to kill someone else. When in those moods, the slightest irritation was likely to set me off.* (Caputo, 1977, pp. 190–191)

Loss of comrades in combat is always a severely traumatic experience for soldiers; survival guilt is one of the main sources of their distress. The following case from the October 1973 Yom Kippur War in the Middle East illustrates this fact.

*A young tank gunner seemed dazed and strained during the first days in the treatment center and did not take part in social and recreational activities. When asked about the things that troubled him, he told the therapist that when his tank was already very close to the Suez Canal they were attacked by strong enemy fire and several crew members were wounded and killed. The tank driver "got hysterical" and was not able to drive any more and, therefore, the tank commander ordered him to take his place, because he knew that he had a driving license, although he had not had any previous experience as a tank driver. "For three hours and a half we were the only tank in the field and during this time I was all alone."* (Sohlberg, 1976, p. 525)

In the course of psychotherapy it became clear that this soldier was haunted by guilt and a feeling of extreme helplessness. These feelings welled up even though he had saved as many wounded as was possible under the circumstances. Similar reactions have been observed in soldiers who were forced to leave burning tanks and were tormented by obsessive thoughts about buddies who they believed might have been saved, although it was quite clear this was a distortion of reality (Grinker and Spiegel, 1945). Survival guilt seems to be part of the coping process by which some people adjust to situations of loss.

**The Effects of Disasters** In order to explore further the psychological side of stress, we will examine in detail the short- and long-term effects of disasters. Research has been able to correct many popular misconceptions about how people behave during disasters. Behavior in a disaster is influenced by several factors, including the disaster's unexpectedness, intensity, and duration. Community morale, experience with previous emergencies, and previous training also influence behavior (see Figure 5-6). More often than one might expect, people respond to disastrous events in a reasonably adaptive manner. In general, they do not lose their heads, and the social integration of the community remains intact.

Mass panic is rare in disasters, particularly when relatives and friends are available to provide social support. The victims generally do not scream and cry uncontrollably. Children usually do not cause special problems in a disaster, especially if they are not sepa-

**FIGURE 5-6**

A mock disaster might help people develop coping skills for an actual event. In Spruce Grove High School in Alberta, Canada, students in a health-services class were called to help 16 students who had been "injured" in an explosion in the automotive shop. There they found drama students realistically made up with simulated injuries ranging from broken legs and backs to concussions and burns. "I was happy with their reaction," their teacher Connie Filipchuk commented. "They didn't just stand around, they used the skills they were taught," "no one panicked." (*Disaster Service News and Notes*, September 1982, p. 5). The helpers did not know that the disaster was a fake until they had aided the victims. The photo shows a "victim" giving first aid to a classmate. (Mark Walters *Stony Plain Reporter*)

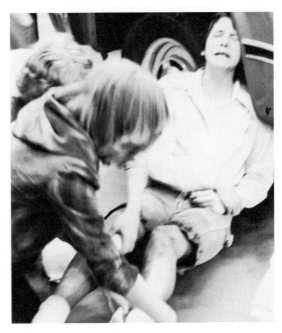

rated from their parents. Although extreme emotional and physical outbursts are fairly widespread, they tend to be temporary. However, when disasters are severe and their effects are protracted, the incidence of severe mental disorder increases.

Although most people adjust rapidly to the effects of disasters, about one-third of the survivors may display what has been called the **disaster syndrome**. During the hours following the disaster, such people are dazed and wander around aimlessly. They often complain of severe physical symptoms such as nausea, insomnia, and "the shakes."

The following case illustrates the long-term effects of the experience of surviving a disaster. In February of 1972 a flood caused by the collapse of a dam occurred at Buffalo Creek, West Virginia. The flood killed 125 people and left 4,000 homeless. According to clinicians who studied the Buffalo Creek residents, more than 80 percent of the survivors suffered from severe psychological maladjustments. Most of these maladjustments could not be traced to preexisting personality characteristics. Among the psychological and social problems observed more than two years after the disaster were anxiety, depression, hostility and belligerence, social isolation, and a variety of physical complaints. The survivors' emotional patterns and social behavior were strikingly similar to those of outpatients at mental health clinics. Five years after the disaster, 30 percent still had symptoms that interfered with their effectiveness (Gleser and others, 1981).

Psychological studies of a large group of survivors left little doubt that everyone who experienced the Buffalo Creek disaster had some or all of the following experiences (Lifton and Olson, 1976).

1. *Death anxiety and a death imprint.* Not only were the survivors preoccupied with fears of sudden death, both during and after the flood, but they also seemed to have indelible imprints or images that evoked intense emotional reactions years later. A host of ordinary life events were capable of arousing strong stress reactions.

   *When it rained hard last week it was like the past came out again. I took the family down to the cellar and [at times like this] I just know the flood is going to come back. . . . It's like you might step out of the trailer and get caught in something. Every time it rains I get the feeling that it's a natural thing for the floods to come.* (Lifton and Olson, 1976, p. 2)

2. *Terrifying dreams.* Years later the survivors' dreams were still marked by terror and a feeling of being trapped.

   *I dream I'm in a car on a pier surrounded by muddy water—or else in a pool of muddy water. I feel like I've got to hold onto the side of the pool. If I do I'm all right. I know that I can't get out. I have to stay in it. I've never been to no funerals except the ones right after the flood. . . . In the dream there is a big crowd at the funeral—the whole family is watching. I'm being buried. I'm scared to death. I'm trying to tell them I'm alive but they don't pay no attention.* (Lifton and Olson, 1976, p. 3)

3. *Death guilt.* The survivors had a sense of painful self-condemnation for having lived while others died.

4. *Psychological numbing.* The survivors suffered a reduced capacity for feelings of all kinds. They showed apathy, withdrawal, and depression. Psychic numbing is perhaps the most common component of the disaster syndrome.

5. *Impaired social relationships.* As a result of the flood, many Buffalo Creek residents were less able to engage in warm social relationships than they had been before the disaster. They were more prone to breakdowns in human bonds and to a rage that made them feel out of control.

6. *Search for meaning.* The survivors seemed compelled to search for some meaning in the disaster. Some sought solace in religion ("It was God's will"), but most could not avoid being preoccupied by the fact that the flood was due to human negligence.

Because the Buffalo Creek flood was caused by human negligence, this disaster was different from natural disasters like earthquakes and most floods. The difference is primarily in the survivors' anger, inability to find meaning in what happened, and feeling of dehumanization. These reactions have also been observed in victims of the atomic bombing of Hiroshima and in those who survived the Nazi concentration camps.

Research on the psychological effects of disasters has shown that they set in motion a cycle of reactions aimed at restoring an equilibrium between the person's self-concept and the new realities of his or her life. Preexisting personality characteristics may interfere with an adaptive response after a disaster. People who see themselves as incompetent, who tend to respond defensively to challenges (for example, by using denial or projection), who have conflicts involving themes similar to some aspect of the disaster, or who believe that their past thoughts might have somehow influenced what happened—such people are likely to have long-lasting maladaptive reactions to traumatic situations. These prolonged reactions usually include feeling dazed and having intrusive thoughts and images about the traumatic event. These thoughts and images may interfere with the ability to sleep (Brett and Ostroff, 1985; Horowitz, 1985).

Disasters show the impact of unforeseen events on human lives. They are characterized by a **prestress** period that usually is not marked by concern about the possibility that the event might occur (the Buffalo Creek community did not expect a flood). When the stressor occurs, it creates an immediate **impact period** marked by excessive excitation, intense anxiety, confusion, and heightened physiological reactivity. The disorientation may continue into the **post-stress period**, but as the disturbing events weaken in intensity the personality is reconstituted. As we have seen, however, this reconstitution may be incomplete. The type of stress and its characteristics, together with the circumstances of the situation and each person's resources and vulnerabilities, determine the long-range influences, if any, of stressful life events. Philip Caputo, whose account of the effects of combat was presented earlier, has also described the intense post-stress anxiety he experienced after leaving the combat area.

> It was a quiet day, one of those days when it was difficult to believe a war was on. Yet, my sensations were those of a man actually under fire. Perhaps I was suffering a delayed reaction to some previous experience. Perhaps it was simply battle fatigue. Whatever the cause, I was outwardly normal, if a little edgier than usual; but inside, I was full of turbulent emotions and disordered thoughts, and I could not shake the weird sensation of being split in two. (Caputo, 1978, p. 297)

## Life Transitions

Whereas disasters are imposed on people from outside, other crises grow out of the individual's own path of personal development. Beginning with birth into a complex, often confusing world and continuing through childhood, adolescence, adulthood, and advanced age, crises build up and are resolved in either adaptive or maladaptive ways. In early childhood the transitions seem to be both momentous and frequent. Lois Murphy's (1974) study of 2-year-old Molly's adjustment to the stress of thunderstorms illustrates how easy it is for adults to underestimate the challenges involved in the growing-up process.

1. As a 2-year-old, Molly cried many times and was completely terrified during thunderstorms or when a jet plane passed overhead.

2. A year later she was able to get into bed with her older sister during a thunderstorm and accept comfort from her.

3. At about the same time Molly began to reassure herself (and her baby brother), saying, "It's just noise and it won't really hurt you a bit."

4. A month after this storm Molly was again terrified as a jet plane flew unusually low overhead; she cried and clung to her sister for comfort. A few hours later she repeated several times to herself, "Thunder really doesn't hurt you; it just sounds noisy. I'm not scared of planes, only thunder."

5. The next month she opened the door to her parents' room during a thunderstorm, saying that her younger brother was afraid (although he was really fast asleep).

6. Nine months later, at four years and two months, she was awakened from a nap during a thunderstorm, but remained quietly in bed. Afterward she said to her sister, "There was lots of thunder, but I just snuggled in my bed and didn't cry a bit."

7. Four months later, at four and a half years, Molly showed no open fear herself during a storm, and comforted her frightened little brother, saying, "I remember when I was a little baby and I was scared of thunder and I used to cry and cry every time it thundered." (Murphy, 1974, p. 76)

As she progressed developmentally, the following factors probably contributed to Molly's successful transition:

1. Expressing her fearfulness and sense of helplessness

2. Seeking comfort from a supporting person

3. Developing comforting things to say to herself, which permitted her to provide her own support

4. Formulating a self-image that emphasized pride in her mastery of her fear

The two-steps-forward–one-step-backward process shown by Molly is also characteristic of later developmental transitions.

Stressful transitions come about because of changes in the operation of biological, personal, cultural, environmental, and historical variables. Adaptation to one life crisis often influences success in adaptation later on. Many people are able to weather these crises, but some develop a clinically significant degree of inappropriate behavior that usually disappears after the transition has been made.

Following are some of the transitions in the life cycle that can cause stress.

1. Birth and attainment of coordination between mother and infant

2. Initial steps toward independence and transition to an out-of-home facility (school, day-care center)

3. Puberty, with all the biological and social changes that mark the adolescent years

4. Major educational transitions, such as going to college

5. Entry into the world of work

6. Marriage

7. Bearing and rearing children

8. Moving to a new place of residence

9. Children's milestones

10. Retirement

We will illustrate transitional stress with three examples: adolescence, job burnout, and old age.

**Adolescence**   The role of cultural factors in adolescence cannot be overestimated. As a reasonably distinct period of life, adolescence might be described as a by-product of the Industrial Revolution. Prior to that event there had been no need to provide a special niche for people who were biologically no longer children but to whom society did not find it convenient to assign adult roles. Since the Industrial Revolution, the age at which individuals are admitted to adult occupational roles has repeatedly been raised, with the result that the period of adolescence has been lengthened. The stress experienced by adolescents has been increased by the lack of agreement about when adolescence ends as well as by the greater number of life choices young people have to make (Adelson, 1980).

Adolescence can be divided into early, middle, and late periods. The dominant theme of early adolescence is the individual's response to changes in sex hormone levels and a general growth spurt. The onset of puberty comes at an increasingly early age—the average age at first menstruation has declined from 16.5 years in 1860 to 12.5 years today. The comparable events of puberty for boys lag approximately two years behind those for girls.

By the end of this early period, the person has acquired a body that is quite different from the one he or she had as a child. Changes in body image have a significant effect on an adolescent's self-concept. How well an adolescent likes his or her body often depends on how other people respond to it. For example, late-maturing boys generally show more personal and social maladjustment at all stages of adolescence than those who mature early. They tend to be characterized by negative self-concepts, prolonged dependency, and feelings of rejection by social groups that are important to them. The picture is different for girls. Early-ma-

turing girls often lack poise and are submissive in their social relationships. Late-maturing girls, on the other hand, seem more outgoing and self-assured (Hamburg, 1974).

The extent to which the unpredictable moodiness, depression, anger, and emotionality often seen in early adolescence are related to changes in sex hormone levels is unclear. It has been shown, however, that adolescence does not neccessarily have to be a stormy and stressful time. Parental interest, reasonable guidelines, and support, particularly from the same-sex parent, play important roles in helping the younger teenager make the necessary developmental transitions.

During midadolescence (roughly 15 to 18 years of age), the individual receives increasing responsibility and more privileges (for example, holding down a part-time job; driving a car). There are also increases in stress created by the fact that the adolescent is in many ways a marginal character: too old to be treated as a child, too young to have the rights of an adult. For example, the percentage of individuals who report that they have engaged in premarital intercourse has increased markedly in the last decade, especially among females. Although there is increasing moral acceptance of premarital intercourse, this does not remove the social issues related to this behavior. Thus, the incidence of venereal disease is at an all-time high, and the increasing number of high school students who are mothers is a source of both personal and social problems.

Perhaps the most noteworthy developmental occurrence in midadolescence is the gradual shift from a here-and-now perspective to a point of view that is oriented toward the future. In addition, the individual becomes less self-absorbed and grows increasingly concerned with values and ideals.

Graduation from high school is usually taken as the high point of late adolescence. Living with the family, which is seen as protection by some adolescents and as restraint by others, can now come to an end. Some individuals move directly into the adult roles of marriage and full-time work, whereas others enter a more or less extended adolescence through college or job-training experience. Major tasks of this period include development of a personal identity, renegotiation of the relationship to the family, and the development of stable and enduring ties to others. Late adolescence can be difficult for a variety of reasons, including high unemployment rates among teenagers and young adults as well as high crime rates and the problems posed by alcoholism and drug abuse.

One of the major events of adolescence occurs when parents are relinquished as primary attachment figures. During this period adolescents often feel isolated and in limbo. In a study of over 9,000 adolescents in ten U.S. cities (Brennan and Auslander, 1979), 54 percent of the subjects agreed with the statement, "I often feel lonely." There was a significant sex difference in this sense of isolation: 61.3 percent of the girls but only 46.5 percent of the boys agreed with the statement. The adolescents' sense of isolation involved relationships with parents, teachers, and peers. Ten percent of the adolescents sampled felt that their parents were not interested in them; 36 percent felt that their parents did not understand their problems; 33 percent felt that their teachers did not understand them well enough; 12 percent felt that they had no one to turn to for help; and 25 percent indicated that they spent less than half an hour a day with their friends.

Various factors contribute to adolescent loneliness (Brennan, 1982). The adolescent experiences new desires and expectations that may not be readily satisfied but that disrupt existing personal relationships. A predisposition to loneliness may originate in such personality characteristics as shyness and low self-esteem and may be intensified by cultural factors such as the social network within the high school.

Because of the inevitable changes that occur during adolescence, some degree of loneliness may be unavoidable. Moreover, the pain of loneliness can have a positive function. Lonely individuals may be more motivated to develop or upgrade social and emotional relationships and to do something about meeting the challenges of becoming an adult. One study of first-year college students found that those who overcome their initial loneliness are able to maintain a positive view of themselves and their future relationships with others despite the stress of moving to a new social environment (Cutrona and others, 1979).

Loneliness is not the same thing as social isolation. It is a subjective experience. A person can be alone without being lonely, and a person can be lonely in the middle of a crowd. Essentially, we are lonely when our current social relationships do not satisfy our needs or do not live up to our expectations. The psychological study of loneliness is growing in importance (Peplau and Perlman, 1982). People go through periods of loneliness at many points in their lives, not just during adolescence. Researchers are intensively studying loneliness as a product of unsatisfying social relationships and interpersonal skills, as an attribute that can be measured and influenced by interventions (such as counseling), and as a state that is precipitated by specific conditions.

**Job Burnout**  Many stressful transitions seem minor and easy to overcome but actually are likely to be more complex than we think. The reason for this complexity is that personal characteristics and situational factors combine to influence how a given transition is handled. This point is illustrated in job burnout, a condition that has been observed among professional workers. With their years of experience, such workers should be at the peak of their powers. However, instead of becoming a more mature leader, a person who is undergoing burnout becomes noticeably less effective.

Burnout is especially common among people in human service occupations such as teaching, nursing, and medicine (see Figure 5–7). It is a syndrome of emotional exhaustion following years of involvement in and commitment to "people work." Burnout is characterized by a diminution of enthusiasm, idealism, and job satisfaction. In one study a questionnaire was developed to assess aspects of burnout (Maslach and Jackson, 1981, pp. 102–103). The following are some of the items that reflect the burned-out syndrome.

- □ *I feel emotionally drained from my work.*
- □ *I've become more callous toward people since I took this job.*
- □ *I feel uncomfortable about the way I have treated some recipients.*
- □ *I feel I'm working too hard on my job.*

In addition to these subjective feelings of emotional exhaustion, frustration, and failure, there are often physical symptoms. Increased fatigue, sleep disturbances, headaches, and lowered resistance to infection are common.

Why should teachers or health care professionals who have pursued their work with dedication for years suddenly burn out? Typically, they go through several phases as they approach the burnout point. An initial phase is marked by enthusiasm, high hopes, and even missionary zeal. Teachers who are susceptible to burnout often overidentify with their students and harbor unrealistic expectations about what they can accomplish. Burnout-prone individuals often skip coffee and lunch breaks and cancel vacations because they feel indispensable. Reality gradually erodes their unrealistic expectations, and they begin to question their goals, methods, and values. They become more irritable and complain more, and they feel unappreciated and depressed. They come to the conclusion that "it can't be me, there's something wrong with the system." At this point anger and then apathy set in. Thus, the people who may begin with the greatest enthusiasm in their work often experience the greatest disillusionment.

Burnout has both external and internal sources. The external sources include bureaucratic practices that cause feelings of powerlessness, along with heavy work loads, difficult or unresponsive clients (students, pa-

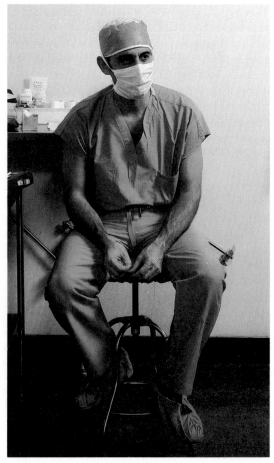

**FIGURE 5-7**
The helping professions and burnout. Workers who provide human services are susceptible to burnout, particularly if they feel their efforts are not leading to desired goals. Teachers whose students don't pay attention and hospital personnel whose patients often die are candidates for burnout. (Richard Hutchings, Photo Researchers; Seth Resnick/Stock, Boston)

tients), and repetitive assignments. Internal sources of burnout include the unrealistic expectations and disillusionment already mentioned. Burned-out workers feel a lack of social support as they perform their duties.

Research on burnout is aimed at clarifying its causes and devising ways of coping with it. One recent finding is that depression is an important component of burnout (Meier, 1984). When people experience depression and burnout, they feel "bad." Many individuals are unable to discriminate their feelings further without additional help.

People who have high levels of job involvement and a sense of satisfaction with their work are least likely to experience burnout. Workers who have good relationships with co-workers and receive feedback from others also are less likely to burn out, as are people who feel that they can influence their work situation (Eisenstat and Felner, 1984; McDermott, 1984).

Efforts to reduce burnout include increasing opportunities for social support (for example, through staff meetings at which mutual problems can be dis-

cussed), increasing staff training, and improving the quality of leadership. Authoritarian or workaholic administrators generate stress; democratic leaders who can pace themselves lessen it.

**Old Age**  As people grow older, they often seem to slow down because of physiological changes. For example, chemical changes in the bone structure make the bones more brittle. Age also seems to cause decreases in adrenal gland secretion, which results in hair loss. Changes in the central nervous system may result from the loss of cells that do not replace themselves, as well as from changes in hormone levels, oxygen deficiencies caused by impaired blood circulation, or changes in cell components. Finally, aging seems to be associated with increased susceptibility to disease.

Increased susceptibility to psychological disorders accompanies the physical debilities of old age. Depression is the most prevalent psychological disorder among older people, and paranoid thinking (for example, the belief that people are eavesdropping on one) seems to increase in the later years. Sleep patterns also change with age. Older people need less sleep and are more likely to awaken spontaneously during the night. A wide variety of physical complaints in the absence of a diagnosed physical problem is also frequent. A significant portion of old people in hospitals and nursing homes have brain disorders that interfere with their psychological and social effectiveness. Elderly people, who often have diminished physical and mental reserves, may face especially strong stressors, including illness and the adverse changes that typically accompany growing old, such as loss of loved ones, forced relocation, and increased dependence on others (*Research on Mental Illness and Addictive Disorders*, 1984).

What makes for good adaptation to old age? People who adjust well to old age appear to have been able to enjoy themselves and to obtain gratification from social relationships throughout their lives. They are also able to express their feelings, have a positive self-image, and feel a sense of purpose in life. Maladjusted elderly people express distress and discontent and are problems for their family and often for their community. The following factors seem to encourage adaptation to old age.

1. Economic security
2. High educational level
3. Social independence (including the capacity for solitary enjoyment)
4. Good health

Certain difficult transitions are inevitable even for people who have these assets. The transitions faced by many old people involve retirement from work, the death of one's spouse, and serious illness. Pining for the lost spouse may continue despite the availability of alternative relationships or even when the spouse was not liked, admired, or respected. This persisting bond to the no-longer-present spouse resembles the attachment bond of children to parents (Bowlby, 1980).

In one recent study, the effects of bereavement on several thousand men and women in semi-rural Washington County, Maryland, were investigated (Helsing and others, 1981). The bereaved subjects were compared with still-married individuals who were similar in such factors as age, sex, race, education, religious interests, and number of bathrooms and animals on the premises. The major finding was that bereavement is much harder on men than on women. The overall mortality rate was 26 percent higher for widowers than for married men, compared with only a 3.8 percent difference between the rates for widows and married women. For widowers aged 55 to 64, the mortality rate was almost 61 percent higher than the rate for married men

in the same age group. In men under 55 who remarried (at least half of them did), the death rate was at least 70 percent lower than for those who did not. In men aged 55 to 64, it was 50 percent lower. Death rates for widowers who remarried were even lower than the rates for men in the same age groups who were married throughout the period of the study. Further research will be needed to find out why wives are less affected by the loss of a spouse than husbands. This study did not support the popular idea that the remaining spouse's risk of dying was significantly greater in the early months after bereavement. Only long-term death rates differed for the widowed and still-married subjects.

Two objectives of recent research have been to identify the behavioral and physiological processes involved in bereavement and to seek patterns in the ways in which people react to bereavement (see Table 5–4). People who feel that they are somehow responsible for the death of a loved one, whether actually, as through neglect, or in some imagined way, are more vulnerable to prolonged reactions to bereavement. They often suffer unremitting feelings of guilt or resentment that are too powerful to be worked out by mourning. Mourning entails a spontaneous, sometimes overwhelming process in which the bereaved person is preoccupied with thoughts of the dead person, even in dreams. As the mourning proceeds, the preoccupation decreases, leaving behind it a realistic assessment of life and death and the ability to go on. When this process goes awry, the rest of life suffers. Over a protracted period, perhaps years, the mourner is so overwhelmed and obsessed that the grief is debilitating and distorts all other aspects of life (Raphael, 1983).

Just as all of us face moral decisions at many points in our lives, all of us will eventually face the approach

□ **TABLE 5–4**
**Behavioral and Physiological Aspects of Bereavement in Adults (based on Hofer, 1984)**

| Behavioral Changes | Physiological Changes |
|---|---|
| crying | muscular weakness |
| agitation, restlessness | sighing |
| preoccupation with image of the deceased | sleep disturbance |
| social withdrawal | immunological changes |
| decreased concentration and attention | endocrine changes |
| depressed mood | cardiovascular changes |
| anxiety | decreased body weight |

of death, that of members of our family and finally our own. One of the pioneers in the effort to understand the psychological implications of the approach of death is Elisabeth Kübler-Ross (see Figure 5–8). In an effort to understand the problems of people who are coping with a serious and probably terminal illness, Kübler-Ross interviewed over 200 dying patients. She found that the typical dying person goes through five stages in the process of coping with approaching death. She stresses that these stages do not always occur in the same order and that several may occur at the same time

**FIGURE 5–8**
Dr. Elisabeth Kübler-Ross is a pioneer in the study of the impact of impending death on dying patients and their families. Her writing and lecturing has focused on the psychological needs of those who know that they are fatally ill. (UPI/Bettmann Newsphotos)

(Kübler-Ross, 1974). The stages of the dying process are as follows.

1. *Denial and isolation.* People who have just been told that they have a terminal illness most often respond with denial: "It can't be true. There must have been a mistake." This response is often followed by a search for any physician who will give a different, more positive diagnosis, or for a faith healer or a miracle cure. Denial eventually gives way to partial acceptance, with fleeting periods of renewed denial.

2. *Anger.* When denial becomes less complete, anger at the unfairness of life often occurs. This anger frequently is directed at anyone available—nurses, physicians, family members, or visitors. It often makes the dying person difficult to deal with. The dying person is asking, "Why me?" (and, implicitly, "Why not you?").

3. *Bargaining.* When anger fails to work, a dying person sometimes turns to bargaining—with God, with the disease itself, or with the medical staff: "I must live until June to see my daughter get her law degree," or "My children are too young to be without a father," or "I promise I'll straighten up, if you'll just let me off this time." Bargaining, of course, is not a very effective way of dealing with illness, except perhaps for a very short time.

4. *Depression.* Many dying patients become depressed, either as a reaction to the loss of some body part, such as the surgical removal of a breast, or in anticipation of the loss of life and all its relationships. Talking about these feelings of depression can lead to the final stage, acceptance.

5. *Acceptance.* This period has been described by patients as almost devoid of feeling. The dying person has worked through his or her feelings of denial, anger, and depression and come to "contemplate his coming end with a certain degree of quiet expectation" (Kübler-Ross, 1969, p. 112). This model has relevance not only for people who are facing their own or another's death but also for very old people who anticipate that their time is limited.

There has been little systematic study of how dying people cope with the approach of death. Some therapists who see many dying patients find a much more varied pattern of responses than that described by Kübler-Ross. Other observers suggest that there are sex differences in the way people adapt to the reality of death. For example, women may be more concerned about the effect of their death on others. Men may be more concerned about the effect of a life-threatening illness on their occupational role, about the possibility of becoming dependent, and about possible pain. Although the idea of a progression of stages may be too simple, Kübler-Ross' theory has been valuable because it has called attention to a long-neglected topic—the stages of development that are related to dying.

## Multiple Stressors

There seems to be some truth to the commonly held belief that everyone has a breaking point. The more stress people experience, the more likely they are to break down either physically or psychologically. Dealing with several stressful situations at the same time obviously places great demands on a person's resources, but stress can also have cumulative effects. The following case illustrates how stresses that accumulate over time can have long-term negative effects.

*Mrs. A. was a 34-year-old woman who came to an outpatient clinic, complaining that the problems of managing her four children, aged 5 through 12, had become intolerable, especially the management of her hyperactive, negativistic 9-year-old son. She found herself either frantically attempting to discipline them or allowing them to do as they pleased while she shut herself up in a room and cried. This situation had distinctly worsened since her husband's death, 11 months earlier.*

*Her husband had been a chronic invalid for five years of the six years of their marriage. Her two older children were by her first husband, who had been discovered to be a bigamist. After this marriage had been annulled, she had a third child out of wedlock and then the fourth child in her second marriage. After her husband's death, she had experienced severely increased economic pressures: she was working a very full schedule and had problems in arranging day care for the children when they were not in school. Except when on her job, she was quite isolated, with few friends and no available relatives. Symptoms of moderate depression, with fears and guilt about impulses to hurt her children, had built up since her husband's death. (Wynne, 1975, p. 1615)*

The clinical assessment of such a case is complicated. Even though the environmental stress experienced by Mrs. A. was undoubtedly substantial, it is difficult to separate her current distress from her longstanding personality problems and difficult life situation.

In other cases, the multiple stresses in a person's life are easily identified. Someone whose mother and husband have died recently and who has just lost a job and had an automobile accident has suffered a combination of terrible blows. Sometimes some of the blows occur only in a person's thoughts. For example, a man who had recently lost his job and whose son had recently become addicted to heroin heard about a man of about his own age who had recently died of a heart attack. Although he hardly knew the other man, he imagined himself collapsing in the street as the heart-attack victim had done. Although simply hearing about the heart attack would not seem to have been a piercing personal blow, the man began to suffer from an intense fear that he was about to die. In this case, the combination of recent stressful life events and personality factors may have so raised the man's stress level that a seemingly minor event brought on an attack of anxiety.

Research has shown that people who have experienced multiple stressors in the recent past are especially susceptible to depression, anxiety, and overreactivity of physiological systems. There is growing reason to believe that mental or physical breakdowns could be predicted if there were a way to quantify how stressful certain life experiences are. For this reason, researchers have sought ways of assessing those experiences. Because recent experiences often exert a more powerful influence and are more easily recalled than those that occurred many years before, efforts have been made to quantify stressful life changes for specific time periods, such as the past year. Table 5–5 contains excerpts from the Life Experiences Survey (Sarason and others, 1978), one of the instruments that have been developed for this purpose.

Even though economics may seem somewhat far removed from psychology, there is growing evidence that economic conditions such as poverty can affect the incidence of stressful life events, which in turn can cause health and behavioral problems. A number of studies have shown that low socioeconomic status is associated with a high frequency of stressful events and the learning of inadequate methods for coping with them (Eron and Peterson, 1982). Thus, it is not necessarily socioeconomic status by itself that causes problems, but rather the life events and poor coping skills that are correlated with this status.

Regardless of socioeconomic status, unemployment can cause psychological as well as economic problems. Brenner (1973) has reported that when employment levels decline, admissions to state mental hospitals rise. He also found that economic reverses are correlated with increases in death rates from a variety of conditions, including suicide, homicide, and cirrhosis of the liver, a disorder that is often associated with heavy alcohol use. From demographic data, Brenner has calculated that over a six-year period a 1 percent rise in unemployment would have the following effects on national statistics.

☐ *36,887 total additional deaths*
☐ *20,240 additional deaths from cardiovascular diseases*

Because life experiences seem to be related to susceptibility to physical or psychological breakdown, assessing them might lead to the development of useful predictive tools. Recent experiences often exert powerful influences and are more easily recalled than those that occurred many years before, so several researchers have sought to quantify stressful life changes for specific time periods, such as the past year. Research has shown that people who had many of what they regard as bad or undesirable experiences in the recent past are especially susceptible to abnormal psychological and physical conditions. The following excerpts from the Life Experiences Survey illustrate this assessment approach to stress (Sarason, Johnson, and Siegel, 1978). Note that whether a given event is judged as desirable or undesirable is left up to the individual. Thus, depending on other factors in the person's life, a pregnancy could be judged as either desirable or undesirable. People with a large number of life events that they regard as *bad* and as having had a *great effect* on their lives are more likely to experience maladaptive stress reactions. The individual's personality characteristics also help to determine the effects of environmental stressors.

### Life Experiences Survey

Listed below are a number of events that may bring about changes in the lives of those who experience them.
Rate each event that occurred in your life *during the past year* as *Good* or *Bad* (circle which one applies).
Show how much the event affected your life by circling the appropriate statement (no effect—some effect—moderate effect—great effect).
*If you have not experienced a particular event in the past year, leave it blank.*
Please go through the entire list before you begin to get an idea of the type of events you will be asked to rate.

| Event | Type of Event | | Effect of Event on Your Life | | | |
|---|---|---|---|---|---|---|
| 1. Minor law violations (traffic tickets, disturbing the peace, etc.) | Good | Bad | no effect | some effect | moderate effect | great effect |
| 2. New job | Good | Bad | no effect | some effect | moderate effect | great effect |
| 3. Change of residence | Good | Bad | no effect | some effect | moderate effect | great effect |
| 4. Being fired from job | Good | Bad | no effect | some effect | moderate effect | great effect |
| 5. Serious injury or illness of close friend | Good | Bad | no effect | some effect | moderate effect | great effect |
| 6. Ending of formal schooling | Good | Bad | no effect | some effect | moderate effect | great effect |
| 7. Breaking up with boyfriend/girlfriend | Good | Bad | no effect | some effect | moderate effect | great effect |
| 8. Failing an important exam | Good | Bad | no effect | some effect | moderate effect | great effect |
| 9. Financial problems concerning school (in danger of not having sufficient money to continue) | Good | Bad | no effect | some effect | moderate effect | great effect |
| 10. Other recent experiences that have had an impact on your life. List each and rate. | Good | Bad | no effect | some effect | moderate effect | great effect |

Sarason and others, 1978, pp. 943–946.

□ *495 additional deaths from cirrhosis of the liver*
□ *920 additional suicides*
□ *648 additional homicides*
□ *4,227 additional first admissions to state mental hospitals*
□ *3,340 additional admissions to state prisons*

These physical and physiological effects of unemployment are not necessarily immediate. The entire impact of a rise in umemployment might not be felt for several years after it occurred. People who have multiple stressors in their lives at the time that they lose their jobs run the greatest risk of some sort of breakdown.

## Treating Stress-Related Problems

People often overcome their maladaptive reactions to stress in the course of time, but help from an expert may speed up the process. The clinician has two broad functions: (1) to provide social support for troubled people, and (2) to strengthen their coping skills. Several procedures are used in treating stress-related problems.

**Supportive Therapy** It is hard to recover from a stress-related disorder if one is or feels socially isolated. Because most stress reactions involve feelings of inadequacy and isolation, many people can be helped by sympathetic listening and encouragement. Though they use different terms, both psychodynamically and humanistically oriented clinicians emphasize the client–therapist relationship as a means of facilitating adaptive coping. Freudians describe their efforts in this regard as strengthening the client's ego. When the ego is able to manipulate reality more effectively, it is able to handle the id's incessant demands with less stress. The Rogerian therapist's acceptance of clients as they are, coupled with recognition of their strengths and deemphasis of their failings, helps clients feel more positive about themselves and creates a supportive climate. Clients who receive supportive therapy often comment with relief that the therapist did not criticize them either directly or indirectly for their handling of difficult situations. Within a supportive environment clients can relax enough to engage in problem solving and the careful consideration of alternatives that had previously seemed impossible.

**Drugs and Sedatives** A variety of anti-anxiety and antidepressive drugs are available to help people who have experienced trauma. While they are not a cure, such drugs can be of considerable value in overcoming panic states and other maladaptive reactions to intense short-term stress. Tranquilizers are often used along with psychological approaches such as supportive therapy.

**Relaxation Training** It is possible for people to learn ways of helping themselves deal with stress. It is a well-known fact that people can learn to regulate voluntarily certain effects of the autonomic nervous system. Such regulation, in turn, can affect their emotional state. For example, anxiety can be caused by the sensation of tension that is experienced when muscle fibers are shortened or contracted, as they are during stress. Conversely, tension cannot be present when muscle fibers are lengthened or relaxed. Relaxation training involves the following steps.

1. Focusing attention on a series of specific muscle groups
2. Tensing each group
3. Maintaining tension for five to seven seconds
4. Telling oneself to relax and immediately releasing tension
5. Focusing attention on each muscle group as it relaxes

Relaxation training is used not only as a technique in its own right but also as a basis for other therapies. It is applicable to a wide variety of stress-related problems and can be readily taught both individually and in groups.

**Systematic Desensitization** This procedure consists of combining relaxation training and a hierarchy of anxiety-producing stimuli to gradually eliminate the fear of a specific situation. The person learns to maintain the relaxed state while imagining anxiety-associated stimuli from the various stages of the hierarchy. In one study, soldiers with fears of airplanes, open places, and blood were treated with systematic desensitization (Kipper, 1977). The result was a significant reduction in their fears.

**Cognitive Modification** Behavioral problems can arise in part because an individual persists in a particular maladaptive line of thought. If someone can be guided to think about a situation in a different, more productive way, adaptive coping may become possible. Cognitive modification involves learning new internal dialogues and new ways of thinking about situations and about oneself. In this sense, cognitive modification is a step toward productive problem solving.

**Social Intervention** Some therapists prefer to treat troubled individuals alone, whereas others feel that they can be more helpful if they treat people within their social contexts. Family therapy, in which all members of the family go into treatment together, is based on the latter idea. In some instances the clinical worker might even decide to make one or more home visits to observe the family's interactions in more natural surroundings.

# ■ CLINICAL REACTIONS TO STRESS

Stress plays a role in most of the conditions that make up abnormal psychology. The three conditions that we will review in this section, while they are dealt with in different ways in DSM-III-R, are all linked to stress arousal and to the resulting clinical symptoms. In adjustment disorders a recent increase in life stress precedes what is usually a temporary maladaptive reaction. Post-traumatic disorders are often more complicated because of the possibility of delayed and recurring reactions to stress. Dissociative disorders are among the most dramatic and puzzling forms of abnormal behavior and are almost always preceded by an upsurge of stress that the individual cannot handle.

## Adjustment Disorder

A person with an **adjustment disorder** is someone who has not adapted well to one or more stressors that have occurred in the previous three months. The stressors might involve a developmental transition (such as marriage, divorce, having a child, or menopause), or they might be situational (such as changing schools, getting a new supervisor at work, or having been socially rejected), or they might be multiple stressors that have accumulated recently. Most of the time a person's maladaptive reactions to these stressors tend to disappear when the stressful circumstances dissipate or when the person learns how to live with new conditions. In the following case, the stressful transition to marriage resulted in an adjustment disorder.

*Mark Catton, aged 23, had recently married. He and his wife had known each other for two years at college and were deeply in love. Their getting married seemed a perfectly logical consequence of their affection for each other. The first several weeks after the wedding were wonderful for the couple. They looked forward to their evenings together and often took short trips on the weekend.*

*One evening at dinner Dorothy talked about a new salesman at her office. She described him as intelligent, handsome, and charming. When Dorothy used the word "charming," something seemed to click inside Mark. He wondered why she had chosen that particular word to describe the new salesman, as well as why she talked so much about someone she had known for only a day. During the next few weeks Dorothy made several additional references to the salesman. Her liking for him was more obvious with each reference. Each time it came up, Mark became increasingly suspicious and depressed. When Dorothy worked until late in the evening twice in one week, his suspiciousness and depression increased. When he confronted her with his suspicion that she was dating the salesman, Dorothy displayed shock and outrage.*

*During the next few weeks Mark became increasingly depressed. His depression was interrupted only by occasional outbursts of venom directed toward Dorothy. Their sex life soon ceased to exist, and their evenings were filled with silence. The problem reached clinical proportions when Mark began to stay in bed all day. It took great effort for Dorothy to get him to see a psychotherapist, although by this time even Mark knew that something was very wrong.*

*During his session with the psychotherapist Mark came to see how unrealistic his expectations about marriage were. He also was able for the first time to bring all of his thoughts and feelings out into the open. One recollection about his parents seemed particularly important. He remembered that when he was about 6 or 7 his parents had quarreled a great deal, apparently over his father's suspicion about his mother's activities at home while he was at work. His father had accused his mother of infidelity and had been very nasty. Mark couldn't remember exactly how the situation had been resolved. Although he had not thought about the incident for years, it became very meaningful to him, and discussing it in psychotherapy seemed to help him.*

Mark Catton's case is interesting because it shows so clearly the interaction between past and present experiences. His own marital problems, created by his irrational suspicions about his wife's activities, seemed to be linked to things his wife had told him about the salesman and to his unrecognized fear that the thing his father had feared was actually being inflicted on him. One additional point about this case is that Mark did not have a history of suspiciousness and depression. Both reaction patterns had apparently been ignited simply by getting married. Mark's going to pieces would be considered an adjustment disorder because his distress was caused by a stressor that was within the range of normal human experiences, not by a stressor of unusual intensity. His psychological functioning deteriorated primarily because of the expectations and concerns he had brought to the marital situation, not because of a traumatic development within the marriage.

The severity of an adjustment disorder is not directly proportional to the severity of the stressor, because personality characteristics as well as cultural or group norms contribute to how well an individual copes with a given set of circumstances. However, one characteristic of adjustment disorders is that the behavior displayed is in excess of what would normally be expected under the circumstances. Depression over the death of a loved one would not be considered an adjustment disorder because such a reaction is expected. Depression over a minor disagreement with a friend, on the other hand, would be considered an adjustment reaction.

An adjustment disorder usually does not involve extremely bizarre behavior and is not part of a lifelong pattern of maladaptation. The chances of complete recovery when the stress level comes down are good. Depression, anxiety, disturbances in conduct (truancy, fighting, reckless driving), disrupted sleep patterns, deterioration in performance at work or school, and social withdrawal are typical behaviors of individuals who have adjustment disorders.

## Post-Traumatic Disorders

Whereas the stressors in adjustment disorder are within the range of common experience, **post-traumatic disorders** involve more extreme experiences (such as disasters) whose effects may extend over a long period. The onset of the clinical condition in post-traumatic disorders varies from soon after the trauma to a long time afterward. These disorders are considered to be acute if the condition begins within six months of the trauma and delayed if it begins more than six months after the event. The chances of complete recovery are better in the acute form than in the delayed form. Although preexisting psychological difficulties may intensify post-traumatic disorders, many people who develop these disorders do not have a history of psychiatric problems.

A frequent characteristic of post-traumatic disorders is a tendency to reexperience the event. Painful and intrusive recollections and recurrent dreams or nightmares are common. The reexperiencing of a traumatic event may have an aura of unreality about it. When this happens, the person feels emotionally numb or anesthetized, and there is an unstoppable flood of thoughts about the event, along with a feeling of estrangement from the content of the thoughts.

In addition to reexperiencing the stressor, people who are suffering from post-traumatic disorders may show excessive autonomic arousal, hyperalertness, difficulty in concentrating on or completing tasks, and difficulty falling asleep. A symptom that often occurs in children who have experienced trauma is an exaggerated startle response. These symptoms may increase when the individual is exposed to cues related to the traumatic event (for example, when a victim of an automobile accident sees a car crash in a movie). Preoccupation with the traumatic event may also lead to decreased interest in social relationships, intimacy, and sexuality. Painful guilt feelings are common, as are depression, restlessness, and irritability. In some cases, there may be outbreaks of impulsive behavior, usually of a nonviolent nature (for example, unexplained absences from work), and abuse of alcohol or drugs. Table 5–6 lists some of the prominent clinical features of post-traumatic disorders.

In the following case, there was a short interval between the stressor and the onset of the post-traumatic condition. The case illustrates how denial can be used to blunt the strong feelings aroused by a stressful event.

*Harry is a 40-year-old truck dispatcher. He had worked his way up in a small trucking firm. One night he himself took a run because he was shorthanded. The load was*

☐ **TABLE 5–6**
**Clinical Features of Post-traumatic Stress Disorders**

Reexperiencing the traumatic event
Intrusive memories
Nightmares
Hyperalertness
Autonomic arousal
Depression
Irritability
Insomnia
Guilt feelings
Poor concentration

*steel pipes carried in an old truck. This improper vehicle had armor between the load bed and the driver's side of the forward compartment but did not fully protect the passenger's side.*

*Late at night Harry passed an attractive and solitary girl hitchhiking on a lonely stretch of highway. Making an impulsive decision to violate the company rule against passengers of any sort, he picked her up on the grounds that she was a hippy who did not know any better and might be raped.*

*A short time later, a car veered across the divider line and entered his lane, threatening a head-on collision. He pulled over the shoulder of the road into an initially clear area, but crashed abruptly into a pile of gravel. The pipes shifted, penetrated the cab of the truck on the passenger's side and impaled the girl. Harry crashed into the steering wheel and windshield and was briefly unconscious. He regained consciousness and was met with the grisly sight of his dead companion.*

*The highway patrol found no identification on the girl, the other car had driven on, and Harry was taken by ambulance to a hospital emergency room. No fractures were found, his lacerations were sutured, and he remained overnight for observation. His wife, who sat with him, found him anxious and dazed that night, talking episodically of the events in a fragmentary and incoherent way so that the story was not clear.*

*The next day he was released. Against his wife's wishes, he returned to work. From then on, for several days, he continued his regular work as if nothing had happened. There was an immediate session with his superiors and with legal advisors. The result was that he was reprimanded for breaking the rule about passengers but also reassured that, otherwise, the accident was not his fault and he would not be held responsible. As it happened, the no passenger rule was frequently breached by other drivers, and this was well known throughout the group.* (Horowitz, 1974, p. 769)

For several days after the accident Harry thought about it occasionally, but he was surprised at how little emotion he felt. However, despite his good performance at work, Harry's wife reported that he thrashed around in his sleep, ground his teeth, and seemed tenser and more irritable than usual. A month after the accident he had a nightmare in which mangled bodies appeared. He awoke in a state of anxiety. During the following days he had recurring, upsetting images of the girl's body. He developed a phobia about driving to and from work, increased his consumption of alcohol, had outbursts of temper at minor frustrations, and began feeling intense guilt about the accident.

In psychotherapy an effort was made to understand the significance of the accident for Harry. Initially Harry resisted describing to the therapist the circumstances surrounding the accident. After this resistance subsided, his strong feelings—the guilt, fears, and anger—emerged and were discussed. Because of complex and defensive motives, Harry could not accept and integrate his traumatic perceptions of the accident. They were stored, but not forgotten. He came to understand that two themes had been most upsetting to him: guilt over his relief at the fact that the girl had been the victim instead of him, as well as guilt over his sexual fantasies about her; and anxiety over the realization that he had come so close to being the victim. Bringing these themes into focus enabled Harry to be more open about himself and to take a problem-solving rather than a defensive stance toward his situation. Psychotherapy enabled him to look at himself in a more realistic way, to feel comfortable doing so within the supportive-therapy situation, and to achieve an improved adaptation.

What happens in post-traumatic stress? In coping with trauma, an individual uses a huge amount of psychological energy to fend off thoughts about it. He or she may feel emotional numbness, which results in loss of interest in social and sexual involvements. Although the event has ended, it is relived daily, and there is an irrational fear that it will happen again. It is this fear that causes hypervigilance and agitation. Intrusive thoughts, images, and dreams may become so preoccupying that the person cannot engage in normal work or love relationships. An example is the case of Mr. C., a violinist who survived a nightclub fire that destroyed the nightclub and resulted in the loss of many lives. Mr. C. functioned well during the fire (he helped rescue people and valuable original musical scores), but six months later he could not work: he became anxious whenever he smelled burning meat or smoke, and he had recurrent visions of people tearing and grabbing at others' clothes.

**The Post-Vietnam Stress Syndrome**  Many of the manifestations that are characteristic of post-traumatic disorders have been observed in Vietnam War veterans. During the Vietnam War 2.5 million people saw combat, 58,000 were killed, and over 400,000 were wounded. The lasting scars and delayed effects of trauma are both illustrated by the postwar experiences of many of these veterans.

Veterans of the Vietnam War are special in several ways. They served in a controversial war. In addition, unlike their counterparts in previous wars, soldiers entered and left the war in Vietnam as individuals, not as cohesive combat units (See Figure 5–9). The Veterans Administration estimates that 20 percent of all Viet-

**FIGURE 5–9**
Combat in Vietnam often involved long periods of waiting and uncertainty. Soldiers who felt close ties to the others in their units were able to stand this stress better than those who felt isolated and alone. (UPI/Bettmann Newsphotos)

nam veterans have had difficulty adjusting to civilian life. Many of these people feel alienated, exploited, and angry. For some, hot, humid weather serves as a trigger for flashbacks, nightmares, and generalized tension. Their suicide rate is higher than that for the general population. Clinicians who have worked with Vietnam veterans often regard them as otherwise well functioning but affected by nightmares, psychic numbing, and other symptoms. While it is difficult to draw firm conclusions concerning the incidence of post-traumatic disorders related to different wars, four psychological and social features stand out among Vietnam veterans: (1) dramatic and dangerous behavior (such as fighting at a bar); (2) social isolation (in part because their behavior frightens other people); (3) a negative self-concept (perhaps related to what the veterans perceive as their brutality during the war); and (4) reexperiencing traumatic war experiences (in dreams, memories, and flashbacks) (Rosenheck, 1985).

Group therapy has been used successfully with Vietnam veterans who have problems in these areas. Therapeutic groups made up entirely of Vietnam veterans help neutralize the "You don't understand what I've been through" attitude that veterans sometimes express. The therapist can help group members develop trust in each other and overcome the guilt feelings that often torment them. The camaraderie and social support found in group therapy decrease veterans' feeling of having been treated as scapegoats. However, because Vietnam veterans may have difficulty forming close emotional ties, group dropouts are a significant problem (see Figure 5–10).

The behavioral therapy technique known as flooding has also been used to help Vietnam veterans rid themselves of the intrusive thoughts, nightmares, and flashbacks that are part of a post-traumatic stress disorder. The following case describes the procedure.

*L., a 31-year-old divorced male, was an honorably discharged Vietnam War veteran who served an extended duty tour of 20 months in combat. He was bothered by nightmares and flashbacks, guilt over behavior necessary for survival, explosive behavior, and social withdrawal, and when seen by the therapist he showed chronic anxiety and depression. Together he and the therapist selected scenes from his flashbacks that he ordinarily avoided thinking about and which increased his anxiety when he had to discuss them.*

*Among them were the following:*

1. *A wounded American died in the subject's arms during an enemy assault.*
2. *The subject viewed the killing of a friend by an enemy combatant whom he subsequently killed with a knife.*
3. *While walking from a bunker to the showers, the subject was injured and his best friend killed by an exploding rocket round.*
4. *When the jeep which the subject was operating was destroyed by a grenade thrown by a child, the subject panicked and fired his revolver into a crowd, killing a woman and child and wounding several other civilians. (Fairbank and Keane, 1982, p. 500)*

*During each session the subject was instructed to imagine one of the scenes as vividly as possible, aided by the*

**FIGURE 5–10**
These Vietnam veterans show their mutual support during a Veterans Day parade. Demonstrations of support are especially important to veterans of what became an unpopular war. (Wesley Bocxe, Photo Researchers, Inc.)

*therapist, who gradually presented detailed cues for each aspect of that scene. When the client reported an increased level of anxiety, he was encouraged to retain that image as long as possible. All scenes ended with cues related to the time immediately following the event, and then switched to positive imagery. A period of relaxation exercises followed. Brief presentations of each of the four scenes, called probes, were also used at each session to test the patient's response. He reported his anxiety level for each, and measures of heart rate and skin conduction were taken. The treatment resulted in lowered anxiety and decreased physiological response, but only to the scenes that had been presented therapeutically. There was also a decrease in intrusive thinking. The results suggest that multiple traumatic experiences must be treated individually because treatment of one may not generalize to the others.* (Adapted from Fairbank and Keane, 1982)

## Dissociative Disorders

The maladaptive behaviors that arise from dissociative disorders provide a striking contrast to those that arise from post-traumatic stress disorders and adjustment disorders. Stress plays a major role in both, yet the reactions involved appear to be poles apart. Once again we see that similar situations can elicit drastically different responses in people with different dispositions and vulnerabilities.

In post-traumatic stress disorders, individuals cannot get the distressing experiences that they have undergone out of their minds. People with adjustment disorders show milder disturbances and decreased ability to cope, but their behavior clears up when the stressor is removed. The disturbance in adjustment disorders comes from overinvolvement with the stress-causing situation. In contrast, people with dissociative disorders use a variety of dramatic maneuvers to escape from the anxieties and conflicts aroused by stress. Their behavior involves sudden, temporary alterations of consciousness that serve to blot out painful experiences.

Many dissociative disorders appear to begin and end abruptly and are precipitated by stressful experiences. They do not seem to be attributable to organic factors. Although these disorders usually occur after childhood, in most cases there is a history of serious family turmoil. Separation from parents in early childhood and abuse by parents have frequently been reported.

The dissociation often involves feelings of unreality, estrangement, and depersonalization, and sometimes a loss or shift of self-identity. Less dramatic, but somewhat similar, examples of dissociation are commonly observed in normal adults and children. When the first impact of bad news or a catastrophe hits us, we may feel as if everything is suddenly strange, un-

natural, and different (estrangement), or as if we are unreal and cannot actually be witnessing or feeling what is going on (depersonalization). Stress can make a person feel stunned or dazed, as if in a dream or in another world. Such feelings of dissociation become abnormal when they become too intense, last too long, or cannot be controlled.

Four conditions classified as dissociative disorders are:

1. Psychogenic amnesia
2. Psychogenic fugue
3. Multiple personality
4. Depersonalization

All of these disorders involve large memory gaps and drastic changes in social roles.

**Psychogenic Amnesia Amnesia,** the most common dissociative disorder, involves extensive, but selective, memory losses. Because some memory losses can also be traced to organic changes (for example, head injuries), the word **psychogenic** is used when no organic causes are discernible. The memory losses that are characteristic of amnesia are too extensive to be explained by ordinary forgetfulness. Some people cannot remember anything about their past. Others can no longer recall specific events, people, places, or objects while their memory for other, simultaneously experienced events remains intact. Amnesia is usually precipitated by a physical accident or an emotionally traumatic event such as an intensely painful disappointment.

*A young man dressed in work clothes came to the emergency room of a hospital in the city in which he lived with the complaint that he did not know who he was. He seemed dazed, was not intoxicated, and carried no identification. After being kept in the hospital a few days, he woke up one morning in great distress, demanding to know why he was being kept in the hospital and announcing that he had to leave immediately to attend to urgent business.*

*With the recovery of his memory, the facts related to his amnesia emerged. The day his amnesia began, he had been the driver in an automobile accident that resulted in the death of a pedestrian. Police officers on the scene were convinced that the driver had not been in the wrong: the accident had been the pedestrian's fault. The police told the driver to fill out a routine form and to plan to appear at the coroner's inquest. The man filled out the form at the home of a friend and accidentally left his wallet there. Later after mailing the form, he became dazed and amnesic. He was led to the hospital by a stranger. The amnesia was probably related to the stress of the fatal accident, fear of the inquest, and worry that he might actually have been responsible for the accident. (Based on Cameron, 1963, pp. 355–356)*

Psychogenic amnesias are seen more often in adolescents and young adults than in children and older people, and occur more often among females than among males. Amnesia was once a favorite plot device in movies, but actually the condition is rare and recovery is usually rapid.

**Psychogenic Fugue** Whereas amnesiacs experience simple memory losses, individuals who are going through **psychogenic fugue states** suddenly lose their sense of identity, give up their customary life and habits, and characteristically wander far from home. Such an individual sets up a new life in some distant place as a seemingly different person. The fugue state, or amnesic flight, usually ends when the person abruptly "wakes up," mystified and distressed at being in a strange place under strange circumstances.

Fugues, like amnesia, are often precipitated by intolerable stresses such as marital quarrels, personal rejection, military conflict, and natural disasters. Fugues are usually of brief duration, with complete recovery and little likelihood of recurrence. After "waking up," the person frequently has no recollection of the events that took place during the fugue. The following case illustrates a fugue state with massive amnesia.

*Samuel O., a graduate student, impoverished and far from home, was invited to dinner at the home of an instructor whom he had known when they were socioeconomic equals in another town. He accepted the invitation because he was lonely and hungry, but he regretted it almost at once because his clothes were shabby. He thought, in retrospect, that the instructor had seemed condescending. That evening he left his rooming house in plenty of time for the dinner, but he failed to show up at the instructor's home. Two days later he was picked up by the police in a neighboring state. He could vaguely remember riding a freight train, talking with strangers, and sharing their food, but he had no idea who he was, where he had come from, or where he was going.*

*Later on, the young man was able to remember the events leading up to the fugue and something of what went on during it. When he started out for the instructor's house, he was still experiencing strong conflict about going there. He was ashamed of his appearance, resentful over the condescension, and afraid to express what he felt and call the dinner off. On his way, he was held up at a grade crossing by a slowly moving freight train. He had a sudden impulse to board the train and get away. When he acted on this impulse,*

*he apparently became amnesic. (Based on Easton, 1959, pp. 505–513)*

Because dissociative reactions are so difficult to believe, one frequently wonders whether the person is faking. As the following case illustrates, it often is not easy to answer this question.

*An enlisted man in the Air Corps had some previous experience as a private pilot. After a disagreement with his wife, he decided to punish her by committing suicide. Choosing the most dramatic method he could think of, he took off in a large, unattended aircraft and made several passes at the local river, each time pulling up before plunging in. Very soon, all other aircraft were diverted to other cities, and the local control tower was concentrating on trying to persuade him to change his mind. He finally agreed, but then he discovered that although he knew how to take off, he did not know how to land the unfamiliar plane. After some tense interchanges with the control tower, however, he managed to get the plane down. When the welcoming party of military police arrived at the plane, he found himself unable to remember his name or anything about his identity, his present situation, or the events leading up to it. (Aldrich, 1966, p. 238)*

From the available information we cannot be sure how well the pilot had planned this escapade. Neither can we be confident about whether his memory loss was feigned or real. These gaps illustrate the uncertainties connected with diagnosing dissociative reactions.

**Multiple Personality** **Multiple personality** is the most dramatic of the dissociative disorders. In a multiple-personality reaction an individual assumes alternate personalities, like Dr. Jekyll and Mr. Hyde. Each personality has its own set of memories and typical behaviors. Frequently none of the personalities has any awareness of the others (see Box 5–2). In other cases, there is a one-way amnesia in which personality A is aware of the experiences of personality B while B remains unaware of A.

Multiple personality occurs rarely. Between 1817, when the first case was reported, and 1969, only 90 cases were reported. Since 1970 at least 50 additional cases have been described (Boor, 1982). Whether this "epidemic" is a real increase or a reflection of greater interest in the disorder is unknown. Many more female than male multiple personalities have been reported, the ratio being about 4 to 1 (Kluft, 1984).

Clinically, the personalities' behavioral differences and disparate self-concepts seem striking and puzzling. They may experience themselves as being of different genders, ages, and sexual orientations. They may have

# ■BOX 5-2 THE TEN FACES OF BILLY

*Christene is a loving 3-year-old who likes to draw pictures of flowers and butterflies. David is a withdrawn little boy who bangs his head against the wall when upset. Adelena is a young lesbian. These distinct personalities, along with at least seven others, presented a bizarre puzzle in a Columbus, Ohio, courtroom; they all exist within the same individual—William Milligan, 23, who was accused of rape. Last week, after a brief trial, the ten faces of Billy were found not guilty by reason of insanity.*

*Milligan's is the second known U.S. case in which a defendant has been acquitted of a major crime because he possessed multiple*

*personalities. The Milligan case started when four women were raped last year near the Ohio State campus. An anonymous tip to police—the call might have come from one of Milligan's "personalities"—led to his arrest. During a jailhouse interview, psychologist Dorothy Fuller began routinely by asking if he were William Milligan. "Billy's asleep," came the reply. "I'm David."*

*Fuller suspected that Milligan was a multiple personality. One of his two females, the lesbian Adelena, is thought to be the "personality" who committed the rapes. Besides Adelena, little Christene and David, and the core personality Billy, there are:*

FIGURE 5–11
William Milligan's art work differed greatly depending on which of his personalities was dominant. Milligan (left) produced the portrait on the right as Christene and the center one as Billy, his core personality.

Why do I gots to say in a cage and cant get out an play
Do you like Icream
I Love you
No Antrei say you going to help us

A giant big hug AN A kiss For Miss Judey

From Christene

separate wardrobes, possessions, interests, and interpersonal styles. Their values, beliefs, and problems may diverge. They may even have different handwritings, handedness, speech patterns, and accents. There seem to be two or more distinctive personalities that alternate in controlling the body. Some, but not necessarily all, of the multiple personalities are unaware of the others.

In the following case, a 38-year-old woman named Margaret B. was admitted to a hospital with paralysis of her legs following a minor car accident that had occurred six months earlier.

*She reported that until three years before her admission to the hospital she had enjoyed smoking, drinking, visiting nightclubs, and otherwise indulging in parties and social activities. At that point, however, she and her husband, who was an alcoholic, were converted to a small, evangelical religious sect. Her husband achieved control of his drinking, she gave up her prior social indulgences, and the two of them became completely immersed in the activities of the church.*

*[The] history revealed that she often "heard a voice telling her to say things and do things." It was, she said, "a terrible voice" that sometimes threatened to "take over completely." When it was finally suggested to the patient that she let the voice "take over," she closed her eyes, clenched her fists, and grimaced for a few moments during which she was out of contact with those around her. Suddenly she opened her eyes and one was in the presence of another person. Her name, she said, was "Harriet." Whereas Margaret had been paralyzed, and complained of fatigue, headache and backache, Harriet felt well, and she at once proceeded to walk unaided around the interviewing room. She spoke scornfully of Margaret's religiousness, her invalidism and her puritanical life, professing that she herself liked to drink and "go partying" but that Margaret was always going to church and reading the Bible. "But," she said impishly*

*and proudly, "I make her miserable—I make her say and do things she doesn't want to." At length, at the interviewer's suggestion, Harriet reluctantly agreed to "bring Margaret back," and after more grimacing and fist clenching, Margaret reappeared, paralyzed, complaining of her headache and backache, and completely amnesiac for the brief period of Harriet's release from her prison.* (Nemiah, 1978, pp. 179–180)

The clash between Margaret B.'s religiosity, on the one hand, and her inclinations to indulge in pleasure, on the other, is a frequent theme in cases of multiple personality. It is noteworthy that as a child Margaret B. had had a playmate, Harriet, to whom she had been very devoted. When they were both 6 years old Harriet had died of an acute infectious disease. Margaret had been deeply upset at her friend's death and wished that she had died in Harriet's place. Perhaps internalizing the image of her dead friend had in some way protected Margaret from prolonged despair and sorrow at her loss. As Margaret grew older, that internalization became the depository for all of her unacceptable impulses and feelings.

Most clinicians think of multiple personality as a psychological adaptation to traumatic experiences in early childhood. These experiences are severe and dramatic; examples are being dangled out of a window or being the victim of sexual sadism. In addition to having experienced harsh trauma in childhood, people with multiple personality seem prone to go into spontaneous hypnotic trances. This temporary defense may become stabilized into multiple personality when the child faces repeated, overwhelming trauma.

Interest in multiple personality has mushroomed. The International Society for the Study of Multiple Personality was founded in 1984, and many case studies and interpretations of this disorder have appeared in recent years (Braun, 1984) (see Figure 5–12). At the

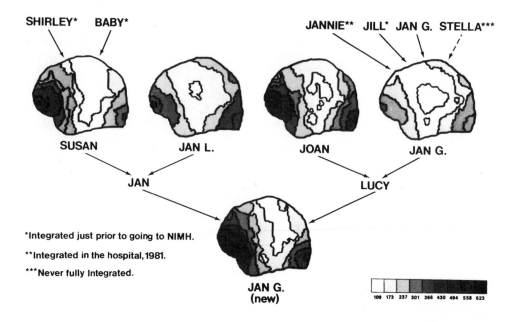

SHIRLEY*   BABY*                    JANNIE**  JILL*  JAN G.  STELLA***

SUSAN          JAN L.          JOAN          JAN G.

JAN                           LUCY

*Integrated just prior to going to NIMH.

**Integrated in the hospital, 1981.

***Never fully Integrated.

JAN G.
(new)

109  173  237  301  366  430  494  558  623

**FIGURE 5-12**
Evoked-potential recordings of a case of multiple personality. Evoked potentials consist of a short train of large slow brain waves measured by placing electrodes on the scalp. This figure shows different evoked potential mappings for the multiple personalities of Jan G. (Braun, 1983, p. 89)

same time, some researchers question whether multiple personality represents anything more than an extreme form of the normal ability to present a variety of distinctive "selves" that are not really separate personalities. An important reason for such disagreements about multiple personality is that cases of this disorder are rare, making it difficult to do good research and to compare cases seen at different times under different circumstances.

**Depersonalization**   Although DSM-III-R includes **depersonalization** among the dissociative disorders, some clinicians question its inclusion because it does not entail memory disturbances. In depersonalization there is a change in self-perception, and the person's sense of reality is temporarily lost or changed. Someone who is experiencing a state of depersonalization might say, "I feel as though I'm in a dream" or "I feel that I'm doing this mechanically." Frequently the individual has a feeling of not being in complete control of his or her actions, including speech. The onset of depersonalization is usually rapid and causes social or occupational impairment. The state of estrangement from oneself gradually disappears.

**Interpreting Dissociative Disorders**   Dissociation seems to represent a process whereby certain mental functions that are ordinarily integrated with other functions presumably operate in a more compart-

mentalized or automatic way, usually outside the sphere of conscious awareness or memory recall. It might be described as a condition in which information—incoming, stored, or outgoing—is actively deflected from its usual or expected associations. This phenomenon results in alteration of the person's thoughts, feelings, or actions so that information is not associated or integrated with other information as it normally or logically would be.

The dissociative disorders are difficult to explain, for several reasons. Often it is unclear whether a given case involves dissociation or is some sort of psychotic manifestation. Also, it is often difficult to obtain the information needed to draw reasonable conclusions. In the case of Margaret B., one wonders about the stressors that led to Harriet's emergence. How important were the loss of the 6-year-old playmate and the recent changes in Margaret's adult life? In most stress disorders the source of stress is usually easy to identify. In the dissociative disorders, however, the source might not be obvious at all. Because human beings are able to distort their memories, considerable probing is often needed to determine the true nature of the stress.

Dissociative disorders are often discussed in psychodynamic and cognitive terms. These disorders help the individual escape from reality and seem to facilitate the expression of a variety of pent-up emotions. They have been interpreted as attempts to escape from excessive tension, anxiety, and stimulation by separating some parts of the personality from the rest. When there are no indications of a recent experience that might have functioned as a stressor, these perspectives raise questions about earlier stressors that might still have symbolic meaning for the individual. (Margaret's loss of Harriet illustrates this possibility.) In treating dissociative disorders, many clinicians seek to uncover the dissociated memories and to help the individual face them and deal with them more directly. Psychoanalysis, behavior therapy, hypnosis, and videotaped interviews combined with sedative drugs have all been useful for this purpose.

# ■ STUDY OUTLINE

## VULNERABILITY, STRESS, AND COPING

1. Whether a situation is stressful or not depends on how the individual appraises it and on his or her ability to deal with it. During **primary appraisal,** individuals interpret a situation as either threatening or harmless. During **secondary appraisal,** they consider the action that is called for and their own resources for coping.

2. **Vulnerability** to stress is reduced by adequate coping skills and social support. There are four types of **behavioral coping,** or what we actually do in reacting to stress: matter-of-fact confronting, anxiety, anger, and defensiveness. **Coping resources** refer to our capability for handling stress. Some stresses may be beyond our ability to cope with them.

3. Stress can be reduced when people know what to expect, have the specific skills needed for stressful situations, and can limit their emotional response. Effective copers know how to probe for information, think constructively, solve problems, behave flexibly, and provide feedback about what tactics work.

4. Social support—*Social support* can be defined as the belief that one is loved and valued and that others are available who can be relied on to provide help or understanding if it is necessary.—may reduce vulnerability and the possibility of maladaptive behavior. The Social Support Questionnaire provides information on the amount of social support people have and how satisfying it is to them.

## STRESS AROUSAL

1. People may react to stress physiologically, psychologically, or behaviorally. Two broad types of stress-arousing conditions are life situations and developmental transitions.

2. Situational stresses can differ in duration, severity, predictability, and suddenness of onset, as well as in the amount of loss of control that they involve. Post-traumatic stress disorders typically result from accidents, natural disasters, and military combat.

3. About one-third of the people who survive a disaster display the **disaster syndrome,** which may be expressed as death anxiety or death imprint, terrifying dreams, death guilt, psychological numbing, impaired social relationships, and a search for the meaning of the disaster. People's reactions to disasters aim to restore an equilibrium between self-concept and the new realities of life. Preexisting personality characteristics may interfere with an adaptive response. Disasters are characterized by a **prestress period,** and **impact period,** and a **post-stress period.** Reconstitution of the personality during the post-stress period may be incomplete.

4. Life transition stresses are associated with stages in development such as birth, puberty, entering college, marriage, career planning, having children, and retirement. Some people adapt to these transitions better than others.

5. Adolescence is a particularly difficult transition. The individual's coping skills are still forming, and the physical changes involved in puberty increase the stress of getting used to new roles and responsibilities. Because of the nature of the changes through which the individual is going, a certain amount of loneliness may be inevitable during adolescence.

6. Job burnout is a syndrome of emotional exhaustion after years of involvement and commitment to work. It is especially common among people in human service occupations such as teaching and medicine. It is characterized by loss of enthusiasm, feelings of frustration and failure, depression, and physical symptoms. The causes are both external (functions of the work environment) and internal (overinvolvement in the job and unrealistic expectations about what can be accomplished).

7. Old age can be a difficult life transition. The accompanying physical changes and psychological disorders can be stressful. Adaptation to old age is enhanced by economic security, high educational level, social independence, and good health. Major problems are presented by retirement from work, forced relocation, increased dependence on others, and loss of a spouse. In addition, elderly people must face the approach of death. Elisabeth Kübler-Ross has identified five stages in the dying process: denial and isolation, anger, bargaining, depression, and acceptance.

8. Stress-related problems can be treated by supportive therapy, which seeks to strengthen clients' self-confidence and thus improve their problem-solving

abilities; by drugs and sedatives, which can be valuable in cases of short-term stress; by relaxation training; by cognitive modification, through which individuals may be guided to think in more productive ways; and by social intervention, in which the therapist treats the individual in his or her social context.

## CLINICAL REACTIONS TO STRESS

1. Disorders in which stress is a major causal factor include adjustment disorders, post-traumatic disorders, and dissociative disorders.

2. In **adjustment disorders,** a recent stressful experience has preceded a maladaptive reaction. Most instances of adjustment disorder tend to improve on their own as the stress that precipitated them dissipates. The sign of an adjustment disorder is a reaction that is not proportionate to the circumstances. Other symptoms include depression, anxiety, misbehavior, disturbed sleep patterns, deterioration in performance at work or school, and social withdrawal.

3. **Post-traumatic disorders** involve more extreme types of stress, which may last for a long period. The reaction may be acute or delayed. Post-traumatic disorders involve a recognizable stressor that would be hard for anyone to deal with. They are characterized by recurrent and intrusive recollections of the trauma; psychological numbing and lack of interest in previously significant people and activities; hyperalertness; an exaggerated startle response; and guilt, depression, restlessness, irritability, and substance abuse.

4. People with **dissociative disorders** use a variety of dramatic maneuvers to escape the anxieties and conflicts aroused by stress. Dissociation often involves feelings of unreality, estrangement, and depersonalization, which can go as far as a loss or shift of self-identity.

5. **Amnesia,** the most common dissociative disorder, involves selective memory losses that are too extensive to be explained by ordinary forgetfulness. The condition is rare, and recovery is usually complete.

6. People who are going through **psychogenic fugue states** suddenly give up their customary ways of life and wander far from home. Often they take new identities because they do not remember their old ones. The fugue state ends when the individual "wakes up." Fugues occur in response to intolerable stress; they do not last long and do not usually recur.

7. In **multiple personality** the individual assumes alternate personalities that may or may not be aware of each other. Most clinicians see multiple personality as resulting from traumatic early-childhood experiences.

8. **Depersonalization** is included among the dissociative disorders although no memory disturbances are connected with it. This disorder consists of a change in self-perception and in the person's sense of reality, and frequently involves a feeling of loss of control.

9. In dissociative disorders certain normally integrated mental functions seem to operate in a more compartmentalized way, usually outside of conscious awareness or memory. It is often unclear whether a given case involves dissociation or is a psychotic manifestation.

# 6

# ANXIETY DISORDERS

## CASE A: SUSAN

*I wish I could tell you exactly what's the matter. Sometimes I feel like something terrible has just happened when actually nothing has happened at all. Other times I'm expecting the sky to fall down any minute. Most of the time I can't point my finger at something specific. Still, I feel tense and jumpy. The fact is that I am tense and jumpy almost all the time. Sometimes my heart beats so fast, I'm sure it's a heart attack.*

*Little things can set it off. The other day I thought a supermarket clerk had overcharged me a few cents on an item. She showed me that I was wrong, but that didn't end it. I worried the rest of the day. I kept going over the incident in my mind, feeling terribly embarrassed at having raised the possibility that the clerk had committed an error. The tension was so great, I wasn't sure I'd be able to go to work in the afternoon. That sort of thing is painful to live with.*

## CASE B: PAUL

*It happened without any warning, a sudden wave of terror. My heart was pounding like mad, I couldn't catch my breath, and the ground underfoot seemed unstable. I was sure it was a heart attack. It was the worst experience of my life.*

## CASE C: SHARON

*I can't tell you why I'm afraid of rats. They fill me with terror. Even if I just see the word "rat," my heart starts pounding. I worry about rats in restaurants I go to, in my kitchen cupboard, and anywhere I hear a noise that sounds like a small animal scratching or running.*

## CASE D: MIKE

*Before I come home from work I spend half my time wondering whether a burglar has broken into the apartment. As soon as I get home I check every room, under the bed, and in the closets. Before going to sleep I probably check the lock on the front door fifty times. I feel better after each check, but then my concern wells up and I have to go check again.*

The problems described in these four cases are different, but they have one feature in common: the experience of strong anxiety, worry, tension, and discomfort. In Susan's case, which illustrates a **generalized anxiety disorder,** the anxiety is chronic and is felt in a variety of situations. Paul is suffering from a **panic disorder,** in which the anxiety is sudden and overwhelming. People who experience one or more panic attacks worry a great deal about whether and where another attack may take place. Sharon has a **phobic disorder,** in which anxiety is aroused by a spe-

cific type of situation, animal, or object. Mike's is an example of an **obsessive compulsive disorder,** in which thinking certain thoughts and not doing certain things (like checking the lock on the front door) arouse intense anxiety and concern.

Everyone has worries and fears. Freud argued that anxiety can be adaptive if the discomfort that goes with it motivates people to learn new ways of approaching life's challenges. But whether it is adaptive or maladaptive, the discomfort can be intense. This chapter focuses on the serious maladaptive aspects of anxiety, but it is useful to remember that anxiety has many causes and that all people experience it at some time in their lives. It is normal for people to experience anxiety when faced with stressful, threatening situations, but it is abnormal to feel strong, chronic anxiety in the absence of a visible cause.

Surveys of the general population have been conducted in an attempt to assess how widespread various aspects of anxiety are. These surveys suggest that as many as one-third of all adults suffer from nervous complaints, especially anxiety (Lader, 1975). The proportion is lower for males, the economically well off, and the young; it is higher for females, the poor, and the elderly. The clinical workers who probably see the greatest number of anxiety symptoms are physicians in general practice, who often prescribe tranquilizing drugs for anxious patients. One tranquilizer, Valium, has become the most frequently prescribed drug in the United States. The statistics for western Europe are similar (Koumjian, 1981).

The characteristics of anxiety include feelings of uncertainty, helplessness, and physiological arousal. A person who experiences anxiety complains of feeling nervous, tense, jumpy, and irritable (see Figure 6–1). Often he or she has difficulty falling asleep at night. An anxious person becomes fatigued easily and has "butterflies in the stomach," as well as headaches, muscle tension, and difficulty in concentrating. Table 6–1 lists common symptoms of anxiety and self-descriptions given by people with high levels of anxiety.

The experience of intense anxiety may occur after an event has taken place, in anticipation of a future event, or when a person decides to resist a preoccupying idea, change an undesirable aspect of behavior, or approach a fear-arousing stimulus. Although the behaviors observed in anxiety disorders vary widely, they have one thing in common: change and the possibility of change are involved in each of the precipitating situations.

In the previous chapter we discussed one kind of anxiety disorder, the post-traumatic stress disorder, which occurs after an intensely traumatic event such as a serious accident or natural disaster. In this chapter

**FIGURE 6-1**
An anxious individual is often apprehensive about aspects of life that are not troubling for most people. This person is tense about leaving her house to do some shopping. (Lawrence Migdale, Photo Researchers)

---

□ **TABLE 6-1**
Common Anxiety Symptoms and Self-Descriptions Indicative of High Anxiety

---

**Symptoms**

1. nervousness, jitteriness
2. tension
3. feeling tired
4. dizziness
5. frequency of urination
6. heart palpitations
7. feeling faint
8. breathlessness
9. sweating
10. trembling
11. worry and apprehension
12. sleeplessness
13. difficulty in concentrating
14. vigilance

---

**Self-Descriptions**

1. I am often bothered by the thumping of my heart.
2. Little annoyances get on my nerves and irritate me.
3. I often suddenly become scared for no good reason.
4. I worry continuously and that gets me down.
5. I frequently get spells of complete exhaustion and fatigue.
6. It is always hard for me to make up my mind.
7. I always seem to be dreading something.
8. I feel nervous and high-strung all the time.
9. I often feel I can't overcome my difficulties.
10. I feel constantly under strain.

---

we discuss four types of disorders in which the causes of anxiety usually are not so clear. A generalized anxiety disorder is marked by chronic anxiety over a long period (at least several months). A panic disorder consists of recurrent, sudden anxiety attacks in which the individual experiences intense terror and dread. In phobic disorders, the anxiety has an identifiable cause—for example, being near dogs or having to speak to a group. When the stimulus is not present, the phobic person's tension level is relatively low. In obsessive compulsive disorder, anxiety results from efforts to prevent undesirable outcomes. The individual is plagued with a recurrent need to ward off disaster by thinking about certain ideas and/or performing certain acts.

Many clinicians would describe people who are suffering from anxiety disorders as neurotic. In DSM-II, a classification system that was strongly influenced by the psychodynamic perspective, the word **neurosis** was used to describe disorders marked by anxiety, personal dissatisfaction, and inappropriate (but not psychotic) behavior. These were grouped together because it was thought that they all arose from somewhat similar unconscious mental processes and motivations. Though this view may some day be substantiated, that day has not yet arrived. Because DSM-III-R is designed to classify maladaptive behavior on the basis of observable characteristics rather than theories about its source, it uses the obvious presence of marked anxiety as the criterion for including disorders in this group.

The DSM-III-R category is called **anxiety disorders.** (The term *neurosis* is still used, but only as an alternative label.) Disorders from the former neurosis category in which anxiety is not so openly expressed, such as depressive neurosis and hysterical neurosis, have been placed in other categories. This chapter is restricted to cases in which the individual is abnormally anxious but still has adequate contact with reality and is rarely incapacitated enough to require institutionalization. The role of anxiety in several other disorders is described in later chapters.

## ■ GENERALIZED ANXIETY DISORDER

**Anxiety** is usually defined as a diffuse, vague, very unpleasant feeling of fear and apprehension. The anxious person worries a lot, particularly about unknown dangers. In addition, the anxious individual shows combinations of the following symptoms: rapid heart rate, shortness of breath, diarrhea, loss of appetite, fainting, dizziness, sweating, sleeplessness, frequent urination, and tremors. All of these physical symptoms accompany fear as well as anxiety. Frightened people, however, can easily state what they are afraid of. People who suffer from anxiety disorders, on the other hand, are not aware of the reasons for their fear. Thus, even though fear and anxiety involve similar reactions, the cause of worry is readily apparent in the former case but is not at all clear in the latter (see Figure 6–2).

In generalized anxiety disorder, anxiety persists for at least a month (usually much longer) and is not attributable to recent life experiences. The symptoms of generalized anxiety disorder are of four types: motor tension, hyperactivity of the autonomic nervous system, dread of the future, and hypervigilance.

1. *Motor tension*. Individuals with this symptom are unable to relax, are keyed up, and are visibly shaky and tense. Strained facial expressions are common,

as are furrowed brows and deep sighs. Such individuals are easily startled.

2. *Autonomic reactivity*. In individuals with this symptom, the sympathetic and parasympathetic nervous systems seem to be working overtime. There is some combination of sweating, dizziness, pounding or racing heart, hot or cold spells, cold and clammy hands, upset stomach, lightheadedness, frequent urination or defecation, lump in the throat, and high pulse and respiration rates.

3. *Apprehensive feelings about the future*. People with generalized anxiety disorders worry about what the future holds for them, for people close to them, or for their valued possessions.

(a)

(b)

**FIGURE 6–2**
Discomfort marks both fear and worry. In fear, the cause of the discomfort is readily apparent. In the case of anxiety, it is vague. In photograph a, worried family members are waiting for news about the condition of a loved one whose medical condition is critical. In photograph b, a person feels tense and frightened while "relaxing" in the living room. (Laimute Druskis)

4. *Hypervigilance.* People who suffer from generalized anxiety adopt a sentrylike stance in their approach to life. They constantly scan the environment for dangers (not necessarily of a physical nature), although often they cannot specify what the dangers might be. This excessive vigilance is related to their hyperaroused state. Because they are always alert to potential threats, they are easily distracted from tasks on which they are working. Their hypervigilance also contributes to difficulty in falling asleep.

Generalized anxiety disorder might best be described as consisting of prolonged, vague, unexplained, but intense fears that do not seem to be attached to any particular object. They resemble normal fears, but there is no actual danger, and in most cases danger is not even imagined to be present (Hibbert, 1984). Although anxiety is a factor in many types of disorders, the term *generalized anxiety disorder* is reserved for cases that are not complicated by other problems such as poor contact with reality.

## ■ PANIC DISORDER

The indicators of panic disorder are similar to those of generalized anxiety disorder except that they are greatly magnified and usually have a sudden onset. People with panic disorder may not be anxious all the time. Instead, they have unanticipated anxiety attacks that recur after periods (perhaps several days) of normal functioning. Severe palpitations, extreme shortness of breath, chest pains or discomfort, trembling, sweating, dizziness, and a feeling of helplessness mark the panic attacks. The victims fear that they will die, go crazy, or do something uncontrolled, and they report a variety of unusual psychosensory symptoms (see Table 6–2).

Panic attacks range in length from a few seconds to many hours and even days. They also differ in severity and in the degree of incapacitation involved. In the following case, frequent panic attacks had a definitely incapacitating effect.

---

□ **TABLE 6–2**
Frequently Reported Psychosensory Symptoms Experienced During Panic Attacks (based on Uhde and others, 1985)

---

Distortion of light intensity
Distortion of sound intensity
Strange feeling in stomach
Sensations of floating, turning, moving
Feelings of unreality and loss of self-identity

---

*A 35-year-old mathematician gave a history of episodic palpitations and faintness over the previous 15 years. There had been periods of remission of up to five years, but in the past year the symptoms had increased and in the last few days the patient had stopped working because of his distress. His chief complaints were that at any time and without warning, he might suddenly feel he was about to faint and fall down, or tremble and experience palpitations, and if standing would cringe and clutch at the nearest wall or chair. If he was driving a car at the time he would pull up at the curbside and wait for the feelings to pass off before he resumed his journey. If it occurred during sexual intercourse with his wife he would immediately separate from her. If it happened while he was lecturing, his thoughts became distracted, he could not concentrate, and he found it difficult to continue. He was becoming afraid of walking alone in the street or of driving his car for fear that the episodes would be triggered by it, and was loath to travel by public transport. Although he felt safer when accompanied, this did not abolish his symptoms. Between attacks the patient did not feel completely well, and a slight tremulousness persisted. The attacks could come on at any time of day or night. The patient felt that he lacked energy but was not depressed. He denied that he experienced fear, anxiety, or panic during his attacks.*

*The patient had had a happy childhood without nervous symptoms, led an active social life when in remission, and had a contented marriage and vigorous professional life.* (Marks and Lader, 1973, p. 11)

Generalized anxiety and panic disorders run in families and occur twice as often among women as among men. There is no evidence that any specific type of childhood experience predisposes people to these states. Problems often arise in classifying these disorders, because many cases are complicated. Several types of maladaptive behavior may occur simultaneously. Obsessions, compulsions, and phobias might all be observed in a given individual. Severe panic states are sometimes followed by periods of psychotic disorganization in which there is a reduced capacity to test reality.

Box 6–1 presents a case of anxiety and panic and classifies it in terms of the DSM-III-R system. A person who has had a panic attack develops anticipatory anxiety: he or she becomes worried and tense, and is afraid that the panic will recur (see Figure 6–3). In some cases, this type of anticipatory anxiety seems to be a quite realistic fear.

Drug research has provided an interesting finding that suggests that panic and anticipatory anxiety have different sources. Imipramine, a drug that is used in the treatment of depression, has been shown to prevent the recurrence of panic attacks (Klein, 1981).

# ■BOX 6-1: AN ANXIOUS, PRECISE, DEMANDING MAN SEEKS HELP

Mr. E., 40 years old and recently married, sought clinical help because he was nervous and worried about his health. These lifelong concerns became worse during his courtship and honeymoon.

*Mr. E. has trouble falling asleep if the room is too dark or too light, if he has eaten too much or too little, if the sheets are cold or wrinkled, if he forgets his nose spray, or if there is any noise. He fears nightmares, nocturnal asthma attacks, or dying in his sleep. He often awakes in a panicky sweat with nightmares, typically of being chased or suffocated. He worries that his lost sleep is shortening his life and ruining his work efficiency.*

*Mr. E. has always been anxious and worried. He expects the worst, dreads each time the phone rings lest it be bad news, and suspects that he has a serious illness. He experiences frequent palpitations, shortness of breath, dizziness, and numb fingers and has had numerous physical exams and electrocardiograms. The negative findings do not reassure him as Mr. E. is convinced that his doctors are withholding information, and he is determined to have additional checkups until his condition is diagnosed. He also has gastrointestinal flutters, frequent diarrhea or constipation, and occasional nausea and vomiting. His father died of heart disease and his mother of cancer, and he feels confident that he already has, or soon will have, one or both conditions.*

*Mr. E. is also extremely anxious about his work. He is a stockbroker responsible for large financial transactions and cannot ever relax his concentration, even on vacations. He has also felt considerable performance anxiety about his recently more active sex life and has suffered from consistent premature ejaculation. There are many specific situations that make him intolerably nervous—waiting in line, sitting in the middle of a row at a movie, riding public transportation, wearing a pair of pants a second time without having them cleaned, having dirty dollar bills, and so forth—but he is able to avoid most of them without great inconvenience. Mr. E. has panic attacks at least every few weeks. They tend to occur whenever something new is expected of him, when he is forced to do one of the things he fears, when he must give a talk, and, at times, for no apparent reason.*

*Mr. E. is a very precise and demanding man who is difficult to live or work with (or to treat). He is controlling, self-absorbed, maddeningly fastidious, and meticulous. He did not marry previously because he had very demanding expectations of a woman, and his worries and habits are intolerable to many women. His wife has begun to complain to him, and he is afraid she may leave unless he is able to change quickly. (Frances and Klein, 1982, p. 89)*

## HOW WOULD DSM-III-R CHARACTERIZE MR. E.?

Because this is a real-life case, it is more complicated than a textbook outline of a disorder. On DSM-III-R's Axis I, Mr. E. might be described in terms of either generalized anxiety disorder or panic disorder. However, because of the definite recurring panic attacks, panic disorder seems the more likely primary diagnosis. Mr. E.'s concerns about being precise and meticulous make obsessive compulsive personality disorder a reasonable Axis II categorization. Despite Mr. E.'s protestations to the contrary, Axis III would note that he suffers from no apparent physical disorder. The Axis IV rating of psychosocial stress (his recent marriage) would seem to be moderately severe, suggesting a rating of 4. On Axis V, Mr. E. might be described as having a fair level of adaptive functioning in the past year (a rating of 6). Despite his superior work performance, his social and leisure-time difficulties now suggest a decreased level of functioning (level 5).

Thus, Mr. E. might be classified in this way:

- □ Axis I: Panic disorder with limited phobic avoidance
- □ Axis II: Obsessive compulsive personality disorder
- □ Axis III: No apparent physical disorders
- □ Axis IV: Moderate severity of stress (4)
- □ Axis V: Moderate difficulty in prior functioning (6) Increased difficulty in present functioning (5).

It is important to remember that experienced clinicians might disagree about this classification either because of gaps in what is known about Mr. E. or because of emphasis on different known facts. With additional information, the classification might change. A clinician treating Mr. E. would want to better understand his sexual problems, his conviction that he has cancer or heart disease, and his somatic complaints, for which no bodily cause has been found.

**FIGURE 6-3**
This attorney, due in court in a few minutes for the summation of the defense's case, feels the beginning of a panic attack—trembling, a rapidly beating heart and a feeling of dizziness—that may make it impossible for him to appear on schedule. (Laimute Druskis)

□ **TABLE 6-3**
Percentages of Patients with Panic Disorder and Generalized Anxiety Disorder Reporting Particular Symptoms (based on Anderson and others, 1984).

| Symptom | Panic Disorder | Generalized Anxiety Disorder |
|---|---|---|
| Sweating, flushing | 58.3 | 22.2 |
| Heart palpitations | 89.5 | 61.1 |
| Chest pain | 68.8 | 11.1 |
| Faintness, light-headedness | 52.1 | 11.1 |
| Blurred vision | 31.2 | 0 |
| Feeling of muscular weakness | 47.9 | 11.1 |

However, it seems to have no effect on the anticipatory anxiety that panic attacks almost always arouse.

Prior to DSM-III relatively few attempts had been made to identify and compare subgroups of anxiety disorders. Because DSM-III focused attention on the subgroups, these topics have now been investigated more intensively. For example, one group of researchers has compared the patterns of symptoms, family characteristics, type of onset, and clinical course in generalized anxiety disorder and panic disorders (Anderson and others, 1984). Their findings support DSM-III's assumption that these conditions are distinct from one another. Table 6–3 compares these disorders with regard to several bodily symptoms. Subjects with generalized anxiety disorder have fewer bodily symptoms than those with panic disorders. Their histories also show an earlier, more gradual onset. A generalized anxiety disorder has a more chronic course and favorable outcome. Members of families in which a person suffers from a panic disorder tend to have a relatively high percentage of panic episodes. The comparable percentage for family members of those with a generalized anxiety disorder is much lower.

## ■ PHOBIAS

Phobos was the Greek god of fear. His likeness was painted on masks and shields to frighten enemies in battle. The word *phobia*, derived from his name, came to mean fear, panic, dread, or fright. Unlike people who have generalized anxiety disorders, people who have phobias know exactly what they are afraid of. Except for their fears of specific objects, people, and situations, phobic individuals usually do not engage in gross distortions of reality. Nothing physical seems to be wrong with them. However, their fears are out of proportion with reality, seem inexplicable, and are beyond their voluntary control.

One question that inevitably arises in discussions of anxiety is why people spend so much time brooding about vague menaces when there are so many real dangers to worry about. Perhaps the degree of fear we feel about a potentially harmful event is linked not primarily to the degree of threat (in terms of the probability that it will actually happen to us) or even to the amount of injury that we imagine we might sustain if the worst did happen, but to the disturbing quality of the event or situation itself. For example, even though there are three times as many traffic fatalities as there are murders, our thoughts are rarely preoccupied by the danger of an automobile accident. Fear of violent crime, on the other hand, touches many of us. Crucial to the experience of fear is whether people feel that they will be able to respond meaningfully to a situation—that is, whether they will be able to cope.

Phobics do not need the actual presence of the feared object or situation to experience intense tension and discomfort. The following account by a psychiatrist with an airplane phobia shows that simply imagining a phobia-related event can elicit strong psychological and bodily reactions.

*I was pampering my neurosis by taking the train to a meeting in Philadelphia. It was a nasty day out, the fog so thick you could see only a few feet ahead of your face, and the train, which had been late in leaving New York, was making up time by hurtling at a great rate across the flat land of New Jersey. As I sat there comfortably enjoying the ride, I happened to glance at the headlines of a late edition, which one of the passengers who had boarded in New York was reading. "TRAINS CRASH IN FOG," ran the banner headlines, "10 DEAD, MANY INJURED." I reflected on our speed, the dense fog outside, and had a mild, transitory moment of concern that the fog might claim us victim, too, and then relaxed as I picked up the novel I had been reading. Some minutes later the thought suddenly entered my mind that had I not "chickened out" about flying, I might at that moment be overhead in a plane. At the mere image of sitting up there strapped in by a seat belt, my hands began to sweat, my heart to beat perceptibly faster, and I felt a kind of nervous uneasiness in my gut. The sensation lasted until I forced myself back to my book and forgot about the imagery.*

*I must say I found this experience a vivid lesson in the nature of phobias. Here I had reacted with hardly a flicker of concern to an admittedly small, but real danger of accident, as evidenced by the fog-caused train crash an hour or two earlier; at the same time I had responded to a purely imaginary situation with an unpleasant start of nervousness, experienced both as somatic symptoms and as an inner sense of indescribable dread so characteristic of anxiety. The unreasonableness of the latter was highlighted for me by its contrast with the absence of concern about the speeding train, which if I had worried about it, would have been an apprehension founded on real, external circumstances.* (Nemiah, 1985a, p. 895)

The onset of many phobias is so gradual that it is difficult to tell whether there were any specific precipitating factors. In other cases, the apparent time of onset, although not necessarily the cause, can be pinpointed (see Figure 6–4).

*I was riding in my husband's car and I suddenly became terrified. I felt as if I would die. I made him turn around and take me home. I ran into the house and suddenly felt safe. I could not understand what had happened. I had never been afraid of cars. The next day it happened again, and it kept getting worse. Finally, just being on the street and seeing a car would bring on a terrible feeling. Now I just stay at home.* (De Nike and Tiber, 1968, p. 346)

Phobias may begin with a generalized anxiety attack, but the anxiety then becomes crystallized around a particular object or situation (for example, elevators, snakes, or darkness). As long as the feared object or situation can be avoided, the anxiety does not reach disturbing proportions. Some objects of phobias—such as cats, cars, and stairs—are considered aspects of everyday life by most of us. Other objects and situations—snakes, death, and heights are disliked to some extent by most people. However, phobias involve levels of fear that, in addition to being overly intense, interfere with normal living patterns. One study of phobic patients showed that their fears fell into five categories related to (1) separations, (2) animals, (3) bodily mutilation, (4) social situations, and (5) nature (Torgersen, 1979). Table 6–4 gives examples of phobic content that falls into these categories.

Phobias tend to grow progressively broader. For example, one woman had a subway phobia that began with an inability to ride an express train between two fairly distant locations. Gradually the phobia developed until she would have to get off the train at each local stop, wait until her anxiety diminished, get on the next train, get off again at the next stop, and so on, until her destination was reached.

People who experience the intense fears that are characteristic of phobias strive to organize their lives in such a way as to minimize exposure to the fear-arousing stimuli. The following account by a professor describes a phobia that effectively confined him to the campus where he taught.

*Let me assume that I am walking down University Drive by the lake. I am a normal man for the first quarter of a mile; for the next hundred yards I am in a mild state of dread, controllable and controlled; for the next twenty yards in an acute state of dread, yet controlled; for the next ten, in an anguish of terror that hasn't reached the crisis of explosion; and in a half-dozen steps more I am in as fierce a panic of isolation from help and home and of immediate death as a man overboard in mid-Atlantic or on a window-ledge far up in a skyscraper with flames lapping his shoulders. The reader who can't understand why I have not merely whistled or laughed or ordered the phobias off my psychic premises, or who thinks that I must be grossly exaggerating a mere normal discomfort, like the initial dread in the dentist's chair, is not the reader for whom I am writing one line of this book. He belongs among the fools, of whom in my phobic career I have met a goodly number already. I would leave him alone. Let him leave me alone. . . . It is as scientific a*

(a)

(b)

**FIGURE 6-4**
Phobias can cause people to lead restricted lives. Some fears, while strong, do not reach phobic proportions. For instance in photo a, although this man is afraid of heights, he endures the discomfort because he cannot afford to have someone fix a clogged gutter and to ask his wife to climb the ladder would be humiliating. If he had a true phobia to heights, he would not climb the ladder no matter how humiliating his refusal would be. An effective therapy for conquering phobic fears is shown in photo b. The patient who has an intense fear of heights is helped to climb the stairs in the presence of her trusted therapist. For many phobic individuals this type of exposure to a feared situation eventually results in extinction of the irrational fears and the ability to cope with formerly frightening situations. (Mimi Forsyth, Monkmeyer; James Wilson, Woodfin Camp & Associates)

fact as any I know that my phobic seizures at their worst approach any limits of terror that the human mind is capable of in the actual presence of death in its most horrible forms. That I have never fainted away or died under them is due to two factors: first, my physical vitality, and second, my skill in devising escapes—psychic surrogates, deflections of attention, or actual retreat to safety—before the exhausting surge has torn me to pieces. But more than once the escape has been at all but the last moment. The fools say nothing ever happened from one of these seizures—so why worry. Nothing ever happened? Well, here is what happens always. First, the seizure happens—as well say nothing happens if a red-hot iron is run down the throat, even though it should miraculously leave no aftereffects. The seizure happens; the acutest agony of the conscious brain happens. Second, the seizure leaves me always far more exposed to

phobic seizures for weeks or months; increases my fear of the Fear; and robs me of a goodly part of what little freedom of movement on street and hillside I have. "Nothing ever happened." This means simply that to date I've lived through seizures and continued for fifteen years to teach school, write books, and make jokes at the University Club across the street. (Leonard, 1927, pp. 321–323)

Phobic individuals usually develop ways of reducing their fears. The professor managed to live with his phobia, and the subway rider mentioned earlier was able to get from one place to another. However, the often cumbersome procedures that phobics devise do not eliminate their fear; indeed, the fear seems always to be one step ahead of them (see Figure 6–5). In one

Separation fears
 crowds
 traveling alone
 being alone at home
Animal fears
 mice
 rats
 insects
Mutilation fears
 open wounds
 surgical operations
 blood
Social fears
 eating with strangers
 being watched writing
 being watched working
Nature fears
 mountains
 the ocean
 cliffs, heights

sense, phobic individuals who cannot cross the thresholds of certain rooms or cannot work may be as incapacitated as people with severe psychotic symptoms. In another sense, they are more fortunate than people who exhibit free-floating anxiety, since at least their fears are directed toward a specific object, and they can reduce their anxiety by simply avoiding that object.

Phobias, like other forms of maladaptive behavior, do not occur in isolation. They are usually intertwined with a host of other problems. In consequence, it is difficult to estimate their frequency accurately. While mild phobias are common, phobias that are serious enough to be clinically diagnosed occur relatively infrequently. They are the main complaint in perhaps 2 to 3 percent of all clinical cases (Kolb and Brodie, 1982). Phobias do not require hospitalization. Professional treatment, when it is given, is usually carried out on an outpatient basis.

One of the most interesting aspects of phobias is that the stimuli that evoke them are not picked at random. The most common fear-arousing stimuli tend to be animals, objects, or events that presented real dangers in earlier stages of human evolution. Although extreme fear of dogs, snakes, and spiders seems maladaptive today, such fear may have been highly adaptive in earlier times. More "modern" phobias are rare. For example, pajama and electric-outlet phobias occur infrequently, even though these objects are often associated with trauma.

Traditionally, phobias have been named by means of Greek prefixes that stand for the object of the fear, as shown in the following examples:

□ acrophobia: fear of heights

□ agoraphobia: fear of open places and unfamiliar settings

□ aquaphobia: fear of water

**FIGURE 6-5**
Phobias are a special maladaptive form of fear which is out of proportion to situational demands, cannot be explained or reasoned away, is beyond voluntary control, and leads to avoidance of the feared situation. One day this woman was suddenly overcome with terror while driving an automobile. Similar experiences in the following weeks contributed to a phobia that required behavioral therapy.
(Laimute Druskis)

□ claustrophobia: fear of closed places

□ xenophobia: fear of strangers

Recently, however, such names have been avoided. People's knowledge of Greek is not what it once was, and in any case, a staggering number of labels would be needed to take account of the great variety of phobias that have been observed. Today, therefore, phobias are grouped into three general categories: simple phobias, social phobias, and agoraphobia.

## Simple Phobias

**Simple phobias** which are relatively rare, are a miscellaneous category comprising irrational fears that do not fall within the other two categories. Examples of simple phobias are intense fear of particular types of animals (for example, snakes, dogs, or rats) and claustrophobia. Although it is not unusual for people with simple phobias to overcome their fear as a result of a positive experience involving contact with the fear-arousing stimulus, simple phobias tend to be chronic. A variety of therapeutic approaches have been used in treating simple phobias. Procedures that promote association between the fear-arousing stimulus and non-anxiety responses, and at the same time provide information that disconfirms mistaken beliefs about the stimulus (for example, that all dogs are ferocious), often have positive effects.

## Social Phobias

**Social phobias** are characterized by fear and embarrassment in dealings with others. Often the individual's greatest fear is that signs of anxiety such as intense blushing, tremors of the hand, and a quavering voice will be detected by people with whom he or she comes into contact (see Figure 6–6). Fear of public speaking and of eating in public are the predominant complaints of socially phobic individuals. These problems often begin in late childhood or early adolescence.

> *I sometimes don't go to class because I think the professor might call on me. My fear doesn't have anything to do with being unprepared if he asks me a question, because I'm almost always well prepared. My grades on exams are always near the top of the class. What I keep thinking about is that the professor and all the students will see how red my face gets whenever I have to say something in a group.*

Most phobias about interpersonal relationships involve one or more of the following fears: fear of asserting oneself, fear of criticism, fear of making a mistake, and fear of public speaking. People who are afflicted in these ways have much in common. They go through life feeling generally inadequate and have many social and interpersonal difficulties. They attempt to compensate by immersing themselves in school and then in their work, never being really sure of their skills and talents. They dismiss their successes,

**FIGURE 6-6**
People who suffer from social phobias are preoccupied with fears of social scrutiny, criticism, and rejection. They overestimate the likelihood that others will respond to them in these ways. This woman is worried about how the people at the party she is about to join will respond to her. She does not yet have a full-blown social phobia. If she did, she probably would be unable to attend the social gathering. (Laimute Druskis)

if any, by saying, "My work isn't really good enough" or "I was just lucky—being in the right place at the right time." They may feel like impostors, fearing that they will be discovered and that the rug will be pulled out from under them.

The incidence of social phobias in two urban populations over a six-month period ranged from 0.9 to 1.7 percent for men and 1.5 to 2.6 percent for women. These figures are derived from self-reports and screening questionnaires in community surveys. The figures for socially phobic people who actually seek clinical help would be lower. Significant depressive symptoms are common in clinical cases of social phobia (Aimes and others, 1983).

## Agoraphobia

The most common phobia is **agoraphobia,** or fear of entering unfamiliar situations. It accounts for 50 to 80 percent of the phobic psychiatric population (Foa and others, 1984). Agoraphobics avoid going into open spaces, traveling, and being in crowds. In severe cases, the individual may have an irrational fear of leaving the familiar setting of the home; in the most extreme cases, the victim is unable even to walk down the street. Like most other phobias, agoraphobia is more common among women than among men. It often begins in the late teens, although it is also observed in older people. Like other phobias, it waxes and wanes, and it is not uncommon for the object of the fear to change. Some cases of agoraphobia are preceded by panic attacks marked by intense anxiety. In most of the cases of agoraphobia seen by clinicians the phobic symptoms are a complication of panic disorder.

Recent research suggests that agoraphobics can be divided into two groups, those with and those without panic attacks. A high percentage of people who experience panic attacks go on to develop agoraphobia unless they are treated early with certain drugs. One theory regarding the panic attack–agoraphobia linkage is that an individual is born with a biological vulnerability to panic attacks. Psychosocial factors, such as a pile-up of stressful life events and upsetting situations, can trigger a panic attack in a vulnerable individual. According to this theory, many patients, unaware of the biological roots of panic attacks, conclude that the situations in which the attacks take place must be the culprit. They become increasingly preoccupied with avoiding such situations and constrict their life styles—often at considerable economic and social expense—in the hope of eluding the attack. One patient confided that she had accumulated hundreds of dollars in fines by parking her car illegally in front of her office rather than face the anxiety associated with walking across the parking lot.

Spontaneous panic attacks, unlike phobic anxiety, can be treated with certain drugs that are effective in treating depression (for example, the tricyclic antidepressants and monoamine oxidase inhibitors). To a significant extent, agoraphobia is a complication of panic attacks that are untreated and therefore are allowed to recur (Thyer and others, 1985). Antidepressants are effective in suppressing panic but not in reducing anticipatory anxiety and agoraphobia. Behavioral techniques, including graduated exposure to the situation the individual is afraid of, are effective in treating agoraphobia.

The following is an account of one incident in the life of an agoraphobic.

*The woman who lives next door is a very nice person and I like her. One day she asked me if I would like to drive over to a big shopping center that had recently opened about 5 miles from where we live. I didn't know how to tell her that there isn't a chance in the world that I'd go to that shopping center or any other place outside our neighborhood. She must have seen how upset I got, but I was shaking like a leaf even more inside. I imagined myself in the crowd, getting lost, or passing out. I was terrified by the openness of the shopping center and the crowds. I made an excuse this time, but I don't know what I'll say next time. Maybe I'll just have to let her in on my little bit of craziness.*

In one study, agoraphobics and normal individuals were compared in terms of the thoughts and ideas that passed through their minds when they were nervous (Chambless and others, 1984). The researchers also inquired into the subjects' bodily reactions to nervousness. Table 6–5 lists items that differentiate the two groups. Agoraphobics report more disturbing thoughts and stronger bodily reactions when nervous than normals do. Thus, they are distinguished by intense fear and physiological overreactivity as well as by their avoidant behavior.

Agoraphobics are often clinging and dependent. Studies of the histories of severely impaired agoraphobics have shown that 50 percent of the patients exhibited separation anxiety in childhood, well before the onset of the agoraphobia (Gittelman and Klein, 1984). The association between childhood separation anxiety and agoraphobia is much stronger in women than in men. Because separation anxiety is almost always measured by means of retrospective self-reports, there is a need for longitudinal studies that allow for the observation of subject's behavior in addition to self-reports.

□ **TABLE 6–5**
Questionnaire Items for Which Agoraphobics
Reported Stronger Reactions When Nervous Than
Normal Subjects (based on Chambless and others,
1984)

### Thoughts

I am going to choke to death.
I will hurt someone.
I am going to act foolish.
I am going to scream.

### Bodily Reactions

heart palpitations
pressure in chest
numbness in arms or legs
nausea
feeling disoriented or confused
wobbly or rubber legs

Perhaps, in some sense, agoraphobia is a delayed outbreak of childhood separation anxiety.

# ■ OBSESSIVE COMPULSIVE DISORDER

A man spends three hours in the bathroom every day, repeatedly washing himself, pursued by the thought that he might pass on a deadly disease to anyone he touches. Another man cannot prevent himself from driving back to reexamine every place on the road where he has hit a bump, because the thought that he has run someone over keeps forcing itself on him. A third man has stopped cooking for fear that he will poison his wife, and has stopped using electrical appliances for fear of causing a fire. A woman feels a recurrent urge to kill her children. Every time a teenage girl is kissed, for several days she is unable to dismiss the thought that she has become pregnant.

All of these people have symptoms of an obsessive compulsive disorder, they are tyrannized by repetitive acts or thoughts. **Obsessive** people are unable to get an idea out of their minds (for example, they are preoccupied by sexual, aggressive, or religious thoughts); **compulsive** people feel compelled to perform a particular act or series of acts over and over again (for example, repetitive hand washing or stepping on cracks in the sidewalk).

Obsessions usually involve doubt, hesitation, fear of contamination, or fear of one's own aggression. The most common forms of compulsive behavior are count-

ing, ordering, checking, touching, and washing. A few victims of obsessive compulsive disorder have purely mental rituals; for example, to ward off the obsessional thought or impulse they might recite a series of magic words or numbers. About 25 percent of people with an obsessive compulsive disorder have intrusive thoughts but do not act on them. The rest are both obsessive and compulsive; compulsive behavior without obsessional thoughts is rare.

Compulsive rituals may become elaborate patterns of behavior that include many activities. For example, a man requires that his furniture never be left an inch out of place, and feels a need to dress and undress, brush his teeth, and use the toilet in a precise, unvarying order, all the time doubting whether he has performed this sequence of actions correctly, and often repeating it to make sure. Some theorists believe that compulsive behavior serves to divert attention from obsessive thoughts. In any case, compulsive rituals become a protection against anxiety, and as long as they are practiced correctly, the individual feels safe.

People who suffer from obsessive compulsive disorder are very cautious. Like victims of phobias and other anxiety disorders, they unreasonably anticipate catastrophe and loss of control. In general, victims of phobias fear what might happen to them, whereas victims of obsessive compulsive disorders fear what they might do. There are mixed cases, however; for example fear of knives might be associated with the obsessional thought that one will hurt someone if one picks up a knife, and fear of elevators might be brought on by a recurrent impulse to push someone down the shaft. An obsessional thought about shouting obscenities during a sermon might lead the victim to avoid attending church, just as a phobia about the sound of church bells would. Normally, the object of a phobia can be avoided while an obsession cannot be, but again there are mixed cases; a dirt phobia may be as intrusive as an obsession, because dirt is everywhere.

Because of their seemingly senseless character, obsessive compulsive reactions, like phobias, are extremely intriguing and challenging to clinical workers, researchers, and lay observers (Insel, 1984). As Figure 6–7 shows, they have also intrigued cartoonists.

The exact incidence of obsessive compulsive disorder is hard to determine. The victims tend to be secretive about their preoccupations and frequently are able to work effectively in spite of them; consequently, their "problems" are probably underestimated. Obsessive compulsive disorder is more common among upper-income, somewhat more intelligent individuals. It tends to begin in late adolescence and early adulthood, and males and females are equally likely to suffer from

**FIGURE 6-7**
Ralph seems to have a problem with at least one obsessional thought. (Copyright 1969. Reprinted by permission of *Saturday Review* World-Censoni.)

it (Rachman and Hodgson, 1980). A relatively high proportion of obsessive compulsives—some surveys report up to 50 percent—remain ummarried.

The most common features of obsessive compulsive disorder are the following.

1. The obsession or compulsion intrudes insistently and persistently into the individual's awareness.
2. A feeling of anxious dread occurs if the thought or act is prevented for some reason.
3. The obsession or compulsion is experienced as foreign to oneself as a psychological being; it is unacceptable and uncontrollable.
4. The individual recognizes the absurdity and irrationality of the obsession or compulsion.
5. The individual feels a need to resist it.

The language used by obsessive compulsives conveys their exaggerated attention to details, their air of detachment, and the difficulty they have in making a decision:

> I seem to be stuck with them—the thoughts, I mean. They seem so unimportant and silly. Why can't I think about things I really want to think about? But I can't stop thinking about trivia like did I lock the garage door when I went to work this morning. I've never not locked it and my wife's home anyway. I get depressed when I realize how much time I waste on nothing.

> I feel under such pressure, but I can't make a decision. I write out on 3-by-5 cards all the pros and cons, then I study them, consider all the complications that perhaps might bear on the decision, and then I do it again—but I never seem to be able to make up my mind.

As the following case illustrates, obsessives are often plagued by repetitive, abhorrent ideas.

> A *newly married young computer programmer sought help in overcoming a single tormenting obsessional rumination that had plagued her for years. It fluctuated in intensity and appeared to be fueled by recurrent depression. She spent many long hours ruminating over whether she had or had not murdered a solitary old lady whom she had visited regularly. This troublesome thought intruded repeatedly, seriously impaired her concentration, and provoked considerable discomfort and guilt. Repeated inquiries, including several visits to the local police station, failed to satisfy her that the woman had in fact died of natural causes some days after the patient had last seen her.* (Rachman and Hodgson, 1980, p. 257)

Obsessional thoughts often seem distasteful and shameful. Their content generally involves harming others, causing accidents to occur, swearing, or having abhorrent sexual or religious ideas. The obsessive's ruminations can be viewed as noxious stimuli that give rise to distress and attempts at avoidance. In a typical case, Joseph D., aged 36, had been hospitalized for a severe obsessional disorder. He was preoccupied about the possibility of bumping into people. One day as he was walking to an appointment with his therapist, he paused momentarily and was overcome with apprehension.

> PATIENT: *Just as we were coming down the stairs and we turned the corner, I had the feeling there was something I wanted to check there. I still have the feeling, and I'm trying to put it out of my mind right now. And I want to walk back and check, but I'm trying to force myself not to. Now I know I couldn't have hurt anybody out there or bumped into anything, or anything like that. I know there's nothing there, and I didn't harm nothing. I just want to go back and check that, to see that there's nothing there. Now I know there's nothing.*

> DOCTOR: *What do you think you might see?*

> P: *I know I'll see nothing.*

> D: *No—but in imagination what do you think is there?*

> P: *I don't know what I would see. It's just there might be something out of place there—something like that.*

> D: *Something out of place—like what?*

P: I don't know—I can't explain it. It sounds crazy, I know, but I can't help it. I've been doing this the last couple of weeks on the street. I'd walk by people, and I'd think that they fell down, or something happened. Not that they fell down—I had to check to see that they got by me all right. Do you understand this? I just have to check to see that they got by me all right. I must have an aggression toward things, and I'm afraid it's going to come out. And when I walk by those people, there must be like a feeling of anxiety there that I could possibly have bumped into them—when I didn't. I must be guarding that aggression. In other words, I'm watching it like a hawk, and when somebody moves by me like that, I think that possibly they—the aggression will come out. Do you think so?

D: Tell me about the aggression that you have.

P: I can't explain it, doctor. I can't seem to analyze it. Whether it's a guilt that I'm responsible for people, and I'm afraid I'm going to do something that I don't know I've done—like indirect aggression. Like suppose you bumped into someone going down the stairs you didn't mean to. You jostled them in the subway as you walked down to the bottom. Well, then, when that person got to the bottom, they might have been a little bit upset by being jostled and they might have tripped at the bottom (which wasn't your fault that they tripped at the bottom), and they might have hurt themselves. Well, now, I would feel guilty because I jostled them at the top. Do you understand? It's like an indirect aggression. (Nemiah, 1985b, pp. 909–910)

Two things are noteworthy in this therapy session. First, the patient describes very clearly the insistent intrusive thoughts that mark his obsession. Second, he provides a hint that he may be struggling with angry feelings and impulses, which many clinicians have noted in obsessive compulsive individuals.

Depending on the situation and the nature of the obsession, the obsessive may feel some pride in his or her unwillingness to make a premature decision, or may feel self-contempt when indecisiveness prevents action and allows others to win acclaim. Only when Charles Darwin faced the possibility of prior publication by a colleague was he able to overcome his obsessive indecisiveness and put On the Origin of Species into the hands of a publisher.

Compared with repetitive upsetting ideas, repetitive images are much less common among obsessives. A typical case is the following.

One of the patient's most distressing images consisted of four people lying dead in open coffins in an open grave. Once this image intruded she was unable to continue with her normal activities unless and until she put matters right by having one or more images in which she saw the same four people standing and walking about, seemingly healthy. Although the images appeared for the most part to be spontaneously (i.e., internally) generated, they could be provoked by exposure to violent or aggressive material of one sort or another—books or television programs. The images were extremely distressing and were capable of provoking her to tears in a matter of minutes. (Rachman and Hodgson, 1980, p. 257)

The variety of obsessive-compulsive rituals and thoughts is practically unlimited, but investigators have identified four broad types of preoccupations: (1) checking, (2) cleaning, (3) slowness, and (4) doubting and conscientiousness. The following statements illustrate each type.

## CHECKING
☐ I frequently have to check things (gas or water taps, doors) several times.

## CLEANING
☐ I avoid using public telephones because of possible contamination.

## SLOWNESS
☐ I am often late because I can't seem to get through everything on time.

## DOUBTING-CONSCIENTIOUSNESS
☐ Even when I do something very carefully, I often feel that it is not quite right.

Most of us have had similar feelings. One study compared the preoccupying thoughts of clinically diagnosed obsessives with those of normal individuals. Although the content of the two groups' thoughts showed many similarities, the clinical group's obsessions occurred more frequently, lasted longer, were more intense, and disrupted their lives more than those of the control group (Rachman and de Silva, 1978).

When the compulsive rituals or obsessive thoughts begin to interfere with important routines of daily life, they become significant problems that require professional attention. Their bases frequently are not well understood, but because all of us have had some persistent preoccupations with particular acts and thoughts, their interfering effects can easily be appreciated. Obsessive-compulsive preoccupations—checking details, keeping things clean, and being deliberate—often increase during periods of stress. They can have undesirable effects when speedy decisions or actions are required. Table 6–6 summarizes the results of a

Ratings by Obsessive Compulsive Patients of Aspects of Their Own Rituals

| How sensible do the rituals seem? | Sensible 22% | Rather Silly 13% | Absurd 65% |
|---|---|---|---|
| Does reassurance from others influence the rituals? | Definitely Yes 27% | Some 15% | Definitely No 58% |
| Does the presence of others affect the rituals? | Occurs When Alone 20% | Company Irrelevant 76% | Occurs in Company 4% |
| How much family distress do rituals cause? | Little or None 29% | Moderate 22% | A Great Deal 49% |
| Do you resist carrying out the rituals? | Definitely Yes 32% | Somewhat 22% | Definitely No 46% |

Adapted from Stern and Cobb, 1978.

study that examined the reactions of obsessive compulsives to their preoccupations and rituals.

Attempts to find out what obsessive-compulsives are afraid of usually fail. Many clinicians believe that fear of loss of control and the need for structure are at the core of the obsessions and compulsions. Whether the disorder reflects the impact of environmental factors or heredity, its incidence is greater among members of some families than among the general population.

A common feature of psychotic behavior is irrational thought, but an obsessive-compulsive person is not considered to be psychotic since he or she is usually aware of the irrationality. In some cases, however, the border between obsessive compulsive disorder and true psychosis is imprecise.

Obsessive thoughts and compulsive rituals shade into phobias to the extent that anxiety accompanies the thoughts or rituals and there is avoidance of situations that evoke them. For example, someone who has a washing ritual will try to avoid dirt, much as a person with a dog phobia avoids dogs. Clinical workers often observe that both obsessive-compulsives and phobics have an unusually high incidence of interpersonal problems. The two disorders differ in that the obsessive-compulsive's fear is directed not at the situation itself but, rather, at the consequences of becoming involved with it—for example, having to wash afterwards. Another difference is that obsessive-compulsives develop a more elaborate set of beliefs concerning their preoccupying thoughts and rituals than phobics do about their fears. Cognitions seem to play a larger role in obsession-compulsion than in phobia. This point is illustrated by the case of a 40-year-old man with a checking compulsion.

*The other night my wife and I went to the movies. It was torture even though the movie was great. For about an hour before going I couldn't stop thinking about this need I have to check the doorknob in order to make sure it's locked. I had to get out of the car four times to check the doorknob. When I do that sort of thing, my wife tries to be understanding, but I know she is thinking, "How come once isn't enough?" On the way to the theater I kept worrying about whether the door was locked. I would bet I had similar thoughts a hundred times while at the theater. You can't enjoy yourself under those circumstances, can you?*

## ■ INTERPRETING AND TREATING ANXIETY DISORDERS

Whether it is general or specific to certain situations, anxiety is a major component of the disorders dealt with in this chapter. Anxiety and the things that people do to keep it at manageable levels have been looked at from several theoretical perspectives.

### The Psychodynamic Perspective

Psychodynamic theorists and many other clinicians believe that the major determinants of anxiety disorders are intrapsychic events and unconscious motivations. They believe that anxiety is experienced by the ego when it is exposed to excessive environmental demands or when there is tension within the id–ego–superego system. They base this interpretation on clinical observations and inferences. Anxiety is interpreted as an alarm reaction that appears whenever the person is threatened. How an individual adapts to the anxiety alarm depends on its intensity, the cue that evokes it, and the person's characteristic response to alarms. It is normal to experience some overt anxiety; the amount of anxiety and the nature of the threat determine whether an instance of anxiety is normal or pathological.

A distinguishing characteristic of clinical anxiety is that an alarm is frequently sounded in the absence of a consciously recognized source of danger. A danger exists, but its basis is vague or totally hidden from view. A tourist may understandably experience overwhelming anxiety while walking through a jungle. However, some individuals experience the same kind of anxiety in their own living rooms, for no apparent reason. According to the psychodynamic view, their defenses are inadequate to control or contain their anxiety. Figure 6-8 indicates that it is possible to develop a defensive posture that effectively masks inner turmoil.

Psychodynamic theorists frequently mention the following as causes of anxiety that reaches clinical proportions: perception of oneself as helpless in coping with environmental pressures, separation or anticipation of abandonment, privation and loss of emotional supports as a result of sudden environmental changes, unacceptable or dangerous impulses that are close to breaking into consciousness, and threats or anticipation of disapproval and withdrawal of love.

The psychodynamic view of phobias stems from two fundamental concepts: (1) psychological conflict and (2) unconscious mental processes. From this standpoint the phobic situation or object has symbolic significance; it can be regarded as a stand-in for something else that one is frightened of, something that is completely beyond one's awareness. It represents an unresolved psychological conflict, a holdover from childhood. For example, a child who reaches school age at the same time that her brother is born might be very angry at her mother for sending her to school. She might feel that her mother is getting rid of her so that she can be alone with the new baby all day. On the way to school each day the little girl passes a house where a vicious German shepherd is chained up. The dog becomes associated with her fantasy about her mother's real reason for sending her to school. The girl manages to get through her childhood all right, but in her twenties she develops a phobia about dogs after her mother has expressed strong disapproval of her future husband.

Obsessive thoughts and compulsive rituals may direct attention away from significant, distressing, unconscious thoughts. Psychoanalysts believe that these thoughts often involve aggression and rage that may have first been aroused in the battle for autonomy between the growing child and the mother. When the mother is especially demanding and has unreasonably high expectations about when the child should meet certain developmental challenges (such as toilet training), the child may be forced to bottle up his or her anger. This unacceptable anger expresses itself deviously later in life.

Freud emphasized the roles of several defense mechanisms in the development of obsessive compulsive disorders. These include isolation, undoing, and reaction formation. Through **isolation,** emotions are separated from a thought or act, which then becomes obsessive or compulsive. However, the emotion is not completely barred from consciousness and constantly threatens to break through the controls that have been imposed upon it. **Undoing** is illustrated by an individual who thinks obsessively, "My father will die" whenever he turns off a light. This thought compels him to turn around, touch the switch, and say, "I take back that thought." The compulsive act could be said to "undo" what he feared might result from the initial obsessive thought, which might be rooted in an underlying aggressive impulse toward the father. **Reaction formation** is illustrated by a mother who compulsively checks her children's rooms dozens of times while they are asleep; she is overly solicitous about her children because of her underlying resentment toward them.

Psychotherapy, the main clinical tool of the psychodynamically oriented clinician, is intended to help people expose and deal with the psychodynamic roots of their maladaptive behaviors. Most psychotherapists believe that such behaviors occur when a person be-

**FIGURE 6-8**
From a psychodynamic standpoint, inconsistencies between Snoopy's overt and covert behaviors would be explained in terms of intrapsychic conflicts and attempts to resolve them [(c) 1964 United Features Syndicate, Inc.]

comes preoccupied with relieving or eliminating anxiety. They feel that by gaining insight into the unconscious roots of anxiety, the person can direct his or her activity toward altering or abandoning unwanted behavior. Chapter 17 reviews some of the major aspects of research on psychotherapy and other therapeutic approaches.

## The Learning Perspective

Instead of speaking of symptoms caused by underlying events, learning psychologists speak of acquired responses and response tendencies. They believe that the general principles of learning can be applied to the understanding of all behavior, including anxiety disorders. According to learning theorists, anxiety that reaches clinical proportions is a learned or acquired response, a symptom that has been created by environmental conditions, often within the home.

B. F. Skinner, a leading behaviorist, objects to any references to mental events (thoughts or feelings) as explanations of behavior; he prefers to rely almost exclusively on observable stimulus and response (S and R) variables. Other theorists emphasize S and R variables but have gone one step beyond Skinner in dealing with internal events as well. Dollard and Miller (1950) were among the earliest theorists to broaden the psychology of learning to include mental events. They went so far as to agree with psychodynamic theorists that there is a history behind the development of neurotic behavior and that psychotherapy (the "talking therapy") is the optimum means of modifying it.

> If neurotic behavior is learned, it should be unlearned by some combination of the same principles by which it was taught. We believe this to be the case. Psychotherapy establishes a set of conditions by which neurotic habits may be unlearned and nonneurotic habits learned. Therefore, we view the therapist as a kind of teacher and the patient as a learner. In the same way and by the same principles that bad tennis habits can be corrected by a good coach, so bad mental and emotional habits can be corrected by a psychotherapist. There is this difference, however. Whereas only a few people want to play tennis, all the world wants a clear, free, efficient mind. (Dollard and Miller, 1950, pp. 7–8)

Learning concepts such as conditioning, reinforcement, and extinction have increasingly been applied to the study of abnormal behavior. Several new, clinically useful techniques, collectively referred to as behavioral therapy, are the most valuable outcomes of these applications. Research using behavioral therapy has been directed at discovering the variables that help defuse highly emotional responses.

A common element in most behavioral therapies is exposing the client to stimuli that evoke discomfort until he or she becomes used to them. Much research has been carried out in which clients are exposed to feared stimuli and are prevented from making an avoidance or escape response. The client is strongly urged to continue to attend to the anxiety-eliciting stimuli despite the stressful effects that usually accompany this effort.

Exposure therapy has been used in treating both phobic and obsessive-compulsive disorders. A critical element of the treatment is motivating the client to maintain contact with the actual noxious stimuli or with their imagined presence until he or she becomes used to them. This might mean, for example, exposing a compulsive hand washer to dirt until the hand washing no longer occurs, or encouraging such a person to think about dirt, perhaps imagined first as household dust and later as particularly noxious dirt such as vomit or feces. The therapist's task is to identify all components of the stimulus that evoke an avoidance or escape response and to continue the exposure until the evoked response no longer occurs.

The following sections describe three types of behavioral therapy based on the exposure principle: systematic desensitization, implosive therapy, and in vivo exposure. In **systematic desensitization** a series of fear-arousing stimuli, carefully graded from mild to strongly fearful, are used. Only when a client is comfortable with one level of fear-producing stimuli is the next, slightly stronger stimulus introduced. **Implosive therapy** refers to therapist-controlled exposure to the imaginal re-creation of a complex, high-intensity fear-arousing situation. **In vivo exposure** means that the individual experiences the actual feared situation rather than imagining it under the therapist's direction. In vivo exposure may be conducted gradually, beginning with low levels of stimulus intensity, or rapidly, by exposing the client immediately to high-intensity and prolonged stimulation. This rapid, intense exposure is called **flooding.**

**Systematic Desensitization** Systematic desensitization, which is used primarily in the treatment of strong fears, is based on conditioning principles. The client is taught to relax and then is presented with a series of stimuli that are graded from low to high according to their capacity to evoke anxiety. Relaxation training is a component of systematic desensitization (Levin and Gross, 1985). The patient may be given instructions like the following.

> All right, lean back comfortably in the chair. Place both hands on your thighs or in your lap. Now, close your eyes and follow my instructions. First of all, I want you to

*relax the muscles of the forehead and the scalp. Just consciously think about your forehead and scalp and begin to relax those muscles. Let all of the muscles in that area go completely limp, become completely tranquil, and become completely at rest. Smooth all the wrinkles out of the forehead and relax the muscles of the forehead and scalp. Now move down to the facial muscles and relax all of the muscles of the face, just letting all of the tension go out of those muscles; letting them become completely limp; letting all the flesh and all of the muscles of the face just relax completely without any pressure or any tension. Relax the tongue, the lips, the cheeks, and the jaws, without any pressure in any of those muscles. Now, move down to the neck and relax all the muscles in the neck, letting them go completely limp, becoming completely relaxed . . . completely calm. Now move down to the shoulders and just relax the shoulders completely, letting them droop, go completely at rest, become completely tranquil, completely limp. And then move down the shoulders to the arms . . . down to the elbows . . . and from there down the forearms to the wrists . . . hands and fingers; relaxing all of these muscles and letting the arms dangle from the frame of your body; letting them hang completely limp. And now move down to the chest. Take a deep breath and, as you exhale, relax every muscle in the chest. Let all the muscles there go completely limp and relax; let all the pressure and all the tightness go out of that area of your body and let the muscles relax completely. Now move down to the stomach. Relax all of the muscles of the stomach; without any pressure or any tension in any of the musculature of the midsection of your body. Now go up and down the spine. Go up one side and down the other, relaxing every muscle in the back. Become completely at rest and completely relaxed. And now move down to the waist . . . and buttocks . . . down to the thighs . . . knees . . . calves of your legs . . . ankles, feet, and toes, relaxing every muscle; letting them become completely limp and completely relaxed. With each breath you may relax just a little bit more and become completely calm, completely tranquil. (Walker, Hedberg, Clement, and Wright, 1981, pp. 66–67)*

The treatment of a death phobia illustrates how systematic desensitization is used. The patient's fears are arranged in a hierarchy, with the items in the hierarchy ranging, in descending order, from human corpses to funeral processions, black clothes, dead dogs, and floral wreaths. The therapy begins with items that are low in the hierarchy, such as seeing a wreath. The therapist tries to teach the client to remain relaxed while imagining or actually seeing a wreath. When the client can maintain a relaxed state consistently, the therapy proceeds with stimuli that are higher in the hierarchy.

A therapist does not try to produce cures overnight with conditioning procedures. Usually, the process of reducing the level of an emotional response to a stimulus that should be neutral is a gradual one. Clinical applications of systematic desensitization have shown that clients who are treated in this way become less upset by previously feared situations and better able to manage their anxiety. It is possible that the most effective part of systematic desensitization is the client's exposure to gradually increasing levels of fear-arousing stimuli under nonthreatening conditions. Individuals who can mentally rehearse being exposed to the upsetting, fear-arousing situations show particularly high levels of improvement (Biran and Wilson, 1981).

**Implosive Therapy**   Implosive therapy is based on the belief that many conditions, including anxiety disorders, are outgrowths of painful prior experiences. For the patient to unlearn them, the original situation must be re-created so that it can be experienced without pain.

Therapists who use implosion ask their clients to imagine scenes related to particular personal conflicts and to recreate the anxiety felt in those scenes. The therapist strives to heighten the realism of the re-creation and to help the patient extinguish the anxiety that was created by the original aversive conditions. In addition, the client is helped to adopt more mature forms of behavior. The following example shows how a therapist might introduce the technique of implosion to the client.

*I'm going to describe a situation which you currently associate with much anxiety. I would like you to imaginatively enact your part in the scene as I describe it to you. You should make every effort to lose yourself in the scene as it is described and live it as if you were actually in the situation, feeling every genuine emotion that you would if it were actually occurring. Every feeling and emotion you experience is an important part of the scene and the treatment procedure being used. I want you to picture yourself in the scene, rather than someone else whom you are watching. If, at any time, you wish to terminate the experience of the scene that I am presenting, please resist and continue to be involved in the scene as I present it. Although in the past you have generally terminated situations that are anxiety producing, this time I want you to stay in the situation all the way through until I terminate the presentation of the scene.*

*In all likelihood, you will experience notable and definite arousal of anxiety with many different bodily sensations being realized, such as increased heart rate, breathing, and muscle tension, as you would in any other anxiety situation. As I continue to describe the scene, this anxiety will increase and maintain itself at a high level for a period of time thereafter. Remember, stay with the scene as long as it is described, and as if it were actually happening. You are to pay attention to all of your body sensations and signs of anxiety, but not to terminate the scene or the treatment session until I do.* (Walker and others, 1981, pp. 121–122)

Implosive therapy uses the methods and ideas of both behavioral and psychodynamic theories. Although it is not uniformly effective in reducing anxiety, research to date suggests that it, like desensitization, can reduce many intense fears.

**In Vivo Exposure** The term **in vivo exposure** means that the exposure is carried out in a real-life setting, not simply in the imaginations of the client and the therapist as they sit in the therapist's office. Desensitization is usually carried out in clinical settings; however, the following case, which was reported by Joseph Wolpe, a leading proponent of the technique, took place in a real-life setting. In this case, desensitization in vivo occurred inadvertently at first and later was deliberately continued.

*The patient, who had an 11-year-old fear of confinement in social situations, was being treated as a demonstration case in front of 20 members of a Behavior Therapy Institute. After training I then told him it would be necessary for us to work with real stimuli. He replied, "Something interesting has already happened, Doctor. During my first session here I was very nervous in this group, but every day my nervousness has decreased; and today I don't feel nervous at all." He had been unwittingly desensitized to the audience of 20. As it happened, 160 psychologists were expected at the Institute the next day, and I decided to make use of them for continuing the treatment. Accordingly, the next morning, in the large lecture hall, I had the patient at first sit with me on the platform while the original 20 Institute members sat in the forward row of seats. The patient reporting no anxiety, I gave a prearranged signal for 20 more people to enter the hall. When they did so, he reported anxiety and was instructed to relax. After a minute he stated that he felt comfortable, and then another 20 people were permitted to enter. Again anxiety appeared and was relaxed away. The same procedure was repeated until all 160 members were seated. The patient spent the remainder of the afternoon seated comfortably in the front row of the audience. Subsequently, further in vivo operations were arranged—such as jamming him in the front row of spectators at a tennis tournament. These measures resulted in marked improvement of his neurosis.* (Wolpe, 1973, p. 160)

The difference between this gradual in vivo exposure and flooding might be compared to the difference between wading into a swimming pool and jumping in at the deep end. For example, an agoraphobic client who experienced intense anxiety anywhere outside her home might be asked to go to a crowded shopping center with the therapist and remain there until her desire to escape disappeared. Using this procedure, someone with a specific fear can lose it in only three sessions (Marks, 1978) (see Figure 6–9).

In the treatment of most anxiety disorders, exposure has produced consistently good results, with improvements lasting for up to several years. The longer the exposure to the critical stimulus, the better the results. How well exposure treatment works depends on the client's motivation and on specific factors in his or her life. For example, when compulsive rituals are triggered by home cues (which is true in many cases), treatment needs to be conducted in the home setting. Failure to improve can usually be traced to failure to comply with treatment instructions, particularly by not

**FIGURE 6–9**
This agoraphobic woman was afraid to visit a shopping center near her home. Her therapist took her there on a series of trips. She became able to visit a supermarket in the center while the therapist went to another store and eventually she was able to go to the shopping center on her own. (Laimute Druskis)

seeking exposure to fear-arousing stimuli. In one study, compulsives received in vivo exposure therapy in their homes. The client's task was to avoid responding compulsively when the evoking stimuli were present. Figure 6–10 shows changes in the clients' ratings of their levels of anxiety when exposed to the evoking stimuli. If the client refrained from compulsive behavior in the presence of the stimuli, the level of anxiety decreased immediately after exposure and the decrease was maintained one and six months later in the presence of the compulsion-evoking stimuli.

An important task for future research is to find out *why* exposure is effective. When a client "gets used to" an upsetting stimulus, what is going on? One possible explanation is that as clients find that they can handle a little exposure to upsetting stimuli and note that their anxiety levels subside, quickly they gain confidence in themselves and develop the courage to persist in their efforts to overcome their problems.

The most effective behavioral technique for treating compulsive rituals is a combination of exposure and response prevention. The therapist asks the patient to disclose all obsessions and compulsive patterns, and then prohibits them. A compulsive washer, for example, is allowed to become dirty, or even made dirty, and then is ordered not to wash. A typical treatment might allow one ten-minute shower every fifth day. Exposure

reduces hypersensitivity to dirt and the associated anxiety; response prevention eventually eliminates the compulsive ritual. Exposure usually has to be done outside the psychotherapist's office, and trained helpers may be needed—wives, husbands, friends, or nurse-therapists. Exposure in fantasy is less effective, but sometimes it is the only possible way—for example, a patient cannot actually run over someone.

Exposure therapy and other behavioral approaches are not highly effective with people who are "pure obsessives," that is, who do not engage in rituals or avoidant behavior. Because depression is a factor in many of these cases, antidepressant drugs are often used in the treatment of obsessions.

**Modeling**   In exposure therapies, emphasis is placed on *removing* some of the overwhelming emotional response that may inhibit people who have anxiety disorders. In **modeling,** another behavioral approach, the emphasis is usually on *acquiring* behavioral skills or a feeling of competence.

Sometimes the two approaches seem quite similar. For example, Peter Carlson (1969) carried out a study that compared four groups of college women, all of whom were intensely afraid of snakes. One group participated in a series of desensitization sessions, a second group observed a model handling a live snake, a third group was lectured about snakes, and a control group received no treatment. The groups were then compared on whether each woman would look at, touch, or hold a tame, nonpoisonous, 3-foot-long boa constrictor. On a pretest, all of the women looked at the snake but none of them would go beyond that point. On the post-test immediately after completion of the experiment, the modeling group appeared to show the strongest approach tendency. Six weeks later, the modeling and desensitization groups were superior to the other two groups in approach tendencies.

Several measures of autonomic arousal, including pulse, respiration, and galvanic skin response, were recorded during Carlson's experiment. One might expect a change in autonomic response correlated with the women's greater willingness to approach the snake. Somewhat surprisingly, the physiological measures were not correlated with the women's motor behavior but, instead, continued to show high arousal. One explanation is that behavioral therapies like modeling create a stimulus situation in which a fearful person feels safe enough to be able to emit a dreaded response but the accompanying physiological changes may come about only when, after repeated exposure to the situation, the feared response has been completely defused of its emotional charge.

We might explain this difference from another per-

**FIGURE 6–10**
Changes in rated anxiety before exposure in vivo (pre), immediately afterwards (post), and at 1- and 6-month follow-up points. Reprinted with permission from *Behavior Research and Therapy, 18,* Emmelkamp, R.M.G., van der Helm, M., van Zanten, B.L., & Plochg, I., 1980, p. 65. Treatment of obsessive compulsive patients: The contribution of self-instructional training to the effectiveness of exposure. Copyright (c) 1980, Pergamon Journals, Ltd.

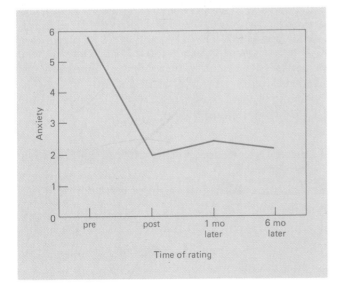

spective by remembering that anxiety may have cognitive, emotional, and behavioral components. Observation of models may initially alter only the cognitive component. The observer may have become convinced that it is possible to pick up a snake without ill effects, but watching the model will not immediately rid the observer of the emotional feeling that "snakes are disgusting" or "slimy" or something associated with bad dreams.

The behavioral component of modeling is also important. In addition to acting as a disinhibitor, modeling can function in the acquisition of new skills and response capabilities. This is especially true in **participant modeling,** which is often more effective than modeling alone. In participant modeling, a therapist models a response and then provides corrective feedback as the client performs the same behavior. In addition to the information provided by the modeled behavior, the client receives guidance on his or her own performance. If Carlson had asked one group of subjects to practice handling the snake as the model did, it is likely that this participant group would have been the least anxious in the test situation because it had had the same experience during the practice sessions. Participant modeling works especially well with complex behaviors, such as those involved in certain social situations.

Modeling plays a role in **guided mastery,** in which the therapist guides the client toward mastery over frightening situations and maladaptive behavior. Guided mastery might involve modeling of adaptive behavior by the therapist, or it might take the form of directions to the client about how to cope with various aspects of a problematic situation. In either case, the guidance helps the client attain a sense of mastery or self-efficacy (Williams and others, 1984).

## The Cognitive Perspective

The methods developed by behavioral therapists, although they are based on learning principles, have important implications for our understanding of cognitive processes, that is, private or internal processes such as imagery and how we think about ourselves and the world. Therapies like systematic desensitization, exposure, and modeling affect not only clients' behavior but also how they think about themselves. Furthermore, cognitive activity is often a specific step in behavioral therapy; for example, in systematic desensitization the client is asked to visualize, think about, or imagine certain fear-arousing situations. Cognitive rehearsal in combination with exposure in vivo has been used successfully with phobics and obsessive-compulsives. Available evidence suggests that this procedure is highly effective in ultimately reducing anxiety, regardless of whether the client feels relaxed or anxious during exposure.

Modeling can also have an important cognitive element. Someone who overcomes intense fears as a result of a behavioral-therapy program like participant modeling acquires more self-confidence and may begin to think about new ways of behaving in situations that were not covered in the modeling program. The way people think about things often changes when they acquire new response capabilities. These cognitive changes can then lead to important behavioral advances. The term **cognitive behavior therapy** refers to clinical procedures based on principles of learning, such as extinction and reinforcement, that emphasize cognitive behavior.

**Cognitive Factors in Maladaptive Behavior**  In addition to the increased interest in cognitive aspects of behavior therapy, there has been a rapid increase in the influence of the cognitive perspective on efforts to understand anxiety. According to cognitive theorists, thinking disturbances that occur only in certain places or in relation to specific problems are the sources of anxiety. These types of thoughts include unrealistic appraisals of situations and consistent overestimation of their dangerous aspects; for example, the *degree* and *likelihood* of harm may both be exaggerated. Thus, a person's train of thought and mental set can be viewed as vulnerability factors that interact with the characteristics of situations. From this point of view, precipitating events (the situation) elicit or magnify an underlying attitude or fear (the vulnerability factor) and give rise to hypervigilance. As this attitude strengthens, danger-related thoughts become more easily activated by less specific, less avoidable situations ("If you look for it, you're sure to find it"). As a result, the anxious individual continually scans internal and external stimuli for danger signals.

An example of this sort of disturbance may be seen in an obsessive person who experiences intense anxiety when having to cross the street and may actually be unable to attempt a crossing. Most people would use the following train of thought.

1. Streets are safe for crossing at green lights or when free of traffic.
2. This street has a green light or is free of traffic.
3. Therefore, this street can be crossed.

The obsessive person's thinking, on the other hand, might go as follows.

1. Streets are safe for crossing at green lights or when free of traffic.

2. This street has a green light or is free of traffic, but if the light suddenly changes or a car appears unexpectedly . . .

3. Then this street is not safe for me to cross.

Studies of obsessives have revealed unreasonable beliefs and assumptions. Obsessives believe that they (1) should be perfectly competent, (2) must avoid criticism or disapproval, and (3) will be severely punished for their mistakes and imperfections. In addition, at some level they seem to believe that thinking certain thoughts or performing certain rituals will help them avoid the disastrous outcomes they imagine are just around the corner. Obsessive compulsives make arbitrary rules that they must follow (for example, stepping on every seventh crack in the sidewalk). Phobics also make up rules for themselves that are not based in reality (for example, "If I go into an elevator, it might get stuck and I might suffocate"). Unfortunately, these "protective" thoughts and rituals become very intrusive and can interfere with normal activity.

**Cognitive Therapy** Cognitive therapists employ a number of techniques. One of these is **cognitive restructuring.** Developed out of the rational–emotive therapy of Albert Ellis, cognitive restructuring calls the client's attention to the unrealistic thoughts that serve as cues for his or her maladaptive behavior. The therapist helps clients review their irrational beliefs and expectations and develop more rational ways of looking at their lives. For example, many people with anxiety disorders are perfectionists who expect too much of themselves and others and become overly emotional when their unattainable goals are not realized. During therapy sessions emphasis is placed on how the irrational things that people say to themselves can affect their emotions and behavior. The baseball player in Figure 6–11 is being advised to do some cognitive restructuring.

By means of cognitive restructuring, people develop more realistic appraisals of themselves and others. For example, when taking an exam a person might think: "This test is hard. Everyone else seems to think it's going to be simple. They all must know a lot more than I do." Such thoughts are likely to lead to a high degree of anxiety. A cognitive therapist would help this client concentrate on a more adaptive type of thought, such as: "I studied hard. I'll just try to answer one question at a time. If I don't know the answer, I'll go on to the next one. No reason for panic. Even people who do well don't know the answer to every question."

**FIGURE 6-11**
"Forget about his six-million-dollar contract—think of him as a guy with tax problems." From *The Wall Street Journal*—Permission, Cartoon Features Syndicate.

**Thought stopping** is another cognitive technique. It works on the assumption that a sudden distracting stimulus, such as an unpleasant noise, will serve to terminate obsessional thoughts. The client is asked to get the thought firmly in mind; then the therapist loudly says "Stop!" This sequence—obsessional thought followed by "Stop!"—is repeated several times with the client, rather than the therapist, yelling "Stop!" Finally, the client simply mentally says "Stop!" If it is successful, this procedure provides the client with a specific self-control technique for removing an obsessional thought when it occurs.

A third cognitive technique is **cognitive rehearsal,** through which the client can mentally rehearse adaptive approaches to problematic situations. Cognitive rehearsal is particularly useful for problems that cannot be conveniently simulated in a clinical setting. For example, behavioral rehearsal of social skills by socially phobic individuals requires the presence of a large group of people. However, someone who suffers from a social phobia can imagine being in a group and can mentally rehearse behaviors and internal statements designed to improve his or her interpersonal relationships.

Aaron T. Beck has developed one of the most influential types of cognitive therapy (Beck and Emery, 1985). He believes that the core psychological problem in anxiety disorders is a vulnerability that grows out of the individual's tendency to devalue his or her problem-solving ability as well as to exaggerate the degree of threat in a problematic situation. Such an individual perceives anxiety-provoking threats to social relationships, freedom, and self-identity.

Beck's cognitive therapy typically consists of five to twenty sessions (see Figure 6–12). A minimal amount of time is spent acquiring background information, searching for the original causes of anxiety, or engaging in unfocused conversation with the patient. Most of the therapy is task-oriented, being devoted to solving problems brought up by the patient. The therapist encourages the patient to talk openly about his or her fears and concerns, and conveys empathy for the patient's anxiety. The Socratic method is used to help the patient become aware of what his or her thoughts are, examine them for cognitive distortions, and substitute more realistic thoughts. Three steps are involved in cognitive therapy: (1) conceptualizing the patient's problem, (2) choosing strategies and tactics to deal with the problem, and (3) assessing the effectiveness of those strategies and tactics.

In a sense, Beck is arguing that each of us has an inner voice. When that voice interferes with our ability to function adequately, the unproductive thoughts that result must be replaced by productive ones. This is done by correcting thinking errors and having the patient work on pertinent homework assignments. Using these techniques, the patient can develop not only improved ways of thinking but also more effective, less anxiety-producing behaviors.

## The Biological Perspective

Over the years several different types of reactions have been found to be caused by the individual's biological state. Some of these discoveries have led to the development of medical treatment methods. Although no direct organic cause has been found for most types of anxiety disorders, in view of the findings of physical causation in other conditions it becomes difficult to deny the possibility that anxiety disorders are somehow correlated with physical defects.

Several studies have revealed some links between anxieties and biophysical functioning. People whose nervous systems are particularly sensitive to stimulation seem more likely to experience severe anxiety. In addition, inbreeding experiments with animals have shown that heredity has a strong influence on such characteristics as timidity, fearfulness, and aggressiveness. Evidence also shows that anxiety disorders tend to run in families. About 15 percent of parents and siblings of people with anxiety disorders are similarly affected (Carey and Gottesman, 1981). Identical or monozygotic twins show more concordance (about 40 percent) for anxiety symptoms than do fraternal or dizygotic twins (about 4 percent). These findings suggest a genetic cause of anxiety; however, the results are not definitive, because the subjects in this type of research not only have identical or similar heredities but usually also live together and thus experience similar environments.

Tranquilizing drugs are the most commonly used somatic therapy in the treatment of anxiety. Well over 50 million prescriptions for these substances are filled each year. Although placebo and enthusiasm reactions may account for some of their effectiveness, psychiatrists and other physicians who prescribe tranquilizers have found them valuable in reducing states of great tension. The literature on the behavioral effects of tranquilizers or anti-anxiety drugs suggests that these agents reduce the intensity of responses to stimuli that signal punishment and frustration.

In 1960 a group of drugs called **benzodiazepines** were introduced. They are marketed under trade names like Librium and Valium and are used for the treatment of anxiety, tension, behavioral excitement, and insomnia. Figure 6–13 shows the effect of one dose of a member of this group, diazepam (Valium), on the anxiety experienced when people who were phobic about cats

**FIGURE 6–12**
Aaron Beck has developed a time-limited therapy that aims at improving the individual's ability to think constructively and solve problems. (Courtesy of Aaron T. Beck)

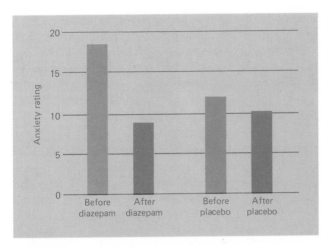

**FIGURE 6-13**
Subjective anxiety ratings when confronted with phobic stimuli. "After" measures were made 2 hours after the subject took either a pill containing diazepam (Valium) or a placebo. (Adapted from Whitehead, Blackwell, and Robinson, 1978, p. 63)

and roaches were exposed to these animals. Similar results were obtained when the dependent measure was how close the person would come to the fear-arousing stimulus. It seems clear that a dose of diazepam made phobics better able to tolerate the animals they were afraid of. One problem with benzodiazepines is their side effects. These include drowsiness, lethargy, motor impairment, and reduced ability to concentrate. The drugs also produce physiological and psychological dependence. Excessive use may lead to undesirable behavior, including disorientation, confusion, rage, and other symptoms that resemble drunkenness.

Several years ago researchers found that benzodiazepines bind to certain receptor sites in the receiving neuron and that the relative potencies of drugs in competing for these binding sites parallel their clinical effects. Receptor sites serve as receiving stations for the brain's nerve cells. They are analogous to locks into which the appropriate chemicals fit like keys. Research has shown that some chemicals open the locks, others simply block the "keyhole" so that nothing else can get in, while still others seem to unlock different but related processes. Accordingly, a whole spectrum of drugs has been developed, some of which act as tranquilizers while others block that action and still others produce the opposite effect—anxiety. One anxiety producer that is being used in animal research is a chemical called beta-CCE, a member of a family of substances that are known to have powerful effects on the nervous system.

Efforts to map receptor sites have shed light on the specific sites in the brain that mediate the effects of different types of drugs (Costa, 1985). One of these

mapping efforts has shown that mice that were inbred for "emotionality" had fewer benzodiazepine receptors than "nonemotional" strains of mice (Robertson, 1979). It has also been found that many receptors are specific to certain chemicals. For example, other drugs, such as alcohol and barbiturates, do not bind to the benzodiazepine receptors. Future research will make clearer the mechanism by which anti-anxiety drugs exert their effects, and may give rise to more effective drugs with fewer side effects.

The discovery of receptor sites for anti-anxiety drugs has set off a widespread search for other details of the brain system to which they are a key. Some experts believe that receptor sites are a key to a natural anxiety system and that anti-anxiety drugs act in the same way as natural body substances, perhaps still undiscovered, that keep anxiety under control. One of the exciting questions that are now being investigated is that of what substances produced within the body attach to which types of receptors.

The biggest recent change in the use of drugs to treat anxiety disorders is the increasing use of antidepressants in treating panic and obsessive compulsive disorders. This and other evidence suggests that the relationships between anxiety and depression need careful study.

### STUDY OUTLINE

1. Although it is normal to experience anxiety occasionally, it is abnormal to feel strong anxiety chronically in the absence of a visible cause. The characteristics of anxiety include feelings of uncertainty, helplessness, and physiological arousal.

2. **Generalized anxiety disorder** is marked by chronic anxiety over a long period. **Panic disorder** consists of recurrent, sudden anxiety attacks leading to feelings of intense terror and dread. In **phobic disorders,** the experience of anxiety is connected to a specific object or situation. In **obsessive-compulsive disorder,** the individual tries to ward off disaster by thinking certain thoughts or performing certain actions.

### GENERALIZED ANXIETY DISORDER

1. The physiological responses to fear and anxiety are the same, but in the case of anxiety the cause of worry is not apparent.

2. The symptoms of generalized anxiety disorder are of four main types: motor tension, hyperactivity of the autonomic nervous system, dread of the future, and hypervigilance. The diagnosis of generalized anxiety disorder is reserved for conditions in which the only problem is the presence of prolonged, vague, unex-

plained, but intense fears that do not seem to be attached to any particular object.

### PANIC DISORDER

1. The indicators of panic disorder are similar to those of generalized anxiety disorders except that they are greatly magnified and occur very suddenly. People with this disorder have a variety of unusual psychosensory symptoms. A source of anxiety in panic disorder is **anticipatory anxiety,** or fear of another panic attack.

### PHOBIAS

1. A **phobia** is a highly specific fear of certain objects, people, or situations. The fear is out of proportion to reality, inexplicable, and beyond the individual's control. Phobics do not need the presence of the feared object to experience discomfort.

2. There are three general types of phobias. **Simple phobias** are a miscellaneous group of irrational fears that do not fall into the other two categories. **Social phobias** are characterized by fear and embarrassment connected with dealings with other people. **Agoraphobia,** the most common type, is fear of entering unfamiliar situations. Agoraphobia is often a complication of panic attacks.

### OBSESSIVE COMPULSIVE DISORDER

1. **Obsessive** people are preoccupied with recurrent ideas; **compulsive** people feel compelled to perform the same action over and over again. These compulsive rituals become a form of protection against anxiety. The individual recognizes the absurdity and irrationality of the obsession or compulsion and feels a need to resist it, but the feelings of anxiety that accompany resistance are usually overwhelming. Four broad types of obsessive-compulsive preoccupations are checking, cleaning, slowness, and doubting and conscientiousness.

### INTERPRETING AND TREATING ANXIETY DISORDERS

1. According to the psychodynamic perspective, the causes of anxiety disorders are intrapsychic events and unconscious motivations. In generalized anxiety and panic disorder, the individual's defenses are inadequate to control or contain anxiety. The psychodynamic view sees the object of a phobia as having symbolic significance, as representing an unresolved psychological conflict. Obsessive compulsive disorders are viewed as developing out of **isolation,** the separation of emotions from thoughts or actions; **undoing,** or ritual actions that "take back" unacceptable thoughts; and **reaction formation,** or compulsively behaving in ways that are opposite to one's thoughts.

2. Learning theorists believe that symptoms of anxiety disorders are learned in the same way that all other behaviors are learned. Whereas Skinner rejects any explanation that refers to internal events, Dollard and Miller include thoughts and feelings in their explanation of how maladaptive behaviors are learned. Therapeutic approaches based on the learning perspective include **exposure therapies** and **modeling.** Three types of exposure therapy are **systematic desensitization,** in which gradually stronger stimuli are introduced; **implosive therapy,** in which the original anxiety-producing situation is re-created in the mind; and **in vivo exposure,** which is carried out in a real-life setting. In vivo exposure may be gradual or may take the form of a rapid, intense exposure called **flooding.** In **modeling,** the patient acquires behavioral skills by watching someone else; in **participant modeling,** the patient then models the desired behavior; in **guided mastery,** the therapist guides the patient toward mastery over frightening situations.

3. Various elements of the cognitive approach can be incorporated in behavioral therapy. According to cognitive theorists, anxiety is a result of faulty, unrealistic, and illogical thoughts and beliefs, especially unrealistic exaggeration of the dangers inherent in a situation. Cognitive techniques that are used to treat anxiety disorders include **cognitive restructuring,** in which the individual recognizes and changes irrational beliefs; **thought stopping,** which helps remove obsessional thoughts; and **cognitive rehearsal,** or mentally rehearsing adaptive approaches to situations.

4. Although no physical cause of anxiety has been found, there are clear associations between anxiety and certain physical functions. The high concordance rate for monozygotic twins may indicate a genetic component. Tranquilizing drugs are the most common biologically oriented treatment for anxiety, although they may produce undesirable side effects. Antidepressants are now being used to treat panic and obsessive compulsive disorders.

# 7

# PSYCHOLOGICAL FACTORS AND PHYSICAL SYMPTOMS

*Perhaps the fact that the Great Depression hit just as she and my father were starting out to raise their family had something to do with it. But no matter. Already as a small child I was aware that in the handling of money my mother was more than simply thrifty; she was downright frugal. Extravagances and luxuries did not exist. She never bought anything, for example, unless she was certain she would use it. And not only use it, but use it to the best purpose and for the longest possible time. The one exception was a new, frilly, never-worn nightgown that she kept in the bottom drawer of the bureau. But even that had its purpose: "In case I should ever have to go into the hospital," she said. And so the nightgown lay there for years, carefully protected in its tissue wrappings.*

*But one day, many years later, the time came. The nightgown with its now yellowed lace and limp ruffles was taken from its wrappings and my mother entered the hospital, seeking an answer to the mysterious fevers, sweats, and malaise that had plagued her like a flu since autumn. The time was early January, in the deepest darkest days of a cold winter, just before her 69th birthday.*

*We did not have long to wait for an answer. It came with the finality of a period at the end of a long sentence of strung-out clauses: lymphoma, disseminated, progressive. Privately, her physician told me he was sorry, there was probably only a matter of two or three weeks left, certainly less than even a month.*

*For days, I agonized over what to do with this information that only I had been told. Should I tell the family? Should I tell my mother? Did she already know? If not, did she suspect? Surely she must after so many months of malaise. Could I talk about it with her? Could I give her any hope? Could I keep up any hope she might have? Was there in fact any hope?*

*Some relief came when I realized her birthday was approaching. The nightgown she had saved all those years she now was wearing, but it was hopelessly dated. I resolved to lift her spirits by buying her the handsomest and most expensive matching nightgown and robe I could find. If I could not hope to cure her disease, at least I could make her feel like the prettiest patient in the entire hospital.*

*For a long time after she unwrapped her birthday present, given early so she would have longer to enjoy it, my mother said nothing. Finally she spoke. "Would you mind," she said, pointing to the wrapping and gown spread across the bed, "returning it to the store? I don't really want it." Then she picked up the newspaper and turned to the last page. "This is what I really want, if you could get that," she said. What she pointed to was a display advertisement of expensive designer summer purses.*

*My reaction was one of disbelief. Why would my mother, so careful about extravagances, want an expensive summer purse in January, one that she would not possibly use until June? She would not even live until spring, let alone summer. Almost immediately, I was ashamed and appalled at my clumsiness, ignorance, insensitivity, call it what you will. With a shock, I realized she was finally asking me what I thought about her illness. She was asking me how long she would live. She was, in fact, asking me if I thought she would live even six months. And she was telling me that if I showed I believed she would live until then, then she would do it. She would not let that expensive purse go unused. That day, I returned the gown and robe and bought the summer purse.*

*That was many years ago. The purse is worn out and long gone, as are at least half a dozen others. And next week my mother flies to California to celebrate her 83rd birthday. My gift to her? The most expensive designer purse I could find. She'll use it well.* (McAdams, 1985)

Is this account of a mother's recovery simply a heartwarming anecdote, or does it provide a clue to why some people recover from illness and others do not? Evidence that psychological and social factors play important roles in health and illness—an idea that has intrigued clinical workers for a long time—is increasing. In this chapter we will review existing theories about the relationships among personality, environment, and illness and examine how psychological and social variables operate in health and illness.

First we will focus on a number of conditions that have often been referred to as **psychosomatic** or **psychophysiological** disorders; they are marked by physical complaints and actual tissue damage or impairment. Later in the chapter we will discuss another group of conditions, those that involve physical complaints with no detectable tissue damage or impairment. These conditions have been referred to as **somatoform disorders** because they suggest somatic impairment when there is no evidence that any exists. A third group of conditions that will be dealt with is **factitious disorders.** "Factitious" means not real, genuine, or natural. People with factitious conditions have physical or psychological complaints that appear to be simulated and under their voluntary control. In other words, they seem to be faking.

Many of the disorders covered in this chapter are thought to result from frequent, intense, and prolonged physiological arousal. Whereas some people respond to stress primarily with bizarre thoughts and behavior, others respond primarily with physical symptoms such as cancer and migraine headaches. But while it is known that there are wide differences in individual patterns of physiological, cognitive, and behavioral reactions to stress, the mechanisms behind those patterns remain unclear. Whatever the mechanisms turn out to be, it is now certain that they involve interactions among personal variables (for example, attitudes and physiological patterns) and situational variables (such as past and recent life experiences and social supports). Illness results from multiple factors.

# ■ CONCEPTS OF PSYCHOLOGICAL, SOCIAL, AND BODILY INTERACTIONS

Awareness that one's state of mind can influence one's body has a long history. In the eighteenth century Mesmer claimed that he could modify the course of physical symptoms by using his personal "magnetism." In the nineteenth century Charcot pioneered the use of hypnosis in the treatment of bodily complaints, and early in this century Freud applied psychoanalytic concepts to physical symptoms. Freud believed that somatic symptoms had symbolic significance; they represented compromises among forbidden impulses, intrapsychic conflicts, and the need to defend oneself from anxiety.

## The Psychosomatic Hypothesis

In the 1930s and 1940s a number of clinicians attempted to integrate Freudian ideas into a growing body of knowledge concerning the bodily aspects of emotional experiences. During this period the **psychosomatic hypothesis** became popular. According to this hypothesis, bodily symptoms can be caused by a blocking of emotional expression. This idea, in turn, gave rise to the concepts of specificity and organ susceptibility.

Numerous psychoanalytic writers argued for **specificity**: specific emotional conflicts and stresses were thought to be associated with particular physical conditions in vulnerable individuals. Whether these conflicts and stresses resulted in bodily dysfunction depended on the individual's characteristics, including personality profile. For example, it was argued that people who chronically suppress their anger are prone to develop rheumatoid arthritis when they are confronted with situations that arouse anger in most people. It was also argued that many individuals have a particularly weak or susceptible organ (such as the lungs) and that certain stresses evoke unconscious conflicts that result in a specific disorder in that organ. This is known as **organ susceptibility.** Most of the evidence supporting the concepts of specificity and organ susceptibility has come from the observations of psycho-

therapists, many of whom were psychoanalysts. Only a few laboratory studies were conducted by early psychosomatic theorists, and the number of patients described in clinical reports was small.

More recent research work has focused on how bodily reactions change when people are exposed to various emotion-arousing stimuli. For example, a psychosomatic symptom, such as high blood pressure, can be viewed as a product of the emotional arousal experienced when a person is exposed to stress over an extended period. Contemporary research on the psychophysiology of emotions and stress has furthered our understanding of this process. For example, emotional tension has been shown to influence the autonomic nervous system and the endocrine glands. One of the endocrine glands, the adrenal medulla, releases its hormones when the situation calls for "fight or flight." As a result, the rates of breathing and heartbeat and muscle tension increase. These and other bodily changes caused by emotional responses to stress prepare the organism to struggle for survival.

Much of the basic research on the endocrines' responses to stress has used animals as experimental subjects. Experimental studies have dealt with two central questions: (1) How does stress affect endocrine function? and (2) How do different levels of biochemical substances influence bodily functioning and behavior?

Over a number of years Hans Selye subjected a variety of laboratory animals to many kinds of stress. He invariably found that the endocrines spring into action when there are bodily or environmental threats of damage to the organism (Selye, 1976). Selye coined the phrase **general adaptation syndrome** to refer to an organism's pattern of reactions to prolonged stress. This pattern begins with an initial shock or alarm response, which is followed by a recovery or resistance phase. During the alarm phase the adrenal glands show particularly striking changes (see Figure 7–1). They become enlarged and discharge their supply of steroids, a process that causes them to change color from yellow to brown. When Selye's animals were removed from stress, the adrenal glands returned to their normal size and seemed to resume normal functioning, but this recovery was only temporary. After several weeks of renewed stress, the glands again enlarged and lost their store of steroids. Selye found that if the stress is very great and continues for a long time, the animal finally dies from exhaustion.

Not surprisingly, demonstration of the general adaptation syndrome in animals has led to research on its existence in human beings. Studies of professional hockey players and of psychiatric patients appearing at staff conferences found increases in subjects' hormonal secretions during emotional stress that were

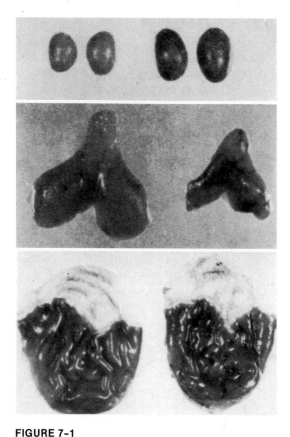

**FIGURE 7-1**
The organs on the left are those of a normal rat. Those on the right are those of a rat that was exposed to the stress of being forcefully immobilized. Note the marked enlargement and dark discoloration of the adrenals (top), caused by congestion and discharge of fatty-secretion granules; the intense shrinkage of the thymus (middle); and the numerous blood-covered ulcers (bottom) in the stressed rat. (Selye, 1952)

similar to those found in Selye's animals (Elmadjian, 1963). Because of such changes in body functioning, severe and prolonged psychological pressures can cause physical diseases such as high blood pressure and stomach ulcers.

## The Biopsychosocial Model

Today most researchers who study psychological processes reject simplified ideas of specificity and organ susceptibility in attempting to explain certain physical symptoms. Instead, they look at physical symptoms from an interactional viewpoint: bodily defects may cause psychological problems, and psychological prob-

lems may in turn cause bodily defects. When psychological factors are involved in illness, their roles are usually indirect. For example, personality characteristics by themselves may not cause an illness like asthma, but in combination with hypersensitive lungs and certain situational stresses, they may play an important role.

Recently emphasis has been placed on the interaction between psychological states and social and biological variables. According to the **biopsychosocial model,** a person can be regarded as a system with interacting biological, psychological, and social subsystems (Engel, 1977). This model can be illustrated by some of the complex activities involved in brain function. The brain processes both physical and nonphysical inputs (environmental events, ideas); it generates thoughts and behavior; and it regulates bodily functions. At any given moment the brain's circuitry permits simultaneous "programming" of data pertaining to the biological, psychological, and social spheres. The challenge facing researchers is to identify the factors and conditions that play roles in this complex type of information processing.

Biopsychosocial problems often arise when people's lives are disrupted by environmental changes, challenges, and constraints. The word **homeostasis** refers to the mechanism by which the organism mobilizes itself to restore a dynamic equilibrium in the face of these disruptions. At present most researchers and clinicians believe that, for any given individual, a host of variables—physical, psychological, and social—contribute to the phenomenon that we call "getting sick." The idea that illness is due simply to the influence of external agents seems outmoded. While it is true that there are individual differences in the vulnerability of bodily organs to disease, these differences must be considered in light of personality characteristics, environmental factors, and the general condition of the body. The biopsychosocial point of view is not limited to the causes of illness. It is also relevant to prevention and treatment.

## ■ PSYCHOLOGICAL FACTORS THAT AFFECT HEALTH

If you have a terrible stomachache and someone says, "Don't worry, it's probably psychosomatic," that doesn't help very much. When people use the word "psychosomatic," they often mean, "It's all in your head." This attitude stems from the vague notion that there are two distinct entities—mind and body—that are locked in a struggle for supremacy. Actually, most psychological and physical problems arise from a multitude of interacting factors. When social relationships and environmental events have special personal meaning and evoke strong emotions, a variety of bodily reactions take place. For example, hearing of a loved one's death or going home to spend Christmas with one's family inevitably leads to at least temporary bodily changes.

The connection between psychological factors and physical health is not a one-way street. One psychological state plays a role in one's susceptibility to physical illness, but getting sick also influences one's state of mind. Depression, anxiety, anger, and feelings of hopelessness and helplessness characterize most people who must live with illness and physical incapacity. A physical illness does not have to be catastrophic to have a psychological impact. Anyone who has had the flu, a sprained ankle, or a toothache knows how much psychological damage these relatively minor problems can cause. Of course, the more serious the physical disorder, the greater the likelihood that it will significantly affect the person's thoughts and feelings. Such effects, in turn, compound the effects of the illness.

Because attitude can affect the speed and extent of recovery from an organic illness, medical researchers are devoting increased attention to the role of psychological complications in physical disorders. It has been estimated that between 25 and 50 percent of patients treated in medical settings have psychological disorders

as well as medical ones (Lipowski, 1977) (see Figure 7–2). The scientific recognition that these interactions exist may not seem to be a major discovery. Each of us has felt the psychological letdown that follows the onset of a physical illness. On the other hand, we might reject the less obvious possibility—also accepted by many scientists—that our psychological condition plays an important role in creating bodily disturbances. Yet a large body of knowledge suggests that certain personality characteristics may be associated with certain types of physical symptoms—for example, those connected with high blood pressure and heart attacks. How specific these associations are and whether they reflect causal (rather than correlational) relationships are explored later in the chapter. First we will examine the evidence for general relationships among psychological factors, health, and specific physical disorders.

## Stress and Illness

Much abnormal behavior can be viewed as ways of dealing with stress—not good or desirable ways, but ways that become understandable on the basis of two factors: meager or distorted psychological resources and the perceived severity of the situation. Stress is created when individuals face difficult situations and have to ask themselves, "How am I going to handle this one?" or "Can I do it?"

We have observed that stress leads to diverse bodily

**FIGURE 7–2**
At least half of these people waiting for medical treatment probably have psychological disorders that may contribute to or cause their symptoms and may also affect their recovery. (Catherine Ursillo, Photo Researchers)

reactions. The heart, lungs, and digestive, endocrine, and nervous systems, among others, work overtime when people experience stress. When these symptoms are consistently overloaded throughout long periods of a person's life, the likelihood increases that some sort of physical weakness or disturbance will occur (see Figure 7–3). It makes good medical sense, therefore, to study the personal characteristics and aspects of life that go along with strong and persistent stress reactions or might predispose a person to psychological or physical breakdown. Psychological, social, community, and biological factors are each important by themselves, and there is every reason to believe that their joint effects are at least equally as important as their individual effects.

Although they do not usually act alone, certain psychological factors do play roles in physical illnesses. Those factors include the following.

1. Inability to adapt to changes in environmental demands
2. Inability to handle strong feelings and emotions, and to express them realistically
3. Inability to interpret demands, constraints, and opportunities correctly
4. Inability to form rewarding, lasting interpersonal ties, particularly love relationships

There are some indications that an individual's temperament and personality early in life may be predictive of his or her susceptibility to illness decades later. For example, for a number of years Rorschach inkblot tests were given routinely to medical students at Johns Hopkins University (Graves and Thomas, 1981). At the time of testing, the students were in good health. The researchers developed special ways of rating Rorschach responses in which figures in the inkblots were described as interacting in some way with each other (for example, "Two small children arguing," "Two bears fighting"). The interaction ratings ranged from warm, affectionate, and close ("People kissing") to violent and destructive ("A witch committing a murder").

Twenty to 25 years later the health status of each of the subjects was assessed. Those whose Rorschachs reflected either a relative lack of well-balanced patterns of social relationships—a relatively restricted capacity for emotional relationships or ambivalence about ties to others—were especially prone to develop cancer later in life. Interestingly, the Rorschachs of subjects who either were healthy or had cardiovascular disorders tended to be similar to each other but different from those of subjects who developed either cancer or mental disorders. The Rorschachs of the latter two groups tended to be similar. These results suggest the value of exploring the linkages between emotional and social orientations and physiological and biological systems.

Several community and social variables also seem to be implicated in physical functioning. For example, urbanization, poverty, rapid social change, and migration can all have negative effects on health. Occupa-

**FIGURE 7–3**
Rush-hour stress. According to the general adaptation syndrome, the body responds to stress by going through three stages: (1) alarm, (2) resistance, and (3) exhaustion. Even such ordinary activities as driving a car or pushing through crowds to catch a packed bus can contribute to the process that ends in the physical wear-and-tear characteristic of the exhaustion phase. The effects of that ordinary activity are multiplied greatly when there are special hazards like snow. (George E. Jones III, Photo Researchers)

tion, workload, working hours, attitudes toward work, morale, and job performance also can play negative roles. Complicating the picture further are biological factors such as individual differences in body type, hormone levels, and cardiovascular functioning.

Only some of the people who are biologically predisposed to a particular condition actually fall ill. Others seem to have a greater capacity to adapt and therefore remain in good health. Psychological contributions to the onset of illness may vary with a number of factors, including age, the particular form of the illness, and what is going on in the person's life. These interacting factors provide a clue to why it is practically impossible to make statements like, "John Jones got pneumonia because he had been working overtime for two months" or "Mary Smith developed ulcers because she is such a nervous person." Many people develop pneumonia without working overtime, and most people can work overtime without becoming sick. Similarly, many people who develop ulcers do not appear to be especially nervous, and most nervous people do not develop ulcers.

Knowledge about how the body reacts to stress is increasing rapidly. As noted earlier, stress stimulates hormonal secretions (particularly those of the pituitary and adrenal glands), activates the autonomic system, brings about biochemical changes, and alters the brain's electrical level. Although all people have these reactions to stress, the strength and pattern of the reactions depend on the nature of the stressful stimulus and the individual's biological characteristics, personality, and life experiences. Recent and past life experiences play important roles in influencing our appraisal of situations and the coping mechanisms we use to deal with stress. Learning that takes place in a social context tends to reinforce or extinguish particular behavioral and physiological reactions.

## Longevity

Ever since Ponce de Leon searched in vain for the Fountain of Youth, human beings have been beating their heads against the wall of old age. Evidence that nonbiological factors play roles in longevity is accumulating. Social isolation, sudden loss of a loved one, death of a parent, and chronic loneliness all seem to shorten the life span. Vulnerability to such stresses may be expressed as anxiety, psychosis, or physical illness. Table 7–1 presents a number of predictors of longevity, only some of which are controllable. In most cases, it is not clear how these variables are related to longevity (Palmore, 1980).

In the United States the mortality rate for all causes of death is higher for certain groups, such as single,

□ **TABLE 7-1**
Predictors of Longevity

### Factors in Longevity that are Wholly or Partly Under Personal Control

1. *Diet.* Too much or too little food reduces longevity. Many people in Western countries would live longer if they ate less, particularly foods that are high in fat.
2. *Exercise.* People who are more active and get more exercise are likely to live longer.
3. *Smoking.* The association between cigarette smoking and greater mortality is well documented.
4. *Retirement and work.* Retired people have higher mortality rates than people of the same age who continue to be gainfully employed.
5. *Marital status.* Aged married people have lower mortality rates than elderly people who are not married.
6. *Social activity.* Social activity (for example, belonging to clubs and religious institutions) is modestly correlated with greater longevity.

### Less Modifiable Factors in Longevity

1. *Heredity.* There is a positive relationship between the longevity of parents and that of their children.
2. *Sex.* Women live longer than men.
3. *Race.* Up to age 75, blacks have higher mortality rates than whites. After age 75, there is a small difference in favor of blacks.
4. *Intelligence.* Higher intelligence or better mental functioning is associated with greater longevity.
5. *Socioeconomic status.* Education and income levels are strong predictors of longevity.

divorced, and widowed people. However, knowing that these groups are more vulnerable to fatal illnesses does not tell us much about the mechanism that actually causes the higher rates. The obvious thing that these groups have in common is the absence or loss of a loved one. Does a love relationship in fact have health-protecting features? There is evidence to support this idea, although longitudinal studies of married and single people are needed to show how personal characteristics influence the course of development, including marriage, illness, and death. Ideally, such research should begin when the subjects are very young. (Early loss of a parent has been related to the subsequent development of various physical illnesses.) In addition, the roles of community factors such as urbanization and neighborliness must be determined. The community, like a loving marital partner, seems to be able to provide social supports that increase an individual's resistance to the negative effects of stress.

It is a well-established fact that women live longer than men (see Table 7–1). However, the cause of this difference is unclear. Probably both genetic and lifestyle factors play roles. Sex differences in longevity are smaller in nonindustrial than in industrial societies. To a large extent this reflects smaller sex differences in mortality for coronary heart disease in nonindustrial societies. In industrialized societies like the United States, higher male mortality rates seem to be related to society's expectations that men will be more aggressive, adventurous, ambitious, and hard-driving than women. If these expectations were changed, would male mortality rates become lower as a result? As more and more women hold jobs and support families, will their mortality rates go up? We do not have definite answers to these questions. Research that compares mortality among men who differ in their need to adopt traditional male roles and among women who differ in their conceptions of female roles may clarify this issue.

The term **psychological hardiness** has been used to refer to individuals who are more resistant to stress and less susceptible to illness than most people (Kobasa and others, 1982). People who are psychologically hardy tend to have a strong sense of personal control over their lives, to feel more involved in whatever they are doing, and to be more open to new ideas and change. Future research may show a link not only between psychological hardiness and illness but also between hardiness and longevity.

## ■ BEHAVIORAL MEDICINE AND HEALTH PSYCHOLOGY

*The care of tuberculosis depends more on what the patient has in his head than what he has in his chest. (Sir William Osler, 1849, the father of modern medicine)*

Although the influence of the mind on the body was well known to ancient healers and has dominated folklore to the present day, until recently the field of medicine has focused almost exclusively on physical causes of bodily illness. New studies strongly indicate that virtually every ill that can befall the body—from the common cold to cancer and heart disease—can be influenced, positively or negatively, by a person's mental state, lifestyle, and social relationships. By unveiling the mechanisms behind these effects, research may point to new ways of preventing and treating disease.

Increasing evidence that psychological factors play a role in health and illness has given impetus to two rapidly developing fields, behavioral medicine and health psychology. **Behavioral medicine** is concerned with ways of improving diagnosis, treatment, and rehabilitation by using psychological techniques that help people adopt healthier ways of living. An important goal of behavioral medicine is the improvement of ser-

vice delivery by providers of health care. Researchers in behavioral medicine are particularly concerned with direct patient evaluation and treatment.

The related field of **health psychology** is directed toward the prevention of disease. Health psychologists seek to reduce health risks by changing people's thinking and living habits. Researchers in health psychology tend to be concerned with broader topics, including the acquisition and modification of behavior that influences health or is guided by concerns about health. Health psychologists seek to strengthen behaviors that contribute to good health, such as getting enough exercise, following a balanced diet, and not smoking. As much as 50 percent of mortality from the leading causes of death can be traced to such behaviors. Health psychologists seek to uncover ways of changing behavior and thought so as to maximize health and well-being (Jenkins, 1985).

Common to both health psychology and behavioral medicine is a philosophy that emphasizes individual responsibility as a means of maximizing health. According to this view, health is a personal achievement, and people's behavior influences whether they attain it or not. Physical, mental, social, and economic factors all influence health and recovery from illness.

Psychologists who are interested in helping people maintain health and recover from illness employ a variety of techniques to modify behavior that is in itself a health problem, to help people stick to prescribed treatment plans that may have unpleasant side effects (such as chemotherapy or a rigid diet), and to help people modify behavior that may increase the risk of disease—for example, the Type A behavior discussed later in the chapter. An additional focus of behavioral medicine is on modifying the behavior of health care providers in order to improve the delivery of their services—for example, by explaining various possible treatments in clear and nontechnical language.

Behavioral medicine and health psychology are interdisciplinary fields that integrate the behavioral and biomedical sciences. We will illustrate work in these fields with four examples: interpretation of bodily symptoms, the role of information about medical procedures, biofeedback, and psychological interactions with the immune system.

### Interpreting Bodily Signals

People go to the doctor when they attend to and are concerned about bodily signals. Their behavior is like that of a driver who does not pay much attention to the sound made by the car engine unless an unusual noise is heard. However, there are significant differences in people's attentiveness to bodily symptoms.

Awareness of symptoms depends on psychological processes and is subject to the same perceptual and cognitive rules that govern the perception of external events. People do not appear to be able to perceive highly specific physiological states with great accuracy (Pennebaker, 1982). Furthermore, a person who may be accurate about one bodily system (for example, the digestive system) is no more likely than another to be accurate about another symptom. Rather than basing beliefs about symptoms and sensations on actual physiological states, people often infer their symptoms, emotions, and other external states from their immediate environment. Accuracy in reporting symptoms is most likely when major physiological changes that result in pain have actually taken place.

Individuals who misperceive or misreport physical symptoms confront completely different types of problems than do people who are not attentive to their bodily state. An error in perceiving the causes of symptoms can result, for example, in a person's thinking that a heart attack is merely a case of indigestion. Failure to interpret symptoms accurately can prove fatal. Over-attention to symptoms can also create problems (for example, with doctors and family members who do not know how to respond to symptoms that have little or no physical basis). For most people, symptoms serve as useful indicators of a problem that requires attention.

There are two major reasons why a person may not report the presence of physical symptoms. First, the symptoms may represent a life-threatening disorder such as cancer. Second, the individual may be afraid that there is no physiological basis for the symptoms and believe that a visit to a doctor will be embarrassing as well as costly.

Physical symptoms can be viewed as problem-solving challenges. Although many cases involve common problems that can be verified objectively, sometimes the physician is unable to substantiate a diagnosis. A number of questions confront the doctor: Is the patient reporting all of the symptoms? Does the patient present symptoms in a way that is misleading? Are the symptoms present all the time or only under certain conditions? Could the reported symptom be an unlabeled emotion? A person who might not be able to express or acknowledge a given emotion may be particularly distressed when emotion-related symptoms appear. From this individual's perspective, the emotion might not seem to be occurring.

The understanding of symptoms is a problem that cuts across a number of psychological and medical disciplines. Changes in bodily functioning are an important aspect of the individual's understanding of the world. Because of the difficulty of measuring various physiological processes, researchers are directing in-creasing attention to the specific stimulus properties inherent in the physiological signals that are being picked up. They are working on assessment techniques to determine the ways in which people react to various stressors, emotions, and other events on both the physiological and psychological levels.

## The Uses of Information

The fact that the information we have and the way we interpret it influence our health and our ability to recover from illness was demonstrated by Irving Janis (1958) in a psychological study of recovery from surgery. Janis found that patients who had a moderate amount of fear before an operation made a better recovery than either patients who had little fear or patients who were very much afraid. Janis believes that worry can be constructive and speed recovery, and his findings suggest that a moderate amount of anticipatory fear is necessary for a person to begin the "work of worrying." By mentally rehearsing potentially unpleasant events and gaining information about what to expect, the patient can develop effective ways of coping with postoperative pain and concern about recuperation. Four kinds of information play important roles in patients' responses to illness and treatment:

1. Information about the nature of the illness and the medical reasons for initiating particular treatments
2. Information describing the medical procedures to be carried out, step by step
3. Information about particular sensations (for example, pain or possible side effects of medication)
4. Information about coping strategies can be used in adjusting to the upcoming threat

Whether or not patients use the information available to them and whether or not they follow medical advice depend on several factors besides the information they get and how it is presented. For instance, people who do not feel that they are in control of their lives may not follow instructions about exercise and medication. Less educated people are more likely than better educated people to break medical appointments and not follow medical advice. Patients who express their concerns to their doctors and receive answers in simple language tend to experience less stress about their physical condition. Researchers in the area of behavioral medicine are investigating the types of information that are medically useful and the best ways of communicating that information to patients. Without free communication between patients and health care providers, patients' fears stay bottled up and their misconceptions cannot be corrected. Self-help groups made up of patients with similar diagnoses can provide needed social support as well as encourage the communication of information.

Audiovisual techniques have been used to aid in recovery from illness and stimulate the promotion of healthful behavior. The use of films and videotapes to convey information to patients is illustrated by Melamed's (1979) research with children who were undergoing painful dental procedures. Melamed showed the children films of other children as they proceeded through the treatment. The children who saw the informative films exhibited fewer disruptive behaviors, reported less apprehension, and showed better clinical progress than children in control groups. In other words, their coping abilities had increased. This sort of preparatory procedure is particularly effective with people who experience high levels of worry and emotional tension before and during medical procedures (Peterson and Ridley-Johnson, 1984).

Films, videotapes, and pamphlets have been used effectively in several community education programs to provide information about health hazards such as smoking and obesity. For example, a team of psychologists and physicians at Stanford University is con-ducting an ambitious study aimed at reducing the incidence of heart attacks. They are using television and radio programs, direct mail, newspaper columns and ads, billboards, bus posters, and recorded telephone messages to influence public attitudes. This mass-media information includes facts about the effects of smoking and obesity, how the heart functions, diet tips (including how to prepare simple, healthful meals), and how to get more exercise (see Figure 7-4). The evidence indicates that this heart disease prevention program is working. Better health habits and reductions in smoking have been noted among the subjects. The best results were found among people who had been exposed to the mass-media campaign and had also participated in special classes (Maccoby and others, 1985).

Health psychologists are especially interested in identifying and strengthening lifestyles that contribute to well-being. The need for improvement in lifestyles is shown by a few statistics. It has been estimated that 40 to 80 million people in the United States are overweight and don't obtain proper nutrition. About 50 million are smokers, and approximately 9 million abuse alcohol. Smoking and drinking are self-destructive behaviors with profound personal, social, and economic

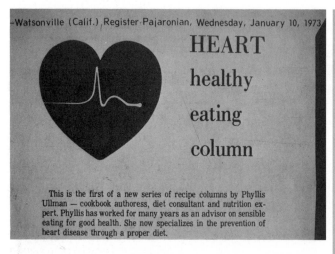

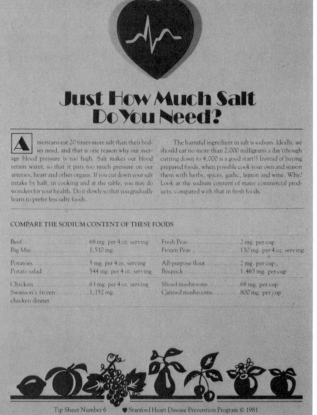

**FIGURE 7-4**

The mass media (newspapers, books, TV) have played an important role in the Stanford heart disease prevention project.

implications. Unfortunately, such behaviors often are not accompanied by unpleasant symptoms in the early stages, and their medical consequences may go unnoticed.

## Biofeedback

**Biofeedback** is a technique that is used in behavioral medicine to treat such problems as hypertension, highly volatile blood pressure, and epilepsy (see Figure 7–5). Biofeedback is a way of extending self-control procedures to deal with a variety of physiological behaviors that were formerly thought to be involuntary responses, such as heart rate, blood pressure, and brain waves. Such behaviors were thought to be beyond conscious control until researchers became aware of individuals who apparently are able to control them. One such person, a Yogi practitioner named Swami Rama, was studied intensively at the Menninger Foundation (Green, 1972). Laboratory tests showed that, among other things, Rama was able to speed up and slow down his heart rate at will, to stop his heart from pumping blood for 17 seconds, to cause two areas of his palm a few inches apart to change temperature in opposite directions until their temperature differed by 10 degrees F (the "hot" side of his palm became rosy whereas the "cold" side became ashen), and to produce widely differing brain wave patterns at will.

Rama is not unique, although the extent of his control is startling. Research has shown that humans and animals can learn to control their heart rate, blood pressure, brain waves, and other behaviors. For humans, no external reinforcement of the behavior seems to be necessary. All that is required is that the individual be given information in the form of feedback from the response system in question. Just as we could never learn to shoot a basketball accurately if we did not receive visual feedback and feedback from our muscles, we cannot learn to control our heart rate or brain waves unless we receive some kind of feedback on physiological changes as they occur. The feedback then serves as a reinforcer for change in the desired direction.

Ordinarily we do not get feedback on responses like blood pressure and brain waves, but by precisely measuring physiological events and converting the electronic signals into visual or auditory feedback, we can be made aware of our own physiological responses. This biofeedback process has been used to train people to control the physiological responses of the brain, muscles, and cardiovascular and glandular systems, and has been applied to an enormous variety of clinical problems, including cardiac disorders, high blood pressure, headaches, anxiety, and neuromuscular disorders like cerebral palsy. For example, over half of a large group

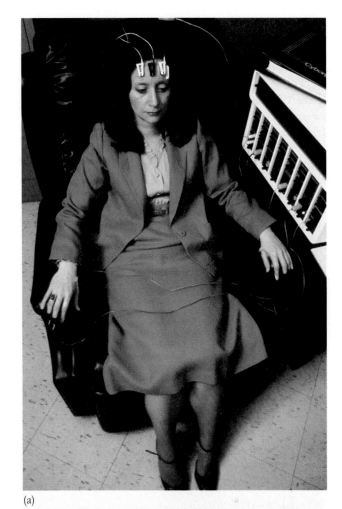
(a)

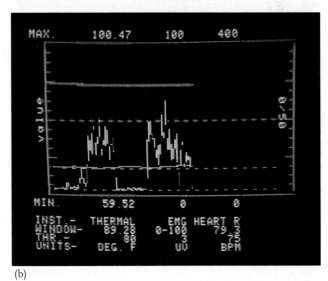
(b)

**FIGURE 7–5**
Biofeedback training can help clients control a variety of physiological responses. Photo (a) shows the biofeedback apparatus. Photo (b) shows the video monitor which visually presents the responses as they occur. (Robert Goldstein, Photo Researchers, Inc.)

of headache sufferers benefited significantly from biofeedback training (Blanchard and others, 1982). This positive effect was found for various types of headaches, including migraines.

There is no longer any question that people can learn to control a wide range of bodily functions. However, there are questions about the overall effectiveness of biofeedback, especially when compared to other techniques that are less expensive and time-consuming. There is evidence that skills learned through biofeedback training are lost rather quickly when training stops. As researchers continue to identify the limitations of biofeedback, it becomes more apparent that these techniques are not the cure-all that overenthusiastic proponents initially believed they would be. But it is equally clear that biofeedback can be successfully applied to certain problems. An important goal of current research is to determine how and when biofeedback techniques can be used most effectively to enhance control over physiological and psychological responses.

## Psychological Processes and the Immune System

The immune system is the body's surveillance system; it protects the body from disease-causing microorganisms. It is integrated with other physiological processes and is sensitive to changes in the functioning of the central nervous system and the endocrine glands. The immune system regulates susceptibility to cancers, infectious diseases, allergies, and auto-immune disorders (diseases in which cells of the immune system attack the normal tissue). There is increasing evidence that stress and emotional arousal can lower the immune system's resistance to disease.

Animal studies have demonstrated the complex relationship between stress and susceptibility to disease. The effects depend on the age of the animal, its stage in the life cycle, and the timing and duration of the stress. Experimental stressors such as physical restraint, overcrowding, electrical shock, or exposure to a predator have been associated with increased susceptibility to numerous viral illnesses. The induction and rate of growth of tumors in experimental animals have also been altered by such stressors (Locke and others, 1984).

There is also evidence that certain early life experiences (for example, daily handling of maternal separation) result in different patterns of cancer susceptibility in rats, with both the nature and the timing of the stressor accounting for significant variability in the response. Another critical factor is the animals'

ability to develop an adaptive coping response: exposure to acute *escapable* stress does not influence tumor growth appreciably; however, the identical amount of *uncontrollable* stress markedly exacerbates tumor growth.

Recent research has provided evidence that psychological, behavioral, and environmental factors influence the functioning of the immune system in humans. Immunological consequences of stressors have been observed in such diverse situations as space flight, sleep deprivation, school examinations, bereavement, and depressive states. Exposure to multiple or chronic life stressors, loneliness, low levels of social support, and poor coping skills all seem to lower the effectiveness of a person's immune system (Jemmott and Locke, 1984; Kiecolt-Glaser and Greenburg, 1984).

There is evidence that many college students show decreased immune system functioning during exam periods (Jemmott and Locke, 1984; McClelland and others, 1985). This may help explain why they have so many illnesses during these periods. Another example of this relationship is a Canadian study of accountants that was conducted during the eight weeks preceding the deadline for filing income taxes and six months thereafter (Dorian and others, 1984). The accountants experienced high levels of psychological distress and declines in immune system measures at the peak tax-filing periods. Studies like these suggest that high performance demands may be significantly associated with alterations in the immune system, which, in turn, may increase susceptibility to disease.

Lack of social support, like major increases in performance demands, may have a negative effect on the immune system or on illness. For example, there is evidence of an association between death of a spouse and risk of death of the surviving spouse. The greatest risk of mortality seems to be during the first 24 months after the loss; this applies for all causes of death and in both sexes. Bartrop and others (1977) studied 33 pairs of bereaved spouses and matched controls, and found a tenfold suppression of certain immune system indexes in the bereaved group. Subsequent research has confirmed this finding (Schleifer and others, 1983).

The importance of social networks in relation to immune function is suggested by a series of studies conducted by Kiecolt-Glaser and her coworkers (1984). These studies demonstrated interactions among life stress, psychiatric symptoms, self-reported loneliness, and immune system changes. In their studies of medical students, the researchers also found that two subgroups are especially susceptible to immune changes: those who experience high levels of stress associated with tests and examinations, and those who perceive their social networks to be poor. Similar results with regard to social networks were obtained with psychiatric in-patients.

The mounting evidence of a relationship between stress and lack of social support, on the one hand, and illness and decrements in immune system functioning, on the other, raises the question of whether ways of weakening the relationship can be devised. Many types of psychological manipulations can have positive effects on indexes of bodily functioning and health. For example, psychological counseling and therapy are powerful tools in reducing the use of medical services (Mumford and others, 1984). While the basis for this effect is not yet clear, evidence from a variety of sources suggests that therapists and counselors may be providing their clients with social support that serves as a stress buffer. It has been shown that the act of discussing a problem or talking about a personal concern to a confidant has a positive effect in maintaining health and reducing the probability of illness (Pennebaker, 1985; Pennebaker and O'Heeron, 1984).

## ■ PSYCHOPHYSIOLOGICAL DISORDERS

Recent research on stress, emotions, and social support suggests that the way we live influences our health and longevity. Several groups of physical disorders in which personality and social factors may play a part have been studied over the years. There is no evidence that these conditions are directly attributable to the mental state of the individual or that a person suffering from one of these disorders has a completely different personality from a person suffering from another disorder or none at all. What is becoming increasingly clear, however, is that people—not just cells or organs—have diseases, and that diseases must be studied in the context of people's psychological, social, and cultural environments.

The term **psychophysiological disorder** has traditionally been applied to physical conditions in which psychologically meaningful events are closely related to bodily symptoms. Psychophysiological disorders might be thought of as end products of biopsychosocial processes. A large number of physical problems have been studied from a psychophysiological standpoint. These include disorders of the cardiovascular, respiratory, gastrointestinal, musculoskeletal, and genitourinary systems, as well as the skin. Both clinical data and informal observations suggest the importance of psychological factors in many of these disorders. Consider the following case.

*A 38-year-old mother of four children had a 5-year history of attacks of hives, a skin condition characterized by itching, burning, and stinging. During these attacks, areas of her face, trunk, waist, thighs, and arms would swell. There would be swelling even on her tongue and inside her respiratory passages. The attacks initially occurred about once a month, but at the time that she sought help, their frequency was closer to once every 4 or 5 days. Each attack was accompanied by depression and nausea.*

*An examination in an allergy clinic yielded negative results. After a psychiatrist placed the patient on tranquilizing drugs, the incidence of hives declined markedly. Further study indicated that her attacks usually occurred when she was experiencing intense stress. For example, when she was having marital difficulties and was forced to face the possibility that her husband might leave her, she had an especially severe series of attacks. At one point she felt so overwhelmed by situational stresses that she was hospitalized. During this period she was protected from family tensions, and her hives disappeared completely.*

*After leaving the hospital the patient entered psychotherapy on a twice-a-week basis. In these sessions she was able to express her frustrations at leading a very restricted life because of her small children's demands and her husband's inability to see why she might need time away from home. Another point that emerged in therapy was the patient's inability to express to her husband how much she needed to have him acknowledge her value as a person, not just as the mother of his children. After several months of therapy, she felt able to tell her husband about her unfulfilled psychological needs as well as her resentment and frustration. At the time that therapy ended, she had been completely free from hives for 4 months.*

A major hurdle for the researcher is figuring out how to proceed from relationships that may be at work in a given case to generalizations that could apply to whole groups of people. The most extensive evidence that physical illness is caused by the interaction of psychosocial and biological factors probably comes from the study of cardiovascular disorders.

### Cardiovascular Disorders

*Every affection of the mind that is attended with either pain or pleasure, hope or fear, is the cause of an agitation whose influence extends to the heart.* (William Harvey, 1628)

Written more than 350 years ago, Harvey's allusion to an intimate association between neural factors and the heart received some attention in anecdote and fable, yet was not subjected to systematic scientific inquiry until the second half of the twentieth century. The heart is a highly specialized muscle that pumps blood to the body. The blood flows through the body in an unending loop of blood vessels called the circulatory system. Each day the heart beats 100,000 times, delivering the equivalent of 4,300 gallons of blood to all parts of the body. The arteries provide food and oxygen to the cells, while the veins remove carbon dioxide and waste products. The term **cardiovascular disorders** refers to pathological conditions that are related to the functioning of the heart and blood vessels. There is growing evidence that psychological and social factors play a role in two major cardiovascular disorders: coronary heart disease and hypertension. These conditions have caused over half of all deaths in the United States for more than 40 years.

**Coronary Heart Disease** **Coronary heart disease** (CHD) is the leading cause of death and disability in the United States. One in five Americans develops CHD before his or her sixtieth birthday; of these, 11 percent die suddenly and another 44 percent suffer nonfatal heart attacks. CHD is produced by lesions of the coronary arteries, the arteries that circulate blood within the heart itself. In CHD one or more of the three coronary arteries are partially or totally obstructed by deposits, called **plaques,** that thicken the arterial wall. When the coronary arteries become rigid and narrow as a result of these plaque deposits, the supply of blood to various portions of the heart muscle is temporarily or permanently cut off.

CHD takes a variety of forms. In **angina pectoris,** people suffer from periodic chest pains caused by an insufficient supply of oxygen-rich blood to the heart. The insufficient blood supply is related to plaque buildup (referred to as **atherosclerosis**) in the arteries. A **myocardial infarction,** also caused by an insufficient blood supply to the heart, is more serious than angina pectoris because it involves a more complete curtailment of the heart's blood supply. When people speak of a heart attack, they are usually referring to a myocardial infarction.

A significant factor in heart attacks is stress. From the Stone Age to the present day, human beings have responded to environmental challenges and threats by releasing larger amounts of adrenal and other stress hormones, followed by increases in heart rate and respiration and dilation of the vessels that transport blood to the muscles. Although these responses are adaptive or even life-saving when the threat is a wolf pack, you would do better without them if you are stuck in a traffic jam. In fact, not only are these primitive physiological responses of little help in dealing with most modern-day problems, but they may actually be related to the development of disease.

Stress seems to contribute to coronary disease through the body's general reactions to aversive stimulation. Under arousing conditions, hormonal substances called **catecholamines** are secreted. Two of the catecholamines, **epinephrine** and **norepinephrine,** accelerate the rate of arterial damage and ultimately can lead to heart attacks. Which people are most likely to have heart attacks under high levels of stress, and what steps lead from psychological stress to cardiac damage, are both topics of current research.

Factors that increase the risk of CHD include age (older people are at greater risk), sex (males are at greater risk), cigarette smoking, high blood pressure, high cholesterol level, and diabetes. Some studies have also implicated such factors as obesity, heredity, and lack of physical exercise. These factors may not be causes of CHD; they may simply be correlated with it. Even the most predictive of the risk factors still fails to identify more than half of the new cases of CHD. How these factors are related to the incidence of heart attack in a given individual is not yet known precisely.

Death due to CHD has decreased more than 30 percent in the last 30 years, and recently this decrease has accelerated. Deaths as a result of heart disease have declined from first to third among all causes of death in people between 25 and 44 years of age, but heart disease remains the leading cause of death in people aged 45 and over (Levy and Moskowitz, 1982). Factors that may be contributing to the decline in mortality are improved medical services, the development of coronary care units in hospitals, advances in surgical and medical treatment of CHD, and improved control of blood pressure. Lifestyle changes, such as less smoking, better eating habits, and increased physical fitness, may also play a role.

*Twin Studies.* A widely used research strategy used to understand the relationship between physical factors and personality involves comparing the life experiences of people with particular physical conditions with those of a matched control group. Twin studies allow the experimenter to control for genetic factors so they are often especially useful. A study conducted in Sweden (Liljefors and Rahe, 1970) provided a unique set of data about the relationship between CHD and personality. The sample consisted of 32 pairs of identical male twins, 42 to 67 years of age, who were discordant for CHD—that is, only one member of each pair had a heart condition. Virtually all the twins had been raised together at least until their early teens. The twins' characteristic behavior patterns in four areas—devotion to work, lack of leisure, home problems, and life dissatisfactions—were assessed through interviews. Although a composite score of behavior in these areas revealed a striking consistency, the twins differed in stressful life experiences, and their life-stress scores were positively correlated with the incidence of CHD. Table 7–2 shows the differences in life experiences in one twin pair. The study's results supported the hypothesis that CHD is related to the amount of stress in an individual's life. A more recent study (Kringlen, 1981) has provided further support for this hypothesis.

### Cross-cultural Comparisons and Social Change

In general, low rates of CHD tend to be found in parts of the world where tradition and family ties are strong. Cross-cultural data have provided a broader perspective on the relationship between psychosocial experience and physical breakdown. Japan, for example, has one of the lowest rates of heart disease in the world, while the United States has one of the highest. The rate of death from CHD for Japanese men between the ages of 35 and 64 is 64 per 100,000 population; the comparable figure for American men is 400 per

100,000. Could the nature of life in the United States be responsible for this high mortality rate? A study in which Japanese living in Japan were compared with Japanese-Americans living in Hawaii and California highlights the importance of cultural factors in the development of CHD (Marmot and Syme, 1976). The Japanese living in Japan had the lowest incidence of CHD; the Japanese-Americans living in Hawaii had a somewhat higher rate; and the Japanese-Americans living in California had the highest frequency of heart disease. Although diet probably accounts for some of these differences, societal and cultural differences also play a substantial role. For example, Japanese-Americans who believed in preserving traditional Japanese culture developed fewer cases of CHD than Japanese-Americans who had strongly accepted American culture.

There are wide regional and cultural differences in a large country like the United States. For example, according to a survey done some years ago, the town of Roseto, Pennsylvania, had a remarkably low death rate, especially from heart attacks. The coronary death rate for men was 100 per 100,000, and the rate for women

---

☐ **TABLE 7–2**
Twin-Pair Members Who Were Discordant for Coronary Heart Disease (CHD)

| Twin Without CHD | Twin With CHD |
|---|---|
| **Devotion To Work** | |
| The subject has been an auto repairman for the past 33 years. His workday is 8 hours long, and he works less than 5 hours per week overtime. At one time during his life for a 5–10-year period he worked about 8 hours per week overtime. | The subject is an owner of a small fur shop. During his high season he works up to 18 hours per day. The rest of the year he averages 9 hours per day. |
| **Lack of Leisure** | |
| The subject visits friends and family less than once per month. He reads the newspapers and watches TV about once per week. In the summer he rents a "sommarstuga," where he goes once a week. In the winter he goes skiing now and then. He takes a 45-minute lunch break along with a 20-minute coffee break during the day, and he usually relaxes then. | The subject visits friends less than once per month and has a hobby in the summer which he follows at a once-per-week frequency. He reads the newspapers and watches TV frequently. He manages to take regular vacations. The subject's lunch periods are 30 minutes long; he sometimes relaxes then and sometimes does not. |
| **Home Problems** | |
| He was married at 27 years of age. His wife is three years younger than he is. They have three children with one still living at home. He recalls having some arguments with his wife and having had some financial difficulties. | He was married at 33 years of age. His wife is eight years younger than he is. There are two children—both still reside in the home. He generally has had a good home life. He has had considerable economic difficulties. |
| **Life Dissatisfactions** | |
| The subject thinks that neither twin dominated. He had a comfortable childhood and was quite happy with his education. The problems in his marriage he sees as primarily due to his alcohol consumption prior to the last eight years. Since then he has not had much alcohol to drink, primarily because it interfered with his sexual relations. He is quite satisfied with his work. | The subject makes no comment about which twin might have dominated. He recalls a good childhood experience and was satisfied with his level of education. Throughout his working life he has felt constantly rushed and never had enough time for himself. He has had considerable trouble with his creditors in his business and feels he has particular difficulty in being tough enough to collect the money owed him. He feels he has strived a good deal to achieve the luxuries of life and has not succeeded very well. |

From Liljefors and Rahe, 1970, pp. 540–541.

was almost half that figure (Wolf, 1969). Moreover, residents of Roseto had low rates of several other stress-related disorders, such as stomach ulcers.

These low rates might seem surprising, since both the men and women of Roseto tended to be overweight and their diets contained as much animal fat as those of people in other communities. Their smoking and exercise patterns were not unusual. What seemed to contribute most to the relatively low death rate was the way in which the people lived. Roseto was distinguished from similar communities in that almost all of its residents were of Italian descent. Family relationships were extremely close and supportive, and the town's neighborhoods were very cohesive. Moreover, in Roseto men were the uncontested heads of their families. Personal and family problems tended to be worked out with the help of relatives, friends, and the local priest.

Although Roseto had several stable features, it was, like all American communities, undergoing constant change. Young men and women were marrying non-Italians from other towns. The birth rate was declining, church attendance was down, and people were moving into more modern suburban neighborhoods. Another, more unfortunate trend was also discovered: by the mid-1970s a striking increase in the rate of heart attacks and sudden death could be noticed, particularly among men under 55 (Greenberg, 1978). Apparently social change was weakening Roseto's sources of social and emotional security, with important consequences for the health and longevity of its inhabitants.

**The Role of Occupation.** The role of occupation in CHD was suggested by a study that found that 25 out of 100 coronary patients had been holding two jobs and that an additional 46 had worked 60 hours or more per week for long periods immediately preceding the onset of symptoms. The patients were compared with an appropriate control group for heredity, diet, occupational pressure, obesity, smoking, and exercise. Although other factors were also involved, occupational stress and strain were most highly correlated with the occurrence of heart disease. The results do not demonstrate a cause-and-effect relationship, but they do suggest that life stress is a significant component of a complex health problem (Russek, 1967). An example is provided by bus drivers in London, who suffer twice as many heart attacks as the conductors who sell tickets on board the bus but do not face the strain of city driving (Fox and Adelstein, 1978).

Another indication of the central role of occupation in CHD comes from a study of patients under 55 years of age who were recuperating from early heart attacks (Theorell and others, 1974). These patients were interviewed in an effort to determine the importance of the work environment as a factor in their cardiac disorders. While the interviews, which dealt with work, family, finances, and other potential problems, were being conducted, the patients' heart rate and blood pressure were monitored. The most consistent differences between cardiac patients and controls occurred during discussions of their work situations.

As part of the same study, cardiac patients and controls were asked to indicate which of a long series of events they had experienced during the year before they had their heart attacks. Change in work schedule, conflict with superiors, and conflict with colleagues were more frequent among the cardiac patients than among the controls. Differences outside the work area seemed minor. However, other research has demonstrated that harmful stress can come in any area of people's lives that is important to them. Social losses and social isolation seem to play particularly important roles in CHD.

**Social Relationships.** The following account is typical of many situations in which separation from or loss of a loved one culminates in a heart attack.

*Harry Allen's wife had suffered from lung cancer for many months. Her death came slowly and painfully. For Allen, aged 54, the loss and grief were overwhelming. Everyone knew that the cancer was incurable and that death was approaching. Yet it came as a terrible shock to Allen. Four months before his wife's death, Harry had had a thorough physical examination that included an electrocardiogram. The electrocardiogram as well as the other studies relevant to heart function were completely negative. Yet 2 days after his wife's death Allen collapsed and died of a massive heart attack.*

Recent research has explored the role of social losses and social isolation in CHD. In one investigation, 2,320 male survivors of myocardial infarctions were studied to identify factors that were predictive of how long they would live after having had a heart attack (Ruberman and others, 1984). One such factor was education, with the better-educated subjects living longer. Life stress and social isolation, both alone and in combination, also emerged as significant predictors of mortality. Life stress was defined by subjects' reports concerning such problems as job difficulties, divorces and separations, accidents, and criminal victimization. Social isolation was defined in terms of contacts with friends and relatives and membership in social, church, and fraternal organizations.

Figures 7–6a and 7–6b show that when the effects of life stress and social isolation were evaluated separately, each of these factors was significantly associated with increased probability of mortality. The risk of death for men who were high in life stress was double

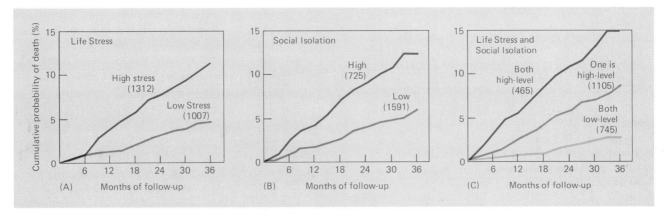

**FIGURE 7-6**
Cumulative probability of death as a function of number of months that subjects were followed up after myocardial infarction. (adapted from Ruberman and others, 1984, p. 555. Reprinted by permission of *The New England Journal of Medicine, 9, 555,* 1984)

the risk for men who were low in life stress. A similar relationship was found when men who were high and low in social isolation were compared. The combined effect of these two factors is shown in Figure 7–6c. For men who were high in both life stress and social isolation, the risk of dying was four times greater than for men who were low in both life stress and social isolation. The middle line in Figure 7–6c presents the risk of dying for men who were high in either life stress or social isolation.

**The Type A Coronary-Prone Behavior Pattern** Is there a heart attack-prone personality? Friedman and Rosenman (1974) have concluded that such a personality exists. These people, called *Type A's* (see Figure 7-7), tend to operate under high pressure and to be very demanding both of themselves and of others. Because of these characteristics, Type A people are believed to run an inordinate risk of suffering heart attacks. The characteristics that seem to typify the Type A person include the following.

1. Talking rapidly and at times explosively
2. Moving, walking, and eating rapidly
3. Becoming unduly irritated at delay (for example, waiting in line)
4. Attempting to schedule more and more in less and less time
5. Feeling vaguely guilty while relaxing
6. Trying to do two things at once

These characteristics are assessed by means of specially designed questionnaires and interviews. The

Type A pattern exists on a continuum, with some people showing more of the characteristics just listed than others. Table 7–3 lists some items from a questionnaire designed to assess the Type A personality.

While the Type A pattern has not been proven to

**FIGURE 7-7**
Type A individuals work rapidly, feel pressured, and frequently try to do two or more things at once. (© 1984 by Sidney Harris–Chicago Magazine)

"CERTAINLY I HEARD YOU. YOU SAID SOMETHING ABOUT BEING A WORKAHOLIC."

Questionnaire Items Designed to Reflect Type A
Characteristics. The subject's task is to rate each
item on a scale ranging from *not at all like me* to
*a great deal like me.*

1. I don't get upset when I have to wait in line at a store or theater.
2. I usually don't find it necessary to hurry.
3. When I play games, winning is very important to me.
4. I like competing with other people.
5. Second best is not good enough for me.
6. I'm often so busy that I have trouble finding the time for things like a haircut, shopping, and household chores.
7. I often feel like letting someone have it.
8. I get tense at work when I am competing for recognition.

cause heart attacks, there are definite links. For example, one study showed that during 8½ years of follow-up Type A men had more than twice as much heart disease as Type B men (Type B's do not show the Type A behavior pattern and are much less driven) (Rosenman and others, 1975). This difference could not be explained simply in terms of traditional risk factors, such as cigarette smoking, because those factors had been equalized for the two groups. Other research has corroborated that a Type A behavior pattern is one of the strongest predictors of recurring heart attacks.

The popular theory that top business executives are especially susceptible to physical breakdowns such as heart attacks has not received widespread empirical support. Often the Type A behavior pattern is stronger among middle-level administrators than among those at the top of the organization. One group of researchers conducted a five-year study of 270,000 male telephone-company employees in the United States and found no evidence that men with high levels of responsibility or those who had been promoted rapidly, frequently, or recently faced any added risk of coronary heart disease. Men who entered the telephone company with a college degree had a lower rate of heart attacks, death, and disability than those who had no degree (Hinkle and others, 1968).

Type A behavior can be identified among college students and even in childhood and adolescence. Type A college students show more involvement in extracurricular activities, better academic performance, and higher aspirations for academic success than Type B's do (Ovcharchyn and others, 1981). High-school students can also be categorized as Type A's and B's (Siegel and others, 1981).

One type of investigation that may help chart the development of Type A tendencies and clarify how known risk factors combine to bring about physical illness is the longitudinal or prospective study. Most clinical problems have been studied retrospectively, that is, after the fact. After someone gets sick, the doctor inquires about past illnesses and experiences that might explain the current problem. More powerful—but also more time-consuming and costly—is the prospective, or before-the-fact, investigation. Such a study gathers information over a relatively long period. Because prospective studies are longitudinal, they can provide a picture of how a person's thinking, behavior, and bodily reactions unfold over time. Depending on the data gathered, this approach permits the researcher to identify interactions between particular personality variables and important life events and the effects of those interactions on the person's health.

*Type A and the Framingham Study.*  An example of a prospective study that points up the strengths and weaknesses of this approach is the Framingham study. A group of 5,127 adult residents of Framingham, Massachusetts, have volunteered to participate in a study on coronary heart disease for the rest of their lives. They have been monitored for the incidence of illness, hospitalization, and death since 1948. Every 2 years each participant is given a physical examination that includes blood tests, electrocardiograms, X rays, and blood pressure readings. Several physical risk factors have been identified by the Framingham study, including elevated blood pressure, cholesterol level, and cigarette smoking. The study has confirmed that weight gains result in elevated blood pressure and thus indirectly increase the risk of coronary heart disease.

A subgroup of 1,674 Framingham participants between the ages of 45 and 77 was assessed for Type A tendencies and then followed up over an eight-year period (Haynes and others, 1980). Women between the ages of 45 and 64 who developed CHD scored significantly higher on the Framingham Type A measure and showed more suppressed hostility (not showing or discussing anger), tension, and anxiety than women who remained free of CHD. Type A women developed twice as much CHD as Type B women. Although working women tended to have higher Type A scores than housewives, being a housewife did not protect Type A women from higher rates of CHD. Figure 7–8a shows that working women under 65 years of age were almost twice as likely to develop CHD if they exhibited Type A rather than Type B behavior. Among housewives in the under-65 age group, CHD incidence among Type A's was almost three times greater than among Type B's. Figure 7–8b shows the association of Type A behavior with CHD incidence among white- and blue-collar men in the 45 to 64 and 65 to 74 age groups. The association was significant only among men holding white-collar jobs.

The results of the Framingham study suggest that the Type A behavior pattern operates independently of the usual coronary risk factors (such as blood pressure, age, and weight). The Type A behavior pattern and suppressed anger seem to be important risk factors for CHD in both men and women (Diamond, 1982).

***Physiological Reactivity of Type A's.*** As part of the effort to understand how the psychological and behavioral characteristics of Type A's translate into heart attacks, research has been carried out on the physiological reactivity of groups with varying degrees of Type A characteristics. One of the most consistent findings is that while there are few baseline physiological differences among these groups, Type A's show greater cardiovascular reactivity than Type B's (Krantz and Manuck, 1984). This difference is greatest when there are highly motivating conditions that elicit the competitive drive.

Researchers are now exploring the possibility that cardiovascular reactivity is the key factor in Type A characteristics and risk of heart attacks. Perhaps there are two groups of people, hot and cool reactors, with the cool reactors showing normal cardiovascular responses (blood pressure, heart rate) to stress and hot reactors displaying abnormally intense cardiovascular responses. Hot and cold reactors might not differ in terms of their overt behavior, but the hot reactors might experience steep blood pressure surges under stress. If this proves to be the case, measurements of the Type A pattern by means of questionnaires and interviews may not be as direct a predictor of cardiac disorders as measurements of actual cardiovascular responses under stressful conditions.

The causes of cardiovascular disease are complex, involving behavior patterns superimposed on genetic makeup in response to specific environmental challenges. The particular type of challenge or stress may be of critical importance. For example, the rates of cardiovascular disorders declined in European countries during World War II. It is possible that this was a result of the scarcity of risk-increasing foods such as eggs and richly marbled meats, as well as cigarettes and other risk-increasing commodities. But psychological factors may also have played a role. The fight against the Nazis generated a mutual support system and a group spirit that are not generally found in today's world. Certainly people who lived in war-torn countries suffered great hardship, but in working cohesively against a common enemy, they had clear-cut goals and a sense that they were doing something of great importance. A Dane who was instrumental in smuggling 7,000 Jews out of Denmark under loads of coal in freight cars with false

bottoms perhaps described it best. When asked whether such risk taking was stressful, he replied, "Heavens, no. We had to save those people's lives and pulled together to do it. We knew exactly what we had to do, we did it, and we're proud of it" (Eliot and Buell, 1983).

***Can the Type A Behavior Pattern Be Modified?*** Type A behavior is elicited in susceptible individuals by stressful situations such as job pressures. Researchers are now exploring the possibility of reducing this susceptibility. They are using a variety of cognitive and behavioral techniques with Type A's, including self-control training, learning to think about situations in less intense ways, and being attentive to the problems created by personal beliefs that emphasize urgency and the need to gain immediate control over events. Available evidence suggests that learning to think and act differently exerts a positive influence on the health of Type A's. For example, one study found that Type A men who had already had a heart attack were less likely to have another attack if they had participated in a cognitive-behavior counseling program after the first heart attack (Thoresen and others, 1982).

Another group of researchers has tried to help healthy successful Army colonels engage in fewer Type A behaviors (Gill and others, 1985). The colonels participated in a series of counseling sessions that dealt with ways of modifying beliefs and attributions that underlie Type A behavior. They were also given advice on how to avoid potentially stressful situations, and engaged in role plays in which they practiced less highly pressured ways of coping with situations. The findings support the conclusion that the Type A attributes of anger, irritation, and impatience are not necessary aspects of the drive, ambition, creativity, and hard work needed by military leaders. The study showed that the colonels became less prone to Type A behaviors but that their ability to function as leaders was in no way impaired. They actually may have become more effective leaders.

**Hypertension** Hypertension is what most people describe as high blood pressure. A blood pressure level that is over 150 (systolic) when the heart contracts and does not fall below 90 (diastolic) when the heart relaxes is usually considered high. High blood pressure indicates that there is resistance to the flow of blood through the cardiovascular system. This places pressure on the arteries and forces the heart to work harder to overcome the resistance. Among younger adults (aged 25 to 44), men have higher blood pressures than women. Among older adults (aged 65 to 74), this pattern is reversed. The blood pressure readings of black adults exceed those of white adults (*Hypertension in Adults*, 1981).

High blood pressure is a major contributor to cardiovascular disorders and is one of the conditions that creates increased risk of heart attacks. Usually it is a silent or symptomless risk because the hypertensive individual might show no observable signs of a medical problem for many years. Hypertension may be the most common major chronic disease in the United States today. In addition, borderline systolic blood pressure elevations occur in about 10 percent of people over the age of 20.

The bodily response to stress falls mainly on the cardiovascular system. Many studies have uncovered an association between prolonged emotional arousal and elevated blood pressure. The persistent effect of stress on blood pressure was shown in a World War II study of 695 men that found hypertension in 27 percent of the men after they had been involved in desert warfare for one year (Graham, 1945). For days on end, even when there was no immediate danger, these soldiers had elevated blood pressures, rapid pulses, pale faces, and enlarged pupils. A high workload, low morale, and the need to make many instantaneous decisions of life-and-death importance are among the factors that may contribute to high blood pressure. However, while highly stressful environments clearly influence many aspects of cardiovascular functioning, little insight has yet been gained into the mechanisms involved.

Clinical observations showing that many hypertensives show wide variability in blood pressure readings and seem emotionally on edge much of the time have led to speculation about the causes and treatment of this disorder. Chronic anger and anxiety have been identified as particularly important factors. It is suggested that prevention or treatment of these factors might result in lower blood pressure. Psychotherapists believe that within the warm acceptance of the psychotherapeutic setting, angry, anxious people can gain insight into and mastery over their tendency to experience strong emotional reactions. However, firm empirical support for this approach is not yet available.

Some support is emerging for a behavioral approach to hypertension that directs attention to the specific types of situations associated with elevated blood pressure. Lack of competence in dealing with situations that call for assertiveness may be a specific behavioral deficit of many hypertensives. Assertiveness, defined as the ability to stand up for one's rights, express feelings, and avoid mistreatment by others, is a vital interpersonal skill and an indicator of social competence. People who are low in assertiveness tend to be mistreated, fail to express their feelings, and are frequently unable to have their needs met. Natural consequences of these experiences are anger over being pushed around and anxiety about the possibility of exposure to threatening situations in the future. Researchers have been able to show that hypertensives respond positively to behavioral training that involves the modeling and role-playing of appropriate assertiveness. As the social competence of these individuals increases, in many cases their blood pressure declines (Manuck and others, 1985); thus, strengthening the social skills of hypertensives may prove to be of clinical value.

Another line of research concerns the relationship between relaxation and blood pressure. If hypertensives could learn how to relax, would their blood pres-

**FIGURE 7–8a**
Eight-year incidence of coronary heart disease among Framingham working women and housewives with Type A and Type B behavior patterns. (Findings from the Framingham study, adapted from S.G. Haynes, M. Feinleib, T.W.B. Kannel, The relationship of psychological factors to coronary heart disease in the Framingham study. *American Journal of Epidemiology, 111*, 37–58, 1980.)

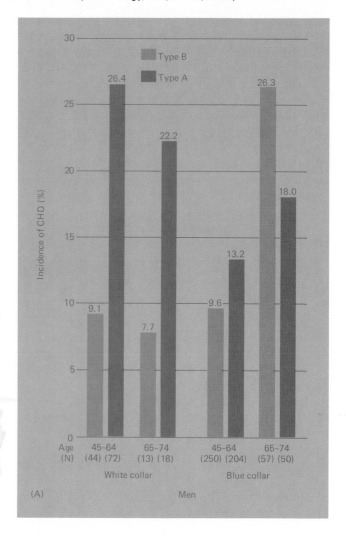

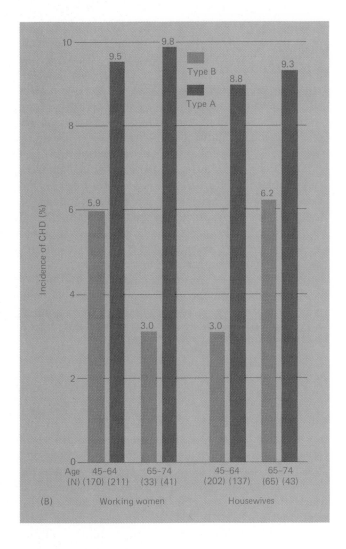

**FIGURE 7–8b**
Eight-year incidence of coronary heart disease among white-collar and blue-collar Type A and Type B men in the Framingham study. (adapted from Haynes and others, 1980, p. 46)

sure levels go down? There is evidence that some reduction in blood pressure can be achieved by teaching relaxation skills to hypertensives. Herbert Benson (1977) has developed relaxation exercises that are more related to meditation techniques than to the muscular-relaxation approach described in Chapter 6. Benson's system involves four elements: a repetitive mental device, a passive attitude, decreased muscle tension, and a quiet environment. His approach uses instructions like the following.

*Sit quietly in a comfortable position. Close your eyes. Deeply relax all your muscles, beginning at your feet and progressing up to your face. Keep them deeply relaxed.*

*Breathe through your nose. Become aware of your breathing. As you breathe out, say the word "one"*

*silently to yourself. Continue for 20 minutes. You may open your eyes to check the time, but do not use an alarm. When you have finished, sit quietly for several minutes, at first with closed eyes and later with opened eyes.*

*Do not worry about whether you are successful in achieving a deep level of relaxation. Maintain a passive attitude and permit relaxation to occur at its own pace. Expect distracting thoughts. When these distracting thoughts occur, ignore them and continue repeating "one."*

*Practice the technique once or twice daily, but not within two hours after a meal, since the digestive processes seem to interfere with elicitation of anticipated changes.* (Benson, 1977, p. 1153)

This simple method leads to lower blood pressure as well as to other bodily changes that accompany relaxation. Figure 7–9 shows the types of results that have encouraged clinicians to use relaxation techniques with hypertensives. The figure shows that relaxation led to lower blood pressure during the day and also while the subjects were asleep. There were similar results for diastolic pressure.

Biofeedback, a method that operantly conditions automatic responses, is another promising approach to the treatment of hypertension. It has long been known that automatic responses can be classically conditioned, but it is now clear that operant conditioning of autonomic responses is also possible. Operant procedures are capable of generating highly specific changes in physiological systems that were previously thought to be involuntary. Though some experiments designed to operantly condition autonomic responses have yielded negative results, the overall pattern of the findings is encouraging.

Even though both relaxation and biofeedback seem to be effective in reducing blood pressure, some cases will probably require the use of several clinical methods together with psychotherapy aimed at clarifying the conditions that gave rise to the disorder. There is evidence that the combined use of relaxation and bio-

feedback has particularly good long-term effects on blood pressure (Taylor, 1980). Although antihypertensive medications have also been shown to be effective in reducing blood pressure, drug treatments have certain drawbacks, including cost, side effects, and difficulty in getting some patients to take the medicines.

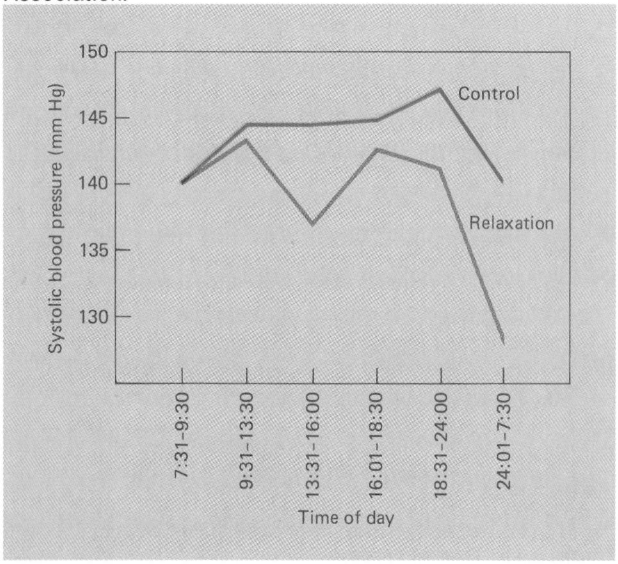

Further research is needed to deal with several specific questions. What is it that hypertensives are doing when their blood pressure goes up or down? Might some of the positive effects of relaxation and biofeedback be placebo effects—that is, might lowered blood pressure following relaxation or biofeedback training be due partly to the expectation that the treatment will be effective? Follow-up studies are needed to determine how lasting the results of behavioral procedures are, and comparative studies are needed that evaluate the effectiveness of several treatment methods (biofeedback, psychotherapy, and so on). Behavioral techniques might prove particularly useful in conjunction with antihypertensive drugs in treating high blood pressure (Wadden and others, 1984).

## Cancer

Stress and personality are emerging as two of the most widely studied psychological factors that may contribute to cancer. Animal studies have shown that uncontrollable stress is related to cancer growth (Sklar and Anisman, 1981). Earlier in the chapter we mentioned the Johns Hopkins University prospective study that found that emotional constrictedness in medical students was related to the incidence of cancer many years later. That study is one of a growing number of efforts to find out whether psychological variables might also be related in some way to the occurrence and growth of cancer and to recovery from the disease.

One emerging hypothesis is that people who deny strong feelings are more prone to develop cancers than people who can appropriately ventilate their emotions. In one psychological study of cancer patients, only about 30 percent of the group admitted feeling any discouragement whatever about the future, although many of them had large tumors for which no treatment was available (Plumb and Holland, 1977). In another study, patients with malignant melanoma, a type of cancer, were asked to rate on a scale of 1 to 100 the amount of personal adjustment needed to handle or cope with a serious illness (Rogentine and others, 1979). All of the patients reported that they had made the rating with their melanomas in mind. One year later each patient's clinical status was evaluated. Patients who had low scores (low ratings of the need for adjustment) were clinically worse off at the one-year follow-up than patients with high scores. This result seems

**FIGURE 7–9**
Systolic blood pressures for hypertensives who were given relaxation training and for an untreated control group. Blood pressure readings were taken during six time periods beginning with 7:31 to 9:30 a.m. (adapted from Agras, Taylor, Kraemer, Allen, and Schneider, *Archives of General Psychiatry, 37,* p. 861. (c) 1980 American Medical Association)

consistent with the view that subjects who score low on the scale are using denial or repression of the impact of the disease (lack of concern), whereas those who report a need for more adjustment are more realistic in their appraisal of the illness.

A study by Greer and Morris (1975) suggests that the way people deal with one strong emotion, anger, may be particularly important. The study dealt with the relationship between personality and breast cancer in women. The day before undergoing exploratory surgery to determine whether their tumors were malignant, the women were interviewed and took psychological tests. The women whose tumors turned out to be malignant seemed either to express anger too directly or to bottle it up too tightly. The researchers who conducted the psychological interviews and administered the tests could not know whether a given woman's tumor was malignant or benign. They—and the subjects—were "blind" with regard to the outcomes of the operations. Although there were significant differences in anger between the women with malignant and benign tumors, there were no significant differences in other variables, such as intelligence and depression.

Another hypothesis that is being investigated concerns the relationship between depression and cancer. In one study, the MMPI was administered to over 2000 middle-aged employed men. Seventeen years later only the MMPI Depression score was associated with increased risk of death due to cancer (Shekelle and others, 1981). Death from cancer was not associated with scores on any of the other standard scales of the MMPI. Whether psychological depression can be described as a direct or indirect cause of increased risk of death from cancer was not answered by this study. To answer that question we would need more information about the biology of psychological depression and its relationship to the growth of cancer cells.

Though we are a long way from identifying a "cancer-prone personality" or using psychological methods in treating cancers, the increasing attention being given to the relationships between personality and cancer is encouraging (Cox, 1984). One of the greatest needs in cancer research is for longitudinal studies that begin before people develop cancer symptoms. Obviously, such studies are difficult to conduct because no one can tell in advance that a person will develop a malignancy. The ideal study would be one in which a large representative sample of apparently healthy people is assessed psychologically and then followed up to determine which individuals develop cancer and whether its incidence can be predicted by psychological data collected before the cancer was identified.

The evidence implicating psychological factors in cancer is still tentative; similar emotional states have been associated with a variety of physical disorders. In much of the available research, methodological limitations make it dangerous to draw firm conclusions. Many studies are characterized by an inadequate or inappropriate control group, vagueness in the definition of psychological factors, use of psychological tests and questionnaires that have been inadequately validated, or dependence on the recollections of patients who already have cancer. Improvements in research methodology may help clarify a number of questions regarding the relationship between psychological factors and cancer.

## Headaches

*My problem was migraine headaches, which threatened to ruin my career. I had gone to several New York specialists, paying the last one six hundred dollars . . . "It is the imponderable that causes much illness," said Draper. Draper eventually psychoanalyzed me and helped me discover and understand the stresses and strains that produced the headaches. Once I faced up to them, the migraines disappeared . . . He was a seminal influence because having discovered that I had been launched in life as a package of fears, he tried to convince me that all fears were illusory. (Douglas, 1974, excerpted from pp. 177–182)*

Few of us would have predicted that the most significant influence in the life of a Supreme Court justice would be that of a psychoanalyst. However, as Justice William O. Douglas' autobiographical account makes clear, his relationship with the psychoanalyst, George Draper, made a unique contribution to his personal development that was highly valued decades later. The stresses and strains mentioned by Justice Douglas came about because of interactions between his particular personality (his needs, motivations, and concerns) and the situations of his life.

Headaches may be the most commonly reported bodily complaint. Every year an estimated 80 percent of Americans suffer from at least one headache, and 10 to 20 percent go to a physician with headaches as their primary complaint. Headaches also are a major reason given for absenteeism from work or avoidance of other undesired social or personal activities (Thompson, 1982). The majority of headaches are not associated with significant organic disease (Thompson, 1982).

The pain of a headache has three components.

1. Physiological changes (usually either muscular contractions or blood vessel dilation)
2. The subjective experience of pain (aching, distress, fatigue, and so on)

3. Behavior motivated by the pain (for example, pill taking, withdrawal from family and social activities, absence from work)

A number of psychological factors affect the degree of correlation between these three components and the effectiveness of treatment. There are wide differences in people's sensitivity to the physiological changes that signal the beginning of a headache. The experience of pain does not always correspond closely with the actual amount of muscle tension present.

**Tension headaches,** distinguished by changes in skeletal muscles, are probably the most common form of head pain. The person reports an aching, dull, pressing feeling; the scalp may feel tender if pressed with the hand; and there are persistent sensations of band-like pain or tightness in the head. Tension headaches develop gradually and may last for hours or weeks.

The exact cause of tension headaches is unclear, but they often seem to occur in response to stress. States of prolonged chronic anxiety are common among headache sufferers, and antianxiety drugs are helpful in providing relief. If stress is related to tension headaches, training in how to handle stress should reduce discomfort. Because the experience of stress is such a personal thing, an individual might be helped by achieving a better understanding of the cognitions (specific worries and preoccupations) involved in headaches.

One experiment attempted to accomplish just that (Holroyd and others, 1977). Tension-headache sufferers who seemed organically healthy participated in a cognitive training program in which it was emphasized that disturbing emotional and behavioral responses are a direct result of maladaptive cognitions. The headache sufferers were encouraged to attribute the cause of their headache to relatively specific cognitions (for example, exaggerating the dangers connected with a specific event). The program also dealt with the cues that trigger tension and anxiety, how anxiety can be dealt with, and the thoughts that precede headaches. Emphasis was placed on the value of monitoring one's own thoughts, being alert for thoughts that arouse strong negative emotions, and replacing them with adaptive ones. For example, when your car will not start in the morning, it is more adaptive to look under the hood or call a taxi than to bang on the steering wheel or burst into tears. The training program directed attention to such questions as "What am I thinking about that induces stress?" and "What are the facts?" Participants were taught to talk to themselves: "Calm down, concentrate on the present—there is no point in catastrophizing."

Tension-headache sufferers who receive this cognitive training were compared with those who did not (see Figure 7–10). The results show that ratings of headache severity were similar for the experimental and control groups at the outset of the experiment. During the training, the experimental group reported that the severity of their headaches declined. This reduction was maintained both immediately after the program had ended and in a later follow-up.

**Migraine headaches,** the type that brought Justice Douglas to Dr. Draper, are headaches that are localized on one side or on the front of the head. They are severe, tend to recur, and are often accompanied by a variety of somatic symptoms. The throbbing, pulsating pain may last for several hours. Nausea and vomiting are common. In some cases, the dilated cranial artery is visible and tender. The cause of the dilation is not known, and there is usually no permanent structural damage. The cranial arteries of people who suffer from migraines seem to be more responsive than those of other people. Unlike tension headaches, migraines are usually preceded by a sensory, motor, or mood disturbance, called an *aura*. There may be ringing in the ears; tingling, numbness, or weakness of a limb; extreme sensitivity to light; visual blurring; distorted depth perception; nausea; or unaccountable emotional changes. The blood vessels constrict and then dilate. Many migraine sufferers have a family history of such headaches, but whether this is due to heredity or to common living experiences is unclear. Migraine attacks may begin with stressful life changes such as puberty, going to college, or starting a job. A person's migraine attacks are often

**FIGURE 7–10**
Effects on the incidence of tension headache of a training program for coping with stress. (From Holroyd et al., 1977, p. 128)

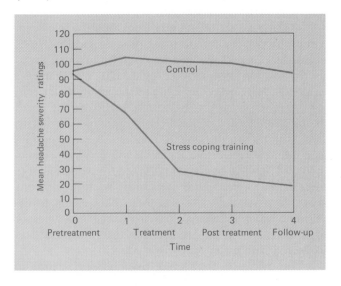

triggered by particular types of events, moods, and experiences. Table 7–4 lists some migraine triggers.

People with migraines have been described as perfectionistic and driving—"I had to get it done," "I was trying to get all these things accomplished"—and the headaches typically occur after the individual has completed a project that is to be evaluated as a success or failure. Some migraine-prone individuals appear outwardly calm and composed, but seem to be hiding anxiety and anger over their inability to achieve perfection.

A published report about a 38-year-old woman with a long history of painful migraines is particularly interesting because it combines features of assertiveness training and cognitive training with an emphasis on personal insight (Lambley, 1976). The patient seemed to have little ability either to assert herself or to express strong feelings like anger. Her treatment consisted of three phases. During Phase A, she and her therapist worked on exercises designed to increase her level of assertiveness. Behavioral rehearsal of self-assertion occupied most of these therapy sessions. During Phase B, the patient's husband agreed to be supportive of her self-assertion at home, and he was taught ways of reinforcing the desired behavior. During Phase BC, as the husband's cooperation continued, the therapist helped the patient explore the relationship between the migraine headaches and her inhibition of anger and resentment. This period was marked by gains in psychodynamic insight into her difficulty in handling negative emotions. During the therapy the patient recorded the intensity of her headaches on a 5-point scale. Figure 7–11 summarizes the changes that took place during the three phases of therapy and upon follow-up. The assertiveness training did not lead to a decrease in headache intensity, but the husband's reinforcement efforts appeared to bear fruit. The greatest decrease in headache intensity came in Phase BC, which emphasized the patient's acquisition of insight.

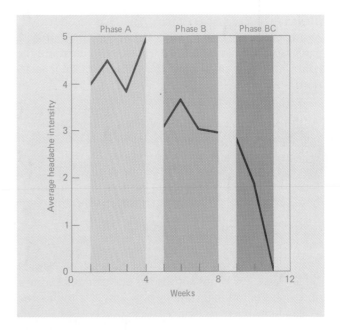

**FIGURE 7-11**
Average weekly intensity of migraine attacks during therapy. (Based on Lambley, 1976, *163*, 61–64 in *Journal of Nervous and Mental Disease*, Williams and Wilkins)

Nine months later the patient had been completely free of severe attacks for 5 months.

Migraine headaches often respond positively to drugs that constrict the arteries in the scalp. Psychotherapists have observed significant improvement in some people who suffer from chronic headaches, but little or no improvement in people who have migraines only occasionally. Behavior therapy, including relaxation, densensitization, and assertiveness training, helps a significant number of headache sufferers. Another helpful technique is biofeedback.

## Allergies

Allergies are a common problem, affecting at least 15 percent of the population. Normally, when an **allergen,** a substance capable of causing an allergic reaction, enters the body, the antibodies produced by the immune system attack it. An allergy is an "abnormal" reaction to an ordinarily harmless substance; it is frequently described as immunity "gone wrong." While most research on allergies is directed toward understanding components of the immune system that are involved in the allergic response, recently there has been interest in the psychological as well as the physical aspects of allergies. One finding of this new line of research is that a person's total stress load, as well as exposure and adaptation to allergens, contributes to allergic reactions

□ **TABLE 7–4**
Migraine Triggers

Anxiety, stress, worry
Menstruation
Oral contraceptives
Glare, dazzling lights
Physical exertion
Lack of sleep or excessive sleep
Certain foods and alcoholic beverages
Weather or temperature changes
Pungent odors
Exposure to high altitude

(Bell, 1982). Because asthma is one of the oldest forms of chronic allergy and has been studied most from a psychological standpoint, we will use it to illustrate the contribution of psychological factors to allergic reactions.

**Asthma** People who have *asthma* chronically wheeze, cough, and have difficulty breathing. The cause of asthma is unknown, though it appears to be an allergic condition that results in reversible obstruction of the bronchial passages. To the patient, asthma means labored breathing, a feeling of constriction in the chest, gasping, and apprehension. About 30 out of 1,000 people in the United States have asthma.

Asthma patients often report that intense emotional states accompany acute attacks of labored breathing. This is not surprising: one can quickly measure one's emotional state by how easy it is to breathe. It has long been recognized that psychological variables contribute to asthma attacks. According to one theory, asthmatics share a common personality type and similar unconscious conflicts. However, there is little evidence to indicate that asthmatics are psychologically any more deviant than the general population. Another theory holds that characteristic personality features are the result, rather than the cause, of the restricted activities of severe asthmatics. According to this view, people become more dependent and fearful because they are asthmatic, not the other way around. Alexander and Solanch (1981), who have worked with asthmatics of all ages, have provided the following sketch of what chronic airway obstruction can do to the asthma sufferer and his or her family.

> *Children with asthma tend to grow up watching other children play from the living-room side of the front window. Poor self-concepts are common. Academic and social development is often detrimentally affected due to the amount of time lost from school and the restricted and specialized contacts with agemates. These youngsters face both peers and adults who are variously overindulgent or lacking sensitive understanding of their difficulties. A chronic illness such as asthma can cause a child to react with shame, embarrassment, and/or demandingness to the extreme. . . . Parents may feel responsible, guilty, and helpless, and at other times angry and resentful. Such feelings can lead to very inconsistent child-rearing practices. A child with asthma can most certainly learn to manipulate others with illness or use sickness to avoid unpleasant activities or situations. Because asthma can be physically restricting, it is often difficult for the asthmatic child to discover his or her true capabilities. Certainly, maladaptive and inappropriate behavior patterns can develop as child and family struggle with the ravages of this disorder. . . .*

> *The late-onset (adolescent or adult) asthma sufferer faces a somewhat different set of problems because the asthma usually disrupts a life style that has become more or less fixed. . . . Like the youthful sufferer, the late-onset asthmatic may become frightened of the symptoms and often very scared by and concerned over the side effects of medications. For the families of both young and old, the financial burdens encountered in continually fighting asthma are almost always oppressive.* (Alexander and Solanch, 1981, pp. 11–12)

Although the search for the cause and cure of asthma continues, a number of psychological and situational factors that seem to maintain or worsen asthmatic attacks have been studied successfully. One group of investigators has given special attention to the relationship between panic and fear, on the one hand, and the severity of asthmatic attacks, on the other (Dirks and others, 1978). To test the hypothesis that panic and fear increase the severity of asthma, the researchers constructed a panic–fear scale whose items were found to correlate with subjective symptoms that accompany asthmatic attacks. People who get high panic–fear scores tend to describe themselves as panicky, frightened, worried, afraid to be left alone, scared, and nervous.

Dirks and his coworkers found that asthmatics who scored high on the panic–fear scale required stronger doses of medication to relieve asthmatic symptoms and longer periods of hospitalization than low scorers did. High scorers tended to exaggerate their subjective symptoms and to report more physical distress. They also seemed to lack adaptive ways of dealing with their illness; instead, they tended to respond to airway obstruction with feelings of helplessness and panic. One interesting outcome of this research was the finding that in certain respects high- and low-scoring asthmatics were more similar than those with moderate panic–fear scores. Both of these groups tended to have higher rehospitalization rates than the moderate scorers.

The value of objective study of clinical cases is suggested by an experiment conducted with asthmatic children in Denver (Purcell and others, 1969). Parents of asthmatic children have been described as overcontrolling people who create an emotionally tense home environment. Clinical evidence has indicated that removing the children from the home and placing them in an institutional setting often reduces their asthmatic symptoms. Purcell and his colleagues wished to discover the effects of separating asthmatic children from their families while keeping the environment relatively constant.

The experimental design involved an initial qualification period during which asthmatic symptoms were assessed, a preseparation period, a separation period, and reunion. During the two-week separation period the child's family lived in a nearby motel or hotel and had no contact with the asthmatic child, who remained within the family home, playing and attending school as usual. A substitute parent cared for the child at home during the separation period. Wheezing declined precipitously during the separation and increased again during reunion (see Figure 7–12). The home environment thus appears to be conducive to asthmatic symptoms, although the psychological mechanism involved is unclear. One possibility is that the breathing obstruction that is characteristic of asthma may be produced by stress-induced activity of the autonomic nervous system, which stimulates mucus secretion, increased blood flow, and constriction of the bronchial tubes. Situational variables and personal vulnerability appear to combine in producing symptoms of asthma.

The importance of psychological factors in the clinical course of asthma is suggested by a recent study of children who died of asthmatic attacks compared to children who did not (Strunk and others, 1985). Especially associated with the deaths were depressive symptoms in the children and conflicts between the children's parents and medical personnel treating the children. The evidence suggested that the psychological features of the cases that resulted in death were not due only to the severity of the disease. More psy-

chological disturbance was noted both in the children who died and in their families.

## Gastrointestinal Disorders

**Gastrointestinal disorders** are abnormalities of the digestive system. The number of television commercials for stomach remedies clearly indicates that many people have trouble with their digestive processes. One such disorder, **diarrhea,** has plagued troops going into battle for as long as wars have been fought. Scientists still do not know exactly how emotional processes are linked to pathological changes in the gastrointestinal tract. There is evidence that anger and hostility increase stomach acidity and that gastric symptoms commonly follow worry, business reverses, family quarrels, and other emotionally disturbing experiences.

Many studies of stress and gastrointestinal disease relate to **ulcers,** which are open sores in the skin or on some mucous membrane such as the lining of the stomach or intestine. Ulcerated tissue disintegrates, and the sores often discharge pus. Peptic ulcers include ulcers in the stomach (gastric ulcers) and in the first part of the small intestine (duodenal ulcers). The incidence of peptic ulcers ebbs and rises. It rose in the 1950s but has declined recently—a seeming paradox if our society is, as many people believe, more stressful now than it was in the past (Murray, 1982).

Cases of peptic ulcer often highlight the interacting roles of a number of relevant variables. The following case of duodenal ulcers in one member of a pair of twins is of particular interest.

*John M., an identical twin, developed a series of severe ulcer symptoms, including bleeding, when he was 46 years old. His condition deteriorated to the point where he required hospitalization. He was described as passive, shy, dependent, and anxious. His wife had had several near-psychotic episodes, and John's ulcer symptoms developed about the time she was experiencing a particularly frightening breakdown. She was having an affair with another man and had threatened to kill her children.*

*John's twin brother Fred was studied because some clinical workers have speculated that psychophysiological disorders may be attributed partly to hereditary features. As in many cases of identical twins, Fred's personality was remarkably similar to John's; he was also shy and dependent. However, he was completely free of ulcer symptoms. The twins had been inseparable until they were 25, when Fred met his future wife; John married three years later. The major difference in the lives of the twins after age 25 was their marriages. Because John, the ulcer victim, had married a disturbed woman, he was forced to live under great tension, which increased his*

**FIGURE 7–12**
Mean daily scores for clinical evidence of wheezing during each period in the Denver asthma study. Reprinted by permisson of Elsevier Science Publishing Co., Inc. from *The effect of asthma in children of experimental separation from the family,* from K. Purcell, K. Brady, H. Schal, J. Muser, L. Molk, N. Gordon, and J. Means, by *Psychosomatic Medicine, 31,* 144–164. Copyright (c) 1969 by the American Psychosomatic Society, Inc.

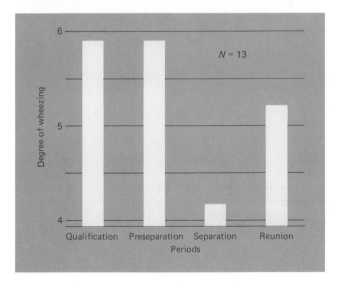

*anxiety level. Fred, on the other hand, had married a motherly woman who managed the family affairs dependably. The ulcer-free identical twin had apparently found a psychosocial situation in which his passivity and dependency needs could be gratified, while his brother found only frustration in his marriage.* (Gottschalk, 1978)

Although John's case does not seem to support a genetic interpretation of duodenal ulcers, the situation is, in fact, equivocal. Ulcers occur mainly in people with high levels of blood pepsinogen (a gastric secretion). Both John and Fred had high blood pepsinogen levels. If they had swapped wives, John might have been cured while Fred got the ulcers. Thus, heredity may be a predisposing factor in ulcer cases, but the level of stress experienced by the individual may determine whether structural damage actually occurs.

In many instances it is impossible to say that psychological stress is the only cause of a physical problem. Yet the high blood pepsinogen levels of both twins and the contrast between their social situations seem consistent with the hypothesis that life experiences contribute to chronic physiological reactions that result in tissue damage. Studies of adolescents have shown that a recent separation or loss is often associated with the onset of peptic ulcers in predisposed individuals (Ackerman and others, 1981).

### Rheumatoid Arthritis

**Rheumatoid arthritis** is a chronic disease of the joints (usually small joints like the wrist) that consists of an inflammatory response involving the immune system. At present rheumatoid arthritis has no known cause or cure. Recently psychologists have become involved in research on the onset and course of the disease. One limitation of this research is that subjects usually have not been studied psychologically until after they become patients. As a consequence, it is difficult to conclude that there is a set of personality characteristics that predispose a person to develop arthritis. It is always possible that certain characteristics emerge after a person has acquired a clinical condition.

There is evidence that many victims of rheumatoid arthritis experience significant psychological stress. One study comparing rheumatoid arthritis patients with matched controls found that the arthritis patients had experienced more life events with potential long-term emotional threat in the 12 months preceding the onset of symptoms (Baker, 1982). Only 4 percent of the arthritis patients failed to report either a negative relationship with their mother or a stressful event before the onset of symptoms. Negative relationships with mothers were particularly prevalent among the female

arthritis patients. Studies of both adult and child arthritis patients suggest that disturbed interpersonal relationships and lowered self-esteem may play significant roles in the onset of the condition, and that the availability of social support (for example, a caring spouse) has a favorable effect on its clinical course (Anderson and others, 1985).

## ■ SOMATOFORM DISORDERS

So far we have been dealing with psychological and social factors associated with actual diagnosed physical conditions. Many of the bodily complaints that physicians are asked to treat suggest physical pathology, but no actual impairment can be found. Although failure to diagnose a case medically might be due to a doctor's lack of knowledge or to a faulty laboratory test, in a large group of cases psychological rather than physiological factors are responsible for the symptoms. These cases, which do not seem to be produced consciously, are characterized in DSM-III-R as **somatoform** disorders. This category includes both somatization and conversion disorders (to be discussed shortly) and psychogenic pain disorders and hypochondriasis.

Severe prolonged pain either without organic symptoms or greatly in excess of what might be expected to accompany organic symptoms is classified as a **psychogenic pain disorder**. There is often a temporal relationship between the occurrence of an actual, threatened, or fantasized interpersonal loss and complaints of pain. The complaints may be used to evoke social responses, such as attention, from others. **Hypochondriasis** is diagnosed if a person shows an unrealistic fear of disease in spite of reassurance that his or her social or occupational functioning is not impaired. Hypochondriacs have an obsessive preoccupation and concern with the condition of their bodily organs and continually worry about their health (see Figure 7–13). They tend to misunderstand the nature and significance of physiological activity and to exaggerate symptoms when they occur (Kellner, 1985).

### Somatization Disorder

**Somatization disorders** are marked by multiple somatic complaints that are recurrent or chronic. This condition is often referred to as *Briquet's syndrome* because a physician by that name described it in detail in 1859. The most common complaints are headaches, fatigue, heart palpitations, fainting spells, nausea, vomiting, abdominal pains, bowel troubles, allergies, and menstrual and sexual problems. With this wide assortment of complaints, it is not surprising that somatizing

**FIGURE 7-13**
This woman seems to be an unusually well-organized hypochondriac. (*Prevention,* September 1982, p. 75)

" THE DOCTOR WILL EXPECT TO HEAR MY SYMPTOMS. "

patients are constantly going to the doctor, changing doctors, and undergoing surgery. Figure 7–14 compares the frequency of major surgical procedures for patients who were classified as somatizers and for normal controls.

Patients with somatization disorders believe that they are sickly, provide long and detailed histories in support of their belief, and take large quantities of medicines. The following case is typical.

*A 74-year-old woman had complained of severe headaches and weakness that persisted for more than 6 months. Her medical history revealed numerous diagnostic evaluations over the course of her life. At the time she was seen for her complaints of headaches and weakness, she was taking six prescription medications regularly as well as several painkillers. She had had over 30 operations often for vague complaints.*

*Her physical examination showed a thin, downcast woman, who seemed remarkably well despite her medical ailments. With the exception of the numerous surgical scars all over her body, her examination yielded results within normal limits. This woman's remarkable medical history and her journey through the medical system for over 50 years leave little doubt that she had an unrecognized somatization disorder. (based on Quill, 1985)*

Almost always, the chronic multiple complaints of somatizers are accompanied by a characteristic personality pattern and by difficulties in social relationships.

**FIGURE 7-14**
The complaints of somatizing patients often lead to unnecessary surgery. These two figures compare the number and location of major surgical procedures in fifty somatizing patients and fifty control subjects. Three times as much body tissue was removed from the somatizing patients as from the controls. (Woodruff, Goodwin, and Guze, 1974, p. 67)

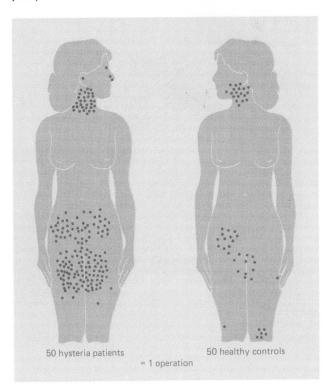

50 hysteria patients              50 healthy controls
= 1 operation

They share many of the features of histrionic personality disorders, including a self-centered attitude and exaggerated expressions of emotion (see Figure 7–15). Anxiety and depression are common features, as is manipulativeness, which may take the form of suicide threats and attempts. Somatizers impress people as being immature and overly excitable.

The complaints in somatization disorders are usually presented in a dramatic, vague, or exaggerated way. Somatizers tend to use vivid images in describing events and their reactions to them. For example:

- □ I wake up in the morning stiff as a board.
- □ My heart felt as if iron bands were being tightened around it.
- □ I throw up every half hour.
- □ I can't even take liquids.
- □ I feel as weak as a cat.
- □ I really can't take it much longer.

Somatization disorders usually have long medical histories that go back at least to early adulthood. They seem to occur mainly in women; approximately 1 percent of women have the condition. It is not uncommon for a family to have more than one somatizer. Since people who are classified as having a somatizing disorder tend to be suggestible, the high prevalence of the disorder in certain families may reflect the influence of a somatizing parent (usually the mother) rather than heredity.

The vagueness of somatization complaints makes it difficult to do good research on the disorder (for example, the researcher is frequently left to wonder about possible organic causes of the symptoms). One interesting approach to this problem defined somatization disorder somewhat arbitrarily, as a characteristic of workers with a lifetime average of two or more sick leaves per year. Somatizers had repeated brief sick leaves with complaints of headache, backache, and abdominal distress. Frequency of somatization was associated with high divorce rates and low occupational

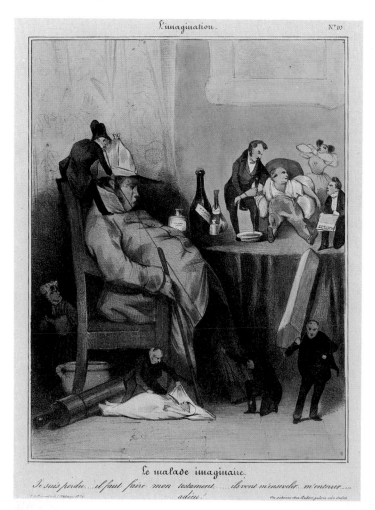

**FIGURE 7–15**
This lithograph by Honoré Daumier, titled "The Imaginary Illness," illustrates the self-centeredness and demanding behavior that may be seen in some somatization disorders. (National Library of Medicine)

status. There seemed to be two types of somatizers: Type 1, high-frequency somatizers whose complaints emphasized abdominal and back problems; and Type 2, workers who described diverse symptoms at each medical consultation and whose disability was less severe than that of Type 1 somatizers. Type 2 somatizers tended to come from families in which alcohol abuse and petty criminality were relatively common among males. Understanding of somatization disorder may improve when the heterogeneous group of somatizers can be subdivided into specific types (Sigvardsson and others, 1984; Cloninger and others, 1984; Bohman and others, 1984).

## Conversion Disorders

People with **conversion disorders** report that they have lost part or all of some basic bodily function. The disturbance does not seem to be under voluntary control and cannot be explained in terms of the principles of medical science. Paralysis, blindness, deafness, and difficulty in walking are among the symptoms reported by these patients. The onset of symptoms in conversion disorders often follows a stressful experience and may be quite sudden. Psychodynamic theorists believe that the symptom represents an underlying psychological conflict.

Conversion symptoms seem to be naive inventions developed without regard for the actual facts of anatomy. In the case of **glove anesthesia,** for example, the individual may be unable to feel anything in one hand, although the arm has normal sensation. This is anatomically impossible. The sensory nerve supply to this part of the body is organized so that glove anesthesia could not be a result of a neurological disorder.

Although conversion symptoms often seem to appear for no apparent reason, they can frequently be traced to specific precipitating events. The problem in the following case was the complaint of blindness by a 28-year-old man soon after he had been in a minor automobile accident. Even though the only visible effects of the accident were a few minor scratches, the man stated that he could no longer see. Medical studies revealed no sign of any physical injury. The accident had occurred while the patient was driving to visit his wife, who had just given birth to their first child. In an interview he stated that he would probably be blind for the rest of his life and that he should divorce his wife in order to avoid burdening her with a blind husband.

*The patient was an only child. The father was physically of slight build, of a meek and dependent type of personality, economically unsuccessful. The mother was the direct antithesis, ample of body and "strong" in character. . . . [The patient's] feelings toward them were ambivalent. He liked the sympathetic and kind father, but pitied his weakness and dependence. He respected the mother, but at the same time hated her and revolted against her domineering attitude. Fearing a fate similar to that of the father, he had determined never to get married. Seeking independence and freedom, he decided to cut away from home and make his own way. He adhered to his original decision not to get married, although . . . he was attracted to members of the opposite sex. He had several affairs which invariably took the same pattern. As long as it was a matter of friendship only or uncompromising sexual contacts, he continued the relationship, but as soon as any hint of marriage appeared, he found some means of dissolving the contact. His present wife was, of course, the last of these affairs. He became very much attached to her and a unique but understandable relationship was established between them. She was very similar in character to his mother, or at least she appeared so to him, and early in their contacts he began to seek her advice in business affairs, and let her make decisions for him. The more he did so, the greater became his discomfort in her presence, but nevertheless he could not find the necessary strength to break the relationship. In the course of events she suggested they get married and in a weak moment he acquiesced. At his instigation they had decided that care should be taken to avoid children.*

*About two years after marriage she became pregnant. A quarrel ensued and he accused her of deliberately allowing this to happen. All through her pregnancy . . . he had hoped that the pregnancy would not mature. . . . He still had hopes of someday breaking away from his wife, but . . . the birth of the child would place an inseparable barrier in this way. When she was taken to the hospital for delivery he spent a few days in his home in great anxiety, conscious of fears that something would happen, either to the wife or the child. Then the news came that he was the father of a normal boy, and that both the child and his wife were in good condition. On his way to the hospital after this news, the accident occurred which resulted in his blindness.* (Malamud, 1944, pp. 834–836)

Complicating the task of diagnosing conversion disorders is the fact that at times they cannot easily be distinguished from somatically rooted symptoms. One of the characteristic features of conversion disorders has been termed *la belle indifférence.* Whereas the individual may experience intense anxiety in other areas of life, his or her lack of concern about what seems to be an incapacitating physical disturbance is remarkable (Ford and Folks, 1985).

Clinical conversion cases usually involve a single disturbance during a given period. Different bodily sites might be affected in subsequent episodes. As mentioned earlier, the episodes tend to follow frustrating or challenging experiences. The symptoms often allow the person to escape from the situation through physical incapacity. When the pressures of these experiences wane, the physical symptoms weaken. Secondary gain may also occur when the person derives something from a physical symptom (such as attention, affection, or a pension) that he or she might not get otherwise.

Because histrionic tendencies and excitability are characteristic of people who have these bodily reactions, their symptoms often tend to be highly dramatic as well as incapacitating. The drama is perhaps most intense in cases of **group hysteria,** outbreaks of conversion symptoms among people who live or work together (see Box 7–1). The mass outbreak of hysteria is a vivid illustration of what social psychologists call group contagion (Colligan and others, 1982).

## ■ BOX 7–1 GROUP HYSTERIA AMONG SCHOOLCHILDREN

*Two hundred twenty-four elementary-school students assembled in their school auditorium in Norwood, Mass., on the morning of May 21, 1979. The program, a play by the sixth graders honoring their graduation, marked the last formal gathering of the student body for the year. The performance came to an abrupt halt. A sixth-grade boy, a class leader, experienced dizziness, fell from the stage, lacerated his chin, and bled profusely. As a few teachers assisted the boy, several students became ill, and their symptoms began to spread rapidly. First, weakness, dizziness, chills, and faintness developed in four girls and one boy, all sixth graders. Then four more sixth-grade girls complained of the same symptoms. As more and more children became ill, teachers hurriedly dismissed the assembly. They directed the afflicted students to the auditorium floor and covered them with blankets. Alarmed and bewildered by these events, school officials summoned the fire department. The firemen, suspecting an environmental contaminant, ordered immediate evacuation of the building.*

*Authorities then moved the stricken children to one area of the school grounds. Sirens of approaching vehicles intensified the chaos. Once police arrived, they directed ambulances to transport the children to a local hospital. Evacuation of the building and isolation of the afflicted students, however, failed to contain the spread of illness; the symptoms struck a new child every few minutes. The illness spread so rapidly that the number of afflicted children exhausted the capacity of the available vehicles. With 34 of the more severely ill already hospitalized, the hospital dispatched a team of physicians and nurses to treat another 40 or 50 mildly symptomatic children lying on the lawn. As the physicians examined and reassured these patients, their symptoms began to subside. Within four hours of its precipitous beginning, the epidemic was over . . .*

*During the outbreak, rumors spread rapidly throughout the school and the surrounding community. For example, two priests arrived to*

FIGURE 7–16
Emergency workers examine one of the afflicted students. (Ted Fitzgerald)

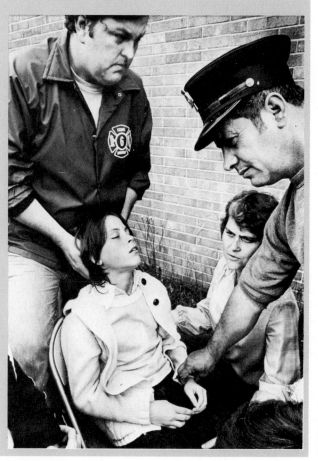

attend the families and friends of the "deceased" as a result of a rumor that 12 children had died of food poisoning. Another rumor circulated among the students that the boy who lacerated his chin underwent open-heart surgery when hospitalized. Mosquito spray, toxic fumes, gas leaks, water contamination, infectious agents, and psychological influences included some of the causes of the epidemic proffered by both professional and laymen. As the epidemic subsided, the more exaggerated rumors subsided. The cause of the outbreak, however, remained controversial in the community: one segment of the population thought "it was only in their minds," others insisted "it was something harmful in the air." (Small and Nicholi, 1982, p. 721)

Although most instances of group hysteria are treated somewhat like curiosities, the Norwood incident was investigated from a research standpoint. The research had to do with two questions: Were the hysterical symptoms related to events in the current lives of the children? Were the symptoms related to events experienced earlier in their lives?

One of the striking features of the Norwood incident was that the sixth grade had by far the highest number of hysterical cases (the preponderant percentage being girls). The researchers (Small and Nicholi, 1982) found that

1. A few days prior to the epidemic, local newspapers had reported that the school principal, who was respected and admired by both children and parents, would be transferred to another school. Many of the families had become disturbed about his transfer and signed a petition protesting his departure.
2. The epidemic began during the sixth graders' play, which marked their impending graduation and departure from school.
3. The sixth graders had planned a camping trip to follow graduation; those attending would sleep away from home for an entire week, many for the first time.

Thus, the sixth graders experienced or were about to experience the loss of their principal, separation from familiar school surroundings, and an exciting trip that included a new experience for many. Most children take such experiences in their stride. Did other features exist in the backgrounds of the affected children that, within the current climate of loss and change, made them more vulnerable to symptoms of mass hysteria?

By administering questionnaires to parents and children, the researchers were able to make some valuable comparisons between the children who required hospitalization and those who did not. They found that 47 percent of the hospitalized children had lost a parent, whereas only 10 percent of those who were not hospitalized had, and that 74 percent of the hospitalized children had experienced a death in the family, whereas only 39 percent of the nonhospitalized children had had such an experience.

The Norwood epidemic had several characteristics that are typical of group hysteria, particularly psychological stress, which in this case took the form of anticipated loss. In addition, there was a significant link between previous loss and hysterical symptoms. Although this does not prove that early loss causes hysterical symptoms, it does suggest that such loss may be an important vulnerability factor in hysteria.

# ■ FACTITIOUS DISORDERS AND MALINGERING

Although somatoform disorders and problems that have traditionally been described as psychophysiological (for example, asthma and peptic ulcers) are different in a number of respects, they have in common the fact that the individual assumes the role of a patient—someone who receives attention and care. Another group of conditions that are characterized by the same feature is **factitious disorders.** However, in these conditions physical and psychological symptoms are voluntarily self-induced by the patient. They may involve a total fabrication or an exaggeration of a preexisting condition.

In a factitious disorder the only apparent goal is the desire to assume the role of patient. The person often has a history of uncontrollable lying, demands for attention from professional people, and dramatic accounts of vague pains. Classifying a set of symptoms as factitious may be quite difficult. The dramatic way in which the patient presents his or her problems usually arouses suspicion; however, many individuals with this disorder have managed to gather quite a bit of medical information and, as a consequence, may be good enough actors to make their symptoms seem credible.

Factitious disorders typically begin during early adulthood and are often stimulated by hospitalization for a genuine physical problem. Because of their dramatically presented but vague symptoms, individuals with factitious disorders undergo frequent hospitalizations during which unnecessary surgery may be performed. Factitious disorders are more common among men than among women.

The term **Munchausen syndrome** refers to an extreme type of factitious disorder that is marked by repeated, knowing simulation of disease for the sole purpose of obtaining medical attention. A patient with this syndrome may travel great distances to appear at hospitals with dramatic and plausible, yet false, histories that convince physicians and staff members that he or she is suffering from an acute illness. The syndrome is named after Baron von Munchausen, an eighteenth-century German cavalry officer who became legendary for concocting elaborate lies. Patients with this syndrome tell incredible tales about their medical histories. They also fake symptoms; for example, they may pretend to be in pain, put blood in a urine sample, or manipulate a thermometer to create an impression of fever. Sometimes they go even further, inflicting real injury on themselves by burning, cutting, taking dangerous drugs, or injecting foreign material into their veins. Often they persuade doctors to perform unnecessary surgery. They may spend most of their lives moving from one hospital to another, trying to be admitted. Once in a hospital, they refuse to comply with its rules and make constant demands for attention.

A particularly disturbing variant of Munchausen syndrome is one in which a mother produces symptoms of disease in her child and then presents the child for treatment. The mother's concern may be convincing because she herself feels a need to be cared for; it is as though she regards the child's body as an extension of her own. The child goes along with the mother because the relationship is so close and intense and the activity so exciting.

Having a factitious disorder is not the same thing as **malingering.** People with factitious disorders simply crave attention and want to be taken care of. Malingerers, on the other hand, seek medical care and hospitalization in order to achieve some specific goal such as compensation, a disability pension, or evasion of the police. Whereas multiple complaints and hospitalizations seem almost a continuous pattern in factitious disorders, malingering often ends abruptly when the patient gets what he or she wants. People with factitious disorders seem incapable of stopping their lying and manufacturing of symptoms, whereas malingering is an entirely conscious process. However, both of these conditions are self-induced, and both increase in response to high levels of stress.

Distinguishing factitious disorder or malingering from other conditions can be difficult. The judgment that a particular symptom is under voluntary control occasionally is made by excluding all other possible causes. Distinguishing between a factitious disorder and malingering also poses problems. When the clinician is not fully aware of the particular purpose for which the malingerer manufactures his or her symptoms, the chances of misdiagnosis increase. An act of malingering might, under certain circumstances, be considered adaptive (for example, when a prisoner of war fakes an illness), but factitious disorders are almost always seen in people with severe, lifelong personality disturbances.

## ■ STUDY OUTLINE

### CONCEPTS OF PSYCHOLOGICAL, SOCIAL, AND BODILY INTERACTION

1. During the 1930s and 1940s the **psychosomatic hypothesis,** which held that the blocking of emotional expression could lead to physical symptoms, became popular. Many psychotherapists supported the theory of **specificity,** believing that specific emotional conflicts and stresses were associated with particular physical conditions. Some adhered to the **organ-susceptibility** theory, believing that under stress a person's body would break down at its weakest point.

2. Research has shown that emotional tension influences the autonomic nervous system and the endocrine glands. Hans Selye uses the term **general adaptation syndrome** to describe the pattern of animals' reactions to continued stress. Similar increases in hormone secretions have been found in humans.

3. Contemporary clinicians emphasize the **biopsychosocial model**—they consider illness to be caused by the interaction of psychological states with social and biological variables. Through a mechanism called **homeostasis** the organism mobilizes itself to restore equilibrium in the face of environmental changes, challenges, and constraints.

### PSYCHOLOGICAL FACTORS THAT AFFECT HEALTH

1. There is a two-way connection between psychological factors and physical health. Psychological factors that play a role in physical illness include inability to adapt to new situations, inability to handle and express strong emotions, inability to interpret the environment correctly, and inability to form close personal relationships. In addition to temperament and personality, community and social factors, job demands, biological predispositions, and other factors interact to affect physical functioning.

2. Many nonbiological factors affect longevity. They include social isolation, chronic loneliness, and particularly the loss or absence of a loved one. People who are characterized by **psychological hardiness**—

have personality characteristics that make them more resistant to stress and less susceptible to illness than those who do not share this trait.

## BEHAVIORAL MEDICINE AND HEALTH PSYCHOLOGY

1. **Behavioral medicine** is concerned with helping people adopt more healthful living habits and with improving the delivery of health care. **Health psychology** seeks to prevent disease by strengthening behaviors that contribute to good health.

2. One area in which the behavioral and biomedical sciences are involved is people's awareness of their symptoms and accuracy in reporting them. Another example is the types of information given to patients and the way it is presented.

3. **Biofeedback** is used in behavioral medicine to give people control over functions that were thought to be involuntary, such as blood pressure and heart rate.

4. Animal and other studies have shown that stress, particularly with lack of social support, can lower the immune system's resistance to disease.

## PSYCHOPHYSIOLOGICAL DISORDERS

1. The term **psychophysiological disorders** refers to physical conditions in which psychologically meaningful events are closely related to bodily symptoms. They include cardiovascular disorders, cancer, headaches, allergies, gastrointestinal disorders, and rheumatoid arthritis, as well as somatoform disorders, factitious disorders, and malingering.

2. There is growing evidence that psychological and social factors play a role in **coronary heart disease.** A significant factor in heart attacks is stress. Societal and cultural differences also play a substantial role, as do occupation and separation from or loss of a loved one.

3. Some researchers have concluded that there is a heart attack-prone personality known as **Type A.** Type A individuals tend to operate under high pressure and to be very demanding both of themselves and of others. It has been found that Type A individuals show greater cardiovascular receptivity than Type B's.

4. **Hypertension** or high blood pressure has been shown to be associated with prolonged emotional arousal. Relaxation and biofeedback seem to be effective in reducing blood pressure.

5. Stress and personality are among the psychological factors that may contribute to cancer. It is thought that people who deny strong feelings are more prone to develop cancers than those who vent their emotions. Depression also seems to be associated with cancer.

6. The exact cause of headaches is unclear, but they often seem to occur in response to stress.

7. Chronic allergies such as asthma are often accompanied by intense emotional states. Among the psychological and situational factors that seem to worsen asthmatic attacks are panic and fear.

8. **Gastrointestinal disorders** such as diarrhea and ulcers appear to be caused by a number of interacting factors, including psychological stress. There is also evidence that many victims of rheumatoid arthritis experience significant psychological stress.

9. **Somatoform disorders** are disorders that take the form of bodily complaints without actual physical pathology. They include psychogenic pain disorders, hypochondrias, somatization, and conversion disorders.

10. Severe prolonged pain either without organic symptoms or greatly in excess of what might be expected to accompany organic symptoms is classified as a **psychogenic pain disorder. Hypochondriasis** is diagnosed if a person shows an unrealistic fear of disease in spite of reassurance that his or her functioning is not impaired.

11. **Somatization disorders** are marked by recurrent, chronic somatic complaints that are usually presented in a dramatic, vague, or exaggerated way. The complaints of somatizers tend to be accompanied by a characteristic personality pattern and by difficulties in social relationships.

12. People with **conversion disorders** report that they have lost part or all of some basic bodily function. The disturbance does not seem to be under voluntary control and cannot be explained in terms of the principles of medical science. Conversion episodes tend to follow frustrating or challenging experiences and allow the person to escape from the situation through physical incapacity.

13. **Factitious disorders** are voluntarily self-induced by a person for the sole purpose of assuming the role of patient. **Malingerers,** on the other hand, seek medical care and hospitalization in order to achieve some specific goal such as compensation or a disability pension.

# 8

# SEXUAL VARIATIONS AND DISORDERS

*In the afternoon, viewers may be titillated with heavy breathing and heavy hissing; at night, stronger allusions to more intimate acts prevail. (Greenberg and others, 1981, p. 88)*

Every weekday, six hours per day, the three major U.S. television networks present a dozen or more soap operas that are watched by 5 to 10 million people. During each hour of viewing time, petting, intercourse, and other sexual acts are referred to at least twice in the average program. Shorter 20-minute programs have an even higher frequency, averaging 1.5 references during each segment. These sexual references run the gamut from petting to intercourse to rape. Most often, unmarried characters are involved. The cartoon in Figure 8–1 illustrates the content of a typical soap opera.

Surprisingly, even everyday foods like Graham crackers and Kellogg's corn flakes had their origins in sexual concerns (Money, 1984). The Reverend Sylvester Graham, author of "A Lecture to Young Men" (1834), was concerned about the effects of masturbation, sexual fantasies, and lust on health. He developed Graham crackers as the ultimate food to discourage sexual feelings. For similar reasons John H. Kellogg, a prominent abdominal surgeon, developed corn flakes as part of his doctrine of diet, exercise, and abstinence from sex. Kellogg believed so strongly in the healthful effects of sexual abstinence that his own marriage was never consummated. Corn flakes were developed as a food that would extinguish sexual desire. These ideas, which focus on the bad effects of semen loss, especially through masturbation, and of sexual thoughts and fantasies, can be traced all the way back to the ancient Greeks.

**FIGURE 8–1**
*Journal of Communication, 31,* p. 89 (Summer 1981), Copyright (c) Arthur Asa Berger.

## ■ CHANGING VIEWS OF SEXUAL BEHAVIOR

Although sexual behavior has never ceased to be a topic of great interest to many people, over the centuries ideas about sexuality and sexual deviance have undergone drastic changes. During the fourth century B.C. the Greeks regarded sex as a pleasurable part of nature, to be enjoyed with partners of either sex. This open view of sexuality contrasts sharply with the prevailing view during the period between the fall of Rome and the fifteenth century, when church authorities were obsessed with the notion of sex as a sin. During that period many thousands of Europeans were tortured into confessing erotic encounters with the devil, after which they were publicly burned alive. Entire villages in southern Germany and Switzerland were exterminated in this way.

The price that women had to pay to be rescued from this fate was to renounce all sexual or erotic thoughts. By the mid-nineteenth century, the idea of women as morally pure, erotically apathetic, and sexually inert had reached a peak. Women were expected to engage in sexual behavior only as a way of satisfying their husbands and carrying out their obligation to become mothers. Despite these expectations, however, pornography, prostitution, and venereal disease flourished during the nineteenth century.

Some brave souls were willing to risk their professional careers to discuss the role of sexuality in human behavior. One of these individuals, Sigmund Freud, used material gathered from many patients to illustrate the negative effects of a repressive view of sexuality. Freud published a wealth of material on sexuality and erotic experiences and traced the sexual deviations of adults to significant events in childhood. His theories of infantile sexuality shocked many people. Although today some aspects of these theories continue to be controversial, Freud, more than any other individual, stimulated a rethinking of the role of sexual feelings in development.

Havelock Ellis was another important influence on views about sexuality. Ellis wrote books and articles that focused on the range of sexual behavior that occurred in the lives of ordinary people. He recognized that it was common for both men and women to masturbate, and emphasized the psychological rather than physical causes of many sexual problems. He believed that many groups and individuals viewed sex as a dirty topic because they were overly preoccupied with sordid tales about sexual criminals and perversions. It was Ellis who suggested that objective surveys be taken to find out what happens in ordinary sexual relationships. This useful suggestion was not acted upon until the 1940s.

# ■ GATHERING OBJECTIVE INFORMATION ABOUT SEXUAL BEHAVIOR

Scientific information about sexual behavior can be gathered in several ways. Among these are surveys, observation, and experiments.

## Surveys

**Kinsey's Survey Research**   Most of the information about the frequency of different sexual practices comes from survey research. Alfred Kinsey was one of the pioneers in this approach to the study of sexual behavior.

In 1938 Kinsey, a biologist, was asked to take charge of a new course on marriage at Indiana University and to give lectures on the biological aspects of sex and marriage. As he prepared for the course, Kinsey was amazed to find that there were only a few statistical studies on sexual behavior and no scientific data that he could pass on to students when they asked such questions as "Is masturbation harmful?" or "Is homosexuality abnormal?" In his class one night he stated that no one knew the answers to these questions because of a lack of information. He asked whether his students would be willing to submit their case histories so that scientists could discover enough about human sexual behavior to be able to answer some of these questions. Their positive response was the beginning of several important research studies and ultimately led to the establishment of the Institute for Sex Research at Indiana University.

Kinsey believed that human sexual behavior could be studied objectively. To find out about people's sex lives, he interviewed them about a wide variety of sexual practices. In each interview he asked hundreds of exceedingly personal questions in an accepting and matter-of-fact manner. One of Kinsey's colleagues, the psychologist Wardell Pomeroy, has provided this account of Kinsey's approach to interviewing.

*We asked our questions directly without hesitancy or apology. Kinsey correctly pointed out that if we were uncertain or embarrassed in our questioning we could not expect to get anything but a corresponding response. Unlike previous researchers, we did not say "touching yourself" when we meant masturbation, or "relations with other persons" when "sexual intercourse" was intended. "Evasive terms invite dishonest answers," was Kinsey's dictum. We also never asked whether a subject had ever engaged in a particular activity; we assumed that everyone had engaged in everything, and so we began by asking when he had first done it. Thus the subject who might want to deny an experience had a heavier burden placed on him, and since he knew from the way the question was asked that it would not surprise us if he had*

*done it, there seemed little reason to deny it.* (Pomeroy, 1972, p. 112)

Although change in public attitudes and legal codes rarely comes about because of a single person or event, it would be difficult to overestimate Kinsey's contribution to knowledge about sexual behavior. In addition to promoting scientific research on human sexuality, Kinsey influenced public attitudes (see Figure 8–2) through his objective reporting of results showing that sexual behaviors that had been considered unusual or abnormal were in fact widely practiced. The following letter, one of many that Kinsey received, suggests that many people experienced a sense of relief at discovering that their behavior was not as unusual as they had thought.

*I am a professional man slightly past middle age and have three grown-up children. I wish that I and others could have read your book years ago. With the exception of homosexualism, for which I have never had the least desire, and extra-marital relations, I believe I have indulged more or less in all of the main class perversions, if they were such, which you describe in your book.*

*As a result of such episodes I have always felt that I was a moral pervert, a pariah or outcast and thereby developed a degree of inferiority complex which has been a deterrant [sic] to me in my profession.*

*Now when I find such a high percentage of others in the same boat, I have been mentally relieved and now can hold my head a bit higher and meet life on a surer basis. I am offering no brief or extenuation for this moot conduct except that the primary urge was more than my inhibitions could withstand. I am deeply grateful to you for presenting to the world facts that are unquestionable.* (Pomeroy, 1972, p. 277)

The first Kinsey Report (Kinsey and others, 1948) presented a detailed statistical picture of the sexual behavior of 5,300 American males ranging in age from 10 to 90. Five years later a second report (Kinsey and others, 1953) provided similar information based on interviews with almost 6,000 women. The reports on homosexuality were issued in 1978 and 1981 (Bell and Weinberg, 1978; Bell and others, 1981).

Although there is no question about Kinsey's pioneering contribution in gathering data about sexual practices, some of Kinsey's critics have noted that the sample of people he interviewed was disproportionately white, educated, well off, and midwestern and hence was not really representative of the general population. Kinsey was aware of this problem, but he believed that an effort to obtain a random sample in this highly controversial area was doomed to failure. He

**FIGURE 8-2**
The Kinsey surveys provided the first scientific view of the variety of sexual behaviors practiced in contemporary life. Probably the most valuable functions of the surveys were making the study of sexual practices respectable and correcting a great deal of guilt-producing misinformation. After the publication of his book on sexual behavior in the human male, Kinsey was invited to address large audiences throughout the country. He is shown here speaking to an overflow crowd at the University of California at Berkeley, 1952. Reprinted by permission of the Kinsey Institute for Research in Sex, Gender, and Reproduction, Inc. (Richard Dellenback)

tried to compensate for sampling bias by interviewing a large number of subjects (12,000 in the first two studies alone) and using what he called 100 percent sampling, by which he meant that he tried to interview virtually all the members of groups, such as clubs and college classes, that agreed to be interviewed. Although neither of these approaches made his sample more representative, Kinsey's findings have been supported by data collected through other means.

Recent large-scale surveys show that the proportion of college-age males and females reporting that they are sexually active has changed over the years. Not only has there been a great increase in the proportion of members of each sex who report having had intercourse, but the proportion of females has increased much more rapidly than that of males. Before 1978, about twice as many men as women reported having had intercourse. Since 1970, the proportions of men and women have been nearly equal (Darling and others, 1984). Figure 8–3 shows the changes since the beginning of the century in the reports of coital relationships among college-age students.

Another change has been in the increase in and acceptance of oral–genital sexual behavior among college-age students. In one survey about oral sex among college women, about two-thirds of the respondents reported that they had experienced it and most reported feeling no guilt about it. The women were just as likely to have performed oral sex as to have received it (Herold and Way, 1983). Kinsey (Kinsey and others, 1953) had found that oral sex was considered more intimate than intercourse and seldom occurred until intercourse had been experienced. Herold and Way (1983) found just the reverse. In their study, two-thirds of the women who were still virgins had experienced oral sex. This suggests a change in attitudes regarding the level of intimacy represented by oral sex as compared to intercourse. Mahoney (1980) found that the sequence of oral sex and coitus may be related to religious conviction. In more religious students, oral sex preceded coitus; in less religious ones, the order was reversed. He suggests that vaginal virginity is a concern of highly religious students and that they therefore feel less guilty about oral sex than about coitus.

**Other Surveys**   Finding a representative sample—one in which the important characteristics of age, educational level, ethnicity, and socioeconomic status match those of the larger population that the investigators would like to study—is always difficult. In a large-scale survey commissioned by the Playboy Foundation in the 1970s (Hunt, 1975), the sample was obtained by randomly selecting phone numbers from telephone book listings in 24 cities. Only 20 percent of the potential respondents agreed to participate in the survey. Surveys that appear in magazines are even less representative of the general population. They produce large numbers of responses, but the total represents only a tiny proportion of the magazine's readership. Again, therefore, the sample is not representative of the population (Brecher, 1983; Wolfe, 1980; Rubenstein and Shaver, 1982).

Another way of obtaining data is illustrated by a large study by Blumstein and Schwartz (1983). These investigators recruited couples mainly through newspaper ads and radio and television announcements that described the study and asked for volunteers. They sent out about 11,000 questionnaires and obtained a return rate of about 55 percent. In addition to 4,300 married and unmarried heterosexual couples, almost 1,000 gay male couples and nearly 800 lesbian couples completed questionnaires. An example of the results is shown in Figure 8–4. This study has many positive elements: a large, diverse national sample; a research design that allowed for comparisons among different types of couples; and a questionnaire that gathered data about nonsexual as well as sexual aspects of relationships. However, this study, too, is not very representative of the general population.

The truthfulness of subjects' answers to any kind of questionnaire is open to question, and this is a particular problem in sensitive areas such as sexual behavior. Questionnaires have an advantage over interviews in that the respondent may feel less embarrassed. However, in either case subjects may brag or exaggerate their sexual experiences or not admit to behaviors that they find embarrassing. These possible sources of inaccuracy must be kept in mind when interpreting survey results.

## Observation

Through the Kinsey study and other surveys, we know a lot more about people's sexual behaviors than we used to. Through observational studies, we know a lot more about the body's responses to those behaviors. The best-known observational studies were carried out by the gynecologist William Masters and the behavior scientist Virginia Johnson. Over a ten-year period Masters and Johnson (1966, 1970) studied the sexual responses of 694 men and women under controlled laboratory conditions (see Figure 8–5). They have been largely responsible for giving the laboratory study of human sex-

**FIGURE 8–3**
Percent of college-age males and females who reported having had sexual intercourse. The data are based on selected studies from 1900 to 1980. (adapted from Darling, Kallen, and Van Dusen, 1984, p. 388)

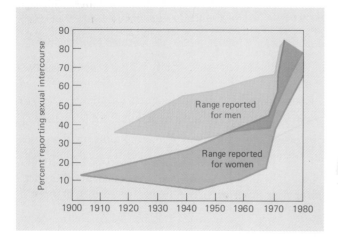

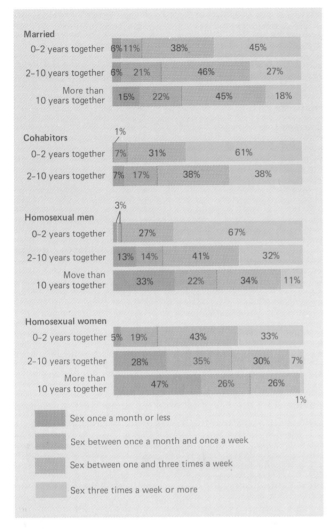

**Married**

0-2 years together 6% 11% 38% 45%

2-10 years together 6% 21% 46% 27%

More than 10 years together 15% 22% 45% 18%

**Cohabitors**

0-2 years together 1% 7% 31% 61%

2-10 years together 7% 17% 38% 38%

**Homosexual men**

0-2 years together 3% 27% 67%

2-10 years together 13% 14% 41% 32%

Move than 10 years together 33% 22% 34% 11%

**Homosexual women**

0-2 years together 5% 19% 43% 33%

2-10 years together 28% 35% 30% 7%

More than 10 years together 47% 26% 26% 1%

Sex once a month or less

Sex between once a month and once a week

Sex between one and three times a week

Sex three times a week or more

**FIGURE 8-4**
Frequency of sexual intercourse reported by individuals in different types of sexual relationships for varying lengths of time. Adaptation of Fig. 27, 196, *American Couples* by Philip Blumstein, Ph.D. and Pepper Schwartz, Ph.D. Copyright (c) 1983 by Philip Blumstein, Ph.D. and Pepper W. Schwartz, Ph.D. By permission of William Morrow & Company.

ual behavior and the treatment of sexual dysfunctions scientific credibility and respectability.

In their research Masters and Johnson observed volunteer subjects who engaged in sexual activity to the point of orgasm while sophisticated measuring instruments monitored their bodily reactions. The study monitored about 10,000 orgasms brought about by masturbation and intercourse. Masters and Johnson carried out much of their research on volunteers from their university community. First, volunteer couples were interviewed to ensure their psychological stability. Before the measurement sessions began, they were asked to have a practice session—to have sexual activ-

ity in the laboratory without observers present and without being hooked up to any equipment. Once the actual sessions began, a variety of sexual activities were measured: self-masturbation, genital stimulation by the partner, oral–genital stimulation, and intercourse. Most of the subjects were studied many times to identify variability in their sexual response.

On the basis of their findings, Masters and Johnson described a four-stage pattern of sexual response for both men and women. The initial **excitement** response to sexual stimulation is marked by vaginal lubrication in the female and penile erection in the male. In the female, this is followed by nipple erection, a thickening of the vaginal walls, and a flattening and elevation of the external genitalia. In the male, there is a slight increase in the size and elevation of the testes.

During the second or **plateau** stage, sexual excitement is reflected in increased heart rate, perspiration, and muscle tension. The male's testes increase in size by about 50 percent and are pulled up high in the scrotum. In the female, the tissues surrounding the bottom third of the vagina swell, reducing the diameter of the vaginal opening by up to 50 percent. The clitoris retracts under the hood that covers it.

In the third stage, **orgasm**, the male's penis begins to throb in rhythmic contractions. Semen collects in the urethral bulb, and during ejaculation, contractions of the bulb and penis project the semen out of the penis. In females, orgasm involves rhythmic muscular contractions of the lower third of the vagina and the uterus. Other muscles, such as the anal sphincter, may also contract in a rhythmic fashion. In both males and females, muscles throughout the body contract, and there is a temporary state of high physiological arousal.

In males, orgasm is followed by the **resolution** phase, in which physiological arousal decreases rapidly and the organs and tissues return to their normal condition. There is also a short **refractory period** following orgasm during which further arousal is impossible. Females may have two or more successive orgasms before the onset of the resolution phase, and may have no refractory period.

In addition to yielding these insights into the physiological aspects of human sexual behavior, many of Masters and Johnson's findings contradicted popular beliefs about sex. For example, they showed that there are no detectable physiological differences between female orgasms produced through stimulation of the clitoris and those brought about by vaginal stimulation. In a later study, no significant physiological differences were found between the sexual responses of heterosexually and homosexually oriented individuals (Masters and Johnson, 1979).

**FIGURE 8-5**
William Masters and Virginia Johnson.
(UPI/Bettmann Newsphotos)

## Case Studies

Case studies use an in-depth approach that may require weeks or months of information-gathering. Single case studies are often interesting, but they have limited scientific value. They can be affected not only by lack of accuracy in the subjects' reports but also by bias on the part of researchers, who may selectively seek information that fits their own theoretical perspectives. Despite these problems, case studies provide real-life examples that may add to our understanding of sexual and other behavior. We use case studies throughout this book. Box 8-1 presents two contrasting case studies of the effects of surgical sexual reassignment.

## Experiments

Much experimental research on sexual behavior has studied the effects of viewing erotic materials both on sexual arousal and on attitudes toward aggressive behavior. The effects of alcohol on sexual response have also been investigated by a number of researchers.

Although folklore suggests that sexual excitement may be increased by alcohol consumption, experimental findings contradict this notion. In one study (Malatesta and others, 1982), female subjects were given one of four differing amounts of alcohol. Each woman's psychological responses were measured during a period in which she was asked to masturbate while watching

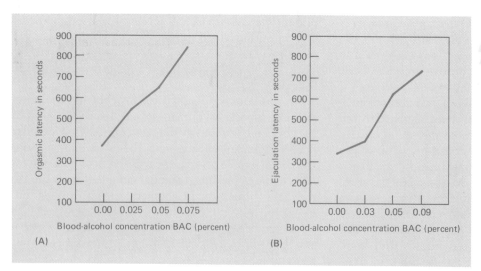

**FIGURE 8-6**
The more alcohol a person drinks, the less likely he or she is to reach orgasm. Figure 8-6a shows length of time before orgasm for women who had received four different doses of alcohol. Figure 8-6b shows that the pattern for men is similar. (Malatesta and others, 1982, Malatesta, 1979)

erotic videotapes in a private, soundproof room. The more alcohol the woman consumed, the more difficulty she had reaching orgasm and the less physiological response she showed. Figure 8–6A presents some of the findings of this experiment. In an earlier study (Malatesta, 1979), the same experimental procedure was used with men as subjects. Figure 8–6B shows that the results were similar to those for women. In this study, almost half the male subjects were unable to reach orgasm at the two highest alcohol blood levels.

Of special interest in understanding the meaning of data obtained using different research methods is the finding that the women who received the highest dose of alcohol also reported more sexual pleasure and arousal than the other groups. Although it is possible to think of explanations for these contradictory results, the actual cause is not clear. This finding illustrates how survey or other methods relying on reports of behavior and feelings may result in different conclusions than studies based on physiological measures. It is important to consider findings obtained in both ways.

## ■ SEXUAL VARIATIONS

Survey research has shown that many individuals have had at least one homosexual experience and that homosexual behaviors are quite common. **Homosexual behavior** is sexual behavior with members of one's own sex. **Homosexuals** are individuals who prefer to engage in sexual activity with members of their own sex over an extended period. Female homosexuality is often called **lesbianism**. Most homosexuals engage in sexual activity only with members of the same sex and are not attracted to members of the opposite sex. However, many homosexuals have heterosexual fantasies and can be sexually aroused by members of the opposite sex. Someone with no sexual experience at all may think of himself or herself as a homosexual (Bell and Weinberg, 1978). In recent years the term *gay* has been used by homosexuals to describe their life style because they feel that the term has fewer negative implications than *homosexual*. Individuals who wish to publicly acknowledge their homosexual orientation usually use the term *gay*.

**Bisexual behavior,** in which partners of either sex may be preferred at different times, is reported by a small but significant number of survey respondents. **Bisexuals** are sexually attracted to members of either sex and often engage in sexual activity with both men and women.

Kinsey and his co-workers believed that there is a continuum extending from heterosexuality to homosexuality. They used a seven-point rating scale to represent this continuum (see Table 8–1). Kinsey's data probably are still the best available on the proportion of the population who have some same-sex erotic experience. They show at the time of the survey, at least 10 percent of white American males had been primarily homosexual for at least three years between the ages of 16 and 65 (Kinsey and others, 1948).

Table 8–2 shows some of the Kinsey survey data. It makes clear that females are much less likely to have homosexual experiences than males. Kinsey and others found that, compared to males, only about one-half to one-third as many females were primarily or exclusively homosexual in any age period. Considering the statistics for both males and females, it is fair to say that the number of people who have same-sex erotic experiences is fairly high but that the number who are exclusively homosexual is quite low (see Table 8–2). Many people who would not be called homosexuals because they do not structure their identities and lives around members of the same sex nevertheless have homosexual desires and fantasies.

One of Kinsey's most surprising findings was the proportion of males and females with any kind of homosexual experience did not change between 1900 and 1950. Again, in spite of the sexual permissiveness that characterized the 1960s and 1970s, there seems to have been little change since the Kinsey studies (Karlen, 1978).

In interpreting Kinsey's findings, it is important to remember that he lumped together in a single category such different behaviors as a single incident of mutual masturbation between teenage boys, exploratory caressing of each other's breasts by girls reaching pu-

---

□ **TABLE 8–1**
**Kinsey's Heterosexual–Homosexual Rating Scale**

| | |
|---|---|
| 0 | Exclusively heterosexual |
| 1 | Predominantly heterosexual; only incidentally homosexual |
| 2 | Predominantly heterosexual; more than incidentally homosexual |
| 3 | Equally heterosexual and homosexual |
| 4 | Predominantly homosexual; more than incidentally heterosexual |
| 5 | Predominantly homosexual; only incidentally heterosexual |
| 6 | Exclusively homosexual |

*Source:* Adapted from Kinsey, Pomeroy, and Martin, 1948. Reprinted by permission of The Kinsey Institute for Research on Sex, Gender & Reproduction, Inc.

Survey Data on Same-Sex Erotic Experience

| | Percent Reporting | | |
| --- | --- | --- | --- |
| Sex of Respondent | Exclusive Homo-sexuality | At Least One Same-Sex Experience Leading to Orgasm | At Least One Same-Sex Erotic Response |
| Male | 4% | 37% | 50% |
| Female | 1-3 | 13 | 20 |

*Source:* Based on Kinsey and others, 1948, 1953.

berty, and frequent oral or anal intercourse by adult males. For many men and women, the homosexual behavior they reported had occurred when they were young, was mainly exploratory, and was brief in duration.

## Homosexuality

A good deal of recent research has challenged the idea that homosexuality is pathological (Meredith and Riester, 1980). One comprehensive study compared the psychopathology of male and female homosexuals to that of heterosexuals (Saghir and Robins, 1973). The types of psychopathology found among homosexuals were in many ways similar to those found among heterosexuals, and their incidence for men was comparable in the two groups. Homosexual women tended to show more psychological disturbance than heterosexual women, but this finding seemed to be related to other problems such as alcoholism. For whatever reason, the vast majority of homosexuals never seek professional consultation.

Some clinicians believe that maladaptive behavior in homosexuals, when it does occur, is often due to the social stigma attached to homosexuality rather than to something pathological in the nature of homosexuality itself. As more information about sexual practices, research findings about sexual response, and data on psychological adjustment have become available, many mental health professionals have changed their views on the implications of homosexuality. In 1973 the American Psychiatric Association removed homosexuality from its list of mental illnesses, and in 1975 the American Psychological Association also took this position. DSM-III-R does not include homosexuality in its list of disorders.

Public attitudes toward homosexuality have also changed. Homosexual and bisexual behaviors have existed throughout history, and in many societies certain forms of homosexual behavior are accepted or expected (Carrier, 1980), although heterosexual behavior is the preferred pattern in most cultures most of the time. Historically, homosexuality has been condemned by the dominant religions of the Western world; in the eighteenth and nineteenth centuries it was considered an illness. In recent years tolerance of homosexuality has increased. Many cities have enacted ordinances that make discrimination on account of sexual orientation illegal. As one author pointed out, "Homosexuals are being slowly redefined in less value-laden terms as practitioners of an alternative lifestyle, members of a new community" (Altman, 1982, p. 35) (see Figure 8–7). This view may be changing, however, because of

**FIGURE 8–7**
Gay Pride activities provide social support for homosexual individuals by visibly demonstrating their numbers. They also provide a way for homosexuals to publicly state their sexual preferences rather than hide them. (Ken Karp)

concern about the deadly disease known as AIDS (acquired immune deficiency syndrome). AIDS, which appears to be sexually transmitted, has a high fatality rate, and the number of cases has grown quite rapidly. Because the disease occurs most frequently among homosexual males, especially those who have many partners, public attitudes toward homosexuality may shift again.

**The Sexual Response of Homosexuals**  Is the sexual experience of homosexuals different from that of heterosexuals? Yes and no. Masters and Johnson (1979) compared the physiological responses of male and female homosexual and heterosexual couples under laboratory conditions. They found no differences in physiological response during sexual activity and orgasm. But they did find that homosexual couples were more leisurely in their sexual activity, communicated more, and were more sensitive to their partners' needs than heterosexual couples.

**Social Behavior and Homosexuality**  Just as there is no single personality type that is characteristic of heterosexuals, there is no such thing as a homosexual personality or behavior pattern. In 1967 the Institute for Sex Research began an intensive ten-year study of homosexuals (Bell and Weinberg, 1978; Bell and others, 1981) based on a large-scale survey of 1,500 individuals in San Francisco and the Bay Area. Bell and Weinberg were the first to study how homosexuals differed from each other, not just from heterosexuals. They found not one but several consistent homosexual life styles.

1. *Close-Coupleds.* Respondents in this category were closely bonded partners whose relationships were similar to those of partners in heterosexual marriages. Close-coupleds did not seek other partners and reported that they had no regrets about their homosexuality (see Figure 8–8).

2. *Open-Coupleds.* These respondents lived with a special partner but reported themselves to be less happy than close-coupled respondents. They had more outside sexual partners, whom they often picked up by cruising.

3. *Functionals.* This noncoupled group consisted of "swinging singles" whose lives were organized around sexual experiences. They engaged in frequent cruising, had many friends, and felt that they were well adjusted.

4. *Dysfunctionals.* The adjustment of respondents in this group was noticeably poorer than that of the functionals. Although they had a high number of partners and a high level of sexual activity, they saw

**FIGURE 8–8**
Close-coupled lesbian partners seem to have more satisfying and stable relationships than close-coupled males according to Bell and Weinberg's study of homosexual life styles.
(Betty Lane, Photo Researchers)

themselves as sexually unappealing and their lives were marked by distress and conflict.

5. *Asexuals.* These people lacked involvements with others. They had few partners and engaged in little sexual activity. People in this group were less likely than those in other groups to say that they were exclusively homosexual. They were lonely and unhappy.

Few homosexual men and women in this study conformed to society's stereotypes. For example, they were not easily identifiable as homosexuals, and few were completely uninvolved with members of the opposite sex. One-third of the female and one-fifth of the male homosexuals interviewed by Bell and Weinberg had been married. One-fourth of the respondents' employers knew that they were homosexuals, as did one-fifth of their neighbors and one-half of their brothers and sisters. Their mothers were the most likely to know.

The sexual problems most frequently mentioned by homosexuals were lack of sexual outlets and difficulty in finding suitable partners. Homosexual males reported having had many more sexual partners than female homosexuals did. Whereas many of the men had had hundreds of partners, the women tended to have had fewer than ten. Lesbians were more likely to have a relationship resembling a marriage than male homosexuals. Men seemed to be more interested in sexual activity, while women emphasized companionship, affection, and emotional support.

This research into the diversity of homosexual behaviors and possible relationships to earlier experiences represents a valuable starting point for further inquiries. However, its limitations should be recognized. The homosexuals in the study were volunteers who had been recruited through public advertising, gay bars, and homosexual organizations. In addition, the homosexual climate in San Francisco is more permissive than that in most other communities in the United States. (Homosexuals living in less permissive places might report a much higher incidence of social difficulties.) Unskilled and semiskilled people accounted for only 18 percent of the people in the study, and 73 percent of the black male respondents reported having had at least some college education—a much higher percentage than that found in the general population of black males. Thus, Bell and Weinberg's subjects may be representative neither of the population as a whole nor of homosexuals in general. For these reasons, without further research we cannot be sure that Bell and Weinberg's conclusions correctly describe the entire homosexually oriented population.

### The Psychological Adjustment of Homosexuals

As noted earlier, homosexuality is no longer considered a mental disorder. A number of studies have provided data that show clearly that there are relatively few differences in psychological adjustment between heterosexual and homosexual groups. The majority of homosexual individuals are well adjusted and productive people (Saghir and Robins, 1973). In a review of dozens of studies, no higher rates of emotional instability or illness were found among homosexuals than among heterosexuals. No psychological tests could discriminate between the two groups (Reiss, 1980). Although homosexuals, like heterosexuals, may be anxious or depressed and are not always emotionally stable, homosexuality is not a form of mental illness (Marmor, 1980).

### Bisexuality

The incidence of bisexuality in Western societies is difficult to estimate. Probably about 5 percent of adults are bisexual if bisexuality is defined as sexual activity with both males and females in the past year (Masters and others, 1985). Patterns of bisexuality differ. Sometimes the bisexual individual has a long heterosexual relationship and then a long homosexual relationship. Or the order might be reversed. Sometimes both relationships go on during the same period. One 23-year-old woman described her bisexual experience as follows.

> I had been dating a guy I was very friendly with for about a year with a good sexual relationship. Then I suddenly found myself making it with my roommate, who slowly but expertly introduced me to how two women make love. I really enjoyed both kinds of sex and both personal relationships, so I continued them for some while until my graduate school career was over and I moved to a new town. (Masters and others, 1985, p. 434)

Some women who are bisexual say that certain emotional needs are best met by men while others are best met by women (Blumstein and Schwartz, 1976).

Bisexuality is most likely to occur under several conditions: during group sex, as a result of sexual experimentation between same-sex friends who are otherwise heterosexual, and when people adopt a philosophy of sexual openness as a sign that they aren't biased against homosexuality (Blumstein and Schwartz, 1977). Bisexual behavior sometimes occurs in situations in which the participants don't think of it as such. Heterosexual individuals may seek same-sex experiences in segregated settings such as prisons, or in isolated military settings (Money and Bohmer, 1980).

Both bisexuals and gays may have conventional heterosexual marriages. Sometimes this happens because the person does not begin to experience other sexual feelings until later in life. It may also be due to a desire to have children or to have a conventional life style.

Sometimes bisexuals are aware of their attraction to members of the same sex before marriage, but relatively few of them reveal this fact to their prospective spouses (Coleman, 1981/1982). If the spouse later discovers the homosexual relationship, an explosive situation may be created. Husbands seem to feel especially threatened because they tend to see the wife's lesbian preferences as a negative statement about the husband's performance as a lover (Masters and others, 1985).

If bisexuality culminates in a move to a homosexual life style, other problems can arise. A substantial number of active homosexuals are also parents (see Figure 8–9). Being both homosexual and a parent may produce two somewhat conflicting identities.

> When I was first coming out I never told anyone that I was a father 'cause I thought I'd be ostracized. But I started telling guys that I'd meet and they were really accepting. And then I gradually realized that it was okay to be gay and a father too. That I could be both. But at first I didn't think I could. I really thought I'd be rejected. But I wasn't. So now I really feel comfortable being a gay father. And boy is that a good feeling. (Bozett, 1981, p. 558)

This double identity may also create problems in the homosexual relationship, especially for partners in close- or open-coupled relationships.

**FIGURE 8–9**
These men, photographed at a Gay Freedom Day parade in San Francisco, live openly as both parents and homosexuals. In a less liberal environment they might be denied not only custody but even access to their children. (Rose Skytta/Jeroboam)

> I know of one man who was frightened off by my daughter. He had a bad experience with a father, and in fact the children didn't even live with this guy that this fellow was seeing. But he didn't want to take up anything with me just because of it. (ibid.)

> Another man who is coupled has two children who live with him six months each year. During this time the lover is exceedingly resentful of his attention to the children, which creates considerable family conflict. Because of this conflict, the men have temporarily separated. (Bozett, 1981, p. 557)

Another problem that sometimes arises is that of child custody. We don't really know how growing up in a household with a homosexual parent (and, in some cases, the parent's lover) can affect a child's development. Although the question has arisen in several court cases, little research on this subject is available. One study found that children of lesbian mothers were no more likely to have problems of gender identity than children of heterosexual single parents (Kirkpatrick and others, 1981).

## How Sexual Preference Develops

**The Biological Perspective** Animal research has shown that prenatal hormone treatments may play a role in later homosexual behavior patterns. There are a few reports that a prenatal excess or deficiency of sex hormones can also affect human sexual behavior. Females who had experienced an excess of prenatal androgen (hormones that develop secondary sex characteristics in males) were more likely to have a lesbian sexual orientation (Money and Schwartz, 1977). However, treating adults with male or female hormones does not alter their sexual orientation in any way. It is possible, although far from proven, that prenatal hormones could predispose individuals to certain patterns of sexual behavior in adulthood.

**The Psychodynamic Perspective** Sigmund Freud believed that all people are innately bisexual. Although psychosexual development usually progresses along a heterosexual course, some circumstances, such as inability to resolve the Oedipus complex, might result in adult homosexual behavior. In general, Freud's view of homosexuality was that it is simply a variation of sexual development. In a letter to a mother who had written to him asking for therapy for her son, he wrote:

> Homosexuality is assuredly no advantage, but it is nothing to be ashamed of, no vice, no degradation, it cannot be classified as an illness; we consider it to be a

*variation of sexual function produced by a certain arrest of sexual development. Many highly respectable individuals of ancient and modern times have been homosexuals, several of the greatest men among them (Plato, Michelangelo, Leonardo da Vinci, etc.). It is a great injustice to persecute homosexuality as a crime, and cruelty too. (Freud, 1951, p. 786)*

Other psychodynamic theorists have stressed parent–child relationships in explaining homosexuality (Bieber and others, 1962; Marmor, 1980). However, research has suggested that, at least for well-adjusted individuals, the family relationships of homosexuals and heterosexuals do not differ (Siegelman, 1974; Bell and others, 1981).

**The Behavioral Perspective**   The view that homosexuality is primarily a learned phenomenon suggests that pleasant early sexual experiences with members of the same sex or unpleasant experiences with members of the opposite sex can condition sexual thoughts and fantasies. This perspective can also be used to explain why some individuals change their sexual preference as adults. Some investigators have found that individuals who have changed their preference may have had unpleasant heterosexual experiences followed by rewarding homosexual ones (Masters and Johnson, 1979).

## What the Data Tell Us

In a large and sophisticated study, Bell, Weinberg, and Hammersmith (1981) concluded that neither a psychodynamic nor a behavioral view of homosexuality was supported by the evidence. Their findings include the following.

1. No evidence that parent–child relationships are important in determining sexual preference.
2. No evidence that homosexuality results from atypical experiences with members of the opposite sex during childhood—experiences such as rape, parental punishment for sex play with members of the opposite sex, seductive behavior by opposite-sex parents, or actual seduction by an older male or female.

The study also provided evidence that sexual preference begins early.

1. Sexual preference is likely to be established by adolescence, even before there is much sexual activity.
2. Sexual feelings of attraction seemed much more important than early sexual activity in the determination of homosexual preference.

3. Adult homosexuals did not lack heterosexual experiences in childhood; however, they did not tend to find these gratifying.
4. Children who did not conform to gender roles in childhood had a somewhat increased probability of homosexual feelings and behavior in adolescence.

*Gender nonconformity in childhood* means that the person was typically interested in activities that are associated with the opposite sex—for example, playing baseball for girls and playing house for boys. However, nonconformity is not a very good clue. At least half the homosexual men were typically masculine in both personal identity and interests while they were growing up, and at least one-fourth of the heterosexual men were nonconforming to male sex roles while growing up. The situation was similar for women. This means that while gender nonconformity in childhood increases the likelihood that the child will be homosexual in adulthood, it does not automatically signal later homosexuality.

Bell and his coworkers conclude that the development of a homosexual preference is probably biologically based. Although their study does not deal with biological data, their findings make that conclusion reasonable. However, as the section on the biological perspective made clear, any biological explanation requires much further research.

## ■ SEXUAL DYSFUNCTION

One of Kinsey's most significant findings was the high incidence of problems of sexual dysfunction. The work of Masters and Johnson and others has supplied information about the causes and treatment of these problems.

## Types of Sexual Dysfunction

Problems people encounter in sexual activity may occur in any of four stages of the sexual response. The stages include the following periods.

1. *Appetitive:* the presence of fantasy about sexual activity and a feeling of desire
2. *Excitement:* a period of subjective pleasure and physiological changes, including penile erection in the male and swelling and lubrication of the female genitals
3. *Orgasm:* the peaking of sexual pleasure and the release of sexual tension, as shown by ejaculation in the male and rhythmic muscle contraction in the pelvic area for both male and females

4. *Resolution:* a sense of relaxation and well-being. Men cannot produce an erection or experience orgasm during the resolution period. Women are able to respond almost immediately to additional stimulation.

Sexual problems can occur during any of these stages. In the appetitive stage, physical conditions such as high blood pressure or diabetes can inhibit sexual desire. Some individuals simply seem to be at the low end of the normal distribution of sexual desire. These problems usually come to the attention of a clinician only when they become a source of concern to the individual or his or her partner.

Sexual problems can also occur at the excitement stage of the cycle. The male may fail to attain or hold an erection until the completion of intercourse. This problem is often called **impotence.** In females, a problem at this stage is inability to attain or maintain the swelling-lubrication response until the sex act is completed. This is usually called **frigidity.**

Both males and females may experience problems in the orgasm phase of the sexual-response cycle. In the male, these take the form of premature ejaculation or delayed or absent ejaculation. In the female, they take the form of a delay or absence of orgasm after a normal excitement phase. **Premature ejaculation,** in which the man is unable to inhibit ejaculation long enough for his female partner to experience orgasm through intercourse, is probably the most common type of male sexual dysfunction. The man's failure to control his orgasm often results in his feeling sexually inadequate. According to one viewpoint, the male experiences anxiety as he reaches high levels of erotic arousal, and the anxiety triggers the involuntary orgasm.

In **retarded ejaculation,** on the other hand, the ejaculatory response is inhibited. Men with this problem respond to sexual stimuli with erotic feelings and a firm erection, but they are unable to ejaculate. In severe cases, the male may prolong intercourse for a long time, engage in fantasy, and drink, all to no avail. Although physical injuries may be responsible for this condition in some cases, a variety of psychological factors that contribute to the occurrence of retarded ejaculation include ambivalence toward the sexual partner, strongly suppressed anger, and a religious upbringing that engenders sexual guilt.

Psychological and situational factors can be an important cause of inhibited female orgasm. Psychological factors include unresolved conflicts over sexual activity and disturbances in the relationship between the partners. In many cases, however, the explanation is simpler: inadequate stimulation during lovemaking

can damage a woman's ability to become sexually responsive. The French have a saying: "There are no inorgasmic women, only clumsy men." In such cases, the therapist attempts to sensitize both partners to each other's sexual needs, explaining, for example, that a woman is more difficult to arouse than a man. Some women are unable to experience an orgasm without manual stimulation of the clitoris, which has a larger number of sensitive nerve endings than the vagina. This may represent a normal variation in sexual response. Most women do not have an orgasm each time they have intercourse, and about 15 percent of women never have orgasms (Frank and others, 1978). Not having orgasms can decrease a woman's overall sexual responsiveness as well as leading to depression and a decreased sense of self-esteem. As one 19-year-old college student said,

> There's so much talk about orgasms that I've been wondering what's wrong with me, that I don't have them. I used to enjoy sex a lot, but lately it's a bad scene because I just get reminded of problems. (Masters and others, 1985, p. 502)

Because many cases never come to a clinician's attention, no one knows how prevalent sexual dysfunction is. One estimate is that half or more of all married couples experience sexual dysfunction of some kind (Masters and Johnson, 1970). In a study of 100 couples who had not sought sex therapy, 60 percent of the women reported difficulties in reaching orgasm, and 40 percent of the men reported problems with erection or ejaculation (Frank and others, 1978). Most of these couples described their marriages as at least moderately satisfying.

Because a woman who has problems of this type can still have intercourse while a male who is unable to maintain an erection cannot do so, most of the attention given to problems of excitement has been directed toward those of the male. According to one estimate, half of all American men have experienced at least occasional episodes in which they could not achieve or maintain an erection (Kaplan, 1974). For this reason, only severe and chronic problems of erection, such as are found in men who have never functioned well, are viewed as serious clinical problems. These dysfunctions may result from psychological or physical causes. One technique that is used in evaluating a man's capacity to have an erection is measurement of changes in penis size during sleep. The ability to have erections during sleep is a clear sign that a man's erectile dysfunction is due to psychological, not physical, causes.

Anxiety stemming from personal conflict or from

concern over a physical problem is often an important factor in erectile dysfunction. Physical causes include early undiagnosed diabetes, hormonal imbalances, and the use of narcotics and alcohol. In the past, hidden psychopathology was believed to be the main psychological cause of this type of sexual dysfunction. More recently, however, recognition has been given to **performance anxiety,** in which the man's preoccupation with sexual adequacy ironically interferes with his performance. One 34-year-old man's comment is typical.

> *After awhile, the problem becomes so predictable that you start to make excuses in advance. It's as though you lose any chance of having sexual pleasure because you become preoccupied with the notion of failure. And that failure hits you right in the gut—you don't feel like much of a man.* (Masters and others, 1985, p. 502)

Erectile dysfunction most commonly occurs early in adult life. Although reliable surveys of representative populations are not available, erectile problems seem to be common, particularly in their milder forms. Like all forms of sexual dysfunction, problems of obtaining or sustaining an erection may be lifelong or may develop after a period of normal functioning. The chances of successful treatment are much better when the dysfunction is recent and when there is reason to believe that the man has had a satisfying sex life in the past. The absence of serious personality problems also increases the likelihood of a favorable response to sex therapy.

Just as failure to achieve or maintain an erection can make sexual intercourse a problem for men, **functional vaginismus** is a problem that can cause women to avoid intercourse. In this disorder the muscles of the outer third of the vagina contract in involuntary spasms so that insertion of the penis becomes difficult or impossible. Males and females can both be affected by another problem, **functional dyspareunia,** in which intercourse is associated with a persistent and sometimes very severe genital pain that may last for minutes or even days. Although this problem is not associated with a physical disorder, it quite naturally causes the individual to fear or actively avoid sexual intercourse.

## The Treatment of Sexual Dysfunctions

**The Masters and Johnson Approach** Since the publication of Masters and Johnson's books in 1966 and 1970, sex therapy has emerged as a discipline in its own right. While they recognize that many sexually dysfunctional people are dysfunctional in other areas of their personal and social lives, Masters and Johnson believe that short-term treatment directed primarily at sexual problems can help most people who experience such dysfunctions. They have observed that becoming sexually functional has a positive influence on a person's anxiety level as well as on his or her self-esteem. A man who is anxious but has a good sex life is probably happier than a man who has to deal with a sex problem in addition to anxiety.

Masters and Johnson treat only couples, not just the individual who seems to have a problem. This does not mean that the partner is seen as the cause of the difficulty, but rather that both members of the relationship are affected by the problem. The Masters and Johnson approach uses a man and a woman working together as therapists. The therapy program is intensive and takes place daily over a two-week period. It emphasizes instruction in the sexual needs of both partners, together with exercises in erotic stimulation. Specific homework assignments are given that are designed to help couples become more aware of their own sexual sensations. The therapy procedure includes basic information about the sexual organs and the physiology of the sexual response for clients who lack this information (i.e., most of the people who come for treatment). The presentation of this basic information often has important therapeutic benefits in itself.

Emphasis is also placed on communication, non-verbal as well as verbal, between partners. Because couples who seek treatment typically place lovemaking exclusively under the man's control, sexual intercourse may be attempted only when he indicates that he is interested. The belief of many women that they will be rejected if they are sexually assertive continues to be widespread. In many cases of sexual dysfunction, the most effective treatment may be not complex physical or psychotherapeutic tactics, but simply the provision of information about sexual relationships and the encouragement of meaningful communication between sex partners.

**Sensate focus** is probably the best known of Masters and Johnson's sexual-retraining techniques. The rationale behind sensate focus is that sexually dysfunctional couples have lost the ability to think and feel in a sensual way because of the various stresses and pressures they associate with intercourse. They therefore have to be reacquainted with the pleasures of tactile contact. Each partner learns not only that being touched is pleasurable, but that exploring and caressing the partner's body can be exciting and stimulating in itself. The basic strategy is to enhance the erotic factors and diminish distractions that inhibit the couple's sexual response. The couple is encouraged to engage in sensate focus under conditions that are dissimilar to those associated with the anxieties, frustrations, and resentments of their former lovemaking. Intercourse is prohibited throughout the early stages of treatment so that sexual communication will come to be regarded as a goal in itself rather than simply as a means to the goal of intercourse. Simply banning intercourse can reduce tension in both sexual and nonsexual areas of the relationship. Many couples report a dramatic increase in their desire for intercourse when it has been expressly forbidden. This deemphasis of intercourse makes sensate focus particularly valuable in treating performance anxiety.

The couples technique is especially appropriate in treating premature ejaculation, since this is often more upsetting to the woman than to the man. If premature ejaculation is the problem, the therapists often introduce a method known as the "squeeze technique" that helps recondition the ejaculatory reflex. The woman is taught to apply a firm, grasping pressure on the penis several times during the beginning stages of intercourse. This technique reduces the urgency of the need to ejaculate.

When the couple's problem is related to an orgasmic dysfunction in the woman, the treatment includes an exploratory discussion to identify attitudes that may be influencing the woman's ability to attain orgasm. Then the couple is given a series of graduated homework assignments. If the woman is willing, she begins by exploring her own bodily sensations, stimulating herself by masturbating. As she becomes more comfortable with this technique, her partner begins to participate in the sessions by "pleasuring" her through kissing and tactile stimulation. There is strong emphasis on the woman's clear and assertive communication of her reactions and desires to her partner.

Masters and Johnson have reported very low failure rates for their treatment programs for both heterosexual and homosexual couples. Their findings have been criticized, primarily because their reports are not completely clear on such topics as who is selected and who is rejected for the program and how success and failure are defined (Zibergeld and Evans, 1980). Nevertheless, their techniques are far superior to earlier methods of treating sexual disorders.

**The Behavioral Approach**   Looked at from a behavioral perspective, the Masters and Johnson technique of sensate focus is reminiscent of systematic desensitization in that it leads to the substitution of a pleasurable response for anxiety. Sex therapists often create a sort of hierarchy in which certain parts of the body initially are designated as "out of bounds" and then are gradually included as progress is made. Although orthodox systematic desensitization can be used to eliminate specific anxieties (such as feeling uncomfortable while looking at a man's genitals), the more global sensate focus appears to be appropriate in dealing with the various diffuse anxieties experienced by sexually dysfunctional individuals.

The methods used by Masters and Johnson have been further refined by many behaviorally oriented therapists (Annon, 1976; LoPiccolo and LoPiccolo, 1978). In one study, relaxation and modeling were combined in treating dysfunctional women whose major problem was sexual anxiety (Nemetz and others, 1978). The anxiety was so disabling that the women could experience neither sexual enjoyment nor sexual activity. Treatment consisted of relaxation training followed by the viewing of videotaped vignettes depicting gradually more erotic sexual behaviors. The clients were encouraged to visualize themselves and their partners in the behaviors they saw depicted in the tapes. Homework assignments were given in which the clients were urged to match the taped scenes. The results showed that women who were treated in this way improved significantly more than an untreated control group. The treated women became less anxious and more assertive and spontaneous in sexual relations with their partners.

Another behavioral approach to the treatment of interpersonal problems related to sexual performance is described in the following case. Notice the importance of cognitive elements in this treatment plan.

*The client was a 24-year-old lawyer who after six months of marriage was upset by his frequent inability to obtain or retain an erection. His history suggested that his mother had been a dominating woman of whom he was fearful and that he was also unwilling to challenge or criticize his wife in any way even though he often felt considerable resentment toward her. He seemed to feel that expressing his feelings was not manly. After several therapeutic sessions directed at his irrational attitudes, he and the therapist composed a carefully worded speech for the client to deliver to his wife.*

*"Grace, I have something very important and very serious to discuss with you. It concerns you, me, our marriage, and life in general. I want you to please hear me out without interrupting me. I've spent a hell of a lot of time mulling over these points, and finally I've straightened out my ideas, and I want very much to share them with you.*

*"Let me put it as clearly as possible. I was raised by my mother to bottle up my feelings, especially in relation to women. In thinking over this attitude, I now realize that this is crazy and even dishonest. I feel, for instance, that if I resent the fact that you turn to your father for advice in matters about which I have more knowledge than he, I ought to express my resentment instead of hiding it from you. I feel that when you order me about and treat me*

*like a child, I ought to tell you how I really feel about it instead of acting like an obedient puppy dog. And most important of all, when you go ahead and make plans for me without consulting me, and especially when you yell at me in front of your parents, maybe I should quit acting as if I didn't mind and let you know how strongly I really react inside.*

*"What I am getting at is simply that in spite of my love and affection for you, I would really rather be unmarried than be a henpecked husband like my father."*

*This little monologue was rehearsed several times during a one-hour session until playbacks on a tape recorder convinced the therapist that the client was ready to confront his wife and that he would do so in a forthright and sincere manner. Rehearsal techniques were used in preparing the patient to cope with tears, interruptions, denials, counterallegations, etc. His assignment was then put into effect. The patient reported that his wife "heard me out without interruption. . . . [She] seemed a little upset, but agreed that I should not withhold or conceal my feelings. I felt incredibly close to her and that night we had very good sex."* (Lazarus, 1971, pp. 156–157)

**The Kaplan Approach**  Some therapists believe that behavioral methods are useful for many sexual problems but that other problems require a combination of behavioral approaches with psychodynamically oriented therapy for one or both partners. One of the foremost proponents of this view is Helen Singer Kaplan (1974, 1979). Kaplan, a psychoanalyst, believes that standard sex therapy methods are effective when sexual problems are based on mild and easily diminished anxieties and conflicts. However, there are many individuals whose symptoms are rooted in more profound conflicts. Kaplan thinks that this is especially true in the cases of men and women who lack sexual desire and men who have difficulty maintaining an erection. For these problems Kaplan and her coworkers have developed a lengthened and more individualized treatment program that involves traditional sex therapy and psychodynamically oriented sessions, sometimes with one of the clients and sometimes with both partners. The case of Sam and Susie illustrates Kaplan's approach.

*Susie, 28, a housewife, and Sam, 30, a high school principal, had been married four years and has 3-year-old twin sons. The chief complaint was Susie's lack of desire. The couple had a good relationship, each felt in love with the other and they were judged to be good parents. During their marriage they had had intercourse only three times. During the last two years they had had no physical contact because any attempt by Sam to hold or kiss Susie resulted in "hysterics," that is, she had an anxiety attack. Sam did not feel rejected or angered by*

*Susie's avoidance, instead he saw it as her problem. The couple were referred to Kaplan after nine months of weekly sessions at a sex therapy clinic had not produced improvement.*

*The ordinary sensate focusing or pleasuring activities threw Susie into an anxiety state. In addition, when there was any improvement Susie would effectively resist or sabotage the treatment by trying to do too much. For example, if the assignment were to lie next to Sam in bed and hold his hand, she might try to have him caress her breast as well. This would then precipitate her anxious feelings. The therapist discussed this behavior with Susie and gave her the job of controlling the progress of desensitizing her anxiety. She was to select only tasks that were within her comfort-zone, that is, those that produced only tolerable anxiety. She realized that if she experienced no anxiety, desensitization could not take place.*

*Susie also had a more general problem with fun and pleasure. Whenever she allowed herself to experience them, she developed sharp headaches. As the desensitizing of her phobic avoidance of sexual contact progressed, Susie had a series of dreams about "dead relatives buried in the basement that needed to be removed." A central threatening figure was her deceased father. After discussions with the therapist about Oedipal feelings toward her father and the transfer of some of these feelings to her husband, Susie's father disappeared from her dreams.*

*After further sessions alone with her husband that focused on guilt over pleasure, Susie's pleasure anxiety had decreased, her relationship with her husband was more open, and the couple was having satisfying intercourse at least once per week.* (adapted from Kaplan, 1979, pp. 73–75)

## The Effectiveness of Sex Therapy

In general, sex therapy leads to improvement for about two-thirds of the clients who are seen at outpatient clinics specializing in such treatment (Crown and D'Ardenne, 1982). The particular treatment approach used does not seem to affect this result. One study compared Masters and Johnson's technique, a modified technique using only one therapist, and a technique that combined efforts to improve communication with behavioral methods such as relaxation training and contracts (Crowe and others, 1981). All three approaches led to improvement lasting at least one year for couples with problems of impotence, anorgasmia, and loss of sexual interest. There was no difference in effectiveness among the various therapies.

Findings like these suggest that research is needed to determine which therapeutic elements are actually helpful and which elements are unnecessary. For instance, decreasing anxiety about sexual performance has been a focus of many approaches to sex therapy. However, anxiety is a complex construct that has behavioral, cognitive, and physiological aspects. The heightened physiological response that is part of anxiety has been shown to increase, not decrease, sexual response (Beck and Barlow, 1984). However, the cognitive aspects—for instance, interfering thoughts and problems of focusing attention—have a negative effect on arousal. Such thoughts may increase because of the demand for performance when the partner is clearly aroused. These findings suggest that attempts to decrease the physiological aspects of anxiety may be ineffective or even counterproductive whereas practice in screening out distracting thoughts might be most helpful.

# ■ GENDER IDENTITY DISORDER

**Gender identity,** a basic feature of personality, refers to an individual's feeling of being male or female. Children become aware that they are male or female at an early age, and once formed, this gender identity is highly resistant to change. Gender identity is different from sexual preference. Sexual preference refers to whether a person desires a sexual partner of the same or the opposite sex, it does not refer to the person's sexual self-concept.

## Gender Identity of Childhood

In **Gender Identity Disorder of Childhood** children before they reach puberty may show considerable distress at being male or female and will express intense desires to be of the opposite sex. For instance a girl may vehemently state her desire to be a boy or even insist that she is a boy. She may refuse to wear ordinary feminine clothing and insist on wearing the clothing typical of males including boys' underwear and other accessories. She may also deny her gender by such behaviors as refusing to urinate while in a sitting position or by the insistence that she either already has or will grow a penis. Boys show the same types of behavior in reverse. In addition to playing with girls' toys and wanting to dress as a girl, a boy may say that he wants to be a woman when he grows up and that his penis and testes are disgusting or that they will disappear as he grows older.

Problems that may relate to gender identity come to clinical attention when parents become concerned because their child's behavior and social relationships are not like those of other children of the same sex and age. For instance, this mother is worried that her son is and will continue to be sexually abnormal.

> *My boy is showing feminine tendencies and has ever since he was two years old. It started out real cute. His sister had dress-up clothes at her grandparents, and when he got to be about two years old, he'd dress up in these clothes and hats and high heels, and he was just real cute. We thought it was something he'd pass. Now he will be eleven years old this month, and he does this in secret. I just felt like now was the time to investigate it.* (Green, 1974, p. xxi)

If a young child's behavior is typical of that of children of the opposite sex, it does not always mean that the child has a gender identity problem. Often parents are not aware of how much their own behavior contributes to the behavior of their children. For example, the mother quoted earlier may have encouraged her son to dress in women's clothes by telling him how cute he was then, and at no other time. When this is the case, counseling may be helpful. Parents can be trained to reinforce sex-appropriate behavior in the home—for example, by giving the child special attention or a material reinforcer when he or she is behaving appropriately—and this approach has been found to be effective in helping children acquire new sex roles (Rekers, 1977).

Despite advances in the study of sexual practices, questions frequently arise as to how maladaptive a certain type of behavior is. Children who act out inappropriate sex roles early in their development may drop this behavior as they get older. The 5-year-old tomboy or sissy may simply be going through a phase. However, when a child's strong desire to be a member of the opposite sex continues into adulthood, transsexualism may result. The problem begins to surface at puberty, when maturational changes in the body emphasize biological gender.

## Transsexualism

Gender identity in adults can take two forms: **transsexualism** and **nontranssexual cross gender disorder.** Transsexuals experience an intense desire and need to change their sexual status, including their anatomical structure. A transsexual's goal is to become a member of the opposite sex through hormonal and surgical treatment.

Although the number of cases of transsexualism is very small (according to one estimate, only 1 per 100,000 people), the behavior has aroused a great deal of curiosity. Scientific interest in transsexualism derives mainly from the light that such cases may shed on the general nature and development of gender identity. Though clinicians agree on the value of studying the lives of transsexuals, the use of medical techniques to bring about bodily changes that conform to the transsexual's gender identity remains controversial.

Changing a male transsexual into a female involves administering female hormones to reduce hair growth and stimulate development of the breasts, removing the male genitals, and creating an artificial vagina. Changing a female into a sexually functioning male is more difficult because the artificially constructed penis cannot become erect by natural means or feel tactile stimulation. In recent years, however, advances in the treatment of primary impotence in men have been applied to transsexual surgery, and an inflation device is sometimes implanted in the penis to make possible artificial erection. The long-term success of this method is still in doubt.

Many of the candidates who apply to clinics for what is called sexual-reassignment surgery show considerable psychological disturbance. In one group of patients who applied to a university gender-identity clinic, only 8 percent of the males and 40 percent of the females showed disturbance in sexual identity alone (Levine, 1980).

Clinicians stress the need to assess each candidate carefully before deciding to carry out the medical steps needed for a sex change. Most reputable centers require a number of preliminary steps for people whom psychological tests reveal to be emotionally stable and likely to adjust well to surgery. Because the surgical procedures are irreversible, this degree of caution is needed.

After patients have been selected, they usually are required to spend one or two years living in the community as a member of the opposite sex. During this period hormone injections are used to alter secondary sex characteristics such as breast size or muscle definition. This period serves as psychological preparation for life as a member of the other sex and also provides a realistic experience of what that life may be like. Psychotherapy is also often required during the presurgical period. Sometimes clients have what might be called "magical" hopes regarding the surgery. The psychotherapeutic sessions can give them a chance to look at their underlying feelings and perhaps become more comfortable as hetero- or homosexuals.

What happens to those who undergo the surgery? Box 8-1 describes two very different outcomes. Early studies of carefully selected patients suggested that the surgery was an effective treatment. The majority of the patients reported they were satisfied with the results, even though professionals did not judge their sexual and social adjustment to be clearly improved (Walinder and Thuve, 1975). Later studies concluded that there was no objectively measurable advantage to individuals undergoing sex-reassignment surgery (Meyer and Reter, 1979), or that the surgery yielded modest results at best (Hunt and Hampson, 1980; Lothstein, 1981). In the 1980s several prominent medical centers stopped doing transsexual surgery because the benefits were doubtful (Beatrice, 1985; Masters and others, 1985).

Transsexualism is a prime example of the interactional point of view. Sex is a matter of anatomy and

# ■BOX 8-1 SUCCESS AND FAILURE IN TRANSSEXUAL SURGERY

Several transsexuals have written about their experiences. One is Jan Morris, whose autobiography is entitled *Conundrum* (1974). James Humphrey Morris was a highly regarded English foreign correspondent. At age 17 he had been an officer in one of Britain's crack cavalry regiments. As a correspondent for *The Times* of London, he covered the successful attempt by Hilary and Tenzing to climb Mount Everest. He covered wars and rebellions the world over and also wrote fifteen books on history and travel. Then James gave way to Jan. Jan Morris refers to her former self as a woman trapped in a man's body.

At age 3 or 4 James Morris realized that he was a girl who had been born into the wrong body. As an adult he enjoyed the company of women but did not desire to sleep with them. He married at 22, and he and his wife had five children. As middle age neared, he became depressed, had suicidal thoughts, and finally sought a transsexual change. Hormones were used to enlarge his breasts and soften his body to more feminine lines. After surgery to complete the process begun by the hormone pills, Morris divorced his wife. Jan Morris reports that she feels like the person she always wanted to be. (See Figure 8-10a-c.) The children of her former marriage treat her as an aunt.

Not all sex-reassignment surgery is as success-

(c)

FIGURE 8–10
(a) James Morris in 1964. (Courtesy of Jerry Bauer) (b) Jan Morris in 1977. (Henry Grossman, *People Weekly* © 1974 Time Inc. (c) A note written by Morris to the authors.

(b)

ful as that of Jan Morris. Recently the Princeton alumni weekly carried a memorial notice that included the following description.

### SUSAN F. (NEE WALTER FAW) CANNON '46

*He was a courtly southern gentleman. He was soft-spoken and intelligent, one of the few authentic geniuses in our class. He was to many of us a drinking companion, a sympathetic listener, a friend.*

*Professionally, he did well. He had a severe stuttering problem, so he became a world-class debater at Princeton. He earned a physics degree. Don Hegstrom, a former*

*graduate and lifelong friend, convinced him that physics, in his context, was dull and he should maybe go for his Ph.D. in the history of science at Harvard. He did.*

*Walter was a scholar, and a certified intellectual (a label he wore with modesty and grace), a voracious reader, a creative thinker, a historian of national note, a teacher, a poet, an author, an editor ("The Smithsonian Journal of History"), and a curator of the Smithsonian Institution.*

*Walter Faw Cannon was also Susan Faye Cannon, a fact that she did not recognize until several years ago. Several years ago, Walter publicly proclaimed that he was a female in a male body. And just last year, he had a surgical sex change against the advice of his doctors. Three months before she died, she called and told a classmate that it had been demonstrated conclusively that genetically she had always been a woman. She was very glad, because she had always suspected it and, in more recent years, known it to be a fact. (Princeton Alumni Weekly, April 5, 1982).*

Cannon began discovering his female identity during his undergraduate days at Princeton and during his stint in the U.S. Navy. At the age of 51 Cannon applied to Superior Court in the District of Columbia to change his first name to Faye, his mother's family name, and during the same period he began dressing as a woman. In an interview with the *Washington Post,* Cannon described his situation. "I don't classify myself as gay, because I don't know what the word means. I define myself as a male woman. Then I know what the words mean" (Levey, 1977, C1).

Cannon's behavior created problems for him in his job at the Smithsonian. In spite of his reputation as a scholar he received a disability retirement in 1979. At the age of 55 he decided to undergo sex-reassignment surgery (see Figure 8–10d and e). Cannon had been a heavy user of painkillers before his surgery because of an arthritic problem. After surgery, her use of these drugs escalated because of the extreme postsurgical pain. In 1981, Susan Cannon was found dead of acute codeine intoxication. It was not clear whether her death was a result of an accidental overdose.

These two cases involving well-educated, successful men who decided in midlife to reconcile their sexual identification with their physical appearance show how hard it is to generalize about the desirability of surgical sex reassignment even for those who clearly seem to be among the small group of true transsexuals.

(d)          (e)

FIGURE 8–10
(d) Walter Cannon before he began receiving hormone treatments. (e) Walter Cannon after receiving hormone treatments and shortly before his sex reassignment surgery.

physiology, but gender identity is strongly influenced by psychological, social, and cultural factors. It is likely that there may be a small group of transsexuals for whom sexual-reassignment therapy is an effective treatment. For many more, who are likely to have significant personality problems and other psychopathology, the surgery does not provide an answer to their mental health problems; instead, the problems may worsen. Some individuals become deeply depressed after surgery, while others have transient psychotic episodes (Levine and Lothstein, 1981).

Nontranssexual cross gender disorder also produces discomfort about one's assigned sex. However, people with this disorder lack the preoccupation for acquiring the sexual organs and other physical characteristics of the opposite sex that is characteristic of transsexuals. Instead they focus on fantasizing that they are of the opposite sex or actually acting out that role through cross-dressing. This cross-dressing differs from that of the transvestites discussed later. Although transvestites obtain sexual gratification from cross-dressing they do not wish to change their sex as people with cross gender disorder do.

# ■ THE PARAPHILIAS

Not everyone is sexually excited by the same stimuli. Some individuals can gain sexual gratification only from particular objects or situations. Most of these sexual behaviors are tolerated by society if they are practiced in private or with consenting adult partners. The behaviors are likely to cause problems only if others are harmed or if social customs are openly flouted. DSM-III-R classifies these disorders as subcategories of **paraphilia,** which means attraction to the deviant. There are three general classes of paraphilias: (1) preference for the use of a nonhuman object for sexual arousal; (2) repetitive sexual activity with humans that involves real or simulated suffering or humiliation; and (3) repetitive sexual activity with nonconsenting partners.

## Fetishism

**Fetishism,** a psychological state in which a nonliving object (fetish) serves as a primary source of sexual arousal and consummation, is an example of a sexual deviation that is not usually addressed by the law. Most fetishists are solitary in their activities, although in some cases they commit crimes to acquire their favorite fetishes (often undergarments, boots, or shoes). Some fetishists seek sexual partners with particular characteristics, usually leg amputations or lameness. Fetishists are almost always male, and the fetish varies widely from the clearly erotic (such as an article of women's underwear, especially underwear that has been worn, stained, and not yet laundered) to objects with little apparent connection with sexuality. Fetishism often begins in adolescence.

Rubber fetishes are particularly popular. In England the Mackintosh Society, named for rubberized raincoats, has over 1,000 members. The group provides reassurance for individuals who feel embarrassed or isolated by their sexual interests. Some rubber fetishists derive sexual excitement from wearing rubber garments themselves. Others dress in them or want their partner to wear them during sexual activity because the garments are necessary for them to become sexually

aroused. One rubber fetishist describes the role played by rubber boots in his sexual behavior.

*I always seem to have been fascinated by rubber boots. I cannot say exactly when the fascination first started, but I must have been very young. Their spell is almost hypnotic and should I see someone walking along with rubber boots, I become very excited and may follow the person for a great distance. I quickly get an erection under such circumstances and I might easily ejaculate. I often will take the boots to bed with me, caress them, kiss them, and ejaculate into them.* (Epstein, 1965, pp. 515–516)

Fetishism is one of the most puzzling of all forms of sexual behavior. It is chronic, and in some cases the collection of fetishistic objects is the main activity in the individual's life. No one has been able adequately to explain fetishists' sexual attachment to diverse objects. Although theories range from those that stress unconscious motivation to those that hypothesize impaired neural mechanisms such as are found among epileptics, the causes of this unusual type of sexual behavior remain shrouded in mystery (Wise, 1985).

Fetishists do not often seek therapy. In one large London hospital only 60 cases were diagnosed in a 20-year period (Chalkley and Powell, 1983). Of these, about 30 percent were referred by the courts, mainly because of their theft of fetishistic objects (see Figure 8–11). About a third of the patients came for treatment because of anxiety about their fetishistic behavior. About 20 percent came for other reasons and the fetish was identified only after they had begun treatment. Treatment based on learning principles has been applied to fetishism with some success. In aversion therapy, for example, the fetishistic object is paired, either actually or in fantasy, with an unpleasant stimulus such as electric shock or a sense of overwhelming embarrassment.

## Transvestism

A transvestite uses clothing as a sexual stimulant or fetish. **Transvestism** literally means "cross-dressing" (see Figure 8–12). Women are not usually considered to be transvestites, probably because society allows them to dress in most masculine styles. References to cross-dressing can be found throughout history. King Henry III of France cross-dressed publicly and wished to be addressed and treated as a woman. Joan of Arc wore her hair short and preferred to dress as a man. Most transvestites are heterosexual men who dress in women's clothes, often starting in adolescence. When not cross-dressed, the transvestite usually exhibits masculine behavior and interests.

**FIGURE 8-11**
The Seattle "shoe bandit" attacked women on the street and stole a single shoe from each. Here some of the shoes found in his apartment are surveyed by police. *(The Seattle Post Intelligencer)*

**FIGURE 8-12**
These male transvestites enjoy playing a female role by dressing as women. (Jean-Claude Lejeune, Stock, Boston)

Although some clinicians have contended that tranvestism and transsexualism are basically similar, there are a number of differences between these two conditions. Transsexuals desire to change their genitals and live as members of the opposite sex. They do not experience sexual arousal when cross-dressing. Transvestites, on the other hand, become sexually aroused when cross-dressing but continue to identify themselves as members of their biological sex.

A male transvestite gave this explanation for his behavior in a letter to his wife.

> The personal masculine attributes that first attracted you to me are, as you know, an integral part of my personality, just as my transvestism is. It has always been a part of me . . . We are only make-believe girls, and we know always that we are really men, so don't worry that we are ever dissatisfied with manhood, or want to change forever into a woman. When we are dressed in feminine clothes and attain as close a resemblance as possible to a real girl, we do certainly pretend that we are girls for that short time, but it is a pretense and definitely not a reality. (Prince, 1967, pp. 80–81)

An unusual study of a nationwide sample of transvestites provided comprehensive descriptions of their behavior and attitudes (Bentler and Prince, 1969, 1970). Compared with a nontransvestite group, the transvestites were more inhibited in their interpersonal relationships, less involved with other individuals, and more independent. In general, they gave evidence of being less able to seek sympathy, love, and help from others and seemed to be happier when they felt no obligations to others. However, in many areas of personality they did not differ significantly from nontransvestites. Another study found that the mothers of transvestites and transsexuals frequently had hoped for a girl prior to the birth of a son (Buhrich and McConaghy, 1978), but there was little evidence that the men in either of these groups had had pathological relationships with their mothers.

Writers have emphasized several perspectives—psychodynamic processes, conditioning, and biological predisposition—in discussing transvestism. Many clinicians believe that transvestism develops in the context of disturbed parent–child relationships. Others see it as a product of aberrant psychosexual development. Behaviorists see it as a conditioned response that is susceptible to aversion therapy in which dressing in women's clothing is paired with an aversive stimulus. Behavioral training aimed at fostering confidence and adequacy in playing a conventional sex role has also been suggested.

Covert sensitization seems to be particularly useful in treating transvestism and other sexual disorders (Little and Curran, 1978). In this procedure clients are first asked to imagine as vividly as possible the sexually arousing behavior that they are trying to eradicate, and to follow these thoughts with equally vivid aversion imagery (for example, being discovered and embarrassed). This approach was used for a 31-year-old transvestite, a married police officer who sought help for uncontrollable urges to dress in women's clothing and appear in public. The client had a 16-year history of transvestism that had begun when he was discharged from the Marine Corps. His wife had threatened to divorce him because of his cross-dressing. In treatment, he was asked to form images of deviant sexual scenes as well as aversive images of their undesirable consequences. The following is an example of the material used in the covert sensitization.

*You are in your house alone, and you are feeling lonely. You get the urge to put on the clothing, so you enter the bedroom and open the closet. You begin to get aroused as you decide what to wear. As you put on the clothing, you can see the colors and feel the clothing on your hands. You really are turned on as you put on the bra, panties, nylons, wig. You feel like playing with yourself as you apply your makeup, but you can't wait to go out. As you leave the house, you get very excited. You are touching your penis through the panties as you're driving.*

*And then you hear sirens! The police pull you over, and it's your fellow policemen. They start to laugh and call for other police cars. A crowd is gathering, and they know you're a man. The officers throw you around and take*

*you to the station. The women are disgusted, and the chief will take your gun and badge. You are humiliated, and they call you "sick." Your kids are crying as they return from school because others tease them about having a perverted father. Look what you've done to yourself!* (Brownell and others, 1977, pp. 1147–1148).

Figure 8–13 shows the average percentages of full erection (measured by penis circumference) during a baseline period, during covert sensitization, and upon follow-up. The figure also shows self-reported changes in sexual arousal to transvestite stimuli. Both the physiological and self-report measures revealed a sizable decrease in sexual arousal. In addition, physiological and self-reported arousal in response to heterosexual stimuli increased. The client, who had received prior treatment for his sexual difficulties, was surprised at the effectiveness of the covert sensitization.

For some transvestites, it is not the clothes themselves that are exciting, but rather the ability to fool the public and be taken for a woman. One transvestite was asked if he would feel happier if social custom allowed people to dress as they wished in public.

*"Heavens, no," he smiled. "Merely to be allowed to wear women's clothes in public is nothing. It is the challenge of being so much like a woman that no one knows I'm a man that turns me on. The combination of doing something that I want to, that everyone says is impossible and is forbidden anyway, produces in me an arousal which, because it is in a sexual context, becomes sexual arousal."* (Gosselin and Wilson, 1980, p. 67)

**FIGURE 8–13**
Mean percentages of full erection and sexual arousal scores (based on actual measurements and self-reports) for a transvestite man during baseline, treatment (covert sensitization), and follow-up periods. (adapted from K.D. Brownell, S.C. Hayes, and D.H. Barlow. Patterns of appropriate and deviant sexual arousal: The behavioral treatment of multiple sexual deviations. *Journal of Consulting and Clinical Psychology,* 1977, 45, 1144–1155, Copyright (c) 1977 by the American Psychological Association. Adapted by permission of the author.)

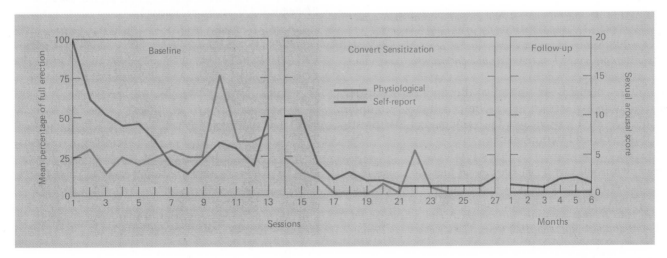

## Sexual Sadism and Masochism

For some people, inflicting or experiencing pain and indignity is linked to sexual gratification. Many people incorporate mildly painful acts—such as biting, nipping, and spanking—into their sexual practices. When both partners enjoy them, these activities can enhance sexual pleasure. However, sadists and masochists often go beyond mild pain and, moreover, cannot enjoy sex any other way. To the **sadist,** achieving orgasm depends on humiliating others or inflicting pain on them. This is often referred to as "discipline." To the **masochist,** sexual satisfaction depends on "bondage"—suffering, humiliation, pain, and ill treatment at the hands of others. Sadism and masochism occur in both heterosexual and homosexual relationships, but, like other sexual deviations, they are poorly understood. Some clinical workers have conjectured that the roots of sadism and masochism are to be found in childhood; others have mentioned possible biological factors. One area that would seem to merit study is the fantasy life of these individuals, for example, the thoughts associated with their sexual activities.

The sexual masochist experiences arousal through his or her own suffering, preferably by being humiliated and beaten. Masochists have fantasies, often beginning in childhood, in which they are bound, tortured, raped, or otherwise abused in ways that they cannot prevent. These fantasies and acts are far more common in males than in females. Five features can be found in most cases of sadomasochism: agreement as to which partner is to be dominant and which one submissive, awareness by both partners that they are role playing, the consent of both participants, a sexual context, and a shared understanding by both participants that their behavior is sadomasochistic (Weinberg and others, 1984).

In sadomasochistic relationships the participants agree on the limits beforehand.

> My wife and I do play dominance and submission games, and maybe we have the marks to prove it on occasion. But the one playing top dog watches like a hawk to make sure we stop when the other one doesn't like it any more.

Often a signal is set up so that the submissive partner can stop the session at any time if the agreed-upon boundaries are exceeded. One sadomasochistic prostitute explained her approach.

> When you have a new client, what I used to do was I used to sit down and I would talk to them first and find out exactly what they wanted. Because sometimes you can get into a session with somebody and get very brutal and that's not what they want. There's heavy dominance

and there's light dominance and there's play acting, roles, all different kinds. So the best thing to do is to sit down and talk to somebody first, initially. (Weinberg, 1978, p. 29)

When sadomasochism is a person's predominant sexual style, the most common way of reaching other sadomasochistic devotees seems to be the use of ads in sadomasochistic magazines. For example:

> Beautiful Dominatrix, 24. A true sophisticate of the bizarre and unusual. I have a well equipped dungeon in my luxurious home. You will submit to prolonged periods of degradation for my pleasure. Toilet servitude a must. I know what you crave and can fulfill your every need.

> A very pretty 30-year-old female has fantasies about receiving hand spankings on bare behind. I've never allowed myself to act out any of the fantasies. Is there anyone out there who'd like to correspond with me about their fantasies or experience with spanking? (Weinberg and Falk, 1980, pp. 385–386)

As these examples show, the ads contain code messages. "Toilet servitude," for instance, refers to handling feces or being defecated on. Sadomasochistic experiences can also be enhanced by hoods, paddles, enema equipment, adult diapers, and other paraphernalia sold in sex shops. For those who wish to pursue such activities at home, this equipment can now be found in "sex boutiques" in middle-class neighborhoods (see Figure 8–14). At one boutique in Florida, for example, police handcuffs and whips are big sellers.

However, masochistic needs can also be satisfied without actually inflicting pain. For many couples, the fantasied aspect of violence is most important.

**FIGURE 8-14**
The leather clothing, restraints, and whips shown in this sex shop display are attractive to many sadists and masochists. (Robert V. Ecker, Jr., Stock, Boston)

*Of course, he doesn't really hurt me. I mean quite
recently he tied me down ready to receive 'punishment,'
then by mistake he kicked my heel with his toe as he
walked by. I gave a yelp, and he said, 'Sorry love—did I
hurt you?' (Gosselin and Wilson, 1980, pp. 54–55)*

*My wife believes in discipline. If she gets angry and yells
at me, I get an erection. If she ever raises her hand as if
to hit me, I get so excited I can't stand it. Actually she
has never hit me. When I have fantasies of her hitting or
slapping me, my penis becomes erect immediately.*

Few studies of fetishists, transvestites, and sadomasochists have been carried out because of the many
difficulties involved in obtaining subjects. The results
of the studies that have been done so far are hard to
interpret because of the unrepresentative samples that
investigators are forced to use. Researchers have become very creative in searching for these hard-to-find
subjects. For example, one recent study utilized the
membership lists of organizations for fetishists, sadomasochists, and transvestites (Gosselin and Wilson,
1980). The subjects, all males, were given the Eysenck
Personality Questionnaire (Eysenck and Eysenck,
1975), a paper-and-pencil test that measures extraversion, neuroticism, and psychotism and includes a "lie
scale" intended to screen out test takers who do not
answer candidly. A questionnaire on life style, sexual
characteristics, sexual fantasies, and childhood and adolescent experiences was also included. On the basis of
these measures, all three sexually deviant groups were
found to be more introverted and more inclined to fantasy than a control group. In the control group, 18 percent of the men could be considered fetishistic on the
basis of their sexual fantasies, but only 2 to 5 percent
could be called sadomasochistic or had transvestite fantasies.

Many of the subjects in one group—for example,
the fetishists—had sexual interests that overlapped
those in the other groups (see Figure 8–15). Thirty-five
percent of any group had all three sets of interests. The
biggest overlaps were between fetishists and sadomasochists and between fetishists and transvestites. This
research suggests that very often sadomasochism and
transvestism are elaborations of an early-learned fetish.
Gosselin and Wilson conclude that these sexually variant behaviors are not the deliberate choice of an individual looking for "kicks," but rather a logical, if
unfortunate, reaction of a shy, introverted, emotionally
sensitive child to a restrictive sexual upbringing.

## Autoerotic Asphyxia

Sometimes sadomasochistic needs are satisfied by dangerous **autoerotic practices** or solo sex-related activities. Unintended deaths may result from these

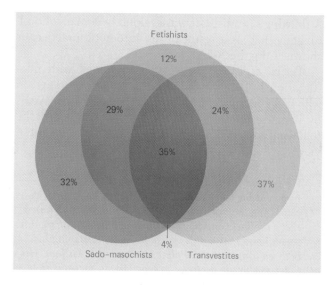

**FIGURE 8-15**
The overlap of sexual interests among groups of male
fetishists, transvestites, and sadomasochists. (Gosselin and
Wilson, 1980, p. 167. Copyright © 1980 by Glenn Wilson
and Chris Gosselin)

practices, but such deaths are rather rare. In the United
States an estimated 500 to 1000 deaths per year result
from autoerotic activities (Hazelwood and others, 1983).
Little research has been done on this group, but a study
of 70 consecutive cases received by the FBI showed
that two-thirds of the victims had died while using materials or devices such as ropes, handcuffs, chains,
hoods, gags, blindfolds, and belts to physically restrain
or mentally humiliate themselves (Hazelwood and others, 1983). The following is a typical case.

*The victim, a 32-year-old married father of three, was
discovered dead on his bed by his 11-year-old daughter.
The victim was dressed in pantyhose, a lady's sweater,
and a brassiere. His hands were restrained to his sides by
a soft belt. A sanitary pad was in his mouth and a pink
brassiere was wrapped over the mouth and around the
head. His scrotum was swollen and exhibited two round
areas resembling old cigarette burns. A similar type burn
was located on the inner aspect of the left thigh near the
scrotum. The cause of death was determined to be
accidental asphyxiation. Because of the slack in the belt
restraining his wrists, it would have been possible for the
victim to slip his feet between his arms, thereby allowing
him to remove the gag. Apparently his judgment was
impaired due to his asphyxial state. (Hazelwood and
others, 1981, p. 131)*

This victim's sadomasochistic needs apparently led him
to inflict burns on his own body as well as to use physical restraints. It seems likely that many individuals who
inflict pain on themselves also have sadistic fantasies.

A drawing of sadistic fantasies done by a man who ultimately died as a result of his autoerotic practices is shown in Figure 8–16.

Partial asphyxiation is often combined with masturbation to heighten sexual excitement. One person who had engaged in autoerotic asphyxia for many years by hanging himself while cross-dressed provided the following information about this practice in an interview.

> He enjoyed the feeling as he lost consciousness and perceived his body going limp. Although he had difficulty expressing the exact nature of the sensation, it appeared that numbness and possibly tingling were part of what he sought, and that a dissociative feeling of watching his body go limp may have played a major role for him. His habit was to use asphyxia as a prelude to masturbation, and he reported that he never ejaculated during asphyxiation. When rushed for time, instead of cross-dressing and hanging himself, he would "give myself a quickie" by applying pressure to both sides of his neck with one hand until losing consciousness. (Hazelwood and others, 1983, p. 84)

The majority of autoerotic deaths occur in teenagers and young adult males, although the reported age range is 9 to 77 and a small number of female deaths have been reported (Brody, 1984). Some health professionals believe that parents should be aware of this behavior. As the mother of one victim commented,

> Yes, I saw the marks, a rashlike redness on his throat—'an allergy,' he said. Yes, he did take long showers but all boys do . . . We saw all the signs . . . and my husband and I ignored them because we had never heard of adolescent sexual asphyxia . . . After our son died, we called his school and told them what really happened. We begged them to warn other students, but nothing was ever done. The next year, another boy in the school died in exactly the same way. (Brody, 1984, p. 20)

Table 8–3 lists some warning signs that may suggest autoerotic asphyxial practices.

## Voyeurism

Some sexual variations are not physically harmful but may be upsetting for the victim. One example is **voyeurism,** the impulse to spy on others, usually strangers. The French word "voyeur" means "watcher." The voyeur is subject to an irresistible, repetitive urge to spy on others through windows or doors, in public toilets, in parks, or on beaches, and particularly enjoys watching other people have sex. Like the exhibitionist (to be described shortly), the voyeur or "peeping Tom" is male and achieves sexual gratification from doing something forbidden. Also like the exhibitionist, the voyeur is usually harmless and will run if he is discovered. In some cases, however, usually after feeling intensely stimulated or provoked, the voyeur will let his presence be known—for example, he may exhibit his genitals and ask his victim to touch him or even to masturbate him. Cases have been known in which the voyeur tried to force the victim to have sexual intercourse with him, but such cases are exceptional.

Voyeurism begins in early childhood. About one-fourth of the men who are arrested for peeping are

**FIGURE 8–16**

Sketches of sadistic sexual fantasies drawn by a victim of autoerotic asphyxia. Reprinted by permission of the publisher, from *Autoerotic fatalities* by Robert R. Hazelwood, Park Elliott Dietz, and Ann Wolbert Burgess. Lexington, MA: Lexington Books, D.C., Heath and Company, Copyright (c) 1983, D.C. Heath and Company.

□ **TABLE 8-3**
Signs of Possible Autoerotic Asphyxial Practices

1. Frequently bloodshot eyes
2. Marks on the neck
3. Disoriented or foggy behavior, especially after having gone off alone for awhile
4. Great interest in or possession of ropes, chains, plastic bags, or gas inhalation devices

*" You don`t often see a real silk lining, these days . . ."*

**FIGURE 8-17**
Exhibitionists receive sexual gratification from the shock and alarm expressed by their victims. A response of this kind would provide no sexual gratification.

married. Fifty percent of those arrested are later re-arrested for similar acts. When voyeuristic acts are related to life stress, the impulse to commit them usually decreases when the stress dissipates. While voyeurs show few signs of serious mental disorders, they usually have unsatisfying heterosexual relationships.

## Exhibitionism

**Exhibitionists,** who are always males, repeatedly expose their genitals to unsuspecting strangers in public places as a way of experiencing sexual arousal. The exhibitionist does not want to harm anyone; his act of exposure is done for his own sexual gratification. His arousal is apparently heightened by seeing people react with amazement or shock when he unexpectedly shows his penis (see Figure 8–17). Exhibitionists expose their genitals mainly to women and children. One-third of all people arrested for sex offenses are exhibitionists, and about 20 percent of these are arrested more than once.

Exhibitionism can begin between preadolescence and middle age, but it occurs most frequently during the twenties. An exhibitionist has an irresistible, compulsive need to expose his genitals, and he does so despite the anxiety, depression, and shame he feels as a result. Acts of genital exposure often seem to be triggered by feelings of excitement, fear, restlessness, and sexual arousal. When overcome by these feelings, the exhibitionist is driven to find relief. Both psychodynamic and behavioral therapies (particularly aversion therapy) have been tried with exhibitionists. Although both methods seem to achieve some success, the results are unpredictable.

## Obscene Telephone Calls

Another way of obtaining sexual gratification with a nonconsenting individual is by making obscene telephone calls. The caller almost always tries to get his victim to give him intimate information, often of a sexual nature, by pretending to be conducting a survey about menstruation, contraception, or sexual practices. In another type of obscene call, the caller masturbates while graphically describing the process to the victim.

## Pedophilia

**Pedophilia** differs from the paraphilias discussed so far. Although it involves the desire for sexual gratification from another nonconsenting human being, in the case of pedophilia that human being is a child. Because of this, pedophilia is considered a much more serious crime than exhibitionism and voyeurism. Pedophiles (who are predominantly male) can be either heterosexual or homosexual, but the odds are two to one that a pedophile is a heterosexual. Girls 8 to 11 years old are the primary targets of pedophiles. In about 90 percent of all cases, the pedophile is someone whom the child knows.

One researcher has classified pedophiles into two groups: fixated and regressed (Groth, 1984). **Fixated pedophiles** begin during adolescence to focus on children as sex objects. They usually remain single and often have their only important sexual relationships with children. **Regressed pedophiles** turn to sexual interest in children only after some serious and negative event in their own lives. These men may be married, and often seem to be seeking a child as a substitute for a woman. They are also likely to have problems of alcohol abuse. Although both groups may choose either boys or girls or both as their sexual targets, a greater proportion of the children sought by regressed pedophiles are girls. In some cases the victim may be frightened or physically harmed, but often children are more upset by their parents' horrified reactions than by the experience itself. Statistics indicate that sexual assault on children is relatively common.

In searching for ways to protect children, some information campaigns have concentrated on children's contacts with strangers—for example, "Never get into a car with anyone you don't know," "Never go with someone who says he or she has some candy for you." However, in the majority of reported assaults children are victimized by people they know. To prevent this kind of assault, children need to be taught to recognize signs of trouble and to be assertive enough to report them to a responsible adult. One novel approach is found in a child's picture book called *Private Zones* (Dayee, 1982). The pictures and text are designed to impress on children in simple, nonthreatening language the concept of private zones, who can touch them, what "good" and "bad" touching is, and the importance of communicating an intrusion to a responsible adult. Figure 8–18 shows an illustration from the book along with some of the text.

Although the range of sexual deviations is very wide and some involve danger to others, they bear intriguing similarities to other disorders discussed in this part of the book. As we have already mentioned, stress, personal conflict, and anxiety contribute to their occurrence. In addition, we frequently see a picture of puzzling, even bizarre, behavior in one area combined with socially acceptable behavior in many other areas of a person's life. In some sexual deviations, such as phobic fears and tyrannizing obsessions, afflicted individuals feel that they lack control over significant portions of their lives. They may be particularly troubled by the compulsive quality of their deviant sexual desires. In addition, they may recognize how bizarre and undesirable their behavior is and may want to change it. Some therapeutic techniques that are useful in treating anxiety disorders can also help people who are sexually deviant.

A psychological approach emphasizing careful observation and objective research methods has much to contribute to our understanding of the range of sexual disorders. This approach is valuable because if its emphasis on explicit definition of the problem under

**FIGURE 8–18**
*Private Zones* is designed to inform even very young children about possible trouble signs in adult behavior toward them. This is Tommy! This is Susie! They are going to the beach. They are wearing bathing suits to the beach. Do you know what bathing suits cover? Bathing suits cover special parts of the body called the PRIVATE ZONE. The parts of *your* body *your* bathing suit covers is *your* PRIVATE ZONE. You have a PRIVATE ZONE. Big people like Mommies and Daddies have PRIVATE ZONES, big kids and small kids that go to school have PRIVATE ZONES. Tommy and Susie have PRIVATE ZONES. Even babies have PRIVATE ZONES.

study, assessment of the problematic behavior, and identification of the factors involved in its development. As we have seen in applications of covert sensitization to deviant sexual behavior, treatment procedures aimed at the specific stimuli and thoughts that are present in the problem situation can yield good results in a short period.

## ■ SEXUAL VICTIMIZATION

Some sexual deviations involve a participant who is either unwilling, uninformed, or vulnerable, or too young to give legal consent. Among the clearest examples of such deviations are rape and incest. When individuals who practice these deviations come into contact with the law, they are usually known as **sex offenders** and are subjected to a variety of treatments as well as to imprisonment. Some cases of rape and incest are examples of paraphilias; others are examples of gratification through aggression or, in the case of incest, desire for an easily obtainable and easily coerced sexual partner.

## Incest

**Incest** is defined as sexual relations between closely related individuals, but the definition of "closely related" varies from one culture to another. One of the most common restrictions on sexual behavior is the prohibition of marriage or sexual relationships between certain members of the same nuclear family. Incest taboos and laws are centuries old and nearly universal. Such taboos have been defended on the grounds that incest would mean the upsetting of age distinctions, the mixing of generations, and drastic role changes within the family. Children who are born as a result of an incestuous relationship also have a greater risk of inheriting recessive genes that may cause birth defects. Despite these taboos, incestuous relations between parents and children and between brothers and sisters do occur.

Most research on incest focuses on father–daughter sexual relationships that end with the father's imprisonment. Much of the time the research doesn't distinguish between father–daughter and father–stepdaughter cases. In one study, about half the cases involved incest with stepdaughters. Men who are involved in father–daughter incest have generally been characterized as poor, unemployed, and poorly educated. However, this stereotype may have developed because such men are more likely to be discovered and jailed.

One extensive study found striking differences between men convicted of incest with older and younger daughters (Gebhard and others, 1965). Most of those whose relationship was with a daughter under 12 were passive, shy men who were experiencing marital difficulties. Most of these men bribed and persuaded their daughters, and they often confined their sexual expression to genital fondling or oral–genital contact. On the other hand, men who had sexual relationships with a daughter over 12 tended to be devout, had conservative social and sexual views, but at the same time had histories of compulsive behavior and excessive drinking. Most of the sexual relationships with these elder daughters involved coitus. Fathers often had a sexual relationship with their oldest daughter first and then with successive daughters as they matured.

Although estimates of the incidence of father–daughter incest range between 1 and 1.5 cases per million, there seems no doubt that incest is a seriously underreported behavior. As treatment becomes more available, the number of reported cases is likely to increase greatly. Indeed, in recent years the topic of in-

cest has received more public discussion and clinics have been set up to help such families. For example, rather than simply being sent to prison, the father may be placed in a work-release situation. He may be allowed to work at his job during the day while being required to spend nights and weekends in a treatment program. At the same time, the offender's wife and children are given counseling and often participate in a support group made up of families with similar problems. The men involved in one such program in Santa Clara County, California, typically came from suburban middle-class families (Rosen and Rosen, 1981).

Little is known about the long-term effects of incest on the child. Some researchers find that victims of incest, whether children or adolescents, often show severe neurotic or sexual conflicts. These conflicts may not become acute or be brought to a therapist's attention until many years later (Meiselman, 1978). Other research findings indicate that the child is harmed less by the event than by the family's reaction (Weinberg, 1976). The age at which the child is molested also seems important: children who were last molested after puberty seem most likely to show negative effects (Tsai and others, 1979). At present, it can only be concluded that incest may or may not have long-term effects, and that those effects depend on a variety of factors.

## Rape

The law also forbids **rape,** or having sexual intercourse forcibly and without the partner's consent. (**Statutory rape** is the crime of having sexual intercourse with a person under the age of consent, regardless of whether force is involved or not.) Rape is a seriously underreported crime because of the emotional trauma experienced by the victim. Probably only about 15 to 20 percent of all forcible rapes are reported to authorities. It is estimated that in the United States a woman is forcibly raped every second of every day (see Figure 8–19). The great majority of convicted rapists are sent to civil prisons for fixed sentences, but some states maintain special treatment facilities for sexual offenders, particularly those who are violent. Many researchers have pointed out that rape usually occurs as an expression of power or anger, not as a result of sexual desire (Hilberman, 1978; Groth, 1979).

Rapes fall into three general categories: power rape, anger rape, and sadistic rape. In a **power rape,** the rapist, who usually feels inadequate and awkward in interpersonal relationships, intimidates the victim with threats of physical harm. In an **anger rape,** the rapist seems to be seeking revenge on women in general and expresses his rage through physical and verbal abuse. He seems to get little or no sexual satisfaction from the

rape. The third and rarest type, **sadistic rape,** seems to combine sexuality and aggression and focuses on the suffering of the victim. Sexual satisfaction seems limited in rape; in one large study, half the rapists had difficulties with erection or ejaculation during the rape itself (Groth and Burgess, 1977).

Rapists are almost always male. The victim may be either male or female, but most of the research on victims has been directed toward women. A female rape victim may experience trauma from the rape long after it has occurred. A victim's functioning in most areas usually returns to an average level after two or three months, but fear and anxiety remain high and sexual satisfaction relatively low for a longer period. Many victims are significantly more anxious, fearful, suspicious, and confused than nonvictims for at least a year after the assault (Kilpatrick and others, 1981). These fears tend to restrict and control the victim's life. Her most prevalent fears are of being alone, of strange men, of going out, and of darkness. Women who have been victims of sudden and violent assaults by strangers are especially likely to remain fearful and depressed for a long time, and they are also more likely to avoid dating for a long period (Ellis and others, 1981).

From the social-learning perspective, a rape is part of an in vivo classical-conditioning situation in which the threat of death or physical damage elicits a strong autonomic arousal, fear. Any stimulus that is present during the rape—darkness, a man with a particular appearance, being alone—becomes associated with the fear response. These cues then become conditioned stimuli that independently evoke fear and anxiety. Because some of these stimuli are often encountered by the victim in her daily life, she may begin to use avoidance behavior to escape them. This decreases the likelihood that the conditioned fear response will dissipate over time. Behavior therapy offers a way of overcoming these problems. By using both cognitive and behavioral techniques, victims can learn to overcome their avoidance behavior and thus extinguish their anxiety (Veronen and Kilpatrick, 1983).

Since an estimated 10 to 20 percent of rape victims have continuing problems of sexual dysfunction several years after the rape, they may also be helped by sex therapy that takes into account anger and resentment toward men, guilt and self-blame, and attitudes toward their partners that may be a residue of the rape.

Rape victims need to know what to do and where to go after the rape in order to obtain medical, mental-health, social, and legal services. They also need immediate and follow-up medical care for physical trauma, collection of medicolegal evidence, prevention of venereal disease, and protection against unwanted pregnancy. Rape victims need to be listened to and helped to talk about their experience, as well as to be given basic information and assistance in making decisions about further steps to be taken. An important source of help for rape victims is rape-relief centers where information and psychological support may be obtained (see Figure 8–20).

It is likely that even fewer male rapes than female rapes are reported because of the stigma attached to

**FIGURE 8-20**
Rape-relief centers, often staffed by volunteers, provide immediate support for rape victims as well as information about what medical and legal services to seek and where to find them. These centers attempt to reduce the social stigma that many rape victims experience. (Sybil Shelton)

*I kept trying to figure out how I could get back at him. I thought of getting a gun and going out to revenge myself.*

*I always thought a guy couldn't get hard if he was scared, and when this guy took me off it really messed up my mind. I thought maybe something was wrong with me. I didn't know what it meant and this really bothered me.* (Groth and Burgess, 1980, p. 809)

**The Rapist**  Rape is usually thought of as a sexually motivated crime, but not all rapists can be diagnosed as paraphilic. In rapes of both males and females, the sense of power and the discharge of anger and aggression often seem much more important than any sexual gratification. Rapists equate manhood with being in control, being aggressive, and carrying out sexual acts. Some also want to degrade and punish their victims.

Many rapists are impulsive and aggressive in their general behavior (Rada, 1978). They tend to be between 16 and 24 years old and to come from lower socioeconomic classes. Most rapes are committed by strangers, but the use of force for sexual purposes may be more common than we would like to think. In a survey of 282 women at Purdue University, more than half reported sexual aggression by their dates that included forcible kissing, fondling of their breasts and genitals, and intercourse. At least one-third of the forcible attempts at intercourse were successful, according to the students' reports (Kanin and Parcell, 1977).

In another research effort, male college students were asked how likely they would be to rape a woman if they could be assured of not being caught. About 35 percent said that there was some likelihood that they would commit rape under such conditions. Men who reported a higher likelihood of committing rape showed greater aggression toward women in a laboratory setting and were also more highly aroused when shown depictions of rape. In fact, their responses closely resembled those of convicted rapists (Malamuth, 1981). These findings suggest that aggression and rape are closely tied together for many individuals and also that the thought of rape does not have completely negative social implications for many young men.

### Treatment of Sexual Offenders

Both the psychological and biological perspectives have been used in treating sexual offenders such as pedophiles and rapists. One psychological technique that is often used is covert sensitization. For instance, this form of therapy has been used successfully in the treatment of some pedophiles. In this form of therapy the client is instructed to visualize a young girl in a specific physical setting and then to imagine experiencing

them. Because society expects men to defend themselves rather than to become victims, a male rape victim may be automatically suspected of homosexuality. The response of male rape victims is similar to that of females. Often their life style is temporarily disrupted, they have trouble eating and sleeping, and their sexual activity may be negatively affected. They may develop fear of men and are also likely to feel long-lasting anger at the assailant. Rapists sometimes succeed in forcing their male victims to ejaculate, and this is likely to be especially disturbing to the victims. The comments of male rape victims highlight some of these issues.

*Even a couple of years after, whenever I'd feel depressed or tired or something, this whole incident would come back to me. I'd think . . . what could I have done to prevent it?*

arousal and a desire to engage in sexual activities with her. The client is then trained to introduce aversive imagery (for example, imagining that a police officer has noticed him approaching the girl) immediately following the imagined sexual arousal. Next, at the cessation of this aversive imagery, the client is encouraged to feel relief (at stopping his approach to the girl and thus avoiding arrest). As the training proceeds, the client is taught to imagine being attracted to adult women and not being anxious about approaching them.

Covert sensitization was used as a therapy for a 39-year-old married man who had been convicted of sexually molesting his 10-year-old niece (Levin and others, 1977). Before and after the covert sensitization training, the client was shown slides with pictures of young girls and of adult women. Figure 8–21 compares the man's subjective ratings of his sexual arousal by slides of girls and his attraction to and anxiety over attraction to slides of women. His attraction to young girls decreased dramatically. Although his attraction to slides of women increased only slightly, there was a decrease in the anxiety aroused by them. A physiological measure, magnitude of penile erection, showed the same pattern of changes in attraction.

The biological perspective has also been applied to the treatment of pedophilia. The earliest biological treatment was surgical castration. However, in addition to being an extreme and abhorrent type of treatment, castration may not be very effective in changing behavior. Researchers surveyed the sexual behavior of re-leased sex offenders who had agreed to undergo surgical castration while in prison in West Germany (Heim, 1981). Although most of the men reported reduced desire and capacity for sexual arousal, about one-third reported that they were still able to engage in sexual intercourse. Rapists in particular were more sexually active after surgery than other groups of sex offenders.

A biological approach of a much less drastic nature is the use of the drug **medroxyprogesterone acetate** (MPA), marketed as Depo-Provera, which temporarily reduces the level of testosterone in the blood. Trials of the drug suggest that it may be effective in reducing compulsive sexual urges. Together with counseling, MPA may help some sex offenders keep their impulses under control. This treatment, which is still highly experimental, does not seem to be effective for sex offenders whose behavior contains a high degree of aggression (Bower, 1981). However, when combined with intensive therapy both in prison and after offenders return to the community, this drug seems to be effective (Groth, 1984).

Some people who engage in deviant sexual practices do not seem unusual in most areas of their lives, whereas others seem to be ridden with personal problems and social inadequacies. For some, the accumulation of worry and stress seems to heighten the need for relief through deviant sexual activity. In our study of psychophysiological disorders, we saw the powerful role of thought patterns in certain bodily changes. Thought patterns also seem to play a role in sexual deviations; preoccupying thoughts can lead to large bodily changes related to sexual arousal.

**FIGURE 8–21**
Changes in a pedophile's ratings of attraction toward girls and toward women, and changes in anxiety toward women before and after therapy. (Levin and others, 1977, p. 907)

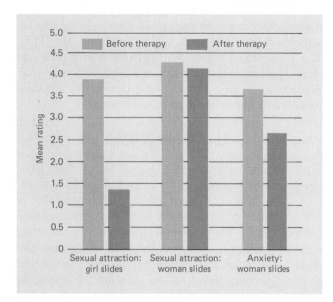

## ■ STUDY OUTLINE

### CHANGING VIEWS OF SEXUAL BEHAVIOR

The ancient Greeks regarded sex as a pleasurable part of nature, to be enjoyed with partners of either sex. During the middle ages, however, church authorities were obsessed with the notion of sex as a sin. By the mid-nineteenth century women were expected to be morally pure and sexually inert. This view began to change in the early twentieth century, partly as a result of the writings of Sigmund Freud and Havelock Ellis.

### GATHERING OBJECTIVE INFORMATION ABOUT SEXUAL BEHAVIOR

1. Alfred Kinsey pioneered in the gathering of scientific data about sexual behavior. He interviewed people about a wide variety of sexual practices and discovered that sexual behaviors that had been considered unusual or abnormal were in fact widely prac-

ticed. He and his coworkers published detailed statistical reports on the sexual behavior of heterosexual and homosexual males and females.

2. Observational studies have provided a great deal of information about the body's responses to sexual stimulation. The best-known observational studies were carried out by William Masters and Virginia Johnson under controlled laboratory conditions. On the basis of their findings, Masters and Johnson described a pattern of sexual response that consists of four stages: excitement, plateau, orgasm, and resolution.

3. Much experimental research on sexual behavior has studied the effects of erotic materials and alcohol on sexual response. The results of this research are contradictory.

### SEXUAL VARIATIONS

1. **Homosexual behavior** is sexual behavior with members of one's own sex; **homosexuals** are individuals who prefer to engage in social activity with members of their own sex over an extended period. Female homosexuality is often called **lesbianism. Bisexuals** are sexually attracted to members of either sex and often engage in sexual activity with both men and women.

2. Homosexuality is not considered a disorder in DSM-III-R. Types of psychopathology found among homosexuals do not generally differ from those found among heterosexuals. Public attitudes toward homosexuality have tended to redefine homosexuality as an alternative life style, but this view may be changing as a result of the link between homosexuality and the often fatal disease known as AIDS.

3. There is no such thing as a homosexual personality or behavior pattern. Homosexuals have been found to have a variety of life styles, ranging from close-coupled to asexual. Male homosexuals report having had many more sexual partners than female homosexuals do.

4. Patterns of bisexuality also differ widely. Bisexuality is most likely to occur during group sex, as a result of sexual experimentation between same-sex friends who are otherwise heterosexual, and when people adopt a philosophy of sexual openness.

5. The role of biological factors in the development of sexual preference is unclear, although a prenatal excess or deficiency of sex hormones may be a factor. So far evidence does not support psychodynamic and behavioral explanations of homosexual preference.

### SEXUAL DYSFUNCTION

1. Among the problems that are included in the category of sexual dysfunction are **impotence, frigid-**ity, **premature ejaculation,** and **retarded ejaculation.** In addition, many women have difficulty experiencing orgasm or never have orgasms. In **performance anxiety,** the man's preoccupation with sexual adequacy interferes with his performance.

2. Masters and Johnson believe that short-term treatment directed primarily at sexual problems can help most people who experience sexual dysfunction. They emphasize instruction in the sexual needs of both partners, together with exercises in erotic stimulation. Emphasis is also placed on communication between partners.

3. Behavioral approaches to the treatment of sexual dysfunction use such techniques as relaxation training and modeling. Some therapists combine behavioral approaches with psychodynamically oriented therapy. Further research is needed to determine which therapeutic elements are helpful and which are unnecessary.

### GENDER IDENTITY DISORDER

**Gender identity disorder in childhood** occurs before puberty. Children with this disorder reject or deny their assigned gender. **Transsexuals** experience an intense desire and need to change their sexual status, including their anatomical structure. They have a disturbance in their **gender identity,** that is, their feeling of being male or female. **Transsexuals** are adults with disturbed gender identity who have an intense desire to change their anatomical structures to those of the other sex. Many of the candidates who apply for sexual-reassignment surgery are also psychologically disturbed in areas other than gender identity.

### THE PARAPHILIAS

1. The term **paraphilia** refers to attraction to deviant objects or situations. Paraphilias may involve the use of a nonhuman object for sexual arousal, repetitive sexual activity with humans that involves suffering or humiliation, or repetitive sexual activity with nonconsenting partners.

2. **Fetishism** is a psychological state in which a nonliving object serves as a primary source of sexual arousal and consummation. It is not usually addressed by the law. Most fetishists are solitary in their activities, and the collection of fetishistic objects may be the main activity in their lives.

3. A **transvestite** uses clothing as a sexual stimulant or fetish. Most transvestites are heterosexual men who dress in women's clothes but continue to identify themselves as members of their biological sex. Covert sensitization has been found to be useful in treating this disorder.

4. To the **sadist,** achieving orgasm depends on humiliating others or inflicting pain on them. To the **masochist,** sexual satisfaction depends on suffering, humiliation, pain, and ill treatment at the hands of others. In sadomasochistic relationships the partners agree on the roles each will play and set limits on their activities beforehand. The sexual interests of fetishists, transvestites, and sadomasochists often overlap.

5. Sometimes sadomasochistic needs are satisfied by **autoerotic** practices, or solo sex-related activities. Among those activities is partial asphyxiation combined with masturbation. The majority of autoerotic deaths occur in teenagers and young adult males.

6. **Voyeurs** obtain sexual gratification from spying on others, usually strangers, especially as they undress or engage in sexual activity. Voyeurs are usually harmless.

7. **Exhibitionists** repeatedly expose their genitals to unsuspecting strangers in public places as a way of experiencing sexual arousal. Another way of obtaining sexual gratification with a nonconsenting individual is by making obscene telephone calls.

8. **Pedophilia** involves the desire for sexual gratification from a child, often a girl between the ages of 8 and 11. **Fixated pedophiles** begin during adolescence to focus on children as sex objects; **regressed pedophiles** turn to sexual interest in children after a serious and negative event in their own lives.

## SEXUAL VICTIMIZATION

1. **Incest** is defined as sexual relations between closely related individuals, but the definition of "closely related" varies from one culture to another. Most research on incest focuses on father–daughter sexual relationships. Often the victim is harmed less by the event than by the family's reaction.

2. **Rape** is having sexual intercourse forcibly and without the partner's consent. In **power rape,** the rapist intimidates the victim with threats of physical harm; in **anger rape,** the rapist seems to be seeking revenge on women in general and expresses his rage through physical and verbal abuse; **sadistic rape** seems to combine sexuality and aggression and focuses on the suffering of the victim.

3. In many rapes, the sense of power and the discharge of anger and aggression seem more important than sexual gratification. Many rapists are impulsive and aggressive in their general behavior. Most rapes are committed by strangers.

4. Behavioral techniques such as covert sensitization may be effective in treating such sexual offenders as pedophiles. Depo-Provera, a drug which temporarily reduces testosterone in the blood, has been used experimentally to treat some sex offenders.

# 9

# PERSONALITY DISORDERS

*Dr. B., a 41-year-old family practitioner, was getting ready to leave his office at 6 P.M. to rush home and have supper before attending his son's final high school basketball game. The hospital called to inform him that one of his obstetric patients had arrived in Labor and Delivery and was currently showing 5 cm of cervical dilation. He knew that one of his partners was covering obstetrics that night, but he felt compelled to run by the hospital to check her before going home. After checking her, he decided to stay through the delivery, necessitating his missing his son's last game. After the delivery, the physician sat in the locker room and wept. He felt terribly guilt-ridden over missing the game, and as he reflected on the evening, he could not understand why he had not simply handed the case over to his partner. He poignantly stated later that he was not even emotionally attached to this particular patient. His own narcissism had gotten the best of him; i.e., he felt that he and he alone had to be the one to deliver the baby, as though his partner could not have performed exactly the same function.* (Gabbard, 1985, p. 2928)

Presumably, most physicians function adequately in conducting their medical practice. Yet as a group, physicians often exhibit a personality style that emphasizes guilt feelings and an exaggerated sense of responsibility (Gabbard, 1985). This style may show itself in both adaptive and maladaptive ways. In one poll of 100 randomly selected physicians, all of them described themselves as "compulsive personalities" (Krakowski, 1982). Twenty percent met all the criteria for Compulsive Personality Disorder and 80 percent came close by meeting three criteria (four are required).

A person's characteristic ways of responding are often referred to as his or her **personality.** Most people's personality styles do not affect their behavior similarly in all situations. Personality styles can be maladaptive if an individual is unable to modify his or her behavior when the environment undergoes significant changes that call for different approaches. If personality characteristics are not flexible enough to allow an individual to respond adaptively to at least an ordinary variety of situations, a personality disorder may be present.

When personality styles become pathological, they can impair an individual's functioning in important situations and can lead to anxiety, feelings of distress, and unhappiness. The point at which a personality style becomes a personality disorder is unclear. **Personality disorders** are longstanding, maladaptive, and inflexible ways of relating to the environment. Such disorders can usually be noticed in childhood or at least by early adolescence, and may continue through adult life. They severely limit an individual's approach to stress-producing situations because his or her characteristic styles of thinking and behavior allow for only a rigid and narrow range of responses.

Personality disorders pose problems for people who construct classification systems, as well as for textbook writers and teachers of abnormal psychology. They seem important, and their existence can easily be recognized even by nonprofessional observers, yet little is known about their origins and development. With the exception of the Antisocial Personality Disorder or psychopathic personality (and until recently the Borderline Personality Disorder), very little research has been done on these problems, probably because they often are not dramatic or severely incapacitating and many people who might fall into these categories never seek help in dealing with their problems. Some writers have speculated that personality disorders are early signs of more disabling conditions, but so far there is no convincing evidence to support this idea.

Although the maladaptive behavior that is typical of personality disorders sometimes causes great distress to the people involved, they find it difficult to change the way they think about and respond to situations. The clinical problems are intensified when, as is usually the case, the person does not regard his or her behavior patterns as maladaptive or undesirable even if the unpleasant and counterproductive consequences of those behaviors are obvious to others. As we will see in this chapter, this is perhaps most evident in cases of antisocial personality.

# ■ CLASSIFYING PERSONALITY DISORDERS

DSM-III and DSM-III-R give new emphasis to the personality disorders by designating Axis II for their diagnosis. The diagnosis is made only when these inflexible maladaptive behaviors cause important problems in social situations or on the job, or when they result in a high level of personal distress. An Axis II diagnosis also requires that these characteristics have been typical of the person's functioning over a long period. In some instances, the classification statements of Axis II are used to provide information that bears on the primary diagnosis of Axis I. In other instances, a personality disorder referred to on Axis II is the individual's major problem.

In the following diagnosis of Henry A., both Axis I and Axis II classifications were made.

AXIS I: Schizophrenia, paranoid, chronic
AXIS II: Schizotypal Personality Disorder (premorbid)

In Henry A.'s case the psychotic symptoms that call for a diagnosis of schizophrenia are present. Before the present schizophrenic episode, however, Henry A. had shown several characteristics—such as odd speech, social isolation, suspiciousness, and hypersensitivity to real or imagined criticism—that had significantly impaired his effectiveness in a variety of situations.

Gerry B. showed similar personality characteristics, but there was no basis for an Axis I diagnosis. Her diagnosis would be as follows.

AXIS I: ———
AXIS II: Schizotypal Personality Disorder

A third individual, Deborah C., had characteristics of the same personality disorder that was seen in Henry A. and Gerry B. However, she had additional characteristics that fit another personality disorder. In this case both personality disorders would be diagnosed.

AXIS I: ———
AXIS II: Schizotypal Personality Disorder, Borderline Personality Disorder

One of the problems in discussing personality disorders is that the distinctions among several of the different types are imprecise. They often overlap and therefore correlate somewhat with one another. If disorders are to be classified into separate types, their criteria should be distinct and mutually exclusive, and the number of ambiguous cases should be relatively few. Some DSM-III-R categories—for example, schizophrenia, the affective disorders, and the organic disorders— are relatively distinct from each other, although there are some fuzzy areas between them. This is not true of personality disorders, many of whose diagnostic criteria overlap.

Another difficulty in deciding on the appropriateness of an Axis II diagnosis is the unclear boundary between those personality characteristics within normal limits and those that represent disordered behavior. Probably for all these reasons, personality disorders produce the least reliable diagnoses of any classification in the DSM III system (Spitzer and others, 1979c). On the positive side, it is possible that the new emphasis on the personality disorders will lead to expanded research and clearer criteria.

Personality disorders can be divided into three groups or clusters.

1. Odd or eccentric behaviors:
   Paranoid Personality Disorder
   Schizoid Personality Disorder
   Schizotypal Personality Disorder
2. Dramatic, emotional, or erratic behaviors:
   Histrionic Personality Disorder
   Narcissistic Personality Disorder
   Borderline Personality Disorder
   Antisocial Personality Disorder
3. Fearful or anxious behaviors:
   Avoidant Personality Disorder
   Dependent Personality Disorder
   Obsessive Compulsive Personality Disorder

Other categories to describe people whose behavior is consistently self-defeating or who gain pleasure from harming others have also been suggested.

The validity of most of these categories has not yet been established. As more research was done using DSM-III criteria, it became increasingly clear that some of the categories overlap a great deal. Rather than being separate disorders, they represent different degrees of the same general behaviors. In one study, for example, the researchers were unable to separate borderline, histrionic, and antisocial personality disorders (Pope and others, 1983). Some personality disorders also overlap Axis I categories. For instance, in the study just mentioned, more than half of the individuals who were diagnosed as borderline also had a major affective disorder.

Another problem caused by the DSM-III categories has arisen when treatment is considered. Because in some personality disorder categories the diagnosis may be made merely if a certain number of items from the list of criteria are met, individuals with the same diagnosis may be quite different. For instance, for a patient to be diagnosed as borderline only five of a list of eight symptoms need to be present; as a result, there are 93 possible combinations of symptoms. Despite these and other problems, DSM-III performed a valuable service by calling attention to personality disorders and providing a vehicle for gathering better information about them.

The behaviors of the personality disorder are long lasting and usually begin in adolescence or early adulthood. As yet, however, it is not clear whether having a particular personality disorder makes a person unusually likely to develop more severe difficulties, such as schizophrenia or an affective disorder, later on. Certain childhood disorders have a logical relationship to personality disorders and may represent part of a continuing process. For example, conduct disorders in childhood or adolescence are similar in character to antisocial personality disorders in adulthood. However, at present the causal factors in these relationships are not clear.

# ■ ODD OR ECCENTRIC BEHAVIORS

## Paranoid Personality Disorder

People with **paranoid personality disorders** have three outstanding characteristics: unwarranted feelings of suspiciousness and mistrust of other people, hypersensitivity, and restricted emotional response. It is very difficult for such people to have close relationships with others because they are constantly expecting treachery.

Paranoid individuals rarely seek clinical help. If the situation becomes so difficult that they are forced to seek help (for example, if they find themselves in a situation that requires them to work closely with other people), the therapist's hardest task is to penetrate the barrier of suspiciousness. They are also hypersensitive to criticism, making it especially difficult for them to function in subordinate positions. They have a strong fear of losing independence and the power to shape events. Just the feeling of being in a position of lower rank or lesser power might be intolerable.

> For example, one such man could not bring himself to address his superiors at work by the title "Mr." He refused, as he put it, to "crawl" or "jump through the hoop." Similarly, he could not bring himself to address his therapist as "Dr." even at their first meeting and used from the outset what he assumed was the therapist's nickname. (Shapiro, 1981, p. 138)

The following example illustrates how such feelings can affect employer–employee relationships.

> A patient felt that his boss "wanted to make him jump through the hoop," and he would have none of it. The patient had a good deal of evidence to prove his point, all of it probably quite factual and some of it quite keenly observed. Yet, to someone else, even these facts did not add up to a particularly unusual boss. True, the boss had insisted that the work be done his way and not the patient's way. He did make a point of promptness, perhaps unnecessarily. He had objected to the patient's apparently cool manner with certain customers. And, quite possibly, he had even done all of this with a certain edge in his voice or the look of a man who didn't mind the opportunity of bringing an independent young fellow

to heel. All these items may have been there, as most of them often are in bosses, because they include a good deal of what bosses are supposed to accomplish. To the patient, however, they were unmistakable clues to the man's real motives: to make him crawl and to emasculate him. Who knows? Perhaps even this motive was not altogether absent. But all these clues appeared in a context that the patient disregarded but that radically alters the significance of them. The fact is, there was work to be done, and the boss was responsible for it; and the difference between a boss who pursues this objective too aggressively and a man whose principal interest is to cut down his subordinate is a very great difference indeed. (Shapiro, 1965, pp. 60–61)

People with paranoid personality disorders often seem cold, humorless, devious, and scheming. These characteristics do not promote close, rewarding relationships. Perhaps because people with this kind of personality keep to themselves and rarely become intimate with others, many of their unusual ideas remain unnoticed. Their performance is often impaired, however, because their preoccupation with searching for hidden motives and special meanings limits their ability to consider and understand whole situations. When problems occur, they are often work-related, since work is an area in which interpersonal contacts are difficult to avoid.

## Schizoid Personality Disorder

Individuals with **schizoid personality disorders** are reserved, socially withdrawn, and seclusive (see Figure 9–1). They prefer solitary work activities and hobbies and

**FIGURE 9-1**
Spending time alone, withdrawn from others, is typical of people with schizoid personality disorders. They often appear quite detached from life around them. (John Running, Stock, Boston)

lack the capacity for warm, close relationships. They rarely express their feelings directly. Not only do they have few relationships with others, but they also seem to have little desire for them. In any case, they often have poor social skills, although their speech and behavior patterns are not unusual or eccentric. They also lack a sense of humor and seem detached from their environment. Perhaps because of this detachment, males with schizoid personality disorder seldom marry. Females are more likely to marry, possibly by accepting a marriage offer rather than seeking it. When, in her novel *The White Album*, Joan Didion uses the phrase "only marginally engaged in the dailiness of life" (p. 121), she could be describing the detachment of people with schizoid personality disorders.

The emotional responses of schizoid individuals seem rather flat as well as cold. The kinds of frustrations that arouse expressions of anger in most people elicit little observable hostility from these individuals. They often seem vague, self-absorbed, absent-minded, and not very aware of or interested in what is going on around them. Some of these people can support themselves if they find socially isolated jobs. Many of them, however, have problems at work because of the contact with other people that most jobs require. Since schizoid people are not bothered by their lack of personal relationships, they are poor prospects for therapy.

## Schizotypal Personality Disorder

People with **schizotypal personality disorders** are characterized by oddities of thinking, perceiving, communicating, and behaving. However, deviations in these areas are never as extreme as those found in cases of full-blown schizophrenia. People with schizotypal personality disorders, like schizoid individuals, are seclusive, emotionally shallow, and socially unskilled, but their speech pattern is quite different. Things that they say in conversation often are not understood because they either use unusual words and phrases or use common words in unusual ways. They also often express ideas unclearly. At times—usually when they are under stress—their thinking deteriorates and they may express ideas that seem delusional. Their behavior at such times may border on the bizarre. Much of the time they seem suspicious, superstitious, and aloof.

Saul, age 28, had had ten years of a variety of therapies but he still felt lonely and isolated, unlovable, undeserving, and unable to experience pleasure. Until he was 12 things seemed fine—he did well in school and made friends. He said, "When I was about 12 years old, I began to get the feeling that I was not like other people . . . , I felt that I was repulsive." He started to keep to himself, and developed a variety of rituals, such as double-checking everything he did. Saul dropped out of college after two years. Shortly afterward his parents sent him to a psychoanalyst; later he saw a behaviorally oriented therapist and also received drugs and went with his parents for family therapy. The only improvement during this long period was during the two times he was admitted to a psychiatric hospital. He functioned very well on the ward, socialized with the other patients, and took a leadership role. Except during these hospitalizations, he continued to be isolated. He spent most of his time alone, refusing even to eat with his parents. He devised various tortures for himself. For example, over a several-year period he starved himself so that he was 40 pounds underweight. Between periods of starvation he would indulge in binge eating and then in self-induced vomiting. Saul read a great deal and had a good vocabulary, but he had an odd manner of speaking that made him sound like a robot. He described himself as a born victim who had no niche in the "fierce competition of the world" and had strong feelings about being repulsive and undeserving. At one point he wrote: "The feeling that I have as I walk through the world filled with people, wanting so much to be in contact with them and yet always remaining apart, can scarcely be described . . . and worst of all is the knowledge that for me there is no reprieve, that I will have to live in this horrible way all my life on this earth." At one point Saul seemed to improve. He got a job in a bookstore, went with his parents to a family function, and even asked someone for a date. After a series of these systematic attempts to make social contact, he quit his job, spent his time in his bedroom, and resumed binge eating. In a letter to his therapist he wrote that he felt his isolation would never end and that he would be better off dead. (adapted from Spitzer and others, 1983, pp. 55–57)

Saul's self-torture may have been related to depression, but he also had a strange sense of being different from other people. His rituals suggest magical thinking. Many of these characteristics are similar to those of people who have recovered from the psychotic period of a schizophrenic disorder. Schizotypal individuals probably have more than the average risk of an episode of schizophrenia later in life. Since many cases of schizophrenia are presumed to have a hereditary, biological component, this would imply that schizotypal individuals share this genetic characteristic.

## ■ DRAMATIC, EMOTIONAL, OR ERRATIC BEHAVIORS

The first group of personality disorders is composed of individuals with withdrawn behavior. The second category contains people who seek attention and whose behavior is often highly noticeable and very unpredictable.

## Histrionic Personality Disorder

For people with **histrionic personality disorders,** getting the attention of others is a high priority (see Figure 9–2). Their motto might be "All the world's a stage"; they often act out a role, such as "the star" or "the victim" as part of an interpersonal relationship. These people strike others as vain and immature and tend to speak in a dramatic, exaggerated, and gushing manner (see Figure 9–3).

This classification is used in cases that are marked by exaggerated expressions of emotion, stormy interpersonal relationships, a self-centered attitude, and manipulativeness. The manipulativeness might manifest itself in suicidal gestures, threats, or attempts, as well as in other attention-getting behaviors such as dramatic physical complaints. Histrionic patients often come to the attention of therapists because of a drug overdose or other form of suicide attempt. Therapy for these individuals commonly includes medication (Widiger and Frances, 1985).

Histrionic individuals often react too quickly to sit-

**FIGURE 9–3**
The speech of those with histrionic personality disorder is characterized by exaggeration and hyperbole. This woman has just seen someone she hardly knows and overreacts by greeting him effusively.

uations that require some analysis and thought. They don't always focus their attention long enough to perceive the details of a situation, and as a result they tend to respond with emotionally tinged generalities. When people with histrionic personalities are asked to describe something, they generally respond with impressions rather than facts. For example, a therapist who was taking a case history from a client and had made repeated efforts to get a description of her father reported that the patient "seemed . . . hardly to understand the sort of data I was interested in, and the best she could provide was, "My father? He was wham-bang! That's all—just wham-bang!" (Shapiro, 1965, p. 111).

Histrionic individuals often operate on hunches and tend to stop at the obvious. Not only are they suggestible and easily influenced by the opinions of others, but they are also easy to distract. Their attention is easily captured and just as easily turned toward something else. This results in behavior with a scattered quality. These problems of attention also lead histrionic people to appear incredibly naive about many commonplace things.

Anthony Storr (1980) has interpreted histrionic behavior as a pattern that is often adopted by individuals who do not feel able to compete with others on equal terms and believe that no one is paying attention to them. Storr thinks that such people may have been disregarded by their parents as children. Although the child repeatedly tried to get the parents to regard him or her as an individual, those attempts failed. The child then became demanding and resorted to all kinds of dramatic behaviors in order to be noticed. The less attention the parents paid to the child, the more the child had to shout or dramatize to get their attention. Histrionic individuals carry these extreme behaviors into adulthood.

**FIGURE 9–2**
Attracting attention by their often affected or unusual behavior and dress is typical of those with histrionic personality disorder. (Bruce M. Wellman, Stock, Boston)

Histrionic people may also feel unlovable and may react to this feeling by trying to make themselves sexually irresistible. Women in particular may dress and behave seductively yet not really desire intimate sexual activity. Women are more likely than men to be diagnosed as histrionic.

## Narcissistic Personality Disorder

The word *narcissism* comes from the Greek myth about a young man, Narcissus, who fell in love with his reflection in a pond. Because he could never grasp the image, which he thought was a water nymph, he sorrowed and ultimately died.

DSM-III-R includes several critical factors in its description of **Narcissistic Personality Disorder:** an extreme sense of self-importance and the expectation of special favors, a need for constant attention, fragile self-esteem, and lack of empathy or caring for others (see Figure 9–4). People with a narcissistic personality dis-

**FIGURE 9–4**
Sometimes performers show narcissistic tendencies that may be encouraged by excessive admiration by their fans. (Chuck Pulin, Star File)

order are often preoccupied with fantasies of unlimited success and brilliance, power, beauty, and ideal love relationships. They may think of their problems as unique and feel that only other equally special people are able to understand them. The case of Robert Graham illustrates many of the characteristics of narcissistic personality disorders.

*Graham, a successful 30-year-old actor, contacted a therapist because he was having trouble with a new stage role. In it he had to play a character who was deeply depressed by the death of his wife. As Graham said, he had trouble portraying "a character who was so involved with a woman that his life essentially ended simply because she died."*

*In his first interview he told the therapist what a good actor he was. "I don't wish to be immodest, but I am uniquely talented." Throughout his life he had been told he was "uniquely cute" and "gifted." He could be charming and entertaining and used these abilities to make other people feel "special" as a way of furthering his career. He seemed to respond to others with a feeling of contempt and remarked that other people were gullible and "easily taken in by experiences."*

*Graham's relations with women puzzled him. He began dating and had sexual activity early and had romances with a series of women as he grew older. However, in each romance after a short period he would gradually lose interest and usually start an affair with another woman before breaking off with the first. He gave little thought to his former partners after breaking off the relationships. "It is almost as if people are playthings and I need lots and lots of new toys." His account of his life sounded as if he had never grieved or been depressed. (adapted from Spitzer and others, 1983, pp. 71–74)*

The category Narcissistic Personality Disorder was introduced in DSM-III because mental health professionals had seen an increase in cases in which the problem seemed to be excessive self-concern and an inflated sense of one's own importance and uniqueness (see Figure 9–5). In addition, in recent years several psychoanalysts have focused on personal development in the early years of life, the development of the self as a separate entity, and narcissism as an aspect of self-development.

Psychoanalysts since Freud have been interested in the idea of narcissism. Freud's views on the topic changed during his lifetime. In his early writings he described narcissism as a developmental stage that occurs very early in life, as soon as the child is able to reliably differentiate him- or herself from the environment. This stage is later replaced by the more mature phase of object love, in which the child is able to "love" in

**FIGURE 9-5**
People with narcissistic personality disorder often spend considerable amounts of time preoccupied with fantasies of fame and power.

the sense of feeling a relationship with another person (Freud, 1914/1925). Freud later suggested that children often remain at the narcissistic stage because they have been cared for by people who do not love dependably. To protect themselves in this situation, children may turn inward so that they will not be rejected. Freud believed that narcissistic individuals could not profit from psychoanalysis because they could not form the necessary transference relationship with the therapist.

More recent psychoanalytic theorists have developed some new ideas about narcissism. One of the most influential of these theorists, Otto Kernberg (1970, 1975), has emphasized the unusual degree of self-reference in the narcissist's interaction with other people and the contrast between the narcissist's apparently inflated self-image and his or her unfulfillable need for approval by others. Although this need for praise and approval may make narcissists seem dependent, according to Kernberg they really are unable to depend on anyone because of their deep distrust of others. Like Freud, Kernberg believes that most narcissistic individuals had parents who were cold and indifferent and at the same time subtly aggressive and spiteful toward their children. Kernberg's views, while they change the emphasis of Freud's ideas, are not a drastic revision of Freudian theory.

Heinz Kohut (1971, 1977), another influential psychoanalyst, had considerably different views on narcissism and suggested a new psychoanalytic approach to this disorder. Instead of seeing narcissistic feelings as characteristic of a particular stage of development, Kohut thought of them as an aspect of personality that permeates our lives from childhood through adult life. Narcissism does not fade away by changing to object love but unfolds throughout a person's lifetime. It is

through this developmental unfolding that the individual gains a sense of self.

Kohut believed that in early childhood the normal child feels grandiose or omnipotent and also idealizes his or her parents. Of course, both of these beliefs are unrealistic, and eventually the child discovers that they are false. If parents do not respond to their child's endearing, praiseworthy, and unique qualities, the child may fail to develop a sense of being worthwhile and valued. He or she may continue unsuccessfully to seek such recognition all through life. If the parents are indifferent or rejecting, and not as wonderful as the child fantasizes, the child may grow into an adult who feels depressed and empty. In these terms, the narcissist is engaged in a hopeless search for an idealized parent surrogate. According to Kohut's view, the chief characteristics of a narcissistic disorder are low self-esteem, periodic self-absorption, minor physical complaints, and feelings of emptiness or deadness. Kohut's ideas, although they are very influential, are not reflected as fully in DSM-III-R as those of Freud and Kernberg.

Kernberg believes that traditional psychoanalysis is the most useful approach to the treatment of narcissism, although he thinks that other, more limited therapies can also be useful. Kohut, on the other hand, believed that the therapist must treat the narcissistic disorder before psychoanalysis can be useful. The therapist does this by imagining him- or herself "into the client's skin" rather than concentrating on interpreting the situation objectively. This procedure is intended to develop the client's sense of being understood and appreciated so that the arrested development of the self can be resumed.

The psychoanalytic perspective presumes that the parents of individuals who have narcissistic personalities were unresponsive to their children's needs and were often cold and rejecting. The social-learning perspective, on the other hand, presumes that narcissism is likely to develop if the parents consistently overrate their children and create self-images for them that cannot hold up in the real world. When early childhood is past and the children are exposed to the more realistic evaluations of others, the clash between the beliefs of importance and talent fostered by the parents and the more realistic responses of outsiders can lead to narcissism (Millon, 1981). Whether any of these viewpoints will be useful in diagnosis and treatment has yet to be determined by research.

## Borderline Personality Disorder

The listing of **Borderline Personality Disorder** in DSM-III represented the first official recognition of this disorder. This category has already become so popular that 20 percent of psychiatric patients are given that diagnosis and it is estimated to occur in 3 to 5 percent of the general population (Grinspoon, 1985). Someone with a borderline personality disorder shows an instability in a number of areas, including mood, interpersonal relationships, and self-image. Since no single characteristic is required to be present in all cases, people with this disorder can differ greatly from one another. Four of the characteristics of borderline personality disorder (impulsivity, unstable/intense relationships, intense/uncontrolled anger, and affective instability) occurred together in 75 percent of one group of borderline patients (Clarkin and others, 1983). The other characteristics were found much less frequently and sometimes were of little help in arriving at a diagnosis.

Sometimes patients who are diagnosed as borderline and those who are diagnosed as schizotypal seem similar. However, the schizotypal and borderline categories have different emphases. The schizotypal category stresses cognitive symptoms: magical thinking, ideas of reference, suspicious thought. The borderline category stresses affective or emotional symptoms: feelings of emotional instability, emptiness, boredom, and inappropriate and intense anger (Gunderson, 1984). Schizotypal individuals are socially isolated; in contrast, borderline individuals cannot stand being alone.

Borderline and narcissistic disorders also seem to overlap. However, the overlap may be due more to the way the DSM criteria are described than to basic similarities between the two types of disorders. The exploitiveness of the narcissistic individual is based on overall arrogance and a sense of being entitled to special privileges, while the borderline person's exploitiveness is manipulative and is based on a need for survival. Both have a strong need for other people, but the narcissistic person is likely to be arrogant or disdainful of others and also to need constant admiration, while the borderline person needs nurturance and the availability of others.

Borderline individuals tend to have intense and unstable interpersonal relationships. A person may be valued as a wonderful friend one day and suddenly cut off the next. Often there is a manipulative quality to these relationships. Borderline individuals are also likely to engage impulsively in a variety of self-damaging behaviors. These may include gambling, shoplifting, overeating, and sexual exploits as well as suicidal gestures, self-mutilation, or fighting. Table 9–1 shows the frequency of self-destructive acts in one group of borderline individuals.

Self-destructiveness is the characteristic of borderline individuals that generates the most discomfort in those who attempt to help them. The therapists' hope

□ **TABLE 9–1**

The total number of self-destructive acts described by 57 people with borderline personality disorder

| Category | Number of Acts | Behavior Pattern |
|---|---|---|
| Suicide threats | 42 | To get attention<br>To cause trouble<br>In rage |
| Overdose | 40 | No usual pattern<br>Barbiturates most frequent |
| Self-mutilation | 36 | Wrist slashing > body banging >> burning, puncturing, hair removal |
| Drug abuse | 38 | Polydrug abuse >> amphetamines, alcohol binges > marijuana |
| Promiscuity | 36 | Usually under the influence of drugs or alcohol |
| Accidents | 14 | Reckless driving |

Adapted from Gunderson, 1984, p. 86.

of saving an endangered life is alternately encouraged and then dashed by the client's spiteful efforts at self-destruction. Therapists often experience intense feelings of responsibility for borderline clients. The therapist's initial efforts to be supportive when the client threatens suicide can lead to increased responsibility for the client's life and increased involvement outside of the therapy sessions. Unless the controlling nature of the client's responses are interpreted in the therapy sessions, the situation may become unworkable for the therapist. It is necessary to make the client understand that the therapist cannot be manipulated by threats of suicide and that the client must work to understand these self-destructive urges without acting them out. If this effort is not successful, the threats of self-destruction will recur and the risk to the client will be even greater if the therapist fails to respond on cue. This danger is illustrated by the following example.

*A borderline patient periodically rented a motel room and, with a stockpile of pills nearby, would call her therapist's home with an urgent message. He would respond by engaging in long conversations in which he "talked her down." Even as he told her that she could not count on his always being available, he became more wary of going out evenings without detailed instructions about how he could be reached. One night the patient couldn't reach him due to a bad phone connection. She fatally overdosed from what was probably a miscalculated manipulation. (Gunderson, 1984, p. 93)*

Marked emotional instability with sudden shifts to anxiety, continued depression, or irritability, which may last only a few hours and never more than a few days, are typical of borderline personality disorder, as is illustrated in the following description by a patient.

> "I was alone at home a few months ago; I was frightened! I was trying to get in touch with my boyfriend and I couldn't . . . He was nowhere to be found. All my friends seemed to be busy that night and I had no one to talk to . . . I just got more and more nervous and more and more agitated. Finally—bang!—I took out a cigarette and lit it and stuck it into my forearm. I don't know why I did it because I didn't really care for him all that much. I guess I felt I had to do something dramatic." (Stone, 1980, p. 400)

Borderline individuals also show disturbance in their concepts of identity: uncertainties about self-image, gender identity, values, loyalties, and goals. They may have chronic feelings of emptiness or boredom and be unable to tolerate being alone. The following anecdote illustrates the behavior of a borderline individual.

> During the night before being brought to the hospital by her parents, Ms. C., a 22-year-old unemployed woman, was assaulted by her boyfriend and had cut both her forearms. Her parents were concerned that her behavior would deteriorate and blamed the boyfriend, a known drug abuser and pusher. Ms. C. and her boyfriend had been at a nightclub the previous evening. He felt she was dancing too seductively, they argued, and he slapped her in the face. She ran from the club, later cut both arms, became fearful something terrible would happen to her boyfriend, and spent the rest of the night looking for him, damaging her car in the process. He went to another bar, got into a fight, and was arrested for assault and possession of illegal drugs. She described the situation, "He didn't understand. I need to dance. I'm a gypsy." In the hospital, with much support, she appeared to understand the advisability of terminating the destructive relationship. As soon as she was free on a pass, however, she would become "desperate" and seek him out again. She observed, "If I have someone else right away I can do it; I can leave him. But it's the only way." (Arkema, 1981, pp. 174–175)

Many psychotherapists report that they are seeing an increasing number of borderline patients, and there has been speculation that the proportion of such people in the population is growing. People like Marilyn Monroe, Lawrence of Arabia, Thomas Wolfe, Adolf Hitler, and Zelda Fitzgerald would probably be classified in this category today (see Figure 9–6). Each of them was famous for unpredictable and often extremely changeable behaviors, intolerance of routine and social conventions, periods of desperation, and the many unusual events that characterized his or her life.

**FIGURE 9–6**
These famous people—the dictator Adolf Hitler, the actress Marilyn Monroe, the writer Thomas Wolfe—all had personality traits that are similar to those found in people with borderline personality disorders. (UPI/Bettmann Newsphotos; Culver Pictures, Inc.)

Some writers believe that the fragmentation and change that characterize contemporary American society create problems in maintaining stable relationships and thereby promote borderline pathology.

## Treatment of Borderline Personality Disorders

Borderline individuals have been described by Freud and many later writers as unsuitable candidates for psychoanalysis. These writers feared that the unstructured nature of the treatment and its encouragement of fantasy would break down the already unstable self-concepts of such individuals and precipitate them into psychotic breakdowns. However, recent developments in psychoanalysis have provided variations that are considered suitable for the borderline person. Otto Kernberg, for example, believes that most borderline individuals can best be treated in intensive face-to-face psychotherapy sessions at least three times a week over a period of several years. In these sessions the therapist plays a more active structuring role than is usual in classical psychoanalysis. At the beginning the emphasis is on present behavior rather than childhood experiences, and rather than allowing the transference relationship to develop fully, the therapist explicitly describes and discusses the client's apparent distortions of reality—for example, the client's perceptions of the therapist.

Kernberg emphasizes the idea of **splitting,** or failure to integrate the positive and negative experiences that occur between the individual and other people. Splitting is Kernberg's theoretical explanation of the extreme changeability that can be seen in the borderline person's relationships to others. Rather than perceiving another individual as a loving person who sometimes accepts and sometimes rejects—for example, a mother who sometimes hugs and sometimes corrects a young child—the borderline individual shifts back and forth between these contradictory images. Kernberg describes this behavior in one of his patients.

*In one session, the patient may experience me as the most helpful, loving, understanding human being and may feel totally relieved and happy, and all the problems solved. Three sessions later, she may berate me as the most ruthless, indifferent, manipulative person she has ever met. Total unhappiness about the treatment, ready to drop it and never come back.* (Sass, 1982, pp. 14–15)

### Drawbacks of the Borderline Category
Some critics believe that the category of borderline personality disorders is unclear and that its name is misleading (Frances, 1980; Loranger and others, 1982; Millon, 1981). The word *borderline* suggests a marginal level of functioning, something that borders on becoming something else. Some researchers argue that borderline patients represent the boundary between personality disorders and mood disorders. About half of the people who are diagnosed as suffering from borderline personality disorder are depressed and can also be diagnosed as having a mood disorder (Pope and others, 1983). (We discuss mood disorders in the next chapter.) This group is also likely to have a family history of mood disorder and to respond well to antidepressive medication.

Another question is whether borderline disorder is really a separate category, since some researchers have been unable to distinguish it from histrionic personality disorder and antisocial personality disorder (Pope and others, 1983). However, other researchers have found that relatives of a person with a borderline personality disorder are ten times as likely to be treated for a borderline or similar disorder themselves than relatives of schizophrenic or bipolar patients (Loranger and others, 1982). These findings provide some support for seeing borderline personality disorder as a true category of pathologies rather than as a combination of several groups.

## Antisocial Personality Disorder

**Antisocial personality disorder** is associated with crime, violence, and delinquency. The essential characteristics of this disorder includes a history of continuous and chronic behavior that violates the rights of others, begins before the age of 15, and continues into adult life. In addition, the following characteristics must be present.

1. Age at least 18.
2. Evidence of a conduct disorder before the age of 15—such things as truancy, school suspension, arrest, running away from home, lying, engaging in sexual intercourse, or using liquor, tobacco, or other nonprescribed drugs unusually early compared to peers, as well as a history of stealing, vandalism, fights, and violation of rules at home or at school.
3. A pattern of irresponsible and antisocial behavior since the age of 15, including inability to sustain a consistent work record; repeated antisocial acts such as stealing, destroying property, and harassing others; repeated fights or assaults; failure to honor financial obligations; failure to plan ahead; recklessness, especially in driving; mistreatment or neglect of children if a parent; sexual promiscuity; and lack of remorse upon harming others.

Gary Gillmore, whose life is described in Box 9–1, fits this description well.

Antisocial Personality Disorder has not been a very useful diagnostic category because it doesn't discriminate well among different types of criminals, at least

The case of Gary Gillmore illustrates many characteristics of antisocial personality disorder. Gillmore was convicted of two murders and sentenced to death. When he was executed, on January 17, 1977, he was the first person to be put to death in the United States in 11 years. Although he refused to appeal his conviction, several appeals were made on his behalf and his execution was delayed three times. During this period, while newspapers featured stories on his "fight for the right to be executed," he attempted suicide twice.

Gillmore displayed an antisocial personality pattern very early. In spite of his high intelligence, his school grades were poor, he was often truant, and he was repeatedly accused of stealing from his schoolmates. At 14 he was sent to a juvenile center for stealing a car; after his release he was sent to jail several times for burglaries; and at 20 he was sent to the state penitentiary for burglary and robbery. After his release from the penitentiary he spent two years in jail for reckless and drunk driving. After this imprisonment he spent 11 years in the state penitentiary for several armed robberies.

Gillmore reported that he had begun drinking at the age of 10 and later had used a variety of illegal drugs—amphetamines, cocaine, and LSD. During his prison stays, he drank when he could and smoked marijuana. He was a talented tattoo artist. Several times he tattooed obscene words and pictures on inmates whom he disliked. "I thought it was a good way to get back at the snitches. I would tattoo them on their bodies where they could not watch what I was doing. It wasn't until they looked at their tattoo in the mirror that they saw what I had done to them." When he was released from prison in April of 1976, Gillmore went to Utah to work in his uncle's shop. When that job didn't work out, he went on to several others. He met a woman and moved in with her the next day. He said that this was the first time he had ever had a close relationship with anyone. It didn't go smoothly. Her two children irritated him, and he often hit them. His drinking and his tendency to get into fights at parties also caused problems.

Before long Gillmore felt increasingly frustrated. He seemed unable to succeed outside prison. He broke parole by getting drunk, but his parole officer decided not to report him. After an argument with the woman he lived with, he walked into a store and forcibly carried out a stereo, but he dropped it and fled when two security guards attempted to grab him. After a chase by the police, he got away. Again through the intervention of his parole officer, no charges were brought. When he went back to his house, his woman friend ordered him out with a gun.

In July he pulled into a gas station, ordered the attendant to give him all his cash, and then took

**FIGURE 9-7**
Gary Gillmore. (Tim Kelly, Liaison)

the attendent into the station restroom and shot him twice in the head as the man knelt before him. The next morning he walked into a motel.

*I went in and told the guy to give me the money. I told him to lay on the floor and then I shot him. I then walked out and was carrying the cash drawer with me. I took the money and threw the cash drawer in a bush and I tried to push the gun in the bush, too. But as I was pushing it in the bush, it went off and that's how come I was shot in the arm. It seems like things have always gone bad for me. It seems like I've always done dumb things that just caused trouble for me. I remember when I was a boy I would feel like I had to do things like sit on a railroad track until just before the train came and then I would dash off. Or I would put my finger over the end of a BB gun and pull the trigger to see if a BB was really in it. Sometimes I would stick my finger in water and then put my finger in a light socket to see if it would really shock me. (Spitzer and others, 1983, p. 68)*

Gillmore was evaluated to determine whether he was competent to stand trial. His IQ was found to be 129, in the superior range. His general knowl-

**FIGURE 9-8a**
Vandalism, such as the damage of these windows, is a typical behavior of children and adolescents who have conduct disorders. When carried out by people who are over 18, it is usually considered to be evidence of an antisocial personality disorder. (Frank Siteman, Stock, Boston)

**FIGURE 9-8b**
Mistreatment of children and other relatively defenseless individuals is a behavior associated with both conduct disorder and antisocial personality disorder. In addition to direct aggressive behavior, mistreatment of children may include neglect of their physical needs for food, cleanliness and adequate supervision. (Wasyl Szkodzinsky, Photo Researchers)

those who are in prison. In one study, 50 percent of the inmates in two prisons were included in this category (Hare, 1983). Moreover, these criteria are often met by many people who grow up in poor areas. They also leave out many people who appear to be antisocial but were not caught by the police before they were adults (Frances, 1980).

When criminals are divided into groups consisting of those who behave as their peers do and those whose antisocial behavior seems to have other causes, only about one-third of all criminals fall into the antisocial-personality category (Hare, 1978). It might be useful to place more emphasis on the personality characteristics of criminals in order to distinguish those who are capable of feeling guilt, anxiety, loyalty, and empathy from those who are not (Miller, 1981). The disorder known as psychopathic personality (to be discussed later) emphasizes the characteristics of lovelessness and guiltlessness. Treatment is likely to affect such individuals very differently.

**Conduct Disorder** Antisocial personality disorder, by definition, occurs only in individuals over 18 years of age. Some other classification is necesary for those below that age. The DSM-III-R category **Conduct Disorder** is used to describe many individuals who are later diagnosed as having an antisocial personality disorder. The conduct disorders are diagnosed on Axis I, not on Axis II as personality disorders are.

The term *conduct disorder* is used to describe children and adolescents whose behavior problems are more serious than the ordinary mischief and pranks often carried out by young people. The term can also be used for adults who do not meet all the criteria for antisocial personality disorders. Conduct disorder is diagnosed when there is a repetitive pattern of actions over a period of six months or more that either violate the basic rights of others or violate social norms or rules appropriate for the patient's age group (see Figure 9–8A and 9–8B). The behaviors that are typical of conduct disorders includes purse snatching, mugging, armed robbery, rape, stealing, drug abuse, vandalism, arson, and cruelty to animals and people, as well as truancy, cheating in school or in games, running away from home, and persistent fighting. Because so many behaviors may be included, people who are diagnosed as having a conduct disorder may be quite different from one another.

*Ever since his parents could remember, Robbie has been in trouble. For example, when he was a young child he pushed his sister down the stairs and turned the switch on the electric garage door when his brother was riding his tricycle under it. As he grew older this behavior*

*continued. At 15 Robbie raped his 6-year-old cousin and beat the elderly lady next door when he demanded her purse and then found only $1 in it. His parents and his teachers were all afraid of him. He never seemed to feel sorry for his victims, and no one around him felt safe whenever he was out of the various institutions to which he had been sent during his adolescence.*

Robbie's behavior is impulsive and aggressive. He seems to have no mercy for his victims and attacks people who have been kind to him as readily as strangers or enemies. Although he dislikes being punished or institutionalized, he shows little concern about the harm his behavior has brought about. Consider another example.

*Tom lied so plausibly and with such utter equanimity, devised such ingenious alibis or simply denied all responsibility with such convincing appearances of candor that for many years his real career was poorly estimated . . . At 14 or 15 years of age, having learned to drive, Tom began to steal automobiles with some regularity. Often his intention seemed less that of theft than of heedless misappropriation. A neighbor or friend of the family, going . . . to where the car was parked . . . would find it missing. Sometimes . . . [Tom] would leave the stolen vehicle within a few blocks . . . of the owner, sometimes out on the road where the gasoline has given out. After he had tried to sell a stolen car, his father consulted advisors and, on the theory that he might have some specific craving for automobiles, bought one for him as a therapeutic measure. On one occasion while driving [Tom] deliberately parked his own car and . . . stole an inferior model which he left slightly damaged on the outskirts of a village some miles away. (Cleckley, 1964, p. 86)*

Tom seems to be influenced not by the behavior of those around him but by a desire for excitement. He differs from Robbie in that his actions are focused not on people but on things and hence lack the violence of Robbie's escapades.

**The Disturbed Adolescent** Sometimes an adolescent commits a single dramatic and very damaging act that surprises people who have known him or her for a long time. Such behavior is not viewed as a sign of a conduct disorder because it is not part of a habitual pattern. Violent behavior of this kind seems to be a manifestation of conflict and anxiety. Harry's case is typical.

*The police received a call from Harry. He told them that he had come home and found his parents and brother murdered. Suspicion first focused on another brother, who was missing. When his body was later found stuffed in a trunk, suspicion finally turned to Harry. At first he seemed an unlikely candidate. He was a first-year student at a prestigious military academy and had been a quiet and somewhat lonely boy in high school. The family had been described as a close one with strong religious beliefs. As the story unfolded, Harry began to appear in a somewhat different light. He wanted to quit school. He hated the hazing the first-year students received. He seemed to have been marked as a loser and was frequently the target of jokes and punishment. His father had refused to allow him to quit school, just as he had earlier refused to allow him to quit Little League baseball even when Harry pleaded. Other students reported that during high school Harry was often teased and mistreated by his classmates.*

*On the night of the murders, Harry, home for Thanksgiving vacation, apparently felt he could stand the frustration no longer. One way to avoid returning to school was to remove the main obstacle to his quitting— his father.* (adapted from *New York Times*, November 29, 1976, pp. 1, 31)

Adolescents like Harry are often found to be psychotic or greatly disturbed. There is usually a long-term pattern of turmoil and emotional hurts that have been held beneath the surface. At last some incident, sometimes very minor, triggers violent behavior.

**The Psychopath**   Adults who suffer from antisocial personality disorders include crime-prone individuals who were formerly called sociopaths or psychopaths. These are men and women whose criminal behavior seems to be based on a rather unique set of personality characteristics. Probably the best definition of a psychopath has been furnished by Hervey Cleckley, whose book *The Mask of Sanity* (1976) has become a classic. Cleckley mentions the following characteristics of psychopaths.

1. Superficial charm and good intelligence.
2. Poise, rationality, absence of neurotic anxiety.
3. Lack of a sense of personal responsibility.
4. Untruthfulness, insincerity, callousness, manipulativeness.
5. Antisocial behavior without regret or shame.
6. Poor judgment and failure to learn from experience.
7. Inability to establish lasting, close relationships with others.
8. Lack of insight into personal motivations.

These are not characteristics that one either has or does not have. With each of them, it is a matter of degree. It is not surprising, therefore, that estimates of the incidence of antisocial psychopathic personality in the U.S. population range from a few million to 10 million. Smith (1978) has noted that particular cultural settings are especially likely to bring out and reward certain psychopathic tendencies. For example, Western society's tendency to glamorize fame and success, together with the psychopath's manipulativeness, superficial charm, and coldness, may aid such individuals in their efforts to get ahead.

*After graduating from high school and having a few dead-end jobs, Bert wanted to go into business for himself. He asked his parents, who had a modest income and some savings for their retirement, to lend him the money he needed to get started. Within 5 months Bert was out of business, his parents' money "lost," as he put it. Several months later, having found a new business opportunity, Bert again pleaded with his parents to borrow the money he needed. They agreed, and again Bert's opportunity fizzled. His parents desperately wanted to help Bert and to believe in him. So great was their need and so successful was Bert in "conning" his parents that they repeatedly helped him engage in activities that were doomed to failure. Bert craved the excitement of going into business for himself, but was able neither to attend to all the details involved in running a business nor to plan ahead. He was magnificent in playing the role of the charming young man on the way up. When he failed, he felt no regrets concerning his failure's implications for his parents and others who had helped him.*

One case study of an antisocial person whom most observers would call a psychopath presented the life of Jackroller, a young mugger, in the 1920s (Shaw, 1930). In his autobiography, written fifty years later, Jackroller reported that his life was no longer high in criminal activity (Jackroller and Snodgress, 1982). Instead, he struggled along, had trouble keeping jobs, and blamed others for most of his difficulties. His life, as he reports it, was a series of injustices. This description fits with research showing that as delinquents grow older, their level of violence decreases (Wolfgang and others, 1974).

Researchers have been hampered by the fact that it is so much easier to identify antisocial personalities among individuals who have been convicted of crimes than among the general population. One researcher approached this problem in a unique way (Widom, 1978): she inserted the following ad in a Boston counterculture newspaper.

*Wanted: charming, aggressive, carefree people who are impulsively irresponsible but are good at handling people and at looking after number one. Send name, address, phone, and short biography proving how interesting you are to . . .* (Widom, 1978, p. 72)

The ad drew 73 responses, of which about two-thirds were from males. About one-third of these seemed to meet the criteria for a diagnosis of psychopathic personality. The respondents were interviewed and given a battery of psychological tests. Some of the characteristics of the group are shown in Table 9–2. The researcher concluded that the main difference between her sample and prison samples was that the people who answered her ad had somehow been able to avoid conviction after arrest or detention by the police. In other respects they seemed very similar to prison inmates.

**Perspectives on Antisocial Behavior** Researchers have looked at many aspects of antisocial individuals—their life histories, psychological and physiological functioning, and personality characteristics—in order to understand why these people behave as they do. The biological perspective has yielded a number of interesting findings. There is increasing evidence that heredity may play a role in both criminality and antisocial behavior. Adopted children who were separated at birth from their antisocial parents show more antisocial behavior later in life than control subjects. Results suggesting a hereditary factor in antisocial behavior have been obtained in adoption studies carried out in Scandinavia as well as in the United States (Crowe, 1974; Hutchings and Mednick, 1977; Bohman and others, 1982).

How antisocial behavior might be inherited is not yet clear. Researchers have connected habitually violent and antisocial tendencies with the neurochemistry of the body. Impulsive physical violence and aggression in humans is related to very low levels of one of the neurotransmitters, serotonin, and one of its metabolites in the spinal fluid (Virkkunen, 1983). Another idea is that left-handedness and right-brain dominance may somehow be associated with antisocial personality disorder, but so far the evidence is not convincing (Hare and Forth, 1985). Other research has focused on patterns of brain wave activity. For example, some researchers have demonstrated a relationship between one type of electrical brain activity, slow alpha waves, and later antisocial behavior (Mednick and others, 1982). In normal individuals alpha-wave frequency is known to decrease with relaxation and drowsiness and to increase with tension, so the slow alpha waves suggest that some antisocial individuals have a lower than normal arousal level. This may mean that sensory inputs that would be disturbing to most people would not be strong enough to excite antisocial individuals. Such people may crave increased stimulation and may therefore seek out unusual forms of excitement.

People who look for a high level of stimulation are called **sensation seekers** (Zuckerman, 1979). Many sensation seekers are not antisocial; they gratify their need in socially acceptable ways—for example, by becoming race car drivers or scuba divers—but others choose antisocial ways of obtaining excitement. Not all imprisoned criminals score high on sensation seeking, but when criminals who meet Cleckley's definition of a psychopath are compared with criminals who are high in anxiety and with "normal" criminals, the psychopaths are highest on sensation seeking. They also engage in more fighting, escape attempts, defiance of regulations, and other impulsive behaviors than other prisoners do (Zuckerman and others, 1980).

Another physiological factor—anxiety—has been studied in antisocial individuals. It had seemed reasonable to assume that people who met the criteria for psychopathic behavior would also show little anxiety compared to other individuals. But this assumption may be true only in a limited sense. Schalling (1978) found that while psychopaths seem to worry less than other people, they nevertheless experience all of the common somatic and muscular indicators of anxiety (high heart rate, shortness of breath, tense muscles). If we divide anxiety into its cognitive part—worry—and its physiological components—the body's responses to fear—antisocial individuals seem to lack the cognitive component of anxiety.

From a cognitive perspective, the study of antisocial behavior focuses on moral development (Kegan, in press). Between the ages of 7 and 11, for example, nor-

□ **TABLE 9–2**
Characteristics of Subjects Interviewed by Widom[a]

| Characteristic | Percentage of Subjects |
|---|---|
| Arrest Records: | |
| Detained | 17.9 |
| Arrested as an adult | 64.3 |
| Convicted as an adult | 17.9 |
| Incarceration: | |
| As a juvenile | 10.7 |
| As an adult | 32.1 |
| Psychiatric Hospitalization: | |
| Hospitalized at some time | 21.4 |
| Treated as an outpatient only | 46.4 |
| Suicide attempts | 28.6 |
| Number with both psychiatric and arrest records | 46.4 |
| Parental separation: | |
| Broken homes | 21.4 |
| Divorce | 7.1 |
| Parental psychopathology | 7.1 |
| Parental alcoholism | 17.8 |

[a]The subjects averaged 25 years of age (from 19 to 47 years old). All except one were white. There were twenty-three males and five females.

mal children can tell when someone else treats them unfairly. If they have been treated unfairly in the past, when an opportunity arises they will "make up" for the past unfairness by striking back when someone else is vulnerable. For example, after being teased for being the shortest player on the peewee basketball team and then growing several inches, instead of feeling empathy for smaller kids the child will think, "Now it's my turn," not, "I'll treat younger kids differently."

In normal children, a new morality begins to develop at about the age of 13. Then children begin to think about the fairness of their own actions rather than concentrating on getting even. Cognitive theorists describe this as the development of the ability to reason in abstract terms and to understand the concept of partnership in relationships. From this point of view, psychopaths are developmentally arrested at the 7–11-year-old level because they are not concerned about the effects of their behavior on others.

Studies of antisocial personality disorder have suggested that both environmental and genetic factors may contribute to its development. So far no treatment seems effective for severe cases of this disorder; at present most of them are dealt with through the criminal justice system.

# ■ ANXIOUS OR FEARFUL BEHAVIORS

Disorders in this group have many characteristics in common with the personality disorders described earlier, but they differ from the other personality disorders in that each has a prominent component of anxiety or fear.

## Avoidant Personality Disorder

The two most outstanding characteristics of **avoidant personality disorder** are extreme sensitivity to rejection or humiliation and low self-esteem. People with this disorder keep away from personal attachments and won't enter into relationships unless the other person provides unusually strong guarantees of uncritical acceptance.

The seclusiveness of avoidant personalities differs from that of people with schizoid personality disorders because avoidant people, unlike schizoids, do want to enter into relationships. The conflict they feel is over wanting affection and, at the same time, doubting their acceptance by others. They cannot seem to rid themselves of the belief that any overtures of friendship will end in pain and disillusion. Some of these feelings come from doubts about their own competence. The primary goal of people in this group is to protect themselves from pain. They are caught between wanting human contact and dreading it.

One coping mechanism that those with avoidant personality disorder are likely to use is hypervigilance (Millon, 1981). They continuously assess all their human contacts for signs of deception, humiliation, and deprecation. As a result, they are able to detect the most minute traces of indifference or annoyance. They literally make mountains out of molehills. This technique of constantly scanning the environment is a self-defeating one, however, because it increases the likelihood that they will pick up just the kind of negative response they expect. In addition, their nervousness can result in making their companions uncomfortable, which can further damage the quality of their relationships with others.

Another maneuver that avoidant personalities use is to narrow their range of activities in order to cut off upsetting stimuli. Someone with an avoidant personality disorder may patronize only a small number of shops and restaurants so as to avoid encountering unfamiliar people or situations, or may even avoid shopping and other everyday activities because they seem too tiring or uncomfortable. Such people may also exaggerate the potential dangers of certain situations; for example, they may refuse to use buses or trains even though others do not doubt their safety. The lives of people with avoidant personality disorders are controlled by fears of looking foolish or being embarrassed or by concern about becoming anxious or crying in public. One unfortunate consequence of this retreat from contact with others and from new experiences is that it gives these individuals more time to be preoccupied with their own thoughts and to relive earlier painful experiences. Thus, a vicious cycle is set up in which the preoccupations make new contacts harder and lead to increased preoccupation.

## Dependent Personality Disorder

People with **dependent personality disorder** have two basic characteristics. First, they passively allow other people to make all the important decisions in their lives because they lack confidence and feel that they are unable to function independently. Second, to ensure that they will not lose this dependent position, such people subordinate their own needs to the needs and demands of others.

Dependent individuals try to make themselves so pleasing that no one could possibly wish to abandon them. They are self-effacing, ever agreeable, and continually ingratiating. If left on their own, they feel empty, extremely anxious, and unable to function. They may feel anxiety even when the dependent relationship is intact because of the pervasive worry that the dominant figure might be lost in some way—for example, through death or divorce.

Dependent individuals feel that they must act meek and obedient in order to hold onto other people. They also behave affectionately and admiringly toward their protectors. In many cases this may actually be an effective coping technique. The dominant partner will then feel useful, strong, and competent and will want to encourage the relationship. Sometimes, however, things go wrong. The dominant individual may tire of the constant need to demonstrate affection and support and seek to be rid of the leechlike attachment of the dependent partner. Sometimes the dominant partner behaves abusively. Battered wives are likely to have dependent personalities. They will accept severe physical abuse again and again rather than leave their partners. As with avoidant personalities, assertiveness training may be useful in treating dependent people. It may be difficult to convince these individuals that their coping styles need to be changed; sometimes a consciousness-raising therapy group is used before direct treatment is attempted.

The causes of dependent personality disorders are unclear. One suggestion is that dependent individuals had overprotective parents who made life so easy for their children that they never learned survival skills. Some theorists have suggested that dependent children were insecurely attached to their mothers or other caregivers or did not have close and trusting relationships with others during childhood. So far both of these ideas are interesting but untested hypotheses.

## Obsessive Compulsive Personality Disorder

Compulsive people have been described as "living machines" (Reich, 1933/1949). As one patient described it, his life was like "a train that was running efficiently, fast, pulling a substantial load, but on a track laid out for it" (Shapiro, 1965, p. 40). An **obsessive compulsive personality disorder** has several characteristics. One is lack of ability to express many warm and tender emotions. Instead, a person with this disorder seems stiff, formal, and unusually serious. Such an individual is likely to be overly conscientious and inflexible about matters of morality. Extreme perfectionism is also a problem because it focuses on small details, lists, and rulemaking rather than on getting the job done. This leads to inability to grasp the "big picture." For instance, in the following example two friends are discussing a house that K is interested in buying. L shows his rigidity in not really listening to what K says but going by his own "rule of house ownership."

K: *So you think I shouldn't buy it?*

L: *Never buy a house with a bad roof. It will cost you its price again in repairs before you're finished.*

K: *But the builder I hired to look it over did say it was in good condition otherwise.*

L: *The roof is only the beginning. First it's the roof and then comes the plumbing and then the heating and then the plaster.*

K: *Still, those things seem to be all right.*

L: *And, after the plaster, it will be the wiring.*

K: *But the wiring is . . .*

L [*interrupts with calm assurance*]: *It will cost double the price before you're finished.* (Shapiro, 1965, p. 25)

This example also illustrates another characteristic of compulsive personalities: insistence that their way of doing things be followed, without any awareness of the feelings this creates in other people. K probably really wants to buy the house, and if L's criticisms are, as we suspect, simply evidence of his compulsive personality without any facts attached, K's self-esteem and his positive feelings toward L are not likely to increase as a result of this encounter.

Another characteristic of the compulsive personality is excessive concentration on work and productivity (see Figure 9–9). Even pleasure becomes work.

*One such person carefully scheduled his Sundays with certain activities in order to produce "maximum enjoyment." He determinedly set about enjoying himself and became quite upset if anything interfered with his schedule, not merely because he missed the activity, but because his holiday had been spent inefficiently. Another compulsive patient always tried hard, in his social life, to be "spontaneous."* (Shapiro, 1965, p. 32)

Finally, obsessive compulsive personality disorder is characterized by indecisiveness. Individuals with this disorder have great difficulty making decisions because they might be wrong. For example, some people cannot bear to throw away anything—even things without sentimental value (see Figure 9–10). Their inability to make decisions can be so extreme that they can accomplish relatively little. Pleasure comes from planning a job, not from doing it. The early psychoanalyst Karl Abraham expressed this problem in the following passage.

*Pleasure in indexing and classifying . . . in drawing up programmes and regulating work by timesheets . . . is so marked . . . that the forepleasure they get in working out a plan is stronger than their gratification in its execution, so that they often leave it undone.* (Abraham, 1921/1927, pp. 378, 388)

**FIGURE 9-9**
Housekeeping routines or other cleaning or straightening rituals occupy a great deal of time for some compulsive people. This person's home library is a source of worry and frustration because of her concern about how to arrange the books. If they are arranged alphabetically by author, then she finds that the different sizes mixed together are visually unpleasing. If she arranges them by size, although they look better, she cannot find a particular book quickly. The result is that she spends a great deal of time both arranging the books and feeling dissatisfied with what she has done. (Laimute Druskis)

The term *obsessive compulsive personality disorder* is similar to *obsessive compulsive anxiety disorder* (discussed in Chapter 6), but the two disorders are different. People with obsessive compulsive personality disorder are rigid and restricted in their behavior, but they do not show obsessional thinking that seems to force itself into consciousness, nor do they engage in the kinds of irrational rituals that are performed by people with obsessive compulsive anxiety disorder. People with the anxiety disorder see their behavior as nonadaptive and distressing, but they cannot stop be-

having that way. People with a personality disorder, on the other hand, usually exhibit behavior that is rigid and unadaptive but that they feel is under their control.

## Passive Aggressive Personality Disorder

People with **passive aggressive personality disorder** habitually resist demands for adequate performance both on the job and in their social life. Although they have the skills to behave more effectively, they sabo-

**FIGURE 9-10**
Obsessive compulsive individuals may have problems parting with anything because it could always be needed later. Sometimes these concerns lead to chaotic accumulations like that shown in this office scene. (Laimute Druskis)

tage their accomplishments through procrastination, intentional inefficiency, stubbornness, and "forgetfulness." As the name suggests, people with passive aggressive personalities resent the demands that are made on them, but rather than expressing these feelings directly, they express their anger through passive resistance. For example, if a supervisor comes in at quitting time and requests a complex report by early the next morning, a passive–aggressive person would be more likely to mislay some of the needed data than to directly tell the supervisor that the request is unreasonable.

Passive aggressive individuals seem to have no awareness of how their own behavior contributes to the situation. The use of passive aggressive coping mechanisms is not usually an effective way of living. A 30-year follow-up study of a group of college men found that the degree to which passive aggressive behavior was used in early adulthood correlated negatively with good adjustment in middle age (Vaillant, 1976). Perhaps because most passive aggressive individuals do not seek clinical help, this category is one of the least used of those in the personality-disorder group (Frances, in press).

Some therapeutic success with passive aggressive patients has been achieved using the behavioral approach, especially assertiveness training. The problems that may be encountered in using this approach are clearly described in the following case:

*Miss Y., a 28-year-old single woman, worked for a governmental agency. The patient was a management information specialist; she appeared submissive and docile. However, the patient was unable to experience and label the affect of anger, had only vague awareness of the multitude of examples of people infringing upon her life, and generally coped with major deficits in self-assertiveness by a compliant and subservient demeanor. She generally resisted more adequate performance by stubbornness and intentional inefficiency.*

*The patient responded well to initial attempts to model, role play, and shape new social behaviors. She became more socially at ease and was pleased that she no longer accepted dates with men she didn't like. Whenever she brought up problems with her boss in therapy, however, she became intransigent. She refused to try new behaviors in dealing with him because, as she said, "He doesn't listen, he won't change. No, I couldn't imagine anything helping with him." Attempts by the therapist to coax the patient to try to change her expectations of him, or even to think that the problems with her boss were workable, were to no avail.*

*The therapist stopped attempting to intervene in the patient's work relationship with the boss, and learning continued in other areas. . . .*

*The therapist determined that the patient's complaints about her boss were realistic. While backing off from attempting to teach assertive skills directed at the relationship with the boss, the therapist did continue to describe certain assertive ways of handling him, which she might be able to use some day. As therapy helped the patient in other areas of life—with the family, roommate, friends, and social life—the patient became more confident of her ability to express her feelings and negotiate meeting her needs. After a year and a half of therapy, she felt confident enough to look for another job, which she obtained after having ascertained that her new boss was more considerate of his employees.* (Perry and Flannery, 1982, pp. 168–169)

The behavior of a passive aggressive individual might be compared to a situation that is often found in childrearing. The child pushes the parents to the limits of their control and then backs off just in time to prevent retaliation. Like the child, the passive aggressive individual is extremely sensitive to the limits of others and goes that far and no farther. Interacting with a passive aggressive person can be immobilizing because it requires one either to give in or to violate one's own beliefs.

## Treatment of Personality Disorders

Personality disorders are like colors. They blend with one another and come in many shades. This makes for unreliability in classifying an individual's predominant personality pattern. Discriminating among the various disorders is often difficult because their characteristics overlap, and all people can see some of these characteristics in themselves. Axis II may not distinguish clearly enough between the basic building blocks of personality that influence all levels of human adaptation and the relatively pure personality styles that lead to personal unhappiness or ineffectiveness. Nevertheless, Axis II does deal with vulnerabilities that lead to maladaptation. Imperfect as it may be, the attempt to include personality factors in psychiatric classification is a step forward. As more information is gained about these disorders, it will be possible to determine which of the present categories are useful ones and how the definitions may be tightened so that there is less overlap between groups.

An important thing to remember about personality disorders is that even these individuals, with their rigid coping styles, may behave appropriately or normally some of the time. However, when coping behaviors are called for, each personality disorder is distinguished by the frequency and intensity with which certain behaviors appear. For example, someone with a paranoid personality disorder does not always appear to be suspicious, but he or she is much more likely than most people to be suspicious and to be inappropriately suspicious. Many people with personality disorders go through life without ever coming into contact with a mental health professional. However, their rigid response styles often lead them to cope ineffectively with their environment. If the environmental stresses become too great, the response style may become clearly ineffective.

Our knowledge of personality disorders is limited because professionals see a restricted sample of people with these disorders. Unless their difficulties become overwhelming, such individuals tend to be satisfied with their behavior, not unhappy the way an anxious or depressed person might be. One important reason for this is that people with personality disorders perceive their environment—not their rigid behavior patterns—as the cause of any difficulties they may encounter.

A variety of therapies have been used in treating personality disorders. Most of these disorders are not very responsive to drugs; however, recently there has been an increase in the use of psychoactive drugs—for example, antipsychotic drugs such as Navane; one group of antidepressant drugs, the MAO inhibitors; and lithium. So far the results of drug therapy are not clear (Widiger and Frances, 1985). Behavioral techniques such as assertiveness training and systematic desensitization may be helpful for avoidant and dependent patients (Pilkonis, in press), and assertiveness training is sometimes useful for passive–aggressive clients. Although cognitive therapies seem to be appropriate for the deviant cognitive styles, little information on their effectiveness is available. Psychodynamic therapy is used especially for borderline, narcissistic, and histrionic personality disorders.

Because personality disorders affect interpersonal relationships, they tend to elicit complementary behavior from family members or friends. These relationships will affect and be affected by any behavior changes that come about through therapy. This means that group or family therapy may be a useful part of the treatment of many individuals with personality disorders (Harbin, 1981). It also means that the therapist must focus the client's attention on the effect of his or her behavior on the behavior of others.

## ■ STUDY OUTLINE

A person's characteristic ways of responding are often referred to as his or her **personality. Personality disorders** are longstanding, maladaptive, and inflexible ways of relating to the environment.

## CLASSIFYING PERSONALITY DISORDERS

DSM-III designated Axis II for the diagnosis of personality disorders. In some cases, the classification statements of Axis II are used to provide information that bears on the primary diagnosis of Axis I. In others, a personality disorder referred to on Axis II is the individual's major problem. Personality disorders can be divided into three groups: odd or eccentric behaviors; dramatic, emotional, or erratic behaviors; and fearful or anxious behaviors.

### ODD OR ECCENTRIC BEHAVIORS

1. People with **paranoid personality disorder** are characterized by unwarranted feelings of suspiciousness and mistrust of other people, hypersensitivity, and restricted emotional response. It is very difficult for such people to have close relationships with others.

2. Individuals with **schizoid personality disorder** are reserved, socially withdrawn, and seclusive. They rarely express their feelings directly, lack a sense of humor, and seem detached from their environment.

3. People with **schizotypal personality disorder** are characterized by oddities of thinking, perceiving, communicating, and behaving that are less extreme than those found in cases of schizophrenia. They often are not understood because they use unusual words and phrases or use common words in unusual ways.

### DRAMATIC, EMOTIONAL, OR ERRATIC BEHAVIORS

1. People with **histrionic personality disorder** place a high priority on getting the attention of others. This classification is used in cases that are marked by exaggerated expressions of emotion, stormy interpersonal relationships, a self-centered attitude, and manipulativeness. It is possible that such individuals do not feel able to compete with others on equal terms.

2. **Narcissistic personality disorder** is characterized by an extreme sense of self-importance and the expectation of special favors, a need for constant attention, fragile self-esteem, and lack of empathy or caring for others. Narcissistic individuals may have had parents who could not love reliably or were cold and rejecting; or their parents may have consistently overrated them.

3. The category **Borderline Personality Disorder** was listed for the first time in DSM-III. It consists of instability in such areas as mood, interpersonal relationships, and self-image. Borderline individuals tend to have intense and unstable interpersonal relationships and may use suicide threats to manipulate others. They also show disturbance in their concepts of identity.

**4. Antisocial personality disorder** is associated with crime, violence, and delinquency. People with this disorder are at least 18 but had a conduct disorder before the age of 15 and have shown a pattern of irresponsible and antisocial behavior since the age of 15.

**5.** Children and adolescents are diagnosed as having a **conduct disorder** when they repeatedly engage in actions that violate the basic rights of others or social norms appropriate for their age group, such as purse snatching, stealing, drug abuse, vandalism, and cruelty to animals and people.

**6.** Some crime-prone adults with antisocial personality disorder are known as sociopaths or psychopaths. They are characterized by charm, intelligence, poise, insincerity, callousness, manipulativeness, poor judgment, and similar traits.

**7.** It is possible that heredity may play a part in antisocial behavior, although it is not clear how antisocial behavior might be inherited. Violent and antisocial tendencies have been associated with slower than normal alpha waves. From a cognitive perspective, antisocial behavior results from arrested moral development.

## ANXIOUS OR FEARFUL BEHAVIORS

**1.** The main features of **avoidant personality disorder** is extreme sensitivity to rejection or humiliation and low self-esteem. Individuals with these disorders are likely to be hypervigilant, continuously assessing all their human contacts for signs of deception, humilia-

tion, and deprecation. They also narrow their range of activities in order to cut off upsetting stimuli.

**2.** People with **dependent personality disorder** passively allow other people to make all the important decisions in their lives and subordinate their own needs to the needs and demands of others. They are self-effacing, ever agreeable, and continually ingratiating.

**3.** People with **obsessive compulsive personality disorder** are characterized by lack of ability to express warm and tender emotions, extreme perfectionism, insistence that their way of doing things be followed, and excessive concentration on work and productivity.

**4.** People with **passive aggressive personality disorder** habitually resist demands for adequate performance both on the job and in their social life. They seem to have no awareness of how their own behavior contributes to the situations in which they find themselves.

**5.** The treatment of personality disorders is difficult for several reasons. One is that classifications of personality patterns tend to be unreliable because their characteristics overlap. Another is that even people with personality disorders may behave appropriately or normally some of the time. Furthermore, knowledge about personality disorders is limited. Nevertheless, such techniques as assertiveness training and systematic desensitization, psychodynamic therapy, and the use of psychoactive drugs may be helpful in specific cases.

# 10

# MOOD DISORDERS

*It is difficult to put into words how I felt at that time. I guess my major reaction was one of despair—a despair of ever being human again. I honestly felt subhuman, lower than the lowest vermin. Furthermore, I was self-deprecatory and could not understand why anyone would want to associate with me, let alone love me. I became mistrustful and suspicious of others and was certain that they were checking up on me to prove that I was incompetent myself . . . I had become increasingly concerned about finances. On one hand, I thought that I was receiving extra money that I didn't deserve and, on the other, I was certain that we were going bankrupt. In any case, I was positive that I was going to wind up in jail. When I received my July salary statement it appeared to me that the total was larger than it should be. This frightened me and I told my wife that we should phone the university immediately and arrange to return the extra money before I got into trouble. Gently, my wife told me that she thought the amount of money was correct and there was nothing to worry about. Of course, she was right . . . I not only pondered my current situation but my whole career as well. I was positive that I was a fraud and a phony and that I didn't deserve my Ph.D. I didn't deserve to have tenure; I didn't deserve to be a Full Professor . . . I didn't deserve the research grants I had been awarded; I couldn't understand how I had written books and journal articles that I had and how they had been accepted for publication. I must have conned a lot of people . . . Not only was my self-esteem low with respect to my academic and intellectual achievements but it was low also with respect to my emotional and social life. I analyzed all the people I knew and felt that each of them could do most things better than I could.* (Endler, 1982, pp. 45–49)

These were the thoughts of a well-known psychologist during a period of severe depression. They illustrate how drastically depression can alter a person's mood and behavior. In contrast, consider the behavior of a well-known writer. He was able to function adequately a good deal of the time, but occasionally manic behavior would break through and his behavior would become quite different.

*One day a play of his was bought by a film company. He was in Florida when he got the news. He promptly bought himself a new Cadillac and some Chivas Regal and went tearing back to New York. On the way, he was picked up for speeding in a small town in Georgia and thrown into the clink. They allowed him one phone call, and whom did he call? He did not call me [his therapist]; he did not call his wife; he did not even call his mistress. He called the Strategic Air Command to bomb the jail.* (Kline, 1977, p. 9)

## ■ DEFINING MOOD DISORDERS

Both **depression,** which is characterized by a feeling of sadness and, in some cases, a decrease in activity, and **mania,** which is a speeded-up state that is often characterized by excitement or exuberance, are included in the category of **Mood** or **Affective Disorders.** Of the two, depression is far more common. Depressive behavior without any manic episodes can be classified under several headings. If the depression occurs as a result of an identifiable event and is expected to disappear when the impact of the event diminishes, the classification is **Adjustment Disorder with Depressed Mood** and the person is not considered to have a mood disorder. If the depression is severe, it is called a **major depressive disorder;** if it is less severe or not quite as incapacitating, it is called a **dysthmic disorder** (also known by the older term **depressive neurosis**). Some researchers refer to mood disorders in which only depression occurs as **unipolar disorders.** A disorder that includes both manic and depressive episodes is called a **bipolar disorder** if it is severe and a **cyclothymic disorder** if it is milder. Bipolar disorders appear to be much more homogeneous than unipolar disorders. However, as researchers learn more about the bipolar group, it is likely that a number of subgroups with different causes will be identified.

## ■ DEPRESSION

### The Depressed Feeling State

The term **depression** is used in everyday language to refer to a feeling state, a reaction to a situation, and a person's characteristic style of behavior. The feeling of depression is usually known as "the blues." It may occur in rainy weather, during an annoying cold, or after an argument with a friend. Often an event that is usually expected to be happy ends with such blue feelings. People may experience the blues after holidays such as Christmas or New Year's Day, after moving to a new home, or following childbirth. Feelings of depression stemming from holidays, new housing, or a major life event usually fade away quickly after the event has occurred or when the person becomes accustomed to the new surroundings.

Another kind of depression is the bereavement or grief reaction, a sadness that comes from a death in the family or the disappointment that accompanies the end of a love affair. After the end of a significant relationship, most survivors experience what is usually called grief. This is entirely normal. In fact, the absence of such a reaction might be bad for the person in the long run. Common features of grief include physical distress such as sighing, tightness of the throat, an empty feeling in the abdomen, and a feeling of muscular weakness. In addition, there may be preoccupation with the visual image of the dead person, along with guilt and hostile reactions. During the process of grieving, the guilt, hostility, feelings of loss, and physical symptoms gradually disappear.

Because feelings of depression have been experienced by almost everyone, these feelings alone are not enough to warrant a diagnosis of depressive mood disorder. Clinical depression is much less common and is a more serious problem than the temporary blues that we all feel once in a while. But where does "normal" depression end and "clinical" depression begin? Some researchers believe that depression can be studied on a continuum from the blues through the severe clinical categories (Blatt and others, 1976). Other researchers, however, think that depression and the blues are two very different things (Akiskal, 1981). For example, unlike the blues, depression is not alleviated by reassurance or helpful advice from friends or family.

Depression is a frequent problem among individuals who seek clinical help for psychological problems. Four hundred thousand people seek treatment for depression every year, and 15 percent of them kill themselves (Ray, 1983). Among patients who see a physician for a physical complaint, at least 18 percent are also depressed, one-third of them moderately or severely (Nielsen and Williams, 1980).

Community surveys show that even among people who do not seek help for their problems, from 6 to 19 percent are depressed (Frerichs and others, 1981; Weissman and others, 1981). In a survey carried out in Los Angeles, women were found to be twice as likely to be depressed as men and people at the lowest income level were found to be three times as likely to be depressed as those at the highest income level (Frerichs and others, 1981).

Depression is a significant problem throughout the world. One longitudinal study kept track of everyone born in Iceland between 1895–1897 (Helgason, 1979). There was one chance in eight that at some time before reaching age 75 these individuals would develop an affective disorder. Results from a number of other studies suggest that the lifetime risk of unipolar depression is 8 to 12 percent for men and 20 to 26 percent for women. For bipolar disorders, which are much less common, the lifetime risk is less than 1 percent; here again, women are at greater risk than men (Boyd and Weissman, 1981).

Women are twice as likely as men to be diagnosed as depressed. This difference has been found not just in the United States and Canada or in western Europe, but throughout the world. It is found whether depression is defined by clinical impressions or patients in treatment, community surveys of people not in treatment, studies of suicide and suicide attempts, or reaction to bereavement (Klerman and Weissman, 1980). A variety of biological reasons have been suggested for this difference, including sex-linked heredity and hormonal differences. However, some researchers believe that the difference may be an artificial one created by the social roles and the behaviors expected of men and women. At present the question of whether the difference is a real one is still open to debate. In two recent studies in which social impairment rather than the presence of particular symptoms was the criterion for the diagnosis, men and women were equally likely to be depressed (Angst and Dober-Mikola, 1984; Egeland and Hostetter, 1983).

Two characteristic features of depression are a **dysphoric mood** (depressed, sad, blue, hopeless, irritable, or worried) and loss of interest or pleasure in almost all of one's usual activities and pastimes. At least one of these must be present to warrant a diagnosis of depression. In addition, at least four of the following behaviors or feelings must be present: poor appetite or weight change (often loss but sometimes gain), difficulty sleeping, loss of energy, psychomotor agitation or increased slowness of response that is obvious enough to be observed by others, fatigue or loss of energy, feelings of self-reproach or inappropriate guilt, complaints of inability to think clearly or concentrate, and frequent thoughts of death or suicide or wishing to be dead. Women who are depressed have a greater number of symptoms than men do. Symptoms like feelings of worthlessness, loss of interest, and appetite disturbances are mentioned much more often by women than by men. Figure 10–1 shows the differences in frequency of various symptoms of depression for men and women.

Depression often seems to begin after some stressful event such as marriage or parenthood. In all of these cases, if depression is present behavior that might have been appropriate under stress continues long afterward instead of returning to normal as time passes, the person often shows inappropriate thought patterns, tending to generalize every event into a calamity and to view the world in the bleakest of terms. This attitude carries over into the individual's self-image; depressed people see themselves as hopeless and worthless.

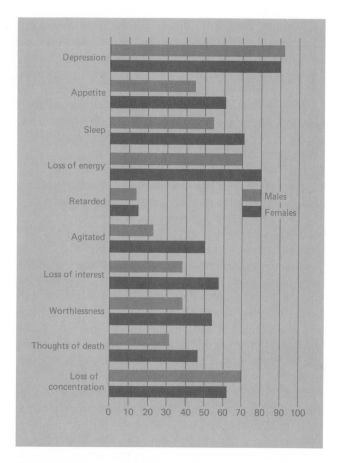

**FIGURE 10-1**
Men who are depressed report fewer symptoms than depressed women do.

## Descriptions of Depression

The following three cases illustrate the variety of behaviors that are characteristic of depressed individuals.

### CASE 1

*A 28-year-old junior executive had obtained a master's degree in business administration and moved to California a year and a half earlier to begin work in a large firm. She complained of being "depressed" about everything: her job, her husband, and her prospects for the future.*

*She had had extensive psychotherapy previously. Her complaints were of persistent feelings of depressed mood, inferiority, and pessimism, which she claims to have had since she was 16 or 17 years old. Although she did reasonably well in college, she consistently ruminated about those students who were "genuinely intelligent." She dated during college and graduate school, but claimed that she would never go after a guy she thought was "special," always feeling inferior and intimidated.*

*Whenever she saw or met such a man, she acted stiff and aloof, or actually walked away as quickly as possible, only to berate herself afterward and then fantasize about him for many months. She claimed that her therapy had helped, although she still could not remember a time when she didn't feel somewhat depressed.*

*Just after graduation, she married the man she was going out with at the time primarily because she felt she "needed a husband" for companionship. Shortly after their marriage, the couple started to bicker. She was very critical of his clothes, his job, and his parents; and he, in turn, found her rejecting, controlling, and moody. She began to feel that she had made a mistake in marrying him.*

*Recently she has also been having difficulties at work. She is assigned the most menial tasks at the firm and is never given an assignment of importance or responsibility. She admits that she frequently does a "slipshod" job of what is given her, never does more than is required, and never demonstrates any assertiveness or initiative to her supervisors. She views her boss as self-centered, unconcerned, and unfair, but nevertheless admires his success. She feels that she will never go very far in her profession because she does not have the right "connections" and neither does her husband, yet she dreams of money, status, and power.*

*Her social life with her husband involves several other couples. The man in these couples is usually a friend of her husband's. She is sure that the women find her uninteresting and unimpressive, and that the people who seem to like her are probably no better off than she.* (Spitzer and others, 1981, pp. 10–11)

### CASE 2

*Mr. T.S., aged 40, married and father of three children, was hospitalized after a consultation between his family physician and a psychiatrist. In the hospital, if left to his own devices, he would spend most of his time sitting on a chair by the side of his bed, moaning and wringing his hands. His facial expression was one of the deepest dejection, and his eyes were reddened from weeping. At times he would get up and pace the floor heavily. All of his muscles seemed to sag, giving him the appearance of a much older man. If left to himself, he would not eat. He was severely constipated. He tended to ignore his personal appearance and hygiene completely. He had trouble sleeping although appearing to be very fatigued.*

*He blamed himself in the harshest terms for having "ruined his family," and said he did not deserve to live, and he also had fears of dying. He was certain he had some incurable disease, the nature of which the doctors were concealing from him.*

Mr. T.S. and his wife had been married for 12 years, and the marriage, for the most part, had been reasonably satisfactory. Mr. T.S., the proprietor of a small business, was a careful, conscientious, and methodical person, very fair in his dealings with others. He placed great emphasis upon routine and was disconcerted by departure from it. He seldom took a vacation, and when he did, he was apt to become restless after a few days, finding it difficult to relax. He was lacking in a sense of humor, although he tried to be a good sport about things.

About three months before his hospitalization, Mr. T.S. had experienced a minor business reverse. A month later, while he was still trying to cope with this situation, his mother died of a heart attack. He became terribly distressed, appeared to grieve deeply, was restless and agitated, lost his appetite, and had trouble sleeping. For a time he strove to carry on his business, but he was quite ineffectual, and had had to turn the management over to an assistant. His self-reproach became increasingly intense and unrealistic. (He spoke of himself as having thrown away the family resources and having caused his mother's death and the impoverishment of his wife and children.) When he began to speak of himself as not deserving to live, his wife had sought medical assistance. (adapted from Hofling, 1968, pp. 360–361)

CASE 3

A 24-year-old, single, female nursery-school teacher terminated brief psychotherapy after ten sessions. She had entered treatment two weeks after she discovered that the man she had been involved with for four months was married and wanted to stop seeing her. She reacted with bouts of sadness and crying, felt she was falling apart, took a week's sick leave from her job, and had vague thoughts that the future was so bleak that life might not be worth the effort. She felt that she must be in some essential way "flawed"; otherwise she would not have gotten so involved with someone who had no intentions of maintaining a long-term relationship. She felt that others "would have seen it," that only she was "so stupid" as to have been deceived. There were no other signs of a depressive syndrome, such as loss of interest or appetite or trouble concentrating. She responded to mixed support-insight psychotherapy and, toward the end of treatment, began dating a law student whom she met at a local cafe. (Spitzer and others, 1981, p. 261)

The first case, that of the junior executive, would be called a dysthymic disorder. The client's life history seems to show consistent, repeating patterns, and feeling depressed seems to be her usual mood. The second case would be classified as a major depressive disorder. Mr. T.S.'s emotions are excessive and clearly are hampering his ability to function in his business and with his family. The third case shows depressed feelings as a short-term reaction to a stressful situation. The nursery-school teacher doesn't have such symptoms as weight loss, sleep disturbance, or loss of pleasure, and she quickly recovered from her depressed mood when her environment improved. Her problem would be classified not as a mood disorder, but rather as an adjustment disorder with depressed mood. These cases illustrate the range of conditions in which depressed mood can exist.

## ■ THEORIES OF DEPRESSION

The causes of depression have been investigated from many theoretical viewpoints. The most popular view at present is that there are distinct groups of depressives whose symptoms have different causes. The bipolar type, which includes both manic and depressive behaviors, is thought to be based on genetic factors. The unipolar category, in which depression occurs alone without manic episodes, probably includes several subgroups, some of which are also related to genetic makeup. Many researchers think of depression as resulting from an interaction between the person's biological characteristics and psychological vulnerabilities and the occurrence of stressful events or difficult ongoing situations in his or her life (Akiskal, 1985).

Despite the view that characteristics of both the person and the situation are important, most studies emphasize one or another of the perspectives that are discussed throughout this book. As is usually the case, the different theoretical approaches to depression have produced different types of studies and different data, all of which may add to our understanding of the causes and treatment of this complex disorder.

### Biological Theories

Biological theories assume that the cause of depression lies either in the genes or in some physiological malfunction that may or may not have an inherited base. The findings of twin studies conducted since the 1930s suggest that hereditary elements figure in some cases of depression. People who are bipolar—that is, who experience both mania and depression—often have at least two generations of relatives who exhibit similar behaviors. More cases of unipolar depression that could be expected by chance also occur in the families of bipolar individuals.

During the twentieth century there has been a progressive increase in rates of depression for groups born in successive periods. Depression also appears to be beginning earlier in each successive group (Klerman and others, 1985). This may be a matter for concern, because the younger people are when their first major depression occurs, the more likely it is that their relatives will also experience periods of depression (Weissman and others, 1984). Figure 10–2 illustrates this difference. Relatives of people who had a major depressive episode before they were 20 had an eight times greater chance of becoming depressed than relatives of normal subjects. Relatives of people who were over 40 when they first had a major depression had little more than the normal risk of depression. This increased risk was found both for relatives of depressed patients who were hospitalized and for relatives of individuals who did not need to be hospitalized (Weissman and others, 1984b).

Although genetic factors seem important in many cases of depression, the exact mechanism by which depression is inherited is not clear and may even vary from one family to another (Lingjaerde, 1983). It is also obvious that nongenetic factors, either physical or related to a person's environment or relationships, may be required to produce depression even in individuals with genetic vulnerability.

**Biochemical Aspects of Depression**   Whatever the mechanism by which the genetic factor is inherited, its influences are biochemical. Depression is probably a result of a lack of chemical neurotransmitters at certain sites in the brain. Before discussing these, a brief review of the neuron and how it functions may be helpful.

The basic building blocks of the nervous system are specialized cells called **neurons**—more than 100 billion of them. Each neuron has three main parts: a **cell body** containing the nucleus that regulates the cell's life process; **dendrites;** and an **axon.** The axon branches at its end to form a number of axon terminals, each of which ends in a terminal button. All of these elements are shown in Figure 10–3.

The neuron can be stimulated either through its dendrites or through its cell body. When the stimulation occurs, an electrical impulse travels along the axon to other neurons, muscles, or glands. To travel from one neuron to another, the impulse must cross the **synapse,** the space or gap between the axon and the dendrites of another neuron. In order to cross this gap, the electrical impulse that travels through the neuron must be transformed into a chemical message.

The axon terminals contain small **synaptic vesicles** or holding containers for chemicals called **neurotransmitters** that make this transformation possible. When the neurotransmitter molecules are released, they travel across the fluid-filled space between the sending (presynaptic) and receiving (postsynaptic) neurons and bind or attach themselves to specific sites on the dendrites or cell body. An area on the semiliquid surface of the postsynaptic neuron's membrane precisely matches the shape of the transmitter molecule; the two fit together with the precision of a key in a lock. The chemical reaction between the neurotransmitter and the receptor molecule causes an electrical impulse to travel through the receiving neutron. After the neurotransmitter molecule has fit into its receptor, it is deactivated or shut off so that its action does not continue too long.

Several types of neurotransmitters have been identified. Each neuron synthesizes and stores only one of these types. Most neurotransmitters are breakdown products of amino acids. Those that are of special interest in the study of the chemical causes of depression have a distinctive amino group in their molecular structure and are called **monoamines.** The most important monoamines are the catecholamines **noradrenaline** (NA) and **dopamine** (DA) and the indoleamine **seratonin** (5HT). An enzyme, monoaminooxidase (MAO),

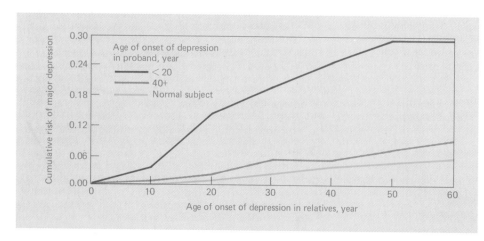

**FIGURE 10–2**
Cumulative risk of major depression in relatives of depressed people varies according to the ages at which the patients become depressed. Weismann and others, 1984, *Archives of General Psychiatry, 41,* p. 1138. Copyright (c) 1984, American Medical Association.

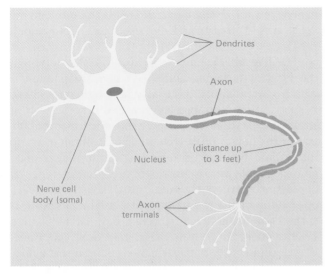

**FIGURE 10-3**
A diagram of a neuron showing some of its most important parts.

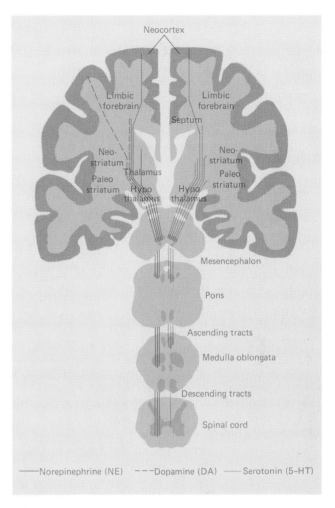

——Norepinephrine (NE)    ---Dopamine (DA)    ——Serotonin (5-HT)

**FIGURE 10-4**
Pathways of neurons that produce specific neurotransmitters are beginning to be identified. Some of these are shown here. From *Depression, Manic-Depressive Illness, and Biological Rhythms* DHHS Pub. No. (ADM)82–889. National Institute of Mental Health, 1979.

causes all of these monoamines to become ineffective.

The three monoamine systems (NA, DA, and 5HT) have somewhat different distributions and functions, but all of them originate in the central part of the brain (Lingjaerde, 1983) (see Figure 10–4). Figure 10–5 shows how the neurotransmitter noradrenaline functions. It is stored in synaptic vesicles and then released into the synaptic cleft by a mechanism that is triggered by an electrical impulse or action potential moving through the axon.

After it crosses the synapse, noradrenaline acts on either an alpha ($\alpha_1$) or a beta ($\beta_1$) receptor. When this has been accomplished, the noradrenaline is inactivated. This is done mainly through the noradrenaline pump, which causes the noradrenaline to be taken back into the presynaptic structure. Noradrenaline also acts on presynaptic $\alpha_2$ receptors in a way that inhibits further noradrenaline release. The presynaptic $\beta_2$ receptors probably have an opposite effect, but not much is known about them.

There are at least six ways in which monoamine production could be altered. These are shown in Figure 10–5. They include (1) a series of chemical changes that determine the amount of the monamine synthesized or produced; (2) storage in the synaptic vesicles; (3) the release into the synapse, which is carried out through the $\alpha_2$ receptors; (4) the reuptake at receptor sites in the presynaptic neuron; (5) metabolism, or chemical inactivation by monoamine oxidase activity from the MAO sites on the neuron; or (6) the responsiveness of the postsynaptic receptors.

For a number of years researchers have used a monoamine hypothesis to explain depression (Schildkraut, 1965). According to this theory, a lack or deficiency of noradrenaline or seratonin is a causal factor in depression. It may be that the receptors ($\alpha_1$ and $\beta_1$ in Figure 10–5) are extremely sensitive and that the low level of monoamine production is the body's way of taking care of this problem. One argument in favor of this explanation is that almost all antidepressants gradually produce lowered sensitivity in the receptors (Charney and others, 1981). Another idea is that depression may be related not to too little or too much activity in the neurotransmitter system, but rather to a failure in the regulation of the system (Siever and Davis, 1985). This means that neurotransmitter activity may be highly variable and may sometimes be an in-

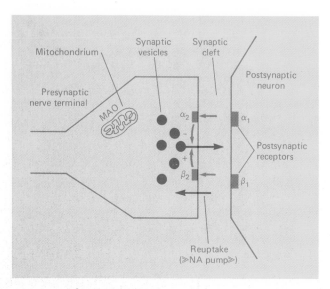

**FIGURE 10-5**
A synapse in the noradrenaline system.

appropriate response to the situation or to the normal cycles of the body. If this idea is correct, individuals who are likely to become depressed have some abnormality at a particular point in the system, for instance, lack of sensitivity in the $\alpha_2$ receptors. This is not enough to cause problems under ordinary circumstances, but under stress the system cannot function normally.

### Biological Response in Depression

Since most scientists agree that not all depressions have similar causes, a great deal of effort has been devoted to finding subgroups of depressed patients that have similar characteristics. The study of such subgroups should not only make it easier to understand the causes of depression but, even more important, provide clues to the most effective treatment for a particular individual. A major focus of research in this area is the effort to develop a test that could be used to identify such subgroups.

*The Dexamethasone Suppression Test.* Although the level of hormone activity in depression often is within normal limits, there may be a reduction in the reaction of the hormonal system to different levels of stress or excitation. This is probably due to some problem in the action of the hypothalamus. In an effort to understand this lack of response and to differentiate among people who seem to have different types of depression, several chemical tests have been developed. One of the most frequently used of these tests is the *Dexamethasone Suppression Test* (DST) (Carroll, 1985). Patients are given the steroid dexamethasone, which suppresses the production of cortisol, a hormone that is produced in the cortex of the brain. Normally dexamethasone suppresses the level of cortisol in the blood for about 24 hours. In some depressed patients, however, the suppression does not last that long (see Figure 10-6).

Although the DST has been enthusiastically accepted by some clinicians, to date research findings have not provided enough evidence to justify its use on a routine basis. One problem is that the test does not differentiate between unipolar depression and the depressed phase of bipolar disorders. Many patients whose depressions appear to be biologically related also show no response. Another problem is that the dexamethasone suppressor response has been reported in many other conditions besides depression—for example, alcoholism, schizophrenia, and eating disorders—as well as in normal individuals who were dieting (Roy and others, 1984). Thus, the DST cannot be viewed as a clear diagnostic sign (Klein and others, 1984).

The development of noninvasive scanning techniques like the PET (positron emission tomography) scan may help investigators understand the biological

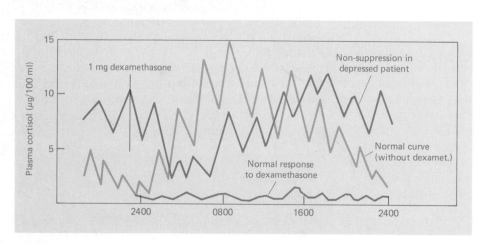

**FIGURE 10-6**
The dexamethasone suppression test identifies individuals whose hormonal systems do not react in a normal way. In most normal people, a dose of dexamethasone will suppress the secretion of blood cortisol. In some depressed people, however, the blood cortisol level does not decrease over a 24-hour period. (Lingjaerde, 1983, p. 44)

changes involved in depression. One advantage of these techniques is their ability to define behavior changes in an objective manner. Figure 10-7 illustrates how scanning techniques can link observed behavioral changes in patients with unipolar disorders to changes in brain activity.

*Biological Rhythms in Depression.* Differences in biological rhythms may be a way to identify subgroups of depressed individuals; this approach may also be a way to clarify how biological functioning differs for people who are depressed and those who are not. Regular rhythms in the functioning of living beings have been recognized for a long time. Of these, the 24-hour or circadian rhythms have been studied most. These rhythms can be shown for a large number of biological functions. Some of them, such as body temperature and sleep activity, are usually synchronized so that their peaks occur at the same time. When these rhythms get out of synchrony, other changes occur. For instance, sleep lasts a long time if a person goes to sleep at the top of the body temperature curve. If, instead, the person goes to sleep near the bottom of the temperature curve, sleep lasts a much shorter time (Czeisler and others, 1980). Sleep disturbance is frequent in depressed individuals. They tend to have trouble going to sleep and staying asleep. They also are likely to waken early in the morning and to feel most depressed in the morning.

Normal sleep has a number of phases that can be measured by monitoring the electrical impulses of the brain. The one that is of most interest from the standpoint of depression is REM sleep, during which the eyes rapidly move from side to side and brain wave patterns indicate a peak in brain activity. One characteristic of some depressed individuals is a shortened period between falling asleep and the beginning of the first REM period (Kupfer and others, 1985). This characteristic, together with early wakening, may be due to an advance in temperature rhythm that causes the person to go to sleep nearer to the bottom than to the top of his or her temperature curve (Czeisler and others, 1980) (see Figure 10-8).

Originally interest in the REM patterns of depressives was aimed at discovering a way to differentiate among various types of depression. However, the study of REM patterns and their relationship to other biological rhythms may give researchers clues about the biological changes that occur in depression. REM research also has significance for therapy. Depriving depressed individuals of REM sleep can decrease their depression (Vogel and others, 1980). This can be done simply by waking the individual whenever REM occurs. This treatment seems to work on the same group of patients who are helped by tricyclic drugs. At least some MAO inhibitors and tricyclic drugs appear to lengthen the cycles in circadian rhythms. The drug lithium, which is used primarily to treat bipolar disorders and will be discussed in a later section, also lengthens the rhythms of the circadian cycle (Wehr and Wirtz-Justice, 1982).

**FIGURE 10-7**

Three series of PT scans of unipolar depression illustrate how this technique can be used as an objective measure of the changes in biological activity that accompany certain behavior changes. The center row illustrates the decreased glucose metabolism found in a unipolar depressed patient. (The darker the area, the greater the metabolic activity.) The top row shows how the glucose metabolism increases as a patient naturally recovers from a period of depression. The lower row shows a similar increase in glucose metabolism when a test drug improves a patient's behavior. (O. Lingjaerde, 1983, The Biochemistry of Depression, *Acta Psychiatrica Scandinavica Supplementum, 302,* 36–51. Copyright (c) 1983 Munksgaard International Publishers Ltd., Copenhagen, Denmark. (University of California, L.A.)

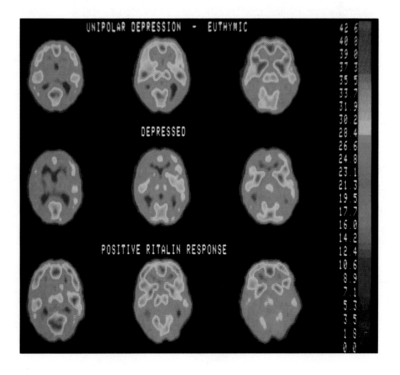

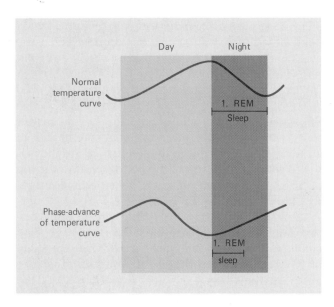

**FIGURE 10-8**
The relationship between duration of sleep and the circadian temperature rhythm. (adapted from Czeisler and others, *Science, 210*, pp. 267. Copyright (c) 1980 by the AAAS.)

**Treatment Based on Biological Theories** The two main groups of drugs that are used to treat depression—the tricyclics and the MAO inhibitors (see Table 10–1)—both increase the amount of norepinephrine, but they produce their effects in somewhat different ways. MAO inhibitors retard the breakdown of norepinephrine so that it remains active longer. The tricyclic drugs increase the amount of available norepinephrine in another way: they slow its reabsorption by the transmitter neuron and thus keep more of it available in the synapse. Which group of drugs and which particular drug within a group will be effective

is usually a matter of trial and error on the part of the physician. Usually one of the tricyclic drugs is preferred because the MAO inhibitors have more potentially dangerous side effects. Use of the MAO inhibitors also requires stricter supervision because when these drugs are taken with foods that contain a substance called tyramine they may produce a toxic reaction and cause blood pressure to rise to a life-threatening level. Because many common foods, including cheese, chocolate, sour cream, and wine, contain tyramine, the use of MAO inhibitors requires careful dietary monitoring.

Bipolar disorders are often treated with lithium. Lithium may change the chemical balance of the body fluids by replacing calcium, magnesium, potassium, and/or sodium, or it may slow down the release or increase the absorption of norepinephrine. Whatever the process, it not only seems effective in calming manic behavior but also serves to prevent the depressed phase of the bipolar cycle.

One of the problems in treating a severe episode of depression with either tricyclics or MAO inhibitors is the time lag between their initial use and the first signs of improvement in the patient's mood. Several weeks may go by before any improvement is seen. If there is concern about suicide, a wait of three weeks or so may seem too great a risk. In such situations, or if drugs are not effective, electro-convulsive therapy (ECT) may be used because it produces a more rapid effect. **Electroconvulsive therapy** involves passing a current of between 70 and 130 volts through the patient's head. First an anesthetic and a muscle relaxant are administered. (The muscle relaxant is given to prevent injury from the convulsion caused by the electric charge.) The current is then administered through electrodes placed on one or both sides of the head. Placement of the electrodes on one side of the head seems to reduce the

□ **TABLE 10-1**
Drugs for Affective Disorders

| *Antidepressant drugs* | | | |
|---|---|---|---|
| Tricyclics | Imipramine | Tofranil | Used to treat relatively severe depressive symptoms of the unipolar type. Variable effectiveness in moderating symptoms. Slow acting. May take up to 3 weeks before response is seen. Many side effects, some dangerous. MAO inhibitors require restrictions in diet because of serious interactive effects with certain food chemicals. |
| | Amitriptyline | Elavil | |
| | Nortriptyline | Aventyl | |
| | Protriptyline | Vivactil | |
| Monoamine oxidase (MAO) inhibitors | Isocarboxazid | Marplan | |
| | Phenelzine | Nardil | |
| | Tranylcypromine | Parnate | |
| *Antimanic drugs* | Lithium carbonate | Eskalith | Used to treat manic episodes and some severe depressions, especially those that alternate with mania. Effective in reducing or preventing manic episodes but variable with depressions. Many possible side effects if use not closely monitored. High toxic potential. |
| | | Lithane | |
| | | Lithonate | |
| | | Lithotabs | |
| | | Phi-Lithium | |

chance of memory loss. One electrode is placed on the temple in front of the ear and the other one three inches higher at an angle from the first. The electrodes are usually placed on the nondominant side of the brain (which for most people is the right side) because that side is believed to be more concerned with nonverbal and emotional behavior as opposed to memory and language functions. Usually a series of six to twelve treatments is given.

ECT is very effective in treating severe depression in which there is a great deal of delusional thinking. **Delusions** are incorrect beliefs that are resistant to change despite evidence that disproves them—for example, the idea that others can read your thoughts or that your best friend is plotting to kill you when that clearly is not true. ECT is also effective for some severe depressions that have not responded to tricyclics or MAO inhibitors. It is not effective for mild depressions (dysthymic disorder and adjustment disorder with depressed mood).

ECT causes many changes. It produces massive discharges of neurons in much of the brain, activates the autonomic nervous system, releases secretions from the endocrine glands, and causes convulsions of many of the muscles. These all cause so many chemical changes in the body that it is difficult to determine which ones have an effect on the depression. It is likely that the seizure activity produces changes in the level of neurotransmitters or changes in the electrical responsiveness of the neuron (Holden, 1985).

ECT can result in memory loss, most of which disappears within a few weeks. The patient's ability to learn and retain information may also be affected for several weeks. Some people who have been treated with ECT report memory lapses several years later. Confusion and memory loss are increased by longer treatments, more frequent treatments, a greater number of treatments, and increased strength of the electrical stimulation (Office of Medical Applications of Research, 1985). In general, although it may be effective, ECT should be used only after other treatments have been tried.

Sometimes ECT can produce dramatic changes in mood. Norman Endler, the psychologist whose description of his own depression (later diagnosed as a bipolar type) appears at the beginning of the chapter, also described his experience with ECT after both tricyclic and MAO-inhibiting drugs had proved ineffective and the depression was still incapacitating him after five months. Endler was faced with a choice between ECT and hospitalization; he reluctantly chose ECT.

*Dr. Persad met us on the sixth floor at seven-forty-five. He tried to calm me down, and I recall his saying that he* *had never seen anyone so agitated as I. The prospect of ECT really frightened me.*

*Beatty (Endler's wife), remained in the waiting area and Dr. Persad and I went into the ECT room. I changed into my pajamas and a nurse took my vital signs (blood pressure, pulse, and temperature). The nurse and other attendants were friendly and reassuring. I began to feel at ease. The anesthetist arrived and informed me that she was going to give me an injection. I was asked to lie down on a cot and was wheeled into the ECT room proper. It was about eight o'clock. A needle was injected into my arm and I was told to count back from 100. I got about as far as 91. The next thing I knew I was in the recovery room and it was about eight-fifteen. I was slightly groggy and tired but not confused. My memory was not impaired. I certainly knew where I was. I rested for another few minutes and was then given some cookies and coffee. Shortly after eight-thirty, I got dressed, went down the hall to fetch Beatty, and she drove me home. At home I enjoyed breakfast and then lay down for a few hours. Late in the morning I got dressed. I felt no pain, no confusion, and no agitation. I felt neither less depressed nor more depressed than I had before the ECT . . . After about the third or fourth treatment I began to feel somewhat better. I started perking up. After the third treatment I went up to Dr. Persad's office and spoke to him briefly. He asked me if I had noticed any improvement and to what degree. I believed that I had improved 35 to 40 percent. Dr. Persad believed that the improvement was more likely to be 70 to 75 percent.* (Endler, 1981, pp. 81–83)

After the fifth and sixth treatments Endler went to his office. A colleague who had been helping to manage the psychology department in his absence was there.

*I asked her to remain. She stated that she would be glad to stay as long as I needed her assistance. By early afternoon Kathy looked at me and said "Norm, you are perfectly fine, you do not need me here." She left and I stayed the rest of the day. As of then I resumed the chairmanship full time. A miracle had happened in two weeks. I had gone from feeling like an emotional cripple to feeling well.* (ibid.)

Like many people who have a bipolar disorder, Endler experienced another depression about a year after the first. This time, although the ECT produced improvement and made it possible for him to work effectively, the depressed mood continued for several months.

Although drug therapy and ECT can be effective, there are still problems with biological treatment of depression. Choosing the right drug can be a hit-or-miss affair (Stern and others, 1980). The effects these drugs may have after many years of use also are not known.

Moreover, some researchers argue that dependence on drugs makes unipolar or bipolar individuals less likely to improve their coping mechanisms and thus increases the chances of their having further affective problems. The attitude of many therapists toward using biological treatment alone is expressed by Silvano Arieti, a well-known psychoanalyst and researcher: "I have never met a patient about whom I could say that his depression came from nowhere and its origin had to be sought exclusively in metabolic disorder" (Arieti and Bemporad, 1978, p. 5).

## The Psychodynamic View

The psychological study of depression was begun by Sigmund Freud and Karl Abraham. Both described depression as a complex reaction to loss (Abraham, 1911/1968; Freud, 1917/1957). In his major work on depression, *Mourning and Melancholia*, Freud described both normal mourning and melancholia (depression) as responses to the loss of someone or something that was loved. However, in contrast to the mourner, the melancholic suffers "an extraordinary diminuation of his self-regard, an impoverishment of his ego on a grand scale" (Freud, 1917/1957, p. 246). Depression was the first disorder described by Freud in which the central causal factor was emotion rather than sexual wish. Melancholy, as Freud called it, was grief gone haywire—excessive, drawn out, often unrelated to the environment, and seemingly unjustified.

Freud believed that a person who is depressed has a strong and punishing conscience or superego. He emphasized the guilt that the conscience creates. He thought that one reason the conscience becomes so strong is to control the anger and aggressive feelings that otherwise might come forth to hurt others (Freud, 1930).

Why do some individuals react with such extreme irrational grief? Psychodynamic theories emphasize unconscious feelings and reactions to new situations based on what has happened earlier in life. Most psychodynamic formulations focus on the history of relationships between the individual and the person on whom he or she was most dependent as a child, usually the mother. Thus, a historical antecedent of depression is a disturbance in early-childhood relationships. The disturbance might be the actual loss of a parental figure or a feared or fantasized loss of such a figure. Because of its anxiety-provoking quality, this early loss is pushed out of awareness. Nevertheless, it exerts an influence and culminates in actual depression when set off by a symbolically significant event.

The importance of parental loss has been studied intensively in animal experiments. Research by Harry Harlow and others has tested the effects on infant monkeys of removal from the mother (Harlow and Suomi, 1974). At first the typical infant shows agitation; this gradually changes to social withdrawal, slow response to stimuli, and slow movement. Eventually the baby assumes a collapsed, self-clasping position that suggests the behavior of a person who is severely depressed. Separation from their mothers also seems to make monkeys more likely to become depressed later in life if they experience a high level of stress. However, there seem to be personality differences among monkeys that cause some of them to react strongly to early separation and later stress while others are unaffected (Suomi, 1983).

John Bowlby, a British psychoanalyst, is one of the more prominent theorists who emphasize the importance of loss or separation in childhood to later development. Bowlby thinks that separation of a child from its mother or another important figure during early childhood, whether because of illness, travel, or other reasons, creates feelings of sadness, anger, and continuing anxiety that may affect the individual's emotional relationships in adult life (Bowlby, 1980).

Researchers have provided data that connect the probability of depression in adults with early experiences of loss. For example, the sociologist George Brown found that women who had lost their mothers before the age of 11 were at greater risk of depression than other women (Brown and others, 1977). In a large study of a Canadian population, people who lost their fathers before age 6 or between ages 10 and 15 had the highest depression scores. In this group there was no effect for early maternal loss (Barnes and Prosen, 1985). Not everyone thinks that early loss has been definitely established as a factor increasing the risk of later depression (Crook and Eliot, 1980), but it remains an important part of the psychodynamic perspective.

The loss that affects a person's self-esteem may be symbolic rather than real, such as loss of love or status as opposed to loss through death. For instance, a middle-aged man became severely depressed after he had lost money in the stock market. First he became morose, irritable, dependent, and self-critical. Then he seemed to collapse emotionally.

*This severe reaction was better understood when it was learned that this man had dreamed of making a sufficient income from stocks so he could resign from his job, which he detested. Therefore, the loss prevented him from obtaining a future lifestyle that he desperately desired. However, this deeper motive still does not explain this man's change in his estimation of himself, transforming his personality from one of moderate confidence and autonomy to one of self-hatred and childish dependency. This change in self-estimation becomes more understandable when his childhood experience is related. He had been raised by a highly critical father and mother, both of whom preferred his brother. Throughout his maturing years he had been repeatedly told that he could never amount to anything, that he was doomed to failure because of his inadequacies, and that he should strive for a secure, if unrewarding, position in life, as this was the best he could hope for. He developed a view of himself as ineffectual and inferior and was plagued with self-doubt and anxiety. As a result, he was unable to perform successfully at school, despite a superior intellect, and went into his family's business, where he continued to be devalued and criticized. He managed to hide his hated self from others and also from himself by exploiting his family's wealth and prestigious place in the community, by pursuing certain hobbies so that he became a somewhat pedantic expert, by criticizing his wife and children, and by fantasizing about becoming a highly successful entrepreneur. His failure to make money in the stock market revived the dreaded childhood self so that he believed that his parents had been correct in their judgment: he was inadequate and stupid. The financial loss was more than an environmental deprivation, the loss caused a drastic alteration in his view of himself, which initiated the depressive process. It is when one's own sense of self is intricately bound up with an environmental loss or failure that depression appears to arise.* (Bemporad, 1983, p. 162)

Psychodynamic therapies are aimed at modifying the existing associations between the client's thoughts and feelings. Long-term psychotherapy is directed at uncovering the unconscious basis of the affective disorder, which is thought to be an unresolved conflict based on childhood experiences. Because such ambitious personality restructuring is not possible in most cases, short-term supportive therapy is often used to give depressed individuals an opportunity to express their thoughts and feelings and encourage them to hope for recovery.

## The Behavioral Perspective on Depression

Learning theorists assume that depression and lack of reinforcement are related. Many learning theorists have been greatly influenced by B. F. Skinner's studies of operant conditioning. Most beginning psychology students are familiar with the behavior change that occurs when a pigeon is reinforced by receiving food when it pecks at a particular spot in its cage or a Skinner box. Experiments have shown that human behaviors can be manipulated in a similar way. The ideas stemming from Skinner's work have been modified by an emphasis on social interaction, specifically on how the behavior of other people can act as reinforcement.

Peter Lewinsohn and his coworkers have been among the leaders in research on depression from the behavioral perspective. In general, they emphasize that the low rate of behavior output and the feelings of sadness or unhappiness associated with depression are due to a low rate of positive reinforcement (Lewinsohn, 1974). According to this perspective, a major cause of the low rate of positive reinforcement is an actual deficiency in social skills (Lewinsohn and Hoberman, 1982). Further, once people are depressed, their behavior makes them less likable, so a kind of vicious cycle is created. Once a person has become depressed, Lewinsohn believes, the depression is maintained because other people find depressed people unpleasant to be with. When acquaintances avoid the depressed person as much as possible, they further decrease the person's rate of reinforcement and in effect intensify the depression (Lewinsohn and Arconad, 1981).

The negative effects that depressed people have on others were demonstrated in a clever experiment by Coyne (1976). Coyne arranged for each of 45 nondepressed people to hold a telephone conversation with a depressed patient, a nondepressed patient, or a normal control. All the participants in the experiment were told that it was a study of the acquaintanceship process. After the conversation, the participants filled in questionnaires about their mood, their perceptions of the other people, and their desire to interact with the others again. Compared to people who spoke to nondepressed patients or to members of the control group, those who spoke to depressed patients described themselves as significantly more depressed, anxious, and hostile after the conversations. Those who spoke to members of the depressed group also had less desire to see or interact with them again than callers who spoke to members of either of the other groups. When the callers were asked to describe the person at the other end of the conversation, the depressed patients were perceived as making less of an effort to present a desirable image and as more depressed than members of the other two groups.

When depressed people find themselves in stressful situations, they tend to cope by delaying (seeking more information before taking any action) and attempting to get emotional support from others (Coyne, 1982; Coyne and others, 1981). Excessive support seeking may make other people feel uncomfortable and guilty (as in Coyne's experiment) and cause them to try to avoid contact with the depressed person. This avoidance response, in turn, may cause the depressed people to doubt others' sincerity and may be why they see themselves as getting less support.

Depressed people may also make many complaints in order to elicit sympathy and affection. Although the person who is on the receiving end of this treatment may respond appropriately at first, after a while he or she may become annoyed or frustrated. Even if the depressed person's associates keep on giving support and making reassuring statements, their feelings of frustration may be expressed in nonverbal behaviors or in other ways. If that anger and frustration are not expressed, negative undertones underlying the reassuring and sympathetic statements may confuse the depressed person so that the unpleasant behaviors are maintained rather than dropped (Coates and Wortman, 1980). Eventually a vicious cycle develops in which the display of symptoms and the frustration of the depressed person's companions increase until the companions begin to say things like, "You could get better if you try" or "No one has to act like that." This, of course, merely serves to worsen an already bad situation. Such feelings, whether expressed or not, are probably one reason people tend to avoid the company of depressed individuals. Perhaps because of such factors, social-skills training may be an effective therapeutic approach to depression.

As we will see in more detail in the next section, one of the characteristics of depressed behavior is negative self-evaluation. Lewinsohn and his coworkers believe that people who are depressed have a negative view of their **self-efficacy** in dealing with situations. This term refers to a person's judgment of his or her own ability to carry out certain courses of action (Bandura, 1977). It may be that the feeling of low self-efficacy is an accurate reflection of a depressed person's lack of social skills and ability to obtain reinforcement. Depressed people show a bigger difference between their ideas of self-efficacy and their behavioral standards than people who are not depressed. Lewinsohn's model predicts that this difference is due to a lower perception of self-efficacy rather than to higher standards of behavior, and it has been demonstrated experimentally that this is the case (see Figure 10–9). This suggests that people who are depressed may not try as hard as others would in situations they see as difficult because they have a negative view of their own abilities, not because they set their goals too high (Kanfer and Zeiss, 1983).

### Treatment Based on Behavioral Theories

In treating clients who are depressed, Lewinsohn and his coworkers first strive to pinpoint the specific interactions and events that are related to the depression. One step in the initial assessment is observation of the person at home (Lewinsohn and Arconad, 1981). This accomplishes several things. It alerts the client to the idea that depression is related to interactions with other people and with the environment, and it gives the ther-

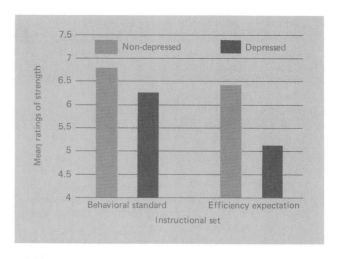

**FIGURE 10–9**
People who are depressed set their performance standards about as high as nondepressed individuals do, but they have less confidence that they will be able to meet those standards. R. Kanfer and A.M. Zeiss, 1983. Depression, interpersonal standard setting, and judgments of self-efficacy. *Journal of Abnormal Psychology, 92*, 319–329. Copyright (c) 1983 by the American Psyhological Association. Reprinted by permission of the author.

apist a productive and relatively unbiased way of learning about the behavior of the client and others in his or her environment.

Another tool used in this social-learning-based treatment is lists of pleasant and unpleasant events. The client notes how often each event has occurred in his or her life and how pleasant or unpleasant it was (or could have been if it had happened), and constructs a tailor-made event list to be used daily. The client also rates his or her mood each day in order to allow both the client and the therapist to become aware of the relationship between events and the client's mood. A summary of these daily monitorings for one client is shown in Figure 10–10. In addition to this daily monitoring, a specific treatment plan is prepared that includes training in the skills that the client lacks. The plan could include such things as assertion training, effective parenting, time management, and relaxation training. This approach is illustrated in the following case.

*Alice was a 37-year-old secretary. She was a single parent with two children, a 14-year-old son and a 9-year-old daughter. Alice's initial complaints included having trouble getting things done, lack of concentration, loss of interest in activities, withdrawal from social life, unreliability, fatigue, and headaches. She complained of feeling depressed. After her initial evaluation Alice started working with her therapist. The treatment was to include twelve sessions. In the first half of the treatment*

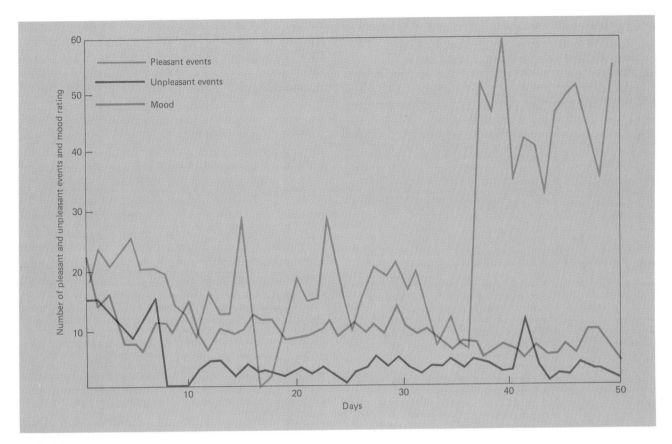

**FIGURE 10-10**
A record of Alice's daily monitoring of pleasant and unpleasant events and moods. (Lewinsohn and others, 1980, p. 330)

*Alice used her listing of pleasant and unpleasant events as a starting point for discussion. She identified finances, household chores, parenting, and social activities as her biggest concerns. Alice didn't know where her money went. She felt her finances were out of control. The therapist helped her prepare a monthly budget and Alice kept a daily log of expenses. Using these techniques made her feel money matters were much less upsetting.*

*Another problem Alice had was her dislike of household chores. She routinely let them pile up and then tried to do them all on the weekend. The therapist helped her organize her chores into small units, pair them with pleasant activities, such as listening to the radio, reward herself for doing them, and assign some of the chores to her children. As a parent, Alice felt totally responsible for any problem her children had. She also had problems disciplining them and relied on punishment which then made her feel guilty. The therapist helped Alice to learn to talk calmly to her children about the reasons for her disciplinary actions, to pinpoint their desirable behaviors and reward them with praise, affection, and allowances. Alice also learned to sort out whether it was "my problem, their problem, or our problem" when thinking about her children's difficulties. (Lewinsohn and others, 1980, pp. 328–332)*

Alice's self-monitoring data (Figure 10–10) showed changes as time went on. The number of pleasant events that she reported increased, the number of unpleasant events decreased, and her mood improved somewhat. The self-monitoring data for the first 21 days of Alice's treatment were analyzed by a computer program that calculated the correlations between each activity and her mood changes. The ten positive and ten negative events that were most highly correlated with Alice's mood are shown in Table 10–2. This list alerted Alice to the relationship of certain events to her mood.

The computer analyses also confirmed Alice's low rate of pleasant activities, especially social activities. The remaining therapy sessions were devoted to this problem. Over time Alice had withdrawn from social activities, especially those involving men. She believed that contacts with men must lead to sex and marriage, and she had difficulty saying no to men's advances. The therapist stressed the importance of friendship and helped Alice practice assertive responses that she might use in potential problem situations. As Alice's daily social interactions increased, the number of pleasant events in her life increased dramatically and the im-

□ **TABLE 10-2**
The Ten Pleasant and Ten Unpleasant Events
Most Highly Correlated with Alice's Mood

| Kind | Specific Event |
|---|---|
| Pleasant events | 1. Buying things for myself.<br>2. Buying things for my family.<br>3. Learning to do something new.<br>4. Planning trips or vacations.<br>5. Going to a party.<br>6. Making a new friend.<br>7. Improving my health (having my teeth fixed, getting new glasses, changing my diet, etc.).<br>8. Wearing expensive or formal clothes.<br>9. Combing or brushing my hair.<br>10. Playing party games. |
| Unpleasant events | 1. Coming home to a messy house.<br>2. Being bothered with red tape, administrative hassles, paperwork, etc.<br>3. Being rushed.<br>4. Having someone I know drink, smoke, or take drugs.<br>5. Having something break or run poorly (car, appliances, etc.).<br>6. Being unable to call or reach someone when it is important.<br>7. Seeing natural resources wasted (trees left to rot, polluted streams, etc.).<br>8. Seeing a dead animal.<br>9. Riding in a car with a poor driver.<br>10. Being socially rejected. |

*Source:* Lewinsohn and others, 1980, p. 331.

provement in her mood continued. At the end of the treatment series, the therapist arranged for a follow-up one month later. At that time Alice continued to report an increased frequency of pleasant events and an improved mood (Lewinsohn and others, 1980).

Lewinsohn and his coworkers (Lewinsohn and others, 1985) have also developed a course in coping with depression to teach techniques and strategies for coping with problems that seem to be related to depression. The course, presented not as therapy but as education, consists of 12 group sessions and covers such topics as making a self-change plan, relaxation techniques, ways of increasing pleasant activities, constructive thinking, social skills, and how to maintain changes in the future.

## The Cognitive Perspective

Probably the most influential psychological theories of depression today are derived from the cognitive perspective. The basis for these theories is the idea that the same experience may affect two people very dif-

ferently. Part of this difference may be due to the way they think about the event, that is, to the cognitions they have about it. One person who does not receive an expected promotion might think: "I am a worthless person. Everyone thinks poorly of me. If they did not, I would have been selected for the job." A second person in the same situation might think: "R. was chosen for that job I wanted because he had more experience in negotiation. I know I could have done the job, but my qualifications didn't look as impressive on paper."

There are several cognitive theories of depression. They include Beck's cognitive-distortion model, attributional theories such as the learned-helplessness theory of Seligman and his coworkers, theories that emphasize the cognitive aspects of stress, and information-processing theories. Moreover, as was pointed out earlier, learning-based theories like Lewinsohn's also have a strong cognitive component.

**Beck's Cognitive-Distortion Model**  Aaron Beck's cognitive-distortion model of depression (Beck, 1967, 1976; Beck and others, 1979) is the most original and influential of the cognitive approaches to depression. Beck argues that depression is primarily a disorder of thinking rather than of mood. He believes that depression can best be described as a **cognitive triad** of negative thoughts about oneself, the situation, and the future. A person who is depressed misinterprets facts in a negative way, focuses on the negative aspects of any situation, and also has pessimistic and hopeless expectations about the future. Table 10–3 illustrates some of these cognitive errors on the part of depressed individuals; Figure 10–11 shows how depressed people tend to emphasize the negative.

A good example of overgeneralization and distortion is provided by Norman Endler's description of his thoughts during his bout of depression (Endler, 1982). Endler went through a period of fear (not at all based on reality) that his family would desert him and that he would be unable to cope with everyday living.

*I recall a time during the end of August when I took the subway with my wife. She had gone through the turnstile before I did and I was positive that she was going to desert me. She probably had had enough of me and my shenanigans and was fed up with my behavior.* (Endler, 1982, p. 49)

After his recovery from this period of depression, Endler recognized the irrationality of such a thought.

*Of course nothing could have been further from the truth. Her kindness and devotion, her concern, compassion, and her love, more than anything else, sustained me during my ordeal. If I had to single out the*

Cognitive Errors and the Assumptions from Which They are Derived
According to Beck's Cognitive Theory

| Cognitive Error | Assumption |
|---|---|
| 1. Overgeneralizing | 1. If it is true in one case, it applies to any case that is even slightly similar. |
| 2. Selective abstraction | 2. The only events that matter are failures, deprivation, etc. Should measure self by errors, weaknesses, etc. |
| 3. Excessive responsibility (assuming personal causality) | 3. I am responsible for all bad things, failures, etc. |
| 4. Assuming temporal causality (predicting without sufficient evidence) | 4. If it has been true in the past, then it is always going to be true. |
| 5. Self-references | 5. I am the center of everyone's attention, especially of bad performances or personal attributes. |
| 6. "Catastrophizing" | 6. Always think of the worst. It is most likely to happen to you. |
| 7. Dichotomous thinking | 7. Everything either is one extreme or another (black or white; good or bad). |

*Source:* Beck and others, 1978, p. 196.

**FIGURE 10-11**
The cartoonist Roz Chast has captured the thinking that is typical of a depressed person.

*one person who was most instrumental in my getting better, it would be my wife. (ibid.)*

Beck believes that a person who is depressed blames any misfortune on his or her personal defects. Awareness of these presumed defects becomes so intense that it completely overwhelms any positive self-concepts. Any ambiguous situation is interpreted as evidence of the defect, even if there are more plausible explanations. For example,

> *Following an argument with her brother, a mildly depressed woman concluded, "I am incapable of being loved and of giving love," and she felt more depressed. When a friend was too busy to chat with her on the phone, she thought, "She doesn't want to talk to me anymore." If her husband came home late from the office, she decided that he was staying away to avoid her. When her children were ill-natured at dinner time, she thought, "I have failed them." (Beck, 1974, p. 10)*

Beck also thinks that depressed people tend to compare themselves with others, which further lowers their self-esteem. Every encounter with another person becomes an opportunity for a negative self-evaluation. For instance, when talking with others the depressed person thinks: "I'm not a good conversationalist. I'm not as interesting as other people." Beck thinks that the tendency to have these negative cognitions may be related to particular ways of evaluating situations that grow out of childhood experiences. These thought patterns, called **schemata,** affect all the elements of the cognitive triad in later life. A list of the characteristics of these schemata is presented in Table 10–4.

Beck has modified his original theory on the basis of evidence collected in later research. He has described two subtypes of people who seem to be vulnerable to depression but respond differently to specific types of stress (Beck, 1982). One type is the **sociotropic** depressive. These people are especially affected by interpersonal negative events because they derive their feelings of well-being from the support of other people. The second type is the **autonomous** depressive. These people, because they get their feelings of self-worth and satisfaction from their achievements, become depressed if they feel that they have failed or have not achieved their goals.

Other research findings have shown that further modifications in Beck's theory are necessary (Hammen, 1985). First, the idea that only people who are depressed distort information needs to be modified. All individuals are biased information processors, although different groups may have different kinds of biases. Second, it has become clear that negative thoughts do not necessarily cause depression but may result from it and may be present only when a person is depressed. However, distorted thinking may cause the depression to continue and intensify in a kind of vicious cycle.

**Cognitive Therapy for Depression** Beck's therapeutic approach includes pointed but friendly questioning designed to make the depressed person aware of the unrealistic nature of his or her thoughts. Another technique that Beck uses is an activity schedule. The client schedules his or her day and then rates each activity on a scale from 0 to 5 for mastery (doing a good job) and pleasure. The following dialog occurred after a severely depressed 38-year-old executive turned in his mastery schedule. One item, "wallpaper kitchen," stood out. This should be an achievement for a severely depressed person, yet the client had given it a 0 for both mastery and pleasure.

THERAPIST: *Why didn't you rate wallpapering the kitchen as a mastery experience?*

PATIENT: *Because the flowers didn't line up.*

THERAPIST: *You did in fact complete the job?*

PATIENT: *Yes.*

THERAPIST: *Your kitchen?*

PATIENT: *No. I helped a neighbor do his kitchen.*

THERAPIST: *Did he do most of the work? [Note that the therapist inquires about reasons for feelings of failure that might not be offered spontaneously.]*

PATIENT: *No. I really did almost all of it. He hadn't wallpapered before.*

THERAPIST: *Did anything else go wrong? Did you spill the paste all over? Ruin a lot of wallpaper? Leave a big mess?*

PATIENT: *No, no, the only problem was that the flowers did not line up.*

THERAPIST: *So, since it was not perfect, you get no credit at all.*

---

□ **TABLE 10–4**
**Schemata Used in Beck's Cognitive Theory of Depression**

---

*Schemata (silent assumptions)*
  Consist of unspoken, inflexible assumptions or beliefs
  Result from past (early) experience
  Form basis for screening, discriminating, weighing, and encoding stimuli
  Form basis for categorizing, evaluating experiences, and making judgments and distorting actual experience
  Determine the content of cognitions formed in situations and the affective response to them
  Increase vulnerability to relapse

---

Source: Beck, 1976.

PATIENT: *Well . . . yes.* [*Note that the irrational belief that "if I don't do everything perfectly, I am useless, inadequate and a failure" is implied by this reasoning. However, the correction of this assumption will be left to a later phase of therapy, when the patient is less depressed. For now, the correction of the cognitive distortion is the objective.*]

THERAPIST: *Just how far off was the alignment of the flowers?*

PATIENT: [*holds out fingers about ⅛ in. apart*]: *About that much.*

THERAPIST: *On each strip of paper?*

PATIENT: *No . . . on two or three pieces.*

THERAPIST: *Out of how many?*

PATIENT: *About 20–25.*

THERAPIST: *Did anyone else notice it?*

PATIENT: *No. In fact, my neighbor thought it was great.*

THERAPIST: *Did your wife see it?*

PATIENT: *Yeh, she admired the job.*

THERAPIST: *Could you see the defect when you stood back and looked at the whole wall?*

PATIENT: *Well . . . not really.*

THERAPIST: *So you've selectively attended to a real but very small flaw in your effort to wallpaper. Is it logical that such a small defect should entirely cancel the credit you deserve?*

PATIENT: *Well, it wasn't as good as it should have been.*

THERAPIST: *If your neighbor had done the same quality job in your kitchen, what would you say?*

PATIENT: *. . . pretty good job!*

(Beck and others, 1978, pp. 85–86. Reprinted with permission of *Psychology Today Magazine*. Copyright © 1978 APA.)

**Attributional Models of Depression**   Another cognitive factor has to do with the attributions a person makes about an event. The term **attribution** is used by social psychologists to refer to the causes a person assigns to things that happen. Beck's cognitive approach predicts that depressed individuals' attributions will be personal—that is, depressed people will blame themselves when anything bad happens. When something good does happen, it is usually attributed to luck. For instance, one woman was not especially pleased when a short story that she had written was accepted for publication; she attributed the acceptance to sheer luck. On the other hand, when one of her articles was rejected (a negative event), she was distressed because she thought the rejection reflected badly on her. Most nondepressed people do the opposite: they accept responsibility for the good in their lives but tend to blame the situation on others when things do not work out. Figure 10–12 illustrates this difference.

*Learned helplessness.*   People who are depressed

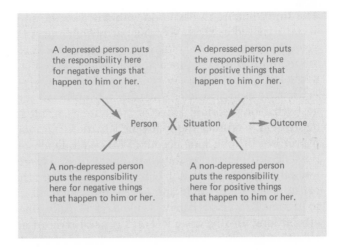

**FIGURE 10-12**
A comparison of the attribution process in depressed and nondepressed people.

seem to feel helpless to control their environment. They think that no matter what they do, they will be unable to affect the way things turn out. It is possible that such people learn to be helpless as a result of certain situations they have encountered in the past. Martin Seligman (1974, 1975) first popularized this concept, which is termed **learned helplessness.**

Early research on learned helplessness showed that sometimes people feel generally helpless and sometimes they feel helpless only in particular situations. The way a person interprets the situation is important in determining whether or not he or she will feel helpless. On the basis of this research, a revised theory of learned helplessness stresses the importance of the attributions people make in determining whether they will become depressed in a particular situation (Abramson and others, 1978). According to the revised theory, depression is more likely when people attribute negative qualities to themselves as a result of having experienced situations in which they felt helpless.

There are three dimensions to these feelings of helplessness. The first has to do with whether the person sees the problem as **external** or **internal**. People are more likely to become depressed or have a low self-image if they attribute the situation to their own inability to control outcomes. Such people see themselves as the only ones who cannot cope with the problem. In this respect they are quite different from people who feel that anyone would have a hard time in the same situation. The second dimension has to do with the **global–specific continuum.** If someone sees a situation as proof that he or she is totally helpless, that person is more likely to be depressed than someone who sees him- or herself as helpless only in a particular situation.

The third dimension has to do with whether the situation is viewed as **stable** (chronic) or **unstable** (acute). People who think their helplessness will go on for years are more likely to be depressed than people who think it will last a short time.

The revised learned-helplessness hypothesis suggests that only certain kinds of attributions result in depression. Consider the following situation. Tim has overdrawn his checking account. We could divide his possible attributions as shown in Table 10–5. The revised theory predicts that if Tim's attribution about the cause of failure is stable and global, he is more likely to become depressed than he would be if he made other attributions. In this case, if Tim's general style of attribution caused him to explain his unbalanced checkbook in terms of stable global factors, whether internal or external, he would have a high chance of becoming depressed. If his attributions were internal, stable, and global, his depressive thinking would be characterized by loss of self-esteem as well. If he perceived the cause as stable, the feelings of depression would be likely to persist. If the cause was seen as unstable, the depressive reaction would be likely to pass away quickly (Abramson and others, 1978).

It appears that people who have low self-esteem in addition to a feeling of helplessness are more likely to be incapacitated by depression. In one study, depressed patients were more likely to attribute bad outcomes to internal, stable, and global causes than either schizophrenic patients or medical patients who were not depressed (Raps and others, 1982).

Some people become depressed in certain situations while others do not. The revised learned-helplessness hypothesis assumes that people who make attributions to internal, stable, and global causes are most likely to become depressed when bad events occur. It also assumes that various individuals have different characteristic ways of explaining events and therefore are consistent across situations in the extent to which their causal explanations are internal, stable, and global. This means that for events for which no clear cause is apparent, these people are likely to give an explanation that comes from habit rather than from an assessment of the situation. However, not all research data support the view that attributional style is consistent for most people in a variety of situations (Hammen, 1985). Another problem with this theory is that only about one-third of all depressed people exhibit this attributional style, and those who do, change their style in periods when they are not depressed (Hamilton and Abramson, 1983). Seligman's attribution model fits best in situations that have to do with achievement, such as college performance or vocational success. Other kinds of negative events, such as a death or a friend moving away, may call up different sets of attributions from the same person.

*Life Stress Models.* Having bad experiences can contribute to depression. In discussing the psychodynamic perspective we mentioned the relationship between negative events, especially early loss of a parent, and depression. Yet it is clear that negative things happen to many people who do not become depressed. The cognitive perspective stresses the importance of a person's **cognitive set** in the interpretation of stressful events (Paykel, 1979). George Brown and his coworkers stress that changes focus a person's attention on the present and thus, since the present is an outcome of the past, stress focuses attention on choices, commitments, and mistakes that have been made. This leads to questions about "what our life might have been, what it is about, and what it will become" (Brown and Harris, 1978, p. 84). For example, if a person's self-es-

□ **TABLE 10–5**
Examples of Causal Explanations for the Event "My Checking Account is Overdrawn"

| Style | Explanation Internal | External |
|---|---|---|
| Stable | | |
| Global | "I'm incapable of doing anything right" | "All institutions chronically make mistakes" |
| Specific | "I always have trouble figuring my balance" | "This bank has always used antiquated techniques" |
| Unstable | | |
| Global | "I've had the flu for a few weeks, and I've let everything slide" | "Holiday shopping demands that one throw oneself into it" |
| Specific | "The one time I didn't enter a check is the one time my account gets overdrawn" | "I'm surprised—my bank has never made an error before" |

Source: Peterson and Seligman, 1984, p. 349.

teem is low before the depression begins, it is unlikely that he or she will be able to picture emerging from the depression. Although loss is important in depression, negative events for which people see themselves as at least partially responsible are also important. In some cases these may be more important than negative events for which there is usually no responsibility, such as death or illness (Hammen and De Mayo, 1982).

*An Information-Processing Analysis.* The information-processing view of depression attempts to combine social-learning theory and the ideas of Beck and Seligman with concepts derived from the work of cognitive psychologists who are interested in learning and memory (Ingram, 1984). The basic idea is that memories are represented by descriptive statements connected by associated linkages. When these linkages are activated beyond certain thresholds, the contents of the system come into conscious awareness in the form of cognitions. But memories are only one set of linkages in the information-processing system. In addition, there may be **primitive emotion nodes** (Bower, 1981). This hypothesis suggests that each specific emotion, such as depression, anger, or joy, is represented by a particular unit or node in memory. Each node connects an autonomic response pattern, the verbal labels used to describe the emotion, a characteristic automatic response pattern, and descriptions of the events that bring forth that particular emotion.

According to this view, the depression unit is activated by the appraisal of a variety of events. Depression is usually related to some event associated with loss, but only losses that are subjectively meaningful will activate the depression node. Once it is activated, its level of excitation gradually decreases until it falls below the threshold level. This may explain why depression is usually time-limited and fades without treatment (Lewinsohn and Hoberman, 1982). Depression can also be maintained through the connections of the depression node to memories of events that have produced depression in the past. For instance, if a person has just lost an important job, this loss will activate the depression node and its network. This means that, in addition to the initial depression, the person will begin thinking about past losses and past depression experiences. As he or she thinks these depressing thoughts, the depression node is reactivated and the depression continues.

The results of some experimental work support the information-processing view. People who are depressed recall more of previously presented negatively self-relevant information than people who are not depressed (Derry and Kuiper, 1981). Research by Rehm (1977) and his coworkers has also shown that depressed individuals give greater attention to negative events, make less accurate attributions about causality, and are less likely to reward and more likely to punish themselves than nondepressed individuals.

*Cognitive Accuracy in Depression.* Many cognitive theories assume that depressed people see situations inaccurately. However, some researchers have found that depressed students were more accurate than nondepressed students in estimating the relationship between their actions and the outcomes of situations (Alloy and Abramson, 1979). These and similar findings suggest that it is not the particular situation that is most important in depression (as the original learned-helplessness hypothesis suggested), but rather the depressed person's attributions about the reasons for the outcome. We noted earlier that people generally attribute good outcomes to themselves and negative outcomes to the situation. This may be true only for nondepressed people (Raps and others, 1982). Whereas those who are not depressive increase their self-esteem through their attributional style, depressive people use a more accurate perception of the situation, which has the opposite effect on their self-esteem.

Both Beck's theory and the revised learned-helplessness hypothesis stress the inaccuracy of self-perception in depression. But, again, the attributions of depressed people may be more accurate than these theories predict. Experimenters studying how well people assessed their own social competence found that depressed patients were quite realistic about their own social skills. In contrast, other psychiatric patients and control subjects tended to see themselves as more competent than other people saw them. Even more interesting, the realism of the depressed patients' self-perceptions tended to decrease as therapy progressed. In short, as they become less depressed, the patients became less realistic about their effects on others; they deluded themselves in the same way that nonpatients do (Lewinsohn and others, 1980). This fits very well with an observation made by Freud.

> When in his [the depressive's] heightened self-criticism he describes himself as petty, egoistic, dishonest, lacking in independence, one whose sole aim has been to hide the weakness of his own nature, it may be, so far as we know, that he has come pretty near to understanding himself; we only wonder why a man has to be ill before he can be accessible to a truth of this kind. (Freud, 1917/1957, p. 246)

The crucial question then becomes, Does depression lead people to become more realistic or are realistic people more vulnerable, more likely to become depressed? As yet, research has not solved this puzzle.

## The Humanistic–Existential Perspective

Whereas psychodynamic theorists emphasize the loss of a loved object as a central cause of depression, existentialist theorists focus on the loss of self-esteem. The lost object can be real or symbolic—power, social rank, or money—but the loss itself is not as important as the change in an individual's self-assessment as a result of the loss. Many people base their self-concepts on who they are or what they have: I'm the leader of the factory assembly team; I'm the boss; I'm a member of the exclusive city athletic club; I'm the wife of a successful lawyer; I'm the husband of a famous movie star. Identifications of this kind offer external verification of people's worth in their own minds. Thus, in our culture a frequent cause of depression in men is loss of their job. The job represents the man's value in his own eyes. For women, at least until the recent great increase in the number of women employed outside the home, a frequent cause of depression was loss of their mate. This represented not only the loss of a loved person but also the loss of a major source of prestige, since a woman's social status was traditionally based on her husband's role.

Humanistic theorists emphasize the difference between a person's ideal self and his or her perception of the actual state of things. Depression is likely to result when the difference between the ideal and the real becomes too great for the individual to tolerate. This idea fits in well with evidence gathered by experimenters who have studied the level of realism in the self-assessments of depressed and nondepressed people.

## Contrasting Psychological Theories of Depression

When one reads about the various psychological theories of depression and the therapies derived from them, it is sometimes difficult to distinguish clearly among them. Learning theories such as Lewinsohn's approach and Beck's cognitive-distortion theory started out quite differently, but as their related therapies developed, many of the techniques used became more similar. The behavioral approach increasingly emphasized social reinforcement and in some cases paid greater attention to cognitive attributions, and Beck included learning-theory techniques like behavioral checklists of events and moods.

The same emphasis on feelings of hopelessness and helplessness is found in the humanistic–existential approach, in which loss of self-esteem and perceived inability to alter the oppressive demands of society are central ideas. The difference from a therapeutic standpoint lies in the less structured approach, especially of existentialist therapists. The therapeutic approach of this group is somewhat more directive than psychoanalysis and, like the learning and cognitive therapies, is centered on the present rather than on the client's past history. It is essentially a talking therapy without the checklists and specific behavioral observations used in learning and cognitive approaches. Psychodynamic therapists stress cognitive distortions, but they tend to focus not only on how these affect present behavior but also on their origins in the client's earlier life. However, as the information-processing perspective shows, cognitive theories are also concerned with a person's past experiences. The thing to remember about the psychological theories and their related therapies is that while they differ in emphasis, some of their basic ideas have become surprisingly similar.

## ■ THE BIPOLAR DISORDERS

**Bipolar disorders,** or manic–depressive disorders, are characterized by phases of both depression and mania. Table 10–6 contrasts manic and depressive behavior. The peak incidence of bipolar disorders is during young adulthood. In one study, the average age of bipolar patients when their symptoms were first recognized was 25 (Roy-Byrne and others, 1985). Many people in this group had shown evidence of the disorder as adolescents.

The occurrence of mania is a prerequisite for the diagnosis of bipolar disorder. Mania is characterized by a flight of ideas, elevated mood, and increased psychomotor activity. Although mania itself represents an extreme type of behavior, it is probably more useful to describe mania as one extreme on a spectrum of elated behavior. This spectrum includes mood states ranging from normal joy and happiness to extreme and hostile overactivity (Klerman, 1981).

### Characteristics of Bipolar Disorders

*Mania.* The very word conjures up an image of the stereotypical crazy person—the maniac, a stock character in many older works of fiction—with frantic behavior, staring eyes, and dramatic gestures. But what is mania really like? The case at the beginning of the chapter illustrates the impairment of judgment and the grandiose ideas that typically accompany mania. Box 10–1 describes the reactions of the child of a bipolar patient to her mother's symptoms. A reaction to a personal experience of mania is described in the following autobiographical account.

*First and foremost comes a general sense of intense well-being. I know of course that this sense is illusory and*

| | Manic Behavior | Depressive Behavior |
|---|---|---|
| Emotional characteristics | Elated, euphoric<br>Very sociable<br>Impatient at any hindrance | Gloomy, hopeless<br>Socially withdrawn<br>Irritable |
| Cognitive characteristics | Racing thoughts, flight of ideas<br>Desire for action<br>Impulsive behavior<br>Talkative<br>Positive self-image<br>Delusions of grandeur | Slowness of thought processes<br>Obsessive worrying<br>Inability to make decisions<br>Negative self-image, self-blame<br>Delusions of guilt and disease |
| Motor characteristics | Hyperactive<br>Does not become tired<br>Needs less sleep than usual<br>Increased sex drive<br>Fluctuating appetite | Decreased motor activity<br>Tired<br>Difficulty in sleeping<br>Decreased sex drive<br>Decreased appetite |

# ■BOX 10-1 THE EFFECTS OF A BIPOLAR PARENT ON ONE CHILD'S DEVELOPMENT

The family life of bipolar patients may be extremely stressful. The most severe impact of the bipolar disorder seems to fall on the children. In one study of twelve families, 45 percent of the children had severe or moderate psychological problems (Mayo, O'Connell, and O'Brian, 1979). Many seemed to have anxiety symptoms that centered on fear of family disintegration. A child with a bipolar parent is more likely to lose that parent either by divorce or suicide than a child in a nonaffected family. In Denmark, a country with excellent treatment facilities, about one of seven of all patients diagnosed as having bipolar disorder ended as a suicide (Joel-Nielsen, 1979). Divorce rates are also higher than average.

Spouses and children almost always prefer that the affected parent be depressed rather than manic. They are constantly alert for signs of mania. Any sign of enthusiasm or liveliness is interpreted in this way and is seen as a threat to family stability (Davenport and others, 1979).

These reactions to her mother's manic and depressive episodes were made by a 30-year-old woman.

*My mother went numerous times to a private mental hospital. She was 21 years old when she started, some months after my brother was born. Dr. A. says it is sometimes easier for children to adjust to parents who are psychotic all the time than only part of the time. This is so true—we kids never knew*

*what to believe. Mother was so completely different when she was well. She listened, she was kind, she was generous, she was fun to be with, she never criticized Dad, and she was always at home. But the big problem was the inconsistency, hearing one thing at one period and something quite different at the next. . . .*

*The inconsistency also does funny things with one's feelings. For instance, when my father got seriously ill and I thought he was going to die, I could not stop laughing. All the time when I was a little girl I would laugh when somebody would get hurt, but what I was really doing was crying on the inside. We seemed to have two sets of everything at that time: two sets of feelings and two sets of thoughts that did not really fit what was actually happening. Life was like a big pretense. . . . We gradually began to learn how to live in our own worlds. Both I and my sister were always looking around for homes outside our own to "adopt" us, and we tried to spend as much time as possible with these families. This helped a great deal, but it also made us realize how differently normal families lived. There was no inconsistency. You could get up in the morning and almost know inside you what was going to happen for the rest of the day. We never knew how any day was going to turn out.*

*The thing she did when she was sick that bugged me the most was never finishing a job, and even while I was still a child it became an obsession for me that I had to finish what I started. At that time, I felt it was my special duty to clean up after her, collect after her, and finish what she left unfinished. It was like being a slave, and you never questioned it.*

*When Mother became ill, I always thought that some terrible show was being put on, but she was never ashamed of what she did and what she said. She always felt that she was the greatest and could not be wrong. My brother was so much like her that today he is extremely difficult to live with, and his wife has frequently threatened to leave him. . . .*

*What effect did all this have on us children? I have already mentioned how fussy I became about tidiness and the need to have everything "just so." But there was also a special danger in my case. Ever since I was small, I have been told that I was just like my mother. I was named after her, and very soon I took to thinking that I was going to be committed when I was 21, like she was. As if it was predetermined, I found myself getting extremely impatient, nervous, muddle-headed, and unable to concentrate. I was sure that they were going to come and haul me away. I felt that I was destined to become exactly like her. . . . I felt as if I were reliving her life. I could not separate her from me inside me. We seemed to be one person inside. (Anthony, 1975, pp. 291–293)*

The children of people with bipolar disorder are much more likely than others to develop bipolar disorder themselves. They also show a high rate of unipolar disorder (Klein and others, 1985). Although heredity may be an important factor, stressful family life may also contribute. Lithium treatment may help the affected parent stabilize mood swings. However, even with this improvement, treatment for the whole family may be useful. Children of a bipolar parent who develop a DSM-III disorder are most likely to live in families in which the parent with bipolar disorder has frequent episodes of mania or depression (LaRoche and others, 1985).

*transient, and that my behavior while it persists is so abnormal that I have to be confined, so that a good deal of the gilt is taken off the gingerbread. It is only when I have been free in the manic state that the ecstatic sensations accompanying it have their full effect, but they are apt to produce dire results in the real world, as will be seen. Although, however, the restrictions of confinement are apt at times to produce extreme irritation and even paroxysms of anger, the general sense of well-being, the pleasurable and sometimes ecstatic feeling-tone, remains as a sort of permanent background of all experience during the manic period. (Custance, 1952)*

Another, somewhat different account of the first phases of a bipolar illness is given by the psychologist Stuart Sutherland, who experienced acute anxiety and inability to concentrate.

*Until I broke down I had always regarded myself as reasonably well-balanced . . . It never occurred to me that one day my existence would disintegrate within the space of a few hours. For half a year I lived in mental anguish, a prey to obsessive and agonizing thoughts. I had neither interest in nor ability to cope with the outside world which formerly I had found so fascinating. I hated myself and I hated others, and so unremitting and painful were my thoughts that I was virtually unable to read: I could not even concentrate sufficiently to peruse the daily paper. For someone accustomed to spending most of the day reading and writing, the complete inability to do either was a singularly refined torture.*

*There were two aspects of the breakdown that were particularly painful. The onset . . . was marked by levels of physical anxiety that I would not have believed possible. If one is almost involved in a road accident, there is a delay of a second or two and then the pit of the stomach seems to fall out and one's legs go like jelly. It was this feeling multiplied a hundredfold that seized me at all hours of the day and night. My dreams were often pleasant, but as soon as I woke panic set in and it would take a few moments to work out what it was all about. The realization brought anguish: an irrevocable and cataclysmic event had occurred from which I could imagine no recovery. Sleep was difficult to come by even with the help of sleeping pills, to which I soon resorted. I would awake in terror twenty or thirty times a night. (Sutherland, 1977, pp. 1–2)*

How do people with bipolar disorders behave when they are not in either the depressed or the manic phase? It has often been assumed that even during a period of remission they behave less adaptively than the average person and are more conforming and dependent. This assumption may not be true, at least for individuals receiving lithium treatment. For instance, in one study, bipolar individuals who were in a remission period did not score differently than a control group on a number of tests designed to measure conformity and dependence (MacVane and others, 1978). The intellectual functioning of bipolar patients may be less effective during periods of depression or mania, but it improves when the symptoms decrease. Intelligence test scores may actually increase during periods of hypomania (mild manic states) (Clark and others, 1985). The personality test scores of many bipolar individuals return to the normal range between episodes of mania or depression (Lumry and others, 1982).

The use of noninvasive methods like PT scans has provided some information about brain metabolism in bipolar disorders. In general, the metabolism rate for glucose increases when a person moves from depression to a more normal state or to mania (see Figure 10–13). It may be that the use of PT scans ultimately will make it possible to distinguish between patients with bipolar and unipolar disorders when their initial state is depression. About 6 percent of those who were originally diagnosed as having unipolar depression will later report an episode of mania and be reclassified as having a bipolar disorder (Schlesser and Altschuler, 1983). Identifying the disorder correctly when it begins is important because the most effective treatments for unipolar and bipolar disorders differ. Bipolar individuals are more likely to be helped by lithium and less likely to be helped by tricyclics.

Manic episodes occur far less frequently than depressions. The chance of an individual's experiencing mania, hypomania (a milder manic state), or a bipolar disorder is about 1.2 percent (Weissman and Myers, 1978). Because so few people experience more than one episode of mania without any noticeable periods of depression, they are classified as having a bipolar disorder with the expectation that a period of depression will ultimately occur. Individual patterns of manic and depressed periods vary considerably. Figure 10–14 shows patterns for several individuals.

## The Effects of Lithium

Lithium has been shown to be effective in treating bipolar disorders as well as some kinds of unipolar illness (Peet and Coppen, 1980). Since this is especially true if the depressed person has a family history of bipolar disorders, some researchers think that some unipolar

**FIGURE 10-13**
PT scans of the brain of a biopolar individual who experienced rapid cycles of mania and depression. The top and bottom rows were taken on depressed days and the middle row on a hypomanic day. The colors of the scans correspond to glucose metabolic rates, which are indicated in the color bar on the right. The overall brain metabolic rates for glucose were 36 percent higher on the hypomanic day than the average rates for depressed days, which were within 10 percent of each other. (Drs. Mazziotta, Phelps, et al., UCLA School of Medicine.)

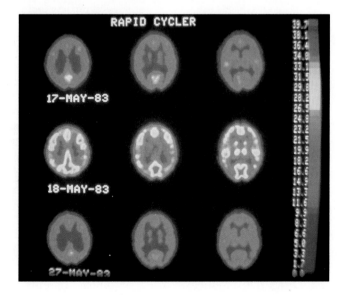

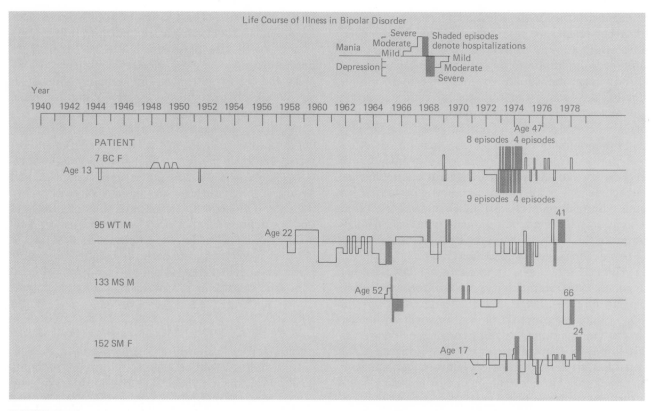

**FIGURE 10-14**
Manic and depressed episodes for four individuals over time. The shaded areas indicate hospitalizations. The height of each rectangle indicates the severity of the episode; the width of the rectangle shows how long the episode lasted.

disorders may have the same causes as bipolar disorders (Winokur, 1980). One problem with the use of lithium for bipolar disorders is that many patients discontinue the drug against medical advice even though lithium usually does a good job of controlling the symptoms of bipolar disorders. There are several possible reasons why this occurs. One may be that lithium is abandoned when the person is in a low, although not depressed, period in the hope that stopping its use will elevate his or her mood. An even more intriguing reason is unwillingness to give up some of the pleasant cognitive and behavioral changes that come with an elevated mood (Jamison and others, 1980). These include increased sensitivity to the environment, sexual intensity, creativity, and social ease. Therapists thus must deal with a client's perceptions of the disorder in addition to prescribing an effective medication.

## The Role of Heredity in Bipolar Disorders

The dramatic aspects of mania continue to fascinate both professionals and the general public. Some drugs can cause people with no history of affective disorders to experience episodes of mania. Drugs that produce this response include steroids, MAO inhibitors and tricyclic drugs used to treat depression, and L-dopa (used to treat Parkinson's disease). Mania can also result from infections, metabolic disturbances, and the growth of tumors. These findings suggest that a manic behavior has a variety of causes. For this reason, researchers have divided bipolar disorders into several subtypes (Klerman, 1981). For example, one group includes people with **cyclothymia,** which can be described as a milder form of bipolar disorder. These individuals have increased risk of mania if they take tricyclic drugs, respond well to lithium, and have a greater than average chance of having other bipolar individuals in their families. Another group contains people who have experienced only depression, not mania, but whose family histories show a high incidence of bipolar disorders. Those in still another group are similar to bipolar individuals except that their manic periods are not severe enough to meet the requirements for that diagnosis. For research purposes this group is often referred to as Bipolar II.

There seems to be a strong hereditary factor in bipolar disorders. For instance, one study found that children of bipolar parents showed significantly higher rates of affective disorders, especially cyclothymia, than children whose parents had other psychiatric diagnoses. The children of bipolar patients did not differ from the other children in their rates of psychiatric disorders other than bipolar disorders (Klein and others, 1985).

One question that has not been settled is whether bipolar and unipolar disorders are genetically related. Some researchers have suggested that the forms of mood disorder differ quantitatively rather than qualitatively; this would mean that different amounts of the same genetically transmitted factor would produce different mood disorders (Gershon and others, 1982). Exactly how the tendency toward mood disorder is inherited is not clear. In bipolar disorders, as in unipolar disorders, women are more frequently affected than men. In addition, the risk for the daughter of a bipolar mother is greater than that for a son (LaRoche and others, 1985). This may mean that, at least for some bipolar disorders, heredity is sex-linked, that is, carried by the X chromosome (Winokur and others, 1972). (Sons receive a Y chromosome from their father and daughters an X chromosome. Members of both sexes receive an X chromosome from their mother. This means that women have a greater chance of inheriting a bipolar X chromosome because they can receive it from either parent.)

## ■ SUICIDE AND PARASUICIDE

Depressed people often have low self-esteem and feel that the future holds no more promise than the past. Such hopelessness is a good predictor of eventual suicide (Beck and others, 1985). The depressed person may not stop at self-condemnation but instead may move from thought to action. Sometimes depressed people threaten to commit suicide. Such threats should always be taken seriously because even though a particular person may not act on such a threat, the best predictor of a suicide attempt is a threat of suicide. Previous suicide attempts are also good predictors; few people kill themselves without some warning. However, sometimes the timing of the suicide makes it seem surprising. Many suicides occur when a depressed individual is beginning to recover or has been discharged from a hospital as improved. Ernest Hemingway, for example, shot and killed himself shortly after he had been released from a hospital after his depressed state had improved.

Suicide is a statistically rare event in the United States; only 13 out of every 100,000 deaths are due to suicide. Yet suicide now ranks ninth among the causes of death in the United States and is responsible for

20,000 to 35,000 deaths per year. Of the total number of people who are clinically depressed, 15 percent will ultimately kill themselves (Murphy, 1983). Another high-risk group consists of people who have a family history of suicide (Ray, 1983), and among college students it is the second most frequent cause of death. About 12 percent of all suicides are committed by people between the ages of 20 and 24.

Since 1949 people born in each successive five-year period have started with a higher chance of suicide than the preceding group, so it seems likely that the overall rate will continue to increase. For example, in 1950 men aged 20 to 24 had a rate of 8.6 suicides per 100,000; in 1955 the rate was 11.9. The increase has continued: in 1975 men aged 20 to 24 had a rate of 26.8 suicides per 100,000 (Murphy and Wetzel, 1980). There is also a sex difference in suicide rates. Twice as many men as women actually kill themselves, although twice as many women as men attempt suicide. Although very few children commit suicide, suicide threats and attempts are common reasons for therapeutic referrals of children.

Suicide and **parasuicide** (suicide attempts that do not end in death) seem to be fundamentally different. People who kill themselves successfully seem to have planned the event carefully. They arrange not to be interrupted and use effective means. Suicide attempters, on the other hand, may act impulsively, make sure they will be rescued, and use a method that is slow to take effect or completely ineffective. The main purpose of parasuicides seems to be to manipulate others. As noted in Chapter 9, individuals who are classified as borderline personalities often use this technique. It is important to remember, however, that a sizable number of people who commit or attempt suicide are not diagnosed as depressed.

There are cultural differences in the way others respond to the act of suicide because different cultures interpret suicide differently. Most Western societies seek to prevent suicide and to interfere with its completion whenever possible. In some other cultures, by contrast, it is thought to be an honorable action, perhaps the only acceptable one for a disgraced person. In still other cultures, suicide is thought of as cowardly.

If the urge to commit suicide is an outgrowth of a profound psychological disturbance, most people would agree that every effort should be made to keep the individual alive so that the problem can be treated. Nevertheless, one may certainly wonder whether there are any circumstances under which no effort should be made to prevent an individual from taking his or her own life. What of the aged, the chronically infirm, and the incurably ill who want to terminate what they feel is a hopeless existence? Although the attention of clinical workers is directed primarily toward suicide as an outgrowth of personal problems and feelings of inadequacy and depression, we should bear in mind that there is a broader, more subjective context within which suicide can be considered.

Suicide is becoming more frequent among adolescents (see Figure 10–15). Most adolescents who attempt suicide are socially isolated (Rohn and others, 1977); this is particularly true of boys. Two-thirds of the girls who commit suicide have one remaining relationship, usually a steady boyfriend. In addition, most adolescent suicides have parents who are divorced or separated, and a large number have parents who are alcoholics. Twenty-five percent are not living at home at the time of their suicide attempt.

The case of Beverly provides an example. Beverly had dropped out of school on the East Coast and traveled to Seattle, as far away from home as she could get. She got a job in a cafeteria and stayed in her apartment the rest of the time. Beverly decided to kill herself on St. Patrick's Day. She considered various methods carefully. She had read about a window washer who fell to his death a short time before. Since she had neither a gun nor drugs at her disposal, she decided to jump from her eighth-floor apartment window. She survived the

fall and later told about some of the feelings that had prompted her to attempt suicide.

> *I hated myself. I felt stupid. I didn't like the way I looked. I wanted to be prettier, to be taller, to have a nicer nose and thicker hair. I stayed in my apartment most of the time . . . I was convinced that I didn't have anything to offer anybody else. I'd only end up getting hurt and rejected . . . I spent a lot of time thinking about what I wanted to do with myself. I saw my choices as going back to high school at night while working, going back to my family, or committing suicide. I thought all the choices were bad, but I thought suicide was the best.* (Seattle Times, June 22, 1978, p. A15)

Most adolescents who commit suicide have exceptionally poor school records. One in five have failed at least one grade, and one-third are dropouts or chronic truants. Another third have engaged in problem behaviors in school. However, not all adolescent suicides fit this description. A profile of adolescents who had attempted suicide found one group to be above average in intelligence, perfectionistic, and self-critical, as well as quiet and "difficult to know." These adolescents shared at least one characteristic with those with poorer

**FIGURE 10–15**
The rates of suicide and suicide attempts among children and adolescents have increased greatly, but suicide can sometimes be prevented by skilled intervention. This 13-year-old, who climbed onto a bridge support and threatened suicide, was calmed by a fire department chaplain who promised help with his problems. (AP/Wide World Photos)

academic records: both groups were socially isolated. This second type of suicide is illustrated by a news story that appeared the same week as the story about Beverly. A pre-med student with straight A's shot and killed his 10-year-old brother and then himself when his medical school application was rejected. He left a note saying that he wanted to save his brother from having to live through the many miserable years ahead of him. The two boys were reported to have had a close and warm relationship.

Many suicides can be prevented if friends and relatives recognize the danger signs. Some of these signs are listed in Table 10–7. Research aimed at developing objective ways to predict suicide indicates that the following variables are useful: a clinician's judgment that the individual is potentially suicidal, precipitating life stress, absence of emotional expressiveness, extreme preoccupation, and socially inappropriate behavior. A quickly administered test for suicide potential would be most useful for both clinical work and research because it could provide not only a way of assessing the danger of suicide but also a quantitative score that would simplify communication about a person's suicidal potential. One such test is the Scale for Suicide Ideation, developed by Aaron Beck and his coworkers

(Beck and others, 1979). It is designed so that an interviewer can assess the extent to which an individual is preoccupied with suicide. Items from the scale are shown in Table 10–8.

## Suicide and the Media

The possibility of suicide is a thought that enters the minds of many people, not just those who are diagnosed as depressed. In a survey of more than 700 people, almost 10 percent reported having had suicidal feelings during the previous year. Specifically, 3.5 percent felt that life was not worthwhile, 2.8 percent wished to be dead, 2 percent had thought of or seriously considered suicide, and 0.6 percent had made an actual suicide attempt (Paykel and others, 1974).

Concern about the possibility of suicide for oneself or a loved one can be seen in an incident that occurred in Seattle. After a 27-year-old woman threw herself from the Space Needle, about 100 anxious people called city authorities. This was not unusual.

*"They always call by the dozens when there has been a sensational suicide. They have someone close whom they feel is that desperate. And they want to know if it's their loved one,"* say local authorities who deal with suicide regularly.

*"What it does is elicit panic, and instead of listening to the full description, bingo, they get right on the phone,"* said Don Marvin, an investigator in the King County Medical Examiner's Office.

*Many of the callers had a relative or friend who had been missing for some time. Or they knew someone who was*

---

☐ **TABLE 10–7**
**Warning Signs of Teenage Suicide**

*Verbal comments*  Statements such as "I wish I'd never been born," and "You'll be sorry when I'm gone," should be taken just as seriously as the direct threat, "I'm going to kill myself."

*Behavior changes*  These cover a wide range and include giving away treasured possessions, taking life threatening risks, and having frequent accidents. Other signs may be complaints of intense loneliness or boredom, a marked increase in agitation or irritability, or getting into trouble with school or the police. There may also be the more customary signs of depression: changes in appetite and sleep habits, suddenly dropping grades, complaints of inability to concentrate, and withdrawal from friends and from favorite activities.

*Situational factors*  Inability to communicate with parents, recent problems at school, end of a love relationship, recent involvement with drugs or alcohol all increase the situational risk.

*What to do*  Parents and friends should take action by asking questions such as "Are you very unhappy?" "Do you have a plan about taking your life?" "Do you think you really don't want to live anymore?" Asking direct questions about suicide doesn't put ideas into someone's head. Instead it may be a lifesaving measure if the answers are taken seriously. Both parents and friends often don't believe that such statements might be carried out or they may be too frightened to take action. Although friends are sometimes sworn to secrecy about suicidal thoughts, they should contact a parent or responsible adult immediately if they suspect thoughts of suicide and professional help should be obtained at once. If the suicidal threat seems immediate, the nearest suicide prevention center (usually listed under "suicide" or "crisis" in the phone book) should be contacted.

---

☐ **TABLE 10–8**
**Items from the Scale for Suicide Ideation**

1. Desire to make active suicide attempt
   0 None
   1 Weak
   2 Moderate to strong
2. Passive suicidal desire
   0 Would take precautions to save life
   1 Would leave life/death to chance
   2 Would avoid steps necessary to save or maintain life
3. Deterrents to active attempt (e.g., family, religion, irreversibility)
   0 Would not attempt because of a deterrent
   1 Some concern about deterrents
   2 Minimal or no concern about deterrents
4. Method: Specificity/planning of contemplated attempt
   0 Not considered
   1 Considered, but details not worked out
   2 Details worked out/well formulated

*Source:* Beck and others, 1979, p. 346.

severely depressed. Some were social workers with troubled or missing clients. And all were shaken by some part of the woman's description, especially her red hair, Marvin said.

"In a word, they were very anxious, especially if they had someone missing for some period of time," he said.

Calls also increased at Crisis Line, a local agency that provides telephone counseling and referrals to troubled residents. But these calls were from those who are considering suicide themselves, said Bill Hershey, the agency's director.

"Any kind of death like this that occurs, makes people think about dying themselves," said Hershey. "Some people who have been ambivalent about themselves call and want to talk things over."

Hershey said there were 10 to 15 callers who discussed suicide in the hours following the Space Needle suicide. (Seattle Times, July 7, 1978, p. E9)

## Causes of Suicide

Ideas about the causes of suicide are divided into two main groups: those that see society as a reason and those that focus on the individual. In a few cases a society literally demands that a person commit suicide. In Japan, for instance, hara-kiri, a ritual suicide, was traditionally an honorable death that atoned for a se-

(a)

**FIGURE 10-16**
Concern over the increasing number of adolescent suicides has led some school districts to hold special programs to inform students and their parents about suicide prevention techniques. Photo (a) shows a human-relations specialist in a White Plains, New York, high school talking with students about suicide. Inset (b) shows one of the illustrative slides he used. Here an actor takes the part of a despondent teenager. (Joyce Dopkeen/NYT Pictures)

(b)

rious personal failure. Sociologists also point out that most suicidal people are socially isolated and have few ties with the community. They lack the social supports that make life bearable and worthwhile. The case of Beverly is an example. And as the death of the pre-med student illustrates, a shocking loss of social standing—an abrupt change in the relationship between the individual and society—may also precipitate suicide.

Psychological theories, on the other hand, tend to stress the role of the individual in the decision to commit suicide. The psychodynamic perspective is the source of most of the prominent psychological theories in the clinical literature on suicide. Psychodynamic theories describe suicide as an extreme case of a person's turning hostile or aggressive impulses toward him- or herself. However, this theory is not supported by research findings, which indicate that hostile motives are infrequent in suicide (Linehan, 1981).

Learning theory emphasizes the importance of suicidal behavior in a person's repertory. Past suicidal behavior and suicide threats, and suicidal behavior on the part of significant people in an individual's environment, all make suicide more likely. Certain reinforcing ideas may also be present—such as revenge, reunion with a deceased partner, or simply peace (Diekstra, 1973).

Cognitive theorists suggest that suicide is an example of problem-solving behavior. A series of negative events beyond the person's control is likely to have occurred during the year before someone makes a suicide attempt. It is likely that several events will have occurred close together just before the suicide or parasuicide. **Exit events,** or events in which a strong source of social support is removed, seem most likely to precede a suicide attempt. Such an event might be a death, a divorce, or a breakup with a partner (Slater and Depue, 1981). According to this view, suicide may result from a person's cognitive assessment of the situation as hopeless and of death as a way of getting rid of problems (Kovacs and others, 1975).

Parasuicides are often quite rigid in their approach to situations (Shneidman, 1980). This rigidity may include narrow perceptions of situations and of behavioral options. For such people, the world appears to be divided into only two parts—good and bad. This recalls the depressed thinking described by cognitive theorists like Beck (1976).

Research suggests that the factors associated with suicide and parasuicide are complex and that an approach that looks at the interaction between the individual and the situation, as well as various mediating factors such as the availability or quality of social support, is a useful way to study these behaviors. An interactionist approach draws upon all the major perspectives but leaves the researcher with a complex set of factors to consider.

When a member of a group has committed suicide, group discussion and intervention can sometimes be helpful. For instance, several suicides by high school students prompted a series of school meetings for parents and students (see Figure 10–16). Both the signs of potential suicide and various ways of dealing with them were discussed. The program was also designed to help students realize that thoughts about self-destruction occur to most people at one time or another and that there are sources of help for people who have such thoughts. Perhaps one of the best ways to prevent suicide is to demonstrate to the person that someone really cares what happens to him or her.

## ■ STUDY OUTLINE

### DEFINING MOOD DISORDERS

The category of **Mood** or **Affective Disorders** includes **depression,** which is characterized by a feeling of sadness and a decrease in activity, and **mania,** a speeded-up state that is often characterized by excitement or exuberance. A depression that occurs as a result of an identifiable event is classified as an **Adjustment Disorder with Depressed Mood.** A severe depression is called a **major depressive disorder;** less severe depressions are referred to as **dysthmic disorders.** A mood disorder in which only depression occurs is **unipolar,** whereas one that includes both manic and depressive episodes is **bipolar.**

### DEPRESSION

Depressed feelings are quite common and are often referred to as "the blues." Clinical depression is much less common and is a more serious problem. It occurs more frequently in women than in men and is found in societies throughout the world. Two characteristic features of depression are a dysphoric mood (sad, hopeless, irritable, or worried) and loss of interest in one's usual activities and pastimes.

### THEORIES OF DEPRESSION

1. Biological theories assume that the cause of depression lies either in the genes or in some physiological malfunction that may or may not have an inherited base. Although genetic factors seem important in many cases of depression, the exact mechanism by which depression is inherited is not clear.

2. Depression is probably a result of a lack of chemical neurotransmitters at certain sites in the brain. According to the **monoamine hypothesis,** lack of nor-

adrenaline or seratonin is a causal factor in depression. The receptors may be extremely sensitive, causing the body to produce low levels of monoamines, or depression may be due to a failure in the regulation of the neurotransmitter system.

3. Depression may be related to abnormalities in the regular rhythms of certain biological functions, such as body temperature and sleep activity. Some depressed individuals have a shortened period between falling asleep and the beginning of REM sleep (the period of peak brain activity during sleep).

4. The main drug groups that are used to treat depression are the tricyclics and the MAO inhibitors; both increase the amount of norepinephrine in the neurotransmitter system. Bipolar disorders are often treated with lithium. If drugs are not effective or if it would be dangerous to wait for their effects to become evident, **electro-convulsive therapy** (ECT) may be used. ECT is very effective in treating severe depression, but because of possible hazards, it should be used only after other treatments have been tried.

5. Psychodynamic theories of depression emphasize unconscious feelings and reactions to new situations based on what has happened earlier in life. For example, depression in adults may be related to parental loss or separation in childhood.

6. Learning theorists assume that depression and lack of reinforcement are related. According to this perspective, a major cause of the low rate of positive reinforcement of depressed individuals is an actual deficiency in social skills. Once people are depressed, their behavior makes them less likable, and this creates a vicious cycle.

7. Treatment based on behavioral theories begins with an assessment of the specific interactions and events that are related to the depression. The client may be asked to list pleasant and unpleasant events and to rate his or her mood each day. In addition, a treatment plan is prepared that includes training in skills such as parenting, time management, and relaxation.

8. Cognitive theories of depression are based on the idea that the same experience may affect two people very differently because of the different cognitions they have about the event. According to Aaron Beck, depression can best be described as a **cognitive triad** of negative thoughts about oneself, the situation, and the future. Cognitive therapy includes questioning designed to make the depressed person aware of the unrealistic nature of his or her thoughts.

9. People who are depressed seem to feel helpless to control their environment. They may learn to be helpless as a result of situations they have encountered in the past. This concept is termed **learned helplessness.** A depressed person can feel varying degrees of helplessness depending on whether he or she views a situation as **external** or **internal, global** or **specific,** or **stable** (chronic) or **unstable** (acute).

10. The information-processing view of depression attempts to combine social-learning and cognitive approaches to depression. It is based on the idea that memories are represented by descriptive statements connected by associated linkages. In addition, memories are connected to emotion nodes. This means that certain memories may touch off a chain of thoughts all of which have the same negative emotional context.

11. Existentialist theorists focus on loss of self-esteem as a cause of depression. Humanistic theorists emphasize the difference between a person's ideal self and his or her perception of the actual state of things.

## THE BIPOLAR DISORDERS

1. **Bipolar** or manic-depressive **disorders** are characterized by phases of both depression and mania. **Mania** includes mood states ranging from normal joy and happiness to extreme and hostile overactivity. Manic episodes occur far less frequently than depressions.

2. Lithium has been shown to be effective in treating bipolar disorders. However, many patients discontinue the drug against medical advice.

3. There seems to be a strong hereditary factor in bipolar as well as unipolar disorders, but it is not clear whether bipolar and unipolar disorders are genetically related.

## SUICIDE AND PARASUICIDE

1. The hopelessness that is characteristic of depression sometimes leads to suicide. Among the predictors of suicide are suicide threats and previous suicide attempts.

2. Suicide and **parasuicide** (suicide attempts that do not end in death) seem to be fundamentally different. People who kill themselves successfully arrange not to be interrupted and use effective means. Suicide attempters may act impulsively, make sure they will be rescued, and use a method that is slow to take effect or completely ineffective.

3. Suicide is becoming more frequent among adolescents. Most adolescents who attempt suicide are socially isolated; this is particularly true of boys. They generally have poor school records.

4. Many suicides can be prevented if friends and relatives recognize the danger signs. Among those signs are a clinician's judgment that the individual is poten-

tially suicidal, precipitating life stress, absence of emotional expressiveness, extreme preoccupation, and socially inappropriate behavior.

5. Ideas about the causes of suicide are divided into two main groups: those that see society as a reason and those that focus on the individual. The former emphasize the fact that most suicidal people lack the social supports that make life bearable and worthwhile, while the latter stress the role of the individual in the decision to commit suicide. People who commit suicide may turn hostile or aggressive impulses against themselves, or may have had experiences that reinforce the idea of suicide, or may be using suicide as a means of solving a problem.

# 11

# SCHIZOPHRENIC DISORDERS

*"All of a sudden things weren't going so well. I began to lose control of my life and, most of all, myself. I couldn't concentrate on my school work, I couldn't sleep, and when I did sleep, I had dreams about dying. I was afraid to go to class, imagined that people were talking about me, and on top of that I heard voices. I called my mother in Pittsburgh and asked for advice. She told me to move off campus into an apartment with my sister.*

*After I moved in with my sister, things got worse. I was afraid to go outside and when I looked out of the window, it seemed that everyone outside was yelling "Kill her, kill her." My sister forced me to go to school. I would go out of the house until I knew she had gone to work; then I would return home. Things continued to get worse. I imagined that I had a foul body odor and I sometimes took up to six showers a day . . . Things worsened—I couldn't remember a thing. I had a notebook full of reminders telling me what to do on that particular day. I couldn't remember my school work, and I would study from 6 P.M. until 4 A.M., but never had the courage to go to class on the following day. I tried to tell my sister about it, but she didn't understand. She suggested that I see a psychiatrist, but I was afraid to go out of the house to see him.*

*One day I decided that I couldn't take the trauma anymore so I took an overdose of 35 Darvon pills. At the same moment, a voice inside me said, 'What did you do that for? Now you won't go to heaven.' At that instant I realized that I really didn't want to die, I wanted to live, and I was afraid. So I got on the phone and called the psychiatrist whom my sister had recommended."*

*When she got to the emergency room, this student, J., refused to see a psychiatrist or admit herself to the hospital because "I thought psychiatrists were only for crazy people and I definitely didn't think I was crazy yet." When her mother arrived, J. was admitted to the hospital. After more than a year on medication, first in the hospital and then out, J. decided she was well and stopped both medication and therapy. She got a job but quickly lost it. "My friends and family said I was behaving strangely, but I took no notice. I went out dancing practically every night to make up for the time lost while being afraid . . . "*

*In the fall she went back to school in Atlanta to finish her senior year. Her parents wanted her to stay in Pittsburgh "in case anything else might occur." "I didn't listen, and somehow thought they were plotting against me." Then she was hospitalized again. "This time things were twice as bad as the first. I no longer heard voices, but the things I saw and dreamed about were far more traumatic. I recall at one point thinking I was Jesus Christ and that I was placed on this earth to bear everyone's sins."*

*After a month in the hospital J. returned home and received both antipsychotic drugs and psychotherapy as an outpatient. Two years later, still on medication, she was back in college, president of her sorority, "more confident and happy than I have ever been in my life."* (adapted from O'Neal, 1984, pp. 109–110).

This young woman seems to have made a good recovery from several schizophrenic episodes. Before they began, she had been functioning at a high level. She was a good student, an officer in her sorority chapter, and president of a campus club, and she had a part-time job and a satisfying relationship with her boyfriend. As we will see later in the chapter, the best predictor of improvement from a schizophrenic disorder is the person's level of adjustment before the symptoms appeared.

Not all people who develop schizophrenia experience such a dramatic recovery, even when they continue to use antipsychotic drugs. The following passage, written by the mother of a schizophrenic son, describes a more common pattern.

*When Dan first began to suffer from schizophrenia, our family thought it was just a case of teenage blues. We sent him off to college. By the time he began attacking the refrigerator for reading his mind and threatening family members for using the word "right," we had learned to recognize the disease. We have six children. The two youngest at that time were six and ten years old. Three are older than Dan. It was a happy family, and I wish I could say it hasn't changed. Our family isn't destroyed, but it is badly damaged.*

*We did everything we could to be helpful to Dan. We signed him up for a specialist in New York, but after we had waited many weeks for the appointment to come due, Dan disappeared the day before we were to leave. We took him weekly to a psychiatrist, and then tried to see that he took his medicine. Whenever he was released from a hospital, we helped him find a job. We took him around until he found a suitable room in the area, and then once more helped him move his drafting table and other belongings to his new home.*

*He never took his medicine once he was away from us. Gradually he began working less and coming home more often for "visits." Each time he finally began breaking things, and we once more brought the drafting table, suitcases, and sometimes cockroaches back home. Eventually, he would be reaccepted by the hospital, and we sat with heavy hearts while heaving sighs of relief. . . . My husband, John, is now 71 and has had two heart attacks. I am 65, in excellent health except for regular unexplainable seizures . . . There has never been a time when we would be surprised to look out the window and see Dan coming up the driveway. This was true especially in the year we were testing adult homes, though we continued calling on Dan, taking him places, and inviting him home for visits. Here is an example of Dan's life during this period:*

*On August 6, 1981, we drove Dan to Richmond, stopping on the way to buy him a new pair of shoes. Ten days later, John suggested we visit Dan for the day—take him out for dinner and go to a museum. We called to find out Dan was in jail. He had eaten a restaurant meal he couldn't pay for and assaulted a policeman.*

*The manager of the adult home explained Dan's problem to the police, and they released him, but Dan was not happy to be back at the home. He thought the food was terrible. Dan is a proud man. He wanted to have only the best. He would do anything to eat in restaurants. He sold his new shoes, pawned his watch, ran up a bill in a friendly Vietnamese cafe, and found new places where he could order a meal only to discover later that he didn't have his billfold. He was constantly asking John to raise his allowance from $20 to $35 a week. Whenever we went to visit him, he would spoil our time together by badgering his father.*

*Within the next few days, Dan was getting more and more upset over people "messing with his mind." He finally threatened to kill his younger brother, who moved out to live temporarily with a friend.*

*It wasn't long before Dan was back in the hospital. Though the doctor said there was nothing wrong with him, his lawyer had talked him into volunteering.*

*While Dan was in the hospital, we once more investigated adult homes, hoping to find one which would please him. By the time he was to be dismissed, we hadn't found anything suitable, and in the end, we presented him with a plan for living at home. He was now 34 years old, and his younger brother, Fred, was away at college, so it would be just the three of us. Here was our proposition:*

> *We welcome you to live at home with us if you take your medicine regularly, eat at meal time, and smoke only in a restricted area. We will give you $30 a week for your expenses, and you will have occasional use of the car after you get your driver's license.*

*For over a year now, he has been going to the clinic to get his shots. He knows a good thing when he sees it. That $30 never makes it to the end of the week, but if he talks hard enough, he can always get a couple more dollars out of his Dad, who would rather toss him the bills than risk building up his blood pressure.* (adapted from Piercey, 1985, pp. 155–157)

**Schizophrenic disorders** are a prominent part of the category of mental disorders known as **psychoses.**

A psychosis is a disorder that involves alterations of perception, thought, or consciousness. Someone who is psychotic makes incorrect inferences about reality based on these alterations, and believes that the inferences are real and actual. When the person can understand that the inferences are not real but are the products of fantasy or misperception, the psychosis is no longer present.

Many of the psychoses produce the kinds of behaviors that were formerly called "madness," "lunacy," or "insanity." Specific causal factors have been found for some disorders with these symptoms. Some of those factors are temporary, such as the effects of some drugs (e.g., amphetamines), reduced availability of oxygen to the brain during high fevers, or extreme vitamin deficiencies. Others are permanent results of infections such as general paresis. But there are several disorders that produce psychoses for which a specific cause has not been found. In addition to schizophrenic disorders, these include some manias, certain severe depressions, paranoid states, and brief psychotic reactions. Despite their similarities, there are many differences in behavior that help identify the various psychoses (see Table 11–1).

Of all the psychoses, the schizophrenias have the most severe impact on people's lives and on the health care system. About 1 percent of the population will be diagnosed as having a schizophrenic illness at some time. Schizophrenia tends to occur early in life, from the late teens to the early thirties, and also is likely to be chronic or persisting. Hence, the total costs of this disorder are high. The economic cost in the United States has been estimated to be $10–$20 billion a year in medical costs and loss of income (Cancro, 1985). A New Zealand study illustrated the high per-person costs of schizophrenia (Hall and others, 1985). Although twelve times as many people had heart attacks as became schizophrenic, the total cost of care for heart attack patients was only one-sixth as high as the cost of care for those with schizophrenic disorders. The chief reason for this was that those who had heart attacks tended to be older and were less likely to be chronically ill afterward.

As an example of the high costs of treating schizophrenia, consider one recent case, that of a 32-year-old American woman who became ill when she was 14. In 18 years the direct costs for her care in inpatient settings or in community outpatient settings totaled more than $636,000 in 1983 dollars (Moran and others, 1984). This figure does not include costs for outpatient therapy, health care, emergency room care, and social services, or the costs to her parents, who supported her financially when she was not in a hospital or halfway house.

At any one time, for every 1,000 adults in the pop-

Differences Among the Acute Psychoses

| Type | Behavioral Characteristics |
|------|----------------------------|
| Schizophrenia | Loose associations<br>Flat affect<br>Bizarre delusions<br>Alert, not dazed or confused<br>Aware of time and place |
| Mania | Hyperactivity<br>Pressured speech<br>Elevated or irritable mood<br>Usually aware of time<br>and place |
| Organic brain syndrome | Loss of intellectual abilities<br>Poor memory<br>Impaired orientation<br>Possible hallucinations<br>or delusions |
| Brief reactive psychosis (response to particular conditions or physiological states) | Sudden onset<br>Dramatic array of hallucinations and delusions<br>Visual hallucinations more common than auditory hallucinations<br>Mood tends to be expansive and effervescent<br>Symptoms decline or disappear in a day or two |
| Psychotic depression | Somatic delusions (e.g., spine being eaten by worms)<br>Hallucinations with negative, critical tone<br>Delusions of guilt and self-reproach<br>Paranoid thinking<br>Biological signs—sleep disturbance, change in appetite, altered sex drive |

ulation, excluding those in psychiatric hospitals, there are approximately 4.6 who have an active schizophrenic disorder and 1.8 whose schizophrenic disorder is in remission. About half of the entire group are not receiving any treatment, although most of them are in need of mental health care (Von Korff and others, 1985). In addition to the cost in money, the social and psychological costs of the schizophrenic disorders are tremendous.

# ■ CHARACTERISTICS OF SCHIZOPHRENIC DISORDERS

The symptoms of schizophrenic disorders include disturbances of attention; problems of perception, including hallucinations and delusions; difficulty expressing thoughts coherently so that others can understand them; inappropriate or flat emotional responses; and

unusual motor behavior. Before and after the overtly psychotic episode, lack of initiative and marked impairment of work at job or school are likely.

## Diagnostic Criteria

To be diagnosed as having a schizophrenic disorder, a person must show deterioration from his or her previous level of functioning in work, social relations, or self-care. Such a person is likely to be characterized by family and friends as "not the same" as before. Continuous signs of illness must be present for at least six months before the diagnosis can be made, and psychotic behavior must be present at some point in the illness. The diagnosic criteria listed in DSM-III-R are shown in Table 11–2.

## Problems of Attention

A review of over 50 autobiographical books and articles by people who had been diagnosed as schizophrenic showed that difficulty in focusing attention and lack of concentration were mentioned more often than any other problem of cognition (Freedman, 1974). For example:

> "At first it was as if parts of my brain 'awoke' which had been dormant, and I became interested in a wide assortment of people, events, places, and ideas which normally would make no impression on me . . . Every face in the windows of a passing streetcar would be engraved in my mind . . . What had happened to me . . . was a breakdown in the filter, and a hodge-podge of unrelated stimuli were distracting me from things which should have had my undivided attention . . . My brain . . . had become sore with a real physical soreness, as if it had been rubbed with sandpaper until it was raw . . . I had very little ability to sort the relevant from the irrelevant . . . the filter had broken down." (MacDonald, 1960, pp. 218–219).

> "Nothing settles in my mind—not even for a second . . . My mind goes away—too many things come into my head at once and I lose control . . . I'm falling apart into bits. My mind is not right if I walk and speak. It's better to stay still and not say a word." (Chapman, 1966, p. 232).

Some people make desperate attempts to control their thinking as they become aware of the onset of psychosis. They often concoct elaborate schemes for character or body building. One 19-year-old made up the following schedule for himself in an attempt to control his anxiety.

□ **TABLE 11–2**
**The DSM-III-R Criteria for Schizophrenia**

A. Active phase: At least one of these categories of behavior must occur for at least two weeks:
  1. At least two of the following:
    a. Delusions
    b. Hallucinations lasting more than a brief time that may occur through the day for several days or several times a week for several weeks
    c. Incoherent thinking or a marked loosening of associations
    d. Catatonic behavior (a disturbance in motor behavior in which the person may "freeze" into an apparently uncomfortable pose or become extremely overactive)
    e. Lack of changes in affect or grossly inappropriate affect
  2. Bizarre delusions such as thought broadcasting or mind control
  3. Prominent auditory hallucinations, such as hearing a voice that keeps up a running commentary on one's behavior, or hearing two or more voices talking to each other

B. Level of functioning in work, social relations, and self-care is clearly below the highest level achieved in the past. If the individual is a child, the level of social functioning does not meet that expected for his or her age group.

C. If severe depression or manic behavior is present, it occurred relatively briefly.

D. There must be continuous signs of illness for six months, including at least two weeks of psychotic symptoms. This period may include phases both before and after the psychotic period and in each case must include at least two of the following behaviors:
  1. Marked social isolation or withdrawal
  2. Marked impairment in functioning at work or in school
  3. Markedly peculiar behavior, for example, collecting garbage or talking to oneself in public
  4. Impaired personal hygiene and grooming
  5. Blunted, flat, or inappropriate emotional expression
  6. Digressive, vague, overelaborate, or circumstantial speech, or poverty of speech or speech content
  7. Odd or bizarre ideation or magical thinking, for example, being able to see the future, having a sixth sense, believing that "others can feel my feelings"
  8. Unusual perceptual experiences, for example, sensing the presence of a force or person not actually present
  9. Apathy or lack of initiative

E. Not due to any organic mental disorder

F. If there is a history of autistic disorder (a developmental disorder discussed in Chapter 16), prominent delusions or hallucinations must also be present before a schizophrenic disorder can be diagnosed. (adapted from DSM-III-R, 1985, pp. E: 1–2)

| TIME | ACTIVITY |
|---|---|
| 7:00–8:00 | Cold bath, toiletries, bed, dress |
| 8:00–8:15 | Encyclopedia (memorize three facts) |
| 8:15–8:30 | Handwriting |
| 8:30–8:45 | Brisk walk |
| 8:45–9:00 | Breakfast (one apple, one dish of bran, two glasses of milk, two glasses of water) |
| 9:00–10:00 | Hearing, sight, and scent |
| 10:00–11:00 | European, financial, and sport news |
| 11:00–12:00 | Wax floors and clean door knobs |
| 12:00–1:00 | Cold bath and exercises |
| 1:00–1:30 | Geometry |
| 1:30–1:45 | Vegetable lunch (very light) |
| 1:45–2:45 | Music |
| 2:45–3:45 | Walk as far as Atwater and then back to library |
| 3:45–4:45 | Study at library |
| 5:00–6:00 | Accounting |
| 6:00–6:20 | Cold bath |
| 6:20–6:35 | Vegetable supper |
| 6:35–8:05 | Accounting |
| 8:05–9:00 | Hearing, sight and scent |
| 9:00–9:30 | "Strength and Health Magazine" |
| 9:30–10:00 | Wardrobe |
| 10:00–10:20 | Cold bath |
| 10:20–10:40 | Study vocabulary (12 words) |
| 10:40–11:00 | Undress and toiletries |
| 11:00–11:15 | Breathing exercise |
| 11:15–11:30 | Note improvement in mental fortitude in diary |

(Lehman and Cancro, 1985, p. 684)

## Problems of Perception— Delusions and Hallucinations

It is clear that people who are labeled as schizophrenic do not perceive situations in the same way that most other people do. What is not clear is whether they focus on too many factors in a situation and become confused by too much information, or whether they notice only certain details and thus become incapable of accurately assessing what is happening.

*I went to the teacher and said to her, "I am afraid...." She smiled gently at me. But her smile, instead of reassuring me, only increased the anxiety and confusion, for I saw her teeth, white and even in the gleam of the light. Remaining all the while like themselves, soon they monopolized my entire vision as if the whole room were nothing but teeth under a remorseless light. Ghastly fear gripped me.* (U.S. Dept. of Health and Human Services, 1981, p. 2)

Many schizophrenic individuals become so preoccupied with internal events that they no longer distinguish between objective reality and fantasy images. These people may experience two characteristic signs of schizophrenia: delusions and hallucinations. A **delusion** is essentially a faulty interpretation of reality that cannot be shaken despite clear evidence to the contrary. The delusions that occur in different disorders tend to have different content (see Table 11–3). Delusions of being controlled by others, delusions of being persecuted and continuing delusions that are not reflected in the person's mood, combined with auditory hallucinations in which voices are heard but are all likely to occur together and can be used as a way to

**□ TABLE 11-3**

Differences in the Content of Delusions in Various Severe Disorders

| Disorder | Delusion |
| --- | --- |
| Paranoid disorder | Delusions of jealousy and persecution |
| Schizophrenia | Delusions of being controlled; bizarre delusions; sometimes delusions of persecution |
| Mania | Grandiose delusions |
| Depression | Delusions of guilt; somatic delusions |
| Organic brain syndrome | Delusions secondary to perceptual disturbances |

*Source:* Walker and Brodie, 1985, p. 753.

distinguish individuals with schizophrenic disorders from others (Cloninger and others, 1985). The artist who painted the picture in Figure 11-1 expressed some of his delusional thinking. One author described a variety of delusions that she had experienced while psychotic. Some delusions were somatic—for example, she believed that she was able to stop her heart on command. Others were grandiose. She believed that people were worshipping her as the Madonna and that her child (not yet born) would be the savior of the world (Thelmar, 1932). In the case at the beginning of the chapter, the patient described her belief that she was Jesus Christ.

Delusions can result in violent behavior that harms others. For instance, a mother severed a hand from each of her two daughters with a butcher knife and then chopped off her own hand. She then ran to neigh-

**FIGURE 11-1**

The artist who created this picture was, at the time, a hospitalized psychiatric patient who was troubled by a variety of tormenting thoughts. Here he represents his negative view of life and some of the topics that were special areas of conflict for him. Talented as an artist, he made painting his vocation after his recovery. (UPI/Bettmann Newsphotos)

bors and told them that she was John the Baptist and was going to be beheaded (*Seattle Times*, April 1, 1979, p. A13). At other times the behavior, although it is based on delusional thinking, is highly organized and requires immense concentration. For example, for eight hours a 22-year-old male student performed surgery deep in his abdomen, in his college dormitory room and carried out the operation with a precision that astonished surgeons (Kalin, 1979). He had spent months preparing for the surgery, which, he said, was intended to "denervate his adrenal glands." He had read surgical texts and acquired instruments. Before the operation he sterilized his dormitory room, anesthetized himself with barbiturates, donned a sterile mask and gloves, and draped his body in sheets.

> *Lying supine and looking into strategically placed mirrors to obtain an optimum view, he began by cleansing his abdomen with alcohol. The incision was made with a scalpel, exposure obtained by retractors, and the dissection carried out with surgical instruments . . .*
>
> *After eight hours he had had a minimal blood loss but was unable to obtain adequate exposure to enter the retroperitoneal space because of the unexpected pain in retracting his liver. Exhausted, he bandaged his wound, cleaned up his room, and called the police for transport to the hospital because of a "rupture."* (Kalin, 1979, p. 2188)

**Hallucinations** are projections of internal impulses and experiences onto perceptual images in the external world. Although they may occur in other disorders—for example, during the delirium associated with a high fever or as a result of the effects of drugs or other chemicals on the nervous system—only in schizophrenia do hallucinations occur when the person is in a clear, conscious state. Hallucinations can be associated with any of the senses. In the case at the beginning of the chapter, J. had the hallucination of hearing voices threatening to kill her. This kind of auditory hallucination is the most common type found in schizophrenia. Many schizophrenics report voices either issuing orders or accusing them of terrible crimes or actions (see Figure 11–2). Hallucinations associated with smell, while less common, are also typical. The individual may believe that foul odors are coming from his or her body as a sign of decay and death or of some sexual change.

Sometimes hallucinations are visual (see Figure 11–3). One account includes the following descriptions.

> *I saw people whom I had entombed in milk bottles, putrefying, and I was consuming their rotting cadavers. Or I was drawing the head of a cat which meanwhile gnawed at my vitals. It was ghastly, intolerable.* (Sechehaye, 1951, pp. 34, 37)

**FIGURE 11–2**
Some hallucinations are extremely unpleasant. This person hears voices accusing her of horrible crimes that she has not committed. (Irene Springer)

Not all hallucinations are accusatory or unpleasant. Sometimes voices provide comfort and companionship. In a description of his psychotic period, one young adult described both pleasant and unpleasant voices.

> *The Voices. Testing one, two, testing one. Checking out the circuits: "What hath God wrought. Yip di mina di zonda za da boom di yaidi yoohoo."*
>
> *By this time the voices had gotten very clear.*
>
> *At first I'd had to strain to hear or understand them. They were soft and working with some pretty tricky codes. Snap-crackle-pops, the sound of the wind with blinking lights and horns for punctuation. I broke the code and somehow was able to internalize it to the point where it was just like hearing voices. In the beginning it seemed mostly nonsense, but as things went along they made more and more sense. Once you hear the voices, you realize they've always been there. It's just a matter of being tuned to them.*
>
> *The voices weren't much fun in the beginning. Part of it was simply my being uncomfortable about hearing voices*

**FIGURE 11-3**
This crayon drawing expresses the artist's perception of his mental illness. Unless he keeps busy, he has visual hallucinations of animals which frighten him greatly. (Schizophrenic Bulletin)

*no matter what they had to say, but the early voices were mostly bearers of bad news. Besides, they didn't seem to like me much and there was no way I could talk back to them. Those were very one-sided conversations.*

*But later the voices could be very pleasant. They'd often be the voices of someone I loved, and even if they weren't I could talk too, asking questions about this or that and getting reasonable answers. There were very important messages that had to get through somehow. More orthodox channels like phone and mail had broken down.* (Vonnegut, 1975, pp. 136–137)

Sometimes schizophrenics find these hallucinations so comfortable that they are unwilling to give them up. They serve as protection from the discomforts of reality.

## Thought Patterns and Speech

The word *autistic* has been used to describe schizophrenic thought patterns. Derived from the Greek word *autos*, meaning self, **autistic thinking** is defined as thinking that is so self-centered that it is fully intelligible only to the person who is doing the thinking. Researchers have found that schizophrenic individuals ask inappropriate questions and get inappropriate answers (Rutter, 1985). What seems to be missing is the predictability and the repetitions of meaning that are present in normal speech. This may be the reason that interviewers who talk to someone with a schizophrenic disorder may come away confused about the meaning of what was said.

It is important to remember that not all schizo-phrenics display peculiar speech. The majority of people with schizophrenic disorders speak coherently most of the time, and peculiar speech is found in other patients about as frequently as it is in schizophrenics (Andreason and Grove, 1979). To appreciate this point, rate the following examples on a five-point scale from 1, schizophrenic, to 5, normal.

a. *Then, I always liked geography. My last teacher in the subject was Professor August A. He was a man with black eyes. I also like black eyes. There are also blue and gray eyes and other sorts, too. I have heard it said that snakes have green eyes. All people have eyes. There are some, too, who are blind. These blind people are led by a boy. It must be terrible not to be able to see. There are people who can't see, and in addition, can't hear. I know some who hear too much. One can hear too much. There are many sick people in Burgholzli; they are called patients.* (Bleuler, 1950, p. 17)

b. *Everybody needs sex . . . I haven't had sex for five years. The clock is in this room because they want patients to learn how to tell time. I know Mary Poppins, and she lives in Massachusetts. I didn't like the movie "Mary Poppins." They messed up the book, so they could try to win the Oscar. Movies come from real life. This morning, when I was at Hillside, I was making a movie. I was surrounded by movie stars. The x-ray technician was Peter Lawford. The security guard was Don Knotts . . . Is this room painted blue to get me upset? My grandmother died four weeks after my eighteenth birthday.* (Sheehan, 1981, p. 69)

c. *Yes, of course, the whole thing wasn't my idea. So, I suppose I'd be perfectly happy if he came back and decided to do it all on his own. If I could make two trips myself, I don't see why he can't. (Laffal, 1965, p. 309)*

d. *Well, I wonder if that part of it can't be—I wonder if that doesn't—let me put it frankly; I wonder if that doesn't have to be continued? Let me put it this way: let us suppose you get the million bucks, and you get the proper way to handle it. You could hold that side? (Gold, 1974, p.117)*

When these excerpts were informally rated by several psychologists, items (a) and (b) were usually rated as schizophrenic. They represent the way people think schizophrenics speak. Item (c) was rated as normal because it is neither bizarre or obscure. Item (d) was rated moderately schizophrenic because, while it is not bizarre, it is repetitious, loose, and difficult to follow (Schwartz, 1982). How do these ratings agree with yours? The results may cause you to readjust your ideas about schizophrenics, because (c) was produced by a patient who was diagnosed as schizophrenic and (d) is from a conversation by former U. S. President Richard Nixon. Many of Nixon's colleagues produced similar speech (Gold, 1974).

Hard-to-follow speech may also come from people who have been given diagnoses other than schizophrenia. The following excerpt was produced by a hypomaniac patient.

*Women of America, it behooves you one and all to help at this, the most interesting epoch of the World's History, in every way possible, the march of civilization, the march of victory! I will play you Beethoven's Great Symphony with its four fateful opening notes—sol, sol, sol, mi . . . V.V.V.V. the Day of the Century has dawned! (R. A. Cohen, 1975, p. 1020)*

Schizophrenic individuals may be highly intelligent, not at all confused, and very painstaking in working out logical solutions to problems. However, their thought processes do not lead to conclusions based on reality or universal logic.

## Unpredictable Motor Behavior

The motor behavior of some schizophrenics is unpredictable. These individuals may remain motionless in strange postures for many hours, to the point at which circulation is impaired and swelling of body parts such as the feet and ankles occurs. At other times they may become wildly aggressive and difficult to control. They may move about constantly, much like a person experiencing a manic episode, stopping only when exhaustion sets in.

## Lack of Appropriate Emotion

Many people who are labeled as schizophrenic, especially those whose behavior is severely disordered, show a characteristic apathy. They display little emotion no matter what the situation. Talking with such a person is very unsatisfactory because it seems that no emotional contact can be made. The interpersonal contacts of this kind of person are characterized by lack of empathy, warmth, and concern about the realities of the situation. Schizophrenics are often described as showing emotional flatness, and this is especially true after the period of acute psychosis has passed. Whereas a depressed patient might show a consistent and intense mood, schizophrenic behavior does not appear to be consistently happy or unhappy; it is this inappropriate and arbitrary quality that stands out.

## Motivational Level

Another change that almost always accompanies a schizophrenic disorder is a change in motivation or interest level. This is most likely in the early phases and again in the period after acute psychosis has passed. Parents often notice the first symptoms of what may become a schizophrenic disorder when their child's school grades begin to fall and the child does nothing but sit around listening to music or TV and often retreats to his or her bedroom and avoids contact with others.

## ■ A HISTORICAL VIEW OF SCHIZOPHRENIC DISORDERS

Brief descriptions of what today would probably be called schizophrenic disorders are found in the Hindu *Ayur Veda*, which dates from 1400 B.C., and in the writings of the physician Aretaeus in the first century A.D. (Kendell, 1983). However, for many centuries descriptions of schizophrenia were much less common and detailed than descriptions of mania. Schizophrenic disorders were not clearly defined until the nineteenth century.

## Dementia Praecox

One of the first writers to classify schizophrenia as a distinct disorder was Emil Kraepelin (1856–1926), who called it **dementia praecox.** Kraepelin was the author of the most influential psychiatric textbook of his period. In the fourth edition of the book, published in 1893, dementia praecox appeared as a heading under

"Psychic Degenerative Processes." In later editions it was treated as a separate disorder. Kraepelin used the term *dementia praecox* because the onset of the disorder occurred early in life, typically in adolescence. He also emphasized that classification depended on the cause of the illness, not just the symptoms observed at a particular time. He believed that recovery was impossible because the cause of dementia praecox was irreversible organic deterioration, which would eventually be found to have a specific organic cause and pathology. However, he noted the great variability in the speed and extent of different individuals' declines and pointed out that there might even be remissions, or periods when the disorder was no longer obvious. In fact, out of 127 cases that Kraepelin studied, 16 seemed to have ended in complete recovery (Kraepelin, 1909, vol 2, p. 865).

Kraepelin paid no attention to the psychological aspects of schizophrenia; his entire focus was on the symptoms of the underlying deterioration. The person's life history, personality, and experiences with the illness were ignored. When he did mention psychological features, Kraepelin considered them temporary expedients, expecting that findings from microscopes and test tubes would make it possible to investigate the disease objectively.

## The Schizophrenias

One of the first people to emphasize the psychological aspects of the disorder was Eugen Bleuler (1857–1939), who was influenced by Freud's work on the neuroses. According to Bleuler, whatever the underlying process might be, many of the symptoms had a psychological cause. He used the term *schizophrenia* instead of *dementia praecox* and broadened the concept of the disorder as well as changing its name. Bleuler spoke of "the schizophrenias"; that is, he believed that the symptoms might represent a group of disorders with different causes and outcomes, not a single cause and outcome as Kraepelin had thought. Bleuler noted that although some people with schizophrenic disorders deteriorate, others remain unchanged and some improve. He divided people with schizophrenic symptoms into two groups: chronic and acute. The acute cases had a good chance of recovery. Bleuler also emphasized the role of the environment in schizophrenic disorders: He believed that some individuals might have the potential for developing these disorders, but because particular types of environmental situations did not occur, the disorder remained latent and the person never showed visible signs of schizophrenia.

Bleuler spoke of this group of disorders as characterized by loss of integration of thinking, emotion, and motivation rather than by gradual deterioration. He summed up the primary characteristics of schizophrenic behavior as the "four A's": alterations in affect, alterations in association, ambivalence, and autism. Associated with these changes, in Bleuler's view, were the secondary symptoms of hallucinations and delusions. Bleuler's ideas became popular in the United States. In Europe, however, Kraepelin's ideas continued to dominate.

One problem with Bleuler's definition was that his criteria were vaguely defined and could be interpreted in a number of ways. This led to increased use of the diagnosis of schizophrenia for behaviors that differed greatly both in kind and in severity. To make things worse, Bleuler's diagnostic guidelines were often interpreted even more broadly than he had intended. For example, even if the individual had only some of the specified characteristics, the diagnosis of schizophrenia was applied frequently by American-trained clinicians. This meant that the label "schizophrenia" was being used to describe a wide variety of behaviors.

If Bleuler's criteria were used, more people would be considered schizophrenic than when Kraepelin's definition was used. Because of this difference, U. S. statistics showed a much higher incidence of schizophrenia than European statistics. As this more generalized concept of schizophrenia became popular, many people were diagnosed as schizophrenic if they showed some of these characteristics. From the 1930s until the 1960s, several important figures in American psychiatry, such as Adolf Meyer and Harry Stack Sullivan, emphasized a broad concept of schizophrenia and psychosis in general, a concern with the psychodynamics of the behavior and emphasis on interpersonal relationships as causal factors. As a result, emphasis on differential diagnosis—discriminating, for example, between affective disorders and schizophrenia—was thought to be of little importance and the proportion of people who were called schizophrenic increased sharply. For example, in the 1930s about 20 percent of patients at the New York Psychiatric Institute were diagnosed as schizophrenic. By the 1950s, the figure had reached 80 percent (Kuriansky and others, 1974). In contrast, the proportion of patients diagnosed as schizophrenic at Maudsley Hospital in London remained at about 20 percent over a long period.

## First-Rank Symptoms

Because such a wide variety of individuals were given the diagnosis of schizophrenia, it became more difficult to do meaningful research on the causes of schizophrenic disorders. One way to deal with this problem was to clarify the definition. Kurt Schneider (1887–1967) was one of the leaders in this effort. Schneider did not deny that Kraepelin's idea of bodily changes was correct, but he believed that since these changes had not been identified, it was important to divide people into types on the basis of their psychological symptoms. Bleuler's four A's seemed too vague to be interpreted reliably; moreover, they had caused people with psychotic symptoms to be grouped with others whose psychoses involved disturbances of thought and perception.

Schneider dealt with this problem by describing a series of **first-** and **second-rank symptoms.** If first-rank symptoms were present and no organic cause was evident, a diagnosis of schizophrenia was justified. Second-rank symptoms, in Schneider's view, could be found in other psychotic disorders, although if they occurred with sufficient frequency and in certain combinations, a diagnosis of schizophrenia could still be made with-

**FIGURE 11-4**
This painting, by an artist who had experienced a period of psychosis, seems to represent the kinds of delusional thinking and the feelings of being watched and influenced that Schneider described. (UPI/Bettmann Newsphotos)

The first-rank symptoms of schizophrenia fall into three groups: special forms of auditory hallucinations, inadequate perception of boundaries between the person and the environment, and normal perceptions with highly personalized delusional interpretation.

1. Auditory hallucinations:
   a. Voices repeating the subject's thoughts out loud or anticipating the subject's thoughts.

   *The voice would repeat almost all the patient's goal-directed thinking—even the most banal thoughts. The patient would think, "I must put the kettle on" and after a pause of not more than one second the voice would say, "I must put the kettle on." It would often say the opposite, "Don't put the kettle on."* (Mellor, 1970, p. 16)

   b. Two or more hallucinatory voices discussing or arguing about the subject, referring to him or her in the third person.
   c. Voices commenting on the subject's thoughts or behavior, often as a running commentary.

2. The sensation of alien thoughts being put into the subject's mind by some external agency, or of his or her own thoughts being taken away (thought insertion or withdrawal).

   *A 22-year-old woman said, "I am thinking about my mother, and suddenly my thoughts are sucked out of my mind by a phrenological vacuum extractor, and there is nothing in my mind, it is empty."* (Mellor, 1970, pp. 16–17)

3. The sensation that the subject's thinking is no longer confined within his or her own mind but instead is shared by or accessible to others (thought broadcasting).

   *A 21-year-old student said, "As I think, my thoughts leave my head on a type of mental ticker-tape. Everyone around has only to pass the tape through their mind and they know my thoughts."* (Mellor, 1970, p. 17)

4. The sensation of feelings, impulses, or acts being experienced or carried out under external control, or the sensation of being hypnotized or having become a robot.

   *A 23-year-old female patient reported, "I cry, tears roll down my cheeks and I look unhappy, but inside I have a cold anger because they are using me in this way, and it is not me who is unhappy, but they are projecting unhappiness into my brain. They project upon me laughter, for no reason, and you have no idea how terrible it is to laugh and look happy and know it is not you, but their emotions."* (ibid.)

5. The experience of being a passive and reluctant recipient of bodily sensations imposed by some external agency.

   *A 38-year-old man had jumped from a bedroom window, injuring his right knee which was very painful. He described his physical experience as follows: "The sun-rays are directed by a U.S. army satellite in an intense beam which I can feel entering the center of my knee and then radiating outward causing the pain."* (Mellor, 1970, p.16)

6. Delusional perception—a delusion arising fully fledged from a genuine perception that others would regard as commonplace and unrelated to the content of the delusion.

out first-rank symptoms. Schneider considered the abnormal inner experiences of the individual to be the most telling characteristics of the illness (see Figure 11–4). His classification system attempted to identify behavioral symptoms that would be readily noticed by an examiner, could be easily agreed upon by several observers, and could occur only in schizophrenia. Those symptoms included one or more of the following: hearing one's voice spoken aloud in one's head; hearing voices that comment on what one is doing at the time; experiences of bodily influence (delusions of passivity); thought withdrawal and other forms of thought interference; thought diffusion; delusional perception; and believing that the feelings or motivation of others are being imposed on one ("made" or "inserted" thoughts or feelings). Table 11–4 lists and illustrates first-rank symptoms. Second-rank symptoms include other forms of hallucinations, confusion, disorders of mood, and emotional blunting.

The first-rank symptoms meet two of Schneider's goals: They are easily noticed and are easy for examiners to agree upon. However, his third goal was not met: Although these signs occur frequently in schizophrenia, they are not unique to it. At least one-fourth of patients with bipolar affective disorders also show some of these symptoms (Hoenig, 1984). In addition, the presence or absence of these symptoms does not seem to be related to later functioning and improvement (Silverstein and Harrow, 1981).

The DSM-III-R criteria presented in Table 11-2 represent a kind of amalgam or bonding together of the criteria suggested by the three theorists—Kraepelin, Bleuler, and Schneider. Kraepelin's influence on DSM-III-R can be seen in its emphasis on the course of the disorder over time. While DSM-III-R does not assume a negative outcome, it does require that the behaviors described last over a certain period. It also reflects Kraepelin's approach in its emphasis on the description of behavior in making the diagnosis. Like Bleuler, DSM-III-R refers to the Schizophrenic Disorders. Schneider's influence is also clear: DSM-III-R includes several of his signs, such as thought broadcasting, thought insertion, and thought withdrawal, in its diagnostic criteria.

## ■ TYPES OF SCHIZOPHRENIA
### Traditional and DSM-III-R Subtypes

Kraepelin described three subtypes of schizophrenia or dementia praecox—**catatonic, hebephrenic,** and **paranoid.** When Bleuler broadened the description of the disorder, he added a fourth category, **simple schizo-**phrenia. These four categories were used for many years. DSM-III-R uses a modification of the traditional groupings for the active phases of disorder: *paranoid, catatonic, disorganized,* and a catchall or *undifferentiated* group. In addition, there is a *residual* category for cases in which the psychotic features are no longer prominent. People who formerly would have been diagnosed as simple or borderline schizophrenics—that is, people who have some of the symptoms without ever experiencing psychotic components such as hallucinations and delusions—now are placed in the category of **Schizotypal Personality Disorder.** This group includes people who exhibit a lifelong pattern of seclusiveness and withdrawal from others. They may show decreasing interest, initiative, and ambition around the time of puberty and then progressively decrease their attempts at social interaction. A person who fits this description of schizotypal personality disorder is described in the following passage.

*Frank is 36 years old and still lives at home with his parents. He held a job in the packing department of a small cannery for a number of years. He never has created any trouble at home, during his school years, or on his job. He spends most of his time at home alone in his room. On his job he rarely had much to say and did not form friendships with the other workers, who thought of him as a little strange. Three years ago, when the plant closed down, Frank was laid off. Since then he has refused to look for another job. He spends most of his time in his room and seems to be taking less interest in his personal appearance. His mother has noticed that when he thinks he is alone he sometimes smiles, gestures, or frowns as though he were talking to someone. When she asks him about this, he pays no attention or denies that he is acting strangely.*

People like Frank usually come to the attention of clinicians only if some dramatic change occurs in their lives. If they lose a job, or if their parent or other caretaker dies or becomes disabled, their lack of self-sufficiency may bring them into contact with the medical or welfare system. Although such people may be eccentric, they do not fit the DSM-III-R definition of schizophrenic disorder. They are distinguished primarily by their lifelong inability to function independently, even though they are not retarded intellectually. They show a marked lack of assertiveness, which prevents them from expressing anger, from making friendly overtures to the people around them, and from having a normal sex life. They also showed marked peculiarities in communication and may use words deviantly.

The diagnostic subgroups listed in DSM-III-R vary in frequency of occurrence. It seems likely that the outcome of the disorder also varies from one category to another, although many researchers and clinicians question whether the subgroups remain stable over time. A person may be diagnosed in one category at one time whereas later, when his or her behavior changes, another category may be more appropriate.

**Disorganized Schizophrenic (Hebephrenic)** The extreme forms of **disorganized schizophrenia** are among the most bizarre varieties of psychosis. Profuse delusions and hallucinations (particularly visual hallucinations), grimacing, and gesturing mark the hebephrenic's behavior. Hebephrenics show a childish disregard for social conventions and may resist wearing clothes, urinate or defecate at inappropriate times, and eat with their fingers. They behave actively but aimlessly and display emotional responses that are inappropriate to the circumstances. Giggling, silly mannerisms, and inexplicable gestures are common.

**Catatonic Schizophrenia** Disturbance in motor activity is the major symptom of the **catatonic schizophrenia**. People with this disorder may remain stiffly immobile or may be extremely agitated. **Waxy flexibility** is an extreme form of immobility in which the catatonic's arm or leg remains passively in the position in which it is placed. At the opposite extreme, the agitated catatonic shows extreme psychomotor excitement, talking and shouting almost continuously. Patients who experience prolonged catatonic excitement may be very destructive and violent toward others. As with manic excitement, there is danger of personal injury or collapse due to exhaustion.

**Paranoid Schizophrenia** The diagnosis that is most often given on first admission to a mental hospital is **paranoid schizophrenia**. This disorder seems to be primarily cognitive. It is characterized by delusions and sustained, extreme suspiciousness. In some cases the content of the delusions and hallucinations may shift dramatically and unpredictably; for example, delusions of grandeur may for no apparent reason replace delusions of persecution. In addition to delusions and inability to trust others, the paranoid schizophrenic displays loose thinking and blunted emotional responses. However, since some aspects of intellectual functioning may be unaffected by the delusional thoughts, under certain circumstances paranoid schizophrenics may seem relatively well put together.

The following account was given by a medical student with a Ph.D. in psychology who developed an acute psychotic reaction in which delusions played a prominent role. His case illustrates not only the delusions that occur in paranoid schizophrenia but also the acute fright that is felt by someone experiencing the

beginning of such an episode. During his acute episode, the student had the haunting notion that there was something wrong with him, that he could not breathe, and that he might die. One morning, after an especially fearful, sleepless night, he reported the following experience.

> I got up at 7 A.M., depressed, and drove to the hospital. I felt my breathing trouble might be due to an old heart lesion. . . . I decided that I was in heart failure and that people felt I wasn't strong enough to accept this, so they weren't telling me. I thought about all the things that had happened recently that could be interpreted in that light. I looked up heart failure in a textbook and found that the section had been removed, so I concluded that someone had removed it to protect me. I remembered other comments. A friend had talked about a "walkie-talkie," and the thought occurred to me that I might be getting medicine without my knowledge, perhaps by radio. I remembered someone talking about a one-way plane ticket; to me that meant a trip to Houston and a heart operation. I remembered an unusual smell in the lab and thought that might be due to the medicine they were giving me in secret. I began to think I might have a machine inside of me which secreted medicine into my blood stream. . . . A custodian's eyes attracted my attention, they were especially large and piercing. He looked very powerful. He seemed to be "in on it," maybe he was giving me medicine in some way. And, as periodically happened throughout the early stages, I said to myself that the whole thing was absurd, but when I looked again the people really were watching me. . . . Conversations had hidden meanings. When someone told me later that I was delusional, though, I seemed to know it . . . One part of me seemed to say, "Keep your mouth shut, you know this is a delusion and it will pass." But the other side of me wanted the delusion, preferred to have things this way. The experience was a passive one; that is, I just sat back as these things happened to me. Getting better was passive too; it just happened, so to speak, as I watched. (Bowers, 1968, p. 353)

Paranoid schizophrenics misinterpret the world around them. Although they are capable of evaluating the situation correctly, they resist the feedback cues that most people use (Gillis and Blevens, 1978). Well-defined systems of delusional paranoid thinking can also occur in people who in other respects show well-integrated behavior. Such people are diagnosed as having paranoid disorders rather than schizophrenia of the paranoid type (see Box 11–1).

## Schizophrenic Spectrum Disorders

When the families of schizophrenic individuals are studied, they seem to include more than the expected number of relatives who are somewhat unusual in their

# ■ BOX 11-1 PARANOID DISORDERS

Everyone engages in paranoid thinking at one time or another. You could probably think of at least one occasion when you have felt that you were being discriminated against or talked about or were suspicious of someone else's motives without adequate proof that such things had actually occurred. We can consider paranoid thinking to be a kind of cognitive style. People vary in how frequently they use it and in how much they let reality influence what they perceive. Paranoid thinking thus can be expressed as a kind of continuum extending from the everyday type to severe delusional thinking that affects all of a person's life (see Figure 11–5).

Sometimes people who have not thought in this way before suddenly begin to do so. Such varied factors as liver failure, vitamin $B_{12}$ deficiency, hearing loss, brain tumors, syphilis, and a variety of drugs may produce paranoid thinking along with other symptoms. At least 65 different conditions have paranoid features (Manschreck and Petri, 1978).

Paranoid thinking is more common in older people. Often it is caused by social isolation and perhaps by a progressive hearing loss or a loss of vision that makes it harder for the person to verify his or her perceptions of what is actually happening. Sometimes the small strokes or bloodclots in the brain that occur in older people can lead to paranoid symptoms. Another possible cause is atrophy or degeneration of brain tissue. Any of these conditions may produce severe enough maladaptive behavior to require that the person be institutionalized.

*A 73-year-old man had lived in the community for years. He was not very sociable but was always thought of as a harmless crank. Then his hearing began to fail and he became afraid that his house was going to be broken into and all his things stolen. He thought his family was after his money and wanted to get rid of him. As a result, he barricaded himself in his house and refused to see anyone. He was finally hospitalized and given antipsychotic drugs. As a result, his hostile angry behavior decreased but his delusional beliefs were unchanged.*

Stress caused by environmental changes can also bring on a temporary episode of paranoid thinking. For example, immigrants experience paranoid disturbances at a much higher rate than native-born citizens. The move to a new place, with all the readjustment involved, usually produces high levels of stress.

*After being told by his recruiting officer not to report his bedwetting problem during his induction physical, an 18-year-old enuretic male from the rural South enlisted in the military. The other recruits began to tease him unmercifully with the discovery of his secret soon after the beginning of basic training. He began to believe that his recruiting officer and drill instructor were plotting to murder him so that his bed wetting would remain undiscovered by higher authorities. When he*

**FIGURE 11–5**
The range of disordered perceptions of reality with paranoid elements.

| MILD | MODERATE | | | | SEVERE |
|------|----------|--|--|--|--------|
| | | Paranoid Disorders | | | |
| Average person Occasional suspicious thoughts | Paranoid personality A suspicious cognitive style. | Paranoid personality disorder A suspicious cognitive style so strong that it impairs effective behavior. There are no delusions. Reality testing is intact. | Paranoid A stable and chronic delusional system. Reality testing good in all other areas | Acute paranoid disorder Usually of sudden onset due to an extreme stress. Lasts less than 6 months. Rarely becomes chronic. | Paranoid schizophrenia Multiple delusions that are likely to be fragmented, accompanied by marked loosening of associations, obvious hallucinations, and other evidence of disorganization. Reality markedly distorted. |

was examined, the patient exhibited hypersensitivity to criticism, paranoid thinking, and ideas of reference. After two months' hospitalization his delusions cleared. On one-year follow-up, although his social contact was minimal and he remained periodically enuretic, he continued to be free of psychotic thinking while he was living and working on his father's farm. (adapted from Walker and Brodie, 1985, p. 751)

Paranoid delusions usually fall into one of several categories: the feeling of being persecuted by others, unwarranted jealousy and suspicion of sexual unfaithfulness by one's lover or mate, the feeling that another person has fallen in love with one when there is no evidence for this, and delusions of illness when none exists. The following descriptions illustrate some of these types.

T.Y. became suspicious that his wife was having an affair with her obstetrician during her pregnancy. The baby did not resemble the father, but he thought it did look like the obstetrician. T.Y. then threatened to kill the physician. After antipsychotic drugs and psychotherapy, his anger and threats of murder disappeared but he continued to believe the child was not his.

B.Z., an accountant, met a famous writer when he came to the accounting firm for advice about his financial planning. Although he was courteous and pleasant, he showed no special attention to her. She became convinced that he was irresistibly attracted to her, and she was soon entirely preoccupied with thoughts about his love and their future life together. Her feelings became so clear that he soon found another accounting firm. Antipsychotic medication was of no help, but after some psychotherapy sessions B.Z. agreed to stop calling the writer and waiting for him in the lobby of his apartment building.

Probably the most interesting kind of paranoia is the shared paranoia disorder that is sometimes called **folie à deux.** In such cases one person is dominant, with fixed delusions, and the other is a suggestible person who adopts the delusional beliefs when the two are together. Usually the suggestible person gives up the belief when the two are separated. Two sisters, a husband and wife, or a mother and her child are the most common pairs involved. In some cases more than two people may take part in the delusion. The following case illustrates folie à deux.

A 34-year-old student was admitted to the hospital after threatening to kill his graduate advisor for perceived discrimination. The student, a Vietnam combat veteran, believed that his professor was turning the college faculty against him because of his war experiences. When contacted by the hospital social worker, the student's widowed mother emphatically insisted that her son's beliefs were correct. A family session revealed that the mother, a passive and ineffectual lady, was completely dominated by her son. . . . She would agree, without hesitation, to his tirades against the university. He had influenced the mother to write numerous letters to the university president, the city's mayor, the chief of police, and the state governor protesting perceived actions of the university. She had written to the mayor after her son convinced her that his tardiness was secondary to a university plot to slow the bus service from the home to school. Her letters to the police chief asserted that the advisor had influenced her son's classmates to pelt him with snowballs. She wrote to the university president to report her son's allegations that his advisor gave better grades to the women in the class because of their sexual favors to him. Her detailed letters to the governor railed against the university for discriminating against her son, the Vietnam veteran. After her son had been hospitalized for several weeks, she began to realize that his thinking was disturbed. He decided not to return to school following discharge from the hospital, and although his delusions remained, he was able to find a job with the forestry service in another community. His mother entered psychotherapy to deal with the separation anxiety engendered by her son's move. (adapted from Walker and Brodie, 1985, p. 75)

Paranoid disorders are rare, affecting only 0.1 to 0.4 percent of all people who are treated for mental disorders. Little is known about their causes or the most effective means of treatment. Antipsychotic medications may be helpful in some crisis situations. Psychotherapy may also be helpful. The most effective way to deal with the delusions seems to be to suggest to the client the ways in which they interfere with his or her goals, rather than attempting to meet them head on. The client can sometimes be taught to recognize and avoid situations that produce or increase the delusions.

behavior. These relatives dress eccentrically, behave in unusual ways, and seem somewhat limited emotionally or somewhat asocial. A greater than anticipated number of relatives of schizophrenics may also show peculiarities in thinking—magical thinking, for instance. Many researchers believe that there may be some genetic relationship between these behaviors and the schizophrenic disorders. They believe that the whole spectrum of disordered behaviors should be investigated together.

**Schizophrenic spectrum disorders** include not only these unusual behaviors but also certain personality disorders. For instance, schizotypal and paranoid personality disorders occur more frequently in the families of people who have schizophrenic disorders (Baron and others, 1985). Other disorders that have sometimes been linked to the schizophrenic spectrum are *schizoaffective disorder* (a category that includes individuals who show significant depression or manic symptoms along with the development of thought disorder), *atypical psychoses*, and *paranoid disorder* (Kendler and others, 1985). The study of the relationships among these disordered behaviors may provide clues to the causes of schizophrenic behavior.

## Type I and Type II Schizophrenias

Because most authorities agree that schizophrenic behavior can be produced by a variety of causes, there have been many attempts to group together patients with different sets of symptoms in the hope that this will help in identifying possible causes of schizophrenic behavior. At present the most popular division for research use is between Type I and Type II schizophrenias (Strauss and others, 1974; Andreasen and Olson, 1982; Crow, 1980). Type I schizophrenia is characterized by positive symptoms or behavioral excesses.

These include hallucinations, delusions, bizarre behavior, and disordered thinking. It is thought to be a result of problems with the chemical neurotransmitter dopamine. Patients with a Type I disorder often respond well to drug therapies and have a better chance of resuming effective functioning than patients with a Type II disorder.

Type II patients show negative symptoms or behavior deficits such as poverty of speech and of speech content, flattened affect, apathy, seclusiveness, and impaired attention (see Table 11-5). They tend to respond poorly to drug therapy and are more likely to be chronically ill. It may be that Type II symptoms are related to structural changes in the brain. (Such changes are discussed in Chapter 12.) Negative symptoms and several behavioral measures are related to each other (see Figure 11-6). However, it seems likely that positive and negative symptoms are not related to each other and represent different processes that may occur at the same time, although this conclusion is still disputed (Crow, 1985).

Table 11-6 summarizes the distinctions between Type I and Type II schizophrenias. Sometimes a person with positive symptoms will eventually develop negative symptoms as well. If both types of symptoms occur together, the positive symptoms may fade and leave just the negative ones. Occasionally, though rarely, the negative symptoms may decrease when treated with antipsychotic drugs (Goldberg, 1985; Pogue-Geile and Harrow, 1985). Some researchers have suggested that negative symptoms may be related to genetic components in schizophrenia whereas there may be little or no hereditary component in cases in which positive symptoms predominate (Dworkin and Lenzenweger, 1984).

Negative symptoms not only are associated with poor functioning after the initial psychotic period but

---

□ **TABLE 11-5**
Examples of Negative Symptom Behaivor

| Poverty of speech | Flat affect | Psychomotor retardation |
| --- | --- | --- |
| 1. Long lapses before replying to questions | 1. Avoids looking at interviewer | 1. Slowed in movements |
| 2. Restriction of quantity of speech | 2. Blank, expressionless face | 2. Reduction of voluntary movements |
| 3. Patient fails to answer | 3. Reduced emotion shown when emotional material discussed | |
| 4. Speech slowed | 4. Apathetic and uninterested | |
| 5. Blocking | 5. Monotonous voice | |
| | 6. Low voice, difficult to hear | |

*Note:* Items are from the Behavior Rating Inventory of the Psychiatric Assessment Interview.
*Source:* Adapted from Carpenter and others, 1976.

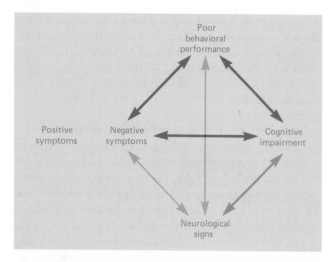

**FIGURE 11-6**
When 500 inpatients with chronic schizophrenia were evaluated several significant relationships among negative symptoms, intellectual impairment, and neurological signs were found. Positive symptoms were not related to any of the other variables. (The heavier the line between variables, the greater the relationship.) (adapted from Owens and Johnstone, 1980)

also are related to poor social and educational functioning before hospitalization. Lack of friends and failure to finish high school both increased the risk that negative symptoms would be present when individuals were followed up after their initial hospitalization (Pogue-Geile and Harrow, 1985). This may mean that these early difficulties are influenced by the same factors as the later negative symptoms, or it may simply mean that early deficits in behavior interact with any genetic vulnerability toward schizophrenia that a person may have. In any case, dividing schizophrenia into

Type I and Type II disorders seems to be useful for research purposes.

## ■ OUTCOME INDICATORS AND LONG-TERM STUDIES

There are two schools of thought regarding the outcome or prognosis for schizophrenia. One is derived from Kraepelin's original concept of dementia praecox. This view of schizophrenia as a nonreversible deteriorative disorder assumes that the prognosis is negative. The second viewpoint stems from Bleuler's concept of the schizophrenias, which emphasizes the symptoms rather than the course of the disease. From this viewpoint, a certain number and kind of symptoms are necessary for the diagnosis, but the outcome may range from complete recovery to permanent and severe disability.

Information about whether or not there ever is or can be a complete recovery from schizophrenia is very important for individuals who have been diagnosed as having a schizophrenic disorder and for their families. The implications are considerable even for those whose behavior seems to have returned to a preschizophrenic level. These points are dramatically illustrated by parts of a letter written by someone who had earlier been diagnosed as schizophrenic.

*A few years ago, during my training in medical school, I was hospitalized at a reputable institution and, at some time during my stay, diagnosed as schizophrenic. Fortunately, I am doing very well now, and am pursuing a career in research on schizophrenia . . . During the years since my hospitalization, however, I have often*

□ **TABLE 11-6**
Differences Between Type I and Type II Individuals

|  | Type I | Type II |
|---|---|---|
| Characteristic symptoms | Delusions, hallucinations (positive symptoms) | Flattening of affect, poverty of speech (negative symptoms) |
| Response to psychoactive drugs | Good | Poor |
| Outcome | Potentially reversible | Irreversible? |
| Intellectual impairment | Absent | Sometimes present |
| Abnormal involuntary movements | Absent | Sometimes present |
| Postulated pathological process | Increased $D_2$ dopamine receptors | Cell loss (including peptide-containing interneurons) in temporal lobe structures |

[1]Modified from Crow and Johnstone, 1985.
*Source:* Crow, 1985, p. 481.

*been fraught with profound guilt over my diagnosis of schizophrenia . . . I felt that for some people I would be forevermore something of a subhuman creature. I grieved and mourned over my loss for several months . . . Returning to work as a fellow in a department of psychiatry, I was repeatedly in contact with psychiatrists, psychologists, and other mental health professionals. Quite frequently amidst such contacts there were derogatory and slanderous remarks of persons labeled as schizophrenic. Dismayed, I soon had repeated dreams in which I had a brain tumor, dreams that were not in the least bit frightening to me. Having an organic disorder seemed far easier to live with then—preferable to experiencing the full psychological impact of this label of schizophrenia . . . But I continually have a need to ask myself certain questions. For example, must I live forever with the doubt, mystery, and ambiguity that permeates the issue of schizophrenia itself? Am I now committed to schizophrenia for life? Or is schizophrenia committed to me?* (Anonymous, 1977, p. 4)

## Predictors of Outcome

Predictions about the outcome of a schizophrenic disorder typically take into account a set of criteria including type of disorder, whether the psychosis appeared suddenly, and level of prepsychotic adjustment. Recently other criteria such as positive and negative symptoms have been added.

**Type of Disorder**  It is generally assumed that hebephrenics have the poorest chance of recovery. Paranoids and catatonics are thought to have a better prognosis, especially if vivid delusions are present during the initial phase.

**Acute Versus Chronic Onset**  Cases in which there is a sudden onset, often related to a situation that is seen by others as obviously stressful or traumatic, seem to have the best prognosis. Cases with a gradual onset marked by no outstanding external precipitating event have less likelihood of a positive outcome.

**Premorbid Adjustment**  Whether the person's life prior to the appearance of schizophrenia showed adequate school and social adjustment, and whether—if the individual is an adult—he or she demonstrated the ability to be self-supporting are very strongly related to the probable outcome after the period of acute psychosis has passed (Stoffelmayr and others, 1983). If there is a long history of relative deviance, including school difficulties, few friends, and little active dating, the prognosis is poorer. This is especially true if the person has typically been uncommunicative, apathetic, inactive, and accepting of his or her condition.

The person's past level of functioning seems to be a much better predictor of outcome than the severity of the symptoms that appear when the first diagnosis of schizophrenia is made. Table 11–7 summarizes some characteristics that are associated with good or poor outcomes.

## Long-term Follow-up Studies

One frequently asked question is, What happens to people who are diagnosed as schizophrenic? Studies that follow individuals over long periods provide important information about the long-term implications of the diagnosis of schizophrenic disorder. However, the definition of schizophrenia has changed over time. Unless we know the particular definition used in the study, the results are hard to interpret. Another drawback of follow-up studies is that, because of their cost, they are often done on the basis of hospital records and the individual is never actually interviewed or personally evaluated. This introduces a good deal of uncertainty—for example, did all the record keepers use the same definition of level of adaptation?

A long-term study that is of particular interest was done by Manfred Bleuler, Eugen Bleuler's son. This study was one of the first to suggest a good outcome for many individuals who had been hospitalized for schizophrenia. What is important about the study is the amount of personal contact Bleuler had with his former patients. Rather than simply following up or recontacting them after a long time, Bleuler followed his patients' progress closely over a 30-year period (Bleuler, 1972). He found that whatever deterioration occurred happened in the first five years of illness. After that the

◻ **TABLE 11–7**
**The Five Best Predictors of Level of Functioning After a Particular (Index) Hospitalization for Schizophrenic Disorder**

| Predictor | Predictive of Good or Poor Prognosis |
|---|---|
| Impairment of work ability (1 year before index admission) | poor |
| More advanced age at first hospitalization | good |
| Poor level of functioning at discharge | poor |
| Length of occupational disintegration in the 5 years before index admission | poor |
| Precipitating factors before first signs of psychosis | good |

*Source:* Möller and others, 1982, p. 105.

proportions of recovered, improved, and unimproved cases remained fairly constant. Research by a number of other clinicians has supported this finding.

Bleuler's information on the patients he saw during his years of practice suggests that the overall recovery rate has remained constant. However, over many years Bleuler observed changes in the symptom patterns exhibited by his patients. Cases of acute onset followed by severe psychosis became rarer. Moreover, the number of milder chronic conditions seemed to increase and the frequency of severe chronic cases to decrease. Other clinical workers have noted the same trends, as well as a decrease in the frequency of excited catatonic states and an increase in the number of people who have periodic disturbances accompanied by periods of remission. The reason for these changes are not clear; however, this pattern is similar to that found in cross-cultural studies conducted in developing countries in Africa (Cooper and Sartorius, 1977).

In another study, all patients who had been diagnosed as schizophrenic over a 38-year period in a rural area in England were reinterviewed by the diagnosing physician, or, if they were no longer alive, their records were studied and relatives contacted (Watts, 1985). Like Bleuler's patients, some of these patients had a good outcome; however, most of the good outcome group had the kinds of symptoms associated with Type I schizophrenia or else would today be diagnosed as having schizotypal personality disorders or bipolar disorders. Of those who had mainly negative symptoms of schizophrenia, about one-third had made a social recovery and were able to work, another third were unemployed and living at home, and the final third were institutionalized.

In a recently reported 30-year study carried out in Vermont (Harding and others, in press), long-term hospitalized patients who had participated in a comprehensive rehabilitation program and deinstitutionalized 30 years earlier were rediagnosed from their records; those who met the DSM-III criteria for schizophrenia were traced and they or their families were interviewed. Between half and two-thirds of these individuals had recovered or were significantly improved. Of these, the majority functioned so well that they could not be identified as former mental patients. A large number no longer took antipsychotic drugs.

Although many of these people had functioned poorly for at least five years after the rehabilitation program, many had returned to their previous level of functioning over time and had even developed further. Some of these, however, functioned well only because they apparently had learned to live with certain symptoms. Some were employed and had good social relationships but still experienced some hallucinations or delusions. Others, who did not work, had nevertheless developed extensive social networks. Because the patients in this study had been hospitalized for up to 25 years and were middle aged when the rehabilitation program began, these results suggest that with younger, more recently hospitalized patients the outcome might be even better.

# ■ THERAPEUTIC APPROACHES

Because the cause or causes of schizophrenic disorders are not well understood, a variety of therapies have been used. Therapies based on the different psychological perspectives are often used together.

## Biological Therapies

Perhaps the most universal treatment for schizophrenia today is the use of antipsychotic drugs. The introduction of these drugs in the 1950s revolutionized the hospital treatment of psychotics because the drugs decreased the unusual and hard-to-control behaviors of many patients. This reduced the number of patients who had to be hospitalized for long periods. The exact way in which the antipsychotic drugs work is not clear, although the ways in which they affect the neurotransmitter system are reasonably well understood. What is known about the role of the neurotransmitter system in producing schizophrenic behavior is discussed further in Chapter 12.

Many people who improve as a result of drug therapy remain on a drug program after being discharged from the hospital. In about half of these cases, withdrawal of antipsychotic drugs will be followed by a return of symptoms. It is not clear whether or how these patients are different from those who do not need continued medication. Some individuals, especially those who have become acutely ill and were adequately adjusted before their illness, seem to recover more completely if drugs are not used. Whether they also should be viewed as a different subgroup within the schizophrenic disorders is not known.

Another, less often used biological therapy for schizophrenia is electro-convulsive therapy (ECT). In a study sponsored by the National Institutes of Health, drugs seemed more effective than ECT in the short run. However, in a follow-up five years after treatment, ECT treatment was as effective as drug therapy (May and others, 1981).

A serious drawback of the use of drug therapies is the potentially irreversible damage to the nervous system that occasionally occurs as a result of overuse of antipsychotic drugs. This damage usually appears in the form of **tardive dyskinesia,** or involuntary movements of the mouth, lips, tongue, legs, or body. The development of tardive dyskinesia is generally related to length of treatment and the amount of drugs given, but at present there is no way to identify people who are at special risk except that the risk seems to increase with age. About 10 to 20 percent of patients in mental hospitals and 40 percent of chronically ill hospitalized and nonhospitalized schizophrenic patients show signs of tardive dyskinesia linked with drug treatment. Because antipsychotic drugs are sometimes given inappropriately or used for too long a time, the risk of these side effects is unnecessarily high for some patients. Because of these concerns, the American Psychiatric Association has recently issued a new warning about the need for "cautious use" of antipsychotic drugs (*Psychiatric News*, May 17, 1985).

Both because of the risk of tardive dyskinesia and because of the effectiveness of lithium and antidepressants in some cases of mood disorders, accurate diagnosis is becoming even more important. The following case illustrates possible consequences of misdiagnosis.

*Mrs. X was referred to a hospital for evaluation of "chronic psychosis." Now age 61, she was first hospitalized at age 40 because of symptoms of withdrawn behavior, inability to function at home, staying in bed, and a marked decrease in speaking to others. Before that hospitalization at 40 she had completed eighth grade, functioned well at home, was happily married, and considered a good mother. For 15 years she was treated with thorazine (an antipsychotic drug). She developed tardive dyskinesia (uncontrolled movements of the lips and tongue) and eventually the thorazine was discontinued. Three months before her present hospitalization she was hospitalized for symptoms of depression. She felt hopeless, wanted to die, had lost her appetite, and had trouble sleeping. [You will recall from Chapter 10 that these are all characteristic symptoms of depression.] Antipsychotic drugs were given, but after two months she was rehospitalized with a severe memory deficit. After her present hospitalization she was given a series of ECT and showed a remarkable improvement. Her family described her as better than she had been in years.* (adapted from Ferrell, 1980, p. 3)

It seems likely that Mrs. X's problem should have been diagnosed as an affective disorder from the start. Not only might she have been able to assume her normal family role again with effective treatment for depression, but she might have escaped the disfiguring effects of tardive dyskinesia brought on by antipsychotic medication.

## Psychodynamic Therapies

In general, the results of psychotherapy with schizophrenics have not been impressive. Studies comparing the results of psychotherapy with those of drug therapies have indicated that when each is used alone, drug therapy is more effective than psychotherapy both in shortening the hospital stay and in preventing future readmissions. It might be speculated that simply being in a hospital for a long time can have negative effects by creating feelings of dependence and cutting off the patient from his or her social relationships. At least one study also suggests that patients who are known to be receiving psychotherapy are somewhat less likely to receive help from other staff members, such as social workers and rehabilitation therapists. They are also less likely to receive drug treatment after they are released than patients who have been treated in other ways during hospitalization (May and others, 1981).

One reason for psychotherapy's lack of success may be that psychodynamically oriented therapy provides too much stimulation for some patients, especially chronic patients. A comparison study of day treatment centers found that more professional staff hours and more group therapy programs were associated with less successful treatment programs. Successful outcomes were more likely at centers that had more occupational therapy and a very nonchallenging environment (Linn and others, 1979).

Despite these disadvantages, some psychodynamic therapists, such as Frieda Fromm-Reichmann and Otto Will, were known for their ability to help schizophrenics, even those with very severe symptoms. They worked mainly with people whose disordered behavior was acute rather than chronic. Also, they worked in excellent private hospitals where the general level of therapeutic treatment is high and the therapist can meet with the patient several times a week over a long period.

## Behavioral and Cognitive-Behavioral Therapies

Two types of therapies using the behavioral perspective have had at least limited success in helping individuals modify schizophrenic behavior. One therapy, known as the **token economy,** is based on reinforcement and has been used primarily with hospitalized patients. Rewarding individuals for desired behaviors can produce dramatic behavior change that makes ward life more pleasant. The second commonly used behavioral therapy, **social-skills training,** is based on social-learning theory. Some social-skills programs focus primarily on behavior, while others stress ways of thinking about problem situations.

**The Token Economy** The main characteristic of the reinforcing environment is that it motivates the patient to acquire new responses. Carefully programmed reinforcement procedures are used to strengthen connections between specific stimuli and responses. The mental hospital might be viewed as an environment in which the patient can learn by doing. One way of providing reinforcement, the token economy, has been tried in several hospital settings. This type of program is effective with chronic, severely disturbed patients.

A token economy has the following basic features.

1. The patient receives tokens as payment for work performed or for behaving appropriately.
2. The number of tokens represents the amount of reinforcement.
3. The reinforcers are received when the tokens are cashed in (for candy, cigarettes, special privileges, and so on).

Ayllon and Azrin (1965), pioneers in the development of token economies, reported the effects of the program on a group of chronic patients in a state hospital. When the economy was in operation, there was a relatively high level of work, but when no tokens were given, output declined drastically. We mentioned earlier that a number of researchers have contended that a major component of the schizophrenic's maladaptation is poor attention to external events. The results of Ayllon and Azrin's project suggest that one effect of a reinforcement regimen is to heighten patients' awareness of their environment and motivate them to respond to it. However, the drop in patients' performance when the reinforcements are withdrawn raises questions about the ability of patients to generalize their behavioral gains beyond the token-economy situation. In other words, a token economy may just teach people how to earn tokens, not to value adaptive behavior for its own sake.

**Social-skills Training** The reinforcer that is most powerful for many people—social relationships—may not be effective or may even be aversive for schizophrenics. Many hospitalized schizophrenics are deficient in social skills (Liberman, 1982). They also seem to lack the motivation to learn them. Schizophrenic patients frequently describe feelings of emptiness or blandness or even a total lack of feelings. Their lack of pleasure in the external world sets up a vicious cycle of withdrawal into fantasy and delusions. Schizophrenics also experience anxiety or distress in social situations, and this too leads to active avoidance of social and even therapeutic relationships. However, through the use of money as a reinforcer, schizophrenic patients can be motivated to participate in social-skills training and to perform the necessary interpersonal activities. In one study, paying patients $2 to attend each five-hour session kept the dropout rate to a minimum (Wallace, 1981).

At present the main focus of the learning perspective in treating schizophrenia is on increasing patients' interactions with other people by helping them develop social skills and overcome anxiety in social situations. The therapy is usually administered in a group setting but is sometimes given on an individual basis. The patient first acts out an interpersonal situation with a trainer or another patient. The trainer then reviews the performance, reinforces the correct behaviors, and models or gives verbal instructions for other behaviors that will lead to a more skilled performance. This procedure is repeated until the patient's performance reaches a desired criterion. The focus is usually on specific behaviors, such as eye contact, smiles, and voice intonation, as well as on more cognitive aspects of behavior such as ways of expressing independence, appreciation, or hostility. Figure 11–7 shows measures taken from the training of one patient who had problems with verbally aggressive behavior. Like token economies, social-skills training does not seem to have a lasting effect on many chronic patients (Wallace and others, 1980). The technique remains a promising one, however.

**Behavioral Self-instruction** Many therapists concentrate on changing the way their clients perceive and interpret situations. In general, people with schizophrenic disorders respond better to modeling of specific behaviors than they do to verbal instructions.

One rather unusual use of cognitive-behavioral therapy is shown in the case of a hospitalized male who was trained to eliminate his psychotic speech (Meyers and others, 1976). The procedure caused such a significant change in his behavior that he was discharged from the hospital. Six months later he had a part-time job and showed only a low level of inappropriate speech. The patient was taught to monitor himself in the following ways.

1. *Don't repeat an answer.*
2. *I must pay attention to what others say. What did they ask me?*
3. *The only sickness is talking sick. I mustn't talk sick.*
4. *I must talk slowly.*
5. *People think it's crazy to ramble on. I won't ramble on.*
6. *Remember to pause after I say a sentence.*

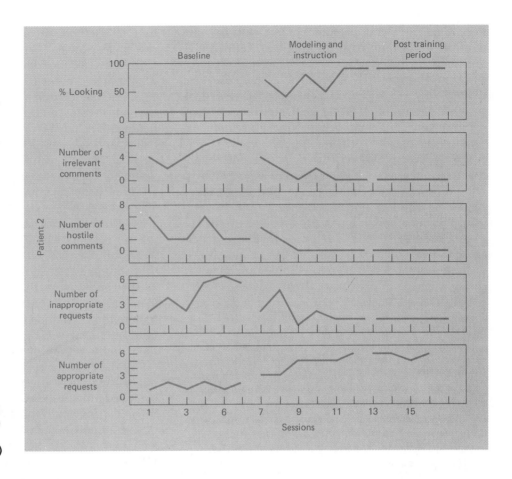

**FIGURE 11-7**
Measures made during the training of a patient who had difficulty suppressing hostile comments. (adapted from Frederiksen and others, 1976)

7. *That's the answer. Don't add anything on.*

8. *I must stay on the topic.*

9. *Relax, take a few deep breaths. (Meyers and others, 1976, p. 481)*

The patient practiced these self-instructions for six 45-minute sessions. Further practice in generalization was given for five additional sessions. At the end of the therapy sessions, the patient's rate of psychotic speech had declined from 65 percent to 8 percent. He attributed the change to "the new self-instructions that stopped me from talking like a crazy man" (Meyers and others, 1976, p. 482).

# ■ THERAPEUTIC COMMUNITIES AND FAMILY EFFORTS

For many patients, the use of antipsychotic drugs has shortened their first hospital stay by shortening the period during which their psychotic symptoms are most evident. This has some very positive effects, since just being hospitalized for a long period, even in the best of institutions, can have negative effects on a person's coping abilities. For that reason, as well as cost factors and concern about civil rights, increased emphasis has been placed on short hospital stays, mainly to begin and assess drug treatment, followed by discharge to aftercare in the community.

The kind of setting to which schizophrenics return and the forms of support available there are crucial to their recovery. One effective source of support can be the patient's family. If the family's attitude toward the patient is judgmental, hostile, and overinvolved, the chances of a relapse are much higher than if the family has a positive attitude (Vaughn and Leff, 1976).

Because families may not have a supportive attitude and many patients may not have a family to return to, other kinds of support programs are often provided. These include halfway houses or group homes, day-care facilities, and mental health clinics that provide both treatment and practical help. Some of these supports may be transitional; they help the discharged patient readjust to life in the community. Others are used to help a person who is functioning at a low level stay out of the hospital. Some research suggests that aftercare treatment is most effective for chronic patients who maintain contact with the program on a long-term basis (Mosher and Keith, 1981). This suggests that most support programs help people maintain the same level of adaptive behavior they had at the time of their hospital discharge but do not increase their level of performance. Unfortunately, good aftercare programs and sheltered living accommodations are in very short supply.

One effective method that helps prevent relapse and rehospitalization is training of family members. The purpose of such training is to modify critical or controlling attitudes toward the person who has reentered the household after being discharged from the hospital, or to find ways of reducing their face-to-face contact. The kind of behavior that can be modified is illustrated in the following portion of an interview.

*He got up one Sunday morning and he sat in the chair and I said, "What's the matter? Don't you feel well?" "No," he said. So I said, "Can I get you a drink?" "No." So I left him. I went back again to see that he was all right. He was still in the same position. This was nearly an hour later. So I thought, it's not very warm, he must be getting cold. So I went out and got a blanket without asking him and put it on him. "I don't want it," he said. And then I did break down because I thought, well, what the devil can I do for him? And that's when it upset me—when I can't do anything to help him like that.* (Hooley, 1985, p. 135)

As this example suggests, some relatives may behave in a controlling way because they are concerned about the former patient's welfare, but their behavior may not be pleasing to the patient.

In one study, families who were rated as critical and controlling participated in a social intervention that had three components: (1) educational sessions that explained symptoms, expected behavior, and ways of dealing with individuals who had a schizophrenic disorder; (2) group meetings for relatives that included families who were rated as accepting and uncontrolling; and (3) family sessions in which mental health workers met with the patient and other family members at home to discuss problems and plan effective ways for the family to interact. All of the patients included in the study continued to take antipsychotic drugs throughout the period. At the end of two years the relapse rate for the experimental group was 14 percent compared to 78 percent for a group of control patients on regular medication (Leff and others, 1985).

Emphasis on both behavioral training and aftercare can be effective in preparing people with schizophrenic disorders to leave the hospital and in helping them function in a community setting. One of the most thorough and carefully controlled studies using a behavioral method was carried out by Paul and Lentz (1977). The project began during the patients' hospitalization. Twenty-eight chronic and severely affected schizophrenic patients were assigned to each of two experimental treatments: social-learning focused behavioral therapy and milieu therapy. The behavioral treatment included training in interpersonal skills, work habits, and self-care. **Milieu therapy** refers to therapy in which all staff members concentrate on providing a therapeutic environment. There was also a control group of patients from the regular hospital program. The patients were evaluated every six months during a 4½ year active treatment period and a 1½ year follow-up. All patients who were discharged were given 26 weeks of aftercare. If they needed rehospitalization, they returned to their original units. At the beginning of the study, more than 90 percent were receiving maintenance doses of medication (i.e., doses intended to keep their condition stable). As the study progressed, drug treatment was discontinued for the majority of the patients without ill effects.

By the end of the 4½ years, over 10 percent of the original social-learning group had been discharged as independently functioning, compared to 7.1 percent of the milieu patients and none of the regular treatment patients. Many other somewhat less improved patients had been placed in the community in sheltered environments; again the social-learning group was superior. Overall more than 95 percent had at least one 90-day stay in the community compared to less than half of the regular hospital group. These findings are remarkable, because at the beginning of the study all of the patients had been rejected for community placement. One finding from this study that is of particular interest is the important role played by aftercare. The aftercare program originally consisted mainly of drug maintenance. However, because during the six months after release, all of the patients experienced a decline in their level of functioning, a consulting service was set up and was maintained for the remainder of the follow-up. The aftercare program was able to reverse the deterioration in the patients' performance after discharge.

Because none of the patients in the study had responded well to drugs in the early stages of their disorder, it may be that they represent a unique group within the general category of schizophrenic disorders. For this reason, the study should not be used to compare drug therapy with the two psychosocial therapies. However, the study does demonstrate that behavioral programs can be effective and that consultation services in an aftercare period are important in preventing deterioration after a return to the stress of life in the community.

# ■ STUDY OUTLINE

**Schizophrenic disorders** are part of the category of mental disorders known as **psychoses,** which involve alterations of perception, thought, or consciousness. This category also includes some manias, certain severe depressions, paranoid states, and brief psychotic reactions.

## CHARACTERISTICS OF SCHIZOPHRENIC DISORDERS

1. To be diagnosed as having a schizophrenic disorder, a person must show deterioration from his or her previous level of functioning in work, social relations, or self-care. Continuous signs of illness must be present for at least six months, and psychotic behavior must be present at some point in the illness.

2. Difficulty in focusing attention and lack of concentration are the most frequently cited problems of cognition associated with schizophrenia.

3. Schizophrenic individuals do not perceive situations in the same way that other people do. Many experience **delusions,** or faulty interpretations of reality that cannot be shaken despite evidence to the contrary. They may also experience **hallucinations,** or projections of internal impulses onto perceptual images in the external world. Only in schizophrenia do hallucinations occur when the person is in a clear, conscious state.

4. Schizophrenic thought patterns are **autistic,** or so self-centered that they are fully intelligible only to the person who is doing the thinking. This often results in peculiar and confusing speech

5. The motor behavior of some schizophrenic persons is unpredictable. They may remain motionless for many hours, or become wildly aggressive and difficult to control.

6. Many people who have a schizophrenic disorder display little emotion no matter what the situation, and most show a decline in motivation or interest from previous levels.

## A HISTORICAL VIEW OF SCHIZOPHRENIC DISORDERS

1. One of the first writers to classify schizophrenia as a distinct disorder was Emil Kraepelin, who called it **dementia praecox.** Kraepelin believed that recovery from the disorder was impossible because it was caused by irreversible organic deterioration.

2. Eugen Bleuler was among the first writers to emphasize the psychological aspects of schizophrenia. He believed that schizophrenic symptoms might represent a group of disorders with different causes and outcomes. The primary characteristics of schizophrenic behavior could be summed up as the "four A's": alterations in affect, alterations in associations, ambivalence, and autism.

3. Since Bleuler's criteria were vaguely defined, the diagnosis of schizophrenia began to be used for behaviors that differed greatly. To deal with this problem, Kurt Schneider described a series of **first-** and **second-rank** symptoms. If first-rank symptoms (primarily abnormal inner experiences) were present and no organic cause was evident, a diagnosis of schizophrenia was justified.

## TYPES OF SCHIZOPHRENIA

1. DSM-III-R groups schizophrenic disorders into four categories: disorganized, catatonic, paranoid, and undifferentiated. There is also a residual category for cases in which the psychotic features are no longer prominent. People who have some symptoms of schizophrenia without ever exhibiting psychotic behavior are placed in the category **Schizotypal Personality Disorder.**

2. **Disorganized schizophrenia** is characterized by profuse delusions and hallucinations, grimacing, and gesturing. People with this disorder behave actively but aimlessly and display inappropriate emotional responses.

3. The major symptom of **catatonic schizophrenia** is disturbance in motor activity. People with this disorder may remain stiffly immobile or may be extremely agitated.

4. **Paranoid schizophrenia** is characterized by delusions and sustained, extreme suspiciousness. Paranoid schizophrenics misinterpret the world around them and resist the feedback cues that most people use.

5. **Schizophrenic spectrum disorders** include unusual behaviors, such as eccentric dress, and certain personality disorders. Among the latter are schizotypal and paranoid personality disorders, schizoaffective disorder, atypical psychoses, and paranoid disorder.

6. Schizophrenias have recently been divided into Type I and Type II disorders. Type I is characterized by behavioral excesses such as hallucinations, delusions, bizarre behavior, and disordered thinking. Type II patients show negative symptoms or behavior deficits such as poverty of speech content, apathy, seclusiveness, and impaired attention. Patients with a Type I disorder have a better chance of resuming effective functioning than patients with a Type II disorder.

## OUTCOME INDICATORS AND LONG-TERM STUDIES

1. Predictions about the outcome of a schizophrenic disorder take into account a set of criteria including type of disorder, whether the psychosis appeared suddenly, and level of prepsychotic adjustment, as well as positive versus negative symptoms. The chances of recovery are greater for paranoids and catatonics, in cases in which there is a sudden onset, and when the individual showed adequate adjustment prior to the appearance of schizophrenia. The severity of the symptoms does not seem to be a good predictor of outcome.

2. Long-term studies of people who have been diagnosed as schizophrenic have found that whatever deterioration occurs happens in the first five years of illness, that there has been an increase in the number of milder chronic conditions, that recovery is less likely when the patient has negative symptoms, and that rehabilitation programs can have a positive effect on the functioning of deinstitutionalized patients.

## THERAPEUTIC APPROACHES

1. Perhaps the most universal treatment for schizophrenia is the use of antipsychotic drugs. Many people who improve as a result of drug therapy remain on a drug program after discharge from the hospital. In some cases overuse of drugs causes damage to the nervous system in the form of **tardive dyskinesia**, or involuntary movements of the mouth or other parts of the body.

2. The use of psychotherapy with schizophrenics has not been very successful. Limited success has been achieved using two behavioral therapies: the **token economy**, which uses carefully programmed reinforcement procedures, and **social-skills training**, which helps patients develop social skills and overcome anxiety in social situations.

## THERAPEUTIC COMMUNITIES AND FAMILY EFFORTS

1. The attitudes of family members can make a difference in a discharged patient's chances of recovery. If the family's attitude is judgmental, hostile, and over-involved, the chances of a relapse are much higher than if the family has a positive attitude. Family members can be trained to modify critical or controlling attitudes.

2. Community support programs include halfway houses or group homes, day-care facilities, and mental health clinics. Such programs seem to be most effective for chronic patients who maintain contact with the program on a long-term basis. The combination of social-learning therapy with consultation services in an after-care period appears to be especially effective.

# 12

# CAUSES AND MARKERS OF SCHIZOPHRENIA

The cause of schizophrenic behavior is not known, although it seems likely that schizophrenia is produced by the interaction of vulnerability factors with stress. Schizophrenic behavior has been investigated from many points of view. Experimental manipulation and observational research have both been used in attempts to determine how people who exhibit schizophrenic behavior differ from those who do not. Such factors as heredity, family structure, and biochemistry have been examined. Recently, attempts have been made to find out why some people who have a hereditary risk of schizophrenia develop it while others do not. This is referred to as the **high-risk** approach. Much current research is focused on **markers** or characteristics that predict vulnerability to schizophrenic disorders. If these can be identified, they may provide clues

to how the disorders come about and how they can be prevented.

## ■ GENETIC FACTORS

The risk of schizophrenia is greater for someone whose relatives have displayed schizophrenic behavior than it is for someone who does not have such relatives. This fact has long been recognized, but it does not definitely establish a hereditary factor in the development of schizophrenia. Merely living with a schizophrenic parent or sibling could create a stressful environment that is conducive to schizophrenic behavior (see Box 12-1). But researchers have struggled with this question for a long time and have established quite clearly that there

---

## ■BOX 12-1 GROWING UP AS THE DAUGHTER OF A PARANOID SCHIZOPHRENIC

This account illustrates some of the stresses experienced by a child with a schizophrenic parent.

*My mother is a paranoid schizophrenic. In the past I was afraid to admit it, but now that I've put it down on paper, I'll be able to say it again and again: Mother, schizophrenic, Mother, paranoid, shame, guilt, Mother, crazy, different, Mother, schizophrenia.*

*I have been teaching inpatient children on the children's ward of Bellevue Psychiatric Hospital in New York City for 13 years, and yet I'm still wary of revealing the nature of my mother's illness. When I tell my friends about my mother, even psychiatrist friends, I regret my openness and worry that they will find me peculiar . . .*

*On the outside our house resembled those of our neighbors, but on the inside it was so different that there was no basis of comparison. Our house was a disaster. Everything was a mess. Nothing matched, furniture was broken, dishes were cracked, and there were coffee rings and cigarette burns clear across our grand piano. I was ashamed of our house. It was impossible to bring friends home. I never knew what my mother might be doing or how she would look.*

*She was totally unpredictable. At best she was working on a sculpture or practicing the piano, chain smoking and sipping stale coffee, with a dress too ragged to give to charity hanging from her emaciated body. At worst she was screaming at my father, still wearing her nightgown at 6 o'clock in the evening, a wild look on her face. I was never popular as a youngster, and I blamed my lack of popularity on my mother . . .*

*Mother was quite interested in music and ballet, and she took me to every ballet and concert in Kansas City. She always looked terrible when she went out, and more than once she arrived at the theatre in her bedroom slippers. I was embarrassed to be seen with her, and before we left home, I would try to convince her to dress properly. She never listened and sometimes became angry, but chic or not, I accompanied her. I loved music and dance as much as she did. I even gave up Saturday afternoons to stay home with her and listen to the Metropolitan Opera broadcasts, and I loved her most and felt closest to her sitting in front of a gas fire, feeling her bony arm around my shoulders as we listened to the music together. Throughout my childhood I was torn between my bizarre, but loving artist-mother and the conventional mothers of my friends . . .*

---

is a hereditary risk factor in schizophrenia (Deutsch and Davis, 1983). Genetic studies of schizophrenia are of three main types: family studies, twin studies, and adoption studies.

## Family Studies

We know, of course, that relatives share a greater proportion of their genes than unrelated people do and that the closer the relationship, the greater the number of shared genes. If a disorder is genetically determined, the individuals who are closest in heredity to the diagnosed person (who is often called the *proband* or *index case*) should be at greatest risk of also showing signs of the disorder. Therefore, a common strategy is to compare the prevalence of a disorder in relatives of affected individuals with its prevalence in the general population. Such comparisons are illustrated in Table 12–1. The data in the table show clearly that the more genes two individuals have in common, the higher the risk of the disorder for one when the other has a schizophrenic disorder. Yet this relationship is not a perfect one. Even twin pairs who share the same heredity do not always share the diagnosis of schizophrenia.

Another interesting finding, also shown in Table 12–1, is that the siblings and children of index cases seem to have a higher risk of becoming schizophrenic than the parents of index cases. The reasons for this are not clear, although the same finding has turned up in several studies. The reason may be simply that many schizophrenic individuals do not become parents.

□ **TABLE 12-1**

Risk of Developing Schizophrenic Disorder for Relatives of a Person with this Diagnosis

| Relationship | Risk (Percent) |
| --- | --- |
| First-degree relatives | |
|   Parents | 4.4 |
|   Brothers and sisters | 8.5 |
|     Neither parent schizophrenic | 8.2 |
|     One parent schizophrenic | 13.8 |
|   Fraternal twins of opposite sex | 5.6 |
|   Fraternal twins of same sex | 12.0 |
|   Identical twins | 57.7 |
|   Children | 12.3 |
|     Both parents schizophrenic | 36.6 |
| Second-degree relatives | |
|   Uncles and aunts | 2.0 |
|   Nephews and nieces | 2.2 |
|   Grandchildren | 2.8 |
|   Half-brothers/sisters | 3.2 |
| First cousins (third-degree relatives) | 2.9 |
| General population | 0.86 |

*Source:* Tsuang and Vandermey, 1980.

Many factors influence whether a person will become a parent. Some of these, such as ability to get and keep a job, form relationships with others, and so on, may tend to be absent in schizophrenic individuals, with the result that they do not have children. Another possible reason is what is called **assortive mating.** This term refers to the tendency for people to mate with others who are more similar to them than would be the case if their choices were random. Assortive mating occurs for physical traits, psychological traits, and behavior disorders. At least one-third of the spouses of chronic schizophrenics are also in the schizophrenic spectrum, and another 20 percent have other psychotic disorders (Parnas, 1985). This means that their children may get "double doses" of genes associated with disordered behaviors.

Family studies focus not only on the overall risks for different family relationships but also on exactly how the hereditary mechanisms work. Early in the history of genetic studies of disordered behavior, it was assumed that what people inherited was simply an increased chance of developing some "mental disease." Current knowledge of heredity suggests that different disorders, or at least groups of them, do not have the same genetic cause. In addition to determining the patterns of heredity for different disorders, family studies provide information about the relationships between schizophrenia and other disorders that may appear in families. If several particular disorders typically occur together in families, this suggests that those disorders may be genetically similar. So far, the evidence about relationships between schizophrenia and affective disorders, schizoaffective disorder, anxiety disorders, and alcoholism is contradictory. Some studies have indicated relationships among these disorders while others have shown them to occur independently.

In one large study, the occurrence of mental disorders in relatives of patients who had been hospitalized for schizophrenia was compared with the rate for relatives of surgical patients from the same hospital (Kendler and others, 1985). When family groups were compared, 9 percent of the families of schizophrenic patients and less than 1 percent of the families of surgical patients contained at least one other schizophrenic member. Overall, the relatives of the patients with schizophrenic disorders had higher rates of nonaffective psychosis, especially schizophrenia and schizoaffective disorders. Relatives of surgical patients had higher rates of alcoholism. Another interesting finding was that although the overall rate of mood disorders was no higher among the relatives of schizophrenic patients than in the control group, relatives of parents who did have these affective disorders were more likely than relatives of control patients to have psychotic symptoms.

## Twin Studies

While family studies can give an overall picture of hereditary risks in schizophrenia and the possible genetic relationships among disorders, twin studies provide a way to focus on the environmental factors that contribute to schizophrenic disorders while keeping the hereditary factors constant. This is possible because identical or monozygotic (MZ) twins are produced from the same fertilized egg and therefore have identical heredity. Fraternal or dizygotic (DZ) twins are produced from two fertilized eggs; they have the same genetic relationship as any other brothers and sisters.

Early studies of twins were flawed because there was no convenient method of determining whether the twins were of the MZ or DZ type. (Of course, twins of opposite sexes are always DZ). Now that such a test is available, one source of error has been removed from twin studies. Another problem was that older studies often used only patients who had been hospitalized on a long-term basis. Recent studies are much more sophisticated: They use consecutive admissions to an institution or data from birth registrations to obtain the twins for study. About a dozen major twin studies have been carried out. All show that MZ twins have a greater chance of being concordant for schizophrenia than DZ twins do. (*Concordance* is a measure of agreement. One way to measure it is to calculate the percent of the time that both twins have the same diagnosis.)

In considering genetic interpretations, the fact that there is less than 100 percent concordance for schizophrenia in monozygotic twins cannot be ignored. This finding makes it clear that heredity alone is not enough to produce a schizophrenic disorder, at least in most people. Researchers therefore are beginning to do joint studies of possible inherited predispositions and environmental variables.

One environmental variable that can differ even for identical twins is the environment experienced before birth. One study compared 100 pairs of MZ twins in which one member had schizophrenia and the other did not. The schizophrenic twin was twice as likely to have weighed less at birth as the nonschizophrenic twin (Stabenau and Pollin, 1967). The differences in birthweight might have been due to a condition in the mother's uterus that influenced one twin but not the other. For example, one twin may have suffered mild brain damage that predisposed it to develop schizophrenia. The twin who became schizophrenic was also more likely to have had an illness in which the central nervous system was affected. In addition, the schizophrenic twins were described as having been less intelligent and outgoing than the nonschizophrenic twins prior to developing the disorder.

Whatever environmental similarities identical twins experience after birth seem to be created more by behavioral similarities in the twins themselves than by aspects of their environment (Kendler, 1983). In contrast to what might be expected, twins who are reared apart are more similar in personality than twins who are reared together (Farber, 1981). The more contact the twins have, the less similar their personalities seem.

Twins do not occur frequently in the population, and twins who are adopted at or near birth—so that they grow up in clearly different environments—are extremely rare. This means that twin adoption studies base their conclusions on scanty evidence. Even rarer are pairs of twins reared apart in which at least one twin develops a schizophrenic disorder. One researcher found only nine such pairs in her review of all the twin studies that had been done (Farber, 1981). In six of these pairs (67%), both twins had schizophrenic disorders, a rate that is very similar to the rate for monozygotic twins reared together. In general, twin studies show that genetic factors are at least as important in the development of schizophrenic disorders as they are in diabetes, hypertension (high blood pressure), coronary artery disease, and ulcers, all of which have a strong genetic component (Kendler, 1983).

## Adoption Studies

Another way of studying the effects of heredity on the development of schizophrenia is through adoption studies. There are three basic kinds of adoption studies: those that compare adopted children whose biological parents were diagnosed as schizophrenic with adopted children whose parents did not have this disorder; those that examine the incidence of schizophrenia in the biological and adoptive families of adopted people who became schizophrenic; and those that study the relatively rare individuals who have nonschizophrenic biological parents but whose adoptive parents became schizophrenic.

One of the first large adoption studies ever conducted was reported by a group of Danish and American researchers working in Denmark (Rosenthal and others, 1968, 1975). First the researchers searched the government adoption register of the Copenhagen area to find the names of parents who had given up their children to nonfamily members for adoption. Then they searched the official psychiatric register to see if they could find the names of any of those parents. The records of those who were found were rated, and those that clearly fit a strict definition of schizophrenia were selected. The children who had been given up for adoption by these parents became the index cases. The control group consisted of the adopted children whose parents had no psychiatric history. Three of the 39 index cases and none of the 47 controls were diagnosed as definitely schizophrenic. This high rate (8 percent compared to 0 percent) in the index group points to a hereditary factor. The children of schizophrenic parents also had a higher risk of other schizophrenic spectrum disorders (26 percent compared to 15 percent).

In another kind of adoption study, Kety and his colleagues (1978) took advantage of the comprehensive records kept by the Danish government to locate people who had been adopted and had later become schizophrenic. They compared the frequencies of schizophrenia or other disturbances in the adoptees' biological and adoptive relatives. They also compared these findings with those for relatives of a control group of adoptees who had not been diagnosed as schizophrenic. They found that about twice as many blood relatives as adoptive relatives of schizophrenics had been diagnosed as definitely or possibly schizophrenic. Both rates were higher than those for the control group.

This study also contained an important subsample: half-brothers and half-sisters of the adopted individual who had the same father. Half-siblings share 25 percent of their genes, rather than 50 percent as full siblings do. However, half-siblings with a common father do not share the environment in the uterus before birth (e.g., chemical factor), nor do they share birth traumas and early mothering experience. These paternal half-brothers and half-sisters were also found to have a greater risk of schizophrenia and schizophrenic spectrum disorders than the control group. This finding gave increased weight to the importance of genetic factors in schizophrenia.

A third kind of adoption study is called a *cross-fostering study*. Such a study asks whether children whose biological parents are nonschizophrenic but who are reared by a schizophrenic foster parent are more likely to become schizophrenic than either of two other groups: children with a schizophrenic biological parent or children with nonschizophrenic heredity who are reared by normal individuals. Wender and others (1974) found that almost twice as many children with schizophrenic heredity as children without such heredity became schizophrenic whether they were reared by schizophrenic or normal adoptive parents. Although the sample size was small, this study suggests that rearing by a schizophrenic adoptive parent does not increase a person's chances of developing schizophrenia.

## A Genetic Model

In studies of heredity, predictions based on theoretical models are compared with the observed frequency of occurrence of various characteristics. If the model is a good one, the agreement between prediction and observation should be close. The two major types of models show the transmission of inherited traits by one gene (monogenic) and by more than one gene (polygenic). A third model involves genetic heterogeneity.

**Monogenic models** are based on the idea that the genetic transmission that occurs at one locus (the place occupied by a gene pair on a particular chromosome) is all that is necessary to produce a particular characteristic. At any one locus, one gene of the pair may be dominant over the other. That means that the characteristic carried by that dominant gene—say, brown eyes — will be *expressed*; that is, the person will have brown eyes. A recessive trait—for example, blue eyes—will not be expressed unless both members of the gene pair carry the characteristic for blue eyes.

In investigating the genetics of schizophrenia, researchers originally looked for distributions based on a monogenic model, but they did not find them. The number of cases of schizophrenia in relatives of schizophrenics is always less than would be expected by monogenic models. One way of explaining this is to use the concept of **penetrance.** According to this idea, a predicted number of individuals will carry the potential for schizophrenia—they will have the right genetic makeup—but not all of them will become schizophrenic because they are not exposed to significant environmental stress. Another way to explain this difference in predicted and observed frequency is to use the **schizophrenic spectrum view** and broaden the criteria to include relatives of schizophrenics who show sufficiently shy, odd, eccentric, or otherwise psychologically abnormal behavior.

**Polygenic models** assume that a number of genes found at specific locations must interact to produce a trait. Many characteristics including height, weight, and skin color, are thought to be influenced by more than one gene. Some models suggest that a limited number of genes and locations are involved. Other polygenic models, called **multifactorial polygenic models,** do not specify the number of gene loci involved in schizophrenia. Instead, they assume that there are many of them and that they are interchangeable. What happens is that genes at all of these loci may have small additive effects on a person's vulnerability to schizophrenia. According to this view, all people have some predisposition to develop schizophrenia. If their predisposition is over a certain threshold, they will develop a schizophrenic disorder; if their liability is below that threshold, they will not (Gottesman and Shields, 1967; Hanson and others, 1977). This kind of polygenic model can be expanded to include two types of liability (Reich and others, 1979). Figure 12–1 illustrates such a model. People to the right of the right-hand threshold would develop a severe form of schizophrenia while those to the left of the left-hand threshold would not be schizophrenic. Those between the two thresholds would develop a mild form of the disorder. Using a complex statistical technique called path analysis, this model

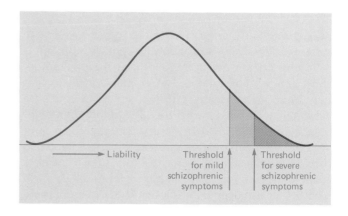

**FIGURE 12–1**
A two-threshold multifactorial polygenic model (from S.V. Faraone and M.T. Tsuang, Quantitative models of the genetic transmission of schizophrenia. *Psychological Bulletin, 98,* 41–66. Copyright (c) 1985 by the American Psychological Association. Reprinted by permission of the author.

seems to predict outcome fairly well for several large sets of data that have been collected to date (McGue and others, in press; Faraone and Tsuang, 1985).

Genetic theorists tend to favor multifactorial polygenic models of heredity over single major locus models, but some combination of the two cannot yet be ruled out. The varying results from one study to another make it seem likely that schizophrenic disorders are not all based on the same genetic transmission. Figure 12–2 suggests one way of organizing the possible subtypes. The solid lines represent divisions that are generally supported by research findings; the dotted lines represent guesses based on what is currently known.

## Genetic Counseling

People seek genetic counseling to learn more about the risk of schizophrenia for themselves, their relatives, or their potential children. This may happen because a relative has been diagnosed as having a schizophrenic disorder or because the individual is thinking of marriage or childbearing. A genetic counselor does not ordinarily give advice but instead presents whatever is known about the risk factors. Because the inheritance of schizophrenia is complex and is not clearly understood at present, a genetic counselor must judge the risks for a particular family on the basis of both theoretical and practical information. Computer programs are available to calculate the exact theoretical risk based on varying combinations of affected and nonaffected

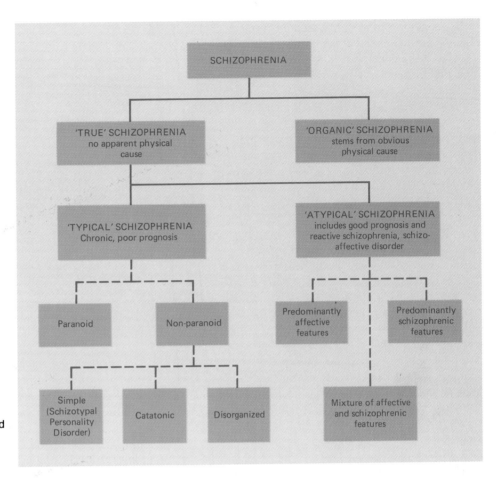

**FIGURE 12-2**
A model showing one possible division of schizophrenia into genetic types (from Tsuang and Vandermey, *Genes and the Mind*, Oxford University Press, 1980.

relatives. However, because this and other models may not be correct, risk figures can be very inaccurate. Even worse, because some individuals may be more vulnerable than others, the amount of risk they bear can vary greatly. The severity of the disorder in the affected relatives, how chronic the behavior is, and the age at which the disorder began all influence vulnerability. Thus, although there is usually a minimal risk of schizophrenia to a potential child of a normal relative of someone who has a schizophrenic disorder, the work of a genetic counselor is complex and should be carried out in connection with other counseling and therapeutic services (Reveley, 1985).

## ■ VULNERABILITY/STRESS FACTORS

Although this model can be applied to all behavior, in the area of schizophrenia it has been particularly clearly defined by Joseph Zubin (Zubin and others, 1982; Zubin and Spring, 1977). Zubin's hypothesis assumes that schizophrenia is not a permanent disorder, but rather

a permanent vulnerability to a disorder. Each person has a certain level of vulnerability to schizophrenia. This level, which may range from no risk to near certainty, is determined by genetic inheritance and pre- and postnatal physical factors, interacting with stressful events or conditions in a person's life (see Figure 12-3). If the combination exceeds a certain critical level, schizophrenic behavior will occur. Zubin's idea of vulnerability is one way of understanding why there isn't 100 percent concordance for schizophrenia among identical twins.

Zubin's model has quite a different emphasis from that of the genetic models discussed earlier. It assumes that when the stressors decrease, the schizophrenic disorder will abate and the person will return to his or her earlier level of functioning (see Figure 12-4). This view contrasts with the traditional view that once the schizophrenia occurs, the person is to be thought of as having the disorder from that time on.

The data from Manfred Bleuler's long-term study support Zubin's approach (Bleuler, 1978). About 80 percent of the schizophrenic individuals in Bleulers'

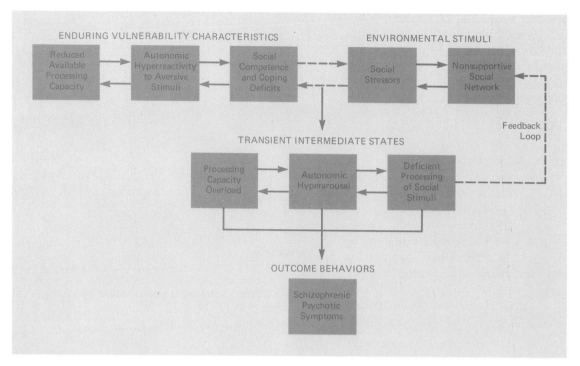

**FIGURE 12-3**
A model showing how stress and vulnerability may interact in the development of schizophrenic psychotic episodes. (from Neuchterlein and Dawson, 1984, p. 304)

**FIGURE 12-4**
The relationship between vulnerability and challenging events. (from Zubin and others, 1982)

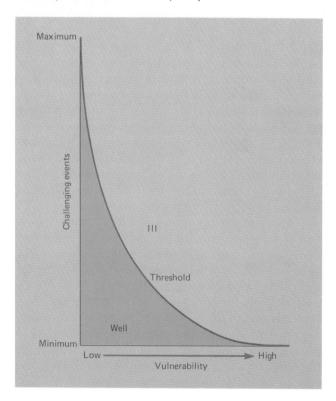

follow-up study had either one or multiple hospitalizations followed by release. About one-third of all former patients were hospitalized, released and never rehospitalized. These findings and those reported in Chapter 11 support the idea that schizophrenia may be an episodic disorder. Most present-day researchers, regardless of whether or not they accept Zubin's statements, would agree that a schizophrenic disorder is almost always a product of several factors, including biological make-up, coping skills, environmental conditions, and life events.

An adoption study carried out in Finland supports this point of view (Tienaro and others, 1985). The study paired adopted children whose biological mothers were schizophrenic with adopted children whose biological parents were not schizophrenic. In the first 91 pairs to be investigated, 26 of the children with schizophrenic biological mothers and only 15 of the children of nonschizophrenic parents had developed serious psychological disorders. Of the 7 who developed psychoses, only 1 was from the control or normal group. However, the most interesting thing about the results was that no seriously disturbed child was found in a healthy or only mildly disturbed adoptive family (rated 1 or 2 on a 5-point scale from health to severe disturbance), and the children who were psychotic had nearly all been brought up in disturbed adoptive families. This study supports the view that genetically transmitted vulnerability may be necessary for a schizophrenic disorder to occur, but that a disturbed family environment may be necessary for that vulnerability to develop into a schizophrenic disorder (see Figure 12–5).

When a person experiences a schizophrenic episode, even if it is clearly brought about by a high stress level resulting from negative environmental conditions, the psychotic episode itself has many negative implications. Figure 12–6 illustrates the complex interactions that may occur after a stressor (b) sets off schizophrenic behavior based on an underlying vulnerability (a). The episode leads to personal and social handicaps (d) that result from the schizophrenic episode. New episodes are likely to occur if there are further psychosocial stresses, or from the added psychosocial handicaps or negative aspects of treatment (b, d, and e). To prevent the disorder from becoming chronic, both hospital treatment policies and social attitudes

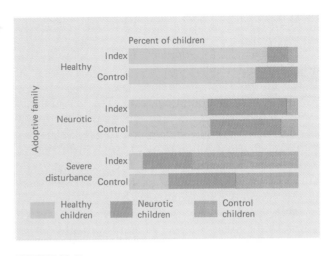

**FIGURE 12–5**
Outcomes for children of schizophrenic (Index) and nonschizophrenic (Control) biological mothers who were reared in differing adoptive families. (adapted from Tienari, and others, 1983, p. 231)

**FIGURE 12–6**
An interactionist model of schizophrenia showing the many ways in which the consequences of a schizophrenic episode continue to affect the individual. (Marzillier and Birchwood, 1981, p. 142)

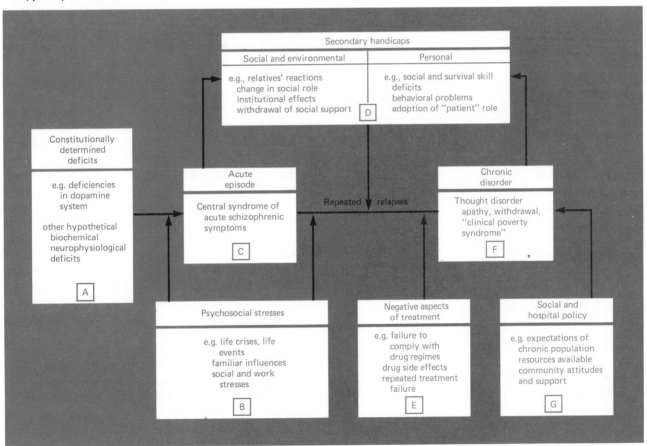

toward people who have been mentally ill need to be improved.

The vulnerability approach to schizophrenia has quite different implications than a strictly biological view, even though it also includes awareness of biological and environmental interactions. The vulnerability approach emphasizes the episodic nature of the disorder, that it may come and go in a vulnerable individual depending on the amount of stress in his or her environment. It seems likely that, because of the varied nature of the schizophrenic disorders, each view may be appropriate for some individuals.

Zubin's vulnerability theory suggests that research efforts in the areas of genetics and psychophysiology can be of great use in pointing out **markers,** or characteristics that can be used to identify vulnerable people. Efforts can then be directed toward helping these individuals avoid the degree of stress that might produce a schizophrenic disorder. This can be done both by providing a supportive environment and by helping vulnerable individuals develop better coping skills so that the unavoidable stressors of life will not affect them so severely. Most of the remainder of this chapter will be devoted to a discussion of the search for markers of vulnerability to schizophrenia.

## ■ HIGH-RISK STUDIES

One way of studying the causal factors in schizophrenia is to study children beginning in infancy or early childhood and compare the records of those who later become schizophrenic with those who do not. This type of research has several advantages.

1. The subjects can be studied before those who develop disorders have experienced hospitalization and drugs.

2. None of the researchers, relatives, teachers, or subjects know who will become schizophrenic. This removes one potential source of bias in their observations and reports.

3. The information obtained is relatively current when it is gathered. Questions about teenage dating patterns and frequency, for example, are answered more accurately by adolescents than they would be by a 30-year-old schizophrenic patient and his or her 55-year-old mother.

4. The data can be obtained uniformly, not by relying on records from various agencies and individuals working in different ways.

This type of study avoids many problems that arise in dealing with an individual who is already schizophrenic. For example, it is not necessary to rely on the patients' and their families' sometimes faulty and selective memories of past events. This is especially important because once a diagnosis of schizophrenic disorder has been made, everyone in the family may see past events in a different light. Studying the person and his or her family after schizophrenia has developed tells more about the consequences of having a schizophrenic disorder than about its causes. The diagnosis of schizophrenia means that the person has already suffered educational, economic, and social failures and may also have experienced hospitalization and extensive drug therapy. These factors alone may explain many of the differences that researchers find between schizophrenic and control groups.

However, there is one severe problem with longitudinal studies that test people before they become ill and later compare the records for those who develop schizophrenia with those who do not. Since only about 1 percent of the population becomes schizophrenic, many thousands of people would have to be tested in order to be sure that the schizophrenic group would make a large enough sample for useful research. One way to cope with this problem is to select for research a group that is thought to have a higher potential or risk of schizophrenia than the population in general. One such group consists of children who have at least one schizophrenic parent. Pioneering research using such children has been carried out in Denmark in a long-term study that began in 1962 (Mednick and Schulsinger, 1968; Mednick and others, 1984). The experimenters have extensively examined 207 of these high-risk children and 104 controls whose families had no hospitalizations for mental illness for three generations.

At the beginning of the study, the children were given intelligence and personality tests, tests of psychophysiological condition, and a psychiatric interview. Their parents were interviewed, and school reports and midwives' reports on pregnancy and delivery were obtained. By 1967, twenty children in the high-risk group showed signs of behavior disorders. Of these, 12 had been hospitalized. Follow-up interviews with most of the subjects were carried out about ten years after the study began. In the high-risk group, 15 schizophrenics were identified; 2 others who had died had also been diagnosed as schizophrenic.

When the group that had developed schizophrenic disorders was compared with the other high-risk subjects, several characteristics distinguished the schizophrenic subjects from the others (Mednick and others, 1984).

1. Their mothers had a more serious disorder.
2. Many of them had been separated from their par-

ents and placed in children's homes early in their lives.

3. They were extremely violent and aggressive in school.

4. Earlier measures of electrical skin conductance predicted later schizophrenia, especially for people who showed hallucinations, delusions, and disordered thought.

So far, the findings of the study support a vulnerability view of schizophrenic disorder. The high-risk subjects who became schizophrenic were much more likely than the remainder of the high-risk group to have experienced two different and unrelated types of stress: complications at birth and difficult living conditions in childhood. The childhood experiences were of two major kinds: The risk of schizophrenia was greater if the mother had experienced a psychotic episode within six months of childbirth or if she had unstable relationships with men.

Since this study began, many other high-risk studies have started. Fifteen such studies are organized in a High-Risk Consortium so that they can share information and not duplicate each other's work. In most of these projects the children being studied have, at most, reached early adulthood, so a long period of risk of schizophrenia lies ahead for them. Most of the studies are longitudinal and compare children of a schizophrenic parent or parents with children of parents with other psychological disorders and with normal children. However, a study being done at the University of Minnesota is cross-sectional with a short-term follow-up, and compares not only children who are vulnerable because they have schizophrenic parents but also children who are vulnerable because they themselves have engaged in aggressive, bullying behavior or hyperactivity (Garmezy and Devine, 1984). A high-risk study being done at the University of Rochester combines cross-sectional and longitudinal approaches by comparing boys in several age groups at initial testing and over time (Wynne, 1984). Some of the results from these studies are presented in Table 12–2.

Another high-risk study with a unique design is being conducted in Israel (Nagler and Mirsky, 1985). This study also compares high-risk children with a schizophrenic parent with matched controls. However, it adds another factor: whether the family lives in a conventional town setting or on a kibbutz, where the children live together and are cared for by a child-care worker. Although kibbutz children visit their parents and eat with them, their parental contacts are much more limited than is usual in a traditional family. One finding of a 15-year follow-up of these individuals is particularly surprising: The only group that showed an

□ **TABLE 12–2**
**Markers of Increased Risk
of Schizophrenia from High-Risk Studies**

Childbirth problems—low birthweight and difficult birth
Poor emotional bonding—lack of a close relationship with the mother in the first three years of life
Poor motor coordination in infancy
Separation from parents—being raised in an institution or foster home
Intellectual deficits—poor performance on intelligence tests, especially in verbal abilities
Cognitive deficits—distractability and problems in focusing attention
Social deficits—aggressive behavior, anger, abrasiveness
Confusion and hostility in parent–child communication

*Source:* Adapted from Watt and others, 1984.

increased risk for some mental disorder was the high-risk group who lived on the kibbutz (See Table 12–3). The reason for this is not clear, but perhaps kibbutz living causes increased stress, for instance, because of lack of privacy, pressure to conform to a common goal, or the greater likelihood that others will know that a person has a schizophrenic parent.

Much research on high-risk subjects has focused on identifying markers for schizophrenia by determining the distinctive early characteristics of children who ultimately become schizophrenic. So far the findings suggest several conclusions (Lewine, 1984).

1. A marker, if it exists, may reflect vulnerability to psychosis in general rather than specifically to schizophrenia. When children whose parents have non-schizophrenic psychoses are included, these children also differ from normal controls.

2. Changes over time, rather than particular traits, may be the most important markers.

3. Among the children in the high-risk group, only some (11 to 14 percent) are clearly deviant.

High-risk studies are making an important contribution to knowledge about schizophrenia. However, they have an important drawback. Since only about 15 percent of all people who become schizophrenic have one or more schizophrenic parents, it may be that the data from these studies apply only to a specific subtype of schizophrenia. As is true of other research carried out on a specific population—such as college students, members of the armed forces, or relatives of hospital patients—it is not clear what general statements can be made from findings based on a particular group. However, because they focus attention on vulnerabil-

□ **TABLE 12-3**
Adult Outcomes of Israeli High-Risk Children from Town and Kibbutz

| | Diagnostic Category | | | |
| Group | Schizophrenia or Schizophrenic Spectrum Disorder | Mood Disorder | Other | No Diagnosis |
|---|---|---|---|---|
| Kibbutz high risk N = 23 | 6 | 9 | 1 | 7 |
| Town high risk N = 23 | 3 | 1 | 3 | 16 |
| Kibbutz control N = 23 | 0 | 1 | 2 | 20 |
| Town control N = 21 | 0 | 0 | 1 | 20 |

*Source:* Adapted from Mirsky and others, 1985.

ities, the results of high-risk studies may play an important role in the design of prevention programs.

## ■ UNDERSTANDING THE SCHIZOPHRENIC PROCESS

### Structural Abnormalities in the Brain

The search for structural abnormalities in the brain that are related to schizophrenia or other disordered behavior has a long history but has produced little in the way of meaningful data. New technology may make this research topic popular again. The computerized axial tomography (CT) scanner makes it possible to look at the structure of the living brain by viewing a series of x-rays of thin sections of the brain. First the patient is placed on a couch within an enclosure containing x-ray generating and detection equipment. Then a narrow x-ray beam is passed through the patient from a variety of directions. Data on the angle of the beam and the initial and final amounts of x-ray energy are stored in a computer. For each brain section, these data are used to solve a series of equations. The radiologist can then use a computer program to produce CT scan images like those in Figure 12–7.

One finding that has emerged from the use of this technique is that some schizophrenics have significantly larger **cerebral ventricles** (cavities that contain cerebrospinal fluid) than those found in the brains of nonschizophrenics (see Figure 12–7). The size of the cerebral ventricle in normal individuals is thought to increase with age. When schizophrenic patients are compared with controls of the same age, between one-quarter and one-half of the schizophrenics have significantly larger ventricles than the controls (Weinberger, 1984). This is true both for younger individuals who have a history of intermittent hospitalization and for older or chronic patients who have been hospitalized a long time. In two studies, patients with schizophrenia were found to have larger ventricles than their brothers and sisters, including monozygotic twins of the patients (Weinberger and others, 1981; Reveley and others, 1982).

A group of schizophrenic patients with ventricles that are much smaller than average has also been identified. The symptoms of this group (in which bizarre behavior, hallucinations, and delusions were prominent) differed from those of patients with unusually large ventricles (primarily flat affect, lack of ambition, and absence of pleasure) (Andreasen and others, 1982). These findings suggest that large ventricles may be related to Type I schizophrenia, which has negative symptoms, while small ventricles are related to Type II schizophrenia, which has positive symptoms. Schizophrenic individuals with large ventricles usually are not helped by antipsychotic drugs, a fact that also indicates a relationship to the Type I category (Weinberger and others, 1980). While it is too soon to be certain that ventricular enlargement is related to schizophrenic illness, the CT scan technique has provided new and possibly important information.

**FIGURE 12-7**
Various degrees of cerebral ventricular enlargement on CT scans. (from Nasrallah and Coffman, 1985, p. 240)

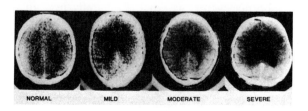

## Biochemical Abnormalities in the Brain

There are strong arguments for the assumption that biochemical factors play a role in at least some of the schizophrenias. An impetus to the search for biochemical clues has been provided by the effectiveness of some antipsychotic drugs, which are known to produce certain biochemical changes. However, most research findings that indicate biochemical differences between schizophrenic patients and control individuals have not been confirmed by later studies. For example, the blood serum of schizophrenic patients was reported to kill tadpoles that were not affected by serum taken from normal people, and the blood of catatonic schizophrenics was reported to cause spiders to build inadequate, bizarre webs. Neither of these findings has been supported by later investigations.

It is not difficult to find organic or biochemical differences between schizophrenics and control subjects. The problem lies in finding an explanation that takes account of all the possible causes of a particular result. Part of the problem is poor experimental design. Often the control group lives under very different conditions than the patient group. For example, many of the people used in earlier studies had been hospitalized for many years, led sedentary lives, ate routine hospital diets, and had been treated with various drugs; they may have been under constant stress, which also has been shown to cause biological changes. The control groups, on the other hand, consisted of college students, hospital nurses, or nonprofessional employees, whose lives obviously differed from those of the patients in many ways. The experimental findings may simply reflect these differences.

Recent research reflects a new and much more sophisticated approach to biological differences. Instead of looking for the presence of some abnormal substance that is unique to schizophrenics, investigators are looking for abnormalities in biochemical *functioning*. Because of the development of new and increasingly sensitive research techniques and the discovery of new neurochemical systems in the body, this research promises to be more productive than past efforts. Although adequate techniques for dealing with unstable, rapidly changing chemical compounds have not yet been developed and many experimental findings cannot be reproduced by other investigators, great progress has been made.

### PT Scans

A technology that may provide breakthroughs in the study of chemical activity in the living human brain is the positron emission tomography (PT) scan. This scan, which is similar to the CT scan, shows what is going on chemically inside the brain by recording radiation from a glucose-like substance injected into the individual's bloodstream. The injected material enters the brain and is used by the working brain cells, and the PT scanner records this activity in a series of thin cross sections of the brain. Initial use of this technique with psychiatric patients suggests that the PT scan can be used to distinguish among the brains of control subjects, patients who have been diagnosed as having bipolar disorders, and patients with a diagnosis of schizophrenia (see Figure 12–8). In addition, the PT scan has been used to observe changes in biochemical action in the brain caused by antipsychotic drugs.

One of the findings of research using PT scans is that people who are chronically schizophrenic tend to have a lower level of metabolism in the frontal and temporal lobes of their brains and a somewhat higher flow at the base of the skull than control subjects. When the schizophrenic patients were given psychoactive drugs, their rate of metabolism was similar to that of the control subjects except in the frontal-lobe area (Wolkin and others, 1985).

### The Dopamine Hypothesis

Just as neurotransmitters are currently thought to be important in at least some types of affective disorders, biologically oriented research on schizophrenia also stresses the importance of neurotransmitter functioning. In the affective disorders, research has centered on norepinephrine; in schizophrenia, current research focuses on dopamine. The **dopamine hypothesis,** simply stated, says that there is an excess of dopamine at certain synapses in the brain. This is thought to be due either to excess production of dopamine or to faulty regulation of the feedback apparatus by means of which the dopamine returns and is stored by vesicles in the presynaptic neuron. However, it might also be due to oversensitivity of the dopamine receptors or to the presence of too many receptors.

The idea that dopamine is involved in schizophrenia comes from two sources. One is the finding that large doses of amphetamine are capable of producing behavior that is very similar to the behavior typical of paranoid schizophrenics in individuals with no history of psychological difficulties. Even more important, low doses of amphetamines make the symptoms of some schizophrenic individuals worse. Biochemically, amphetamines increase the amounts of both the catecholamines, dopamine and norepinephrine, that are present at the synapse.

The second reason to suspect that dopamine is involved comes from knowledge of the effects of the antipsychotic drugs used to treat schizophrenia. The effectiveness of the drugs in reducing psychotic symptoms is directly related to their effectiveness at binding

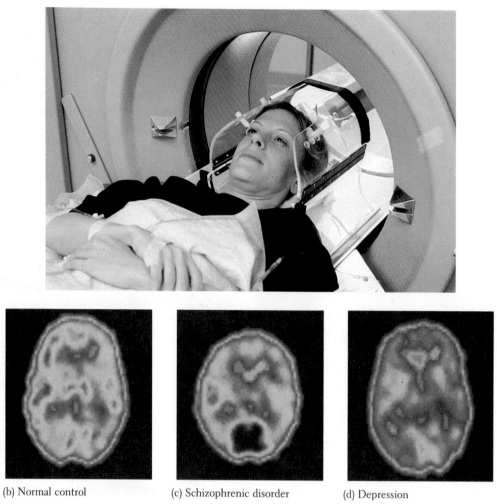

(b) Normal control    (c) Schizophrenic disorder    (d) Depression

**FIGURE 12-8**
PT scan photos show brain metabolism and function. Photo (a) shows how a patient is prepared for a PT scan. (National Institute of Health) Photo (b) shows the brain of a normal individual. Photos (c) and (d) show PT scans of individuals with schizophrenia, and depression, respectively. (Brookhaven National Laboratories)

(or blocking) postsynaptic dopamine receptors (Creese and others, 1976). The story cannot be as simple as this, however, because antipsychotic drugs typically do not produce a quick behavioral improvement; instead, they produce a gradual improvement over a period of about six weeks. This suggests that the biochemistry of schizophrenia is more complicated than the dopamine hypothesis suggests. What appears to happen is that initially the blockage of the dopamine receptor results in feedback that increases the activity of the dopamine neurons in the midbrain. However, after some time the neurons are firing so quickly that their effectiveness is actually decreased (Paul, 1985).

Although most of the research on dopamine has been done with animals, studies of the brains of patients who have died have shown that treatment with antipsychotic drugs is related to an increase in the number of dopamine receptors (Lee and others, 1978). It is also possible to measure changes in dopamine activity by measuring the amount of a chemically related product, homovanillic acid, in the blood (Pickar and others, 1984). In addition, dopamine receptors can now be identified by PT scans; this may provide another way of investigating the dopamine hypothesis (Wagner and others, 1983).

## Psychophysiological Abnormalities

The study of the psychophysiology of behavior concentrates on the relationship between behavior and variations in the functioning of the central and peripheral nervous systems, as well as on the ways in which these systems mediate the responses of other systems (for example, the cardiovascular system). Psychophysiological measurement includes methods of recording and processing bioelectric signals from the surface of the skin.

Psychophysiological responses can be studied using a variety of techniques, including measures of the electrical conductance of the skin, analysis of brain wave patterns by means of an electroencephalograph, and analysis of heart rate by means of an electrocardiograph. But researchers in this area still face many technical problems. For example, some measures of nervous system activity are especially sensitive to the drugs used to treat schizophrenic patients. Since many patients are started on these drugs when they first come to clinical attention, untreated patients are rare. In addition, it is not yet known whether differences in psychophysiological response between schizophrenics and controls are due to the underlying biology of the schizophrenic person or to the effects of being a patient.

Psychophysiological experimentation was formerly very tedious and time-consuming because the responses were recorded as tracings on polygraph paper, which had to be analyzed by hand. Today computers not only can present a complex series of visual or auditory stimuli but can convert the subject's responses from wiggly lines into numbers that can be analyzed using sophisticated computer programs. Under these conditions, research on psychophysiological responses has grown rapidly.

**Brain Electrical Activity Mapping**  One new technique, brain electrical activity mapping (BEAM), summarizes EEG and evoked electrical potential in the form of color maps (see Figure 12–9). In one study, schizophrenic subjects had more slow wave activity (delta waves), especially in their frontal brain regions, than controls (Morihisa and others, 1983). This response may be an indication of overarousal. The unusually high level of delta waves can be corrected by antipsychotic medication and has been reproduced in normal individuals by giving them the psychomimetic drug LSD-25 (Itil and others, 1974; Itil, 1977). The BEAM technique may provide another way to identify markers of vulnerability to schizophrenia.

**The Orienting Response**  The **orienting response** is defined by psychophysiological changes that occur when the person notices and is prepared to receive some information from the environment. The frequency and size of the orienting response and the time needed to return to one's normal attention level are the most frequent measures used. Over a series of trials, the size of the orienting response in most people de-

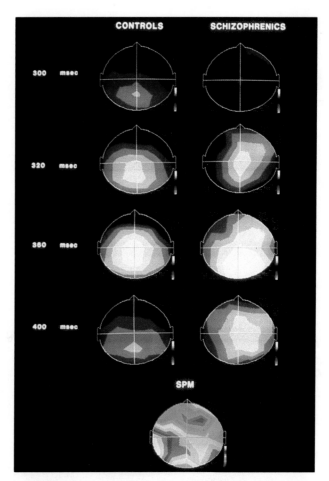

**FIGURE 12-9**
Brain electrical activity mapping (BEAM) provides a new way of studying electrical activity in the brain. The left column shows the average activity at 4 time intervals for 10 control (normal) subjects. The right hand column represents the averaged data of 10 schizophrenic subjects. In all these records, the lowest level of activity is represented by blue, with higher values represented by yellow, red, and white in that order. The single record at the bottom center illustrates the differences between the control and schizophrenic groups. Blue represents the smallest difference and white the greatest. (Archives of General Psychiatry)

creases or *habituates*. Most studies of individuals who have been diagnosed as schizophrenic have shown that about half of them are more responsive to stimuli than normal subjects while the other half do not respond. Moreover, among those who do respond, most fail to habituate; that is, their responses stay at an elevated level after many stimulus presentations (Rubens and Lapidus, 1978).

Research using animals suggests that the limbic system controls the orienting response. Researchers have noticed that schizophrenic individuals who give orienting responses show higher-amplitude responses with the right hand than with the left hand. Because of what is known about how the two hemispheres of the brain control behavior, this finding suggests that the problem may lie in the limbic area of the left hemisphere of the brain (Venables, 1979). This focus on the left brain hemisphere is supported by data from the intelligence test performance of schizophrenic individuals. Their ability on verbal tests (which is thought to be controlled by the left hemisphere of the brain) is more impaired than their ability on performance tests (which is related to right-hemisphere activity). Although these ideas about left-hemisphere dysfunction are highly speculative at present, they are supported by a reasonable amount of research data and clearly deserve further investigation.

## Attention

Anyone who has contact with schizophrenics is struck by their attentional deficits. Kraepelin had noted that schizophrenics lose both the inclination and the initiative to keep their attention fixed for any length of time. A great deal of psychophysiological research has focused on understanding these attentional problems.

**Eye Movements**   One way of studying schizophrenics' responses to external stimulation is through the study of eye movements. Two kinds of eye movements have been studied. **Saccadic movements,** which are under voluntary control, are quick jerks with steady fixations. **Smooth-pursuit movements,** which, strictly speaking, are not voluntary, occur when a person tracks a moving target such as a pendulum. Saccadic movements are so complex and sensitive to outside distractions that researchers have been frustrated in trying to study them. Smooth-pursuit movements, however, occur only when a person tracks a slowly moving target, and they cannot be faked. About 85 percent of schizophrenics show abnormal patterns of smooth-pursuit movements (Siever and Coursey, 1985). Figure 12–10 illustrates this difference between normal and schizophrenic individuals. About 50 percent of close relatives of schizophrenics also show this deviant pattern, but only 13 percent of relatives of other types of patients do (Holzman and others, 1984). Deviant tracking patterns also have been shown by people who have bipolar disorders, brain lesions, brain damage, and some drug intoxications. In a study of college students, poor trackers were likely to have at least two of the four characteristics of schizotypal personality disorder and also showed interpersonal difficulties, especially remoteness, and neurological impairment (Siever and Coursey, 1985).

The smooth-pursuit performance of both schizo-

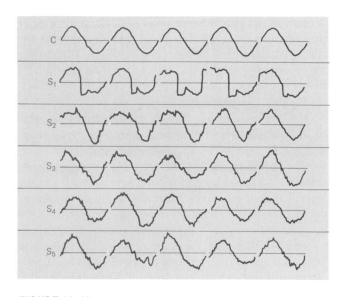

**FIGURE 12-10**
Samples of visual tracking performance by a control subject (C) and five patients with schizophrenia (S1–S5). (The target transcribed 20 degrees of visual arc; each cycle represents 2.5 sec of performance.) (Iacono and Koenig, 1983, p. 39)

phrenic and normal subjects can be improved by placing numbers on a pendulum and requiring that the numbers be read as the pendulum revolves during its swing (Shagass and others, 1976). Although the schizophrenics' deviant tracking patterns can be modified by altering the task conditions, even under the new conditions the schizophrenics' performance is not at the same level as that of controls.

**The Continuous Performance Test**   The Continuous Performance Test (Rosvold and others, 1956) measures sustained visual attention for periods of up to 20 minutes. The subject is exposed to a series of different stimuli after he or she has been instructed to respond to one particular type of stimulus by pressing a key. Schizophrenic individuals make more errors both by pressing the button for the wrong stimulus and by not pressing the button when it would have been correct to do so. This poor performance may be related to a dysfunction in the ascending reticular system in the brain stem (Mirsky and Bakay Pragay, 1984).

Children of schizophrenic mothers who were part of a high-risk study also scored more poorly on the continuous-performance task than either children of mothers with other disorders or other children in their classrooms (Nuechterlein, 1983). It appears that a general measure made up of tasks measuring attention may be a useful marker in high-risk groups. In one high-risk study, among children with a schizophrenic parent those children who scored poorly on measures of attention were most likely to show behavioral difficulties in adulthood that might be early signs of schizophrenia (Cornblatt and Erlenmeyer-Kimling, 1985).

## Cognitive Functioning

**Memory** People with schizophrenic disorders seem to have a relatively intact network of information in long-term memory. Problems arise when they are asked to recall the material. For example, their recall of previously learned information is poor, but their *recognition* of the same information is much better and in some cases may be comparable to or even the same as the performance of a control group. Figure 12–11 shows that even chronic schizophrenic patients who are hospitalized show much less of a difference from control subjects when recognition rather than recall is used as a measure (Calev, 1984).

Studies of long-term memory suggest that the problems of thinking that occur in schizophrenia may not be due to difficulty in filtering stimuli (as was suggested by the observations of former schizophrenic patients in Chapter 11) or to the problems of attention discussed earlier. Instead, the problem seems to be one of coding the material in the memory system so that it can be found and used again when appropriate (Schwartz, 1982). Some schizophrenic individuals also have problems with short-term memory (George and Neufeld, 1985). These seem to be related to failure to use the kinds of active rehearsal processes that most people use to remember such things as telephone numbers between the time of looking them up and dialing the telephone. In general, however, most cognitive researchers believe that the cognitive deficits of schizophrenics are more likely to occur on the output side in recalling and reproducing the material rather than in originally perceiving it (Grove and Andreasen, 1985).

Research on memory can also help us understand delusions, a form of disturbed thinking that is found most frequently in paranoid schizophrenics. When paranoid, nonparanoid, and normal control subjects were tested on their processing of information for short- and long-term storage in memory, the normal subjects had the highest scores and the paranoid group the lowest (Broga and Neufeld, 1981). At the same time, although they remembered less of the actual material, the paranoid group was the most likely to draw broad, general conclusions from the material. They seemed to evaluate the situation incorrectly largely because they were depending on their own rigid cognitive system for information instead of processing the new material itself. Paranoid thinking is very similar to a "jump-to-conclusions" response style.

**Disordered Thinking** Although schizophrenia is often described as thought disorder, disordered thinking is not unique to schizophrenia. Disordered thinking is part of a continuum that includes normal thinking. In one study, a number of groups were compared by means of tape recordings of their verbalizations on an intelligence test (the Wechsler Adult Intelligence Scale) and a personality test (the Rorschach). The responses were all rated on a thought disorder index. Mildly peculiar responses were given a low weight, loose associations and queer responses a moderate weight, and confusion and other serious disturbances a high weight. Although schizophrenics had the highest score, no group was entirely free from thought disorders (see Figure 12–12). Of special interest was the finding that parents of schizophrenic patients showed more disordered thinking than parents of nonschizophrenic patients (Johnson and Holzman, 1979).

Researchers have attempted to determine whether thought disorder is a permanent trait of people with schizophrenia or whether it is a symptom of acute psychosis. Disordered thinking accompanies acute psychotic episodes in mania as well as in schizophrenia (Andreasen, 1979). However, some degree of disordered thought may be a permanent characteristic of people who are schizophrenic and may show up long before other signs of the disorder appear. For instance, in the Danish high-risk study of children of severely schizophrenic mothers, a significantly larger percent of

**FIGURE 12–11**
Mean performance on recall and recognition for 10 schizophrenics and 10 control subjects. (from A. Calev (1984) Recall and recognition in chronic nondemented schizophrenics, *Journal of Abnormal Psychology, 93,* 172–177. Copyright (c) 1984 by the American Psychological Association. Reprinted by permission of the author.

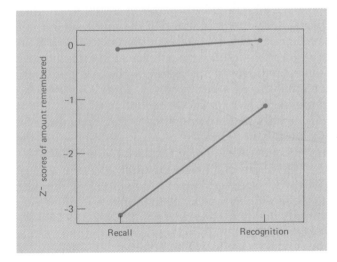

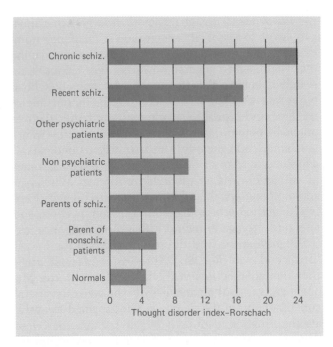

**FIGURE 12-12**
Mean Thought Disorder Index of several groups of subjects. Schizophrenic individuals have the highest level; normal subjects have the lowest level. (Holzman, 1978, p. 369)

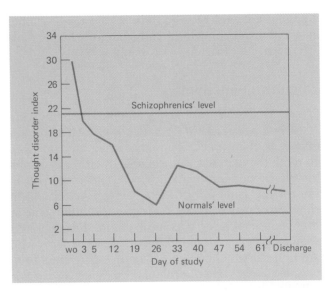

**FIGURE 12-13**
Mean Thought Disorder Index of 18 schizophrenic patients during their hospital stays. Effects of antipsychotic medications appear quickly and the index reaches a stable level that is higher than the level for normal individuals (W.O. = end of drug-free wash-out period to remove effects of previous medication). (Holzman, 1978, p. 367)

children who later developed one of the schizophrenic spectrum disorders had shown cognitive disturbance when they were tested at age 15 compared to the control subjects (Parnas and others, 1982).

A measure of thought disorder can be useful in assessing the effects of antipsychotic medication. For example, in one study, the responses of schizophrenic patients were evaluated on a thought disorder index before the patients began drug treatment and then again several times during the treatment. The results showed that thought disorder as measured by the index dropped dramatically (see Figure 12–13). The maximum effect was reached in about three weeks, after which a relatively stable level was maintained. This suggests that the drug therapy was effective in maintaining better cognitive performance, although it is important to note that there was a limit to the effectiveness of the treatment. The level of disordered thinking shown by the schizophrenic patients remained higher than that of nonschizophrenic individuals. At least a subgroup of schizophrenics continue to show bizarre and idiosyncratic speech even after their condition improves (Harrow and others, 1983).

## Language

The speech of some schizophrenic individuals is difficult to follow, but this does not seem to be due to lack of knowledge of grammatical rules. What is per-

ceived as abnormal seems to lie in the thought communicated by the speech, not in the language used in the communication.

Schizophrenic speech has been described as disruptive by normal listeners. In addition to making inappropriate responses, the schizophrenic individual often fails to provide necessary information, uses ambiguous phrases, and omits logical links between sentences (Rutter, 1985). One way in which the disordered speech of manic phase bipolar patients can be distinguished from that of schizophrenics is by the presence of these cohesive links: Manics have them; schizophrenics don't. Clinicians often intuitively think they can understand the disordered speech in mania better than that in schizophrenia, and that the difference can aid in diagnosis. However, under experimental conditions a group of clinicians were not able to use this intuitive approach to separate patients into the correct diagnostic groups using speech samples alone. After the clinicians were given a short description of the sorts of ties or links that are absent in schizophrenic speech, their ability to use a speech sample to differentiate the patients improved dramatically (Wykes, 1981).

By experimentally studying various aspects of schizophrenics' language, cognitive theorists look for clues to the specific ways in which schizophrenics differ from controls and how conditions can be varied to improve schizophrenics' performance. Through these procedures, they hope to obtain a better understanding of the thought processes that characterize schizophrenia.

## Family Relationships

One source of stress that may interact with a person's vulnerability to schizophrenia may be created by profoundly frustrating interpersonal relationships during the early years of life, accompanied by a lack of emotional ties to people. The schizophrenic seems to go through life with no expectation of support and warmth from the social environment. He or she regards other people as uninterested or critical. The drawing shown in Figure 12–14 conveys some of these feelings. Research on high-risk children points to some markers related to family environment that may increase the stress experienced by children.

## Family Communication Deviance

**Communication deviance** refers to the inability of the parent or parents to maintain a shared focus of attention during interactions with another person. Cross-sectional studies have shown that high communication deviance is associated with schizophrenia in the children of such parents (Wynne and others, 1977). However, some of the research on communication deviance

has raised questions about the meaning of the findings. One study found that analysis of the Rorschach test results of adoptive parents as well as those of biological parents could be used to predict which parents had schizophrenic children (Wynne and others, 1977). This suggests that parental communication in families of schizophrenic children can be reliably identified and that such communication occurs whether or not there are biological parent-child relationships. Other investigators have used laboratory tasks such as a 20-questions game or other problem-solving tasks in which family members participate together. In at least one study, the parents' communication problems seemed to be a response to unclear communications from the children (Liem, 1974).

One way to understand the causes and effects of communication problems is through long-term prospective studies. In the high-risk study carried out at the University of California at Los Angeles, the participating families each contained a mild to moderately disturbed teenage member (Goldstein, 1985). All of the families had contacted the university-based psychological clinic for help. At the time that they were originally seen, the parents were given the Thematic Apperception Test, which was scored for communication deviance. Fifteen years later the children were rediagnosed and grouped according to the original assessment of parental deviance. The number of cases of schizophrenia and schizophrenic spectrum disorders was clearly related to the earlier assessments of communication deviance (see Figure 12–15). Fifty percent of the children in the families with high communication deviance had a diagnosis in the schizophrenic spectrum, compared

**FIGURE 12–14**
This drawing depicts the isolation felt by a 25-year-old schizophrenic patient. (UPI/Bettmann Newsphotos)

**FIGURE 12–15**
When families were divided into three levels of communication deviance (CD), the number of children who were diagnosed as having a schizophrenic spectrum disorder was clearly different for each type of family. (adapted from Goldstein, 1985, p. 12)

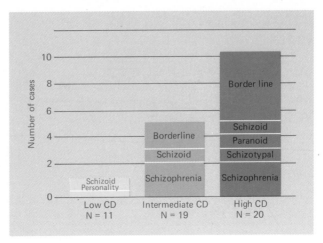

to 26 percent in the intermediate families and 9 percent in the low-deviance families.

### Expressed Emotion and Negative Affective Style

In addition to how clearly families communicate, the emotional impact of what they communicate is important. **Expressed emotion** is a measure of the attitudes of criticism or emotional overinvolvement expressed by family members when talking about the person whose behavior is disturbed (Vaughn and Leff, 1976). Negative expressed emotion includes criticism, hostility, and emotional overinvolvement (exaggerated emotional response to the illness or extreme protectiveness). Relatives who were rated high in expressed emotion made remarks like the following.

> *I always say, "why don't you pick up a book, do a crossword or something like that to keep your mind off it." That's even too much trouble.*
>
> *I've tried to jolly him out of it and pestered him into doing things. Maybe I've overdone it, I don't know.*
>
> *He went round the garden 90 times, in the door, back out the door. I said "Have a chair, sit out in the sun." Well, he nearly bit my head off. (Hooley, 1985, p. 134)*

Relatives who were low in expressed emotion were likely to make very different comments.

> *I know it's better for her to be on her own, to get away from me and try to do things on her own.*
>
> *Whatever she does suits me.*
>
> *I just tend to let it go because I know that when she wants to speak she will speak. (ibid.)*

As noted in the preceding chapter, whatever the role of the family in precipitating the initial schizophrenic behavior, the family environment may be important in a former patient's chances of recovering from a schizophrenic episode and staying out of the hospital. Criticism, hostility, and overinvolvement on the part of family members have been shown to be related to the frequency of relapse and rehospitalization (Vaughn and Leff, 1976). Patients who returned to families who were high in expressed emotion were not likely to stay out of the hospital as long as patients whose families were less critical. This was true whether or not the patient was also taking antipsychotic drugs (Vaughn and Leff, 1976; Leff and Vaughn, 1981) (see Figure 12–16). Studies carried out in England and Los Angeles produced similar results (Vaughn and others, 1984).

**Parental affective style** is measured in directly observed interactions when family members are discussing problems that tend to upset the family. (Expressed emotion is measured when a family member talks about

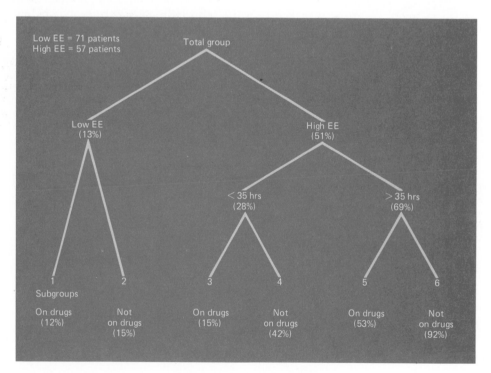

**FIGURE 12–16**
The relapse rates (after nine months) of 128 schizophrenic patients grouped by whether their families were high or low in expressed emotion (EE) and whether or not the patient was taking antipsychotic drugs. From C. E. Vaughn and J. P. Leff, 1976, *British Journal of Psychiatry, 129*, p. 132. Copyright (c) 1976 by *The British Journal of Psychiatry*. Reprinted by permission.

the patient to someone else.) Although negative expressed emotion and negative parental affective style may coexist in many individuals, they are not perfectly correlated. In the UCLA research project described earlier, analysis of the interactions of parents and children showed a complex pattern when the affective style of the parent pairs was studied (Valone and others, 1983).

Figure 12-17 shows that when the parents interact with each other, their behavior is modified by this interaction. When one parent was high and one low in expressed emotion, the criticisms directed at the child tended to be less harsh. The presence of the parent who was low in expressed emotion seemed to temper the criticisms made by the other parent. Overall, the number of harsh criticisms for this mixed pair did not differ from the number for parents who were both low in expressed emotion. The adolescent child's manner in reacting to the parent and the kinds of problems for which the family had come to the clinic also were not related to the parents' expressed emotion levels. This suggests that a parent's level of expressed emotion may be a stable characteristic and not simply a reaction to a child who exhibits problem behaviors.

When both parents were high in expressed emotion, the family interaction was also more emotional (as measured by electrical skin conductance) than when the parents were low or mixed in expressed emotion (Valone and others, 1984). This arousal was shown not only by both parents but also by the adolescent child, who seemed most aroused when anticipating what the parents' next comments would be. This high level of arousal shows that families with high levels of ex-

pressed emotion experience a great deal of stress in their interactions.

**Disturbed Family Interactions**  In the 1950s the popularity of psychoanalytic theory prompted researchers to extend their interest in family–child relationships to their possible role in the development of schizophrenia. Two concepts that were used to characterize the marriage of parents of a schizophrenic child were marital schism and marital skew (Lidz and others, 1965). **Marital schism** is an overt conflict in which each parent tries to enlist the child as an ally against the other parent. In **marital skew,** one dominant parent shows serious psychopathology that the other parent passively accepts. These concepts tie in to the observation that schizophrenics tend to choose mates who have some type of maladjustment (Parnas, 1985). Both sorts of marriages would be highly stressful for children, and such families might act as transmitters of irrationality: The children grow up seeing their parents' daily denials and distortions of reality and learn to accept them as normal. In a high-risk study carried out at St. Louis University, the skew factor contributed very highly to accurate prediction of later psychopathology, but the schism factor did not aid in prediction (Altman, 1980).

Like other research of this type, these studies raise the question of why some children of these marriages do not become schizophrenic and whether families in which there are no schizophrenic offspring might also show some very deviant characteristics if they were studied closely. The humanistic–existentialist psychiatrist R. D. Laing has examined some cases that have led him to believe that what seem to be psychotic symptoms are actually the person's attempt to adapt to the "insane" situation in his or her family. The following case is an example (Laing, 1964).

**FIGURE 12-17**
Expressions of affective style by parents grouped by their expressed emotion (EE).

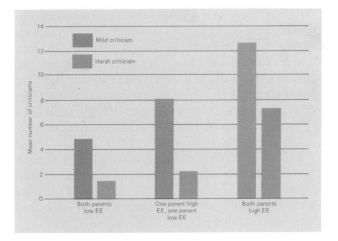

*Maya Abbott was an only child who, at 28, had spent 9 of her last 19 years in a hospital. Her diagnosis was paranoid schizophrenia. She had lived with her parents until she was 8, when she was evacuated to a rural area because of bombing danger during World War II. Laing set out to determine whether Abbott's auditory and visual hallucinations, occasional catatonia, withdrawal, feelings of being controlled by others, and decreased emotional expression could be made intelligible through an understanding of her family situation.*

*He concluded that Abbott's parents were upset by her efforts to behave independently. They contrasted her closeness, especially to her father, before she was evacuated from the city at age 8, with her desire for independence when she returned at age 14. What seemed to Laing to be the normal signs of growing up were interpreted by the parents as the first signs of illness.*

*"She wanted to study. She did not want to go swimming, or to go for long walks with her father any more. She no longer wanted to pray with him. She wanted to read the Bible herself, by herself. She objected to her father expressing his affection for her by sitting close to her at meals. She wanted to sit further away from him. Nor did she want to go to the cinema with her mother. In the house, she wanted to handle things and do things for herself, such as washing a mirror without first telling her mother"* (Laing, 1964, p. 18).

*Abbott also had paranoid ideas that people were talking about her. In the interviews, it became clear that her parents did talk about her to each other and to neighbors, and then denied that they had been speaking about her if she overheard them and asked about it. They also developed a nonverbal code of facial grimaces and gestures that they used to communicate with each other in Abbott's presence. Yet when she asked about this obvious behavior, they denied it as well. Abbott began to "mistrust her own mistrust." Believing her parents, she could not believe that what she thought she saw was going on.*

In Abbott's case and others, Laing found that the patient's behavior made sense in terms of the family's interactions and that in many cases its origin was not pathological but was in fact a rational response to an irrational situation. In Laing's view, the preschizophrenic copes with an undesirable family environment by denying its pathological features. The development of the psychotic behavior takes place when the defense of denial is abandoned. The psychotic behavior appears pathological only to people who are unaware of the environment that gave rise to it.

## The Role of the Community

More than 50 studies conducted in Canada, Denmark, Finland, Great Britain, Norway, Sweden, and Taiwan, as well as in the United States, have found that lower-class people are diagnosed as schizophrenic more frequently than people from the middle or upper classes. However, no one has been able to discover why social class is related to schizophrenia. Two theories—social selection and the social-causation or increased-stress theory—have been used to explain the greater incidence of schizophrenia among lower-class individuals. The **social-selection theory** assumes that people who cannot make it in society gradually become part of the lower class because of their poor coping skills, in contrast to the idea that people who experience the stress of lower-class living develop poor coping skills. A re-

view of research on the community and interpersonal functioning of people who have had a schizophrenic disorder shows that in at least one subgroup, poor functioning in these areas can be found before the disorder is noticed (Wallace, 1984). Poor functioning also is related to poor outcome after the disorder has been diagnosed. This means that, for at least some people, poor social functioning may be a marker of vulnerability to schizophrenia.

Whereas the social-selection theory points to flaws in the individual as the cause of schizophrenia, an alternative explanation for the greater incidence of schizophrenia in the lower class points to flaws in the society itself. The **increased-stress theory** refers to the amount of stress experienced by people in different socioeconomic classes. Living in areas with high crime rates, run-down housing, and inadequate schools may be more difficult and stressful than living in more affluent areas. At the same time, lower-class people have little money or power to cope with the stresses they encounter. Thus, in a study of schizophrenics and matched controls who lived in conditions of terrible poverty in the slums of San Juan, Puerto Rico, it was found that, although all the participants could be said to live under great stress according to the usual standards, those who were schizophrenic had experienced greater stress than the control group in the period before their symptoms became obvious (Rogler and Hollingshead, 1965).

High density, or the presence of a large number of people in a living unit or neighborhood, has often been thought to be related to psychopathology. However, a recent analysis of the living conditions of people who were admitted for the first time to mental hospitals in Chicago in the years 1960 and 1961 showed that, after differences in socioeconomic status and racial differences were taken into account, most of the cases came from areas where there were both a higher proportion of people living alone and a low population density (Magaziner, 1980).

It may seem that people who are vulnerable to schizophrenia often choose to live alone because they find personal interactions stressful. However, living alone may be a disadvantage in a crisis. People who live alone lack the social interaction and supports that give meaning to life. They also lack input and structure in their daily affairs, and this may lead to withdrawal from others and too much concentration on personal problems (Gove and Hughes, 1980).

This chapter has discussed what is known about schizophrenia, drawing upon research based on a variety of perspectives. Box 12–2 illustrates how focusing on a unique group of people from several perspectives can produce a fuller picture of schizophrenic disorders.

## ■ BOX 12-2 INVESTIGATING A SINGLE CASE FROM A VARIETY OF PERSPECTIVES

Investigation of schizophrenic behavior from several perspectives can help in understanding both the disorder and its symptoms. The case of the Genain sisters illustrates how investigations of heredity, brain anatomy and activity, psychophysiological measures, and family interactions can complement one another.

The sisters who were identical quadruplets, shared the same heredity. Because the odds for identical quadruplets are one in 16 million births, they became celebrities in their home town. During their childhood, they performed song and dance routines and were so popular that they had a police escort on one early local tour. As they grew older, however, it became clear that they were not developing in a normal way. One sister dropped out of high school. The other three graduated but had trouble holding jobs. During their 20s, all four sisters developed schizophrenic disorders.

Because of the uniqueness of this case (four individuals with identical heredity who all showed schizophrenic behavior could be expected to occur only once in tens of billions of births), a local physician alerted scientists at the National Institute of Mental Health. The sisters came to Washington, D.C., and were hospitalized there for intensive study. During the three years that they spent at NIMH, they were examined from a number of perspectives. To protect their privacy, the sisters were given pseudonyms corresponding to NIMH's initials—Nora, Iris, Myra, and Hester—and the family was given the name Genain, from the Greek words meaning "dire birth."

Several of the quadruplets' family members had histories of psychological problems. Not only was their father's behavior often bizarre, but his brother, his mother, and his paternal uncle had each had a nervous breakdown sometime in the past.

Even though they were genetically identical and may all have had the same hereditary risk factor, the sisters' schizophrenia could have been at least partly the result of environmental factors. For example, as is usual in multiple births, they were all small at birth. All of them spent time in incubators and did not go home from the hospital until they were six weeks old. They grew up in the glare of publicity and constantly heard comments about their similarity. Their father restricted their interactions with other people by refusing to allow them to play with other children or, later, to take part in school activities or to date.

The girls' father also objected to their stay at NIMH and often threatened to take them out of the hospital. Although he was cooperative and cordial at times, he also had considerable hostility toward

people. His wife reported that he had tried to choke her several times and said that she had considered leaving him. At times, he accused his wife of having sexual relationships with his daughters' psychiatrists. During the quadruplets' third year at the hospital, he died.

The following report, which reflects the psychodynamic perspective, describes the family relationships in more detail:

Mrs. Genain's unfulfilled needs for maternal nurturing found expression in her closeness to Nora. It was the symbiotic tie of mother and infant, one in which the mother does not see the infant as a separate individual but as part of herself. . . . In her adult psychosis, she [Nora] caricatured her mother's friendly facade and stereotyped sweetness. The closeness between them supported a report that Nora was not only her father's "favorite," but her mother's also. The earliest evidence for this was that Nora was always the first of the babies to be burped after feeding. The most recent evidence was that Nora was the daughter Mrs. Genain took home for trial visits from the hospital, although Iris' adjustment was also appropriate for home visits.

The central role for Myra was the "independent positive." Mrs. Genain identified Myra with her own independent strivings and actions. . . . Myra was the daughter upon whom Mrs. Genain was prone to lean in times of stress, who often strove for the favored position (which in this family was the protected one) with her mother. . . . She tried to live out the role her mother assigned to her of becoming independent, and the dependent–independent conflict became acute for her when she tried to move out on her own.

The central theme of the role Mrs. Genain assigned to Iris was the "repressed" one. She identified in Iris her own feeling that she must put up with anything and in her psychosis, Iris caricatured this aspect of her mother's personality. Later, when she improved, she made occasional sarcastic remarks to her mother which Mrs. Genain described as being like Iris' prepsychotic behavior and as being hostile to her. . . . In areas that concerned Iris as an individual, e.g., her abilities and appearance, Mrs. Genain was neither concerned nor interested.

The central theme assigned to Hester was the "negative" one. It was as though Hester personified that which Mrs. Genain regarded as undesirable—hostility and sexuality, for example. The perception of these feelings in Hester appeared to have blocked her mother's perception of other human qualities in her. She was the last to be regarded as sick (she had been "bad") and she was not hospitalized before coming to the Clinical Center. Later

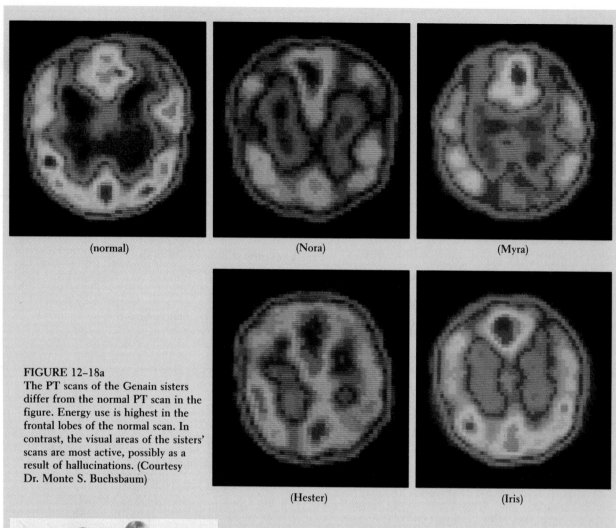

(normal)       (Nora)       (Myra)

(Hester)       (Iris)

**FIGURE 12–18a**
The PT scans of the Genain sisters differ from the normal PT scan in the figure. Energy use is highest in the frontal lobes of the normal scan. In contrast, the visual areas of the sisters' scans are most active, possibly as a result of hallucinations. (Courtesy Dr. Monte S. Buchsbaum)

**FIGURE 12–18b**
The Genain sisters as young children. (Courtesy Dr. Monte S. Buchsbaum)

Mrs. Genain did not even consider a time when Hester might come for home visits from the hospital. Hester had the end position on the continuum. (Rosenthal, 1963, pp. 463–465)

Twenty years after the Genains had first been studied at NIMH, they were invited back for a fol-low-up. During that period Myra had lived the most normal life. She went to business college and later worked as a secretary. She was the only one of the four sisters to marry and have children. Nora was next best in adjustment. She had worked at least seven years, at least partly in government training programs. Hester and Iris had each spent at least 15 years in hospitals and had received more antipsychotic drug treatment than either Myra or Nora.

Researchers wondered whether scanning techniques, developed after the early study of the sisters, could shed light on the differences in their behavior. The sisters' CT scans appeared normal, but their PT scans, made when the women were resting, showed activity in the visual areas (see Figure 12–18). Scientists wondered whether this was an indication of hallucinations. The PT scans of Myra and Nora, the two sisters who had made the best adjustment, were closer to the normal PT scans than those of the two sisters whose behavior was less adaptive. The Genains also showed much less alpha brain wave activity than is normal. Since alpha waves appear when people relax or let their minds go blank, the low frequency of alpha waves may also suggest hallucinations. These findings, when matched with the sisters' behavioral histories and with the earlier test data, may prove a help in relating specific behaviors with environmental factors and biological functioning.

# ■ STUDY OUTLINE

## GENETIC FACTORS

1. The more genes two individuals have in common, the higher the risk of a schizophrenic disorder for one when the other has such a disorder. The siblings and children of schizophrenic individuals seem to have a higher risk of becoming schizophrenic than the parents of those individuals.

2. Twin studies have found that monozygotic twins have a greater chance of being concordant for schizophrenia than dizygotic twins, but the concordance is less than 100 percent. This suggests that environmental variables interact with inherited predispositions to produce schizophrenia.

3. Adoption studies have found that children of schizophrenic parents who are given up for adoption are more likely to develop schizophrenia than adopted children whose biological parents had no psychiatric history. This is true even when children are raised by schizophrenic adoptive parents.

4. **Monogenic models** are based on the idea that genetic transmission at one locus is all that is necessary to produce a particular characteristic. Such models are not adequate to explain the transmission of schizophrenia. **Polygenic models** assume that a number of genes found at specific locations must interact to produce a trait. **Multifactorial polygenic models** assume that there are many gene loci involved in schizophrenia and that genes at all of these loci may have small additive effects on a person's vulnerability to schizophrenia.

## VULNERABILITY/STRESS FACTORS

Joseph Zubin has suggested that every individual has a certain level of vulnerability to schizophrenia, which is determined by genetic inheritance and pre- and postnatal physical factors, interacting with stressful events or conditions in the person's life. If a certain critical level is passed, schizophrenic behavior will occur. In this view, schizophrenia is an episodic disorder; it may come and go depending on the amount of stress in the individual's environment.

## HIGH-RISK STUDIES

High-risk studies focus on groups that are thought to have a higher risk of schizophrenia than the general population. One such group consists of children with at least one schizophrenic parent. Studies of such children support a vulnerability view of schizophrenia: They find that complications at birth and difficult living conditions in childhood are related to the incidence of schizophrenia in children of schizophrenic parents.

## UNDERSTANDING THE SCHIZOPHRENIC PROCESS

1. CT scans have found that some schizophrenics have significantly larger **cerebral ventricles** than non-schizophrenics, while others have much smaller than average ventricles. The symptoms of the two groups differ and appear to be related to the differences between Type I and Type II schizophrenia.

2. Efforts to link schizophrenia with the presence of abnormal substances in the brain have had little success, partly because of poor experimental design. Today researchers are looking for abnormalities in biochemical functioning, aided by the development of new techniques like the PT scan. The **dopamine hypothesis** states that there is an excess of dopamine at certain synapses in the brain. The effectiveness of antipsychotic drugs is related to their effectiveness at blocking postsynaptic dopamine receptors.

3. The study of psychophysiological responses uses such techniques as **brain electrical activity mapping** and measurement of the **orienting response**. This research has found differences between schizophrenic

and nonschizophrenic patients that may serve as **markers** of vulnerability to the disorder.

4. The study of schizophrenics' responses to external stimulation focuses on eye movements. Schizophrenic individuals have been found to have more difficulty than normal individuals in tracking a moving target such as a pendulum. They also make more errors on the Continuous Performance Test, which involves responding to specific visual stimuli by pressing a key.

5. Studies of cognitive functioning in schizophrenics have found that people with schizophrenic disorders have difficulty *recalling* material from long-term memory, although they can *recognize* the same information reasonably well. Some schizophrenic individuals also have problems with short-term memory.

6. Although disordered thinking occurs in other disorders besides schizophrenia, it appears that some degree of disordered thought may be a permanent characteristic of people who are schizophrenic and may show up before other signs of the disorder appear.

7. High **communication deviance** (inability to maintain a shared focus of attention during interactions) in parents appears to be associated with schizophrenia in their children. However, the parents' communication problems could be a response to unclear communications from the children.

8. Such factors as **expressed emotion, parental affective style,** and disturbed family interactions appear to play a role in the development of schizophrenia and in the chance that a former patient will recover from a schizophrenic episode. R. D. Laing believes that what seems to be psychotic symptoms are actually attempts to adapt to an "insane" family situation.

9. Two theories attempt to explain the greater incidence of schizophrenia in the lower class than in the middle and upper classes. The **social-selection theory** assumes that people with poor coping skills (who are more vulnerable to schizophrenia) gradually become part of the lower class. The **increased-stress theory** holds that living in poor areas may be more stressful than living in more affluent areas (and thus increases vulnerability to schizophrenia).

# 13

# BRAIN DISORDERS AND CHANGES RELATED TO AGING

*Ann Martin used to have an enviable memory. Now, at age 58, she forgets recent events and shows poor judgment. (She recently threw out a pair of valuable sterling silver salt and pepper shakers.) Because she can no longer balance her household budget, plan her meals, and take care of herself in other ways, she now lives in a retirement home, even though she is still relatively young.*

*Martin's condition was diagnosed as Alzheimer's disease, which is caused by physical degeneration in the brain. Alzheimer's disease results in loss of intellectual ability and changes in personality and behavior.*

*Robert Case had a long history of alcoholism. His drinking binges followed a fairly regular course, as did his drying-out periods. Beginning at about 40 years of age, something new, a progressive memory impairment, entered the picture. Case could easily recall details of his youth and his war experiences, but he had difficulty remembering more recent events. In a recent clinical evaluation, he could not remember the names of five objects for 5 minutes and thought that Richard Nixon was still president of the United States.*

*His memory impairment led to other problems. He would forget that he had left the water running in the sink or bathtub. He became upset at his "stupidity" and sometimes would "fill in" gaps in his memory with details that were untrue. As time passed, he was hospitalized a number of times. When he was admitted, he was usually unable to provide the details of his previous hospitalizations.*

*Case's condition was diagnosed as Korsakoff's syndrome, a type of brain disorder in which an irreversible memory deficit emerges following a history of excessive drinking.*

These two cases show both similarities and differences. The main similarity is that the abnormal behaviors from which both individuals are suffering are caused by organic brain disorders. Our knowledge of these conditions is increasing, not only because of new discoveries about how the brain functions but also because of information about the interaction between organic functioning and personal characteristics and environmental variables. The main difference between the two examples is that Martin's condition does not seem to be attributable to external or environmental causes. Case's condition, on the other hand, seems to be directly attributable to the effects of chronic alcoholism.

Estimating the incidence of specific brain conditions is difficult because their diagnosis is often based on the presence of symptoms rather than on any identifiable organic causes. In one study, it was possible to identify a specific brain dysfunction in only 52 out of

238 hospitalized patients with diagnoses that implied some sort of organic mental impairment (Seltzer and Sherwin, 1978). For the remaining 186 patients, the label *"organic brain syndrome"* was used, mainly because their behavior was similar to that of individuals with known brain damage or deterioration.

## ■ VULNERABILITY TO BRAIN DISORDERS

Three areas of brain research seem especially pertinent to an understanding of both normal and abnormal behavior.

1. Specifying how the brain grows and maintains itself
2. Identifying the mechanisms by which the brain acquires, stores, and uses information at the cellular and molecular levels, as well as the level of behavior and social interaction
3. Making clear the role played by the brain in monitoring and regulating internal bodily processes

In the past, people looked for physical causes for all forms of maladaptive behavior. If people behaved in odd ways, it was because there was something physically wrong with them. People could be "born criminals" or have "bad blood." Then scientists became aware of the psychological and social causes of behavioral problems. Physical explanations came to be seen as inadequate and even as somewhat simple-minded. Today, however, psychologists are developing a more complete picture of how intertwined the psychological, social, and physical domains of human life are.

We learn social skills, interact with others, and acquire personal attitudes within a framework of physical development. Human functioning is influenced by organic events that occur during intrauterine life, the birth process, and the long period of development outside the uterus. The brain may become damaged suddenly, for example, when a person has a stroke or receives a head injury in an accident (see Figure 13-1). In other cases certain diseases cause slow deterioration in the brain. These changes in the brain's physical nature, whether they happen quickly or slowly, and whether they involve large or small areas, are often the cause of unusual behavior. Damage to the brain can lead to a wide variety of behavioral problems, depending on what part of the brain is affected and how much of it is damaged.

What is known today about brain disorders is consistent with what we have already said about the interaction among personal and environmental factors,

(a)

(b)

**FIGURE 13-1**
Automobile accidents often cause head injuries that affect the victim's mental functioning. This person sustained a head injury in a car crash (a). (Peter Menzel/Stock, Boston) The injury resulted in large and permanent losses in ability to attend to stimuli, concentrate, and solve different kinds of problems, even simple things such as counting out correct bus fare (b). (Laimute Druskis)

vulnerability, and stress. It would simplify the lives of clinicians and researchers if they could assume that certain types of maladaptation are due to personal variables and others to situational pressures. Unfortunately, such an assumption would be incorrect. Behavior is a joint product of individual differences and environmental variables. The particular mix of these variables determines how people act and what they think about. There is no standard type of psychological effect for each type and degree of brain defect. The same amount of brain damage or deterioration can have varying effects, depending on the affected individual's personality and abilities and the social supports available to cushion the organic blow. Thus, there are many cases in which the psychological and behavioral effects of brain injuries and tumors do not conform to what would be expected on the basis of the amount of brain damage suffered.

The following are among the factors that influence vulnerability to brain damage and brain disorders:

1. *Age.* The age at which a brain condition develops can have both long- and short-term effects. Although in some instances an infant brain is better able to compensate for an injury than an adult brain, the infant brain may also be more susceptible to a variety of pathological conditions. Many behavioral deficits that are caused by damage to the brain in infancy are not noticed until considerably later.

2. *Social Support.* The presence of caring, accepting people on whom the individual can rely usually eases adjustment to a brain condition. Social isolation, on the other hand, increases cognitive deficits and, thus, abnormal behavior.

3. *Stress.* The greater the stress, the greater both the cognitive and behavioral deficits will be. Elderly people with chronic brain conditions often show marked deterioration following a piling up of stressful life events such as retirement or the death of a spouse.

4. *Personality factors.* It is a common clinical observation that some people react with intense anxiety, feelings of depersonalization, paranoid thinking, defensiveness, and hallucinations to any condition that causes even mild clouding of consciousness and impairment of cognitive and perceptual functioning.

5. *Physical condition.* The site of the brain disorder, the rate of onset of the disorder, and the duration of the disorder all influence the clinical picture. In addition, the individual's general level of health plays a role in his or her adjustment.

An individual's psychological state and social relationships at the onset of an organic condition can influence the impact of the condition on his or her behavior. A person with a stable personality usually responds differently, and more adaptively, to treatment than someone in the throes of marital turmoil or financial reversal. When personal problems complicate an organic condition, both medical and psychological treatment may be necessary. In addition to its personal effects, impairment of brain function has a profound influence on interpersonal relationships. For example, people with epilepsy suffer from undesirable social consequences as well as from the seizures themselves.

Because determining the presence and extent of brain damage is complicated by the need to isolate its effects from those caused by personal and social factors, clinicians must avoid overly simple diagnoses. Clearly, a person who is noticeably disoriented, has trouble solving problems, and displays shallow or very changeable moods and emotions is suffering from some sort of behavioral problem. But the primary aspects of the diagnosis—an estimate of the roles played by organic damage, personality, and life stress in causing the disturbance—are not so easily determined.

## ■ ASSESSING BRAIN DAMAGE

A variety of procedures are used in assessing the extent of damage or deterioration of the brain. In addition to a general physical evaluation, clinical tests may include a mental-status examination, neuropsychological testing, and both traditional x-rays and newer radiological techniques such as PT and CT scans that provide information on the brain's soft tissues and chemical activity.

The **mental-status examination** consists of an interview, which is useful for clinical observation as well as for any statements the individual might make. The mental-status examination is often supplemented by psychological testing and a neurological examination. Clinicians use the mental-status examination to elicit the following information.

1. Level of consciousness. How aware is the individual of what is going on?
2. General appearance (behavior, dress, cooperation).
3. Attention span.
4. Orientation with regard to time and place.

**FIGURE 13–2**

Computerized axial tomography (CT scans). The basic technique is to scan the patient's brain 160 times with a narrow beam of x-rays along a tangent of the skull and to analyze the result with a computer. (a) in CT scanning, x-rays are taken of different "slices" of the brain. (b) A CT scan of an 82-year-old senile man with extensive brain atrophy. Areas of decreased density of brain tissue are the dark areas shown in the scan. (c) A CT scan of a 35-year-old woman with a brain hemorrhage (stained black) and enlarged ventricles. Her symptoms included visual deficits and memory impairment. Surgical removal of a brain malformation that was contributing to the hemorrhaging resulted in noticeable clinical improvement.

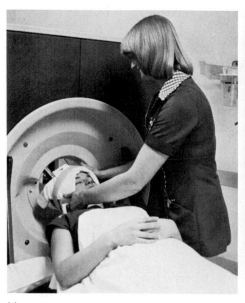
(a)

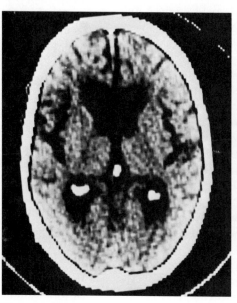
(b)

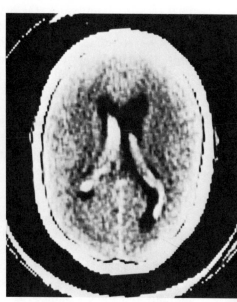
(c)

5. Short-term memory (events of past life or common knowledge).
6. Language (spontaneous speech, comprehension, repetition, reading, writing).
7. Stream of thought. (Do the individual's ideas fit together logically?)
8. Mood.
9. Judgment and insight.

**Neurologists,** or physicians who specialize in diseases of the nervous system, use various techniques to assess brain damage and its cause. **Neuropsychology** is a relatively new branch of psychology that deals with relationships between behavior and the condition of the brain. Clinical neuropsychologists are particularly interested in the effects of brain lesions on behavior. Neuropsychological tests are used to assess impairment in such areas as awareness of and responsiveness to sensory stimulation, ability to understand verbal communication and to express oneself, and emotional expression. Neuropsychological testing is sensitive to impaired functioning of various regions of the brain.

Progress in constructing tests to measure disturbances in various regions of the brain has been limited by the lack of direct information about what actually goes on in the brain. As we saw in Chapter 12, new technology using a variety of brain-imaging techniques is rapidly changing this situation. For example, the CT scan is 100 times more sensitive than conventional x-rays and provides information about the brain's soft tissues that cannot be obtained by means of x-rays. CT scans provide films that show where injuries or deterioration have occurred (see Figure 13–2). This technology should contribute to clarifying the relationship between damage to specific regions of the brain and its effects on psychological functioning.

The PT scan which was also discussed in earlier chapters, allows researchers to visualize the activity of different parts of the human brain. A PT scan is a color or black-and-white reconstruction of x-ray pictures that show patterns of glucose utilization—an index of brain activity—in different parts of the brain. Much as weather maps show various levels of rainfall, a PT scan shows the levels of glucose metabolism in different parts of the brain as they vary with the person's mental state and behavior. The PT scan enables scientists to study biochemical changes in the brain that could never be charted before. Whereas the CT scan shows the brain's anatomy, the PT scan reveals the varying strength of biochemical processes that occur in different areas of the brain. A PT scanner and some PT scans were shown in Figure 12–8.

## ■ ORGANIC MENTAL DISORDERS

Many of the organic mental disorders are basically physical disorders that have psychological symptoms associated with them. Because DSM-III-R uses Axis III to describe physical disorders and conditions, many of the traditional names have disappeared from the two main axes (Axis I and II) of the psychiatric diagnostic system. The classification scheme used in Axis III of DSM-III-R puts emphasis on the clusters of symptoms that accompany brain damage. A **syndrome** is a group of symptoms that tend to appear together. Clusters of psychological and behavioral symptoms that are connected with temporary or permanent brain dysfunction are called **organic brain syndromes.** Cognitive loss is generally thought to be the hallmark of these organic brain syndromes. This loss can affect perception, memory, imagination, thought processing, problem-solving skills, and judgment. Of these, the most common syndromes are delirium, dementia, intoxication, and withdrawal. Delirium and dementia are emphasized in this chapter; intoxication and withdrawal are discussed in Chapter 14.

Organic brain syndromes are most often marked by delirium (which affects the person's state of consciousness or attention) or by dementia (which causes loss of intellectual ability), or by a combination of both. Delirium is often a short-term condition that is reversible, whereas dementia generally implies a nonreversible and often progressive condition. People with organic brain syndromes are likely to die earlier than people in the general population, especially if they are under 40 years of age (Black and others, 1985).

### Delirium

**Delirium** is marked by relatively global cognitive impairment, disorientation, and confusion. In delirium, an individual has difficulty mobilizing, focusing, shifting, and sustaining attention. A wide and changeable range of strong emotions that do not seem related to environmental events may be evident. The presence of two or more of the following symptoms permits diagnosis of this condition.

1. Perceptual disturbances (for example, misinterpreting what is happening in a situation)
2. Incoherent speech
3. Insomnia or daytime sleepiness
4. Increased or decreased psychomotor activity (for example, hyperactivity)
5. Disorientation and memory impairment

The case of Mr. D. is typical.

*Mr. D., a man 30 years of age, is on a medical ward with the diagnosis of lobar pneumonia. He is somewhat dehydrated and has a fever of 104 degrees. Aside from the chest findings, fever, and an increased cardiac rate, the physical examination is essentially normal. There is a past history of mild, chronic alcoholism.*

*Routine treatment measures for pneumoccocal pneumonia are instituted with the patient's full cooperation.*

*Toward evening of the first hospital day, Mr. D. becomes restless. When the nurse urges the patient to drink more fluids, he asks her for a glass of beer. In response to a few moments of explanation, the patient accepts a glass of water and temporarily becomes calmer.*

*At 8:00 P.M., when receiving medication, Mr. D. appears tremulous and agitated and says that he is afraid that he will be late for work. Again a brief explanatory conversation is sufficient for the patient to abandon the idea.*

*Lights on the ward are turned down at 9:00 P.M. Shortly afterward the patient is seen by the nurse on duty to get out of bed and begin searching for something. In response to her question, Mr. D. says that his clothes have evidently been stolen, refers to the hospital as a "boarding house," and insists that he be provided with street clothes and be allowed to leave for work. (Hofling, 1975, pp. 277–278)*

Delirium can occur as a result of either an acute or a chronic brain condition. Mr. D.'s delirium was acute. In a few days, when his fever went down, it ceased entirely and did not return. While he was in the state of delirium, however, he perceived his environment inaccurately, reacted inappropriately to stimuli, and lost control of his impulses. A significant percentage of acutely ill patients in medical hospitals show some degree of delirium (see Figure 13–3).

Delirium generally accompanies some other serious physical problem. Mr. D.'s brain ceased to function normally because cells at 104 degrees need much more oxygen than cells at normal body temperature. A person who is hospitalized after a heart attack may become delirious because the amount of oxygen supplied to the brain may depend on whether the patient is sitting up or lying down. Inadequate excretion of body wastes can also cause delirium. For example, if the kidneys fail to function, the toxins that are usually filtered out by the kidneys will accumulate in the bloodstream and the blood will have less room for oxygen. As a result of such physical disturbances, the brain begins to starve for oxygen, and symptoms of delirium may occur. As in Mr. D.'s case, these symptoms generally disappear shortly after the condition that led to their appearance has been corrected.

Psychological stress, sleep and sensory deprivation, prolonged immobilization, and severe fatigue are likely to contribute to the onset of delirium and to increase its severity. It is believed that a general derangement of brain metabolism coupled with an imbalance in the

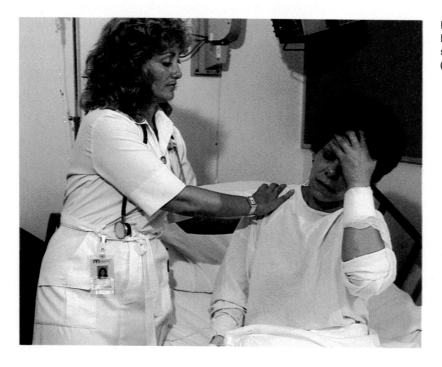

**FIGURE 13-3**
Delirium may occur following the stress of surgery and the post-surgical period.
(Laimute Druskis)

neurotransmitters underlies all cases of delirium. Delirium can also take place because of intoxication or the sudden withdrawal of alcohol or other drugs.

One of the most dramatic examples of delirium can be seen in an acute brain condition called **delirium tremens** (or "the DTs") that may sometimes result from excessive alcohol consumption. People with the DTs may be unable to follow directions like "stick out your tongue" or to attend to events going on around them. In addition to delirium, the DTs are characterized by tremors and visual hallucinations that result in a state of terror. The following excerpt from *Huckleberry Finn* is a vivid description of the DTs.

*I don't know how long I was asleep, but all of a sudden there was an awful scream and I was up. There was Pap looking wild, and skipping around every which way and yelling about snakes. He said they was crawling up his legs; and then he would give a jump and scream, and say one had bit him on the cheek—but I couldn't see no snakes. He started running round and round the cabin, hollering, "Take him off, take him off; he's biting me on the neck." I never see a man look so wild in the eyes. Pretty soon he was all fagged out, and fell down panting; then he rolled over and over wonderful fast, kicking things every which way, striking and grabbing at the air with his hands, and screaming and saying there was devils a-hold of him. He wore out by and by, and laid still awhile, moaning. Then he laid stiller, and didn't make a sound. I could hear the owls and wolves away off in the woods, and it seemed terrible still. He was lying over by the corner. By and by he raised up part way and listened, with his head to one side. He says, very low: "Tramp-tramp-tramp; they're coming after me but I won't go. Oh, they're here, don't touch me—don't! Hands off—they're cold; let go. Oh, let a poor devil alone." Then he went down on all fours and crawled off, begging them to let him alone, and he rolled himself up in his blanket and wallowed in under the old pine table, still a-begging; and then he went to crying. I could hear him through the blanket.* (Clemens, 1923)

The symptoms of delirium tremens usually are not evident until after the person has stopped drinking. Several aspects of the mechanism that causes it symptoms are not well understood, but the DTs seem to be due to the prolonged interference of alcohol with the metabolism of neurons. The condition occurs in about 5 percent of alcoholics. Regardless of the cause (alcohol, infection, and so on), diffuse slowing of brain-wave patterns is a regular finding.

Delirium tremens can last for a week or longer and must be treated in a hospital. During an episode of the DTs, the patient's physical condition deteriorates and he or she becomes highly susceptible to infections. Tranquilizing drugs and a quiet and orderly environ-ment are essential, since even routine conversations among hospital personnel may frighten the patient and heighten his or her hallucinatory experiences. Renewed ability to sleep and rest usually indicates that an episode of DTs is coming to an end. However, recovery depends on restoration of metabolic equilibrium. In some cases equilibrium cannot be restored and death occurs.

Although every person has the potential to develop delirium, there appear to be wide variations in susceptibility (Wells, 1985). Some people become delirious in response to metabolic changes or medications that do not produce delirium in others, whereas others fail to become delirious under metabolic conditions that are likely to produce delirium in most people. The incidence of delirium is highest among old people. It is not known to what extent this is a function of age itself rather than the frequency of organic brain disease and systemic disease in old age.

Patients with organic brain lesions are especially liable to develop delirium, as are people with long histories of alcohol or drug addiction. Delirium is frequent following surgery, either immediately or after a lucid period of several days, and seems to be due to the physical stress of the surgery itself and to the psychological stress of the surgery and the postoperative period. In a sense, delirium is a threshold phenomenon; that is, each individual probably has a specific threshold for this condition. Preexisting brain damage, addiction, and certain chronic medical disorders probably bring people close to this threshold even if they do not exceed it; relatively small metabolic changes may then push the patient over the threshold.

## Dementia

The essential feature of **brain deterioration,** or **dementia,** is a gradual loss of intellectual abilities that is sufficient to interfere with social or occupational functioning. Memory impairment, decline in ability to exercise good judgment and engage in abstract thinking, loss of self-control, and personality changes also occur. Dementia may be progressive, static, or even reversible if an effective treatment is available. Because individuals with dementia are not able to think clearly and often have difficulty making rational judgments, they are particularly vulnerable to physical, psychological, and social stress. Demented individuals are more likely than other people to experience delirium.

The onset of dementia is insidious, and the course of the disorder is gradual. The term **senile dementia** is often used to refer to the condition when it occurs in people over 65. Autopsies show that most senile dementias have the characteristics of **Alzheimer's dis-**

ease. If dementia occurs in younger individuals, it is termed **presenile dementia.** In people with this condition there is a progressive atrophy (degeneration) of brain tissue, and their brain-wave patterns are almost invariably abnormal. The individual becomes increasingly subject to lapses of memory, poor judgment, and disorientation. Deterioration in personal habits is common, and behavior may become unpredictable and impulsive. Because the person often remembers past events better than recent ones, he or she seems to live in the past much of the time.

The rate at which behavior is affected and the manner in which it changes are influenced by many factors, not the least of which is the individual's reaction to the physical and psychological deterioration. A sizable percentage of senile people undergo profound personality changes. Reconstruction of their earlier personalities usually uncovers the presence of maladaptive behavior patterns before the onset of senility, including actual and severe psychotic or neurotic reaction patterns or, more likely, tendencies in those directions. These tendencies are made worse by the onset of senility, but they are not caused by it. Over half of the cases that are diagnosed as senile dementia show various combinations of agitation, paranoid and schizophreniclike reactions, and depression. One common symptom is **confabulation:** When faced with loss of particular memories, the individual fills in memory gaps with detailed, but inaccurate, accounts of his or her activities. The case described at the beginning of the chapter illustrates this tendency.

The following case illustrates symptoms that are often seen in primary degenerative dementia. These include a progressive memory deficit, at first for recent events but later for remote ones, along with narrowing of interests, loss of initiative, sluggishness of thought, apathy, irritability, and restlessness at night.

*A talented artist was referred by his wife; he had become anxious and mildly depressed when his first symptoms emerged. In many respects he was very fortunate. At the age of 65 he had achieved a national, even international, reputation as an illustrator . . . [he] had devised a special process used to produce color covers and prints. . . . Recognition of his work gained him election to one of the distinguished clubs of artists in the city.*

*There had been some beginning failure in his memory. He complained of some difficulty in the use of his hands and arms, a clumsiness and lack of precision that did not exist before. When first seen, he advised that his father had become senile . . . and had had a slowly progressive course of increasing mental impairment, which the patient feared for himself, abhorring the thought. He was accompanied on his first visit by his wife, who had been*

*his model. They had been married 30 years and had two daughters, both married.*

*She declared that at home he had become critical and querulous. He seemed to avoid going out to meet his artist friends. Furthermore, in contrast to his usual self-assurance at his work he seemed anxious and upset when requested to take on a new contract. His concern over his abilities, his doubts, and even refusal of work were reflected in his relations with his wife. Over the succeeding months it was learned that she had been nagging him. He complained that she had commenced to drink and did not seem as interested in the care of the house. Also, he said his daughters were hounding him. Although he was able to talk most interestingly of his past work and life, it was clear that he had difficulty in recalling his earlier visits with his physician, when they occurred, or what had been discussed. The course was slowly progressive. As time went on, the tension and near panic he felt over inability to perform, on the recognition of his slowly progressive impairment of perception and skill, accompanied by much anxiety in meeting his business and social acquaintances, continued to increase.*

*The therapeutic efforts were devoted to discussion of the events of the recent past, prescribing medication (thorazine) which most effectively damped his mounting anxiety, explanation of the probable course of his illness to his wife, and the ways in which she could respond most helpfully. She had to know that he could not be held responsible, that the course would be progressive, that he would become increasingly unable to care for himself, even to the point of being unable to understand where he was, to dress, or to maintain his cleanliness. She was assured that her feelings of frustration and anger were justified, and that their control required that she be relieved at times and get away. Hospitalization was discussed. . . . [but] she wished to maintain the patient at home.*

*The failure in his mental functioning proceeded slowly. Periods of disorientation were first noticed at night when he arose to go to the bathroom. Some six years after onset he became seriously disturbed, had the delusion that men were attempting to kill him, and hallucinated voices. By increasing the dose of thorazine and reducing other medication, this acute and overtly psychotic paranoid reaction subsided and hospitalization was avoided, but only through the warm and understanding attendance of his wife and his daughters in her relief.*

*The periods of anxiety and panic with breaks went on for another year or so, to be succeeded by increasing apathy and disinterest. He could no longer tell his wife of the difference between Picasso and Braque. He tried to draw, attempting to improve old sketches, but without creativity. He would talk to her of planning a Christmas card, but would forget that his daughters were married. His death, in a local general hospital, occurred quickly from cardiac arrest seven years after he was first seen.* (Kolb and Brodie, 1982, pp. 238-239)

**Alzheimer's Disease** **Alzheimer's disease** is an insidious, heartbreaking malady that is associated with advancing age. Its memory lapses, confusion, and dementia inevitably get worse. People with Alzheimer's disease forget how to cook, go on wild spending sprees, lose the ability to balance their checkbooks and count change, and forget how to drive a car. Nearly total bodily and behavioral deterioration is typical in its final stages.

By far the leading cause of mental deterioration among the elderly, Alzheimer's disease affects between 5 and 10 percent of all people over 65. In one family out of three, one parent will die of the disease. The disease tends to run in families and to be more frequent among females than among males. Because most Alzheimer's patients must eventually be placed in institutions, the disease (which has an average duration of about seven years) places tremendous demands on the nation's health-care resources. Alzheimer's victims constitute 50 to 60 percent of the 1.3 million people in nursing homes, accounting for more than half of the over $25 billion spent annually on nursing home care. The disease will become more common and take an even greater toll as the average age of the U.S. population continues to increase.

Alzheimer's disease is also the most common form of presenile dementia. In these cases also, it usually causes gradual intellectual deterioration with growing lapses of memory (see Table 13-1). The progressive destruction of nervous tissue leads to slurring of speech, involuntary movements of arms and legs, and in some cases, seizures. When the disease manifests itself primarily in the intellectual sphere, the individual may experience great anxiety about the deterioration of his or her abilities. It is not yet known why the neural degeneration that is fairly common among old people occurs in some people who are much younger.

*Clues to the cause.* Alzheimer's disease was first identified in 1906 by a German physician, Alois Alzheimer. His patient, a 51-year-old woman, suffered loss of memory, disorientation, and later, severe dementia. After her death, Alzheimer performed an autopsy on her brain and found the two distinctive characteristics of the disease: tangled clumps of nerve cells and patches of disintegrated nerve-cell branches. Because Alzheimer's patients were relatively young, the disease was thought to be a disease of middle age; similar symptoms in elderly people were regarded as a natural consequence of aging. Today this view has been discarded. Nerve cells that resemble those noticed by Alz-

---

□ **TABLE 13-1**

Phases in the Cognitive Decline Accompanying Alzheimer's Disease

| Phase | Examples |
|---|---|
| 1. Complaints of memory deficit | Forgetting names that one formerly knew well |
| 2. Increased cognitive decline and signs of confusion | Losing or misplacing an object of value |
| 3. Moderately severe cognitive decline and intensified confusion (early dementia) | Inability to recall major aspects of one's life, such as the names of close family members |
| 4. Severe cognitive decline and confusion (middle dementia) | Largely unaware of all recent events and experiences |
| 5. Very severe cognitive decline and confusion (late dementia) | Loss of all verbal abilities, need for assistance in eating and toileting |

*Source:* Based on Reisberg, 1985.

---

heimer have been found to contain two abnormal rigid structures called *plaques* and *tangles*. The greater the number of plaques and tangles, the more severe the intellectual disability of the patient. Thus, dementias of the Alzheimer's type seem to involve a specific pathological process rather than being a normal consequence of aging.

The cause of the degenerative process is not yet known, but recent research gives reason to believe that it may be discovered in the foreseeable future. Research to date has shown that there is a loss of neurons, especially in the frontal and temporal lobes of the cerebral cortex. Other clues to understanding the disorder are being provided by research on the chemical messengers in the affected parts of the brain (Coyle and others, 1983). *Acetylcholine,* a chemical that nerves in the brain use to signal to one another is known to be involved in learning and memory. There is some evidence that an acetylcholine deficiency might contribute to the learning and memory deficits of senility. Autopsy of the brains of patients who have died shows that *choline acetylcholine transferase,* an enzyme that forms acetylcholine, is greatly reduced in the cerebral cortex and hippocampus regions of the brains of patients dying with senile dementia. It appears that impairment in acetylcholine production is a fundamental and relatively specific defect in the brains of patients with Alzheimer's dementia. Accordingly, one focus of current research is the development of drugs that will increase the formation of acetylcholine, prevent its destruction, or directly stimulate the acetylcholine receptors.

Little progress has been made in the treatment of

Alzheimer's disease since Alzheimer's day, and even diagnosis remains difficult. The only way to be absolutely certain that a patient has the disorder is to examine the brain after death. While the patient is alive, the diagnosis must be arrived at by a careful process of elimination. Through CT scanning and other tests, it is possible to determine that the patient has not suffered a series of small strokes and does not have Parkinson's disease, a brain tumor, depression, an adverse drug reaction, or any other disorder that can cause dementia. If all tests are negative, Alzheimer's disease is diagnosed by default. This conclusion may be further verified using psychological tests.

Alzheimer's disease would be far easier to treat and detect if its cause were known. The fact that the disease often occurs in several members of the same family suggests that a genetic factor is at work. Screening for hereditary influences might reveal genetic markers, and it might be possible to identify environmental factors that influence the age of onset and the progress of the disease.

***Effects on the family.*** In addition to searching for the causes of Alzheimer's disease, researchers are attempting to find ways of treating not only the patient but caregivers as well. Those who care for people with Alzheimer's disease often experience severe stress. Marian Roach (1983) has provided the following description of her reactions and those of her sister, Margaret, to their mother's deterioration as a result of Alzheimer's disease.

> I noticed that she had stopped taking phone messages. One friend said she sounded "jealous and hostile." She would abruptly hang up on people. She became obsessed with the plumbing: She would look under the sinks and start to take apart the pipes, convinced there was a drip. She would walk away in the middle of conversations. She became repetitive, depressed. (p. 23)

As the deterioration continued, the pressures and emotional strain worsened.

> Margaret and I have no relatives but my mother. The decisions we make are made together. Margaret works until 11 at night and on weekends. We have a young woman who lives in the house from Monday through Friday. Another woman comes on Friday and Saturday nights. Yet another takes my mother out—for rides or to the movies—three afternoons a week. But the burden of care is on my patient sister, who manages the schedules and sees my mother daily. I work during the day. I am with my mother on Sundays.

> As I have gotten to know this disease, I have felt ashamed at my own embarrassment. I find myself explaining her condition to people, to excuse her behavior. Sometimes I do this in front of her and, for an instant, my mother will look terribly embarrassed. I see it in her face and I feel very unlike a daughter. I feel like a traitor. And then she will forget my explanation of her "memory problem," and her questions and repetitions, along with my embarrassment, will continue. Alzheimer's victims are likely to say or do anything during the stages just before they can do literally nothing for themselves. It is difficult to know what to expect. The anticipation is sometimes the worst part.

> I sometimes dread the weekends. I try not to cry in front of Margaret, who tries not to cry in front of me. Margaret and I have discussed the possibility of our contracting the disease. If I get it, I have said that I'd want Margaret to kill me; she has said the same. (p. 31)

Research on the aspects of caring for Alzheimer's victims that are particularly stressful for people like Marian and Margaret Roach has shown that the sense of lack of control over what will happen next is of great importance (Pagel and others, 1985). In addition, caregivers feel isolated, unable to deal effectively with the continuing stress, and confused about their own reactions. Support groups and group therapy can be valuable in allowing family members to express their feelings, particularly those that they consider unacceptable (for example, anger and disappointment). The opportunity to compare their experiences with those of other people who are going through the same trial often makes them aware that such feelings are normal and understandable (see Figure 13–4).

**Pick's Disease** **Pick's disease** is much less common than Alzheimer's disease. Whereas the risk of Alzheimer's disease increases steadily through adult life, Pick's disease is most likely to develop between the ages of 60 and 70. After that period the risk decreases (Heston and Mastri, 1982). Its symptoms are so similar to those of Alzheimer's disease that it takes an autopsy to tell the two disorders apart. People who have died from Pick's disease show a characteristic form of brain atrophy. Among people over age 40, 24 out of 100,000 can be expected to die of the disease. Women are affected more often than men.

There are no known cures for any of these senile and presenile dementias. Their treatment consists mainly of emotional support and sedative drugs. Efforts are made to structure the individual's life so that his or her days are uncomplicated and routinized so as to avoid pressure and tension. Various types of biophysical treatments (for instance, the use of cerebral stimulants, vitamins, and inhalation of oxygen) have been tried. Although research on these treatments continues, no cure for dementia has yet been found.

(a)

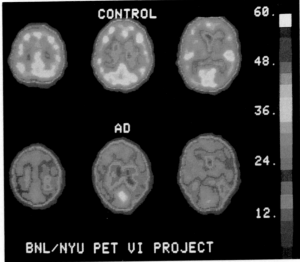

(b)

**FIGURE 13-4**
Alzheimer's disease has a profound effect, not only on the person who develops it, but also on the lives of all the members of the family. Photo (a) shows reminder signs which are useful to lessen the memory problems Alzheimer's disease creates. (Lynn Johnson, Black Star) The PT scans in photo (b) show the lower glucose metabolism in the brain of an Alzheimer's patient (bottom) compared to that of an age and sex matched control (top). (Peter Arnold, Inc.)

**Multi-Infarct Dementia** Another less common dementia, which is more likely to occur after age 65 than before, is **multi-infarct dementia.** This disorder is caused by a series of minor strokes that occur at different times. The onset is abrupt and the course of the disorder is fluctuating rather than uniformly progressive. The pattern of deficits is "patchy," depending on which areas of the brain have been destroyed. As the condition worsens, the relatively intact areas of intellectual functioning decrease and there is increased disturbance in several functions, including memory, abstract thinking, judgment, and impulse control. Hypertension may be a major factor in multi-infarct dementia. Controlling high blood pressure helps prevent this type of dementia and reduces the likelihood of minor strokes when multi-infarct dementia is already present.

### Other Organic Brain Syndromes

Other organic brain syndromes that are discussed in DSM-III-R not only are less common than delirium and dementia but also do not involve as great a change in overall functioning. In an **amnestic syndrome,** for instance, there is a memory disturbance marked by inability to learn new material or recall information acquired in the past. Table 13-2 describes the three main diagnostic features of amnestic syndromes.

Amnestic syndromes are marked by neither the confusion and clouding of consciousness seen in delirium nor the general loss of intellectual abilities seen in

□ **TABLE 13-2**
Diagnostic Features of Amnestic Syndrome

1. *Anterograde amnesia*—impaired ability to learn, retain, and reproduce new information.
2. *Retrograde amnesia*—impaired ability to recall memories that were established prior to the onset of the disorder.
3. *Confabulation*—expression of inaccurate and at times inappropriate answers to straightforward and simple questions.

dementia. The most common forms of amnestic syndrome result from thiamine deficiency and chronic alcohol use. The syndrome may also follow head injuries, surgery, or anything else that interferes with the flow of blood through the brain. The treatment depends entirely on the cause; no specific treatment is available for most of the disorders that cause this condition.

The diagnosis of **organic delusional syndrome** applies when there are delusions that seem to be attributable to an organic process. Intellectual impairment is absent or slight, and the confusion of delirium is absent. A number of substances discussed in Chapter 14 (for example, amphetamines, cannabis, and psychedelics) may cause this syndrome.

**Organic hallucinosis** refers to a syndrome that is characterized by recurrent or persistent hallucinations experienced in a state of clear awareness. This diagnosis is used when an organic factor is believed to be involved. Use of psychedelics is a common cause of this

| Feature | Examples |
| --- | --- |
| 1. Emotional instability | Temper outbursts, sudden crying |
| 2. Impaired impulse control | Poor social judgment, shoplifting |
| 3. Marked apathy and indifference | No interest in usual hobbies |
| 4. Paranoid thinking | Extreme suspiciousness |

syndrome. The types of hallucinations manifested are often related to the substance involved. For example, alcohol tends to induce auditory hallucinations.

The **organic affective syndrome** features an abnormal mood, either depressive or manic, that is judged to be a consequence of a brain disorder rather than a personal response to an event or situation. The syndrome is often caused by toxic or metabolic factors. Disorders of the endocrine system can also play a role.

The **organic anxiety syndrome** is marked by recurrent panic attacks or generalized anxiety. This diagnosis is made when there is evidence from the patient's medical history, physical examination, or laboratory tests that a specific organic factor is causally related to the disturbance.

In an **organic personality syndrome** there are changes in the person's motivation, emotions, and impulse control. He or she may seem uncharacteristically apathetic, irritable, or euphoric. As with the other syndromes, the diagnosis of organic personality syndrome is used when an organic factor is believed to be involved in the personality change. Structural damage to the brain—caused, for example, by a tumor or head injury—is common in this syndrome. Table 13-3 describes the diagnostic criteria for organic personality syndrome. The clinical picture depends to a great extent on the size and location of the brain lesion. The syndrome is more likely to be diagnosed in people who are over 50 years of age, who have no history of mental disorder, and in whom a personality change takes place abruptly over a relatively short period.

## ■ BRAIN DISORDERS WITH A VARIETY OF CAUSES

To illustrate the range of problems that produce symptoms or organic brain disorder, we will discuss a number of additional disorders that alter behavior, emotions, and cognitive functioning. These include disorders that are related to heredity, to the lack of a particular neurotransmitter, to infection, to a nutritional deficiency, or to brain damage caused by outside forces, the growth of a tumor within the brain, or cerebrovascular problems.

## Huntington's Disease: A Genetically Based Disorder

**Huntington's disease,** or **Huntington's chorea,** is a rare hereditary disorder that is transmitted by a single dominant gene and is characterized by progressive degeneration of brain tissue (see Figure 13-5). It can begin at any time from childhood to late in life, but most commonly the onset occurs between the ages of 30 and 50. The offspring of affected fathers often experience the disorder earlier than their fathers. Four types of symptoms are observed in Huntington's disease: dementia, irritability and apathy, depression, and hallucinations and delusions (Folstein and Folstein, 1983). In addition, there are choreiform movements—involuntary, spasmodic jerking and twisting movements of the neck, trunk, and extremities, and much facial grimacing. (The word *chorea* refers to these movements.)

The psychological and behavioral symptoms of Huntington's disease are even more devastating than the physical ones. As the disease develops, the person experiences increasing difficulty in memory storage and retrieval. There is also evidence that intelligence test scores get progressively lower in the period just before the appearance of the characteristic choreiform movements (Lyle and Gottesman, 1979). This suggests that the gene for Huntington's disease does not suddenly "turn on" at the time that the involuntary movements appear.

Impulsiveness in behavior and paranoid and depressive thinking are likely to occur as the disorder progresses and family life becomes disrupted. It is not clear whether these behavioral components of Huntington's disease are organically caused or whether they are psychological reactions to physical deterioration. Recently it has become known that people with Huntington's disease have a deficiency of one neurotransmitter, GABA (gamma-amino-butyric-acid).

The disorder usually begins in middle life, although the onset can occur much earlier. The folksinger and composer Woody Guthrie died in 1967 after suffering from Huntington's disease for 13 years. As a result of a misdiagnosis, Guthrie had been considered an alcoholic and had been placed in a series of mental hospitals for years before the correct diagnosis was made. Guthrie had eight children, one of whom has already died of Huntington's disease.

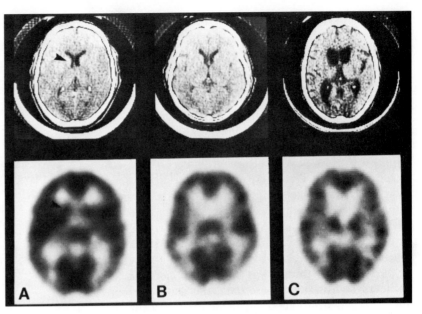

**FIGURE 13-5**
Both computerized axial tomography (CT) and positron emission tomography (PT) scans are valuable in studying aspects of Huntington's disease. Column A shows scans of a normal individual. Column B shows scans of a patient with early signs of clinical disease. Although the structural appearance is still normal, an abnormal pattern of glucose metabolism is already occurring. The scans in Column C, illustrating an advanced case of Huntington's disease, show both structural changes (brain atrophy) and an abnormal metabolic pattern. Comparison of the two types of scans demonstrates the loss of function preceded significant structural cell loss in Huntington's disease. (Kuhl and others, 1981)

Since the disease is inherited through a single dominant gene, each child of an affected parent has a 50 percent chance of inheriting the disorder. There is no skipping of generations, and there is no way of distinguishing carriers of the gene from noncarriers until the symptoms appear. The fact that Huntington's disease does not manifest itself until the middle decades of life means that members of a family that might be affected by it must spend their childhood, adolescence, and early adult years not knowing whether they will develop the disorder or not.

In the San Luis region of Venezuela, the prevalence of Huntington's disease is 700 times higher than in the United States. Within a population of about 3,000, about 150 people have been stricken by the disease and 1,500 more have a substantial risk of developing it. This is because San Luis is the home of a handful of families with many affected members. By far the largest of these families is the Soto family, which has the highest known concentration of Huntington's disease of any family in the world. This is bad news for the Soto family but good news for science. By carefully studying the blood of Iris del Valle Soto and other members of her extended family of almost 4,000 people covering eight generations, researchers achieved a startling breakthrough. They pinpointed the specific location in the specific chromosone pair (chromosome pair 4) at which the gene for Huntington's disease is located (Wexler and others, 1985). This was an important first step toward developing a diagnostic test for the disease and perhaps, eventually, a treatment.

**Genetic Counseling** As noted in Chapter 12, the purpose of **genetic counseling** is to alleviate problems related to the occurrence or possible recurrence of a genetically influenced mental disorder. Twin, adoption, and family studies have shown that these disorders include schizophrenia, affective disorders, presenile dementias, and alcoholism. The most obvious use of genetic counseling is to help a couple decide whether they want to have children when a serious mental illness appears to run in one of their families. A genetic counselor may also relieve parents' anxiety about the future health of already born children by providing reliable information or clarifying a diagnosis of mental disorder through analysis of the family's history. The counselor may also talk to unaffected family members about their fears of developing the illness, and may give advice about how and when to inform children that they are at risk.

Genetic counseling involves seven steps: (1) diagnosis of any symptoms currently present; (2) taking a family history; (3) establishing the risk of mental illness; (4) evaluating the needs of the client; (5) weighing burden, risk, and benefit; (6) forming a plan of action; and (7) follow-up. Every possible source of information is used. In uncertain cases the counselor may abstain from risk analysis rather than offer estimates that might be inaccurate.

The family history, derived from records and personal recollections, establishes the number and order of relatives as well as information on abortions, stillbirths, miscarriages, deaths, and the ethnic background, age, sex, and health of parents, brothers, sisters, and children. Disorders within the immediate family are of greatest concern, but the health of grandparents, uncles, aunts, and cousins is also pertinent.

In the case of Huntington's disease, the counselor

can calculate exact risk figures based on current knowledge of genetics. In disorders in which the mechanism of genetic transmission is not as well understood, estimates will be based on studies of mental illness in the families of patients with that specific disorder. These estimates of lifetime risk must be modified for family members who have passed through part or all of the period of greatest risk for the illness in question.

Three basic types of information are used in a risk estimate: (1) scientific information based on data collected in controlled studies, which may concern morbidity rates, average age of onset, or rate of gene mutations in the population; (2) information based on a theoretical understanding of the way a certain trait or complex of traits is inherited; and (3) particular information contained in the family history of the person or persons whose heredity is being examined. Having gathered and assessed these data, the counselor considers the client's ability and readiness to accept and make use of it. The counselor must bear in mind whether the mental health of living children is in question, whether future childbearing is a concern, whether the client understands the meaning of the diagnosis, and so on. He or she must take into account the genetic relationship between the client and the ill relative. Intelligence, compassion, confidence, candor, and flexibility are important qualities in a counselor, especially when the client is deciding whether to have a child.

## Parkinson's Disease: A Neurotransmitter Deficit

Like Huntington's disease, **Parkinson's disease** is progressive and may begin by the age of 50. Its symptoms include tremor, rigidity, an expressionless, masklike facial appearance, and loss of vocal power. Its cause is unknown, although some researchers believe it is caused by an acquired defect in the brain mechanism. There is evidence that the brains of Parkinson's patients are deficient in dopamine. Unlike the dementias discussed so far, this disorder can be treated. A drug called L-dopa is used to relieve some of the symptoms. One study found that Parkinson's patients treated with L-dopa showed clinical improvement that persisted over a ten-year period (Bauer and others, 1982).

A person with Parkinson's disease typically exhibits social withdrawal, reduced intellectual ability, and rigidity in coping with his or her problems. Most Parkinson's patients seem emotionally overcontrolled. It is difficult to determine how much of the behavioral maladaptation associated with Parkinson's disease is due to organic processes and how much is due to the patient's psychological reaction to them.

## General Paresis: An Infectious Disease

Infectious disorders often have an acute onset, although the possibility of slow-acting viral infections should not be ruled out. The central nervous system often is more susceptible to bodily infections than other tissues of the body. Some of these infections do not last long, and successful treatments have been worked out for many of them. If left untreated, however, some infections can lead to irreversible brain disorders.

Untreated **syphilitic infections** are an example of this type of condition. If syphilis is diagnosed before its terminal stages, it can be treated with drugs, usually penicillin. The aim of the drugs is to return the cerebrospinal fluid to normal, which may require many months. These drugs may cure the patient, but the degree of improvement depends on how many neurons were destroyed before the treatment began. When the destruction is great, losses in intellectual functioning cannot be restored. Another factor that influences recovery is the individual's preinfection personality. The kind of deterioration that occurs depends partly on lifelong personality characteristics. The more stable the personality, the greater the chance of recovery.

One of the results of untreated syphilis in its late stage is **general paresis**, or **dementia paralytica**, a progressive deterioration in psychological and motor functioning that results in paralysis, psychosis, and death. Among the symptoms of general paresis are loss of cognitive functions, slurring of speech, tremors of the tongue and lips, and poor motor coordination. These symptoms are progressive and eventually lead to a helpless condition. Before the cause and treatment of syphilis were discovered, patients with general paresis represented between one-tenth and one-third of all admissions to mental hospitals.

Because of the negative relationship between the degree of possible improvement and the extent of irreversible brain damage, prompt diagnosis and medical treatment of syphilitic infections is clearly the best approach to reducing the incidence of general paresis.

There is increasing evidence that transmissible viral infections may cause certain types of dementia. One such dementia, Creutzfeldt-Jakob disease, begins between ages 40 to 60. It results in a quickly progressing dementia that usually ends in death within 3 to 12 months. The incubation period for the disease may vary from 1 1/2 years to nearly 50 years. Although the Creutzfeldt-Jakob virus can be isolated, it has not yet been possible to determine how it is transmitted. D. Carleton Gajdusek, winner of a 1976 Nobel Prize, has uncovered more than 5,000 cases of transmissible viral dementias that are fatal and, at this time, incurable (*Psychiatric News*, 1985). Studies of these cases may provide clues to the process by which viral infections can cause brain deterioration.

## Pellagra and Korsakoff's Syndrome: Nutritional Deficiencies

Vitamin and other nutritional deficiencies can affect the nervous system. For example, **pellagra** is a reversible disease that is caused by a deficiency of the vitamin niacin (nicotonic acid) or its derivatives. The deficiency affects cells in the area of the cerebral cortex that controls body movement and in other parts of the brain. There are a variety of symptoms, including a skin disorder (the skin looks as if it had been severely sunburned), diarrhea, and psychological deterioration. The signs of psychological impairment are similar to those of anxiety disorders and depression: anxiety, irritability, loss of recent memory, and difficulty in concentration. Untreated cases may manifest delirium, hallucinations, and a variety of psychotic behaviors.

The incidence of pellagra has declined sharply in the United States as a result of improved diet, but it is still common in many underdeveloped countries. Chronic alcoholics who have poorly balanced diets may show symptoms of pellagra. On the basis of behavior alone, it is difficult to distinguish between pellagra and conditions like anxiety or schizophrenia, but when a niacin deficiency is suspected (usually on the basis of skin and digestive symptoms), diagnosis is relatively simple. Except in very severe cases, nutritional therapy is highly effective. The individual is placed on a protein-rich diet that is also rich in vitamins (niacin, thiamine, and vitamin B complex). Mild cases improve noticeably within 48 hours.

Nutritional deficiencies sometimes combine with toxic substances to produce substantial and irreversible damage to brain tissue. **Korsakoff's syndrome,** which occurs in some chronic alcoholics, results from a combination of alcoholism and vitamin $B_1$ (thiamine) deficiency. Recent and past memories are lost, and the person seems unable to form new memories. In addition, there are perceptual deficits, loss of initiative, and confabulation. Delirium tremens frequently is part of the patient's medical history. The longer the vitamin deficiency has persisted, the less responsive the individual will be to vitamin therapy.

## Brain Injuries and Tumors

Head injuries and intracranial growths (brain tumors) can lead to both acute and chronic disorders (see Figure 13–6). In many cases it is difficult to determine the extent to which abnormal behavior is a result of dam-

**FIGURE 13-6**
On Christmas Day, 1985, James McDonnell came home to his wife in Larchmont, New York, after 14 years of amnesia. He had lost his memory after suffering head injuries in two automobile accidents, had gone to Philadelphia, and had found a job in a restaurant. McDonnell said that his memory had returned on Christmas Eve when he bumped his head. (*Seattle Times,* December 28, 1985, p. A3) (New York Daily News Photo)

age and how much represents a lifelong behavior pattern or simply a reaction to knowledge of the injury. These factors can interact in many ways. A startling or traumatic event, whether or not it involves physical injury, usually has some specific and symbolic significance for the individual. The term **traumatic neurosis** has been used to describe reactions that follow such an event. A blow to the head that caused little physical damage might be exploited by the injured person, as in some hysterical disorders. The reaction may be reinforced by secondary gains, such as sympathy or permission to quit one's job. Table 13–4 lists some of the factors that influence the effects of a brain injury.

Brain injuries are usually classified into three groups: **concussions,** or transient states that momentarily change the physical condition of the brain but do not cause structural damage; **contusions,** in which diffuse, fine structural damage—for example, the rupturing of tiny blood vessels—takes place; and **lacerations,** which involve major tears or ruptures in the brain tissue.

Although a concussion might include a temporary

1. Age
2. Site of injury
3. Extent of damage
4. Emotional reactions to resulting physical and mental deficits
5. Personality and social competence
6. Social support available after injury

loss of consciousness, the person can be expected to recover completely within 24 to 48 hours. Sometimes it is difficult to diagnose precisely the extent of brain injury and its potential effect on brain functioning. A variety of tests and observations are used to analyze each case, including x-ray evidence of skull fracture, a CT scan to determine tissue damage, a test for blood in the spinal fluid, and observation of symptoms such as bleeding from the skull orifices (for example, the ears), throbbing headaches, prolonged loss of consciousness, and sluggish cognitive behavior. Head injuries can lead to highly specific losses in motor or cognitive functioning, with the extent of the loss depending on the kind of injury and where it is located. Although perhaps 1.5 million people suffer head injuries in automobile accidents each year, less than 1 percent of first admissions to mental hospitals are attributable to head injuries.

Sometimes the brain is injured not by an accident or a blow but by pressure inside the skull, perhaps from a tumor. In such cases the speed with which the intruding body develops also influences the amount of loss. A tumor might grow slowly for a long time before there is evidence of intracranial pressure or behavioral change. A good prognosis in cases of brain injury or tumor depends on how early and how accurately the condition is diagnosed and whether a treatment for the condition exists.

The behavioral effects of brain injuries and tumors are often puzzling and sometimes dramatic. For example, the evening of July 31, 1966, Charles Whitman, a student at the University of Texas, wrote the following note.

*I don't really understand myself these days. I am supposed to be an average, reasonable, and intelligent young man. However, lately (I can't recall when it started) I have been the victim of many unusual and irrational thoughts. These thoughts constantly recur, and it requires a tremendous mental effort to concentrate on useful and progressive tasks. In March when my parents made a physical break I noticed a great deal of stress. I*

*consulted Dr. Cochran at the University Health Center and asked him to recommend someone that I could consult with about some psychiatric disorders I felt I had. I talked with a doctor once for about two hours and tried to convey to him my fears that I felt overcome by overwhelming violent impulses. After one session I never saw the doctor again, and since then I have been fighting my mental turmoil alone, and seemingly to no avail. After my death I wish that an autopsy would be performed on me to see if there is any visible physical disorder. I have had some tremendous headaches in the past and have consumed two large bottles of Excedrin in the past three months.* (UPI)

Later that night Whitman killed his wife and his mother. The next morning he went to the tower on the university campus with a high-powered hunting rifle and opened fire. Ninety minutes later he was shot to death, but by that time he had shot 38 people, killing 14, and had even managed to hit an airplane (see Figure 13–7).

Because of the shocking nature of this incident, it attracted widespread attention. There were many attempts to explain Whitman's murderous acts. The letter that Whitman had written provided a number of clues. It referred to intense headaches, and a postmortem examination revealed a highly malignant tumor in a region of the brain that is known to be involved in aggressive behavior. Some experts suggested that Whitman's actions had been caused by brain damage. Others viewed them as products of the "unusual and irrational thoughts" to which he referred in his letter. A study of Whitman's life revealed that he had had many positive experiences with guns, and some authorities on violent behavior pointed to these experiences as a possible causal factor. Still others cited Whitman's reference to "overwhelming violent impulses" and suggested that those impulses had been bottled up for many years and had finally exploded into action because of the recent life stresses described in his letter.

We cannot be certain which of these potential causes was most important. Perhaps all of them contributed to his actions to varying degrees. The Whitman case dramatically illustrates the many perspectives from which a single act can be viewed and explained.

In some cases in which there is known physical damage, only minor behavioral deficits develop. Apparently some people adapt to minor brain damage better than others. Thus, while brain damage can cause maladaptive behavior, the opposite can occur: An individual can respond maladaptively to the knowledge of having a damaged brain. Furthermore, any type of major injury or traumatic condition might set off a maladaptive psychological reaction such as a psychosis.

**FIGURE 13-7**
Emergency workers rush one of
Whitman's victims to the hospital.
(AP/Wide World Photos)

**Posttraumatic psychoses** are similar to other psychoses. They involve confusion, delirium, and temporary catatonic, manic, or depressive reactions. A posttraumatic psychosis might develop abruptly when a person begins to regain consciousness after receiving a head injury.

Unfortunately, it is usually unclear whether a latent psychosis existed before the traumatic event occurred. The patient cannot, of course, remember the period of unconsciousness following brain trauma, and recollections of the confused state that occurs just after regaining consciousness usually are hazy. In addition, there may be amnesia (loss of memory) for some time prior to the injury. Even after relatively minor injuries, many patients complain of headaches, dizziness, fatigue, lack of concentration, and anxiety. In most cases these complaints are of short duration.

Tumors produce a variety of physiological and psychological changes because their presence causes a rise in intracranial pressure or interferes with the blood supply to the brain. Their symptoms depend on their location in the brain. For example, tumors growing in or near the frontal lobe frequently lead to a gradual onset of mental changes, but again, the symptoms depend on the site of the tumor. One group of people with frontal-lobe tumors may become exuberant and euphoric; their conversation is punctuated by laughter and jokes. Another group may show general apathy and slowness in responding.

Memory disorders are very common in people with cerebral tumors and are often the first noticeable indication that a problem exists. The nature of the memory impairment varies widely. For example, people with left-hemisphere lesions may have difficulty with material that they hear, but they may be able to cope with the same material if they can see it. Researchers are investigating the degree to which training in attentional and cognitive skills can aid in the rehabilitation of brain-damaged individuals (Gummow and others, 1983).

Early in their development some brain tumors result in changes that neurologists can assess. However, in the absence of other evidence to suggest the presence of a tumor, personality and behavioral changes often result in misdiagnosis and are attributed to nonorganic factors. The role of organic factors may become evident later. For example, the composer George Gershwin underwent psychoanalysis because he suffered severe headaches. It was not until shortly before his death that the diagnosis of a brain tumor was made.

## Epilepsy: Multiple Causal Factors

**Epilepsy** has inspired awe, fear, a sense of mystery, and puzzlement throughout history. The Greek physician Hippocrates argued that epilepsy was a naturally caused disease, but for most of modern history it was seen as a sign of demonic possession. Many famous people, including Julius Caesar, the elder William Pitt, and Fyodor Dostoyevsky, were epileptics (see Figure 13–8).

The illness of Vincent van Gogh (1853–1890) is an example of the complex mental changes associated with epilepsy. Van Gogh, the son of a Dutch preacher, was the product of a difficult birth. As a child he was unruly and required special schooling. Later he failed as an art dealer, a teacher, and a preacher. He described himself as "a man of passion, capable and prone to undertake more or less foolish things which I happen to repent more or less." Shunned by the few women he loved, he pursued his mission as an evangelist to a miserably poor mining district with such extreme devotion that he was dismissed by the church. Only then, at the age of 27, did he begin his career as a painter—a career

that he pursued with singular intensity for the last ten years of his short life.

Beginning in his mid–20s, Van Gogh suffered from peculiar sensations in his stomach, episodes of terror, and lapses of consciousness. The illness may have been precipitated partly by the use of absinthe, an alcoholic drink that heightens susceptibility to epileptic episodes. He underwent unpredictable mood shifts—"attacks of melancholy" alternating with ecstatic states or "indescribable anguish." He became argumentative and reclusive. He lost sexual interest, fell victim to violent rages, and complained of poor circulation and a weak stomach. After an outburst of anger at a friend, he cut off an earlobe and was hospitalized in an acute hallucinatory psychotic state. He had no memory of the events preceding his hospitalization. Although he never suffered major seizures, the attending physicians correctly diagnosed him as epileptic. Two weeks after entering the hospital, he had already recovered enough to paint his serene "Self-Portrait with Bandaged Ear and Pipe" (see Figure 13–9). But there were further psychotic episodes, often provoked by drinking bouts, and he remained in an asylum for a full year. A few months after his release, although he apparently was

**FIGURE 13–8**
Fyodor Dostoyevksy, one of the world's great novelists, suffered from epileptic seizures. His first attack came while he was in prison in Siberia. He believed that the agony of living in chains, the stench, and hard labor had precipitated the seizures, which persisted for years even after he was permitted to leave the prison. (New York Public Library Collection)

**FIGURE 13–9**
Van Gogh's "Self-portrait with Bandaged Ear and Pipe." (Giraudon/Londres, Institut Courtauld)

no longer suffering from either psychoses or lapses of consciousness, he committed suicide.

It was the English neurologist Hughlings Jackson who first accounted for epileptic seizures in terms of brain lesions. He believed that the seizures resulted from excessive discharging by nerve cells in the gray matter of the brain and that irritation of specific areas of the brain caused the particular symptoms manifested by epileptics. However, many questions remain. The causes of the brain lesions found in epilepsy are not clear; moreover, brain lesions are not the only cause of epilepsy.

Most forms of epilepsy are not believed to be hereditary, but there seems to be a predisposition toward epilepsy in some families. Although it is difficult to give a precise estimate, perhaps half of all cases of epilepsy may be preventable because they result from head injuries at birth, infectious diseases of childhood, or brain infections and injuries later in life. The clinical problem of epilepsy is particularly challenging because its solution usually requires establishing the particular combination of causes at work in a given case.

Current epidemiological research shows that the incidence of epilepsy varies from one country to another. In the United States, repeated spontaneous seizures occur in 0.5 to 1.0 percent of the population. The disease is more common in less affluent countries because minor or moderate central nervous system infection and trauma are more likely to be neglected.

Epilepsy is best looked at as a group of related disorders rather than as a single disorder. *Acquired* or *symptomatic epilepsy* refers to seizures for which the cause is known. The causes include brain infections, head wounds, metabolic disorders, and tumors. Many other forms of epilepsy have no apparent cause.

**Grand Mal and Petit Mal Seizures**   An epileptic seizure is a result of transient electrical instability of some cells in the brain, which sometimes triggers an "electrical storm" that spreads through part or all of the brain. This culminates in a seizure, which can take one of many forms. Many epileptics have only one type of seizure, but a sizable minority experience two or more types. The major types include grand mal and petit mal seizures and psychomotor epilepsy. The brain-wave patterns that are characteristic of each type are shown in Figure 13–10.

The most severe form of epileptic disorder is the **grand mal seizure,** which typically lasts from two to five minutes. This type of attack leaves a painful

**FIGURE 13-10**
EEG patterns of various types of epileptic seizures. (Gibbs, Gibbs, and Lennox, 1939, p. 1112)

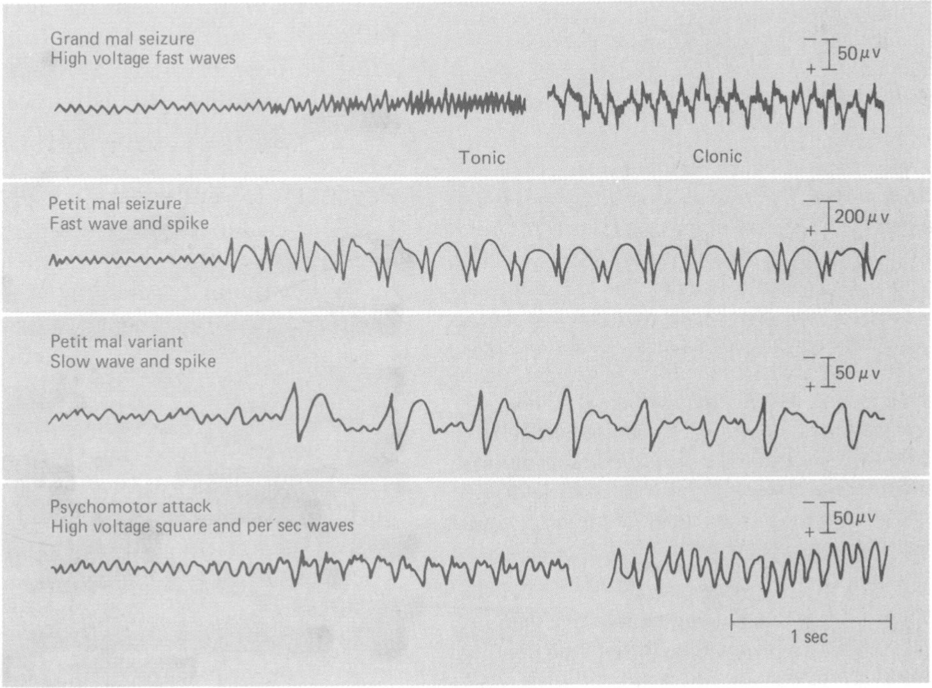

impression on anyone who witnesses it. The victim of a grand mal seizure displays a set of very striking symptoms. The seizure often begins with a cry, followed by loss of consciousness, falling to the floor, and extreme spasms. These uncontrollable spasms can cause serious harm to the victim. Among the greatest dangers are head injuries and severe biting of the tongue or mouth. The muscular movements of a grand mal seizure are usually preceded by an *aura*, in which the individual experiences a clouded state of consciousness, including feelings of unreality and depersonalization (feelings of strangeness about oneself). The aura may last only a few seconds, but it is often remembered very vividly.

Following the aura, the *tonic phase* of the seizure begins. The body is in an extended position, the eyes remain open, the pupils are dilated, and the corneal and light reflexes are absent. The tonic phase lasts for 15 to 30 seconds and is followed by the *clonic phase*, during which the body alternates between marked muscular rigidity and relaxation. Bladder and bowel control may be lost. Following the convulsive part of a grand mal seizure, there may be a deep sleep that lasts for an hour or two. As the victim regains consciousness, he or she may be bewildered and amnesic. While some grand mal epileptics have daily attacks, cases have been reported in which there were only a few seizures in an entire lifetime. The following case illustrates the impact of an initial grand mal seizure.

> It was Christmas morning and the children had come into our room to open presents. They sat all three bouncing around on the foot of our bed, the younger girl in the middle, Jonathan and his older sister on each side.
>
> Suddenly one of them shouted "Mummy, something's wrong with Jonathan," and we all looked at him. He sat quite still, with a fixed stare in his eyes. Slowly his head turned to the left and his eyes moved sideways. His body stiffened, and as he began to slide off the bed, I jumped out and supported him. For seconds he seemed to get tighter and tighter, and his color became pallid and then a horrible blue. Then small convulsive movement began in his arms and legs, which although they were not violent were very forceful and not to be restrained. He grunted, as if he were making a great physical effort with each jerk. This seemed to go on for an eternity, although it cannot have been much more than half a minute, with his color getting worse all the time.
>
> Then it stopped, fairly quickly, and he lay there with his eyes turned up, once again motionless, not even seeming to breathe. I felt for his pulse and it was still there. As I held his wrist, Jonathan gave a few deep gasping breaths, and his color began to come back, and the blueness disappeared. He coughed and spat, and my wife wiped his

> lips with a handkerchief because he seemed to have much more saliva than usual.
>
> When he was breathing normally again, and murmuring to us, we carried him back to his bed, where he slept for a quarter of an hour. When he got up, he was a bit silent, but soon back to normal and returned to his very subdued sisters for more opening of presents.
>
> I suppose the whole incident could only have lasted less than half an hour, but those thirty minutes changed our family life. (Laidlaw and Rickens, 1976, p. 2)

Jonathan's epileptic seizure might be thought of as an interaction between his personal characteristics and the situation. It resulted from events occurring in his brain in combination with other factors, such as the excitement he felt about opening his Christmas presents.

In the **petit mal seizure** which is particularly common in children, there is no convulsion. Rather, there is a lapse of consciousness characterized by blank staring and lack of responsiveness lasting up to about half a minute. The individual usually does not lose consciousness. These seizures may occur many times a day.

Petit mal attacks may be difficult to identify unless the person is known to be epileptic or an attack is actually observed. They commonly start in early childhood. Some children have so many attacks daily that they have difficulty attending to what is going on around them. Most petit mal attacks result from disturbances in subcortical brain structures, although the cause of these disturbances is usually unknown. A significant proportion of children with petit mal epilepsy have low levels of intelligence.

**Psychomotor Epilepsy** In **psychomotor epilepsy,** a type that includes 15 percent of epilepsy cases and is rarely seen in children, the patient retains control of his or her motor functioning but loses the ability to exercise good judgment in carrying out activities. During a psychomotor attack, the individual is in a kind of trance and carries out movements that may be repetitive and highly organized but are in fact semiautomatic. Psychomotor seizures may resemble those of petit mal epilepsy, but they last longer (up to two minutes), involve muscle movements related to chewing and speech, and show more clouding of consciousness. The occasional visual hallucinations and the confused state that characterize psychomotor epilepsy are similar to some symptoms of psychosis.

In some cases fear, terror, rage, and depression are among the emotional side effects of psychomotor seizures. These outbursts of emotion come on suddenly. They are apparently automatic and unpremeditated, and they cannot be recalled later. Another feature of this syndrome is inability to shift attention to new objects and situations. There is some evidence suggesting that this syndrome may be associated with temporal lobe lesions; hence, it is referred to as **temporal lobe epilepsy.**

**Psychological Factors** Over the years there has been much conjecture about the role of psychological factors in epilepsy. Are epileptics helpless victims of their condition, or is it possible that the disease is part of their psychological adjustment to some other aspect of their lives? Clinicians have observed that epileptics' seizures tend to become more frequent when they are confronted with challenges and problems they do not feel competent to handle. A buildup of pressures in daily living increases vulnerability to seizures (Temkin and Davis, 1984). On the other hand, perhaps epileptics receive some sort of gratification (for example, secondary gain) from their seizures and, in fact, can learn to control them. A number of clinical studies suggest that more than a few epileptics are capable of inducing seizures. Some learn to do this by carrying out certain bodily maneuvers or by seeking out certain stimuli. For example, some people can induce a seizure by looking at flickering lights.

From a psychological point of view, the disease often creates overwhelming stress for epileptics and their families. Much of this stress is related to lack of knowledge about epilepsy, its causes, and its treatment. Other important factors are the role of general life stresses in bringing on seizures and the effect of the stress caused by the ever-present possibility of a seizure, the need to lead a somewhat restricted life, and the stigma that attaches itself to people who are known to be epileptic.

There is increasing recognition of the developmental problems posed by epilepsy. For example, approximately 60 percent of all epileptics experience their first seizure before they are 10 years old. This represents a major handicap during a formative period of physical and psychological growth.

**Treatment of Epilepsy** There are three major ways to treat epilepsy: drugs, surgery, and psychological management. Certain drugs, such as Dilantin and phenobarbitol, can reduce the frequency and severity of seizures. Unfortunately, there is considerable variation in the way people react to these drugs. The only way to establish the optimal dosage is through trial and error. In some cases the epileptic may use substances (e.g., alcohol) that interfere with the effectiveness of anticonvulsive drugs.

If the seizures are a result of some identifiable structural defect and drugs either are not effective or have strong side effects, surgical intervention may be considered. The seizures of temporal lobe epilepsy are especially difficult to control by means of medication, but some studies have reported successful results following removal of parts of the temporal lobe. Because brain surgery entails obvious risks, it is used only when it is clear that some abnormality of brain tissue is causing the seizures. However, because the brain is such a complex structure, it is not always possible to be absolutely certain where the abnormality is. In some cases diagnosed as temporal lobe epilepsy, the temporal lobe has been removed and has been found to have no lesions. For this reason, surgery is seen as a treatment of last resort, to be attempted only after drugs and psychological approaches have failed.

A variety of psychological methods have been used in treating epileptics. Operant conditioning procedures have been tried successfully with some epileptics who cannot be helped by medication. For example, epileptic children have been rewarded with attention and care following seizure-free periods. After a seizure occurs, these reinforcers are withdrawn or reduced in strength. Avoiding or changing certain cognitive cues can also be helpful because it is known that the aura preceding a grand mal seizure can be induced by thinking certain thoughts. Epileptics who have this form of the disorder can be trained to direct their attention to pleasant thoughts when they feel an aura coming on. Desensitization and relaxation training have been found to be helpful in reducing the frequency of epileptic attacks. Biofeedback, in which patients receive visual or auditory information about their brain-wave patterns, can also be an effective treatment.

Many epileptics need help to cope with their condition. Because the disorder frequently begins before adulthood, the emotional responses of the epileptic's family must also be dealt with. Often the patient and the family see epilepsy as a kind of disgrace and react to it with shame and guilt. Because an atmosphere of emotional tension and frustration can increase the severity of an epileptic's seizures, psychotherapy and counseling are frequently recommended both for the victim and for members of his or her family. Many people still see epilepsy as frightening and mysterious. As a result of such attitudes, an epileptic often feels socially stigmatized. Organizations like the Epilepsy Foundation work to provide information about epilepsy and to decrease occupational, social, and legal discrimination against epileptics. They publicize facts like the following.

1. Epileptics have the same intellectual capabilities as the general population.

2. Between seizures an epileptic suffers no disturbance in psychological function.

3. Most cases of epilepsy (about 80 percent) can be controlled with anticonvulsive drugs.

4. The genetic factor in epilepsy is probably no greater than in many other common diseases. A person with epilepsy who marries a nonepileptic may expect a 2 percent risk of having a child who also has the disorder. In many cases the risk is even less, especially if the epilepsy is associated with a birth injury or later accident or infection.

## Cerebrovascular Accidents: Blockage of Blood Supply

**Cerebrovascular accidents** (CVAs), or **strokes,** are blockages or ruptures of the blood vessels in the cerebrum. When these blood vessels break or are blocked by a clot, a portion of the brain is deprived of its supply of oxygen and blood. Extensive damage to the brain and obvious changes in behavior may result. When the affected blood vessels are small and the interference with blood flow is temporary, the symptoms are milder—perhaps only confusion, unsteadiness, and excessive emotionality. Some of the behavioral effects of a stroke may be similar to the dementia that occurs in cases of brain deterioration. However, the symptoms of stroke characteristically have an abrupt onset.

Eric Hodgins, an editor and author, suffered a severe stroke that resulted in **aphasia,** a disturbance in the ability to use words, and paralysis of the left side of his body. He recovered from the aphasia. His account of his stroke vividly portrays the psychological as well as the physical side of the stroke experience.

*The first thing to be said about it, is that it is like nothing else on earth . . . The victim-patient is confused, or stunned, or shocked, or unconscious. Whatever his state he is not in good condition to give any fellow layman a clear and coherent account of what happened. Perhaps he can talk—perhaps not. Even with speech, he can't say "It hurts"—because it probably doesn't. So, stroke exists in no focal plane the uninitiated layman can understand or recognize, or on which he can practice his own brand of differential diagnosis. Thus, as with the traffic accident, a variable period of total confusion elapses after the stroke has struck before the cry goes up, "Somebody get a doctor!" . . .*

*Unlike other patient types I can think of, the stroke patient goes to the hospital with profound relief, and gladly. Although he is probably not in pain, he is in considerable fear—more than he can express. Something has gone very, very wrong, but "Somebody will fix it":*

*this child-like phrase describes the depth of the patient's need for support and reassurance . . .*

*In my own case I found it both depressing and infuriating that I encountered no physician with the willingness or capacity to say, as my acute symptoms subsided, "I freely concede you are in a jam—in fact, in several jams. I have no ready-made solutions—but I will help you think your way out of your jams, because I conceive it part of my job, my medical job." Perhaps it is a contentious suggestion that medicine should reach this far out from its examination rooms and its prescription pads to help the stroke patient. But in that case, whose job is it?* (Eisenson, 1973, pp. 204–207)

Strokes are the third-ranking cause of death after heart attacks and cancer. There are approximately 500,000 new strokes and 200,000 deaths due to strokes in the United States each year. Over 80 percent of these involve people over the age of 65. In addition to age, high blood pressure plays a major role in strokes. The single most important way in which strokes can be prevented is through the treatment and control of high blood pressure. Many clinicians have observed that strokes occur especially often in people who live pressured lives. However, it is not clear why these people tend to have their strokes while they are relaxing or vacationing.

## ■ AN INTEGRATIVE APPROACH TO BRAIN DISORDERS

Because the conditions discussed in this chapter involve actual organic defects, it is tempting to see them as purely medical problems. Why do we consider brain disorders to be different from other organic problems, such as broken arms or gallstones? A physical defect lies at the root of all of these conditions, but the brain has a complex effect on our behavior as well as on our body. This effect is not as clear and predictable as the effects of damage to other parts of the body. Once a broken arm has been set and healed, the person can return to the condition he or she was in before the accident. This is not the case with brain injuries, and it is for this reason that they are of interest to psychologists.

To comprehend the effects of a brain injury on behavior, we require information about the person's life history, personality, and environmental and biophysical factors. Purely physical conditions such as broken arms can be treated successfully without such data. Although brain disorders can be treated medically, psychodynamic, learning, cognitive, and community concepts are also important. Thus, from both the scientific and clinical standpoints, the most fruitful approach to brain disorders is one that integrates knowledge from these diverse fields.

From a psychodynamic perspective, although certain forms of maladaptive behavior may be organically caused, the way people respond to their condition involves psychological factors such as personality, earlier experience and ways of coping. For example, the more outgoing a person is, the greater the likelihood of improvement in his or her condition. Many cases of brain disorder indicate that an individual's personality at the time of the organic damage has an effect on the degree and form of his or her behavioral deterioration. For example, the content of hallucinations and the ease with which they are expressed depend on personality characteristics.

Behavioral psychologists are less interested in the effects of personality and experience than psychologists who emphasize other perspectives. They focus on people's ability to adapt to even the most drastic situations. Teaching new responses to compensate for those that have been lost is seen as more important for adjustment than simply helping people accept their new lot in life. Moreover, the way people respond to such training can provide more relevant information about their present psychological state than an examination of their personality before the illness occurred. Because of their emphasis on revising people's maladaptive responses as quickly as possible, behavioral psychologists have a major contribution to make in the treatment of organic brain disorders.

Cognitively oriented psychologists have contributed a variety of techniques to help people in the early stages of dementia deal with the deterioration in their abilities. Memory-aiding techniques such as list making are practical examples. Cognitive techniques are also useful in counteracting the depression that often accompanies the development of physical problems and declining intellectual competence.

Damage to the brain and central nervous system would not seem to be a condition that is influenced by community variables. Yet, from all indications, central nervous system dysfunction is not randomly distributed. Cases of brain damage are highly concentrated in the poor white and black segments of the population. Such problems seem to be most prevalent among black children of lower socioeconomic status. This is true for sociological, not biological, reasons. Black infants are not biologically inferior at the moment of conception, but they may become so shortly thereafter. Inadequate nutrition and prenatal care result in complications of pregnancy, which take their toll in high rates of premature births and congenital defects. These abnormalities include neurological damage that results in impaired intellectual functioning and in behavioral difficulties such as hyperactivity and short attention span. No single complication of pregnancy is more clearly associated with a wide range of neurological dysfunctions than premature birth. For these reasons, those who focus on the community perspective emphasize the prevention of brain disorders through preventive medical care, especially good prenatal care.

The stigma attached to many of the behavioral maladaptations stemming from brain damage often makes the situation worse. People tend to avoid and isolate individuals who are markedly deviant. The behavior of old people provides one of the clearest illustrations of the effects of this social rejection. Mild brain deterioration in a socially rejected older person may lead to greater behavioral maladaptation than moderate deterioration in a person who lives in a friendlier, more accepting environment. From the community perspective, changing people's attitudes toward those who behave differently because of brain disorders can sometimes lessen the behavioral effects of these biological changes.

## ■ AGING AND PERSONALITY CHANGE

Although loss of intellectual abilities due to brain deterioration can be detected in childhood, it is most easily observed late in life (see Figure 13–11). Twenty-five percent of first admissions to public mental hospitals are people over 65, and 80 percent of these patients are diagnosed as having some type of dementia. The growing number of elderly people means that senile dementia will increase as a social problem in the years ahead. More than 6 million individuals will suffer organic mental disorders by the year 2030. If we add to that number the 15 percent of older people who are estimated to have psychological problems that are not organically caused, the total number of elderly people with serious behavioral problems is over 13 million.

For many years most of the problems of older people were lumped together under the heading of senile disorders. We now know that several different types of psychological and behavioral problems occur among old people. The elderly are vulnerable to serious consequences of brain changes such as senile dementia as well as certain other psychological conditions in which the role of organic factors is much less clear-cut. For example, depressive episodes increase in both frequency and depth in the later years of life. Transient depressions, which usually are without suicidal risk or intolerable distress, may occur in 30 percent or more of elderly people.

There is a strong and consistent relationship be-

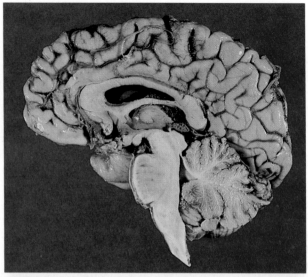

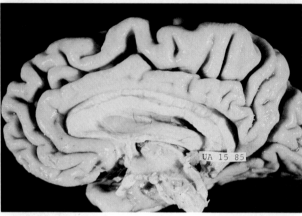

**FIGURE 13-11**
The intellectual and personality changes that are sometimes seen in old age may be reflected in dramatic changes in brain tissue. Part (a) shows a healthy brain. Note the marked contrast to (b), which shows the changes that take place in dementia, in this case Alzheimer's disease. Not only does the physical appearance of the brain change, but the structure of the brain cells is also radically altered. (Martin M. Rotker, Taurus Photos)

tween depression and physical illness. Such correlations may be as high as .40 to .50 in elderly populations (Gurland and Cross, 1982). Depression is likely to be provoked by the beginning of an illness or disability, but given time, most people adjust to these changes in their health status. The majority of severe depressions in old age are relapses, although new cases may occur even after the age of 75.

Although individuals over the age of 65 make up only 11 percent of the total population, over 16 percent of all suicides are committed by people over 65. The rate of suicide in elderly white men is especially high. There is little doubt that the presence of an incapacitating physical illness is a factor in these suicides. Those who are most likely to commit suicide include people who are widowed, living alone, physically ill, abusing alcohol, unemployed, inactive, or depressed. The onset of early symptoms of what appears to be organic brain disease is also thought to be associated with suicide (Busse, 1981).

Paranoid thinking increases in old people and is most likely to occur in individuals who have been sensitive and suspicious throughout their lives. Paranoid reactions are frequently coupled with defects of sight and hearing; these sensory problems make it easier to slip into this kind of thinking. Aged people who are experiencing paranoid reactions often rely on the defense mechanisms of projection and denial. Unable to face or deal with biological losses that are taking place within them, they may deny them, project them onto the outside world, and insist that they are victims of people who are lying, cheating, and stealing.

New cases of schizophrenia continue to arise in old age, and those who receive this diagnosis in their later years constitute about 10 percent of elderly schizophrenics (Gurland and Cross, 1982). However, the largest group of elderly schizophrenics acquired the disorder during the first half of their lives. Those with late-onset schizophrenia are less likely to have a family history of schizophrenia than those who develop the disorder earlier, but they are more likely to have such a history than elderly people in the general population.

Hypochondria, a somatoform disorder in which the individual is preoccupied with fears of serious illness and problems related to sleep, is common in the elderly and results in frequent clinical contacts. Hypochondria in late life is complicated by the fact that many elderly people have chronic physical disabilities, and although their complaints appear to be grossly exaggerated, the actual existence of organic problems cannot be dismissed. In addition to chronic disabilities and biological changes, stress—in the form of economic insecurity, loss of meaningful social roles, and fear of decline in mental functioning—plays a role in the elderly person's vulnerability to hypochondria. When stress decreases—for example, when favorable changes occur in the individual's life—hypochondriacal concerns often decrease as well.

Important changes in sleep patterns accompany increasing age. Spontaneous interruptions of sleep, which are relatively infrequent through adolescence, become more frequent with age, and the amount of time spent awake in bed increases after age 40. Older people sleep better if they engage in physical activity—for example, going for walks—every day. Studies of people over 60 suggest that 7 to 10 percent use sleeping pills habitually and 20 to 40 percent use them on occasion (Busse, 1981). Pain, particularly from arthritis, is a common contributor to insomnia. Among elderly people who are free from physical pain, those who use sleeping pills excessively have been found to be poorly adjusted socially.

Overall, the major clinical challenge facing the elderly is the greater likelihood of disorders in which there is brain degeneration. However, the problems of the elderly also reflect a number of other psychological problems that often accompany increased age. These problems seem to be outgrowths of personal insecurities evoked by such life changes as having to live alone or being supported by others. With advancing age, the social niche in which the individual lives often changes drastically. At the same time, physiological changes may create additional stress as the person seeks to maintain self-esteem and competent, satisfying interactions. It would not be an exaggeration to say that the daily stresses the elderly have to cope with are so numerous and so severe that they would probably tax the coping resources of young adults.

Three points need to be kept in mind about the elderly. One is that there are many examples of successful old people—people who are active, feel that they have something to offer, and make contributions to their families and communities (see Figure 13-12). These people may suffer the physical declines that are frequent among the elderly, but they have found ways to work around them (see Box 13-1). A second point is that there is every reason to believe that most people can adapt successfully to the developmental transitions they encounter throughout life (see Chapter 5). Through public-education programs, society could do a much better job of preparing people for these changes. The third point is that there has been an unfortunate clinical neglect of older people. This is particularly true with regard to their psychological needs. Counseling and psychotherapy for the aged have often been dismissed as a waste of time. Yet many older people need opportunities to express their reactions to the variety of problems they face and to receive the support and advice of trusted clinicians.

**FIGURE 13-12**
The social stimulation and a sense of usefulness or competence that older people receive from a variety of activities such as those shown in photos (a) and (b) may not ony make old age more pleasant but also help prevent a rapid decline in intellectual skills. (Karen Preuss, Taurus Photos and Hugh Rogers, Monkmeyer Press)

(a)

(b)

The later years of life are marked by gradual, irreversible physical decline and by psychological and social changes. However, there is ample evidence that social stimulation, interest in meaningful activities, and feeling that one is needed by other people prolong the ability to lead a happy, productive life (see Figure 13-12). Recent studies have shown that noninstitutionalized older adults do not necessarily report more psychological distress than people in other age groups (Feinson, 1985), their sense of well-being can be relatively high and their rate of psychiatric disorders lower than it is for people under 45 years of age. Although after age 74 in women and age 79 in men there is a significant increase in psychiatric disorders (Weissman and others, 1985).

One of the few longitudinal studies of the relationship between age and intellectual functioning is the Seattle Longitudinal Study, conducted by K. Warner Schaie and his associates (Schaie, 1983). The original subjects, who ranged in age from 18 to 67, have now been tested 4 times over a 21-year period. The results have given a reasonably good picture of longitudinal change in cognitive abilities (see Figure 13-13). The data show that there are only small changes in the kinds of abilities measured by intelligence tests before the age of 60, and no reliable decrease can be shown in these abilities before the age of 74. Although there is some decrease in measured ability beginning in the late 60s, it is not until age 81 that the average person falls below the middle range of performance for young adults. The data from the Seattle Longitudinal Study also suggest that there are very great individual differences in intellectual change throughout adulthood.

Some ways in which older people can cope better with the challenges they face are suggested in the following article about B.F. Skinner, which was written in 1982. At this writing, Skinner is still going strong (see Figure 13-14).

*Burrhus Frederick Skinner—better known as B.F.—is 78, a circumstance that does not seem to cause him any concern. Skinner, it is evident, has spent some time doing some personal application of his theories of behavior to aging and specifically to his own experience. He shared his experiences—he declined to call it research—with an appreciative audience yesterday at the American Psychological Association.*

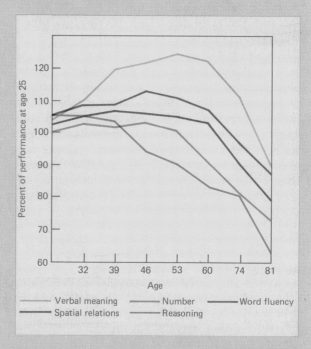

**FIGURE 13-13**
Performance on a variety of tasks used to measure intelligence is shown as a percent of performance at age 25. (adapted from data presented by Schaie, 1983, p. 114)

*If drawing power is any gauge, then Skinner can still be considered to be in his prime. He attracted a standing-room-only crowd of more than 600 persons who gathered in the International Ballroom West of the Washington Hilton yesterday to hear him talk on "Intellectual Self-Management in Old Age."...*

*"If many of the problems of old people are due to shortcomings in their environments," [Skinner said], "the environments can be improved ... If you cannot read, listen to book-recordings. If you do not hear well, turn up the volume on your phonograph (and wear headphones to protect your neighbors). Food can be flavored for aging palates. Paul Tillich, the theologian, defended pornography on the ground that it extended sexuality into old age.*

**FIGURE 13-14**
B.F. Skinner. (Courtesy of B.F. Skinner)

*you are skillful at that sort of thing, forgetting may even be a pleasure."*

*On forgetting ideas: "The problem in old age is not so much how to have ideas as how to have them when you can use them . . . A pocket notebook or recorder helps to maximize one's intellectual output by recording your behavior when it occurs. The practice is helpful at any age but particularly so for the aging scholar. In place of memories, memoranda."*

*On forgetting what you were going to say: "One solution is to keep saying it to yourself (his audience laughs appreciatively); another is to appeal to the privilege of old age and interrupt the speaker; another is to make a note (perhaps pretending it is about what the other person is saying). The same problem arises when you are speaking and digress. You finish the digression and cannot remember why you embarked on it or where you were when you did so. The solution is simply not to digress—that is, not to interrupt yourself." . . .*

*Although Skinner has his own share of afflictions—he wears a hearing aid and reads only with great difficulty—he seems to get by well enough. Though he walks to his office in William James Hall every morning—"striding down Brattle Street"—he admits to getting tired. Without blushing, he confesses that he does watch Archie Bunker nightly. It "comes on at 5:30—right before dinner. I usually get a good laugh out of it. I'm frank to say I enjoy it."*

*He reads detective novels, somewhat indiscriminately to hear him tell it. He likes to watch pro-football games on television, along with the Red Sox and programs on public television. He had to give up playing the piano when his eyes got too bad, he says, because he could never memorize music and he couldn't read the music and watch his hands.*

*He also expressed elegant scorn for the kind of patronizing that younger people bestow on the elderly:*

*"Those who help those who can help themselves can work a sinister kind of destruction by making the good things in life no longer contingent on behavior. If you have been very successful, the most sententious stupidities will be received as pearls of wisdom, and your standards will instantly fall." (Meyer, 1982, pp. B1, B9)*

*And there is always the possibility, secondhand though it may be, of living the highly reinforcing lives of others through literature, spectator sports, the theater and movies, and television." . . .*

*Skinner was not embarrassed to admit that he suffers from the conventional maladies of old age: a bad memory, especially for names; failing eyesight; fatigue, both mental and physical. He had helpful hints to offer on how to combat these problems.*

*On forgetting names: "Appeal to your age . . . Or flatter your listener by saying that you have noticed that the more important the person, the easier it is to forget the name. Recall the amusing story about forgetting your own name when you were asked for it by a clerk. If*

# ■ STUDY OUTLINE

## VULNERABILITY TO BRAIN DISORDERS

In the past, people looked for physical causes for all forms of maladaptive behavior. Today, psychologists believe that the psychological, social, and physical domains of human life are intertwined. Behavior is thought to be a joint product of individual differences and environmental variables. Among the factors that influence vulnerability to brain disorders are age, social support, stress, personality factors, and physical condition.

## ASSESSING BRAIN DAMAGE

The procedures used in assessing brain damage include a mental-status examination, neuropsychological testing, and radiological techniques. The **mental-status examination** provides information about the patient's level of consciousness, attention span, short-term memory, and the like. Neuropsychological tests are used to assess impairment in such areas as awareness of and responsiveness to sensory stimulation, while CT and PT scans are used to measure injuries or deterioration in specific regions of the brain.

## ORGANIC MENTAL DISORDERS

**1.** Clusters of psychological and behavioral symptoms that are connected with temporary or permanent brain dysfunction are called **organic brain syndromes.** Of these, the most common are delirium, dementia, intoxication, and withdrawal.

**2. Delirium** is characterized by relatively global cognitive impairment, disorientation, and confusion. It generally accompanies another serious physical problem. **Delirium tremens** is an acute brain condition that sometimes results from excessive alcohol consumption.

**3.** Brain deterioration, or **dementia,** is a gradual loss of intellectual abilities that is sufficient to interfere with social or occupational functioning. The term **senile dementia** is often used to refer to the condition when it occurs in people over 65. In younger individuals it is termed **presenile dementia.** A common symptom is **confabulation,** or filling in memory gaps with detailed, but inaccurate, information.

**4. Alzheimer's disease** is a disorder associated with advancing age. It is characterized by memory lapses, confusion, and dementia, and has an average duration of about seven years. The nerve cells of Alzheimer's victims contain abnormal rigid structures called plaques and tangles. There is also evidence of neurotransmitter deficiencies in patients with Alzheimer's disease.

**5. Pick's disease** is similar to Alzheimer's disease except that it is most likely to develop in the sixth decade and involves a form of brain atrophy.

**6. Multi-infarct dementia** is caused by a series of minor strokes that occur at different times and cause disturbances in memory, abstract thinking, judgment, and impulse control.

**7.** Other organic brain syndromes include **amnestic syndrome,** which is characterized by severe memory disturbance; **organic delusional syndrome,** in which there are organically caused delusions; **organic hallucinosis,** or hallucinations caused by an organic factor; **organic affective syndrome,** in which an abnormal mood is caused by a brain disorder; **organic anxiety syndrome;** and **organic personality syndrome,** which refers to personality changes that appear to be caused by an organic factor.

## BRAIN DISORDERS WITH A VARIETY OF CAUSES

**1. Huntington's chorea** is a rare hereditary disorder that is characterized by progressive degeneration of brain tissue. The symptoms include dementia, irritability and apathy, depression, and hallucinations and delusions. In addition, there are **choreiform movements,** or involuntary, spasmodic jerking and twisting movements. The disease is inherited through a single dominant gene.

**2. Parkinson's disease** is a progressive disorder that is characterized by tremor, rigidity, and loss of vocal power. It is believed to be caused by an acquired defect in the brain mechanism. Some of the symptoms can be relieved by the use of the drug L-dopa.

**3.** Infectious disorders such as **syphilis** can lead to **general paresis** or **dementia paralytica,** a progressive deterioration in psychological and motor functioning that results in paralysis, psychosis, and death. Prompt diagnosis and treatment is the best approach to reducing the incidence of this condition.

**4.** Vitamin and other nutritional deficiencies can affect the nervous system. **Pellagra** is caused by a deficiency of niacin; **Korsakoff's syndrome** results from a combination of alcoholism and thiamine deficiency.

**5.** Brain injuries can be classified into three groups: **concussions, contusions,** and **lacerations.** Such injuries can lead to specific losses in motor or cognitive functioning, as well as psychological reactions. Tumors in the brain can also produce behavioral changes. **Posttraumatic psychoses** involve confusion, delirium, and temporary catatonic, manic, or depressive reactions.

**6. Epilepsy** refers to a group of disorders involving seizures caused by transient electrical instability of some cells in the brain. The most severe form of epileptic disorder is the **grand mal seizure,** which includes loss of consciousness and extreme spasms. In a **petit mal seizure** there is a lapse of consciousness but no convulsion. **Psychomotor** or **temporal lobe epilepsy** is a trancelike state in which the individual carries out repetitive, semiautomatic movements. It is possible that psychological as well as organic factors play a role in epilepsy.

7. The methods used to treat epilepsy are drugs (e.g., Dilantin and phenobarbitol), surgery, and psychological management. Surgery consists of removal of parts of the temporal lobe and is attempted only after drugs and psychological approaches have failed.

8. **Cerebrovascular accidents,** or **strokes,** are blockages or ruptures of the blood vessels in the cerebellum. They can cause extensive damage to the brain and obvious changes in behavior. In some cases the effects are similar to those of dementia.

## AN INTEGRATIVE APPROACH TO BRAIN DISORDERS

Brain disorders can be treated psychologically as well as medically. Psychodynamic approaches emphasize the role of personality in people's responses to organic conditions. Behavioral psychologists focus on teaching new responses to compensate for those that have been lost. The cognitive perspective has contributed techniques to help people deal with declining intellectual competence.

## AGING AND PERSONALITY CHANGE

The elderly are vulnerable to serious consequences of brain disorders as well as psychological conditions in which the role of organic factors is less clear-cut. The latter include depression, suicidal tendencies, schizophrenia, paranoid thinking, hypochondria, and insomnia.

# 14

# PSYCHOACTIVE SUBSTANCE DEPENDENCE DISORDERS

The gentleman in the corner had been regarded as a true American success, lanky and deep-voiced, brilliant and beloved, the master of all he surveyed. Now, he gazed out defiantly, as if still on the summit, too high to see the cat feces at his feet or the unopened mail or the mirror that would have told him he was master of nothing but his own delusions.

Those who were to thrust the mirror in front of the 62-year-old man, whom I will call James B., were his daughter Isabel, myself, and three of the friends who loved him best.

If James B. had denied his problem, so had we. He had been depressed over the death of his wife and the loss of his architectural business. He had been presenting different excuses to each of us for his growing isolation. He had kept us at bay by clever use of the telephone, until it was cut off for nonpayment of a bill he had never opened.

Yet at last we had gathered into a crisis intervention team and surprised him, hung over, before he could perfect his alibis . . .

"Daddy, we are here because we love you." Isabel's voice wavered, but the 9-month-old baby on her knee stared at her grandfather unblinkingly. James B., very gingerly, poured out coffee. "I can understand your concern," he said. He had thrown on a shirt—even a tie—but below his bathrobe, his thin, red legs had the look of arms flung down in defeat. "I've had this local flu. I've been going to my doctor for shots every day."

"I checked with your doctor, Daddy, and he hasn't seen you for two years. We think your disease is alcoholism."

All of James B.'s roles now seemed to collide and fall away, revealing the obsession which shone in his eyes like unrequited love. "That's preposterous! My problems have nothing to do with alcohol."

Mel, his former business partner, said he had watched the most brilliant man he had ever known become addled into dull predictability. George, his former chess opponent, blushed and said that James B. had begun to cheat at the game. Lisa, his former lover, tremulously said she was going to marry a man she didn't love because the one she did had not preferred her to the bottle. I reminded him of the stars, and all of the people, including my baby and Isabel's, who could still learn from him.

Coached about the new science of alcohol and the liver, we tried to convince James B. that there was no shame in being an alcoholic.

"Look, can't you understand?" James B. said. "I'm sick, yes; depressed, yes; getting old, yes. But that's all."

"Jim," Mel said, in a voice that resonated with the tension we all felt, "it sounds like you would rather be anything at all than an alcoholic."

After 14 hours of this scenario, some of us began to question whether he really was an alcoholic. Maybe it was some other illness. Then he let spill a few words. "Geez, if I couldn't go down to the pub for a few, I think I'd go nuts!"

"Aaah," Isabel said. "You just admitted it." She put the baby on her father's knee. "Look at your granddaughter. This is your immortality, Daddy, and she needs you. Please don't die. Please choose life, for us."

James B. put his face, the color of gravel, in his hands. No one spoke. When he looked up, he said he would go to a local hospital. (Franks, 1985, p. 48)

Alcohol is one of a group of substances that have ruined the lives of countless numbers of people. Although there are many differences among them, all of these substances are *psychoactive*; that is, they affect thought, emotions, and behavior. As the case of James B. shows, they are capable of causing serious physical symptoms. This case also illustrates the tendency of abusers to deny that the substance they are using excessively is a major factor in their problems.

DSM-III-R classifies the behavioral and psychological effects associated with regular use of substances that affect the central nervous system as **psychoactive substance dependence disorders.** To distinguish recreational and medical use of these substances from pathological abuse, this category refers to behavioral and psychological changes that would be considered undesirable in almost any subculture—for example, impaired social or occupational performance, inability to stop taking the substance, and development of physiological or psychological symptoms if its use is discontinued.

People who use these substances may have periods of intoxication or withdrawal symptoms. **Intoxication** leads to a substance-specific syndrome that follows recent ingestion of the psychoactive substance. The syndrome includes various types of maladaptive behavior, such as belligerence and poor judgment. In **withdrawal,** a substance-specific syndrome follows cessation of or reduction in intake of a psychoactive substance that was previously used regularly to induce a state of intoxication. A generalized reduction in goal-directed behavior (for example, going to school or work), together with cognitive deficits (such as inability to concentrate), is a common consequence of prolonged heavy use of a psychoactive substance. There may also be *flashbacks* in which the person reexperiences one or more of the perceptual symptoms, such as hallucinations, that were originally experienced while intoxicated.

Some mood and behavior-modifying substances have medical uses. Physicians prescribe these substances to reduce pain, relieve tension, or aid in limiting food intake by suppressing appetite. Although the use of these substances is common in many cultural groups, there are some subcultural differences. Some religious groups, such as Moslems, frown on the use of alcohol. Mormons are expected to avoid not only alcohol but also coffee, tea, and other products that contain caffeine. On the other hand, some subcultural groups not only use alcohol but view the use of illegal substances such as marijuana or cocaine as a legitimate recreational activity.

Throughout history people have used a variety of substances to modify their moods and behavior. The use of some substances has become so common that it is considered normal and even appropriate; examples include champagne toasts for the New Year and a cigar for the new baby. A majority of adults use alcohol as a recreational drink; many individuals, from children to elderly people, use caffeine in the form of coffee, tea, or cola drinks as a stimulant; and a great many teenagers and adults use nicotine in the form of cigarettes. Reflecting on the many paths to paradise that people have explored or at least sought, the novelist Aldous Huxley came to the following somewhat pessimistic conclusion.

> That humanity at large will ever be able to dispose with artificial paradises seems very unlikely. Most men and women lead lives at the best so monotonous, poor, and limited that the urge to escape, the longing to transcend themselves if only for a few moments, is and has always been one of the principal appetites of the soul. (Huxley, 1954, p. 62)

## ■ SUBSTANCE DEPENDENCE

In order to justify the diagnosis of a **psychoactive substance dependence disorder,** the impairment in functioning that results from the substance use must be severe and long-lasting. Some of the symptoms must continue for at least a month or they must occur frequently for a period of at least six months. Getting drunk at the company New Year's Eve party would not qualify; neither would a single drunken binge after a family quarrel. Instead, there must be significant, ongoing maladaptive behavior that interferes with social functioning or effectiveness on the job and continues even though the person knows that use of the substance is having important negative consequences.

Another characteristic of substance dependence is that when not actually using the substance, the person spends a lot of time looking forward to using it and devotes a great deal of effort to making it available. For example, an office worker might have a three-martini lunch and keep the glow going by nipping at a bottle he keeps hidden in his desk. He would be unable to restrict his use of alcohol to certain times of the day, such as after working hours, even though his accuracy in preparing reports had slipped and he had received several warnings from the boss. A factory worker might know that her safety depended on being alert around a drill press, yet she might still drink on the job. A retired engineer might continue to drink even though he knew that the resultant damage to his liver was creating a life-threatening situation. All of these examples involve alcohol, but we could have substituted marijuana, heroin, or Valium. The critical factor is not the particular substance used but its effects on the person's life.

Physiological dependence on a substance can be shown in one of two ways: tolerance or withdrawal. Withdrawal refers to a particular set of physical symptoms that occur when a person stops or cuts down on the use of a psychoactive substance. The physical reaction that occurs when the use of heroin is stopped is probably the best-known form of withdrawal. **Tolerance** means that the person has to use more and more of a substance to get the same effect, or that the same-sized dose has progressively less effect as time goes by. For example, the pain-reducing power of morphine decreases if the drug is given over a long period. As alcoholics consume increasing amounts of alcohol, their cell membranes are altered so that less and less of the alcohol permeates the membranes. If less alcohol is actually penetrating cell membranes, an alcoholic may have less alcohol in his or her brain than a normal person with the same blood level of alcohol would. This is interesting in view of the fact that some alcoholics can perform well after consuming an amount of alcohol that would put a nonalcoholic into a coma.

The substances that can produce physiological dependence include alcohol, amphetamines, barbiturates, opioids, and tobacco. Four types of substances are related to psychological dependence only (i.e., have never been shown to produce physiological dependence). They are cannabis, cocaine, psychedelics, and PCP. Table 14–8 gives more information about these substances.

Psychologists are interested in substance dependence because a person's response to drugs seems to be due to a combination of physiological and psychological factors. Some people can control their use of many of these substances; others seem unable to do so.

Some individuals who are addicted have severe withdrawal symptoms; others do not. The effects that drugs produce also differ from one user to another. Freud noted this when he described the effects of cocaine.

> After a short time (10–20 minutes), he feels as though he had been raised to full height of intellectual and bodily vigor, in a state of euphoria, which is distinguished from the euphoria after consumption of alcohol by the absence of any feeling of alteration. . . . One can perform mental and physical work with great endurance, and the otherwise urgent needs of rest, food, and sleep are thrust aside, as it were. During the first hours after cocaine, it is even impossible to fall asleep. This effect of the alkaloid gradually fades away after the aforesaid time, and is not followed by any depression. . . . I could not fail to note, however, that the individual disposition plays a major role in the effects of cocaine, perhaps a more important role than with other alkaloids. The subjective phenomena after ingesting coca differ from person to person, and only few persons experience, like myself, a pure euphoria without alteration. Others already experience a slight intoxication, hyperkinesia, and talkativeness after the same amount of cocaine, while still others have no subjective symptoms of the effects of coca at all. (Freud, 1963)

Probably both the personality and physiological characteristics of the user and the environment or setting in which the substance is used influence the reaction observed. This is another case in which the interaction between the person and the situation, which has been referred to so often throughout the book, is important in understanding individual behavior. However, although these individual characteristics have a major influence on a person's response to a mood- or behavior-modifying substance, such substances do have certain general effects that are experienced by most people who use them.

# ■ ALCOHOL

Negative effects of overuse of alcohol have been considered a social problem for many years (see Figure 14–1). About 70 percent of adults in America drink alcohol on occasion; 12 percent of them are heavy drinkers, people who drink almost every day and become intoxicated several times a month. More men than women are heavy drinkers. For both men and women, the prevalence of drinking is highest and abstention is lowest in the 21- to 34-year age range (Goodwin, 1985). Table 14–1 provides estimates of the percent of alcohol in the blood as a function of amount of alcohol consumed and body weight.

Abuse of alcohol or other psychoactive substances means using them in a way that has negative effects on a person's life. Alcohol abuse shows several typical patterns: regular daily intake of a large amount, regular heavy drinking confined to weekends, and unpredictable binge drinking (long periods without alcohol interrupted by episodes of heavy drinking lasting for weeks or months). Alcohol abuse is often referred to as **problem drinking** while alcohol dependence or addiction is referred to as **alcoholism.** Problem drinking should not be viewed as a step on the way to alcoholism, though some individuals do progress from one to the other.

Many college administrators feel that the use of alcohol and other drugs on their campuses is increasing. As a result many schools have established programs to educate students about the effects of alcohol. Table 14–2 shows the results of a survey of college deans concerning alcohol use and abuse on their campuses. The excessive use of alcohol by many high school students is also considered a major problem. A recent survey in New York state found that 27 percent of secondary school students drink more than moderately (see Table 14–3). Evidence that substance use begins at early grade levels suggests that intervention efforts should begin prior to junior high school, perhaps as early as the fourth or fifth grade (Keyes and Block, 1984).

## Alcohol and Health

Alcoholism is one of the most common mental disorders in the United States, and abuse of alcohol is strongly associated with increased risk of dying. People who drink heavily even on occasion face an increased risk of death associated with accidents, especially those caused by drunken driving. This is because alcohol acts like a general anesthetic, thereby impairing driving skills. Drivers aged 16 to 24 have the highest rate of alcohol-related crashes. Figure 14–2 shows the relationship between blood alcohol concentration and the probability that the person will cause a fatal automobile accident.

Research data show that alcohol is also involved in a high percentage of nontraffic accidents: Almost 50 percent of people who died from falls had been drinking; 52 percent of the fires that led to adult deaths involved alcohol; and 50 to 68 percent of drowning victims had been drinking (*Special report to Congress on alcohol and health*, 1981).

Highway accidents in which alcohol is involved are the primary cause of death for young people. After 18-year-olds received the right to vote in 1971, the legal drinking age was lowered in many states. Studies of auto accident statistics from these states produced con-

(a)

(b)

**FIGURE 14-1**
The negative social effects of alcohol have concerned reformers for centuries. The nineteenth-century illustration in (a) was part of a series on the evils of drink. The caption reads, "Quarrels between Mr. and Mrs. Latimer, and brutal violence between them, were the natural consequences of the too frequent use of the bottle." The illustration in (b), "Gin Lane," first published in 1751, shows some of the evils of alcohol as seen by William Hogarth. (Engravings by Hogarth, NY Dover, 1973)

## Are You Drunk?

This table shows the estimated percent of alcohol in the blood according to body weight and the number of drinks consumed. One drink equals one ounce of 100-proof alcohol, a 4-ounce glass of wine, or a 12-ounce bottle of beer. Alcohol in the blood decreases over time. To calculate how much time decreases blood-alcohol level, subtract .015 for each hour that has passed since the first drink.

### PERCENT ALCOHOL IN BLOOD

| Body Weight | Drinks | | | | | | | Interpreting the Results | |
|---|---|---|---|---|---|---|---|---|---|
| | 1 | 2 | 3 | 4 | 5 | 6 | | *Blood alcohol* | *Intoxicated?* |
| 100 lbs. | .038 | .075 | .113 | .150 | .188 | .225 | | .000 to .050% | No |
| 120 | .031 | .063 | .094 | .125 | .156 | .188 | | .050 to .100 | Maybe[a] |
| 140 | .027 | .054 | .080 | .107 | .134 | .161 | | .100 to .150 | Probably |
| 160 | .023 | .047 | .070 | .094 | .117 | .141 | | .150 and above | Yes |
| 180 | .021 | .042 | .063 | .083 | .104 | .125 | | | |
| 200 | .019 | .038 | .056 | .075 | .094 | .113 | | | |
| 220 | .017 | .034 | .051 | .068 | .085 | .102 | | | |
| 240 | .016 | .031 | .047 | .063 | .078 | .094 | | | |

[a]In most states, .100 is proof of illegal intoxication.

*Source:* Government of the District of Columbia.

---

□ **TABLE 14-2**
## Alcohol Use among College Students as Reported by College Deans

| | |
|---|---|
| Percent of students who drink: | |
| Excessively[a] | 16.1 |
| Socially[b] | 52.1 |
| Experimentally[c] | 26.3 |
| Not at all | 24.7 |
| Percent of students needing treatment for alcohol abuse | 5.6 |
| Percent of students leaving college because of alcohol | 2.3 |
| Percent of institutions reporting increases in the last five years: | |
| In excessive drinking by students | 35.9 |
| In student use of marijuana | 17.1 |
| In student use of cocaine | 40.9 |
| In faculty and staff use of alcohol | 22.1 |
| In number of students seeking help for alcohol abuse | 44.2 |
| Percent of institutions reporting increases in alcohol-related problems in the last five years: | |
| Bad hangovers | 21.0 |
| Drinking before or while driving | 23.8 |
| Drinking before class | 15.5 |
| Missing class | 22.1 |
| Getting lower grades | 23.8 |
| Fighting | 26.5 |
| Damaging property | 29.8 |
| Loss of memory | 19.9 |
| Doing something later regretted | 24.3 |

[a]Occasional to frequent drinking resulting in intoxication.

[b]Drinking in social settings and usually in moderation, as a secondary reason rather than main reason for the occasion.

[c]Infrequent drinking that may include such first-time experiences as patronizing a bar, drinking to the point of intoxication, or getting sick.

*Source:* 1982 Chronicle of Higher Education Survey from John Minter Associates, *New York Times,* August 22, 1982, p. 20E. Copyright © 1982 by the New York Times Company. Reprinted by permission.

□ **TABLE 14-3**
Drinking Rates Among Secondary School Students in New York State (N = 1,542,000).

| Drinking Classification | Percent |
|---|---|
| Abstainers | 27% |
| Infrequent drinkers | 14 |
| Light drinkers | 16 |
| Moderate drinkers | 14 |
| Moderate/heavy drinkers[a] | 14 |
| Heavy drinkers[a] | 13 |

[a]Heavy drinkers drank a very large amount once a week; moderate/heavy drinkers drank a large amount once a week.
*Source:* Barnes, 1984.

vincing evidence that the age reduction had resulted in an increased proportion of auto crashes and fatalities involving youthful drivers. Since 1976, therefore, many states have raised the drinking age. In the 12 months after Michigan raised the drinking age, accidents resulting in death or injury among 18-to-20-year-olds dropped by 28 percent.

**FIGURE 14-2**
The relative probability of being responsible for a fatal crash rises with rising blood alcohol concentrations. (Council on Scientific Affairs, American Medical Association, 1986, p. 523)

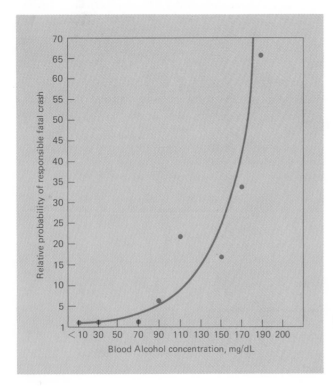

Other health risks associated with overuse of alcohol are high blood pressure and several types of cancer. People who both smoke and use alcohol are especially vulnerable to certain forms of cancer (Tuyns, 1979). Cirrhosis of the liver, which can be fatal, is often associated with overuse of alcohol. Even one or two years of heavy drinking may bring on this disorder (Turner and others, 1977), although it is most frequently seen after long-term heavy use.

Alcohol may also have some beneficial effects. Moderate use of alcohol (2 ounces, or two drinks, per day) may lessen the chances of a heart attack (Hennekens and others, 1979). It is not clear why this should be the case, but researchers have suggested a number of possibilities. Alcohol may reduce psychological stress, or it may promote the formation of substances that help prevent or remove the plaque that can clog the coronary arteries. Some researchers worry that announcing positive effects of alcohol use will be interpreted as a suggestion that drinking is desirable for everyone. They point out that it is premature to recommend alcohol as a heart-attack preventative. A moderate amount for one person may be too much for another because of individual differences in tolerance for alcohol.

When alcohol is abused extensively, brain damage can result. For example, CT scans of young chronic alcoholics showed reductions in the density of their left brain hemispheres compared to those of nonalcoholic individuals (Golden and others, 1981). Brain dysfunction is present in from 50 to 70 percent of detoxified alcoholics at the beginning of treatment. Certain cognitive abilities of people who use alcohol only moderately in social situations have been found to be impaired even 24 hours after they last used alcohol (Eckhardt and others, 1981).

One of the most dramatic findings concerning the effects of alcohol has been the identification of **fetal alcohol syndrome.** This syndrome, which produces mental retardation and a number of physical malformations, results from heavy use of alcohol by pregnant women. Even light to moderate alcohol use is now thought to have negative effects on the unborn child. (Fetal alcohol syndrome is discussed in Chapter 16.)

A recent study permitted estimates of the years of potential life lost (YPLL) as a result of alcohol-related causes of death. Table 14–4 shows the YPLL rates for whites, blacks, and Native Americans, and for males and females, in relation to alcohol abuse and alcohol dependence. Native Americans have the highest rate of YPLL, and men of all races have a higher rate than women. Targeting groups with high risk of premature death from alcohol misuse can be useful in planning educational and other intervention programs aimed at reducing the risk.

## TABLE 14-4
Years of Potential Life Lost (YPLL) Rates per 100,000 Population for Alcohol-Related Causes of Death, by Race and Sex

| Cause | Race | YPLL rates per 100,000 | |
|---|---|---|---|
| | | Male | Female |
| Alcohol abuse | White | 72.9 | 19.7 |
| | Black | 131.5 | 32.2 |
| | Native American | 458.8 | 97.3 |
| Alcohol dependence | White | 117.2 | 32.8 |
| | Black | 459.1 | 158.8 |
| | Native American | 769.8 | 372.0 |

*Source:* Adapted from *Morbidity and Mortality Weekly Report,* 1985.

## Perspectives on Alcohol Abuse

**The Biological View**  Ingestion of alcohol is associated with numerous behavioral, biophysical, and psychological changes. After the first drink, the average person experiences a lessening of anxiety. As more alcohol is consumed, the depressant action of alcohol affects brain functions. The individual staggers, and his or her mood becomes markedly unstable. Sensory perception is seriously impaired.

Influenced by evidence that heavy drinking leads to a variety of bodily changes, writers have often characterized alcoholism itself as a disease. E. M. Jellinek (1960), often referred to as the father of the modern study of alcoholism, believed that alcoholism is a permanent and irreversible condition and that alcoholics are essentially different from nonalcoholics. Alcoholics, he contended, experience an irresistible physical craving for alcohol. Satisfaction of this craving leads to loss of control as a result of increasing physical dependence on alcohol. Alcoholic individuals feel compelled to continue drinking even after ingesting only a small amount of alcohol. Jellinek believed that the only way alcoholics can return to a normal life is through complete abstinence.

Some of Jellinek's ideas have been questioned on the basis of research findings that seem inconsistent with them. However, Jellinek's disease concept of alcoholism has succeeded in changing people's attitude toward alcoholics from one of condemnation and blame to one of concern. In addition, it has focused researchers' attention on the biological aspects of alcohol abuse.

*Genetic Factors in Susceptibility to Alcohol*  Studies using animals have shown that it is possible to breed strains of mice or rats that differ in their metabolism of alcohol. Some of these strains prefer dilute alcohol solutions to water, while others avoid alcohol at all costs. It has been demonstrated many times that alcoholism runs in human families as well. One-third of all alcoholics report that one or more of their parents were alcoholic, compared to 5 percent of the general population (Schuckit, 1981).

An extensive study of the medical and social records of adopted children in Sweden has identified two different forms of inherited alcohol problems (Cloninger and others, 1981). One type is called **male limited** because it is passed only from fathers to sons. The son of an affected father is very likely to show alcohol problems regardless of the environment in which the child grows up. This condition seems to occur only in men whose fathers have extensive criminal records in addition to histories of alcohol abuse. The fathers of these sons usually began drinking in adolescence. Alcohol abuse often interfered with their work and marriage, and they were often arrested for violent crimes such as wife beating and assault. About one-fourth of the sons of these men developed alcohol problems even though they were reared by adoptive parents. The kind of environment provided by the adoptive parents was related to the severity of the abuse problem in the adopted children but not to whether they became abusers or not.

The other type of inherited alcohol problem is called **milieu limited** because in this group, although susceptibility seemed to be hereditary, environmental factors significantly affected the frequency and severity of the drinking problem. The milieu-limited type of alcohol problem accounted for three-quarters of the men and all of the women in the study. Their biological parents showed both mild alcohol abuse and mild forms of criminal behavior compared to the fathers in the male-limited type. Women whose mothers had alcohol problems seemed more susceptible to difficulties related to alcohol use than women whose fathers were alcohol abusers.

Studies of genetic susceptibility to alcohol have led researchers to think about the specific physical pathways that lead to the alcoholic behavior pattern. Box 14-1 describes some recent research on the roles of enzymes and of neurochemical and neurophysiological factors in susceptibility to alcohol.

*Markers of Susceptibility to Alcohol.*  There is little doubt that heredity plays an important role in an individual's susceptibility to alcohol abuse and alcoholism. By itself, however, this knowledge is of little value in the prevention of alcoholism. The urgent need is to identify genetically based physiological or biochemical markers that show unequivocally the existence of an inherited susceptibility to alcohol abuse (Goodwin, 1985).

# ■ BOX 14-1. ENZYMES, NEUROCHEMICAL AND NEUROPHYSIOLOGICAL MECHANISMS, AND SUSCEPTIBILITY TO ALCOHOL.

Individual sensitivity to the effects of alcohol varies greatly. Some people can remain conscious after drinking a quantity of alcohol that would cause others to "pass out," become comatose, or even die. Others are so sensitive to alcohol that just one or two drinks can produce acute discomfort accompanied by facial flushing, elevated skin temperature, and a rapid pulse. These individual variations are probably due to differences in the ability to metabolize alcohol, to innate differences in the central nervous system's sensitivity to alcohol, or to differences in the capacity to adapt rapidly to the presence of alcohol (acute tolerance).

The body's major chemical pathway for the metabolism of alcohol requires the action of two enzymes—alcohol dehydrogenase (ADH) and acetaldehyde dehydrogenase (ALDH). The process, which occurs mostly in the liver, involves three steps. First, alcohol is converted into acetaldehyde by the action of ADH; second, acetaldehyde is converted into acetic acid by the action of ALDH; finally, acetic acid is converted by a series of enzymes into carbon dioxide and water. Considerable scientific attention is being focused on the molecular structure and function of ADH and ALDH to determine how genetic variations in their properties might account for individual differences in sensitivity to alcohol and susceptibility to alcoholism.

A major area of study is the comparison of alcohol metabolism in different races (*Alcoholism: an inherited disease,* 1985). There is evidence of a high prevalence of sensitivity to alcohol among people of Oriental derivation (Chinese, Japanese, Koreans, Native Americans, and Eskimos). Signs of sensitivity—rapid facial flushing, elevated skin temperature, and increased pulse rate—after consuming moderate amounts of alcohol appear to be common among these groups but are seen in only 5 percent of Caucasians. Recent studies suggest that these differences are based on genetic variations in the enzymes involved in alcohol metabolism. Distinct molecular differences have been found in ADH and ALDH of Orientals and Caucasians.

Another important area of research on susceptibility to alcohol is the role of neurochemical and neurophysiological factors. Alcohol affects every system of the body, but its greatest, most immediate, and most visible effects are on the central nervous system. The chemical processes involved in the transmission of neural impulses are carried out at the synapse by neurotransmitters that are released from the axon and join with specific receptors in the dendrites of nearby neurons. (Figure 3-2 illustrates this process.) The propagation of an electrical signal along a nerve cell is based on the movement of sodium and potassium ions back and forth through the membrane that encloses the cell. The movement of these ions through the membrane is regulated by the enzyme sodium-potassium ATPase, whose molecules are embedded in the cell membrane.

All of the complex features of the self—thoughts, emotions, actions—are based on these chemical and electrical processes, which occur in billions of nerve cells at any instant. Several features of this system could be involved in inherited predisposition to alcoholism. Alcohol could interfere with numerous processes involved in nerve cell function, and if there is inherited variation in these processes it could result in either neurochemical vulnerability or resistance to alcoholism. Among the leading neurochemical hypotheses are the following.

- Individuals who are predisposed toward alcoholism might have nerve cell membranes that are less sensitive to the permeability-altering effects of alcohol, which would affect the movement of sodium and potassium ions and the propagation of nerve impulses.

- Predisposition toward alcoholism might be based on inherited variations in the sensitivity of sodium-potassium ATPase and other membrane enzymes to inhibition by alcohol. This also would affect the transmission of nerve impulses, which depend on the enzyme's regulation of the flow of ions through the nerve cell membrane.

- Predisposition toward alcoholism may be based on inherited variations in the neurotransmitter release and uptake systems involved in the chemical propagation of nerve impulses between nerve cells.

- People who are predisposed to alcoholism may produce abnormal amounts of certain morphine-like compounds that may be involved in alcohol addiction.

- Predisposition toward alcoholism may be based on inherited variations in the brain's neurochemical mechanisms for reinforcing certain behaviors.

It seems plausible that the genetic susceptibility to alcoholism might be expressed in alterations of certain neurobehavioral functions that can be measured in the laboratory. Scientists exploring this new area of research are coming up with encouraging findings. For example, an individual whose body produces a variant of the enzymes ADH or ALDH that causes acetaldehyde to accumulate can be said to have a genetic marker—in this case, a genetic marker of relative nonsusceptibility to alcoholism. Researchers are exploring other possible markers of genetic susceptibility among the variant forms of ADH and ALDH.

In view of the neurochemical basis of reinforcement, it seems very likely that an individual's genetic predisposition toward alcoholism could be due to inheritance of neurochemical mechanisms that are abnormally responsive to alcohol. Such individuals may become alcoholic because alcohol is abnormally stimulating and rewarding to them. But it is important to realize that even if heredity is involved in alcoholism, this is not a reason to adopt a fatalistic attitude. Environment is also involved, and while we cannot alter our heredity, we can alter our environment. A proper environment or an appropriate intervention can prevent milieu-limited alcoholism in spite of the existence of a genetic component, and even if the more serious male-limited form of hereditary alcoholism cannot be prevented, its effects can be made less serious. (Gabrielli and Plomin, 1985).

Knowledge that alcoholism has both genetic and environmental components can have important practical applications. Prevention of alcohol abuse and alcoholism would certainly be an important application of this new and growing knowledge. If reliable biological indicators of a predisposition toward alcoholism can be found, individuals who have those indicators can know the risks they face and can make informed choices about drinking.

Another practical application is improved treatment. It is already clear that alcoholism is not a single disease entity. By clarifying the nature of various subcategories of alcoholism, genetic studies can point the way to more specific and effective therapies based on the genetic uniqueness of individuals.

**The Psychodynamic View** Psychodynamic theorists often describe the typical person who develops an alcohol problem as an **oral-dependent personality**. They believe that such a person's basic need for oral gratification was not satisfied early in life. This lack of satisfaction resulted in the development of an individual who is driven to secure oral satisfaction through such devices as drinking, smoking, and eating, and

whose personality is characterized by s_ sivity, and dependence.

To investigate this possibility, Georg_ used data from a longitudinal study of men w_ first contacted in their college years. Vaillant con_ cluded that an unhappy childhood and personality problems in college are related to oral-dependent behavior but not to alcoholism. A longitudinal study of another, quite different group—adolescent boys from an inner-city environment—suggested that emotional problems and family difficulties in childhood are not related to alcohol abuse (Vaillant, 1976; Vaillant and Milofsky, 1982). If cultural factors related to ethnic background and the number of alcoholic relatives were taken into account, childhood characteristics were not useful in predicting alcoholism in middle adulthood. From these two studies, Vaillant concluded that the average alcohol-abusing adult does not drink because he or she had an unhappy childhood. Instead, the alcohol abuser is unhappy in adulthood as a result of abuse of alcohol.

Although there is no conclusive evidence that personality factors are involved in the development of alcoholism, a study reported by Jones (1981) demonstrated a consistent set of personality attributes among some alcoholics. The study drew upon data from a longitudinal research project that had begun when the subjects were 10½ years old. In middle age the subjects were interviewed about their drinking patterns. Jones found that as adults, male problem drinkers were likely to be described as relatively hostile, submissive, socially unsuccessful, and anxious. In general, these men had been rated as rather extraverted in adolescence. However, at that time they also described themselves as having less satisfactory social relationships and greater feelings of inferiority than other males in the study. Jones believed that these men were rather impulsive and unsure of themselves in adolescence and that they had difficulty forming deeper, more lasting friendships.

Jones' finding of some childhood personality correlates of adult problem drinking would appear to conflict with Vaillant's finding that childhood personality is unrelated to adult problem drinking. Additional longitudinal studies are needed to clarify the issue, since Vaillant and Jones studied two quite different samples of subjects.

**Learning Factors** Some people drink as a way of coping with problems of living. They learn this behavior through reinforcement (being accepted by friends who value drinking), modeling (seeing others "solve" their problems with alcohol), and other learning mechanisms. Short-term use of alcohol may be reinforcing for many people because of the pleasurable feeling of relaxation it produces. But since drinking is not an effective coping mechanism, their life situation does not improve. Feeling even less able to cope constructively, they increase their maladaptive coping behavior.

It is also possible that alcohol is sought for its short-term excitatory actions and is reinforcing because it makes people "feel good." Like all psychological phenomena, reinforcement has underlying neurochemical mechanisms. Most researchers agree that alcohol is a reinforcer, that its reinforcement arises from specific mechanisms within the brain, and that these mechanisms, which constitute the brain's reward system, are probably located in a specific cluster of nerve cells.

Several studies have implicated certain neurochemicals in the reinforcing properties of alcohol. Alcohol may make many people "feel good" because it alters the levels of dopamine and norepinephrine, as well as opioid peptides, in a specific brain region. Subjectively, these neurochemical changes are experienced as excitation, and because that experience can be pleasurable, both people and animals will seek alcohol again (*Alcoholism: an inherited disease*, 1985).

**Cognitive Factors**  Behavior is influenced by expectations about the consequences of behaving in a particular way as well as by what actually does happen. Behavior thus can be shaped and maintained by cognitive appraisals of what has happened and what is likely to happen. A problem drinker learns to expect

positive effects from drinking and interprets the experience in that way, despite the fact that the predominant quality of the actual experience is negative.

The importance of expectancy is illustrated by an experiment reported by Marlatt and others (1973). These investigators used a taste-rating task to determine whether drinking rates are affected by the actual presence of alcohol or merely by the expectancy of alcohol. The taste-rating task was an unobtrusive measure of drinking because the person's attention was focused on the taste of the drinks. The drinks used were vodka and tonic, and tonic alone. The subjects were permitted to drink as much of the beverages as they wished in the time allotted. The researchers found that the only significant determinant of the amount of alcohol consumed was the subject's expectations regarding what they were drinking; those who expected alcohol drank more. This finding supports a cognitive interpretation of drinking. (Later in the chapter we discuss the applications of this cognitive perspective to therapy for problem drinkers.) Figure 14–3 shows a naturalistic setting for experiments on drinking behavior.

There is evidence that a person's belief about the alcohol content of a drink, regardless of its actual content, can be a significant determiner not only of alcohol consumption but also of various behaviors that may accompany or result from drinking such as depression, delay of gratification, social anxiety, and sexual responsiveness in men. This evidence comes from studies using the *balanced placebo design*, in which half of the

**FIGURE 14–3**
Behavioral Alcohol Research Laboratory (BARLAB), a University of Washington research facility is designed for direct observation of drinking behavior in a seminaturalistic setting. (John A. Moore, Office of Information Services, University of Washington)

subjects are given a drink containing alcohol and half are given a nonalcoholic beverage. By varying both drink content and expectancy set, this design permits joint and separate evaluation of the behavioral consequences of a subject's belief that he or she has consumed alcohol and the consequences of actual alcohol consumption.

**Social and Community Factors**   The problem of excessive use of alcohol has sociocultural as well as psychological dimensions. The values and customs of the community influence attitudes toward drinking. In the past, problems of alcohol use were extremely frequent among certain ethnic groups, such as the Irish and Swedish, relatively infrequent for Italians, and particularly infrequent for Jews. Today, however, alcoholism is decreasing among Irish- and Swedish-Americans but rising among second- and third-generation Italian-Americans and Jews. Changing social customs within the cultural group seem to be a significant factor in these patterns of alcohol consumption.

Rates of alcoholism are low in groups in which the drinking customs, values, and sanctions are well known, agreed to by all, and consistent with the rest of the culture (see Figure 14-4). Among the sociocultural conditions that minimize alcohol problems are the following.

1. Exposure of children to alcohol at an early age in a strong family or religious setting. The alcoholic beverage is served in diluted form (wine as opposed to distilled spirits, for example) and in small quantities.
2. The beverage is considered a food and is served mainly at meals.
3. Drinking is not considered either a virtue—for example, a proof of manhood or virility—or a sin.
4. Abstinence is socially acceptable but excessive drinking or drunkenness is not.

A variety of social and interpersonal factors also influence alcohol consumption. These include the level of stress in the community and in the individual's personal life. Among the personal factors are friendships, family situation, and employment and financial status (Linsky and others, 1985).

## Treatment

The first step in treating an addicted alcohol user is usually detoxification, or "drying out." Physiological withdrawal symptoms often begin 6 to 24 hours after heavy drinking has stopped, although they can occur when alcoholics simply reduce their intake of alcohol.

Withdrawal signs can include tremors, delirium, sweating, confusion, increased blood pressure, and agitation. Once detoxification is complete, insomnia, depression, and anxiety may persist for weeks or months. Most people with alcohol-related problems do not receive treatment for them after the detoxification period. In the following section we describe several treatment programs for problem drinkers and detoxified alcoholics.

**The Biological Approach**   Earlier in the chapter we mentioned that biological theories regarding susceptibility to alcohol might someday lead to effective physical therapies for alcoholism. Such therapies have not yet been developed, but one outgrowth of the view that alcoholism is a disease, caused perhaps by an allergy or physiological sensitivity to alcohol, is the belief that the alcoholic needs to avoid alcoholic beverages completely. According to the disease model, losing control of drinking is an involuntary manifestation of an internal addictive disorder. If one drink is enough to set off a drinking binge in alcoholics who want to rehabilitate themselves, that drink must not be taken. Because Alcoholics Anonymous (AA) attempts to help the alcoholic resist taking that one drink, the AA program is widely recommended by adherents of the disease model.

AA is a self-help program for alcoholics that emphasizes the need for spiritual awakening. Its members are expected to admit their powerlessness to solve their drinking problem and to confess their personal defects. They must resolve to devote themselves to helping others in need without regard to personal prestige or material gain.

One study estimated that of the alcoholics who stay in AA, about half are abstinent after 2 years, 15 percent drink lightly to moderately, and at least 13 percent drink abusively. Because 21 percent could not be traced after two years, the number of failures may be higher (Alford, 1980). These figures are somewhat difficult to interpret because many alcoholics drop out of the program, presumably as failures, yet are not counted in the statistics. However, a comprehensive review of research on the topic supports the conclusion that AA is an effective source of help for many alcoholics (Leach, 1973). One of AA's most important rehabilitative ingredients is the social support it provides for members. Members know that they can call upon fellow members at any time for aid in resisting the temptations of alcohol. Although AA may not be the right approach for every alcoholic, for those who find it congenial it can be a valuable source of support, belongingness, and security.

Another biological approach to alcohol problems is

(a)

(b)

**FIGURE 14-4**
The context in which alcoholic beverages are consumed is an important factor in alcoholism. Drinking wine at family gatherings, like this Jewish Passover ceremony (a), is much less likely to lead to problem drinking than drinking in situations in which there is pressure for the individual to "excel at drinking" (b). (Sybil Shackman, Monkmeyer Press and Robert E. Murowchick, Photo Researchers).

the use of disulfiram to alter the body's response to alcohol. Disulfiram is a drug that causes extreme and sometimes violent discomfort (nausea, vomiting, cold sweats) when a person drinks alcohol within 12 hours of taking it. Since disulfiram is self-administered, the success of this technique depends on the individual's motivation to reduce or eliminate drinking. If the person wants to drink, disulfiram therapy will fail. It may be useful, however, as part of a therapeutic approach that also deals with motivations or situational cues that lead to alcohol use.

**The Psychodynamic Approach** Clinicians who take a psychodynamic perspective advocate psychotherapy for alcoholics. Although there have been some encouraging clinical reports on the usefulness of psychotherapy, research on the topic has not yet produced definitive conclusions. Most studies of psychotherapy with alcoholics are not comparable with respect to such important variables as the setting in which the treatment was applied, the duration of the therapy, and the criteria by which the therapy was evaluated.

The following case illustrates the psychodynamic

approach to alcoholism. It concerns Mr. R., a 37-year-old alcoholic who was married and had two preschool-age sons. In psychotherapy sessions much time was devoted to his obsessive desire to tell his wife to be quiet.

*Mr. R.: I don't know—I just get so up-tight with Ann; it's driving me crazy!*

*Therapist: I wonder if the "up-tightness" could be caused by a holding-in? Is there something you're trying not to say to Ann?*

*Mr. R.: Maybe . . . I guess I do keep wanting to tell her to shut up! . . . to shut up and stop her nagging and pushing.*

*Therapist: So what would happen if you told her to shut up?*

*Mr. R.: She couldn't take it . . . I know she couldn't. She'd . . . she'd, God! . . . She might even pack up and leave.*

*Therapist: Leave? Just because you tell her to shut up?*

*Mr. R.: Sure. She's not used to being told to do anything; she does all the telling.*

*Therapist: So you've never told her to shut up?*

*Mr. R.: Only when I've had a few.*

*Therapist: Only when you've been drinking?*

*Mr. R.: Yeah, like last Friday; I came home late and she started in right away—wanted me to drive her to the store. Shopping's her avocation and one I don't want to share. If she had her way, I'd drive her to one store or another, seven days a week.*

*Therapist: What did you say to her?*

*Mr. R.: Well, I'd stopped for a few drinks so I just told her to forget it and went out again.* (Triana and Hinkle, 1974, pp. 287–288)

The therapist discussed with Mr. R. the ways in which he might confront his wife about her excessive demands. One step that Mr. R. took was to arrange a schedule whereby his wife would go shopping and he would pick her up. The therapist helped him put his relationship with his wife in perspective by clarifying and accepting the conscious anger he felt. Mr. R. then was able to experiment with ways of expressing his anger more appropriately.

The use of psychotherapy to help people with alcohol problems may be limited by the fact that they often need help at odd hours in their efforts to stay sober. The low self-esteem of some overusers of alcohol may be even further lowered by having to depend on people who do not have an alcohol problem.

**The Learning Approach**  Aversive conditioning is based on the principles of classical conditioning. If a glass of alcohol (conditioned stimulus) regularly precedes an aversive stimulus such as a nausea-producing drug (uncontrolled stimulus), the alcohol will eventually elicit some part of the unconditioned response—in this case, vomiting. Once the unpleasant response has been conditioned to alcohol, the habit of avoiding alcohol will be established through operant conditioning. The response of abstinence is strengthened because it reduces the unpleasant feeling (nausea) that the conditioning situation has associated with alcohol. Electric shock is sometimes used in place of nausea-producing drugs in this procedure, but it seems to be less effective. Aversive-conditioning approaches often require "booster sessions" because the threat of an unpleasant reaction tends to weaken over time. Long-term follow-up studies are needed to establish the success rate of aversive conditioning.

Another learning approach, covert sensitization, uses aversive images and fantasies rather than actual shocks and chemicals. Alcoholic patients are told that they can eliminate their "faulty habit" by associating it with unpleasant stimuli. They are instructed to close their eyes and imagine that they are about to drink an alcoholic beverage. They are then taught to imagine the sensations of nausea and vomiting. If it is repeated often enough, the association between nausea and the sight, smell, and taste of alcohol is presumed to establish a conditioned aversion to alcohol.

**The Cognitive Approach**  In the cognitive approach, clients are oriented toward monitoring their own behavior by noting the situational and environmental antecedents and consequences of heavy drinking. Their past learning in relation to drinking is reviewed, and their expectations about the effects of alcohol are discussed. Participants in controlled-drinking programs are encouraged to ask themselves questions like the following.

- At what places am I most likely to overdrink?
- With which people am I most likely to overdrink?
- When am I most likely to overdrink?
- How do I feel emotionally just before I begin to overdrink?

Special emphasis is placed on drinking as a response to stress. This approach makes sense, since a high percentage of people with alcohol problems report that their heavy drinking often begins when they are faced with unpleasant, frustrating, or challenging situations. Improved problem-solving skills, particularly in the area of interpersonal relationships, learning how to anticipate and plan for stressful experiences, and acquiring the ability to say "No, thanks" when offered a drink have been shown to have therapeutic value for alcoholics (Marlatt and Gordon, 1985).

One reason that learning approaches may not be effective is that the short-term effects of alcohol often are positively reinforcing. Only the effects of overconsumption ending in intoxication, dangerous or socially frowned-upon behavior, or a period of binge drinking have negative-reinforcement properties. The cognitive perspective deals with this problem by focusing the client's thoughts on the consequences of the drinking behavior as well as on the specific situations in which drinking is most likely to appear tempting. The client and the therapist work together to develop cognitive coping techniques to deal with these situations.

*Relapse Prevention.* While the goal of therapeutic efforts is to help alcoholics stop drinking, maintaining sobriety over the long term is also of great importance. Alcoholics who undergo treatment have a high relapse rate. Many go through treatment a number of times or through a number of treatments and still relapse into uncontrolled drinking.

For those who view alcoholism as a disease, a relapse is a failure that the victim is powerless to control. From the cognitive viewpoint, a relapse is a slip or error. Such a lapse might be prevented in the future by strengthening the person's coping skills. The cognitive approach views a relapse as a fork in the road. One fork leads back to the abusing behavior, the other toward the goal of positive change.

**Relapse-prevention programs** combine a cognitive approach with a variety of treatment procedures designed to change the individual's drinking pattern (Marlatt and Gordon, 1985). The programs are equally useful whether the goal is abstinence or controlled drinking. The only requirement is that the client make a voluntary decision to change. The relapse-prevention approach assumes that the person experiences a sense of control over his or her behavior as long as the treatment program continues. If the person encounters a high-risk situation, this sense of control is threatened and a relapse is likely. High-risk situations include negative moods such as frustration, anger, or depression; interpersonal conflicts such as an argument with an employer or family member; and social pressure to indulge in drinking (see Figure 14–5). If the person is able to make an effective coping response—for example, behaving assertively when friends suggest "just one drink"—the probability of a relapse decreases.

An important factor in relapses is the **abstinence-violation effect.** When a relapse occurs, the individual has two kinds of cognitive and emotional responses.

One is conflict and guilt; the other is self-blame. An alcoholic who breaks abstinence for the first time may continue to drink after the lapse in order to relieve the conflict and guilt related to the first drink. The individual may also reduce the conflict between the drinking behavior and the goal of avoiding relapses by thinking: "This just proves I'm an alcoholic. I can't control my drinking once I start it." Rather than attributing the lapse to the difficult situation, people who use these cognitions are likely to blame themselves for lack of willpower or inability to resist temptation. Such thoughts increase the probability that a single drink may snowball into a full-strength alcoholic binge and a total relapse. Table 14–5 summarizes the steps that lead to relapses.

In addition to viewing any slip into drinking as a lapse and not necessarily a relapse, one of the primary goals of the relapse-prevention program is to train the individual to recognize the early-warning signals that may precede a relapse and to plan and carry out a series of intervention or coping strategies before it is too late to do anything about it. The relapse-prevention technique holds promise not only for alcohol abuse but also for drug use, smoking, and other problems of self-control such as dieting. Its main ingredients—identifying high-risk situations and learning pertinent coping and behavioral skills—are applicable to many types of situations. There is a need for research that explores its short-and long-term effects and its limitations (Carey and Maisto, 1985).

**Abstinence Versus Controlled Drinking** Critics of the disease approach argue that while abstinence can work well for some individuals, it is very hard to live up to; moreover, recovery from alcoholism may not require such a drastic step. One study that suggested that alcohol abusers can recover without abstinence is known as the Rand study (Polich and others, 1980). Over 900 individuals with severe alcohol problems were studied for four years after they had been admitted to one of eight federal alcoholism treatment centers. The researchers found that at the end of four years almost half of the subjects were either abstaining from alcohol or drinking in a controlled manner. One of the most interesting findings was that alcoholics over age 40 who were highly dependent on alcohol when they were admitted to the program had lower relapse rates when they abstained completely. In contrast, those under 40 who had low levels of dependence when they entered the program were less likely to relapse if they practiced controlled drinking rather than abstinence.

Another longitudinal study also found that some alcohol abusers can return to drinking on a controlled basis without abusing alcohol (Vaillant and Milofsky,

(a)

(b)

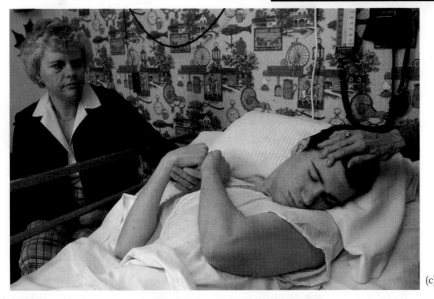
(c)

**FIGURE 14-5**
Situations and emotional states can put a person at high risk of relapse. The person in (a) is socially insecure when meeting strangers. The person in (b) is receiving a six-month work performance evaluation from his supervisor. The person in (c) is worried by the illness of someone she loves. In each case increased stress heightens the risk of relapse. (Laimute Druskis, Mike Kagan, Monkmeyer Press, and N. Alexanian/Stock, Boston)

□ **TABLE 14-5**
Steps in the Relapse Process

1. Entry into a high-risk situation (a particular environmental setting, interpersonal encounter, emotional state).
2. Lack of an adequate coping response.
3. Decreased expectations of self-efficacy because of failure to cope.
4. Use of substance.
5. Further decrease in feelings of self-efficacy when the goal had been total abstinence.

1982). However, subjects who were alcohol dependent and/or had many alcohol-related problems generally achieved successful results only if they became abstinent (see Figure 14–6).

These findings suggest that there may be two groups of alcohol abusers. Some can successfully resume drinking on a controlled basis. Others must abstain entirely if they are to cope with their alcohol problem. Both studies show that level of abuse before treatment plays an important role in the success of various treatment strategies. However, most researchers in this area would agree that the success rates of treatment procedures are not high enough. Further research on such issues as the value of abstinence versus

**FIGURE 14–6**
A return to controlled social drinking has a greater chance of success if the person has only a few symptoms of alcohol abuse. Only four men who had six or more symptoms were able to return to social drinking. Most of those who did not resume alcohol abuse eventually became abstinent. (Vaillant and Milofsky, 1982, p. 129)

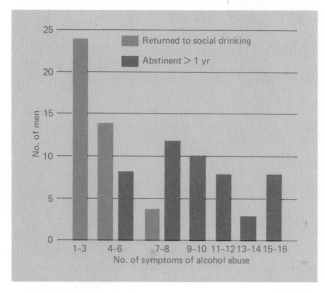

controlled drinking needs to be sufficiently complex to take account, not only of subjects' drinking histories, but also motivations and expectations about what would constitute success in coping with their drinking problems (Miller, 1985; Peele, 1984, 1985).

## ■ OTHER DRUGS

Strictly speaking, alcohol is a drug—it is a chemical substance that leads to physiological and psychological changes when ingested. But for most people the word *drugs* means pills, powders, and pot. Psychoactive drugs may be classified into several groups: barbiturates and tranquilizers, the opioids, cocaine, amphetamines, psychedelics, phencyclidine (PCP), marijuana, and nicotine.

### Barbiturates and Tranquilizers

Barbiturates (such as phenobarbitol) and tranquilizers (such as Valium) are grouped together because they both have a depressing effect on the central nervous system. They probably do this by interfering with synaptic transmission. Either they inhibit the secretion of excitatory neurotransmitters or they cause the release of inhibitory transmitter substances. Both types of drugs reduce anxiety and insomnia and affect a wide range of bodily functions. They are both very popular. Each year Americans consume over 300 tons of barbiturates; tranquilizers are an even bigger business.

**Barbiturates,** or derivatives of barbituric acid, are prescribed by physicians for relief of anxiety or to prevent convulsions. Illicit use of barbiturates often occurs in conjunction with the use of other drugs, notably alcohol and heroin. Mild doses of barbiturates are effective as sleeping pills, although they may actually cause sleep disorders if used over a long period. Higher doses, such as those used by addicted individuals, trigger an initial period of excitement that is followed by slurred speech, loss of coordination, severe depression, and impairment of thinking and memory.

The body quickly develops a tolerance for many of the effects of barbiturates and tranquilizers. As tolerance develops, the amount of the substance needed to maintain the same level of intoxication is increased. The margin between an intoxicating dose and a fatal one also becomes smaller (see Figure 14–7). These drugs can cause both physical and psychological dependence. After addiction has developed, sudden abstinence can cause withdrawal symptoms including delirium, convulsions, and death. People who are addicted to barbiturates often eat the drugs like candy during the day and take a massive dose at bedtime.

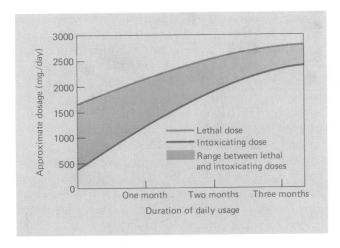

**FIGURE 14-7**
The relative relationship between lethal and intoxicating doses of short-acting barbiturates in the blood as tolerance develops. (Dosages are approximate because of individual differences in tolerance to the drug and patterns of use. (Adapted from Wesson and Smith, 1977, p. 35)

There are three types of barbiturate abuse.

1. *Chronic intoxication,* in which people obtain prescriptions, often from more than one physician. Initially they seek barbiturates to reduce insomnia and anxiety. Chronic use leads to slurred speech and decreased effectiveness on the job.

2. *Episodic intoxication,* in which teenagers and young adults take barbiturates to produce a "high" or state of well-being.

3. *Intravenous injections,* in which the drug is injected, often in combination with other drugs (such as heroin). Intravenous use produces a "rush" of pleasant, warm, drowsy feelings. Many complications are associated with prolonged use of the drug in this manner.

Barbiturates in home medicine cabinets are second only to aspirin as a cause of childhood death from accidental drug overdose. They are second to alcohol as a cause of lethal accidents in adults, and they are the drugs that are most commonly taken with suicidal intent. Relapses are common among barbiturate users because the drug is an easy way of escaping tension, anxiety, and feelings of inadequacy.

Some **tranquilizers** act like barbiturates, while others act quite differently. Overuse of tranquilizers is common. They are frequently prescribed to reduce anxiety, and perhaps half a million Americans use them for nonmedical purposes. As with barbiturates, the body develops a tolerance to many tranquilizers. Phys-

ical and psychological dependence and serious withdrawal symptoms may occur. Apparently unaware that they are addictive or that they can cause death, many people use tranquilizers freely. The undesirable effects of these substances increase when they are used in combination with alcohol and other drugs. Tranquilizers are involved in about one-quarter of all drug-related deaths (Vischi and others, 1980).

Valium is a member of the *benzodiazepine* group of tranquilizers. Drugs in this group produce less euphoria than other tranquilizing drugs, so the risk of dependence and abuse is relatively low. Nevertheless, tolerance and withdrawal can develop.

## The Opioids

The word **opioid** describes all drugs with morphine-like effects. These drugs bind to and act upon opioid receptor sites in the brain. The opioids include a variety of substances, some of which occur naturally while others are synthetic.

**Natural Opioids**  Several forms of opioids that resemble opium and heroin in their effects are manufactured by the brain and the pituitary gland. These substances, called **endorphins**, can also be made artificially for experimental use. Research using these endorphins may provide insights into the mechanisms of pain, pleasure, emotion, and perception. There is already some evidence that when individuals suffering from chronic spinal pain are treated effectively with acupuncture, endorphins are released into the spinal fluid. The endorphin levels seem to peak at the moment when the pain-relieving effects of the acupuncture are most pronounced.

Study of the endorphins has led to the mapping of the entire opioid-receptor system. The nerves of the brain and spinal cord have been found to contain specific sites to which opioids must bind in order to produce their effects. Morphine and similar drugs block pain signals to the brain because they fit into these sites like a key into a lock.

Work on the possibility that drug addiction may yield to endorphin therapy has begun in several laboratories. Some scientists suspect that addiction is a deficiency disease: The addict's craving for and dependence on opioids may be caused by chronic underproduction of natural endorphins. If this is the case, it may be possible to use synthesized endorphins to correct the underlying cause of addiction. Two possibilities might account for endorphin deficiencies. One is that the opioids themselves suppress endorphin production; the other is that some people have a genetically caused deficiency in endorphin production.

While the endorphins have been isolated and examined directly by biochemists, behavioral researchers have been able to study their action either by injecting endorphins into subjects and observing their analgesic effects or by injecting a drug called *nalaxone,* which blocks the effects of the endorphin. If a procedure produces analgesia when nalaxone is not used but does work when nalaxone is present, there is indirect evidence that endorphins mediate the pain-reducing effects of the procedure. For example, research done in China has shown that injections of nalaxone greatly reduce the analgesic effects of acupuncture.

**The Opiates**   The word **opiate** refers only to drugs of this type that are derived from the juice of the opium poppy, *Papaver somniferum.* Archaeologists think that the opium poppy's seemingly miraculous powers were first discovered by Neolithic farmers on the eastern shores of the Mediterranean Sea. This knowledge spread from Asia Minor across the ancient world. In the seventeenth century opium was praised by a prominent physician as God's greatest gift to humanity for the relief of its sufferings.

In 1804 the most important active ingredient of opium, **morphine,** was identified. Physicians applauded it as a painkiller of known reliability. Opium and its derivatives were also used to treat coughs, diarrhea, fever, epilepsy, melancholy, diabetes, skin ulcers, constipation, and a variety of other ills well into the 1800s. They were popular as home remedies, and until the 1860s there were few restrictions on who might sell or purchase them. One of the largest abuses of the drug was to sedate infants. Working mothers and women who tended babies for pay used these home remedies to keep infants sleepy and calm. Many people became addicted to opium and its derivatives after it was given to them for medicinal purposes; the nineteenth-century English writers Thomas DeQuincy and Samuel Coleridge are examples. By the late 1800s many physicians were becoming concerned about the problem of opium addiction.

Just as morphine was at first considered a safe substitute for opium, **heroin,** which was produced for the first time in 1874 by boiling morphine in acetic acid, was at first hailed as a safe and effective substitute for morphine. This soon proved to be horribly untrue, and today heroin is involved in over 90 percent of narcotic-addiction cases.

Heroin can be injected, smoked, or inhaled. Heroin addicts go through a characteristic sequence of experiences. After the drug is injected, the user feels a "rush" or "flash" as the nervous system reacts to its presence. Addicts describe the rush as an extraordinarily pleasurable sensation, one that is similar in many ways to sexual orgasm, only more intense and involving the whole body. Following the rush, the user experiences the "nods," a lingering state of euphoric bliss. Fatigue, tension, and anxiety fade away. Feelings of inadequacy are replaced by relaxed contentment. One young addict reported that after experiencing his first heroin high he had exclaimed to himself: "Why didn't they tell me such wonderful feelings existed?" A significant number of heroin addicts have stated that unless the world could provide them with a feeling to compensate for the loss of the high, they would never be able to give up heroin.

The following dreams of two addicts suggest the central role these drugs play in their lives.

> *The cops were chasing me (I was in a car). While they were chasing me I was trying to cook up some dope. They finally caught up to me when I had the dope all cooked up and in the syringe and I'm begging them to please let me get off before I go to jail. They're banging at the windows and I'm begging and then I woke up.*

> *The dope is in a syringe on a table and I can pick it up, but it takes ages to get it to my arm. I can see it coming closer but it always seems to be just as far as ever. When at last it reaches the vein, I see blood mixing into the dope and coming up in swirls like a mushroom cloud, and it's like I'm looking at it very closely because that's all I can see and it's large. I usually wake up because I can't get the spike out of my arm.* (Looney, 1972, p. 25)

**The Effects of Opioids**   The term *opioid* refers to any natural or synthetic substance that acts on the body in a way that is similar to the action of derivatives of the opium poppy. Opioids have both sedative (sleep-inducing) and analgesic (pain-relieving) effects. The opioids are sometimes called *narcotics,* but because this term is used differently by those who study drugs and by the legal system, it does not always have the same meaning to law enforcement personnel, laypeople, physicians, and scientists.

The opioids cause mood changes, sleepiness, mental clouding, constipation, and slowing of the activity of the brain's respiratory center. An overdose may cause death due to cessation of breathing. The withdrawal reaction can be severe and is manifested by sweating, muscle pains, nausea, vomiting, diarrhea, and other symptoms that may last for two or three days; less severe symptoms may persist for four to six months. Heroin use is likely to be associated with serious deterioration of the individual's social life and family relations.

Many American service personnel in Vietnam became users of opium products, especially heroin (see Figure 14–8). But only a relatively small number of

**FIGURE 14–8**
A GI in Vietnam holds an empty vial of heroin against his nose. In 1970 more than 11,000 service personnel in Vietnam were apprehended for drug use. For each individual caught, it is estimated that five escaped detection. (AP/Wide World Photos)

these individuals continued to use the drugs after they returned to the United States. This was true whether they had become physically dependent on the drugs or not; whether they had injected, smoked, or "snorted" them; and whether they had been in a detoxification program or not. The amount of heroin they had used in Vietnam, their ethnic background, and their social class had little bearing on whether they continued to use drugs after returning to the United States. Behavior before entering the military was the best predictor of continued drug use after discharge. Veterans who continued to use drugs had not finished high school, had a criminal record, or had used a combination of addictive drugs while in Vietnam.

**Causes of Opioid Addiction**    The finding that many veterans who used opiates in Vietnam were able to abstain upon returning home stimulated interest in the

idea that controlled use of at least some addictive substances is possible for some people. Additional support for this view was provided by reports of people who have used opioids in a controlled manner for long periods. Although some users require drugs in increasingly large dosages every day, other daily users seem able to limit their intake. Perhaps the reason that controlled use of opioids has received relatively little attention is that people who are able to achieve such use do not come to the attention of clinicians. In any case, a better understanding of the process of opioid addiction is necessary so that effective social policies—for example, drug use laws and treatment procedures—can be formulated.

At present there are two competing views of opioid addiction: the exposure orientation and the adaptive orientation. According to the **exposure orientation,** the cause of addiction is simply exposure to opioids. When a person experiences stress, endorphins are secreted and produce a stress-induced analgesia (increased tolerance for pain). Some researchers have suggested that use of heroin and other opioids may cause a long-term breakdown in the biochemical system that synthesizes the endorphins (Jaffee, 1985). According to this view, an addict continues to use opioids because drug use has broken down the body's normal pain-relief system. It is also thought that opioid drugs are reinforcing because they postpone painful withdrawal symptoms. This view does not explain the Vietnam experience, nor does it explain why some addicts have severe withdrawal symptoms while others do not. Moreover, some people become seriously addicted to drugs that do not produce severe withdrawal symptoms, such as nicotine and coffee.

The **adaptive orientation** is an interactional one in which both the person and the situation are considered to be important factors in the development of addiction: People's characteristics (their expectations, worries, etc.) and the situations they face in life, particularly those that create stress, jointly influence their need for and reactions to drugs. The available evidence is consistent with this interpretation. This view can explain why some military personnel could so easily leave heavy drug use behind when they returned to the United States. In Vietnam, they were faced with strange people and places, boredom, danger, feelings of helplessness, and other emotions and situations that made their coping mechanisms appear inadequate. Once they had returned home, the situational cues that were related to a craving for opioids were absent.

Animal experiments also support the interactional view. In one such experiment rats were individually housed in translucent cages. Each cage was kept in an unlighted drawer of a filing cabinet with air supplied by a relatively noisy ventilating fan. For one group the drawer was opened in a lighted room and the fan turned off. This procedure was the conditioned stimulus (CS). While the drawer was open the rats were injected with morphine (the unconditioned stimulus or UCS). In the other group the CS and UCS were not paired. The morphine was injected while the drawer was opened quickly in a dimly lit room with the fan still on. Then four hours later the drawer was opened in a lighted room with the fan turned off. After 15 of these daily trials all the rats were given three test sessions. They were injected with morphine (the UCS) paired with the CS; 45 minutes later they were tested for response to pain. The measure was the length of time a rat remained on a hot surface before licking its paw.

Both groups of rats showed increasingly short response times over the three test sessions. This indicated that the injection was having less effect (they were becoming drug tolerant). However, tolerance developed at different rates in the two groups. The rats that were in new situations (that is, had not previously had the CS and the UCS paired) were slower to develop tolerance (Siegel and others, 1981) (see Figure 14–9). This experiment demonstrates that, regardless of the physical effects of a drug, experiences with the

drug itself and with an environment related to its administration are important factors in the effectiveness of the drug. The results support an interactive view of addiction.

Clinicians do not agree on how opioid addiction should be treated. Since the nineteenth century treatment has consisted primarily of hospitalization for withdrawal from the drug. Aside from being expensive, hospitalization generally seems to be ineffective, although positive findings have been reported in a 20-year follow-up study of hospitalized addicts (Vaillant, 1973). Although 23 percent had died (mostly from unnatural causes) and 25 percent were still known to be using drugs, somewhat more than one-third had achieved stable abstinence, mainly as a result of strict supervision after discharge from the hospital.

One recurring finding of research on opioid addicts is that they frequently have severe personality problems. Table 14–6 shows the results of one study of this subject. Might psychotherapy that deals with addicts' complex psychological problems contribute to their rehabilitation? Psychodynamically and cognitively oriented therapies have been found to be helpful with opioid addicts, particularly those with longstanding addictions and severe psychiatric disorders (Woody and others, 1984).

**Treatment for Opioid Dependence** Methadone maintenance is the most widely used treatment for opioid addicts. Methadone is a synthetic substance whose action is pharmacologically similar to that of other opioids, including heroin; however, methadone's effects last from 24 to 48 hours rather than 6 to 12. When taken orally in constant doses, methadone does not produce the intense euphoria that is produced by heroin. Its withdrawal effects are also less intense (though somewhat more prolonged) than those of heroin, and their appearance is delayed. In sufficient doses methadone blocks the action of heroin so that the dependent person does not experience its euphoric ef-

**FIGURE 14-9**
The time elapsing before response to pain by rats previously given morphine paired with a situational stimulus and by rats for which the two stimuli were separate. The results suggest that tolerance to morphine develops in response both to the drug itself and to cues conditioned to the administration of the drug. (adapted from Siegal, Hinson, and Krank, 1981, p. 1543)

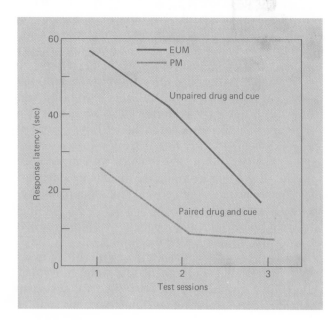

□ **TABLE 14-6**
Percentages of Male and Female Opioid Users Who Also Had Other Diagnosis.

|  | Males | Females |
| --- | --- | --- |
| Affective disorder | 70.7% | 85.4% |
| Anxiety disorder | 13.2 | 25.4 |
| Alcoholism | 37.0 | 26.9 |
| Antisocial personality disorder | 29.5 | 16.9 |

*Source:* Adapted from Rounsaville and others, 1982.

fect. At lower doses it will not block heroin's effects but will suppress "heroin hunger." While the biochemical and physiological properties of methadone are not fully understood, it apparently blocks all the ordinary effects of morphinelike drugs by competing with them at receptor sites in the central nervous system. Through the use of methadone, the craving for heroin is relieved. Methadone prevents withdrawal and allows a heroin-dependent person to function in society.

Methadone-maintenance programs seem suitable to a wide range of opoid-dependent individuals, and since they can be carried out on an outpatient basis, they cost less than institutional treatment. However, despite its relative effectiveness methadone maintenance is not universally supported. Critics claim that it does not really cure addicts but merely transfers their dependence from one drug to another.

Dealing with drug addicts and with the traffic in illegal drugs is a major problem in many countries. The British tried to control heroin abuse through a system of outpatient drug-dependence clinics. These clinics gave addicts daily maintenance doses not only of methadone but even of heroin and cocaine. By providing a legal daily maintenance dose, the clinics hoped to draw the addicts into contact with the helping system and to make it unnecessary for them to support their habit through crime. The ultimate goal was to gradually wean addicts from the drugs if possible, or at least to stabilize them on a fixed dose of heroin or methadone in a lifetime program. In a 10-year follow-up study of the effectiveness of the system, investigators found that 40 percent of a group of addicts who had attended the clinics in 1969 were still attending a clinic and receiving heroin or methadone (Wille, 1981). The majority of these continuing users had been socially stable for at least 10 years. Most of them were employed and were not currently in trouble with the law. Of the group who were no longer attending the clinics, at least half had become abstinent.

There are few follow-up studies from other countries with which these data may be compared. However, the data that exist suggest that the British program was at least as effective as approaches used in other countries (Jaffee, 1985). Moral objections to the government's providing heroin and cocaine for addicts has been a constant threat to the existence of the British program as more than a methadone-maintenance plan.

## Cocaine

Whereas the opioids are "downers" that quiet the body's responses, **cocaine** is an "upper" that increases heartrate, raises blood pressure and body temperature, and decreases appetite. Cocaine puts the body in an emergency state in much the same way that a rush of adrenaline would in a stressful situation. Although it is not clear how cocaine produces this effect, it is likely that it is produced by the release of large amounts of dopamine in the brain. Cocaine also affects at least three parts of the brain itself: the cerebral cortex, which governs reasoning and memory; the hypothalamus, which controls appetite, body temperature, sleep, and emotions such as fear and anger; and the cerebellum, which regulates motor activities such as walking and balance.

The coca bush grows on the eastern slopes of the Andes Mountains in South America. The Indians of Peru and Bolivia have used its leaves for centuries to increase endurance and decrease hunger so that they can cope better with the rigors of their economically marginal, high-altitude existence. In 1860 cocaine, the main active drug in the leaves, was isolated and purified.

Like heroin, cocaine initially had a positive, even benign image. In 1884 Sigmund Freud, who periodically used cocaine himself, recommended it for use in treating depression and other conditions, including morphine withdrawal. Its use as a local anesthetic led to the discovery of synthetic substitutes with low toxicity, while its use in treating morphine withdrawal indirectly led to self-administration of the drug. From about 1880 to 1900 cocaine was actually an ingredient in some popular brands of soda pop.

Cocaine can be "snorted" or sniffed, smoked (often in a water pipe), or injected directly. Today cocaine is the drug of choice for many conventional and often upwardly mobile citizens—young professionals, executives, politicians—and is used rather openly in spite of its illegal status (see Figure 14–10). It produces feelings of wittiness and hyperalertness and is often praised by users as being almost risk free: no hangovers like those produced by alcohol, no injection scars like those caused by heroin use, and no lung cancer, which is associated with use of marijuana and tobacco. Unfortunately, its action is more complex and less benign than most users believe. Table 14–7 lists the effects of cocaine use.

High doses or repeated use of cocaine can produce a state resembling mania, with impaired judgment, incessant rambling talk, hyperactivity, and paranoia that may lead to violence or accidents. There is also an acute anxiety reaction that is sometimes severe enough to be called panic. Serious acute physical reactions are also possible. By constricting blood vessels and increasing the heart rate, cocaine can produce cardiac symptoms, including irregular heartbeat, angina, and myocardial infarction. High doses may also cause nausea, headache, cold sweats, tremors, and fast, irregular, shallow

**FIGURE 14–10**
A middle-class New Yorker openly snorts cocaine during his lunch break. (Photo by Ginger Wall, *Time*, July 6, 1981, p. 60)

breathing. People who have high blood pressure or damaged arteries may suffer strokes as a result of cocaine use. Death usually results from convulsions followed by paralysis of the brain centers controlling respiration, followed by cardiac arrest; in serious cases an acute overdose must be treated with oxygen and an-

---

☐ **TABLE 14–7**
Effects of Cocaine[a]

1. Euphoria
2. Increased energy
3. Enhanced mental acuity and alertness
4. Increased sensory awareness (sexual, auditory, visual)
5. Decreased appetite
6. Decreased need for sleep
7. Increased self-confidence
8. Delusions
9. Constricted blood vessels and increased heart rate
10. Convulsions

---

[a]The effects depend on dosage and degree of habitual use.

ticonvulsant drugs. A common cause of death is intravenous injection of a "speedball"—a combination of heroin and cocaine.

Cocaine presents serious problems when it is taken habitually in large doses. As long as only a limited quantity is consumed, cocaine can be taken daily for years with no apparent ill effects. But since it is one of the most powerful drug reinforcers, desire for it is hard to control. A damaging habit usually develops over a period of several months to several years. Compulsive users cannot turn the drug down; they think about it constantly, dream about it, spend all their savings on it, and borrow, steal, or deal to pay for it.

Short-term tolerance for cocaine develops very fast with repeated doses during a single session; users often say that they never quite recapture the euphoria of the first snort. After months of use, long-term tolerance may also develop, although this happens less strikingly and consistently.

Whether cocaine can be said to produce a withdrawal reaction depends partly on definitions. It does not cause physiological addiction like that associated with alcohol, sedatives, and opioids, in which the central nervous system becomes hyperexcitable when deprived of the drug. Therefore, abstinence does not usually result in acute physical discomfort. A common pattern of cocaine abuse consists of binges or runs followed by crashes. A week-long run produces extreme acute tolerance and exhaustion from lack of food and sleep. The user becomes agitated and depressed, and then falls into several days of severe depression, excessive sleep, overeating, and sometimes chills, tremors, or muscle pains.

The crash is more like a hangover than an alcohol or opioid withdrawal reaction; during the acute phase there is no desire for cocaine. Afterward the abuser may go through a period of unhappiness and lethargy that stimulates further craving. Even many months or years later, a passing but intense craving can reemerge, especially when certain moods or situations have come to evoke a conditioned response.

Cocaine use is increasing rapidly in the United States. A recent survey showed that more than 4 million Americans have used cocaine (*Cocaine use in America*, 1985). Among young adults between the ages of 18 and 25, 28 percent have used it. Emergency-room admissions associated with cocaine use tripled between 1981 and 1984. Today cocaine is the most frequently used drug after marijuana.

**Treating Cocaine Dependence** The cocaine dependent person must first become convinced that treatment is necessary. As in all types of drug and alcohol dependence, more or less subtle forms of denial are common; for example, abusers may want relief for some of the side effects without giving up the habit itself. Sometimes they are induced to come in for treatment only by pressure from family members, employers, or the law. People seek treatment at different stages of dependency, and the severity of the symptoms varies greatly.

Sometimes cocaine users can help themselves. One way of doing so is through aversive conditioning. The user resolves not to use cocaine at certain times and places, with explicit self-imposed penalties if the promise is broken. Contingency contracting is a variant of this technique that requires the cooperation of a professional. The cocaine abuser deposits a letter with a psychotherapist that is to be sent if a sample of the client's urine reveals evidence of cocaine use or a sample is not produced for inspection. The letter contains an admission that is likely to be embarrassing or damaging either professionally or financially. Since the penalty is severe and public, the motivation to fulfill the contract is strong. Unfortunately, many people who are offered contingency contracts decline, and almost all who decline eventually drop out of treatment or resume cocaine use. Possibly abusers who refuse contingency contracts have more serious problems, while those who sign such contracts are already prepared to give up the drug anyway.

Psychotherapy alone rarely solves drug problems, but it can be an important part of treatment. Supportive psychotherapy is a relationship with a sympathetic professional who provides comfort and encourages the abuser to stay away from sources of cocaine. Interpretive or exploratory psychotherapy can help abusers understand what functions cocaine has been fulfilling in their lives and find other ways of coping.

Many cocaine users have also joined mutual-help groups: Alcoholics Anonymous, Cocaine Anonymous, and Narcotics Anonymous. All of these programs use more or less the same approach: They encourage their members to confide in others who have the same problem, to share their feelings, to make a resolution to overcome dependency, and to support the resolutions of other members. Members admit their powerlessness to control their drug use and seek help from a higher power while taking a "moral inventory" of themselves and pledging abstinence one day at a time.

## Amphetamines

**Amphetamines,** like cocaine, are potent psychomotor stimulants. Various drugs in this group are called speed, crystal, pep pills, bennies, meth, and many other names, depending on the specific active agent. Despite their dissimilar chemical structures, amphetamines and cocaine have many similar properties. They both probably act by influencing the norepinephrine and dopamine receptor systems. Antipsychotic drugs block not only the dopamine receptors but some of the norepinephrine receptors as well. If antipsychotics are given prior to amphetamine or cocaine use, most of the behavioral effects of these two drugs are inhibited (Snyder and others, 1974).

Moderate amphetamine use results in increased wakefulness, alertness, and elevation of mood. Psychomotor performance is improved temporarily, but the improvement may be followed by a compensatory rebound or letdown in which the user feels fatigued, less alert, and somewhat depressed.

The medical uses of amphetamines include suppression of appetite and improvement of mood in mild depressions. Amphetamines are also helpful in treating certain neurological and behavioral disorders. College students who use amphetamines when "cramming" for exams not only notice increased energy and tolerance for sleeplessness but also increased productivity on the next day's exam. Although this may be useful at times, even the "improved" performance may not be truly better. Many students have the disillusioning experience of looking at their wondrous performance later and finding it to be of poor quality. The drug impaired their critical thinking at the same time that it increased their output.

High doses of amphetamines have significant effects on the central nervous system and the cardiovascular system; they lead to nervousness, headache, dizziness, agitation, apprehension, confusion, palpitations, and elevated blood pressure. Regular use of large amounts leads to greater tolerance for the drug and increased intolerance for being without it. Users become malnourished, exhausted, careless, and indifferent to normal responsibilities. Often their thinking is characterized by a paranoia that may develop into a full-blown psychosis accompanied by hallucinations. Withdrawal symptoms, if they occur, are mild compared with those that often accompany cessation of opioid use; they also differ qualitatively. Since tolerance for amphetamines develops rapidly, many users inject it into a vein to obtain more intense effects. This high-dose, long-term use of amphetamines is dangerous and self-destructive. Since the initial effects are stimulating and pleasant, unwary individuals often proceed to higher doses and eventually to a state of dependence. Aversive conditioning and token economies have been used with some success in treating amphetamine addicts.

## Psychedelics

**Psychedelics** or **hallucinogens** act on the central nervous system to produce alteration of consciousness. They change the user's perceptions of both the internal and the external world. There is usually sensory displacement, which can drastically alter color perception and hearing. Auditory, visual, and tactile hallucinations accompany the experience, along with a changed perception of self. Among the natural psychedelic substances are mescaline, psilocybin, and dimethyl tryptamine (DMT). Synthetic psychedelics include diethyltryptamine, STP, and d-lysergic acid diethylamide (LSD).

In many cultures psychedelics have been used for hundreds of years. Mescaline, which is derived from the peyote cactus, and psilocybin, which is obtained from "magic mushrooms," are used for religious ceremonies by Indians in Mexico and Central America. West Africans and Congolese have traditionally chewed the ibogaine root, which contains tryptamine, to "release the gods." In the 1950s and 1960s extensive research was conducted on the biochemical, psychological, and therapeutic effects of such drugs. At the same time, some people became interested in the psychedelics as a way of obtaining religious insight. Timothy Leary and others who promoted this view touched off a craze for psychedelics among college students.

LSD (popularly called "acid") is a colorless, odorless, and tasteless material. Effects are produced by as little as 50 micrograms (a microgram is a millionth of a gram), an amount that in pure form would not be visible to the naked eye. No legally manufactured LSD is available to the general public, and the output of illegal, often amateur, laboratories is rarely pure LSD.

The immediate effects of LSD usually last about 8 to 12 hours. The mechanism of its action is not well understood, but it is known to stimulate the sympathetic nervous system and to produce physiological changes like those seen in a person who is aroused, excited, or under stress. The most common subjective effects are euphoria, quick shifts from one mood to another, and altered awareness of the color, size, and shape of stimuli. Time perception is so altered that minutes may seem like hours. Bizarre sensations may be experienced, frequently including feelings of separation or disintegration of some part of the body. The user is usually aware that these effects are due to the drug and are not "out there." Some users experience bewilderment, disorganization, personal and sexual identity confusion, and fears of losing control. They may experience intense emotions that they cannot label. In fact, one of the most unfortunate effects of LSD is the feeling of being overwhelmed by confusing emotions that cannot be sorted out because they are going by so fast. For example:

*A 25-year-old woman used some LSD because a friend had had a number of "great" LSD experiences and convinced her that it would make her less inhibited sexually. About a half hour after ingesting the LSD, she became confused and disoriented. The walls, floor, and ceiling became wavy, "as if an earthquake were taking place." She became panicky when she could not distinguish her body either from the chair she was sitting in or from her friend's body. Her panic heightened when she came to feel that she would never return to normal. She felt overwhelmed with a flood of emotions. When she became hyperactive, laughed inappropriately, and could not stop talking, another friend brought her to a community mental-health center.*

LSD sometimes produces extreme anxiety or panic reactions. Such "bad trips" are generally short-lived and can often be modified by supportive reassurance. Bad trips may be terminated by appropriate medication and occasionally by hospitalization. The most serious effects of LSD are paranoid symptoms (feelings of being followed, spied on, or persecuted), psychosis resembling that found in schizophrenia, and severe depression that occasionally leads to suicide attempts. Negative effects of a large dose of LSD may persist for months, require long hospitalization, and resist the usual forms of treatment. The frequency of such reactions is difficult to determine but is probably less than 1 percent. When such problems arise, it is often difficult to separate the effects of LSD from those of prior drug use, personality characteristics, and a variety of other factors.

A more common effect of LSD use is "flashbacks": spontaneous recurrences of parts of the LSD experience long after the action of the drug has ceased. Such recurrences can take place in the first few weeks and have been reported as long as two years following the last dose of the drug. It is not clear why these flashbacks occur. One possibility is that LSD causes biochemical changes in the body that last long after drug use. The aftereffects may have serious consequences if they occur in situations that require attentive thinking and decision making.

Most of the hallucinogens are fairly easy to produce chemically, and their use spread rapidly in the 1960s despite widespread reports of severe drug reactions, including homicide, suicide, and acute panic attacks. It is likely that many users thought these reports were propaganda to discourage drug use. LSD use declined in the early 1970s, perhaps in part because of reports of genetic damage to users and to their offspring.

Treatment for abuse of psychedelics depends on the severity of the reaction. Severely affected people must have medical attention to prevent cardiovascular or respiratory collapse. If psychotic behavior is present, antipsychotic drugs of the type used to treat schizophrenia may be helpful, although about 10 percent of acutely psychotic drug users never recover. Psychologically based therapy, particularly group psychotherapy and supportive drug-free groups, can be helpful because users of psychedelic drugs often have feelings of low self-worth and use the drugs to improve their relationships with other people. Many of these abusers need help with their social responses so that they can substitute reinforcing social experiences for the reinforcement they get from drugs.

## Phencyclidine (PCP)

**Phencyclidine** or PCP (often called "angel dust") is relatively cheap and easy to synthesize in an amateur laboratory. It is classified as a dissociative anesthetic. It may cause hallucinations, but it also makes the individual feel dissociated or apart from the environment. In small doses, it produces insensitivity to pain; in large doses, it produces a comalike state and blank stare. PCP can be smoked, sprinkled, swallowed, or injected. No matter how it is taken, it increases systolic blood pressure, quickens the pulse, increases sweating, and may produce nausea and vomiting. People who take larger doses feel as if they are being bombarded by stimuli. They may lose the ability to test reality and suffer severe intellectual and emotional disorganization. PCP users sometimes develop severe depression or a severe psychotic state that is not easily reversible. Whether these outcomes are a result of the drug alone or of underlying personality characteristics is not clear.

PCP use seems to be increasing, particularly in several large metropolitan areas. Hospital emergency-room visits due to PCP use increased by 60 percent from 1981 to 1983, and there was also a large increase in PCP-related deaths. However, many PCP deaths are not due to overdose but rather are direct results of some external event, such as homicide, suicide, an automobile accident, or a fall or cut. These events are consistent with the symptoms of PCP use, which include disorientation and violent, aggressive behavior. It is not clear what proportion of psychotic reactions to PCP occur in people with a predisposition toward psychosis. Many people who appear at hospitals with PCP psychoses return later with acute psychotic reactions that are not related to the drug.

## Marijuana

The cannabis plant has been harvested throughout history for its fibers, oils, and psychoactive resin. **Marijuana,** which consists of the dried leaves and flower tops of the plant, is the form in which it is most often used in the United States. The solidified resin, called **hashish** (or, colloquially, hash), can also be used to produce psychoactive effects.

Marijuana is the most commonly used illegal drug in the United States. One out of every five Americans has used it at least once, in spite of the fact that it is classified as an illegal substance and its cultivation, possession, distribution, and use are prohibited. Despite these prohibitions and the controversy over its safety, the use of marijuana increased sharply during the 1960s and 1970s. Since 1971 the number of people who have used it has doubled in every age group from 12 to 24.

Peer pressure is the strongest factor influencing adolescents toward marijuana use. Marijuana use by high school students appears to have peaked in 1978 and has declined significantly since then, perhaps because the fashion shifted toward alcohol. Because of the prevalence of its use and the public controversy about whether it should be decriminalized, over 20 percent of the states have dropped criminal penalties for minor marijuana offenses in the last few years. Several other states permit the use of marijuana for certain medical purposes.

Marijuana is not pharmacologically a narcotic, although it has been legally classified as one since 1937. The mechanism of its action is not well understood, but its more common effects have been identified. (Table 14–8 compares the properties of marijuana with those of other drugs.) An important advance was the isolation of the major active ingredient in marijuana, THC (delta-9-tetrahydrocannabinol). Only barely detectable concentrations of THC are present in the brain of a rat after one dose. But with repeated administration THC and the products of its metabolism gradually build up and are detectable as long as eight days after the administration of a single dose.

THC can be taken by either eating or smoking parts of the cannabis plant. Smoking is the fastest way to feel the drug's effects. When the smoke is inhaled, it is spread across the surface of the lungs, quickly absorbed into the bloodstream, and carried to the brain in a few seconds. When THC is eaten, the chemical enters the bloodstream from the digestive system and is carried to the liver. There enzymes break it down into other substances, which are carried to the brain by the circulatory system.

The psychological effects of marijuana use are illustrated in the following descriptions.

*Usually the first puff doesn't affect me, but the second brings a slight feeling of dizziness and I get a real "buzz" on the third. By this I mean a sudden wave of something akin to dizziness hits me. It's difficult to describe. The best idea I can give is to say that for a moment the whole room, people, and sounds around me recede into the distance and I feel as if my mind contracted for an instant. When it has passed I feel "normal" but a bit "airy-fairy."*

*The first time I smoked I had the feeling of being entirely outside of my body, hovering above it and as it*

| | **Typical Effects** | **Effects of Overdose** | **Tolerance/Dependence** |
|---|---|---|---|
| *Depressants* | | | |
| Alcohol | Biphasic: tension reduction "high," followed by depressed physical and psychological functioning | Disorientation, loss of consciousness, death at extremely high blood-alcohol levels | Tolerance; physical and psychological dependence; withdrawal symptoms |
| Barbiturates Tranquilizers | Depressed reflexes and impaired motor functioning, tension reduction | Shallow respiration, clammy skin, dilated pupils, weak and rapid pulse, coma, possible death | Tolerance; high psychological and physical dependence on barbiturates, low to moderate physical dependence on such tranquilizers as Valium, although high psychological dependence; withdrawal symptoms |
| *Stimulants* | | | |
| Amphetamines Cocaine Caffeine Nicotine | Increased alertness, excitation, euphoria, increased pulse rate and blood pressure, sleeplessness | For amphetamine and cocaine: agitation, and with chronic high doses, hallucinations (e.g., "cocaine bugs"), paranoid delusions, convulsions, death | For amphetamine and cocaine: tolerance; psychological but probably not physical dependence |
| | | For caffeine and nicotine: restlessness, insomnia, rambling thoughts, heart arrythmia, possible circulatory failure. For nicotine: increased blood pressure | For caffeine and nicotine: tolerance; physical and psychological dependence; withdrawal symptoms |
| *Opioids* | | | |
| Opium Morphine Heroin | Euphoria, drowsiness, "rush" of pleasure, little impairment of psychological functions | Slow, shallow breathing, clammy skin, nausea, vomiting, pinpoint pupils, convulsions, coma, possible death | High tolerance; physical and psychological dependence; severe withdrawal symptoms |
| *Psychedelics and PCP* | | | |
| LSD PCP (dissociative anesthetic) | Illusions, hallucinations, distortions in time perception, loss of contact with reality | Psychotic reactions, particularly with PCP; possible death with PCP | No physical dependence for LSD, degree unknown for PCP; psychological dependence for PCP, degree unknown for LSD |
| *Marijuana* | | | |
| | Euphoria, relaxed inhibitions, increased appetite, possible disorientation | Fatigue, disoriented behavior, possible psychosis | Psychological dependence |

*was lying on the bed, I was exceptionally conscious of my body for part of the time, realizing how, and feeling how, each individual part was working.* (Berke and Hernton, 1974, pp. 96, 97)

Marijuana became popular as a recreational drug partly because it is cheap and readily available but also because many people believe that when used in moderation it is not a risk to physical or mental health. Despite this widespread attitude, the federal government has conducted a vigorous and costly campaign to prevent the entry of marijuana into the country. As a result, a great deal of marijuana is grown illegally in the United States and Canada. Several authoritative reports have been issued on the effects of marijuana on health, but scientific controversy and public confusion still exist as to whether marijuana should be legalized or whether the laws against it should be strengthened.

In the early 1980s a committee of the National Academy of Science was asked to make a critical review of current knowledge about the effects of marijuana on health (National Academy of Sciences, 1982). The committee's report concluded that marijuana has a variety of effects, some of which are harmful to human health. Marijuana use causes changes in the heart and circulation that are similar to those caused by stress. These changes might be a threat for individuals with high blood pressure or heart disease. Marijuana smoke causes changes in the lungs that may lead to respiratory problems, but cancer-producing agents in marijuana smoke are even more of a problem. Marijuana smoke contains about 50 percent more carcinogens than tobacco smoke.

In males, marijuana suppresses the production of male hormones, decreases the size and weight of the prostate gland and testes, and inhibits sperm production, although these effects appear to be reversible. Such specific effects have not been found for nonpregnant women. In pregnant women, however, THC crosses the placental barrier and may harm the unborn child. It can also be secreted in breast milk, thereby affecting nursing infants. Various studies have shown that marijuana blocks ovulation and can cause birth defects in animals. The belief that marijuana use is associated with chromosome breaks, which are thought to be indicators of genetic damage, does not appear to be correct. Contradictory evidence exists as to whether the drug causes atrophy or other gross changes in the brain.

One area in which definite conclusions about marijuana use have been reached is its effects on the functioning of the brain and nervous system. Marijuana impairs motor coordination and perception and makes driving and machine operation more hazardous. It also impairs short-term memory and slows learning. One particularly important point is that the impairment lasts for four to eight hours after the feeling of intoxication is over. This means that behavior may be affected even when the user is no longer aware of the presence of the drug.

One positive aspect of marijuana and its chemical derivatives is its therapeutic potential. Evidence suggests that marijuana is useful in the treatment of glaucoma, an eye disorder that may cause blindness, and that it helps control the severe nausea and vomiting that accompany chemotherapy for cancer. It may also be useful in treating asthma and certain types of epileptic seizures. However, the stress it puts on the cardiovascular system may make marijuana an inappropriate drug for treating older people.

Government agencies are reluctant to legalize the sale and use of marijuana because of vocal public opposition. Some opponents argue that the most potent deterrent of marijuana use is the possibility of arrest and imprisonment. However, while enforcement of marijuana laws is a major drain on the resources of the criminal justice system, it does not seem to be effective. Some people have proposed licensing the sale of marijuana, as is done with alcohol, and writing laws regulating its potency. Endangering the lives or well-being of others—for example, by operating a motor vehicle while intoxicated—would be penalized, but safe recreational use would not be illegal. Other writers have suggested eliminating criminal penalties for users but not for sellers of marijuana. These proposals reflect the trend toward increasing acceptance of marijuana use.

There is a great need to base laws and social policies concerning marijuana and other drugs on facts rather than on opinions and fears. Laboratory research and studies of the longer-term effects of drugs and therapies are a first step toward providing the facts.

## Nicotine

Nicotine use is believed to be physically hazardous, not only by professionals but by many smokers themselves (see Figure 14–11). Despite this knowledge, many people continue smoking; some experience psychological distress in the form of anxiety and guilt because they cannot stop smoking. The difficulty of giving up tobacco use on a long-term basis may be due to the unpleasant nature of the withdrawal experience, the importance of social or environmental cues, and the highly overlearned nature of the habit (the pack-a-day smoker is reinforced by the rapid effects of nicotine in each of about 75,000 puffs per year). Withdrawal symptoms—irritability, anxiety, headache, and difficulty in concentrating—do not occur in all smokers, but in some heavy smokers withdrawal symptoms can be detected within 2 hours after the last cigarette. Since many smokers use cigarettes as a way of coping with stress, it is not clear whether these symptoms are related to the withdrawal of nicotine or whether some of them may be related to psychological characteristics that helped start the addictive behavior. Tobacco withdrawal is also associated with a number of physiological changes, including decreased heart rate and blood pressure, and with impaired performance on tasks that require vigilance.

Most professionals agree that addiction to cigarette smoking is hard to overcome on a long-term basis. The results of one survey of therapeutic success are shown in Figure 14–12. Although these data were gathered some time ago, they remain accurate. When these data are combined with data for people who attempt to stop smoking on their own, the picture is brighter. Of the

**FIGURE 14-11**
"Phil suddenly decided to give up everything that was bad for him—no more smoking, drinking, or junk food—and he feels absolutely *terrific!*"
(Drawing by Handelsman, © 1985 The New Yorker Magazine, Inc.)

latter group, from half to two-thirds eventually succeed (Schachter, 1982; U.S. Department of Health, Education and Welfare, 1979).

Therapeutic efforts to help people stop smoking take several forms. Some of these efforts use the biological perspective. From this viewpoint, the problem is not so much that smoking calms the nerves as that nonsmoking sets up the negative reinforcement of withdrawal symptoms, which can be ended by having another cigarette. By resuming the use of cigarettes, the individual is attempting to regulate the nicotine level in his or her body. This may have important physiological effects because nicotine stimulates the release of *central peptides*, hormones that have a powerful effect on key mental and physical functions. This suggests that smokers who are heavily dependent but want to quit smoking may require, on a temporary basis, some pharmacological substitute for the nicotine they are deriving from cigarettes.

In 1984 nicotine-containing chewing gum was approved by the Food and Drug Administration for prescription use in the United States. The gum was developed to ease withdrawal from tobacco by providing both an alternate source of nicotine and a substitute oral activity. Nicotine gum probably does not give the same positive pleasure as smoking a cigarette because nicotine is absorbed more slowly through the lining of the mouth than through the lungs. However, the gum may enable a smoke to break the habit in two stages. First the smoker can focus on overcoming the behavioral and psychological components of tobacco dependence without having to cope with nicotine withdrawal at the same time. Linked with each smoker's puffing habits are the many other actions involved in handling cigarettes and responding to cues that call for lighting up. Once these behavior patterns are controlled, withdrawal from the nicotine gum might be accomplished more easily.

Because smoking is a complex behavior, all components of that behavior need to be addressed in helping a person stop smoking. The gum may be more effective when used as part of a smoking cessation program or with counseling. Some clinicians feel that without a treatment that is capable of reducing with-

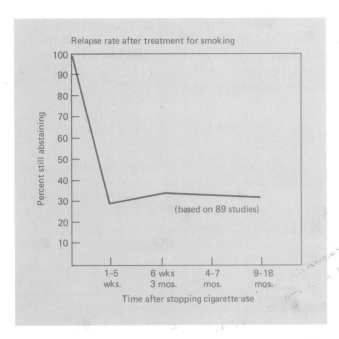

Relapse rate after treatment for smoking

(based on 89 studies)

Time after stopping cigarette use

**FIGURE 14-12**
The relationship between relapse rates and time after stopping cigarette use. [adapted from Hunt, W.A., & Bespalec, D.A. An evaluation of current methods of modifying smoking behavior, *Journal of Clinical Psychology*, 1974, *30*, 430–438, (c) 1974, Clinical Psychology Publishing Co. (Reprinted with permission)]

drawal symptoms, therapists become drained by having to provide constant encouragement and support to help their clients tolerate withdrawal. The rapid and tangible effect of the nicotine gum in relieving withdrawal symptoms may be a boost to the morale and confidence of both the client and the therapist (Grabowski, 1985).

Research is needed to evaluate the effects of nicotine gum by itself and in combination with other factors. For example, one recent experiment evaluated the gum using a balanced placebo design (Gottlieb, 1985). An advantage of this design is that it permits an answer to the question, What is the effect of receiving a drug alone and in combination with the subject's expectancies about the drug's effects? Gottlieb found that nicotine gum helped people stop smoking, but he also found that its effects were weaker than those of smokers' positive expectancies. Many smokers who were given a placebo but were told that it was nicotine gum showed a strong positive effect. Thus, cognitive factors are an important influence on the success of efforts to stop smoking.

One cognitive approach to smoking involves a training program in which smokers are helped to identify the situation in which they are most likely to smoke. They then learn cognitive coping techniques as alternatives to smoking and use self-reinforcement when they are successful in resisting the temptation to smoke.

Cognitive methods seem to be effective for many ex-smokers. One study assessed the way callers to a relapse-counseling hotline described how they dealt with the temptation to smoke (Shiffman, 1982). The relapse crises were usually brought on by situational factors: either positive feeling states related to other smokers, eating, or alcohol consumption, or (more frequently) negative feelings, especially anxiety, anger, and depression. Ex-smokers who performed any coping response in these situations were more likely to avoid a relapse (see Table 14–9). Behavioral responses such as getting up and leaving the situation were useful, but a combination of behavioral and cognitive coping responses worked best, especially in situations involving alcohol. Cognitive coping consisted of such things as reviewing the reasons for not smoking.

☐ **TABLE 14-9**
Effects of Cognitive Coping, Behavioral Coping, or Both on the Outcome of Smoking Relapse Crises

| OUTCOME | No Coping | | Behavioral Coping Only | | Cognitive Coping Only | | Behavioral and Cognitive Coping | | Total | |
|---|---|---|---|---|---|---|---|---|---|---|
| | n | % | n | % | n | % | n | % | n | % |
| Did not smoke | 6 | (21) | 24 | (62) | 21 | (58) | 43 | (71) | 94 | (59) |
| Smoked | 22 | (79) | 15 | (38) | 15 | (42) | 13 | (23) | 65 | (41) |
| Total | 28 | (18) | 39 | (24) | 36 | (23) | 56 | (35) | 159 | (100) |

*Source:* Shiffman, 1982, p. 80.

Behavioral methods often combine aversive stimuli, such as mild electric shock, with smoking. In another technique, **rapid smoking,** the subject smokes cigarettes at such a high frequency that the desire to smoke decreases. However, rapid smoking can increase blood pressure significantly. Research on this technique indicates that it causes a substantial short-term decrease in smoking behavior but that after a while smokers are likely to return to their previous behavior. The long-term effectiveness of this technique might be enhanced if it were used as part of a multicomponent program with cognitive elements like those mentioned earlier (Lowe, 1985).

Substance dependence continues to be a major problem throughout the world. Recent developments in the study of pain regulators and pain receptors in the body are providing some valuable clues, particularly in the area of opioid abuse. Information about the health consequences of using some substances—for example, marijuana and tobacco—have decreased their overall use. Some therapeutic procedures, especially those that emphasize cognitive techniques for relapse prevention, show promise as treatments for alcohol and tobacco abuse. Still unanswered, however, is the question of whether social policy should be changed—for example, to decriminalize marijuana or provide maintenance doses for heroin addicts in government clinics. In part because of lack of knowledge about the consequences of these actions—such as whether they would increase or decrease use of the substance—and in part because of philosophical differences among citizens, lawmakers, and scientists, these policy issues seem likely to remain unresolved.

# ■ STUDY OUTLINE

The behavioral and psychological effects associated with regular use of substances that affect the central nervous system are referred to as **psychoactive substance dependence disorders.** People who use these substances may have periods of intoxication or withdrawal. **Intoxication** leads to a substance-specific syndrome that includes various types of maladaptive behavior. In **withdrawal,** a substance-specific syndrome follows reduction of intake of a psychoactive substance that was previously used regularly.

### SUBSTANCE DEPENDENCE

In **substance dependence,** significant, ongoing maladaptive behavior occurs as a result of use of the substance, interfering with social functioning or effectiveness on the job and extending over a period of at least a month or recurring over at least a six month

period. Physiological dependence can be shown by tolerance or withdrawal. **Tolerance,** means that the person has to use more effect. **Withdrawal** means that certain physical symptoms occur if the use of the substance is decreased or stopped.

### ALCOHOL

1. Abuse of alcohol or other psychoactive substances means that their use has negative effects on a person's life. Alcohol abuse is often referred to as **problem drinking,** while alcohol dependence or addiction is referred to as **alcoholism.** Problems with alcohol are strongly associated with increased risk of dying in an accident, especially one caused by drunken driving. Other health risks associated with overuse of alcohol are high blood pressure, cancer, and cirrhosis of the liver. Extensive abuse can cause brain damage.

2. From a biological perspective, alcoholism is a permanent, irreversible condition in which the individual experiences an irresistible physical craving for alcohol. The only treatment that can succeed, in this view, is complete abstinence. Some research findings indicate a genetic basis for alcohol problems, perhaps expressed in alterations of certain neurobehavioral functions. However, it is clear that environmental factors are also involved.

3. According to psychodynamic theorists, a person with an alcohol problem has an **oral-dependent personality** as a result of lack of satisfaction of the need for oral gratification in childhood. There is no conclusive evidence that personality factors are involved in the development of alcoholism.

4. Learning theorists point out that some people drink as a way of coping with problems of living. This behavior is learned through reinforcement, modeling, and other learning mechanisms.

5. Cognitive theorists emphasize the effects of expectancy on the behavior of people who consume alcohol. There is evidence that a person's belief about the alcohol content of a drink can be a significant determiner of such behaviors as depression, delay of gratification, and social anxiety.

6. The biological approach to the treatment of alcoholics calls for complete abstinence from alcohol. This approach is used by Alcoholics Anonymous, a self-help program for alcoholics that emphasizes the need for spiritual awakening. Another biological approach is the use of disulfiram, a drug that causes extreme discomfort when a person drinks alcohol after taking it.

7. Psychotherapy is sometimes useful in treating alcoholics, but there are no definitive conclusions on

the subject. Learning techniques such as aversive conditioning and covert sensitization have been used with some success, as have cognitive techniques in which clients are oriented toward monitoring their own behavior in relation to alcohol use.

8. **Relapse-prevention programs** combine a cognitive approach with a variety of treatment procedures designed to change the individual's drinking pattern. They help the alcoholic identify high-risk situations and learn pertinent coping and behavioral skills.

### OTHER DRUGS

1. **Barbiturates** are derivatives of barbituric acid that trigger an initial period of excitement followed by slurred speech, loss of coordination, severe depression, and impairment of thinking and memory. Some **tranquilizers** act like barbiturates and can cause physical and psychological dependence and serious withdrawal symptoms.

2. The **opioids** (sometimes called **narcotics**) include both naturally occurring and synthetic substances. Several forms of opioids, known as **endorphins,** are manufactured by the brain and the pituitary gland. **Opiates** are opioids that are derived from the juice of the opium poppy. Their most important active ingredient is **morphine,** which is used primarily as a painkiller. **Heroin** was originally used as a substitute for morphine, but today it is involved in the vast majority of narcotic-addiction cases.

3. The opioids cause mood changes, sleepiness, mental clouding, and other physical effects. An overdose may cause death due to cessation of breathing. Withdrawal symptoms include sweating, muscle pains, nausea, vomiting, and diarrhea.

4. According to the **exposure orientation,** the cause of opioid addiction is exposure to the drugs. The **adaptive orientation** considers both the person and the situation to be important factors in the development of addiction. The available evidence is consistent with the latter orientation. The most widely used treatment for opioid addicts is **methadone maintenance,** which involves substituting another drug that does not produce the euphoria that accompanies heroin use but relieves the craving for heroin.

5. **Cocaine** is derived from the leaves of the coca bush. Its effects include increased heart rate, blood pressure, and body temperature and decreased appetite, together with feelings of wittiness and hyperalertness. High doses can produce a state resembling mania and sometimes cause strokes. Since cocaine is one of the most powerful drug reinforcers, desire for it is hard to control. Treatment of cocaine abuse requires that the abuser be convinced that treatment is necessary.

6. **Amphetamines** are potent psychomotor stimulants whose use results in increased wakefulness, alertness, and elevation of mood. High doses lead to nervousness, headache, dizziness, agitation, and other symptoms. Regular use of large amounts causes users to become malnourished, exhausted, careless, and indifferent to normal responsibilities.

7. **Psychedelics** or **hallucinogens** act on the central nervous system to produce alteration of consciousness. They change the user's perceptions of both the internal and the external world. The most frequently used psychedelic drug is LSD (d-lysergic acid diethylamide). Treatment for abuse of psychedelics depends on the severity of the reaction; severely affected people must have medical attention to prevent cardiovascular or respiratory collapse.

8. **Phencyclidine** or **PCP** is a dissociative anesthetic that causes the user to feel dissociated from the environment. Users sometimes lose the ability to test reality and suffer severe intellectual and emotional disorganization. Many PCP deaths are not due to overdose but are direct results of homicide, suicide, or accidents.

9. **Marijuana,** the dried leaves and flower tops of the cannabis plant, is the most commonly used illegal drug in the United States. It is not pharmacologically a narcotic, although it has similar psychological effects. The effects of marijuana use on health are unclear, but there is no doubt that it impairs motor coordination and perception, short-term memory, and learning.

10. **Nicotine** is contained in tobacco smoke. Smoking is believed to be physically hazardous; however, it is extremely difficult for users to give up the habit. Therapeutic efforts to help people stop smoking take several forms, including the substitution of nicotine gum, the use of cognitive techniques, and **rapid smoking,** in which the subject smokes cigarettes at such a high frequency that the desire to smoke decreases.

# 15

# MALADAPTIVE BEHAVIORS OF CHILDHOOD AND ADOLESCENCE

"*Karl was a five-year-old boy whose parents had been asked to remove him from kindergarten. From the teacher's report, it seemed that Karl was characterized by a multitude of deviant behaviors. For example, when separated from his mother, he became intensely aggressive—biting, kicking, throwing toys, screaming, and crying. The teacher's legs were a mass of black and blue marks; on several occasions he had tried to throttle her . . . Much of the time he ignored the other children. When he did interact with them, there was an awkward and frequently aggressive quality to his behavior which led the teacher to be concerned about their safety. As a result, much of the time he was followed about the room by an adult."*

*Karl's mother also reported that he sometimes wet his bed and that she had trouble getting him to feed or dress himself. She wondered if he were retarded. (His IQ was in the normal range.) She thought it was very unlikely that he would change because he was "strongheaded" and his disturbed behavior had gone on for a long time. She mentioned how upset she had been the week before when she brought him to school and he held her dress with his teeth to prevent her from leaving.* (adapted from Patterson and Brodsky, 1966, pp. 278–279)

Children's emotions take a long time to acquire the veneer of civilization, and since they do not yet understand the consequences of their actions, children sometimes act out behavior that adults feel uncomfortable even thinking about. But usually such behaviors simply drop out of the child's repertoire as he or she grows up.

Deciding to do something about unwanted behavior in a child can be much more agonizing than making a similar decision about an adult. Parents often feel responsible for everything their children do, and they feel especially guilty about admitting that their child has a problem that is serious enough to require professional help. When parents or other adults intervene, they may make things worse by emphasizing a problem that might disappear if it were ignored. On the other hand, many behavioral problems are easier to treat in children, since their behavior patterns and interaction styles have not yet become firmly established.

Even more important, behavioral problems sometimes interfere with a child's development by delaying the learning of all kinds of school and social skills. Moreover, many children with psychological problems are brought to the attention of mental-health workers only when some crisis occurs. By then the problem may be difficult to treat because it has become so severe that the child has been labeled as a "problem."

What would happen if Karl's difficulties went untreated? Certain types of childhood disturbances certainly contribute to adult psychiatric disabilities.

Antisocial and acting-out behavior and severe reading problems in children are often correlated with adult disorders. On the other hand, such childhood problems as shyness, fear, tics, nervousness, hypersensitivity, speech defects, and anxiety reactions may have no discernible effect on later development, although adults who had these problems in childhood may be described as at least mildly maladjusted compared to the average person (Rutter and Hersov, 1985).

Psychological disorders that affect children run the gamut from extremely serious to minor. Some of these disorders are unique to childhood, whereas others may be experienced by both children and adults. Some, such as depression and schizophrenia, include behaviors that would be abnormal at any developmental stage. Others, such as phobias of early childhood, represent exaggerations of normal developmental trends. These disorders can affect the child's mood (as in anxiety disorders or depression) or behavior (as in hyperactivity or conduct disorders). They can also produce physical symptoms, as in eating disorders like anorexia nervosa or bulimic disorder. In addition, there are more severe disorders, such as mental retardation and autism, in which the child does not develop normally over a long period and the outlook for significant change is poor. These severe developmental disorders are discussed in Chapter 16.

## ■ THE SCOPE OF THE PROBLEM

In the United States today, 15,000 children are living in residential treatment units because of psychological problems (Blotcky and others, 1984). Six million or more children between the ages of 5 and 19 have psychological problems that are severe enough to interfere with their learning in school and to require some kind of professional contact. At least 13 percent of all children in the United States have severe psychological problems. In some groups the rate of problem behavior is even higher. For example, preschool children from poor families may have a 30 percent chance of having a mental-health problem (Berlin, 1975).

Efforts to help troubled youngsters often fail, for several reasons. Lack of understanding of the nature of childhood disorders and their causes is one important factor. For example, it is not known whether some disorders of childhood, such as psychoses, depression, and anxiety disorders, are extensions of the adult categories or whether they have different causes. One piece of evidence that suggests that many childhood disorders are distinct from their adult versions is the difference in the sex ratios of these disorders for children and adults. In childhood, boys are affected more often than

**FIGURE 15-1**
Learning to write requires a certain degree of coordination and cognitive skill. Children develop these skills at different rates. Those who develop them later than average often are at a disadvantage in kindergarten and in later school years. (Bill Binzen, Photo Researchers)

girls in almost all categories. Beginning in adolescence, however, affective disorders and anxiety disorders are more frequently diagnosed in women, and there is no sex difference in schizophrenic disorders (Rutter and Garmezy, 1983).

Some maladaptive behavior in childhood results from the fact that in the normal course of things children do not all develop at the same rate. Children who develop later than their age-mates often carry feelings of inadequacy and inferiority into adulthood. Personalities of children who are late in maturing physically may be permanently affected. Problems can also result from lateness in acquiring cognitive skills. Children who are unable to master academic work when their classmates are ready for it are at a serious disadvantage both in school and in later life, even if they catch up afterward (see Figure 15-1).

## ■ DISRUPTIVE BEHAVIORS

Two kinds of children who behave disruptively are of special concern to adults: children who do not pay attention and seem exceptionally active, and children who behave aggressively, break rules, and may cause significant harm to other people or their property. The former are diagnosed as having attention deficit–hyperactivity disorder, while the latter have conduct disorders.

### Attention Deficit–Hyperactivity Disorder

Children vary in their motor activity. Most children may seem overactive to adults, but some children seem never to stop moving. During their preschool years, they run, climb, and crawl incessantly and without apparent purpose. As they become older, they show a marked inability to sit still, and they have a tendency to fidget excessively. An observer would conclude that they are more active than the average child and that their activity has a purposeless, random quality.

Overactive children are not well liked by parents or teachers. Even when such children are intelligent and creative, their hyperactivity is hard to tolerate. Thomas Edison and Winston Churchill were hyperactive children. As a child Edison was constantly in trouble with most of the adults he knew. He was always asking questions, exploring, and creating minor disasters. His mother finally had to withdraw him from school and teach him herself. Churchill was called an impossible and incorrigible child by his first governess, who resigned in fury. He went on to alienate a series of other teachers. At one school he was allowed to leave the classroom at regular intervals to run around the school grounds in the hope that this activity would wear off some of his energy.

Restless behavior of students is a major complaint of school personnel. When teachers rate children in their school classes, 10 percent of all boys and 1 percent of all girls are classified as hyperactive (Lambert and others, 1978). Some of these children may not be considered hyperactive by their parents or by mental-health professionals. The structure of classroom activities or the frustrations encountered in learning may cause these children to behave with less control or may make their high activity levels more noticeable while they are in school. Nevertheless, hyperactivity is the most frequent reason that children are referred to mental-health facilities (Ross and Ross, 1982).

Some of the problems connected with hyperactivity are social: interrupting other children or adults, talking out of turn in class, or making distracting noises when others are trying to work or listen. Children who behave in these ways frequently leave tasks uncompleted and work in a disorganized manner. In addition, they behave impulsively and have difficulty taking turns in group situations. Most of them have trouble getting along with their parents and teachers, and with other children as well. When students are asked to name classmates whom they do not prefer as work or play partners, the names of overactive children tend to be very high on their lists (Pelham and Bender, 1982)

Some children who are called hyperactive also show other, more serious behavior deficiencies. These are the children for whom the term **attention deficit–hyperactivity disorder** is appropriate. Perceptual and learning difficulties may be even more of a problem for these children than social situations. They may have deficiencies in visual and auditory discrimination, reading, writing, and language development. Children who have this disorder are likely to fail in school and also to fail in social situations, both outcomes that cause them to have a low opinion of themselves. As a result, they make few friends and are likely to develop various physical complaints as well as emotional problems, especially depression (Ross and Ross, 1982).

In a study comparing the behavior of hyperactive boys and their nonhyperactive brothers, mothers were asked to rate the severity of various behavior problems in both sons (Tarver-Behring and others, 1985). For all the behaviors rated, the hyperactive sons created more severe problems (see Figure 15–2). This was especially true in interpersonal situations involving play with other children or when the mother's attention was focused on other things such as talking on the phone, entertaining visitors, taking the child to public places, or driving.

In order to see whether the mothers interacted differently with their two sons, the mothers were ob-

served alone with each son in two kinds of situations: free play and a series of structured tasks. During free play the hyperactive boys were less likely than their brothers to answer their mothers' questions and were more likely to be distracted. Their behaviors differed in the same way during the structured task; in addition, the hyperactive sons were less likely to follow instructions from their mothers. In this study, the mothers' behavior toward their two sons did not differ, but it is likely that over time the hyperactive sons' lack of responsiveness might lead their mothers to interact with them less.

Children who are hyperactive may grow out of it, but most of them improve only partially as they grow older. In adolescence they continue to be impatient, belligerent, difficult to discipline, and uninterested in school. Often their parents consider sending them away to school. Up to half of all adolescents with this disorder end up in court for theft or truancy (*Harvard Mental Health Letter*, 1985). These problems are likely to continue when they become adults. Nearly one-fourth of all children who have attention deficit–hyperactivity disorder may develop into adults with a mild form of antisocial personality disorder (Loney and others, 1981).

**Possible Causes**  The causes of attention deficit–hyperactivity disorder are unknown. Most children who have the disorder show no evidence of actual brain damage. Complications during pregnancy or birth and illnesses in early infancy have been found to be associated with hyperactive behavior, but the relationship is not strong enough to be used in predicting future school or behavior problems (Hartsough and Lambert, 1985). Another possible cause may be hereditary. Often the father of a child with attention deficit–hyperactivity disorder had a troubled childhood, was a school dropout, and remains restless and short-tempered. In addition, some researchers have found high rates of antisocial personality disorder in male relatives and histrionic personality disorder in female relatives (Rie and Rie, 1980).

Stimulant drugs such as methylphenidate (Ritalin) or dextroamphetamine (Dexedrine) are often effective in reducing some of the problems of attention deficit and hyperactivity. This suggests that the disorder may be a result of a deficiency of dopamine or norepinephrine because many stimulant drugs increase the effects of these neurotransmitters.

**Treatment**  By far the most common treatment for hyperactive children is the use of psychostimulant drugs like Ritalin. A large number of studies show that

**FIGURE 15-2**
Mean rating of severity of child behavior problems in 14 situations from the Home Situations Questionnaire as completed by mothers for both their hyperactive and nonhyperactive sons. (Tarver-Behring and others, 1985, p. 207)

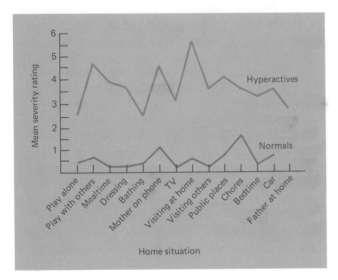

these drugs have positive short-term effects: Many children show improved behavior and decreased disruptiveness in the classroom (Ross and Pelham, 1981). However, some problems have been created by the ease of administration and apparent effectiveness of stimulant treatment. The definition of hyperactivity tends to be stretched to cover any child who is annoying or disrupts classroom activities.

Stimulants have some side effects that may cause problems if they are used over a long period. They may cause insomnia, headaches, nausea, and tearfulness. Some children also develop incessant talking or explosive outbursts of rage when they are treated with psychostimulants. In some cases the drugs depress the appetite so that weight gain is below normal. Dextroamphetamine may also suppress growth and decrease the child's adult height by as much as one and one-half inches. It is also difficult to predict how long the improvement produced by the drugs will last. In many cases changes in behavior last only as long as the medication is being taken. As the effect of each dose wears off, the child's behavior returns to its premedication baseline rather quickly. In one study, deterioration of behavior was serious enough to require renewed use of medication in almost all cases (Abikoff and Gittelman, 1984).

Extensive reliance on drugs may also reduce the interest of parents and teachers in finding other ways to help. About 30 to 40 percent of children who use stimulant medication do not improve or have unpleasant side effects (Whalen and others, 1985). Many parents refuse stimulant therapy for their children, while others discontinue it prematurely, often because the children dislike taking the drugs (Brown and others, 1984). These problems, together with the growing awareness that attention deficit–hyperactivity disorders may have lifelong effects, have encouraged researchers to look at other therapeutic possibilities.

Traditional operant-conditioning methods are often used in efforts to treat hyperactive children. In one experiment (O'Leary and Pelham, 1977) seven elementary school boys who had been receiving medication were given a behavioral-therapy program instead. The program included daily reports on the boys' social and academic achievements, which were reinforced by rewards from their parents. Both parents and teachers were taught to reinforce desired behaviors and to discourage misbehavior by withdrawing attention or removing the child for a brief "time-out" period. When the medication was terminated, behavior that was not task related increased dramatically. But four weeks after the last therapeutic session, the children's behavior was comparable to that of children whose drug regimen had not been terminated (See Figure 15–3).

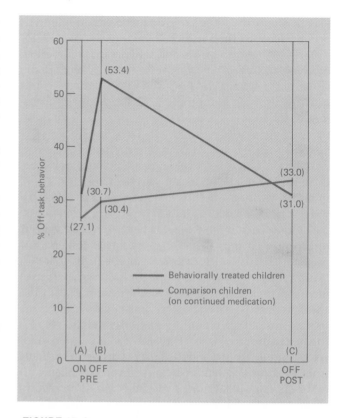

**FIGURE 15–3**
Amount of time spent in undesirable behavior by children during medication with stimulant drugs (a), when drugs were withdrawn (b), and after behavioral training had been completed (c). (O'Leary and Pelham, 1977, p. 215)

Most behavioral interventions produce changes that last less than two months, and their effects usually are not strong enough to bring behavior into the normal range (Whalen and others, 1985). For that reason, researchers have studied cognitive procedures such as self-control training or verbal self-instruction as possible therapeutic approaches. These approaches emphasize the child's role in overcoming the problem of hyperactivity; they are often useful when combined with drug therapy.

One problem that occurs in drug therapy is that the medication, rather than any personal action, may be seen as the sole reason for any changes in the child's behavior. As a result, the child may feel no responsibility for his or her behavior. Social psychologists might see this as a demonstration of attribution theory, which emphasizes the importance of self-statements about cause on the behavior that follows. The importance of attribution can be seen in the following example, in which stimulant therapy for a 9-year-old boy was terminated.

*The result was marked behavioral deterioration accompanied by such spontaneous attributional statements as "My pills help me get done with the work" and "I get angry without my pill." After four days, Tom was given pills again, but this time they were placebos. Even so, task attention and productivity returned to high levels, and the teacher attempted "reattribution therapy" by emphasizing that Tom, not the pills, was controlling his behavior. When he was allowed to earn his way off medication by finishing his work four days in a row, Tom met this criterion and continued to perform well in the classroom with neither medication nor placebo. (Whalen and others, 1985, p. 404)*

One reason for the appeal of cognitive–behavioral therapy is that it gives children the message that they can control their own behavior, although it is important that the child not be made to feel responsible for more change than he or she is able to accomplish. Researchers have used cognitive–behavioral therapy as a way to enhance the effectiveness of treatment and also to increase the transfer of adaptive behavior to other areas. So far this approach seems promising, judging from the results of some individual case studies.

Other approaches to the treatment of attention deficit–hyperactivity disorder have been tried but have not been effective. Traditional psychotherapy, for instance, is helpful only as a secondary measure to deal with emotional problems resulting from the reactions of others to the child's behavior and the child's frustration over lack of academic success. Another approach that has received a great deal of publicity is based on the theory that hyperactivity is caused by hypersensitivity to certain food additives and to chemicals that occur naturally in food. This view, suggested by Feingold (1975), has adherents among many parents and some professionals, but so far research has not provided sufficient evidence to support it (*Harvard Mental Health Letter*, 1985). The chemical additives used in food dyes may have negative effects on learning in one subgroup of hyperactive children who are especially sensitive to those chemicals (Swanson and Kinsbourne, 1980). However, until such findings are repeated and better understood, the question of chemical causes of hyperactive behavior remains open.

## Conduct Disorders

**Conduct disorders** are another category of child and adolescent behavior that frequently comes to the attention of clinicians. Children and adolescents whose behavior is classified in this way go far beyond the pranks and mischief that are characteristic of their age group. Their behavior seriously violates the basic rights of others or the major rules of society. Children who have conduct disorders are often truant and may lie, steal, run away from home, and molest animals and other people. They may begin voluntary sexual activity very early and regularly use illegal drugs.

Conduct disorders are far more common in males than in females; they are also more common in families in which antisocial personality disorders or alcohol problems affect one or both parents. Up to half of all children with conduct disorders are also considered hyperactive (Rutter and Garmezy, 1983).

**Predicting Future Behavior** The category of conduct disorders includes varied types of individuals, but experts do not agree on how this category can be meaningfully subdivided. A study of data from three long-term longitudinal studies suggested that all of these behaviors may be part of a single group (Robins and Ratcliff, 1980). Although specific types of deviant behavior in children can be used to predict later deviance, the overall childhood deviance measure is the best predictor of deviance in adults. Many studies have shown that children who engage in antisocial behaviors, except for some minor sex offenders, do not behave in very specialized ways and that little is gained by dividing them into subgroups (Rutter and Giller, 1984).

It is clear, however, that there are important differences between occasional minor delinquency, which is common, especially among inner-city boys, and persistent antisocial behavior that causes severe harm to the victim. Conduct disorders should not be confused with socialized delinquency, which ordinarily tends to increase from about age 8 to about age 19 or 20 and then decreases. In conduct disorders there is remarkable consistency over time.

The long-term outcome of conduct disorders is clearly worse than that of emotional disorders. Children who engage in antisocial behavior and hyperactivity are much more likely to engage in criminal behavior, become alcoholic, or develop a personality disorder in adult life than children with purely emotional disorders (Rutter and Garmezy, 1983).

Many children and adolescents who have a conduct disorder also are emotionally disturbed. They are especially likely to be depressed (Rutter, 1984). Children with social problems whose peers think of them negatively tend to feel good about aggressive solutions to problems (Asarnow and Callan, 1985). They rate trouble-causing peers as "fun to be with." Responses like these suggest that the children lack the skills to become popular with most of their peers. One way of dealing with this skill deficit is preschool education.

In a project that was designed to enhance preschool children's cognitive development, a follow-up was carried out when the children reached adolescence

(Schweinhart and Weikart, 1980). Although the intelligence test scores of children who had been in the preschool group did not differ from those of children who had been in the control group, their motivation and achievement in school and their classroom behavior were superior to those of the controls. Even more important in terms of the treatment of conduct disorders, their self-reports of delinquent behavior showed a much lower level than was reported by the controls. This suggests that skill building may be an important tool for modifying the aggressive behavior that is typical of conduct disorders.

**Attributions and Aggressive Behavior** For skill building to be helpful, the way the child customarily evaluates situations must be taken into account. One interesting difference between aggressive and nonaggressive children is that the aggressive children show more bias in interpreting the causes of social interactions (Milich and Dodge, 1984). In situations in which the cause was not obvious—for example, being hit on the back with a ball—they are more likely to interpret the act as hostile. Sometimes this response may be caused by past experiences. For example, a psychologist reported the following incident.

> I was treating an aggressive adolescent boy named Rocky twice per week on a long-term basis. We had built a good, warm relationship. One day I saw Rocky in the hallway and approached him from behind as he talked to a peer. I touched him on the shoulder and began to say hello when he turned around and impulsively punched me in the jaw. As soon as he realized whom he had hit, he apologized profusely saying that he thought I must have been another patient on the ward. It was painfully clear to me that Rocky had been perceptually ready to perceive an attack from another. (Dodge, 1985, p. 93)

One study compared aggressive and nonaggressive boys who were chosen on the basis of ratings by teachers and fellow students. The boys read a series of brief stories like the following.

> Let's imagine that you are sitting in the lunchroom at school, eating your lunch with a bunch of kids from your classroom. You look up and see ——— (the name of a boy in the subject's peer group) walking toward your table with his lunch tray. You look back at your table and begin eating. The next thing you know,———'s lunch tray has spilled all over your back. The other kids laugh, and your back is all wet. Now, how do you think that might have happened? What would you do if this really happened? (Dodge, 1985, p. 78)

The boys were then asked what the peer's intention was and what they would do to retaliate. The aggressive subjects made hostile attributions 50 percent more frequently than the nonaggressive boys did; in addition, they were more likely to say they would retaliate. The hostile attributions were clearly responsible for the higher tendency toward retaliation. This difference in attributional bias also occurs in real life.

One way of dealing with these aggressive responses might be to devise interventions that aim at debiasing perceptions. For instance, the child might be taught to use "think aloud" procedures like the following.

> Uh oh, my pencil is missing. There, I see that Ronald has it. Now before I go and get it back, let me think about what happened. I'll do it out loud, like my skills leader has told me. Let's see, first I'll say to myself "What happened?" Well, I lost my pencil and Ronald has it. Ronald could have stolen it. Or maybe he just found it and was using it. Or maybe he doesn't know that it is mine. I wonder what Ronald is thinking. I guess I could ask him. I'm not sure which of these is right, but I don't want to get into a fight. I'd rather stay friends with Ronald, because we play basketball together. So I'll give him the benefit of the doubt. Maybe he just found it. I'll go ask him to return it. (Dodge, 1985, p. 101)

For this kind of approach to be effective, the child must have a warm working relationship with a clinician or some other person with whom he or she can have a series of positive social encounters. The positive encounters must happen over and over again to demonstrate to the child that his or her initial negative expectations were not accurate. Even then it may be difficult for the child to generalize the experience to other people, especially peers.

## ■ EMOTIONAL DISTURBANCES

Emotional disturbances and the behavioral disorders discussed in this chapter are two quite different kinds of problems. The behavioral disorders described in the last section often continue, perhaps in changed form, in adulthood. Most emotional disorders of childhood do not continue into adult life, and emotional disorders in adults do not seem to be connected to the same disorders in childhood (Zeitlin, 1982). Childhood emotional disorders occur about equally in boys and girls, although they tend to be somewhat more frequent in girls. In contrast, behavioral disorders are much more frequent in boys. Behavioral disorders are also quite strongly related to problems in reading and to school achievement. This is not true of emotional disorders.

In general, emotional disorders respond better to treatment and are less likely to continue into adolescence and adulthood than childhood behavioral disorders. Only about one-third of children with emotional disorders still have those disorders four or five years later (Richman and others, 1982). There is some continuity in emotional disorders, however. For instance, children who are very high in anxiety, although they may no longer have an anxiety disorder, seldom move to the opposite end of the scale and become low in anxiety.

The emotional disorders that are most common in children include several kinds of anxiety disorders—including separation anxiety, generalized anxiety, phobias, obsessive compulsive disorders—and depression. All of these tend to overlap when they occur. Unlike the anxiety disorders, however, depression becomes more frequent in adolescence and tends to overlap with behavioral disorders, especially conduct disorders (Rutter and Garmezy, 1983).

Although specific fears become fewer as children grow older, there are changes in many fear patterns that seem to be related to development. Some fears occur so frequently in infancy that they are not considered abnormal. These include fear of noises, falling, and strange objects or people. These fears reach a peak at about the age of 2 and usually decline rapidly after that.

When children are very young, their level of cognitive functioning does not always allow them to make sense of the world. Research on child development has shown that children's logic is not the same as that of adults. For example, young infants do not seem to recognize that when objects or people are out of sight they still exist. Probably for this reason, young children are often afraid when their caretakers leave the room. After infancy other fears develop, but usually they are intense only during the preschool years. Fear of the dark and fear of animals are examples.

As children grow older, they acquire the ability to think about the past and anticipate the future. When this happens, their fears are likely to change. Instead of being afraid of what is happening in a given situation, children begin to anticipate and to worry about what may happen.

## Anxiety Disorders of Childhood

Anxiety in children takes many forms. Some children are preoccupied with thoughts about terrible (and unlikely) things that might happen to them or their families; others show a general social anxiety in which they shrink from contact with people or even refuse to speak for long periods. Still others have phobias, or unrealistic fears of specific objects or places, that may greatly interfere with their everyday living. Some children develop obsessive–compulsive behaviors. In this section

we describe several of these problems. Some are unique to children; others occur in adults as well.

**Fears and Phobias** Most children's fears disappear as they grow older, even without treatment. On the other hand, some children's fears are intense and disturbing and are appropriate objects of professional concern even if they may disappear spontaneously later. To appreciate the impact of a childhood phobia on the child and his or her family, imagine Cindy, who has an unreasonable fear of dogs. She will not go out to play even in her own fenced yard because a dog might come near. She is unable to walk to school or go on errands, so she must be chauffeured everywhere.

Animal phobias and other fears that continue beyond the age at which they normally would disappear can usually be treated effectively using some kind of behavioral approach such as systematic desensitization or modeling (see Figure 15–4). At the beginning of therapy the fearful child observes another child or adult interacting in the feared situation. Then, after a number of sessions, the fearful child is encouraged to approach the feared object gradually until finally he or she interacts with it as the model does. This adaptation of social-learning theory, stimulated by the work of Albert Bandura and others (Bandura and Menlove, 1968), is often used successfully in treating frequently occurring fears.

Modeling of a somewhat different sort (*symbolic modeling*) can be used to prepare children for frightening and unfamiliar situations such as surgical and dental procedures. This procedure typically uses a realistic film that shows the child what to expect. Studies have shown that symbolic modeling may be an effective aid in reducing anxiety (Melamed and Siegel, 1975).

Psychodynamic and learning theorists have very different views of phobias. Compare Freud's description of the case of Little Hans (Freud, 1909/1950) with later explanations of the same case by behaviorally oriented theorists.

The case of Little Hans is one of the most famous examples of a phobic disorder. When he was 5 years old, Hans refused to go out into the street because he was afraid of horses. He was especially fearful that he would be bitten by them. Because of the increasingly constricted life that his phobia forced him to lead (horse-drawn vehicles were the automobiles of that era), Hans' father discussed the case with Freud. The father interpreted Hans' phobia as being due to a "nervous disorder." Freud had only indirect contact with the boy; Hans' treatment was carried out by his father.

Hans' father had often played "horsie" with him, and Freud believed that horses' bridles reminded Hans of his father's dark moustache. Freud thought that

**FIGURE 15–4**
Modeling is often used in treating phobic behavior. After seeing that no unpleasant results occur when another child pets a dog, a child who is fearful of dogs may be able to make an approach. (Bill Binzen, Photo Researchers)

Hans harbored aggressive fantasies and thoughts toward his father because he was the boy's only rival for his mother's love. At the same time, Hans loved his father. In his fantasies Hans expected retaliation from his father for the primitive hostility he felt toward him. To avoid this fantasied punishment, Hans "forgot about" his aggressive feelings and shifted his fantasies of retaliation onto horses. This resulted in the fear that horses would bite him. From one point of view, this was a convenient resolution of the conflict because Hans could avoid horses more easily than he could avoid his father.

Freud portrayed Little Hans as presenting a classic conflict of love and hatred directed toward the same person. He maintained that Hans' ego dealt with the conflict through repression of his ambivalent and incestuous impulses, together with the mechanism of displacement. Apparently as a result of the therapy, Hans recovered from his phobia.

A number of behaviorally oriented theorists reviewed the case of Little Hans and argued that Hans' behavior was simply an instance of classical conditioning (Bandura, 1969; Wolpe and Rachman, 1960). They noticed that three major elements seemed to be present whenever Hans had a phobic response: a large horse, a heavily loaded transport vehicle, and a high travel speed for both horse and vehicle. Freud had noted that Hans became afraid of horses after he was frightened by a serious accident involving a horse. The behavioral theorists believed that this experience,

rather than displaced hostility toward his father, was the cause of Little Hans' reactions. They argued that Little Hans underwent a classical-conditioning process when he saw the accident, and that this was the cause of his continued fear of horses.

It is clear that the perspective from which a phobia is viewed is important in determining both the cause of its development and the kind of therapy used. A psychodynamically oriented clinician would help a phobic child identify the feelings that may have aroused the phobic reaction. A behaviorally oriented clinician would concentrate on helping the child tolerate the feared object by exposing him or her to the fear-producing situation. A cognitive therapist would be interested in the history of the fear, at least in order to determine what thoughts the feared stimulus evokes. Cognitive therapy would teach the child to be aware of the irrationality of these thoughts and help him or her substitute more adaptive ways of thinking in the phobic situation.

**Separation Anxiety Disorder**  Another disorder that occurs mainly in childhood is **separation anxiety disorder.** Children with this disorder show excessive anxiety or even panic when they are not with major attachment figures, usually parents, or in familiar surroundings. Such children may be unable to stay in rooms by themselves and may refuse to go to school or visit friends' homes. When such children are asked why they are afraid, they may express fear of getting lost and never finding their parents again. Or they may be afraid that accidents or illness may strike them or their parents. Very often such children complain of nausea, headaches, abdominal pains, or rapid heart rate. Sometimes overt signs of anxiety or panic are seen when the time for the separation approaches.

Of all the separation fears that bring children to the attention of professionals, refusal to attend school is the most common. In **school refusal** the child's fear is not of school but of separation. Such children may be preoccupied with morbid fears of what will happen to their parents or themselves if they leave home. Although these fears usually are rather specific, sometimes they are simply ill-defined thoughts about death and other dangers, both real and unreal.

The problem of fear of school is interpreted differently by theorists who approach it from different psychological perspectives. Psychodynamically oriented theorists often stress anxiety about separation from the parents or fear of what may happen at home while the child is gone. For example, John Bowlby (1973) believes that four main family-interaction patterns can account for school refusal.

1. The mother or father is an anxious person who keeps the child at home as a companion.
2. The child is afraid that if he or she leaves for school something dreadful may happen to one or both of the parents.
3. The child believes that he or she will experience something dreadful as a result of leaving home.
4. The mother or father fears that something dreadful may happen to the child as a result of leaving home.

These possibilities emphasize the unusual and neurotic interaction patterns that are often found in the families of school refusers. In contrast, a behavioral theorist might stress the fact that some children receive more reinforcement at home than at school. And from a community perspective the disorder might be caused by the negative aspects of the school experience itself. For example, programs that emphasize middle-class values and speech patterns and assume certain basic skills may be unpleasant for children from minority or poverty backgrounds or for those whose home lives have poorly prepared them for the demands of the classroom. The problem with this explanation is that children who are absent because of school refusal tend to be middle-class children with good academic skills who enjoy reading and similar tasks as long as they can do them at home. (There is probably also a very small group of children who fear school, not being away from home or their parents. This fear would be a true *school phobia*, not a separation anxiety disorder.)

Secondary problems develop as a result of continued absence from school. Missed schoolwork and loss of school friends make returning to school more difficult as time goes by. At the same time, the pleasure and reinforcement value of being at home may increase. As a result, some treatment procedures emphasize returning the child to school as soon as possible, even if severe pressure must be used. Other therapists argue that a rapid return to school may reduce the chance that the underlying conflict that gave rise to the situation will be resolved. They believe that placing too much pressure on the child might increase the chance of a panic reaction or even a suicide attempt.

Whatever treatment is used, it is usually successful. Two-thirds or more of the children who are treated for school refusal return to school. However, the older the child, the lower the chances of success. More serious pathology is often seen in children over 11, and in their families, than in younger children. As a group, children who fear school do well when they grow up, although some seem rather dependent and live in socially restricted ways (Waldron, 1976).

**Reactive Attachment Disorders**   The process by which a child becomes attached to its mother or caretaker usually takes place in the earliest years of life. Many theorists believe that the establishment of a secure attachment is important in preventing later psychological disorders, especially depression (Bowlby, 1980). Research on children who are securely attached shows that as they grow older they become more independent and better able to form good social relationships than other children.

**Reactive attachment disorders** may develop when a child has been physically abused or neglected, has been cared for by a caregiver who is emotionally withdrawn and ignores the child, or has experienced frequent changes of caregivers, for example, by being constantly moved from one foster home to another. Children with such disorders are unresponsive in most social interactions. They seem fearful and watchful despite comforting by the person who is caring for them. At the same time, they may show excessive and indiscriminate sociability toward people they hardly know. Box 15-1 describes some of the consequences of disordered attachment.

**Obsessive Compulsive Disorders**   Many children engage in mild rituals and obsessions as part of their normal development. Bedtime and dressing rituals are common in toddlers, preschool children, and younger grade school children. Compulsions, such as trivial motor acts, are also common. A young child may stroke a blanket continuously before falling asleep or may suck

## ■BOX 15-1 EFFECTS OF CHILD ABUSE AND NEGLECT

Parents who neglect their children may fail to provide food, clothing, warmth, a clean environment, and the supervision necessary to keep the child safe. Or they may provide these things but express no interest in their children and fail to interact with them more than is absolutely necessary. Abusive parents, on the other hand, may use severe physical punishment and even permanently harm their children, or they may use psychological forms of abuse that leave their children feeling like innately bad people who are unworthy of love.

Neglected children show the effects of lack of parental stimulation. They talk less and make fewer social responses. In addition, they engage in little exploratory or inquisitive behavior. They also are likely to be depressed.

Child abuse can leave both psychological and physical scars. Physically abused children are often seriously damaged. Many suffer neurological damage, and one-third of these have problems that are severe enough to handicap them in everyday life (Martin, 1976). Children who have been physically abused tend to be deficient in motor skills such as those involved in running, skipping, or riding a tricycle. This may be caused by their fear of exploring and taking risks, but poor motor development has been noted as early as 4 months of age, so lack of exploratory behavior is not a complete answer. Abused children also show delayed development of speech and language. Preschool children may be abused for talking, so they simply don't practice speaking. Instead, much of their communication is nonverbal.

The IQs of abused children are lower than might be expected (Salter and others, 1985). The delay in their cognitive development might be due to the unpredictable and dangerous environment in which such children live. Instead of concentrating on learning, they are anxious, preoccupied by fantasy, and concerned with ways of surviving. Fear of fail-

**FIGURE 15-5a**
Frequency of different types of behaviors of abusive, neglectful and control group mothers when interacting with their children. (adapted from Bousha and Twentyman, 1984, p. 110)

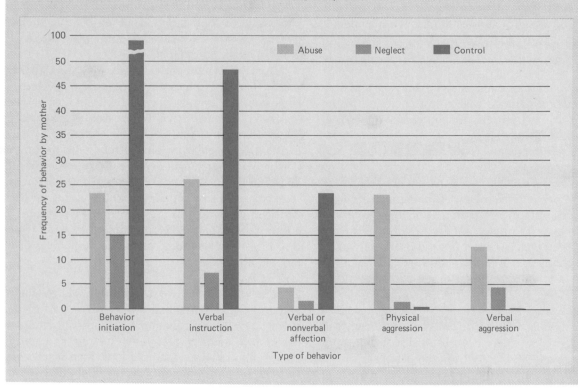

ure and difficulty in paying attention to instructions seem to handicap abused children in testing situations.

For abused children, the world is an unpredictable and hateful place. The adults they live with may be hostile and impatient and can become violent without warning. These children must be prepared to anticipate and meet the needs of their parents and are constantly afraid of harsh punishment and verbal abuse. As a result, the children look unhappy and take little pleasure in their surroundings. They may have sleep disturbances, wet their bed, be apathetic, fearful, or phobic, and underachieve in school (Blumberg, 1981). They are also likely to be depressed, to have low self-esteem, and to think of themselves as innately bad (Kazdin and others, 1983).

Much research on child abuse and neglect has lumped both kinds of parents together. However, although they overlap somewhat, these two groups differ in important respects. In one study, abusive, neglectful, and control-group mothers were observed in their homes for 90 minutes on each of 3 consecutive days (Bousha and Twentyman, 1984). The abusive mothers showed the highest rates of physical and verbal aggression and neglectful mothers the lowest rate of interaction. Figure 15–5a shows some of the differences among the three groups of mothers. The children of these mothers also behaved differently (see Figure 15–5b.) The control children showed less aggressive verbal and physical behavior and more initiations of social behavior than either of the other two groups. The neglected children initiated very little social behavior.

Some researchers have wondered whether the cognitions of the two types of mothers differ when they evaluate situations involving their children. In one study, mothers were shown several sets of pictures (Larrance and Twentyman, 1983). Each set of pictures showed both the mother's own child and a similar child engaging in some activity. The third picture portrayed the result of the activity. In the example shown here, the result is crayon marks on the wall. Other sets portrayed a good outcome, such as a completed puzzle or a prize for winning a game. In all the pictures the children's faces were hidden so that the mothers could not see their expressions.

The results showed that both the abusing and the neglectful mothers had more negative expectations regarding their children's behavior than the control mothers did. If the results were bad, they blamed their children, believed that they had acted intentionally to annoy them, and did not look at situational cues in evaluating the children's behavior.

Research on child abuse and neglect suggests

FIGURE 15–5b
Frequency of different types of behaviors by children when they interacted with their mothers who were abusive, neglectful or from a control group. (adapted from Bousha and Twentyman, 1984, p. 110)

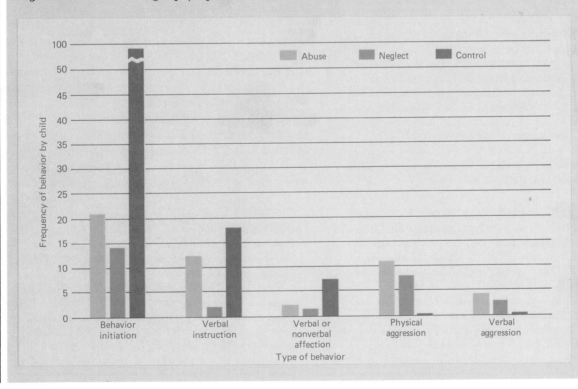

that parents who behave in this way may follow a four-stage pattern (Twentyman and others, in press):

1. The parent has unrealistic expectations for the child.
2. The child acts in a way that does not confirm these expectations.
3. The parent misattributes the child's actions to intentional and negative motivations.
4. The parent overreacts and excessively punishes the child.

Child abuse and neglect may have implications for the child's development, behavior, and mental health both in childhood and as an adult. Researchers are beginning to try to understand the behaviors and thoughts that lead to abuse and to devise ways of helping abused and neglected children and their parents.

his or her thumb only at bedtime. Even children's games reflect these rituals. Children often feel compelled to avoid certain objects, such as sidewalk cracks, or to chant rhymes or songs in a repetitive fashion. Such behaviors rarely are maladaptive in childhood. Sometimes, however, they develop into more disruptive **obsessive compulsive** and **ritualistic** behaviors that require treatment. In the following case a behavioral approach was used successfully.

*Byron was a 5-year-old child who had an obsessive compulsive fascination with electrical devices. He also had a ritual of being unable to sleep except in his parents' bed and a negativistic attitude, which was expressed in a refusal to follow his parents' instructions.*

*He roamed through the house turning lights on and off and staring at them and unplugging the refrigerator and other appliances. At the grocery store, he cut off power to the meat counter. At neighbors' houses, he unscrewed lightbulbs, dismantled lamps, and unplugged clocks and other appliances. In the evening, it sometimes took his parents two or three hours to get him to bed. The evening was punctuated by requests for water for his thirst and cookies for his hunger. During the night, he continued to get up and would lie down between his parents in their bed. Despite their efforts to remove him, he was usually found asleep there the next morning.*

*Byron's parents were taught how to make his maladaptive behaviors less rewarding and how to reward his adaptive behaviors. They were instructed to stop all attempts to spank him, reason with him, or attempt to understand his behavior. They were to meet all his requests for food prior to bedtime. If he stayed in bed all night, he would receive eight tokens in the morning. These tokens could then be exchanged on a daily basis for activities such as snacks, watching TV, or visiting friends. If Byron did get into his parents' bed, they were to pretend to be asleep and make it uncomfortable for him by taking up more room themselves. If this failed, his mother was to lead him matter-of-factly back to bed.*

*When Byron played with switches, he was required to pay half the tokens in his account for each episode, and in addition his parents were instructed to put him in his room for a 30-minute time period. Since he gained tokens during the day only by following instructions, this meant he lost his opportunity to earn tokens. Within three or four weeks of behavior therapy, Byron began to develop friendships with other children and, since his obsession with electrical items was controlled, he was again invited into their homes. He stopped sleeping with his parents, and slept in his bed instead.* (adapted from Ayllon and others, 1977, pp. 316–321)

Figure 15–6 illustrates the dramatic improvement that behavior therapy produced in Byron's behavior.

Despite the success of therapy in Byron's case, in general the outlook for children who engage in severe obsessive compulsive behavior is not promising; about 50 percent do not make a substantial recovery (Elkins and others, 1980). They spend most of their day in rituals and obsessive thoughts, and this severely restricts their functioning. Fortunately, severe obsessive compulsive behavior in childhood is rare. It involves less than 1 percent of all children who come to the attention of mental-health professionals (Rapoport and others, 1981). Two such cases, adolescent patients who were hospitalized because of the severity of their problems, are described in the following excerpt.

*Patient A was a 14-year-old boy who began washing eight to ten times a day after his family moved to a new neighborhood when he was 4. After that, he had only occasional episodes until about two years ago, when he began washing excessively because of fear of sperm on the body. He also had obsessive thoughts of death and compulsively checked light switches. He had been treated both by psychotherapy and with antipsychotic drugs. At school, he was quiet and unaggressive, participated in many activities, and was a good student. His parents had a mutually supportive relationship and were of middle class in socioeconomic status. All his siblings were well; however, his father was mildly depressed.*

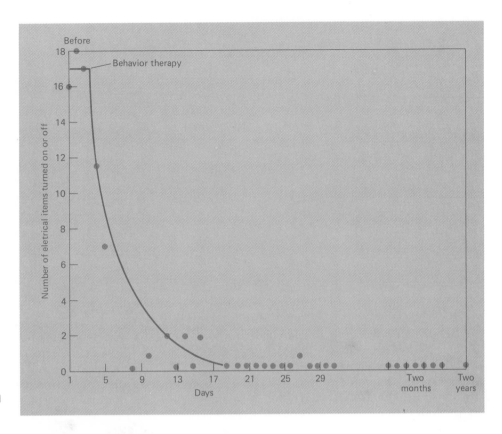

**FIGURE 15–6**
The number of electrical items turned on or off by Byron before, during, and at the end of behavior therapy, and at follow-ups 2 months and 2 years later. (Ayllon, Garber, and Allison, 1977)

*Patient B was also 14 years old. For the last two years, she had washed herself excessively, and was preoccupied by number rituals, such as the compulsion to perform all her daily acts in multiples of six. Until her symptoms developed, she had no obsessive traits, was a good student, and had many friends. She had been treated by psychotherapy for one year. Her symptoms began suddenly at a time when her father's business failed. Both parents, socioeconomically middle class, were alcoholic.* (adapted from Rapoport and others, 1981, p. 1548)

These adolescents were among nine children who were studied by Judith Rapoport and her coworkers (Rapoport and others, 1981). Although none of the children could function effectively because of the severity of their obsessive compulsive problems, none showed any signs of disordered thinking and all were able to discuss their problems sensibly. All of the children showed some depressive symptoms. Only three met the DSM-III criteria for major depressive disorder at the time of hospitalization, but all would have met those criteria at some time in the past. Before their symptoms began, their development had not been particularly unusual. In general, they were good, but not outstanding, students, and they seemed somewhat timid, although they were not excessively withdrawn.

## Depression in Children and Adolescents

Childhood is often pictured as a happy time with little responsibility, much play, and infinite enjoyment. Why is it, then, that children often think: "I'm dumb, ugly, and stupid," "I wish I were dead," and "You don't love me" (see Figure 15–7).

**Frequency of Mood Disorders** Many children often feel sad or depressed. In one large group of families who participated in a family health plan, more than 17 percent of the children showed clinically significant evidence of sadness or depression (Kashani and Simonds, 1979). Although less than 2 percent of these sad children met the DSM-III criteria for affective disorders, they were significantly different from children who were not sad. They had more physical complaints, were more likely to be overactive, had lower self-esteem, and were more likely to be involved in fights and to refuse to go to school. In another study, about 10 to 12 percent of the 10-year-olds in a school district population were described by their parents and teachers as often appearing miserable, unhappy, tearful, or distressed. When the children were interviewed, their responses created the same impression (Rutter and others, 1981).

**FIGURE 15-7**
Although adults seldom think of children as depressed, many children describe their own thoughts in ways that would suggest depression in adults. This boy could be thinking about whether he should go home to watch TV, but he might also be thinking that he doesn't know how to do anything or that no one cares about him or that he wishes he were dead. (Mimi Forsyth, Monkmeyer Press)

Depression is frequent among children who come to clinical attention. Between 30 and 60 percent of child mental-health outpatients meet the DSM-III criteria for depression (Kashani and others, 1981). Depression in childhood may be relatively long lasting. In one study of children 8 to 13 years old (Kovacs, 1985), children who met the criteria for major depressive disorder (see Chapter 10) were depressed for an average of about 7 1/2 months; 92 percent were no longer depressed after a year and a half (see Figure 15-8). However, the chances of another occurrence of depression were high. Seventy-two percent of these children had a second episode within five years.

Children in the study who had a dysthymic disorder had a longer period of depression. On the average, they

**FIGURE 15-8**
Duration of depressive disorders in children. (Data from Kovacs, 1985)

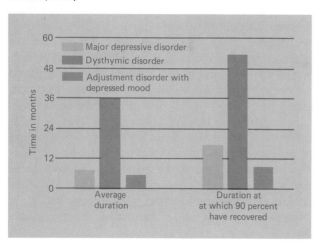

had the symptoms for three years, and at the end of 6 1/2 years 89 percent had recovered. Some of these children had become depressed by the time they were 6 years old. During the period when the children had the dysthymic symptoms, their risk of developing a major depressive disorder was also quite high.

Least severely affected were school-age children who had adjustment disorders with depressed mood. These disorders lasted an average of 5 1/2 months; after 9 months, 90 percent of the children had recovered. None of these children developed a more severe depressive disorder. In this study, boys and girls had equal rates of depression, although many studies have found depression to be more common in boys before puberty.

**Changes in Adolescence** Major changes in mood disorders seem to take place in adolescence (Rutter, 1984). There is a large shift in the sex ratio—during adolescence mood disorders become much more common in girls than in boys. Mood disorders also become generally more common in adolescence. In one study, about 1 out of 9 children had depressive feelings before adolescence and 2 out of 5 had them after adolescence (Rutter, 1980). The higher incidence of depression seems to be related to puberty rather than simply to age. After puberty other mood disorders may also occur. Hypomania, a disorder in which there is an unusual elevation of mood, and bipolar disorders begin to occur in this period. One study found about 25 percent of adolescents with primary major depression also had manic episodes and were reclassified as having a bipolar disorder (Strober and Carlson, 1982).

Rates of suicide and parasuicide also increase sharply during adolescence. Younger children do kill themselves, but suicide before age 10 is rare. From ages

10 to 14 the rate of suicide increases a hundredfold, and between 15 and 19 there is an additional tenfold increase (National Center for Health Statistics, 1984).

Thoughts of suicide and even suicide attempts do occur in young children. In one group of children between the ages of 6 and 12 who were seen at a mental-health outpatient clinic, more than one-third had thought about suicide or had threatened or attempted suicide (Pfeffer and others, 1980). The suicide methods tried or considered included jumping from high places, hanging themselves, running in front of cars, stabbing themselves, and swallowing pills.

Not all children who kill themselves are depressed. Children who are angry or have personality disorders and problems of impulse control also are likely to kill themselves. Feelings of hopelessness increase the probability of suicide more than feelings of depression do (Kazdin and others, 1983).

**Characteristics of Childhood Depression** Depression is hardest to assess in very young children, since they have difficulty describing their emotional state. While fear can be inferred from behavior, facial expressions, and physiological responses, depression is harder to assess because of the importance of its cognitive components. Some of the characteristics of depressed children are shown in Table 15–1. Even in adolescents whose cognitive development should allow them to communicate these feelings, many parents and teachers fail to note depression until the symptoms become quite severe (Rutter and Garmezy, 1983).

Some children experience depression through a large part of their lives. In one longitudinal study, several children showed differing but long-continuing patterns of depression (Chess and others, 1983).

□ **TABLE 15–1**
**Behaviors that are Characteristic of Depressed Children 4 to 11 Years of Age**

Complains of loneliness
Fears he/she might think or do something bad
Feels he/she has to be perfect
Feels or complains that no one loves him/her
Feels others are out to get him/her
Feels too guilty
Feels worthless or inferior
Self-conscious or easily embarrassed
Sulks a lot
Too fearful or anxious
Unhappy, sad, or depressed
Worrying

*Source:* Achenbach and Edelbrock, 1983.

*At 8 years of age, Harold had been having behavioral problems for a year. He disliked school, was shy, and had few friends. He was moody, quiet, and afraid of new situations. Because there had been several problems in his life—his parents had separated when he was 6 and his mother had been briefly hospitalized for severe depression—it was unclear whether his depression was due to these events or to other causes. Things improved, but at 12 Harold became depressed again and disliked school intensely. At 17 he reported that he could "step into an unhappy mood for no apparent reason" and then would feel tired and irritable and would avoid people. Shortly after this he became severely depressed for about two weeks and was treated with antidepressant drugs. At 22 he had moved to his own apartment. He made some money mopping floors but was basically supported by his mother. He spent most of his time practicing music—he had taught himself to play the piano, banjo, and guitar. He summarized his existence as going from "slow deadness to acute crisis" and described recurrent depressions at ages 9, 15, 18, and 19, each of which lasted months even when treated with antidepressant drugs. (adapted from Chess and others, 1983, pp. 413–414)*

*Sylvia's depression was not noted until she was 21, after months of an intense obsessive preoccupation that her skin and hair were terribly ugly, which was not true. She threatened to drop out of college, and although she had top grades and was attending a top-level school she had changed colleges twice. She was hospitalized briefly and for the next year made many suicidal threats and a few suicidal attempts and then gradually improved.*

*During her therapy sessions she reported that she had been depressed even as far back as age 8 and had always covered it over with a veneer of cheerfulness and friendliness. This was substantiated by some poems she had written from ages 12 to 15 which were filled with melancholy and hopelessness. She did not report any life events that could explain the cause of her depression, although she did have several family members who had been depressed. (adapted from Chess and others, 1983, p. 415)*

From these cases and others the researchers concluded that the reasons for the depressive disorder did not seem to be related to the child's early temperament, to the way the parents and child interacted, or to stresses in the child's environment. They thought that the basic cause of these depressions was probably biological. This conclusion is supported by evidence that relatives of children who are depressed have a higher risk of depression than of some other disorders (see Figure 15–9).

Although some childhood depressions seem to have a biological base and there is evidence of a genetic

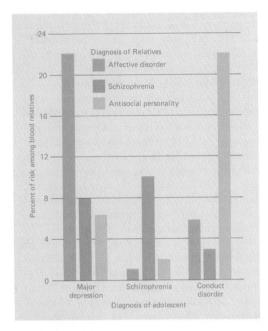

**FIGURE 15-9**
Risk for psychiatric illness among blood relatives of adolescents with depression, schizophrenia, or conduct disorder. (Data from Strober, 1985)

component, exactly what is inherited is not clear. The role of stress and vulnerability in many cases of depression is an interactive one. Bowlby's (1980) research on the attachment of mothers and infants suggests that an insecure mother–child relationship early in life, the child's perception that he or she is not loved, and loss of a parent during childhood, may all cause depression in childhood. The following case shows how feelings of loss can arise from events other than parental death or divorce.

*Michael, who had been seen for some time, was displeased with himself and withdrawn from other people. He suddenly told the therapist about a repetitive dream. "I have this dream coming up all the time. Ever since I have been little it has come up." Michael had been born to an unmarried mother. His father had deserted her before Michael's birth. After five years, during which she and Michael lived alone together, she had married. The family now consisted of two parents and six children. Suddenly Michael had a real family, although he had "lost" his exclusive relationship to his mother. In reporting his dream, he said:*

*"In the dream, I have money, a lot of money, and I lose my money. Well, I don't lose it, but I give it to my mother for her to keep, and then when I ask her for it because I want to buy something for myself she tells me that she has already given it to somebody else, that she has given it to my brothers and sisters, and they have spent it . . . And this dream comes up over and over." He said he had this dream almost every month. Once he*

related that dream and cried, the depression began to become very obvious. Nobody had mentioned the word depression before, but when we looked back we could see that he was struggling with depressive affect most of the time, and after he related his dream, it became manifest. (adapted from Anthony, 1977, pp. 63, 64)

**Treating Childhood Depression** Psychodynamically oriented therapy has traditionally been used in treating depressed children. More recently, behavioral therapy and family therapy have also been frequent choices. Behavioral therapy is often oriented toward helping the child learn social skills or assertive behavior. In many cases researchers have found that depressed children have depressed parents; this suggests that they have learned to cope with stress in the same way that their depressed parents do. One way to provide models of nondepressed coping styles is through therapy in which the therapist models effective behavior for the child (Petti, 1981).

Antidepressant drugs are also used to treat depression in children and adolescents. Tricyclic medication is as readily prescribed for adolescents as it is for adults. Among younger children, only those who are severely depressed seem to respond to tricyclics in the same way that adults do (Toolan, 1981). Because of the lack of information about the effects of such drugs during these crucial years of physical and cognitive development, most clinicians use them with great care.

## ■ PROBLEMS WITH PHYSICAL SYMPTOMS

Childhood and adolescent disorders with physical symptoms include movement disorders (rapid, involuntary movements or voluntary stereotyped movements such as rocking of the entire body), as well as stuttering, bedwetting, sleepwalking, and eating disorders. Among the eating disorders that occur in childhood and adolescence are **pica,** in which the child persistently eats nonfood substances such as paint, string, leaves, or pebbles; **rumination disorder of infancy,** in which the infant regurgitates partially digested food; **anorexia nervosa,** in which adolescents become preoccupied with "feeling fat" and may diet until they die from malnutrition; and **bulimia nervosa** or binge eating that is often followed by purging through self-induced vomiting or the use of large doses of laxatives or diuretics. The two disorders that we discuss in this section, anorexia nervosa and bulimia, are especially prevalent throughout adolescence as well as young adulthood, and are more likely to be found in females than in males.

## Anorexia Nervosa

Although anorexia nervosa has been recognized since the late 1700s and was given its present name in 1874, only recently have its psychological features become a subject of clinical interest. For many years medical opinion held that anorexia nervosa was a result of an endocrine disturbance, and the possibility remains that the condition is due to a disorder of the hypothalamus. (Certain hypothalamic tumors are known to give rise to a distaste for food.)

**Characteristics of Anorexics** Although the term **anorexia nervosa** means nervous loss of appetite, researchers have found that anorexics are indeed hungry. They have both physiological and cognitive feelings of hunger, together with a strong preoccupation with food. Anorexics are likely to discuss recipes and cook elaborate meals for their families or friends, but somehow they never have time to eat what they prepare. If they do eat with others, most of their time is spent cutting food into tiny pieces and moving it around on the plate. If they actually eat, it is usually when they are alone.

Research on starvation has shown that when people are starving, for whatever reason, as long as they eat more than 200 calories a day they will experience hunger. If the consequences of starvation are so unpleasant, why do anorexics find reinforcement in partially starving themselves? There are some basic differences between anorexics and people who starve involuntarily (see Table 15-2).

People with anorexia nervosa have an intense fear of becoming fat even when they are obviously underweight. They claim to "feel fat." To be considered anorexic, a person must refuse to eat to such an extent that his or her body weight is at least 15 percent below the normal level, or fail to gain weight during a period of growth so that his or her body weight is 15 percent below what would be expected. For women, the weight loss must be great enough to result in the absence of at least three consecutive menstrual cycles.

Anorexia is most common in middle- and upper-class adolescent females. The first case of anorexia in a black female was not reported until relatively recently (Jones and others, 1980). Anorexia nervosa is also found in men, but it is much rarer. In a study conducted at a large hospital over a 20-year period, only 9 percent of the patients diagnosed as anorexic were men (Crisp and Burns, 1983).

**Sociocultural Pressures** The incidence of anorexia appears to be increasing, perhaps as a result of sociocultural pressures. The "ideal" weight for females has decreased in recent years. For example, a team of researchers found that the average bust and hip measurements of models in *Playboy* magazine centerfolds decreased over a 20-year period (Garner and others, 1980). They also found that the average weight of contestants in the Miss America pageant had decreased over the same period. Meanwhile the discrepancy between ideal and reality increased because the average weight of American women under 30 increased by 5 pounds. The same cultural pressures can be seen in occupational groups where thinness is especially desirable. Female ballet dancers and models are more likely to be anorexic than other women of their age (Garner and Garfinkel, 1980). For ballet dancers, the more competitive their ballet school, the more likely they are to be anorexic.

**Other Factors** Only one in every 100-150 teenage girls age 15 and over becomes anorexic, and the rate is even lower for younger girls. This suggests that other factors besides sociocultural pressures play a role in the development of anorexia.

In their attempts to understand this disorder, researchers have divided anorexics into subgroups: those who were thin primarily because of restricted food intake (the restrictor group) and those who, in addition to restricting food intake, use vomiting and purging

---

□ **TABLE 15-2**
Comparison of Psychological and Behavioral Changes in Starvation and Anorexia Nervosa

### *Mood or Feeling State*

Starvation: Lack of initiative; quarrelsome; indecisive; loss of concern about physical appearance
Anorexia nervosa: High initiative; strong-willed; pride in personal appearance; frequent periods of feeling exuberant

### *Mental Content*

Starvation: Thinking, dreaming, and daydreaming about eating food
Anorexia nervosa: Same as in starvation, but preoccupation with thoughts of gaining weight continues after eating resumes

### *Activity Level*

Starvation: Fatigue, avoidance of physical exertion
Anorexia nervosa: Seemingly inexhaustible energy; physical exercise sought; overactivity

### *Sexual Activity*

Starvation: Decrease in sexual fantasies, feelings of interest; inability to maintain erection (males); cessation of menstruation (females)
Anorexia nervosa: Same

*Source:* Adapted from Casper and Davis, 1977, pp. 977–978.

with laxatives to control their weight (the bulimic anorexic group). (Not all bulimics are anorexic. Some are of average weight and use purging only to compensate for the extremely high calorie intake during binges.) There are a number of differences between the two subgroups. Those in the bulimic anorexic group are more likely than those in the restrictor group to abuse alcohol or drugs and to have other problems of impulse control, such as stealing (Leon and Phelan, 1984). The families of the bulimic anorexics are less stable, have more parental discord and physical health problems, and have experienced more negative events in the recent past. These families of bulimic anorexics have much higher rates of mood disorders and substance abuse disorders than the families of restrictors (Kog and Vandereycken, 1985). Thus, it is possible that genetic factors play a role in the development of anorexic disorders.

**Consequences of Anorexic Behavior** Both types of anorexics show obsessive preoccupations and feel a great deal of stress. Test results from the MMPI also indicate that anorexics are likely to be depressed (Leon and others, 1985). Even after successful treatment for their weight problem, anorexics are likely to remain depressed (Hudson and others, 1982). A long-term follow-up study of 151 former anorexia patients found that 9 had died an average of 7 years after their first medical contact for anorexia, 7 of them by suicide (Tolstrup and others, 1985).

In addition to the increasing risk of suicide, anorexia disturbs the body's functioning in many ways, including retarded bone growth, anemia, dry skin, low body temperature and basal metabolism rate, slow heart rate, and lack of tolerance for cold (Matthews and Lacey, 1983). Anorexia results in at least a temporary absence of menstrual periods. In addition, a number of physiological changes are likely to accompany anorexia, especially if there is vomiting. One of these, a low level of serum potassium, may cause cardiac arrhythmia, a tendency toward changes in heart rate that can result in death (see Figure 15–10).

Some researchers believe that while many of these changes may be caused by extreme weight loss or malnourishment, others may be due to malfunctioning of the hypothalamus, which may precede the development of the anorexic behavior (Halmi and others, 1983). This hypothalamic malfunction may also be related to impairment in dopamine regulation and, thus, to the development of depression.

**Therapy for Anorexia** Although anorexia is a serious disorder, many anorexics recover. In a long-term study of the outcome of treatment for anorexia, half of the former patients who were still living were considered

**FIGURE 15–10**
Karen Carpenter, shown here with her brother, died from a heart attack in her early thirties. Physicians thought the recording star's long battle with anorexia nervosa was an important factor in her death. (Steve Shapiro, Sygma)

to be free of mental illness (Tolstrup and others, 1985). One-quarter were still anorexic, and one-quarter had other disorders.

The two major therapeutic approaches used in treating anorexics are behavioral methods and family therapy; these approaches are often used together. In behavioral programs hospital privileges are made dependent on weight gain. While this technique often leads to increases in body weight, it has some negative features. If the weight gain required is too great (some programs have required a half-pound gain per day), patients may develop bulimia and use laxatives and vomiting as a method of weight control (Leon and Phelan, 1984). They are also likely to show poor social adjustment.

Cognitive–behavioral approaches to anorexia have also been tried. These focus on the faulty thinking that seems to contribute to the faulty body image of some anorexics. Cognitive interventions are usually combined with other approaches. So far their usefulness has not been demonstrated clearly (Leon and Phelan, 1984).

Because behavioral therapy has met with limited long-term success, some researchers have focused on family therapy, especially for younger anorexics. One family therapist who has taken a special interest in anorexic adolescents is Salvador Minuchin (Minuchin and others, 1978). Minuchin has found four predominant characteristics in families with an anorexic child: enmeshment, overprotectiveness, rigidity, and lack of conflict resolution. The enmeshed family is one in which no one can be an individual or have a separate identity and the insistence on togetherness results in a lack of privacy. Family members are overprotective; they frequently express concern for each other's welfare and respond protectively to the least sign of distress. Families of anorexics also tend to be very rigid and to resist change. They have what amounts to a storybook image of themselves, and the growth of individuality in an adolescent child is a threat to this picture of perfection. Tolerance for conflict is extremely low in these families. Some deny that any differences exist among their members; others deal with differences by shifting the conversation to other topics. When such tactics are used, conflicts within the family are not resolved. Instead, natural differences accumulate and stress builds up.

Minuchin and his coworkers followed most of their first 50 anorexic cases for at least 2 1/2 years after treatment began. They reported a recovery rate of 86 percent, with recovery defined as no symptom of eating disturbance or psychosocial difficulty at home, at school, or with peers (Minuchin and others, 1978). This study focused on young girls (average age 14) who had very recently begun to show anorexic symptoms. It is possible that this high recovery rate might not occur with older anorexics with more established eating (or noneating) habits.

## Bulimia Nervosa

In bulimia nervosa, or binge eating, the person is aware of his or her abnormal eating patterns, afraid of being unable to stop eating, and likely to be depressed and self-critical about this behavior. In bulimia, binge eating occurs at least twice a week for at least three months and is often accompanied by laxative use, self-induced vomiting, or rigorous dieting in order to compensate for the binge behavior. Many anorexic patients have symptoms of bulimia, but the problem is also common among people of average or above-average weight.

**An Analysis of the Binge Cycle**   Binge eaters are generally on some sort of weight-reduction diet, and the binge represents their falling "off the wagon." They may binge only at certain times rather than continuously, and many hide food and eat in secret. They may consume prodigious amounts of food during one of these binges. Between 2000 and 5000 calories are usually consumed per binge, up to twice as many calories as most people consume in a day (Johnson and others, 1983). Most binge eaters consume easily prepared, high-

calorie foods such as chips, fast food, bread, and sweets, and many focus their binges on particular foods (Mizes, 1985). Binges often occur while the person is at home alone watching TV or browsing through a magazine, or in a car or a fast-food restaurant. If food runs out during a binge, the bulimic may rush out to buy more. Bulimics tend to eat in an unsystematic manner; they binge, do not eat for a day, and then binge again.

Binging is quite common among college women. About two-thirds of college women report eating binges, but these are not as severe or frequent as those of bulimics and are not usually accompanied by self-induced vomiting or the use of laxatives. About 5 percent of college women and 1 percent of young women who work report bulimic-style binging (Hart and Ollendick, 1985).

Attempts to explain bulimia have focused on the role of negative cognitive/emotional states in bringing on binge episodes. Pressure at work or school and problems with personal relationships often precede binges, and most bulimics feel anxious, depressed and somewhat guilty before a binge. They also report that their binges are prompted by contact with certain people, most frequently their mothers but sometimes their boyfriends, fathers, or sisters (Carrol and Leon, 1981). During their binges most bulimics feel immediate relief from anxiety and depression. Bulimics may be using binging as a means of coping with stress. If this is the case, teaching them alternative coping skills should be an important part of therapy.

In the post-binge period most bulimics feel disgust and anger at their lack of self-control, guilt over having eaten "forbidden" foods that violate their strict and unrealistic diet standards, and depression at their inability to stop binging. These negative post-binge feelings are thought to serve as a cue for purging, which "undoes" the eating act and leads to a decrease in negative feelings (Rosen and Leitenberg, 1982). Post-binge purging in the form of vomiting has been reported by over 90 percent of bulimics (Mizes, 1985). Purging alone often is not enough to produce a better mood, however. In one study, 70 percent of bulimic individuals reported thoughts about suicide at the conclusion of the binge–purge cycle (Abraham and Beaumont, 1982). This negative state can serve as a precipitating factor for another cycle.

Bulimia is not just an eating problem. It is associated with poor overall adjustment (Johnson and Berndt, 1983). This means that not only do bulimics have poor skills for coping with depression and anxiety but they also experience these feelings unusually strongly.

**Consequences of the Binge–Purge Cycle**   In addition to the psychological consequences of anxiety, depression, and guilt, the binge–purge cycle can also have distressing physical results. The most serious of these are due to the potassium imbalance from frequent vomiting, which can lead to muscle weakness and heart problems. Vomiting can also damage the esophagus, increase tooth decay and damage tooth enamel.

**Treatment of Bulimia**   Treatment of bulimia can be focused either on preventing binges or on preventing purging. Many of the studies that have been reported deal with single subjects, so a clear picture of the general process is lacking. Relaxation training seems to be helpful in preventing the binge from starting (Mizes and Fleece, 1984). Treatment to prevent purging involves exposure and response prevention. For instance, in one study, subjects were asked to eat until a strong urge to vomit occurred (Leitenberg and others, 1983). While they were eating, the therapist focused their attention on negative thoughts about feeling full, fat, ugly, and rejected. The therapist also helped them focus on three positive thoughts: (1) The physical sensations after eating were abnormal and could be relieved without vomiting; (2) the strict diets they set for themselves were unrealistic and set them up to "blow it" and binge; and (3) the post-binge anxiety would decrease and not be as unpleasant as they feared. After eating, the patients stayed with the therapist for at least an hour until they felt sure that they were not going to vomit. Four of the five patients treated either stopped vomiting or showed a definite improvement. One patient showed no change.

Antidepressant drugs are sometimes used to treat bulimia. In some cases these are initially helpful in reducing the rate of binging, but relapses may occur when the medication is stopped. In some cases binges occur even when the drug therapy is continued (Stewart and others, 1984).

Bulimia may be related to mood disorders, as is suggested by the higher incidence of both mood disorders and alcoholism in relatives of bulimic individuals. However, it seems likely that other psychological factors contribute to bulimic behavior. Therefore, a behavioral treatment may be more effective than the use of antidepressant drugs in enhancing coping skills and thereby preventing relapse.

# ■ THERAPY WITH CHILDREN AND ADOLESCENTS

## Results of Therapy

The results of therapy with children are about the same as those of therapy with adults. This means that treated children experience outcomes about two-thirds of a standard deviation better than those experienced by untreated children. This conclusion and others come from an analysis of 75 studies of the effectiveness of therapy with children (Casey and Berman, 1985). As in therapy with adults, the largest effect of therapy with children was on measures of fear and anxiety. Unlike adults, however, children tended to show relatively little change in self-esteem, overall adjustment, and social adjustment.

Reports of the effects of therapy from parents and therapists have been encouraging. In contrast, reports from teachers and classmates seem more restrained. Another indicator of therapeutic outcome shows up when children's behavior changes are compared with their self-reports. Although their actual performance is often better, positive self-reports from the children are rare. One reason for this may be that children have difficulty engaging in introspection, or thinking about how they see themselves.

## Differences in Therapeutic Techniques

Therapy with children often differs from therapy with adults. There are several reasons for this, including the following.

1. Children rarely initiate treatment for themselves and typically do not understand the purpose of mental-health services. Therefore, some children actively resist being taken for treatment.

2. Children's problems tend to be more closely related to the family situation than the problems of adults.

3. The goals and methods of treatment for children are often more complex than those of treatment for adults. Not only must the child's parents initiate, continue, and finance treatment, but they usually must modify their own behavior in certain respects.

4. A child's deviation from developmental norms may be an important factor in convincing his or her parents to seek help. When this happens, treatment focuses on helping the child reach certain developmental milestones.

Many therapies that are used with adults have been adapted for use with children, and some methods that are uniquely suited to young children have been developed as well. Play therapy, storytelling techniques, and parent-administered behavior-modification programs are examples of therapies specially tailored for children. Until behavioral therapy became popular, much therapy for children was psychoanalytic in its orientation. Because young children's limited verbal skills made traditional talking therapy inappropriate (see Fig-

**FIGURE 15–11**
Traditional psychodynamic therapy is not appropriate for young children. (From Roche Report: *Frontiers of Psychiatry*, April 1, 1982, p. 11)

ure 15–11), many therapists began using play therapy. They met with the child in a playroom and used the child's play activities or play interactions between the child and the therapist as a therapeutic vehicle (see Figure 15–12). Psychodynamically trained therapists use play as a substitute for the free-association approach

they use with adults. Nondirective therapists use play to help the child act out his or her feelings, face them, and learn to control them.

The following examples contrast the nondirective and psychodynamic aspects of play therapy. The first example illustrates the nondirective approach.

*Joann, age 6, comes into the playroom and begins to play with the clay. This is her fourth play therapy session. She is usually very quiet and does very little talking. Every time she comes in she plays with the clay and makes the same thing—a figure of a man carrying a cane. Each time, after he is finished, awful things happen to him. He is punched full of holes, beaten with a stick, run over by the toy truck, buried under a pile of blocks. The fourth time the clay figure emerges, the therapist says, "Here comes that man again."*

*Joann: Yes. (Her voice is tense, determined.)*

*Therapist: The man with the cane.*

*Joann: Yes. (She begins to punch him full of holes.)*

*Therapist: You're putting holes in the clay man.*

*Joann: Stab! Stab! Stab!*

*Therapist: You're stabbing him.*

*Joann (in small voice): Ouch. You hurt me. (Voice changing) I don't care. I want to hurt you.*

*Therapist: The clay man is crying because he is hurt.*

*Joann (interrupting): I want to hurt him.*

**FIGURE 15–12**
Children often communicate better through play than through speech. Play therapy is designed to take advantage of this fact and to give children a symbolic way to express their fears, aggressions, and insecurities. (Michael Heron, Monkmeyer Press)

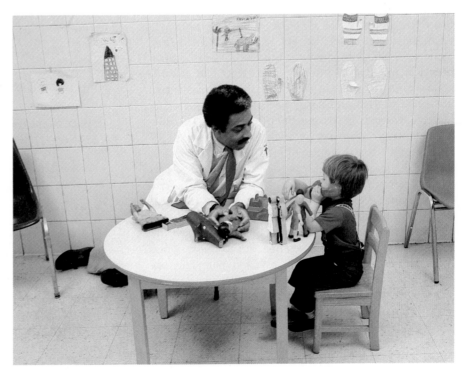

*Therapist: You want to hurt him.*

*Joann (emphatically): I don't like him.*

*Therapist: You don't like him.*

*Joann: I don't like him. I hate him. Look. This hole went clear through him. It went in his front and out his back.*

*Therapist: He gets holes punched clear through him. You fixed him.*

*Joann: Yes. I'll tear his head off.*

*Therapist: You'll even tear his head off.*

*Joann: I know, I know. I'll put him clear down in the bottom of the jar and then I'll put the clay in on top of him and he'll smother. (She tears him into little pieces and gouges her thumb through the clay and carefully puts the pieces down in the bottom of the jar and then covers it with all the rest of the clay.)*

*Therapist: You tore him into little pieces and buried him in the bottom of the jar.*

*Joann nods—and smiles at the therapist. Then she goes over to the baby doll, pretends to feed it, holds it tenderly in her arms, puts it in bed, sets the table, and plays house very quietly.*

*This was the pattern of Joann's behavior while in the playroom. She always made the clay man, tore him up, got rid of him, and then played with the baby doll. This continued through the seventh interview, and then she stopped making the clay man. She sometimes played with the clay, but made cats or toy dishes or candles. She was very fond of the doll and continued with this play. (Axline, 1947, pp. 179–180)*

In the course of the therapy, Joann's nervous, tense, withdrawn behavior greatly improved. The therapist later learned that Joann's mother, who had been a widow for three years, was considering remarriage to a man who limped and carried a cane. Expressing her feelings without discussing them had apparently enabled Joann to accept her mother's marriage plans.

Note that the therapist offered no interpretations. Simply being able to express these negative thoughts in the presence of an accepting adult seemed beneficial to Joann. A psychodynamically oriented therapist might have handled this situation differently. Using the play behavior as a base, the therapist might have interpreted the behavior to the child. For example, when Joann stabbed the clay man, a psychodynamically oriented therapist might have begun by saying, "You're angry with the man. You want to hurt him." Eventually, after many play-therapy sessions, Joann would have come to understand why she felt as angry as she did about her mother's proposed remarriage.

Sometimes the self-understanding by psychody-namic therapists can be achieved through more direct interchanges with children. The following dramatic incident produced the same kind of insight that an adult might gain by verbally analyzing his or her reactions with the help of a therapist.

*John was a 12-year-old boy who had a history of delinquent behavior. In the preceding session, he had asked the therapist to get him a penknife so that he could carve some balsa wood . . .*

*When John came into the playroom, he immediately looked on the table, found the knife, picked it up, snapped open the blade.*

*"Oh, you fool, you," he cried. "I asked you to get me a knife to carve with, and you walked into the trap. Now you've given me a knife, and I'll cut your wrists." He suddenly reached out, grabbed the therapist's hand and placed the open blade against the vein. "Now what are you going to do?" he demanded.*

*"It seems to me that is my question," the therapist replied. "You're the one with the knife. What are you going to do?" . . .*

*"You know what will happen if I get mad enough right now?" John asked threateningly.*

*"What will?" asked the therapist.*

*"I'd cut your damn wrists. Then how would you like that? I'd cut that vein right there. What would you do? Tell me that. What would you do?"*

*"I'd probably bleed," the therapist answered, after some quick thinking.*

*"And then what would happen?" John demanded.*

*"I don't know," the therapist said. "That would be your problem."*

*"My problem? You'd be the one bleeding to death!" John yelled.*

*"You'd be the one who did it, though," the therapist said.*

*"Why don't you try to pull loose?" John demanded.*

*"Why don't you let go and put away the knife?"*

*"You were a fool to get me this knife for in here, you know," John said. "You realize what a fool you were? You brought this all on yourself."*

*"You asked for the knife to carve balsa wood," the therapist replied . . .*

*John suddenly released the therapist's wrists, closed up the knife, tossed it on the table.*

*"Some people are too damn dumb to be turned loose," he said. "You're so stupid you could get your very throat cut and wouldn't know what happened. Why did you get this knife? Why did you give it to me?"*

*"You said you wanted to carve wood. I believe what you say."*

*Suddenly he sat down with his back to the therapist.*

*"Some people shouldn't be let out alone," he said. "Some people are too damn dumb. How can I fight you if you won't fight back? How can I cut your wrists if you won't even struggle? All the time here it's like this. It's me against all the people in the world that I hate and despise. You make it turn out again and again that it's me against myself. All of a sudden I feel all my feelings—and sudden like I just wish I'm not the way I am. I wish I had a feeling of being strong deep inside of me without threats and being afraid really. I feel like I'm too little or too big a world. I don't want to always make war with myself"* (Axline, 1955, pp. 625–626).

Cognitive therapy, which has a behavioral rather than a psychodynamic orientation, is becoming increasingly popular in work with children and adolescents. In this chapter it is illustrated by some of interventions for hyperactivity and for bulimia.

Probably the most often used treatments for children involve behavioral methods of various kinds. An example can be seen in the following case.

> *Valerie, an 8-year-old girl from a low-income area, started to miss school in the second grade and in third grade the problem became worse. Whenever her mother attempted to take her to school, Valerie threw a temper tantrum or said she felt sick, so her mother left her at the neighbor's. The therapists concluded that Val was getting reinforcement for staying away from school. By staying home, she gained extra contact with her mother and fun at the neighbor's house while her mother was at work. Some of the things Val liked most—chewing gum, ice cream, soda pop, and having her cousin stay all night— were combined as reinforcers to reward Val for going to school. Her mother no longer took Val to the neighbor's. Instead she reinforced Val by leaving home early before the children left for school and meeting her at the school door each morning, and by giving her candy when she returned from school and special treats when she had completed a week of school attendance. She also ignored Val's complaints of illness. The effect of this treatment on Val's school attendance is shown in Figure 15–13. In addition, Val's grade-point average changed from C's before the treatment to A's and B's. (adapted from Ayllon and others, 1970)*

A unique aspect of behavioral therapy for children is that one or both parents can be trained as "therapists" so that behavior modification can be carried out at home. The case of Valerie and that of Byron described earlier are examples of therapy in which parents carried out the actual treatment. Although in many cases a clinician must plan the behavioral inter-

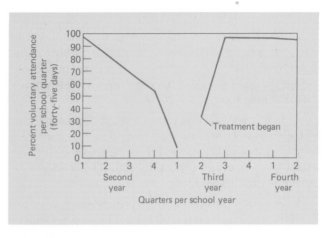

**FIGURE 15-13**
Valerie's voluntary school attendance. The behavioral intervention (including positive reinforcement) was initiated during the second quarter of the third year of school. (Ayllon and others, 1970, p. 135)

ventions and train the parents to carry them out, in some instances, particularly for less severe but still disruptive behaviors, class sessions can be used to teach parents how to develop successful home treatment programs.

## ■ STUDY OUTLINE

### THE SCOPE OF THE PROBLEM

Six million or more children in the United States have psychological problems that are severe enough to interfere with their learning in school and require professional contact.

### DISRUPTIVE BEHAVIORS

1. Restless behavior of students is a major complaint of school personnel, but some children who are considered hyperactive by teachers may not be classified as such by mental-health professionals. Children with **attention deficit–hyperactivity disorder** not only are overly active but also have perceptual and learning difficulties. The most common treatment for this disorder is the use of psychostimulant drugs, but some cognitive–behavioral techniques have also been attempted.

2. Children with **conduct disorders** engage in behaviors that seriously violate the basic rights of others or the major rules of society. Many such children are also hyperactive. Children with conduct disorders often engage in criminal behavior, become alcoholic, or develop personality disorders as adults.

## EMOTIONAL DISTURBANCES

1. Most children's fears disappear as they grow older, but some children have intense, disturbing fears that require treatment. Such fears can be treated effectively using behavioral techniques such as systematic desensitization or modeling.

2. Children with **separation anxiety disorder** show excessive anxiety when they are not with major attachment figures or in familiar surroundings. One form of separation anxiety is **school refusal**. This disorder is usually treated successfully.

3. **Reactive attachment disorders** may develop when a child has been physically abused or neglected or has experienced frequent changes of caregivers. Children with such disorders are unresponsive in most social interactions.

4. Children sometimes develop **obsessive compulsive** and **ritualistic** behaviors that require treatment. These disorders are rare and are difficult to treat successfully.

5. Depression is frequent among children who come to clinical attention. Childhood depression is more common in boys than in girls and may be relatively long lasting. During adolescence mood disorders become more common in girls than in boys and may take the form of hypomania or bipolar disorder. Mood disorders become generally more common in adolescence, as do suicide and parasuicide.

6. Some researchers believe that the basic cause of childhood depression is biological, and there is evidence of a genetic component. Stress appears to interact with vulnerability to produce depression. Treatment often consists of behavioral therapy or family therapy.

## PROBLEMS WITH PHYSICAL SYMPTOMS

1. **Anorexia nervosa** means nervous loss of appetite, but anorexics have both physiological and cognitive feelings of hunger and a strong preoccupation with food. People with this disorder have an intense fear of becoming fat even when they are obviously underweight. Sociocultural pressures may have contributed to the increase in the incidence of anorexia in recent decades. Genetic factors may also play a role in the development of anorexia.

2. Some anorexics stay thin by restricting food intake. Others combine food restriction with periodic binges and purges. Anorexia is related to depressed mood and has a variety of effects on the body, including retarded bone growth, anemia, dry skin, low body temperature, and other symptoms. Many anorexics recover when treated with a combination of behavioral methods and family therapy.

3. In **bulimia nervosa,** binge eating occurs at least twice a week for at least three months and is often accompanied by laxative use, self-induced vomiting, or rigorous dieting. Binge episodes appear to be brought on by negative cognitive/emotional states such as pressure at work or school and problems with personal relationships. Negative feelings after the binge are thought to serve as a cue for purging to "undo" the effects of the binge.

4. Treatment of bulimia can be focused either on preventing binges or on preventing purging. Relaxation training may help prevent binges, while treatment to prevent purging involves exposure and response prevention.

## THERAPY WITH CHILDREN AND ADOLESCENTS

Many therapies that are used with adults have been adapted for use with children. In addition, some methods have been developed specifically for use with young children. The latter include play therapy, storytelling techniques, and behavior-modification programs. Play therapy may be either nondirective or psychodynamically oriented. A unique aspect of behavioral therapy for children is that parents can be trained to carry out interventions at home.

# 16

# DEVELOPMENTAL DISORDERS

*Peter nursed eagerly, sat and walked at the expected ages. Yet some of his behavior made us vaguely uneasy. He never put anything in his mouth. Not his fingers nor his toys—nothing. More troubling was the fact that Peter didn't look at us, or smile, and wouldn't play the games that seemed as much a part of babyhood as diapers. While he didn't cry, he rarely laughed, and when he did, it was at things that didn't seem funny to us. He didn't cuddle, but sat upright in my lap, even when I rocked him. But children differ and we are content to let Peter be himself. We thought it hilarious when my brother, visiting us when Peter was 8 months old, observed that "that kid has no social instincts, whatsoever." Although Peter was a first child, he was not isolated. I frequently put him in his playpen in front of the house, where the school children stopped to play with him as they passed. He ignored them too. . . .*

*Peter's babbling had not turned into speech by the time he was 3. His play was solitary and repetitive. He tore paper into long thin strips, bushel baskets of it every day. He spun the lids from canning jars and became upset if we tried to divert him. Only rarely could I catch his eye, and then saw his focus change from me to the reflection in my glasses. It was like trying to pick up mercury with chopsticks.* (Eberhardy, 1967, pp. 257–258)

Peter's case is an example of one of the most serious developmental disorders: autistic disorder. Mental retardation and autistic disorder (autism) are two developmental disorders that have an overall effect on children's patterns of development. Other developmental disorders are more specific: they affect speech (stuttering or difficulties in pronunciation), academic skills (reading disorder, expressive-writing disorder, or arithmetic disorder), or motor skills (coordination disorder). However, none of these disorders has as great an impact on other children and their families as autism and mental retardation. This chapter therefore is devoted to these two major developmental disorders.

## ■ AUTISTIC DISORDER

Autistic disorder occurs in 2 to 4 children out of every 10,000 under the age of 15. Boys are three to four times as likely to be autistic as girls (Campbell and Green, 1985). Autism is not common, but its effects are devastating.

### Characteristics of Autistic Behavior

Children with **autistic disorder** show several kinds of impairment—in social relationships, communication,

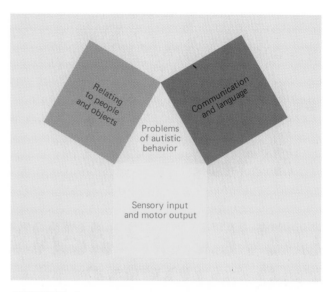

**FIGURE 16–1**
Problem areas of autistic behavior.

and activities (see Figure 16–1). Their social interactions are highly unusual. In general, such children have a noticeable lack of awareness of the existence or feelings of others. They may treat people as though they were objects and are likely to have no empathy for the feelings of others. They do not seek out an adult for comfort if they are hurt or upset. They don't like to be held and they avoid eye contact. Autistic children prefer solitary play and have a poor understanding of social conventions.

Even as young children, autistic children do not enjoy the usual parent–child kiss-and-cuddle routines. They do not wave goodbye or play peek-a-boo. As toddlers, they do not follow their parents around the house or run to meet them when they come home.

Communication impairment is even more dramatic than impaired social behavior in autism (see Figure 16–2). About half of all autistic children do not develop speech at all. Even their babbling as infants is not intended as communication. If they do learn to talk, their speech is likely to be unusual. For instance, they may simply repeat what is said to them (*echolalia*) or repeat commercials they have heard on television. They also tend to reverse "you" and "I"; thus, when asking for a drink they might say "You want a drink" instead of "I want a drink." In addition, their tone of voice may be unusual—singsong or monotonous.

Autistic children have a very narrow range of in-

**FIGURE 16-2**
Autistic children show deficits in communication skills. In this therapy session the clinician plays a body-contact game in an effort to improve the child's skills in communicating with others. (Mimi Forsyth, Monkmeyer Press)

1. Did you ever suspect the child was very nearly deaf?
   + 1. Yes
   ___ 2. No

2. (Age 2–5) Is he cuddly?
   ___ 1. Definitely, likes to cling to adults
   ___ 2. Above average (likes to be held)
   + 3. No, rather stiff and awkward to hold
   ___ 4. Don't know

3. (Age 3–5) How skillful is the child in doing fine work with his fingers or playing with small objects?
   + 1. Exceptionally skillful
   ___ 2. Average for age
   ___ 3. A little awkward, or very awkward
   ___ 4. Don't know

4. (Age 3–5) How interested is the child in mechanical objects, such as the stove or vacuum cleaner?
   ___ 1. Little or no interest
   ___ 2. Average interest
   + 3. Fascinated by certain mechanical things

5. (Age 3–5) Does the child get very upset if certain things he is used to are changed (like furniture or toy arrangements, or certain doors which must be left open or shut)?
   ___ 1. No
   + 2. Yes, definitely
   ___ 3. Slightly true

6. (Age 3–5) Does the child typically say "Yes" by repeating the same question he has been asked? (Example: You ask "Shall we go for a walk, Honey?" and he indicates he does want to by saying "Shall we go for a walk, Honey?" or "Shall we go for a walk?")
   + 1. Yes, definitely, does not say "Yes" directly
   ___ 2. No, would say "Yes" or "OK" or similar answer
   ___ 3. Not sure
   ___ 4. Too little speech to say

**FIGURE 16-3**
Some items from a questionnaire to collect behavioral data on autistic and other developmentally disturbed children are shown here. The responses marked with pluses are more characteristic of autistic children than of the others. From Rimland, 1974, p. 55, © 1974 by John Wiley & Sons, Inc. Reprinted by permission.

terests and activities; they may spend a great deal of time flicking their fingers, twisting, rocking, or spinning. Sameness and routine are very important to them. Moving a piece of furniture or changing the daily routine in any way can be terribly distressing to an autistic child.

As they grow older, autistic children may spend their time repetitively feeling or smelling objects or lining up items in a row. Bus timetables and the like may be fascinating to them, and they sometimes spend hours studying such items. Figure 16–3 represents one effort to systematically collect data on the behavior of autistic children.

## Prospects for Change

Although their intelligence scores range from highly superior to severely retarded, about 80 percent of autistic children are retarded. In adulthood about two-thirds of autistic individuals are severely handicapped and unable to care for themselves, but 5 to 17 percent hold their own in the community, work, and have some kind of social life (Rutter and Garmezy, 1983). As with other children, the intelligence test scores of autistic children predict their school achievement, later occupations, and social status. One key predictor of later outcome is whether the child has developed fairly good language skills by the age of 5.

A few autistic children who have made a good adjustment later in life have written about their experiences and provided some insight into what it must feel like to be autistic.

*Tony was referred to a children's clinic when he was 26 months old. He did not speak at all and he did not seem to respond to his parents or the clinic staff in the way a young child might be expected to do; instead he ignored their approaches. His parents said he had always seemed* stiff and hard to hold, he never smiled back at them, and he spent most of his time spinning objects or watching his hands as he moved his fingers.

Tony spent several years in a therapeutic nursery school and by age 3 had learned to communicate although he was severely echolalic. By the time he was 6 his intelligence test score was just slightly below average. During high school he was very aware of his feelings of being different. He quit high school in 10th grade and joined the army but was quickly discharged for fighting. Then he worked as an assembler in a manufacturing plant. He tried to get a girlfriend, but had been unsuccessful. He said he has difficulties with anxiety, periodic overuse of alcohol, and unusual sensory experiences. This is a portion of what Tony wrote about himself:

"I was living in a world of daydreaming and Fear revolving aboud my self I had no care about Human feelings or other people. I was afraid of everything! I was terrified to go in the water swimming, (and of) loud noises; in the dark I had severe, repetitive Nightmares and occasionally hearing electronic noises with nightmares. I would wake up so terrified and disoriented I wasnt able to Find my way out of the room for a few miniuts. It felt like I was being dragged to Hell. I was afraid of simple things such as going into the shower, getting my nails cliped, soap in my eyes, rides in the carnival—except the Spook house I love it, I also like Hellish envirments such as spookhouses at the Carnival, Halloween, and movies—horror. I daydreamed a lot and tryed to activly communicate and get into that world. . . .

In school I learned some things very quickly but others were beyond learning comprehenshion. I used to disrupt the whole class and love to drive the teachers nuts. When I first started talking—5 years old—I started talking about an inccendent that happened a year befor. I was obsessed with certain things and played in my own way. I make things with Garbage or Junk and Play with them. I like mechanical Battery Power toys or electronic toys . . . IN tenth grade I quit school and worked washing cars and work(ed) many other Jobs too. I was verry derpressed and Hyper at wok. I got along with my boss at all my Jobs. I tend to get lazy and had trouble getting along with other people. So in (an) effort to keep my Jobs I avoided many people. I found It a lot easeyer to get along with older people and FEARED People my age because of school. I went into to the army and got in lots of Fights with people. So I got dicarged (discharged). I allso have great Troub(l)e getting thing(s) organized and missunderstand allmost everything.

I dont or didnt trust anybody but my self—that still (is) a problem today. And (I) was and still (am) verry insucure! I was very cold Harted too. I(t) was impossible for me to Give or Receive love from anybody. I often Repulse it by

turning people off. That is still a problem today and relating to other people. I liked things over people and dint care about People at all. I was Verry Fussy about everything and damanded comfort and pleasure and (was) Very Hyperactive and smelled thi(n)gs all the time. I spent hours Flicking books and was thirst(y) all the time and drank a lot—not booze . . .

And had and still have some mental blocks and great difficulty paying attention and listening to people and was verry eas(i)ly distracted. I damanded to be amused by people and got board verry eas(i)ly and cant deal with stress. And had great difficulty fullfilling oblagations. I woudl hear electronic Noises and have quick siezious (seizures) in bed and many other ph(y)sical problems. Often I have to be Force to get things done and (was) verry uncoordinated. And was verry Nervous about everything. And Feared People and Social Activity Greatly . . . I never got Fired from a job. My problems havn't changed at ALL from early childhood. I was Just able to Function. And it still (is) the same today."
(Volkmar and Cohen, 1985, pp. 49–52)

Another person who was autistic in childhood but was above average in intelligence had fewer difficulties than Tony but still has some characteristics of autism.

I am now 36 years old and work as a consultant, designing livestock facilities for feedlots, ranches, and meat plants throughout the U.S. and abroad. I have also authored articles in both national and international livestock publications. At the present time I am doing research on animal behavior and neurophysiology and working on my doctorate in animal science at the University of Illinois. . . .

At the age of 1 1/2 to 3, I had many of the standard autistic behaviors such as fixation on spinning objects, refusing to be touched or held, preferring to be alone, destructive behavior, temper tantrums, inability to speak, sensitivity to sudden noises, appearance of deafness, and an intense interest in odors. . . .

At the age of 3 to 3 1/2 my behavior greatly improved, but I did not learn to speak until 3 1/2. At the age of 3 to 4 my behavior was more normal until I became tired. When I became tired, bouts of impulsive behavior would return. . . .

In college I was on the Dean's honor list, but getting through the foreign language requirement was difficult. I scraped by with Ds and Cs. Learning sequential things such as math was also very hard. My mind is completely visual and spatial work such as drawing is easy. I taught myself drafting in six months. I have designed big steel and concrete cattle facilities, but remembering a phone number or adding up numbers in my head is still difficult. I have to write them down. Every piece of *information I have memorized is visual. If I have to remember an abstract concept I "see" the page of the book or my notes in my mind and "read" information from it. Melodies are the only things I can memorize without a visual image. I remember very little that I hear unless it is emotionally arousing or I can form a visual image. In class I take careful notes, because I would forget the auditory material. When I think about abstract concepts such as human relationships I use visual similes. For example, relationships between people are like a glass sliding door. The door must be opened gently, if it is kicked it may shatter. If I had to learn a foreign language, I would have to do it by reading, and make it visual. (Grandin, 1984, pp. 144–145)*

Successful adjustment is achieved by only a small proportion of autistic children. More typical is the case of Bruce.

*During his preschool years he was involved in extensive therapy but he remained mute, bizarre, and socially isolated. During Bruce's school years no special program was available, so his mother took special courses to prepare herself to teach him. Through her efforts he learned about 100 words. He never used them voluntarily and relied on simple signs for communication.*

*At 20 Bruce is physically healthy. He remains mute, but does use signs to express his wishes. As a child, he had unusual skill at assembling puzzle pieces. He still has this ability which helps him in his prevocational training. If left alone he still rocks his body for hours and twirls objects in front of his face, much as he did when was a preschooler. (adapted from Cohen and others, 1978, pp. 68–69)*

## Therapy

Behavior-modification programs have often been used with children who are severely autistic. These programs have shown promise in improving such children's language and self-help skills, which, in turn, improve their chances for social adjustment (see Figure 16–4).

At the beginning of a behavior-modification program, it may take 15 to 30 minutes to get a correct response from the child, even for simple tasks such as looking at the instructor on command. Once the child can consistently follow simple commands, he or she may be asked to perform imitative behavior, first by following visual instructions (such as raising an arm when the instructor does) and then by following verbal instructions (such as raising an arm when the instructor asks for that movement). The entire program takes several hours a day for months at a time. For this reason, at least one parent is trained to work with the child

between visits to a professional. As the child progresses, the parent takes over a great deal of the training. The case of Jason is typical.

*Soon after he was 1, Jason was tuned out on everything. He didn't talk. He didn't respond to his name. His behavior grew worse. He cried all night. His parents had to take turns sitting up with him. Every time they tried to pick him up his body became rigid and he pushed them away. Jason and his parents made the round of experts. After several false starts they contacted a psychologist who used operant-conditioning techniques. The psychologist explained that behavioral training might make it possible for Jason to live at home as a more acceptable member of the household, or at least help him develop enough skills to get into a better institution. For several months Jason worked with teachers trained in behavior modification who slowly taught him a few words. Using bits of cereal, Jason's favorite food, they worked with him. When he made a "J" sound, he got a piece of cereal. Eventually he was able to say his name and then a few more words. Using the same technique they began to teach him to dress himself. Then his parents took over at home. After three years of this training, Jason, now 5 years old, can say about twenty words, dress himself, and is toilet trained.*

This may seem like a pathetically poor group of skills for a 5-year-old, but for an autistic child as severely affected as Jason was, it represents a huge success.

Although they help autistic children with specific skills, behavioral approaches to autism have met with limited success (Franks, 1985). One of the biggest problems is the child's inability to generalize the responses that have been learned to other situations.

Autistic children's unusual social behaviors and low level of academic achievement have made it difficult to educate them in a regular school setting. However, at least one secondary school program has been successful (Gaylord-Ross and others, 1984). In this operant-learning program, students may start with edible reinforcers, then move to token reinforcers such as listening to records, and finally respond to verbal praise. The students use the school gym and cafeteria and are trained to visit stores and restaurants. Those who can do so are allowed to participate in vocational training.

## Research on Autism

Autism was first described by Leo Kanner, a child psychiatrist, in 1943. Kanner presented cases of children who exhibited a unique pattern of behavior in which they were unable to relate in an ordinary way to people and situations from the beginning of life. In addition to this "extreme autistic aloneness," he stressed the children's "obsessive desire for the maintenance of

(a)

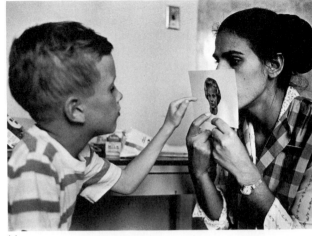
(c)

(b)

(d)

**FIGURE 16-4**
Autistic children receive special learning programs. (a) The therapist is hand-prompting a mute child to make the ''wh'' sound. (b) The therapist is using food as a reinforcer for attending to him and making eye contact. (c) The therapist is teaching a child to identify parts of the face from a picture after he has learned to name the parts from his face and hers. She uses verbal reinforcement. (d) Autistic children have difficulty playing with other children. The therapist is using food to reinforce joint play activity. (Allan Grant)

sameness." Kanner thought of autism as a child psychosis and believed that most autistic children were basically very intelligent.

We now know that in the majority of cases autism is connected with global mental retardation. Although research on autism usually groups all autistic children together, such children seem to fall into at least two groups: those who are normal or near normal in intelligence and those who function at a retarded level (Prior, 1984). One important area for future research is the separate study of these two groups, which may be very different despite the similarities in their social functioning.

**The Cognitive Perspective** A cognitive deficit seems to be central to autism. Most autistic children can see and hear normally, but they respond to sensory input in a distorted way. From a very early age they are either under- or overresponsive to all kinds of stimuli. Often both ways of responding can be seen in the same person. Some of the perceptual disturbances of autistic children seem to decrease with age, especially if the child responds well to treatment for the overall disorder, but there seems to be no doubt that early cognitive development in autistic children is abnormal.

The most universal symptom of autistic disorder is language disturbance. More than half of all autistic children remain mute, and for those who do speak, specific aspects of language disorder remain. Autistic language is deviant; it includes echolalia and reversal of pronouns. The social language of autistic children is inappropriate, and they do not engage in spontaneous vocal speech. Autistic children also have problems in comprehension. Their speech seems to be a repetition of what was heard rather than a form of communication. They don't seem to have difficulty with short-term recall; instead, the problem has to do with meaning. For instance, when asked to repeat strings of words, autistic children can repeat random meaningless strings as well as they can repeat meaningful sentences. This is not true of normal children. A few autistic children can make use of meaning to help their recall (Fyffe and Prior, 1978). These children have some ability to comprehend what they read, but their language use is likely to remain literal and concrete (Snowling and Firth, 1982).

In general, research on cognition suggests that autistic children, while their basic input and simple memory may not be impaired, have a problem with higher-level cognitive processing in which stimuli are organized by meaning. Autistic children seem to have more problems with symbolic thought than with real-life examples. For instance, one group did better at puzzles that required thinking about alternatives if the material they used was three-dimensional (colored wooden shapes) instead of two-dimensional (line drawings) (Prior and McGillivray, 1980). These cognitive deficiencies are probably related to the absence of symbolic or representational play in autistic children (Wulff, 1985).

**The Biological Perspective** Because of the pattern of cognitive disabilities found in autism, researchers have focused on problems in the left hemisphere of the brain, where language and symbolic material are assumed to be processed. One problem with this idea, however, is that when very young children have some left-hemisphere maldevelopment or destruction, the plasticity of their nervous systems seem to allow the right hemisphere to take over many of the functions of the damaged left hemisphere. Since autistic behavior is observed very early, this probably means that both hemispheres are affected in autistic children.

The cognitive problems, especially the language problems, of autistic children seem different from those that occur in either left-hemisphere or bilateral damage to the brain. It has been suggested that these problems are caused by early damage to the limbic system, which then affects other parts of the nervous system (Prior, 1985). Another possibility is that the symptoms of autism can be explained in terms of a dysfunction of behavioral systems in the brain stem that is further distorted by the functioning of the midbrain and the cortex (Ornitz, 1985).

Some form of brain pathology seems likely in autistic individuals, since at least one-fifth of autistic children develop epileptic seizures in adolescence (Deykin and MacMahon, 1979). The risk of seizures is much greater for those who are severely retarded than for those who are not. Some kind of brain injury at or after birth is also a possibility. In a study of 17 sets of identical twins in which only one of each twin pair was autistic, in 12 sets it was likely that the affected twin had experienced brain damage (for example, from convulsions shortly after birth) (Folstein and Rutter, 1977).

So far there have been no specific findings in either brain anatomy or brain metabolism that differentiate autistic individuals from other groups (Rumsey and others, 1985). PT scans of a group of autistic adults show a higher rate of glucose metabolism than that found in a group of normal subjects, but there is a large overlap between the groups.

Some researchers have wondered about the possibility that there is a hereditary factor in autism. Autism is a rare disorder, and autistic individuals rarely marry and have children. Hence, a family history of autism would not be expected. However, research has turned up some findings that suggest a genetic link. Two percent of the brothers and sisters of autistic children are also autistic. Although this percentage is low, it is 50 times greater than would be expected by chance (Rutter, 1967). Moreover, a family history of delayed speech is much more common in autism (25 percent of all cases) than in the average family (Bartak and others, 1975). Another clue comes from the finding that when one of a set of twins was autistic, whether the twins were monozygotic or dizygotic greatly affected the probability that the other twin would also be autistic (see Figure 16–5). Knowledge about the genetics of autism suggests that what is inherited is probably not autism but some general tendency toward language or cognitive abnormalities (Rutter and Garmezy, 1983).

It has also been suggested that the parents of autistic children share HLA antigens (human leukocyte antigens), which may increase the likelihood that the unborn child will be attacked by its mother's immune system (Stubbs and others, 1985). Mothers of autistic children report a greater frequency of both spontaneous abortions and bleeding during pregnancy; these also may be due in part to immune system attacks. If the antigens of the two parents differ, they may stimulate blocking antibodies that protect the fetus from immune system attacks. Although this idea is still somewhat speculative, a comparison of HLA antigen samples from two groups of parents with autistic children with examples from control parents showed the predicted differences: Seventy-five percent of the parents of autistic children shared antigens, but only 25 percent of the control parents did so.

## Autism Versus Childhood Schizophrenia

Although autism was originally thought of as a psychosis, it is now considered to be a developmental disorder. However, psychosis can occur in children, and some childhood psychosis may be the same as schizophrenia in adults. It is not clear whether schizophrenia that occurs before age 15 has the same consequences and outcome as schizophrenia in adulthood; however, the symptoms are similar and include hallucinations, bizarre fantasies, ideas of reference, and paranoid ideas (Beitchman, 1983).

Childhood schizophrenia is even rarer than autism and much rarer than schizophrenia in adulthood. When they were followed up later, about 20 percent of children with childhood schizophrenia seemed completely recovered and another 30 percent were making at least a satisfactory social adaptation. All the children in the group who became psychotic before age 10 had a poor outcome. Although childhood schizophrenia seems different from autism, whether it also differs from adult schizophrenia is not known.

## ■ MENTAL RETARDATION

**Mental retardation** means a significantly below-average level of intellectual functioning as measured by an individually administered intelligence test. To be classified as mentally retarded, a person's social as well as intellectual functioning must be impaired (see Figure 16–6).

Mental retardation is a chronic, irreversible condition that begins before the age of 18. If intellectual functioning drops to retarded levels after age 18, the

**FIGURE 16–5**
Differences between monozygotic and dizygotic twin pairs in which at least one twin is autistic.

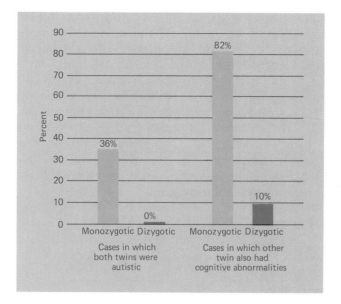

**FIGURE 16–6**
Only people who are significantly below average in both intellectual functioning and adaptive behavior are classified as mentally retarded.

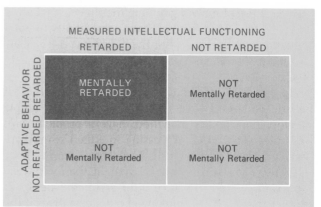

# ■BOX 16-1 HOW FAMILIES ADAPT TO RETARDED CHILDREN

From the parents' point of view, the birth of a mentally retarded child is a stressful and often tragic event. For nine months they have looked forward to the arrival of a healthy, normal child. When those expectations are shattered, they often go through a grieving process similar to that following the death of a family member. In the past, many professionals emphasized the parents' need for help until they could accept the situation. They viewed the process as time limited. One parent of a retarded child comments on this view.

*Parents of retarded people, the theorists tell us, learn to live with their children's handicaps. They go through stages of reaction, moving through shock, guilt, and rejection to the promised land of acceptance and adjustment.*

*My own experience as the father of a retarded child did not fit this pattern. Instead, it convinced me that most people seriously misunderstand a parent's response to this situation. The standard view does not reflect the reality of parents' experience or lead to helpful conclusions.'*

*Professionals could help parents more—and they would be more realistic—if they discarded their ideas about stages and progress. They could then begin to understand something about the deep, lasting changes that life with a retarded son or daughter brings to parents. And they could begin to see that the negative feelings—the shock, the guilt, and the bitterness—never disappear but stay on as a part of the parents' emotional life.*

*Most parents, I believe, never fully resolve the complexity of feelings about their child's retardation. They don't "adjust to" or "accept" that fact, at least not in the way psychology books describe it."* (Searl, 1978, p. f27).

Many parents of retarded children retain some optimism about their child's future progress while the child is still young. For example, they may overestimate the child's learning potential and underestimate problems in learning. This is illustrated by the observation that parents of young children are more supportive of the concept of mainstreaming (combining children of all abilities into one school program) than parents of older children, who see a greater need for special-education programs

(Suelzle and Keenan, 1981). In general, just as the grieving process goes on over a lifetime, the parents' acceptance of the severity of their child's disability is not steady and gradual. Instead, problems of acceptance flare up acutely at particular stages in the child's development.

Families of retarded children go through a series of crises as the child reaches various developmental stages. In one survey, three-quarters of the parents described life with their retarded child as a series of ups and progressively greater downs. Only one-quarter described their grief as being healed by time (Wikler and others, 1981). The parents were asked to evaluate the extent to which they were upset at a number of points, including early events such as the time of diagnosis, the time for walking and talking, and decisions on school placement, and later events such as the onset of puberty, the twenty-first birthday, and discussion and decisions about the care of the child after the parents' death.

When the parents' responses were compared with the predictions of social workers, the results showed that the social workers tended to overestimate the extent to which the parents' were upset over the earlier experiences and to underestimate the extent to which they were upset over the later experiences. For example, the social workers overestimated the extent to which parents were upset at the times when the child would normally have been expected to walk, when the child entered a special-education class rather than the regular school program, and when younger siblings surpassed the retarded child in functioning. They markedly underestimated how upsetting the child's twenty-first birthday was to the parents.

The unmet needs of parents seem to form a U-shaped curve. They are high among parents of preschoolers, drop off when the children enter some kind of school program, and rise again, even beyond the original levels, when the children become young adults.

In the past, parents of severely retarded children were urged to institutionalize such children shortly after birth, before they had had a chance to become attached to them. More recently, they have been urged to care for their children at home. However, the presence of a retarded child puts great stress on a family. Parents report a sense of loss and hopelessness, a decrease in self-esteem, and increases in shame, guilt, and marital disharmony (Lobato, 1983). The father of one autistic and retarded child wrote movingly in his diary about the stresses that his son's problems imposed on him and his wife, Foumi.

*I notice that I have become more distrustful of Foumi, have lost some of my faith in her, so necessary for our marriage, or any marriage, because she has borne me Noah. Even though genetically, I suspect, it is I who am the wreck. But worse than cheating or mutual suspicion when it comes to unfixing the mystique that glues a marriage, I guess, is to have a disturbed kid. At first I thought it would draw us closer together, necessarily cement our relationship. Now Foumi and I have to be wary that it doesn't draw us apart. We have to be intelligent enough to realize there is a strain on any marriage whenever a baby is sick. And we always have a sick baby.*
(Greenfeld, 1970, pp. 66–67)

Very little research has been done on how parents cope with these stresses. A study of parents whose children were in a preschool program found that some parents, especially those who were younger and less well educated, used religion as a coping device (Friedrich and others, 1986). These parents believed that "God specifically chose me to be the parent of this special child." This belief appeared to give them comfort and increase their feeling that things were under control. Another group of parents believed that they were in control of their lives and could deal with the situation. These parents tended to be older and better educated. The results of this study suggest that the belief that someone or some force is in control can be helpful in withstanding the stress of having a retarded child. These feelings could be enhanced through support groups formed by the families themselves. Such groups could not only provide emotional support but increase feelings of control by sharing advice about parenting techniques and information about the availability of community facilities.

The brothers and sisters of retarded children may also be affected by the child's presence. Again, there has not been much research on these effects. What we do know suggests that the parents of a retarded child often place increased demands on their other children. They are expected to care for the retarded child and to subordinate their needs to those of their sibling. Their parents expect more of them and at the same time often have less time and attention to give them. These children sometimes feel pressure to excel in order to "make up" for their retarded sibling.

The children who are most negatively affected by the presence of a retarded child in the family are younger brothers and sisters. They are most likely to show problems in psychological adjustment. Older sisters are also negatively affected, perhaps because they are given additional responsibilities. The siblings seem most affected in two-child families and in unusually large families (Lobato, 1983).

Much of the research on the effects of a retarded child on other family members was done some years ago, when many children were institutionalized, and in many cases there were no control groups. This is an area where more facts are needed. What is known at present is that, not surprisingly, the parents' attitudes toward the retarded child and their ways of dealing with the situation have an important effect on their other children's adjustment (Brody and Stoneman, 1984).

---

problem is classified as dementia rather than as mental retardation.

## Degrees of Mental Retardation

There are four categories of mental retardation based on intelligence-test scores: **mild, moderate, severe,** and **profound** (see Table 16–1). The following cases illustrate these categories and Table 16–2 summarizes the characteristics of each group.

Mild Retardation. *Alice is 16 and has been in special classes since preschool. She can feed and dress herself well, but she needs help in deciding on appropriate clothes to wear. She can write simple letters and use the telephone. She can carry on an ordinary conversation, but*

---

□ **TABLE 16–1**
Levels of Mental Retardation

|  | IQ | Percent of All Retardation |
| --- | --- | --- |
| Mild mental retardation | 50–70 | 80% |
| Moderate mental retardation | 35–49 | 12% |
| Severe mental retardation | 20–34 | 7% |
| Profound mental retardation | Below 20 | Less than 1% |

Behavior of Retarded Individuals at Various Stages of Development.[1]

| Level of Retardation | Highest Level of Adaptive Behavior | | |
| --- | --- | --- | --- |
| | 3 Years of Age | 9 Years of Age | 15 Years of Age and Over |
| Profound | Drinks from a cup with help, sits unsupported or pulls self up, imitates sounds, repeats Ma-Ma. Indicates knowing familiar people and interacts with them nonverbally. | Tried to feed self but spills, can pull off pants and socks, walks alone, uses 4–10 words, may play with others briefly. | Feeds self, can dress except for small buttons and zippers; toilet trained but may have accidents. Can climb steps and throw a ball. Vocabulary of up to 300–400 words and uses grammatically correct sentences or if nonverbal may use gestures for communcation. Understands simple questions and directions. Participates in simple group games. |
| Severe | Feeds self with finger foods. Can remove clothes, but often does so inappropriately, stands alone or walks unsteadily. Says 1 or 2 words, plays "patty cake" or with toys. | Feeds self with spoon. May be messy. Drinks unassisted. May indicate need for toilet, runs and jumps. Speaks 2–3 word sentences. Interacts with others in simple play. | Feeds self adequately with spoon and fork, can dress with zippers and buttons, is toilet trained. Can run, go up and down stairs alternating feet. May communicate in complex sentences, participates in group activities, does simple tasks and errands. |
| Moderate | Tries to feed self but spills, can pull off pants and socks, walks alone, uses 4–10 words, may play with others briefly. | Feeds self, can dress except for small buttons and zippers, toilet trained but may have accidents. Can climb steps and throw a ball. Vocabulary of up to 300–400 words and uses grammatically correct sentences or if nonverbal may use gestures for communication. Understands simple questions and directions. Participates in simple group games. | Feeds, bathes and dresses self. Selects daily clothing, can wash and iron own clothes, good body control, can carry on simple conversation and can interact cooperatively with others. Can go on errand without a list. Can assume responsibility for simple household tasks. |
| Mild | Feeds self with spoon. May be messy. Drinks unassisted. May indicate need for toilet, runs and jumps. Speaks 2–3-word sentences. Interacts with others in simple play. | Feeds self adequately with spoon and fork, can dress with zippers and buttons, is toilet trained. Can run, go up and down stairs alternating feet. May communicate in complex sentences, participates in group activities, does simple tasks and errands. | Cares for own personal grooming, sometimes with reminders. Can go around own neighborhood easily. Carries on everyday conversation. Writes simple letters and uses telephone. Can go shopping, prepare simple meals and initiate most of own activities. |

[1]Areas with the same shading describe identical behavior. This illustrates how the same behaviors appear at different ages depending on the level of retardation.

she does not seem aware of important current events and is unable to talk or write about abstractions. She rides a bicycle and seems well coordinated. She can find her way around her neighborhood but can't go farther without aid. She can cook simple meals and go shopping for specific items by herself.

Moderate Retardation. *Bob, age 17, has been in a special-educational program since he was 6. He can dress himself but needs to be checked over to be sure he is completely dressed before going out. He can go to a nearby store by himself but cannot tell if he has been given the correct change. He cannot take buses alone. In his group home he makes his bed, helps set the table, and sweeps the floor. He works in a sheltered workshop stuffing envelopes. His speech is barely understandable, but he responds to directions and requests.*

Severe Retardation. *Jason, age 21, has been in educational programs since he was 6. He can feed himself with a spoon and can dress himself if the clothing is not too difficult to get on. He gets lost if he goes more than a block from home. He can talk, but his speech is repetitive and his vocabulary small. He enjoys going to the store with others but has no concept of making purchases. He cannot select three objects from a group. Jason has been enrolled in two different sheltered workshop programs but has been unable to learn the job routine.*

Profound Retardation. *Peggy is 30. She has been slow in development since birth and has been in a special educational program since preschool. She cannot dress herself completely. She can use a spoon but not a knife and fork. She does not interact much with other people except by smiling or laughing; she does not talk. She can respond to simple commands like "Come here" and to her name. She spends a great deal of time rocking her body back and forth. Although she watches TV, she pays attention for only brief periods and seems to be watching only the movements.*

Mental retardation has many causes, but these may be grouped into two general categories. Children who are **psychosocially disadvantaged** may show no specific disabilities but may resemble their parents in intellectual achievement and may be from lower socioeconomic levels. Thus, their heredity and/or environmental experiences may cause their intelligence-test scores to fall in the lower end of the distribution.

If only this group were included, the distribution of intelligence-test scores would look like the theoretical curve in Figure 16–7 and only 2.3 percent of the population would be mentally retarded. However, there are more retarded individuals than would be predicted; about 3 percent of the children born each year are retarded. This is because some children are retarded as a result of some kind of pathology—disease, injury, chromosomal abnormality, or specific genetic disorder. The IQs of this group are usually lower than those of retarded children for whom there is no obvious causal factor.

The differences between these two groups also show up in the intelligence-test scores of other children in the family. In one study of retarded children, the IQ scores of their brothers and sisters were also measured. None of the siblings of the severely retarded children were retarded, but 20 percent of the siblings of mildly retarded children were also retarded (see Figure 16–8). These findings indicate that although there is some overlap, mild and severe cases of mental retardation probably have different causes.

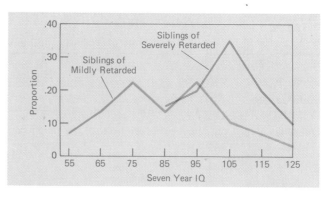

**FIGURE 16-8**
IQ distribution for siblings of severely retarded (IQ less than 50) and mildly retarded (IQ 50–69) white children. (Nichols, 1984, p. 163)

## Biological Causes

Whenever nonenvironmental causes of retardation are discussed, a number of overlapping terms are used. Figure 16–9 explains the differences among these terms. The predictable gene-based qualities that are transmitted from the parents to the children are *hereditary*. However, some of the genes available at the moment of conception are not quite like those of either parent and are called *mutants*. In addition, sometimes each nonaffected parent contributes enough pathologically related genes to move the child over the threshold from nondisordered to disordered. This is what is thought to happen in polygenic disorders such as schizophrenia.

**FIGURE 16-9**
Definitions of nonenvironmental contributors to psychopathology.

**FIGURE 16-7**
The theoretical curve of intelligence scores. If this curve were a correct predictor, the percent of retarded individuals would be lower than is actually the case.

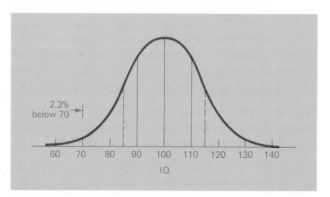

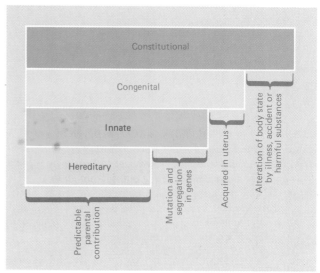

These mutations and superthreshold doses of affected genes are added to the predictable parental contribution and the total is referred to as *innate*. In addition, certain disorders can be acquired in the uterus, for example, as a result of chemical substances passed to the child through the placenta. These factors together with the innate factors make up what are called *congenital* factors. Finally, *constitutional* factors include congenital factors and any factors that are due to illness or injury after birth.

## Hereditary Disorders

*Disorders Caused by Specific Dominant Genes.* The number of known dominant genes that cause severe retardation is small because people who are afflicted by these disorders do not usually have children. Often a mutation, or spontaneous variation in a gene, seems to be responsible for the first case of a dominant-gene disorder recognized in a family. In many of these disorders the symptoms do not become apparent immediately after birth. One such disorder is **tuberous sclerosis.** In addition to severe retardation and seizures, this condition produces small fibrous tumors, often beside the nose, as well as internal tumors and skin abnormalities. The seizures may not begin until the child is 3, and the tumors may not appear until several years later. In some mild cases the tumors appear but retardation is minimal or absent.

*Disorders Caused by Specific Recessive Genes.* A parent may carry only one recessive gene in a particular gene pair without showing symptoms of the problem transmitted by the gene. If both parents carry the same recessive gene, one in four of their children may be affected by the problem and two in four may become carriers like their parents. Many of these inherited problems involve disorders of metabolism, or the way the body utilizes various chemicals. In **phenylketonuria** (PKU), for example, the body cannot oxidize the chemical phenylalanine, which therefore accumulates in the body. If this accumulation is allowed to continue, severe mental retardation may result. Very few untreated PKU victims have IQs above 50. If treatment, which involves a restrictive diet, is started early, most of these changes can be prevented, although earlier damage cannot be reversed. Children who received treatment at an early age are usually in the normal range on intelligence tests and neurological examinations, although they score lower on intelligence tests than their siblings did at comparable ages.

Newborn infants can be tested for PKU, although because only 1 in 17,000 children has PKU, the costs of such testing are high per case actually identified. However, the costs of caring for the retarded are also high. In one program the saving from detecting and treating each infant with PKU and thus preventing retardation was over $200,000 (Barden and others, 1984).

A group of PKU women who were treated in their early years but are now on normal diets are approaching childbearing age. It is likely that the majority of the children born to these women will not have PKU, but they will be retarded unless the mother follows a special diet during pregnancy. Without such a diet, the high level of phenylalanine in the blood of the mother will almost certainly result in severe brain damage to the fetus (Kirkman, 1982).

**Tay-Sachs disease,** another inherited metabolic disorder, is inevitably fatal. This condition, which is caused by a recessive gene, occurs most often in Ashkenazi Jews whose ancestors came from a small area in Eastern Europe. It causes progressive degeneration of the nervous system, degeneration of the brain, and death, usually before the age of 4.

## Disorders Due to Mutations

In one study (Kaveggia and others, 1972), nearly 50 percent of children with IQs below 50 had a genetically related disorder. Most of these children did not have a disorder transmitted directly through specific dominant or recessive genes. Instead, almost half of them had chromosomal abnormalities, and about one-third had single-gene mutations. Recent research has greatly increased our knowledge about the specific causes of some of these genetic disorders.

About 10 percent of all conceptions have some **chromosomal abnormality.** Since most of these abnormal fetuses are aborted through miscarriage, only about 1.5 percent of all newborns have chromosomal abnormalities. If the abnormality affects the nonsex chromosomes, or **autosomes,** mental retardation is almost always present. If the abnormality occurs in the sex cells, it does not usually produce as severe defects as those caused by abnormalities in the autosomal cells. A female who has only one X chromosome but lacks a Y chromosome (XO) will be short in height, will not attain adult sexual development, and may be mildly retarded. Males who have an XXY or XXXY pattern **(Klinefelter's syndrome)** are likely to be below average in intelligence but not severely retarded.

*Down Syndrome.* The most frequent autosomal abnormality is **Down syndrome,** which occurs about once in every 700 births. The likelihood of this condition increases as the age of the mother increases (see Figure 16–10). In most cases Down syndrome results from the presence of an extra chromosome. There are three number 21 chromosomes instead of the usual two. For this reason, Down syndrome is also called *trisomy 21* (see Figure 16–11).

Children who are affected by Down syndrome have

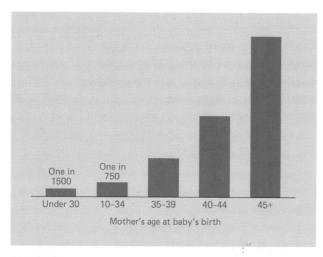

**FIGURE 16-10**
The chances of giving birth to a child with Down syndrome increases as the mother's age increases. (Smith and Wilson, 1973, p. 17)

many characteristic physical features that make this disorder easy to recognize (see Figure 16-12). Some of the most striking physical features are a flat face and a small nose, eyes that appear to slant upward because of small folds of skin at the inside corners, small ears, and small square hands with short fingers and a curved fifth finger. Children with Down syndrome tend to be shorter than average, with especially short arms and legs in proportion to their bodies. They also are likely to be somewhat obese in childhood and adolescence. In addition to being retarded, such a child is likely to have a congenital heart abnormality.

Children with Down syndrome show considerable variability in level of retardation, which may range from mild to severe. They seem especially weak in tactile perception, higher-level abstraction and reasoning, and auditory perception. As infants, they explore their environment in the same ways that other children do (MacTurk and others, 1985). As they grow older, however, the discrepancy between their performance and that of nonretarded children widens. The average adolescent or adult with Down syndrome has the abilities of a young child.

Programs to provide increased stimulation to very young Down syndrome children have attempted to modify the typical early downward trend of developmental progress. Intervention often begins a few days after birth with physical-therapy programs. Older chil-

dren who cannot yet speak can be taught to communicate with sign language. Programs for young children provide a variety of activities to help develop both physical and cognitive skills (see Figure 16-13). Parents are also trained to take part in activities to stimulate their children.

Perhaps because of the availability of such programs, some Down syndrome children have higher intelligence scores than would have been thought possible in the past. In one study, more than 5 percent of a group of 180 Down syndrome children had IQs above 70 (Connolly, 1978). According to the classification system presented earlier, these children would not be considered retarded at all. Since most of the children in the study were 5 years old or less, it remains to be seen whether or not this progress continues. It is clear, however, that the intellectual potential of some Down syndrome children has been underestimated.

Mental development for people with Down syndrome can continue into their 30s and 40s if they are in a stimulating environment (Berry and others, 1984); however, for many such people aging seems to bring a decrease in cognitive abilities. This may occur because they have fewer neurons in the brain than normal people, with the result that aging affects them unusually severely. Researchers have discovered that the brains of young adults with Down syndrome tend to show changes like the lesions found in Alzheimer's disease. By age 30 they have plaques and tangles (see Figure 16-14) (Kolata, 1985). As in Alzheimer's disease, these changes seem to be concentrated in the hippocampus, the area of the brain that plays a selective role in learning and memory. About 25 to 40 percent of Down syndrome adults actually become demented, that is, lose their memories and the ability to care for themselves.

In addition to Down syndrome, there are other trisomies that are related to retardation: *trisomy 13* and *trisomy 18*. These conditions, which are much rarer than Down syndrome, cause much more severe retardation and a shorter life expectancy. The parents of an infant with one of these other trisomies face an increased risk of trisomy in future pregnancies.

***Amniocentesis.*** Help is available for parents who believe their unborn child is at risk for trisomy or a disorder caused by dominant or recessive genes. One way of determining whether the new fetus has such a defect is **amniocentesis** (see Figure 16-15), a technique in which amniotic fluid is removed from the mother and examined. Microscopic analysis of fetal cells in the fluid shows whether a chromosomal abnormality is present in the unborn child. A biochemical analysis may reveal the presence of other defects that are associated with retardation or physical malformations.

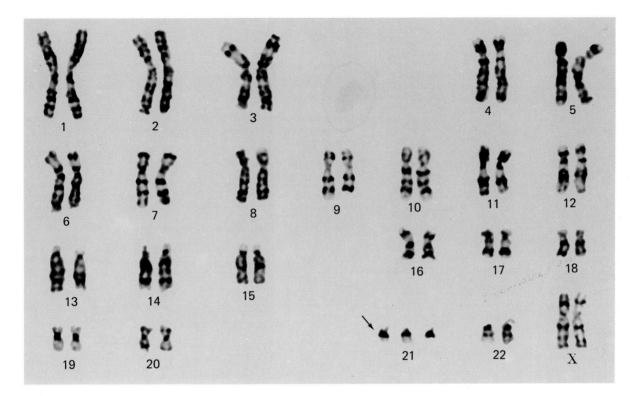

**FIGURE 16-11**
Chromosomal abnormalities are detected with relatively high frequency. Many human fetuses abort spontaneously because of chromosomal abnormalities. The most common abnormality in children who are born alive is trisomy 21, which causes Down syndrome. In more than 95 percent of Down syndrome cases, there are 47 chromosomes, with three, rather than two, twenty-first chromosomes. In other cases one member of this chromosome pair is defective. This photo shows the chromosomal analysis of a girl with Down syndrome. Trisomic chromosome 21 is indicated by the arrow.

Amniocentesis may be suggested if the risk of a retarded or otherwise genetically damaged child is high, for example, if the mother is over 35 or if there is another child with genetic problems in the family. The results, together with information about the parents' genetic history, are used to counsel parents regarding the probable outcome of the pregnancy. Given this knowledge, the prospective parents can decide to terminate the pregnancy, or they can prepare themselves for the birth of a child with a specific problem. In the majority of cases the procedure reveals that the fetus does not have the defect and the parents are spared months of needless anxiety.

### Disorders Caused by Prenatal Environmental Factors

The environment of the fetus before birth is a frequent cause of below-average intellectual functioning. In fact, mental retardation of prenatal origin is the most common of all birth defects. Prenatal factors that have been linked to mental retardation include maternal infections, blood incompatibilities and chronic maternal conditions, chemicals in the fetal environment, radiation, malnutrition, the age of the parents, and maternal stress.

*Maternal Infections.* The placental sac surrounding the unborn infant acts as a barrier that prevents many infections from being transferred from the mother to the fetus, but a number of viruses may cross this barrier. Three viruses that are known to cause congenital malformations are *rubella virus* (German measles), *cytomegalovirus,* and *herpes virus hominus (herpes simplex).*

About half of all fetuses whose mothers contract rubella in the first three months of pregnancy are also infected. The virus destroys cells and may interfere with the fetal blood supply. In one group of children of mothers who had had rubella, about one-third were retarded (Chess, 1978). Retardation can also result if the mother has a bacterial infection such as syphilis or a chronic viral illness like herpes. Syphilis in the mother causes miscarriages and stillbirths as well as mental retardation, blindness, deafness, and other birth defects.

(a)

(b)

**FIGURE 16-12**
The physical characteristics associated with Down syndrome cause people, like the boy in (a) and the older woman in (b) to have a resemblance similar to what might be expected among members of the same family. (Bruce Roberts, Photo Researchers, and Mimi Forsyth, Monkmeyer Press)

**FIGURE 16-13**
Enrichment activities for young Down syndrome children may help them achieve far more as they grow older than would have been previously expected. (National Institutes of Health)

Herpes infections in adults and older children are usually quite mild, but in a fetus or newborn child the same virus can cause a widespread infection that can result in death. Although the herpes virus can pass through the placenta and infect the fetus, the most common way in which herpes is passed from mother to child is through direct contact during the birth process.

Rubella can be controlled by a general vaccination program. Syphilis can be treated with penicillin, preferably given to the mother, although damage may still occur if treatment is not begun as soon as the infection is discovered. Herpes simplex has no known cure, but since the child is usually infected by contact with the virus during the birth process, a Caesarean section may avoid this contact and lower the risk of infection to the child.

***Blood Incompatibilities and Chronic Maternal Conditions.*** Sometimes biochemical substances in the fetus cause the mother to develop an antibody response to the baby. These antibodies may damage fetal tissues in much the same way that people reject organ

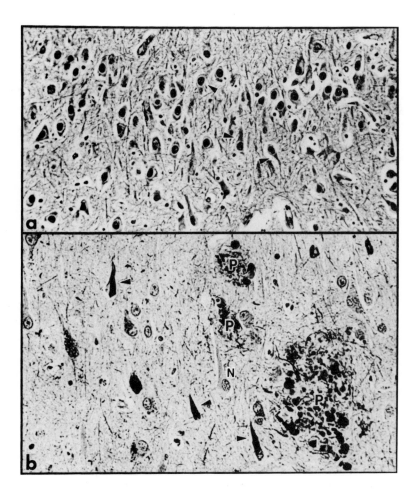

**FIGURE 16-14**
Almost all adults with Down syndrome who live to be 30 or older develop brain lesions like those seen in patients with Alzheimer's disease. Only a a minority of the Down syndrome group become demented as Alzheimer's patients do. Photo (a) shows brain tissue from a normal adult. The neurons are marked with arrows. Photo (b) shows brain tissue from an adult with Down syndrome. Arrows show neurons with neurofibrillary tangles. Plaques are marked with a P and normal neurons with an N. (Courtesy National Syndrome Society)

transplants. Incompatability of several different blood factors may have this result. The most familiar of these is **Rh incompatibility.** This occurs if the child has Rh positive blood, inherited from the father, while the mother has Rh negative blood. If the Rh negative mother has previously been sensitized to Rh positive blood, either by a blood transfusion or as a result of an earlier pregnancy, she will produce antibodies against the baby's Rh positive cells. The production of Rh positive antibodies can be prevented by means of an injection that destroys the Rh positive cells in the mother's blood prior to her new pregnancy.

Some medical conditions in the mother may also cause retardation in the fetus. Hypertension (high blood pressure) and diabetes are examples of disorders that may interfere with fetal nutrition and lead to brain damage.

*Drugs.* Drugs taken by the mother can pass through the placenta to the fetus. The average pregnant woman probably uses at least four drugs during pregnancy, including aspirin, tranquilizers, antihistamines, and other popular medications. Even mild tranquilizers such as Librium are associated with an increase in the rate of serious fetal malformations. In addition, chemicals in the air, food, and water may affect the child before birth.

Children born to mothers who are chronic alcoholics often exhibit **fetal alcohol syndrome,** a specific set of characteristics that includes mental retardation (see Figure 16–16). About 40 percent of the children born to alcoholic mothers have serious abnormalities (Jones and others, 1974). Frequently the children are small in weight and height and have unusual facial features such as small eye slits, a flattened nasal bridge, and malformed ears. Smaller-than-average head size is also common. Many of these children are moderately retarded, and as they grow older their intellectual performance decreases further. At age 7 they perform more poorly compared to children of the same age than they did at 4.

Two out of every 1000 babies born alive have fetal alcohol syndrome, and three others show some signs of it (Hanson and others, 1978). This is probably a significant underestimate of the number of children whose

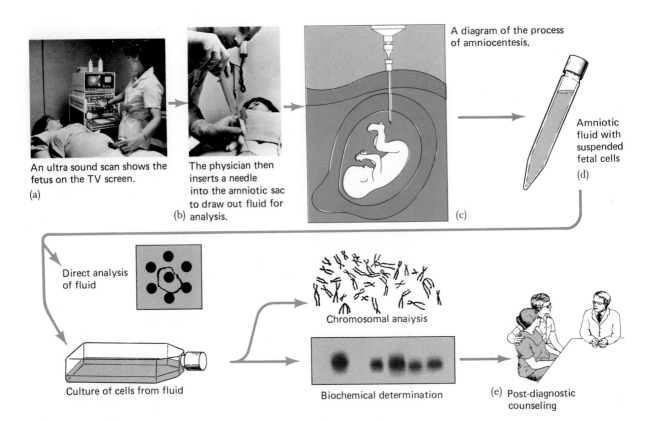

**FIGURE 16-15**
The process of amniocentesis: (a) An ultrasound scan shows the fetus on the TV screen. (b) The physician then inserts a needle into the amniotic sac to draw out fluid for analysis. (c) A diagram of the process of amniocentesis. (d) Amniotic fluid with suspended fetal cells; direct analysis of fluid; culture of cells from fluid; chromosomal analysis; biochemical determination. (e) Postdiagnostic counseling.

development is affected by alcohol. For example, although most children born to alcoholic mothers do not show physical signs of fetal alcohol syndrome, one study showed that 44 percent of these children had IQs below 79, compared to 11 percent of a control group (Jones and others, 1974). Because the controls were matched to the experimental group in socioeconomic status, age, and other factors, the mothers of the children in both groups were mainly high-risk women. This probably explains the unusually high frequency of lower-IQ children among the controls.

In recent years alcohol use during pregnancy has become recognized as an important cause of retardation. Even women who drink moderately during pregnancy may have children who are affected to some degree. So far no safe limits of alcohol use during pregnancy have been established.

**Problems at Birth and After Birth** Certain conditions occurring at birth are known to increase the probability of mental retardation, although these are not nearly as frequent causes of retardation as some of the

prenatal causes. Two of the most common birth complications are asphyxia and prematurity. Some infants do not get enough oxygen during or before the birth process. If death does not result from this asphyxia, seizures, retardation, and other problems are likely to occur. Premature infants usually are low in birth weight. When a child weighs three pounds or less at birth, the risk of retardation as well as health problems becomes much greater. Because adolescents often give birth to small infants and—especially in the case of unmarried mothers—often do not have adequate medical care, their infants are at high risk for retardation and other problems. For this reason alone, the increase in pregnancies among adolescent girls should be viewed with concern.

Damage to the central nervous system after birth can also cause retardation. Among the causes of such damage are infections, blows to the head, tumors, asphyxiation, and poisons. Some poisonous substances damage the brain cells by depriving them of oxygen. Carbon monoxide, barbiturates, and cyanide work in this way. Other poisons damage specific sites in the

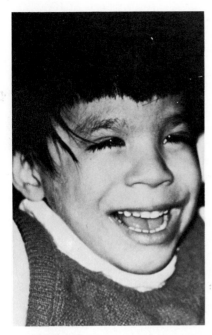

**FIGURE 16–16**
This 6-year-old child showed the physical characteristics of fetal alcohol syndrome at birth. Although from early infancy he has lived in a foster home that provides a high level of care, his intellectual development is at the moderately retarded level. (Streissquth, Herman, & Smith, 1978)

brain. Of these, lead, arsenic, and mercury are the most common.

Severe meningitis or encephalitis, which sometimes develops as a complication of mumps, measles, or chicken pox, can cause inflammation of the brain and the surrounding tissue. Often this results in retardation, seizures, or both. Some ear and blood infections can also damage brain tissues. Probably the most frequent causes of head injury are automobile accidents and child abuse. In an English institution for the retarded, researchers found that 11 percent of the children were handicapped because of brain damage associated with abuse (Buchanan and Oliver, 1977).

## Psychosocial Disadvantage

About three-quarters of all retarded people are mildly retarded. In the majority of these cases, there are no clear causal factors like the biological ones just discussed. In most instances these mildly retarded individuals cannot be singled out on the basis of their appearance, and often they are not identified as retarded until the early years of school. A very large number of children in this group come from families of low socioeconomic status. Because in many cases their parents' IQs also fall in the mildly retarded range, the question is often asked whether heredity is the predominant factor in their retardation. Rather than having specific problems in learning, these children often appear to be generally slower in learning and development. From this point of view, this group is simply at the bottom of the distribution and has no unusual characteristics. If intelligence is a normally distributed characteristic, there must always be a lowest 2 or 3 percent. Children who fall in this lowest group because of psychosocial disadvantage rather than pathology would technically not be considered to have a developmental disorder. While they may be disadvantaged and deficient in certain intellectual activities many of them become self-sufficient.

**The Role of Heredity** There have been a number of investigations of the hereditary and environmental aspects of intelligence. In one such study, the researchers were interested in whether the social class of a child's adoptive family or the IQ of his or her biological parent was the better predictor of the child's intelligence (Scarr and Weinberg, 1978). They studied adopted and biologically related adolescents in families ranging from working class to upper middle class. The intelligence-test scores of the biological parent–child pairs were significantly more similar than those of the adoptive parent–child pairs. When children in a family were compared at age 18½, the adopted siblings hardly resembled each other at all in intelligence, whereas biological siblings did resemble each other. The adopted children's average IQ was 106. This is higher than the average of 100 estimated for their biological mothers but below their adopted siblings' average of 112. Thus, at least in the socioeconomic range studied, "intellectual differences in the children at the end of the child rearing period have little to do with environmental differences among families" (Scarr and Weinberg, 1978, p. 691). In interpreting the results of this study, it is important to remember that most of the children in the study were adopted into homes that were superior in child-rearing skills. If some of the homes had provided extremely negative environments, a stronger environmental effect might have been noted.

Environment has been referred to as a threshold variable (Jensen, 1969), meaning that once a certain minimal quality of environment has been reached, further environmental stimulation is unimportant compared to inherited capability. To put it another way, heredity provides a range of possibilities for the developing child, but the child's level of achievement within that rather wide range might be attributable to the environment in which he or she grows up. The results of many studies show that between 50 and 80 percent of the variation in intelligence scores is due to genetic factors and the remainder to environmental influences (Zigler and others, 1984).

***Effects of Environmental Change.*** Some investigators have tried to manipulate the environment to determine the effects on children who are thought to have low intellectual potential. In a program carried out in North Carolina, pregnant women with IQs averaging 80 were recruited for study (Ramey and Haskins, 1981). After their babies' births, half of the infants were cared for during the day at an educational day-care center and half were reared at home by their mothers. Both groups of children received medical care and dietary supplements, and their families were given social services if they requested them.

At the age of 3, the experimental children had significantly higher IQs than the control group. This difference seemed to be due to a decline in the IQs of the control infants during the 12- to 18-month age period. By the time the children were 5 years old, 39 percent of the control group had IQs below 85, whereas only 11 percent of the experimental group had IQs in this range. This study suggests that educational day care beginning before 3 months of age results in normal intellectual development, at least until the age of 5, for children of high-risk families.

Whether interventions that enrich the environment of economically deprived children who are at risk for retardation have a long-term effect on their intellectual performance is still an open question. Some investigators believe that interventions that begin in the very early years of life are most likely to succeed. Others believe that the early period of life is not uniquely critical and that later interventions also have a good chance of success (Clarke and Clarke, 1979). Most investigators would agree that work with the parents of young children, as well as with the children themselves, enhances the likelihood of success for any program.

Typically, intervention programs produce improved scores during and immediately after the program. The same effect can be seen in the increased intelligence-test scores of culturally deprived children after their first year in school. However, in both cases these at-risk children seem to lose their early gains, and in later grades their performance worsens relative to that of other children. This change might be a function of the changing demands of school programs as children grow older. Greater emphasis is placed on abstract thinking in the higher grades. This is also true of the content of intelligence-test questions aimed at older children. Perhaps many at-risk children are deficient in the ability to think abstractly. On the other hand, perhaps the special help in cognitive skills that the children obtained in the program was not complete enough to enable them to use those skills independently or to apply them to more complex levels of problem solving. This area of research is filled with many unanswered questions.

## Cognitive Functioning

In the past, retarded people were usually institutionalized for life. However, as more has been learned about their capabilities and institutionalization has become less popular, a variety of training programs have been developed to help retarded people live as independent lives as possible.

**Identification of Retardation** People who are profoundly, severely, or moderately retarded are often identified soon after birth. Such individuals are more likely than the average person to have multiple, easily identifiable physical abnormalities or poor responsiveness at birth, or to have seizures or speech or hearing disorders later. In some cases screening programs may prevent the development of retardation. For instance, many states require the test to detect PKU in newborns.

In contrast, most children who are mildly retarded, especially those who come from economically deprived families in which many members are of low intelligence, are not identified as retarded until they have been in school for several years. Because they appear physically similar to other children and have social or manual skills that partially mask their inability to handle intellectual tasks, it may be years before a teacher raises the question of retardation and asks for psychological testing. Many children whose test scores would classify them as retarded are never even tested. One study of a large number of schoolchildren found that almost 5 percent had intelligence-test scores that classified them as retarded and almost 10 percent had IQs below 80. Despite this fact, these children apparently fit well into the classroom setting. None had been referred for suspected learning problems (Mercer, 1971).

Some mildly retarded children escape testing and labeling, but even people who are labeled as retarded while in school are able to fade into the general public as they grow older. As adults, these people can function adequately because the emphasis on intellectual attainment that is characteristic of the school years has been replaced by a need for other skills on the job.

**Developmental and Difference Models** Understanding differences in learning abilities is important not only from a theoretical standpoint but also in developing efficient teaching methods for use with retarded children and adults. Two basic models are used to describe the intellectual functioning of retarded individuals: the developmental model and the difference model.

The **developmental model** assumes that the process of cognitive development is no different, at least for mildly retarded people, than it is for people with higher IQ scores. This theory stems from Jean Piaget's idea of cognitive development as a process in which stages occur in a fixed order but are attained at different rates. The thing that distinguishes mentally retarded people from others is that they progress more slowly through the stages and do not attain the higher stages. From this viewpoint, two people at the same developmental level would be able to handle a problem in the same way whether their chronological age was 3 or 16. Sometimes this developmental level is referred to as **mental age.**

Some research findings support this idea. Work with retarded children has shown a correspondence between Piaget's stages of cognitive development and the classifications of retardation: A severely retarded adult performs at Piaget's lowest level, the sensorimotor stage; a moderately retarded adult performs at the preoperational level; and so on (Inhelder, 1968). Retarded children may also show a fixation or slowing down of cognitive development as they grow older.

The **difference model,** on the other hand, suggests that the cognitive functioning of retarded people differs from that of normal individuals in other ways besides rate of development and level attained. For example, when compared to children of the same mental age, Down syndrome children are particularly deficient in tasks that require abstractions, but they do not have marked difficulties in concrete language usage and tasks requiring eye-hand coordination. Children whose retardation is related to an identifiable defect such as an extra chromosome appear to differ in the structure of their intelligence from children whose retardation is familial. They are likely to show specific areas of poor intellectual performance rather than a generally lower level of intelligence. Thus, when retarded children who were matched in mental age to normal children were compared on certain tasks that are used to test intellectual performance, there were few differences between nonretarded and familially retarded children, but there were differences when children with organic retardation were included in the group (Weisz and others, 1982).

Some researchers have studied the role of cognition in mental retardation by focusing on specific memory processes. In one such study, college students and retarded adults were compared on a number of short-term memory tasks (Baumeister and others, 1984). The results showed that the college students could hold more in short-term memory. They were also faster at processing information, and these differences increased as the information load increased. Despite training, the retarded subjects showed deficiencies both in short-term memory and in the time required to make judgments about a very simple task. These findings suggest that retarded individuals have basic limitations in short-term memory.

The developmental and difference models have important implications for the teaching of mildly retarded children. Should unique educational methods be used because of differences in cognitive processes between normal and retarded children, or can the methods and materials used in regular teaching programs, elaborated and presented more slowly, be used to teach retarded children? So far we do not have a clear answer to this question.

## Public Educational Programs

School programs for the retarded have changed greatly over the last 20 years. Special classes have been established for severely and moderately retarded students who previously were totally excluded from school programs, and many slow-learner classes for mildly retarded children have been abolished. The children from such classes have been "mainstreamed," or integrated into regular classes. Both of these changes have come about as a result of court decisions in cases dealing with the civil rights of the retarded.

The Education for All Handicapped Children Act of 1975 required public schools to provide free appropriate education to all handicapped children. Because of this law and recent court decisions, school districts are obligated to provide training even for severely and profoundly retarded children. Such programs concentrate on basic communication and social skills. Although it is too early to assess whether they improve the child's performance, these programs seem to prevent many severely and profoundly retarded children from being institutionalized in early childhood. Instead, a large number are cared for at home, sometimes through adolescence or longer.

School classes for slow learners have been affected by a series of legal decisions, beginning with the *Brown v. Board of Education* case in 1954. In that decision, which marked the end of legally segregated schools and "separate but equal" education, the Supreme Court ruled that discrimination based on race or color is prohibited in public education. Although students were usually placed in classes for slow learners on the basis of intelligence tests, a high proportion of those students were from minority groups. Critics argued that intelligence tests were unfair to lower-class or minority children because they were heavily loaded with socially and culturally biased items. These items would be familiar to middle-class children but might not be part of the experience of a child from a lower-class or minority family.

Special-education classes have been criticized as offering poor education. In one court case such classes were referred to as "dead ends" by nine expert witnesses. Pressure to place mildly retarded children in regular classrooms has also come from laws requiring the "least restrictive" placement possible for any given child. There is a growing movement to avoid identifying and labeling children as retarded because of concern that such labels may stigmatize them. For minority children in particular, it is feared that such labels may be a result of test bias rather than valid estimates of their abilities.

Education in a mainstreamed or regular class is believed to be desirable for retarded children because exposure to normal role models and the absence of labeling might help them improve their achievement level and social adjustment. So far, however, this belief has not been supported by research findings. There seems to be little difference in performance between children who have been mainstreamed and those who have been placed in special classes. In one large study, both groups scored in the lowest 1 percent on standardized tests of reading and arithmetic (Kaufman and others, 1982). Nor does mainstreaming by itself improve the social status of a retarded child. In a study of more than 300 mainstreamed classrooms, the stu-

dents were asked to rate each other's behavior. The mean rating for the retarded children was one standard deviation below that for their nonretarded classmates (Gottlieb and others, 1978). The basis of the ratings was not the label "retarded" but the behavior of the retarded children.

**New Approaches to Intelligence Testing**  In response to legal pressures and the efforts of parents and civil rights groups, many schools have given up the use of intelligence testing in assigning students to classes. Yet because intelligence testing is important for some purposes, several new approaches to such testing have been developed. One of these, the System of Multicultural Pluralistic Assessment (SOMPA) (Lewis and Mercer, 1978), includes a traditional children's intelligence test, the Wechsler Intelligence Test for Children (WISC), but also gathers information about the child's health and social competence and information about his or her social and economic background. This information is used to construct a measure of estimated learning potential (see Figure 16–17). The second test is the Kaufman Assessment Battery (K-ABC) (Kaufman and Kaufman, 1983). This test, discussed in Chapter 4, attempts to combine traditional intelligence-test tasks with recently developed cognitive tasks in order to measure abilities that are relatively unaffected by cultural and environmental factors. Some sample items are shown in Figure 4–3.

So far neither of these test batteries seems to have

**FIGURE 16–17**
A portion of the SOMPA scoring sheet shows the difference in one child's scores between estimated learning potential and present school funhctioning level.

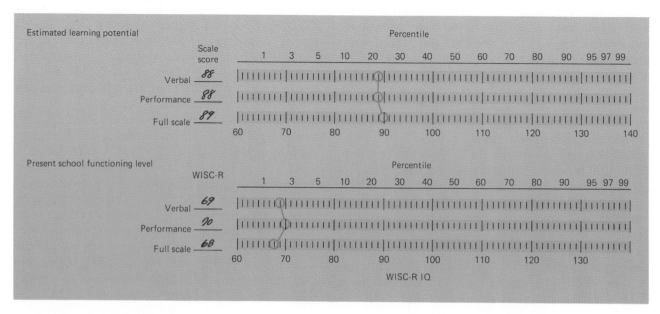

solved the problem of test bias. However, the K-ABC has prompted a flood of research that may be useful in providing better tests for use in making both educational and clinical decisions (Kamphaus and Reynolds, 1984).

One of the purposes for which the K-ABC was constructed was to aid in the diagnosis of specific cognitive deficits so that teachers could concentrate on those deficits. This approach to teaching mildly retarded children was pioneered in Israel and the United States by Reuven Feuerstein (Feuerstein and others, 1980). Although Feuerstein's ideas have stimulated teachers and others to work to improve their teaching of retarded students, many researchers question whether improvement in specific cognitive skills affects overall classroom performance (Bradley, 1983).

## Deinstitutionalization

Emphasis on normalizing the lives of the retarded has increased in recent years. Changes in the law have required that even severely retarded individuals receive the least restrictive care possible. As a result, many people who have been in institutions for many years have been discharged. Young children who formerly would have been sent to institutions often live at home and attend special school programs that include job training. Currently less than 19 percent of all mentally retarded people live in institutions.

Deinstitutionalization can have a major impact not only on retarded individuals but on their families as well. In one case residents of a large institution were moved into small community-based living groups because of a court order (Latib and others, 1984). Initially most of their families opposed deinstitutionalization. Many of them had made the decision to institutionalize their relatives many years earlier, often under great stress. In general, they believed that their relatives had reached their highest level of development and had little chance of learning new skills. They thought they were adequately cared for and worried that they would not be protected in small residential settings. They also wondered how long funding would be available for community-based homes.

Before the move, the families were surveyed about their expectations. Six months later they were interviewed again. Figure 16–18 shows the results. These results are especially impressive in view of the fact that the families' initial expectations were so negative.

For retarded individuals who are discharged from large institutions, several kinds of living arrangements are possible. The most frequent choice is a group home for up to 15 residents. Other possibilities are a return to the retarded person's own family or to a foster home,

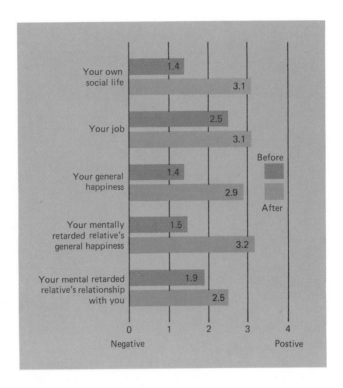

**FIGURE 16–18**
Expected and actually perceived changes in family life after deinstitutionalization of a family member. (adapted from Latib and others, 1984, p. 81)

or, less frequently, a move to a medium-sized institution or a nursing home (Craig and McCarver, 1984).

Group homes for the retarded function both as a permanent home for those who are unable to live independently and as a transition point for those who are learning skills that will help them live on their own. (See Figure 16–19.) Staff members work to broaden the residents' experiences—for example, by taking them on excursions. One problem in opening new group homes is the opposition of potential neighbors. Once the home is established, the opposition generally decreases and the neighbors' unrealistic fears about crime, property values, and quality of life dissipate (Okolo and Guskin, 1984).

An important part of community-living programs is the job training offered to residents through sheltered workshops or special training programs (see Figure 16–20). The women described in the following excerpts illustrate how such programs enhance the lives of retarded individuals.

*Linda had been in an institution for nearly 17 years before coming to the Community Residential Facility just two years ago. At 25, she has an estimated IQ of 21 and is physically handicapped. The home she lives in is*

near a large city and is a contemporary family house which has very homey and personalized living areas. Linda's home responsibilities include making her own bed and cleaning her own room; occasionally she helps clean the rest of the house and helps with the gardening. Linda works in a sheltered workshop doing piecework and other small jobs such as collating, assembling, and

**FIGURE 16-20**
A sheltered workshop offers both a place to learn job skills and a working environment for people who cannot compete for jobs on an equal basis. (David M. Grossman, Photo Researchers)

stapling, and she has been working for over one year. For working a half-day, two days per week, she earns over $20, which she puts into an account for clothing and recreation. Thirty hours a week, Linda attends an adult education class where she learns basic living skills. Linda gets along very well with other residents, but the facility operator doubts she will ever be able to live without supervised care. (O'Connor, 1976, pp. 46–47)

Carolyn has lived in a community residence for three years after moving from her family home at the age of 28. She lives with four other women residents who rent and maintain a six-bedroom house in a residential area. They essentially run the house in an independent manner and have their own rooms and housekeeping responsibilities. There is a counselor/advocate available for assistance whenever needed. Carolyn had been working in a sheltered workshop for two years and now has a job assisting in a thrift store. She works full time and handles her money herself. She has contact with friends outside the home and uses public transportation to visit them. Carolyn feels she is about ready to live on her own, possibly with another resident of the facility. (O'Connor, 1976, p. 48)

## Vocational and Social Skills Training

Knowledge and use of appropriate vocational and social skills are key factors in success both in competitive job environments and in sheltered workshops. Skills training through modeling has been found to be more effective than coaching in the same skills. In one study, several problem situations were modeled so that prospective workers could learn to identify both problem behaviors and appropriate ways of dealing with such situations (LaGreca and others, 1983).

*You come to work in the morning and can't find one of the materials you need to do your job (for example, the napkins). Inappropriate: walk around, talking to co-workers; sit at table and do nothing. Appropriate: request help from supervisor politely.*

*You are working in the morning and the person working next to you is being very loud, talking and laughing. You are finding it hard to concentrate on your work because of the noise. Inappropriate: yell at co-worker to "shut up"; throw something at co-worker; insult co-worker; threaten co-worker. Appropriate: politely request quiet behavior; ignore co-worker. (LaGreca and others, 1983, p. 272)*

The effectiveness of modeling is shown by a comparison with both a coaching group and a control group. After seven weeks on the job only 1 of the 11 people in the modeling group had been fired. Half of the coaching group had been fired; in the control group, 10 had been fired and only 2 were still on the job.

Another important aspect of retarded people's lives is a supportive network of people. One way to increase the amount of support available is to help the individual learn social skills. Another is to make sure that decisions about living and working conditions take friendships into account. If friendship networks are kept in mind when residents of facilities for the retarded have to be relocated, the outcome is likely to be much better. In one study, residents who had moved to a new home with chosen friends were more sociable several years later than residents who had been separated from friends (Romer and Heller, 1983). They were also better able to care for themselves.

While mentally retarded individuals are being integrated into the community, they are vulnerable to personal, sexual, and financial exploitation. One source of problems of this nature is their tendency to answer "yes" to all questions, regardless of their content. This tendency can be measured using the reverse-question technique: Within the same interview two opposite questions are asked, such as "Are you usually happy?" and "Are you usually sad?" In one study, almost half of the retarded people interviewed answered "yes" to both questions (Sigelman and others, 1981). This tendency to say "yes" is correlated with IQ: the lower a person's IQ, the greater the tendency to agree. Such readiness to agree clearly can have negative consequences. For one thing, it means that retarded people are likely to agree to inappropriate or unfair requests.

One way to prevent exploitation of retarded individuals is to pay special attention to teaching them what is expected of a person and how to say "no" (Schilling and Schinke, 1984). For example, participants in a training program for food service workers were taught how to handle their earnings and how to say "no" to people who asked to borrow money. Another problem area is sexual behavior. Training programs have taught retarded people how to recognize and escape from sexually exploitive situations. Mentally retarded individuals also need to be trained to understand what society views as appropriate sexual behavior and to avoid such acts as public masturbation and inappropriate sexual approaches.

## Psychological Problems

Retarded individuals are likely to experience psychological problems as well as intellectual retardation. In one study, up to 40 percent of retarded children were rated by their parents or teachers as psychologically disturbed (Rutter and others, 1970). Severely retarded children exhibit an even higher rate of disturbance: Nearly half may be diagnosed as having a behavior disorder. The same range of disorders is seen in retarded children as in nonretarded children, although the frequencies of different types of disorders differ in the two groups. Those who are severely retarded are more likely to have a psychosis or to be hyperactive and less likely to have a conduct disorder (Rutter and others, 1975). This difference is probably explained by the likelihood that severely retarded children also have central nervous system damage.

Retarded children living with their parents may have more problems during adolescence than nonretarded children do. In one study, 84 percent of retarded children developed emotional or behavioral problems during adolescence (Zetlin and Turner, 1985). These included temper tantrums, violent or destructive behavior, and use of drugs and alcohol for some, and an increase in withdrawal behavior for others. Many of these problems seemed to be related to the young people's growing awareness of the gap between themselves and other teenagers in terms of expectations for the future and ability to be independent. The retarded adolescents' desire for dating relationships was another source of problems. When these young people became adults, only one-third were still in conflict with their parents. The rest either had adjusted to dependence on their parents or had been able to establish fairly independent life styles that gave them satisfaction.

Retarded individuals often have a low opinion of themselves. When they live in the community, this problem becomes more severe because there are more opportunities for comparisons with nonretarded people. In one study, retarded individuals living in an institution were more likely to rate themselves as smart and attractive than retarded people living in a community setting. Since the intellectual level of those in the institution was lower and the rated attractiveness no different, the community group's exposure to and self-comparisons with nonretarded individuals probably accounted for the difference (Gibbons, 1985).

Another problem for many retarded individuals is that they often have a low opinion of the attractiveness of other retarded people and of the desirability of this group as friends and dating partners. Since their best chance of friendship and romantic attachments is with people similar to themselves, these attitudes may interfere with their social adjustment if they live in the community.

The kinds of problems these adolescents and adults face can be helped by psychotherapy. Family therapy is often used for adolescents. Individual psychotherapy can be useful in the same way that it may be helpful for nonretarded adolescents. Social-skills training and job preparation also contribute to adjustment. Such techniques have helped many retarded people to adjust well, marry, and live semi-independent lives (see Figure 16–21).

## Training for Leisure-Time Enjoyment

Even severely retarded individuals may be helped to become more independent and to enjoy some of the everyday experiences that nonretarded people enjoy. This is illustrated by a study of four adult males who had lived in an institution for an average of 25 years and had IQs that placed them in the middle of the severely retarded range. Each pair of subjects spent a to-

**FIGURE 16–21 ·**
This photo shows Victor, 30, and Kathy, 29, after they had announced their marriage plans. A few years ago such an announcement would have been almost unthinkable because both Kathy and Victor are retarded.

tal of 35 hours with a trainer. They learned how to take a bus to a shopping center, find a fast-food restaurant, order and pay for their food, and behave appropriately in the restaurant. A sequence of target behaviors for the bus rides and food purchases had been prepared by the trainer, who used graduated prompting, corrective feedback, rehearsal, social reinforcement for success, modeling, and occasional removal of social reinforcement. For example:

*Suppose the travel teacher asked the subject a question from the restaurant sequence, "Where do we eat?," and the subject failed to respond or responded incorrectly. The travel teacher would then prompt as follows, "No" (corrective feedback), "We go to Mm . . . " (no response), "We go to Mc . . . " (no response), "We go to McDon . . . " (response, "McDonald's"). The travel teacher would then praise the subject and ask him the question again (rehearsal). "Where do we eat?" (response, "McDonald's"). The travel teacher would then confirm the response and reward the behavior with praise, smiles, and a headnod (for example "Good, we eat at McDonald's"). Some behaviors were modeled by the travel teacher. At McDonald's, following unsuccessful prompting of an item ("states what he wants to waitress"), a travel teacher might model the correct response for the subject (e.g., "I'll have a Big Mac, large fries, large coke, and apple pie"). If the subject failed to imitate the modeled response but appeared to be attending to the travel teacher, the sequence would then be broken down into smaller component steps. For example, if a subject did not imitate, "I'll have a Big Mac, large fries, large coke, and apple pie," he would be asked to perform only the response "Big Mac," then "Big Mac and large fries," and so on. If, however, the subject did not appear to be attending to the travel teacher's modeled response and emitted some irrelevant behavior (for example, a response of "5 cents" to the travel teacher's question of "What do you want to eat?"), the travel teacher would say "No" and turn 180 degrees away from the subject for 5 seconds. After this timeout, the travel teacher would repeat the previously modeled response. If the subject still failed to imitate the modeled behavior, the sequence would be broken down into even smaller steps. When the subject emitted the modeled response, the behavior would be praised and behavioral rehearsal would follow. (Marholin and others, 1979, pp. 239, 241)*

At the end of the training, the subjects were taken to another shopping center in the trainer's car. In this transfer test, the subjects had to walk through the shopping center, find the fast-food restaurant, and carry out the rest of the sequence. They continued to perform at the same level, confirming that training of this type can be transferred to a new setting. Although 35 hours of training time for each pair of men and a cost of approximately $450 in trainer's salary and other expenses may seem a large price to pay for fast food, this study is impressive. In evaluating the results it is important to remember both the severe retardation of the subjects and the fact that they had lived in an institution for a quarter of a century. Viewed in this light, the study shows the power of behavioral methods for training retarded individuals.

# ■ STUDY OUTLINE

### AUTISTIC DISORDERS

1. Children with an **autistic disorder** show impairment in social relationships, communication, and activities. They have a noticeable lack of awareness of the existence or feelings of others. They have a very narrow range of interests and activities, and about half do not develop speech at all.

2. In adulthood about two-thirds of autistic individuals are severely handicapped, but some are able to make a good adjustment to life in the community. Efforts to provide therapy for autistic children have met with limited success.

3. In the majority of cases autism is connected with global mental retardation. Autistic children seem to have a cognitive deficit, especially in relation to language and comprehension. These problems may be caused by early damage to the limbic system or a dysfunction of behavioral systems in the brain stem. There is also some evidence of a hereditary factor in autism.

### MENTAL RETARDATION

1. **Mental retardation** means a significantly below-average level of intellectual functioning as measured by an individually administered intelligence test. There are four categories of mental retardation based on intelligence-test scores: **mild, moderate, severe,** and **profound.**

2. The causes of mental retardation can be grouped into two general categories. Children who are **psycho-socially disadvantaged** may show no specific disabilities but may have low intelligence-test scores because of their heredity and/or environmental experiences. Other children are retarded as a result of disease, injury, chromosomal abnormality, or a specific genetic disorder.

3. Some cases of retardation are caused by specific dominant genes and some by specific recessive genes. The latter often cause disorders of metabolism such as **phenylketonuria** and **Tay-sachs** disease. Many other cases of retardation are due to **chromosomal abnormalities.** The most frequently occurring of these is **Down syndrome,** which results from the presence of an extra chromosome. Children with Down syndrome have many characteristic physical features and show considerable variability in level of retardation.

4. Mental retardation can be caused by a variety of prenatal environmental factors. Among these are maternal infections (e.g., by the rubella or herpes virus), blood incompatibilities (especially **Rh incompatibility**), and drugs taken by the mother. In recent years alcohol use during pregnancy has become recognized as an important cause of retardation. Mental retardation can also be caused by problems at birth and after birth, such as damage to the central nervous system or inflammation of the brain due to meningitis or encephalitis.

5. In the majority of cases of mild retardation, there are no clear causal factors. A large number of children in this group come from families of low socioeconomic status. It appears that the intellectual potential of the individual is determined by heredity, but that environmental stimulation can make a difference in whether a person reaches his or her full potential. Changes in environment have been shown to affect IQ, but it is not clear whether such changes have a long-term effect on intellectual performance.

6. The **developmental model** of retardation assumes that the process of cognitive development is no different for retarded people than it is for people with higher IQs, but that it occurs more slowly. The **difference model** suggests that the cognitive functioning of retarded people differs in specific ways from that of normal individuals.

7. In recent years many retarded children have been "mainstreamed," or placed in regular public school classrooms, as a result of court decisions dealing with the civil rights of the retarded. The results to date suggest that mainstreaming does not improve a child's achievement level or social adjustment.

8. Efforts to normalize the lives of the retarded have also led to the discharge of many retarded people from institutions. Deinstitutionalized individuals may live with their own family, in group homes, in a foster home, or in a medium-sized institution or a nursing home. Job training is an important part of community-living programs.

9. Modeling is often used to teach vocational and social skills to retarded people. Special training is required to teach them ways of avoiding sexual and financial exploitation.

10. Retarded individuals are likely to experience psychological problems as well as intellectual retardation. This is especially true of adolescents living with their parents and adults living in the community. These problems can be helped by psychotherapy.

# 17

# THERAPY AND ITS EVALUATION

*Betty Rouse, housewife and mother of three adolescent children, had been in psychotherapy for two years. She had sought therapy because she felt herself to be an unhappy, inadequate person, who, as she put it, "was not good for much besides cooking dinner and chauffeuring the kids around to Scout meetings."*

*During the first several months of therapy, she talked mainly about herself. As time passed, however, her husband Fred was mentioned with increasing frequency and strong emotion. By the end of therapy, Betty concluded that, while many of her problems were of her own making, Fred had consistently made them worse by showing that he saw her as "just a housewife and mother," not as someone who was admirable for her own sake. After trying fruitlessly to talk with Fred about how he always belittled her, Betty concluded that her self-esteem was more important to her than she had ever realized and that Fred would only hinder its strengthening. With great pain and guilt, mainly because of the effect it might have on the children, Betty decided to get a job, live apart from Fred, and eventually get a divorce. She hoped one day to meet a man who would both love her and value her as a person.*

Was the outcome of Betty Rouse's psychotherapy good or bad? The answer depends on a number of things, including her past life and our own values. Therapy situations involve a special relationship between a professional clinician and a person with a problem. Therapy is difficult to do and hard to evaluate because each person's problem is unique and because the various therapeutic approaches differ greatly. Would the outcome of Betty Rouse's therapy have been different if she had been seeing a behavior therapist, a biologically oriented psychiatrist, or a family therapist? So many factors are involved that we cannot answer this question, but it is possible to make comparisons among the therapeutic approaches used for different types of cases.

It is important to keep in mind the similarities as well as the differences among the various therapeutic approaches. All therapeutic relationships are aimed at providing clients with certain ingredients that are missing from their lives. Regardless of their therapeutic orientation, all clinicians must deal with the patient's demoralized state and with his or her expectation of receiving help. All therapists must attempt to form some sort of supportive therapeutic relationship. All clinicians must communicate their views of the problems that have been presented, and possible solutions to those problems must be devised.

In preceding chapters we have described major therapeutic approaches to specific types of maladaptive behavior. We have discussed the "talking therapies," such as psychoanalysis and client-centered counseling, in which conversations between the client and the therapist are the vehicle for achieving change; cognitive–behavioral therapies, such as systematic desensitization and token economies, which involve applications of learning and cognitive principles in specially structured clinical situations; and somatic therapies, such as the use of antipsychotic, antidepressive, or tranquilizing drugs and electro-convulsive treatments, which are aimed at achieving behavior change through physical means.

Although we have talked about these approaches in relation to specific disorders, it is useful to summarize what we know about the various therapeutic methods in general. Reviewing these methods toward the end of the book will highlight how much we have learned along the way and also lay the groundwork for a discussion of how different therapies can be evaluated and compared. Do most or all of the different therapeutic approaches have common elements? Is a particular therapy effective for certain types of problems but not for others? What gaps exist in current knowledge about therapies and their rates of success?

## ■ PSYCHOTHERAPY

All forms of psychotherapy involve interchanges between a client and a therapist. These interchanges, which are nonverbal as well as verbal, are aimed at understanding what is on the client's mind. This understanding is then used as a basis for efforts to change the client's maladaptive ways of thinking, reacting to situations, and relating to others.

Most psychotherapists adhere to some type of psychodynamic or cognitive theory. Psychodynamic orientations emphasize the role of unconscious conflict in causing personal problems, whereas cognitive orientations emphasize the role of unrealistic or irrational thinking. Many psychotherapists utilize both psychodynamic and cognitive concepts in working with clients.

In the course of their work, and regardless of their theoretical orientations, psychotherapists must perform three tasks: (1) listen, (2) understand, and (3) respond. The therapist listens to the patient in order to find out about his or her preoccupations, worries, and concerns. Listening serves two functions: It lets the therapist hear about topics that the client brings up spontaneously and it provides information that is pertinent to the therapist's hypotheses about the client's problems. Listening provides a basis for the therapist's understanding of the client's self-concept and view of the world.

Through listening and understanding, the therapist

becomes able to respond. The response might be a question aimed at eliciting more information, or it might be a comment. The comment might be an interpretation of what has been going on in the session or in the client's interpersonal relationships (see Figure 17–1). Those relationships are of three types.

1. Current in-treatment relationships
2. Current out-of-treatment relationships
3. Past relationships

Current in-treatment relationships have to do with what is going on between the therapist and the client. (Do they like each other? Is there tension between them?) Current out-of-treatment relationships involve significant others such as the client's spouse, friend, or employer. (Is the patient experiencing less tension at work? Are there opportunities for good social relationships?) Psychodynamically oriented therapists in particular attempt to explore past relationships in order to uncover clues to the causes of current difficulties. (Are current difficulties with friends consistent with or a continuation of undesirable relationships in early childhood?)

Therapists are interested in determining the degree to which these three types of relationships may be related; for example, are conflicts between the client and the therapist similar to the client's earlier conflicts with parents or current conflicts between the client and a spouse or friend? In addition to searching for continuities in interpersonal relationships, the therapist is

**FIGURE 17–1**
Psychotherapists deal with what is going on in their sessions with clients and with clients' present and past relationships. (Laimute Druskis)

attentive to themes that recur over several sessions. How similar is the way the client and the therapist relate to each other in the twentieth session to the way they related during their first therapeutic meeting? Are similar or different emotions and motives expressed as the therapy progresses?

## Psychoanalysis and Psychodynamic Therapy

**Psychoanalysis** is a specific subtype of psychodynamic therapy. Because psychoanalysis takes a long time and is expensive, only a small fraction of the people who desire it can experience it. However, psychoanalytic concepts and techniques are widely used by nonpsychoanalytic therapists.

Before they can analyze others, psychoanalysts must undergo analysis themselves. The number of analytic interviews included in a psychoanalyst's training can range from fewer than 200 sessions to about 2,000. On the average, most analyses, whether they are conducted for training or therapeutic reasons, require between two and five years. The American Psychoanalytic Association recommends at least four analytic sessions each week. Over the years, the total number of sessions in a typical psychoanalysis has increased.

Psychoanalysis makes extensive use of **free association,** in which the client expresses thoughts and feelings in as free and uninhibited a manner as possible. This results in a natural flow of ideas unencumbered by interruptions or explanations. One psychologist has provided the following description of free association as it occurred in his own psychoanalysis.

*I learned to be profoundly impressed with my unconscious. Some hours seemed to be little short of miraculous. Without any plan or preparation on my part, my free associations would apparently adopt a theme, which might also be the theme of a dream the preceding night. Many times it was possible to connect this theme with certain experiences of that day or of the day before, experiences with emotional content and which, not being wholly resolved, had left a residue of tension. The remarkable thing was the way in which my free associations would weave in and around this theme, coming back to it again and again, instead of just flitting on and on like a butterfly from one theme to another. I gained the impression that the episode of the day before pertained to deep-seated grievances going way back to early childhood and infancy—wrongs which had never been completely resolved; and that my associations were like outcroppings of rock which reveal the possibility of a continuity of structure between the surface exposure and submerged strata. (Symonds, 1940, p. 14)*

The examination of dreams and fantasies is also important in psychoanalysis. Although the following example is not drawn from a psychoanalytic session, it illustrates the therapeutic use of fantasy material.

*A 26-year-old patient reported that he was feeling rejected by his fiancee although she had done nothing to justify his reaction. He then reported that the feeling had started the previous day when he had been at a picnic with his fiancee and his best friend. Although his fiancee and his friend had been attentive to him, he felt uncomfortable. He then recalled that during the picnic he had experienced the following daydream. "Jane (his fiancee) and Bob (his friend) began to look at each other in a loving way. They passed signals back and forth of getting rid of me. They arranged to get together later that night. I got the old feeling of being rejected—wanting to be in but kept out and not wanted. They sneaked off at night and necked and had sex. Then they told me about it and I gave her up although I felt a deep loss at the same time." After having experienced this fantasy, he had felt rejected by his fiancee even though in reality she continued to be very affectionate to him.*

*After recounting the fantasy in the therapeutic hour, the patient had a stream of associations. "I feel sad and low, almost as though she actually was unfaithful. Bob reminds me of competing with my brother. I was always second fiddle to him. . . . I never made it up to his level. I was always losing out. . . . He was always better than me. Everybody liked him more than me."*

*The patient was then able to view his unpleasant reaction at the picnic as analogous to his early pattern of expecting to be pushed to one side by his brother. He visualized Bob's displacing him as his brother had previously triumphed over him. It became clear to him that his current reactions of jealousy and vulnerability were not justified on the basis of the reality situation. With this realization, his feelings of estrangement from his fiancee disappeared. (Beck, 1970, pp. 6–7)*

In the course of telling the therapist about a fantasy, the client may acquire some insight into the relationship between his or her early experiences and a current tendency to distort reality. **Insight,** or understanding of one's inner life, is a goal of most psychotherapies.

*After months of talking about her husband as a demanding, overbearing man who was always gloomy, Rose Francis, aged 50, remarked to her therapist: "You know, I guess I really don't like him." There was a tone of wonder and surprise in her voice when she said this. After recognizing her strong negative feelings toward her husband, Mrs. Francis found it possible to identify and sympathize with some of her husband's worries and concerns. She became better able to see the world through his eyes. Being able to say out loud "You know, I guess I really don't like him" made her more aware of just how angry she felt toward her husband. Somehow that insight enabled her to see herself in relation to her husband in a new way.*

Whereas in principle the agenda of a psychoanalytic session is determined by the free associations of the patient, psychodynamically oriented psychotherapy usually focuses on a fairly specific problem or group of problems rather than on a general reshaping of the personality. Many people seek clinical help because of something that has happened to them. Stressful situations often call for readjustments in an individual's life, and the therapist helps by listening, supporting, and clarifying. Many of the principles and mechanisms that operate in psychoanalysis are believed also to play a role in psychotherapy. One of the most important of these is the relationship between the person seeking help and the helper.

Freud noticed that his patients' attitudes toward him changed as their analysis proceeded. He also noticed that his own attitudes toward his patients changed. As the relationship between patient and therapist develops, it comes to involve feelings and patterns of behavior that originally were experienced earlier in life, often in relation to significant figures of one's childhood. For example, during psychotherapy feelings toward one's father may be transferred to the therapist. A key aspect of psychoanalysis is the use of this **transference** as a vehicle for resolving interpersonal conflicts and revealing the meaning of anxiety. In **positive transference,** the patient feels predominantly friendly and affectionate toward the analyst. However, in **negative transference** hostility predominates. **Counter-transference** refers to the therapist's emotional reactions to his or her patients. Psychoanalysts must be analyzed themselves because of the belief that their self-insight will reduce the occurrence of countertransference reactions.

The case of Bill Jenkins, a 40-year-old construction supervisor who sought psychotherapy because of the increasing number of arguments he was having with his wife, provides an example of transference.

*During the first twenty sessions he described in detail to the therapist frustrations connected with his marital and work situations. In these sessions, he never referred to any thoughts he might have had about the therapist. In the twenty-first session, Jenkins noticed a small crack in one of the walls of the therapist's office. He said to the therapist: "It looks like the construction company that put up that wall didn't do a very good job." After several uncomfortable pauses, he went on, "You know, Doc, I*

*feel embarrassed saying this but somehow I keep feeling sorry for you, feeling like, in a way, you've been a loser. Like that lousy construction job over there (pointing to the crack in the wall). Some of those construction guys are pretty smart fellows who don't mind taking advantage of innocent people."*

*The characteristic Jenkins was attributing to the therapist (being a loser) could not have been based on facts available to him because Jenkins knew little about the therapist's background. What he said was the first outward expression of his developing relationship with and fantasies concerning the therapist. In subsequent sessions, Jenkins himself observed the similarity between his pictures of the therapist and his father, who was an alcoholic and a "loser." At one point he said, "It doesn't make sense, does it, for me to see you as being like my father?"*

In asking that question, Jenkins showed insight and came close to making an interpretation of his behavior toward the therapist (seeing him as a loser like his father). Interpretations of behavior that arise during psychotherapy sessions may be made by either the therapist or the client. Many people go into psychotherapy expecting to be told what is wrong with them and what to do about it, but psychotherapists usually limit their intervention to making interpretations. Actually, most therapists prefer that clients evolve their own interpretations and achieve self-understanding with the help of the therapist. But many therapists will offer interpretations when they seem especially appropriate and the client seems unable to make or express them. Through these interpretations, therapists seek to expose areas of conflict, portions of which have been unconscious, and to help the client understand past psychological events. During therapy, individuals may be confronted with an interpretation that they have an interest in not acknowledging. They may become irritated with the person who has confronted them, and in an effort to protect themselves they may try to think of more acceptable, but incorrect, explanations for their behavior. Psychoanalytic treatment is aimed at helping the client place his or her motivations in perspective and redirect their influence on everyday life.

In psychoanalysis, transference and countertransference reactions are ultimately dealt with. In other forms of psychotherapy, interpretations of these processes might be less important than dealing with the pressing problems in the client's day-to-day life. This does not mean that transference and countertransference do not occur or that the therapist doesn't think they are important. It means that the therapist has decided to give the highest priority to the problems that the client feels are most crucial. In some cases psychotherapists wish that they could explore certain aspects of the client's thinking but conclude that the client isn't ready to engage in such exploration.

In the initial stages of psychotherapy, tentative answers must be sought to a number of questions:

□ Why did the client come to me?

□ What are the pressing problems from the point of view of the client?

□ What underlying problems is the client not aware of?

□ Will it be possible to help the client explore these underlying problems?

The answers to these questions help the therapist set objectives and decide on tactics for later stages of therapy. Clients often feel that as a result of their therapy experience they are able to see themselves, their past lives, and the people in their lives in a more objective light. Identifying the subjective reactions of both clients and therapists to what goes on in therapy sessions is an important research task.

Illustrative of how this task can be approached is the study of "good" and "poor" psychotherapy sessions, sessions that either the therapist or the client or both feel were particularly valuable. For example, Hoyt and others (1983) had psychotherapists and independent observers rate the quality of therapy sessions. The ratings were then related to what had gone on in the sessions. One finding was that therapists and independent observers often disagreed about the relationship between specific occurrences in the sessions and their degree of "goodness" or "badness." Therapists seemed to believe that a session was not particularly "good" if the client seemed resistant or difficult to relate to. On the other hand, outside observers often felt that a session was productive if the client was difficult and the therapist had to take a more active role as a result. Table 17–1 lists factors that independent observers rated as contributing to either "good" or "bad" sessions.

**Hypnosis** Hypnosis is used for a variety of purposes: to suggest specific changes in thinking or behavior, as an aid in psychotherapy (for example, to help a client overcome anxiety or deal with upsetting ideas), and to enhance relaxation. Although the technique has been used clinically for years, research on hypnosis is in its infancy. There is considerable controversy over what hypnosis actually is and whether it really involves a special trancelike state. Because of its success in inducing states that appear to involve relaxation, it has aroused

□ **TABLE 17–1**
**Factors Contributing to "Good" and "Bad" Psychotherapy Sessions as Rated by Independent Observers**

**Factors Contributing to "Good" Sessions**
1. The patient was encouraged to express thoughts and feelings.
2. The meaning of the patient's behavior was discussed.
3. The patient's avoidance of painful material was discussed.
4. The patient's responsibility for what went on in the session was discussed.

**Factors Contributing to "Poor" Sessions**
1. There were long silences.
2. The therapist used humor in discussing topics.

*Source:* Adapted from Hoyt and others, 1983.

the interest of behavior therapists as well as psychotherapists.

It is now known that hypnosis is an altered state of consciousness—not sleep, but an intense alertness in which the mind can screen out extraneous matters and focus on particular details. The hypnotic trance is characterized by extreme relaxation and heightened susceptibility to suggestion. It allows people to suspend logical reasoning and draw upon psychological strengths that they do not normally command voluntarily. The focused concentration and heightened suggestibility of the trance state help the individual accept the therapist's directions and come to grips with problems more rapidly. When used with people who are suffering from great pain, hypnosis seems to mask the discomfort. The person still "feels" the pain at some level, but conscious awareness is blocked. Just how the trance state enables one to "disconnect" pain from awareness is not known.

Hypnotists typically begin their sessions by asking subjects to stare at an object, suggesting in a soothing voice that their eyelids are becoming heavy, that they are relaxing and becoming hypnotized, and that they will find it easy to comply with the hypnotist's suggestions (see Figure 17–2). In experimental settings this "hypnotic induction" typically lasts for about 15 minutes. If the subjects are willing to be hypnotized, they appear relaxed and drowsy and become responsive to test suggestions from the hypnotist. Afterward they report changes in bodily sensations and claim that they have been hypnotized. People who are susceptible to hypnosis have beliefs and expectations that motivate them to adopt the hypnotic role. They usually have better than average ability to focus attention as well as a vivid imagination.

**FIGURE 17-2**
The soothing voice of the hypnotist, together with a voluntary focus of attention on a particular object, can produce a relaxed and suggestible state in subjects willing to be hypnotized. (Leonard Kausler, Medichrome)

## Humanistic and Existential Therapies

Several forms of psychotherapy either disagree with the assumptions of psychodynamic theory or modify them in certain ways. The neo-Freudians accept most psychodynamic principles but reject the emphasis placed by psychoanalytic theory on instinctual unconscious impulses. **Humanistic therapies** emphasize people's desire to achieve self-respect. Existential therapists, whose viewpoints often overlap those of humanistic therapists, emphasize the need to confront basic questions of existence, such as: What is the meaning of my life? Am I hiding from myself?

**Client-Centered Therapy**  Carl Rogers, the founder of **client-centered therapy,** sees the individual as seeking personal growth but needing the support of an appreciative, accepting therapist. The therapist is a nondirective facilitator who encourages the client's self-exploration and efforts to achieve greater maturity and self-confidence. Whereas in psychoanalysis the therapeutic relationship—transference and countertransference—and the analyst's interpretations help clients solve personal problems, in client-centered therapy a nonjudgmental therapist facilitates the process of self-understanding by serving as a mirror for the client.

As a group, client-centered therapists have been among the leaders in research about what actually goes on in psychotherapy. Rogers saw psychotherapy as a growth process and encouraged objective study of the events that occur as therapy progresses. He recognized that people's ideas and ways of looking at the world influence their emotional lives.

The client-centered therapist believes that perceptions and cognitions determine whether an individual has warm, positive interpersonal relationships or strained relationships that stir up unpleasant emotions. As the client restructures his or her view of the world, troubling emotions such as anxiety and anger become less potent. For example:

> When I started coming here, I saw my problem as anger—toward other people as well as myself. There were times I felt like a seething inferno. You sat there as I ranted and raved and I really appreciated the fact that you listened so attentively to everything I said. Sometimes you would reflect back to me what I had just said, sometimes you would just ask a question about a comment I had made. I don't really know how it happened but I began thinking about why I get so angry at home. Then a lot of things fell into place. I was angry because I was doing things I didn't want to do. I was doing those things out of guilt and obligation. Why should I think I had to be nice to people I can't stand? When I finally realized that I didn't have to do certain things, I became more spontaneous and less angry.

Rogers believes that people are basically good and that no feelings are intrinsically destructive. What appear to be destructive feelings reflect externally imposed distortions that resemble the contortions of a plant trying to grow under a brick. For Rogers, therapy is present-oriented and existential. Labels and diagnoses are not useful. What is needed is **unconditional positive regard,** reflected in the therapist's nonjudgmental, empathetic listening. Whereas a behavior therapist would concentrate on getting clients to change their behavior, a Rogerian therapist would concentrate on supplying an environment in which the client feels free to express thoughts and feelings. The Rogerian therapist assumes that unconditional positive regard will increase the client's self-acceptance and self-knowledge, which, in turn, will lead the client to change his or her behavior.

**Existential Therapy**  Existential therapies also emphasize the present and the need to recognize the uniqueness of each client. Existential therapists work as partners with their clients. Many combine humanistic and psychodynamic approaches in dealing with anxiety, its causes, and the defenses that the client erects to cope with it. In this sense the existential approach is a therapeutic hybrid.

The emphasis of existential therapy is on helping

clients come to terms with basic issues concerning the meaning and direction of their lives and the choices by which they shape their own destinies. Like the majority of clinicians who see nonhospitalized clients, most existential therapists work with people who are troubled by anxiety and depression. Existential therapists see their primary role as helping lonely people make constructive choices and become confident enough to fulfill their unique selves rather than repressing or distorting their experiences.

**Gestalt Therapy** **Gestalt therapy** focuses on clients' perceptions of themselves and the world. It is based on the recognition that people unconsciously organize their perceptions as a *Gestalt:* a meaningful, integrated whole. A Gestalt therapist uses a variety of techniques, including role playing, in an effort to stimulate the client to express strong emotions.

Fritz Perls, the founder of Gestalt therapy, stressed the relationships among distorted perceptions, motivations, and emotions. Perls's therapy was a function of his personality. He could be inspiring and manipulative, perceptive and hostile. He says in his autobiography, "I believe I am the best therapist for any type of neurosis in the States, maybe in the world. . . . At the same time I have to admit that I cannot work successfully with everybody" (Perls, 1969). Unlike most humanistic therapists, who stress the importance of unconditional positive regard for the client, Perls believed that the therapist's main task was to frustrate the client, to make him or her angry enough to fight out conflicts with authority and thereby develop enhanced feelings of self-worth. Perls believed that instead of trying to reconstruct the history of the client's relationships with others, the therapist should stress the client's moment-to-moment experiences as each session progresses.

Gestalt therapists believe that anxiety and personality disorders arise when people dissociate parts of themselves, particularly their need for personal gratification, from awareness. Because dreams often contain clues to dissociated parts of the self, Gestalt therapists encourage discussion and acting out of dreams.

## ■ COGNITIVE AND BEHAVIORAL THERAPIES

Whereas in traditional psychotherapy conversations between the client and the therapist are the primary vehicle for achieving clinical improvement, most cognitive and behavioral therapies rely heavily on a growing number of other techniques such as modeling and role playing. We will review some of these techniques

later in this section. First, however, we will describe some cognitive approaches to psychotherapy that are distinguished not so much by the use of novel techniques as by the hypothesis that faulty beliefs and assumptions are the primary causes of maladaptive behavior.

### The Cognitive Psychotherapies

The cognitive psychotherapies seek to correct misconceptions that contribute to maladjustment, defeat, and unhappiness. Imagine someone who, as a result of the vicissitudes of life, develops a faulty belief to the effect that "no one could possibly like me if I reveal my true self." Such people are likely to spend time endlessly avoiding others, avoiding spontaneous behavior, and eating their hearts out in loneliness. Another set of circumstances may convince someone that a series of incidents of "bad luck" mean that whatever happens next is likely to be disastrous. Thereupon the individual becomes fearful of the immediate future. Or, after many frustrations and conflicts, a person becomes so anxious that he or she is convinced that a "nervous breakdown" is imminent. The person then tries to avoid all stress even though the best approach would probably be subjection to normal stresses since success in handling them would provide the only convincing evidence of mental well-being.

Since opinions, beliefs, or conceptions are ordinarily formed on the basis of evidence, adequate or inadequate, we can also assume that beliefs are modified by evidence, adequate or inadequate. Thus, in order to modify their misconceptions clients must review the evidence in some way. Psychotherapy may, in fact, provide one of the few situations in which individuals are encouraged to think somewhat systematically about their beliefs, particularly their beliefs about themselves (Raimy, 1985). A number of psychotherapeutic approaches share the assumption that maladaptive behavior is a product of unrealistic perceptions and conditions. The various cognitive therapies use different tactics in redirecting the way people see and interpret their experiences, but they all generally reject the Freudian emphasis on the powerful role of unconscious drives.

An early cognitive approach to therapy was developed by George Kelly. Kelly's (1955) **psychology of personal constructs** led him to ask clients to examine the roles they played in interacting with others and the assumptions underlying those roles. In his **fixed-role therapy** Kelly encouraged his clients to practice new roles and relationships. Kelly saw people as problem-solvers whose faulty beliefs and assumptions often lead to undesirable solutions to the problems of living. According to Kelly, by discussing the client's personal constructs and social roles, the therapist helps the client question and reevaluate aspects of his or her life that arouse anxiety.

Another clinical approach based on cognitive theory is Albert Ellis's **rational–emotive therapy.** Ellis (1970) believes that self-defeating thinking is at the root of maladaptive behavior. Such thinking is based on arbitrary, inaccurate assumptions about oneself and others. It is often marked by a preoccupation with "musts": "I *must* always be friendly to people," "I *must* not disappoint my parents," "I *must* be a big success." In rational–emotive therapy these musts are seen as causes of emotional arousal, which, if maintained at too high a level for too long a time, causes psychological and physical wearing down. Most of these and other self-defeating musts were pounded into our heads as children, and we tend to accept them without question. Thus, rational–emotive therapy has two goals: to get people to question these fundamental, but mistaken, beliefs, and then to exchange them for more constructive ones.

During the course of therapy the cognitive therapist actually demonstrates the ways in which unrealistic self-verbalizations can create or worsen emotional problems. The therapist also actively questions and contradicts faulty, unreasonable assumptions by the client and suggests alternative ways of thinking. Role playing is often used, with the therapist demonstrating the behavioral consequences of different types of beliefs.

Aaron Beck's (1976) cognitive therapy is also directed toward the thoughts that underlie intense, persistent emotional reactions. Beck's technique involves frequent, gentle questioning of the client about the basis for what he or she is saying. Beck speaks of "automatic thoughts" that seem to arise by themselves, without reasoning. These thoughts are accepted as valid even though they are not the products of rational consideration of alternatives. Children who simply accept their parents' values without questioning them are engaging in automatic thought. According to Beck, therapy should be aimed at terminating automatic thinking and replacing it with thoughts that result from rational consideration of alternatives.

Beck's cognitive therapy has been used with various forms of maladaptive behavior, but he has specialized in work with depressed people. In this work, emphasis is placed on the irrational ideas that contribute to feelings of depression and thoughts of suicide.

## Cognitive–Behavioral Interventions

Few clinical approaches have shown such rapid development as **behavior therapy.** In contrast to the various psychotherapies that had their origins in Freud's work, the roots of behavior therapy can be found in operant and classical conditioning; cognitive and psychodynamic events were intentionally ignored. The operant elements led to techniques for directly changing behavior, an approach that came to be known as **behavior modification.** The classical-conditioning elements led to a variety of techniques, notably systematic desensitization, that are used to reduce people's fears of specific objects or situations.

In recent years increased recognition has been given to the simultaneous influences of environmental manipulations, such as those used in behavior modification programs, and cognitive processes. Cognitive–behavioral interventions aim to correct people's misconceptions, strengthen their coping skills and feelings of control over their own lives, and facilitate constructive self-talk. Whereas cognitive therapists like Ellis and Beck use the conversational format of psychotherapy, clinicians who use cognitive–behavioral therapies are more likely to use structured training sessions that require the client to practice prescribed exercises.

There is growing evidence that cognitive–behavioral training can be quite effective in helping people overcome fears and inhibitions and increase their coping skills. While the mechanism by which this training leads to improvements in behavior has not been completely described, an important factor seems to be the client's sense of self-efficacy, that is, the client's belief that he or she is effective at carrying out tasks. Feelings of self-efficacy increase when individuals acquire new skills, and this encourages them to strengthen their skills even further.

**Efficacy expectations** refer to the belief that one is able to execute successfully the behavior required to produce a particular outcome. If people possess the necessary skills and there are adequate incentives, efficacy expectations can be major determinants of whether coping behavior will be initiated, how much effort will be expended, and how long that behavior will be sustained in the face of stress-arousing circumstances. Efficacy expectations may be altered through performance accomplishments, vicarious experiences, verbal persuasion, and emotional arousal. Of these, performance accomplishments have the most positive effect on efficacy expectations (Bandura, 1982, 1986). It seems possible that efficacy expectations are among the most important contributors to behavioral change (see Figure 17–3).

**Relaxation Training**  **Relaxation training** often helps people who are tense and generally anxious. In one approach, emphasis is placed on learning to contrast muscular tension with muscular relaxation. In another,

(a)

(b)

**FIGURE 17-3**
Efficacy expectations influence an individual's performance. These two individuals both know that being outgoing and cheerful contributes to the enjoyment of social relationships. Yet the unfavorable efficacy expectations of the person in photo (a) contribute to ineffective social behavior, whereas the favorable expectations of the one in photo (b) contribute to effectiveness and a feeling of being at ease. (Abigail Heyman, Archive and Richard Hutchings, Photo Researchers)

meditation procedures are employed. In yet another method, known as autogenic training, self-suggestion is the key ingredient.

***Muscular Relaxation.*** Muscular relaxation involves tensing and then relaxing various muscle groups. The individual is encouraged to note the differences between feeling tense and feeling relaxed. Relaxation training is used in many methods of natural childbirth and in yoga. People who have difficulty falling asleep often find that relaxation exercises help them get to sleep more quickly. At first individuals use relaxation exercises mainly in the therapy situation. But as their ability to relax themselves improves, they are encouraged to relax themselves in stressful situations that they encounter in everyday life.

***Meditation.*** In relaxation training using meditation procedures, the individual learns to concentrate on a thought, a sensation, a word, an object, or some mental state. Some techniques are very active and require that the person make a strenuous effort to focus on a specific thing. Certain yoga techniques, for example, require that the practitioner maintain specific postures and deliberately control his or her breathing or other bodily functions. Other meditation techniques, such as transcendental meditation (TM), are passive approaches. Practitioners simply remain in a quiet atmosphere and make a relaxed attempt to achieve a state of inner peace. The individual concentrates on a *mantra* (a specially selected word) and tries, but does not strain, to exclude all other thoughts. Most passive techniques are practiced for 20-minute periods each day, once in the morning and again before dinner.

***Autogenic Training.*** Strictly speaking, autogenic training is not exclusively a relaxation technique. Rather than training people to achieve a state of low arousal, autogenic training aims at a state of psychophysiological equilibrium. Although this often involves decreasing physiological arousal, autogenic training does not try to produce complete relaxation. The autogenic method teaches the individual to assume an attitude of "passive concentration" on a series of "formulas," or self-suggestions, pertaining to various physical, emotional, and mental sensations. The following are standard formulas (one limb at a time for those related to the limbs).

1. My arms are heavy.
2. My legs are heavy.

3. My arms are warm.
4. My legs are warm.
5. My forehead is cool.
6. My heartbeat is calm and regular.

The individual is encouraged to imagine feelings, sensations, or scenes that may make the sensation more vivid, but is warned not to *try* to make the sensation occur. Concentration on the formula must remain a passive experience, whether or not the sensation is perceived.

There is evidence that progressive relaxation has greater effects on the muscles whereas autogenic training has greater effects on the autonomic nervous system (Lehrer and Woolfolk, 1984). Relaxation therapies appear to be helpful for a variety of psychosomatic disorders, particularly tension headaches and migraine headaches. However, they usually are not sufficient by themselves. Life styles, social environments, and views of the world can create or compound people's problems in living. Such factors as the quality and nature of available social support and the individual's goals, attitudes, and values often must be dealt with. Table 17–2 lists a number of factors that bear on the advisability of using relaxation techniques in a given case.

Research on relaxation skills requires answers to two questions: Has the individual learned the relaxation skill? Does use of the skill lead to beneficial clinical results? Obviously, if the skills were never learned, there would be little reason to expect positive results from relaxation training. Appropriate control groups are needed to provide an adequate basis for judging the effectiveness of the training. There is also a need for studies that explore the effectiveness of relaxation training both alone and in combination with other types of therapy.

---

□ **TABLE 17–2**
**Factors in Successful Use of Relaxation Training**

---

1. The individual's problems do not have an organic basis.
2. The individual is not psychotic, depressed, or subject to panic attacks.
3. The individual is able to assume responsibility for active participation in treatment, with special emphasis on home practice.
4. Family members are cooperative with and supportive of the individual's treatment.
5. The individual has reasonable expectations (i.e., does not expect a miracle).

---

**Systematic Desensitization** **Systematic desensitization** combines behavioral training (muscular relaxation) with cognitive activity. It begins with the induction of a relaxed state. While the person is relaxed, he or she imagines scenes that are related to his or her specific fear. Desensitization begins with scenes or images that are only mildly fear arousing. The individual is encouraged to concentrate on perpetuating the relaxed state while imagining those situations. Once the person is able to remain relaxed, progressively more upsetting scenes are imagined.

The theory behind systematic desensitization is that the relaxation response competes with previously learned anxiety responses, such as fears and phobias. (Other responses, such as eating, sexual arousal, or animated conversation, might also compete with anxiety-arousing thoughts.) Research has shown that practicing relaxation when the fear-arousing stimulus is actually present (*in vivo* desensitization) yields superior results to simply imagining the stimulus. Desensitization works best with people who habitually show noticeable increases in physiological arousal (e.g., accelerated heart rate, moist palms) when exposed to the fear-arousing stimulus.

**Exposure Therapies** **Exposure therapies** are based on the principle that continued exposure to anxiety-provoking stimuli (for example, exposing a person who is afraid of dirt or dirty objects) will decrease anxiety. *Exposure* consists of a gradual approach to an anxiety-provoking situation. Under such conditions the distress experienced in the situation is kept at a relatively low level.

Exposure to fear-arousing situations is one of the most effective ways of overcoming fear. However, there are positive results only if clients are willing to expose themselves to the situations they are afraid of. Although **in vivo exposure** (actually being in the situation) usually works best, **fantasized exposure** (thinking about being in the situation) is also effective. Exposure treatment is appropriate for many unpleasant or disadvantageous emotional responses. If the treatment is effective, improvement can usually be observed within five or six sessions.

**Flooding** is a form of exposure therapy in which the client is exposed to a flood of fear-arousing stimuli that is not terminated simply because the client experiences a high level of tension. In flooding, the clinical session is saturated with frightening thoughts and images in the hope that emotional responses to them will be extinguished through burnout. If this happens, **extinction** is said to have occurred.

In **implosive therapy** the client experiences higher

and higher levels of anxiety through imaginal presentation of scenes depicting behavior and situations that he or she has strenuously avoided in the past. The imagery used in treatment is intended to represent conflict areas that are thought to be the source of the avoidance behavior. Implosion is based on the therapist's interpretation of the psychodynamics underlying the avoidance behavior. The imaginal material used in implosion therapy tends to be much more intense than that used in flooding.

**Modeling** Often people are unaware that habit controls much of their behavior. Through **modeling,** they can be shown that there are other ways of doing things. Although modeling can take place when an individual observes someone demonstrating specific social skills, it also occurs informally, for example, when children imitate the heroes of television shows. In clinical applications of modeling, demonstrations by models are often combined with **guided rehearsals,** in which the individual is encouraged to imitate the behavior of the model with the model helping whenever necessary. When people imitate the adaptive behavior of models, their new responses are strengthened by positive reinforcement. The success of a modeling program depends on several factors.

1. How carefully the observer attends to the modeled behavior.
2. How well what was observed is retained.
3. The observer's ability to reproduce the modeled behavior.
4. How motivated the observer is to use the modeled behavior.

**Live modeling** involves direct observation of a model. **Symbolic modeling** refers to observation of a model who is presented indirectly through film, video or audio tape, or printed word. **Covert modeling** is a logical extension of symbolic modeling in which the individual is asked to imagine observing a model and a particular consequence. For example, a male cross-dresser was asked to imagine the following scene.

*You are standing behind a one-way mirror. You see a bare room except for two single beds with clothes on them. One bed has male clothes on it and the other has female clothes on it. Straight ahead at the other end of the room, you see a door open and a naked man about your age walks into the room. He walks toward the beds which are next to each other about four feet apart. He starts to go toward the bed with the female clothes on it. He looks at the clothes; suddenly you can see a painful expression*

*on his face. He sits down on the bed. Now he starts to sweat and looks sick. He reaches for a bra and he starts to gag. As he puts the bra on he starts to vomit all over the clothes and on himself. He groans in agony as he doubles over and falls down to the ground. He is lying with the bra on and wallowing in vomit.* (Cautela, 1985, p. 93)

A covert modeling scene was then presented in which the model puts on the male clothes and looks happy.

In general, covert modeling involves constructing scenes or situations in which the client can picture the behavior that is to be changed. Although this is a relatively new technique and requires more research, available evidence suggests that it is a promising clinical tool (Kazdin and Mascitelli, 1982).

Like other cognitive and behavioral therapies, modeling is often combined with other approaches. For example, while reinforcing adaptive overt behavior, the therapist might help the client acquire more realistic ideas about problem areas. In treating a complex problem such as intense anger in a child, the therapist might: (1) teach the parents to be more effective in reacting to temper tantrums (modeling might be used to accomplish this); (2) help the child identify the situations and thoughts that evoke the tantrums; (3) model cognitive and behavioral responses to stress and frustration that are more effective than anger; and (4) use guided rehearsal and praise to strengthen the child's adaptive behavior.

**Assertiveness Training** **Assertiveness training** is specifically designed to enhance the interpersonal skills one needs to stand up for one's rights, such as refusing unwanted requests, expressing opinions, and making requests. Assertiveness training is preceded by a careful assessment of the client's responses in certain types of situations. The assessment is designed to answer these questions: What situations are of concern to the client? What does the client typically do in these situations? What are the personal and environmental blocks to more assertiveness in these situations?

Lack of assertive behavior is often related to deficits in social skills or to interfering emotional reactions and thoughts. If appropriate behaviors are available but are not performed because of anxiety, the focus may be on enhancing the client's anxiety management skills. Modeling and behavioral rehearsal play important roles in assertiveness training programs (see Figure 17-4). Positive feedback is offered after each rehearsal, and prompting is provided when needed. Homework assignments are used if, as is desirable, the client agrees to carry out tasks that require assertiveness outside the training sessions. If the assertiveness deficits extend

(a)          (b)          (c)

**FIGURE 17-4**
Modeling can be an effective technique in assertiveness training. In this series of photos, (a) the therapist demonstrates an introduction for a shy client, (b) the client practices with others, and (c) the client uses her new skills in the stress-producing setting of a job interview. (Irene Springer)

over a broad range of social behaviors, a number of training sessions may be needed. However, if the problem is fairly specific, a few sessions may be sufficient.

**Paradoxical Intention** Paradoxical intention is a technique in which the therapist instructs the client to perform behaviors that appear to be in opposition to the client's therapeutic goal. For example, an individual who complains of inability to fall asleep within a satisfactory interval might be asked to remain awake as long as possible. An agoraphobic who cannot go into crowded places for fear of suffering severe heart palpitations might be instructed to go into crowded places and try to become anxious. Paradoxical intention is a relatively new technique that requires more research. It is not yet clear when it is appropriate or why it seems to be effective in particular cases. Perhaps it is effective because it requires the client to maintain the very behavior that he or she seeks to change under conditions that cannot support continuation of that behavior. Exposure to anxiety-provoking situations is an element of paradoxical intention and may contribute to its effectiveness.

**Behavior Modification** Operant methods use schedules of reinforcement and shaping to gradually achieve a desired response. Special prompts might be employed to highlight a situation that calls for a particular response. **Fading** refers to gradual elimination of these special cues when they are no longer needed. Positive reinforcers (such as praise or money) are used to strengthen desired responses. The token economy is one of the most common applications of operant principles to modify maladaptive behavior. Extinction procedures and punishment might be used to eliminate undesirable responses. When punishment is employed to eliminate a response, it is a good idea to

positively reinforce an alternative, more desirable response at the same time.

Reinforcement and cognitive approaches may be combined in some cases. For example, both environmental and cognitive factors usually play important roles in therapy for depressed people. A depressed person might be helped to do things that lead to positive reinforcement from others. At the same time, the therapist would help the individual become aware of and change internal events, such as negative self-statements, that enhance his or her feelings of pessimism and worthlessness. Simultaneously strengthening social skills and modifying thoughts and attitudes can be a very valuable therapeutic approach.

Another major development of recent years is the use of biofeedback procedures in which the individual is reinforced whenever a designated change in bodily functioning takes place. Through biofeedback the individual becomes better able to control internal processes, such as body temperature and heart rate, that are related to maladaptation.

## ■ GROUP THERAPY

Group approaches to psychotherapy are used not only because they are less costly but because many clinicians believe that therapy can be at least as effective with groups as it is with individuals. One appealing feature of group psychotherapy is that clients can learn both by observing other group members' adaptive and maladaptive attempts to solve personal problems and by comparing their own relationship with the therapist with those of the other members.

Group therapy is usually seen as a means of broadening the application of psychotherapeutic concepts. Some advocates of group psychotherapy believe it may actually produce better results than individual therapy. There is evidence that groups are particularly effective when they give participants opportunities to acquire new social skills through modeling (Curran and Monti, 1982). Opportunities to rehearse or practice these skills in the group increase the chances that the participants will actually use their newly acquired skills in everyday life.

From a psychodynamic point of view, group psychotherapy represents an opportunity to deal with transference in a social situation and to compare one's attitude toward participation in a group with those of other group members. The group is often seen as an extension of the family. For example, a frequent topic that arises in group therapy is the competition of group members for the therapist's attention. A psychoanalyst might see echoes of the members' relationships to parents and siblings in their performances in the group. A cognitively oriented clinician, on the other hand, would be interested primarily in the often irrational ideas of group members concerning what goes on, or should go on, in social situations. Client-centered therapists see the therapist's role in groups as basically the same as in individual counseling; in both situations the therapist is a facilitator of personal growth. Cognitive–behavioral therapists are increasingly using techniques such as modeling and behavior rehearsal in groups.

## Family Therapy

**Family therapy** is a specialized clinical approach that is used in treating family groups. Instead of treating family members individually, the therapist encourages the family to deal as a group with the members' attitudes and feelings toward one another and their resistance to cooperation and sharing (see Figure 17–5). Family therapy often begins when one member of the family is labeled as having a problem. When it becomes clear that the family, not just the individual, has the problem, a group approach is considered. The following example shows how a problem that was originally presented as involving only one member of a family came to be viewed from a broader perspective.

*A mother called a therapist in private practice and said, "Cindy needs therapy. She is having problems. She can't communicate with us anymore. Cindy says the problem is with the family, but I know it's her problem." The therapist made the appointment for Cindy, as requested by her mother, but extended an invitation to the entire family to come so that he might get to know the Cindy's family. He took care to clearly show the mother that he respected her view of the problem, but he also put out tentative feelers to learn if perhaps a little bit more could be gained at the start. The entire family agreed to come. When they arrived at the therapist's office, the therapist made a few mental notes: the mother was very well dressed, wore a rigid smile, and appeared to be very strained; the 18-year-old son and 16-year-old daughter (the index patient) followed behind their mother, both nice-looking, somber youngsters; behind mother and children, and at a much slower pace, came the father, on crutches. All four family members quickly explained that the crutches were regarded matter-of-factly; father had been using them since he had polio when Cindy was just 15*

**FIGURE 17–5**
During this family-therapy session the therapist observes how the members of the family interact. In this photo the therapist is using what has just been said by a family member to help the others see how one person's behavior affects other members of the family. (Linda Ferrer/Woodfin Camp & Associates)

months old. Almost the first words Cindy said to the therapist were, "Dad and I learned to walk together."

*The therapist first talked things over individually with each family member. The family's story emerged gradually. Cindy wanted to join a drug-abuse group at school; she complained, "but Mom won't let me. She doesn't want her baby in with those drug fiends, or with the nice counselor." The 18-year-old boy was planning to leave for an out-of-state college within six months. He expressed much concern for his mother and considerable awareness of her emotional distress. He was also very anxious to get away from it all and to live his own life. "I am leaving," he stated firmly. "Even if she's all upset, I need to go away." Both children let the therapist know that their father worked up to 20 hours a day at his own little company. "His job is his life," the mother said, echoing her children. She added, "But that's o.k., I have accepted that." (McPherson and others, 1974, pp. 80–81.)*

As he worked with this family, the therapist sensed the anger, sadness, and depression underneath the mother's veneer of forced cheerfulness. She felt that her husband had already deserted her and that her children were about to do so. It also became apparent that her husband was using his work as a means of avoiding intense involvement with his wife. To the therapist it seemed clear that Cindy's was not the only problem in the family.

Family therapy often provides a valuable forum for airing hostilities, reviewing emotional ties, and dealing with crises. Every family must pass through a series of stages, each of which is potentially a crisis—changes in behavior are required, relationships shift, and everyone feels pressured and disorganized. Behavioral problems often arise when the life cycle of the family is interrupted. It is not the task of the child, alone, to get through the changes brought by stages of development such as becoming an adolescent or going to college. It is a job for the whole family, with implications for each member. Maladaptive behavior in the family as a whole can be triggered by a child's attempt to handle a phase that is still a source of conflict for one of the parents. Facilitating the family's transition from one developmental phase to another is the basic goal of the family therapist (Minuchin, 1985).

## Psychodrama

Although most group therapy is essentially an expanded, more complicated, and more realistic version of individual therapy, a number of approaches have been designed especially for groups. One of these is **psychodrama**, which was created by Jacob Moreno in

the 1920s. Moreno led impromptu activity groups of children in the public gardens of Vienna. He noticed that when the children were encouraged to act out stories instead of merely reading or listening to them, they often displayed unexpected depths of feeling and understanding. He later experimented with a form of theater, the "theater of spontaneity," in which players were encouraged to draw upon their inner resources in creating the dramatic action rather than following a script.

In psychodrama a group of individuals assembles under the leadership of a therapist (often called the director). The group enacts events of emotional significance in order to resolve conflicts and release members from inhibitions that limit their capacity for spontaneous and creative activity, particularly social activity. Behavior therapists use role playing to give clients practice in new social skills, but in psychodrama role playing tends to be more spontaneous and oriented toward expressing strongly felt emotions (see Figure 17–6).

Moreno saw psychodrama as a vehicle for expressing strong emotions, acquiring insight into one's own behavior, and realistically evaluating the behavior of others. Psychodrama is a directive treatment in that the therapist controls the mechanics of the therapy situation. However, it is nondirective in that the emotional content of sessions arises spontaneously from the activities of the participants.

## Cognitive–Behavioral Group Therapy

Although group therapy has traditionally been carried out from a psychodynamic perspective, cognitive and behavioral therapists are developing their own group techniques. The focus of cognitive–behavioral group therapy is on increasing the skills and comfort of people in social situations. Group members role-play specific social situations that they find difficult. The themes of particular sessions are often programmed by the therapist from prior knowledge of the members' problems. The therapist may model alternative ways of handling these situations. The role playing is accompanied by social reinforcement and feedback, and homework tasks are assigned. Other techniques are used as well, including graded task assignments, examination of specific types of distortions that may arise in social interactions (such as overgeneralization and catastrophizing), and discussion of types of cognitions that have negative and positive influences in group situations.

Cognitive–behavioral group therapy is more highly structured than group therapy conducted along psychodynamic lines. Although it is a relatively new approach, group members not only seem to value the task-

**FIGURE 17-6**
Acting out emotionally significant events can help people deal with strong emotions that they may have been afraid to acknowledge. (Richard Hutchings, Photo Researchers)

oriented sessions but also exhibit improved behavior. (Falloon, 1981; Steuer and others, 1984).

## ■ INTEGRATION OF THERAPEUTIC APPROACHES

When therapists who base their techniques on different perspectives discuss their work, there are inevitable differences of opinion. The issues that separate the various schools of thought seem substantial. Should therapists actively direct patients toward behavioral change, or should they focus on the development of insight? Should therapy delve into the past or examine the present? Should its duration be long or short? Despite the different ways in which these questions are answered, there is evidence of a movement toward the integration of therapeutic approaches. "Talking therapies," such as psychoanalytically oriented psychotherapy, are placing more emphasis on the need of patients to take responsibility for themselves and develop self-mastery. Behavioral therapies are giving increased attention to the cognitive underpinnings of behavioral change. Often this means helping patients acquire insight into their misconceptions about themselves and their social relationships. Many cognitive–behavioral therapists rely heavily on imagery as a means of achieving therapeutic goals. The use of imagery for treatment purposes clearly acknowledges the potentially crucial role of private events.

There is growing evidence that performance-based therapies, in which individuals actually deal with problematic situations, can be very effective. However, cognitive processes, such as insight, may play an important role in helping people develop more adaptive performance orientations to their problems of living. As more therapists attend to the relative roles of cognition, emotion, and behavior, steps toward greater integration of therapeutic approaches are becoming noticeable.

## ■ RESEARCH ON THE PSYCHOLOGICAL THERAPIES

Many groups have a stake in the evaluation of therapeutic effectiveness. Patients, their families, therapists, researchers, insurance companies, legislators, and planners of mental-health services all want to know which therapy is most effective. Given the number of psychological therapies, it is obvious that researchers who study these areas have their work cut out for them. Obtaining information about therapeutic effectiveness is not easy for a number of reasons. For example, therapists differ in their ability to carry out particular therapies. Furthermore, some therapies may be more effective with certain types of patients than others. Psychological therapy is not a unitary process applied to a unitary problem. Research on therapy is improving because studies are becoming more complex and incorporating more relevant factors into their research designs. Some of the practical differences between laboratory experiments and research on psychotherapy are summarized in Table 17–3.

Comparison of a particular therapy with a control

□ **TABLE 17-3**

Differences Between Experimental Laboratory Studies and Therapy

| Factor | Laboratory Study | Psychotherapy |
|---|---|---|
| 1. Independent variables | Usually quite clearly defined | Complex, often difficult to define clearly |
| 2. Dependent variables | Usually quite clearly defined | Often involve complex set of responses that change over time |
| 3. Experimental situation | Well-controlled | Not possible to eliminate unexpected events |
| 4. Other situations | Researchers usually not concerned about what happens to subject outside experimental situation | Therapist is interested in what happens outside therapy situation |

condition is useful, but studies that compare the effectiveness of several treatment approaches for similar groups of clients are even more significant. Most clinicians agree that the same therapy will have varying effects on different types of patients. There is a need for experiments in which the independent variable is a specific therapeutic procedure (such as group therapy and systematic desensitization) and the dependent variable is some aspect of behavior (such as frequency of suicidal thoughts).

Before a research project is carried out, there must be agreement on how to measure the results. For example, suppose a researcher intends to assess the effectiveness of different therapies designed to reduce the tendency to hallucinate. One way to measure the dependent variable would be to count the number of times people report having hallucinatory experiences. But people might have hallucinations that they did not report, or might make up such experiences just to have something to report. Thus, whereas some clinicians might contend that frequency of reported hallucinations is a reasonable index of the general tendency to hallucinate, others might not be satisfied with this conclusion.

In any research, all groups of subjects must be as similar or equal as possible before the experiment begins. The therapists in the various groups should also be comparable. Many other factors must also be controlled. For instance, suppose the staff on the ward of a mental hospital believe that their program is a significant therapeutic innovation. Their enthusiasm for the program might, *by itself,* influence the patients in their care. Actually, there is evidence that such an **enthusiasm effect** operates in a variety of situations, including hospitals, schools, and private consulting rooms.

Most studies of therapy techniques compare a group of people who receive treatment with one or two groups of people who do not. But such comparisons do not show how individuals within the groups are affected by specific aspects of the treatment. Clinicians also need to know how changes in the client's behavior are related to what the clinician does or says. Some behavior therapists see single-subject research, which is described in Box 17–1, as an important source of information.

## Outcome Studies

There are disagreements about the relative effectiveness of the different psychological therapies. In evaluating psychotherapy a common procedure has been to compare two groups, one that is treated clinically and one that is not. Researchers with different criteria and expectations have obtained different results in such comparisons. For example, after reviewing the literature, Eysenck (1952, 1961) concluded that psychotherapy was an ineffective clinical method. He argued that many apparent successes could be explained by **spontaneous remissions,** in which the client's symptoms would have disappeared in time with or without treatment. Bergin and Lambert (1978) found that psychotherapy had an effect but that the effect was not necessarily positive. Some patients actually seemed to deteriorate because of psychotherapy.

Whether a given patient would have shown a spontaneous remission if left untreated is a tantalizing question. Just what is a spontaneous remission? Scientists usually do not put any store in spontaneous events. They believe that things happen for reasons. What causes the recovery when untreated cases get better? As research on spontaneous remissions has become

# ■BOX 17-1 SINGLE-SUBJECT RESEARCH

Single-subject research differs in an important respect from the traditional case study. Although case studies may provide insights about treatment, they generally rely on anecdotal information and impressions, which may be misleading. In single-subject studies, on the other hand, behavior is observed directly, either in the actual problem situation or in a simulated laboratory environment. The behavior is also measured continuously, before, during, and in some cases after treatment. Immediate information about whether the treatment is having the desired effects can be obtained. This allows the therapist to make decisions about the treatment while it is going on.

The most common test of the effect of a clinical procedure with a single client involves the A-B-A-B research design. This design is used most often to determine whether operant-conditioning procedures are effective in bringing about behavioral changes. It consists of obtaining a baseline measure of the target behavior (A), instituting reinforcement-contingency procedures (B), removing the contingency so that the conditions that were present during the baseline period are reinstated (A), and reintroducing the phase-B contingency (B). This repeated-measures design is a very powerful method for isolating the conditions that control behavior.

An A-B-A-B design was used in operant therapy with a 19-year-old man who had been admitted to a hospital with complaints of pain in the lower back, hips, and both legs, and great difficulty in walking, sitting, and standing. An exhaustive medical study determined that his symptoms were unrelated to physical causes, and the case was diagnosed as a psychological disorder.

The operant therapy consisted of visits by a young assistant to the patient's room three times daily. During these visits the assistant spent approximately 10 minutes talking to the patient about topics unrelated to his psychiatric disorder. During an initial 3-day period she encouraged him to walk but provided him with no reinforcement for doing so. During the next 3-day sequence she instructed the patient to walk and reinforced him when this happened. Reinforcement consisted of comments such as "Good," "That's great," and "You're doing fine," accompanied by attention, friendliness, and smiling. Reinforcements were not given during the following 3-day period, but they were reinstituted during the final 3 days of the experimental therapeutic program.

Figure 17-6 summarizes the results of the program. During the instruction period there was no increase in walking. The addition of reinforcement resulted in increased walking. When reinforcing contingencies are discontinued, there is usually a

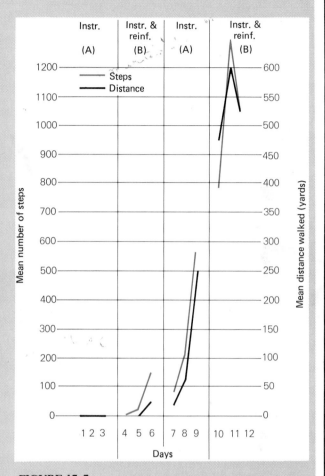

FIGURE 17-7
The chart shows changes in walking behavior during the four conditions of the repeated-measures design. Mean number of steps and distance are shown as a function of instructions and reinforcements.

decrement in the target behavior. In this case, contrary to what might be expected, improvement continued during the period when no reinforcement was given. Uncontrolled and unscheduled reinforcement by other patients may have contributed to this continued improvement. The greatest improvement occurred during the final phase of the program.

Single-subject A-B-A-B designs are useful in monitoring a particular type of behavior (such as temper tantrums or inappropriate verbal responses) over time. Effective treatment strategies can be developed by adding therapeutic components to facilitate behavior change in a cumulative manner.

This process is greatly aided by the continual, ongoing assessment of treatment outcome. A limitation of single-subject research designs is that it may be difficult to control such factors as the occurrence of reinforcement during noncontingent periods. It is also difficult to know whether the findings can be generalized until the same procedures are carried out with many clients. Yet for clinicians and researchers who are interested in behavioral measurements and the specifics of cause and effect relationships, single-subject designs are an effective tool.

more sophisticated, it has become clear that people who are turned down for treatment at a clinic or are put on a waiting list often do not stop seeking help. They may approach nonprofessionals—family members, friends, teachers, and members of the clergy, among others—and these people may be able to help.

Everyday life is full of examples of people who are helped by informal or chance contacts with others. Even though no money changes hands, such contacts often contribute to personal growth. In the following example an exceptionally effective young college graduate was found to have had a chaotic, stress-inducing family life. Yet an informal relationship with a neighboring family gave him valuable opportunities for personal growth.

*He came from an extremely disturbed home setting in which every member of his family except himself had been hospitalized for severe mental illness; and yet he had graduated from a renowned university with honors, had starred on the football team, and was unusually popular. During his government training he was held in the highest esteem by staff members and was rated as best liked and most likely to succeed by his peers.*

*In examining this young man's history we discovered that during his elementary school years he had essentially adopted a neighborhood family as his own and spent endless hours with them. Certain characteristics of this family appear most significant. They were a helping family in the sense that love emanated from them and was freely available to all. Of special significance for the fellow under consideration was his relationship with a boy in the family, a year older than he, who formed for him a positive role model with whom he closely identified and whom he followed to his considerable satisfaction.*

*An even more crucial factor was his relationship with the mother in this family, who became his guide, counselor, and chief source of emotional nurturance. His reports indicate that while this relationship was intense, it was not symbiotic, and seemed to foster his independence and self-development. Although there are probably few like her, she represents a dimension of socially indigenous therapy that may be more significant than is usually recognized. Her home became a neighborhood gathering place. It might be characterized as an informal therapy agency, a kitchen clinic.* (Bergin and Lambert, 1978, pp. 149–150)

Clearly, personal growth can take place in a variety of settings. It follows that identifying the elements of personal growth and the factors that foster it will contribute to the development of better formal and informal therapies. In this regard, the observations of people who have had successful therapy can be enlightening. Box 17–2 contains comments about psychotherapy by a group of clients who were asked to evaluate their experiences.

It is not unusual for clients to see themselves as cured while their therapists see them as unimproved or even as being worse. Studies of improvement therefore should include three independent measures: the client's evaluation of the progress made; the therapist's evaluation; and the judgments of people who know the client well, such as family members and friends.

Another approach to evaluating the effectiveness of therapy is to assess the resultant behavior change. Although one of the goals of psychotherapy is enhancement of the client's self-awareness and insight, most people would consider therapy a failure if the person's behavior remained the same. One psychotherapist has argued that the therapist's most significant function is to motivate clients to modify their behavior. It is not enough to be a source of insight.

Changes in overt behavior are easier to describe and assess objectively than changes in attitudes, feelings, and beliefs. But questions remain. To what degree should behavioral change be used as a criterion? Who should determine the kinds and amounts of change desired? How lasting should the change be? How longstanding and disabling has the patient's condition been? It seems reasonable that criteria for success should be related to the difficulty of the hurdle to be overcome. Implicit in this conclusion is the recognition that criteria that are appropriate in one case may be inappropriate in others.

# ■BOX 17-2 CLIENTS' COMMENTS ABOUT PSYCHOTHERAPY

Each paragraph contains the reactions of a different client.

*I have accepted "me." I know now everyone experiences anxiety and uses an individual mechanism to accommodate this. I understand my own particular pattern and can adjust accordingly. . . .*

*I have rid myself of the greatest inferiority complex possible. I feel I am now a fairly attractive, competent person, who can handle the necessary crises of life that I will encounter. My fear of people in crowds and my fear of being alone have both been overcome almost entirely. I thoroughly enjoy people, my life, and those about me. . . .*

*I am a great deal more self-sufficient, so that my relationships are not based merely on need, but I can now be a part of a reciprocal situation. I can assume much more responsibility for my own actions and thus am better able to act rather than just react. My anger at my family has subsided, and I no longer feel that they are to blame for my unhappiness in any present sense. Most importantly, I am able to feel joy and pain, which even with the latter is good, because I'm living, and not just being parasitic. I can trust another person enough to care, and to risk the consequences of the caring. . . .*

*Although problems still exist, I run no more. I find myself thinking back to my therapy sessions and trying to use what I learned there. I try to determine why certain situations cause problems for me and then determine what is the best way to handle them as they*

*come. I now realize that nothing is really as "earth shattering" as it may seem at the time, and after I have done all I can, I stand.*
(Strupp, Fox, and Lessler, 1969, pp. 69–72)

That the impact of psychotherapy may be felt years after its completion is reflected in these paragraphs written by psychologist Sandra L. Harris after the death of her therapist.

*A friend died recently. I am still assimilating the loss and taking stock of all that he meant. Jim was no ordinary friend. He was my therapist some twenty years ago and a central figure in my transition from adolescence to adulthood. He had an important influence on my decision to become a clinical psychologist. Although we saw each other rarely in the intervening years, the fact of his existence remained a tangible, if peripheral, fact to me.*

*His death has led me once again to reflect on what it is that matters in therapy and how enduring changes are wrought. When I think about the girl I was in my freshman year at the University of Maryland, and the young woman I was when I graduated four years later, it is clear that it was not only the issues Jim and I discussed, but how we talked that made the difference. The intangibles of trust, respect, and caring were at least as important as the active problem solving which transpired in our weekly meetings. It was not a dramatic transformation, rather it was a slight shifting of a path by a few degrees on the compass. Over the years that shift has had a cumulative effect and I walk a very different road than I would have without him.* (Harris, 1981, p. 3)

## Comparing Therapies

There is a growing support for the conclusion that psychological therapies are worthwhile for many people. But are the different therapeutic approaches equally effective? In one widely cited comparative study (Sloane and others, 1975), the subjects were college students who had applied for treatment—mostly for anxiety and personality disorders—at a psychiatric outpatient clinic. The goal of the study was to compare the relative effectiveness of behavioral therapy (desensitization, assertiveness training, and so on) and more traditional, short-term, psychodynamically oriented therapy. In addition to these two groups, there was a control group whose members were told that they would have to wait about 4 months to receive treatment.

The clients were followed up 4 and 12 months after completing therapy. The measures used in the treatment comparisons were derived from interviews with the clients at these times, from the clients' ratings of their own improvement, and from improvement ratings made by an independent assessor. At 4 months, the psychotherapy and behavioral-therapy groups had improved equally, and significantly more than the waiting-list group. At the 1-year follow-up, the behavioral-therapy clients, but not the psychotherapy group, showed some significant improvement with regard to the problems that had led them to seek therapy. However, there were no significant differences between the two groups with regard to social adjustment. The 1-year follow-up results were complicated by the fact that some of the clients continued to receive treatment even though the therapy sessions were supposed to end after 4 months. The researchers concluded that their study provided no clear evidence that behavioral therapy was superior to psychotherapy.

The same researchers reported an interesting additional set of comparisons for some of the subjects in their treatment study (Sloane and others, 1977). One year after beginning treatment, the subjects were mailed questionnaires in which they were asked to rate the importance of 32 factors in the success of their treatment. What was most striking about their responses was the similarity between the psychotherapy and behavioral-therapy groups. Both groups emphasized the importance of gaining insight into one's problems, the client–therapist relationship, the opportunity to give vent to emotions, a sense of trust in the therapist, and the development of confidence. Thus, even though the two treatment approaches are based on different assumptions and use different methods, they were described similarly by the clients. This similarity held both for the sample as a whole and for subgroups of clients who were judged to have responded most positively to the treatments offered them.

Psychological therapies are most useful in treating milder, nonpsychotic disorders (which are more common than severe ones). Psychotherapy seems to be well suited for treating mild disorders in which feelings of unhappiness are a major feature, as well as anxiety disorders (generalized fears, phobias) and some nonpsychotic forms of depression. Behavioral and cognitive–behavioral therapies are also effective in treating many of these types of cases, especially anxiety disorders. Of the group approaches, family therapy seems to be most effective (Epstein and Vlok, 1982). Relatively short-term psychotherapy and behavioral therapy can produce significant improvements that last at least a year (Andrews and Harvey, 1981; Cross and others, 1982).

There is growing evidence that the various psychological approaches to treating cases that do not involve extreme psychopathology are often effective. However, one should not conclude that it makes no difference which techniques are employed in clinical work. There is a need for more information on which treatments are especially effective with particular problems, and on the similarities and differences in the techniques and results of psychological therapies (Parloff, 1982; Wilson, 1982).

Psychological therapies have been less successful with serious conditions such as schizophrenia, some types of affective disorders, alcoholism, and drug abuse. However, such therapies can play an important role in treating some of these conditions when used in combination with somatic methods like drug therapy and ECT. The value of the psychological component of these combinations frequently lies in helping the patient deal realistically with problems of day-to-day living. For example, social-skills training has been used effectively to help psychotic individuals taking antipsychotic drugs to adjust better to hospital or community settings. Perhaps as more is learned about the distinctive features of particular therapies, it will be possible to combine them in ways that are optimal for clients (see Figure 17–8).

Evaluating the effectiveness of therapeutic efforts requires carefully planned large-scale projects. Conclusions about the relative effectiveness of these different techniques cannot be drawn from research that is too limited in scope or methodologically weak. We noted earlier that there is no best index of clinical outcome. That being the case, research studies should conclude several measures of outcome, such as clients' self-reports and behavioral measures gathered before and after therapy, as well as expert judgments of clinical

**FIGURE 17–8**
Treating abnormal behavior often requires the therapist to combine different therapeutic procedures to create the best treatment for a given client. (From *The Wall Street Journal*, permission Cartoon Features Syndicate)

"I UTILIZE THE BEST FROM FREUD, THE BEST FROM JUNG AND THE BEST FROM MY UNCLE MARTY, A VERY SMART FELLOW."

progress. There might be significant differences between therapeutic approaches to specific problems with respect to some outcome measures but not others. Furthermore, a therapeutic procedure may be valuable even if it doesn't bring about a complete cure. A person who is less anxious after therapy will be grateful for that benefit despite the failure to achieve a total release from anxiety. Anthony Storr, a leading British psychotherapist, has offered an example of an "unsuccessful" success.

> Some time ago I had a letter from a man whom I had treated some twenty-five years previously asking whether I would see, or at any rate advise treatment for, his daughter. He assumed, wrongly, that I would not remember him, and, in the course of his letter, wrote as follows: "I can quite truthfully say that six months of your patient listening to my woes made a most important contribution to my life style. Although my transvestism was not cured, my approach to life and to other people was re-oriented and for that I am most grateful. It is part of my life that I have never forgotten."
>
> Looked at from one point of view, my treatment of this man was a failure. His major symptom, the complaint which drove him to seek my help, was not abolished. And yet I think it is clear that he did get something from his short period of psychotherapy which was of considerable value to him. A man does not write to a psychotherapist asking him to see his daughter, twenty-five years after his own treatment was over, using the terms employed in this letter, unless he believes that what happened during his period of treatment was important. (Storr, 1980, p. 146)

Arguments over the effectiveness of therapeutic programs can be expected to continue for several reasons: People's problems, expectations, and the extent to which their lives can be changed vary; therapists use different methods and have different expectations; and there are no uniform criteria for judging therapeutic effectiveness. Many people are helped by therapy, but some get worse. Even though psychological therapies are not for everyone, they seem to help a sizable number of people sort out their problems and develop new ways of handling stress and the challenges of life.

## Meta-Analysis

Recently the technique known as **meta-analysis** has been used in research on therapeutic outcome. Smith, Glass, and Miller (1980) pioneered this technique in their comprehensive review of the research literature. Their results led them to conclude that the average client receiving therapy was generally better off in a measurable way than 75 percent of people who receive no treatment, and was also better off with respect to the alleviation of fear and anxiety than 83 percent of untreated controls. Whether meta-analysis, a way of quantifying outcome measures so that they can be combined over many studies, is the best way to answer questions about therapeutic effectiveness is still being debated (Glass and Kliegl, 1983; Wilson and Rachman, 1983).

Meta-analysis involves (1) grouping studies in which treatment conditions have been compared with an untreated control condition on one or more measures of outcome; (2) statistically determining the therapeutic effects on different groups using the available measures; and (3) averaging the sizes of the effects across the studies that the researcher wants to compare. In this way groups receiving psychotherapy can be compared with untreated control groups and groups receiving other therapeutic approaches, such as systematic desensitization and behavior modification. Figure 17–9 provides an example of a meta-analysis of 475 studies of the effects of psychotherapy.

The number of meta-analytic studies is increasing, and so is their complexity. Greater complexity is needed, in part, because researchers do not want to be criticized for mixing apples and oranges. The results of

**FIGURE 17–9**
Meta-analysis involves the statistical combination of many separate and often very different studies. This figure illustrates the general findings of an analysis that combined 475 controlled studies of therapeutic effectiveness. The average person in the treated group was 0.85 standard deviations above the mean for the control group on the measures used to evaluate therapeutic outcome. This difference is a large one when compared to the effects of many experimental interventions used in psychology or education. For example, cutting the size of a school class in half causes an increase in achievement of 0.15 standard deviation units. The effect of nine months of instruction in reading is an improvement in reading skills of 0.67 standard deviation units. (Smith and others, 1980, p. 88)

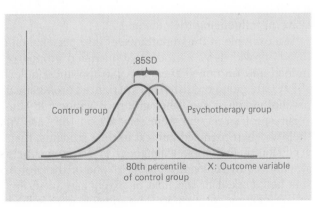

meta-analysis are harder to interpret if the effect sizes from fundamentally different types of studies are lumped together. Perhaps the sharpest criticism of meta-analysis is that comparisons of studies that are methodologically weak can add little to an ultimate evaluation of therapeutic effects. On the other hand, meta-analysis of tighter, more homogeneous studies could prove very enlightening (Kendall and Maruyama, 1985; Strube and others, 1985).

## The Ingredients of Effective Therapy

There is evidence that therapeutic effectiveness may be more closely related to therapists' personalities than to their theories. This suggests that we need to increase our understanding of what clients and therapists do during therapy sessions and how they react to one another. The therapeutic situation merits investigation, regardless of its measurable results, because each contact between a client and a therapist involves a unique interpersonal experience composed of complex events. This is true not only in traditional psychotherapy but in the newer behavioral and cognitive therapies as well.

Research on the nature of psychological therapies has explored the characteristics, attitudes, and behavior of the client and therapist in addition to the therapeutic technique used. What goes on in therapy sessions can be characterized in terms of the operation of two sets of factors. **Technique factors** are the procedures employed by the therapist, which may or may not match the descriptions of those procedures found in books and manuals. **Interpersonal factors** refer to the social chemistry of the relationship between the therapist and the client. To minimize the effects of individual differences among therapists, Freud struggled hard to establish technique factors as the single most important therapeutic influence in psychoanalysis. More recently, behavioral theorists have also emphasized the need to specify the procedures they employ. While it would be convenient if technique factors were the only ingredients in therapy, interpersonal factors not only are important but in some cases may be decisive in influencing the outcome.

An example of the importance of interpersonal factors is provided by a study that included groups of trained and untrained therapists (Strupp and Hadley, 1979). One group consisted of experienced professional psychotherapists; the other group of Vanderbilt University professors who were selected on the basis of their widely recognized interest in their students, their accessibility, and their willingness to listen and help students solve personal problems. None of the professors had worked in the field of psychology or in any other "helping" profession. The subjects were college students, most of whom complained of anxiety. Each student was assigned to either a professional or a nonprofessional therapist. A third group of subjects constituted a control group. Each control subject went through an assessment procedure, but the start of therapy was delayed.

The study found no significant differences that could be attributed to the type of therapist to which a given client had been assigned. Clients who were treated by either psychotherapists or professors showed more improvement than the control subjects. The measures of change included the students' own ratings, judgments by independent experts, MMPI scores, and clinicians' evaluations of their clients' progress. Favorable outcomes were most prevalent among clients whose therapists actively provided them with information, encouragement, and opinions. The therapists whose clients improved were those who made special efforts to facilitate the discussion of problems, focused on the here and now rather than on early-childhood experiences, and encouraged the client to seek new social activities. Thus, the personal qualities of the therapist clearly are a very important factor in therapeutic process.

If psychological therapies are effective in treating specific clinical problems, an important question is, Which events in therapy sessions are the active ingredients, the ones that actually bring about change? Evidence from studies like the one just described suggests that the active ingredients might be interpersonal factors and not the therapeutic process as usually described in textbooks. The following characteristics of therapists may influence the process of personality change and, thus, the outcome of therapy: warmth, friendliness, genuineness, interpersonal style, beliefs, values, and prejudices. In addition to the therapist's personality, his or her age, sex, and socioeconomic background may also play a role in the therapeutic process (see Figure 17–10). The means by which therapists' characteristics are communicated to the public include the therapist's appearance and his or her verbal and nonverbal behavior. The following account illustrates the subtle way in which the therapist's value system can influence the therapeutic process.

*Many years ago—which is not to say that this event could not happen now—a young man improved from a state of deep regression. He was on his way to what we call good health when he became increasingly bitter and turned against me more forcibly and violently than he had before. He brought to me tracts of a (to me) strange religion, saying that his goal in life was to convert me to this way of thought. I resisted and finally said, with impatience, "I do not want to be converted by you." He replied: "And I shall not be converted by you." We*

**FIGURE 17-10**
There is evidence that what goes on early in the patient-therapist relationship may be an important predictor of outcome. Although a patient who has an early negative reaction to his or her therapist may eventually be able to work productively with the therapist, a successful therapeutic outcome is more likely if the reaction is warm and positive (Frances, Sweeney, and Clarkin, 1985). One factor in positive or negative reactions to the therapy situation is the patient's first impression of the therapist. Which of these therapists would you prefer to go to? (SIU, Photo Researcher; Jim Wilson, Woodfin Camp & Associates; Michael Heron, Monkmeyer Press)

*parted, and for a time I did not understand his words. Then I learned the lesson. I thought that for him "getting well" was to return to the college courses which he had left, receive his degree in business, work at some job, marry, raise children, buy a house, and so on. These were middle-class standards so much a part of me—although I often failed to meet them—that they seemed to be a "natural" part of life. I did not then realize that I was attempting in the guise of therapy to convert someone to a system of values that were not his—and not truly mine either.* (Will, 1981, p. 210)

## Improving the Design of Psychotherapy Research

We have seen that in addition to technique factors such as the type of therapy practiced by the clinician, researchers must consider client and therapist factors and the tone or quality of the therapeutic relationship. Table 17-4 summarizes the research and clinical ques-

tions raised by these factors. The design of therapy research will improve as these questions stimulate methodological advances.

A number of clues are already available to permit the strengthening of research designs. These pertain to sample size, patient specificity, treatment specificity, and outcome measures.

1. *Sample size.* Because of the need to incorporate a large number of factors in the design of therapy research, large enough sample sizes are needed to allow for appropriate statistical analyses and justifiable inferences from results.

2. *Patient specificity.* Firm conclusions are more likely if subjects are relatively homogeneous in terms of factors that are not the target of the treatment intervention. So many factors may influence outcome that it is important to control as many extraneous variables as possible.

□ **TABLE 17-4**
Questions Raised by Client, Therapist, and Relationship Factors

| 1. Client factors | What role do the personal characteristics of clients play in the outcome of therapy? Among the factors that often play important roles are the attitudes of clients toward therapy, their educational and socioeconomic levels, their levels of psychological distress, the social supports available to them in their environment, and the nature of the problem for which they are seeking help. |
|---|---|
| 2. Therapist factors | What contribution do the characteristics of the therapist make to the process of therapy and its outcome? Among the important therapist variables are training, experience, clinical orientation, and personal qualities. The therapist's sex, age, ethnicity, and cultural background may also play important roles. |
| 3. The therapeutic relationship | Does the therapist–client relationship make a difference? Available evidence suggests that the psychological chemistry that takes place when a therapist with a particular personality meets a client with a particular personality is an important factor in several types of therapy. Although therapist–client relationships have been explored more deeply in psychotherapy, there is evidence that they are also very important in other forms of therapy. |

3. *Treatment specificity.* The more clearly defined the treatment or treatments, the more likely it is that reasonable inferences can be drawn from the research. This requires careful specification of the therapeutic techniques used in the research.

4. *Outcome measures.* The more relevant the outcome measures are to the type of case being treated, the more useful the study will be. For example, since obsessive compulsives rarely hallucinate, there would be little value in using the frequency of hallucinations as an outcome variable. A more useful variable would be the frequency of obsessive thoughts and compulsive behaviors.

**Control and Comparison Groups** Control and comparison groups are needed in therapy studies because many influences beyond those that are of special interest to the researcher may be at work during the period covered by therapeutic intervention. Without adequate control or comparison groups, researchers cannot rule out the possibility of alternative explanations such as spontaneous remission.

□ **TABLE 17-5**
Types of Control Groups in Therapy Outcome Research

| Untreated controls | A group that theoretically receives no treatment. No-treatment control groups are ethically questionable if the subjects are people who have come to a clinic seeking help for personal problems. |
|---|---|
| Dropout/wait-list controls | People who request treatment and either do not attend sessions or are offered treatment but only after a waiting period. |
| Attention-placebo controls | Patients who see a therapist on the same schedule but receive a presumably inactive treatment. |
| Crossover controls | For a set period, one group serves as the control while the other receives treatment; then the conditions are reversed. |
| Patients as own controls | Changes in a patient's behavior during a baseline period of no treatment are contrasted with behavioral changes occurring after treatment (see Box 17-1). |

*Source:* Based on Schacht and Strupp, 1985.

No single control group is appropriate for testing all hypotheses. The control group or groups for a particular study must be chosen on the basis of the particular question under investigation. Table 17–5 describes some types of control groups that have been used in therapy outcome research. The type of control group or groups used in a given study depends on the number of subjects available and on the nature of the setting in which the research is carried out.

## ■ BIOLOGICAL THERAPIES

In Chapter 3 we discussed the biological orientation to maladaptive behavior and the therapies that have been generated by this point of view. The most widely used biological therapies today are **electro-convulsive therapy (ECT)** and a growing variety of drugs that influence psychological functioning.

### Electro-Convulsive Therapy

Although ECT is still an important biological therapy, its use has declined in the past 20 years. ECT is particularly effective in treating cases of severe depression in which rapid recovery is essential (for example, where a suicide attempt seems likely). It is also effective in treating acute mania and, to a lesser extent, catatonic states and some forms of schizophrenia. Available evidence suggests that ECT is a relatively safe procedure, particularly when used with anesthetics and muscle relaxants that substantially lessen the traumatic effects of the treatment. Risks are further reduced by applying the electric current to only one side of the head. However, there is concern about the cognitive consequences of passing an electric current through a person's head. The major risk is memory loss, although this can be reduced by using ECT on the nondominant side of the brain and in the lowest possible dose.

Even though it has been used for many years, the mechanism by which ECT works is not yet clear. It is thought that the active ingredients in ECT are the electrical–biochemical events that follow the seizures triggered by the electrical impulses. The lack of precise knowledge about how ECT works, together with its occasional adverse effects and the availability of effective drugs, has contributed to the decline in its use.

A psychiatrist who was treated with ECT has described its positive effects on him.

*After the first treatment in both series, I felt a blunting of the acute sadness of the depression. Whereas before treatment I became tearful with very little provocation, and felt intensely sad out of all proportion to the*

*stimulus. After one single treatment I was no longer crushed by any chance sadness. The troublesome symptom of irritability also subsided early in the course of treatment. Before treatment, I was very easily irritated by trifles and expressed, on more than one occasion, an irrational belief that people were doing stupid things intentionally to annoy me.*

*I hope that this account will help to dispel the erroneous belief that ECT is a terrifying form of treatment, crippling in its effects on the memory and in other ways. The technique today is so refined that the patient suffers a minimum of discomfort, and the therapeutic benefits are so great in those cases when it is indicated that it is a great pity to withhold it from mistaken ideas of kindness to the patient. (Anonymous, 1965, pp. 365–367)*

The following case illustrates some of the infrequently occurring undesirable effects of ECT.

*A 30-year-old woman, overwhelmed with depression and thoughts of suicide, received four ECT treatments, after which she became cheerful, felt "normal," and was once again able to engage in rewarding social relationships. The therapy consisted of applying an electric current to both sides of her brain. Following the treatments, the woman experienced intense grand mal seizures once or twice a week and had to be given anticonvulsive drugs.*

A clinician who is considering the use of ECT must perform a risk–benefit analysis. On the benefit side is the likelihood of rapid improvement and, for depressives, the reduced likelihood of death due to suicide. On the risk side, however, are the possibility of death in the course of receiving ECT (this risk is low, with an incidence of about one in 10,000 treatments), the chance of memory impairment (which is short-term and becomes less noticeable with time), and the risk of spontaneous seizures (which are infrequent). In weighing the advantages against the risks, clinicians might reasonably consider ECT when there is severe depression or a possibility of suicide, or when drugs and other therapies are ineffective or seem inappropriate (see Figure 17–11).

### Drug Therapies

Many drugs have been used clinically and in research. They fall into three broad categories based on whether they are used with people who are depressed, schizophrenic, or anxious. The drugs that are used in the treatment of depression include the tricyclics, monoamine oxidase inhibitors (MAO inhibitors), stimulants, and more recently, lithium. The neuroleptics, particularly the phenothiazines, are used with schizophrenics. Anxiolytic drugs (minor tranquilizers) are used to treat

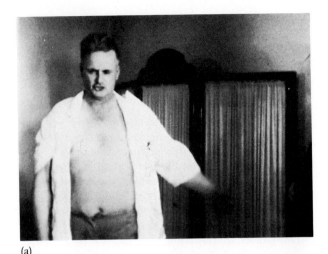

(a)

(b)

**FIGURE 17-11**
The dramatic positive effects that ECT can have are shown by the contrast between these two photos. Photo (a) shows a depressed patient's agitation and inability to sit still or think constructively. In photo (b), after a series of ECT treatments, the same patient thinks more clearly and can enjoy a social interaction. In recent years the use of ECT has decreased because of the increasing number of drugs available to treat depression. (Lester V. Bergman & Associates)

people who are suffering from anxiety. These drugs include benzodiazepines such as diazepam (Valium).

There are many unanswered questions about these drugs. Even though their safety has improved over the years, a number of risks must still be considered, including the risk of physical and psychological side effects. An extreme example of a psychological side effect is the vegetablelike state into which some patients sink when they have taken some of these drugs. Depending on the drug employed, other side effects may include drowsiness, confusion, nightmares, poor appetite, in-

somnia, blurred vision, and heart palpitations. On balance, however, the psychoactive drugs have helped many people live normal or almost normal lives.

Like those of psychological therapies, the effects of drug therapy are not always predictable. Factors such as age, sex, and genetic background can influence a person's response to a drug. The effectiveness of a particular drug may also depend on how it is metabolized, whether the patient takes it as prescribed, and whether other drugs are being taken at the same time.

**Drug Research**  Physicians who prescribe drugs want to maximize their therapeutic effects and minimize their undesirable consequences. These goals require the use of carefully designed research procedures. First, extensive preliminary research is done to study the effects of varying doses of a drug on laboratory animals. If these tests suggest that the drug is effective and does not have harmful side effects, the drug is administered to human beings under carefully controlled conditions. If these results are also positive, the drug may be approved for large-scale clinical trials and scientifically compared with other treatment methods. If it passes these tests successfully, it may be approved for use in clinical practice.

*Clinical Trials.*  **Clinical trials** involving drugs and other therapeutic procedures can be complex and costly, and may extend over many years. They often include samples of subjects located throughout the country and even the world. The following are some of the steps in a clinical trial.

1. Planning the research design and statistical analyses.
2. Deciding on the dependent measures to be used in evaluating the trial.
3. Organizing procedures for gathering data.
4. Assigning subjects to treatments.
5. Assuring that clinical personnel are "blind" to the assigned treatment whenever possible.

In the course of conducting clinical trials, scientists must be careful to rule out alternative explanations for the results they get. In addition to the enthusiasm effect discussed earlier, researchers have to be aware of **placebo effects**. A placebo (often referred to as a "sugar pill") is an inactive substance that has no pharmacological effects but under certain conditions may produce noticeable improvements in patients (see Figure 17-12). When a placebo is effective, it is because it has some of the same suggestive properties as a real treatment. Physicians know that the confidence with which they prescribe given medicines can influence their pa-

**FIGURE 17–12**
"Find out who set up this experiment. It seems that half of the patients were given a placebo, and the other half were given a different placebo." (© 1983 by Sidney Harris–Johns Hopkins Magazine)

tients' reactions. Suggestible patients often show great improvement if a drug, even a chemically inactive one, is presented to them as a "wonder drug."

It might seem sufficient to evaluate the effectiveness of drugs by comparing placebo groups with groups that are given chemically potent drugs. Actually, this is not the case, because the knowledge of which patients have received active substances and which ones have not can have a considerable influence on a physician's behavior or evaluations. Thus, the double-blind method is used to ensure that none of the participants knows whether the drug given to a particular patient is active or inert.

**Comparative Studies.** When we received the psychological therapies, we mentioned the need to compare different approaches in order to identify the ones that are likely to be most effective in treating particular disorders. The same need exists for drug therapies. Unfortunately, the number of well-controlled comparative studies, while growing, is still small.

An example of a comparative study is one that was carried out over several years at California's Camarillo State Hospital (May, 1968). The subjects were 228 schizophrenic patients who had been admitted to the hospital for the first time. These men and women had not had extensive clinical care before they were hospitalized. Clinical psychiatrists agreed that the patients were about average in terms of their prospects for recovery.

Each patient was assigned to one of five treatment groups. After a treatment period of 6 to 12 months, the patients were categorized on the basis of whether they were discharged from the hospital because of improvement or whether they were judged to be unresponsive to therapy. Before and after treatment each patient was given a comprehensive multidisciplinary evaluation by psychiatrists, psychologists, nurses, and social workers. The five conditions in the experiment were as follows.

1. *Milieu therapy.* Patients in this group received basic ward care at a level that was judged to be good to superior for a public hospital. The patients received nursing care, hydrotherapy, and occupational, industrial, and recreational therapies. Nurses conducted weekly community ward meetings, and a social worker was assigned to each patient.

2. *Electro-convulsive therapy (ECT).* These patients were given ECT three times a week. (The frequency was decreased if the patient showed severe confusion or memory loss.) The average number of treatments was 19 for males and 25 for females.

3. *Drug therapy.* These patients were given antipsychotic drugs (either trifluoperazine or chlorpromazine).

4. *Individual psychotherapy.* Patients in this group received support therapy aimed at fostering a better awareness of reality. This therapy varied according to the characteristics of the patient and the therapist. Relatively little emphasis was placed on indepth interpretation; the primary focus was on working through the patient's current problems. The number of interviews ranged from 12 to 106.

5. *Individual psychotherapy plus drug therapy.* Each patient in this group received both psychotherapy and a drug.

One measure of the success of a hospital program is its discharge rate. In the Camarillo study, not all of the subjects showed sufficient improvement to allow release. Considering only those who were successfully released, we find that the drug-alone, ECT, and psychotherapy-plus-drug groups had mean hospital stays of 130, 135, and 138 days, respectively. The average stay of the psychotherapy-alone group was 185 days, while the average for the milieu group was 163 days. Among the unimproved patients, the psychotherapists persisted much longer before giving up than clinicians using other forms of treatment. When both successfully and unsuccessfully treated cases were combined, the drug-alone treatment was highly superior in shortening hospital stay. Only two drug-alone patients were not improved enough to be discharged.

In the Camarillo study, the drug-alone and psychotherapy-plus-drug approaches provided the best treatments for the average schizophrenic admitted to that state hospital. There were no substantial differences in effectiveness between these two groups. However, from the standpoint of economics, the drugs were the least expensive form of effective treatment. The psychotherapy and milieu approaches seemed far less effective. ECT occupied an intermediate position. A follow-up carried out several years after completion of the research suggested that the same pattern of results had persisted (May and others, 1981).

Even though the Camarillo project appears to argue strongly for the use of antipsychotic drugs with schizophrenics, not all of the results can be interpreted so readily. Psychotherapy alone may indeed be ineffective with hospitalized schizophrenics; however, its ineffectiveness may have been due to the particular forms or styles of psychotherapy used at Camarillo. Or perhaps the frequency of the psychotherapeutic sessions was too low. One uncontrolled factor was the variability of the approaches used by the psychotherapists. Perhaps it is significant that patients in the psychotherapy-alone condition had fewer, but longer, contacts with their doctors than patients in the other conditions. The apparent failure of the psychotherapy and milieu conditions may have been due to failures of the particular methods used at Camarillo and not to inherent weaknesses in these approaches.

A methodological weakness of the Camarillo study is the fact that it could not use a blind or double-blind technique. Thus, there is a limit to the extent to which the results can be generalized. Nevertheless, the results provide a practical basis for using drugs to improve the functioning of schizophrenics, together with a caution against assuming that psychotherapeutic and milieu approaches are always effective. Recent evidence suggests that although psychotherapy without drugs may not yield favorable results within the hospital, the picture is different after patients have been discharged. Psychotherapy seems to play a positive role after discharge (Davis, 1985). Perhaps the main effect of drugs is to alleviate symptoms and disordered thought while psychological interventions improve the patient's interpersonal functioning.

The nature of the problem to be treated is an important consideration in comparing therapies. For ex-

ample, although in treating schizophrenia the use of psychotherapy alone often compares unfavorably with the use of drugs alone or drugs plus psychotherapy, some studies have reported that cognitive–behavioral therapy produces better outcomes with depressed outpatients than treatment with the antidepressant drug imipramine. Figure 17–13 shows that depressed patients who were treated with a version of Beck's cognitive therapy had fewer feelings of hopelessness about the future than a group of patients who were given imipramine (Rush and others, 1982). In one study of therapy with depressed patients (McLean and Hakstian, 1979), the psychological therapy consisted of graduated practice and modeling in communication, social interaction, assertiveness, decision making, problem solving, and cognitive self-control. This treatment package resulted in better personal and social adjustment than the use of imipramine alone.

Findings like these have increased interest in doing large-scale studies that compare different therapeutic approaches. An ambitious project that is currently under way is sponsored by the National Institute of Mental Health. It is intended to compare four therapeutic approaches to depression: cognitive–behavioral therapy, psychodynamic therapy, tricyclic drug therapy, and a placebo control. Comparisons among these groups are being made at three different clinical centers around the country. Besides helping to identify the most ef-

**FIGURE 17–13**
Mean hopelessness scale scores of depressed patients treated with cognitive therapy or imipramine. (Rush and others, 1982, p. 864)

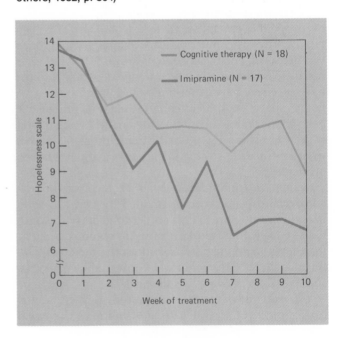

fective therapeutic approaches, this type of research may suggest ways in which different approaches might be optimally combined.

## ■ HOSPITALIZATION

Serious physical illness may require hospitalization not only because the hospital provides round-the-clock care but also because it can offer all the complex therapies that a patient might need. Some comprehensive mental hospitals provide an enriched program of therapies. Patients at expensive private hospitals may receive psychotherapy, drug therapy, and active social, educational, and recreational programs. The budgets of most state hospitals do not permit such varied fare. As a result, many patients in state hospitals receive drugs but few psychological therapies, and live in a relatively impoverished, unstimulating social environment. This is unfortunate because a hospital can be a place that helps a person cope with a crisis and experience personal growth.

No matter what kind of hospital is available, the major reasons for psychiatric hospitalization are as follows.

1. Thought or behavior that poses a threat to self or others.
2. Thought or behavior that is intolerable to members of the patient's community.
3. Failure of outpatient treatment and the hope that inpatient treatment will reverse the process.
4. A treatment procedure that requires a degree of control that is possible only in a hospital.
5. Withdrawal from alcohol or drugs.
6. Physical illness that is complicated by a mental disorder that requires continuous care.

When complete hospitalization is not required, partial hospitalization may be employed. This may include either day or night hospitalization and, perhaps, evening and weekend care in the hospital. Evening, night, and weekend programs are designed primarily to help hospitalized patients make the transition from the hospital to the community. Such programs are especially useful for people who are able to return to their jobs, schools, or training programs but do not have adequate family or social supports to go from inpatient to outpatient status without a partially protected transition period. The concept of night hospitals has gained some acceptance, but relatively few such hospitals have been established on a formal basis. Day hospitals are used to provide treatment for patients who can live at home but need the structure and social interaction available in the treatment center. Day hospitals also allow members of the patients' families to function more normally because they can carry on their usual activities during the day. Day hospitals often concentrate on teaching social and interpersonal behaviors as well as helping patients learn practical skills such as how to use the bus system or a pay telephone. They may also include training in basic work skills so that patients can get jobs in sheltered workshops that will provide the satisfaction of doing useful work and some payment as well.

Researchers have studied the kinds of hospital activities that are helpful to patients when they are not in an acute phase of their disorder. One experiment compared a fairly traditional mental-hospital routine with a routine based on social-learning principles (Paul and Lentz, 1977). Under the traditional routine, patients spent 6 percent of their time taking drugs, 4.9 percent in classes and meetings, and 63.4 percent in unstructured activities. This last percentage represents a great deal of boredom and a waste of therapeutic opportunities. Under the social-learning routine, however, 58.9 percent of the patients' time was devoted to classes, meetings, and structured activities. Only 11.6 percent of their time was spent in unstructured activities. The ward employed a token economy to motivate the patient to engage in productive behavior. A comparison of the effects of the two approaches showed that the social-learning group had a significantly higher percentage of discharges to the community than the traditional group. However, regardless of the treatment used, only a small percentage of the patients were able to function in a self-supporting way.

A striking example of the positive effects of the social-learning program can be seen in the following case.

*Thelma, a 42-year-old single woman, had lived continuously in mental institutions for more than half of her adult life. Before she was hospitalized, she lived in her sister's home, where she served as an unpaid housekeeper and babysitter. Upon entering the program, Thelma was generally less withdrawn than most other patients in the project, but she was badly groomed and regularly displayed a variety of intermittent "crazy" mannerisms. Hospital staff characterized her behavior with others as "nagging, tattling, complaining, and lying," and noted her marked stammering and facial grimaces.*

*Thelma's response to treatment was remarkable. Eleven weeks after treatment began, she was performing well in all areas of functioning, including interpersonal skills, and was indistinguishable from normal on 90 to 100 percent of all hourly observations. She was admitted to a prerelease group and was taught alternative means of expressing her concerns, methods for establishing friendships, techniques for pacing speech to overcome stammers and grimaces, as well as vocational and money management skills. She was released within 30 weeks, having "dramatically improved from the obnoxious patient who had entered the program to a pleasant, socially appropriate woman."*

*Since her relatives would have nothing to do with her and even made an attempt to keep her institutionalized, a woman who hired Thelma as a live-in domestic and babysitter agreed to act as her sponsor upon her release. This job did not last because of turmoil in the employer's family. Nevertheless, Thelma continued to find employment, living quarters, and friends on her own, and became exceptionally active socially. By the time the project ended, Thelma had supported herself over five years and showed no indication of any need for reinstitutionalization in the future.* (Science Reports, 1981, pp. 6–7)

Research on the process of resocialization may contribute answers to such questions as, What steps could help chronic patients adjust successfully to the community? Gordon Paul (1969) has suggested ten steps that mental hospitals might take to provide greater happiness and effectiveness among patients, higher morale among staff members, and a more positive social-rehabilitation role for the institution.

1. *Emphasize a "resident" rather than "patient" status through informal dress of staff, open channels of communication in all directions, and broad (but clear) authority structure.*

2. *Make clear, through a set of rules and attitudes, that the residents are responsible human beings; are expected to follow certain minimal rules of group living; and are expected to do their share in participating in self-care, work, recreational, and social activities.*

3. *Utilize step systems which gradually increase the expectations placed on the residents in terms of their degree of independence and level of responsibility, with community return emphasized from the outset.*

4. *Encourage social interactions and skills and provide a range of activities as well as regular large and small group meetings.*

5. *Emphasize clarity of communication, with concrete instruction in appropriate behavior and focus on utilitarian "action" rather than "explanation."*

6. *Provide opportunity to practice vocational and housekeeping skills, with feedback, and specific training in marketable skills when needed.*

7. *Reacquaint residents with the "outside world" by exposing them to the community and bringing in community volunteers for discussions.*

8. *Identify the specific unique areas for change and support in concrete terms for each individual.*

9. *Prepare residents and significant-others to live in mutually supportive ways in the community through prerelease training and scheduled aftercare.*

10. *When no significant-other exists, train and release residents in groups of 2–3 as a "family" to provide significant-others for one another.* (Paul, 1969, p. 91)

The effectiveness of a hospital depends on the needs of its residents, the quality and scope of its programs, and the community and family resources available to the patient. Because of variations in all of these areas, it is not surprising that there are strong differences of opinion about the effectiveness of hospitalization. When all factors are considered, it seems reasonable to conclude that some severely disturbed people can benefit from life in a socially active, therapeutic hospital. The precise percentage of currently institutionalized individuals who might benefit from this experience is very difficult to estimate.

If a ward is run mainly to satisfy the staff, or if a latent goal of the hospital is to maintain order and stability in the institution, the patients get the message. No therapy takes place if patients are regimented and prevented from experimenting with their social-response repertoires. Their behavior is aimed at minimizing conflict with the system and disruption of routine.

An unfortunate hospitalization is a special kind of experience whose mark may be visible long after its completion. It can increase patients' sense that they bear a stigma and make it easy for them to acquire "sick roles"—that is, to come to see themselves as sick people who will always have to be taken care of. It can also lead to a weakening of social and work skills. When these things happen, patients become less able to function in the community.

Over the past few decades hospitalizations have become less frequent while the use of outpatient services has mushroomed. Patients are being discharged after shorter periods of hospitalization, largely because of the effectiveness of psychoactive drugs and an increase in efforts to return patients to the community as quickly as possible. This **deinstitutionalization** process can be a boon to personal development if the individual has a good place to live, sufficient social support, and supervision when needed. Unfortunately, many people who have been discharged from mental hospitals live in furnished rooms in undesirable neighborhoods, are socially isolated, and receive little professional help beyond brief contacts with physicians who prescribe antipsychotic drugs.

It is hazardous to make unqualified statements

about the value of either hospitalization or deinstitutionalization. A good hospital can help disturbed people; a bad one can harm them. Similarly, a good community placement can help deinstitutionalized patients and a bad one can hurt them. A former resident of a California mental hospital put it well when she made the following comments to a state legislative body.

*"We need both types of care," she emphasized. "And both kinds of services need to be improved."*

*According to the former patient, myths have developed about both kinds of care . . . "I think that saying that state hospitals always have an 'institutionalizing' effect falls into this myth category," Ms. Allen said. "Some people assume that the state hospital of today resembles the fearsome 'snakepit' of yesteryear. On the contrary, it has been my experience that a well-run ward in a state hospital can provide many constructive and therapeutic influences."*

*On the other hand, according to Ms. Allen, many expatients living in board and care homes cannot rightly be said to be "living in the community." Some who could walk freely in the grounds of a state hospital find city streets threatening, and so for the most part live within the confines of the walls of the board and care home. For others freedom means going to the corner store and back.* (California Department of Health, *Health News*, September 1973, p. 4)

## ■ STUDY OUTLINE

### PSYCHOTHERAPY

1. All forms of psychotherapy involve interchanges between a client and a therapist that are aimed at understanding what is on the client's mind. This understanding is used as a basis for efforts to change the client's maladaptive ways of thinking, reacting to situations, and relating to others.

2. **Psychoanalysis** is a subtype of psychodynamic therapy that makes extensive use of **free association,** in which the client expresses thoughts and feelings in as free and uninhibited a manner as possible. The examination of dreams and fantasies is also important in psychoanalysis. The goal is to help the client gain **insight** into the relationship between his or her early experiences and a current tendency to distort reality.

3. A key aspect of psychoanalysis is the use of **transference** as a vehicle for resolving interpersonal conflicts and revealing the meaning of anxiety. In **positive transference,** the patient feels predominantly friendly toward the analyst; in **negative transference,** hostility predominates. **Countertransference** refers to the therapist's emotional reactions to the patient.

4. **Humanistic therapies** emphasize people's desire to achieve self-respect. In **client-centered therapy** the individual is seen as seeking personal growth but needing the support of an appreciative, accepting therapist. This form of therapy emphasizes **unconditional positive regard** for the client.

5. **Existential therapies** also focus on the present and stress the uniqueness of each client. Their emphasis is on helping clients come to terms with basic issues concerning the meaning of their lives and the choices by which they shape their own destinies.

6. **Gestalt therapy** focuses on clients' perceptions of themselves and the world. It is based on the recognition that people organize their perceptions as a meaningful, integrated whole.

### COGNITIVE AND BEHAVIORAL THERAPIES

1. The **cognitive psychotherapies** seek to correct misconceptions that contribute to maladjustment, defeat, and unhappiness.

2. George Kelly's **psychology of personal constructs** led him to ask clients to examine the roles they play in interacting with others and the assumptions underlying those roles. In his **fixed-role therapy** he encouraged clients to practice new roles and relationships.

3. Albert Ellis' **rational–emotive therapy** is based on the belief that self-defeating thinking is at the root of maladaptive behavior. Its goals are to get people to question their mistaken beliefs and to exchange them for more constructive ones.

4. Aaron Beck's approach to therapy involves frequent, gentle questioning of the client about the basis for what he or she is saying. It is aimed at eliminating thoughts that are not products of rational consideration of alternatives.

5. **Behavioral therapy** has shown rapid development in recent years. **Behavior modification** consists of using environmental manipulations to directly change behavior. This approach has increasingly been combined with cognitive processes designed to help people correct their misconceptions, strengthen their coping skills, and facilitate constructive self-talk.

6. **Relaxation training** uses a variety of techniques, including **muscular relaxation, meditation,** and **autogenic training.** In the latter technique the individual is taught to assume an attitude of passive concentration on a series of physical, emotional, and mental sensations.

7. **Systematic desensitization** combines behav-

ioral training with cognitive activity. The patient is induced to relax and then exposed to scenes or images that are progressively more fear arousing.

8. **Exposure therapies** are based on the principle that continued exposure to anxiety-provoking stimuli will decrease anxiety. **In vivo exposure** (actually being in the situation) works best, but **fantasized exposure** is also effective. In **flooding**, the client is exposed to a flood of fear-arousing stimuli. In **implosive therapy**, the client experiences higher and higher levels of anxiety through imaginal presentation of scenes depicting situations that have been avoided in the past.

9. Through **modeling**, clients can be shown that there are alternative ways of doing things. Demonstrations by models are often combined with **guided rehearsals**, in which the individual is encouraged to imitate the behavior of the model. **Live modeling** involves direct observation of a model; **symbolic modeling** refers to observation of a model presented through film or another medium. In **covert modeling**, the client is asked to imagine observing a model and a particular consequence.

10. **Assertiveness training** is designed to enhance the interpersonal skills one needs to stand up for one's rights.

11. **Paradoxical intention** is a technique in which the therapist instructs the client to perform behaviors that appear to be in opposition to the client's therapeutic goal.

### GROUP THERAPY

1. In **group therapy**, clients can learn both by observing other group members' attempts to solve their problems and by comparing their relationship with the therapist with those of other members. **Family therapy** is a specialized clinical approach that is used in treating family groups.

2. **Psychodrama** is an approach that was designed especially for groups. In this technique a group of individuals led by a therapist enacts events of emotional significance in order to resolve conflicts and release members from inhibitions.

3. The focus of cognitive–behavioral group therapy is on increasing the skills and comfort of people in social situations. Group members role-play situations that they find difficult, and the therapist may model alternative ways of handling those situations.

### RESEARCH ON THE PSYCHOLOGICAL THERAPIES

1. In research on the effectiveness of psychological therapies, all groups of subjects must be as similar or equal as possible before the experiment begins. The therapists should also be comparable, and other factors must also be controlled. Among the latter are the **enthusiasm effect,** in which clinicians' enthusiasm for a treatment method influences the patients in their care.

2. Studies of the outcome of therapy have found that some patients appear to experience **spontaneous remission,** in which their symptoms would have disappeared in time with or without treatment. In some of these cases nonprofessionals such as family members, friends, teachers, and members of the clergy appear to contribute to the personal growth of the individual.

3. Comparative studies have found that psychological therapies are most useful in treating milder, nonpsychotic disorders. Behavioral and cognitive–behavioral therapies are especially effective in treating anxiety disorders. Psychological therapies have been less successful with serious conditions such as schizophrenia, but can play an important role when used in combination with drug therapy or electro-convulsive therapy.

4. Recently the technique known as **meta-analysis** has been used in research on therapeutic outcomes. This involves grouping studies in which treatment conditions have been compared with an untreated control condition, statistically determining the therapeutic effects on different groups, and averaging the sizes of the effects across the studies to be compared.

5. Studies of what actually goes on in therapy sessions have focused on **technique factors,** or the procedures employed by the therapist, and **interpersonal factors,** or the relationship between the therapist and the client. Such studies have found that the personal qualities of the therapist are a very important factor in the therapeutic process.

### BIOLOGICAL THERAPIES

1. The use of **electro-convulsive therapy** has declined in the past 20 years because it is not clear exactly how it works and because it occasionally has adverse effects. It might reasonably be used when there is severe depression or a possibility of suicide, or when drugs and other therapies are ineffective.

2. Drugs are frequently used in treating people who are depressed, schizophrenic, or anxious. The safety of these drugs has improved, but their use still entails the risk of physical and psychological side effects. In addition, their effects are not always predictable.

3. **Clinical trials** of new drugs can be complex and costly, and may extend over many years and include samples of subjects at many locations. In conducting such trials, scientists must rule out alternative explanations for the results they get. To avoid the **placebo**

effect, in which patients show great improvement because they believe in the effectiveness of a drug, the double-blind method is used.

4. There have been few well-controlled comparative studies of drug therapies. The available evidence suggests that antipsychotic drugs are the least expensive form of effective treatment for schizophrenia. It appears that although psychotherapy without drugs may not yield favorable results in a hospital setting, psychotherapy can play a positive role after discharge.

### HOSPITALIZATION

1. Psychiatric hospitalization is appropriate in cases in which the patient's thought or behavior poses a threat to self or others or the patient requires a treatment procedure that is possible only in a hospital. When complete hospitalization is not required, partial hospitalization may be employed.

2. Research on hospital activities has found that hospital routines based on social-learning principles can result in a significantly higher percentage of discharges to the community than traditional mental-hospital routines.

3. Over the past few decades hospitalizations have become less frequent and there has been an increase in efforts to return patients to the community as quickly as possible. **Deinstitutionalization** can enhance personal development if the individual has a good place to live, sufficient social support, and supervision when needed.

# 18

# SOCIETY'S RESPONSE TO MALADAPTIVE BEHAVIOR

*Ann Jackson had taught at Buchanan High School for eight years. She was 33 years old, still had some ideals, and had a reputation among both students and faculty of being a nice person. She was also a discouraged person who too often felt she wasn't able to reach several of her students. One who fell into this group was 16-year-old Bill Hadley. Bill paid little attention in class, did not complete assignments, and frequently did not show up at all. But what worried Ann Jackson the most was what she knew about Bill's activities outside class. Other students were afraid of him because of his imposing size, his bullying attitude, and his history of antisocial behavior. He had had numerous contacts with the police for a variety of reasons. He had been accused of puncturing the tires of a dozen cars parked along a street, extorting money from other students, and shoplifting at neighborhood stores. The most serious offense was a severe beating Bill had given to another student. According to those present at the fight, Bill was in such an uncontrollable rage that he couldn't stop hitting and kicking the other student even though it was evident that the student was helpless and in pain, and he started fighting with the spectators when they intervened. Ann Jackson couldn't get Bill out of her mind. She continually worried about what was going to happen to him.*

Small problems have a way of becoming big problems if nothing is done about them. Ann Jackson wished that something could be done to redirect Bill Hadley's life while he was still young, but she didn't know what she, the school, or the community could do now or what could have been done earlier to prevent Bill's current unhappiness, anger, and counterproductive behavior. Many well-meaning and intelligent people feel helpless when confronted with obvious mental distress in another individual. In this chapter we discuss the role played by society in dealing with deviance and preventing problems of living.

## ■ SITUATION-FOCUSED AND COMPETENCY-FOCUSED PREVENTION

Throughout this book we have considered methods of assessing, treating, and caring for individuals with behavior problems, but we have only briefly mentioned the possibility that the actual occurrence of maladaptive behavior in the population can be reduced. This is the focus of prevention.

Prevention can be approached from two perspectives. **Situation-focused prevention** is aimed at reducing or eliminating the environmental causes of disordered behavior, while **competency-focused prevention** is concerned with enhancing people's ability to cope with conditions that might lead to maladaptive behaviors. Situation-focused approaches seek to change the environment, for example, by making it less stressful. Competency-focused approaches seek to strengthen people's coping skills so as to make them more resistant should various types of stress-arousing situations arise (Cowen, 1985).

Divorce is an example of a common stress-arousing situation. Its occurrence has increased dramatically over the last several decades and has resulted in changes in life styles and in the environments in which children are brought up. (Nearly half of all children can expect to spend some time—an average of about six years—living in a single-parent family.) Divorce and parental discord are related to impaired functioning and social behavior in children. Divorced people are likely to be overrepresented among people who make suicide attempts, become alcoholics, go through periods of depression, and seek help from mental-health professionals.

There is a need for programs that can reduce the likelihood of maladjustment in divorced couples and their children. Preventive work related to this problem is just getting under way. An example is a program for newly separated individuals that provided the participants with psychological support and special training over a six-month period after the separation (Bloom and others, 1982). Staff members made themselves available to participants when advice and counseling were needed. Training was provided in such practical areas as how to find employment, change jobs, and deal with child-rearing problems. Compared with newly separated people who did not participate in the program, the participants experienced less anxiety, fatigue, and physical illness, along with improved coping ability. There was some evidence that the intervention program was more effective for women than for men. Participants' comments after the program ended suggested that the knowledge that interested people and special services were available may have been the most powerful ingredient in the program. Future research will be needed to determine the long-term effects on both parents and children of programs that are designed to reduce the traumatic effects of an inevitably distressing situation.

The program just described was activated only after the participants had already taken steps toward divorce. A competency-focused approach might aim to strengthen skills that are important in interpersonal relationships, particularly with one's spouse, long before thoughts of divorce might arise. The idea behind such an effort would be to increase coping skills and thereby enable couples to handle the stresses of marriage in more effective ways. Research on this type of preventive intervention is under way (Barker and Lemle, 1984). For example, Markman and his colleagues (1983) are seeking to strengthen skills that seem to help couples weather the stresses that challenge a marriage. Their program emphasizes communication skills. For example, the couples are taught to focus on one topic at a time and to make their concerns and irritations clear, as in "I may seem angry because I had a bad day at work." They are also trained to "stop the action" until the partners cool down when repetitive cycles of conflict begin. One of the major signs of distress in a couple is escalating hostility, often in the form of nagging that provokes an angry response.

Early-education programs also illustrate competency-focused prevention. Their aim is to prevent or reduce problems in subsequent years. One project began with the frequent observation that maladapted children (and adults) tend to have weak interpersonal cognitive problem-solving skills (Shure and Spivack, 1982; Spivack, Platt, and Shure, 1976). These skills include the ability to identify problems and feelings (in oneself and others), to think of alternative solutions to a problem, to see relationships between alternative approaches and the achievement of goals, and to appreciate the consequences of one's actions. Interpersonal problem-solving skills can be thought of as mediating effective behavioral adjustment as well as fostering academic competence (see Figure 18-1).

The following is an excerpt from one of the lessons used by Spivack and his coworkers in teaching young children to be more sensitive to their feelings and those of others.

> Now this is just a game. *Have each child hold a toy previously used from trinket box.* Peter, you snatch Kevin's toy from him.
>
> Kevin, how do you feel about that? *Kevin responds.*
>
> Peter, now let him have it back.
>
> Now, how do you feel, Kevin? *After child answers, repeat with other pairs.*
>
> *Use a picture of a firetruck.* Larry, how would going for a ride on this firetruck make you feel? *Let child respond.*
>
> Let's pretend that a man came and drove the truck away and you could NOT have a ride. How would you feel now? *Same child responds.*
>
> Now let's pretend he came back and said, "Okay, now you can go for a ride." How would that make you feel? *Same child responds.*

**FIGURE 18-1**
Children often act directly—when they want something they take it or they express displeasure by hitting another child. Cognitive games of the kind used by Spivack, Platt, and Shure attempt to create greater empathy with others and in this way change the self-centered aggressive behavior that is often seen in childhood. (Freda Leinwand, Monkmeyer Press)

> *Use a picture of a ball.* How do you think Steven might feel if we let him play with this ball? *Group answers.*
>
> Maybe he would feel happy and maybe he would not feel happy. Let's find out. How can we find out? *Encourage children to ask.*
>
> Let's pretend someone came along and threw the ball out the window so Steven could not play with it anymore. Now how do you think Steven might feel?
>
> He might feel sad or he might feel mad. How can we find out?
>
> *Encourage children to ask. (Spivack and others, 1976, pp. 183–184)*

These researchers found that behavioral adjustment was positively influenced by training in cognitive and social skills. This positive effect was greatest for children who originally seemed most maladjusted, and positive results were still evident a year later. In a related project inner-city mothers who were given training in interpersonal cognitive problem-solving skills were able to pass their training on to their children. Research with older children and adults supports the idea that the skills involved in academic and social effectiveness are learnable. Furthermore, it has been shown that improved teacher training—for example, teaching them to reinforce students' adaptive behavior—contributes to a more productive learning environment in the classroom.

## ■ TYPES OF PREVENTION

If we all know that an ounce of prevention is worth a pound of cure, why aren't preventive measures more common? In some cases it is not clear what steps are needed to achieve the goal of prevention, and in others society does not seem willing or able to take the needed steps.

Prevention can take place on three levels. **Primary prevention** is concerned with the reduction of new cases of mental or physical disorder in a given population. Scientific information about cause and effect is very important in primary prevention. For example, knowledge of the possibility of harm to the unborn child has persuaded many women not to smoke or drink during pregnancy. Physicians are much more careful about prescribing medication for pregnant women because of information linking even seemingly harmless drugs with birth defects. Psychologists are conducting research on ways to discourage children from beginning to smoke cigarettes (Flay and others, 1985). Another example of primary prevention is premarital counseling. Marital problems and divorce are highly correlated with maladaptive behavior. Premarital counseling is aimed at encouraging couples to anticipate any problems and to develop ways of coping with them before marriage.

The aim of **secondary prevention** is to reduce the duration, intensity, and disability of an existing abnormal condition. If a child with phenylketonuria (PKU) is identified early, a special diet can prevent serious retardation. Enrichment programs for infants from homes where little stimulation is available can improve children's intellectual functioning and their level of achievement in school.

Whereas secondary prevention refers to the diagnosis and treatment of disorders as soon as possible, **tertiary prevention** is aimed at reducing the impairment that may result from a given disorder or event. This is achieved through rehabilitation and resocialization. For example, behavioral therapy for a hyperactive child may help him or her become more attentive in school and more accepted by other children. Counseling or group therapy after a traumatic event such as the death of a spouse or a rape may provide the social supports that reduce a person's vulnerability to stress.

Preventive measures have been developed in many cases in which biophysical factors are known to cause maladaptive behavior. However, the effects of detrimental social factors have frequently been ignored or neglected. It is much easier to detect and control the effects of an enzyme deficiency in newborn infants than it is to detect and control the pervasive influence of poverty and racism. But ignoring these causes and correlates of maladaptive behavior will not decrease their influence.

When prevention methods are successful, risk factors that lead to abnormal behavior are reduced or eliminated. In general, priority in efforts to achieve prevention is given to serious conditions that have high rates of incidence, and for which effective methods are available. For example, one of the most serious and prevalent maladaptive behaviors of childhood is juvenile delinquency. Delinquent behavior seems to have many causes, ranging from poor living conditions to a psychopathic or antisocial personality disorder to psychosis. It is sobering to realize that one out of nine children will be referred to juvenile court for an act of delinquency before his or her eighteenth birthday and that perhaps one-third of all cases of delinquency involve repeat offenders.

One study found that one of every three boys born in Philadelphia in 1945 was arrested at least once before he was 19 years old (Wolfgang, Figlio, and Sellin, 1974). For black youths, the ratio was one in two. Race and socioeconomic status were frequently related to whether a boy became an offender. While 48 percent of white boys who committed serious crimes were arrested, the figure was 68 percent for nonwhites. It seems possible that the social and economic problems of life in the deteriorated core of a large eastern city could be used to explain this high rate of delinquency. But similar rates of involvement in delinquent behavior have been shown in boys from nonmetropolitan counties in Oregon. One in four of these boys had an official record with the county juvenile department before the age of 18. Almost half of them had encountered the law more than once (National Institute of Mental Health, 1974).

Obviously, not all delinquents are arrested for their crimes. Thus, when juveniles are asked about their delinquent activities, the percentage of young people who have been involved in delinquency becomes even higher. For example, in a long-term study of youths in central London, the number of self-reported delinquencies was twice as high as the number listed on official records (Farrington, 1979).

As noted earlier, delinquent behavior can have many causes. Some of the following conditions have often been identified with delinquency.

1. Poor physical and economic conditions in the home and neighborhood.
2. Rejection or lack of security at home.
3. Exposure to antisocial role models within or outside the home, and antisocial pressures from peer-group relationships.
4. Lack of support for social achievement in school.
5. The expectation of hostility on the part of others.

Juvenile delinquency can be approached at different levels of prevention. Primary prevention often takes the form of programs aimed at improving living conditions and school achievement. Sometimes primary prevention comes about more informally. There is some evidence that if children growing up in high-crime areas have a positive figure to copy or model themselves after, their behavior may be more influenced by that person than by their antisocial peers. The value of a model is shown in the following example.

Caesar and Richard are two brothers who lived in a high-crime community. Neither has become delinquent. Talking with them gives us some clues to why this is so. Caesar has had one year of community college. He quit because he had to support the family, but at present he is unemployed. He spends his time with gang members but does not participate in their antisocial activities. He thinks he is able to do this because the others admire him for his skill at restoring old cars (see Figure 18–2a). This admiration makes it possible for him to know them without participating in their activities, to dress differently, and to see himself as a potentially achieving person who will contribute to the community. Caesar attributes his goals and behavior to his efforts to be like an older, retired gang member, Hood.

> Hood's been through it all. He's lived here all his life— he's done time—he's been a user but now he's clean. He is harassed by the cops so much that he had to get a letter from a judge saying that he was clean and that he should be left alone. He helps all of us in the barrio. He tells it like it really is, takes us to the ball game, helps raise money for bail, whatever. He does it all for nothing. Not even teachers and counselors work for nothing. (Aiken and others, 1977, p. 217)

Richard, a younger boy, thinks Caesar, his older brother, was instrumental in the development of his own prosocial behavior.

> My mother told my brother when my father left that he was responsible for me, she wasn't. My brother counseled me, looked out for me, and told me what to do. He told me never to steal—that if I wanted something to come to him and he'd try to get it for me or see if I could earn it. If my brother thought that I was getting into trouble, he would probably kick my butt. (Aiken and others, 1977, p. 217)

Richard is classified as a slow learner in school and has problems in math and reading. But he has learned how to repair bicycles and sees this as a way to gain status in the community.

Some adolescents develop their own cognitive mechanisms to help them resist peer pressure. Linda Carmichael, who lives in a Chicago tenement inhabited by winos, junkies, and petty hustlers, is going to college this fall. Linda wants to get out of the ghetto (see Figure 18–2b). This is how she describes the cognitions that helped her keep on her track when her peers sneered and when she "wanted to be out partying and goofing off like everyone else": "I'd start thinking about all those people on the street with nothing to look forward to and where would I be without school. That kept me going" (Goldman and Williams, 1978, p. 34).

Secondary prevention progams concentrate on young people who have shown early signs of delinquency. An example of this approach is a project aimed at rehabilitating predelinquent boys in a homelike setting (Kirigin and others, 1982). This project focuses not only on teaching social and vocational skills but also on helping boys to behave less impulsively. The project has been carried out at Achievement Place, a group home in Lawrence, Kansas, for 12- to 14-year-old boys who have committed minor nonviolent offenses (such as theft or truancy) but seem to be on the road to more serious crimes. House-parents at Achievement Place identify target behaviors and employ token reinforcement systems to strengthen prosocial tendencies. The emphasis is on social and academic skills as well as on self-care.

The points that boys receive for achieving can be used to obtain permission to go downtown, stay up past bedtime, play games, and watch television. The economy is arranged so that a boy who performs the tasks that are expected of him obtains the greatest number of points. The token-economy program has been successful in modifying aggressive behavior and improving bathroom tidiness, homework preparation, grammar, and punctuality. The program seems also to have succeeded in strengthening the boys' repertories of prosocial responses: this might reasonably be expected to reduce their antisocial tendencies.

Sometimes changing delinquent behavior might be classified as tertiary prevention. For example, the youth might be involved in seriously maladaptive behavior. For instance, a 14-year-old boy was referred to a ther-

(a)

(b)

(c)

**FIGURE 18–2**
Primary and secondary prevention of delinquency can take many forms. (a) Sometimes an interested adult can serve as a role model. Both the skills learned and the feeling that someone cares can be important in the primary prevention of delinquency. (b) Sometimes goals can be achieved by cognitive coping strategies that help a person resist peer pressure for delinquent behavior. (c) Family therapy can often be effective for secondary prevention of delinquent behavior. (Rhoda Sidney, Monkmeyer Press; Rob Nelson/Stock, Boston; Judy S. Gelles/Stock, Boston)

apist by the court because he had set several large grass fires that had endangered houses. He could not explain his behavior, and neither could his parents since he had always behaved responsibly at home.

The boy's family was seen for six family-therapy sessions (see Figure 18–2c). These sessions revealed that the family could not discuss problems openly but tended to communicate nonverbally. Several recent family crises had caused tension. The father seemed to handle his unhappiness by withdrawing from the family into club activities. The son seemed to express his anger at family problems by setting fires. Once they began to meet in therapy sessions and these problems became evident, all of the family members were able to change their behavior. One year later there had been no more fire-setting (Eisler, 1972).

At all levels of prevention, the problems of delinquency and the therapeutic treatment of delinquents are far from solved. The number of delinquents who go on to commit more antisocial acts is high. Different approaches work best with different types of cases, but as yet all methods produce more misses than hits. Understanding delinquency requires a better grasp of the variables involved in the interaction between the person and the situation.

## ■ SITES OF PREVENTION

In this chapter we are especially interested in research that is relevant to the prevention of maladaptive behavior. Where data are lacking, we speculate about the use of social experimentation. We do not attempt a comprehensive analysis of all the components of a complex social structure; instead, we direct our attention toward three areas that definitely affect the growth and development of children and adults: the family, the school, and the community.

## The Family

Parents are important because of the genes they contribute and the environment they provide for their children. This environment begins in the uterus during the nine months before birth. Whatever can improve prenatal care and thus reduce the incidence of premature birth and other foreseeable difficulties might help reduce several types of problems, such as low intelligence. Improved prenatal and neonatal care can be expected to reduce brain damage, which, among other conditions, is related to certain types of epilepsy.

From the standpoint of prevention, the family is important because much of the child's earliest learning and development takes place within the family setting. One of the most common observations of clinicians who specialize in treating childhood disorders is that treating the child is not enough. The parents are usually part of the problem. The following are some extreme examples: Children of psychotic parents are slow in developing speech and bladder control, have more eating and sleeping problems, and are more likely to be delinquent than other children. Alcoholic parents have a disproportionately large number of hyperactive children, and alcoholic mothers are overrepresented among mothers of babies with low birthweight and low IQs. There is also a relationship between criminality in parents and delinquency in their children. Children who have been physically abused, malnourished, and neglected by their parents are more prone to various forms of maladaption than other children. Under certain circumstances even "normal" parents—that is, parents who are not obviously disturbed—can have negative effects on their children's development.

**Child Abuse** Parental failure is most blatant when parents physically harm their children. There are varying estimates of the number of children who are physically mistreated in the United States each year. It is difficult to make such an estimate, because **child abuse** varies in degree and is often hidden from view by embarrassed and ashamed parents. But thousands of children, many under 3 years of age, are seriously—often fatally—mistreated each year. When emotional abuse is included as well as physical abuse, the figure becomes much larger. A sizable percentage of abuse cases involve sexual assault.

Abusive parents tend to be less intelligent and more aggressive, impulsive, immature, self-centered, tense, and self-critical than nonabusive parents. They are more likely to have been abused themselves as children; thus, child abuse is a vicious cycle. Complicating the situation is the fact that despite frequent and severe abuse by their parents, many children are deeply attached to them and resist efforts to remove them from their homes.

Some aspects of the physical and psychological damage done to children by abusive parents can be observed immediately.

*One of the jurors covered her mouth in horror at the sight of 7-year-old Daniel Brownell. Tears dampened the eyes of other jurors and many of the spectators.*

*The blond-haired boy was curled unresponsive in the fetal position in a crib that was wheeled into the courtroom.*

*Doctors recited the abuse the child had endured: a beating which caused gangrene and permanent brain damage; and having the words "I cry" burned into his back with a cigarette.*

*Dr. Wallace Fagan added the postscript to Daniel's case.*

*"We can get very few demonstrable responses. He is unable to move any finger on command. He has primitive reflexes. He blinks at the sound of a snap in his ear. He is in the 203rd postoperative day. He's not going to get any better."*

*The jury Wednesday convicted Daniel's stepfather of child abuse and sentenced him to the maximum 20 years in prison. The boy's mother will stand trial later on charges she failed to report the abuse.*

*Lozier Pickering, a 25-year-old construction worker, showed no emotion at the jury's verdict of guilty but he wept earlier at the appearance of his stepson.*

*"Only when he lost consciousness did they take the boy to the hospital," Prosecutor Hogan Stripling said. "A surgeon didn't even know what he was looking at because it was a mass of rotten flesh, days old."*

*Pickering's defense attorneys presented no witnesses and rested their case immediately after the state. Pickering told police he had spanked the boy, but he denied abusing him.*

*Fagan, who operated on the child when he was hospitalized by his parents October 13, 8 days after the beating, testified Daniel suffered a ruptured colon due to insertion of some object in his anus.*

*An ensuing gangrenous infection led to permanent brain damage.*

*Fagan said the infection was so advanced by the time he opened the child's abdomen that he was unable to recognize internal organs.*

*He also found unusual marks on the child's back.*

*"They looked like an abrasion at first. Later, it took the form of certain letters as scabs forming the letters 'I—C-R-Y'."*

*The doctor said the letters apparently were burned with a cigarette.* (UPI, 1977)

Less observable than the bodily damage done to Daniel Brownell are the long-term effects on people who have been abused as children. The following report describes Rick, a 26-year-old college junior who sought psychotherapy. The case is interesting because it suggests how problems of adult life may be related to the experience of childhood abuse. Rick seemed to be able to function effectively. Unfortunately, many victims of child abuse do not turn out so well.

*When he was two months old, he was hospitalized in traction with multiple broken bones in his legs, hips, and rib area. His mother claimed he had fallen from her lap to the floor, an impossible story in view of the extent of the injury. He remained immobilized in the hospital for six months. Then he was sent home in a partial body cast, and two weeks later was returned to the hospital with a similar set of fractures and put back in traction. This time the doctor suggested to his father that Rick should be placed in a foster home or his mother should be admitted to a mental hospital. The father refused and Rick returned home. Three times during the next four years Rick's father took him to the doctor when he appeared sick and the doctor diagnosed starvation, saying the child clearly wasn't being fed. These events are known to Rick through his father, his father's relatives, and his family physician. Rick himself has only one memory before age 10—that is of at age 7 playing with his grandfather whom he saw only a few times in his life. From the time Rick can remember, his mother totally ignored him, never talked to him or fed him, nor did she strike him again. His only sibling is a brother 16 months older than Rick, who suffered similar malnutrition but no violent injuries. Rick recalls believing his brother was the mother's favorite because he can recall her fixing the brother a meal once, which he claims she never did for him.*

*Rick's presenting complaints were anxiety during tests (although he does quite well on them) and a recurring nightmare which he had no insight into although it was found to be strikingly transparent: He is driving along in a car and passes a terribly injured man in a ditch—the injury varies, most commonly his leg is cut off. He drives into a nearby town and approaches people asking them to help the man in the ditch, and each one gives him an excuse why they cannot. A feeling of horror surfaces, not upon first seeing the man but when he realizes no one will help. At this point Rick awakens.* (Barrett and Fine, 1980, p. 290)

Rick's nightmares suggest that he is still reliving his childhood situation, in which he was helpless and no one would help him.

An abusive parent is usually a very troubled person who seems to be a victim of uncontrollable impulses and frustrations. The following is an excerpt from a group therapy session in which the participants were mothers who had abused their children.

MOTHER 1 *(comparatively new to the group): I was just at my breaking point and I knew if I didn't get help somewhere, it would just go on and on and end up a vicious circle. I think that everyone who has had this problem at one time has thought 'my goodness, I must be the only person in the world that feels this way.' And when I found out that I wasn't, that was a load off my mind.*

THERAPIST: *Feels what way?*

MOTHER 1: *Desperation with their children. Not knowing how to cope. Afraid that you would just lose control completely and knock their head off, you know. I think we were all brought up to believe that women are supposed to have children and they're supposed to have the mother-instinct and if you don't have it, there is something definitely wrong. And I think it took this group to make me realize that women just aren't born with the mothering instinct . . . that has helped me.*

ANOTHER MOTHER: *If you're going to pound your child, the best thing to do is separate yourself from your child.*

MOTHER 1: *That's fine to say, but what if you're like me and you can go on beautifully for a month, two months, three months and all of sudden like last week I was feeling just fine and I cleaned house like I do every Monday . . . I got all them damn floors waxed and —— wakes up from her nap and she couldn't get her body shirt undone so she got all upset and she wet all over my new waxed floor. And I just went berserk and I threw her around like she had killed somebody, because right at that moment I just snapped, I didn't feel it coming. I was fine, everything was hunky-dory, nothing was wrong, I wasn't in a bad mood, there was no warning . . .*

This type of behavior is typical of abusive parents. Behavioral training in impulse control and coping skills can be helpful for parents who want to change their behavior (Isaacs, 1982). Numerous kinds of preventive programs have been attempted. These include parental education and the use of parents as therapists. A promising mutual-aid approach is Parents Anonymous (PA), an organization that is concerned with the problems of parents who abuse their children.

An example of preventive research on abuse is a study in which abusing parents received training in parenting skills (Wolfe and others, 1981). The parents' training consisted of reading about effective parenting techniques, observing modeled demonstrations of how to handle common child-rearing problems, and learning relaxation and other coping skills. In addition, project staff members made weekly home visits to help the parents implement what they had learned. When parents who participated in this program were compared with a control group of abusers, the parents in the special program showed significant improvement in parenting skills. A follow-up showed that none of the specially treated abusers harmed their children during the year after their participation in the program. This study suggests that effective child management skills can be taught to abusive parents with a relatively small investment of time and labor.

**Spouse Abuse**  "To have and to hold . . . to love and to cherish . . . " This sentiment reflects the feelings of most people toward marriage—but these feelings are not shared by everyone. In the 1970s, largely as a result of the women's movement, attention was drawn to the plight of abused women—those who are browbeaten psychologically as well as those who are physically assaulted—who cower in bedrooms and kitchens, are patched up in emergency rooms, and, not infrequently, are beaten, shot, or stabbed to death in their own livingrooms.

A woman who has been abused over a long period is afraid. Fear might be a woman's first and most immediate feeling during or after a beating, but other negative feelings may surface when she is not in physical danger. The abused woman is likely to develop doubts about herself. She might wonder whether she is justified in fearing for her life and calling herself an "abused wife." Most likely, however, a woman who thinks or feels that she is being abused is probably correct.

An abused woman may also feel guilty, even though she has done nothing wrong. An abused wife may feel responsible for her husband's violence because she believes she may have provoked him in some way. She then places the shame and blame on herself instead of on her abuser. Along with the feelings of being a failure, both as a woman and in her marriage, may come a real feeling of being trapped and powerless.

A wife abuser tends to be filled with anger, resentment, suspicion, and tension. He also, underneath all his aggressive behavior, can be insecure and feel like a loser. He may use violence to give vent to the bad feelings he has about himself or his lot in life. Home is one place where he can express those feelings without punishment to himself. If he were angry with his boss and struck him, he would pay the price; but all too often he gets away without any penalty when he beats his wife. One study found that compared with nonabusive husbands, abusive husbands were less assertive in social relationships than their wives, more likely to have been abused as children, and more likely to have witnessed spouse abuse between their own parents (Rosenbaum and O'Leary, 1981).

Efforts to help abused spouses include not only emergency care, safety, and shelter but also long-range planning. Because abused spouses need to develop better feelings about themselves—that is, change their self-image—they need to strengthen their self-related positive cognitions. Counseling often emphasizes the following types of self-statements.

☐ I am not to blame for being beaten and abused.

☐ I am not the cause of another person's violent behavior.

☐ I do not have to take it.

☐ I deserve to be treated with respect.

☐ I do have power over my own life.

☐ I can use my power to take good care of myself.

☐ I can make changes in my life if I want to.

☐ I am not alone. I can ask others to help me.

☐ I deserve to make my own life safe and happy.

The three types of prevention can all be applied to spouse abuse. Premarital counseling illustrates primary prevention; marital counseling to reduce discord illustrates secondary prevention; and providing abused spouses with safety, shelter, and counseling illustrates tertiary prevention.

**Effects of Divorce on Children**  When we mentioned divorce earlier in the chapter, most of the emphasis was on minimizing maladjustment in the couple. There is also a sizable literature on the negative effects of divorce on children, and growing evidence that these effects can be reduced by taking certain preventive steps.

Each year about a million American children experience the disruption of their homes by the separation or divorce of their parents. It is estimated that by the end of the 1980s nearly one-third of all children in the United States will have experienced parental divorce. Despite its frequency, from a cultural standpoint divorce is still considered to be an unusual event with many negative implications for the people involved. It is also one of the most stressful and disorganizing events that may occur in a person's life, one for which most people, both children and adults, are not psychologically prepared.

The degree to which divorce is upsetting to children has been recognized for a long time. Children of divorced parents show up much more frequently in psychiatric outpatient clinic populations than their proportion in the population would predict. Even children in nonclinical samples are likely to exhibit dramatic divorce-related changes in play behavior and relationships with others (Hetherington and others, 1979; Wallerstein and Kelly, 1980). Not only do children have to deal with their own stress, but they must cope with parents who are also experiencing high levels of stress and whose own physical and emotional health may have significantly deteriorated.

Since divorce seems to play an increasing role in our culture, psychologists have thought it important to take a look, not only at how divorce affects children and adults at the time but also at how it affects their later development and adjustment. One of the most important decisions made concerning children of divorced parents involves custody.

***The Effects of Divorce Over Time.***   The California Children of Divorce Project (Wallerstein and Kelly, 1980) followed 60 divorcing families and their 131 children, initially ages 3 to 15, through the first five years after the separation. A major purpose of the investigation was to understand how the children experienced the divorce itself and to see what factors made the experience more manageable for them. Another aim of the study was to look at the children over time to see what developmental processes were impeded or accelerated by the changes brought about by the divorce (see Figure 18–3).

The initial period after the parents' decision to divorce was experienced as extremely stressful by the children, both for its own sake and because they were able to obtain less psychological support from the parents, who were undergoing high degrees of stress themselves. After about a year many of the acute responses had decreased or disappeared. Many of the children recovered their previous level of functioning faster than their parents, although girls seemed to recover much faster than boys. The changes that still remained after a year tended to become chronic. The transition period following the period of acute stress lasted as long as two or three years in many of the families. In the third stage most of the families had stabilized either as a postdivorce family or in a new marriage.

The children and the parents frequently had different attitudes about the divorce that lasted throughout the five-year period. Many of the marriages that had been unhappy for the parents were experienced as gratifying or even happy by the children. More than half of the children did not think of the divorced family as an improvement over the predivorce family even after five years had passed; in contrast, less than 20 percent of the adults thought the divorce had been ill advised, and many felt that the situation was greatly improved. After five years about one-third of the children were well adjusted and adapting well, and about the same number were still unhappy, felt deprived or rejected, and were angry at one or both parents.

The age of the child at the time of the divorce did not seem to predict his or her later adjustment. The factors that predicted good adjustment were related to the quality of the child's relationship with both parents, the quality of life of the divorced family, and the degree to which the divorce resolved the problems that brought it about. But the major factors in determining whether or not the child adjusted well to the divorce were the personalities and parenting styles of both the mother and the father. A continued close relationship with the noncustodial parent (in this study usually the father) was also important in the child's later adjustment. Children who lacked such a relationship were likely to continue to feel depressed and to have impaired self-esteem.

***The Custody Decision.***   Until recently courts have usually awarded custody of children to the mother unless she was obviously unfit to care for them. A mother who for some reason wished the father to have custody was regarded with disapproval by society; she was seen as uncaring and not what a mother "should be." It was clear that better information on the results of custody awards was needed. One study that was designed to supply some of this information is the Texas Custody Research Project (Warshak and Santrock, 1983). The study compared the adjustment of male and female children whose custody was granted to the father after divorce with that of children whose custody was awarded to the mother and that of children who lived in intact families. Children living with the same-sex parent were found to show more competent social development. When comparisons were made among all the children, a sex difference appeared only for children who were in the custody of the father. The boys in the father-custody homes were rated as more mature than boys from intact families. Girls from father-custody homes were rated lower in maturity than girls from intact families. Ratings of children from the mother-custody homes did not differ from those of children who lived with both parents. In general, though, chil-

**FIGURE 18-3**
After the family turmoil that precedes a divorce, children must deal with dislocations and discontinuities associated with the postdivorce period. One of these discontinuities is infrequent, and perhaps artificial, contacts with the parent who has not been given custody. (Randy Matusow, Monkmeyer Press; Bruce Roberts, Photo Researchers; Richard Hutchings, Photo Researchers)

dren living with the same-sex parent seemed to be faring better than children living with the opposite-sex parent. This study, while certainly not a sufficient basis for custody decisions in itself, nevertheless suggests that there is something very important about an ongoing relationship between a child and its same-sex parent.

Although longitudinal research data on ways to moderate the effects of divorce on children are scarce, the clinical experience of many therapists and counselors has provided some ideas that may help parents soften the blow for their children.

1. *Tell the children ahead of time.* This lets them prepare for one parent's moving out.

2. *Tell the children the reasons that the decision was made.* This helps prevent children's frequent belief that they were the cause of the breakup. Make the explanation brief but honest and suitable for the age of the child.

3. *Emphasize that the divorce is a permanent decision.* Many children harbor the belief that their parents will eventually get back together.

4. *Explain what changes there will be in the child's life.* These may include moving, a new school, and much less money to spend. Emphasize the positive challenge of adapting to the new situation.

5. *Let the children be free to express their anger.* This is an effective way to prevent long-term problems. At the same time, the parents should avoid using their children as a dumping ground for their own sense of anger or despair. Instead, they should share their negative feelings with an adult friend or with a therapist or counselor.

6. *Avoid forcing the child to choose between the parents or to take sides.* Custody and visitation rights that are fair to both parents should be agreed upon. Both parents should make continued contact with the children a high priority.

**Parents as Therapists**   While parents sometimes fail to help their children develop optimally, there are numerous instances in which they play very positive roles. For example, there is growing evidence that parents can be trained to respond therapeutically to their children's behavioral problems (Moreland and others, 1982). The main techniques for bringing this about are modeling, behavioral rehearsal, and reinforcement (see Figure 18–4).

Many demonstrations of the use of parents as therapists have focused on extreme forms of behavior such as autism and some forms of mental retardation. Parents of autistic children have been taught to observe behavior, to identify responses that need to be strengthened or weakened, and to use reinforcers skillfully. The following is an interchange between a mother and a psychologist who was training her to deal more effectively with her 6-year-old son Dorian. The mother had already learned several principles of behavioral therapy in preparation for her conference with the psychologist. She had listed the behaviors that she felt Dorian had to learn, as well as a number of points that she and her husband would have to learn simultaneously.

> MRS. COOPER: *We would like Dorian to respond to instructions in various arts and crafts activities which would eventually lead to his learning of reading, writing, numbers, colors, and appropriate behavior in the classroom. In order to achieve this broad objective, he has to learn the following. The following are most of his problems. . . .*
> a) *The proper use of objects, such as crayons, paste, paper, pencils, and books.*
> b) *Sit still and pay attention. (They are not necessarily in that order. That is how they came to my mind.)*
> c) *Focus his vision on what we point out.*
> d) *He has to perceive the whole picture rather than focusing or fixating on a small part of it. (Perception, I feel, is somewhat of a problem.)*
> e) *I would like him to learn to take pride and enjoy his success. Pride in his own achievement will, I hope, be his strongest reinforcer as he grows. These are his problems as well as what I feel our goals are and what we have to work for.*
>
> DR. W.: *The implication when you list all of these behaviors is that the behaviors are there, either too weakly . . .*
>
> MRS. COOPER: *Yes, I feel they are there and could be brought out, but he's not willing to do it, as of now, so this is what I feel are his problems.* (Walder and others, 1967, pp. 57–58)

Mrs. Cooper became skillful at recognizing environmental events that might reinforce appropriate responses emitted by Dorian. She planned and wrote up records of her "reinforcement experiments" with him.

*We know the following about Dorian already:*

A. *He imitates what we say and with some positive reinforcement, successfully learned a great deal of behavior.*

B. *He loves chocolate in any way, shape, or form. He imitates what we say and because of this, and in addition, with positive reinforcers such as the chocolate he has successfully learned a great deal of verbal behavior. This we know.*

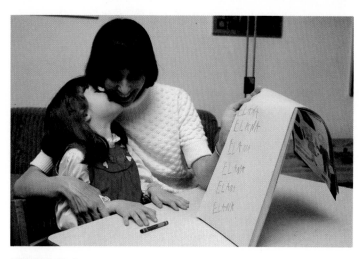

**FIGURE 18-4**
This mother is teaching her child, who is slow at learning in school, how to write her name. Notice how she uses modeling, how the child practices what the mother has modeled, and the mother's reinforcement of the child's progress. (Paule Epstein)

*C. He loves chocolate and trains, lights, vacuum cleaners, cleaning objects, dearly.*

*D. He fixates on certain pages of books, and verbalizes quite accurately what he sees there.*

*E. He is beginning to explore the environment and loves to walk, looks into people's homes, and occasionally stops to talk to them.* (Walder and others, 1967, p. 59)

Mrs. Cooper's experiments became more and more successful, and her son's autistic behavior, although it was not eliminated, became less a problem.

Other studies have demonstrated that through special tutorial programs parents can become more effective in fostering desirable behavior in children who exhibit the more common types of problem behavior. For example, one child had learned how to command and control the behavior of his parents ("You go over

there and I'll stay here"). When his parents learned to identify and differentially respond to his autocratic behavior, its frequency declined. The child became more socially cooperative when his parents ignored his commands; they also gave him special attention when he cooperated. Parents and teachers of highly aggressive boys have been taught to note the occurrence of particular types of undesirable behavior and to reduce their frequency through the use of reinforcement and other appropriate behavioral techniques (Patterson, 1982).

## The School

School districts, schools, and classrooms are larger and more complex social systems than families. Often they seem unwieldy and unmanageable. However, in some respects it is more feasible to attack problems of behavior in the school situation than in the home. Dorian's mother invited a behavior modification specialist to visit her home and observe what went on there, but many parents, even while admitting that their families have problems, would be neither eager nor willing to have their privacy invaded by observers.

Teachers, school psychologists, and social workers can cite many instances in which longstanding family problems are not identified until the child reaches school age. But even when a problem is recognized at school, it may not be possible to deal with it effectively. The parent may refuse to cooperate with the school, or the realities of the child's life may make any significant change in his or her condition impossible—for example, if the child's home is unstable because of continual fighting between the parents or because the parents are immature and irresponsible.

Despite such barriers, early-detection projects in schools have attempted to identify children who are likely to have adjustment problems later in life. The results of these projects show that early observation of the child, together with data available to school mental-health workers (for example, nurses' notes, teachers' reports, and test scores), can predict later psychological casualties. In addition, classmates' ratings of each other seem to have predictive value. On the basis of such information, intervention studies have been carried out to help vulnerable children before their problems become serious enough to require clinical help. For example, in one project nonprofessional aides worked under close professional supervision for an entire school year with children who were judged to be at risk for school maladjustment. The children who received this one-to-one contact showed significant changes in a number of areas, including social and academic skills and overall adjustment (Chandler and others, 1984). Special training for teachers, workshops to help parents develop their child-rearing skills, and carefully planned in-school and after-school activity programs can help prevent a significant number of behavior disorders in children.

**Dropping Out**   Some children are never comfortable in school, and by the time they reach high school they are ready to leave. The dropout problem is a social problem as well as an educational one. In prosperous times, when jobs are not difficult to obtain, the economic cost to the dropout may not seem great. However, when competition in the job market intensifies, poorly educated, unskilled people tend to fall by the wayside.

An example of primary prevention is a study aimed at teaching cognitive and social skills to high school students (Sarason and Sarason, 1981). The school in which the research was carried out had a history of high drop-out and delinquency rates and a low percentage of graduates who went on to college. The research was carried out in class sessions as part of a regular course. The basic procedure involved using modeling to demonstrate social and cognitive skills, followed by rehearsal of the modeled behavior. The subjects saw demonstrations of the cognitive antecedents of effective behavior (for example, deciding between alternative courses of action) and effective overt responses (such as how to ask a teacher a question). Repeated emphasis was placed on the links between thought and action. The following is an excerpt from a videotape that was used in the experimental program ("Jim's cognitions" refers to voiceovers).

TOM: *Hey Jim, you want to go down to Green Lake fourth period?*

JIM: *What are you gonna do down at Green Lake?*

TOM: *A bunch of us are gonna take the afternoon off and party it up.*

Jim: *I don't think I can go. Sixth period Mr. Smith is reviewing for the algebra exam.*

TOM: *What about coming over and staying until sixth?*

JIM: *Well, I kind of like Mr. Jones's class. Besides, it's too hard to get to Green Lake and back in an hour and forty minutes. I could come after school.*

TOM: *You know Lydia is going to be there.*

JIM (with noticeable interest): *She is?*

TOM: *Yeah. And by the time school is over, who knows if the party will still be there. We might go over to someone's house.*

JIM'S COGNITIONS: *Gee, I really want to go to that party. Maybe I can get up the nerve to ask Lydia out. But I should stay for that algebra review, at least. The test will be hard enough without missing the review.*

TOM: *You know, it is Friday afternoon and a beautiful day.*

JIM'S COGNITIONS: *I wish Tom would let me make my own decision. This isn't easy. Maybe I could study hard this weekend. Then I won't need to go to the review. But will I really study on Saturday?*

TOM: *Well, are you going to come?*

JIM: *I don't know, Tom. I'll have to think about it some more. Maybe I'll see you there fourth. If not, I'll probably come later.*

TOM: *Okay, I hope you come.*

One year after the completion of the study, the experimental subjects had better school-attendance records, less tardiness, and fewer referrals to school counselors and psychologists because of behavioral problems than similar students who did not participate in the program.

## The Community

After people leave school they are pretty much on their own. Most of their activities are not supervised by authority figures, and a certain degree of independence is expected of them. They are also expected to fit into the community by working and by adhering to its laws, values, norms, and priorities.

Work is the major postschool activity for most people. Finding employment that is satisfying and sufficient to earn a livelihood is obviously a major ingredient in an individual's satisfaction with life. How can maladaptive work behavior be prevented?

A study by Ross and Glaser (1973) compared several variables related to childhood experiences and the home environments of successful and unsuccessful male residents of a ghetto in a large city. Both groups grew up under decidedly disadvantaged circumstances, but while half continued to live in poverty, the other half managed to change their lives for the better in significant ways. There were two successful (A) groups consisting of blacks and Mexican-Americans, and two unsuccessful (B) groups of the same ethnic makeup. The A groups had worked more or less steadily during the two years preceding the study; the B groups had been unemployed or underemployed. The investigators hypothesized that parental attitudes and aspirations made the difference between people who did and did not overcome the developmental barriers posed by poverty and discrimination.

Interviews with respondents in the two groups uncovered a number of differences that supported the hypothesis and were consistent for both blacks and Mexican-Americans. Members of the A groups received greater support, encouragement, and discipline at home. They also had developed a sense of self-esteem through involvement in productive activities. The results indicate the need to help relatively unsuccessful people overcome low self-esteem and self-confidence. Another personality characteristic of members of the B groups that might be modified through imaginative programs is their dependence on approval from peers. We might expect that many unproductive people would benefit from a close relationship with nonpeers—teachers, athletic coaches, or employment counselors, for example—who would make demands, motivate achievement, provide information about productive skills, and act as both models and reinforcers of good performance.

**Community Agencies**   Every person is influenced by the way in which society and its institutions are organized. Although some institutions are concerned with specific segments of the population (for example, day-care centers, schools, social centers for senior citizens), several are capable of reaching all of the society's members. Because of our tendency to take these institutions for granted, we may lose sight of their potential for contributing to personal growth and reducing the likelihood of maladaptation. For example, a public library can be a powerful force in a person's life, and if it provides positive models, it can indirectly contribute to the prevention of maladaptive behavior. Kenneth Clark, an influential educator who grew up in Harlem, found such a model in a librarian at the New York Public Library.

> I met Schomburg when I was about twelve years old, a crucial period in my life. It was at this time I clearly recognized that I was not ever going to be able to compete with my classmates in athletic skills.
>
> I went to the library not only to escape the athletic competition, but also to escape the streets.
>
> On one of my trips to the library, I decided that I was going to go upstairs to the third floor to the forbidden and mysterious area reserved for adults. I fully expected to be turned away unceremoniously. As I climbed the last flight of stairs, I felt the excitement of an interloper. I was prepared for the risk of either a polite or a more direct rejection. When I entered the room, a large man, whom I later came to know as Arthur Schomburg, got up from his desk and came over to me and smiled. He didn't ask me what I wanted. He merely put one arm around my shoulder and assumed that I was interested in the books. We went over to a table and sat down and began to talk. . . . We talked about books. We talked about wonderful things: about the history of human beings, about the contributions of Negroes which were to be found in books. He showed me portraits of Negroes who had contributed something important.
>
> On that first day of meeting Schomburg, I knew I had met a friend. He accepted me as a human being and through his acceptance helped me to share his love of, and his excitement in, the world of books. (Clark, 1965)

Most people deal with everyday crises in the best way they can using available resources. Just as we don't go to the doctor every time we have a sniffle, we don't run to the clinical psychologist every time we are upset. The availability of nonprofessional "therapists" may be one reason for this. For example, people like hairdressers and bartenders do a lot of therapeutic listening to the troubles of their customers (Cowen, 1982). However, some social institutions have been specifically assigned the task of handling crises.

Although they are not usually included in lists of mental-health workers, police officers frequently modify behavior—whether for good or ill and whether they are aware of it or not. Police officers are not in a position to remove the causes of crime, but as their skills in human relations develop, their contributions to the prevention of crime could increase. A crime prevention experiment in New York City has provided some information about the effects of increasing police officers' psychological sophistication and expertise (Bard, 1970). The focus of training and preventive work was on handling family disputes, since a high percentage of violent crimes are committed by close relatives. Another reason for developing more skill in handling family disturbances is that 22 percent of fatalities and 40 percent of injuries to police officers occur while they are intervening in these situations (see Figure 18–5). Psychological training does help police officers handle violence more effectively. In addition, it can help them handle many other problems, such as the usually harmless but often bizarre behavior of former mental-hospital patients, with more tact and discretion.

Aside from the police, in many communities there is a need for specialized programs directed toward people who are going through a personal crisis or share particular types of problems. For example, suicide and crisis prevention centers have been established in many communities (see Figure 18–6). The purpose of these centers is to encourage troubled people to seek help, either through telephone contact or in person. Such efforts may provide a means of reducing social isolation and bringing destructive and self-destructive thoughts out into the open. However, because it usually is not possible to conduct well-controlled studies of sudden crisis events such as potential suicides, there is continuing debate about the nature and effectiveness of crisis prevention centers. One recent study presented evidence suggesting that suicide-prevention centers do lower suicide rates, particularly among young white females (Miller and others, 1984).

**Treatment in the Community**  Whether people receive mental-health services in the community or in institutions, society has a definite interest in how those services are provided, their effectiveness, and their cost. The mix of available services can influence not only the recipients' sense of well-being but also their economic productivity. In one study, matched groups of schizophrenic patients in Portland, Oregon, and Vancouver, British Columbia, were compared approximately one year following discharge from a mental hospital (Beiser and others, 1985). Whereas Vancouver had a rich network of accessible community services for the chronically mentally ill, Portland's services at the time of the study were limited. One year after discharge, the Vancouver group experienced fewer readmissions, were more likely to be employed, and reported a higher level of well-being than was the case for the former patients in Portland. These results suggest that the effects of deinstitutionalization depend on the resources available to help former patients.

Many people who would otherwise have to be hospitalized could remain in the community if facilities that provide additional social support and supervision

**FIGURE 18–5**
Police officers frequently must intervene in family disputes. This officer is trying to calm an emotionally disturbed person who might harm himself or others. (Gerard Davis, Woodfin Camp & Associates)

**FIGURE 18-6**
Crisis hotlines and suicide-prevention centers provide help for people who feel unable to cope with events in their lives. Sometimes just talking to an understanding listener is all that is needed. If more help is required, those who staff the hotlines can provide the callers with additional numbers to call for assistance. (Charles Kennard/Stock, Boston)

were available. An example of such a facility is the half-way house or community lodge. In one study, a group of institutionalized patients who had volunteered to do so moved from the mental hospital to a lodge in the community (Fairweather and others, 1969). The members decided who their leaders would be and the work that each would perform. Initially, extensive supervision was needed, and the group frequently found it necessary to seek help. However, as time passed, the lodge patients significantly increased their employment level and the length of time they were able to be out of the hospital. The median percentage of time in full employment for the lodge group was as high as 70 percent, while virtually all of the control subjects were totally unemployed.

***The Case of Sylvia Frumpkin.*** The story of Sylvia Frumpkin shows how the community's "help" can sometimes be anything but helpful (Sheehan, 1982). Frumpkin (the name is fictitious, but the story is true) had a long and disheartening journey through what is commonly called "the system." In fact, she encountered the disjointed, fragmented, and ineffective system at every turn. Following her first psychotic break in 1964 at the age of 15, she was repeatedly hospitalized or placed in various types of institutions. At different times she was diagnosed as manic-depressive or as schizophrenic, either undifferentiated or paranoid type. At one time or another she was given individual psychotherapy, antipsychotic medications, lithium, insulin coma therapy, electro-convulsive therapy, "Chris-

tian psychotherapy," and megavitamin therapy. Over the years she saw a constantly changing variety of therapists, often for very short periods. These therapists treated her with nearly every available medication, sometimes without reference to her history, and they sometimes changed, suddenly decreased, or altogether stopped her medication in a seemingly arbitrary manner.

Sylvia Frumpkin is not the kind of patient most therapists enjoy; she is slovenly, unappreciative, and uncooperative. She drains the energies of clinical personnel by being loud, abusive, and even violent during the acute phases of her illness. Even when she was not acutely ill, Frumpkin was characterized by a staff member as "arrogant, nasty, and demanding." Nevertheless, as Figure 18–7 shows, Sylvia Frumpkin experienced 45 changes of treatment settings. She was repeatedly bounced back and forth between her family home, various hospital settings, and community residential facilities. She was admitted 27 separate times to 8 different hospitals (state, municipal, general, voluntary, and private), where she spent a total of 9 years. She spent almost 7 years in a state hospital. For slightly less than 6 years she lived with her family, cycling in and out of their home 9 different times. She spent a total of 3 years in several different types of community settings, such as halfway houses, a foster home, a YWCA residence, and a religious community. The cost of her care would be estimated at $636,000 if the effects of inflation are taken into account.

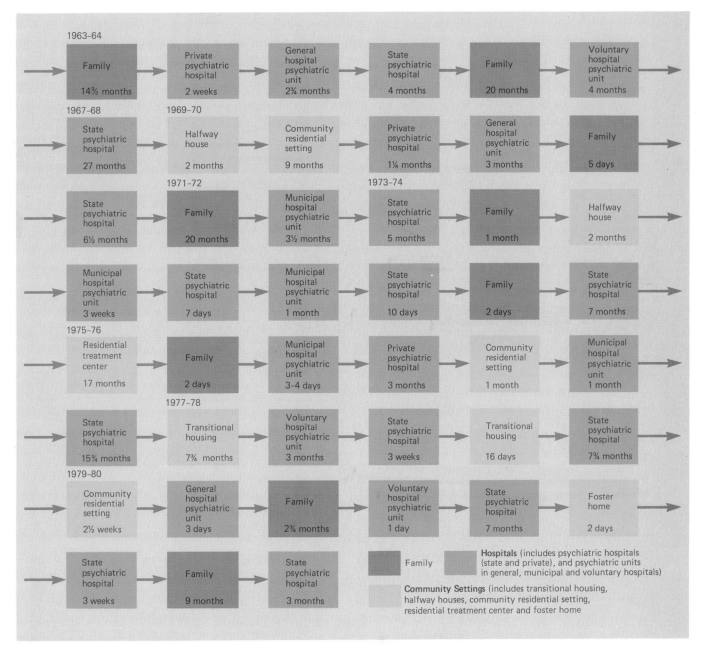

**FIGURE 18-7**
Sylvia Frumpkin's odyssey as a chronic mental patient, 1963–1980 (based on Moran, Freedman, and Sharfstein, 1984, p. 889)

Unfortunately, Sylvia Frumpkin's story is not unique. There are an estimated 1.7 to 2.4 million chronically mentally ill people in the United States. Policy makers and the public can learn a great deal from the experiences of people like Sylvia Frumpkin. Her story clearly illustrates the profound impact of chronic mental illness on patients, families, and communities, as well as on the staggering costs of providing care. It may well be that Frumpkin would have continued to deteriorate even if the conditions of her treatment had been more favorable, but the behavior of the system

certainly seems to have been a contributing factor. In her various hospitalizations, Frumpkin never experienced a prolonged relationship with a caring person. She perceived no one as having her interests continuously at heart during a period of 17 years. Cases like Frumpkin's have led mental-health workers, judges, and other government officials to think about ways to reform both the system and the laws that place disturbed individuals in public institutions.

***Improving Treatment Programs.*** Experiments designed to improve the mix of available mental-health services are under way in a number of states. For example, the Massachusetts Mental Health Center provides an alternative for patients who traditionally would have been admitted and retained on inpatient services. In the new system all patients who are thought to need inpatient hospitalization are first admitted to a day hospital. Those who do not require residential facilities return to their homes or community living situations at night and on weekends. Those who are admitted for day hospitalization but require 24-hour inpatient care because they are dangerous or unable to care for themselves are transferred to an acute intensive-care unit within the hospital. As soon as is warranted by the clinical situation, these patients are returned to the day hospital or to a day hospital and dormitory-inn. The dormitory-inn is a special facility that provides care for patients for whom the intensive-care unit is no longer appropriate, who need treatment in the day hospital, and who have no other place to sleep. It is a time-limited residence with an anticipated 3-week length of stay (Gudeman and others, 1985). Whether dormitory-inns will provide an effective alternative to inpatient hospitalization is a question that requires further investigation. However, the development of this type of facility clearly reflects growing awareness of the need for an expanded array of treatment facilities in the community.

Long-term mental-hospital patients do not usually fare well when they return to the community unless effective aftercare programs are available to them. The Vancouver–Portland and community-lodge studies mentioned earlier, as well as other evidence, suggest that long-term patients can help themselves attain an impressive degree of autonomy through carefully planned aftercare programs both in hospitals and in the community. The opportunity for resocialization is an important element of these programs. Of importance, also, is the ability of the program to adapt to the special needs of its residents and workers. Halfway houses can, at a lower cost to society, increase the personal freedom and self-confidence of many former mental-hospital patients and decrease the stigma attached to mental illness.

Although the concept of community care for the chronically mentally ill is a good one, most deinstitutionalized people have simply been dumped into communities that fear them because of their eccentric behaviors and do not look after them in any systematic way. Few deinstitutionalized people are given the vocational training, guidance in self-care, recreation, or opportunities for socializing that are required for any sort of meaningful existence (Braun and others, 1981; Kiesler, 1982). The need for follow-up care, the hard realities of insufficient funding, the impact of patients on communities, and the uncertainties as to what constitutes effective community programs have all been largely ignored. As a result, a growing number of people who would otherwise be enthusiastic about deinstitutionalization have become at least somewhat disillusioned.

For some individuals, hospitalization denies them their freedom and further decreases their ability to cope with their problems. For others, the psychiatric hospital provides a haven where, in a protected atmosphere, they can regroup their defenses for reentry into the community (see Figure 18–8). The following excerpt from a Seattle newspaper illustrates how the deinstitutionalization movement may result in inadequate protection and help.

*Rubie Label rapped gently at the door of the small housekeeping unit in the Frye Apartments, which he manages.*

*There was no answer.*

*Label pushed open the door and stepped inside. No one was in the kitchenette. He looked in the sitting room. Empty.*

*He glanced toward the open bathroom door. A young woman, without clothing, was standing rigid and*

**FIGURE 18–8**
Deinstitutionalization may not live up to its potential if the trade-off for not being hospitalized is inadequate housing, isolation, and lack of therapeutic contact.

*transfixed in front of the mirror, her back to the doorway, apparently in deep shock.*

*Label sighed. He wrapped a robe around her, coaxed her gently to a chair and talked constantly to her, "This is Rubie. You're all right now. No one is going to hurt you. Rubie is here now."*

*She looked at him, wide-eyed, questioning. She began to sob and the tears dampened long, dark hair cascading around her face. Label put his arms around her, comforting her.*

*Afterward, after he had drawn her out of her trance and promised to return, Label stepped outside and leaned a sagging shoulder against the corridor wall. His eyes, too, were wet.*

*He knew that for this young woman there were no solutions, only problems. She was one of dozens, perhaps hundreds of people with mental problems who are in downtown Seattle now.*

*Few can be taken in for hospital care. More refused to commit themselves to a hospital. Most are not considered dangerous to themselves or others, the criteria for an involuntary commitment. (Seattle Times, December 16, 1977, p. A17)*

This article stimulated the following letter from a reader.

*After reading the article in the paper about the little psychotic lady who is living in abject misery in the hotel on First Avenue (The Times, December 16), I feel compelled to write this letter.*

*It is not an easy letter to write, as my past history of hospitalization in a mental institution is not one I am proud of or like to recall.*

*However, I must speak out on the issue of the commitment law in the State of Washington.*

*The crux of the whole problem of voluntary versus involuntary commitment to a mental hospital seems to lie in the simple fact that a person in the midst of a mental crisis is not capable of making the decision to commit himself to a hospital for treatment.*

*In a state of mental confusion or breakdown, one's mental processes are in such a muddle that one is unable to make any rational decision about life. Also, most times a mentally confused person has the feeling that if "so-and-so would only keep me, I could make it." Well, so-and-so doesn't have the time, the interest, or the expertise to do or say the things you may need.*

*Most of the time, one's family and friends are just as confused as you are about what is best to do.*

*One of the things one is painfully aware of in any mental hospital is that the staff is being paid to care. But at least they care, and if they are up to snuff, they know how to help you.*

*A large mental hospital is not a happy place to be, but tell me this—what's so great about being in a flea-bitten hotel room where no one knows you exist or cares? Freedom and rights are great rhetoric, but what is freedom to one who is unable to use it for one's own best interests?*

*Is the right to starve to death in a wretched hotel room, and be so zonked out of your mind that you don't know who you are, really all that precious? (Seattle Times, December 25, 1977, p. A13)*

The incident described in the newspaper article reflects the lack of community help and supervision for the mentally disturbed; the letter explains why the mental hospital remains a needed haven for some people.

One consequence of the large number of failures of deinstitutionalization has been an increase in readmissions to state hospitals. Patients now stay in the hospital for shorter periods but, because of their inability to function in the community, return more often. About half of the patients who are released from state hospitals are readmitted within a year of discharge.

What lessons can be learned from the way deinstitutionalization has been practiced up to now? Perhaps the most important lesson of the bad experiences of the past decade is that deinstitutionalization as it is now being carried out is not helpful to many individuals. As happens so often, society neglects many of the nuts and bolts needed to reach a worthy objective. More money and more trained personnel are needed. However, there is an increasing tendency to place people with criminal records in mental hospitals, and people with previous arrest records are likely to be arrested again after they are discharged from mental hospitals (Steadman, 1981).

More education is also essential. Public-information programs about mental illness and retardation and more citizen involvement in planning for the reentry of former patients into the community can help make deinstitutionalization a positive experience for both the patients and the community. The entry of formerly institutionalized patients into the neighborhood has frequently been perceived as a threat, even though the overwhelming majority of ex-mental patients and retarded individuals are harmless (Rabkin, 1979). Nothing can arouse negative feelings in a neighborhood more effectively than the proposed establishment of a half-way house or aftercare center in the vicinity. Yet there is no evidence that simply being a discharged mental patient makes a person more likely to commit crimes or endanger the community.

## ■ LEGAL ASPECTS OF TREATMENT AND PREVENTION

In this and the previous chapter we have discussed ways to help people to avoid having problems and, if that isn't possible, to overcome them to the extent possible. What could be more humane, more noncontroversial? Because people live in groups, the community has an interest in preventing behavior that is maladaptive. Although historically it has not always been the case, governmental units now have laws that deal with both helping people who behave deviantly and protecting the public from the dangers posed by certain types of deviant individuals (for example, murderers). Actually, trying to help someone can create problems if our judgment of what constitutes help happens to be wrong or the person doesn't want to be helped (at least by us).

### Institutionalization

The process of placing a person in an institution is called **commitment.** Prisoners are committed to prisons for punishment, and mental patients are committed to mental hospitals for treatment. **Criminal commitment** of an individual to a mental hospital may occur when a criminal act is legally declared to be a result of insanity and that the interests of society and the individual would be best served by commitment to a mental hospital rather than to a prison. Some mental patients voluntarily commit themselves, but others are involuntarily hospitalized through a legal procedure called **civil commitment.** Civil commitment can only be carried out if a person is judged to be a risk to him or herself or to others. The forced institutionalization of a person poses serious problems. On the one hand, civil commitment aims at providing help, but to do that, it must deprive the person of basic human rights.

Anna May Peoples has made the Public Safety Building her home for two years, but authorities have had to dismiss trespassing charges against her. She is not competent to stand trial and not dangerous enough to institutionalize (see Figure 18–9).

> But the 64-year-old transient was arrested again last night, charged again with criminal trespass for being in the Public Safety Building after hours. Officers escorted her out of the building at 10:45 P.M., then arrested her five minutes later when she came back in.

> To the consternation of the Police Department, Peoples insists on making her home in the building at Third Avenue and James Street. She bathes in the restroom sinks, dresses in the elevators, and sleeps on the rock-hard floors.

> One night, police found her naked in an elevator. Another time, she fell asleep and plunged through a plate-glass door.

**FIGURE 18–9**
Anna May Peoples, caught between the technicalities of legal incompetence and lack of dangerousness, waits to hear her fate during a court appearance. (Cole Porter, *Seattle Times*)

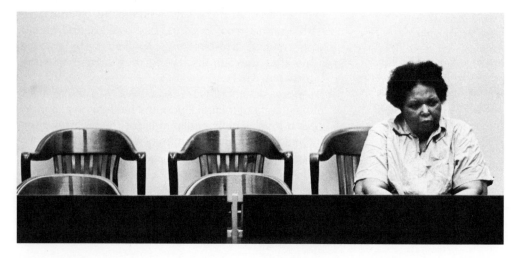

*Social workers tried to find the woman a home, but Peoples refused help. She preferred the Public Safety Building, despite being dragged out by police on various occasions. (Adapted from Guillen, 1982, p. B1)*

Peoples is a paranoic schizophrenic who believes people are out to shoot her. Because of that, she said, she takes refuge in the Public Safety Building. She could not be committed involuntarily because she was not a danger to herself or others.

**Criminal Commitment**   To convict a person of a crime, the state must establish beyond a reasonable doubt not only that the person committed the prohibited act but also that the act was committed with criminal intent. If it cannot be proven that the person meant to do harm, the insanity defense becomes possible. The aim of the insanity defense is to show that the defendant did not have a "guilty mind" at the time that the crime was performed.

The concept of insanity is often confused with that of competence to stand trial. Insanity refers to a person's state of mind at the time that an act was carried out, while competency refers to the person's state of mind at the time of a judicial proceeding. In a legal sense, an **incompetent person** is one who lacks the capacity to consult with a lawyer and to understand what legal proceedings are about. Both insanity and competency are legal terms whose applicability in a given case is determined by a judge after considering all evidence, including the opinions of expert witnesses.

During the late nineteenth and early twentieth centuries, it was recognized that a crime did not necessarily have to be seen as a deliberate defiance of social norms; it might be an unconscious response to personal conflicts. The offender might be psychologically disturbed rather than simply wicked. As belief in this interpretation grew, statutes were introduced that permitted the court to defer sentencing decisions until the offender could be studied and recommendations made to the judge. Psychiatrists, psychologists, social workers, and probation officers became advisers to the court. Sentencing became more flexible, and parole was used increasingly. Along with these developments came the possibility that an accused individual could plead insanity, by which was meant mental incompetence and inability to distinguish right from wrong at the time that a crime was committed.

The number of insanity defenses that are successful is very small. In the entire state of New York, for example, there are on the average fewer than 50 successful insanity defenses each year. Thus, the insanity defense can be contributing only a tiny fraction to the problem of crime in the United States. In part, this is because juries have difficulty applying the fine legal points involved in the insanity defense. The following excerpt from a news article illustrates this point.

*Roderick Stoudamire, whose previous trial ended in a hung jury three months ago, was found guilty in Superior Court today of first-degree murder in the stabbing death last summer of a woman jogger at Seward Park.*

*A jury of six women and six men announced its verdict for the second trial at 10:40 A.M. in a courtroom packed with spectators. They deliberated about five hours.*

*The jury also found Stoudamire guilty of assaulting two other women joggers.*

*Stoudamire, 16, had pleaded not guilty by reason of insanity. It was his insanity defense that caused the deadlock in the first trial. After deliberating more than two days, jurors in that case said they were confused by the definition of criminal insanity, and could not decide whether it applied to Stoudamire.*

*The tall, slender youth sat quietly, usually with a vacant look on his face, as witnesses testified during both of the long and often dramatic trials. He wore the same look this morning when the decision against him was read.*

*A mistrial was declared in the youth's first trial after jurors announced they were deadlocked. In that trial, 10 said they did not believe Stoudamire was legally insane, while the 2 others said they were convinced the youth was schizophrenic and voted to acquit him (Horne, 1979, p. C11).*

One of the toughest problems with the insanity defense is what to do with those who are acquitted—how to deal humanely with the criminally insane on the one hand and protect the public on the other. At one time the criminally insane were simply committed indefinitely and warehoused along with the rest of the mentally ill. Recently, however, a nationwide trend toward deinstitutionalization, tighter commitment laws, and guaranteed right to treatment have made it almost impossible to imprison the criminally insane in hospitals for long periods.

**Insanity** is a legal term, not a psychiatric diagnosis. Early English law did not recognize insanity as an excuse for criminal behavior. However, by the thirteenth century proof of criminal intentions was necessary to convict a person of a felony. If accused individuals could prove that they were completely "mad," they could successfully defend themselves against a criminal charge. In 1843 Daniel M'Naghten, a Scottish woodturner, assassinated Edward Drummond, secretary to the prime minister of England (see Figure 18–10). He

**FIGURE 18-10**
Daniel M'Naghten.

of a defendant's mental illness and include the following ideas.

*1. A person is not responsible for criminal conduct if at the time of such conduct as a result of mental disease or defect he lacks substantial capacity either to appreciate the criminality (wrongfulness) of his conduct or to conform his conduct to the requirements of law.*

*2. . . . The terms "mental disease or defect" do not include an abnormality manifested only by repeated criminal or otherwise antisocial conduct.* (American Law Institute, 1962, p. 66)

With each passing year, the ALI guidelines have gained increased acceptance throughout the country. In 1983, in the case of *Jones v. United States,* the Supreme Court ruled that people who are found not guilty by reason of insanity can be held indefinitely in a mental hospital under a less rigorous standard of proof of dangerousness than is required for civilly committed individuals. The Court ruled that acquitted insanity defendants "constitute a special class that should be treated differently."

John Hinckley's acquittal by reason of insanity from charges of attempting to assassinate Ronald Reagan caused many people to question the fairness of the insanity defense. The American Psychiatric Association argued that people should be acquitted for insanity only if they have a serious mental disorder such as a psychosis. Those who have personality disorders—for example, antisocial personality disorder—or abuse drugs or alcohol should be held responsible for their actions. The Association further stated that expert witnesses should not be allowed to testify about whether the defendant was able to control his or her behavior (*Psychiatric News,* February 4, 1983). The use of expert opinion poses profound interpretive problems (see Box 18-1). So far none of the guidelines that have been proposed for dealing with the problem of insanity have provided a completely satisfactory solution.

Thomas Szasz (1970), a psychiatrist, believes that a verdict of "mentally ill" rather than "guilty" or "not guilty" is dehumanizing because it denies personal responsibility. In one survey, over 80 percent of a sample of people living in midtown Manhattan were judged to be mentally ill to some extent (Srole and others, 1962). Does this mean that over 80 percent of the population is therefore immune from having to accept the consequences of their actions? Perhaps the criminal-justice system should be revised to deal separately with the determination of guilt and with the appropriate type of sentence. In this way a person might be judged guilty

was found not guilty because the judges stated that he was "labouring under such a defect of reason, from disease of the mind, as not to know the nature and quality of the act he was doing; or, if he did know, that he did not know he was doing what was wrong" (M'Naghten case, 1843).

This rule, the **M'Naghten rule,** because the "right and wrong" test of insanity and was widely adopted. An example of an attempt to invoke this rule occurred in the trial of Jack Ruby, who was convicted of the murder of President Kennedy's assassin, Lee Harvey Oswald, in 1964. In appealing his death sentence, Ruby claimed that he suffered from psychomotor epilepsy and that this prevented him from determining right and wrong. However, this claim was rejected by the judge and Ruby was found legally sane. He eventually died in prison.

The M'Naghten rule and subsequent court decisions have been controversial largely because of the difficulty defining precisely what knowing right from wrong really means. In 1962 the American Law Institute (ALI) proposed a set of guidelines that have since been incorporated into the laws of several states. The ALI's guidelines focus on impairment that grows out

# ■BOX 18-1 THE DEBATE OVER THE INSANITY DEFENSE

(a)

(b)

(c)

(d)

FIGURE 18-11
Edmund E. Kemper, III (a) was acquitted by reason of insanity from the charge of murdering his grandparents in 1964, and was released from a mental hospital in 1969 as "cured"; he later murdered six college students, his mother, and one of her friends—for which he was found sane and guilty. Dennis Sweeny (b) was sent to the Mid-Hudson Psychiatric Center when a judge accepted his plea of "not guilty by reason of mental disease" of killing Congressman Allard Lowenstin in 1980. After the slaying of his parents, Gregory Shaddy (c) was acquitted by reason of insanity; he spent two years in a hospital and was then pronounced cured and released. The case of John W. Hinckley, Jr. (d) revived debate over the insanity defense after he was acquitted from the charge of attempting to assassinate President Ronald Reagan, and committed to a mental hospital.

Will the insanity defense be retained in, or banished from, the federal and state criminal codes throughout the country? Legal and clinical experts—abolitionists and retentionists—continue to disagree. Throughout the controversy, however, one major point seems clear: Whatever happens to the insanity defense, the judicial system cannot ignore the mental aberrations that a defendant may have experienced at the time of an unlawful act. The public outcry against "criminals getting away with murder" also cannot be ignored, even though the insanity defense is only infrequently successful (see Figure 18-11). Understandably, the public remembers highly publicized cases in which the in-

sanity defense is invoked and someone who has clearly committed a crime is found not guilty by reason of insanity, is released after a short hospitalization, and later commits another crime.

During the trial of John W. Hinckley, Jr., the man who shot Ronald Reagan and an aide, the barrage of contradictory expert testimony damaged the image of psychiatry in the public mind. Those who would abolish the insanity defense believe that one way to end this type of spectacle would be to restrict psychiatric testimony to evidence of mental abnormality that bears on the defendant's conscious awareness and perception—his or her "intent" to commit the crime. Other testimony concerning more subtle impairments of understanding, judgment, or behavior control would no longer be relevant at the guilt stage of the trial, but could be introduced at the time of sentencing. Another proposal calls for a pool of expert witnesses to be selected by the court. These experts would no longer testify for the prosecution or the defense. Instead, the impartial panel would attempt to arrive at a conclusion regarding the defendant's mental state when the crime was committed.

yet still be sent to a hospital for treatment instead of prison. The state of California is unusual in that it does provide for two trials—a guilt trial and a penalty trial.

Two factors have restricted this type of judicial innovation. In the first place, the judicial system is already overloaded with cases and so far behind in its work that there is little time to plan and carry out the experiments on which reforms might be based. Second, the decisions of judges and juries are based on varied and often conflicting goals, including rehabilitation of offenders, isolation of offenders who pose a threat to community safety, discouragement of potential offenders, expression of the community's condemnation of the offender's conduct, and reinforcement of the values of law-abiding citizens.

### Civil Commitment

All fifty states have civil commitment laws. These laws are based on the doctrine of *parens patriae*, according to which the state can act in what it takes to be the best interest of a minor or of an adult who is incapacitated. The principal features of the process are a petition, a hearing, and a decision about the place to which the individual is to be committed. In some states, the judgments of psychiatrists are decisive in reaching commitment decisions. In others, physicians who are not psychiatrists play dominant roles. Until a short time ago standards for commitment were loosely worded and protections for the patient either did not exist or were ignored. Then, in a 1979 decision (*Addington v. Texas*), the Supreme Court ruled that people may not be committed to mental institutions unless the state has presented "clear and convincing" evidence that they require hospitalization.

Growing awareness of abuses like the one described in the following newspaper article led to reforms of commitment codes in many states. The patient in this article had been sent to a medical hospital during a severe attack of asthma in 1956. Twenty days later she was committed to a county mental hospital. She was not discharged until 1960, even though the staff of the mental hospital had considered her sane since 1957. *The New York Times* gave the following report of the proceedings at her release trial.

At today's hearing in Judge Pindar's court, Dr. John J. Scott, assistant medical director of the county mental hospital, testified that as far back as 1957, at a hospital staff conference, Miss Dean had been adjudged sane.

Asked why she had not been released in view of her many requests for her freedom since that time, Dr. Scott said that the woman was without relatives and it had been feared that she would become a public charge.

When a patient at the hospital, Miss Dean performed the duties of a registered nurse, without pay.

Miss Dean's release was effected through the effort of a friend, who remembered that Raymond H. Chasan, a lawyer, had won the release of another mental patient in 1947, under somewhat similar circumstances. (New York Times, July 17, 1960, p. 59)

All civil-commitment laws involve two judgments: whether the individual is suffering from a disabling mental illness and whether he or she is dangerous. The first criterion is relatively easy to establish. The second is more of a problem. Dangerousness refers to the potential to inflict harm on other people as well as on oneself. Because dangerousness involves a prediction of future behavior, its application to individual cases creates enormous problems. Can a clinical expert tell the court whether a person is dangerous and when he or she has stopped being dangerous?

In 1985 a 22-year-old accountant was pushed in front of a speeding subway train at rush hour. A team of some 200 doctors, nurses, and technicians operated on her for 22 hours, trying to save her life and repair her severe head injuries and numerous broken bones. Her assailant, who had been held by another subway rider until police arrived, turned out to be a 19-year-old unemployed woman with a history of mental problems. She had been released from a psychiatric ward less than a month before her crime, despite violent behavior while incarcerated and a psychiatrist's warning that she was dangerous. On two occasions she had attacked fellow patients and had to be subdued by means of a straitjacket.

Although the psychiatrist in this case was correct in

thinking that the 19-year old woman was dangerous, available evidence suggests that clinicians' predictions of whether a given individual will do something dangerous in the future are often inaccurate. As a group, former mental patients do have a higher arrest record for all types of crime than the general population, but patients who did not have an arrest record *before* hospitalization have a lower arrest rate than the general population. The higher rate of violent crimes committed by released mental patients can be accounted for entirely by patients with a record of criminal activity before hospitalization. Thus, a record of past violence is the best predictor of future violence. By itself, the mental status of released patients does not raise their risk of arrest for committing violent crimes (Monahan, 1981).

Involuntary hospitalization will be controversial as long as the dangerousness criterion is used in civil-commitment proceedings. Recent reforms require that the individual's constitutional rights be protected in a commitment proceeding as they would in any other court action. Steps in that direction include providing the person with a lawyer to protect those rights, limiting the length of confinement, and reviewing the person's progress at specified intervals.

The goal of protecting the rights of people who might be committed to an institution against their will is accepted by all. However, it is by no means clear how to protect those rights while simultaneously assuring the welfare of the individual and of society. Civil-commitment procedures and the concepts underlying them are in a state of flux, and humane procedures in which both lawyers and clinicians play defined roles are needed. At present, civil commitments seem to be increasing in frequency. This trend is being reinforced by recent court decisions that have emphasized the *parens patriae* role of the state in treating a patient for his or her own good. Also contributing to the trend is the failure of many states to develop community treatment networks to supplement hospital systems, as well as health insurance programs that provide only marginal subsidies for outpatient care.

**The Rights of Patients**   In the not-so-distant past, people were treated as if admission to a mental hospital justified taking away all their rights. However, according to recent court decisions patients' rights must be upheld and adequate treatment must be provided. In a 1971 case that attracted national attention (*Wyatt v. Stickney*), the court ruled that a state must provide adequate treatment for mental hospital patients who are confined involuntarily. Beyond recognizing the patient's right to treatment, the court specified basic hospital staffing ratios and qualifications and also required individualized treatment plans.

In a 1975 Supreme Court decision (*O'Connor v. Donaldson*), Kenneth Donaldson was awarded compensatory and punitive damages of $38,500 against two staff psychiatrists at the Florida State Hospital because they had not provided adequate treatment for him during the 14 years of his involuntary commitment. The significance of the *O'Connor v. Donaldson* ruling was its recognition that hospitalized people who are not dangerous have a constitutional right to treatment. Whether or not a dangerous patient has a similar right has not yet been decided. The *O'Connor v. Donaldson* decision strengthened the rights of involuntarily hospitalized patients, but it did not make the task of determining whether or not a patient is dangerous any easier.

The courts have opened the door to long-overdue improvement in the treatment of the mentally ill. A federal judge in New Jersey has ruled that an involuntarily committed mental patient who objected to the drug therapy administered to him may not be forced to take the medicine (*Rennie v. Klein*, 1978). Since drugs now constitute the primary mode of behavior control in institutions, and virtually all involuntarily committed patients are routinely given antipsychotic medications, this and similar rulings may have widespread effects on the way in which treatment is defined in state institutions. In addition to strengthening their right to get treatment (and their right to refuse it), the courts have also supported patients' right to receive the least restrictive treatment available. The "least restrictive treatment" is only as restrictive and confining as is necessary to achieve the purposes of the commitment.

Increasingly, both patients and judges are questioning the safety and effectiveness of present-day treatment methods. Physical treatments such as drugs and electro-convulsive therapy do have the potential to cause permanent injury. Some experts also believe that behavior-modification procedures such as token economies may obliterate individuality. In addition, certain patients appear to deteriorate as a result of receiving psychotherapy. Some critics believe that merely being institutionalized is therapeutically counterproductive, regardless of the quality of the institution. Until recently a hospital's power to deny patients the right to examine their own files was taken for granted. Now patients can see their charts, but some hospitals do not voluntarily tell patients that they are entitled to do so.

As the rights of patients have been extended, the requirement of informed consent has been strengthened. **Informed consent** requires that patients receive adequate information about the nature of a planned treatment before they agree to submit to it. The physician must communicate this information in language that is meaningful to the patient, rather than in "doctor talk," and must clearly explain the potential risks and benefits, including any discomfort that might arise from the treatment. Frequently, if the patient is incompetent to evaluate the information provided (for example, because of a psychotic condition), a lawyer assigned to look out for the patient's interests plays a role in the decision-making process. The requirement of informed consent applies to people who serve as subjects in experiments as well as to patients who are undergoing treatment. Patients and experimental subjects both have the right to terminate their participation in treatment or research even if they had previously consented to participate.

Should patients have the right to discontinue treatment that most people would agree was helping them? The difficulty of answering this question can be seen in this daughter's account of her mother's changed behavior after discontinuing the use of antipsychotic medication. Her mother came to New York to join her children after being discharged from a mental institution. She was talking Haldol, an antipsychotic drug.

*On Haldol Mother's behavior improved tremendously, and we even harbored false hopes of her return to normal living. We never suspected that she might cease taking medication and regress. . . .*

*Not only did Mother rediscover art and music in New York, but she soon became familiar with the liberal New York laws regarding "patients' rights." She refused to continue to take Haldol and slowly began the reverse trip to "No Man's Land," where she now dwells. The first sign of her decompensation was a refusal to come to my apartment, and then she rejected me completely. Next the manager of her middle class apartment hotel asked us to remove her. She was annoying the guests with her outbursts. She had become known to all the shopkeepers on the block as "The Crazy Lady of West 72nd Street." Looking like a zombie, she paraded down West 72nd Street, accusing aunts, uncles, and brother of stealing her father's fortune, screaming at people who frightened her. . . .*

*Whether or not it's preferable for her to be forcefed Haldol and incarcerated in Kansas or allowed to do as she pleases in liberal New York, as destructive as her life is now, is paradoxical. She was not able to enjoy life and pursue her artistic interests in the former situation, but she is even less able to do so in the latter. Without medication, she can only exist. I believe that basically she is less free in her present life, a prisoner of her delusions and paranoia. My brother, however, disagrees. He thinks that Mother is better off having the choice to live as she wishes, wandering aimlessly in the streets, constructing the world to fit her delusions.* (Adapted from Lanquetot, 1984, p. 471)

The courts are only beginning to deal with the special problems that arise in the institutionalization of children. Among the questions that must be considered are: How much freedom may parents exercise in seeking to institutionalize a son or daughter? When, and under what conditions, can the state institutionalize children against their will? What procedures are needed to protect the child's rights? What are those rights? The United States Supreme Court has ruled that parents may commit their children to state institutions as long as "neutral fact-finders" approve.

The quality of the treatment provided is an important factor in approving institutionalization for children as well as for adults. For example, questions have been raised concerning the constitutionality of institutions for the mentally retarded that provide little or no special training. It has been argued that all such institutions are unconstitutional because they do not conform to the standard of least restrictive treatment. Retarded people can be helped in much less restrictive environments.

Although it may be a less obvious problem than protection of the rights of institutionalized people, the need to preserve the dignity of those who seek the help of mental-health specialists on an outpatient basis is also important. The need to assure the confidentiality of the interaction between therapist and client is just as great in a community clinic as it is in a state hospital.

Another area in which ethical issues arise is the selection of treatment methods and the goals of treatment. Informed consent is needed before therapeutic programs are begun. The issue of informed consent in therapy has been recognized most clearly in the case of organic or aversive treatments such as electroconvulsive therapy, but it is also relevant to the psychological therapies. Whenever possible, the goals of therapy should be determined jointly by the therapist and the client, without undue influence exerted by the therapist. Should a therapist encourage a young man to go to college because the client's parents, who are paying the therapy bills, want him to? The client should be the main concern of the therapist, but external influences like the parents' desires might become coercive factors in treatment. Clinicians also must not unduly impose their personal values on the therapy they offer to clients. A respectful attitude toward the client, an undogmatic approach, and healthy questioning of therapeutic tactics are important ingredients in all types of treatment.

# ■ THE CHALLENGE OF PREVENTION

At the beginning of the chapter we said that prevention can take more than one form. It can involve taking the steps needed to keep a disorder from arising in the first place as well as efforts to limit its impact on the life of the individual. In this sense prevention and treatment are closely related. Common to both is the concept of vulnerability. Vulnerability arises when an individual's personal characteristics are insufficient to deal with characteristics of the situation. We have just seen how the mentally disturbed can deteriorate when placed in situations that lack social supports and opportunities to learn needed skills. The challenges of deinstitutionalization and prevention are the identification of opportunities for growth and stability and the provision of such opportunities to people who need them. These opportunities differ depending on the nature of the people to be served. For example, as they grow older, children need situations that give them increasing opportunities to be on their own. On the other hand, the aged usually need increasing care and attention.

Society inevitably must be involved in meeting the challenge of prevention because it controls or influences so many of the situations of modern life. We have seen many examples of the impact of community and social forces on our lives. Certain types of maladaptive behavior (for example, phobias and delusions) can be attacked on an individual basis with the clinical methods we have described (psychotherapy, behavioral therapy, drugs). But lasting solutions to many problems of living require social change. Slum children living in crowded apartments have only limited opportunities to generalize from what they learn in a stimulating school or preschool program. Medication may help deinstitutionalized patients hallucinate less frequently, but they still need a supportive environment and a chance to acquire new social and occupational skills.

Preventing maladaptive behavior and responding therapeutically to it when it does occur require an examination of society, its components, and how they are interrelated. This examination should include elements that a community lacks as well as positive steps that it may take. Examples of such steps are houses for runaway children, drop-in centers for teenagers, and crisis centers. Virtually all such programs have been started by citizens without government support, and,

at least initially, on a nonprofessional basis. As a result of such efforts, professionals in many areas have broadened the scope of their clinical services and have increased their involvement in community programs.

## Paraprofessionals

Programs have also been created to train and use nonprofessionals and paraprofessionals for significant roles in a variety of community settings. A wide culture-related gap often exists between middle-class professional workers (clinical psychologists, psychiatrists, and social workers) and people from low socioeconomic strata who need help. Much of the success of paraprofessionals seems to be due to similarities between their backgrounds and those of their clients. For this reason, some community psychologists devote a major portion of their activities to training paraprofessionals.

Paraprofessionals vary widely in age, education, and cultural background. They often make up a large part of the staff in neighborhood service centers, residential youth centers, and mental-health programs in both urban and rural areas. There they may serve as bridges between an established agency and a target group in the community that the agency has failed to serve effectively. Although relatively little research has been done on how to select, train, and evaluate the effectiveness of these workers, it has been shown that in some situations paraprofessionals may be as effective as professionals (Hattie and others, 1984). The responsibilities of paraprofessionals and their role in professional and community power structures need to be defined.

## Self-Help Groups

**Self-help groups** can also contribute to prevention. For many human problems there are no easy answers or easy cures, but there is an alternative to coping with them alone. Millions of people whose problems and needs are not met through formal health care, social services, and counseling programs can find the hope and personal support they need in self-help groups. Within these groups, whose members share common concerns, they are offered the understanding and help of others who have gone through similar experiences. People like those in the following examples might find the help they need by contacting the appropriate group.

*Margaret and Bill are parents of a young child with cancer. For two years they have shared suffering, dashed hopes, and heartbreak. In spite of caring friends and professional support, they feel alone in their grief.*

*Jean is a divorced mother who has custody of her three children. She now finds herself overwhelmed by the problems of single parenthood. Her teenage son has become difficult to handle and she is increasingly discouraged in trying to provide for her children's needs and the demands of her job.*

*Roger has a serious drinking problem. He has been fired from two jobs in the last year and is deeply in debt. He has lost the respect of his family and friends. He entered treatment at an alcoholic clinic but began to drink again two months after the treatment ended. He realizes that his addiction is ruining his life but feels helpless to control it.*

Table 18–1 lists some of the ways in which self-help groups help their members.

As social beings, all of us need to be accepted, cared for, and emotionally supported; we also find it satisfying to care for and support those around us. Within the most natural "self-help networks"—families and friends—we establish the one-to-one contact so important to our happiness and well-being. This informal support is such a basic part of our social character that we tend to take it for granted, but it clearly influences our ability to handle distressing events in our lives. Many of our daily conversations are actually mutual counseling sessions in which we exchange the reassur-

□ **TABLE 18–1**
**Ways in Which Self-Help Groups Help Their Members**

1. Emotional support and understanding
2. An accepting reference group that reduces social isolation
3. Information and advice
4. Models on how to cope effectively with stress
5. Enhancement of members' awareness of alternatives available in dealing with problems

*Source: Based on Levy, 1976.*

ance and advice that help us deal with routine stresses. In fact, research scientists have found that there is a strong link between the strength of our social-support systems and our health (see Figure 18–12). Further research is needed to determine when, under what conditions, and for which types of problems self-help groups are effective (Videck-Sherman and Lieberman, 1985). Research is also needed to identify the reasons for success when self-help groups are effective.

## Community Psychology

**Community psychology** is concerned with the role of social systems in preventing human distress and maladaptive behavior. Community psychologists attempt to work in settings that have an impact on prevention.

**FIGURE 18–12**
Self-help groups are not intended to replace skilled professionals. Rather, they are based on the belief that some problems of living go beyond the bounds of formal care services. Some self-help groups avoid formal professional guidance or counsultation, although many groups have benefited from the informal help of professionals. (Baron Wolman, Woodfin Camp & Associates)

For example, they might serve as human-relations consultants to a police department, work to increase the skills of individuals who staff welfare offices, or develop prevention programs in homes or schools. Outreach programs are aimed at either preventing breakdowns or dealing with problems in the community before more drastic treatment programs, such as hospitalization, become necessary. Making communities livable requires good ideas about social planning as well as awareness that various segments of the population, including the aged, minorities, and the unemployed, have special needs. Community psychologists are interested in the environmental facts of life in particular communities as well as the impact of those facts on individual lives.

However, if pitfalls and problems cannot be anticipated, tampering with the mechanisms of society could do more harm than good. As a result, there is an urgent need for indexes of current social and psychological conditions in a community, roughly similar to the economic indicators that public and private officials use in setting economic goals. Some of these indicators are more visible than others. For example, national income statistics provide a measure of the level of material well-being; crime and accident statistics provide clues to the moral condition of society; and infant-mortality figures tell us something about the level of health care. Indicators that are less easily indexed are the effectiveness of an educational system, the influence of mass media on behavior, and the cohesiveness of a neighborhood.

A reliable group of social and psychological indicators would not only tell us where society is at a given time but also provide useful dependent measures of the effects of social, political, and economic programs. The community exerts potent psychological influences on its members, and the task of community planners and behavioral scientists is to make those influences as adaptive as possible for the community's residents.

# ■ A FINAL WORD

In Chapter 2 we traced the history of abnormal psychology and noted the enormous conceptual changes that have taken place over the centuries. This concluding chapter, perhaps more than any other in the book, illustrates the optimistic outlook of many researchers and therapists today. It is easy to point out the gaps in our knowledge: Why does schizophrenia occur in the late teens and early twenties? What causes panic attacks? What can be done about senility? But perhaps more significant than the lack of knowledge implied by these questions is the current consensus that (1) the scientific method can fruitfully be applied to

them and (2) the resulting knowledge can be used to reduce the occurrence of maladaptive behavior.

There are many leads to effective prevention, but systematic research is needed to develop effective interventions. While the preventive approaches reviewed in this chapter seem promising, only scientific studies can validate them.

The formula for achieving prevention might be written $P = K \times W$. Prevention (P) is achieved when the needed knowledge (K) is available and society has the will (W) to use that knowledge to prevent unwanted outcomes. One of the great achievements of the present era is the widespread awareness that little good and much harm is done by blaming or stigmatizing people for their abnormalities, whether physical or behavioral. One of the great challenges is finding a way to motivate both individuals and society to do things to increase happiness, personal effectiveness, and the common good of the human family. The social need for prevention is, and will continue to be, one of the most powerful motivations of objective research in abnormal psychology.

# ■ STUDY OUTLINE

### SITUATION-FOCUSED AND COMPETENCY-FOCUSED PREVENTION

**Situation-focused prevention** is aimed at reducing or eliminating the environmental causes of disordered behavior, while **competency-focused** prevention is concerned with enhancing people's ability to cope with situations that might lead to maladaptive behaviors.

### TYPES OF PREVENTION

1. **Primary prevention** is concerned with the reduction of new cases of mental or physical disorder in a given population. The aim of **secondary prevention** is to reduce the duration, intensity, and disability of an existing abnormal condition. **Tertiary prevention** is aimed at reducing the impairment that may result from a given disorder or event.

2. One of the most serious maladaptive behaviors of childhood is juvenile delinquency. Efforts to prevent delinquency may take the form of programs aimed at improving living conditions and school achievement (primary prevention). Secondary prevention programs teach social and vocational skills to young people who have shown early signs of delinquency, while tertiary prevention involves efforts to change seriously maladaptive behavior.

## SITES OF PREVENTION

1. Preventive programs that are carried out in a family setting focus on **child abuse,** or physical and psychological harm inflicted on children by their parents. Behavioral training in impulse control and coping skills can be helpful for parents who want to change their behavior.

2. Another area in which preventive programs have been attempted is **spouse abuse.** Efforts to help abused spouses include not only emergency care, safety, and shelter but also counseling to strengthen their self-related positive cognitions.

3. Divorce often has negative effects on children, who not only have to deal with their own stress but also must cope with parents who are experiencing high levels of stress. The possibility of a good adjustment depends on the quality of the child's relationship with both parents, the quality of life of the divorced family, and the degree to which the divorce resolved the problems that brought it about. Research on custody arrangements has found that children living with the same-sex parent seem to fare better than children living with the opposite-sex parent.

4. Prevention programs in school settings have focused on efforts to keep children from dropping out by teaching them cognitive and social skills.

5. Institutions in the community have tremendous potential for contributing to personal growth and reducing the likelihood of maladaptation. Police officers in particular are in a position to modify behavior. In addition, in many communities there are specialized programs directed toward people who are going through a personal crisis or share particular types of problems.

6. The mix of services available in the community can influence not only the recipients' sense of well-being but also their economic productivity. Many people who would otherwise have to be hospitalized could remain in the community if facilities that provide additional social support and supervision were available.

7. Efforts to improve treatment programs include the use of aftercare programs in day hospitals and halfway houses. However, very often deinstitutionalized mental patients are simply released into the community without effective follow-up care.

## LEGAL ASPECTS OF TREATMENT AND PREVENTION

1. The process of placing a person in an institution is called **commitment. Criminal commitment** of an individual may occur when a criminal act is legally declared to be a result of insanity. Some patients are involuntarily hospitalized through a legal procedure called **civil commitment.**

2. **Insanity** refers to a person's state of mind at the time that an act was carried out. The number of insanity defenses that are successful is very small. The American Psychiatric Association has suggested that people should be acquitted for insanity only if they have a serious mental disorder such as a psychosis.

3. Civil-commitment laws are based on the doctrine of **parens patriae,** which permits the state to act in what it takes to be the best interest of a minor or of an adult who is incapacitated. In 1979 the Supreme Court ruled that people may not be committed to mental institutions unless the state has presented "clear and convincing" evidence that they require hospitalization. All civil-commitment laws involve two judgments: whether individuals are suffering from disabling mental illness and whether they are dangerous to themselves or others.

4. Recent court decisions have upheld the rights of patients to adequate treatment, specified hospital staffing ratios, and individualized treatment plans. They have also strengthened the requirement of **informed consent,** meaning that patients must receive adequate information about the nature of a planned treatment before they agree to submit to it. The question of whether patients should have the right to discontinue treatment is extremely difficult to answer.

## THE CHALLENGE OF PREVENTION

1. Society must be involved in meeting the challenge of prevention because it controls or influences so many of the situations of modern life. Certain types of maladaptive behavior can be attacked on an individual basis, but lasting solutions to many problems of living require social change.

2. Efforts to prevent maladaptive behavior include programs to train and use nonprofessionals and **paraprofessionals,** as well as **self-help groups** whose members benefit from the understanding and help of others who have gone through similar experiences.

3. **Community psychology** is concerned with the role of social systems in preventing human distress and maladaptive behavior. Making communities livable requires good ideas about social planning as well as awareness that certain segments of the population have special needs.

# GLOSSARY

**Abnormal psychology**   Study of deviant and maladaptive behaviors.

**Abstinence violation effect**   The reaction of conflict and guilt when an individual fails to resist the temptation to indulge in a behavior that he or she is trying to stop—for example, using alcohol. This response often triggers a binge or total relapse.

**Acetylcholine**   Chemical involved in the transmission of nerve impulses.

**ACTH**   *See* Adrenocortico-trophic hormone.

**Adaptation**   Dynamic process by which an individual responds to his or her environment and the changes that occur within it. Ability to modify one's behavior to meet changing environmental requirements. Adaptation to a given situation is influenced by one's personal characteristics and the type of situation. Term often used in a biological, Darwinian sense.

**Adjustment**   An individual's ability to harmonize with the environment.

**Adjustment disorder**   Maladaptive reaction to a particular stressful condition that results in impaired functioning and symptoms in excess of what might be a normal response to the stressor. The reaction must occur soon after the beginning of the stress and the reaction can be expected to decrease when the stressor ceases.

**Adjustment disorder with depressed mood**   Depression that occurs as a result of an identifiable life event and that is expected to disappear when the event's impact ceases. (Not classified as mood disorder.)

**Adoption studies**   An attempt to understand the genetics of a disorder and separate them from the effects of environment. Children adopted in infancy whose biological parents were affected by a disorder are compared with adopted children without such heredity.

**Adrenaline**   Secretion of the adrenal glands; also called epinephrine.

**Adrenal medulla**   One of the two principle parts of the adrenal glands, the part of the endocrine system located just above the kidneys. A principle function is the secretion of hormones in emergency-type situations.

**Adrenocortico-Trophic Hormone (ACTH)**   Hormone secreted by the pituitary gland that goes to the adrenal cortex to release adrenal corticosteroids, chemicals that stimulate the body's responses to stress.

**Affect**   Emotion, feeling, or mood: pleasant or unpleasant, intense or mild. Tone of feeling accompanying a thought.

**Affective disorder**   *See* Mood Disorder.

**Agoraphobia**   Pathological fear of open spaces.

**Alcohol amnestic disorder**   Another term for Korsakoff's disease.

**Alcoholism**   Alcohol dependence or addiction.

**Allergen**   A substance that precipitates an allergic reaction.

**Alpha receptor ($\alpha$)**   Postsynaptic ($\alpha_1$) and presynaptic ($\alpha_2$) receptors involved in noradrenaline inhibition.

**Alpha wave**   A particular kind of electrical brain activity often seen when a person is tense, and the frequency of which decreases with drowsiness or relaxation.

**Alzheimer's disease**  Chronic brain disorder, occurring as early as the fourth decade of life and involving a progressive destruction of nervous tissue that results in slurring of speech, involuntary muscular movements, and gradual intellectual deterioration with growing lapses of memory. No known causes or cures.

**Amnesia**  Total or partial memory loss, often acute, following emotional or physical trauma.

**Amnestic syndrome**  A memory disturbance without confusion or delirium in which there is both inability to learn new material and to remember information learned in the past.

**Amniocentesis**  Technique of removing a sample of amniotic fluid from a pregnant woman and analyzing it to determine whether there are chromsomal defects in the fetus.

**Amphetamines**  Nonaddicting nervous-system (particularly cerebral cortex) stimulants, such as dexedrine, which bring a sense of well-being and exhilaration. The stimulation effect is succeeded by fatigue and depression.

**Anal stage**  Stage of psychosexual development in which the child derives intense pleasure from activities associated with elimination.

**Angina pectoris**  Periodic chest pains resulting from an insufficient supply of oxygen to the heart. A type of coronary heart disease.

**Anorexia nervosa**  An intense and irrational feeling of being fat that leads to excessive restriction of food intake and weight loss that may be life threatening. Usually occurs in adolescence or early adulthood and is much more common in females than in males.

**Antianxiety drugs**  Commonly called tranquilizers. Used to calm anxious people.

**Antidepressant drugs**  General term for a number of drugs used to relieve depression and to elevate mood.

**Antigens**  Foreign substances that, when introduced into the body, induce the formation of antibodies and then react with these antibodies in a specifiable manner.

**Antipsychotic drugs**  Group of chemical compounds used to treat individuals who show severely disturbed behavior and thought processes, especially in cases of schizophrenia.

**Antisocial personality disorder**  Characterized by continuous, chronic antisocial behavior, beginning before the age of 15 and continuing into adult life.

Before the age of 18 such behavior is called a conduct disorder. Behavior tends to impair the rights of others and to be characterized by an impaired capacity for close relationships.

**Anxiety**  An affect with both a psychological and a physiological side. Generally, an unpleasant emotional state accompanied by physiological arousal and the cognitive elements of apprehension, guilt, and a sense of impending disaster. Distinguished from fear, which is an emotional reaction to a specific or identifiable object.

**Anxiety disorder**  Formerly called neurosis or neurotic disorder. Characterized by some form of anxiety as the most prominent symptom. Includes panic disorders, phobic disorders, obsessive-compulsive disorder, generalized anxiety disorders, and reactions to stressors.

**Asexual**  Characterized by lack of response to sexual stimulation and of interest in sexual activity.

**Asphyxia**  Unconsciousness or death caused by a lack of oxygen. May result in retardation or seizures as a result of brain damage.

**Assertiveness training**  Combined cognitive and behavioral approach designed to increase the frequency of aggressive behavior that is socially desirable.

**Assessment**  Information gathering aimed at describing and predicting behavior. Assessment specialists devise tests that measure various aspects of behavior.

**Assessment interview**  Same as diagnostic interview.

**Assortive mating**  The tendency for people to marry those who have characteristics similar to their own. For instance, chronic schizophrenics tend to marry individuals who have a schizophrenic spectrum disorder or other psychotic disorder. This additional genetic loading must be taken into account when estimating genetic risk for a variety of disorders.

**Asthma**  Disorder of a chronic nature, often psychophysiological in nature, characterized by coughing, wheezing, breathing difficulty, and a feeling of suffocating.

**Atherosclerosis**  A disorder caused by a buildup of plaque (deposits on the blood-vessel walls) that narrow the vessels and result in insufficient blood supply to the heart.

**Attention deficit-hyperactivity disorder**  Inability to focus attention together with an impulsive behavior pattern, which could not be expected from the child's developmental level. Often referred to as hyperactivity or by other similar labels.

**Attribution**  Term used by social psychologists to describe the way a person assigns responsibility for cause and effect.

**Aura**  Clouded state of consciousness, accompanied by feelings of unreality, which precedes an epileptic attack. Sensory, motor, or mood disturbance preceding a migraine headache.

**Authentic behavior**  Term used by some existential theorists to describe behavior dictated by a person's own goals rather than by the goals of society.

**Autistic**  Term used to describe a certain type of schizophrenic thought pattern characterized by self-centered thinking understandable only to the individual.

**Autistic disorder**  Developmental disorder usually occurring early in childhood characterized by severe impairment in social relationships, communication, and activity. Frequently includes mental retardation.

**Autoerotic practices**  Sexual stimulation practiced by an individual on him- or herself.

**Autogenic training**  Gaining psychophysiological equilibrium through passive concentration on a series of self-suggestions of various sensations.

**Autonomic system**  Part of the nervous system concerned with visceral activities, smooth muscles, and endocrine glands. Functional division of the nervous system. Name comes from the fact that it was formerly thought to function independently of the central nervous system.

**Autosome**  Chromosome that does not determine the sex of the individual.

**Aversion therapies**  (Aversive conditioning). Group of behavior therapies which attempt to condition avoidance responses in patients by pairing the behavior to be extinguished with punishing stimuli—for example: electric shock, social criticism, and drugs that cause vomiting.

**Avoidance response**  Attempt to leave a situation in which an aversive stimulus is expected to occur.

**Avoidant personality disorder**  Characterized by social withdrawal based on fear of social rejection.

**Axon**  Part of the cell that transmits impulses away from the cell body and across the synapse to the dendrite of another cell.

**Baquet**  A water-filled tub used by Mesmer as a focus for treatment of hysterical complaints.

**Barbiturates**  Family of drugs that depress central nervous-system action and may be addictive.

**Baseline observation**  Operant conditioning procedure in which an initial rate of some response is established. Can be used for descriptive purposes or as a control condition before introducing behavior-modification procedures and subsequent response-rate comparisons.

**Behavioral assessment**  The objective recording of particular categories of observable behavior prior to beginning behavior therapy. The assessment may take place in specially-contrived situations or under real-life conditions.

**Behavioral coping**  What a person actually does when confronted by a stressor.

**Behavioral medicine**  An area focused on ways to improve diagnosis, treatment, and rehabilitation by using behavioral techniques to help people adopt generally healthier ways of living and to follow treatment plans for specific problems. Also focuses on helping health-care providers improve their service delivery.

**Behavior-change experiment**  The test of a therapeutic manipulation to determine whether the individual's maladaptive behavior is lessened.

**Behavior genetics**  Study of the transmission of certain kinds of behavior through selective mating.

**Behaviorism**  School of psychology whose adherents contend that the study of overt and observable behaviors provides the only legitimate data of science.

**Behavior modification**  Type of therapy based on the principles of operant conditioning.

**Behavior therapy**  Includes several techniques of behavior modification based on laboratory-derived principles of learning and conditioning. Behavior therapies focus on modifying overt behaviors with minimal reference to internal or covert events.

**Belle indifference, La**  Marked lack of concern about one's disability, seen in patients with conversion disorder.

**Benzodiazepines**  Group of drugs used primarily to treat anxiety. Examples are Librium and Valium.

**Beta receptor ($\beta$)**  Postsynaptic ($\beta_2$) and presynaptic ($\beta_1$) receptors for noradrenalin.

**Binet tests**  Intelligence tests, developed by Alfred Binet, that yield a quantitative estimate of a person's intelligence.

**Biofeedback**  Method for inducing behavioral change in which the client learns to alter autonomic nervous-system responses by monitoring them on recording instruments.

**Biological perspective**  Theoretical perspective that suggests that all disorders, physical or behavioral, have biological causes. Causes may lie in heredity, genetic accident, or bodily infection or trauma.

**Biopsychosocial model**  Interactional view that emphasizes the interaction among biological, psychological, and social factors in determining behavior and body functioning.

**Bipolar disorder**  Mood disorder in which the individual experiences both periods of mania and periods of depression. Formerly called manic-depressive disorder.

**Bisexuality**  Attraction to and sexual activity with people of both sexes.

**Borderline personality disorder**  Characterized by impulsive and unpredictable behavior and marked shifts in mood. Instability may affect personal relationships, behavior, mood, and image of self.

**Brain deterioration**  *See* Dementia.

**Brain electrical activity mapping**  (BEAM) A technique for study of electrical brain activity in which the electrical impulses are summarized in color maps.

**Brain reward system**  Activation of this system produces intense sensations of pleasure, made up of the limbic system and hypothalamus.

**Brainstem**  Portion of the central nervous system that includes the hindbrain, midbrain, and forebrain up to the thalamus.

**Briquet's syndrome**  Another name for somatization disorder.

**Bulimia**  Episodes of binge eating with the awareness that this behavior is abnormal. Vomiting is often self-induced by the individual at the end of the individual's eating session.

**Burnout**  Condition found most often among people in the helping professions whose work involves intense interpersonal contact. Symptoms include loss of effectiveness and self-confidence and the general feeling of inability to deal with particular situations.

**Caffeine**  Crystalline compound that is found in coffee, tea, and kola nuts. It acts as a stimulant of the central nervous system and also as a diuretic.

**Cannabis**  Plant whose resin produces a psychoactive substance. In solid form the resin is called hashish.

**Cardiovascular disorder**  Disorder affecting the blood vessel system and the heart.

**Case-study method**  *See* Clinical method.

**Catatonic schizophrenia**  Type of schizophrenic disorder characterized by psychomotor disturbance. Often takes the form of body rigidity or posturing. Other behavior may include waxy flexibility or mutism.

**Catecholamines**  Group of hormones, including epinephrine, norepinephrine, and dopamine, that are important in the response to stress. Some catecholamines are produced in the brain, where they are important in nerve transmission.

**Cell body**  Part of the cell that contains the nucleus.

**Central nervous system (CNS)**  Brain and spinal cord. Does not include the nerve trunks and their peripheral connections.

**Cerebellum**  Portion of the brain consisting of two hemispheres located behind and above the medulla. Coordinates motor activities and maintains bodily equilibrium.

**Cerebral cortex**  Convoluted layer of gray matter of the brain; outer layer of the cerebrum.

**Cerebral hemispheres**  One of the two lateral halves of the cerebrum or upper part of the brain.

**Cerebral ventricles**  Cavities in the brain that are connected to the central canal of the spinal cord and contain cerebrospinal fluid.

**Cerebrovascular accident (CVA)**  Rupture or blockage of blood vessels in the cerebrum that disrupts or prevents blood flow. Commonly referred to as a stroke.

**CHD**  *See* Coronary Heart Disease.

**Child abuse**  Harm, usually physical, deliberately inflicted on children by their parent(s), often by repeated beatings.

**Choline acetylcholine transferase**  Enzyme that forms acetylcholine.

**Chromosomal abnormality**  Abnormality in chromosome structure or number of chromosomes in body cells.

**Chromosomes**  Gene-bearing structures within cells.

**Civil commitment**  *See* Commitment, civil.

**Classical conditioning**  Pavlov's experimental method by which a conditioned stimulus is paired with an unconditioned stimulus. Procedure involves presenting the two stimuli in close temporal proximity. The first, or unconditioned, stimulus elicits a reflex. After a number of trials the second, or conditioned, stimulus acquires the potentiality of evoking a similar reflex.

**Classification**  The establishment of a hierarchical system of categories based on the relationship or presumed relationship among the things to be classified, for instance, disorders of behavior and cognition.

**Client-centered therapy**  Carl Rogers' therapeutic approach, which views the subject matter of psychotherapy as the client's world of immediate experience that should be approached from the client's frame of reference. In the Rogerian system, the therapist's main task is to create the opportunity for the individual to achieve a reorganization of his or her subjective world and to reach self-actualization.

**Clinical method** Case study of the individual through observation. May rely heavily upon intuitive judgments of the clinician rather than upon experimentation and systematic measurement.

**Clinical psychologist** Psychologist, usually with a Ph.D., who has special training and skills in assessing and treating maladaptive behavior.

**Clinician** Professional who deals directly with the examination or treatment of patients or clients.

**Clitoris** In females, a small organ at the front of the vulva that is highly sensitive to sexual stimulation. The analogue of the penis in the male.

**Clonic phase** An aspect of seizure activity in which there is rapid alternation of muscle contractions and muscle relaxation.

**Cocaine** Stimulant with a number of characteristics in common with the amphetamines.

**Codeine** Derivative of opium that is less potent than morphine.

**Cognitive assessment** Specification and enumeration of the typical thoughts that precede, accompany, and follow behavior. Used in research and by cognitive behavior therapists especially in working with depressed individuals.

**Cognitive-behavior therapy** Psychotherapeutic approach that emphasizes the importance of cognitions or thoughts as behavior to be changed. Modifying "self-talk" is the most usual approach.

**Cognitive coping skills** Particular ways of thinking that aid in behaving effectively in stressful situations.

**Cognitive distortion model** (of depression) Proposed by Aaron Beck; suggests that depression is a disorder of thought.

**Cognitive modification** Technique whereby individuals learn to modify maladaptive thought patterns or to substitute new internal dialogues for old maladaptive ones.

**Cognitive perspective** Point of view that considers behavior to be the result of information processing and problem solving. Emphasis is on mental processes of which the individual is aware or can easily become aware.

**Cognitive psychology** Study of human beings as information processors and problem solvers. The focus of cognitive psychology has recently been extended from the traditional studies of memory, attention, and problem solving to include the effects of personality factors and emotions on learning and performance.

**Cognitive rehearsal** Procedure in which a client learns to rehearse ways to handle problem situations mentally. Such rehearsal makes it easier for the client to behave effectively in the actual situations.

**Cognitive restructuring** A technique used by Albert Ellis and other cognitive therapists in which clients are made aware of a connection between unrealistic thoughts and the maladaptive behaviors these evoke. Clients are helped to develop more rational ways of looking at their behavior.

**Cognitive set** A person's habitual way of viewing the world and distorting it in terms of his or her personality characteristics and expectations.

**Cognitive triad** Description of depression in terms of negative thinking about oneself, the current situation, and the future. Part of Beck's cognitive distortion model.

**Coming out** Term used by homosexuals to indicate the occasion of openly declaring their sexual orientation.

**Commitment, civil** Commitment based on judgment that a person is a potential danger to him- or herself and/or to others.

**Commitment, criminal** Commitment based on a judgment that a person is guilty of a criminal act and is also legally insane.

**Communication deviance** Term referring to the inability of a person to maintain a shared focus of attention with another. Studied in parent-child communications in families with a schizophrenic child.

**Community perspective** Viewpoint that much maladaptive behavior results from poor living conditions, discrimination, and so on. Emphasis is on preventive activities.

**Community psychology** Branch of applied psychology concerned with modifying both the individual and the structure of the social system to produce optimal benefits for both society and the individual. Community psychologists are often primarily interested in preventing maladaptive behavior.

**Compulsive behavior** Characterized by an individual's need to repeat a series of acts again and again even though he or she perceives them as senseless and interfering with desirable activities.

**Computerized axial tomography (CT)** Technique

that uses a narrow beam of X-rays to photograph an area of the body from many angles. A computer then analyzes this information to provide a clear picture of soft tissues as well as the conventional X-ray findings.

**Concordance**  Term describing the degree of relationship between twins and other family members with respect to a given characteristic or trait. They are referred to as concordant if they both show a particular trait. If they do not, the pair is described as discordant for that trait.

**Concussion**  Head injury that does not cause lasting structural damage. Rate of recovery is proportional to the severity of the injury.

**Conditioned response (CR)**  In classical conditioning, the response that occurs after training has taken place and after the conditioned stimulus has been presented.

**Conditioned stimulus (CS)**  In classical conditioning, the neutral stimulus that does not elicit a response prior to training.

**Conditioning**  See Classical conditioning, Operant conditioning.

**Conduct disorder**  DSM-III-R classification for those under 18 who commit antisocial acts. Adults may also be classified this way if they do not meet the criteria for antisocial personality disorder.

**Confabulation**  Type of thinking characterized by the filling of memory gaps with false and irrelevant information and details.

**Congenital**  Characteristics that are either innate or acquired, usually through chemical action, while the child is in the uterus.

**Conscious**  Aspects of one's mental life of which a person is aware at any particular time.

**Constitutional**  Any characteristics acquired by heredity, uterine environment, or illness or injury at or after birth.

**Continuous Performance Test**  Test of sustained visual attention in which the subject is required to indicate whenever a certain stimulus is presented and to ignore all other stimuli.

**Contusion**  Brain condition in which diffuse structural damage has occurred (e.g., rupture of blood vessels). Typically, cerebrospinal fluid pressure is raised, causing such symptoms as coma and stupor.

**Conversion disorder**  Type of somatoform disorder in which there is a loss or change in physical functioning that suggests a physical disorder but seems to be a direct expression of a psychological conflict.

**Cool reactor**  Someone who shows normal cardiovascular response to stress. Contrast with Hot reactor.

**Coping**  Contending with difficulties and overcoming them.

**Coping resources**  Capabilities that a person has available to call into play in a stressful situation.

**Coping skills**  Techniques an individual uses to deal with a variety of challenging situations. Often related to personality characteristics.

**Coping style**  Characteristic way a person deals with the stimuli in his or her environment.

**Copying**  Replicating the actions of another.

**Coronary heart disease (CHD)**  Disorder in which one or more of the coronary arteries is partially or totally obstructed by deposits. This results in a temporary or permanent cut off of blood to portions of the heart muscle.

**Correlation**  Degree of correspondence between two variables; a statistical index of covariation that varies from $+1.00$ to $-1.00$.

**Correlational study**  Type of research in which the relationship of two or more characteristics is measured. No statement about cause and effect can be made from correlational research.

**Cortex**  Outer layer of an organ such as the cerebrum, cerebellum or adrenal gland.

**Corticotrophin-Releasing Factor (CRF)**  Substance secreted by the hypothalamus that releases the chemical ACTH when it reaches the pituitary gland.

**Countertransference**  Psychoanalytic term that refers to the therapist's emotional reactions to the patient. See Transference.

**Covert**  Behavior which is internal and not directly observable. Includes unexpressed thoughts and feelings and other conscious and unconscious mental phenomena.

**Covert modeling**  Learning to change behavior through imagining a model's behavior and its consequences.

**Covert sensitization**  Behavioral therapy in which anxiety is created toward a particular stimulus situation that is likely to produce undesirable behavior. Usually the stimulus is paired with cognitions relating to the possible negative consequences if the person continues a given behavior. A treatment often used in changing the focus of sexual excitement.

**Criminal commitment**  See Commitment, criminal.

**Cross-cultural approach**  Method of studying the causes of various psychological and physical problems by studying their occurrence in a variety of cultures and then attempting to identify factors that are correlated with high and low frequency of the problems.

**Cross-fostering study** Method of evaluating hereditary factors in behavioral disorders.

**Cross-sectional study** Research design in which different groups are sampled at the same time and the results compared. Technique often used to study human development.

**CAT scan** *See* Computerized axial tomography.

**Culture** General values, attitudes, achievements, and behavior patterns shared by members of the same society.

**Cyclothymia** *See* Cyclothymic disorder.

**Cyclothymic disorder** Disorder that includes both mania and depressive episodes, neither of which meets the criteria for major episodes. Lasts for at least 2 years.

**Cytomegalovirus** One of a number of viral diseases which, if present in a pregnant woman, may result in retardation and other congenital problems in the child.

**Defense mechanism (ego defense)** Psychoanalytic term for various psychic operations used by the ego to avoid awareness of unpleasant and anxiety-provoking stimuli. The ego selectively uses defense mechanisms to ward off anxiety originating in the id, the superego, or dangers in external reality.

**Deficiency needs** According to Maslow, the most basic needs of life, which must be met before higher needs, such as social and intellectual needs, can be considered.

**Deinstitutionalization** Movement whose purpose is to remove patients from large mental hospitals and to obtain treatment and sheltered living conditions for them in the community.

**Delirium** Condition characterized by a confused mental state, usually resulting from shock or fever, accompanied by alterations in attention and by hallucinations, delusions, and incoherence.

**Delirium tremens** Acute delirium caused by overdoses of alcohol and consisting of severe alterations in consciousness and attention. Also referred to as the D.T.s.

**Delusion** Incorrect belief maintained despite clear evidence to the contrary.

**Dementia** Progressive atrophy of brain tissue that results in lapses of memory, poor judgment, and disorientation. Called presenile dementia if it occurs before age 65, and senile dementia if it begins after age 65.

**Dementia paralytica** Another term for general paresis.

**Dementia praecox** Older term for schizophrenia. Used by Kraepelin to emphasize the early onset and irreversibility of the disorder as he defined it.

**Dendrite** Branched part of a cell that serves as a receptor for nerve impulses from the axons of other cells and transmits them toward the cell body.

**Denial** Defense mechanism which allows rejection of elements of reality that would be intolerable if they became conscious. Negation of experiences or reality through unacceptance.

**Deoxyribonucleic acid** *See* DNA.

**Dependent personality disorder** Characterized by an inability to make major decisions and a belittling of a person's own abilities and assets. Intense discomfort is experienced if the person remains alone for more than a brief period.

**Dependent variable** Aspect of behavior which changes according to manipulation of the independent variable in an experiment.

**Depersonalization** Feelings of unreality or a loss of personal identity; often experienced as one's being someone else or as watching oneself in a movie.

**Depression** Pervasive feeling of sadness that may begin after some loss or stressful event, but that continues long afterwards. Inappropriate thought patterns that generalize every event as a calamity are characteristic.

**Depressive neurosis** Older term for dysthymic disorder.

**Developmental disorder** One of a group of disorders that involve distortions in the development of basic psychological functions that are involved in social skills, language, perception, and motor behavior. The disorder can be pervasive and involve many functions (e.g., autism) or specific and involve only a single aspect of development (e.g., developmental arithmetic disorder).

**Developmental model** Viewpoint that the process of cognitive development of a retarded person is no different than that of a nonretarded individual. Only the speed of development and the level reached differentiate the two groups. Contrast with *Difference model.*

**Dexamethasone Suppression Test** Chemical test thought to be able to differentiate depressed individuals who may be helped by different treatments.

**Dexedrine** *See* Dextroamphetamine.

**Dextroamphetamine (e.g., Dexedrine)** Stimulant

drug sometimes used in the treatment of hyperactivity.

**Diagnosis**  Classification of behavior disorders in terms of relatively homogeneous groups based on similar behaviors or correlates. Shorthand description of the behavioral and personality correlates associated with a particular classification. In medicine, the act or process of deciding the nature of a diseased condition.

**Diagnostic and Statistical Manual,**  3rd Edition, Revised, (DSM-III-R) Classification system for abnormal behavior published by the American Psychiatric Association. The system is generally used in the United States for official diagnostic and record-keeping purposes.

**Diagnostic interview**  Interview designed to gather information and assess behavior, usually for the purpose of determining seriousness and outcome or deciding what treatment approach would be appropriate.

**Diagnostic Interview Schedule (DIS)**  Standardized interview format designed to yield information necessary to make a DSM-III diagnosis. At present the schedule covers only a few disorders.

**Diastolic**  Term used to describe the blood-pressure reading at the time the heart dilates to allow more blood to enter.

**Diazepam**  One of the benzodiazepines, a group of antianxiety tranquilizers. Known by trade name, Valium.

**Difference model**  Viewpoint that the intellectual functioning of retarded individuals is not only less efficient than that of others but also different. Those who hold this view advocate different teaching approaches for retarded children, not merely simplification of standard methods. Contrast with *Developmental model.*

**Disaster syndrome**  Condition occurring immediately after a disaster. Characterized by dazed feelings and a sense of unreality and purposelessness and often accompanied by nausea, insomnia, or tremulousness.

**Discordant**  Term often used in twin studies to describe particular characteristics in which the twins differ. Characteristics which are the same for both are referred to as concordant.

**Disorganized schizophrenia**  (hebephrenic) Type of schizophrenia distinguished by incoherent speech and flat, incongruous, or silly affect. Often associated with extreme oddities of behavior such as gesturing or grimacing.

**Displacement**  Defense mechanism in which an emotional attitude is transferred from one object to a substitute object.

**Dissociative disorder**  Sudden, temporary alteration in the functions of consciousness, identity, or motor behavior in which some part of one or more of these functions is lost. If consciousness is affected, the person cannot remember important personal events. If identity is affected, a new identity which dominates behavior is temporarily assumed. If motor behavior is affected, then consciousness and/or identity is also affected. Wandering away is the most common resulting motor behavior.

**Dizygotic twins**  Fraternal twins developed from two fertilized eggs. The two individuals have the same genetic relationship as any pair of siblings.

**DNA**  Abbreviation for deoxyribonucleic acid, a complex chemical found in chromosomes within living cell nuclei. The sequence of its units determines genetic inheritance.

**Dominant gene**  Member of the gene pair that determines whether the individual will show the trait controlled by that gene. Other member of the pair may be the same (also dominant) or different (recessive).

**Dopamine**  Neurotransmitter thought to be involved in schizophrenia.

**Dopamine hypothesis**  Idea that schizophrenia involves an excess of the neurotransmitter dopamine at certain sites in the brain.

**Double-blind method**  Experimental design used in drug research. Neither the subjects nor the experimenters know which groups receive medication and which receive placebos (inert substances).

**Down syndrome**  Condition related to some inequality in the chromosome pair designated as number 21. Usually associated with a trisomy, or presence of an extra chromosome in addition to the usual pair. Also called *Trisomy 21.*

**Drug therapy**  Use of a variety of psychoactive drugs to treat different types of maladaptive behavior. Drugs are most often used to treat schizophrenia, bipolar disorder, some depressions, and anxiety. Drug treatment is often combined with other types of therapy.

**DSM-III-R**  *See* Diagnostic and Statistical Manual.

**DTs**  *See* Delirium tremens.

**Dyspareunia**  (functional) Type of sexual dysfunction in which persistent and recurrent genital pain without any apparent physical cause is associated with coitus.

**Dysphoria** Feelings of anxiety, depression, and restlessness.

**Dysphoric mood** Characterized by symptoms of depression, sadness, and feeling blue and hopeless.

**Dysthmic disorder** Chronic depressed mood or loss of pleasure in most usual activities; lasts at least 2 years. Does not meet the criteria for a major depressive episode.

**Echolalia** Meaningless repetition of words.

**EEG** *See* Electroencephalogram.

**Efficacy expectation** The belief that one can successfully carry out a particular behavior.

**Ego** In psychoanalytic theory, the part of the psyche which makes up the self or the "I." Part of the psyche that is conscious and most closely in touch with reality, and that functions as the executive officer of the personality.

**Electro-convulsive therapy (ECT)** Treatment for depression in which electrical current is passed through a patient's head. Used if a quick treatment is needed because of a high suicide risk or if antidepressant drugs have not been effective.

**Electroencephalogram (EEG)** Graphic record of minute electrical impulses arising from brain cells. Measured by an electronic device called an electroencephalograph.

**Encephalitis** Inflammation of the white matter of the brain. Symptoms include visual failure, mental deterioration, and spastic paralysis.

**Endocrine** Referring to any of the ductless glands of the body. These pass their secretions directly from the gland cells to the bloodstream.

**Endorphin** Pain-killing substance that occurs naturally in the brain.

**Enthusiasm effect** False appearance of effectiveness of a particular procedure or treatment that results only from the beliefs of both the recipient and the treatment giver that the procedure is effective.

**Epidemiology** Scientific study of the social or ecological distribution of physical disorders or behavioral deviations.

**Epilepsy** Transitory disturbance of brain function which is characterized by a sudden onset and loss of consciousness, and which may involve tonic and clonic muscle spasms. Epileptic seizures may be minor (petit mal) or major (grand mal) and tend to recur.

**Epinephrine** One of the hormones secreted by the adrenal medulla, active in emotional excitement and in response to stress.

**Erectile dysfunction** (impotence) Type of sexual dysfunction in which the male is occasionally or chronically unable to achieve or maintain a penile erection. The condition may have physical or psychological causes.

**Erogenous zones** Parts of the body sensitive to sexual stimulation.

**Escape response** The attempt to get out of an unpleasant or adverse situation.

**Etiology** Assignment of a cause. Scientific study of causes and origins of maladaptive behavior.

**Excitement** (sexual) The initial response to sexual stimulation marked by vaginal lubrication or penile erection.

**Exhibitionism** Exposure of the genitals in public for purposes of obtaining sexual pleasure and gratification.

**Exhibitionist** One who practices exhibitionism.

**Existential therapy** Type of psychotherapy which uses both humanistic and psychodynamic approaches. Emphasis is placed on each person's ability to affect his or her life course by the particular choices made.

**Exorcism** Expelling of evil spirits.

**Experiment** A study using the experimental method.

**Experimental** Process of using tests to demonstrate the truth or falsity of a theory or hypothesis.

**Experimental method** Study of the factors influencing a result by the manipulation of one or more experimental variables rather than simply observing what occurs naturally.

**Exposure in vivo** Part of cognitive therapy or desensitization in which the individual practices adaptive cognitions or relaxation behavior in the actual presence of the anxiety-producing object or situation.

**Exposure orientation** (in drug addiction) Idea that addiction is brought about by an environment that provides availability of drugs.

**Exposure therapy** Behavioral therapy that has as its basic element maintaining contact with or imagining contact with the feared stimulus.

**Expressed emotion** (EE) A measure of emotional involvement and critical attitudes of family members when talking about a behaviorally-disturbed family member.

**External locus of control** Tendency to see events as caused not by oneself but by outside forces. *See also* Locus of control. *See also* Locus of control

**Extinction** Weakening of a response following removal of reinforcement.

**Eye-tracking movements** Study of smooth pursuit

and saccadic eye movements as an individual attempts to visually follow a rhythmically moving stimulus. One goal of such study is to uncover genetic markers of vulnerability.

**Eysenck Personality Questionnaire** A paper and pencil personality questionnaire that measures extraversion, neuroticism, and psychoticism.

**Factitious disorder** Symptoms, either fabricated or self-induced, that are designed to produce attention and care from medical personnel.

**Fading** Technique for gradually eliminating cues; used in behavior modification after an individual begins to achieve a desired response.

**Family study** Study of characteristics of a group of related individuals to uncover genetic patterns.

**Family therapy** Specialized type of group therapy in which the members of the client's family all participate in group-treatment sessions. The basic idea is that the family, not just the individual client, has to alter behavior to solve the problem.

**Fantasized exposure** Exposure therapy in which the upsetting stimuli are presented in fantasy rather than in actuality.

**Fetal alcohol syndrome** Condition that may occur in the children of alcoholic mothers or mothers who used excessive alcohol during pregnancy. Characterized by retardation and unusual physical characteristics.

**Fetishism** Sexual deviation in which sexual interest is centered upon some body part or inanimate object which becomes capable of stimulating sexual excitement.

**First rank symptoms** Group of symptoms described by Kurt Schneider in an attempt to establish clear behavioral criteria for schizophrenia. One of the bases of the DSM-III-R definition of schizophrenic disorders.

**Fixation** Inappropriately strong attachment for someone or something. Often refers to an abnormal arrest of development during infancy or childhood which persists in adult life as an inappropriate constellation of attitude, habits, or interests.

**Fixed-role therapy** Cognitive approach developed by George Kelly in which the client is asked to practice or try out new roles in interpersonal relationships.

**Flooding** Behavioral therapeutic technique used particularly in the treatment of phobias. Treatment consists of exposing the client to the feared stimulus until the fear response has extinguished.

**Follow-up study** A method in which individuals listed at one point in time are contacted again at a later time to reassess behavior so that any changes can be noted.

**Free association** Basic technique of the psychoanalytic method by which a patient expresses his or her thoughts as freely and in as uninhibited a manner as possible. Free associations provide a natural flow of thoughts unencumbered by interruptions or explanations.

**Frigidity** Sexual problems in which a female either does not have swelling-lubrication response when sexually excited or cannot maintain that response until orgasm is reached.

**Frontal lobe** Portion of each cerebral hemisphere involved in abstract thinking processes.

**Fugue state** Flight from reality in which the individual may leave his or her present environment and life situation and establish a new lifestyle in another geographical location. Such a person is usually totally amnesic concerning his or her past life, although other abilities remain unimpaired; he or she may appear essentially normal to others.

**Fully functioning person** Term used by Carl Rogers to describe the optimal level of adjustment at which an individual can function with minimal anxiety.

**GABA** Term for gamma-amino-butyric-acid, a neurotransmitter. A deficiency of GABA, associated with hereditary causes, is thought to be involved in Huntington's disease.

**Galvanic skin response (GSR)** Change in the electrical resistance of the skin. This response serves as a dependent variable in conditioning and is used in lie-detector tests.

**Gastrointestinal disorders** Disorders of the digestive system, the stomach, and the intestines.

**Gay** Term used to describe a homosexual lifestyle by those who feel the term homosexual has too many negative connotations.

**Gender identity** Basic feature of personality encompassing an individual's conviction of being male or female.

**Gender identity disorder of childhood** A disorder occurring before puberty in which the child shows intense distress over its assigned sex. Such children may deny their assigned sex or assert that they will develop the genital characteristics of the opposite sex.

**Gender identity disorders** A group of disorders that have in common a persistent discomfort and sense of inappropriateness of one's sexual assignment.

**Gender nonconformity in childhood** Situation in which the child is primarily interested in the activities culturally associated with the opposite sex. Not necessarily associated with later sexual deviance.

**Gene** Microscopic structure in the chromosome; physical unit of hereditary transmission.

**General adaptation syndrome** Concept proposed by Selye. Three-stage reaction of an organism to excessive and prolonged stress, including (1) an alarm or mobilization reaction; (2) a resistance stage; and (3) a final stage of exhaustion.

**Generalized anxiety disorder** Persistent anxiety that lasts at least 1 month and includes several of the following: motor tension, autonomic hyperactivity, apprehensive expectation, vigilance, and scanning. The symptoms do not include phobias, panic attacks, obsessions, or compulsions.

**General paresis** *See* Paresis.

**Genetic counseling** The giving of information about risk for inheritance of certain disorders based on general information about heredity, knowledge of family history, and genetic characteristics of the person or couple seeking information.

**Genetic heterogeneity** In genetics, the idea that more than one gene is necessary for the inheritance of a characteristic. However, the genes each have a separate effect, not an additive one.

**Genital stage** According to Freud, if maturation proceeds without problems, after adolescence the individual reaches this stage in which the focus of pleasure is on a mature heterosexual relationship.

**Gestalt therapy** Humanistic approach that emphasizes removing distortions in self-perception and in the perception of others. Originated by Perls.

**Glove anesthesia** Condition in which a person cannot move or feel the part of the arm and hand that a glove would normally cover.

**Grand mal** Severe form of epilepsy involving major convulsive attacks and loss of consciousness.

**Group home** A sheltered living environment that may be either transitional or permanent. Often used for retarded persons and those with chronic schizophrenia. Emphasis is on self-care and self-regulation to the extent the individual's ability and condition permit.

**Group hysteria** Hysterical symptoms, often of a conversion disorderlike nature, that seem to spread contagiously through a group of individuals.

**Group therapy** Psychotherapy of several persons at the same time in small groups.

**Guided rehearsal** Aspect of modeling in which the client practices the previously modeled behavior and is coached by the therapist in order to improve the performance.

**Gyri** Raised portions of the brain's surface between the sulci; plural of gyrus.

**Habituation** Decrease of the orienting response after the repeated presentation of a stimuli.

**Halfway house** Transitional living facility that accommodates, for a short period of time, newly discharged psychiatric patients or those who have functioned maladaptively.

**Hallucination** Sensory perception in the absence of an external stimulus. Hallucinations are usually visual ("seeing things") but may occur in other sensory modalities as well.

**Hallucinogen** General name for a group of drugs or chemicals capable of producing hallucinations.

**Halo effect** Tendency to rate an individual improperly high on a particular factor because of a generally favorable impression of the individual.

**Hashish** Hallucinogenic substance. Solidified resin of *cannabis sativa* (marijuana).

**Health psychology** Area of psychology concerned both with calling attention to ways that disease can be prevented by changing living habits and with helping people modify behavior that increases health risks.

**Hebephrenic schizophrenia** *See* Disorganized schizophrenia.

**Helplessness** *See* Learned helplessness.

**Heredity** The process by which characteristics of an organism are basically determined by genes received from the parents.

**Heroin** Extremely addictive opiate derived from morphine.

**Herpes virus hominus (herpes simplex)** Chronic viral illness which, if present in a pregnant woman, may cause retardation and other congenital malformations in her child.

**Heterosexual** Characterized by attraction to the opposite sex.

**Hierarchy of needs** View, especially as described by Abraham Maslow, that certain basic needs of the individual must be met before the person becomes interested in such topics as personal growth and self-actualization.

**High-risk study** Research strategy entailing the longitudinal study of persons who might be vulnerable to breakdown.

**Histrionic personality disorder** Characterized by overly reactive behavior of a histrionic, exhibitionistic type. Individuals with this disorder are egocentric and self-absorbed and usually have poor sexual adjustment. Often called hysterical personality.

**Homeostasis** Maintenance of equilibrium and constancy among the bodily processes.

**Homosexuality** Sexual activity between persons of the same sex.

**Hormones** Glandular secretions which function as coordinates of bodily reactions to external events and body growth and development.

**Hot reactor** Person who shows dramatic increase in blood pressure under stress. Contrast with *Cool reactor.*

**Humanistic-existentialist perspective** Idea that all individuals are unique and should be free to make their own choices about life directions. Emphasizes the creative freedom and potential of the individual.

**Humanistic therapies** Psychotherapies with special emphasis on human beings' fundamental desire to obtain self-respect and their need for it. Carl Rogers' approach is an example.

**Huntington's disease/Huntington's chorea** Uncommon degenerative disease occurring in families. Symptoms include jerking and twisting movement, and facial grimaces.

**Hyperactivity** *See* Attention deficit-hyperactivity disorder.

**Hypertension** High blood pressure, often considered a psychophysiologic disorder.

**Hypervigilance** Tendency to constantly survey the environment for negative stimuli. A coping mechanism often used by avoidant personalities and by anxious individuals.

**Hypnosis** Altered state of consciousness induced by suggestion. Ranges from mild hypersuggestibility to deep, trancelike states.

**Hypochondriasis (Hypochondria)** Disorder in which a person is preoccupied by fear of disease and worries a great deal about his or her health without any realistic cause.

**Hypomania** A disorder characterized by unusual elevation in mood that is not as extreme as that found in mania.

**Hypothalamus** Part of the brain that lies below the thalamus. Controls various activities of the autonomic nervous system, including regulation of body temperature.

**Hypothesis** A statement of relationship or cause and effect stated in terms that allow a scientific test.

**Hypothesis-testing experiment** Evaluation of the correctness of an idea by experimental test.

**Hypothetical construct** Inferred intermediate mechanism; a concept conceived of as having properties of its own (e.g., a memory trace).

**Hysteria** Presence of a physical problem without any physical causes. A person with hysteria is called an hysteric.

**Hysteric** Term used by Charcot to describe an individual who complained of organic symptoms such as pain, blindness, or paralysis for which no organic cause could be found.

**Id** In psychoanalysis, that division of the psyche which is a repository of all instinctual impulses and repressed mental contents. Represents the true unconscious or the "deepest" part of the psyche.

**Identification** Feeling of association with another person or group such that an individual takes on the viewpoint and behavior of the other(s).

**Idiot** Term formerly used for a retarded individual whose intelligence fell in the lowest measurable range.

**Imipramine** One of the tricyclic drugs used in the treatment of some depressed individuals.

**Immune system** Body system that fights disease through inactivation of foreign substances by means of lymphocyte cells.

**Implosive therapy** Behavior-therapy technique based on the principle of extinction. Client is repeatedly presented with strong anxiety-provoking stimuli until he or she no longer reacts in an anxious manner.

**Impotence** Failure of a male to attain or maintain a penile erection.

**Inauthentic behavior** According to existential theorists, the determination of behavioral goals by others, not one's self.

**Incest** Sexual relations between close family members, such as brother and sister.

**Incidence data** Incidence concerning the number of new cases that begin during a certain period of time. A term used in epidemiology. Contrast with *Prevalence data.*

**Incompetent** Legal term used to describe individuals who are not able to understand the meaning of legal proceedings in which they are involved and who are unable to consult with an attorney in a way that might assist their defense.

**Increased-stress theory** Idea that the negative impact of the condition of poverty and crime make mental illness, especially schizophrenia, more likely because of the increased pressures of living. Contrast with *Social-selection theory.*

**Independent variable**  Experimental factor (e.g., time of food deprivation) that is manipulated or altered in some manner while others are held constant.

**Index case**  *See* Proband.

**Indoleamine**  Type of neurotransmitter of the mono-amine group that appears especially closely related to mood. An example is *Serotonin.*

**Infantile sexuality**  View held by Sigmund Freud that children as well as adults have sexual feelings and experience erotic stimulation.

**Inflexibility**  Difficult to change. In personality, those coping styles habitually used even if they are unsuitable to a given situation.

**Information processing**  A view of cognitive behavior that compares the human senses and brain function and behavior to a computer.

**Informed consent**  Requirement that patients must be given adequate information about the benefits and risks of planned treatments before they agree to the procedures.

**Insanity**  Legal term connoting mental incompetence, inability to distinguish "right from wrong," and one's inability to care for him- or herself.

**Insight**  Self-knowledge. Understanding the significance and purpose of one's motives or behavior, including the ability to recognize inappropriateness and irrationality.

**Intelligence test**  Standardized test used to establish an intelligence-level rating by measuring an individual's ability in a variety of tasks including information, word meaning, concept formation, and various performance skills.

**Interactional view of behavior**  Viewpoint that directs attention to the joint effects or interactions of many of the variables emphasized by different theoretical viewpoints in producing abnormal behavior.

**Internal locus of control**  Tendency to see the self rather than the environment as the cause of events. *See also* Locus of control.

**Intervening variable**  Inferred variable functionally connected with antecedents and consequences. Intervening variables are abstractions and have no properties other than those defined by the empirical data.

**Interview**  *See* Diagnostic interview, Therapeutic interview.

**Intoxication**  Mental disorder and the presence of maladaptive behavior due to the use and present effect on the body of some substance. The most common behavior changes are inattention and impaired thinking, judgment, emotional control, and motor activity.

**Intrapsychic conflict**  Lack of acceptance of certain areas of thought or emotion that make it necessary for an individual to attempt to keep some material out of awareness.

**Irrational thought**  Ideas and beliefs that are derived from emotional response rather than from reasoning.

**Isolation**  Defense mechanism by which inconsistent or contradictory attitudes and feelings are walled off from each other in consciousness. Similar to repression, except that in isolation the impulse or wish is consciously recognized, but is separated from present behavior; in repression, neither the wish nor its relation to action is recognized. Intellectualization is a special form of isolation.

**Juvenile delinquency**  Violations of the law committed by adolescents (usually defined as persons 18 years of age or younger).

**Kaufman Assessment Battery for Children**  (K-ABC) Intelligence test designed to reduce cultural bias by use of measures from cognitive psychology and neuropsychology.

**Kinsey Report**  First detailed statistical report that attempted to present the variations in human sexual behavior from a descriptive, scientific view.

**Klinefelter syndrome**  Condition characterized by the presence of an XXY or XXXY pattern of sex chromosomes. Occurs in males; is usually accompanied by below-average intelligence.

**Korsakoff's syndrome**  Chronic brain disorder precipitated by a vitamin deficiency stemming from alcoholism. Characterized by marked disorientation, amnesia, and falsification of memory.

**Labeling**  Cognitive device by which a person classifies his or her own emotional responses as a way of controlling behavior, especially in stress-producing situations. Also a way people are categorized by others, a way of stereotyping.

**La belle indifference**  *See* Belle indifference.

**Laceration**  Gross tear or rupture in tissue. Cerebral lacerations may occur through head injuries.

**Latency period**  According to Freud the period from age 5 until adolescence during which the child's sexual impulses are not a primary focus of his or her pleasure-seeking activities.

**Learned helplessness**  Acquired belief in one's helplessness to deal with a situation or control one's environment. Concept has been applied to explain depression in humans.

**Learning perspective**  Idea that what one experiences is the most important aspect of behavior. Behavior is considered as a product of stimulus-response relationships. Behaviorists are one group of learning theorists.

**Lesbianism**  Female homosexuality.

**Libido**  Psychoanalytic term referring to the general instinctual drives of the id. Motivational force related to the concepts of psychic energy and drive. Libidinal energy or drive is composed of libidinal impulses, which Freud felt were genetically determined. In a narrow sense, some writers have equated libido with sexual drive, although it more appropriately refers to an organism's total quest for pleasure and gratification.

**Librium**  (chlordiazepoxide) Tranquilizer often prescribed for anxiety problems.

**Limbic system**  Part of the brain that controls visceral and bodily changes associated with emotion; also regulates drive-motivated behavior. Lower parts of the cerebrum.

**Lithium**  (lithium carbonate) Chemical salt used in the treatment of bipolar disorder.

**Locus, gene**  The characteristic position within a chromosome where a particular gene pair is located.

**Locus of control**  Personality characteristic described by Julian Rotter in which an individual believes either that he or she has the power to affect the outcome of situations (internal locus of control) or that he or she has little control over what happens (external locus of control).

**Longitudinal study**  Research strategy based on observing and recording the behavior of people over periods of time. Involves obtaining measures on the same people either continuously or at specific or regular intervals.

**LSD (Lysergic acid dimethylamide)**  Chemically produced synthetic hallucinogen with psychotomimetic properties.

**Lunatic**  Term used in the past to describe the insane. The word luna (moon) refers to the old belief that those who were insane were moonstruck.

**Lycanthropy**  Term for the magical change believed to overcome individuals and cause them to behave like wolves.

**Lymphocyte**  A general term that includes several types of cells in the immune system that fight disease.

**Magical forces**  Supernatural powers used to control natural events.

**Mainstreaming**  Practice of assigning retarded and other handicapped children to classes with all ability levels and with nonphysically impaired children rather than segregating them with others who are similar to themselves.

**Major depressive disorder or episode**  A severe depression characterized by dysphoric mood, poor appetite, sleep problems, feelings of restlessness or of being slowed down, loss of pleasure, loss of energy, feelings of inability to concentrate or of indecisiveness, and recurrent thoughts of death or suicide attempts. These occur without mood-incongruent delusions or hallucinations and are not due to schizophrenia, paranoid disorder, organic mental disorder, or recent death of a loved one.

**Maladaptive behavior**  Behavior that deals inadequately with a situation, especially one that is stressful.

**Male limited**  Hereditary pattern which seems to be transmitted only from fathers and only to male offspring.

**Malingering**  Behavior designed to get financial or other rewards by pretending to have some disorder. Contrast with *Factitious disorder*.

**Mania**  Euphoric, hyperactive state in which an individual's judgment is impaired.

**Manic depressive psychosis**  *See* Bipolar disorder.

**Mantra**  *See* Meditation.

**MAO inhibitor**  *See* Monoamine oxidase inhibitor.

**Marijuana**  Substance derived from the leaves or flowering tops of the cannabis plant. Smoking it leads to a dreamy or altered consciousness in which ideas are disconnected, uncontrollable, and plentiful. Under the influence of marijuana, behavior is impulsive and mood is elevated.

**Marital schism**  Term used by T. Lidz to describe a marriage of open conflict in which each parent tries to gain the child as an ally against the other.

**Marital skew**  Term used by T. Lidz to describe a situation in which overtly pathological behavior by one parent is accepted by the other parent as normal.

**Markers**  Biological characteristics that may make it

possible to identify people who are vulnerable to certain disorders.

**Masochism** Deviation in which sexual pleasure is attained from pain inflicted on oneself, from being dominated, or from being mistreated.

**Masochist** One who practices masochism.

**Masturbation** Self-stimulation of the genitals for the purposes of deriving sexual pleasure.

**Mediator** A link—for example, between a stimulus and the resulting behavior.

**Meditation** The technique of relaxing through concentrating on a thought, sensation, or special word or mantra.

**Medroxyprogesterone acetate (MPA)** A chemical used to reduce the level of male sex hormone in the blood. In experimental use for treating some of the paraphilias. Trade name Depo-Provera.

**Meningitis** Inflammation of any or all of the meninges of the brain and spinal cord. Usually caused by a bacterial infection.

**Mental age** The age equivalent at which a person's intellectual behavior places him or her. Contrasted to chronological age, the person's actual age as determined by birth date. The ratio between the two (MA/CA $\times$ 100) was the original formulation of the intelligence quotient.

**Mental retardation** Intellectual functioning significantly below average. Generally defined as an intelligence test score of 70 or below together with a poor level of social functioning. The degree of retardation is further defined. Scores of 50 to 70 are called mild retardation, 35 to 49 moderate, 20 to 34 severe, and below 20 profound retardation.

**Mental-status examination** An interview, sometimes supplemented with psychological and neurological tests, used to assess an individual's intellectual function and ability to interact appropriately with the environment.

**Meta-analysis** Technique used to investigate the effects of psychotherapy on clients. The results are studied by a process of combining the data from many studies in a meaningful way.

**Metacognition** A person's knowledge of his or her own cognitive processes and the products of these processes.

**Methadone** Synthetic chemical whose action is similar to that of morphine. Because its use allegedly does not lead to escalation of dosage, it is prescribed by some authorities as a treatment for heroin addiction.

**Methadone maintenance** Use of methadone as a substitute for heroin. Methadone prevents withdrawal and suppresses the desire for heroin, although it itself has undesirable side effects.

**Methylphenidate** (e.g., Ritalin). Stimulant drug sometimes used in the treatment of hyperactivity.

**Migraine headache** Severe headache caused by a constriction followed by a dilation of the cranial artery. Usually preceded by some sensory or emotional cues called an aura. The disorder is thought to have some stress-related components.

**Milieu-limited** Term for a hereditary pattern in which a disorder seems to appear only under certain environmental conditions.

**Milieu therapy** Effort to provide a totally therapeutic environment within an institution by enlisting the efforts of all staff members as providers of some form of therapeutic contact.

**Mind** Human consciousness as shown in thought, perception, and memory. Reflects the artificial dichotomy often made between mind and body.

**Minnesota Multiphasic Personality Inventory (MMPI)** Self-report personality questionnaire designed to facilitate psychiatric diagnosis.

**M'Naghten rule** Legal precedent in English law, originating in 1843, which provides for acquittal if an accused person is found to be not responsible for the crime—that is, if he or she could not distinguish between "right and wrong." Rule did not take into account that a person might be held to be insane even though he or she knew the difference between right and wrong.

**Modeling** Behavior learned or modified as a result of observing the behavior of others. Learner does not have to make the observed response him- or herself, or be reinforced for making it, to learn the new behavior. Term used interchangeably with observational learning.

**Monoamine** Type of neurotransmitter with a distinctive single amino acid ($NH_2$) in its molecular structure. There are two types of monoamines: catecholamines and indoleamines.

**Monoamine hypothesis** An explanation of how depression is produced by a lack of noradrenalin or serotonen.

**Monoamine oxidase (MAO)** Enzyme in the neuron receptors that inactivates the various amines, including the catecholamines.

**Monoamine oxidase (MAO) inhibitor** One of a group of drugs used to treat depression. Works by preventing the degrading of monoamines and thus allowing more norepinephrine and serotonin to collect at the receptor sites.

**Monogenic (single-gene) theory**   Refers to theory of inheritance in which a gene at one particular locus (e.g., one site on a chromosome) is sufficient to produce an inherited characteristic.

**Monozygotic twins**   Identical twins developed from one fertilized egg.

**Mood disorder**   One of a group of disorders primarily affecting emotional tone. Can be depression, manic excitement, or both. May be episodic or chronic.

**Moral treatment**   Technique of treating mental-hospital patients which prevailed in the nineteenth century. Emphasized removal of restraints, allowing religious conviction, and ensuring humanitarian treatment.

**Morphine**   Principle derivative of opium, which has been used extensively to relieve pain.

**Multiaxial classification system**   System that rates an individual separately on a number of different criteria or axes. The DSM-III-R is an example.

**Multifactorial polygenic model**   Theory that a number of genes from a variety of loci may combine to produce a particular characteristic or disorder.

**Multi-infarct dementia**   Intellectual deficit resulting from a series of minor strokes that occur over a period of time.

**Multiple personality**   Rare form of dissociative disorder characterized by development and existence of two or more relatively independent and coexisting personality systems within the same individual.

**Munchausen syndrome**   A factitious disorder in which the person pretends to have a particular disorder in order to get medical treatment. Involves faking of symptoms, and often self-injury.

**Musts**   Term used by Albert Ellis to define unrealistic, self-defeating demands that many people make of themselves because they feel that society expects such behavior.

**Mutant**   A cell in which the hereditary material has been altered. This mutation may be spontaneous (occurring naturally) or induced by internal factors such as radiation and certain chemicals.

**Mutation**   Sudden change in the composition of a gene, which usually causes abnormal characteristics in the progeny.

**Myocardial infarction (commonly called a heart attack)**   Tissue damage to the heart muscle from a drastic decrease in the amount of blood that reaches the heart.

**Naloxone**   A drug that blocks the pain-relieving effects of endorphins.

**Narcissism**   Term for self-love or self-absorption derived from the Greek myth about Narcissus who fell in love with what he thought was a water nymph but was in reality his own reflection in a pond.

**Narcissistic personality disorder**   Characterized by a sense of self-importance and a preoccupation with fantasies of unlimited success. Individuals are preoccupied with how well they are doing and how well others think of them. Disorder is often accompanied by depressed mood.

**Narcotics**   Addicting drugs, the most common of which are the opiates, derived from the Oriental poppy.

**Natural disaster**   Overwhelming event caused by the forces of nature rather than human intervention—for example, a tornado, earthquake, or flood.

**Natural fool**   Old term for a retarded person. It means one who is born deficient in judgment.

**Nature-nurture controversy**   Argument concerning the relative influences of heredity and environment in the development of individuals.

**Negative reinforcer**   *See* Reinforcer.

**Negative symptoms**   (in schizophrenia) *See* Type II schizophrenia.

**Negative transference**   Feelings of hostility a client transfers from earlier relationships into his or her relationship with a therapist.

**Neoanalyst**   Therapist who agrees with a revised version of Freud's concepts.

**Neo-Freudian**   Pertaining to former followers of Freud who departed in several major doctrinal ways from orthodox psychoanalysis. Prominent among the neo-Freudians are Adler, Jung, and Sullivan. Their writings emphasize the social and cultural determinants of behavior.

**Neuroleptic drugs**   Name for a group of psychoactive drugs that are used to treat schizophrenic disorders. These reduce psychotic symptoms but may have neurological side effects.

**Neurologist**   Specialist in the diagnosis and treatment of disorders of the nervous system.

**Neuron**   Individual nerve cell.

**Neuropsychology**   Branch of psychology dealing with brain-behavior relationships.

**Neurosis**   Older term for what are now called anxiety disorders.

**Neurotic depression**   Older term for dysthmic disorder.

**Neurotransmitter** Chemical product of the nervous system that makes possible the movement of the nerve impulse across the synapse.

**Nicotine** Volatile psychoactive substance that is the chief active chemical in tobacco.

**Non compus mentis** Latin term meaning not of sound mind and therefore not legally responsible.

**Nontranssexual cross gender disorder** Persistent discomfort about one's assigned sex. Frequent cross dressing or fantasies about cross dressing. Differs from transsexualism in that there is no persistent preoccupation to acquire the primary and secondary sexual characteristics of the other sex.

**Norepinephrine** Hormone also called noradrenalin, produced by the adrenal medulla. One of the catecholamine group.

**Observational research** A method in which no variables are manipulated and relationships are studied as they naturally occur. Contrast with *Experimental method.*

**Obsessive behavior** Characterized by preoccupation with a particular type of thought which keeps recurring repetitively.

**Obsessive-compulsive personality disorder** Distinguished by lack of ability to express warmth, a stiff and formal way of relating to others, and extreme perfectionism that leads an individual to focus on details rather than on the whole picture.

**Obsessive-compulsive disorder** Characterized by recurrent obsessions and/or compulsions, often accompanied by depression or anxiety.

**Occipital lobe** The part of the cerebral cortex lying at the back of the head; contains the primary sensory areas for vision.

**Oedipus complex** Freudian term for a constellation of motives and behaviors occurring among male children at approximately the fifth year of life; characterized by the development of an intense fantasized love relationship with the mother and accompanied by the wish to assume the role occupied by the father. The equivalent process in female children is termed the Electra complex. Both are hypothesized to be resolved by identification with the same-sex parent.

**Operant conditioning** (instrumental conditioning) Form of conditioning in which a desired response occurs and is subsequently reinforced to increase its probability of more frequent occurrence.

**Operant response** Response originally occurring rarely, that has been increased in frequency through reinforcement.

**Opiate** Natural or synthetic substance that is similar in action to morphine or other derivatives of the opium poppy.

**Opioid** Drug with a morphine-like action. Can be derived from either a natural or synthetic substance.

**Oral dependent** Psychodynamic term to describe individuals who secure a major part of their psychological gratification from such activities as eating, drinking, and smoking, and who may show dependent personality characteristics.

**Oral stage** First developmental stage of infancy, during which pleasure is derived from lip and mouth contact with need-fulfilling objects (e.g., breast).

**Organic affective syndrome** Abnormal changes in mood thought to be the result of changes in brain metabolism or toxic conditions.

**Organic anxiety syndrome** Panic attacks or generalized anxiety thought to be causally related to some specific organic factor.

**Organic brain syndrome** Group of symptoms characteristic of acute and chronic brain disorders.

**Organic defect theory** Idea that a particular bodily organ that is working improperly is the cause of maladaptive behavior.

**Organic delusional syndrome** Delusional thinking that occurs as the result of some organic condition, often associated with abuse of a variety of substances including amphetamines, cannabis, and hallucinogens.

**Organic hallucinosis** Hallucinations caused by some organic factor. Often the result of use of hallucinogenic drugs or large quantities of alcohol.

**Organic mental disorder** Brain dysfunction based on either aging or the ingestion of substances that affect brain activity. May be temporary or permanent.

**Organic personality syndrome** Diagnosis used when major personality changes occur that are believed to be the result of some change in or injury to brain tissue.

**Organismic point of view** Pertaining to the organism as a whole rather than to particular parts. Behavior is considered an interrelated and interactive function of the integrated organism.

**Organ-susceptibility hypothesis** Idea that emotional stress might cause a psychophysiological problem in a bodily organ in a particular individual because that organ had some inherent weakenss.

**Orgasm** Third stage of sexual response, which involves rhythmic muscular contractions and high physical arousal. In the male, ejaculation of semen takes place during this stage.

**Orienting response**  Measurable psychophysiological changes that come about when a person notices an environmental stimulus and prepares to receive some information from it.

**Overgeneralization**  According to Aaron Beck, characteristic way of thinking found in some depressed individuals. Tendency to exaggerate the meaning of an event into a general principle.

**Panic disorder**  Type of anxiety disorder characterized by recurring panic or anxiety attacks and extreme nervousness not necessarily related to exposure to threatening situations.

**Paradigm**  A model or example.

**Paradoxical intention**  Therapeutic technique in which the client is instructed to perform behaviors that seem to be counter to the therapeutic goal. For instance, someone who is afraid of crowds may be instructed to go into a crowd and concentrate on feeling as fearful as possible.

**Paranoid disorder**  Disorder characterized by the persistence of delusions that are usually well organized; does not include prominent hallucinations, incoherent speech, thought derailment, or many of the delusions associated with schizophrenia.

**Paranoid personality disorder**  Personality disorder similar in some ways to schizoid personality disorder, but notable for extreme sensitivity in interpersonal relationships; suspicious, jealous, and stubborn behavior; and a tendency to use defense mechanism of projection.

**Paranoid schizophrenia**  Type of schizophrenia characterized by persistent delusions, often either grandiose or accusatory.

**Paraphilia**  Sexual deviation that involves either inappropriate sex partners or inappropriate goals for the sex act. Pedophilia, sadism, and voyeurism are examples.

**Paraprofessional**  Term used to describe workers who have received certain basic training that enables them to perform routine tasks formerly performed by professional workers. Paraprofessionals often come from the same communities and educational backgrounds as the people whom they treat or aid.

**Parasuicide**  Term used to describe any act which does not end in death in which a person deliberately causes self-injury or takes a drug overdose with the apparent intention of suicide.

**Parens patriae**  Legal doctrine that gives the state power to act in what it believes to be the best interest of an incapacitated adult or a minor.

**Parental affective style**  A measure of negative feelings expressed by family members as the family discusses upsetting problems together. Compare with *Expressed emotion.*

**Paresis**  Chronic and progressively deteriorating brain condition caused by syphilitic infection and characterized by loss of cognitive and motor functions, speech disorder, and eventual death.

**Parietal (lobe)**  Middle division of each cerebral hemisphere of the brain, behind the central sulcus, above the fissure of Sylvius and in front of the parieto-occipital fissure.

**Parkinson's disease**  Chronic and progressive neurological disorder characterized by motor tremor, rigidity, and loss of vocal power. Believed to be caused by an acquired defect in brain metabolism.

**Partial hospitalization**  Use of either day, night, or weekend hospital care for patients who do not need 24-hour care. Designed particularly to aid transition back to the community. Also used to prevent complete hospitalization if the family can provide partial care, for instance, outside of their own working hours.

**Participant modeling**  Therapeutic procedure in which the response is first demonstrated for the client, who then produces the same response with suggestions from the therapist.

**Passive-aggressive personality disorder**  Usually characterized by aggressive behavior exhibited in passive ways (e.g., pouting). Three types are often distinguished: (1) passive-aggressive type: hostility and aggression expressed by passive means such as obstructionism, stubbornness, inefficiency, and procrastination; (2) aggressive type: hostility and aggressiveness expressed directly through temper tantrums, destructive behavior, argumentativeness, and negativism; and (3) passive-dependent type: characterized by overdependency, helplessness, indecisiveness, and the childlike tendency to cling to others. Reactions are grouped together on the basis that they seem to represent different reactions to common-core conflicts over dependency and aggression.

**Pathology**  Disease or abnormal physical condition.

**PCP (phencyclidine)**  Hallucinogenic drug popularly known as "angel dust."

**Pedophilia**  Sexual deviation in which an adult desires or engages in sexual relations with a child. May be either homosexual or heterosexual in nature.

**Pellegra**  Chronic disease caused by niacin deficiency.

Symptoms include skin eruptions, digestive disturbances, and disturbances of the nervous system which may cause psychoticlike behavior.

**Penetrance**   Percentage of cases in which, regarding a specific gene, a particular trait or characteristic will manifest itself in subsequent organisms of the species.

**Pepsinogen**   Substance found in the gastric system that is converted to a digestive enzyme by hydrochloric acid in the digestive system. Individuals with high natural pepsinogen levels are prone to develop ulcers under stressful conditions.

**Performance anxiety (sexual)**   High degree of concern in males about the ability to maintain an erection until orgasm. The anxiety has a negative effect on sexual performance.

**Performance I.Q.**   One of the two subscores of the Wechsler intelligence-test series. Reflects ability to solve puzzles, copy designs, and perform other similar tasks.

**Peripheral nervous system**   System which includes all outlying nerve structures not included in the central nervous system.

**Personal constructs**   A term originated by George Kelly for personal categories and labels.

**Personality**   Particular constellation of attributes that defines one's individuality.

**Personality disorder**   Deeply ingrained, inflexible, maladaptive patterns of thought and behavior which persist throughout a person's life.

**Personality growth needs**   According to Maslow, the highest level of needs, to be considered only after all other levels are fulfilled. Includes needs for creativity and intellectual stimulation and achievement.

**Personality inventories**   Paper-and-pencil tests in which the person describes him- or herself by answering a series of true–false questions or by rating a series of self-descriptive phrases. Most personality inventories yield several scores, each of which is intended to describe an aspect of personality.

**Personality maladaptation**   Perception by an individual of personal dissatisfactions and concerns that interfere with happiness but not significantly with social adjustment or work achievement.

**Petit mal**   Mild form of epilepsy which involves partial alteration of consciousness.

**Phallic stage**   Stage of psychosexual development during which a child begins to perceive his or her body as a source of gratification. Feelings of narcissism are heightened during this period.

**Phenobarbital**   Barbiturate sometimes used as a sedative and in the control of epileptic-seizure activity.

**Phenothiazine**   One of a family of antipsychotic drugs.

**Phenylketonuria (PKU)**   Form of mental retardation caused by a metabolic deficiency.

**Phobia**   Excessive or inappropriate fear of some particular object or situation which is not in fact dangerous.

**Phobic disorder**   Type of anxiety disorder mainly characterized by irrational and highly specific fears (for example, of dirt, water, high places).

**Phrenology**   Obsolete theory that different psychological behaviors were related to the presence and shape of bumps on the surface of the skull.

**Physical disorder**   Term used to refer to a medical as opposed to a psychological problem.

**Physiotherapy**   Treatment of disorders by mechanical means—for example, exercise, heat, light, or massage.

**Pica**   Repeated eating of non-nutritive substances such as paint, clay, animal droppings, or laundry starch at a time when there is no evidence of hunger, malnutrition, or aversion.

**Pick's disease**   Type of progressive dementia caused by atrophy of the cerebral cortex.

**Placebo**   Inactive or inert substance that is presented as effective remedy for some problem in order to determine what role suggestibility plays in symptom change.

**Placebo effect**   Changes in behavior as a result of the expectancy that a placebo, or inactive substance, administered in place of an active or "real" drug, has had an actual effect. Type of suggestion effect.

**Plaque**   Abnormal structure found in nerve cells of individuals who have Alzheimer's disease.

**Plateau stage (sexual)**   Second stage of sexual response, which includes increases in heart rate and muscle tension as well as swelling of genital tissue.

**Play therapy**   Treatment approach used with children; based on the assumption that young children can express thoughts and fantasies more directly in play than through verbal means.

**Pleasure principle**   Psychoanalytic term for the regulatory mechanism for mental life that functions to reduce tension and gain gratification. Principle which governs the functioning of the id to obtain gratification without regard to reality consideration.

**Polygenic**   (many genes) Theory in genetics that several genes at different loci must interact to produce a particular inherited characteristic.

**Polygraph**  Instrument that measures emotional responses through physiological reactions, such as blood pressure and galvanic skin response. Commonly called a lie detector.

**Population genetics**  Study of the ways genes are distributed in a population through the mating of individuals.

**Positive reinforcer**  *See* Reinforcer.

**Positive symptoms**  (in schizophrenia) *See* Type I schizophrenia.

**Positive transference**  Carrying over of positive feelings about other relationships into the therapist-client relationship.

**Positron emission tomography (PT)**  Technique for studying the dynamic chemical activity of the brain by using a scanning device that produces a series of cross-section images of the brain.

**Posttraumatic stress disorder**  Development of symptoms in response to events of such severity that most people would be stressed by them. Symptoms often include a feeling of numbness in response or psychological reexperiencing of the event in thoughts, dreams, or nightmares.

**Preconscious**  Thoughts which are not held in a person's mind at a particular time but which can easily be brought into awareness.

**Premature ejaculation**  Inability of the male to inhibit ejaculation long enough for his female partner to experience orgasm.

**Premorbid adjustment**  Achievement level and adjustment to interpersonal activities shown by an individual earlier in life before a disorder becomes apparent.

**Presenile dementia**  *See* Dementia.

**Prevalence data**  Information concerning the number of cases of a particular disorder that are ongoing at any particular time. Contrast with *Incidence data*.

**Primary appraisal**  First stage of assessing the meaning of a situation. In this stage the situation is interpreted as threatening or harmless. In the following stage, secondary appraisal, the individual decides how to deal with the situation.

**Primary prevention**  Efforts at preventing the development of maladaptation by removing factors that cause it to develop.

**Primary process thinking**  Primary cognitive mode, characteristic of infants and children, that is not based on rules of organization or logic. The presence of primary process thinking, free association in its purest form, is characteristic of the id. Primary process thought is illogical, is entirely pleasure oriented, has no sense of time or order, and does not discriminate between reality and fantasy. Compare with *secondary process thinking*.

**Primative emotion node**  A hypothetical memory unit that organizes memories related to a particular mood.

**Proband**  Term used in the study of genetics to indicate the individual with a disorder whose heredity is under study.

**Problem drinking**  Term for the pattern of alcohol abuse that does not include alcohol dependence or physiological addiction.

**Prognosis**  Forecast. Probable course and outcome of a disorder.

**Projection**  Defense mechanism which involves attributing to others the undesirable characteristics or impulses which belong to but are not acceptable to the individual.

**Projective technique**  Ambiguous stimulus materials which elicit subjective responses of an associative or fantasy nature. So named because an individual is believed to "project" aspects of his or her personality into the task. Tasks may include inkblot interpretation (Rorschach Test), and various associative completion techniques (word association, incomplete sentences).

**Psilocybin**  One of the two psychoactive substances isolated from the psilocybin mushroom.

**Psychedelic drugs**  *See* Hallucinogens.

**Psychiatric beds**  The number of hospital beds and accomodations reserved for people with mental-health problems that require inpatient treatment.

**Psychiatric social work**  Field of social work in which the worker specializes in treating maladaptive behaviors in a clinical, usually medical, setting.

**Psychiatrist**  Physician with postgraduate training in the diagnosis and treatment of emotional disorders.

**Psychic determinism**  Principle of causality, one of the basic assumptions of psychoanalysis, which states that all events, overt and covert, are determined by prior and often multiple mental events.

**Psychoactive drug**  Term including several types of drugs that may reduce maladaptive behavior. Includes antipsychotic, antianxiety, and antidepressant drugs.

**Psychoanalysis**  Term has three meanings: (1) theory of psychology and psychopathology developed by Freud from his clinical experiences with patients; (2) procedure for investigating the mental life, conflicts, and coping processes, which employs the techniques of free association, dream analysis, and interpretation of transference and resistance phenomena; and (3) form of therapy that uses the psychoanalytic procedure and the theories of personality and psychopathology just described.

**Psychodrama** Method of group therapy in which individuals both act out their emotional responses in situations they find difficult and also practice new, constructive roles.

**Psychodynamic perspective** Point of view that emphasizes thoughts and emotions as the most important determiners of behavior. Basic ideas come from the work of Sigmund Freud.

**Psychogenic** Adjective referring to symptoms for which an organic cause cannot be specified.

**Psychogenic amnesia** Disturbance in the ability to recall important personal information in the absence of an organic disorder and without the assumption of a new identity such as that found in a psychogenic fugue.

**Psychogenic fugue** *See* Fugue state.

**Psychogenic pain disorder** Characterized by severe pain that does not have an identifiable physical cause.

**Psychoimmunology** Study of the relationship between changes in immune system functioning and psychological events.

**Psychological dependence** Habit or need that requires continued or repeated administration of a drug to produce pleasure or to avoid conflict.

**Psychological hardiness** Term used by Kobasa and other researchers to describe people who are more resistant to stress and illness than most people. Research on hardiness is directed toward understanding precisely what characteristics are involved.

**Psychological numbing** Reduced capacity for emotion, and symptoms of apathy, withdrawal, and depression. These are likely to occur after a disaster.

**Psychology of personal constructs** The approach of George Kelly, who was interested in helping his clients understand the unique way in which they viewed themselves and other people and also to see that their behavior was designed to fill certain roles. Kelly urged his clients to try out new roles rather than be stuck in nonadaptive ways of interacting.

**Psychological perspective** View that maladaptive behavior is caused by problems of perception, cognition, or emotion rather than by biological causes.

**Psychological tests** Procedures to measure in a standardized way some aspect of behavior such as intelligence or personality characteristics.

**Psychometric** Refers to measures of psychological functioning.

**Psychomotor** Term used to describe muscular action resulting from prior mental activity, especially conscious mental activity.

**Psychomotor epilepsy** Trancelike state with recurring episodes of confusion during which repetitive and semiautomatic muscle movements occur. Often accompanied by confusion and visual hallucinations.

**Psychopath** Term used by Hervey Cleckley to describe antisocial individuals who met a certain set of characteristics including charm, lack of anxiety or guilt, poor judgment and failure to learn from experience.

**Psychopharmacology** Study of the effects of drugs on psychological functioning and behavior.

**Psychophysiological assessment** Measurement of various body functions such as blood pressure, heart rate, breathing, and galvanic skin response in an attempt to understand feelings and emotions. One commercial use is the polygraph or lie detector.

**Psychophysiological (psychosomatic) disorder** Physical pathology and actual tissue damage that results from continued emotional mobilization of the body during periods of sustained stress.

**Psychophysiology of behavior** Study of the relationship between observed behavior and the functions of the central and peripheral nervous systems.

**Psychosexual disorder** Deviant sexual thoughts and/or behavior that are either personally anxiety-provoking, or are injurious to others.

**Psychosexual stage** One of several developmental stages of life as defined by Sigmund Freud. These differ in terms of the source of primary gratification and include oral, anal, phallic, and genital stages.

**Psychosis (plural is psychoses)** Disorder that includes any of the following: delusions, hallucinations, incoherence, repeated derailment of thought, marked poverty of thought content, marked illogicality, and grossly disorganized or catatonic behavior.

**Psychosocial disadvantage** Growing up in an intellectually, culturally, and financially impoverished environment.

**Psychosocial stressor** Feeling of stress arising from relationships with other people in the environment.

**Psychosomatic disorder** *See* Psychophysiological disorder.

**Psychosomatic hypothesis** Idea popular in the 1930s and 1940s that physical symptoms can be caused by an inability to express strong emotions.

**Psychotherapy** General term referring to psychological, verbal, and expressive techniques used in treating maladaptive behavior. The client works on resolving inner conflicts and modifying his or her behavior by means of verbal interchanges with the therapist. Insight into feelings and behavior is the goal of most psychotherapy.

**Psychotic** An adjective indicating the presence of psychosis.

**PT scan** *See* Positron emission tomography.

**Punishment** Aversive stimulus given as a result of an undesired behavior in an attempt to suppress that behavior in the future.

**Radical behaviorists** Group of learning theorists who think of behavior as entirely a response to environmental stimuli.

**Rape** Sexual intercourse accomplished by force and without the partner's consent.

**Rape, statutory** Crime defined as having sexual intercourse with someone below the age of legal consent. Force is not necessarily involved.

**Rape-relief center** Organization, often composed in part of volunteers, designed to provide information about medical and legal services for those who have been raped and also to offer psychological support for the victims.

**Rapid smoking** Behavioral method to help people stop smoking. The client smokes cigarettes with a very high frequency until the experience becomes a negative one and desire for further smoking decreases. Dangerous because it may result in significant increases in blood pressure.

**Rating scale** Type of test in which a person can indicate on a scale the degree of his or her agreement with each item.

**Rational approach** Idea that only the use of reason and not experimental evidence or observation is the prime source of truth.

**Rational-emotive therapy** Therapy developed by Albert Ellis to modify unrealistic and illogical thought.

**Rational thinking** Based on reasoning and logic, not on observation or experimental evidence.

**Reaction formation** Defense mechanism which enables the individual to express an unacceptable impulse by transforming it into its opposite.

**Reactive attachment disorder** Characterized by either lack of response or indiscriminate sociability in interpersonal situations by children who have been physically abused or neglected.

**Recall** A measure of information retention in which the subject is asked to reproduce as many parts of a previous stimulus as possible.

**Recessive gene** Member of a gene pair which determines the characteristic trait or appearance of the individual only if the other member of the pair matches it. Compare to *dominant gene*.

**Recognition** A measure of information retention in which the subject is asked to select which of several stimulus items have been presented previously.

**Refractory period (sexual)** In males, the period after orgasm when no additional arousal can occur. Females may or may not have a refractory period.

**Regress** To go backward or return to an earlier level of functioning. Interpreted in psychoanalytic theory as a defense mechanism. *See* Regression.

**Regression** Defense mechanism characterized by a return to earlier and more primitive modes of responding. Through regression, the ego returns to an earlier developmental phase of functioning which had met with some success.

**Reinforcement** Any event (stimulus) which, if contingent upon response by an organism, increases the probability that the response will be made again. Reinforcements may be positive (reward) or negative (aversive) and may be presented according to a prescribed schedule (continuous, intermittent). May also be primary (drive reducing—e.g., food) or secondary (derived from prior association with a primary reinforcer—e.g., money, praise).

**Reinforcer** A consequence of behavior that makes it more likely the behavior will occur again. A *positive reinforcer* achieves this result by provoking a reward or pleasure. A *negative reinforcer* is a stimulus that ceases when the desired behavior is performed. *See also* Punishment.

**Relapse prevention** In treatment of alcohol problems from a cognitive viewpoint, the emphasis on identifying problem situations and helping the client to identify coping devices that may give him or her a feeling of control over such situations.

**Relaxation training** Series of specified exercises that the client learns to perform in order to remove a tension response that may be characteristic in certain situations.

**Reliability** The tendency of a measure or procedure to produce the same results when administered on two different occasions. Also refers to the internal homogeneity of a multiple-item test.

**Remission** Ending of the symptoms of a disorder. Implies that the basic problem may still exist.

**REM sleep** Stage of sleep characterized by rapid eye movements and a characteristic brain-wave pattern. Reducing the amount of REM sleep may help decrease some types of depressive symptoms.

**Repression** Psychoanalytic defense mechanism which involves a stopping-thinking or not-being-able-to-remember response. Repression actively forces traumatic events, intolerable and dangerous impulses, and other undesirable mental affects out of consciousness into the less-accessible realm of the unconscious.

**Retardation** Level of intellectual functioning that is significantly below average and is accompanied by an inability to behave adaptively in society because of this lack of cognitive ability.

**Retarded ejaculation** Inhibition of the sexual response of males that results in an inability to eject semen even when sexually excited.

**Rheumatoid arthritis** Chronic joint disease with inflammation caused by immune-system activity.

**Rh incompatibility** Presence of incompatible substances on the surfaces of red blood cells of a pregnant woman and her fetus. The mother's blood will produce antibodies that may harm the unborn child unless preventative measures are taken.

**Ritalin** *See* Methylphenidate.

**Ritualistic behavior** Behavior that follows a series of prescribed actions that are repeated even though they may be maladaptive. Thought to be a way of reducing anxiety.

**Role playing** In psychotherapy, a technique which requires an individual to enact a social role other than his or her own, or to try out a new role. In sociology, an individual's assumption of the role expected of him or her in a particular type of situation.

**Rorschach inkblots** Projective test developed by Hermann Rorschach in which the individual is shown a series of ambiguous inkblots and asked to describe what is seen in them.

**Rubella** (commonly called German measles) Virus which, if present in a pregnant woman, particularly during the first 3 months of pregnancy, can cause retardation and other congenital disorders in her child.

**Rumination disorder of infancy** Disorder in which partially digested food is brought up into the infant's mouth without nausea or vomiting. The infant loses weight or fails to gain weight after a period of normal functioning.

**Saccadic eye movement** Quick jerks of the eye interspersed with steady fixations that are under voluntary control.

**Sadism** Sexual deviation in which sexual gratification is obtained through inflicting physical pain on other people.

**Sadist** One who practices sadism.

**Schemata** Cognitive clusters that serve as a person's organizing system for knowledge and experience.

**Schizoaffective disorder** Separate category from either schizophrenia or affective disorders for individuals who show depressive or manic symptoms as well as those of thought disorder.

**Schizoid personality disorder** Classification used for withdrawn individuals who are not disturbed by their lack of social relationships. These people have flat emotional responses and often seem cold and detached.

**Schizophrenias** Term used by Eugen Bleuler to indicate that schizophrenia probably represented a group of disorders that might have different causes and outcomes.

**Schizophrenic disorders** Group of disorders that always involves at least one of the following at some time: delusions, hallucinations, or certain characteristics of thought disorder.

**Schizophrenic spectrum disorder** One of a group of disorders including schizotypal and paranoid personality disorders, and sometimes schizoaffective disorder, atypical psychosis and paranoid disorder, which are thought by some researchers to be produced by the same genetic factors as schizophrenia. Used as an explanation for the fact that the incidence of narrowly defined schizophrenia alone is less than would be expected by monogenetic theory.

**Schizotypal personality disorder** Shows some of the symptoms of schizophrenia, but not in as extreme a form. People with this disorder include those formerly classified as simple schizophrenic. Differs from schizoid personality disorder in that it includes eccentricities of communication and behavior not seen in that group.

**School phobia** Irrational fear of the school situation. Contrast with *School refusal.*

**School refusal** Separation anxiety that results in the child's complete unwillingness to leave home for school.

**Secondary appraisal** Second stage of appraisal of a situation in which an individual considers the kind of action necessary and whether he or she has the skills to deal with the situation.

**Secondary prevention** Efforts directed toward detecting early signs or symptoms to prevent a more serious condition.

**Secondary process thinking** Psychoanalytic concept referring to organized, logical, and reality-oriented adult thinking. Whereas primary process thinking is characteristic of the id and is based on the pleasure principle, secondary process thought is an ego function based on the reality principle.

**Self-actualization** Synonymous with self-fulfillment. Process by which the development of one's potentials and abilities is achieved.

**Self-determination** Viewpoint of existential theorists that individuals have control of their own lives through the choices they make.

**Self-efficacy** The belief held by someone about his or her own personal effectiveness in acting in specific or general types of situations.

**Self-instruction** A cognitive behavioral approach in which clients are taught to monitor their behavior and give themselves direction either by repeating aloud or in audibly prelearned instructions with which to direct their behavior.

**Self-monitoring** Keeping detailed records of one's behavior.

**Self-observation** A method of determining the effects of variables on behavior by asking the individual to monitor and record particular behaviors or reactions and the circumstances in which they occur.

**Self-regulation** Technique of controlling one's own behavior through internal reinforcement often in the form of cognitions.

**Senile dementia** *See* Dementia.

**Sensate focus** Approach to sex therapy advocated by Masters and Johnson in which an individual learns to focus on erotic sensation to the exclusion of other stimuli.

**Sensation seeker** Term used by Zuckerman to describe people who look for and enjoy highly stimulating and exciting situations.

**Sensorimotor** Pertaining to the functions of the sensing and motor activities of the individual—for example, the sensorimotor nerves.

**Sentence-completion test** Projective test in which the client is presented with a series of incomplete sentences and is asked to complete each one.

**Separation anxiety disorder** Some children's irrational fear of being apart from the parent(s) because of worries of what will happen to themselves or to their parent(s) in their absence.

**Serotonin (5HT)** One of a group of chemical neurotransmitters that implement neural transmission across the synapse. Thought to be involved in some types of depression.

**Sex offender** Term used for individuals who come into contact with the legal system because of practice of sexual deviations that are prohibited by law.

**Sex-reassignment surgery** Surgery in which male or female genital organs are removed and facsimiles of genital organs of the opposite sex are created. Surgery is usually combined with hormone treatment to modify secondary sexual characteristics.

**Sexual dysfunction** Problems in one or more phases of sexual intercourse that make it impossible to carry out or that decrease the pleasure derived by the participants.

**Shaman** Inspired priest or medium who can summon up and communicate with good and evil spirits.

**Shaping** Basic process of operant conditioning involving the reinforcement of successively closer approximations to a desired behavior.

**Sibling** Individual sharing the same parents with another; one's full brother or sister.

**Simple phobia** Relatively rare type of phobia that involves irrational fear not related to either unfamiliar situations or social interactions. Fear of shut-in places (claustrophobia) and of specific animals are examples.

**Simple schizophrenia** *See* Schizotypal personality disorder.

**Skinner box** Apparatus designed by B.F. Skinner and used to study operant conditioning. Organism makes a simple response—for example, presses a bar—to obtain a reinforcement.

**Smooth pursuit eye movements** Type of essentially involuntary movement that occurs when an individual visually follows the movements of a rhythmically moving object such as a pendulum.

**Social causation** Theory that maladaptive behavior is a result of poor economic circumstances, poor housing, and inadequate social services.

**Social facilitation** Acquisition of skills through observing the behavior of others.

**Social intervention** Treatment approach that involves not only interacting with the client but also attempting to modify the client's environment at home or at work.

**Social-learning theories** Refers to several similar theoretical viewpoints which hold that social behavior and inner thoughts and feelings are learned through social interactions.

**Social phobia** Type of irrational fear of situations in which a person will be exposed to the scrutiny of others. Most common types are fear of blushing, public speaking, eating in public, writing in public, and using public toilet facilities.

**Social role** Function a particular person plays in society, which is determined by the particular role he or she fills. Most people have a variety of overlapping social roles, such as an occupational role, several family roles, and perhaps some recreational roles as well.

**Social-selection theory** Idea that the lower socioeconomic class contains many people who drifted there from higher classes because of their poor functioning. Higher incidence of maladaptive behavior in the lower class is explained in this way.

**Social-skills training** Behavioral or cognitive-behavioral therapeutic approach that emphasizes learning more effective ways of interacting with other people in a variety of situations.

**Social support** Perception that one is loved and valued by others who are prepared to provide help and emotional backing if these become necessary.

**Somatic system** Part of the peripheral nervous system that sends nerve impulses from the sense organs to the muscles that determine voluntary movement.

**Somatic therapy** Treatment, such as drugs, surgery, or electro-convulsive therapy, that directly affects a person's physical state.

**Somatization disorder** (Briquet's syndrome) Disorder characterized by a variety of dramatic but vague complaints that are often chronic and which have no discernible physical cause.

**Somatoform disorders** (formerly called hysterical neurosis or conversion reaction) Characterized by physical symptoms that suggest a physical disorder but for which there are (1) no organic findings to explain the symptom and (2) strong evidence or suggestion that the symptoms are linked to psychological factors or conflicts. These disorders include somatization, conversion and pain disorders, and hypochondriasis.

**Specific developmental disorder** Problems in specific areas of development not due to another more general disorder such as retardation or autism. Examples are reading disorder, arithmetic disorder, and inability to articulate certain sounds clearly.

**Splitting** Term used to describe the inability of the borderline individual to integrate the positive and negative experiences he or she has with another individual into a coherent relationship.

**Spontaneous remission** Disappearance of symptoms or maladaptive behaviors in the absence of therapeutic intervention.

**Spouse abuse** Physical harm done to wives or husbands by their marital partners. Physical assaults by husbands on wives are most common. Abuse may also be psychological.

**Squeeze technique** Technique used in sex therapy to assist the male in retarding ejaculation by gently squeezing the end of the penis when ejaculation is imminent.

**Stanford-Binet** Modification of the Binet test developed at Stanford University by Louis Terman. The Binet format most often used in North America.

**Statistics, descriptive** Scores or other numerical measures that allow the group or groups studied to be characterized in terms of one or several factors. Also refers to mathematical descriptions of the relationship among variables.

**Statistics, inferential** Numerical statements about the probability that a given result may have occurred by chance rather than as a result of the variables under study.

**STP (2, 5 dimethoxy-4-methyl amphetamine)** Hallucinogenic agent similar to LSD.

**Straight jacket** Confining garment used to bind the arms tightly against the body. Often used for violent patients.

**Stress** Feeling or reaction individuals have when faced with a situation that demands action from them, especially action that may be beyond their capabilities.

**Stressor** Source of stress, pressure, or strain. Something that upsets the equilibrium of an organism.

**Stroke** *See* Cerebrovascular accident.

**Sublimation** Defense mechanism and developmental concept which involves the refinement or redirection of undesirable impulses into new and more socially acceptable channels. Whereas displacement involves an alteration in choice of object, sublimation alters both the aim (unacceptable drive) and the object to a personally acceptable one.

**Substance abuse** Use of a psychoactive substance to the degree that a severe and long-lasting impairment in function results.

**Substance dependence** Category of disorder involving the use of mood- or behavior-modifying substances to the degree that physiological tolerance or withdrawal symptoms can be demonstrated.

**Substance induced organic mental disorder** Result of direct effects on the central nervous system of mood- or behavior-modifying substances. Examples are intoxication or drug-withdrawal symptoms.

**Substance-use disorder**  Condition in which regular use of one or more substances that affect the central nervous system produces clear effects in behavior or mood.

**Sulci**  Shallow valleys on the surface of the brain separating the convolutions. (Singular form is sulcus.)

**Superego**  Structure of the psyche in psychoanalytic theory which is developed by internalization of parental standards and by identification with parents. Contains two parts: the ego-ideal and the conscience. The ego-ideal represents the total of positive identifications with accepting and loving parents and desired standards of excellence and good conduct. The conscience includes those attitudes and values which are moralistic (good-bad) in nature.

**Supernatural forces**  The origins of miraculous happenings not attributable to natural law.

**Support group**  Group of individuals with the same or similar problems who meet to discuss their problems and how they deal with them.

**Supportive therapy**  Brief form of psychotherapy in which the therapist provides acceptance for the patient and affords him or her some opportunity to be dependent.

**Survey research**  The use of questionnaires or interviews to determine group attitudes and reported frequencies of various behaviors.

**Survival guilt**  Feeling that it is unfair to be alive when others in the same situation have died. Overwhelming feelings of guilt, unworthiness, and helplessness.

**Symbolic modeling**  Using a film or other media to provide information to an individual about a new and potentially stressful situation before he or she experiences the situation.

**Synapse**  Point at which a nerve impulse passes from an axon of one neuron to the dendrite of another neuron.

**Synaptic vesicle**  Container on the axon terminal button that serves as a storage point for a chemical neurotransmitter.

**Syndrome**  A group of symptoms that often appear together.

**Syphilitic infection**  Chronic infectious venereal disease, transmitted through direct contact, caused by a spirochete, Treponema pallidum.

**Systematic desensitization**  Learning-theory-based therapeutic technique in which a client is first trained in muscle relaxation and then imagines a series of increasingly anxiety-provoking situations until

he or she no longer experiences anxiety while thinking about the stimuli. Learning principle involved is reciprocal inhibition, according to which two incompatible responses (e.g., anxiety and relaxation) cannot be made simultaneously by one person.

**Systolic**  Term used to describe the blood-pressure reading at the time the heart contracts to drive the blood through. Compare to *Diastolic.*

**Tactile**  Referring to the sense of touch.

**Tangles**  Abnormal structure found in nerve cells of individuals who have Alzheimer's disease.

**Tarantism**  Uncontrollable urge to dance, believed to be the result of the bite of a tarantula. This was frequent in Southern Italy from the fifteenth to seventeenth centuries.

**Tardive dyskinesia**  Disorder involving uncontrolled body movements, often of the lips and tongue, that may result from treatment with antipsychotic drugs.

**Tay-Sachs disease**  Inherited metabolic disorder, inevitably fatal, that causes progressive deterioration of the nervous system.

**Temporal lobe**  Part of the cerebral hemisphere lying behind the temples and below the lateral fissure in front of the occipital lobe.

**Tension headache**  Probably the most common form of headache; characterized by bandlike pains and tender scalp. Gradual in onset and often long lasting. Thought to be a result of stress.

**Teritary prevention**  Efforts aimed at reducing the impairment that may result from a given disorder.

**Test anxiety**  Unusually apprehensive response to evaluative situations. Often a factor in poor performance because of worry and interfering thoughts.

**THC (tetrahydrocannabinol)**  Major active ingredient in marijuana.

**Thematic Apperception Test (TAT)**  Projective test consisting of somewhat ambiguous pictures. Subject is asked to tell a story about each picture. From these stories personality dynamics are inferred.

**Theoretical perspective**  The particular set of beliefs or ideas that determine what people notice in behavior, how they interpret what they observe, and how they believe problems should be approached.

**Therapeutic interview**  Interaction between a client and therapist although perhaps including other family members as well. Designed to help promote change in behavior and attitudes.

**Thorazine**  Trade name for chlorpromazine, one of a group of phenothiazine drugs used in the treatment of schizophrenia.

**Tic** Involuntary, repetitive, rapid muscle contractions often occurring in the face. Thought to be related to tension and anxiety.

**Token economy** Programmed therapeutic environment based on learning-theory principles in which patients must earn tokens (reinforcers) to obtain various privileges.

**Tolerance (drug)** Condition in which an individual must use increasing doses of a substance to produce the same physiological effect.

**Tonic phase** Phase of seizure in which the body is extended and stiff and during which reflexes to light and to pressure on the cornea are absent. *See also* Clonic phase.

**Tranquilizing drugs** Drugs (for example, of the chloropromazine and phenothiazine families) which are used to reduce agitation and anxiety. Drug action inhibits the activities of the hypothalamus.

**Transference** Psychoanalytic term which refers to the displacement of affect from one person to another. Patterns of feelings and behavior originally experienced with significant figures in childhood are displaced or attached to individuals in one's current relationships (e.g., a psychotherapist). Current person is reacted to as if he or she were some significant other from the respondent's past. Transference reactions may be positive or negative.

**Transsexualism** A gender identity disorder in which the person believes that the assigned sex is inappropriate and he or she is persistently preoccupied with changing both primary and secondary sexual characteristics to those of the other sex so as to gain a new sexual identity.

**Transvestism** Sexual deviation in which an individual derives gratification from wearing the clothing of the opposite sex.

**Traumatic neurosis** Psychological symptoms that occur after a traumatic event but which are not a direct result of physical injury.

**Trephination** Process of making a circular hole in the skull. In early times this was done to allow evil spirits to escape.

**Tricyclics** Group of drugs used to treat depression. An example is imipramine. Common trade names of tricyclic drugs are Tofranil and Elavil.

**Trisomy** Occurrence in an individual of three chromosomes of one kind rather than the usual pair. Usually associated with an abnormality of some type.

**Trisomy 13** Presence of three number 13 chromosomes rather than the usual pair. Occurs in one of every 5000 births and causes severe mental retarda-

tion and a number of specific physical defects. Only about 18 percent of affected infants survive the first year.

**Trisomy 18** Presence of three number 18 chromosomes rather than the usual pair. The next most common trisomy after trisomy 21. Occurs in one of every 3000 births. Most such infants die before birth; only 10 percent of those born alive survive to age 1. Results in severe retardation and many physical abnormalities.

**Trisomy 21** *See* Down syndrome.

**Tuberous sclerosis** Disorder caused by a dominant gene and characterized by severe retardation, seizures, and the appearance of small, fibrous tumors.

**Type I schizophrenia** Characterized by positive symptoms or behavior excesses including hallucinations, delusions, and disordered thinking. Believed to be caused by problems of dopamine transmission. Prognosis with drug therapy is relatively optimistic.

**Type II schizophrenia** Characterized by negative symptoms and behavior deficits such as poverty of speech, flattened affect, and apathy. Responds poorly to antipsychotic drugs and is likely to be chronic. Possibly related to structural changes in the brain.

**Type-A behavior** Term used to describe a personality type hypothesized to be heart-attack prone.

**Type-B behavior** Term used to describe people who do not show the characteristics of Type-A personality. Type Bs are less pressured and hard driving than Type As.

**Ulcer** Sore on the skin or internal mucous tissue that results in the death of the tissue involved.

**Unauthentic behavior** According to existentialist theory, that behavior governed not by an individual's desires but by the desires of other people.

**Unconditional positive regard** Term used by Carl Rogers to emphasize the importance of a therapist's unqualified acceptance of a client as a person of worth.

**Unconditioned response** (UR) In classical conditioning, the response that occurs automatically, before training, when the unconditioned stimulus is presented.

**Unconditioned stimulus** (US) In classical conditioning, the stimulus that automatically elicits the desired response before training has taken place.

**Unconscious** Out of awareness. Mental contents that can be brought to awareness only with great difficulty (or not at all).

**Undifferentiated type schizophrenia** Clearly psychotic symptoms that either do not fit any of the other categories of schizophrenia or that meet the requirements for more than one category.

**Undoing**  Defense mechanism aimed at negating or atoning for some disapproved impulse or act.

**Unipolar disorder**  Term for an affective disorder in which only depression occurs. There can be no episodes of mania.

**Vaginal**  Pertaining to the vagina, the passage leading from the external genital opening to the uterus in female mammals.

**Vaginismus (functional)**  Type of sexual dysfunction in women in which an involuntary spasm of the muscles of the outer third of the vagina interferes with sexual activity.

**Valium**  One of the tranquilizing drugs often prescribed to reduce anxiety.

**Venereal disease**  Contagious disease contracted through sexual intercourse. Examples are syphilis and gonorrhea.

**Ventricles**  Communicating cavities in the brain that are linked with the central canal of the spinal cord.

**Verbal I.Q.**  One of the two subscores of the Wechsler intelligence-test series. Tests reflecting information and the ability to make abstractions.

**Vicarious learning**  Learning that occurs merely by watching the behavior of others.

**Voyeur**  One who practices voyeurism.

**Voyeurism (scopophilia)**  Attaining sexual gratification from observing the sexual behavior of others. Synonymous with *Peeping Tomism*.

**Vulnerability**  Tendency to react maladaptively, to be insufficiently defended especially in particular situations.

**Waxy flexibility**  Term used to describe the extreme immobility often characteristic of catatonic schizophrenia. In this condition a person's arm or leg can be arranged in contorted or uncomfortable poses and will remain there for long periods of time.

**Wechsler tests (WAIS, WISC, WPPSI)**  Tests of intelligence for adults and children; composed of subtests which tap verbal and nonverbal aspects of intelligence.

**Withdrawal**  Physiological changes that take place after an individual's discontinuation of a habit-forming substance. These symptoms vary from mild to extremely unpleasant. The symptoms of heroin withdrawal are perhaps best known.

**Word-association test**  Projective technique in which a list of words is presented one by one. Client is asked to respond to each item with the first word that comes to mind.

**X-linked dominance**  Genes carried on the X sex chromosome that determine a characteristic by their presence. Females have two X chromosomes. Males have one X and one Y chromosome. This means that characteristics that are a result of X-linked dominance can occur in males only through inheritance from the mother. In females they can be inherited from either parent.

# REFERENCES

ABIKOFF, H. (in press) Efficacy of cognitive training interventions in hyperactive children: A critical review. *Clinical Psychology Review.*

ABIKOFF, H. & GITTELMAN, R. (1984) Does behavior therapy normalize the classroom behavior of hyperactive children. *Archives of General Psychiatry, 41,* 449–454.

ABRAHAM, K. (1921) Contributions to the theory of the anal character. In *Selected papers on psychoanalysis.* London: Hogarth.

ABRAHAM, K. (1968) Notes on the psychoanalytic investigation and treatment of manic-depressive insanity and allied conditions (1911). In K. Abraham, *Selected papers of Karl Abraham.* New York: Basic Books.

ABRAHAM, S. F. & BEAUMONT, P. J. V. (1982) How patients describe bulimia or binge-eating. *Psychological Medicine, 12,* 625–635.

ABRAMS, D. B. & WILSON, G. T. (1979) Effects of alcohol on social anxiety in women: Cognitive versus physiological processes. *Journal of Abnormal Psychology, 88,* 161–173.

ABRAMS, S. (1973) The polygraph in a psychiatric setting. *American Journal of Psychiatry, 130,* 94–98.

ABRAMSON, L., SELIGMAN, M. E. P., & TEASDALE, J. D. (1978) Learned helplessness in humans: Critique and reformulation. *Journal of Abnormal Psychology, 87,* 49–74.

ACHENBACH, T. M. (1980) DSM-III in light of empirical research on the classification of child psychopathology. *Journal of the American Academy of Child Psychiatry, 19,* 395–412. Copyright © by American Academy of Child Psychiatry, 1980.

ACHENBACH, T. M. & EDELBROCK, C. S. (1983) *Manual for the child behavior checklist and revised child behavior profile.* Burlington: University of Vermont.

ACKERMAN, S. H., MANAKER, S., & COHEN, M. I. (1981) Recent separation and the onset of peptic ulcer disease in older children and adolescents. *Psychosomatic Medicine, 43,* 305–310.

ADELSON, J. & DOEHRMAN, M. J. (1980) The psychodynamic approach to adolescence. In J. Adelson (ed.), *Handbook of Adolescent Psychology,* New York: John Wiley.

AGRAS, W. S., TAYLOR, O. B., KRAEMER, H. C., ALLEN, R. A., & SCHNEIDER, M. S. (1980) Relaxation training: Twenty-four hour blood pressure reductions. *Archives of General Psychiatry, 37,* 859–863. Copyright © 1980, American Medical Association.

AIKEN, T. W., STUMPHAUZER, J. S., & VELOZ, E. V. (1977) Behavioral analysis of non-delinquent brothers in a high juvenile crime community. *Behavioral Disorders, 2,* 212–222.

AIMES, P. L., GELDER, M. G., and SHAWN, P. M. (1983) Social phobia: A comparative clinical study. *British Journal of Psychiatry, 141,* 174–179.

AKISKAL, H. S. (1981) Concepts of depression. In E. Friedman, J. Mann, & S. Gershon, (eds.), *Depression and antidepressants: Implications for cause and treatment.* New York: Raven Press.

AKISKAL, H. S. (1985) Interaction of biologic and psychologic factors in the origin of depressive disorders. *Acta Psychiatrica Scandinavica,* Supplementum, No. 319, 131–139.

*Alcoholism: An inherited disease* (1985). National Institute on Alcohol Abuse and Alcoholism. Rockville, MD.

ALDRICH, C. K. (1966) *An introduction to dynamic psychiatry.* New York: McGraw-Hill, 1966.

ALEXANDER, A. B. & SOLANCH, L. S. (1981) Psychological aspects in the understanding and treatment of bronchial asthma. In J. M. Ferguson & C. B. Taylor (eds), *The comprehensive handbook of behavioral medicine* (Vol. 2). New York: S. P. Medical & Scientific Books, 3–40.

ALFORD, G. S. (1980) Alcoholics anonymous: An empirical outcome study. In W. R. Miller (Ed.) *Addictive behaviors* (Vol. 5). Oxford: Pergamon Press.

ALLOY, L. B. & ABRAMSON, L. Y. (1979) Judgment of contingency of depressed and nondepressed students: Sadder but wiser. *Journal of Experimental Psychology, 108,* 441–485.

ALTMAN, D. (1982) *The homosexualization of America.* Boston: Beacon Press.

ALTMAN, H. (1980) Family schism and skew and their relation to psychiatric treatment in children at risk. Unpublished dissertation, St. Louis University.

American Law Institute (1962) *Model penal code: Proposed official draft.* Philadelphia: American Law Institute.

ANDERSON, D. J., NOYES, R., Jr., & CROWE, R. R. (1984) A comparison of panic disorder and generalized anxiety disorder. *American Journal of Psychiatry, 141,* 572–575. Copyright © 1984, the American Psychiatric Association. Reprinted with permission.

ANDERSON, K. O., BRADLEY, L. A., YOUNG, C. O., & McDANIEL, L. K. (1985) Rheumatoid arthritis: Review of psychological factors related to etiology, effects, and treatment. *Psychological Bulletin, 98,* 358–387.

ANDREASEN, N. C. (1979) Thought, language and communication disorders II: Diagnostic significance. *Archives of General Psychiatry, 36,* 1325–1330.

ANDREASEN, N. C. & GROVE, W. (1979) The relationship between schizophrenic language, manic language, and aphasia. In J. Gruzelier & P. Flor-Henry, (Eds.) *Hemisphere symmetries of function in psychopathology.* Amsterdam: Elsevier/North Holland.

ANDREASEN, N. C. & OLSEN, S. (1982) Negative v positive schizophrenia: Definition and validation. *Archives of General Psychiatry,* 39, 789–794.

ANDREASEN, N. C., OLSEN, S. A., DENNERT, J. W., & SMITH, M. R. (1982) Ventricular enlargement in schizophrenia: Relationship to positive and negative symptoms. *American Journal of Psychiatry,* 139, 297–302.

ANDREWS, G. & HARVEY, R. (1981) Does psychotherapy benefit neurotic patients? *Archives of General Psychiatry,* 38, 1203–1208.

ANGST, J. & DOBLER-MIKOLA, A. (1984) The definition of depression. *Journal of Psychiatric Research,* 18, 401–406. Reprinted with permission from the *Journal of Psychiatric Research,* Copyright © 1984. Pergamon Press, Ltd.

ANNON, J. S. (1976) *The behavioral treatment of sexual problems: Brief therapy.* New York: Harper & Row.

ANONYMOUS (1965) A practicing psychiatrist: The experience of electroconvulsive therapy. *British Journal of Psychiatry,* 111, 365–367.

ANONYMOUS (1977) Psychosocial implications of schizophrenic diagnoses (personal account). *Schizophrenia Bulletin,* 3, 4(b).

ARKEMA, P. H. (1981) The borderline personality and transitional relatedness. *American Journal of Psychiatry,* 138, 172–177.

ANTHONY, E. J. (1975) The influences of a manic-depressive environment on the developing child. In E. J. Anthony & T. Benedek (Eds.), *Depression and human existence.* Boston: Little, Brown.

ANTHONY, E. J. (1977) Depression and children. In G. D. Burrow (Ed.), *Handbook of studies of depression.* Amsterdam: Excerpta Medica.

ANTHONY, J. C., FOLSTEIN, M., ROMANOSK, A. J., VANKORFF, M. R., NESTADT, G. R., CHAHAL, R., MERCHANT, A., BROWN, H., SHAPIROS, S., KRAMER, M., GRUENBERG, E. M. (1985) Comparison of the lay Diagnostic Interview Schedule and a standardized psychiatric diagnosis: Experience in Eastern Baltimore. *Archives of General Psychiatry,* 42, 667–675.

ARIETI, S. & BEMPORAD, J. (1978) *Severe and mild depression.* New York: Basic Books.

ASARNOW, J. R. & CALLAN, J. W. (1985) Boys with peer adjustment problems: Social cognitive processes. *Journal of Consulting and Clinical Psychology,* 53, 80–87.

AXLINE, V. M. (1947) *Play therapy: The inner dynamics of childhood.* Boston: Houghton Mifflin.

AYLLON T., & AZRIN, N. H. (1965) The measurement and reinforcement of behavior of psychotics. *Journal of the Experimental Analysis of Behavior,* 8, 357–383.

AYLLON, T., GARBER, S. W., & ALLISON, M. G. (1977) Behavioral treatment of childhood neurosis. *Psychiatry,* 40, 315–322.

AYLLON, T., SMITH, D., & RODGERS, M. (1970) Behavioral management of school phobia. *Journal of Behavior Therapy and Experimental Psychiatry,* 1, 124–138. Reprinted with permission. Copyright 1970, Pergamon Press, Ltd.

BAKER, G. H. (1982) Life events; before the onset of rheumatoid arthritis. *Psychotherapy and Psychosomatics,* 38, 173–177.

BANDURA, A. (1969) *Principles of behavior modification.* New York: Holt, Rinehart & Winston.

BANDURA, A. (1977) Self-efficacy: Toward a unifying theory of behavior change. *Psychological Review,* 84, 191–215.

BANDURA, A. (1978) The self-system in reciprocal determinism. *American Psychologist,* 33, 344–358.

BANDURA, A. (1982) Self-efficacy mechanism in human agency. *American Psychologist,* 37, 122–147.

BANDURA, A. (1986) *Social foundations of thought and action: A social cognitive theory.* Englewood Cliffs, NJ: Prentice Hall.

BANDURA, A. & MENLOVE, F. L. (1968) Factors determining vicarious extinction of avoidance behavior through symbolic modeling. *Journal of Personality and Social Psychology,* 8, 99–108.

BARD, M. (1970) Alternatives to traditional law enforcement. In F. Korten, S. W. Cook, & J. I. Lacey (Eds.) *Psychology and the Problems of Society.* Washington, D.C.: American Psychological Association, 128–132.

BARDEN, H. S., KESSEL, R. & SCHUETT, V. E. (1984) The costs and benefits of screening for PKU in Wisconsin. *Social Biology,* 31, 1–17.

BARKER, C. & LEMLE, R. (1984) The helping process in couples. *American Journal of Community Psychology,* 12, 321–326.

BARON, M., GRUEN, R., KANE, J. & AMIS, L. (1985) Modern research criteria and the genetics of schizophrenia. *American Journal of Psychiatry,* 142, 697–701.

BARNES, G. M. (1984) *Alcohol use among secondary school students in New York State.* Buffalo: Research Institute on Alcoholism.

BARNES, G. E. & PROSEN, H. (1985) Parental death and depression. *Journal of Abnormal Psychology,* 94, 64–69.

BARRETT, D. & FINE, H. (1980) A child was being beaten: The therapy of battered children as adults. *Psychotherapy: Theory, Research and Practice,* 17, 285–293.

BARTAK, L., RUTTER, M., & COX, M. (1975) A comparative study of infantile autism and specific developmental receptive language disorder. I. The children. *British Journal of Psychiatry,* 126, 127–145.

BARTROP, R. W., LUCKHURST, E., LAZARUS, L. KILOH, L. G., & PENNY, R. (1977) Depressed lymphocyte function after bereavement. *Lancet,* 1, 834–836.

BAUER, R. B., STEVENS, C., REVENO, W. S., & ROSENBAUM, H. (1982) L-Dopa treatment of Parkinson's disease: A ten year follow-up study. *Journal of the American Geriatric Society,* 30, 322–325.

BAUMEISTER, A. A., RUNCIE, D., & GARDEPE, J. (1984) Processing of information in iconic memory: differences between nonretarded and retarded subjects. *Journal of Abnormal Psychology,* 93, 433–447.

BAXTER, L. J., JR, PHELPS, M. E., MAZZIOTTA, J. C., SCHWARTZ, J. M., GERNER, R. H., SELIN, C. E., & SUMIDA, R. M. (1985) Cerebral metabolic roles for glucose in mood disorders. *Archives of General Psychiatry,* 42, 441–447.

BAYER, R. & SPITZER, R. L. (1985) Neurosis, Psychodynamics, and DSM-III. *Archives of General Psychiatry,* 42, 187–195.

BEATRICE, J. (1985) A psychological comparison of heterosexuals, transvestites, preoperative transsexuals, and post operative transsexuals. *The Journal of Nervous and Mental Disease,* 173, 358–365.

BECK, A. T. (1967) *Depression: Clinical, experimental and theoretical aspects.* New York: Hoeber.

BECK, A. T. (1970) Role of fantasies in psychotherapy and psychopathology. *Journal of Nervous and Mental Disease,* 150, 3–17.

BECK, A. T. (1974) The development of depression: A cognitive model. In R. J. Friedman & M. M. Katz (Eds.), *The psychology of depression: Contemporary theory and research.* Washington, D.C.: V. H. Winston.

BECK, A. T. (1976) *Cognitive therapy and the emotional disorders.* New York: International Universities Press. Copyright 1976 by Aaron T. Beck, M.D. Reprinted by permission of the publisher.

BECK, A. T. (1982) Cognitive therapy of depression: New perspectives. In P. Clayton & J. Barrett (Eds.) *Treatment of depression: Old controversies and new approaches.* New York: Raven Press.

BECK, A. T. & EMERY, G. (1985) *Anxiety disorders and phobias: A cognitive perspective.* New York: Basic Books.

BECK, A. T., KOVACS, M., & WEISSMAN, A. (1979) Assessment of suicidal ideation: The scale for suicide ideation. *Journal of Consulting and Clinical Psychology,* 47, 343–352.

BECK, A. T., RUSH, A. J., SHAW, B., & EMERY, G. (1979) *Cognitive therapy of depression.* New York: Guilford.

BECK, J. G. & BARLOW, D. H. (1984) Current conceptualizations of sexual dysfunction: A review and an alternative perspective. *Clinical Psychology Review, 4,* 363–378.

BEERS, C. (1908) *A mind that found itself.* Garden City, NY: Doubleday. Copyright 1907, 1917, 1921, 1923, 1931, 1932, 1934, 1935, 1937, 1939, 1940, 1942, 1944, 1948, 1953 by the American Foundation for Mental Hygiene, Inc. Used by permission of Doubleday & Company, Inc.

BEISER, M., SHORE, J. H., PETERS, R., & TATUM, E. (1985) Does community care for the mentally ill make a difference? A tale of two cities. *American Journal of Psychiatry, 142,* 1047–1105.

BEITCHMAN, J. H. (1983) Childhood schizophrenia: A review and comparison with adult onset schizophrenia. *The Psychiatric Journal of the University of Ottawa, 8,* 25–37.

BELL, A. P., & WEINBERG, M. S. (1978) *Homosexualities: A study of diversity among men and women.* New York: Simon & Schuster.

BELL, A. P., WEINBERG, M. S., & HAMMERSMITH, S. F. (1981) *Sexual preference.* Bloomington: Indiana University Press.

BELL, I. R. (1982) *Clinical ecology: A new medical approach to environmental illness.* Bolinas, CA: Common Knowledge Press.

BELSKY, J. (1980) Child maltreatment: An ecological integration. *American Psychologist, 35,* 320–335.

BEMPORAD, J. R. (1983) Cognitive, affective and psychologic changes in the depressed process. *Journal of the American Academy of Psychoanalysis, 11,* 159–172.

BENSON, H. (1977) Systemic hypertension and the relaxation response. *New England Journal of Medicine, 296,* 1152–1156.

BENTLER, P. M., & PRINCE, C. (1969) Personality characteristics of male transvestites. *Journal of Abnormal Psychology, 74,* 140–143.

BERCEL, N. A. (1960) A study of the influence of schizophrenic serum on the behavior of the spider: Zilla-X-Notata. In D. D. Jackson (Ed.), *The etiology of schizophrenia.* New York: Basic Books.

BERGIN, A. E., & LAMBERT, M. J. (1978) The evaluation of therapeutic outcomes. In S. L. Garfield & A. E. Bergin (Eds.), *Handbook of psychotherapy and behavior change: An empirical analysis* (2nd ed.). New York: John Wiley.

BERKE, J. & HERNTON, C. (1974) *The cannabis experience.* London: Peter Owen.

BERLIN, I. N. (1975) *Advocacy for child mental health.* New York: Brunner/Mazel.

BERRY, P, GROENEWEG, G., GIBSON, D., & BROWN, R. I. (1984) Mental development of adults with Down syndrome. *American Journal of Mental Deficiency, 89,* 252–256.

BIEBER, I. (1980) *Cognitive psychoanalysis.* New York: Jason Aronson.

BIEBER, I., DAIN, H. J., DINCE, P. R., DRELLICH, M. G., GRAND, H. G., GUNDLACH, R. H., KREMER, M. W., RIFKIN, A. H., WILBER, C. B., and BIEBER (1962) *Homosexuality: A psychoanalytic study.* New York: Basic Books.

BIRAN, N., & WILSON, G. T. (1981) Treatment of phobic disorders using cognitive and exposure: A self-efficacy analysis. *Journal of Consulting and Clinical Psychology, 49,* 886–899.

BLACK, D. W., WARRACK, G. & WINOKUR, G. (1985) The Iowa Record-Linkage Study: II. Excess mortality among patients with organic mental disorders. *Archives of General Psychiatry, 42,* 78–81.

BLANCHARD, E. B., ANDRASIC, F., NEFF, D. F., ARENA, J. G., AHLES, T. A., JURISH, S. E., PALLMEYER, T. P., SAUNDERS, N. L., & TEDERS, S. J. (1982) Biofeedback and relaxation training with three kinds of headache: Treatment effects and their prediction. *Journal of Consulting and Clinical Psychology, 50,* 562–575.

BLATT, S. J., D'AFFLITTI, J. P., & QUINLAN, D. M. (1976) Experiences of depression in normal young adults. *Journal of Abnormal Psychology, 85,* 383–389.

BLEULER, E. (1950) *Dementia praecox or the group of schizophrenias (1911).* (J. Zinkin, trans.). New York: International Universities Press.

BLEULER, M. (1972) *The schizophrenic psychoses in the light of long-term case and family histories.* Stuttgart: Georg Theime Verlag.

BLEULER, M. (1978). *The schizophrenic disorders: Long term patient and family studies.* New Haven: Yale University Press.

BLOOM, B., HODGES, W., & CALDWELL, R. (1982) A preventative program for the newly separated: Initial evaluation. *American Journal of Community Psychology, 10,* 251–264.

BLOTCKY, M. J., DIMPERIO, T. L., & GOSSETT, J. T. (1984) Follow-up of children treated in psychiatric hospitals: A review of studies. *American Journal of Psychiatry, 141,* 1499–1507.

BLUMSTEIN, P. W., & SCHWARTZ, P. (1976) Bisexuality in women. *Archives of Sexual Behavior, 5,* 171–181.

BLUMSTEIN, P. W., & SCHWARTZ, P. (1977) Bisexuality: Some social psychological issues. *Journal of Social Issues, 33(2),* 30–45.

BLUMSTEIN, P. W. & SCHWARTZ, P. (1983) *American Couples.* New York: William Morrow. Adaptation of Figure 27, 196, *American Couples.* Copyright © 1983 by Philip Blumstein, M.D. and Pepper W. Schwartz, M.D. By permission of William Morrow & Company.

BLUMBERG, M. L. (1981) Depression in abused and neglected children. *American Journal of Psychotherapy, 35,* 332–335.

BOHMAN, M., CLONINGER, R., VON KNORRING, A., & SIGVARDSSON, S. (1984) An adoption study of somotoform disorders: III. Cross-fostering analysis and genetic relationship to alcoholism and criminality. *Archives of General Psychiatry, 41,* 872–878.

BOHMAN, M., CLONINGER, C. R., SIGVARDSSON, S., VON KNORRING, A. L. (1982) Predisposition to petty criminality on Swedish adoptees I. Genetic and Rh environmental heterogeneity. *Archives of General Psychiatry, 39,* 1233–1241.

BOOR, M. (1982) The multiple personality epidemic. *Journal of Nervous and Mental Disease, 170,* 302–304.

BOUSHA, D. M., & TWENTYMAN, C. T. (1984) Mother-child interactional style in abuse, neglect, and control groups: Naturalistic observations in the home. *Journal of Abnormal Psychology, 93,* 106–114.

BOWER, B. (1981) The Treatment of sex offenders. *Psychiatric News, 16(14)* 1, 12.

BOWER, G. H. (1981) Mood and memory. *American Psychologist, 36,* 129–148.

BOWERS, B. (1981) The treatment of sex offenders. *Psychiatric News, 16,* 1, 12.

BOWERS, K. S. & MEICHENBAUM, D. (Eds.) (1985) *The unconscious reconsidered.* New York: Wiley Interscience.

BOWERS, M. B., Jr. (1968) Pathogenesis of acute schizophrenic psychosis. *Archives of General Psychiatry, 19,* 348–355.

BOWLBY, J. (1973) *Separation: Anxiety and anger.* New York: Basic Books.

BOWLBY, J. (1980) *Loss, sadness and depression.* New York: Basic Books.

BOYD, J. H. & WEISSMAN, M. M. (1981) Epidemiology of affective disorders. *Archives of General Psychiatry, 38,* 1039–1046.

BOZETT, F. W. (1981) Gay fathers: Evolution of the gay-father identity. *American Journal of Orthopsychiatry, 51,* 552–559.

BRADLEY, T. B. (1983) Remediation of cognitive deficits: A critical appraisal of the Feuerstein model. *Journal of Mental Deficiency Research, 27,* 79–92.

BRAUN, B. G. (1983) Neurophysic changes in multiple personality due to integration: A preliminary report. *American Journal of Clinical Hypnosis, 26,* 84–92.

BRAUN, B. G. (1984) Toward a theory of multiple personality and other dissociative phenomena. *Psychiatric Clinics of North America, 7,* 171–193.

BRAUN, P., KOCHANSKY, G., SHAPIRO, R., GREENBERG, S., GUDEMAN, J., JOHNSON, S., & SHORE, M. (1981) Overview: Deinstitutionalization of psychiatric patients, a critical review of outcome studies. *American Journal of Psychiatry,* 736–749.

BRECHER, E. M. and Consumer Reports Books' Editors (1983) *Love, Sex, and Aging: A Consumer Union Report.* Boston: Little Brown.

BRENNAN, T. (1982) Loneliness at adolescence. In L. A. Peplau & D. Perlman (Eds.), *Loneliness: A source book of current theory, research, and therapy.* New York: John Wiley, 219–290.

BRENNAN, T. & AUSLANDER, N. (1979) *Adolescent loneliness: An exploratory study of social and psychological pre-dispositions and theory* (Vol. 1). Boulder, CO: Behavioral Research Laboratory.

BRENNER, M. H. (1973) *Mental illness and the economy.* Cambridge, MA: Harvard University Press.

BRETT, E. A. & OSTROFF, R. (1985) Imagery and posttraumatic stress disorder: An overview. *American Journal of Psychiatry, 142,* 417–424.

BRODY, G. H. & STONEMAN, Z. (1984) Children with atypical siblings. In B. B. Lahey, & A. E. Kazdin (Eds.) *Advances in child clinical psychology,* (Vol. 6). NY: Plenum.

BRODY, J. E. (1984) Autoerotic death of youths causes widening concern. *New York Times,* March 27, pp 17, 20.

BROGA, M. I. & NEUFELD, R. W. (1981) Multivariate cognitive performance variables and response styles among paranoid and non-paranoid schizophrenics. *Journal of Abnormal Psychology, 90,* 495–509.

BROWN, G. W., BHROLCHAIN, M. N., & HARRIS, T. (1975) Social class and psychiatric disturbance among women in an urban population. *Sociology, 9,* 225–254.

BROWN, G. & HARRIS, T. (1978) *Social origins of depression: A study of psychiatric disorder in women.* New York: Free Press.

BROWN, G. W., HARRIS, T., & COPELAND, J. R. (1977) Depression and loss. *British Journal of Psychiatry, 130,* 1–18.

BROWN, R. T., BORDEN, K. A., & CLINGERMAN, S. R. (1984) Adherence to methylphenidate therapy in a pediatric population: A preliminary investigation. Paper presented at the meeting of the NIMH New Clinical Drug Evaluation Unit Program. Key Biscayne, FL.

BROWNELL, K. D., HAYES, S. C., & BARLOW, D. H. (1977) Patterns of appropriate and deviant sexual arousal: The behavioral treatment of multiple sexual deviations. *Journal of Consulting and Clinical Psychology, 45,* 1144–1155. Copyright © 1977 by the American Psychological Association. Adapted by permission of the author.

BUCHANAN, A. & OLIVER, J. F. (1977) Abuse and neglect as a cause of mental retardation. *British Journal of Psychology, 131,* 458–467.

BUHRICH, N., & MCCONAGHY, N. (1978) Parental relationships during childhood in homosexuality, transvestism, and transsexualism. *Australian and New Zealand Journal of Psychiatry, 12,* 103–108.

BURCHFIELD, S. R. (Ed.) (1985) *Stress: Psychological and physiological interactions.* Washington, D.C.: Hemisphere.

BUSSE, E. W. (1981) Therapy of mental illness in late life. In S. Arieti & H. K. H. Brodie (Eds.), *American handbook of psychiatry* (Vol. 7). New York: Basic Books.

CALEV, A. (1984) Recall and recognition in chronic nondemented schizophrenics: Use of matched tasks. *Journal of Abnormal Psychology, 93,* 172–177. Copyright © 1984 by the American Psychological Association. Reprinted by permission of the author.

CAMERON, N. (1963) *Personality development and psychopathology.* Boston: Houghton Mifflin.

CANCRO, R. (1985) Schizophrenic disorders. In H. I. Kaplan & B. J. Sadock (Eds.) *Comprehensive textbook of psychiatry,* (4th Ed.) Vol. 1. Baltimore: Williams & Wilkins.

CAPUTO, P. A. (1977) *A rumor of war.* New York: Holt, Rinehart & Winston.

CAREY, G. & GOTTESMAN, I. I. (1981) Twin and family studies of anxiety, phobic, and obsessive disorders. In D. F. Klein & J. Rabkin (Eds.), *Anxiety: New research and changing concepts.* New York: Raven Press, 117–136.

CAREY, K. & MAISTO, S. A. (1985) A review of the use of self-control techniques in the treatment of alcohol abuse. *Cognitive therapy and research, 9,* 235–251.

CARLSON, P. M. (1969) An analysis of the motor, cognitive, and physiological components of psychotherapeutically induced changes in phobic behavior. Unpublished doctoral dissertation, University of Washington.

CARPENTER, W. T., JR., SACKS, M. H., STRUASS, J. S., BARTKO, J. J., and RAYNER, J. (1976) Evaluating signs and symptoms: Comparisons of structured interview and clinical approaches. *British Journal of Psychiatry, 128,* 397–403.

CARRIER, J. (1980) Homosexual behavior in cross cultural perspective. In J. Marmor (Ed.) *Homosexual behavior.* New York: Basic Books.

CARROLL, B. J. (1985) Dexamethasone Suppression Test: A review of contemporary confusion. *Journal of Clinical Psychiatry, 46,* 13–24.

CARROLL, K. & LEON, G. R. (1981) The bulimia-vomiting disorder within a generalized substance abuse pattern. Paper presented at the 15th Annual Convention of the Association for the Advancement of Behavior Therapy, Toronto, November, 1981.

CASEY, R. J. & BERMAN, J. S. (1985) The outcome of psychotherapy with children. *Psychological Bulletin, 98,* 388–400.

CASPER, R. C., & DAVIS, J. M. (1977) On the course of anorexia nervosa. *American Journal of Psychiatry, 134,* 974–978.

CASPER, R. C., HALMI, K. A., GOLDBERG, S. C., ECKERT, E., and DAVIS, J. M. (1979) Disturbances in body image estimation as related to other characteristics and outcome in anorexia nervosa. *British Journal of Psychiatry, 134,* 60–66.

CAUTELA, J. R. (1985) Covert modeling. In A. S. Bellack & M. Hersen (Eds.), *Dictionary of behavior therapy techniques.* New York: Pergamon.

CHALKLEY, A. J. & POWELL, G. E. (1983) The clinical description of forty-eight cases of sexual fetishisms. *British Journal of Psychiatry, 142,* 292–295.

CHAMBLESS, D. L., CAPUTO, G. C., BRIGHT, P., & GALLAGHER, R. (1984) Assessment of fear of agoraphobics: The Body Sensations Questionnaire and the Agoraphobic Cognitions Questionnaire. *Journal of Consulting and Clinical Psychology, 52,* 1090–1097.

CHAMBLESS, D. L., CAPUTO, G. C., CRAIG, G., JASIN, S. E., EDWARD, J. G., & WILLIAMS, C., (1985) The mobility inventory of agoraphobia. *Behavior Research and Therapy, 23,* 35–44.

CHANDLER, C. L., WEISSBERG, R. P., COWEN, E. L., & GUARE, J. (1984) Long-term effects of a school-based secondary prevention program for young maladapting children. *Journal of Consulting and Clinical Psychology, 52,* 165–170.

CHAPMAN, J. (1966) The early symptoms of schizophrenia. *British Journal of Psychiatry, 112,* 225–251.

CHARNEY, D. S., MENKES, D. B., & HENINGER, G. R. (1981) Receptor sensitivity and the mechanism of action of antidepressant treatment. *Archives of General Psychiatry, 38,* 1160–1180.

CHAST, R. (1982) "Donna and the Disastrettes" from *Unscientific Americans.* New York: Dial. Copyright © 1982 by Roz Chast. Reprinted by permission.

CHESS, S. (1978) The plasticity of human development. *American Academy of Child Psychiatry, 17,* 80–91.

CHESS, S., THOMAS, A. & HASSIBI, M. (1983) Depression in childhood and adolescence: A prospective study of six cases. *The Journal of Nervous and Mental Disease, 171,* 411–420.

CLARK, D. C., CLAYTON, P. J., ANDREASON, N. C., LEWIS, D., FAWCETT, J., & SCHEFTNER, W. A. (1985) Intellectual functioning and abstraction ability in major affective disorders. *Comprehensive Psychiatry, 26,* 313–325.

CLARK, K. A. (1973) A role for librarians in the relevant war against poverty. Wilson Library Bulletin, Sept. 1965 (Quoted in A. MacLeod, *Growing up in America.*) Rockville, MD: National Institute of Mental Health.

CLARKE, A. M. & CLARKE, A. D. D. (1979) *Early experience: Myths and evidence.* New York: Free Press.

CLARKIN, J. F., WIDIGER, T. A., FRANCES, A., HURT, S. W., and GIL-

MORE, M. (1983) Prototypic typology and the borderline personality disorder. *Journal of Abnormal Psychology, 92,* 263–275.

CLECKLEY, H. (1964) *The mask of sanity* (4th ed.). St. Louis: Mosby.

CLEMENS, S. (Mark Twain) (1923) *Huckleberry Finn.* New York: Harper & Row.

CLONINGER, C. R., BOHMAN, M., & SIGVARDSSON, S. (1981) Inheritance of alcohol abuse. *Archives of General Psychiatry, 38,* 861–868.

CLONINGER, C. R., MARTIN, R. L., GUZE, S. B., and CLAYTON, P. J. (1985) Diagnosis and prognosis in schizophrenia. *Archives of General Psychiatry, 42,* 15–25.

CLONINGER, C. R., SIGVARDSSON, S., von KNORRING, A., & BOHMAN, M. (1984) An adoption study of somotoform disorders: II. Identification of two discrete somotoform disorders, *Archives of General Psychiatry, 41,* 863–871.

COATES, D. & WORTMAN, C. G. (1980) Depression maintenance and interpersonal control. In A. Baum & J. E. Singer (Eds.), *Advances in environmental psychology,* (Vol. 2). Hillsdale, NJ: Lawrence Erlbaum Associates.

*Cocaine use in America: Epidemiologic and clinical perspectives* (1985) National Institute on Drug Abuse, Rockville, MD.

COHEN, D. J., CAPARULO, B. K., & SHAYWITZ, B. A. (1978) Neurochemical and developmental models of childhood autism. In G. Serban (Ed.), *Cognitive defects in the development of mental illness.* New York: Brunner/Mazel.

COHEN, R. A. (1975) Manic-depressive illness. In A. M. Freedman, J. I. Kaplan, & B. J. Sadock, *Comprehensive textbook of psychiatry* (2nd ed.). Baltimore, MD: Williams & Wilkins.

COLEMAN, E. (1981–82) Developmental stages of the coming out process. *Journal of Homosexuality, 7,* (2/3), 31–43.

COLLIGAN, M. J., PENNEBAKER, J. W., & MURPHY, L. R. (1982) *Mass psychogenic illness: A social psychological analyses.* Hillsdale, NJ: Lawrence Erlbaum Associates.

CONNOLLY, J. A. (1978) Intelligence levels of Down's syndrome children. *American Journal of Mental Deficiency, 83,* 193–196.

COOPER, J. E., KENDALL, R. E., GURLAND, B. J., SHARPE, L., COPELAND, J. R. M., & SIMON, R. J. (1972) *Psychiatric diagnosis in New York and London: A comparative study of mental hospital admissions* (Maudsley Monograph #20). London: Oxford University Press.

COOPER, J. & SARTORIUS, M. (1977) Cultural and temporal variations in schizophrenia: A speculation on the importance of industrialization. *British Journal of Psychiatry, 130,* 50–55.

COOPER, W. H. (1981) Ubiquitous halo. *Psychological Bulletin, 90,* 218–244.

CORFMAN, E. (1979) *Depression, Manic-depressive illness, and biological rhythms.* DHHS Pub. No. (ADM) 82-889. Rockville, MD: National Institute of Mental Health.

CORNBLATT, B. A. & Erlenmeyer-Kimling, L. (1985) Global attentional deviance as a marker of risk for schizophrenia: Specificity and predictive validity. *Journal of Abnormal Psychology, 94,* 470–486.

CORSON, S. A., CORSON, E. O., ARNOLD, L. E., & KNOPP, W. (1976) Animal models of violence and hyperkinesis. In G. Serban & A. Kling (Eds.) *Animal models in human psychology,* New York: Plenum.

COSTA, E. (1985) Benzodiazepine-GABA interactions: A model to investigate the neurobiology of anxiety. In A. H. Tuma & J. Maser (Eds.) *Anxiety and the anxiety disorders.* Hillsdale, N.J.: Lawrence Erlbaum Associates.

Council on Scientific Affairs, American Medical Association (1986) Alcohol and the driver. *Journal of the American Medical Association, 255,* 522–527.

COWEN, E. L. (1982) Help is where you find it: Four informal helping groups. *American Psychologist, 37,* 385–395.

COWEN, E. L. (1985) Person-centered approaches in primary prevention in mental health: Situation-focused and competence enhancement. *American Journal of Community Psychology, 13,* 31–48.

COX, T. (1984) Stress: A psychophysiological approach to cancer. In C. L. Cooper (Ed.) *Psychological Stress and Cancer,* Chichester, England: John Wiley.

COYLE, J. T., PRICE, D. L. C., & DeLONG, M. R. (1983) Alzheimer's disease: A disorder of cortical cholinergic innervation. *Science, 219,* 1184–1190.

COYNE, J. C. (1976) Depression and the responses of others. *Journal of Abnormal Psychology, 85,* 186–193.

COYNE, J. C. (1982) A critique of cognitions as causal entities with particular reference to depression. *Cognitive Therapy and Research, 6,* 3–13.

COYNE, J. C., ALDWIN, C., & LAZARUS, R. S. (1981) Depression and coping in stressful episodes. *Journal of Abnormal Psychology, 90,* 439–447.

CRAIG, E. M. & McCARVER, R. B. (1984) Community placement and adjustment of deinstitutionalized clients: Issues and findings. *International Review of Research in Mental Retardation, 12,* 95–122.

CREESE, I., BURT, D. R., & SNYDER, S. H. (1976) Dopamine receptor binding predicts clinical and pharmacological potencies of antischizophrenic drugs. *Science, 192,* 481–483.

CRISP, A. H. & BURNS, T. (1983) The clinical presentation of anorexia nervosa in the male. *International Journal of Eating Disorders, 2,* 5–10.

CROOK, T. & ELIOT, J. (1980) Parental death during childhood and adult depression: A critical review of the literature. *Psychological Bulletin, 87,* 252–259.

CROSS, D., SHEEHAN, P., & KHAN, J. (1982) Short- and long-term follow-up of clients receiving insight-oriented therapy and behavior therapy. *Journal of Consulting and Clinical Psychology, 50,* 103–112.

CROW, T. J. (1980) Positive and negative schizophrenia symptoms and the role of dopamine. *British Journal of Psychiatry, 137,* 383–386.

CROW, T. J. (1985) The two syndrome concept: Origins and current status. *Schizophrenia Bulletin, 11,* 471–486.

CROWE, M. J., GILLAN, P., & GOLOMBOK, S. (1981) Form and content in the conjoint treatment of sexual dysfunction: A controlled study. *Behaviour Research and Therapy, 19,* 47–54.

CROWE, R. (1974) An adoption study of antisocial personality. *Archives of General Psychiatry, 31,* 785–791.

CROWN, S. & D'ARDENNE, P. (1982) Symposium on sexual dysfunction: Controversies, methods, results. *British Journal of Psychiatry, 140,* 70–77.

CUMMINGS, E. M., IANNOTTI, R. J., & ZAHN-WAXTER, C. (1985) Influence of conflict between adults on the emotions and aggression of young children. *Developmental Psychology, 21,* 495–507.

CURRAN, J. P., & MONTI, P. M. (Eds.). (1982) *Social skills training: A practical handbook for assessment and treatment.* New York: Guilford.

CUSTANCE, J. (1952) *Wisdom, madness and folly.* New York: Pelligrini & Cuddahy.

CUTRONA, C. E., RUSSELL, D. W., & PEPLAU, L. A. (1979) *Loneliness and the process of social adjustment: A longitudinal study.* Paper presented at the American Psychological Association, New York.

CZEISLER, C. A., WEITZMAN, G. D., MOORE-EDE, M. C., ZIMMERMAN, J. C., & KNAUER, R. S. (1980) Human sleep: Its duration and organization depend on its circadian phase. *Science, 210,* 1264–1267. Copyright © 1980 by the AAS.

DARLING, C. A., KALLEN, D. J., & VanDUSEN, J. E. (1984) Sex in transition, 1900–1980. *Journal of Youth and Adolescence, 13*(5), 385–399.

DAVENPORT, Y. B., ADLAND, M. L., GOLD, P. W., and GOODWIN, F. K. (1979) Manic-depressive illness: Psychodynamic features of multigenerational families. *American Journal of Orthopsychiatry, 49,* 24–35.

DAVIS, J. M. (1985) Antipsychotic drugs. In H. I. Kaplan & B. J. Sadock (Eds.) *Comprehensive textbook of psychiatry*, (4th ed.), Vol. 2. Baltimore, MD: Williams & Wilkins.

DAYEE, F. S. (1982) *Private zones*. Copyright © 1982 by Frances S. Dayee. Warner Books Inc.

DEMOS, J. P. (1982) *Entertaining Satan: Witchcraft and the culture of early New England*. New York: Oxford University Press.

DE NIKE, L. D. & TIBER, N. (1968) Neurotic behavior. In P. London & D. Rosenhan (Eds.), *Foundations of abnormal psychology*. New York: Holt, Rinehart & Winston.

DERRY, P. A. & KUIPER, N. A. (1981) Schematic processing and self reference in clinical depression. *Journal of Abnormal Psychology*, 90, 286–297.

DEUTSCH, A. (1948) *The shame of the states*. New York: Arno.

DEUTSCH, S. I. & DAVIS, K. L. (1983) Schizophrenia: A review of diagnostic and biological issues II. Biological Issues. *Hospital and Community Psychiatry*, 34, 423–437.

DEYKIN, E. Y. & MacMAHON, B. (1979) The incidence of seizures among children with autistic symptoms. *American Journal of Psychiatry*, 136, 1310–1312.

DIAMOND, E. L. (1982) The role of anger and hostility in essential hypertension and coronary heart disease. *Psychological Bulletin*, 92, 410–433.

DIDION, J. (1979) *The white album*. New York: Simon & Schuster.

DIEKSTRA, R. A. (1973) *A social learning theory approach to the prediction of suicidal behavior*. Paper presented at the Seventh International Congress on Suicide Prevention, Amsterdam, 1973.

DIRKS, J. F., KINSMAN, R. A., HORTON, D. J., FROSS, K. H., & JONES, N. F. (1978) Panic-fear in asthma: Rehospitalization following intensive long-term treatment. *Psychosomatic Medicine*, 40, 5–13.

*Disaster Service News and Notes*, Sept. 1982.

DODGE, K. A. (1985) Attributional bias in aggressive children. *Advances in Cognitive Behavioral Research and Therapy*, 4, 73–110.

DOHRENWEND, B. P. & DOHRENWEND, B. S. (1982) Perspectives on the past and future of psychiatric epidemiology. *American Journal of Public Health*, 72, 1271–1279.

DOLLARD, J. & MILLER, N. (1950) *Personality and psychotherapy*. New York: McGraw-Hill.

DORIAN, B., GARFINKEL, P. E., KEYSTONE, E., GORCINSKI, R., BROWN, G. M., DARBY, P., & GARNER, D. (1984) Occupational stress and immunity. University of Toronto: Unpublished research.

DOUGLAS, W. O. (1974) *Go east, young man*. New York: Random House.

DWORKIN, R. H. & LENZENWEGER, M. F. (1984) Symptoms and the genetics of schizophrenia: Implications for diagnosis. *American Journal of Psychiatry*, 141, 1541–1546.

EASTON, K. (1959) An unusual case of fugue and orality. *Psychoanalytic Quarterly*, 28, 505–513.

EATON, W. W., HOLZER, C. E., III, VONKORFF, M., ANTHONY, J. C., HELZER, J. E., GEORGE, L., BURNHAM, M. A., BOYD, J. H., KESSLER, L. G., & LOCKE, B. Z. (1984) The design of the epidemiologic catchment area surveys, *Archives of General Psychiatry*, 41, 942–948.

EBERHARDY, F. (1967) The view from "the couch." *Journal of Child Psychology and Psychiatry*, 8, 257–263.

ECKARDT, M. J., HARFORD, T. C., KAELBER, C. T., PARKER, E. S., ROSENTHAL, L. S., RYBACK, R . S., SALMOIRAGHI, G. C., VANDERVEEN, E., & WARREN, K. R. (1981) Health hazards associated with alcohol consumption. *Journal of the American Medical Association*, 246, 648–666.

EGELAND, J. A. & Hostetter, A. M. (1983) Amish study-I. Affective disorders among the Amish, 1976-1980. *American Journal of Psychiatry*, 140, 56–61.

EISENSON, J. (1973) *Adult aphasia: Assessment and treatment*. Englewood Cliffs, NJ: Prentice-Hall.

EISENSTAT, R. A. & FELNER, R. D. (1984) Toward a differentiated view of burnout: Personal and organizational mediators of job satisfaction and stress. *American Journal of Community Psychology*, 12, 411–430.

EISLER, R. M. (1972) Crisis intervention in the family of a firesetter. *Psychotherapy: Theory, Research and Practice*, 9, 76–79.

ELDRED, S. H., BELL, N. W., LONGABAUGH, R., & SHERMAN, L. J. (1964) Interactional correlates of chronicity in schizophrenia. *Psychiatric Research Report 19*, Dec. 1-12. Washington, D.C.: American Psychiatric Association.

ELIOT, R. S. & BUELL, J. C. (1983) The role of the CNS in cardiovascular disorders. *Hospital Practice*, May, 189–199.

ELKINS, R., RAPOPORT, J. & LIPSKY, A. (1980) Childhood obsessive-compulsive disorder: A neurobiological perspective. *Journal of the American Academy of Child Psychiatry*, 19, 551–554.

ELLENBERGER, H. F. (1970) *The discovery of the unconscious*. New York: Basic Books.

ELLIS, A. (1962) *Reason and emotion in psychotherapy*. New York: Lyle Stuart.

ELLIS, A. (1970) Rational-emotive therapy. In L. Hersher (Ed.), *Four psychotherapies*. New York: Appleton-Century-Crofts.

ELLIS, E. M., ATKESON, B. M., & CALHOUN, K. S. (1981) An assessment of long-term reaction to rape. *Journal of Abnormal Psychology*, 90, 263–266.

ELMADJIAN, E. (1963) Excretion and metabolism effect in epinephrine and norepinephrine in various emotional states. *Proceedings of the Fifth Pan-American Conference of Endocrinology*, Lima, Peru.

ENDICOTT, J. & SPITZER, R. L. (1978) A diagnostic interview: The Schedule for Affective Disorders and Schizophrenia. *Archives of General Psychiatry*, 35, 837–844.

ENDLER, N. S. (1982) *Holiday of darkness*. New York: Wiley-Interscience.

ENGEL, G. L. (1977) The need for a new medical model: A challenge for biomedicine. *Science*, 196, 129–136.

EMMELKAMP, P. M. G., VAN DER HELM, M., VAN ZANTEN, B. L., & PLOCHG, I. (1980) Treatment of obsessive-compulsive patients: The contribution of self-instructional training to the effectiveness of exposure. *Behavior Research and Therapy*, 18, 61–66. Reprinted with permission from *Behavior Research and Therapy*, Copyright © 1980, Pergamon Journals Ltd.

EPSTEIN, A. W. (1965) Fetishism. In R. Slovenko (Ed.), *Sexual behavior and the law*. Springfield, IL: Thomas.

EPSTEIN, N. & VLOK, L. (1981) Research on the results of psychotherapy: A summary of evidence. *American Journal of Psychiatry*, 138, 1027–1035.

ERDELYI, M. (1985) *Psychoanalysis: Freud's cognitive psychology*. New York: W. H. Freeman.

ERIKSON, E. H. (1975) *Life history and the historical moment*. New York: W. W. Norton.

ERON, L. D. (1982) Parent-child interaction, televised violence, and aggression of children. *American Psychologist*, 37, 197–211.

ERON, L. D. & PETERSON, R. A. (1982) Abnormal behavior: Social approaches. In M. R. Rosenzweig & L. W. Porter (Eds.), *Annual Review of Psychology*. Palo Alto, CA: Annual Reviews.

EYSENCK, H. J. (1952) The effects of psychotherapy: An evaluation. *Journal of Consulting Psychology*, 16, 319–324.

EYSENCK, H. J. (1961) The effects of psychotherapy. In H. J. Eysenck (Ed.), *Handbook of abnormal psychology*. New York: Basic Books.

EYSENCK, H. J. & EYSENCK, S. B. G. (1975) *Manual of the Eysenck Personality Questionnaire*. London: University of London Press.

FAIRBANK, J. A. & KEANE, T. M. (1982) Flooding for combat-related stress disorders: Assessment of anxiety-reduction across traumatic memories. *Behavior Therapy*, 13, 499–510.

FAIRWEATHER, G. W., SANDERS, D. H., MAYNARD, H., CRESSLER, D. L.,

& BLECK, D. S. (1969) *Community life for the mentally ill: An alternative to institutional care.* Chicago: Aldine.

FALLOON, I. (1981) Interpersonal variables in behavioral group therapy. *British Journal of Medical Psychology, 54,* 133–141.

FARAONE, S. V. & TSUANG, M. T. (1985) Quantitative models of the genetic transmission of schizophrenia. *Psychological Bulletin, 98,* 41–66.

FARBER, S. L. (1983) *Identical twins reared apart: A reanalysis.* New York: Basic Books.

FARBER, S. S., FELNER, R. D., & PRIMAVERA, J. (1985) Parental separation/divorce and adolescents: An examination of factors mediating adaptation. *American Journal of Community Psychiatry, 13,* 171–185.

FARINA, A., GHILA, D., BOUDREAU, L. A., ALLEN, J. G., & SHERMAN, M. (1971) Mental illness and the impact of believing others know about it. *Journal of Abnormal Psychology, 77,* 1–5.

FARRINGTON, D. P. (1979) Environmental stress, delinquent behavior, and convictions. In I. G. Sarason & C. D. Spielberger (Eds.), *Stress and anxiety* (Vol. 6). Washington, D.C.: Hemisphere.

FEINGOLD, G. F. (1975) *Why your child is hyperactive.* New York: Random House.

FEINSON, M. C. (1985) Aging and mental health. *Research on Aging, 7,* 155–174.

FERREL, R. B. (1980) Schizophrenia: The diagnoses and misdiagnoses. *Carrier Foundation Letter, 65,* (Nov.) 1–5.

FEUERSTEIN, R., RANDY, Y., HOFFMAN, M. B., & MILLER, R. (1980) *Instrumental Enrichment.* Baltimore, MD: University Park Press.

FLAY, B. R., RYAN, K. B., BEST, J. A., BROWN, K. S., KERSELL, M. W., D'AVERNAS, J. R., ZANNA, M. P. (1985) Are social psychological smoking prevention programs effective? The Waterloo study. *Journal of Behavioral Medicine, 8,* 37–59.

FOA, E. B., STEKETKE, G., & YOUNG, M. C. (1984) Agoraphobia: Phenomenological aspects, associated characteristics, and theoretical considerations. *Clinical Psychology Review, 4,* 431–457.

FOLSTEIN, S. E. & FOLSTEIN, M. F. (1983) Psychiatric features of Huntington's disease: Recent approaches and findings. *Psychiatric Developments, 2,* 193–206.

FOLSTEIN, S. & RUTTER, M. (1977) Infantile autism: A genetic study of 21 twin pairs. *Journal of Child Psychology and Psychiatry, 18,* 297–321.

FORD, C. V., & FOLKS, D. G. (1985) Conversion disorders: An overview. *Psychosomatics, 26,* 371–374, 380–383.

FOX, A. J., & ADELSTEIN, A. M. (1978) Occupational mortality: Work or way of life. *Journal of Epidemiology and Community Health, 32,* 73–78.

FRANCES, A. (1980) The DSM-III personality disorders section: A commentary. *American Journal of Psychiatry, 137,* 1050–1054.

FRANCES, A. (in press) A critical review of four DSM-III personality disorders: The borderline, avoidant, dependent, and passive-aggressive. In G. Tischler (Ed.) *DSM-III: An interim appraisal.* Washington, D.C: American Psychiatric Press.

FRANCES, A., & KLEIN, D. F. (1982) Anxious, precise, demanding man seeks help soon after marriage. *Hospital and Community Psychiatry, 33,* 89–90.

FRANCES, A., SWEENEY, J., & CLARKIN, J. (1985) Do psychotherapies have specific effects? *American Journal of Psychotherapy, 39,* 159–174.

FRANK, E., ANDERSON, C., & RUBENSTEIN, D. (1978) Frequency of sexual dysfunction in "normal" couples. *New England Journal of Medicine, 299,* 111–115.

FRANK, J. D. (1969) Common features account for effectiveness. *International Journal of Psychiatry, 7,* 122–127.

FRANKS, C. (1985) Behavior therapy with children and adolescents. *Annual Review of Behavior Therapy, 10,* 236–290. With permission of the Guilford Press.

FRANKS, L. (1985) The Story of "James B." *New York Times Magazine,* Oct. 20.

FREDERIKSEN, L. W., JENKINS, J. O., FOY, D. W., & EISLER, R. M. (1976) Social skills training to modify abusive verbal outbursts in adults. *Journal of Applied Behavior Analysis, 9,* 117–127.

FREEDMAN, B. J. (1974) The subjective experience of perceptual and cognitive disturbances in schizophrenia: A review of autobiographical accounts. *Archives of General Psychiatry, 30,* 333–340.

FRERICHS, R. R., ANESHENSEL, C. S., & CLARK, V. A. (1981) Prevalence of depression in Los Angeles County. *American Journal of Epidemiology, 113,* 333–340.

FREUD, A. (1937) *The ego and the mechanisms of defense.* London: Hogarth Press.

FREUD, S. (1925) (originally published 1914) On narcissism: An introduction. In J. Strachey (Ed.), *The standard edition of the complete psychological works of Sigmund Freud* (Vol. 4). London: Hogarth.

FREUD, S. (1930) Civilization and its discontents. In J. Strachey (Ed.), *The standard edition of the complete psychological works of Sigmund Freud* (Vol. 21). London: Hogarth.

FREUD, S. (1950) (originally published 1909) Selected papers. In J. Strachey (Ed.), *The standard edition of the complete psychological works of Sigmund Freud* (Vol. 3). London: Hogarth.

FREUD, S. (1951) A letter from Freud (April 9, 1935). *American Journal of Psychiatry, 107,* 786–787.

FREUD, S. (1957) (originally published 1917) Mourning and melancholia. In J. Strachey (Ed.), *The standard edition of the complete psychological works of Sigmund Freud* (Vol. 14). London: Hogarth.

FREUD, S. (1963) *The cocaine papers.* New York: Dunquin.

FREUD, S. (1964) (originally published 1936) A disturbance of memory on the Acropolis. In J. Strachey (Ed.), *The standard edition of the complete psychological works of Sigmund Freud* (Vol. 22). London: Hogarth.

FRIEDMAN, M., & ROSENMAN, R. (1974) *Type A behavior and your heart.* New York: Knopf.

FYFFE, C. & PRIOR, M. R. (1978) Evidence of language recoding autistic children: A reexamination. *British Journal of Psychiatry, 136,* 1310–1312.

GABBARD, G. O. (1985) The role of compulsiveness in the normal physician. *Journal of the American Medical Association, 254,* 2926–2929.

GABRIELLI, W. F. J. & PLOMIN, R. (1985) *Alcoholism: An inherited disease.* Rockville, MD: National Institute on Alcohol Abuse and Alcoholism.

GARDNER, H. (1983) *Frames of mind.* New York: Basic Books.

GARMEZY, N. & DEVINE, E. (1984) Project competence: The Minnesota studies of children vulnerable to psychopathology, pp. 289–303. In N. F. Watt, E. J. Anthony, N. F. Wynne, E. J. Anthony, L. C. Wynne, & J. E. Rolf, (Eds.). *Children at risk for schizophrenia: A longitudinal perspective.* Cambridge: Cambridge University Press.

GARNER, D. M. & GARFINKEL, P. E. (1980) Socio-cultural factors in the development of anorexia nervosa. *Psychological Medicine, 10,* 647–656.

GARNER, D. M., GARFINKEL, P. E., SCHWARTZ, D., & THOMPSON, M. (1980) Cultural expectations of thinness in women. *Psychological Reports, 47,* 438–491.

GAYLORD-ROSS, R. J., HARING, T. G., BREEN, C., and PITTS-CONWAY, V. (1984) The training and generalization of social interaction skills with autistic youth. *Journal of Applied Behavior Analysis, 17,* 229–247.

GEBHARD, P. H., GAGNON, J. H., POMEROY, W. B., & CHRISTENSON, C. V. (1965) *Sex offenders: An analysis of types.* New York: Harper & Row.

GEORGE, L. & NEUFELD, R. W. J. (1985) Cognition and symptomatology in schizophrenia. *Schizophrenia Bulletin, 11,* 264–285.

GERBNER, G., GROSS, L., MORGAN, M., & SIGNORIELLI, N. (1981) Health and medicine on television. *New England Journal of Medicine, 305,* 901–904.

GERSHON, E. S., HAMOVIT, J., GUROFF, J. J., DIBBLE, E., LECKMAN, J. F., SCEERY, W., TARGUM, S. D., NURNBERGER, J. I., GOLDIN, L. R., & BUNNEY, W. E., Jr. (1982) A family study of schizoaffective, bipolar I, bipolar II, unipolar and normal control probands. *Archives of General Psychiatry, 39,* 1157–1167.

GIBBONS, F. X. (1985) Stigma perception: Social comparison among mentally retarded persons. *American Journal of Mental Deficiency, 90,* 98–106.

GIBBS, F. A., GIBBS, E. L., & LENNOX, W. G. (1939) Influence of the blood sugar level on the wave and spike formation in petit mal epilepsy. *Archives of Neurology and Psychiatry, 41,* 1111–1116. Copyright 1939, American Medical Association.

GILL, J. J., PRICE, V. A., FRIEDMAN, M., THORESEN, C. E., POWELL, L. H., ULMER, D., BROWN, B., DREWS, F. R. (1985) Reduction in Type-A behavior in healthy middle-aged American military officers. *American Heart Journal, 110,* 503–514.

GILLIS, J. S., & BLEVENS, K. (1978) Sources of judgmental impairment in paranoid and nonparanoid schizophrenics. *Journal of Abnormal Psychology, 87,* 587–596.

GITTELMAN, R. & KLEIN, D. F. (1984) Relationships between separation anxiety and panic and agoraphobic disorders. *Psychopathology, 17,* (supplement), 56–65.

GLASS, G. V. & KLIEGL, R. M. (1983) An apology for research integration in the study of psychotherapy. *Journal of Consulting and Clinical Psychology, 51,* 28–41.

GLESER, G. C., GREEN, B. L., & WINGET, C. (1981) *Prolonged psychosocial effects of disaster.* New York: Academic Press.

GOFFMAN, E. (1959) *The presentation of self in everyday life.* New York: Doubleday.

GOLD, G. (1974) *The White House transcripts.* New York: Bantam Books.

GOLDBERG, S. C. (1985) Negative and deficit symptoms in schizophrenia do respond to neuroleptics. *Schizophrenia Bulletin, 11,* 453–456.

GOLDEN, J. C., GRAVER, B., BLOSE, I., BERG, R., COFFMAN, J., & Bloch, S. (1981) Differences in brain densities between chronic alcoholic and normal control patients. *Science, 211,* 508–510.

GOLDEN, K. M. (1977) Voodoo in Africa and the United States. *American Journal of Psychiatry, 134,* 1425–1427.

GOLDMAN, P. & WILLIAMS, D. A. (1978) Black youth, a lost generation? *Newsweek,* August 7, 22–34.

GOLDSTEIN, M. J. (1985) Family factors that antedate the onset of schizophrenia and related disorders: The results of a fifteen-year prospective longitudinal study. *Acta Psychiatrica Scandinavica Supplementum,* No. 319, 71, 7–18.

GOLEMAN, D. (1985) Three new psychiatric syndromes spur protest. *New York Times,* Nov. 19, p. 11.

GOODWIN, D. W. (1981) Alcoholism and alcoholic psychoses. In H. I. Kaplan & B. J. Sadock (Eds.) *Comprehensive textbook of psychiatry III,* (4th ed.), (Vol. 1). Baltimore: Williams and Wilkins.

GOSSELIN, C., & WILSON, G. (1980) *Sexual variations.* New York: Simon & Schuster.

GOTTESMAN, I. I. & SHIELDS, J. (1967) A polygenic theory of schizophrenia. *Proceedings of the National Academy of Sciences, 58,* 199–205.

GOTTESMAN, I. I. & SHIELDS, J. (1982) *Schizophrenia: The epigenetic puzzle.* New York: Cambridge University Press.

GOTTLIEB, A. (1985) Nicotine chewing gum, smoking withdrawal symptoms and relapse: A controlled study. Seattle, WA: Unpublished Ph.D. thesis, University of Washington.

GOTTLIEB, B. H. (1985) Theory into practice: Issues that surface in planning interventions which mobilize support. In I. G. Sarason & B. R. Sarason (Eds.) *Social support: Theory, research and applications.* Dordrecht, The Netherlands: Martinus Nijoff.

GOTTLIEB, J., SEMMEL, M. I. & VELDMAN, D. J. (1978) Correlates of social status among mainstreamed mentally retarded children. *Journal of Educational Psychology, 70,* 396–405.

GOTTSCHALK, L. A. (1978) Psychosomatic medicine today: An overview. *Psychosomatics, 19,* 89–93.

GOVE, W. R. & HUGHES, M. (1980) Reexamining the ecological fallacy: A study in which aggregate data are critical in investigating the pathological effects of living alone. *Social Forces, 58,* 1157–1177.

GRAHAM, J. D. P. (1945) High blood pressure after battle. *Lancet, 1,* 239–240.

GRANDIN, T. (1984) My experiences as an autistic child and review of selected literature. *Journal of Orthomolecular Psychiatry, 13,* 144–174. Reprinted with permission.

GRAVES, P. L. & THOMAS, C. B. (1981) Themes of interaction in medical students' Rorschach responses as predictors of midlife health or disease. *Psychosomatic Medicine, 43,* 215–225.

GRAWBOWSKI, J. (Ed.) (1985) *Pharmacological adjuncts in smoking cessation.* Rockville, MD: National Institute on Drug Abuse.

GREDEN, J. F. (1985) Caffeine and tobacco dependence. In H. I. Kaplan & B. J. Sadock (Eds.) *Comprehensive textbook of psychiatry,* (4th ed.) (Vol. 1). Baltimore, MD: Williams & Wilkins.

GREEN, R. (1974) *Sexual identity conflicts in children and adults.* New York: Basic Books.

GREEN, B. S., ABELMAN, R., & NEVENDORF, K. (1981) Sex on the soap operas: Afternoon delight. *Journal of Communication, 31:3,* 83–89.

GREEN, E. (1972) Biofeedback for mind/body self-regulation: Feeling and creativity. *Biofeedback and self-control.* Chicago: Aldine.

GREENBERG, B. S., GRAEF, D., FERNANDEZ-COLLADO, C., KORZENNY, F., & ATKIN, C. K. (1980) Sexual intimacy on commercial television during prime-time. *Journalism Quarterly, 57* (2), 30–37.

GREENBERG, J. (1978) The Americanization of Roseto. *Science News, 113,* 378–382.

GREENFELD, J. A. (1970) A child called Noah. *Life,* October 23, 60–72.

GREER, S. & MORRIS, T. (1975) Psychological attributes of women with breast cancer: A controlled study. *Journal of Psychosomatic Research, 19,* 147–153.

GRINKER, R. R. & SPIEGEL, J. P. (1945) *Men under stress.* New York: McGraw-Hill.

GRINSPOON, L. (1985) (Ed.) Borderline personality disorder--Part I. *The Harvard Medical School Mental Health Letter, 2,* (6), 1–3.

GROTH, A. N. (1979) *Men who rape.* New York: Plenum Press.

GROTH, A. N. & BURGESS, A. W. (1977) Sexual dysfunction during rape. *The New England Journal of Medicine, 297,* 764–766.

GROTH, A. N. & BURGESS, A. W. (1980) Male rape: Offenders and victims. *American Journal of Psychiatry, 137,* 806–810.

GROVE, W. M. & ANDREASEN, N .C. (1985) Language and thinking in psychosis. *Archives of General Psychiatry, 42,* 26–32.

GROVE, W. M., ANDREASEN, N. C., McDONALD-SCOTT, P., KELLER, M. B., & SHAPIRO, R. W. (1981) Reliability studies of psychiatric diagnosis. *Archives of General Psychiatry, 38,* 408–413.

GUDEMAN, J. E., DICKEY, B., HELLMAN, S., & BUFFETT, W. (1985) From inpatient to inn status: A new residential model. *Psychiatric Clinics of North America, 8,* 461–469.

GUILLEN, T. (1982) Competency ruling frees Safety Building squatter. *Seattle Times,* Jan. 27, B1.

GUMMOW, L., MILLER, P., & DUSTMAN, R. E. (1983) Attention and brain injury: A case for cognitive rehabilitation of attentional deficits. *Clinical Psychology Review, 3,* 255–274.

GUNDERSON, J. G. (1984) *Borderline Personality Disorder.* Washington, D.C.: American Psychiatric Press.

GURLAND, B. J. & CROSS, P. S. (1982) Epidemiology of psychopathology in old age. *Psychiatric Clinics of North America, 5*(1), 11–26.

HACKETT, T. P. & CASSEM, N. H. (1975) The psychologic reactions of patients in the pre- and post-hospital phases of myocardinal infarction. *Postgraduate Medicine, 57,* 43–46.

HALL, W., GOLDSTEIN, G., ANDREWS, G., LAPSLEY, H., BARTELS, R., & SILOVE, D. (1985) Estimating the economic costs of schizophrenia. *Schizophrenia Bulletin, 11,* 598–610.

HALMI, K. A., OWEN, W., LASKY, E., & STOKES, P. (1983) Dopaminergic regulation in anorexia nervosa. *International Journal of Eating Disorders, 22,* 129–134.

HAMBURG, B. A. (1974) Coping in early adolescence. In S. Arieti (Ed.), *American handbook of psychiatry* (Vol. 2.) New York: Basic Books.

HAMILTON, E. & ABRAMSON, L. (1983) Cognitive patterns and major depressive disorders: A longitudinal study in a hospital setting. *Journal of Abnormal Psychology, 92,* 173–184.

HAMMEN, C. L. (1985) Predicting depression: A cognitive-behavioral perspective. In P. C. Kendall (Ed.) *Advances in cognitive-behavioral research and therapy,* (Vol. 4). Orlando, FL: Academic Press.

HAMMEN, C. & DeMAYO, R. (1982) Cognitive correlates of teacher stress and depressive symptoms: Implications for attributional models of depression. *Journal of Abnormal Psychology, 91,* 96–101.

HANSON, D. R., GOTTESMAN, I. I., & MEEHLE, P. (1977) Genetic theories and the validation of psychiatric diagnoses: Implications for the study children of schizophrenics. *Journal of Abnormal Psychiatry, 86,* 575–588.

HANSON, J. W., STREISSGUTH, A. P., & SMITH, D. W. (1978) The effects of moderate alcohol consumption during pregnancy on fetal growth and morphogenesis. *Journal of Pediatrics, 92,* 457–460.

HARBIN, H. T. (1980) Episodic dyscontrol and family dynamics. *Advances in Family Psychiatry, 2,* 63–170.

HARDING, C. M., BROOKS, G. W., ASHIKAGA, T., STRAUSS, J. S., & BREIER, A. (In press) The Vermont longitudinal study: II. Long-term outcome for DSM-III schizophrenia. *American Journal of Psychiatry.*

HARE, R. (1978) Psychopathy. In H. von Praag, H. Leder, & O. Rafaelson (Eds.), *Handbook of biological psychiatry.* New York: Marcel Dekker.

HARE, R. D. (1983) Diagnosis of antisocial personality disorder in two prison populations. *American Journal of Psychiatry, 140,* 887–890.

HARE, R. D. (1985) Comparison of procedures for the assessment of psychopathy. *Journal of Consulting and Clinical Psychology, 53,* 7–16.

HARE, R. D. & FORTH, A. E. (1985) Psychopathy and lateral preference. *Journal of Abnormal Psychology, 94,* 541–546.

HARLOW, H. F. & SUOMI, S. J. (1974) Induced depression in monkeys. *Behavioral Biology, 12,* 273–296.

HARRIS, S. L. (1981) A letter from the editor on loss and trust. *The Clinical Psychologist, 34*(3), 3.

HARROW, M., SILVERSTEIN, M., & MARENGO, J. (1983) Disordered thinking: Does it identify nuclear schizophrenia? *Archives of General Psychiatry, 40,* 765–771.

HARSHFIELD, G.A., PICKERING, T. G., KLEINERT, H. D., BLANK, S., and LARAGH, J. H. (1982) Situational variances of blood pressure in ambulatory hypertensive patients. *Psychosomatic Medicine, 44,* 237–245.

HART, K. J. & OLLENDICK, T. H. (1985) Prevalence of bulimia in working and university women, *American Journal of Psychiatry, 142*(7), 851–854.

HARTSOUGH, C. S. & LAMBERT, N. M. (1985) Medical factors in hyperactive and normal children: Prenatal, developmental and health history findings. *American Journal of Orthopsychiatry, 55,* 190–201.

Harvard Mental Health Letter (1985) *Attention deficit disorder, 2*(3), 1–4.

HATHAWAY, S. R. & McKINLEY, J. C. (1967) *Minnesota multiphasic personality inventory: Manual for administration and scoring.* New York: Psychological Corporation.

HATTIE, J. A., SHARPLEY, C. F., & ROGERS, H. J. (1984) Comparative effectiveness of professional and paraprofessional helpers. *Psychological Bulletin, 95,* 534–541.

HAYNES, S. G., FEINLEIB, M., & KANNEL, W. B. (1980) The relationship of psychological factors to coronary heart disease in the Framingham study: III. Eight-year incidence of coronary heart disease. *American Journal of Epidemiology, 111,* 37–58.

HAZELWOOD, R. R., BURGESS, A. W., & GROTH, A. N. (1981) Death during dangerous autoerotic practice. *Social Science Medicine, 15E,* 129–133.

HAZELWOOD, R. R., DEITZ, P. E., and BURGESS, A. W. (1983) *Autoerotic fatalities.* Lexington, MA: Lexington Books, D. C. Heath and Company. Copyright © 1983, D. C. Heath and Company.

*Health News* (1973) California Department of Health, Sept., p. 4.

HEIM, N. (1981) Sexual behavior of castrated sexual offenders. *Archives of Sexual Behavior, 10,* 11–19.

HELGASON, T. (1979) Prevalence and incidence of mental disorders estimated by a health questionnaire and psychiatric case register. *Acta Psychiatrica Scandinavica, 58,* 256–266.

HELSING, K. J., SZELO, M., & COMSTOCK, G. W. (1981) Factors associated with mortality after widowhood. *American Journal of Public Health, 71,* 802–809.

HELZER, J. E., ROBINS, L. N., McEVOY, L. T., SPITZNAGEL, E. L., STOLZMAN, R. K., & FARMER, A. (1985) A comparison of clinical and diagnostic interview schedule diagnoses. *Archives of General Psychiatry, 42,* 657–666.

HENNEKENS, C. H., WILLETT, W., ROSNER, B., COLE, D. S., & MAYRENT, S. L. (1979) Effects of beer, wine and liquor in coronary deaths. *Journal of the American Medical Association, 242,* 1973–1974.

HENNIGAN, K. M., HEATH, L., WHARTON, J. D., DELROSARIO, M. L., COOK, T. D., & CALDER, B. J. (1982) Impact of the introduction of television on crime in the United States: Empirical findings and theoretical implications. *Journal of Personality and Social Psychology, 42,* 461–477.

HEROLD, E. S. & WAY, L. (1983) Oral-genital sexual behavior in a sample of university females. *The Journal of Sex Research, 19,* 327–338.

HESTON, L. L. & MASTRI, A. R. (1982) Age of onset of Pick's and Alzheimer's dementia: Implications for diagnosis and research. *Journal of Gerontology, 37,* 422–424.

HETHERINGTON, E. M., COX, M., & COX, R. (1979) Play and social interaction in children following divorce. *Journal of Social Issues, 35,* 26–49.

HIBBERT, G. A. (1984) Ideational components of anxiety: Their origin and content. *British Journal of Psychiatry, 144,* 618–624.

HILBERMAN, E. (1978) The impact of rape. In M. Notman & C. Nadelson (Eds.) *The woman patient.* (Vol. 1). New York: Plenum.

HINKLE, L. E., JR., WITNEY, L. H., LEHMAN, E. W., FLEAHINGER, B. (1968) Occupation, education, and coronary heart disease. *Science, 161,* 238–246.

HOENIG, J. (1984) Schneider's first rank symptoms and the tabulators. *Comprehensive Psychiatry, 25,* 77–87.

HOFER, M. A. (1984) Relationships as regulators: A psychobiologic perspective on bereavement. *Psychosomatic Medicine, 46,* 183–197.

HOFLING, C. K. (1968) *Textbook of psychiatry for medical practice,* (2nd ed.). Philadelphia: Lippincott.

HOLDEN, C. (1985) A guarded endorsement for shock therapy. *Science, 228,* 1510–1511.

HOLROYD, K. A., ANDRASKI, F., & WESTBROOK, T. (1977) Cognitive control of tension headache. *Cognitive Therapy and Research, 2,* 121–133.

HOLZMAN, P. S. (1978) Cognitive impairment and cognitive stability: Toward a theory of thought disorder. In G. Serban (Ed.), *Cognitive defects in the development of mental illness.* New York: Brunner/Mazel.

HOLZMAN, P. S., SOLOMON, C. M., LEVIN, S., & WATERNAUX, C. S. (1984) Pursuit eye movement dysfunctions in schizophrenia: Family evidence for specificity. *Archives of General Psychiatry, 41,* 136–139.

HOOLEY, J. M. (1985) Expressed emotion: A review of the critical literature. *Clinical Psychology Review, 5,* 119–139.

HORNE, J. (1979) Defendant found guilty of murdering jogger. *Seattle Times,* May 31, C11.

HOROWITZ, M. J. (1974) Stress response syndromes. *Archives of General Psychiatry, 31,* 768–781.

HOROWITZ, M. J. (1985) Disasters and psychological responses to stress. *Psychiatric Annals, 115,* 161–167.

HORWITZ, A. V. (1984) The economy and social pathology. *Annual Review of Sociology, 10,* 95–119.

HOUGHTON, J. F. (1980) One personal experience: Before and after mental illness. In J. G. Rabkin, L. Gelb, & J. B. Lazar (Eds.), *Attitudes toward the mentally ill: Research perspectives.* Rockville, MD: National Institute of Mental Health.

HOUGHTON, J. F. (1982) First person account: Maintaining mental health in a turbulent world. *Schizophrenia Bulletin, 8,* 548–552.

HOYT, M. F., XENAKIS, S. N., MARMAR, C. R. & HOROWITZ, M. J. (1983) Therapists' actions that influence their perceptions of "good" psychotherapy sessions. *The Journal of Nervous and Mental Disease, 171,* 400–404.

HUDSON, J. I., LAFFLER, P. S., & POPE, H. G., JR. (1982) Bulimia related to affective disorder by family history and response to the dexamethasone suppression test. *American Journal of Psychiatry, 139,* 685–687.

HUNT, D. D. & HAMPSON, J. L. (1980) Follow-up of 17 biologic male transsexuals after sex-reassignment surgery. *American Journal of Psychiatry, 137,* 432–438.

HUNT, M. (1974) *Sexual behavior in the 1970s.* Chicago: Playboy Press.

HUNT, W. A. & BESPALIC, D. A. (1974) An evaluation of current methods of modifying smoking behavior. *Journal of Clinical Psychology, 30,* 430–438. Copyright © 1974. Clinical Psychology Publishing Co. Reprinted with permission.

HUTCHINGS, B. & MEDNICK, S. A. (1977) Criminality in adoptees and their adoptive and biological parents: A pilot study. In S. A. Mednick & K. O. Christensen (Eds.), *Biosocial bases of criminal behavior.* New York: Gorner Press.

HUXLEY, A. L. (1954) *The doors of perception.* London: Chatto & Windus.

IANOCO, W. C. & KOENIG, W. G. R. (1983) Features that distinguish the smooth-pursuit eye-tracking performance of schizophrenic, affective disorder and normal individuals. *Journal of Abnormal Psychology, 92,* 29–41.

INGRAM, R. E. (1984) Toward an information-processing analysis of depression. *Cognitive Therapy and Research, 8,* 443–478.

INHELDER, B. (1969) *The diagnosis of reasoning in the mentally retarded* (2nd ed.) (W. B. Stephens et al. trans.). New York: Chandler.

INSEL, T. R. (Ed.) (1984) *New findings in obsessive compulsive disorder.* Washington, D.C.: American Psychiatric Press.

ISAACS, D. C. (1982) Treatment of child abuse: A review of the behavioral interventions. *Journal of Applied Behavior Analysis, 15,* 273–294.

ITIL, T. M. (1977) Qualitative and quantitative EEG findings in schizophrenics. *Schizophrenia Bulletin, 3,* 61–79.

ITL, T. M., SALETU, B., & DAVIS, R. (1974) Stability studies of schizophrenics and normals using computer-analyzed EEG. *Biological Psychiatry, 8,* 321–325.

JACK-ROLLER & SNODGRASS, J. (1982) *The jack-roller at seventy.* Lexington, MA: Lexington Books.

JACOBSON, N. S., WALDRON, H., & MOORE, T. (1980) Toward a behavioral profile of marital distress. *Journal of Consulting and Clinical Psychology, 48,* 696–703.

JAFFEE, J. H. (1985) Opioid dependence. In H. I. Kaplan & B. J. Sadock (Eds.) *Comprehensive textbook of psychiatry,* (4th ed.) (Vol. 1). Baltimore: Williams & Wilkins.

JAMISON, K. R. GERNER, R. H., HAMMEN, C., & PADESKY, C. (1980) Clouds and silver linings: Positive experiences associated with primary affective disorders. *American Journal of Psychiatry, 137,* 198–202.

JANIS, I. L. (1958) *Psychological stress: Psychoanalytic and behavioral studies of surgical patients.* New York: Wiley.

JANISSE, M. P. (1977) *Pupillometry: The psychology of the pupillary response.* Washington, D.C.: Hemisphere.

JELLINEK, E. M. (1960) *The disease concept of alcoholism.* New Haven: Hillhouse Press.

JEMMOTT, J. B. III & LOCKE, S. E. (1984) Psychosocial factors, immunologic mediation, and human susceptibility to infectious diseases: How much do we know? *Psychological Bulletin, 95,* 78–108.

JENKINS, C. D. (1985) New horizons for psychosomatic medicine. *Psychosomatic Medicine, 47* (1), 3–25.

JENSEN, A. R. (1969) How much can we boost IQ. and scholastic achievement? *Harvard Educational Review, 39,* 1–123.

JOEL-NIELSON, N. (1979) Suicide risk in manic-depressive disorder. In M. Schov & E. Stromgren (Eds.), *Origin, prevention and treatment of affective disorders.* London: Academic Press.

JOHNSON, C. T. & BERNDT, D. J. (1983) Preliminary investigation of bulimia and life adjustment. *American Journal of Psychiatry, 140,* 774–777.

JOHNSON, M. H. & HOLZMAN, P. S. (1979) *Assessing schizophrenic thinking.* San Francisco: Jossey-Bass.

JONES, D. J., FOX, M. M., BABIGAN, H. M., & HUTTON, H. E. (1980) Epidemiology of anorexia nervosa in Monroe County, New York: 1960–1976. *Psychosomatic Medicine, 42,* 551–558.

JONES, J. M., HUDSON, J. I., COHEN, B. M., & GUNDERSON, J. G. (1983) *Archives of General Psychiatry, 40,* 23–30.

JONES, K. W., SMITH, D. W., STREISSGUTH, A. P., & MYRIANTHOPOULOS, N. C. (1974) Outcomes in offspring of chronic alcoholic women. *Lancet, 1,* 1076–1078.

JONES, M. C. (1981) Midlife drinking patterns. Correlates and antecedents. In D. H. Eichorn (Ed.), *Present and past in middle life.* New York: Academic Press, 223–242.

KALIN, N. H. (1979) Genital and abdominal surgery: A case report. *Journal of the American Medical Association, 241,* 2188–2189.

KAMPHAUS, R. W. & REYNOLDS, C. R. (1984) Development and structure of the Kaufman Assessment Battery for Children. *The Journal of Special Education, 18,* 213–228.

KANFER, R. & ZEISS, A. M. (1983) Depression, interpersonal standard setting, and judgments of self-efficacy. *Journal of Abnormal Psychology, 92,* 319–329. Copyright © 1983 by the American Psychological Association. Reprinted by permission of the author.

KANIN, E. J. & PARCELL, S. R. (1977) Sexual aggression: A second look at the offended female. *Archives of Sexual Behavior, 6,* 67–76.

KANNER, L. (1943) Autistic disturbances of affective contact. *Nervous Children, 2,* 217–250.

KAPLAN, H. S. (1979) *Disorders of sexual desire.* New York: Simon & Schuster.

KAPLAN, H. S. (1974) *The new sex therapy: Active treatment of sexual dysfunctions.* New York: Quadrangle Books.

KARLEN, A. (1978) Homosexuality: The scene and students. In J. Henslin & E. Sagarin (Eds.), *The sociology of sex: An introductory reader.* New York: Schocken.

KASHANI, J. H., ARSHARD, H., SHEKIM, W. O., HODGES, K. K., CYTRYN, L., & McKNEW, D. H. (1981) Current perspectives on childhood depression: An overview. *American Journal of Psychiatry, 138,* 143–153.

KASHANI, J. & SIMONDS, J. P. (1979) The incidence of depression in children. *American Journal of Psychiatry, 136,* 1203–1205.

KAUFMAN, A. S. (1979) *Intelligence testing with the WISC-R.* New York: John Wiley.

KAUFMAN, A. S. & KAUFMAN, N. L. (1983) *Kaufman Assessment Battery for Children: Interpretive manual.* Circle Pines, NM: American Guidance Service.

KAUFMAN, M. J., AGARD, J. A., & SEMMEL, M. I. (1982) *Mainstreaming: Learners and their environments.* Baltimore: University Park Press.

KAVEGGIA, E. G., OPITZ, J. M., & PALLISTER, P. D. (1972) Diagnostic genetic studies in severe mental retardation. In *The Proceedings of the 2nd Congress of the International Association for the Scientific Study of Mental Retardation.* Primrose: Swets & Zeilingen, 305–312.

KAZDIN, A. E., FRENCH, N. H., UNIS, A. S., ESVELDT-DAWSON, K., & SHERICK, R. B. (1983) Hopelessness, depression and suicidal intent among psychiatrically disturbed impatient children. *Journal of Consulting and Clinical Psychology, 51,* 504–510.

KAZDIN, A. E. & MASCITELLI, S. (1982) Covert and overt rehearsal and homework practice in developing assertiveness. *Journal of Consulting and Clinical Psychology, 50,* 250–258.

KEGAN, R. (in press) Pathology in moral development. In W. H. Reid (Ed.) et al. *Unmasking the psychopath.* New York: Norton.

KEISLER, D. (1982) Mental hospitals and alternative care. *American Psychologist, 37,* 349–360.

KELLNER, R. (1985) Functional somatic symptoms and hypochrondrias: A survey of empirical studies. *Archives of General Psychiatry, 42,* 821–833.

KELLY, G. A. (1955) *The psychology of personal constructs* (Vols. 1 & 2). New York: W. W. Norton.

KENDALL, P. C. (Ed.) (1985) *Advances in cognitive-behavioral research and therapy.* Orlando, FL: Academic Press.

KENDALL, P. C. & MARUYAMA, G. (1985) Metanalysis: On the road to synthesis of knowledge? *Clinical Psychology Review, 5,* 79–89.

KENDALL, P. C., & WILCOX, L. E. (1978) Self-control in children: Development of a rating scale. *Journal of Consulting and Clinical Psychology, 47,* 1020–1029.

KENDELL, R. E. (1975) *The role of diagnosis in psychiatry.* Oxford, Eng.: Journal of Consulting and Clinical Psychology, Blackwell Scientific Publications.

KENDELL, R. E. (1983) Schizophrenia. In R. E. Kendell & A. K. Zealley (Eds.) *Companion to psychiatric studies.* Edinburgh: Churchill Livingstone.

KENDLER, K. S. (1983) Overview: A current perspective on twin studies of schizophrenia. *American Journal of Psychiatry, 140,* 1413–1425.

KENDLER, K. S., GURENBERG, A. M., & TSUANG, M. T. (1985) Psychiatric illness in first-degree relatives of schizophrenic and surgical control patients. *Archives of General Psychiatry, 42,* 770–779.

KERNBERG, O. F. (1970) A psychoanalytic classification of character pathology. *Journal of the American Psychoanalytic Association, 18,* 800–822.

KERNBERG, O. F. (1975) *Borderline conditions and pathological narcissism.* New York: Jason Aronson.

KETY, S. S., ROSENTHAL, D., WENDER, P. H., SCHULSINGER, F., & JACOBSON, B. (1978) The biological and adoptive families of adopted individuals who become schizophrenic: Prevalence of mental illness and other characteristics. In L. C. Wynne, R. L. Cromwell, & S. Matthysse (Eds.) *The nature of schizophrenia: New approaches to research and treatment.* New York: Wiley.

KEYES, S. & BLOCK, J. (1984) Prevalence and patterns of substance use among early adolescents. *Journal of Youth and Adolescence, 13,* 1–14.

KIECOLT-GLASER, J. K. & GREENBERG, B. (1984) Social support as a moderator of the aftereffects of stress in female psychiatric inpatients. *Journal of Abnormal Psychology, 93,* 192–199.

KIECOLT-GLASER, J. K. RICHER, D., GEORGE, J., MESSICK, G., SPEICHER, C. E., GARNER, W., & GLASER, R. (1984) Urinary cortisol levels, cellular immunocompetency, and loneliness in psychiatric inpatients. *Psychosomatic Medicine, 46,* 15–23.

KIESLER, C. A. (1982) Mental hospitals and alternative care. *American Psychologist, 37,* 349–360.

KILPATRICK, D. G., RESICK, P. A., & VERONEN, L. J. (1981) Effects of a rape experience: A longitudinal study. *Journal of Social Issues, 37,* 105–122.

KINSEY, A. C., POMEROY, W. B., & MARTIN, C. E. (1948) *Sexual behavior in the human male.* Philadelphia: W. B. Saunders. Reprinted by permission of the Kinsey Institute for Research in Sex, Gender, and Reproduction, Inc.

KINSEY, A. C., POMEROY, W. B., MARTIN, C. E., & GEBHARD, P. H. (1953) *Sexual behavior in the human female.* Philadelphia: W. B. Saunders. Reprinted by permission of the Kinsey Institute for Research in Sex, Gender, and Reproduction, Inc.

KIPPER, D. A. (1977) Behavior therapy for fears brought on by war experiences. *Journal of Consulting and Clinical Psychology, 45,* 216–221.

KIRKMAN, H. N. (1982) Projections of a rebound in frequency of mental retardation from phenylketonuria. *Applied Research in Mental Retardation, 3,* 319–328.

KIRKPATRICK, M., SMITH, K., & ROY, R. (1981) Lesbian mothers and their children. *American Journal of Orthopsychiatry, 51,* 545–551.

KLEIN, D. F. (1981) Anxiety reconceptualized. In D. F. Klein & J. G. Rabkin (Eds.), *Anxiety: New research and changing concepts.* New York: Raven Press.

KLEIN, D. N., DEPUE, R. A., & SLATER, J. F. (1985) Cyclothymia in the adolescent offspring of parents with bipolar affective disorder. *Journal of Abnormal Psychology, 94,* 115–127.

KLEIN, H. E., BENDER, W., MAYR, H., NIEDER SCHWEIBERER, A., & SCHMAUSS, M. (1984) The DST and its relationship to psychiatric diagnosis, symptoms and treatment outcome. *British Journal of Psychiatry, 145,* 591–599.

KLERMAN, G. L. (1981) The spectrum of mania. *Comprehensive Psychiatry, 22,* 11–20.

KLERMAN, G. L. (1984) The advantages of DSM-III. *American Journal of Psychiatry, 141,* 539–542.

KLERMAN, G. L., LAVORI, P. W., RICE, J., REICH, T., ENDICOTT, J., ANDREASEN, N. C., KELLER, M. D., & HIRSCHFIELD, R. M. A. (1985) Birth-cohort trends in rates of major depressive disorder among relatives of patients with affective disorder. *Archives of General Psychiatry, 42,* 689–693.

KLERMAN, G. L. & WEISSMAN, M. M. (1980) Depressions among women: Their nature and causes. In M. Guttentag, S. Salasin, & D. Belle (Eds.), *The mental health of women.* New York: Academic Press.

KLINE, N. S. (1977) Depression. *Swarthmore College Bulletin,* July, 8–11.

KLUFT, R. P. (1984) An introduction to multiple personality disorder. *Psychiatric Annals, 14,* 19–24.

KNOWLES, P. A. L. & PRUTSMAN, T. D. (1968) *The case of Benjie.* Unpublished manuscript, Florida Atlantic University.

KOBASA, S. C., MADDI, S. R., & KAHN, S. (1982) Hardiness and health:

A prospective study. *Journal of Personality and Social Psychology, 42,* 168–177.

KOG, E. & VANDEREYCKEN, W. (1985) Family characteristics of anorexia nervosa and bulimia: A review of the research literature. *Clinical Psychology Review, 5,* 159–180.

KOHUT, H. (1971) *The analysis of the self.* New York: International Universities Press.

KOHUT, H. (1977) *The restoration of the self.* New York: International Universities Press.

KOLATA, G. (1985) Down syndrome-Alzheimer's linked. *Science, 230,* 1152–1153.

KOLB, L. D. & BRODIE, H. K. H. (1982) *Modern clinical psychiatry* (10th ed.). Philadelphia: W. B. Saunders.

KOUMJIAN, J. (1981) The use of Valium as a form of social control. *Social Science Medicine, 15E,* 245–249.

KOVACS M. (1985) The natural history and course of depressive disorders in childhood. *Psychiatric Annals, 15,* 387–389.

KOVACS, M., BECK, A. T., & WEISSMAN, A. (1975) The use of suicidal motives in the psychotherapy of attempted suicides. *American Journal of Psychotherapy, 29,* 363–368.

KRAEPELIN, E. (1909–1913) *Psychiatrie* (8th ed.) Leipzig: J. A. Barth.

KRAKOWSKI, A. J. (1982) Stress and the practice of medicine: II. Stressors, stresses, and strains. *Psychotherapy and Psychosomatics, 38,* 11–23.

KRANTZ, S., & HAMMEN, C. L. (1979) Assessment of cognitive bias in depression. *Journal of Abnormal Psychology, 88,* 611–619.

KRANTZ, D. S. & MANUCK, S. B. (1984) Acute psychophysiologic reactivity and risk of cardiovascular disease: A review and methodologic critique. *Psychological Bulletin, 96,* 435–464.

KRINGLEN, E. (1981) Stress and coronary heart disease. *Twin Research 3: Epidemiological and clinical studies.* New York: Alan R. Liss.

KUBLER-ROSS, E. (1969) *On death and dying.* New York: Macmillan.

KUBLER-ROSS, E. (1974) *Questions and answers on death and dying.* New York: Macmillan.

KUPFER, D. J., ULRICH, R. F., COBLE, P. A., JARRETT, D. B., GROCHOCINSKI, V. J., DOMAN, J., MATTHEWS, G., & BORBELY, A. A. (1985) Electroencephalographic sleep of younger depressives. *Archives of General Psychiatry, 42,* 806–810.

KURIANSKY, J. B., DEMING, U. E., & GURLAND, B. J. (1974) On trends in the diagnosis of schizophrenia. *American Journal of Psychiatry, 131,* 402–408.

LADER, M. (1975) The nature of clinical anxiety in modern society. In C. D. Spielberger & I. G. Sarason (Eds.) *Stress and anxiety* (Vol. 1). Washington, D.C.: Hemisphere.

LAFFAL, J. (1965) *Pathological and normal language.* New York: Atherton.

LAGRECA, A. M., STONE, W. L., & BELL, C. R., III. (1983) Facilitating the vocational-interpersonal skills of mentally retarded individuals. *American Journal of Mental Deficiency, 88,* 270–278.

LAIDLAW, J. & RICKENS, A. (Eds.) (1976) *A textbook of epilepsy.* Edinburgh: Churchill & Livingtone.

LAING, R. D. (1964) Is schizophrenia a disease? *International Journal of Social Psychiatry, 10,* 184–193.

LAMBERT, N. M., SANDOVAL, J., & SASSONE, D. (1978) Prevalence of hyperactivity in elementary school children as a function of social system defenses. *American Journal of Orthopsychiatry, 48,* 446–463.

LAMBLEY, P. (1976) The use of assertive training and psychodynamic insight in the treatment of migraine headache: A case study. *Journal of Nervous and Mental Disease, 163,* 61–64.

LANGER, E. J., & ABELSON, R. P. (1974) A patient by any other name...: Clinician group difference in labeling bias. *Journal of Consulting and Clinical Psychology, 42,* 4–9.

LANQUETOT, R. (1984) First person account: Confessions of the daughter of a schizophrenic. *Schizophrenia Bulletin, 10,* 467–471.

LAROCHE, C., CHEIFETZ, P., LESTER, E. P., SHIBUR, L. D., TOMMASO,

E. & ENGELSMANN, F. (1985) Psychopathology in the offspring of parents with bipolar affective disorders. *Canadian Journal of Psychiatry, 30,* 337–343.

LARRANCE, D. L. & TWENTYMAN, C. T. (1983) Maternal attributions and child abuse. *Journal of Abnormal Psychology, 92,* 449–457.

LATIB, A., CONROY, J., & HESS, C. M. (1984) Family attitudes toward deinstitutionalization. *International Review of Research on Mental Retardation, 12,* 67–93.

LAUDENSLAGER, M. L. & REITE, M. L. (1984) Losses and separations: Immunological consequences and health implications. In P. Shaver (Ed.) *Review of Personality and Social Psychology.* Beverly Hills, CA: Sage Publications.

LAZELL, E. W. & PRINCE, L. H. (1929) A study of the causative factors of dementia praecox. *U.S. Veterans Bureau Medical Bulletin, 114,* 241–248.

LAZARUS, A. A. (1971) *Behavior therapy and beyond.* New York: McGraw-Hill.

LEACH, B. (1973) Does Alcoholics Anonymous really work? In P. G. Bourne & R. Fox (Eds.) *Alcoholism: Progress in research and treatment.* New York: Academic Press, 245–284.

LEAF, P. J., WEISSMAN, M. M., MYERS, J. K., TISCHLER, G. L., AND HOLZER, C. E., III (1984) Social factors related to psychiatric disorder: The Yale Epidemiological Catchment Area Study. *Social Psychiatry, 19,* 53–61.

LEFF, J., KUIPERS, L., BERKOWITZ, R., AND STURGEON, D. (1985) A controlled trial of social intervention in the families of schizophrenic patients: Two-year follow-up. *British Journal of Psychiatry, 146,* 594–600.

LEFF, J. & VAUGHN, C. (1981) The role of maintenance therapy and relatives' expressed emotion in relapse schizophrenia: A two-year follow-up. *British Journal of Psychiatry, 139,* 102–104.

LEE, T., SEEMAN, P., TOURTELLOTTE, W. W., FARLEY, I. J., & HORNYKEIWICZ, O. (1978) Binding of $^3$H-neuroleptics and $^3$H-apomorphine in schizophrenic brains. *Nature, 274,* 897–900.

LEHMAN, H. E. & CANCRO, R. (1985) Schizophrenia: Clinical features. In H. I. Kaplan & B. J. Sadock, *Comprehensive textbook of psychiatry* (4th ed.) (Vol. 1). Baltimore: Williams and Wilkens.

LEHRER, P. M. & WOOLFOLK, R. L. (1986) Are all stress-reduction techniques interchangeable, or do they have specific effects? A review of the comparative empirical literature. In R. L. Wollfolk and P. M. Lehrer (Eds.), *Principles and practices of stress management.* New York: Guilford Press.

LEITENBERG, H., GROSS, J., PETERSON, J., & ROSEN, J. (1984) Analyses of an anxiety model and the process of change during exposure plus response prevention treatment of bulimia nervosa. *Behavior Therapy, 15,* 3–20.

LEON, G. R. & PHELAN, P. W. (1984) Anorexia nervosa. In B. Lahey & A. Kazdin (Eds.) *Advances in clinical child psychology, 8,* 81–111. New York: Plenum.

LEON, G. R., LUCAS, A. R., COLLIGAN, R. C., FERINANDE, R. J., & KAMP, J. (1985) Sexual, body image, and personality attitudes in anorexia nervosa. *Journal of Abnormal Child Psychology, 13,* 245–257.

LEONARD, W. E. (1927) *The locomotive god.* New York: Appleton-Century-Crofts.

LEVIN, R. B. AND GROSS, A. M. (1985) The role of relaxation in systematic desensitization. *Behavioral Research and Therapy, 23* (2), 187–196.

LEVIN, S. M., BARRY, S. M., GAMBARO, S., WOLFINSOHN, L., & SMITH, A. (1977) Variations of covert sensitization in the treatment of pedophilic behavior: A case study. *Journal of Consulting and Clinical Psychology, 45,* 896–907. Copyright © 1977 by the American Psychological Association. Reprinted by permission of the author.

LEVINE, S. B. (1980) Psychiatric diagnosis of patients requesting sex reassignment surgery. *Journal of Sex and Marital Therapy, 6,* 164–173.

LEVINE, S. B. & LOTHSTEIN, L. (1981) Transsexualism and the gender dysphoria syndromes. *Journal of Sex and Marital Therapy*, 7, 85–113.

LEVY, L. (1976) Self-help groups: Types and psychological processes. *Journal of Applied Behavioral Science*, 12, 310–323.

LEVY, R. F. (1977) "Male woman" finds self. Washington Post, May 11, C1, C3.

LEVY, R. I. & MOSKOWITZ, J. (1982) Cardiovascular research: Decades of progress, a decade of promise. *Science*, 217, 121–129.

LEWINE, R. R. J. (1984) Stalking the schizophrenia marker: Evidence for a general vulnerability model of psychopathology. In N. F. Watt, E. J. Anthony, L. C. Wynne, & J. E. Rolf (Eds.). *Children at risk for schizophrenia: A longitudinal perspective*. Cambridge: Cambridge University Press.

LEWINSOHN, P. M. (1974) A behavioral approach to depression. In R. J. Friedmann & M. M. Katz (Eds.). *The psychology of depression: Contemporary theory and research*. Washington, D.C.: V. H. Winston.

LEWINSOHN, P. M., & ARCONAD, M. (1981) Behavioral treatment in depression: A social learning approach. In J. Clarkin & H. Glazer (eds.), *Behavioral and directive treatment strategies*. New York: Garland Press.

LEWINSOHN, P. M. & HOBERMAN, H. M. (1982) Depression. In A. S. Bellack, M. Hersen, & A. E. Kazdin (Eds.) *International handbook of behavior modification and therapy*. New York: Plenum.

LEWINSOHN, P. M., MISCHEL, W., CHAPLAIN, W., & BARTON, R. (1980) Social competence and depression. The role of illusory self-perceptions. *Journal of Abnormal Psychology*, 89, 203–212. Copyright © 1980 by the American Psychological Association. Reprinted by permission of the author.

LEWINSOHN, P. M., STEINMETZ, J. L., ANTONUCCIO, D., & TERI, L. (1985) Group therapy for depression: The Coping with Depression Course. *International Journal of Mental Health*, 13, 8–33.

LEWIS, J. F., & MERCER, J. R. (1978) The system of multicultural pluralistic assessment: SOMPA. In W. A. Coulter & H. W. Morrow (Eds.) *Adaptive behavior: Concepts and measurement*. New York: Grune & Stratton.

LIBERMAN, R. P. (1982) Assessment of social skills. *Schizophrenia Bulletin*, 8, 62–83.

LIDZ, T., FLECK, S., & CORNELISON, A. (1965) *Schizophrenia and the family*. New York: International Universities Press.

LIEM, J. H. (1974) Effect of verbal communications of parents and children: A comparison of normal and schizophrenic families. *Journal of Consulting and Clinical Psychology*, 42, 438–450.

LIFTON, R. J. & OLSON, E. (1976) The human meaning of total disaster. *Psychiatry*, 39, 1–18.

LILJEFORS, I. & RAHE, R. H. (1970) An identical twin study of psychosocial factors in coronary heart disease in Sweden. *Psychosomatic Medicine*, 32, 523–542. Copyright © 1970 by the American Psychosomatic Society, Inc.

LINEHAN, M. M. (1981) A social-behavioral analysis of suicide and parasuicide. In J. F. Clarkin & H. I. Glazer (Eds.) *Depression: Behavioral and directive intervention strategies*. New York: Garland STPM Press.

LINGJAERDE, O. (1983) The biochemistry of depression. *Acta Psychiatrica Scandinavica Supplementum*, No. 302, 69, 36–51. © 1983 Munksgaard International Publishers Ltd., Copenhagen, Denmark.

LINN, M. V., CAFFEY, E. M., KLETT, C. J., HOGARTY, G. E., & LAMB, H. R. (1979) Day treatment and psychotropic drugs in aftercare of schizophrenic patients. *Archives of General Psychiatry*, 36, 1055–1066.

LINSKY, A. S., STRAUS, M. A., & COLBY, J. P., JR. (1985) Stressful events, stressful condition and alcohol problems in the United States: A partial test of Coles' theory. *Journal of Studies on Alcohol*, 46, 72–80.

LIPOWSKI, Z. J. (1977) Psychosomatic medicine in seventies: An overview. *American Journal of Psychiatry*, 134, 233–244.

LITTLE, L. M. & CURRAN, J. P. (1978) Covert sensitization: A clinical procedure in need of some explorations. *Psychological Bulletin*, 85, 513–531.

LOBATO, D. (1983) Siblings of handicapped children: A review. *Journal of Autism*, 13, 347–364.

LONEY, J., KRAMER, J., & MILICH, R. (1981) The hyperkinetic child grows up: Predictors of symptoms, delinquency, and achievement at follow up. In K. D. Gadrow & J. Loney (Eds.) *Psychosocial aspects of drug treatment for hyperactivity*. Boulder, CO: Westview Press.

LOONEY, M. (1972) The dreams of heroin addicts. *Social Work*, 17, 23–28.

LOPICCOLO, J. & LOPICCOLO, L. (eds.) (1978) *Handbook of sex therapy*. New York: Plenum Press.

LORANGER, A. W., OLDHAM, J. M., & TULIS, E. H. (1982) Familial transmission of DSM-III borderline personality disorder. *Archives of General Psychiatry*, 39, 795–799.

LOTHSTEIN, L. (1980) The post surgical transsexual. *Archives of Sexual Behavior*, 9, 547–564.

LOWE, M. (1985) Rapid smoking. In A. S. Bellack & M. Hersen (Eds.) *Dictionary of behavior therapy techniques*. New York: Pergamon Press.

LUMRY, A. E., GOTTESMAN, I. I., & TUASON, V. B. (1982) MMPI State dependency during the course of bipolar psychosis. *Psychiatry Research*, 7, 59–67.

LYKKEN, D. T. (1981) *A tremor in the blood*. New York: McGraw-Hill.

LYLE, O. E. & GOTTESMAN, I. I. (1979) Psychometric indicators of the gene for Huntington's disease: Clues to "ontopathogenesis." *Clinical Psychologist*, 32, 14–15.

LYNN, R. & HAMPSON, S. (1970) National anxiety levels and prevalence of alcoholism. *British Journal of Addiction*, 64, 305–306.

MACCOBY, E. & MACCOBY, N. (1954) The interview: A tool of social science. In G. Lindzey (Ed.) (pp. 449–487) *Handbook of social psychology*, Cambridge, MA: Addison Wesley.

MACCOBY, N., FARQUAHAR, J. W., & FORTMAN, S. P. (1985) The community studies of the Stanford Heart Disease Prevention Program. In R. M. Kaplan & M. H. Criqui (Eds.) *Behavioral Epidemiology and Disease Prevention*. New York: Plenum.

MACDONALD, N. (1960) Living with schizophrenia. *Canadian Medical Association*, 82, 218–221.

MACTURK, R. H., VIETZE, P. M., McCARTHY, M. E., McQUISTON, S. T., YARROW, L. J. (1985) The organization of exploratory behavior in Down's syndrome and nondelayed infants. *Child Development*, 56, 573–581.

MACVANE, J. R., LANGE, J. D., BROWN, W. A., & ZAYAT, M. (1978) Psychological functioning of bipolar manic-depressives in remission. *Archives of General Psychiatry*, 35, 1351–1354.

MAGAZINER, J. (1980) *Density, living alone, age and psychopathology in the urban environment*. Unpublished doctoral dissertation, University of Chicago.

MAHONEY, E. R. (1980) Religiosity and sexual behavior among heterosexual college students. *The Journal of Sex Research*, 16, 97–113.

MALAMUD, W. (1944) The psychoneuroses. In J. McV. Hunt (Ed.), *Personality and the behavior disorders* (Vol. 2). New York: Ronald Press.

MALAMUTH, N. M. (1981) Rape proclivity among males. *Journal of Social Issues*, 37, 138–157.

MALATESTA, V. J. (1979) Alcohol effects on the orgasmic-ejaculatory response in human males. *The Journal of Sex Research*, 15, 101–107.

MALATESTA, V. J., POLLACK, R. H., CROTTY, T. O., & PEACOCK, L. J. (1982) Acute alcohol intoxication and female orgasmic response. *Journal of Sex Research, 18*, 1–16. Reprinted by permission of *The Journal of Sex Research*, a publication of the Society for the Scientific Study of Sex.

MANSCHRECK, T. & PETRI, M. (1978) The paranoid syndrome. *Lancet, 2*, 251–253.

MANUCK, S. B., MORRISON, R. L., BELLACK, A. S., & POLEFRONE, J. M. (1985) Behavioral factors in hypertension: Cardiovascular responsivity, anger, and social competence. In M. A. Chesney & R. H. Rosenman (Eds.) *Anger and hostility in cardiovascular and behavioral disorders*. Washington, D.C.: Hemisphere.

MARHOLIN, D., O'TOOLE, K. M., TOUCHETTE, P. E., BERGER, P. L., & DOYLE, D. A. (1979) I'll have a big mac, large fries, large coke and apple pie—or teaching adaptive community skills. *Behavior Therapy, 10*, 236–248. Copyright © 1979 by the Association for Advancement of Behavior Therapy. Reprinted by permission of the publisher and the author.

MARKS, I. M. (1978) *Living with fear*. New York: McGraw-Hill.

MARKS, I. M. & LADER, M. (1973) Anxiety states (anxiety neurosis): A review. *Journal of Nervous and Mental Disease, 156*, 3–18.

MARKMAN, H. J., JAMIESON, K., & FLOYD, F. (1983) The assessment and modification of premarital relationships: Preliminary findings on the etiology and prevention of marital and family distress. In J. Vincent (Ed.) *Advances in family interventions, assessment and theory* (Vol. 3). Greenwich, CT: JAI Press.

MARLATT, G. A., DEMMING, B., & REID, J. B. (1973) Loss of control drinking in alcoholics: An experimental analogue. *Journal of Abnormal Psychology, 81*, 233–241.

MARLATT, G. A., & GORDON, J. R. (1985) *Relapse prevention: Maintenance strategies in the treatment of addictive behaviors*. New York: Guilford.

MARMOR, J. (1980) *Homosexual behavior*. New York: Basic Books.

MARMOT, M. G. & SYME, S. L. (1976) Acculturation and coronary heart disease in Japanese-Americans. *Journal of Epidemiology, 104*, 225–247.

MARTIN, H. P. (1976) *The abused child*. Cambridge, MA: Ballinger.

MARZILLIER, J. S. & BIRCHWOOD, M. J. (1981) Behavioral treatment of cognitive disorders. In L. Michelson, M. Hersen, & S. M. Turner (Eds.), *Future perspectives on behavior therapy*. New York: Plenum Press.

MASLACH, C., & JACKSON, S. E. (1981) The measurement of experienced burnout. *Journal of Occupational Behavior, 2*, 99–113.

MASLOW, A. H. (1968) *Toward a psychology of being* (2nd ed.). Princeton, NJ: Van Nostrand.

MASTERS, W. H. & JOHNSON, V. E. (1966) *Human sexual response*. Boston: Little, Brown.

MASTERS, W. H. & JOHNSON, V. E. (1970) *Human sexual inadequacy*. Boston: Little, Brown.

MASTERS, W. H. & JOHNSON, V. E. (1979) *Homosexuality in perspective*. Boston: Little, Brown.

MASTERS, W. H., JOHNSON, V. E., & KOLODNY, R. C. (1985) *Human sexuality* (2nd ed.). Boston: Little, Brown.

MATTHEWS, B. J. & LACEY, J. H. (1983) Skeletal maturation, growth and hormonal and nutritional status in anorexia nervosa. *International Journal of Eating Disorders, 2*, 145–150.

MAY, P. R. A. (1968) *Treatments of schizophrenia: A comparative study of five treatment methods*. New York: Science House.

MAY, P. R. A. & TUMA, A. H. (1976) A follow-up study of the results of treatment of schizophrenia. In R. L. Spitzer & D. F. Klein (Eds.) *Evaluation of psychological therapies*. Baltimore: Johns Hopkins University Press.

MAY, P. R. A., TUMA, A. H., & DIXON, W. J. (1981) Schizophrenia: A follow-up study of the results of five forms of treatment. *Archives of General Psychiatry, 38*, 776–784.

MAY, R. (1958) The origins and significance of the existential movement in psychology. In R. May, E. Angel, & H. F. Ellenberger (Eds.). *Existence: A new dimension in psychiatry and psychology*. New York: Basic Books.

MAYO, J. A., O'CONNELL, R. A., & O'BRIAN, J. D. (1979) Families of manic-depressive patients: Effect of treatment. *American Journal of Psychiatry, 136*, 1535–1539.

MCADAMS, J. A. (1985) Messages. *Journal of the American Medical Association, 254*, 1222. Copyright © 1985, American Medical Association.

MCCLELLAND, D. C., ROSS, G., & PATEL, V. (1985) Exam stress and immunoglobulin levels. *Journal of Human Stress, 11*, 52–59.

MCDERMOTT, D. (1984) Professional burnout and its relation to job characteristics, satisfaction and control. *Journal of Human Stress, 10*, 79–85.

MCGUE, M., GOTTESMAN, I. I., & ROA, D. C. (in press). Resolving genetic models for the transmission of schizophrenia. *Genetic Epidemiology*.

MCGUFFIN, P., REVELEY, A., & HOLLAND, A. (1982) Identical triplets: Non-identical psychosis? *British Journal of Psychiatry, 140*, 1–6.

MCLEAN, P. D. & HAKSTIAN, R. A. (1979) Clinical depression: Comparative efficacy of outpatient treatments. *Journal of Consulting and Clinical Psychology, 47*, 818–836.

MCPHERSON, S. R., BRACKELMANNS, W. E., & NEWMAN, L. E. (1974) Stages in the family therapy of adolescents. *Family Process, 13*, 77–94.

MEDNICK, S. A., CUDECK, R., GRIFFITH, J. J., TALOVIC, S. A., & SCHULSINGER, F. A. (1984) The Danish high-risk project: Recent methods and findings. In N. F. Watt, E. J. Anthony, L. C. Wynne, & J. E. Rolf. *Children at risk for schizophrenia*. Cambridge: Cambridge University Press.

MEDNICK, S., MOFFIT, T., POLLACK, V., TALOVIC, S., & GABRIELLI, W. (1982) *The inheritance of human deviance*. Paper presented at Conference on Human Development from Perspective of Person-Environment Interaction, Stockholm, Sweden, June.

MEDNICK, S. A. & SCHULSINGER, F. (1968) Some premorbid characteristics related to breakdown in children with schizophrenic mothers. *Journal of Psychiatric Research, 6*, 267–291.

MEIR, S. T. (1984) The construct validity of burnout. *Journal of Occupational Psychiatry, 57*, 211–219.

MEISELMAN, K. (1978) *Incest*. San Francisco: Jossey-Bass.

MELAMED, B. G. (1979) Behavioral approaches to fear in dental settings. In M. Hersen, R. M. Eisler, & P. M. Miller (Eds.), *Progress in behavior modification* (Vol. 7). New York: Academic Press.

MELAMED, B. G. & SIEGEL, L. J. (1975) Reduction of anxiety in children facing hospitalization and surgery by use of filmed modeling. *Journal of Consulting and Clinical Psychology, 43*, 511–521.

MERCER, J. R. (1971) The meaning of mental retardation. In R. Koch & J. C. Dobson (Eds.), *The mentally retarded child in his family: A multidisciplinary handbook* (pp. 23–47). New York: Brunner/Mazel.

MELLOR, C. S. (1970) First rank symptoms of schizophrenia. *British Journal of Psychiatry, 177*, 15–23.

MEREDITH, R. L. & RIESTER, R. W. (1980) Psychotherapy, responsibility and homosexuality: Clinical examination of socially deviant behavior. *Professional Psychology, 11*, 174–193.

MEYER, J. K., & RETER, D. J. (1979) Sex reassignment: Follow-up. *Archives of General Psychiatry, 36*, 1010–1015.

MEYER, L. B. F. (1982) Skinner on behaving his age. *Washington Post*, Aug. 24, B1, B9.

MEYERS, A., MERCATORIS, M., & SIROTA, A. (1976) Case study: Use of covert self-instruction for the elimination of psychotic speech. *Journal of Consulting and Clinical Psychology, 44*, 480–482.

MILICH, R. & DODGE, K. A. (1984) Social information processing in child psychiatric populations. *Journal of Abnormal Child Psychology, 12*, 471–490.

MILLER, H. L., COOMBS, D. W., LEEPER, J. D., & BARTON, S. N. (1984)

An analysis of the effects of suicide prevention facilities on suicide rates in the United States. *American Journal of Public Health, 74,* 340–343.

MILLER, W. R. (1985) Motivation for treatment: A review with special emphasis on alcoholism. *Psychological Bulletin, 98,* 84–107.

MILLON, T. (1981) *Disorders of personality: DSM III, Axis II.* New York: Wiley.

MINUCHIN, P. (1985) Families and individual development: Provocations from the field of family therapy. *Child Development, 56,* 289–302.

MINUCHIN, S., ROSMAN, B., & BAKER, L. (1978) *Psychosomatic families: Anorexia nervosa in context.* Cambridge, MA: Harvard University Press.

MIRSKY, A. F. & BAKAY PRAGNAY, E. (1984) Brainstem mechanisms in the processing of sensory information: Clinical symptoms, animal models and unit analysis. In D. E. Sheer (Ed.), *Attention: Theory, brain functions and clinical applications.* Hillsdale, NJ: Erlbaum.

MIRSKY, A. F., SILBERMAN, E. K., LATZ, A., & NAGLER, S. (1985) Adult outcomes of high risk children: Differential effects of town and kibbutz rearing. *Schizophrenia Bulletin, 11,* 150–154.

MIZES, J. S. (1985) Bulimia: A review of its symptomatology and treatment. *Advances in Behavior Research and Therapy, 1,* 91–142.

MIZES, J. S. & FLEECE, E. L. (1984) The effect of progressive relaxation on the urge to binge and actual binges in a bulimorexic female. Paper presented at the *5th Annual Meeting of the Society of Behavioral Medicine.* Philadelphia, May.

MOLLER, H. J., VON ZERSSEN, D., WERNER-EILERT, K., & WUSCHNER-STOCKHEIM, M. (1982) Outcome in schizophrenic and similar paranoid psychoses. *Schizophrenia Bulletin, 8,* 99–108.

MONAHAN, J. (1981) *Predicting violent behavior: An assessment of clinical techniques.* Beverly Hills: Sage.

MONEY, J. (1984) Food, fitness and vital fluids: Sexual pleasure from graham crackers to Kellogg's cornflakes. *British Journal of Sexual Medicine, 11,* 127–130.

MONEY, J. & BOHMER, C. (1980) Prison sexology: Two personal accounts of masturbation, homosexuality, and rape. *Journal of Sex Research, 16,* 258–266.

MONEY, J. & SCHWARTZ, M. (1977) Dating, romantic and nonromantic friendships and sexuality in 17 early-treated adrenogenital females, age 16–25. In Palee, et al (Eds.), *Congenital adrenal hyperplasia.* Baltimore: University Park Press.

MORAN, A. E., FREEDMAN, R. I., & SHARFSTEIN, S. S. (1984) The journey of Sylvia Frumpkin: A case study for policymakers. *Hospital and Community Psychiatry, 35,* 887–893.

Morbidity and Mortality Weekly Report (1985) Alcohol-associated premature mortality-United States, 1980. *Journal of the American Medical Association, 254,* 1134.

MORELAND, J., SCHWEBEL, A., BECK, S., & WELLS, R. (1982) Parents as therapists. *Behavior Modification, 10,* 250–276.

MORIHISA, J. M., DUFFY, F. H., & WYATT, R. J. (1983) Brain electrical activity mapping (BEAM) in schizophrenic patients. *Archives of General Psychiatry, 40,* 719–728.

MORRIS, J. (1974) *Conundrum.* Harcourt, Brace, & Jovanovich.

MOSHER, L. R. & KEITH, S. J. (1981) Psychosocial treatment: Individual, group, family and community support approaches. In *Schizophrenia 1980.* Rockville, MD: U.S. Department of Health and Human Services.

MUMFORD, E., SCHLESINGER, H. J., GLASS, G. V., PATRICK, C., & CUERDEN, T. (1984) A new look at evidence about reduced cost of medical utilization following mental health treatment. *American Journal of Psychiatry, 141,* 1145–1158.

MURPHY, G. E. (1983) The problems in studying suicide. *Psychiatric Developments, 4,* 339–350.

MURPHY, G. E., & WETZEL, R. D. (1980) Suicide risk by birth cohort in the United States, 1949 to 1974. *Archives of General Psychiatry, 37,* 519–523.

MURPHY, L. B. (1974) Coping, vulnerability, and resilience in childhood. In G. V. Coelho, D. A. Hamburg, & J. E. Adams (Eds.), *Coping and adaptation.* New York: Basic Books.

MURRAY, H. A. (1943) *Thematic Apperception Test: Pictures and manual.* Cambridge, Mass.: Harvard University Press.

MURRAY, J. B. (1982) The psyche and stomach ulcers. *Genetic Psychology Monographs, 105,* 182–212.

MUSLIN, H. L., THURNBLAD, R. J., & MESCHEL, G. (1981) The role of the clinical interview: An observational study. *American Journal of Psychiatry, 138,* 822–825.

MYERS, J. K., WEISSMAN, M. M., TISCHLER, G. L., HOLZER, C. E., III, LEAF, P. J., ORVASCHEL, H., ANTHONY, J. C., BOYD, J. H., BURKE, J. D., JR., KRAMER, M., & STOLTZMAN, R. (1984) Six-month prevalence of psychiatric disorders in three communities. *Archives of General Psychiatry, 41,* 959–967.

National Academy of Sciences (1982) *Marijuana and health.* Washington, D.C.: National Academy Press.

NAGLER, S. & MIRSKY, A. F. (1985) Introduction: The Israeli high-risk study. *Schizophrenia Bulletin, 11,* 19–29.

NASRALLAH, H. A. & COFFMAN, J. A. (1985) Computerized tomography in psychiatry. *Psychiatric Annals, 15*(4), 239–249.

National Center for Health Statistics. *Monthly Vital Statistics Report* 32, Sept. 21, 1984. Hyattsville, MD.

National Institute of Mental Health. (1974) *Teenage delinquency in small town America* (Research Report 5). Rockville, MD: Alcohol, Drug Abuse, and Mental Health Administration (DHEW Pub. No. [ADM] 75–138).

NEMETZ, G. H., CRAIG, K. D., & REITH, G. (1978) Treatment of female sexual dysfunction through symbolic modeling. *Journal of Consulting and Clinical Psychology, 46,* 62–73.

NEMIAH, J. C. (1978) Psychoneurotic disorders. In A. M. Nicholi (Ed.), *Harvard guide to modern psychiatry.* Cambridge, MA: Harvard University Press.

NEMIAH, J. C. (1985) Phobic disorders (phobic neuroses). In H. I. Kaplan and B. J. Sadock (Eds.) *Comprehensive textbook of psychiatry* (4th ed.). Baltimore, MD: Williams and Wilkins.

NEMIAH, J. C. (1985) Obsessive-compulsive disorder (obsessive-compulsive neurosis). In H. I. Kaplan & B. J. Sadock (Eds.) *Comprehensive textbook of psychiatry* (4th ed.). Baltimore, MD: Williams & Wilkins.

NESS, R. C. & WINTROB, R. M. (1981) Folkhealing: A description and synthesis. *American Journal of Psychiatry, 138,* 1477–1481.

NEUGEBAUER, R. (1979) Medieval and early modern theories of mental illness. *Archives of General Psychiatry, 36,* 477–483.

NICHOLS, P. L. (1984) Familial mental retardation. *Behavior Genetics, 14,* 161–170. Plenum Publishing Corporation.

NIELSEN, A. C., III, & WILLIAMS, T. A. (1980) Depression in ambulatory medical patients: Prevalence by self-report questionnaire and recognition by non-psychiatric physicians. *Archives of General Psychiatry, 37,* 999–1004.

NOVACO, R. (1975) *Anger control: The development and evaluation of an experimental treatment.* Lexington, Mass.: Heath.

NUCKOLLS, K. B., CASSEL, J., & KAPLAN, B. H. (1972) Psychosocial assets, life crisis and the prognosis of pregnancy. *American Journal of Epidemiology, 95,* 431–441.

NUECHTERLEIN, K. H. (1983) Signal detection in vigilance tasks and behavioral attributes among offspring of schizophrenic mothers and among hyperactive children. *Journal of Abnormal Psychology, 92,* 4–28.

OATLEY, K. & BOLTON, W. (1985) A social-cognitive theory of depression in reaction to life events. *Psychological Review, 92,* 372–388.

O'CONNOR, G. (1976) *Home is a good place: A national perspective of community residential facilities for developmentally disabled persons.* Washington, D.C.: American Association on Mental Deficiency.

O'DONOGHUE, E. G. (1914) *The story of Bethlehem Hospital from its foundation in 1247.* London: T. Fisher.

OKOLO, C. & GUSKIN, S. (1984) Community attitudes toward community placement of mentally retarded persons. *International Review of Research in Mental Retardation, 12,* 25–66.

O'LEARY, S. G. & Pelham, W. E. (1977) Behavior therapy and withdrawal of stimulant medication with hyperactive children. *Pediatrics, 61,* 211–223.

O'NEAL, J. M. (1984) First person account: Finding myself and loving it. *Schizophrenia Bulletin, 10,* 109–110.

ORNITZ, E. M. (1985) Neurophysiology of infantile autism. *Journal of the American Academy of Child Psychiatry, 24,* 251–262.

OVCHARCHYN, C. A., JOHNSON, H. H. & PETZEL, T. P. (1981) Type A behavior, academic aspirations, and academic success. *Journal of Personality, 49,* 247–256.

OWENS, D. G. C. & JOHNSTONE, E. C. (1980) The disabilities of chronic schizophrenia: Their nature and factors contributing to their development. *British Journal of Psychiatry, 136,* 304–395.

PAGEL, M. D., BECKER, J. & COPPEL, D. B. (1985) Loss of control, self-blame, and depression: An investigation of spouse caregivers of Alzheimer's disease patients. *Journal of Abnormal Psychology, 94,* 169–182.

PALMORE, E. (1980) Predictors of longevity. In S. G. Haynes & M. Feinleib (Eds.), *Second conference on the epidemiology of aging* (pp. 163–182). Bethesda, MD: National Institute of Health.

PARKE, R. D. & SLABY, R. G. (1983) The development of aggression. In P. H. Mussen (Ed.) *Handbook of child psychology,* (4th ed.) (Vol. 4). New York: Wiley.

PARLOFF, M. (1982) Psychotherapy research evidence and reimbursement decisions: Bambi meets Godzilla. *American Journal of Psychiatry, 139,* 718–727.

PARNAS, J. (1985) Mates of schizophrenic mothers: A study of assortive mating from the American-Danish high-risk project. *British Journal of Psychiatry, 146,* 490–497.

PARNAS, J., SCHULSINGER, F., SCHULSINGER, H, MEDNICK, S. A. & TEASDALE, T. W. (1982) Behavioral precursors of schizophrenic spectrum: A prospective study. *Archives of General Psychiatry, 39,* 658–664.

PATTERSON, G. R. (1982) *Coercive family processes.* Eugene, OR: Castilia Press.

PATTERSON, G. R. & BRODSKY, G. A. (1966) Behavior modification program for a child with multiple problem behavior. *Journal of Child Psychology and Psychiatry, 7,* 277–295.

PAUL, G. L. & LENTZ, R. J. (1977) *Psychosocial treatment of chronic mental patients: Milieu versus social-learning programs.* Cambridge, MA: Harvard University Press.

PAUL, L. G. (1969) Chronic mental patient: Current status-future directions. *Psychological Bulletin, 71,* 81–93.

PAUL, S. M. (1985) Toward the integration of neuroscience and psychiatry. In H. A. Pincus & H. Pardes (Eds.), *The integration of neuroscience and psychiatry* (pp. 39–52). Washington, D.C.: American Psychiatric Press, Inc.

PAYKEL, E. S. (1979) Recent life events in the development of the depressive disorders. In R. A. Depue (Ed.) *The psychobiology of the depressive disorders: Implications for the effects of stress.* New York: Academic Press.

PAYKEL, E. S., MYERS, J. K., LINDENTHAL, J. J., & TANNER, J. (1974) Suicide feelings in the general population. *British Journal of Psychiatry, 124,* 460–469.

PEELE, S. (1984) The cultural context of psychological approaches to alcoholism: Can we control the effects of alcohol? *American Psychologist, 39,* 1337–1351.

PEELE, S. (1985) The meaning of addiction: Compulsive experience and its interpretation. Lexington, Massachusetts.

PEET, M. & COPPEN, A. (1980) Lithium treatment and prophylaxis in unipolar depression. *Psychosomatics, 21,* 303–313.

PELHAM, W. E. & BENDER, M. (1982) Peer relationships in hyperactive children: Description and treatment. In K. Gadow & I. Bialer (Eds.), *Advances in learning and behavioral disabilities* (Vol. 1). Greenwich, CN: JAI Press.

PENNEBAKER, J. W. (1985) Traumatic experience and psychosomatic disease: Exploring the roles of behavioral inhibition, obsession, and confiding. *Journal of Canadian Psychology, 26,* 82–95.

PENNEBAKER, J. W. (1982) *The psychology of physical symptoms.* New York: Springer-Verlag.

PENNEBAKER, J. W. & O'HEERON, R. C. (1984) Confiding in others and illness rate among spouses of suicide and accidental-death victims. *Journal of Abnormal Psychology, 93,* 473–476.

PEPLAU, L. A. & PERLMAN, D. (Eds.). (1982) *Loneliness: A sourcebook of current theory, research and therapy.* New York: John Wiley.

PERLS, F. S. (1969) *Gestalt therapy verbatim.* Lafayette, CA: Real People Press.

PERRY, J. C. & FLANNERY, R. B. (1982) Passive aggressive personality disorder: Treatment implications of a clinical typology. *Journal of Nervous and Mental Disease, 170,* 164–173.

PERSONS, J. B. (in press) The advantages of studying psychological phenomena rather than psychiatric diagnosis. *American Psychologist.*

PETERSON, C. & SELIGMAN, M. E. P. (1984) Causal explanations as a risk factor for depression: Theory and evidence. *Psychological Review, 91,* 347–374.

PETERSON, L. & RIDLEY-JOHNSON, R. (1984) Preparation of well children in the classroom: An unexpected contrast between the academic lecture and filmed modeling methods. *Journal of Pediatric Psychiatry, 9(3),* 349–361.

PETTI, T. A. (1981) Depression in children: A significant disorder. *Psychosomatics, 22,* 444–447.

PFEFFER, C. R., CONTE, H. R., JERRETT, I., & PLUTCHIK, R. (1980) Suicide behavior in latency age children. *Journal of the American Academy of Child Psychology, 19,* 703–710.

PICKAR, D., LABAREA, R., LINNOILA, M., ROY, A., HOMMER, D., EVERETT, D., & PAUL, S. M. (1984) Neuroleptic-induced decrease in plasma homo-vanillic acid and antipsychotic activity in schizophrenic patients. *Science, 225,* 954–957.

PIERCEY, B. P. (1985) First person account: Making the best of it. *Schizophrenia Bulletin, 11,* 155–157.

PILKONIS, P. A., IMBER, S. D., LEWIS, P., & RUBINSKY, P. (1974) A comparative outcome study of individual, group, and conjoint psychotherapy. *Archives of General Psychiatry, 41,* 431–437.

PINEL, P. (1969) *Traite' medico-philosophique sur l'alienation mentale* (2nd ed.). Paris: Brossen, 1809, as quoted in W. Riese, *The legacy of Philippe Pinel.* New York: Springer.

PLUMB, M. M. & HOLLAND, J. (1977) Comparative studies of psychological function in patients with advanced cancer. I. Self-reported depressive symptoms. *Psychosomatic Medicine, 39,* 264–276.

POGUE-GEILE, M. F. & HARROW, M. (1985) Negative symptoms in schizophrenia: Their longitudinal course and prognostic importance. *Schizophrenia Bulletin, 11,* 427–439.

POLICH, J. M. & AMOR, D. J. (1980) *The course of alcoholism: Four years after treatment.* Santa Monica, CA: Rand.

POMEROY, W. B. (1972) *Kinsey and the Institute for Sex Research.* New York: Harper & Row.

POPE, H. G., JONAS, J., HUDSON, J. et al. (1983) The validity of DSM-III borderline personality disorder. *Archives of General Psychiatry, 40,* 1319–1323.

POPE, H. G. & LIPINSKI, J. F. (1978) Diagnoses in schizophrenia and manic-depressive illness. *Archives of General Psychiatry, 35,* 811–828.

PRINCE, V. C. (1967) *The transvestite and his wife.* Los Angeles: Argyle Books.

PRIOR, M. (1984) Developing concepts of childhood autism: The influence of experimental cognitive research. *Journal of Consulting and Clinical Psychology, 52,* 4–16.

PRIOR, M. R. & McGILLVRAY, J. (1980) The performance of autistic children on three learning set tasks. *Journal of Child Psychology and Psychiatry, 21,* 313–324.

*Psychiatric News* (May 17, 1985) APA to send summary on TD to all members.

*Psychiatric News* (June 21, 1985, pp. 31–32) Nobel Laureate tells psychiatrists to be on lookout for transmissible viral dementias.

PURCELL, K., BRADY, K., SCHAL, H., MUSER, J., MOLK, L., GORDON, N., & MEANS, J. (1969) The effect on asthma in children of experimental separation from the family. *Psychosomatic Medicine, 31,* 144–164. Reprinted by permission of Elsevier Science Publishing Co., Inc. Copyright © 1969 by the American Psychosomatic Society, Inc.

QUILL, T. E. (1985) Somatization disorder: One of medicine's blind spots. *Journal of the American Medical Association, 254,* 3075–3079.

RABKIN, J. G. (1979) Criminal behavior of discharged mental patients: A critical appraisal of the research. *Psychological Bulletin, 86,* 1–27.

RACHMAN, S. J., & DeSILVA, P. (1978) Abnormal and normal obsessions. *Behavior Research and Therapy, 16,* 223–248.

RACHMAN, S. J. & HODGSON, R. J. (1980) *Obsessions and compulsions.* Englewood Cliffs, NJ: Prentice Hall.

RADA, R. T. (1978) *Clinical aspects of the rapist.* New York: Grune & Stratton.

RAIMY, V. (1985) Misconceptions and the cognitive therapies. In M. J. Mahoney & A. Freeman (Eds.) *Cognition and psychotherapy.* New York: Plenum.

RAPHAEL, B. (1983) *The anatomy of bereavement.* New York: Basic Books.

RAMEY, C. T. & HASKINS, R. (1981) The modification of intelligence through early experience. *Intelligence, 5,* 43–57.

RAPOPORT, J., ELKINS, R., LANGER, D. H., SCEERY, W., BUCHSBAUM, M. S., GILLIN, J. C., MURPHY, D. L., ZAHN, T. P., LAKE, R., LUDLOW, C. & MENDELSON, W. (1981) Childhood obsessive-compulsive disorder. *American Journal of Psychiatry, 138,* 1545–1554.

RAPS, C. S., PETERSON, C., REINHARD, K. E. & ABRAMSON, L. Y. (1982) Attributional style among depressed patients. *Journal of Abnormal Psychology, 91,* 102–108.

RAY, O. (1983) *Drugs, society and human behavior.* St. Louis: Mosby.

REDICK, R. W. & JOHNSON, C. (1974) Marital status, living arrangements, and family characteristics of admissions to state and county mental hospitals and outpatient psychiatric clinics, United States, 1970. *Mental Health Statistical Note,* No. 100 (U.S. National Institute of Mental Health). Washington, D.C.: U.S. Government Printing Office.

REDICK, R. W., SITKIN, M. J., & BETHEL, H. (Sept. 1984) Distribution of psychiatric beds, United States and each state, 1982. *Mental Health Statistical Note,* No. 167, U.S. Department of Health and Human Services, National Institute of Mental Health, Washington, D.C.: U.S. Government Printing Office.

REHM, L. P. (1977) A self-control model of depression. *Behavior Therapy, 8,* 787–804.

REICH, W. (1949) (originally published 1933) *Character analysis.* New York: Orgone Institute Press.

REISBERG, B. (1985) Alzheimer's disease updated. *Psychiatric Annals, 15,* 319–322.

REISS, B. F. (1980) Psychological tests in homosexuality. In J. Marmor (Ed.) *Homosexual behavior.* New York: Basic Books.

REKERS, G. A. (1977) Assessment and treatment of childhood gender problems. In B. B. Lahey & A. E. Kazdin (Eds.) *Advances in clinical child psychology* (Vol. 1). New York: Plenum.

Research on mental illness and addictive disorders (1985). *American Journal of Psychiatry, 142,* 9–41, supplement.

*Research on mental illness and addictive disorders: Progress and prospects* (1984). Washington, D.C.: National Academy Press.

REVELEY, A. M. (1985) Genetic counseling for schizophrenia. *British Journal of Psychiatry, 147,* 107–112.

REVELEY, A. M., REVELEY, M. A., CLIFFORD, C. A., & MURRAY, R. M. (1982) Cerebral ventricular size in twins discordant for schizophrenia, *Lancet, 1* (8271), 540–541.

REICH, T., RICE, J., CLONINGER, C. R., WETTE, R., & JAMES, J. W. (1979) The use of multiple thresholds and segregation analysis in analyzing the phenotypic heterogeneity of multifactorial traits. *Annals of Human Genetics, 42,* 371–389

RICHMANN, N., STEVENSON, J. & GRAHAM, P. J. (1982) *Preschool to school: A behavioral study.* London: Academic Press.

RIE, H. & RIE, E. (Eds.) (1980) *Handbook of minimal brain dysfunctions: A critical view.* New York: Wiley.

RIMLAND, B. (1974) Infantile autism: Status and research. In A. Davids (ed.), *Child personality and psychopathology.* New York: John Wiley, 137–168.

ROACH, M. (1983) Another name for madness. *New York Times Magazine,* Jan. 16, pp. 22–31.

ROBERTSON, H. A. (1979) Benzodiazepine receptors in "emotional" and "non-emotional" mice: Comparison of four strains. *European Journal of Pharmacology, 56,* 163.

ROBINS, L. N., HELZER, J. E., CROGHAN, J., & RATCLIFF, K. S. (1981) National Institute of Mental Health Diagnostic Interview Schedule. *Archives of General Psychiatry, 38,* 381–389.

ROBINS, L. N. & RATCLIFF, K. S. (1980) The long-term outcome of truancy. In L. A. Hersov & I. Berg (Eds.) *Out of School: Modern perspectives on truancy and school refusal.* Chichester, Eng.: Wiley.

ROGENTINE, G. N., VanKAMMEN, D. P., FOX, B. H., DOGHERTY, J. P., ROSENBLATT, J. E., BOYD, S. C., & BUNNEY, W. E., JR. (1979) Psychological factors in the prognosis of malignant melanoma: A prospective study. *Psychosomatic Medicine, 41,* 647–655.

ROGERS, C. R. (1951) *Client-centered therapy.* Boston: Houghton Mifflin.

ROGERS, C. R. (1959) A theory of therapy, personality, and interpersonal relationships as developed in the client-centered framework. In S. Koch (Ed.) *Psychology: A study of a science.* (Vol. 3). New York: McGraw-Hill.

ROGERS, C. R. (1980) *A way of being.* Boston: Houghton-Mifflin.

ROGLER, L. H. & HOLLINGSHEAD, A. B. (1965) *Trapped: Families and schizophrenia.* New York: John Wiley.

ROHN, R. D., SARTES, R. M., KENNY, T. J., REYNOLDS, B. J., & HEALD, F. P. (1977) Adolescents who attempt suicide. *Journal of Pediatrics, 90,* 636–638.

ROMER, D. & HELLER, T. (1983) Social adaptation of mentally retarded adults in community settings: A social-ecological approach. *Applied Research in Mental Retardation, 4,* 303–314.

ROSEN, J. C. & LEITENBERG, J. (1982) Bulimia nervosa: Treatment with exposure and response prevention. *Behavior Therapy, 13,* 117–124.

ROSEN, R. & ROSEN, L. R. (1981) *Human sexuality.* New York: Knopf.

ROSENBAUM, A. & O'LEARY, K. D. (1981) Marital violence: Characteristics of abusive couples. *Journal of Consulting and Clinical Psychology, 49,* 63–71.

ROSENHECK, R. A. (1985) Malignant post-Vietnam stress syndrome. *American Journal of Orthopsychiatry, 55,* 166–176.

ROSENHAN, D. L. (1973) On being sane in insane places. *Science, 179,* 250–257.

ROSENMAN, R. H., BRAND, R. J., JENKINS, C. D., FREIDMAN, M., STRAUS, R., & WURM, M. (1975) Coronary heart disease in the Western Collaborative Group Study. *Journal of the American Medical Association, 233,* 872–877.

ROSENSTEIN, M. J. & MILAZZO-SAYRE, (1981) *Characteristics of admissions to selected mental-health facilities.* Rockville, MD: U.S. Dept. of Health and Human Services.

ROSENTHAL, D. (Ed.) (1963) *The Genain quadruplets: A case study and theoretical analysis of heredity and environment in schizophrenia.* New York: Basic Books.

ROSENTHAL, D., WENDER, P. H., KETY, S. S., SCHULSINGER, F., WELNER, J., & OSTERGAARD, L. (1968) Schizophrenics' offspring reared in adoptive homes. In D. Rosenthal & S. S. Kety (Eds.), *The transmission of schizophrenia.* Oxford: Pergamon Press.

ROSENTHAL D., WENDER, P.H., KETY, S. S., SCHULSINGER, F., WELNER, J., & REIDER, R. (1975) Parent-child relationships and psychopathological disorder in the child. *Archives of General Psychiatry, 32,* 466–476.

ROSS, A., & PELHAM, W. E. (1981) Child psychopathology. *Annual Review of Psychology, 32,* 243–278.

ROSS, D. M. & ROSS, S. A. (1982) *Hyperactivity: Research, theory, and action.* New York: John Wiley.

ROSS, H. L. & GLASER, E. M. (1973) Making it out of the ghetto. *Professional Psychology, 4,* 347–356.

ROUNSAVILLE, B. J., WEISMAN, M. M., KLEBER, J., & WILBER, C. (1982) Heterogeneity of psychiatric diagnosis in treated opiate addicts. *Archives of General Psychiatry, 39,* 161–166.

ROY, A., PICKAR, D., & PAUL, S. (1984) Biological tests in depression. *Psychosomatics, 25*(6), 443–451.

ROY-BYRNE, P., POST, R. M., UHDE, T. W., PORCU, T., & DAVIS, D. (1985) The longitudinal course of recurrent affective illness: Life chart data from research patients at the NIMH. *Acta Psychiatrica Scandinavica Supplementum, 71,* 317.

ROSVOLD, H. E., MIRSKY, A. F., SARASON, I. G., BRANSOME, E. D., & BECK, L. H. (1956) A continuous performance test of brain damage. *Journal of Consulting Psychology, 20,* 343–350.

ROWLAND, M. (Ed.) (1981) Hypertension of adults twenty-five to seventy-four years of age: United States, 1971–1975. Hyattsville, Md.: *National Center for Health Statistics.*

RUBENS, R. L., & LAPIDUS, L. B. (1978) Schizophrenic patterns of arousal and stimulus barrier functioning. *Journal of Abnormal Psychology, 87,* 199–211.

RUBENSTEIN, C. & SHAVER, P. (1982) *In search of intimacy.* New York: Random House.

RUBERMAN, J. W., WEINBLATT, E., GOLDBERG, J. D., & CHAUDHARY, B. S. (1984) Psychological influences on mortality after myocardial infarction. *New England Journal of Medicine, 311,* 552–559. Reprinted by permission of *The New England Journal of Medicine.*

RUMSEY, J. M., DUARA, R., GRADY, C., RAPOPORT, J. L., MARGOLIN, R. A., RAPOPORT, S. I., & CUTLER, N. R. (1985) Brain metabolism in autism. *Archives of General Psychiatry, 42,* 448–455.

RUSH, A. J., BECK, A. T., KOVACS, M. J., WEISSENBURGER, M. A., & HOLLON, S. D. (1982) Comparison of the effects of cognitive therapy and pharmacotherapy on hopelessness and self-conceit. *American Journal of Psychiatry, 139,* 862–866. Copyright © 1982, the American Psychiatric Association. Reprinted by permission.

RUSSEK, H. I. (1967) Role of emotional stress in the etiology of clinical coronary heart disease. *Diseases of the Chest, 52,* 1–9.

RUTTER, D. R. (1985) Language in schizophrenia. *British Journal of Psychiatry, 146,* 399–404.

RUTTER, M. (1967) Psychotic disorders in early childhood. In A. J. Coppen & A. Walk (Eds.), *Recent developments in schizophrenia.* Oxford, Eng.: Headley Bros.

RUTTER, M. (1980) *Changing youth in a changing society.* Cambridge: Harvard University Press.

RUTTER, M. (1984) The developmental psychopathology of depression: Issues and perspectives. In M. Rutter, C. E. Izard, & P. Read (Eds.) *Depression in childhood: Developmental perspectives.* New York: Guilford Press.

RUTTER, M., COX, A., TUPLING, C., BERGER, M., & YULE, W. (1975) Attainment and adjustment in two geographical areas: I. The prevalence of psychiatric disorder. *British Journal of Psychiatry, 126,* 493–509.

RUTTER, M. & GARMEZY, N. (1983) Developmental psychopathology. In P. Mussen (Ed.), *Handbook of child psychology,* (Vol. 4). New York: John Wiley.

RUTTER, M. & GILLER, H. (1984) *Juvenile delinquency: Trends and perspectives.* Harmondsworth, Eng.: Penguin.

RUTTER, M., GRAHAM, P., & YULE, W. (1970) A neuropsychiatric study in childhood. *Clinics in Developmental Medicine,* Nos. 35/36. London: Heinemann.

RUTTER, M. & HERSOV, L. (1985) *Child and adolescent psychiatry: Modern approaches.* Oxford: Blackwell Scientific Publications.

RUTTER, M. & QUINTON, D. (1984) Parental psychiatric disorder: Effect on children. *Psychological Medicine, 14,* 853–880.

RUTTER, M. & SHAFFER, D. (1980) DSM-III: A step forward or back in terms of the classification of child psychiatric disorders. *Journal of the American Academy of Child Psychiatry, 19,* 371–394.

RUTTER, M., TIZARD, I., & WHITMORE, K. (Eds) (1981) (originally published in 1970) *Education, health and behavior.* Huntington, NY: Krieger.

RUTTER, M., TIZARD, J., YULE, W., GRAHAM, P., & WHITMORE, K. (1976) Isle of Wight studies 1964–74. *Psychological Medicine, 6,* 313–332.

SAGHIR, M. T. & ROBINS, E. (1973) *Male and female homosexuality: A comprehensive investigation.* Baltimore: Williams & Wilkins.

SALTER, A. C., RICHARDSON, C. M., & KAIRYS, S. W. (1985) Caring for abused preschoolers. *Child Welfare, 64,* 343–356.

SARASON, B. R., SARASON, I. G., HACKER, T. A., & BASHAM, R. B. (1985) Concomitants of social support: Social skills, physical attractiveness, and gender. *Journal of Personality and Social Psychology, 49,* 469–480.

SARASON, I. G. (1979) Three lacunae of cognitive therapy. *Cognitive Therapy and Research, 3,* 223–235.

SARASON, I. G., JOHNSON, J. M., & SIEGEL, J. M. (1978) Assessing the impact of life stress: Development of the Life Experiences Survey. *Journal of Consulting and Clinical Psychology, 46,* 932–946.

SARASON, I. G., LEVINE, H. M., BASHAM, R. B., & SARASON, B. R. (1983) Assessing social support: The Social Support Questionnaire. *Journal of Personality and Social Psychology, 44,* 127–139.

SARASON, I. G. & SARASON, B. R. (1981) Teaching cognitive and social skills to high school students. *Journal of Consulting and Clinical Psychology, 49,* 908–919.

SARASON, I. G. AND SARASON, B. R. (Eds.) (1985) *Social support: Theory, research and applications.* Dordrecht, The Netherlands: Martinus Nijhof.

SARASON, I. G., SARASON, B. R., POTTER, E. H. III, AND ANTONI, M. H. (1985) Life events, social support, and illness. *Psychosomatic Medicine, 47,* 156–163.

SARASON, I. G. & STOOPS, R. (1978) Test anxiety and the passage of time. *Journal of Consulting and Clinical Psychology, 46,* 102–109.

SASS, L. (1982) The borderline personality. *The New York Times Magazine,* August 22.

SCARR, S., & WEINBERG, R. A. (1978) The influence of "family background" on intellectual attainment. *American Sociological Review, 43,* 674–692.

SCHACHT, T. E. & STRUPP, H. H. (1985) Evaluation of psychotherapy. In H. I. Kaplan & B. J. Sadock, (Eds.) *Comprehensive textbook of psychiatry* (4th ed.) Vol. 2. Baltimore: Williams & Wilkins.

SCHACHTER, S. (1982) Recidivism and self-care of smoking and obesity. *American Psychologist, 37,* 436–444.

SCHAFER, R. (1948) *Clinical application of psychological tests.* New York: International Universities Press.

SCHAIE, K. W. (1983) The Seattle longitudinal study: A 21-year exploration of psychometric intelligence in adulthood. In K. W. Schaie (Ed.) *Longitudinal studies of adult psychological development.* New York: Guilford Press.

SCHALLING, D. (1978) Psychopathy-related personality variables and the psychophysiology of socialization. In R. D. Hare & D. Schalling (Eds.), *Psychopathic behavior: Approaches to research.* Chichester, Eng.: John Wiley.

SCHILDKRAUT, J. J. (1965) The catecholamine hypothesis of affective disorders: A review of supporting evidence. *American Journal of Psychiatry, 122,* 509–522.

SCHILLING, R. F. & SCHINKE, S. P. (1984) Maltreatment and mental retardation. In J. M. Berg (Ed.) *Perspectives and progress in mental retardation* (Vol. 1). Baltimore, MD: University Park Press.

SCHLEIFER, S. J., KELLER, S. E., CAMERINO, M., THORNTON, J. C., & STEIN, M. (1983) Suppression of lymphocyte stimulation following bereavement. *Journal of the American Medical Assoc., 250,* 374–377.

SCHLESSER, M. A. & ALTSHULER, K. Z. (1983) The genetics of affective disorder: Data, theory, and clinical applications. *Hospital and Community Psychiatry, 34,* 415–422.

SCHOENMAN, T. J. (1984) The mentally ill witch in text books of abnormal psychology: Current status and implications of a fallacy. *Professional Psychiatry, 15,* 299–314.

SCHUCHTER, S. R. & ZISSOK, S. (1984) Psychological reactions to the PSA crash. *International Journal of Psychiatry in Medicine, 14,* 293–301.

SCHUCKIT, M. A. (1981) Twins studies in substance abuse: An overview. In L. Gedda, P. Paris, & W. Nance (Eds.), *Twin research* (Vol. 3). New York: Alan R. Liss.

SCHWARTZ, S. (1982) Is there a schizophrenic language? *The Behavioral and Brain Sciences, 4,* 579–588.

SCHWEINHART, L. J. & WEIKART, D. P. (1980) *Young children grow up.* Ypsilanti, MI: High/Scope.

Science Reports: National Institute of Mental Health (1981) *Treating and assessing the chronically mentally ill.* Rockville, MD: U.S. Dept. of Health and Human Services.

SEARL, S., JR. (1978) Stages of parent reaction to the birth of a handicapped child. *Exceptional Parent,* (April), 23–27.

SECHEHAYE, M. (1951) *Autobiography of a schizophrenic girl.* New York: Grune & Stratton.

SELIGMAN, M. E. P. (1974) Depression and learned helplessness. In R. J. Friedman & M. M. Katz (Eds.), *The psychology of depression: Contemporary theory and research.* Washington, D.C.: V. H. Winston.

SELIGMAN, M. E. P. (1975) *Helplessness: On depression, development, and death.* San Francisco: W. H. Freeman.

SELYE, H. (1976) *The stress of life.* (revised ed.) New York: McGraw-Hill.

SELTZER, B. & SHERWIN, I. (1978) Organic brain syndromes: An empirical study and critical review. *American Journal of Psychiatry, 135,* 13–21.

SHAGASS, C., ROEMER, R. A., & AMADEO, M. (1976) Eye-tracking performance and engagement of attention. *Archives of General Psychiatry, 33,* 121–125.

SHAPIRO, D. (1965) *Neurotic styles.* New York: Basic Books.

SHAPIRO, D. (1981) *Autonomy and rigid character.* New York: Basic Books.

SHAPIRO, S., SKINNER, E. A., KESSLER, L. G., VON KORFF, M., GERMAN, P. S., TISCHLER, G. L., LEAF, P. J., BENHAM, L. COTTLER, L., & REGIER, D. A. (1984) Utilization of health and mental health services. *Archives of General Psychiatry, 41,* 971–978.

SHAW, C. R. (Ed.) (1930) *The Jack Roller.* Chicago: University of Chicago Press.

SHEEHAN, S. (1981) A reporter at large (Creedmoor, Part 1). *New Yorker,* 25, May.

SHEEHAN, S. (1982) *Is there no place on earth for me.* Boston: Houghton Mifflin.

SHEKELLE, R. B., RAYNOR, W. J., OTSFELD, A. M., GARRON, D. C., BIELIAUSKAS, L. A., LIV, S. C., MALIZA, C., & OGLESBY, P. (1981) Psychological depression and 17-year risk of death from cancer. *Psychosomatic Medicine, 43,* 117–125.

SHIFFMAN, S. (1982) Relapse following smoking cessation: A situational analysis. *Journal of Consulting and Clinical Psychology, 50,* 71–86.

SHIPLEY, R. H., BUTT, J. H., HORWITZ, B., & FARBRY, J. E. (1978) Preparation for a stressful medical procedure: Effect of amount of stimulus preexposure and coping style. *Journal of Consulting and Clinical Psychology, 46,* 499–507.

SHNEIDMAN, E. S. (1980) *Voices of death.* New York: Harper & Row.

SHURE, M. B. & SPIVACK, G. (1982) Interpersonal problem-solving in young children: A cognitive approach to prevention. *American Journal of Community Psychology, 10,* 341–356.

SIEGEL, J. M., MATHEWS, K. A., & LEITCH, C. J. (1981) Validation of the Type A interview assessment of adolescents: A multidimensional approach. *Psychosomatic Medicine, 43,* 311–321.

SIEGEL, S., HINSON, R. E., & KRANK, M. D. (1981) Morphine-induced attenuation of morphine tolerance. *Science, 212,* 1533–1534.

SIGELMAN, C. K., BUDD, E. C., SPANHEL, C. L., & SCHOENROCK, C. J. (1981) When in doubt say yes: Acquiescence in interviews with mentally-retarded persons. *Mental Retardation, 19,* 53–58.

SIGVARDSSON, S., VON KNORRING, A., BOHMAN, M., & CLONINGER, R. (1984) An adoption study of somatoform disorders: I. *Archives of General Psychiatry, 41,* 853–859.

SIEGELMAN, M. (1974) Parental background of male homosexuals and heterosexuals. *Archives of Sexual Behavior, 3,* 3–18.

SIEVER, L. J. & COURSEY, R. D. (1985) Biological markers for schizophrenia and the biological high risk approach. *Journal of Nervous and Mental Disease, 173,* 4–16.

SIEVER, L. J. & DAVIS, K. L. (1985) Overview: Toward a dysregulation hypothesis of depression. *American Journal of Psychiatry, 142,* 1017–1031.

SILVERSTEIN, M. L. & HARROW, M. (1981) Schneiderian first-rank symptoms in schizophrenia. *Archives of General Psychiatry, 38,* 288–293.

SKLAR, L. S. & ANISMAN, H. (1981) Stress and cancer. *Psychological Bulletin, 89,* 369–406.

SLATER, J., & DEPUE, R. A. (1981) The contribution of environmental events and social support to serious suicide attempts in primary depressive disorder. *Journal of Abnormal Psychology, 90,* 275–285.

SKULTANS, V. (1979) *English madness.* London: Routledge & Kegan Paul.

SLOANE, R. B., STAPLES, F. R., CRISTOL, A. H., YORKSTON, N. J., & WHIPPLE, K. (1975) *Short-term analytically oriented psychotherapy versus behavior therapy.* Cambridge, MA: Harvard University Press.

SLOANE, R. B., STAPLES, F. R., WHIPPLE, K., & CRISTOL, A. H. (1977) Patients' attitudes toward behavior therapy and psychotherapy. *American Journal of Psychiatry, 134,* 134–137.

SMALL, G. W. & NICHOLI, A. M. (1982) Mass hysteria among school children. *Archives of General Psychiatry, 39,* 89–90. Copyright © 1982, American Medical Association.

SMITH, D. W., & WILSON, A. A. (1973) *A child with Down's syndrome (mongolism).* Philadelphia: W. B. Saunders. Reprinted by permission.

SMITH, M. L., GLASS, G. V., & MILLER, T. I. (1980) *The benefits of psychotherapy.* Baltimore: Johns Hopkins University Press.

SMITH, R. E., SARASON, I. G., & SARASON, B. R. (1986) *Psychology: The frontiers of behavior* (3rd ed.). New York: Harper & Row.

SMITH, R. N. (1982) *Dewey and his times.* New York: Simon & Schuster.

SMITH, R. J. (1978) *The psychopath in society.* New York: Academic Press.

SMITH, T. W. (1982) Irrational beliefs on the cause and treatment of emotional distress: A critical review of the rational-emotive model. *Clinical Psychology Review, 2,* 505–522.

SNOWLING, M. & FIRTH, U. (1982) A comparison of reading in autistic and dyslexic children. Paper presented at the fifth International Neuropsychological Society Conference, Deauville, France.

SNYDER, S. H., BANERJEE, S. P., YAMAMURA, H. I., & GREENBERG, D. (1974) Drugs, neurotransmitters and schizophrenia. *Science, 184,* 1243–1254.

SOHLBERG, S. C. (1976) Stress experiences and combat fatigue during the Yom Kippur War (1973). *Psychological Reports, 38,* 523–529.

SPANOS, N. P. (1978) Witchcraft in histories of psychiatry: A critical analysis and an alternative conceptualization. *Psychological Bulletin, 85,* 417–439.

SPITZER, R. L., ENDICOTT, J., & GIBBON, M., (1979) Crossing the border into borderline personality and borderline schizophrenia: The development of criteria. *Archives of General Psychiatry, 36,* 17–24.

SPITZER, R. L., FORMAN, J. B., & NEE, J. (1979) DSM-III field trials: I. Initial inter-rater diagnostic reliability. *American Journal of Psychiatry, 136,* 815–817.

SPITZER, R. L., & FORMAN, J. B. (1979) DSM-III field trials: II. Initial experience with the multiaxial system. *American Journal of Psychiatry, 136,* 818–820.

SPITZER, R. L., SKODAL, A. E., GIBBON, M., & WILLIAMS, J. B. W. (1981) *DSM-III casebook.* Washington, D.C.: American Psychiatric Association.

SPITZER, R. L., SKODAL, A. E., GIBBON, M., & WILLIAMS, J. B. W. (1983) *Psychopathology: A casebook.* New York: McGraw-Hill.

SPIVACK, G., PLATT, J. J., & SHURE, M. B. (1976) *The problem-solving approach to adjustment.* San Francisco: Jossey-Bass.

STABENAU, J. R., & POLLIN, W. (1967) Early characteristics of monozygotic twins discordant for schizophrenia. *Archives of General Psychiatry, 17,* 723–734.

STEADMAN, H. (1981) Critically reassessing the accuracy of public perceptions of the dangerousness of the mentally ill. *Journal of Health and Social Behavior, 22,* 310–316.

STERN, R. S. & COBB, J. P. (1978) Phenomenology of obsessive compulsive neuroses. *British Journal of Psychiatry, 182,* 233–239.

STERN, S. L., RUSH, A. J., & MENDELS, J. (1980) Toward a rational pharmacotherapy of depression. *American Journal of Psychiatry, 137,* 545–552.

STEUER, J. L., MINTZ, J., HAMMEN, C. L., HILL, M. A., JARVIK, L. F., MCCARLEY, T., MOTOIKE, P., & ROSEN, R. (1984) Cognitive-behavioral and psychodynamic group psychotherapy in treatment of geriatric depression. *Journal of Consulting and Clinical Psychology, 52,* 180–189.

STEWART, J. W., WALSH, T., WRIGHT, L., ROOSE, S. P., & GLASSMAN, A. H. (1984) An open trial of MAO inhibitors in bulimia. *Journal of Clinical Psychiatry, 45,* 217–218.

STOFFELMAYR, B. E., DILLAVOU, D., & HUNTER, J. E. (1983) Premorbid functioning and outcome in schizophrenia: A cumulative analysis. *Journal of Consulting and Clinical Psychology, 51,* 338–352.

STONE, M. H. (1980) *The borderline syndromes.* New York: McGraw-Hill.

STORR, A. (1980) *The art of psychotherapy.* New York: Methuen.

STRAUSS, J. S., CARPENTER, W. T., JR., & BARKTO, J. J. (1974) Speculations on the processes that underlie schizophrenic symptoms and signs. *Schizophrenia Bulletin, 11,* 61–69.

STROBER, M. & CARLSON, G. A. (1982) Bipolar illness in adolescents with major depression: Clinical, genetic and psychopharmacologic predictors in a three-to-four-year prospective follow-up investigation. *Archives of General Psychiatry, 39,* 545–555.

STRUNK, R. C., MRAZEK, D. A., FUHRMANN, A. S. W., & LaBRECQUE, J. F. (1985) Physiologic and psychological characteristics associated with deaths due to asthma in childhood: A case-controlled study. *Journal of the American Medical Association, 254,* 1193–1198.

STUBBS, E. G., RITVO, E. R., & MASON-BROTHERS, A. (1985) Autism and shared parental HLA antigens. *Journal of Child Psychiatry, 24,* 182–185.

SUELZE, M. & KEENAN, V. (1981) Changes in family support networks over the life cycle of mentally retarded persons. *American Journal of Mental Deficiency, 86,* 267–274.

STRUBE, M. J., GARDNER, W., & HARTMANN, D. P. (1985) Limitations, liabilities, and obstacles in reviews of the literature: The current status of meta-analysis. *Clincial Psychology Review, 5,* 63–78.

STRUPP, H. H. & HADLEY, S. W. (1979) Specific versus non-specific factors in psychotherapy: A controlled study of outcome. *Archives of General Psychiatry, 36,* 1125–1136.

SUELZLE, M., & KEENAN, V. (1981) Changes in family support networks over the life cycle of mentally retarded persons. *American Journal of Mental Deficiency, 86,* 267–274.

SULLOWAY, F. J. (1979) *Freud: Biologist of the mind.* New York: Basic Books.

SUOMI, S. J. & HARLOW, H. F. (1972) Social rehabilitation of isolation-reared monkeys. *Developmental Psychology, 6,* 487–496.

SUOMI, S. J. & HARLOW, H. F. (1978) Early experience and social development in Rhesus monkeys. In M. E. Lamb (Ed.) *Social and personality development.* New York: Holt, Rinehart and Winston.

SUOMI, S. J. (1983) Models of depression in primates. *Psychological Medicine, 13,* 465–468.

SUTHERLAND, S. (1977) *Breakdown.* London: Granada.

SWANSON, J. M. & KINSBOURNE, M. (1980) Food dyes impair performance of hyperactive children on a laboratory learning test. *Science, 207,* 1485–1487.

SYMONDS, P. M. (1940) Psychoanalysis, psychology, and education. *Journal of Abnormal and Social Psychology, 35,* 139–149.

SZASZ, T. S. (1970) *Ideology and insanity: Essays on the psychiatric dehumanization of man.* Garden City, NY: Anchor Books.

TALBOTT, J. A. (1985) Medical humanism: A personal odyssey. *Psychiatric News, 2,* 31.

TARVER-BEHRING, S., BARKLEY, R. A., & KARLSSON, J. (1985) The mother-child interactions of hyperactive boys and their normal siblings. *American Journal of Orthopsychiatry, 55,* 202–208. Reprinted with permission. Copyright © 1985 by the American Orthopsychiatric Association, Inc.

TAYLOR, C. B. (1980) Behavioral approaches to hypertension. In J. M. Ferguson & C. B. Taylor (Eds.) (1980) *The comprehensive handbook of behavioral medicine, 1,* 55–88. New York: S. P. Medical and Scientific Books.

TEMKIN, N. R. & DAVIS, G. R. (1984) Stress as a risk factor for seizures among adults with epilepsy. *Epilepsia, 25,* 450–456.

TERMAN, L. M. & MERRILL, M. A. (1937) *Measuring intelligence.* Boston: Houghton Mifflin.

TERMAN, L. M. & MERRILL, M. A. (1960) *Stanford-Binet Intelligence Scale: Manual for the 3rd revision, Form -M.* Boston: Houghton Mifflin.

TERMAN, L. M. & MERRILL, M. A. (1973) *Stanford-Binet Intelligence Scale: 1972 norms edition.* Boston: Houghton Mifflin.

THELMAR, E. (1932) *The maniac: A realistic study of madness from a maniac's point of view* (2nd ed.). London: C. A. Watts.

THEORELL, T., LIND, E., LUNDBERG, J., CHRISTENSON, T., & EDHOG, O. (1974) *The individual and his work in relation to myocardial infarction.* Paper presented at the Symposium on Society, Stress, and Disease: Working Life. Stockholm, Sweden.

THOMAS, C. B. & DUSZYNCKI, K. R. (1974) Closeness to parents and the family: Constellation in a prospective study of five disease states: Suicide, mental illness, malignant tumor, hypertension and coronary heart disease. *Johns Hopkins Medical Journal, 134,* 251–270.

THOMPSON, T. L., II (1982) Headache. In H. I. Kaplan & B. J. Sadock (Eds.) *Comprehensive Textbook on Psychiatry* (4th Ed.) (Vol. 2). Baltimore, Md.: Williams & Wilkins.

THORESEN, C. E., FRIEDMAN, M., GILL, J. K., & ULMER, D. K. (1982) The recurrent coronary prevention project: Some preliminary findings. *Acta Medica Scandinavica, 68,* 172–192.

THYER, B. A., NESSE, R. M., CAMERON, O. G., & CURTIS, G. C. (1985) Case histories and shorter communications. Agoraphobia: A test of the separation anxiety hypothesis. *Behavior Research and Therapy,* 23, 75–78.

TIENARO, P., SORRI, A., LAHTI, I., NAARALA, M., WAHLBERG, K. E., KONKKO, T., POHJOLA, J., & MORING, J. (1985) The Finnish adoptive family study of schizophrenia. *The Yale Journal of Biology and Medicine,* 58, 227–237.

TOLSTRUP, K., BRINCH, M., ISAGER, T., NIELSEN, S., NYSTRUP, J., SEVERIN, B. & OLESEN, N. S. (1985) Long-term outcome of 151 cases of anorexia nervosa. *Acta Scandinavica Psychiatrica,* 71, 380–387.

TOOLAN, J. M. (1981) Depression and suicide in children: An overview. *American Journal of Psychotherapy,* 35, 311–322.

TORGERSEN, S. (1979) The nature and origin of common phobic fears. *British Journal of Psychiatry,* 134, 343–351.

TRIANA, R. R. & HINKLE, L. M. (1974) Psychoanalytically oriented therapy for alcoholic patients. *Social Casework, May,* 285–291.

TSAI, M., FELDMAN-SUMMERS, S., & EDGAR, M. (1979) Child molestation: Variables related to differential impacts on psychosexual functioning in adult women. *Journal of Abnormal Psychology,* 88, 407–417.

TSUANG, M. T. & VANDERMAY, R. (1980) *Genes and the Mind.* Oxford, Eng.: Oxford University Press.

TSUANG, M. T., WOOLSON, R. R., WINOKUR, G., & CROWE, R. R. (1981) Stability of psychiatric diagnoses. *Archives of General Psychiatry,* 38, 535–539.

TURK, D. C. & SALOVEY, P. (1985) Cognitive structures, cognitive processes, and cognitive-behavior modification: II. Judgments and inferences of the clinician. *Cognitive Therapy and Research,* 9, 19–134.

TURNER, T. B., MEXEY, E., & KIMBALL, A. W. (1977) Measurement of alcohol-related effects in man: Chronic effects in relation to levels of alcohol consumption, Part A. *Johns Hopkins Medical Journal,* 141, 235–248.

TUYNS, A. J. (1979) Epidemiology of alcohol and cancer. *Cancer Research,* 39, 2840–2843.

TWENTYMAN, C. T., ROHRBECK, C. H., & AMISH, P. A. (In press) A cognitive-behavioral model of child abuse. In S. Sanders (Ed.), *Violent individuals and families: A practitioner's handbook.* Springfield, Ill.: Charles Thomas.

UHDE, T. W., BOULENGER, J. P., ROY-BYRNE, P., GERACI, M. F., VITTONE, B. J., & POST, R. M. (1985) Longitudinal course of panic disorder: Clinical and biological considerations. *Progress in Neuropsychopharmacology and Biological Psychiatry,* 9, 39–51.

U.S. Department of Health Education, and Welfare, Public Health Service. (1979) *Smoking and Health: A report of the Surgeon General.* Washington, D.C. U.S. Government Printing Office, (DHEW Pub. No. [PHS]79-50066).

U.S. Department of Health and Human Services. (1981) *Schizophrenia, is there an answer?* Rockville, MD: U.S. Dept. of Health & Human Services (a).

U.S. Department of Health and Human Services (1981) *Special report to Congress on alcohol and health.* Washington, D.C.: Government Printing Office (DHHS Pub. No. [ADM]81-1080 (b).

VAILLANT, G. E. (1973) A 20 year follow-up of New York narcotic addicts. *Archives of General Psychiatry,* 29, 237–241.

VAILLANT, G. E. (1976) History of male psychological health: V. The relation of choice of ego mechanisms of defense to adult adjustment. *Archives of General Psychiatry,* 33, 535–545.

VAILLANT, G. E. (1980) Natural history of male psychological health VIII, Antecedents of alcoholism and orality. *American Journal of Psychiatry,* 137, 181–186.

VAILLANT, G. E. (1983) *The natural history of alcoholism: Causes, patterns, and paths to recovery.* Cambridge, Mass.: Harvard University Press.

VAILLANT, G. E. (1984) The disadvantages of DSM-III outweigh its advantages. *American Journal of Psychiatry,* 14, 542–545.

VAILLANT, G. E. & MILOFSKY, E. S. (1982) Natural history of male alcoholism IV. Paths to recovery. *Archives of General Psychiatry,* 39, 127–133.

VALONE, K., GOLDSTEIN, M. J., & NORTON, J. P. (1984) Parental expressed emotion and psychophysiological reactivity in an adolescent sample at risk for schizophrenia spectrum disorders. *Journal of Abnormal Psychology,* 93, 448–457.

VALONE, K., NORTON, J. P., GOLDSTEIN, M. J., & DOANG, J. A. (1983) Parental expressed emotion and affective style in an adolescent sample at risk for schizophrenia spectrum disorders. *Journal of Abnormal Psychology,* 92, 399–407.

VAUGHN, C. E. & LEFF, J. P. (1976) The influence of family and social factors on the course of psychiatric illness. *British Journal of Psychiatry,* 129, 125–137. Copyright © 1976 by The British Journal of Psychiatry. Reprinted by permission.

VAUGHN, C. E., SNYDER, K. S., JONES, S., FREEMAN, W. B., AND FALLOON, I. R. H. (1984) Family factors in schizophrenic relapse. *Archives of General Psychiatry,* 41, 1169–1177.

VENABLES, P. H. (1979) The psychophysiology of schizophrenia. In R. Gaind & B. Hudson (Eds.) *Current themes in psychiatry,* (Vol. 2). London: MacMillan Press.

VERONEN, L. J. & KILPATRICK, D. G. (1983) Stress innoculation training as a treatment for rape victims' fears. In D. Meichenbaum and M. Jaremko (Eds.) *Stress Reduction and Prevention.* New York: Plenum.

VIDEKA-SHERMAN, L. & LIEBERMAN, M. (1985) The effects of self-help and psychotherapy intervention on child loss: The limits of recovery. *American Journal of Orthopsychiatry,* 55, 70–82.

VIRKKUNEN, M. (1983) Insulin secretion during the glucose tolerance test in antisocial personality. *British Journal of Psychiatry,* 142, 598–604.

VISCHI, T. R., JONES, K. R., SHANK, E. L., & LIMA, L. H. (1980) *The alcohol, drug abuse and mental health national data book.* Rockville, MD: Alcohol, Drug Abuse and Mental Health Administration.

VOGEL, G. W., VOGEL, F., MCABEE, R. S., & THURMAND, A. J. (1980) Improvement of depression by REM sleep deprivation. *Archives of General Psychiatry,* 37, 247–253.

VOLKMAR, F. R. & COHEN, D. J. (1985) The experience of infantile autism: A first-person account by Tony W. *Journal of Autism and Developmental Disorders,* 15, 47–54, Plenum Publishing Corporation.

VONKORFF, M., NESTADT, G., ROMANOSKI, A., ANTHONY, J., EATON, W., MERCHANT, A., CHAHAL, R., KRAMER, M., FOLSTEIN, M., & GROENBERG, E. (1985) Prevalence of treated and untreated DSM-III schizophrenia. *The Journal of Nervous and Mental Disease,* 173, 577–581.

VONNEGUT, M. (1975) *The Eden express.* New York: Bantam Books.

WADDEN, T. A., LUBORSKY, L., GREER, S. & CRITS-CHRISTOPHE, P. (1984) The behavioral treatment of essential hypertension: An update and comparison with pharmacological treatment. *Clinical Psychology Review,* 4, 403–429.

WAGNER, H. H. JR., BURNS, H. P., DANNALS, R. F., WONG, D. F., SANGSTRUM, B., DUELFER, T., FROST, J. J., RAVERT, H. T., LINKS, J. M., ROSENBLOOM, S. B., LUKAS, S. E., KRAMER, A. V., & KUHAR, M. H. (1983) Imaging dopamine receptors in the brain by positron tomography. *Science,* 221, 1264–1266.

WALDER, L. O., COHEN, S. L., & DASTON, P. G. (1967) *Teaching parents and others principles of behavior control for modifying the behaviors of children.* Report to U.S. Office of Education, Washington, D.C.

WALDRON, S. (1976) The significance of childhood neuroses for adult mental health: A follow-up study. *American Journal of Psychiatry,* 133, 532–538.

WALINDER, J. & THUWE, T. (1975) *A social psychiatric follow up on 24 sex reassigned transsexuals.* Copenhagen: Scandinavian Books.

WALKER, C. E., HEDBERG, A., CLEMENT, P. W., & WRIGHT, L. (1981) *Clinical procedures for behavior therapy,* pp. 66–67. © 1981, reprinted by permission of Prentice-Hall, Englewood Cliffs, NJ.

WALKER, J. I. & BRODIE, H. K. H. (1985) Paranoid disorders. In I. H. Kaplan and B. J. Sadock (Eds.) *Comprehensive textbook of psychiatry* (4th ed.). Baltimore: Williams & Wilkins.

WALLACE, C. J. (1981) The social skills training project of the Mental Health Clinical Research Center for the study of schizophrenia. In J. P. Curran & P. M. Monti (Eds.) *Social skills training: A practical handbook for assessment and treatment.* New York: Guilford Press.

WALLACE, C. J. (1984) Community and interpersonal functioning in the course of schizophrenic disorders. *Schizophrenia Bulletin, 10,* 233–257.

WALLACE, C. J., NELSON, C. J., LIBERMAN, R. P., AITCHISON, R. A., LUKOFF, D., ELDER, J. P., & FERRIS, C. (1980) A review and critique of social skills training with schizophrenic patients. *Schizophrenia Bulletin, 6,* 42–62.

WALLERSTEIN, J. S., & KELLY, J. B. (1980) *Surviving the breakup: How children and parents cope with divorce.* New York: Basic Books.

WARSHAK, R. A. & SANTROCK, J. W. (1983) Children of Divorce: Impact of custody disposition on social development. In E. Callahan & K. McKlusky (Eds.). *Life span developmental psychology: Nonnormative life events.* New York: Academic Press.

WATSON, J. B. (1925) *Behaviorism.* New York: Norton.

WATT, N. F. (Ed.) (1984) *Children at risk for schizophrenia: A longitudinal perspective.* New York: Cambridge University Press.

WATTS, C. A. H. (1985) A long-term follow-up of schizophrenic patients: 1946–1983. *Journal of Clinical Psychiatry, 46,* 210–216.

WECHSLER, D. (1955) *Manual for the Wechsler Adult Intelligence Scale.* New York: Psychological Corporation.

WECHSLER, D. (1958) *The measurement and appraisal of adult intelligence* (4th ed.). Baltimore: Williams & Wilkins.

WEHR, T. A. & WERTZ-JUSTICE, A. (1982) Circadian rhythm mechanisms in affective illness and in antidepressant drug action. *Pharmacopsychiatry, 15,* 31–39.

WEINBERG, K. (1976) *Incest behavior* (rev. ed.). Secaucus, NJ: Citadel.

WEINBERG, T. S. (1978) Sadism and masochism: Sociological perspectives. *Bulletin of the American Academy of Psychiatry and Law, 6,* 284–295.

WEINBERG, T. S. & FALK, G. (1980) The social organization of sadism and masochism. *Deviant Behavior, 1,* 379–393.

WEINBERG, T. S., WILLIAMS, C. J., & MOSER, C. (1984) The social constituents of sadomasochism. *Social Problems, 31,* 379–389.

WEINBERGER, D. R. (1984) Computed tomography (CT) findings in schizophrenia: Speculation on the meaning of it all. *Journal of Psychiatric Research, 18,* 477–490.

WEINBERGER, D. R., BIGELOW, L. B., & KLEINMAN, J. E., (1980) Cerebral ventricular enlargement in chronic schizophrenia: An association with poor response to treatment. *Archives of General Psychiatry, 37,* 11–13.

WEINBERGER D. R., DELISI, L. E., NEOPHYTIDES, A. N., AND WYATT, R. J. (1981) Familial aspects of CT abnormalities in chronic schizophrenic patients. *Psychiatric Research, 4,* 65–71.

WEINER, D. B. (1979) The apprenticeship of Philippe Pinel: A new document "Observations of citizen Pussin on the insane," *American Journal of Psychiatry, 136,* 1128–1134.

WEINER, R. D. (1979) The psychiatric use of electrically induced seizures. *American Journal of Psychiatry, 136,* 1507–1517.

WEISSMAN, M. M., GERHON, E. S., KIDD, K. K., PRUSSOF, B. A., LECKMAN, J. F., DIBBLE, E., HAMOVIT, J., THOMPSON, W. D., PAULS, D. L., AND GUROFF, J. J. (1984) Psychiatric disorder in the relatives of probands with affective disorders. *Archives of General Psychiatry, 41,* 13–21.

WEISSMAN, M. M. & MYERS, J. K. (1978) Affective disorders in a U.S. urban community: The use of research diagnostic criteria in an epidemiological survey. *Archives of General Psychiatry, 35,* 1304–1311.

WEISSMAN, M. M., MYERS, J. K., & THOMPSON, W. D. (1981) Depression and its treatment in a U.S. urban community, 1975–1976. *Archives of General Psychiatry, 38,* 417–421.

WEISSMAN, M. M., MYERS, J. K., TISCHLER, G. L., HOLZER, C. E., LEAF, P. J., ORVASCHAEL, H. & BRODY, J. A. (1985) Psychiatric disorder (DSM-III) and cognitive impairment among the elderly in a U.S. urban community. *Acta Psychiatrica Scandinavica, 71,* 366–379.

WEISSMAN, M. M., WICKRAMARATNE, P., MERIKANGAS, K. R., LECKMAN, J. F., PRUSOFF, B. A. CARUSO, K. A., KIDD, K. K., & GAMMON, G. D. (1984) Onset of major depression in early adulthood. *Archives of General Psychiatry, 41,* 1136–1143. Copyright © 1984, American Medical Association.

WEISZ, J., YEATES, K., & ZIGLER, E. (1982) Piagetian evidence and the developmental-difference controversy. In E. Zigler & B. Balla (Eds.), *Mental retardation: The developmental difference controversy.* Hillsdale, NJ: Erlbaum.

WELLS, C. E. (1985) Organic syndromes: Delirium. In H. I. Kaplan and B. J. Sadock (Eds.) *Comprehensive textbook of psychiatry* (4th ed.) (Vol. 1). Baltimore: Williams and Wilkins.

WENDER, P. H., ROSENTHAL, D., KETY, S. S., SCHULSINGER, F., & WELNER, J. (1974) Cross-fostering: A research strategy for clarifying the role of genetic and experiential factors in the etiology of schizophrenia. *Archives of General Psychiatry, 30,* 121–128.

WERNER, E. E. & SMITH, R. S. (1982) *Vulnerable but invincible: A study of resilient children.* New York: McGraw-Hill.

WESSON, D. R. & SMITH, D. E. (1977) *Barbiturates: Their use, misuse, and abuse.* New York: Human Services Press.

WEST, J. B. (1984) Human physiology at extreme altitudes on Mt. Everest, *Science, 223,* 784–788.

WEXLER, N. S., GUSELLA, J. F., CONNEALLY, P. M., & HOUSMAN, D. (1985) Huntington's disease and the new genetics: A preview of the future for psychiatric disorders. In H. A. Pincus and H. Pardes (Eds.) *The integration of neuroscience and psychiatry.* Washington, D.C.: American Psychiatric Press.

WHALEN, C. K., HENKER, B., & HINSHAW, S. P. (1985) Cognitive-behavioral therapies for hyperactive children: Premises, problems and prospects. *Journal of Abnormal Child Psychology, 13,* 391–410.

WHITEHEAD, W. E., BLACKWELL, B., & ROBINSON, A. (1978) Effects of diazepam on phobic avoidance behavior and phobic anxiety. *Biological Psychiatry, 13,* 59–64.

WIDIGER, T. A. & FRANCES, A. (1985) Axis II personality disorders: Diagnostic and treatment issues. *Hospital and Community Psychiatry, 36,* 619–627.

WIDOM, C. S. (1978) A methodology for studying noninstitutionalized psychopaths. In R. D. Hare & D. A. Schalling (Eds.), *Psychopathic behavior: Approaches to research.* Chichester, Eng.: John Wiley.

WIKLER, L., WASOW, M., & HATFIELD, E. (1981) Chronic sorrow revisited. *American Journal of Orthopsychiatry, 51,* 63–70.

WILL, O. A., JR. (1981) Values and the psychotherapist. *American Journal of Psychoanalysis, 41,* 203–212.

WILLE, R. (1981) Ten year follow-up of a representative sample of London heroin addicts: Clinic attendance, abstinence, and mortality. *British Journal of Addiction, 76,* 259–266.

WILLIAMS, J. B. W. (1985) The multiaxial system of DSM III: Where did it come from and where should it go? II. *Archives of General Psychiatry, 42,* 181–186.

WILLIAMS, J. G., BARLOW, D. H., & AGRAS, W. S. (1972) Behavioral measurement of severe depression. *Archives of General Psychiatry, 27,* 330–333.

WILLIAMS, L. S., DOOSEMAN, G., & KLEIFIELDE, E. (1984) Comparative effectiveness of guided mastery and exposure treatments for intractable phobias. *Journal of Consulting and Clinical Psychology,* 52, 505–518.

WILSON, G. T. (1982) Psychotherapy process and procedure: The behavioral mandate. *Behavior Therapy, 13,* 291–312.

WILSON, G. T. & RACHMAN, S. J. (1983) Meta-analyses and the evolution of psychotherapy outcome: Limitations and liabilities. *Journal of Consulting and Clinical Psychology, 51,* 54–64.

WING, J. K. (1983) Use and misuse of the PSE. *British Journal of Psychiatry, 143,* 111–117.

WING, J. K., COOPER, J. E., & SARTORIUS, N. (1974) *Measurement and classification of psychiatric symptoms.* Cambridge, Eng.: Cambridge University Press.

WINOKUR, G. (1980) Is there a common genetic factor in bipolar and unipolar affective disorders? *Comprehensive Psychiatry, 21,* 460–468.

WINOKUR, G., MORRISON, J., CLANCY, J., CROWE, R. (1972) The Iowa 500: Familial and clinical findings favor two kinds of depressive illness. *Comprehensive Psychiatry, 14,* 99–107.

WINSON, J. (1985) *Brain and psyche: The biology of the unconscious.* New York: Anchor Press.

WISE, T. N. (1985) Fetishism--etiology and treatment: A review from multiple perspectives. *Comprehensive Psychiatry, 26.* 249–257.

WITTCHEN, H., SEMLER, G., AND VON ZERSSEN, D. (1985) A comparison of two diagnostic methods. *Archives of General Psychiatry, 42,* 667–684.

WOLF, S. (1969) Psychosocial factors in myocardial infarction and sudden death. *Circulation, 39*(4), 74–83.

WOLF, S. & WOLFF, H. G. (1947) *Human gastric function* (2nd ed.). New York: Oxford University Press.

WOLFE, D. A., SANDLER, J., & KAUFMAN, K. (1981) Competency-based parent training program for child abusers. *Journal of Consulting and Clinical Psychology, 49,* 633–640.

WOLFE, L. (1980) The sexual profile of that Cosmopolitan girl. *Cosmopolitan, 189,* 254–257.

WOODY, G. E., McLELLAN, A. T., LUBORSKY, L., O'BRIEN, C. P., BLAINE, J., FOX, S., HERMAN, I., & BECK, A. T. (1984) Severity of psychiatric symptoms as a predictor of benefits from psychotherapy: The Veterans Administration-Penn study. *American Journal of Psychiatry, 141,* 1172–1177.

WULFF, S. B. (1985) The symbolic and object play of children with autism: A review. *Journal of Autism and Developmental Disorders, 15,* 139–147.

WOLFGANG, M., FIGLIO, R. M., & SELLIN, T. (1974) *Delinquency in a birth cohort.* Chicago: University of Chicago Press.

WOLKIN, A., JAEGER, J., BRODIE, J. D., WOLF, A. P., FOWLER, J., ROTROSEN, J., GOMEZ-MONT, F., AND CANCRO, R. (1985) Persistence of cerebral metabolic abnormalities in chronic schizophrenia as determined by positron emission tomography. *American Journal of Psychiatry, 142,* 564–571.

WOLPE, J. (1973) *The practice of behavior therapy* (2nd ed.). New York: Pergamon Press.

WOLPE, J. & RACHMAN, S. J. (1960) Psychoanalytic "evidence": A critique based on Freud's case of Little Hans. *Journal of Nervous and Mental Disease, 131,* 135–147.

WOODRUFF, R. A., JR., GOODWIN, D. W., & GUZE, S. B. (1974) *Psychiatric diagnosis.* New York: Oxford University Press.

Work group to revise DSM-III. American Psychiatric Association (1985) Draft DSM-III-R in development: 10-5-85. Washington, D.C. *American Psychiatric Association.*

WYKES, T. (1981) Brief communication. Can the psychiatrist learn from the psycholinguist? Detecting coherence in the disordered speech of manics and schizophrenics. *Psychological Medicine, 11,* 641–642.

WYNNE, L. C. (1975) Adjustment reaction of adult life. In A. M. Freedman, H. I. Kaplan, & B. J. Sadock (Eds.), *Contemporary textbook of psychiatry* (Vol. 2) (2nd ed.). Baltimore: Williams and Wilkins.

WYNNE, L. C. (1984) The University of Rochester child and family study: Overview of research plan. In N. F. Watt, E. J. Anthony, L. C. Wynne, & J. E. Rolfe (Eds.), *Children at risk for schizophrenia: A longitudinal perspective.* Cambridge: Cambridge University Press.

WYNNE, L. D. SINGER, M. T. BARTKO, J. J., & TOOKEY, M. L. (1977) Schizophrenics and their families: Research on parental communication. In J. M. Tanner (Ed.), (pp. 254–286) *Developments in psychiatric research.* London: Hodder and Stoughton.

ZETLIN, A. G. & TURNER, J. L. (1985) Transition from adolescence to adulthood: Perspectives of mentally retarded individuals and their families. *American Journal of Mental Deficiency, 89,* 570–579.

ZEITLIN, H. (1982) The natural history of psychiatric disorder in children. Unpublished M. D. thesis. University of London.

ZIGLER, E., BULLA, D., & HODAPP, R. (1984) On the definition and classification of mental retardation. *American Journal of Mental Deficiency, 89,* 215–230.

ZILBERGELD, B., & EVANS, M. (1980) The inadequacy of Masters and Johnson, *Psychology Today, 14,* 28–43.

ZILLMANN, D. (1979) *Hostility and aggression.* New York: Halsted Press.

ZUBIN, J., MAGAZINER, J., & STEINHAUER, S. R. (1982) *The metamorphosis of schizophrenia. From chronicity to vulnerability:* Unpublished paper.

ZUBIN, J. & SPRING, B. (1977) Vulnerability--a new view of schizophrenia. *Journal of Abnormal Psychology, 86,* 103–126.

ZUCKERMAN, M. (1979) *Sensation seeking.* Hillsdale, NJ: Lawrence Erlbaum Associates.

ZUCKERMAN, M., Buchsbaum, M. S., & Murphy, D. L. (1980) Sensation-seeking and its biological correlates. *Psychological Bulletin, 88,* 187–214.

# NAME INDEX

# SUBJECT INDEX

Behavioral assessment, 101
  of marital difficulties, 103
Behavioral coping, 112
Behavioral medicine, 176–181
Behavioral perspective, 67–72
  and brain disorder, 367
  and depression, 273–276
  on sexual dysfunction, 219–220
  and sexual preference, 216
  on suicide, 289–291
  on treatment of depression, 274–276
  see also learning perspective
Behavioral self-assessment, 103
Behavioral self-instruction, 314–315
Behavioral therapy, 478, 503–504
  for children, 429
  and hyperactive behavior, 410
  in schizophrenia, 313–315
Behavioral training, 499–500
Behavior-change experiment, 52
Behavior genetics, 52
Behaviorism, 71
Behavior modification, 466, 470
  and retardation, 435
Behavior Rating Scale for Children, 99
Behavior sample, 91
Behavior therapy, 466–470
  and anorexia, 424
  and anxiety disorder, 160–164
  and childhood depression, 422
  in obsessive-compulsive disorder, 418, 419
Belle indifference, 45, 199
Benzodiazepine
  see also tranquilizing drugs
Bereavement, 127–129
Beta receptor, 267
Bethlehem Hospital, 38, 39
Bicetre, 38
Binet tests, 94
Binge cycle, 425–426
Biochemical brain abnormalities, 331–332
Biofeedback, 106, 179–180, 470
  and hypertension, 190
Biological factors
  in abnormal behavior, 57–60
  in alcoholism, 385–386
  in intelligence, 95
  of retardation, 442–449
Biological perspective, 44–45, 51–60
  of alcoholism, 381–383
  on antisocial behavior, 254
  on anxiety disorder, 166–167
  and autism, 437–438
  and brain disorders, 367
  and depression, 265–272
  and hyperactivity, 411
  in schizophrenia, 342–343
  on sexual deviation, 236
  on sexual preference, 215, 216
Biological rhythms, 268–269
Biological therapies, 483–487
  for depression, 270–272
  in schizophrenia, 312–313
Biopsychosocial model, 172
Bipolar disorder, 262, 265, 282–287
  in adolescence, 420
  heredity in, 286–287
Birthweight
  and retardation, 448–449
  and schizophrenia, 322
Bisexuality, 211, 214–215
Blood alcohol, 379, 380
Blood pressure as assessment, 105, 106
Body temperature rhythm, 269–270
Borderline personality disorder, 246–249
Brain, 53–56
  abnormalities in schizophrenia, 330–334
Brain atrophy, 354
Brain damage
  and alcohol, 380

from child abuse, 449
  effects of, 346
  and violent behavior, 360
Brain degeneration and aging, 369
Brain disorders, 356–366
Brain electrical activity mapping (BEAM), 333
Brain injury, 359–361
Brain lesions, 363
Brain reward system, 56
Brain tumors, 359–361
Briquet's syndrome, 196
Brown v. Board of Education, 451
Bulimia nervosa, 422, 425–426
Burnout, 125–129

Caffeine, 400
Camarillo study, 485–486
Cancer, 58
  stress and, 190–191
Cardiovascular disorder, 181–190
Case studies, 210
Catatonic schizophrenia, 306
Catecholamine, 182, 266–267
Central nervous system, 448–449
Cerebral cortex, 353
Cerebral ventricles, 330
Cerebrovascular accident, 366
Cerebrum, 53
Checking behavior, 157
Child abuse, 416–418, 498–500
  brain damage from, 449
Childhood
  disorders of, 402–427
  psychological problems in, 407–408
  see also developmental disorders
Childhood schizophrenia and autism, 438
Child neglect, 416–418
Chromosomal abnormality, 443–444
Chromosomal anomaly, 52
Chromosome, 52
  and Huntington's disorder, 357
Chronic disorders, 508–509
Cigarette smoking, 401–404
Civil commitment, 516–517
Classical conditioning, 67–68, 414
Classification, 83–84
  research on, 88–90
  systems of, 83
Client-centered therapy, 464, 471
Clinical contacts, 8–9
Clinical judgment
  factors in, 89–90
  trends in, 88–89
Clinical trial, 484–485
Clinician, 15
Cocaine, 395–397, 400
Cognitive accuracy, 281
Cognitive assessment, 103–105
Cognitive-behavioral therapy, 466–470, 478
  and anorexia, 424
  in anxiety disorders, 164
  with groups, 472–473
  in schizophrenia, 313–315
Cognitive distortion, 276–279
Cognitive functioning
  in elderly, 370
  in retardation, 450–451
  in schizophrenia, 335–336
Cognitive Interference Questionnaire, 104
Cognitive modification
  in depression, 470
  in stress, 131
Cognitive perspective, 72–74
  and alcohol abuse, 384–385, 387–388
  on antisocial behavior, 254–255
  in anxiety disorders, 164–166
  on autism, 437
  and brain disorders, 367
  in depression, 276–282
  on suicide, 291

Cognitive processes, 51
Cognitive psychotherapy, 465–466
Cognitive rehearsal, 165
Cognitive restructuring, 165
Cognitive set, 280
Cognitive skills
  for coping, 115–116
  and delinquency, 412
  development of, 408
Cognitive style, 307–308
Cognitive therapy, 165–166, 429
  for anxiety disorders, 165–166
  for depression, 278–279
  for smoking, 403
Cognitive trioa, 279
College students
  alcohol use in, 379
  suicide
Combat stress, 120–121
Combined therapies, 485–486
Commitment, 512–518
Communication in autism, 432–433
Communication deviance, 337–340
Community living program, 453
Community perspective, 77–79
  and alcohol abuse, 385
  and brain disorders, 367
  and prevention, 506–507
  and schizophrenia, 340
Community psychology, 520–521
Comparative studies of therapy, 485–487
Competency, 33–34
Compulsive rituals, 155
Computerized axial tomography, 330, 348, 349, 354, 360
  of alcoholics, 380
  in schizophrenia, 330
Concordance, 52, 322
Concussion, 359
Conditioned stimulus, 68
Conduct disorder, 252, 411–412
Confabulation, 352
Conflict, 61
Congenital factors, 252
  and retardation, 443
Consciousness state, 463
Constitutional factors and retardation, 443
Continuous Performance Test, 334
Control group, 482–483
Controlled drinking, 388, 390
Contusion, 359
Conversion disorder, 199–200
Coronary heart disease, 182–190
Coping, 6–8, 84
  and aging, 370–371
  with anger, 116
  behavioral, 403
  in children, 123
  cognitive, 403
  information and, 115
  resources, 112
  skills, 7, 111–116, 340, 425
  with terminal illness, 127–129
Coping skill training, 500
Coping style, 258–259
Coping techniques, 115–116
Coronary heart disease, 182–187
  and alcohol use, 380
  liver studies in, 186–187
  and Type A, 186–187
Correlational study, 20–21
Cortex, cerebral, 53
  adrenal, 57
Corticotrophin-releasing factor, 57
Costs
  of Alzheimer's disease, 353
  of schizophrenia, 296
Couples sexual patterns, 208
Covert modeling, 469
Covert sensitization, 227, 387
  for pedophilia, 235–236

Creutzfeldt-Jakob disease, 358
Criminal commitment, 513–516
Crisis Center, 519
Cross-cultural studies
    and diagnosis, 89–90
    and heart disease, 183–184
Cross dressing
    see transvestism
Cross-fostering study, 323
Cross sectional study, 21
CT scan
    see computerized axial tomography
Custody of children, 501–502
CVA
    see cerebrovascular accident
Cyclothymia, 262, 286

Day hospital, 487
Death, 127–129
Death imprint, 122
Defense mechanisms, 63–64, 65
Deinstitutionalization, 14, 488, 507–512
    and retardation, 453–457
Delinquency, 411–412, 495–497
Delirium, 349–351
Delirium, tremens, 351
Delusion, 299, 310
    paranoid, 307–308
    in schizophrenia, 298–301
Dementia, 351–355
    senile, 367
Dementia paralytica, 358
Dementia praecox, 303
Denial, 112–113, 128
    in disasters, 122
Density living, 340
Dependence
    cocaine, 396–397
    physiological, 376–377
    disorder, 375
Dependent personality disorder, 255–256
Depersonalization, 140
Depressant drugs, 400
Depressed feeling state, 262–263
Depression, 113, 262–282, 412
    and aging, 368
    biological rhythms in, 269
    and cancer, 191
    in childhood, 419–422
    cognitive assessment in, 104
    delusions in, 299
    genetic factors in, 265–266
    in Huntington's disorder, 356
    prevalence, 263
    sex differences in, 263
    in somatization, 198
    theories of, 265–282
    see also mood disorder
Depressive neuroses
    see dysthymic disorder
Determinism, 67
Development
    in retardation, 441
    transitions in, 123–125
Developmental disorders of childhood, 85–86, 432–457
Developmental model, 450–451
Developmental rate, 408
Deviant behavior
    see maladaptive behavior
Dexamethasone Suppression Test, 268
Diabetes and retardation, 447
Diagnosis, 11, 83
    study of, 17–18
    transnational differences in, 89–90
Diagnostic interview, 90
Diagnostic Interview Schedule, 93–94
Diarrhea, 195
Difference model, 450–451
Disasters, 119–120, 121–123
Disaster syndrome, 122

Disorganized schizophrenia, 306
Dissociative disorder, 86, 136–141
Disulfiram, 386
Divorce, 493–494
    children and, 500–503
DNA, 52
Dopamine, 266–268
Dopamine hypothesis, 331–332
Double-blind study, 23
Down syndrome, 443–445, 446, 447, 451
Drinking rates, 379, 380
Drop-in center, 519
Dropouts, 505
Drug abuse, 10
    mutual help groups for, 397
Drugs, 395–405
    characteristics of, 400
    and hyperactive behavior, 409–411
    and retardation, 447–448
Drug therapy, 483–487
DSM-III, 84–88, 147, 148, 149
    evaluation of, 86–88
DMM-III-R, 84–88, 148, 298
    Axis III, 349
DTs
    see delirium tremens
Dyspareunia, 218
Dysphoric mood, 263
Dysthmic disorder, 262
    in childhood, 420

Early detection projects, 505
Early education, 494–495
Echolalia, 432, 437
ECT
    see electro-convulsive therapy
Education as prevention, 494–495
Education for All Handicapped Children
    Act, 451
EEG
    see electroencephalogram
Efficacy, 466
Ego, 62, 63
Ejaculation, 217
Electro-convulsive therapy, 483, 485
    and depression, 270–271
    and psychotherapy, 478
    in schizophrenia, 312
Electroencephalogram, 54, 56, 333, 363
Emotion
    primitive nodes for, 281
    psychophysiological assessment of, 106–107
    in schizophrenia, 302
Emotional disorder in childhood, 412–415, 418–422
Endocrine glands, 56–57, 59
    and emotion, 171–172
Endorphin, 56, 391–392
Environment
    in intelligence, 450
    in schizophrenia, 322–323
Epidemiology, 9–14
Epilepsy, 54, 348, 361–366
    and autism, 437
    treatment of, 365–366
Ethics of research, 24–25
Exhibitionism, 231
Exorcism, 28
Expectancy, 384–385
Experimental research, 21–24
Exposure orientation, 393
Exposure therapy, 468
    and anxiety disorders, 162–163
    in vivo, 162–163
Expressed emotion, 338–339
Extinction, 67, 68, 468–469
Eye movement, 334
Eysenck Personality Questionnaire, 229

Factitious disorder, 86, 170, 201–202
Fading, 470
Family
    and alcoholism, 375
    and Alzheimer's disease, 354
    impact of bipolar disorder, 11
    and paranoid schizophrenia, 320–321
    in prevention, 497
    in schizophrenia, 337–340
    and schizophrenic aftercare, 315–316
Family adjustment, 455
    to retardation, 439–440, 453
Family conflict and anorexia, 425
Family disputes, 507
Family environment
    and schizophrenia, 337–340
    and attention deficit-hyperactive behavior, 409
Family relationships in schizophrenia, 337
Family therapy, 471–472, 497
    and anorexia, 425
Fantasy, 461–462
Fear
    in childhood, 413–414
    in phobia, 149–155
Fetal alcohol syndrome, 380, 447–448, 449
Fetishisms, 225
First-rank symptoms, 303–305
Fixation, 62
Fixed-role therapy, 465–466
Flashback, 375–376, 398
Flooding, 160
    in post Vietnam syndrome, 135
Folie adeux, 308
Follow-up study, 21
    of alcohol abuse, 395
    of divorce effects, 501–502
    of intellectual development, 450
    of therapy, 477–478
Food additives, 411
Fool, 33
Foster home care, 453
Framingham Study, 186–187, 188–189
Free association, 64, 461
Frigidity, 217
Frontal lobes, 55
Fugue, 137

GABA, 356
Galvanic skin response (GSR), 105–106
Gastrointestinal disorder, 195–196
Genain quadruplets, 341–343
Gender identity disorder, 221–225
Gender nonconformity in childhood, 216
Gene, 52–53
    dominant, 443
    recessive, 443
General adaptation syndrome, 171–172
Generalized anxiety disorder, 145–147
    and phobia, 150
General paresis, 358
Genetic counseling, 324–325, 357
Genetic disorder, 356–358
Genetic factors
    in alcohol abuse, 381, 382, 383
    in epilepsy, 366
    in schizophrenia, 320–325
Genetic heterogeneity, 323–324
Gestalt therapy, 465
Glove anesthesia, 199
Gran mal epilepsy, 363–364
Group home, 496
    for retarded, 453–454
Group therapy, 470–472
    for abusive parents, 499
    for post Vietnam stress syndrome, 135
GSR
    see galvanic skin response
Guided mastery therapy, 164
Guided rehearsal, 469

Prognosis
   see outcome
Projective techniques, 99–101
Psychedelic drugs, 397–399, 400
Psychic determinism, 61
Psychoactive drugs, 58–59
   research on, 483–484
   see also
      antipsychotic drugs
      antianxiety drugs
      antidepressant drugs
Psychoactive substance dependence disorders, 375–405
Psychoanalysis, 64–65, 461–462
Psychodrama, 472–473
Psychodynamic perspective, 50, 60–67, 413–414, 415
   and alcohol abuse, 383, 386–387
   of anxiety disorder, 158–160
   and brain disorder, 367
   on depression, 272–273
   group therapy, 471
   histrionic personality disorder, 244
   and narcissism, 245–246
   in schizophrenia, 341–343
   on sexual dysfunction, 220
   and sexual preference, 215–216
Psychodynamic therapy, 427, 428–429, 461–463
   for childhood depression, 422
   in schizophrenia, 313
Psychogenic pain disorder, 196
Psychoimmunology, 57–59
Psychological perspective, 29
   in epilepsy, 365
Psychological tests, 94–101
Psychomotor epilepsy, 364–365
Psychopath, 253–254
Psychopathology, 2–3, 9–14
   in opioid users, 394
   of retarded, 455–456
Psychopharmacology, 58–59
Psychophysiological assessment, 105–107
Psychophysiological disorder, 170, 181–196
Psychosexual development, 62
Psychosexual disorder, 86
Psychosis, 296–297, 335, 362
   difference among types, 297
   family effect on, 498
   heredity in, 53
   posttraumatic, 361
   in retarded, 455
Psychosocial disadvantage, 449–450
   and retardation, 442
Psychosocial stressor, 85
Psychosomatic disorder
   see psychophysiological disorder
Psychotherapy, 459–465, 473–483, 485
   and aging, 369
   and alcohol abuse, 386–387
   for drug abuse, 397
   reactions to, 477
   research design, 481–483
   in sexual reassignment surgery, 222
Psychotic behavior
   in acute psychosis, 297
   in brain disorder, 359
   characteristics of, 297–302
Psychotic episode, 327–328
PT scan
   see positron emission tomography
Public education
   and prevention, 504–505
   for retarded, 451–455
Public information programs, 511–512
Punishment, 67
Pupil dilation, 105

Rape, 233–235
   effects on victim, 234–235
   of males, 234–235

Rape relief center, 235
Rapid eye movement, 269
Rating scale, 98–99
Rational-emotive therapy, 74–75, 466
Rational thinking, 43
Reaction formation, 159
   see also defense mechanisms
Reactive attachment disorders, 415, 418
Reactor, 187
Realistic preview, 115
Receptor sites, 167
Reform movement, 40–43
Regression, 62
   see also defense mechanisms
Rehearsal processes, 335
Reinforcement, 67, 470
   in brain, 56
Relapse prevention, 388
Relaxation techniques, 467–468
   and hypertension, 188–190
Relaxation training, 131, 162, 466–467
   in bulimia, 426
   for sexual dysfunction, 219
Remission, 18
Renaissance, 34
Rennie v. Klein, 517
Repression, 63–64, 65
   see also defense mechanisms
Research
   on abnormal behavior, 15–25
   precedure in, 19–20
   on psychological therapy, 473–483
Resocialization, 487, 510
Response prevention, 163
Retardation, 438–457
   and autism, 435
   classification of, 440
   mild, 450
Rheumatoid arthritis, 196
Rh incompatability, 446–447
Rights of patients, 517–519
Risk factors
   in health, 176
   in schizophrenia, 324
Ritalin, 409
Ritual, 157–158
Role play, 70
Romanticism, 43–44
Rorschach inkblots, 99–100
Rubella, 445
Rumination, 156
Rumination disorder, 422

Saccadic eye movement, 334
Sadism, 228–229
Sadomasochism, 229–230
Schemata, 278
Schizoaffective disorder, 309
Schizoid personality disorder, 242–243
Schizophrenias, the, 303
Schizophrenic disorder, 85, 294–344
   and aging, 368
   changing definitions of, 303
   diagnostic criteria, 297–298
   frontal lobe activity, 55
   high-risk studies of, 328–330
   prevalence, 11
   relationship to other disorders, 321, 322
   subtypes of, 305–306
   thinking in, 301–302, 335–336
Schizophrenic spectrum, 306, 309, 324, 337–338
Schizotypal personality, 247
Schizotypal personality disorder, 243, 305, 334
   see also personality disorders
School
   and prevention, 504–505
   problems in, 408
   refusal, 415
Screening programs, 450

Secondary process thinking, 62
Self, 76
Self-actualization, 75
Self-concept
   in humanistic perspective, 75–77
   in retarded, 455
Self-destructiveness
   in antisocial personality disorder, 250–251
   in borderline personality, 247
Self-efficacy, 72
   and depression, 274
Self-esteem, 272–273
Self-help groups, 177–178, 519–520
Self-monitoring, 274–276
Self-observation, 17
Self-regulation, 74
Senile dementia, 351–354
Sensate focus, 218–219
Sensation seeking, 254
Sentence completion test, 101
Separation, 23
Separation anxiety, 87, 154–155, 414–415
Seratonin, 266
Sex differences
   in adjustment, 501–502
   in bipolar disorder, 287
   in childhood disorders, 407
   in depression, 263
   in hypertension, 187
   in longevity, 175–176
Sex therapy, 220–221
Sexual assault, 498
Sexual behavior
   changing attitude toward, 206–207
   of college students, 207–208
   experimental research on, 210–211
   historical views of, 205
Sexual dysfunction, 216–221
   in marriage, 217
   treatment of, 218–221
Sexual exploitation, 455
Sexual offenders, 235–236
Sexual preference, 215–216
   and pupil dilation, 105
Sexual reassignment surgery, 222–225
Sexual response, 209
Sexual variations, 211–215
Sexual victimization, 232–236
Sexuality, 62
Shaman, 28
Shaping, 69
Sheltered workshop, 487
Short-term memory, 451
Simple phobia, 153
Single-subject research, 475–476
Sleep
   and aging, 368–369
   in depression, 269
Smoking, 178
   and coronary heart disease, 182
Smooth-pursuit eye movement, 334
Social causation theory, 77
Social change
   and coronary heart disease, 183–184
   and bipolar disorder, 12
Social competence, 188
Social facilitation
   see modeling
Social factors and alcoholism, 385, 386
Social intervention, 131
Social isolation, 340
Social learning, 71–72, 73
   and narcissism, 246
Social learning therapy, 316, 487
   for depression, 274–276
Social phobia, 153
Social relationships, 58, 117
   and coronary heart disease, 184–185
Social role, 78
Social selection theory, 77, 340

Social skills training
    and alcoholism, 386–387
    for retarded, 454–455
    in schizophrenia, 314
Social support, 58
    and brain damage, 347
    and coping, 116–118
    and immune systems, 180–181
    and retarded, 455
Social Support Questionnaire (SSQ), 117
Somatization disorder, 86, 170, 196–201
SOMPA, 452–453
Special education, 451–452
Speech
    incoherency in, 349
    poverty of, 309–310
    in schizophrenia, 301–302, 336
Splitting, 249
Spontaneous remission, 474
Spouse abuse, 500
Squeeze technique, 219
Stanford-Binet, 94
Starvation, 423
Statistics
    descriptive, 19
    inferential, 19
Stimulant drugs, 400
    and hyperactivity, 409–411
Stimulus-response relationships, 67–71
Stress, 6–8, 84, 111–131, 307–308
    and arousal, 118–123
    and brain damage, 346–347
    and cardiovascular system, 188
    clinical reactions in, 131–141
    and coronary heart disease, 182–187
    and delirium, 350
    and depression, 263
    and endocrine response, 171–172
    for family of retarded, 439–440
    and illness, 173–175
    and immune system, 180–181
    job related, 125–126
    and mortality, 185
    in occupation, 183, 184
    response to, 57
    and schizophrenia, 325
    and seizures, 365
    situational factors in, 118–123
    and tension headache, 192–193
Stressful life events, 122
Substance use disorder, 85
Suicide, 287–291
    in adolescence, 420–421
    and aging, 368
    and anorexia, 424
    and epilepsy, 362
Superego, 62, 63
Supernatural forces, 28–29, 30
Support groups, 354
Support seeking, 273
Survey research, 206–208
Survivor guilt, 119–120, 121
Symbolic modeling, 413, 469
Syndrome, 349
Syphilis, 51
Systematic desensitization, 68, 131, 160–161, 468
    for personality disorders, 259
System of Multicultural Pluralistic Assessment
    see SOMPA

Tardive dyskinesia, 313
Task orientation, 116
Tay-Sachs disease, 443
Television, 205
Temporal lobe epilepsy
    see psychomotor epilepsy
Tension headache
    see headache
Test-anxiety, 96
THC, 399
Thematic Apperception Test, 99–101, 337
Theoretical perspectives, 50–79
Theory
    functions of, 19
    role of, 18–19
Therapeutic community, 315–316
Therapist
    characteristics of, 480
    parents as, 503–504
Therapy, 458–491
    adolescent, 426–429
    for anorexia, 424–425
    for anxiety disorders, 158–167
    and autism, 435
    child, 426–429
    cognitive, 74
    comparison of, 477–481
    for depression, 274–276
    effectiveness of, 480–481
    evaluation of, 473, 480, 484–486
    fixed role, 75
    integration of techniques, 473
    for pedophelia, 235–236
    for personality disorders, 258–259
    rational-emotive, 74
    relationship factors in, 482
    for school refusal, 415
    for sexual dysfunction, 218–221
    for smoking, 402–404
    for stress-related problems, 130–131
    supportive, 131
    technique factors in, 480
    Type A, 187
Thinking
    in depression, 262, 276–280
    in mania, 262
    in paranoid disorder, 307–308
    in schizophrenia, 301–302, 335–336
Thought disorder, 336
Thought stopping, 165
Token economy, 314
    and amphetamine use, 397
Tolerance
    for cocaine, 396
    drug, 394
Training
    for family of schizophrenic, 315–316
    of retarded, 456
Tranquilizers, 144, 166–167, 390–391, 400, 483–484
Transference, 462
Transitions, 123–125
Transnational differences in diagnosis, 88
Transsexualism, 221–225
    see also gender identity disorder
Transsexual surgery, 222–224
Transvestism, 225–227
Treatment
    for alcoholism, 385–390
    of bulimia, 426
    of hyperactivity, 409–411

lack of in schizophrenia, 297
legal aspects, 512–518
of opioid dependence, 394–395
Treatment facilities, 12–15
Treatment programs, 507–512
Trephination, 29
Tricyclic drugs, 270
Trisomy, 13, 18, 444
Tuberous sclerosis, 443
Tumor, 359–361
Twin studies, 52–53
    of autism, 438
    of schizophrenia, 322–323, 330
Type A, 185–187
    and Framingham study, 186–187
Type I schizophrenia, 309–310, 330

Ulcers, 195–196
Unconditional positive regard, 464
Unconditional response, 68
Unconscious, 61
Unconscious dimension, 60
Unconscious mental processes in phobia, 159
Undoing, 159
    see also defense mechanisms
Unemployment, 129–130
Unipolar disorder, 262
Unreliability in diagnosis, 84

Vaginismus, 218
Valium, 390
Variable
    dependent, 19
    independent, 19
    intervening, 72
Ventricles
    see cerebral ventricles
Vicarious learning
    see modeling
Vietnam
    battle stress in, 120, 121–122
    drug use in, 392–393
    Post-Vietnam stress syndrome, 134–136
Violence, 516–517
    multiple causation of, 360
Viral dementias, 358
Vocational training
    see job training
Vomiting, 425–426
Voyeurism, 230
Voodoo, 29
Vulnerability, 6–8, 84, 111–115, 340
    to brain disorder, 346–348
    and depression, 422
    and schizophrenia, 325–328, 329–330
    in stress, 175–176
Vulnerability-stress model, 325–328

Waxy flexibility, 306
Wechsler tests, 94–95
Witch, 33
Withdrawal, 375
Word-association test, 101
Worry, 146
    and recovery, 177–179

Thomas O. Nelson

As is evident from their being coauthors of an Abnormal Psychology book that has gone through five editions, the Sarasons have a deep interest in the things that go wrong in human lives and result in psychological pain and behavioral problems. In addition to their textbook writing, the Sarasons have done extensive research on training and therapeutic programs that have proven useful for people who have several types of personal and social problems. They have worked with juvenile delinquents, high school students with poor academic motivation, and college students who experience uncomfortably high levels of test anxiety.

Irwin G. Sarason received his B.A. degree from Rutgers University; Barbara R. Sarason received her B.A. degree from Depauw University. The Sarasons met while graduate students at the University of Iowa. Each of them was awarded a Ph.D. degree with a specialization in Clinical Psychology from Indiana University. They moved to Seattle in 1956, after completing internships at the West Haven, Connecticut, Veteran's Administration Hospital. At present, Irwin is a professor and Barbara is a research associate professor in the Psychology Department at the University of Washington.

In their current research, the Sarasons are investigating how our relationships with family and friends help us to cope with the stresses and strains of daily life. This topic of social support has implications for understanding individual development, abnormal behavior and health status, as well as aspects of the psychotherapeutic relationship that contributes to positive clinical outcomes. The Sarasons' work suggests that people who feel accepted and valued by others are more likely to be good stress copers. They believe that an important ingredient of psychotherapy is the therapist's communication of acceptance and positive evaluation of the patient.

The Sarasons have contributed extensively to the psychology literature. They have written and edited several books and have published numerous scholarly articles. Irwin, a past president of the Western Psychological Association, has written articles on anxiety, coping skills useful in dealing with stress, and the assessment of life stress. Barbara has written articles dealing with the acquisition and strengthening of social skills and the use of television techniques in analyzing interpersonal relations. The Sarasons have lectured extensively about their work in the United States, England, Germany, the Netherlands, Belgium, France, and Sweden. A portion of this edition was written while they were visiting scholars at the Netherlands Institute for Advanced Study.